A Sourcebook of Canadian
MEDIA
Law

Carleton Library Series No. 151

A Sourcebook of Canadian MEDIA Law

Robert Martin & G. Stuart Adam

Carleton University Press
Ottawa, Canada
1989

ISBN 0-88629-076-7 paperback
0-88629-094-5 casebound

Printed and bound in Canada

Carleton Library Series # 151

Canadian Cataloguing in Publication Data

Adam, G. S. (Gordon Stuart), 1939-
A sourcebook of Canadian media law

ISBN 0-88629-076-7

1. Freedom of the press—Canada. 2. Freedom of information—Canada. 3. Freedom of speech—Canada. I. Martin, Robert, 1939- . II. Title.

KE4422.A78 1988 342.71'0853 C88-090291-4

Distributed by: Oxford University Press Canada,
70 Wynford Drive,
Don Mills, Ontario,
Canada M3C 1J9
(416) 441-2941

Cover design: Chris Jackson

Acknowledgements

Carleton University Press gratefully acknowledges the support extended to its publishing programme by the Canada Council and the Ontario Arts Council.

To

Ivan and Dawson,

Mark, Julia and Sara

TABLE OF CONTENTS

Preface 19
Acknowledgements 23

Chapter One: Freedom of Expression and the Canadian Constitution 25

1.1 A Note on the Meaning of Freedom of Expression 25
1.2 The Structure of the Constitution 29
1.3 Judicial Interpretation under the Constitution Act, 1867 29
1.3.1 The Constitution Act, 1867 31
Preamble 31
Section 91 31
Section 92 31
1.3.2 *Re Alberta Legislation* [1938] 2 D.L.R. 81 (S.C.C.) 35
1.3.3 *Switzman* v. *Elbling and Attorney-General of Quebec* [1957] S.C.R. 285 (S.C.C.) 41
1.3.4 *Re Nova Scotia Board of Censors and McNeil* (1978), 84 D.L.R. (3d) 1 (S.C.C.) 47
1.3.5 *Attorney General of Quebec* v. *Kellogg's of Canada* (1978), 83 D.L.R. (3d) 314 (S.C.C.) 52
1.3.6 *Gay Alliance Toward Equality* v. *Vancouver Sun* (1979), 97 D.L.R. (3d) 577 (S.C.C.) 56
1.3.7 *Re Public Service Board, Dionne and Attorney-General of Canada* (1978) 83 D.L.R. (3d) 178 (S.C.C.) 67
1.3.8 Notes on the Implied Bill of Rights 69
1.3.9 The Canadian Bill of Rights (1960) 70
1.4 The Canadian Charter of Rights and Freedoms, 1982 and Current Judicial Practice 72
1.4.1 A Note on the Structure of the Charter 72
1.4.2 Constitution Act, 1982 74
1.4.3 Section 2(b): The Scope and Meaning of Freedom of Expression 75
1.4.3.1 *Re Ontario Film and Video Appreciation Society and Ontario Board of Censors* (1983), 41 O.R. (2d) 583 (Ont. Div. Ct.) 75

1.4.3.2 *Koumoudouros* v. *Municipality of Metropolitan Toronto* (1984), 8 C.R.R. 179 (Ont. H.C.) 76
1.4.3.3 *Re Information Retailers Association of Metropolitan Toronto Inc. and Municipality of Metropolitan Toronto* (1985), 52 O.R. (2d) 449 (C.A.) 77
1.4.3.4 *Re Klein and Law Society of Upper Canada; Re Dvorak and Law Society of Upper Canada* (1985), 50 O.R. (2d) 118 (Ont. Div. Ct.) 77
1.4.3.5 A Note on Advertising and Free Expression 86
1.4.3.6 *National Citizens Coalition* v. *Attorney-General for Canada* (1984), 11 D.L.R. (4th) 481 (Alta. Q.B.) 88
1.4.3.7 *Re New Brunswick Broadcasting Co. Ltd. and CRTC* (1984), 13 D.L.R. (4th) 77 (F.C.A.) 89
1.4.3.8 *Irwin Toy Ltd.* v. *Attorney-General Que.* (1986), 32 D.L.R. (4th) 641 (Que. C.A.) 89
1.4.3.9 *Committee for the Commonwealth of Canada* v. *The Queen in Right of Canada* (1986), 25 D.L.R. (4th) 460 (F.C.T.D.) 90
1.4.3.10 *International Fund for Animal Welfare Inc.* v. *The Queen* (1986) 30 C.C.C. (3d) 80 (F.C.T.D.) 92
1.4.3.11 *Retail, Wholesale and Department Store Union, Local 580* v. *Dolphin Delivery Ltd.*, [1986] 2 S.C.R. 573 93
1.4.3.12 *R.* v. *Zundel* (1987), 35 D.L.R. (4th) 338 (Ont. C.A.) 96
1.4.3.13 *R.* v. *Kopyto* (1988), 24 O.A.C. 81 (C.A.) 97

1.4.4 Applying Section 1 97
1.4.4.1 Reasonable limit 98
1.4.4.1.1 *Re Klein and Law Society of Upper Canada; Re Dvorak and Law Society of Upper Canada* (1985), 50 O.R. 118 (Div. Ct.) 98
1.4.4.1.2 *Re Information Retailers Associations of Metropolitan Toronto Inc. and Municipality of Metropolitan Toronto* (1985), 52 O.R. (2d) 449 (C.A.) 99
1.4.4.2 Prescribed by Law 102
1.4.4.2.1 *Re Ontario Film and Video Appreciation Society and Ontario Board of Censors* (1983), 41 O.R. (2d) 583 (Div. Ct.) 102
1.4.4.2.2 *Re Ontario Film and Video Appreciation Society and Ontario Board of Censors* (1984), 45 O.R. (2d) 80 (C.A.) 103
1.4.4.2.3 An Act to Amend the Theatres Act, 1984, S.O. 1984, c.56 104
1.4.4.2.4 O.Reg. 56/85. Regulation to Amend Regulation 931 of Revised Regulations of Ontario, 1980, Made Under the Theatres Act 105
1.4.4.3 Demonstrably Justified in a Free and Democratic Society 105
1.4.4.3.1 *Re Ontario Film and Video Appreciation Society and Ontario Board of Censors* (1983), 41 O.R. (2d) 583 (Div. Ct.) 105

1.4.4.3.2 *National Citizens Coalition* v. *Attorney-General for Canada* (1984), 11 D.L.R. (4th) 481 (Alta. Q.B.)...... 106
1.4.4.3.3 "Corporate Political Activity" by Ron Atkey, (1985) 23 *The University of Western Ontario Law Review* 129 108
1.4.4.3.4 *International Fund for Animal Welfare* v. *The Queen* (1986) 30 C.C.C. (3d) 80 (F.C.T.D.) 109
1.4.4.3.5 Constitution Act, 1982, s.52......................... 112
1.4.4.4 A General Approach to Section 1: *R.* v. *Oakes,* [1986] 1 S.C.R. 103 112
1.4.5 G. Stuart Adam. "Why Should the Press Be Free? A Journalist's Reflections on the Charter" 113

Chapter Two: Security, The Public Order and Democratic Institutions: Legal Limitations to Protect the State's Rights, Prerogatives and Responsibilities, Part I 121

2.1 A Note on Legitimacy and the Scope of State Power.................. 121

2.2 National Security... 122
2.2.1 Emergencies Act, S.C. 1988, c.29............................ 122
2.2.2 Section 33(1) of the Constitution Act, 1982..................... 123
2.2.3 A Note on the Application of the War Measures Act 123
2.2.4 Official Secrets Act, R.S.C. 1985, c.0-5 133
2.2.5 Notes on the Official Secrets Act 137
2.2.5.1 Excerpts from Walter Tarnopolsky "Freedom of the Press", in *Newspapers and the Law,* Ottawa, Minister of Supply and Services Canada, 1981, ix, 19-21......................... 137
2.2.5.2 Law Reform Commission of Canada, *Crimes Against the State,* Working Paper 49, (Ottawa, 1986), 30, 33-34........ 139

2.3 Access to Information 140
2.3.1 Access to Information Act, R.S.C. 1985, c.A-1, ss.2, 4, 10, 13-27.. 140
2.3.2 *The Information Commissioner* v. *The Minister of Employment and Immigration* (1986), 3 F.C. 63 147
2.3.3 "What Newsrooms Need to Know", Canadian Daily Newspaper Publishers Association, September, 1984 150
2.3.4 John McCamus. "Freedom of Information in Canada", *Government Publications Review,* 1983, Vol. 10, p. 51........... 156
2.3.5 Provincial Access to Information Laws 163

2.4 Public Order and Criminal Libel.................................. 174
2.4.1 A Note on Criminal Libel 174
2.4.2 Criminal Code, ss.59-62 (Seditious libel)...................... 175
2.4.3 *Boucher* v. *The King,* (1950) 1 D.L.R. 657 (S.C.C.)............ 177
2.4.4 Law Reform Commission of Canada, *Crimes Against the State,* Working Paper 49 (Ottawa, 1986) 32, 35-36.................... 191
2.4.5 Criminal Code, ss.297-317 (Defamatory libel) 192

2.4.6 *R.* v. *Georgia Straight Publishing Ltd.* (1969), 4 D.L.R. (3d) 383 (B.C. Co. Ct.) 197
2.4.7 Robert Martin, "Law Reform Commission of Canada, Working Paper 35: Defamatory Libel", (1984) 22 *U.W.O. Law Review*, p. 249 200

Chapter Three: Judicial Proceedings: Legal Limitations to Protect the State's Rights, Prerogatives and Responsibilities, Part II 203

3.1 A Note on the Protection of Judicial Proceedings 203

3.2 The Principle of Openness 204
3.2.1 *Re Southam Inc. and the Queen* (No. 1) (1983), 41 O.R. (2d) 113 (Ont. C.A.) 204
3.2.2 *Edmonton Journal* v. *Attorney-General of Alberta and Attorney-General of Canada* (1983), 28 Alta. L.R. (2d) 369 (Q.B.) 215
3.2.3 *R.* v. *Robinson* (1983), 41 O.R. (2d) 764 (Ont. H.C.) 216
3.2.4 *Re Regina & Unnamed Person* (1985), 22 C.C.C. (3d) 284 (Ont. C.A.) 218
3.2.5 Criminal Code, s.487.2 220
3.2.6 *Canadian Newspapers Co. Ltd.* v. *Attorney General of Canada* (1986), 32 D.L.R. (4th) 293 (Ont. H.C.J.) 220
3.2.7 Courts of Justice Act, 1984, S.O. 1984, c.11, s.46 227
3.2.8 *R.* v. *Rowbotham (No. 3)* (1976), 2 C.R. (3d) 241 (Ont. Co. Ct.) 228
3.2.9 Patricia Chisolm, "No Cameras in Court", *Ontario Lawyers Weekly*, 20 January 1984, p. 1 229
3.2.10 Law Reform Commission of Canada, *Public and Media Access to the Criminal Process, Working Paper 56* Ottawa: Minister of Supply and Services Canada, 1987 230

3.3 Contempt of Court Generally 232
3.3.1 *Attorney-General* v. *Leveller Magazine Ltd. and Others* [1979] A.C. 440 (H.L.) 232
3.3.2 Criminal Code, ss.9, 10 249
3.3.3 *R.* v. *Kopyto*, (1988) 24 O.A.C. 81 (C.A.) 250

3.4 Scandalizing the Court 250
3.4.1 *Ambard* v. *Attorney General Trinidad and Tobago* [1936] A.C. 322 (J.C.P.C.) 251
3.4.2 *Re Nicol* [1954] 3 D.L.R. 690 (B.C.S.C.) 255
3.4.3 *Re Oullett* (1976), 72 D.L.R. (3d) 95 (Que. C.A.) 261
3.4.4 *R.* v. *Kopyto*, (1988) 24 O.A.C. 81 (C.A.) 268
3.4.5 Robert Martin, "Criticising the Judges", 28 *McGill Law Journal* 1, pp. 13-20 274

3.5 The Sub Judice Rule 276
3.5.1 Robert Martin, "Contempt of Court" in Anisman and Linden (eds.), *The Media, The Courts and the Charter*, (Toronto: Carswell, 1986), pp. 208-210 276

3.5.2 Statutory Sub Judice 278
3.5.2.1 Sexual Offences 278
3.5.2.1.1 Criminal Code, ss.166, 271, 272, 273, 276, 486 278
3.5.2.1.2 *Canadian Newspapers Co. Ltd.* v. *Attorney-General for Canada* (1985), 49 O.R. (2d) 557 (C.A.) 280
3.5.2.2 Young Offenders 281
3.5.2.2.1 Young Offenders Act, R.S.C. 1985, c.Y-1 281
3.5.2.2.2 *Southam* v. *R.* (1984), 42 C.R. (3d) 336, at 354-60 (Ont. H.C.) 284
3.5.2.3 Preliminary Inquiries 288
3.5.2.3.1 Criminal Code, ss.537(1)(h), 539, 542 288
3.5.2.3.2 *R.* v. *Banville* (1983) 45 N.B.R. (2d) 134 (Q.B.) 289
3.5.2.3.3 Criminal Code, s.542 293
3.5.2.4 Bail Hearings 293
3.5.2.4.1 Criminal Code, s.515 293
3.5.2.5 Jury Trials 295
3.5.2.5.1 Criminal Code, ss.648, 649 295
3.5.3 Common Law Sub Judice 295
3.5.3.1 *Attorney-General* v. *Times Newspapers Ltd.* [1973] 3 All E.R. 54 (H.L.) 295
3.5.3.2 *Zehr* v. *McIsaac et al* (1982), 39 O.R. (2d) 237 (Ont. H.C.) 304
3.5.3.3 *R.* v. *CHEK TV Ltd.* (1985) 23 C.C.C. (3d) 395 (B.C.S.C.) 309
3.5.3.4 *Bellitti* v. *Canadian Broadcasting Corp.* (1973), 2 O.R. (2d) 232 (Ont. H.C.) 317
3.5.3.5 *Bielek* v. *Ristimaki* (1979, Ont. H.C., unreported) 320
3.5.3.6 *Re Church of Scientology of Toronto* v. *The Queen (No. 6)* (1986) 27 C.C.C. (3d) 193 (Ont. H.C.) 324
3.5.3.7 Aide-memoire on the sub-judice rule in Stuart Robertson, *Courts and the Media,* (Toronto: Butterworths, 1981), p. 25 325
3.5.3.8 Criminal Records Act, R.S.C. 1985, c.C-47, s.6 326

3.6 Disobeying a Court Order 326
3.6.1 Criminal Code, s.545 326
3.6.2 William H. Kesterton, W.H., *The Law and the Press in Canada,* (Toronto: McClelland and Stewart in association with the Institute of Canadian Studies, Carleton University, 1976), pp. 32-39 327
3.6.3 John Sawatsky, "John Sawatsky Stakes Out the High Ground", (1986) 29 *Bulletin of the Centre for Investigative Journalism* 11 ... 332
3.6.4 Sawatsky's Notes 334
3.6.5 *Re Legislative Privilege* (1978), 83 D.L.R. (3d) 161 (Ont. C.A.) 338
3.6.6 *Attorney General* v. *Mulholland; Attorney General* v. *Foster,* [1963] 2 W.L.R. 658 (C.A.) 350
3.6.7 *Re Canada Post Corporation and Canadian Union of Postal Workers (Varma)* (1985), 19 L.A.C. (3d) 361 (Can. Arb. Bd.) 354
3.6.8 *Moysa* v. *Labour Relations Board and Attorney-General of Alberta* (1987), 52 Alta. L.R. (2d) 193, (Alta. C.A.) 357

3.7 Procedure in Contempt Cases 358

3.7.1 Robert Martin, "Contempt of Court: The Effect of the Charter" in Anisman and Linden (eds.), *The Media, the Courts and the Charter* 358

3.8 Reforming the Law 359
3.8.1 Robert Martin, "An Open Legal System" (1985), 23 *U.W.O. Law Review* 169 359

3.9 Dealing with Material that Might Become Evidence in a Judicial Proceeding 362
3.9.1 Criminal Code, ss.139, 487 362
3.9.2 Harold Levy, "What Should We Do When the Cops Arrive?" (1979), *Content* 95 366
3.9.3 *Pacific Press* v. *The Queen* (1977), 38 C.R.N.S. 295 (B.C.S.C.) 371
3.9.4 A Note on Taking Photographs Against Instructions of the Police 377

Chapter Four: Legal Limitations Protecting Social Values and Social Groups 379

4.1 A Note on the Law and the Protection of Beliefs, Morals and Minorities 379

4.2 Blasphemy 380
4.2.1 Criminal Code, s.296 380
4.2.2 *Rex* v. *Rahard* (1935) 65 C.C.C. at 344 381
4.2.3 *R.* v. *Gay News Ltd.* [1979] All ER 898 386

4.3 Expressions of Racism 400
4.3.1 Criminal Code, ss.318, 319, 320 400
4.3.2 *R.* v. *Buzzanga and Durocher* (1979), 101 D.L.R. (3d) 488 (Ont. C.A.) 401
4.3.3 Law Reform Commission of Canada, *Hate Propaganda Working Paper 50* (Ottawa, 1986), pp. 39-41 412
4.3.4 *R.* v. *Keegstra* (1988) 60 Alta. L.R. (2d), (Alta. C.A.) 414
4.3.5 Criminal Code, s.181 433
4.3.6 H.R.S. Ryan, "The Trial of Zundel, Freedom of Expression and Criminal Law", (1985), 44 C.R. (3d) 334 434
4.3.7 *R.* v. *Zundel,* (1987), 35 D.L.R. (4th) 338 (Ont. C.A.) 442
4.3.8 Canadian Human Rights Act, R.S.C. 1985, c.H-6, s.13 443
4.3.9 J. Patrick Boyer, *Political Rights: The Legal Framework of Elections in Canada* (Toronto: Buttersworth, 1981) pp. 308-9 443
4.3.10 Ontario Human Rights Code, S.O. 1981, c.53, ss.1-8, 12 444
4.3.11 *Regina* v. *Buffalo Broadcasting Co. Ltd.* (1977), 36 C.P.R. (2d) 170 (Sask. Magistrates' Ct.) 446
4.3.12 Regulations Respecting Radio Broadcasting, 1986, s.3 457

4.4 Obscenity 457
4.4.1 Criminal Code, ss.163-169 457
4.4.2 Law Reform Commission of Canada, *Limits of Criminal Law; Obscenity: A Test Case, Working Paper 10* (Ottawa: Information Canada, 1975), pp. 39-49 461

4.4.3 Ian A. Hunter, "Obscenity, Pornography and Law Reform", (1975) 2 *Dalhousie Law Journal*, pp. 482-483, 498 466
4.4.4 Bill C-239, An Act to Amend the Criminal Code. First Reading, 31 October 1977 470
4.4.5 Standing Committee on Justice and Legal Affairs, "The Third Report to the House (Report on Pornography)", March 22, 1978, pp. 7-10 471
4.4.6 Bill C-19, An Act to Amend the Criminal Code, ss.159(8), 163.1 473
4.4.7 Canada, Special Committee on Pornography and Prostitution, *Report* (1985) (Fraser Report) 473
4.4.8 Bill C-114, An Act to Amend the Criminal Code, s.138, 1986 479
4.4.9 Bill C-54, An Act to Amend the Criminal Code, ss.1 and 2, 1987 479
4.4.10 *Brodie* v. *The Queen,* [1962] S.C.R. 681 482
4.4.11 *R.* v. *Red Hot Video Ltd.* (1985), 45 C.R. (3d) 36 (B.C.C.A.) 493
4.4.12 S. Noonan, "Annotation to *R.* v. *Wagner*", (1985) 43 C.R. (3d) 318-320 503
4.4.13 *Towne Cinema Theatres Ltd.* v. *R.* (1985), 45 C.R. (3d) 1 (S.C.C.) 504
4.4.14 *Popert et al.* v. *R.* (1981), 19 C.R. (3d) 393 (Ont. C.A.) 523
4.4.15 Canada Post Corporation Act, R.S.C. 1985, c.O-5, s.43 526
4.4.16 *Luscher* v. *Deputy Minister, Revenue Canada, Customs and Excise* (1985), 45 C.R. (3d) 81 (F.C.A.) 526
4.4.17 Customs Tariff, R.S.C. 1970, c.C-41 as am. 1984-85, c.12, ss.1 and 2 529
4.4.18 Broadcasting Act, Radio Broadcasting Regulations, C.R.C. 1970, c.379, r.5(1) as am. SOR/84-786 529
4.4.19 A Note on Film Censorship Laws in Canada 530

Chapter Five: Legal Limitations Arising From Private Rights 539

5.1 A Note on the Law, Reputation and Privacy 539

5.2 Defamation 540
5.2.1 Anne Skarsgard, "Freedom of the Press", (1980-81) 45 *Saskatchewan Law Review* pp. 296-99 540
5.2.2 The Plaintiff's Case 543
5.2.2.1 *Brannigan* v. *S.I.U.*, (1964), 42 D.L.R. (2d) 249 (B.C.S.C.) 543
5.2.2.2 *Thomas* v. *CBC* [1981] 4 W.W.R. 289 (N.W.T.S.C.) 545
5.2.2.3 *Murphy* v. *LaMarsh* (1970), 73 W.W.R. 114 (B.C.S.C.) 552
5.2.2.4 *Vogel* v. *CBC* (1982), 21 C.C.L.T. 105 556
5.2.2.5 *E. Hulton and Co.* v. *Jones,* [1910] A.C. 22 (H.L.) 557
5.2.2.6 *Booth et al.* v. *BCTV* (1983), 139 D.L.R. (3d) 88 (B.C.C.A.) 560
5.2.2.7 *Planned Parenthood Federation* v. *Fedorik* (1982), 135 D.L.R. (3d) 714, at 718 (Nfld. Sup. Ct., Trial Div.) 565

5.2.2.8 *Whitaker* v. *Huntington* (1981), 15 C.C.L.T. 19, at 21-22 (B.C.S.C.) 565
5.2.2.9 *Stark* v. *Toronto Sun* (1983), 42 O.R. (2d) 791, at 794-5 566
5.2.2.10 The Defamation Act, Manitoba R.S.M. 1970, c.60, s.19 567
5.2.2.11 An Act to Amend the Defamation Act S.M. 1980, c.30, ss.2,7 568
5.2.2.12 Ontario Libel and Slander Act, R.S.O. 1980, c.237, ss.1,2 568
5.2.2.13 *Basse* v. *Toronto Star Newspapers Ltd. et al.* (1984), 37 C.P.C. 213, at 216-17 (Ontario H.C.) 570
5.2.2.14 *Farrell* v. *St. John's Publishing Co.* (1986), 58 Nfld. & P.E.I.R. 66 (Nfld. C.A.) 571

5.2.3 The Defendant's Case 572
5.2.3.1 Anne Skarsgard, "Freedom of the Press", pp. 302-03 572

5.2.3.1.1 Justification 573
5.2.3.1.1.1 *Brannigan* v. *S.I.U.* (1964), 42 D.L.R. (2d) 249 (B.C.S.C.) 573
5.2.3.1.1.2 *Baxter* v. *CBC* (1974), 30 N.B.R. (2d) 102, at 113-118 (C.A.) 575
5.2.3.1.1.3 *Munro* v. *Toronto Sun* (1982), 21 C.C.L.T. 261, at 292-4 (Ont. H.C.) 578
5.2.3.1.1.4 *Gordon* v. *Caswell* (1984), 33 Sask. R. 202 (Q.B.) 579
5.2.3.1.1.5 Ontario Libel and Slander Act, R.S.O. 1980, c.237, s.23 580
5.2.3.1.1.6 A Note on the Law in Nova Scotia 580

5.2.3.1.2 Fair Comment 581
5.2.3.1.2.1 Alexander Stark, *Dangerous Words* (Toronto, Ryerson Institute of Technology 1985), p. 15 581
5.2.3.1.2.2 *Pearlman* v. *CBC* (1982), Man. L.R. (2d) 1, at 21 (Q.B.) 581
5.2.3.1.2.3 Anne Skarsgard, "Freedom of the Press", pp. 307-16 581
5.2.3.1.2.4 *Vander Zalm* v. *Times Publishers* (1980), 18 B.C.L.R. 210 (C.A.) 590
5.2.3.1.2.5 *Farrell* v. *St. John's Publishing Co.* (1986) 58 Nfld. & P.E.I.R. 66 (Nfld. C.A.) 597
5.2.3.1.2.6 *Pound* v. *Scott* [1973], 4 W.W.R. 403 (B.C.S.C.) 598
5.2.3.1.2.7 *Mack* v. *North Hill News Ltd.* (1964), 44 D.L.R. (2d) 147 (Alta. S.C.) 604
5.2.3.1.2.8 Ontario Libel and Slander Act, R.S.O. 1980, c.237, s.24 605
5.2.3.1.2.9 *Cherneskey* v. *Armadale Publishers* (1979), 90 D.L.R. (3d) 321 (S.C.C.) 605
5.2.3.1.2.10 Robert Martin, "Libel and Letters to the Editor", (1983) *Queen's Law Journal* 188 616
5.2.3.1.2.11 *Masters* v. *Fox* (1978), 85 D.L.R. (3d) 64 (B.C. S.C.) 621

5.2.3.1.2.12 *Vogel* v. *CBC* (1982), 21 C.C.L.T. 105, at 165 .. 629
5.2.3.1.3 Privilege 629
5.2.3.1.3.1 *Shultz* v. *Porter and Block Bros. Ltd.* (1979), 9 A.R. 381 (S.C.) 629
5.2.3.1.3.2 Absolute Privilege 631
5.2.3.1.3.2.1 Ontario Libel and Slander Act, R.S.O. 1980, c.237, s.4 631
5.2.3.1.3.2.2 Notes on Other Provincial Statutes 631
5.2.3.1.3.2.3 *Tedlie* v. *Southam,* [1950] 4 D.L.R. 415 (Man. K.B.) 632
5.2.3.1.3.3 Qualified Privilege 638
5.2.3.1.3.3.1 Anne Skarsgard, "Freedom of the Press", pp. 303-7 638
5.2.3.1.3.3.2 Ontario Libel and Slander Act, R.S.O. 1980, c.237, s.3; and Notes on Statues in Other Provinces 641
5.2.3.1.3.3.3 *Cook* v. *Alexander and Others,* [1973] 3 All E.R. 1037 (Eng. C.A.) 644
5.2.3.1.3.3.4 *Hefferman* v. *Regina Daily Star* [1930] 3 W.W.R. 656 (Sask. K.B.) 650
5.2.3.1.3.3.5 *Banks* v. *Globe and Mail* (1961), 28 D.L.R. (2d) 343 (S.C.C.) 653
5.2.3.1.3.3.6 *Stopforth* v. *Goyer* (1978), 4 C.C.L.T. 265 (Ont. H.C.) 660
5.2.3.1.3.3.7 *Stopforth* v. *Goyer* (1979), 23 O.R. (2d) 696 (C.A.) 667
5.2.3.1.3.3.8 *Parlett* v. *Robinson* (1986), 30 D.L.R. (4th) 247 (B.C.C.A.) 668
5.2.3.1.3.3.9 *Camporese* v. *Parton* (1983), 150 D.L.R. (3d) 208 (B.C. S.C.) 674
5.2.3.1.3.3.10 *Shultz* v. *Porter and Block Brothers* (1979), 9 A.R. 381 (S.C.) 680
5.2.3.1.3.3.11 *Farrell* v. *St. John's Publishing Co.* (1986), 58 Nfld. & P.E.I.R. 66 (Nfld. C.A.) 682
5.2.3.1.3.3.12 *Vogel* v. *CBC* (1982), 21 C.C.L.T. 105, at 132,133 and 193 685
5.2.3.1.4 Consent 686
5.2.3.1.4.1 *Syms* v. *Warren* (1976), 71 D.L.R. (3d) 558 (Man. Q.B.) 686
5.2.4 Remedies 690
5.2.4.1 Damages 690
5.2.4.1.1 *Munro* v. *Toronto Sun* (1982), 21 C.C.L.T. 261, at 294 690
5.2.4.1.2 *Walker and Walker Brothers Quarries Ltd.* v. *CFTO Limited et al.* (1987), 19 O.A.C. 10 at 16 (Ont. C.A.) 690
5.2.4.1.3 *Farrell* v. *St. John's Publishing Co.* (1986) 58 Nfld. & P.E.I.R. 66 (Nfld. C.A.) 692
5.2.4.1.4 Julian Porter, Q.C., "Tangents" *Canadian Lawyer,* April 1981, p. 24 693

5.2.4.1.5 Factors Related to the Plaintiff 694
5.2.4.1.5.1 *Barltrop* v. *CBC* (1978) 25 N.S.R. (2d) 637 (C.A.) 694
5.2.4.1.5.2 *Leonhard* v. *Sun Publishing* (1956), 4 D.L.R. (2d) 514 (B.C.S.C.) 698
5.2.4.1.5.3 *Walker and Walker Brothers Quarries Ltd.* v. *CFTO Limited et al.* (1987), 19 O.A.C. 10 at 16 (Ont. C.A.) 701
5.2.4.1.6 Factors Related to the Defendant 701
5.2.4.1.6.1 *Vogel* v. *CBC* (1982), 21 C.C.L.T. 105, at 198 .. 701
5.2.4.1.6.2 *Baxter* v. *CBC* (1980), 30 N.B.R. (2d) 102, at 121-2 702
5.2.4.1.6.3 *Munro* v. *Toronto Sun* (1982), 21 C.C.L.T. 261, at 306 702
5.2.4.1.6.4 *Vogel* v. *CBC* (1982), 21 C.C.L.T. 105, at 202-9 703
5.2.4.1.6.5 *Walker and Walker Brothers Quarries Ltd.* v. *CFTO Limited et al.* (1987), 19 O.A.C. 10 at 16 (Ont. C.A.) 707
5.2.4.1.6.6 *Gerald M. Snyder* v. *Montreal Gazette Ltd.* (1988), Supreme Court of Canada (unreported) 708
5.2.4.1.6.7 Ontario Libel and Slander Act, R.S.O. 1980, c.237, ss.5(2), 5(3), 8,9,19 and 22 as am. 1984, c.11, s.191(2) 712
5.2.4.1.6.8 Notes on Statutes in Other Provinces 713
5.2.4.1.6.9 *Hoste* v. *Victoria Times Publishing Co.* (1889), 1 B.C.R. (Pt.2) 365 716
5.2.4.1.6.10 *Brannigan* v. *S.I.U.* (1964), 42 D.L.R. (2d) 249 (B.C.S.C.) 717
5.2.4.1.6.11 John G. Fleming, "Retraction and Reply: Alternative Remedies for Defamation", (1978) 12 *U.B.C. Law Review* 15 718
5.2.4.1.7 Notes on Damages: Appendix to *Snyder* v. *Montreal Gazette Ltd.* (1978), 87 D.L.R. (3d) 5 (Quebec Superior Court) 723
5.2.4.2 Injunctions 728
5.2.4.2.1 *Canada Metal Co. Ltd.* v. *CBC* (1974), 44 D.L.R. (3d) 329 (Ont. H.C.) 728
5.2.4.2.2 Robert Martin, "Interlocutory Injunctions in Libel Actions", (1982) 20 *U.W.O. Law Review* 129 733
5.2.5 Procedural Questions 738
5.2.5.1 Ontario Libel and Slander Act, R.S.O. 1980, c.237, s.51 ... 738
5.2.5.2 Notes on Procedures in Other Provinces 738
5.2.5.3 *Grossman* v. *CFTO* (1983), 139 D.L.R. (3d) 618, at 625-6 (Ont. C.A.) 739
5.2.5.4 Crown Liability Act, R.S.C. 1985, c.C-50, s.23 740
5.2.5.5 Ontario Libel and Slander Act, R.S.O. 1980, c.237, ss.6, 7 and 8 740
5.2.5.6 Notes on Statutes in Other Provinces 741
5.2.5.7 Ontario Legal Aid Act, R.S.O. 1980, c.234, s.15 742

5.2.5.8 Notes on the Use of Juries in Civil Proceedings in the Common Law Provinces 742
5.2.5.9 Ontario Libel and Slander Act, R.S.O. 1980, c.237, s.15; Notes on Other Provinces 745
5.2.5.10 *McLoughlin* v. *Kutasy* (1979), 26 N.R. 242 (S.C.C.) 745
5.2.5.11 *Burnett* v. *CBC (No. 2)* (1981), 48 N.S.R. (2d) 181, at 196-7 (S.C. Trial Div.) 746
5.2.5.12 Crown Liability Act, R.S.C. 1985, c.C-50, s.26 747
5.2.5.13 Ontario Libel and Slander Act, R.S.O. 1980, c.237, s.16 747
5.2.5.14 Notes on Libel Insurance 747
5.2.5.15 Ontario Supreme and District Court Practice, Rule 49 748
5.2.5.16 Ontario Libel and Slander Act, R.S.O. 1980, c.237, ss.12-14 751
5.2.5.17 Notes on Statutes in Other Provinces 752

5.2.6 General Questions 753
5.2.6.1 Robert Martin, "Libel and Class", (1983) 9 *Canadian Journal of Communication* 1 .... ???
5.2.6.2 Robert Martin, "Does Libel Have a 'Chilling Effect' in Canada?" 757

5.3 The Right to Privacy 771

5.3.1 The Charter 771
5.3.1.1 Section 7, The Canadian Charter of Rights and Freedoms 771
5.3.1.2 *R.* v. *Nicolucci and Papier* (1985) 22 C.C.C. (3d) 207 (Que. S.C.) 771

5.3.2 Privacy at Common Law 771
5.3.2.1 *Robbins* v. *CBC* (1957), 12 D.L.R. (2d) 35 (Que. S.C.) 771
5.3.2.2 *Krouse* v. *Chrysler Canada,* (1973), 1 O.R. (2d) 225 (Ont. C.A.) 778
5.3.2.3 *Burnett* v. *The Queen in Right of Canada* (1979), 23 O.R. (2d) 109 (Ont. H.C.) 779
5.3.2.4 *Motherwell* v. *Motherwell* (1976), 73 D.L.R. (3d) 62 (Alta. S.C.) 780
5.3.2.5 *Capan* v. *Capan* (1981), 14 C.C.L.T. 191 (Ont. H.C.) 792
5.3.2.6 *Saccone* v. *Orr* (1982), 19 C.C.L.T. 37 (Ont. Co. Ct.) 796
5.3.2.7 Annotation to *Saccone* v. *Orr* 800
5.3.2.8 Notes on Photography and Rights of Privacy 802

5.3.3 Privacy Statutes 807
5.3.3.1 Notes on Provincial Privacy Acts 807
5.3.3.2 Privacy Act, R.S.C. 1985, c.P-21 809
5.3.3.3 *Silber and Value Industries Ltd.* v. *British Columbia Television Broadcasting System Ltd., Hick and Chu* [1986] 2 W.W.R. 609 (B.C. S.C.) 817

PREFACE

The study of law has been recognized for centuries as a basic intellectual discipline in European universities. However, only in recent years has it become a feature of undergraduate programs in English-Canadian universities. Traditionally, legal learning has been viewed in such institutions as the special preserve of lawyers, rather than a necessary part of the intellectual equipment of an educated person. Happily, the older and more continental view of legal education is establishing itself in a number of Canadian universities and some have even begun to offer undergraduate degrees in law.

If the study of law is beginning to establish itself as part and parcel of a general education, its aims and methods should appeal directly to journalism educators. Law is a discipline which encourages responsible judgment. On the one hand, it provides opportunities to analyze such ideas as justice, democracy and freedom. On the other, it links these concepts to everyday realities in a manner which is parallel to the links journalists forge on a daily basis as they cover and comment on the news. For example, notions of evidence and fact, of basic rights and public interest are at work in the process of journalistic judgment and production just as in courts of law. Sharpening judgment by absorbing and reflecting on law is a desirable component of a journalist's intellectual preparation for his or her career.

But the idea that the journalist must understand the law more profoundly than an ordinary citizen turns on an understanding of the established conventions and special responsibilities of the news media. Politics or, more broadly, the functioning of the state, is a major subject for journalists. The better informed they are about the way the state works, the better their reporting will be. In fact, it is difficult to see how journalists who do not have a clear grasp of the basic features of the Canadian Constitution can do a competent job on political stories.

Furthermore, the legal system and the events which occur within it are primary subjects for journalists. While the quality of legal journalism varies greatly, there is an undue reliance amongst many journalists on interpretations supplied to them by lawyers. While comment and reaction from lawyers may enhance stories, it is preferable for journalists to rely on their own notions of significance and make their own judgments. These can only come from a well-grounded understanding of the legal system.

Finally, the study of law requires an understanding of freedom of expression. The law is full of traps for the unwary. Neither being prosecuted for contempt of court nor getting sued for defamation is attractive. Some reporters end up in trouble. However, what seems to happen most often is that the fear of unpleasant legal consequences results in stories never being broadcast or published. The trepidation of the reporter or editor or publisher is generally reinforced by the caution of the lawyer.

The study of law cannot be viewed as providing the reporter with the skills necessary to be a legal advisor. But it should be possible to equip the reporter with sufficient legal knowledge to enable him or her to exploit the possibilities which the law provides. In this fashion, the working journalist comes to possess the tools necessary to ensure the most ample freedom of expression.

This book is devoted primarily to the latter task although, as will be seen, the method of presentation reflects a dedication to the broader intellectual goals of legal education.

Our primary aim is to equip journalists with the technical knowledge to recognize and interpret the laws that affect their work. This sourcebook contains an inventory of the statutes and case law which circumscribe journalistic practice. Official Secrets, contempt, criminal and civil libel, obscenity, racism and privacy are some of the subjects described and discussed in what follows. However, in addition to equipping apprentice journalists with an understanding of rules and warning signs, we have other goals in mind. We have sought to use the necessity that journalism students master specific legal rules as an opportunity to explore law as an organized system of judgment and intellectual discrimination. In other words, the method of presentation reflects an ambition to elevate the study of law beyond the memorizing of statutory rules to a level of intellectual exploration which reflects the general aims of university legal education.

Finally, we have sought to show how freedom of expression is incorporated into the Canadian legal system. This has been achieved through the book's structure. We have organized the materials in a manner which shows how the Canadian legal tradition has absorbed and expressed the ideas of freedom of expression, press and media.

Accordingly, Chapter One explores the Canadian Constitution and features cases involving freedom of speech and the press from before and after the adoption of the Canadian Charter of Rights and Freedoms in 1982. The chapter concludes with an exploration of the Canadian theory of freedom of expression.

Chapters two to five explore the legal limitations, sanctioned by Section 1 of the Charter, on freedom of expression. Section 2(b) declares that freedom of expression, press and the media are fundamental freedoms that Canadians possess. Section 1 says that these fundamental freedoms may be subject to reasonable limitations prescribed by law which can be demonstrably justified in a free and democratic society. Such limitations on free expression may be grouped into three broad categories. Chapter Two is concerned with the limitations which protect the state's rights, obligations and prerogatives such as the obligation to maintain secrets and public order. Chapter Three, which represents a continuation of the same theme, looks at the limitations protecting the judicial system. Chapter Four is concerned with legal limitations intended to protect certain social values. Thus, the law prohibits forms of obscenity and seeks to protect minority groups against racist attacks. Chapter Five is concerned with limitations intended to protect individuals against attacks on their reputations. The law of civil defamation is its principal subject.

Media law embraces elements from criminal, civil and even administrative law. It is complex and extraordinarily rich. However, what makes it especially important is that its study reveals both the character and limitations of Canadian democracy.

Robert Martin
Professor of Law and Journalism

G. Stuart Adam
Professor of Journalism
Chair, Centre for Mass Media Studies

The University of Western Ontario

September, 1988

ACKNOWLEDGEMENTS

The authors would like to acknowledge the assistance of a number of former law students at the University of Western Ontario who have contributed their work to this sourcebook. They are: Shelley Appleby-Ostroff, Karen Douglas, Nathan Golas, D. James Newland, Lynda Rogers and Michael Rumball.

Special thanks are due to Kathryn Hazel, journalist and research assistant in the Centre for Mass Media Studies, for her editorial assistance and Gordon Mogenson, Dean of the Faculty of Graduate Studies at Western, for providing financial support at a critical stage in the preparation of the manuscript. Particular thanks go to Kay Adair of the Law Faculty at Western. She has typed and re-typed portions of this sourcebook since 1976.

Thanks are also due to Pauline Adams of Carleton University Press who patiently supervised the final editing and production of the text.

The project was also supported by funds provided by the Centre for Mass Media Studies in the Graduate School of Journalism at the University of Western Ontario.

As well the authors gratefully acknowledge and thank:

The editors of Butterworths Legal, Professional and Academic Publishers, and Mr. Patrick Boyer for permission to reproduce pp. 308-309 of *Political Rights: The Legal Framework of Elections in Canada*, by Patrick Boyer (Toronto: 1981); and the editors of Butterworths for permission to reproduce p. 25 and pp. 287-292 of *Courts and the Media*, by Stuart Robertson (Toronto: 1981);

The Canadian Daily Newspaper Publishers Association for permission to reproduce "What Newrooms Need to Know", CDNPA (Toronto: 1984);

The editor of *The Canadian Journal of Law and Jurisprudence* for permission to reproduce an excerpt from "Corporate Political Activity", by Ronald Atkey which appeared in (1985) 23 *The University of Western Ontario Law Review*, 129, the Journal's predecessor;

The publisher of *Canadian Lawyer* for permission to reproduce an excerpt from "Tangents" by Julian Porter, *Canadian Lawyer*, April 1981, p. 24;

The editor of Carleton University Press for permission to reproduce pp. 32-39 of *The Law and the Press in Canada*, by Wilfred H. Kesterton, (Toronto: McClelland and Stewart in association with the Institute of Canadian Studies, Carleton University, 1976);

The editors of Carswell Legal Publications and Peter W. Hogg for permission to reproduce "Notes on the Implied Bill of Rights" from Prof. Hogg's *The Constitutional Law of Canada* (Toronto: 1977); the editors of Carswell Legal Publications and Prof. H.R.S. Ryan for permission to reproduce an excerpt of "The Trial of Zundel, Freedom of Expression and Criminal Law'', *C.R.* (3d) (1985); the editors of Carswell Legal Publications for permission to reproduce excerpts from annotation to *Saccone* v. *Orr* (1982) 19 C.C.L.T. by John Irvine, annotation to *R.* v. *Wagner* (1985), 43 *C.R.* (3d) 318 by S. Noonan, and annotation to *Luscher* v. *Deputy Minister, Revenue Canada, Customs and Excise* (1985), 45 *C.R.* (3d) 81 by Don Stuart;

The executive director of The Centre for Investigative Journalism and John Sawatsky for permission to reprint ''John Sawatsky Stakes out the High Ground'' in the *Bulletin* of the Centre for Investigative Journalism, 11, 1986;

The Editor of *Content for Canadian Journalists* and Mr. Harold Levy for permission to reproduce ''What Should We Do When the Cops Arrive?'' (1979) *Content* 95;

The Minister of Supply and Services Canada for permission to reproduce ''Freedom of the Press'' by Walter Tarnopolsky in *Newspapers and the Law* 1981, ix, 19-21;

The Law Reform Commission of Canada for permission to reprint excerpts from Working Paper #49, *Crimes Against the State* (1986), p. 30, pp. 33-36; Working Paper #56, *Public and Media Access to the Criminal Process*, (1986), pp. 89-91; Working Paper #50, *Hate Propaganda*, (1986), pp. 39-41; and Working Paper #10, *Limits of Criminal Law: Obscenity, a Test Case* (1975), pp. 39-49.

The chairman of the Ryerson School of Journalism for permission to reprint an excerpt from Alexander Stark's *Dangerous Words*;

The editor of the Saskatchewan Law Review and Ann Skarsgard for permission to reproduce excerpts from ''Freedom of the Press, (1980-81) *Sask. L. R.*, pp. 296-99, 302, 307-16.

The editor of the *University of British Columbia Law Review* and John G. Fleming for permission to reproduce ''Retraction and Reply: Alternative Remedies for Defamation,'' (1978) 12 *U.B.C.L. Rev.* 15.

The editor of *Lawyers Weekly* for permission to reproduce an excerpt from ''No Cameras in Court'', by Patricia Chisolm, *Ontario Lawyers Weekly*, 20 January 1984;

The publisher of Pergamon Press for permission to reproduce excerpts from ''Freedom of Information in Canada'', by John McCamus in *Government Publications Review*, 1983, vol. 10;

Prof. Ian Hunter for permission to reprint excerpts from ''Obscenity, Pornography and Law Reform'', (1975), 2 *Dalhousie Law Journal*.

CHAPTER ONE

Freedom of Expression and the Canadian Constitution

1.1 A Note on the Meaning of Freedom of Expression

John Milton asked in his pamphlet *Areopagitica,* published in England in 1644, for "the liberty to know, to utter and to argue freely, according to conscience, above all liberties".[1] Freedom of expression continues to be directed towards these goals. The democratic tradition recognizes the right to know, to speak and to express opinions without first seeking the permission of authorities and without the risk that the law will be used to forbid or punish the exercise of the right. The understanding is that free expression is so fundamental to democratic societies that it can be limited only for clear and pressing reasons. There cannot be democracy if the right to criticize is not secure; nor can there be democracy if governments possess the power to define the meaning of events and values. Accordingly, the notion of freedom of expression in liberal democracies includes the belief that the state has no right to abrogate this fundamental freedom.

The constitutions of the United States, Canada and Great Britain reflect in different ways these beliefs. The constitution of the United States includes the First Amendment which says that Congress may not pass a law "abridging the freedom of speech, or of the press". Section 2(b) of the Canadian Charter of Rights and Freedoms declares that "freedom of thought, belief, opinion and expression, including freedom of the press and other media of communication" is a fundamental freedom. Both Canada and the United States have established rights in their constitutions which are protected by the courts. By contrast, the largely unwritten British constitution posits liberties or conventions protected by Parliament. The British Parliament has traditionally recognized liberties, including liberty of the press.

The distinction between the right to know, on the one hand, and the rights to utter and express opinions on the other may be blurred. But it can be usefully maintained in order to consider the work of journalists. People who make their living as reporters are exercising the right to know. They are exercising the right to know what goes on in Parliament, or in the courts, or in public institutions generally on behalf of a public which is distant from the centres of political and public action. Although the journalist may be actively exercising the right to know, his or her rights are the same as those of the ordinary citizen. The knowledge communicated by the journalist is one element in forming the political consciousness of citizens.

The right to know — that is, the right to gather information — is one thing; the rights to pass it on and express opinions about it are another. There have been occasions in, for example, the United States where individuals have been silenced by political pressure or by law itself. The blacklisted Hollywood producers and writers in the period during which Senator Joseph McCarthy was at the height of his influence were denied the exercise of both rights.[2] The South African journalist, Donald Woods, who was placed under banning orders when he was the editor of the *East London Dispatch* in 1977 was similarly denied the rights to utter or express opinions. He had published an account of the death of the African nationalist Steven Biko at the hands of the security police.[3] Banning orders silence individuals. They deprive them of the right to utter and there have been many legal instruments developed over the years for such purposes. Banning powers were incorporated into Alberta's Act to Ensure the Publication of Accurate News and Information which was ruled unconstitutional by the Supreme Court of Canada in 1938.[4]

The right to express radical opinions has led to the most dramatic events in the development of the democratic tradition. As late as the early eighteenth century an English printer's apprentice was executed for publishing a document in which it was argued that the Pretender's claim to the throne was legitimate.[5]

Attempts by the state to punish the expression of radical opinions have continued. Section 98 of the old Canadian Criminal Code was used until 1935 to prosecute Communists. The Quebec Padlock Law (An Act to Protect The Province Against Communistic Propaganda) was enacted under the Duplessis government in Quebec in 1937 and enforced for 20 years until the Supreme Court of Canada ruled it unconstitutional in 1957. That act made it an offence to publish and circulate communist opinions.[6]

While there have always been powerful advocates of the notion of freedom of expression — from John Milton to George Orwell who said in his essay, "The Prevention of Literature" that the debate over freedom of the press is a debate about the "desirability of telling lies" — none has attacked the idea of law itself.[7] The early advocates of freedom may have attacked the law of seditious libel, but they would have accepted at the same time a notion that originated with the eighteenth-century British jurist Mansfield who said freedom of the press means freedom "subject to the consequence of the law".[8] In the twentieth century, we would say we ought to be free to speak and publish and broadcast without prior restraint, subject to the laws (or at least some of the laws) with which this book is concerned.

However, the consensus on what social harms should be the concern of the laws has shifted considerably. For example, in the seventeenth and eighteenth centuries when printing and publishing were coming of age, the British government used the law of seditious libel to protect itself from critics in the belief that if the public did not believe that government was good, neither the government nor the institutions of state could survive. To those in power, it was reasonable to limit political speech to safe or, at the most, mildly critical utterances and to punish everything else.

The limitations in the twentieth century on the exercise of the rights to utter, know and argue, must, in the words of the Canadian Constitution, be reasonable. Section 1 of the Canadian Charter says that its guarantees are "subject only to such reasonable limits prescribed by law as can be demonstrably justified in a free and democratic society". Attempts are made to justify the limitations in the laws of civil and criminal libel, or contempt of court, by referring to such harms — for example, the possible loss of reputation arising from libel, or the assumed peril to human lives because of incitements to riot, or the fear that an accused person may be denied a fair trial because of the publication, before the trial, of possibly prejudicial material.

Just as there are several variants of democratic theory, there are several ways in which freedom of expression has been justified. The dominant theory is part and parcel of liberal democratic theory in which the analytic starting point is the individual. The theory puts the individual citizen into the foreground and, in a manner of speaking, subordinates the rights of the state and society to the will or desires and, ultimately, the freedom of the individual. Much of legal theory in the common law jurisdictions is based on the philosophical method and arguments of the British philosophers Jeremy Bentham and James and John Stuart Mill.[9]

But many people are not comfortable with an approach to freedom of expression which takes the individual as its analytical starting point. Other democratic approaches are possible. They include a collectivist or socialist conception in which freedom of expression is viewed as a necessary pre-condition to the realization of important collective values and aims. Such an approach sees freedom of expression not merely as a commodity possessed by individuals, but as an essential pre-condition to the creation and maintenance of democracy itself.

The Canadian tradition has absorbed and confirmed the political and democratic values embedded in both traditions. For example, Chief Justice Lyman Duff said in the Alberta Press Act case that the "right to free public discussion of public affairs ... is the breath of life for parliamentary institutions.[10] In that case, the court did not offer constitutional protection to freedom of expression on the basis of a notion of individual rights. Rather the court was seeking to protect the social institution of parliamentary democracy. It affirmed that parliamentary democracy could not function without free expression.

But there is a broader sense in which freedom of expression may be considered. Democracy is not solely a matter of parliaments and elections. A democratic society must not only permit, but encourage, the widest possible participation of all its members in its economic, social and cultural affairs. The creation of the means and the institutions to make this possible constitutes an obligation affecting society as a whole. Freedom of expression is, once again, essential to these processes.

While individualistic justifications for freedom of expression are the norm in Canadian society, pressing the individualistic approach too far may have a contradictory effect. By focussing on the individual, the notion may develop that freedom of expression has to do largely, or exclusively, with the proprietary rights of the individual owners of newspapers, or radio or television stations.

There is a sense in which this issue commanded the attention of the Kent Royal Commission, which studied Canada's newspaper industry in 1980-81.[11] The commissioners noted, for example, that the right of the editor of the newspaper to express his opinions was subordinated in law to the right of the owners and publishers to hire and fire. It has been noted elsewhere that there are occasions when a journalist's right to free expression may be subordinated to codes of professional conduct and thereby to freedom of the press itself. An example would occur when an employer reprimands a journalist for engaging in political activity such as joining a political party or making partisan speeches. Journalists may denounce the government in newspaper columns, but they may not, according to some employment codes, join and campaign for political parties.[12]

Freedom of expression is, then, an idea which may be considered in more than one way and from differing philosophical starting points. However, regardless of the philosophical underpinnings, it is everywhere seen to be fundamental to the political architecture of a genuine democracy.

Endnotes

1. "Areopagitica: A Speech for the Liberty of Unlicensed Printing to the Parliament of England (1644)" in George Sabine, ed., *John Milton, Areopagitica and of Education with Autobiographical Passages from other Prose Works,* (Chicago, 1985), p. 49.
2. See, for example: Richard H. Rovere, *Senator Joe McCarthy,* (New York, 1959), and Victor S. Navarky, *Naming Names,* (New York, 1980).
3. Donald Woods, *Biko,* (New York, 1978), and *Asking for Trouble: Autobiography of a Banned Journalist,* (London, 1980).
4. The judgment in this reference is reprinted in section 1.3.2.
5. See Laurence William Hanson's *Government and the Press, 1695-1763,* (Oxford, 1967).
6. The judgment of the Supreme Court is reprinted in section 1.3.3.
7. Orwell's essay may be found in *The Complete Works of George Orwell,* (London, 1986), p. 327.
8. T.B. Howell, *A Complete Collection of State Trials,* Vol. XXI, (London, 1813), p. 1040.
9. John Stuart Mill, *On Liberty,* (London, 1974).
10. That decision is reported in full in section 1.3.2 of the text.
11. *Report of the Royal Commission on Newspapers,* (Ottawa, 1981), Vol. 1.
12. See "Political Activity and The Journalist: A Paradox" by Andrew MacFarlane and Robert Martin, *Canadian Journal of Communication,* Vol. 10, No. 2, 1984, pp. 1-35.

1.2 The Structure of the Constitution

The three principal components of the Canadian Constitution are the unwritten conventions and practices inherited from the United Kingdom, the Constitution Act, 1867 or, as it used to be called, The British North America Act, 1867, and the Constitution Act, 1982.

That the inspiration for Canadian political and legal practices is British may be inferred from the utterance in the preamble to the Constitution Act, 1867, that Canada is to have a constitution "similar in principle" to that of the United Kingdom. The statement means that fundamental principles of British democracy such as the supremacy of Parliament, the freedom of the press, and the rule of law protected by an independent judiciary are basic to Canada's Constitution.

However, from the beginning Canada was a federal rather than a unitary state and, accordingly, the Constitution Act, 1867, established principles of federalism by defining the jurisdictional limits within which the Federal Parliament and provincial legislatures could make laws.

The Constitution Act, 1867, served as the principal constitutional document from 1867 until 1982 when a new element was added to the constitutional structure. In that year the U.K. Parliament enacted the Canada Act, 1982. One of its purposes was to give to Canadian institutions the ownership, so to speak, of the Canadian Constitution. Until 1982, the B.N.A. Act had remained an act of Westminster and as a result could only be amended there. The curious legal anomaly of the Parliament of one modern sovereign state acting as the custodian of the constitution of another modern sovereign state was ended when the Canada Act was passed.

The Canada Act also permitted the incorporation into Canada's legal foundations of a set of declarations on the basic rights of Canadian citizens. These declarations are contained in the Canadian Charter of Rights and Freedoms which puts in statutory form values which have long been part of the democratic tradition.

1.3 Judicial Interpretation under the Constitution Act, 1867

The British North America Act defined and gave legal sanction to Canada's political system and institutions. The Senate, the House of Commons, the offices of the Governor General and Lieutenants Governor, the legislatures of the federating provinces and the judiciary were authoritatively described.

Because Canada was to be a federation, the Act divided power between the Federal Parliament and the provincial legislatures. Section 91 of the Act conferred on Parliament a general power to "make Laws for the Peace, Order and good Government of Canada" and enumerated 29 headings under which the Parliament of Canada had "exclusive legislative authority". The headings were extensive and varied. They included such items as trade and commerce, postal services, marriage and divorce, money and banking, and criminal law.

Section 92 conferred on the legislatures the exclusive right to legislate in areas defined by 16 headings including direct taxation, municipal institutions, local works, property and civil rights and, as section 16 said, "Generally, all Matters of a merely local or private Nature in the Province".

The location of the boundary between the two jurisdictional territories may seem obvious from a plain reading of the document. It was carefully drafted. However, the legislative practices and ambitions of both levels of government led to disputes. It became the responsibility of the courts to draw that boundary. Constitutional law in Canada from 1867 until 1982, when the Constitution Act, 1982 was approved, was composed mainly of the record of adjudications by the Supreme Court of Canada and, until 1949, the Judicial Committee of the Privy Council, on the practical ambiguities of the British North America Act.

Until 1949 Canadian appeals could be taken to the Judicial Committee. Historians and constitutional lawyers in Canada have concluded from their studies that that court tilted the balance of power in the direction of the provincial legislatures and away from Parliament. However, as influential as the Judicial Committee once was, the procedures governing judicial review in cases involving sections 91 and 92 were established mainly by the Supreme Court of Canada. Typically, the Court would examine "the pith and substance" or "true intent" of contested legislation and then align it under the appropriate heading within section 91 or 92. If, for example, the legislature of a province passed a bill which appeared to regulate banks (sections 91(15) and (16)) but claimed that it was an appropriate exercise of the power to regulate property or a purely local matter (sections 92(10) and (13)), the Court would examine the bill and decide under which of the headings it properly belonged.

Curiously, the Alberta Press Act case which led to the first and perhaps most influential discussion in the Supreme Court of freedom of the press involved such issues. The Court ruled in 1938 that a bill to regulate part of the contents of Alberta's newspapers was not constitutional or *ultra vires* because it was interpreted to be part and parcel of an attempt by the province to impose a Social Credit economic scheme. The Court concluded that the legislative methods of constructing the scheme led to bills which invaded the jurisdiction of Parliament established in section 91. The Court went on to rule that "ancillary and dependent" legislation such as the Press Act was also unconstitutional.

Put differently, the pathway to the issue of freedom of expression in constitutional law under the B.N.A. Act required a first step around jurisdictional obstacles. The old statute did not provide for a direct and unambiguous legal route, although in the Quebec Padlock Law case, which was heard in the Supreme Court in 1957, the Court had an easier time of it.

The legislature of Quebec passed an Act Respecting Communistic Propaganda in 1937. When a case involving that statute was finally heard in the Supreme Court 20 years later, the Court ruled that the province had disguised its true purpose of making expressions of communist sentiment a crime — section 91(27) granted the right to pass criminal law to Parliament — by claiming a right to regulate the use of buildings under section 92(13) and 92(16). The Government of Quebec had simply padlocked houses and buildings in which left-wing propaganda was being produced and argued that their regulation of such buildings was akin to the regulation of brothels. The Court rejected that claim and located the statute's purpose and application in the federal parliament's jurisdiction. It was, accordingly, *ultra vires* the power of the legislature.

The Alberta Press Act case and the case of the Quebec Padlock Law demonstrate that the Court's power to rule on questions of freedom of expression under the B.N.A. Act was circumscribed. In order to rule on such questions the Court had to deal first with the issue of jurisdiction. The *ratio* — that is, the reason for the decision in both cases — was necessarily based on a conclusion about the location of the boundary dividing the jurisdictions of the levels of government. The expressions from the bench about the importance of freedom of the press were uttered as *dicta* or non-binding observations. Still, the statements by Justices Rand and Duff in the Alberta Press Act and Quebec Padlock Law cases remain highly influential.

Although the Canadian Charter of Rights and Freedoms extends the scope of judicial review to substantive questions involving fundamental freedoms and civil liberties, the question of jurisdiction remains important. If, for example, the terms of a statute limiting freedom of the press were contested, the judges would ask first if the statute were legally enacted. In other words, before addressing questions of value, the Court would ask if Parliament, or a legislature, possessed the power to enact the disputed statute. The terms of the Constitution Act, 1867, remain an important source of constitutional law.

1.3.1 The Constitution Act, 1867

Preamble
Section 91
Section 92

An Act for the Union of Canada, Nova Scotia, and New Brunswick, and the Government thereof; and for Purposes connected therewith.

(29th March, 1867.)

WHEREAS the Provinces of Canada, Nova Scotia and New Brunswick have expressed their Desire to be federally united into One Dominion under the Crown of the United Kingdom of Great Britain and Ireland, with a Constitution similar in Principle to that of the United Kingdom:

And whereas such a Union would conduce to the Welfare of the Provinces and promote the Interests of the British Empire:

And whereas on the Establishment of the Union by Authority of Parliament it is expedient, not only that the Constitution of the Legislative Authority in the Dominion be provided for, but also that the Nature of the Executive Government therein be declared:

And whereas it is expedient that Provision be made for the eventual Admission into the Union of other Parts of British North America:

VI. — DISTRIBUTION OF LEGISLATIVE POWERS

Powers of the Parliament

Legislative Authority of Parliament of Canada

91. It shall be lawful for the Queen, by and with the Advice and Consent of the Senate and House of Commons, to make Laws for the Peace, Order, and good Government of Canada, in relation to all Matters not coming within the Classes of Subjects by this Act assigned exclusively to the Legislatures of the Provinces; and for greater Certainty, but not so as to restrict the Generality of the foregoing Terms of this Section, it is hereby declared that (notwithstanding anything in this Act) the exclusive Legislative Authority of the Parliament of Canada extends to all Matters coming within the Classes of Subjects next hereinafter enumerated; that is to say, —

1. Repealed.

1A. The Public Debt and Property.

2. The Regulation of Trade and Commerce.
2A. Unemployment insurance.
3. The raising of Money by any Mode or System of Taxation.
4. The borrowing of Money on the Public Credit.
5. Postal Service.
6. The Census and Statistics.
7. Militia, Military and Naval Service, and Defence.
8. The fixing of and providing for the Salaries and Allowances of Civil and other Officers of the Government of Canada.
9. Beacons, Buoys, Lighthouses, and Sable Island.
10. Navigation and Shipping.
11. Quarantine and the Establishment and Maintenance of Marine Hospitals.
12. Sea Coast and Inland Fisheries.
13. Ferries between a Province and any British or Foreign Country or between Two Provinces.
14. Currency and Coinage.
15. Banking, Incorporation of Banks, and the Issue of Paper Money.
16. Savings Banks.
17. Weights and Measures.
18. Bills of Exchange and Promissory Notes.
19. Interest.
20. Legal Tender.
21. Bankruptcy and Insolvency.
22. Patents of Invention and Discovery.
23. Copyrights.
24. Indians, and Lands reserved for the Indians.
25. Naturalization and Aliens.
26. Marriage and Divorce.
27. The Criminal Law, except the Constitution of Courts of Criminal Jurisdiction, but including the Procedure in Criminal Matters.
28. The Establishment, Maintenance, and Management of Penitentiaries.
29. Such Classes of Subjects as are expressly excepted in the Enumeration of the Classes of Subjects by this Act assigned exclusively to the Legislatures of the Provinces.

And any Matter coming within any of the Classes of Subjects enumerated in this Section shall not be deemed to come within the Class of Matters of a local or private Nature comprised in the Enumeration of the Classes of Subjects by this Act assigned exclusively to the Legislatures of the Provinces.

Exclusive Powers of Provincial Legislatures

Subjects of exclusive Provincial Legislation

92. In each Province the Legislature may exclusively make Laws in relation to Matters coming within the Classes of Subject next hereinafter enumerated; that is to say, —

1. Repealed.
2. Direct Taxation within the Province in order to the raising of a Revenue for Provincial Purposes.
3. The borrowing of Money on the sole Credit of the Province.
4. The Establishment and Tenure of Provincial Offices and the Appointment and Payment of Provincial Officers.
5. The Management and Sale of the Public Lands belonging to the Province and of the Timber and Wood thereon.
6. The Establishment, Maintenance, and Management of Public and Reformatory Prisons in and for the Province.
7. The Establishment, Maintenance, and Management of Hospitals, Asylums, Charities, and Eleemosynary Institutions in and for the Province, other than Marine Hospitals.
8. Municipal Institutions in the Province.
9. Shop, Saloon, Tavern, Auctioneer, and other Licences in order to the raising of a Revenue for Provincial, Local, or Municipal Purposes.
10. Local Works and Undertakings other than such as are of the following Classes: —
    (*a*) Lines of Steam or other Ships, Railways, Canals, Telegraphs, and other Works and Undertakings connecting the Province with any other or others of the Provinces, or extending beyond the Limits of the Province;
    (*b*) Lines of Steam Ships between the Province and any British or Foreign Country;
    (*c*) Such Works as, although wholly situate within the Province, are before or after their Execution declared by the Parliament of Canada to be for the general Advantage of Canada or for the Advantage of Two or more of the Provinces.
11. The Incorporation of Companies with Provincial Objects.
12. The Solemnization of Marriage in the Province.
13. Property and Civil Rights in the Province.
14. The Administration of Justice in the Province, including the Constitution, Maintenance, and Organization of Provincial Courts, both of Civil and of Criminal Jurisdiction, and including Procedure in Civil Matters in those Courts.
15. The Imposition of Punishment by Fine, Penalty, or Imprisonment for enforcing any Law of the Province made in relation to any Matter coming within any of the Classes of Subjects enumerated in this Section.
16. Generally all Matters of a merely local or private Nature in the Province.

Non-Renewable Natural Resources, Forestry Resources and Electrical Energy

Laws respecting non-renewable natural

92A. (1) In each province, the legislature may exclusively make laws in relation to resources, forestry resources and electrical energy

(*a*) exploration for non-renewable natural resources in the province;

(*b*) development, conservation and management of non-renewable natural resources and forestry resources in the province, including laws in relation to the rate of primary production therefrom; and

(*c*) development, conservation and management of sites and facilities in the province for the generation and production of electrical energy.

Export from provinces of resources

(2) In each province, the legislature may make laws in relation to the export from the province to another part of Canada of the primary production from non-renewable natural resources and forestry resources in the province and the production from facilities in the province for the generation of electrical energy, but such laws may not authorize or provide for discrimination in prices or in supplies exported to another part of Canada.

Authority of Parliament

(3) Nothing in subsection (2) derogates from the authority of Parliament to enact laws in relation to the matters referred to in that subsection and, where such a law of Parliament and a law of a province conflict, the law of Parliament prevails to the extent of the conflict.

Taxation of resources

(4) In each province, the legislature may make laws in relation to the raising of money by any mode or system of taxation in respect of

(*a*) non-renewable natural resources and forestry resources in the province and the primary production therefrom, and

(*b*) sites and facilities in the province for the generation of electrical energy and the production therefrom,

whether or not such production is exported in whole or in part from the province, but such laws may not authorize or provide for taxation that differentiates between production exported to another part of Canada and production not exported from the province.

"Primary production"

(5) The expression "primary production" has the meaning assigned by the Sixth Schedule.

Existing powers or rights

(6) Nothing in subsections (1) to (5) derogates from any powers or rights that a legislature or government of a province had immediately before the coming into force of this section.

Education

Legislation respecting Education

93. In and for each Province the Legislature may exclusively make Laws in relation to Education, subject and according to the following Provisions: —

(1) Nothing in any such Law shall prejudicially affect any Right or Privilege with respect to Denominational Schools which any Class of Persons have by Law in the Province at the Union:

(2) All the Powers, Privileges, and Duties at the Union by Law conferred and imposed in Upper Canada on the Separate Schools and School Trustees of the Queen's Roman Catholic

Subjects shall be and the same are hereby extended to the Dissentient Schools of the Queen's Protestant and Roman Catholic Subjects in Quebec:

(3) Where in any Province a System of Separate or Dissentient Schools exists by Law at the Union or is thereafter established by the Legislature of the Province, an Appeal shall lie to the Governor General in Council from any Act or Decision of any Provincial Authority affecting any Right or Privilege of the Protestant or Roman Catholic Minority of the Queen's Subjects in relation to Education:

(4) In case any such Provincial Law as from Time to Time seems to the Governor General in Council requisite for the due Execution of the Provisions of this Section is not made, or in case any Decision of the Governor General in Council on any Appeal under this Section is not duly executed by the proper Provincial Authority in that Behalf, then and in every such Case, and as far only as the Circumstances of each Case require, the Parliament of Canada may make remedial Laws for the due Execution of the Provisions of this Section and of any Decision of the Governor General in Council under this Section.

Use of English and French Languages

133. Either the English or the French Language may be used by any Person in the Debates of the Houses of the Parliament of Canada and of the Houses of the Legislature of Quebec; and both those Languages shall be used in the respective Records and Journals of those Houses; and either of those Languages may be used by any Person or in any Pleading or Process in or issuing from any Court of Canada established under this Act, and in or from all or any of the Courts of Quebec.

The Acts of the Parliament of Canada and of the Legislature of Quebec shall be printed and published in both those Languages.

1.3.2 *Re Alberta Legislation* [1938] 2 D.L.R. 81 (S.C.C.)

SIR LYMAN P. DUFF, C.J.C.: — The three Bills referred to us are part of a general scheme of legislation and in order to ascertain the object and effect of them it is proper to look at the history of the legislation passed in furtherance of the general design.

It is no part of our duty (it is, perhaps, needless to say) to consider the wisdom of these measures. We have only to ascertain whether or not they come within the ambit of the authority entrusted by the constitutional statutes (the *British North America Act* and the *Alberta Act*) to the Legislature of Alberta and our responsibility is rigorously confined to the determination of that issue. As Judges, we do not and cannot intimate any opinion upon the merits of the legislative proposals embodied in them, as to their practicability or in any other respect. ...

We now turn to Bill No. 9.

This Bill contains two substantive provisions. Both of them impose duties upon newspapers published in Alberta which they are required to perform on the demand of "the Chairman," who is, by the interpretation clause, the Chairman of "the Board constituted by s. 3 of the *Alberta Social Credit Act*."

The Board, upon the acts of whose Chairman the operation of this statute depends, is, in point of law, a non-existent body (there is, in a word, no "board" in existence "constituted by section 3 of the *Alberta Social Credit Act*") and both of the substantive sections, ss.3 and 4, are, therefore, inoperative. The same, indeed, may be said of ss.6 and 7 which are the enactments creating sanctions. It appears to us, furthermore, that this Bill is a part of the general scheme of Social Credit legislation, the basis of which is the *Alberta Social Credit Act;* the Bill presupposes, as a condition of its operation, that the *Alberta Social Credit Act* is validly enacted; and, since that Act is *ultra vires,* the ancillary and dependent legislation must fall with it.

This is sufficient for disposing of the question referred to us but, we think, there are some further observations upon the Bill which may properly be made.

Under the constitution established by the *B.N.A. Act,* legislative power for Canada is vested in one Parliament consisting of the Sovereign, an upper house styled the Senate, and the House of Commons. Without entering in detail upon an examination of the enactments of the Act relating to the House of Commons, it can be said that these provisions manifestly contemplate a House of Commons which is to be, as the name itself implies, a representative body; constituted, that is to say, by members elected by such of the population of the united Provinces as may be qualified to vote. The preamble of the statute, moreover, shows plainly enough that the constitution of the Dominion is to be similar in principle to that of the United Kingdom. The statute contemplates a Parliament working under the influence of public opinion and public discussion. There can be no controversy that such institutions derive their efficacy from the free public discussion of affairs, from criticism and answer and counter-criticism, from attack upon policy and administration and defence and counter-attack; from the freest and fullest analysis and examination from every point of view of political proposals. This is signally true in respect of the discharge by Ministers of the Crown of their responsibility to Parliament, by members of Parliament of their duty to the electors and by the electors themselves of their responsibilities in the election of their representatives.

The right of public discussion is, of course, subject to legal restrictions; those based upon considerations of decency and public order, and others conceived for the protection of various private and public interests with which, for example, the laws of defamation and sedition are concerned. In a word, freedom of discussion means, to quote the words of Lord Wright in *James* v. *Commonwealth of Australia,* [1936] A.C. at p. 627, "freedom governed by law."

Even within its legal limits, it is liable to abuse and grave abuse, and such abuse is constantly exemplified before our eyes; but it is axiomatic that the practice of this right of free public discussion of public affairs, notwithstanding its incidental mischiefs, is the breath of life for parliamentary institutions.

We do not doubt that (in addition to the power of disallowance vested in the Governor General) the Parliament of Canada possesses authority to legislate for the protection of this right. That authority rests upon the principle that the powers requisite for the protection of the constitution itself arise by necessary implication from the B.N.A. Act as a whole (*Fort Frances Pulp & Paper Co.* v. *Manitoba Free Press Co.,* [1923] 3 D.L.R. 629); and since the subject matter in relation to which the power is exercised is not exclusively a provincial matter, it is necessarily vested in Parliament.

But this by no means exhausts the matter. Any attempt to abrogate this right of public debate or to suppress the traditional forms of the exercise of the right (in public meeting and through the press) would, in our opinion, be incompetent to the Legislatures of the Provinces, or to the Legislature of any one of the Provinces, as repugnant to the provisions of the *B.N.A. Act,* by which the Parliament of Canada is established as the legislative organ of the people of Canada under the Crown, and Dominion legislation enacted pursuant to the legislative authority given by those provisions. The subject matter of such legislation could not be described as a provincial matter purely; as in substance exclusively a matter of property and civil rights within the Province, or a matter private or local within the Province. It would not be, to quote the words of the judgment of the Judicial Committee in *Great West Saddlery Co.* v. *The King,* 58 D.L.R., at p. 26, legislation "directed solely to the purposes specified in s.92;" and it would be invalid on the principles enunciated in that judgment and adopted in *Caron* v. *The King,* [1924] 4 D.L.R. 105, at pp. 109-10.

The question, discussed in argument, of the validity of the legislation before us, considered as a wholly independent enactment having no relation to the *Alberta Social Credit Act,* presents no little difficulty. Some degree of regulation of newspapers everybody would concede to the Provinces. Indeed, there is a very wide field in which the Provinces undoubtedly are invested with legislative authority over newspapers; but the limit, in our opinion, is reached when the legislation effects such a curtailment of the exercise of the right of public discussion as substantially to interfere with the working of the parliamentary institutions of Canada as contemplated by the provisions of the *B.N.A. Act* and the statutes of the Dominion of Canada. Such a limitation is necessary, in our opinion, "in order," to adapt the words quoted above from the judgment in *Bank of Toronto* v. *Lambe,* "to afford scope" for the working of such parliamentary institutions. In this region of constitutional practice, it is not permitted to a Provincial Legislature to do indirectly what cannot be done directly *Great West Saddlery Co.* v. *The King,* 58 D.L.R., at p. 6.

Section 129 of the *B.N.A. Act* is in these words: —

"129. Except as otherwise provided by this Act, all Laws in force in Canada, Nova Scotia or New Brunswick at the Union, and all Courts of Civil and Criminal Jurisdiction, and all legal Commissions, Powers, and Authorities, and all Officers, Judicial, Administrative, and Ministerial, existing therein at the Union, shall continue in Ontario, Quebec, Nova Scotia, and New Brunswick respectively, as if the Union had not been made; subject nevertheless (except with respect to such as are enacted by or exist under Acts of the Parliament of Great Britain or of the Parliament of the United Kingdom of Great Britain and Ireland,) to be repealed, abolished, or altered by the Parliament of Canada, or by the Legislature of the respective Province, according to the Authority of the Parliament or of that Legislature under this Act."

The law by which the right of public discussion is protected existed at the time of the enactment of the *B.N.A. Act* and, as far as Alberta is concerned, at the date on which the *Alberta Act* came into force, the 1st of September, 1905. In our opinion (on the broad principle of the cases mentioned which has been recognized as limiting the scope of general words defining the legislative authority of the Dominion) the Legislature of Alberta has not the capacity under s.129 to alter that law by legislation obnoxious to the principle stated.

The legislation now under consideration manifestly places in the hands of the Chairman of the Social Credit Commission autocratie powers which, it may well be thought, could, if arbitrarily wielded, be employed to frustrate in Alberta these rights of the Crown and the people of Canada as a whole. We do not, however, find it necessary to express an opinion upon the concrete question whether or not this particular measure is invalid as exceeding the limits indicated above.

The answer to the question concerning this Bill is that it is *ultra vires*.

• • •

CANNON, J.: ... The third question put to us is the following:

Is Bill No. 9, entitled "An Act to ensure the Publication of Accurate News and Information" or any of the provisions thereof and in what particular or particulars or to what extent *intra vires* of the Legislature of the Province of Alberta?

The order-in-council represents that it has been and is the avowed object of the present Government of the Province of Alberta to inaugurate in the said Province a "new economic order" upon the principles or plan of the theory known as the "Social Credit;" and that the said Government has since secured the enactment of several statutes more or less related to the policy of effectuating the said object. The preamble of the bill, which I will hereafter call the Press bill recites that it is "expedient and in the public interest that the newspapers published in the Province should furnish to the people of the Province statements made by the authority of the Government of the Province as to the true and exact objects of the policy of the Government and as to the hindrances to or difficulties in achieving such objects to the end that the people may be informed with respect thereto."

Section 3 provides that any proprietor, editor, publisher or manager of any newspaper published in the Province shall, when required to do so by the Chairman of the Board constituted by s.3 of the *Alberta Social Credit Act,* publish in that newspaper any statement furnished by the Chairman which has for its object the correction or amplification of any statement relating to any policy or activity of the Government of the Province published by that newspaper within the next preceding 21 days.

And s.4 provides that the proprietor, etc., of any newspaper upon being required by the Chairman in writing shall within 24 hours after the delivery of the requirement "make a return in writing setting out every source from which any information emanated, as to any statement contained in any issue of the newspaper published within sixty days of the making of the requirement and the names, addresses and occupations of all persons by whom such information was furnished to the newspaper and the name and address of the writer of any editorial, article or news item contained in any such issue of the newspaper."

Section 5 denies any action for libel on account of the publication of any statement pursuant to the Act.

Section 6 enacts that in the event of a proprietor, etc., of any newspaper being guilty of any contravention of any of the provisions of the Act, the Lieutenant-Governor-in-Council, upon a recommendation of the Chairman, may by order prohibit, (*a*) the publication of such newspaper either for a definite time or until further order; (*b*) the publication in any newspaper of anything written by any person specified in the order; (*c*) the publication of any information emanating from any person or source specified in the order.

Section 7 provides for penalties for contraventions or defaults in complying with any requirement of the Act.

The policy referred to in the preamble of the Press Bill regarding which the people of the Province are to be informed from the Government standpoint, is undoubtedly the Social Credit policy of the Government. The administration of the Bill is in the hands of the Chairman of the Social Credit Board who is given complete and discretionary power by the Bill. "Social Credit," according to s.2(*b*) of c.3, 1937, 2nd sess., of the *Alberta Social Credit Amendment Act* is "the power resulting from the belief inherent within society that its individual members in association can gain the objectives they desire;" and the objectives in which the people of Alberta must have a firm and unshaken belief are the monetization of credit and the creation of a provincial medium of exchange instead of money to be used for the purposes of distributing to Albertans loans without interest, per capita dividends and discount rates to purchase goods from retailers. This free distribution would be based on the unused capacity of the industries and people of the Province of Alberta to produce goods and services, which capacity remains unused on account of the lack or absence of purchasing power in the consumers in the Province. The purchasing power would equal or absorb this hitherto unused capacity to produce goods and services by the issue of Treasury Credit certificates against a Credit Fund or provincial credit account established by the Commission each year representing the monetary value of this "unused capacity" — which is also called "Alberta credit."

It seems obvious that this kind of credit cannot succeed unless every one should be induced to believe in it and help it along. The word "credit" comes from the Latin: *credere,* to believe. It is, therefore, essential to control the sources of information of the people of Alberta, in order to keep them immune from any vacillation in their absolute faith in the plan of the Government. The Social Credit doctrine must become, for the people of Alberta, a sort of religious dogma of which a free and uncontrolled discussion is not permissible. The Bill aims to control any statement relating to any policy or activity of the Government of the Province and declares this object to be a matter of public interest. The Bill does not regulate the relations of the newspapers' owners with private individual members of the public, but deals exclusively with expressions of opinion by the newspapers concerning government policies and activities. The pith and substance of the Bill is to regulate the press of Alberta from the viewpoint of public policy by preventing the public from being misled or deceived as to any policy or activity of the Social Credit Government and by reducing any opposition to silence or bring upon it ridicule and public contempt.

I agree with the submission of the Attorney-General for Canada that this bill deals with the regulation of the press of Alberta, not from the viewpoint of private wrongs or civil injuries resulting from any alleged infringement or privation of civil rights which belong to individuals, considered as individuals, but from the viewpoint of public wrongs or crimes, i.e., involving a violation of the public rights and duties to the whole community, considered as a community, in its social aggregate capacity.

Do the provisions of this Bill, as alleged by the Attorney-General for Canada, invade the domain of criminal law and trench upon the exclusive legislative jurisdiction of the Dominion in this regard?

The object of an amendment of the criminal law, as a rule, is to deprive the citizen of the right to do that, apart from the amendment, he could lawfully do. Sections 130 to 136 of the Criminal Code deal with seditious words and seditious publications; and s.133 (as amended by 1930 (Can.), c.11, s.2) reads as follows: —

"No one shall be deemed to have a seditious intention only because he intends in good faith, —

"(*a*) to show that His Majesty has been misled or mistaken in his measures; or

"(*b*) to point out errors or defects in the government or constitution of the United Kingdom, or of any part of it, or of Canada or any province thereof, or in either House of Parliament of the United Kingdom or of Canada, or in any legislature, or in the administration of justice: or to excite His Majesty's subjects to attempt to procure, by lawful means, the alteration of any matter in the state; or,

"(*c*) to point out, in order to their removal, matters which are producing or have a tendency to produce feelings of hatred and ill-will between different classes of His Majesty's subjects."

It appears that in England, at first, criticism of any Government policy was regarded as a crime involving severe penalties and punishable as such; but since the passing of Fox's Libel Act in 1792, the considerations now found in the above article of our Criminal Code that it is not criminal to point out errors in the Government of the country and to urge their removal by lawful means have been admitted as a valid defence in a trial for libel.

Now, it seems to me that the Alberta Legislature by this retrograde Bill is attempting to revive the old theory of the crime of seditious libel by enacting penalties, confiscation of space in newspapers and prohibitions for actions which, after due consideration by the Dominion Parliament, have been declared innocuous and which, therefore, every citizen of Canada can do lawfully and without hindrance or fear of punishment. It is an attempt by the Legislature to amend the Criminal Code in this respect and to deny the advantage of s.133(A) to the Alberta newspaper publishers.

Under the British system, which is ours, no political party can erect a prohibitory barrier to prevent the electors from getting information concerning the policy of the Government. Freedom of discussion is essential to enlighten public opinion in a democratic State; it cannot be curtailed without affecting the right of the people to be informed through sources independent of the Government concerning matters of public interest. There must be an untrammelled publication of the news and political opinions of the political parties contending for ascendancy. As stated in the preamble of the British North America Act, our constitution is and will remain, unless radically changed, "similar in principle to that of the United Kingdom." At the time of Confederation, the United Kingdom was a democracy. Democracy cannot be maintained without its foundation: free public opinion and free discussion throughout the nation of all matters affecting the State within the limits set by the Criminal Code and the common law. Every inhabitant in Alberta is also a citizen of the Dominion. The Province may deal with his property and civil rights of a local and private nature within the Province; but the Province cannot interfere with his status as a Canadian citizen and his fundamental right to express freely his untrammelled opinion about Government policies and discuss matters of public concern. The mandatory and prohibitory provisions of the Press Bill are, in my opinion, *ultra vires* of the Provincial Legislature. They interfere with the free working of the political organization of the Dominion. They have a tendency to nullify the political rights of the inhabitants of Alberta, as citizens of Canada, and cannot be considered as dealing with matters purely private and local in that Province. The Federal Parliament is the sole authority to curtail, if deemed expedient and in the public interest, the freedom of the press and the equal rights in that respect of all citizens throughout the Dominion. These subjects were matters of criminal law before Confederation, have been recognized by Parliament as criminal matters and have been expressly dealt with by the Criminal Code. No Province has the power to reduce in that Province the political rights of its citizens as compared with those enjoyed by the citizens of other Provinces of Canada. Moreover, citizens outside the Province of Alberta have a vital interest in having full information and comment, favourable and unfavourable, regarding the policy of the Alberta Government and concerning events in that Province which would, in the ordinary course, be the subject of Alberta newspapers' news items and articles.

I would, therefore, answer the question as to Bill No. 9 in the negative.

1.3.3 *Switzman* v. *Elbling and Attorney-General of Quebec* [1957], S.C.R. 285 (S.C.C.)

KERWIN C.J.: This appeal was brought by John Switzman pursuant to leave granted by the Court of Queen's Bench (Appeal Side) for the Province of Quebec from its judgment [[1954] Que. Q.B. 421] confirming that of the Superior Court cancelling and annulling a certain lease between the plaintiff, Freda Elbling, and the defendant Switzman and maintaining the intervention of the Attorney-General of the Province of Quebec and declaring An Act to Protect the Province against Communistic Propaganda, R.S.Q. 1941, c.52, to be *intra vires* of the Legislature of the Province of Quebec. It is quite true that if no *lis* exists between parties this Court will decline to hear an appeal, even though leave has been granted by a provincial Court of Appeal: *Coca-Cola Co. of Can. Ltd.* v. *Mathews* [1944] S.C.R. 385, [1945] 1 D.L.R. 1, where the earlier cases are collected. While, in the present case, it is suggested that the time has elapsed when the appellant had any interest in the lease to him from Freda Elbling, and therefore as between those two parties it is argued that there was nothing left in dispute except the questions of costs, the intervention of the Attorney-General of the Province of Quebec, pursuant to Art. 114 of the Quebec Code of Civil Procedure, raises an issue between him and the present appellant as to the constitutionality of the statute mentioned....

Section 1 provides: "This Act may be cited as *Act Respecting Communistic Propaganda.*"

Sections 3 and 12 read:

> 3. It shall be illegal for any person, who possesses or occupies a house within the Province, to use it or allow any person to make use of it to propagate communism or bolshevism by any means whatsoever.
>
> 12. It shall be unlawful to print, to publish in any manner whatsoever or to distribute in the Province any newspaper, periodical, pamphlet, circular, document or writing whatsoever propagating or tending to propagate communism or bolshevism.

Sections 4 to 11 provide that the Attorney-General, upon satisfactory proof that an infringement of s.3 has been committed, may order the closing of the house; authorize any Peace Officer to execute such order and provide a procedure by which the owner may apply by petition to a Judge of the Superior Court to have the order revised. Section 13 provides for imprisonment of anyone infringing or participating in the infringement of s.12. In my opinion it is impossible to separate the provisions of ss.3 and 12.

The validity of the statute was attacked upon a number of grounds, but, in cases where constitutional issues are involved, it is important that nothing be said that is unnecessary. In my view it is sufficient to declare that the Act is legislation in relation to the criminal law over which, by virtue of head 27 of s.91 of The B.N.A. Act, the Parliament of Canada has exclusive legislative authority. The decision of this court in *Bédard* v. *Dawson & A.-G. Que.*, [1923] S.C.R. 681, 4 D.L.R. 293, 40 Can. C.C. 404, is clearly distinguishable. As Mr. Justice Barclay points out, the real object of the Act here under consideration is to prevent propagation of Communism within the Province and to punish anyone who does so — with provisions authorizing steps for the closing of premises used for such object. The *Bédard* case was concerned with the control and enjoyment of property. I am unable to agree with the decision of Greenshields C.J. in *Fineberg* v. *Taub*, (1939), 77 Que. S.C. 233, [1940] 1 D.L.R. 114, 73 Can. C.C. 37. It is not necessary to refer to other authorities, because, once the conclusion is reached that the pith and substance of the impugned Act is in relation to criminal law, the conclusion is inevitable that the Act is unconstitutional.

The appeal should be allowed....

TASCHEREAU J. (dissenting) (translation): ... There can be no doubt that by virtue of s.91 of The B.N.A. Act (head 27), criminal law is a matter within the federal authority, and upon which it has exclusive power to legislate. And in a case such as this, the theory of the ''unoccupied field'' cannot find its application, and cannot justify a provincial Legislature to assume a right which is barred by the Constitution itself; *Fisheries Case* [*A.-G. Can.* v. *A.-G. Ont., Que. & N.S.*], [1898] A.C. 700 at 715; *Reference re Debt Adjustment Act, 1937 (Alta.), A.-G. Alta.* v. *A.-G. Can.*, [1943] A.C. 356 at 370, 2 D.L.R. 1 at 8-9.

The appellant contends that this legislation is exclusively within the domain of the criminal law, and that consequently it is without the legislative competency of the provincial authority. I would willingly agree with him, if the Legislature had enacted that Communism was a crime punishable by law, because there would then be clearly an encroachment on the federal domain, which would make the legislation *ultra vires* of the Province. But such is not the case that we have before us. The Legislature did not say that any act constituted a crime, and it did not confer the character of criminality upon the Communistic doctrine. If the provincial Legislature has no power to create criminal offences, it has the right to legislate to prevent crimes, disorders, as treason, sedition, illegal public meetings, which are crimes under the Criminal Code, and to prevent conditions calculated to favour the development of crime. In order to achieve its aims, I entertain no doubt that it may validly legislate as to the possession and use of property, as this is exclusively within the domain of civil law, and is by virtue of s.92 of The B.N.A. Act (head 13) within the provincial competency....

I am clearly of opinion that if a Province may validly legislate on all civil matters in relation to criminal law, *that if it may enact laws calculated to suppress conditions favouring the development of crime,* and control properties in order to protect society against any illegal uses that may be made of them, if it has the undeniable right to supervise brokers in their financial transactions in order to protect the public against fraud, if, finally, it has the right to impose civil incapacities as a consequence of a criminal offence, I cannot see why it could not also have the power to enact that all those who extol doctrines, calculated to incite to treason, to the violation of official secrets, to sedition, etc., should be deprived of the enjoyment of the properties from where are spread these theories, the object of which is to undermine and overthrow the established order.

Experience, and it is within our power to take judicial notice of it, teaches us that Canadians, less than 10 years ago, in violation of their oath of allegiance, did not hesitate for the sake of Communism, to reveal official secrets and thus imperil the security of the state. The suppression of the spreading of these subversive doctrines by civil sanctions is, to my mind, as important as the suppression of disorderly houses. I remain convinced that the domain of criminal law, exclusively of federal competency, has not been encroached upon by the impugned legislation, and that *the latter merely establishes civil sanctions for the prevention of crime and the security of the country.*

It has also been contended that this legislation constituted an obstacle to the liberty of the press and the liberty of speech. I believe in those fundamental liberties: they are undeniable rights which, fortunately, the citizens of this country enjoy, but these liberties would cease to be a right and become a privilege, if it were permitted to certain individuals to misuse them in order to propagate dangerous doctrines that are necessarily conducive to violations of the established order. These liberties, which citizens and the press enjoy of expressing their beliefs, their thoughts and their doctrines without previous authorization or censure, do not constitute absolute rights. They are necessarily limited and must be exercised within the bounds of legality. When these limits are overstepped, these liberties become abusive, and the law must then necessarily intervene to exercise a repressive control in order to protect the citizens and society.

The same reasoning must serve to meet the objection raised by the appellant, to the effect that the impugned law is an obstacle to the free expression of all individuals, candidates in an election. Destructive ideas of social order and of established authority by dictatorial methods, do not have more rights in electoral periods than in any other times. In the minds of many, this law may appear rigid (it is not within my province to judge of its wisdom), but the severity of a law adopted by a competent power, does not brand it with unconstitutionality....

RAND J.: The first ground on which the validity of s.3 is supported is head 13 of s.92 of The B.N.A. Act, ''Property in the Province'' and Mr. Beaulieu's contention goes in this manner: by that head the Province is vested with unlimited legislative power over property; it may, for instance, take land without compensation and generally may act as amply as if it were a sovereign state, untrammelled by constitutional limitation. The power being absolute can be used as an instrument or means to effect any purpose or object. Since the objective accomplishment under the statute here is an act on property, its validity is self-evident and the question is concluded.

I am unable to agree that in our federal organization power absolute in such a sense resides in either Legislature. The detailed distribution made by ss.91 and 92 places limits to direct and immediate purposes of provincial action. Under head 13 the purpose would, in general, be a ''property'' purpose either primary or subsidiary to another head of the same section. If such a purpose is foreign to powers vested in the Province by the Act, it will invade the field of the Dominion. For example, land could not be declared forfeited or descent destroyed by attainder on conviction of a crime, nor could the convicted person's right of access to provincial Courts be destroyed. These would trench upon both criminal law and citizenship status. The settled principle that calls for a determination of the ''real character'', the ''pith and substance'', of what purports to be enacted and whether it is ''colourable'' or is intended to effect its ostensible object, means that the true nature of the legislative act, its substance in purpose, must lie within s.92 or some other endowment of provincial power. That a power ostensibly as here under a specific head cannot be exercised as a means directly and immediately to accomplish a purpose not within that endowment is demonstrated by the following decisions of the Judicial Committee: *Union Colliery Co. of B.C. Ltd.* v. *Bryden,* [1899] A.C. 580 holding that legislative power in relation to employment in a coal mine could not be used as a means of nullifying the civil capacities of citizenship and, specifically, of persons qualifying under head 25 of s.91, Naturalization and Aliens;

Reference re Validity of Section 5(a) of Dairy Industry Act, Can. Federation of Agriculture v. *A.-G. Que.*, [1951] A.C. 179 [1950] 4 D.L.R., 689, holding that the Dominion, under its power in relation to criminal law, could not prohibit the manufacture of margarine for the purpose of benefiting in local trade one class of producer as against another. The heads of ss.91 and 92 are to be read and interpreted with each other and with the provisions of the statute as a whole, and what is then exhibited is a pattern of limitations, curtailments and modifications of legislative scope within a texture of interwoven and interacting powers.

In support of the legislation on this ground, *Bédard* v. *Dawson,* [1923] S.C.R. 681, 4 D.L.R. 293, 40 Can. C.C. 404, was relied on. In that case the statute provided that it should be illegal for the owner or occupier of any house or building to use or allow it to be used as a disorderly house; and procedure was provided by which the Superior Court could, after a conviction under the Criminal Code, grant an injunction against the owner restraining that use of it. If the use continued, the Court could order the building to be closed for a period of not more than one year.

This power is seen to have been based upon a conviction for maintaining a public nuisance. Under the public law of England which underlies that of all the Provinces, such an act was not only a matter for indictment but in a civil aspect the Court could enjoin its continuance. The essence of this aspect is its repugnant or prejudicial effect upon the neighbouring inhabitants and properties.

On that view this Court proceeded in *Bédard....*

That the scene of study, discussion or dissemination of views or opinions on any matter has ever been brought under legal sanction in terms of nuisance is not suggested. For the past century and a half in both the United Kingdom and Canada, there has been a steady removal of restraints on this freedom, stopping only at perimeters where the foundation of the freedom itself is threatened. Apart from sedition, obscene writings and criminal libels, the public law leaves the literary, discursive and polemic use of language, in the broadest sense, free.

The object of the legislation here, as expressed by the title, is admittedly to prevent the propagation of Communism and Bolshevism, but it could just as properly have been the suppression of any other political, economic or social doctrine or theory; and the issue is whether that object is a matter "in relation to which" under s.92 the Province may exclusively make laws. Two heads of the section are claimed to authorize it: head 13, as a matter of "Civil Rights", and head 16, "Local and Private Matters".

Mr. Tremblay in a lucid argument treated such a limitation of free discussion and the spread of ideas generally as in the same category as the ordinary civil restrictions of libel and slander. These obviously affect the matter and scope of discussion to the extent that it trenches upon the rights of individuals to reputation and standing in the community; and the line at which the restraint is drawn is that at which public concern for the discharge of legal or moral duties and government through rational persuasion, and that for private security, are found to be in rough balance.

But the analogy is not a true one. The ban is directed against the freedom or civil liberty of the actor; no civil right of anyone is affected nor is any civil remedy created. The aim of the statute is, by means of penalties, to prevent what is considered a poisoning of men's minds, to shield the individual from exposure to dangerous ideas, to protect him, in short, from his own thinking propensities. There is nothing of civil rights in this; it is to curtail or proscribe these freedoms which the majority so far consider to be the condition of social cohesion and its ultimate stabilizing force.

It is then said that the ban is a local matter under head 16; that the social situation in Quebec is such that safeguarding its intellectual and spiritual life against subversive doctrines becomes a special need in contrast with that for a general regulation by Parliament. A similar contention was made in the *Reference re Saskatchewan Farm Security Act, 1944, Section 6,* [1947] S.C.R. 394, 3 D.L.R. 689, affirmed in the Judicial Committee [*sub nom. A.-G. Sask.* v. *A.-G. Can.*], [1949] A.C. 110, 2 D.L.R. 145. What was dealt with there was the matter of interest on mortgages and a great deal of evidence to show the unique vicissitudes of farming in that Province was adduced. But there, as here, it was and is obvious that local conditions of that nature, assuming, for the purpose of the argument only, their existence, cannot extend legislation to matters which lie outside of s.92.

Indicated by the opening words of the preamble in the Act of 1867, reciting the desire of the four Provinces to be united in a federal union with a Constitution "similar in Principle to that of the United Kingdom", the political theory which the Act embodies is that of parliamentary Government, with all its social implications, and the provisions of the statute elaborate that principle in the institutional apparatus which they create or contemplate. Whatever the deficiencies in its workings, Canadian Government is in substance the will of the majority expressed directly or indirectly through popular assemblies. This means ultimately government by the free public opinion of an open society, the effectiveness of which, as events have not infrequently demonstrated, is undoubted.

But public opinion, in order to meet such a responsibility, demands the condition of a virtually unobstructed acces to and diffusion of ideas. Parliamentary Government postulates a capacity in men, acting freely and under self-restraints, to govern themselves; and that advance is best served in the degree achieved of individual liberation from subjective as well as objective shackles. Under that Government, the freedom of discussion in Canada, as a subject-matter of legislation, has a unity of interest and significance extending equally to every part of the Dominion. With such dimensions it is *ipso facto* excluded from head 16 as a local matter.

This constitutional fact is the political expression of the primary condition of social life, thought and its communication by language. Liberty in this is little less vital to man's mind and spirit than breathing is to his physical existence. As such an inherence in the individual it is embodied in his status of citizenship. Outlawry, for example, divesting civil standing and destroying citizenship, is a matter of Dominion concern. Of the fitness of this order of Government to the Canadian organization, the words of Taschereau J. in *Brassard* v. *Langevin* (1877), 1 S.C.R. 145 at 195 should be recalled: "The object of the electoral law was to promote, by means of the ballot, and with the absence of all undue influence, the free and sincere expression of public opinion in the choice of members of the Parliament of Canada. This law is the just sequence to the excellent institutions which we have borrowed from England, institutions which, as regards civil and religious liberty, leave to Canadians nothing to envy in other countries."

Prohibition of any part of this activity as an evil would be within the scope of criminal law, as ss.60, 61 and 62 of the Criminal Code dealing with sedition exemplify. Bearing in mind that the endowment of parliamentary institutions is one and entire for the Dominion, that Legislatures and Parliament are permanent features of our constitutional structure, and that the body of discussion is indivisible, apart from the incidence of criminal law and civil rights, and incidental effects of legislation in relation to other matters, the degree and nature of its regulation must await future consideration; for the purposes here it is sufficient to say that it is not a matter within the regulation of a Province.

Mr. Scott, in his able examination of the questions raised, challenged also the validity of ss.4 *et seq.* which vest in the Attorney-General the authority to adjudicate upon the commission of the illegal act under s.3 and to issue the order of closure; but in view of the conclusions reached on the other grounds, the consideration of this becomes unnecessary.

I would, therefore, allow the appeal, set aside the judgments below, dismiss the action and direct a declaration on the intervention that the statute in its entitety is *ultra vires* of the Province. The appellant will be entitled to the costs of the action in the Superior Court against the respondent Elbling and the costs occasioned by the intervention in all courts against the Attorney-General.

CARTWRIGHT J.: The question in this appeal is whether c.52 of R.S.Q. 1941, formerly c.11 of the Statutes of Quebec, 1937, entitled An Act to protect the Province against Communistic Propaganda, hereinafter referred to as the Act, is *intra vires* of the Legislature. The relevant circumstances and the nature of the arguments addressed to us sufficiently appear in the reasons of other members of the Court.

In my opinion the Act is invalid *in toto,* as being in pith and substance legislation in relation to the criminal law, a matter assigned by s.91, head 27, of The B.N.A. Act to the exclusive legislative authority of the Parliament of Canada.

The nature and purpose of the legislation clearly appear from the words of the Act. The propagation of Communism or Bolshevism is regarded as an evil and such propagation, by any means whatsoever in a house within the Province and by any writing whatsoever elsewhere in the Province, is forbidden under punitive sanctions.

The circumstance that the penalty prescribed for a breach of the provisions of s.3 is the closing of a house within the Province has not the effect of making the enactment one in relation to property and civil rights in the Province, and I find myself unable to relate the Act to any provincial purpose falling within heads 13 or 16 of s.92 of The B.N.A. Act. The purpose and effect of the Act are to make criminal the propagation of Communism or Bolshevism which the Legislature in the public interest intends to prohibit. It is legislation in relation to what is conceived to be a public evil not in relation to civil rights or local matters....

ABBOTT J.: ... The first question to be determined is whether the impugned legislation, in pith and substance, deals with the use of real property or with the propagation of ideas. As Mr. Scott put it to us in his very able argument: (1) the *motive* of this legislation is dislike of Communism as being an evil and subversive doctrine, motive of course, being something with which the courts are not concerned; (2) the *purpose* is clearly the suppression of the propagation of Communism in the Province and (3) one *means* provided for effecting such suppression is denial of the use of a house.

In my opinion the Act does not create two illegalities which are separate and independent, as was suggested to us by Mr. Beaulieu, it creates only one, namely, the propagation of Communism in the Province. Both s.3 and s.12 are directed to the same purpose, namely, the suppression of Communism, although different means are provided to achieve that end. The whole Act constitutes one legislative scheme and in my opinion its provisions are not severable.

Since in my view the true nature and purpose of the Padlock Act is to suppress the propagation of Communism in the Province, the next question which must be answered is whether such a measure, aimed at suppressing the propagation of ideas within a Province, is within the legislative competence of such Province.

The right of free expression of opinion and of criticism, upon matters of public policy and public administration, and the right to discuss and debate such matters, whether they be social, economic or political, are essential to the working of a parliamentary democracy such as ours. Moreover, it is not necessary to prohibit the discussion of such matters, in order to protect the personal reputation or the private rights of the citizen. That view was clearly expressed by Duff C.J.C. in *Re Alberta Legislation,* [1938] S.C.R. 100 at 132-4, 2 D.L.R. 81 at 107-8, ...: [For Duff's words, see s.1.3.2.]

The *Canada Elections Act,* R.S.C. 1952, c.23, the provisions of The B.N.A. Act which provide for Parliament meeting at least once a year and for the election of a new Parliament at least every 5 years, and the Senate and House of Commons Act, R.S.C. 1952, c.249, are examples of enactments which make specific statutory provision for ensuring the exercise of this right of public debate and public discussion. Implicit in all such legislation is the right of candidates for Parliament or for a Legislature, and of citizens generally, to explain, criticize, debate and discuss in the freest possible manner such matters as the qualifications, the policies, and the political, economic and social principles advocated by such candidates or by the political parties or groups of which they may be members.

This right cannot be abrogated by a provincial Legislature, and the power of such Legislature to limit it, is restricted to what may be necessary to protect purely private rights, such as for example provincial laws of defamation. It is obvious that the impugned statute does not fall within that category. It does not, in substance, deal with matters of property and civil rights or with a local or private matter within the Province and in my opinion is clearly *ultra vires*. Although it is not necessary, of course, to determine this question for the purposes of the present appeal, the Canadian Constitution being declared to be similar in principle to that of the United Kingdom, I am also of opinion that as our constitutional Act now stands, Parliament itself could not abrogate this right of discussion and debate. The power of Parliament to limit it is, in my view, restricted to such powers as may be exercisable under its exclusive legislative jurisdiction with respect to criminal law and to make laws for the peace, order and good Government of the nation.

For the reasons which I have given, I would allow the appeal....

1.3.4 *Re Nova Scotia Board of Censors and McNeil* (1978), 84 D.L.R. (3d) 1 (S.C.C.).

RITCHIE J.: The respondent's application was for a declaration that certain sections of the *Theatres and Amusements Act,* R.S.N.S. 1967, c.304, as amended, and certain Regulations made thereunder were *ultra vires* and beyond the legislative competence of the Province of Nova Scotia.

The exciting cause of the application appears to have been the exercise by the Nova Scotia Amusements Regulation Board (hereinafter referred to as "the Board") of the authority which the Act purports to confer on it, to prevent a film entitled "Last Tango in Paris" from being exhibited in the theatres of Nova Scotia.

It is the statutory provisions purporting to authorize the Board to regulate and control the film industry within the Province of Nova Scotia according to standards fixed by it, which are challenged by the respondent on the ground that the citizens of Nova Scotia are thereby denied, on moral grounds, their right to exercise their freedom of choice in the viewing of films and theatre performances which might otherwise be available to them, and it is further alleged that the legislation constitutes an invasion of fundamental freedoms...

In all such cases the Court cannot ignore the rule implicit in the proposition stated as early as 1878 by Mr. Justice Strong in *Severn v. The Queen,* 2 S.C.R. 70 at p. 103, that any question as to the validity of provincial legislation is to be approached on the assumption that it was validly enacted...

When the Act and the Regulations are read as a whole, I find that to be primarily directed to the regulation, supervision and control of the film business within the Province of Nova Scotia, including the use and exhibition of films in that Province. To this end the impugned provisions are, in my view, enacted for the purpose of reinforcing the authority vested in a provincially appointed Board to perform the task of regulation which includes the authority to prevent the exhibition of films which the Board, applying its own local standards, has rejected as unsuitable for viewing by provincial audiences. This legislation is concerned with dealings in and the use of property (*i.e.,* films) which take place wholly within the Province and in my opinion it is subject to the same considerations as those which were held to be applicable in such cases as *Shannon et al. v. Lower Mainland Dairy Products Board et al.,* [1938] 4 D.L.R. 81, [1938] A.C. 708, [1938] 2 W.W.R. 604; *Home Oil Distributors Ltd. et al. v. A.-G. B.C.,* [1940] 2 D.L.R. 609, [1940] S.C.R. 444, and *Caloil Inc. v. A.-G. Can. et al.* (1971), 20 D.L.R. (3d) 472, [1971] S.C.R. 543, [1971] 4 W.W.R. 37...

It will be seen that, in my opinion, the impugned legislation constitutes nothing more than the exercise of provincial authority over transactions taking place wholly within the Province and it applies to the "regulating, exhibition, sale and exchange of films" whether those films have been imported from another country or not.

We are concerned, however, in this appeal with a decision of the Appeal Division of the Supreme Court of Nova Scotia in which the majority quite clearly struck down the legislation as *ultra vires* on the sole ground that it was concerned with morality and as such constituted an invasion of the criminal law field reserved to the exclusive legislative authority of Parliament under s.91(27) of the *British North America Act, 1867...*

Although no reasons were given by the board for the rejection of "Last Tango in Paris", all members of the Appeal Division, were satisfied that its exhibition was prohibited on moral grounds and under all the circumstances I think it to be apparent that this was the case. In any event, I am satisfied that the Board is clothed with authority to fix its own local standards of morality in deciding whether a film is to be rejected or not for local viewing.

Simply put, the issue raised by the majority opinion in the Appeal Division is whether the Province is clothed with authority under s.92 of the *British North America Act, 1867* to regulate the exhibition and distribution of films within its own boundaries which are considered unsuitable for local viewing by a local board on grounds of morality or whether this is a matter of criminal law reserved to Parliament under s.91(27)...

Under the authority assigned to it by s.92(27), the Parliament of Canada has enacted the *Criminal Code,* a penal statute the end purpose of which is the definition and punishment of crime when it has been proved to have been committed.

On the other hand, the *Theatres and Amusements Act* is not concerned with creating a criminal offence or providing for its punishment, but rather in so regulating a business within the Province as to prevent the exhibition in its theatres of performances which do not comply with the standards of propriety established by the Board.

The areas of operation of the two statutes are therefore fundamentally different on dual grounds. In the first place, one is directed to regulating a trade or business where the other is concerned with the definition and punishment of crime; and in the second place, one is preventive while the other is penal.

As the decision of the Appeal Division depends upon equating morality with criminality, I think it desirable at this stage to refer to the definitive statement made by Lord Atkin in this regard in the course of his reasons for judgment in *Proprietary Articles Trade Ass'n v. A.-G. Can.*, [1931] 2 D.L.R. 1 at pp. 9-10, 55 C.C.C. 241, [1931] A.C. 310 at p. 324, where he said:

> Morality and criminality are far from co-extensive; nor is the sphere of criminality necessarily part of a more extensive field covered by morality — unless the moral code necessarily disapproves all acts prohibited by the State, in which case the argument moves in a circle. It appears to their Lordships to be of little value to seek to confine crimes to a category of acts which by their very nature belong to the domain of ''criminal jurisprudence''...

I share the opinion expressed in this passage that morality and criminality are far from co-extensive and it follows in my view that legislation which authorizes the establishment and enforcement of a local standard of morality in the exhibition of films is not necessarily ''an invasion of the federal criminal field'' as Chief Justice MacKeigan thought it to be in this case...

As I have already said, however, I take the view that the impugned legislation is not concerned with criminality. The rejection of films by the Board is based on a failure to conform to the standards of propriety which it has itself adopted and this failure cannot be said to be ''an act prohibited with penal consequences'' by the Parliament of Canada either in enacting the *Criminal Code* or otherwise. This is not to say that Parliament is in any way restricted in its authority to pass laws penalizing immoral acts or conduct, but simply that the provincial Government in regulating a local trade may set its own standards which in no sense exclude the operation of the federal law.

There is, in my view, no constitutional barrier preventing the Board from rejecting a film for exhibition in Nova Scotia on the sole ground that it fails to conform to standards of morality which the Board itself has fixed notwithstanding the fact that the film is not offensive to any provision of the *Criminal Code;* and, equally, there is no constitutional reason why a prosecution cannot be brought under s.163 of the *Criminal Code* in respect of the exhibition of a film which the Board of Censors has approved as conforming to its standards of propriety...

It will be seen that in my view the impugned legislation ''has for its true object, purpose, nature and character'' the regulation and control of a local trade and that it is therefore valid provincial legislation...

As I have said, I take the view that the legislation here in question is, in pith and substance, directed to property and civil rights and therefore valid under s.92(13) of the *British North America Act, 1867* but there is a further and different ground on which its validity might be sustained. In a country as vast and diverse as Canada, where tastes and standards may vary from one area to another, the determination of what is and what is not acceptable for public exhibition on moral grounds may be viewed as a matter of a "local and private nature in the Province" within the meaning of s.92(16) of the *British North America Act, 1867*, and as it is not a matter coming within any of the classes of subject enumerated in s.91, this is a field in which the Legislature is free to act...

As I indicated at the outset, I have taken note of the lengthy judgment of Mr. Justice Macdonald in the Appeal Division in which he finds that the impugned legislation is *ultra vires* as infringing on the fundamental freedoms to which he refers, which include freedom of association; of assembly; of speech; of the press; of other media in the dissemination of news and opinion; of conscience and of religion.

Mr. Justice Macdonald's approach appears to me to be illustrated by the following comment which he makes after referring to censorship legislation relating to morals in other provinces [at p. 55]:

> The foregoing criteria are of the usual "sex, morals and violence" type that are normally associated with film censorship. In the present case, however, the censorship criterion, being left to the *Board* to determine, *could* be much wider and encompass political, religious and other matters. In my opinion censorship relating to party politics cannot be tolerated in a free society where unfettered debate on political issues is a necessity, subject, of course, to the criminal law, particularly those provisions of the *Criminal Code*, relating to sedition, treason and incitement to crime.

(The emphasis is added.)

It is true that no limitations on the authority of the board are spelled out in the Act and that it might be inferred that it *could* possibly affect some of the rights listed by Macdonald, J.A., but having regard to the presumption of constitutional validity to which I have already referred, it appears to me that this does not afford justification for concluding that the purpose of the Act was directed to the infringement of one or more of those rights. With the greatest respect, this conclusion appears to me to involve speculation as to the intention of the Legislature and the placing of a construction on the statute which is nowhere made manifest by the language employed in enacting it.

For all these reasons, I would allow this appeal, set aside the judgment of the Appeal Division of Nova Scotia and substitute for the declaration made thereunder a declaration that Regulation 32 made pursuant to the *Theatre and Amusements Act* of Nova Scotia is null and void.

LASKIN, C.J.C. (dissenting): — ...What is involved, as I have already noted, is an unqualified power in the Nova Scotia Board to determine the fitness of films for public viewing on considerations that may extend beyond the moral and may include the political, the social and the religious. Giving its assertion of power the narrowest compass, related to the film in the present case, the Board is asserting authority to protect public morals, to safeguard the public from exposure to films, to ideas and images in films, that it regards as morally offensive, as indecent, probably as obscene.

The determination of what is decent or indecent or obscene in conduct or in a publication, what is morally fit for public viewing, whether in films, in art or in a live performance is, as such, within the exclusive power of the Parliament of Canada under its enumerated authority to legislate in relation to the criminal law. This has been recognized in a line of cases in which, beginning with the seminal case of *A.-G. Ont. v. Hamilton Street R. Co.*, [1903] A.C. 524 (where it was said that it is the criminal law in the widest sense that falls within exclusive federal authority), the criminal law power has been held to be as much a brake on provincial legislation as a source of federal legislation...

It is beside the point to urge that morality is not co-extensive with the criminal law. Such a contention cannot of itself bring legislation respecting public morals within provincial competence. Moreover, the federal power in relation to the criminal law extends beyond control of morality, and is wide enough to embrace anti-social conduct or behaviour and has, indeed, been exercised in those respects.

Films have been held to fall within s.159 of the *Criminal Code,* dealing with obscene publications: see *R. v. Fraser et al.* (1965), 51 D.L.R. (2d) 408, [1966] 1 C.C.C. 110, 52 W.W.R. 712; affirmed 59 D.L.R. (2d) 240, [1967] 2 C.C.C. 43, [1967] S.C.R. 38; *R. v. Goldberg and Reitman* (1971), 4 C.C.C. (2d) 187, [1971] 3 O.R. 323; *Daylight Theatre Co. Ltd. v. The Queen* (1973), 48 D.L.R. (3d) 390, 17 C.C.C. (2d) 451, 24 C.R.N.S. 368. Indeed, the very film, "Last Tango in Paris", out of which this case arose, was the subject of a prosecution under s.159 which was unsuccessful: see *R. v. Odeon Morton Theatres Ltd. et al.* (1974), 45 D.L.R. (3d) 224, 16 C.C.C. (2d) 185, [1974] 3 W.W.R. 304. I draw attention as well to s.163 of the *Criminal Code* dealing with the presentation or giving of immoral, indecent or obscene performances, entertainments or representations, and it seems to me that if films are within s.159 they are a *fortiori* within s.163...

This is not a case where civil consequences are attached to conduct defined and punished as criminal under federal legislation, as in *McDonald v. Down,* [1939] 2 D.L.R. 177, 71 C.C.C. 179; affirmed [1941] D.L.R. 799, 75 C.C.C. 404 (Ont. C.A.), but rather a case where a provincially authorized tribunal itself defines and determines legality, what is permissible and what is not. This, in my view, is a direct intrusion into the field of criminal law. At best, what the challenged Nova Scotia legislation is doing is seeking to supplement the criminal law enacted by Parliament, and this is forbidden: see *Johnson v. A.-G. Alta.*, [1954] 2 D.L.R. 625 at p. 636, 108 C.C.C. 1, [1954] S.C.R. 127 at p. 138, *per* Rand, J. (see also *St. Leonard v. Fournier, supra,* at p. 320).

It was contended, however, by the appellant and by supporting intervenants that the Nova Scotia Board was merely exercising a preventive power, no penalty or punishment being involved, no offence having been created. It is true, of course, that no penalty or punishment is involved in the making of an order prohibiting the exhibition of a film, but it is ingenuous to say that no offence is created when a licensee who disobeyed the order would be at risk of a cancellation of his licence and at risk of a penalty and any one else who proposed to exhibit the film publicly would likewise be liable to a penalty. Indeed, the contention invites this Court to allow form to mask substance and amounts to an assertion that the provincial Legislature may use the injunction or prohibitory order as a means of controlling conduct or performances or exhibitions, doing by prior restraint what it could not do by defining an offence and prescribing *post facto* punishment.

It does not follow from all of the foregoing that provincial legislative authority may not extend to objects where moral considerations are involved, but those objects must in themselves be anchored in the provincial catalogue of powers and must, moreover, not be in conflict with valid federal legislation. It is impossible in the present case to find any such anchorage in the provisions of the Nova Scotia statute that are challenged, and this apart from the issue of conflict which, I think, arises in relation to ss.159 and 163 of the *Criminal Code*. What is asserted, by way of tying the challenged provisions to valid provincial regulatory control, is that the Province is competent to licence the use of premises, and entry into occupations, and may in that connection determine what shall be exhibited in those premises. This hardly touches the important issue raised by the present case and would, if correct, equally justify control by the Province of any conduct and activity in licensed premises even if not related to the property aspect of licensing, and this is patently indefensible. Moreover, what is missing from this assertion by the appellant is a failure to recognize that the censorship of films takes place without relation to any premises and is a direct prior control of public taste.

It is not enough to save the challenged prohibitory provisions of the Nova Scotia statute, if they are otherwise invalid, that they are part of a legislative scheme which embraces licensing of theatres and of motion picture projectionists. As I have already noted, the provisions now challenged go beyond the licensing provisions and engage the public directly.

For all the foregoing reasons I would dismiss this appeal and answer the constitutional question in the negative.

MARTLAND, J., concurs with RITCHIE, J.
JUDSON, J., concurs with LASKIN, C.J.C.
SPENCE, J., concurs with LASKIN, C.J.C.
PIGEON, J., concurs with RITCHIE, J.
DICKSON, J., concurs with LASKIN, C.J.C.
BEETZ and DE GRANDPRÉ, J.J., concur with RITCHIE, J.

Appeal allowed in part.

1.3.5 *Attorney-General of Quebec* v. *Kellogg's of Canada* (1978), 83 D.L.R. (3d) 314 (S.C.C.)

MARTLAND J.: — Paragraph (*o*) of s.102 of the *Consumer Protection Act*, 1971 (Que.), c.74, empowered the Lieutenant-Governor in Council to make Regulations "to determine standards for advertising goods, whether or not they are the object of a contract, or credit, especially all advertising intended for children". In pursuance of this authority O.C. 3268-72 was enacted dated October 11, 1972, to amend the General Regulations enacted as O.C. 1408-72, dated May 24, 1972, by adding Division XI-A entitled "Advertising intended for children". Paragraph (*n*) of s.11.53, contained in this Division, provided that:

> 11.53 No one shall prepare, use, publish or cause to be published in Quebec advertising intended for children which:
> (*n*) employs cartoons:

The French version of para. (*n*) reads:

> (*n*) emploie un dessin animé ou une bande illustrée (cartoon);

Four complaints were filed by the appellant against the respondent Kellogg's Company of Canada which, along with the respondent Kellogg's of Canada Limited, are hereinafter jointly referred to as "Kellogg", alleging breaches of this regulation in connection with televised advertisements of Kellogg's products over Channel 7 in Sherbrooke and Channels 6 and 12 in Montreal. The appellant sought an injunction to restrain the commission of further infractions.

In the petition for the issuance of an injunction order the appellant alleged that Kellogg (translation) "did prepare, use, publish or cause to be published advertising intended for children which employed a cartoon, namely, an advertisement for a Kellogg product shown on the same channel". Kellogg's solicitors made certain admissions, which included the statement that several paragraphs of the petition should be modified (translation) "by inserting the words 'in the province of Ontario and for T.V. broadcasting in the province of Quebec' after the word 'did' in each of them, and the same are admitted as modified".

Kellogg opposed the issuance of an injunction order on the ground that para. (*n*) was unconstitutional or inoperative to the extent that it applied to the use of cartoons on television in advertising intended for children.

The trial Judge ordered the granting of the injunction. His decision was reversed on appeal by a majority of two to one.

The constitutional issues raised on the appeal to this Court were defined as follows:

(1) Is s. 11.53(*n*) of the General Regulation (O.C. 1408-72 of May 24, 1972) adopted pursuant to the *Consumer Protection Act* as amended by Regulation O.C. 3268-72 of October 31, 1972, unconstitutional, *ultra vires* or inoperative to the extent that it applies to the publication and to the use of cartoons on television in advertising intended for children?...

The Attorney-General of Canada has intervened to support the judgment, holding the impugned enactments *ultra vires;* the Attorneys-General for Ontario, Nova Scotia, British Columbia, Saskatchewan and Alberta intervened to support the appeal.

Two points should be noted at the outset. The first is that the injunction was sought, not against the television stations which televised the advertisements, but as against Kellogg, the manufacturer of the goods which it sought to advertise by means of animated cartoons. The second is that the attack against para. (*n*) is limited. The power of the Province to enact this provision is not questioned, except to the extent that it would apply to the use of cartoons on television.

This being so, it is not necessary to consider the general power of a Province to exercise control over advertising in Quebec intended for children. The provincial power to enact such legislation under s.92(13) and (16), if not under s.93, of the *British North America Act, 1867* would appear to be clear. The basic issue is as to whether a provincial law restricting the type of advertising intended for children which may be used by a manufacturer or vendor of goods within the province can preclude him from advertising, by means of television, in breach of the restriction.

The majority of the Court of Appeal took the view that the regulation in question was an attempt to legislate on the content of broadcasting, that this was a matter exclusively within federal legislative power and that the appellant was not entitled to its injunction. Reference was made to *Re Regulation and Control of Radio Communication; A.-G. Que. v. A.-G. Can.*, [1932] 2 D.L.R. 81, [1932] A.C. 304, [1932] 1 W.W.R. 563, in which the Privy Council held that the legislative power of the federal Parliament extended to radio communication under s. 91(29) of the *British North America Act, 1867* as being an undertaking connecting one Province with another.

Reference was then made to the judgment of the Ontario Court of Appeal in *Re C.F.R.B. and A.-G. Can et al.* (1973), 38 D.L.R. (3d) 335, 14 C.C.C. (2d) 345,

[1973] 3 O.R. 819, which decided that the scope of the Privy Council decision was not limited to the physical means of communication, but extended to programme content. That case was concerned with the constitutional validity of s.28 of the *Broadcasting Act,* R.S.C. 1970, c.B-11, which prohibited a broadcaster from broadcasting a programme, advertisement or announcement of a partisan character in relation to a provincial election on the day of an election or on the day preceding it. The case is concerned with the extent of federal control over a broadcast undertaking licensed under federal legislation.

Reference was also made to the judgment of the Federal Court of Appeal in the case of *Re Capital Cities Communications Inc. et al. and Canadian Radio Television Com'n* (1975), 52 D.L.R. (3d) 415, [1975] F.C. 18, 7 N.R. 18, in which, relying upon the *C.F.R.B.* case, it is stated, at p. 421 D.L.R., p. 25 F.C.: "The legislative authority of Parliament extends over the content of broadcasts as well as over the physical undertaking of the television reception unit."

Subsequent to the judgment of the Court of Appeal in the present case, this Court dismissed an appeal from the judgment of the Federal Court of Appeal in the *Capital Cities* case. The constitutional issues involved in the *Capital Cities* case were as to the power of Parliament to regulate cable distribution systems and to empower the Canadian Radio-Television Commission to regulate the reception of television signals emanating from a source outside Canada and the regulation of the transmission of such signals within Canada. It was held that Parliament had such power. The judgment of this Court is not yet reported [now reported 81 D.L.R. (3d) 609, 18 N.R. 181].

The federal power to regulate cable distribution systems was also considered in the case of *Re Public Service Board et al.; Dionne et al. v. A.-G. Can.* In that case it was held by the Court of Appeal of Quebec that the regulatory powers of the Quebec Public Service Board under the *Public Service Act,* R.S.Q. 1964, c.229, did not extend to the regulation of a cable distribution system in Quebec. This judgment was upheld on an appeal to this Court in a decision which is not yet reported [now reported, *ante,* p. 178].

The judgment of the majority of the Court of Appeal in the present case concludes with the following statement (translation):

> This means that television, including the intellectual content of the programmes, is one of the subject-matters of legislation enumerated in s. 91 of the Constitution, and consequently, any provincial legislation on the subject is of necessity inoperative: *Commission du Salaire Minimum v. Bell Telephone Co. of Canada* (1966), 59 D.L.R. (2d) 145, [1966] S.C.R. 767.

The cases to which I have referred specifically above all dealt with the legislative power to regulate and control broadcast undertakings engaged in the transmission and reception of radio or television signals. That power is not in issue in the present case. What is in issue here is the power of a provincial Legislature to regulate and control the conduct of a commercial enterprise in respect of its business activities within the Province. The majority of the Court of Appeal appears to hold the view that the federal power in respect of the broadcast undertaking is decisive. I do not think that it is.

The object of the Regulation in Division XI-A made under the *Consumer Protection Act* is clear. It is sought to protect children in Quebec from the harmful effect of the kinds of advertising therein prohibited. The power of a provincial Legislature to legislate so as to restrict or prohibit certain kinds of advertising was recognized by this Court in *Cowen et al. v. A.-G. B.C. et al.,* [1941] 2 D.L.R. 687, [1941] S.C.R. 321.

Legislation restricting the advertising of liquor in Ontario was upheld by Schatz, J., in *R. v. Telegram Publishing Co. Ltd.* (1960), 25 D.L.R. (2d) 471, 129 C.C.C. 209, [1960] O.R. 518 *sub nom. R. v. Toronto Magistrates, Ex p. Telegram Publishing Co. Ltd.* Hinkson, J., in *Benson & Hedges (Canada) Ltd. et al. v. A.-G. B.C.* (1972), 27 D.L.R. (3d) 257, 6 C.P.R. (2d) 182, [1972] 5 W.W.R. 32, upheld two provincial statutes which prohibited the advertising of liquor and of tobacco in British Columbia.

As its name indicates, the purpose of the *Consumer Protection Act* is the protection of consumers in Quebec by regulating the commercial conduct of persons engaged in the sale of goods in that Province. Part of this regulation involves the control of the advertising which is used in effecting such sales. Paragraph (*n*), under attack in this case, is one of several restrictions imposed in connection with advertising intended for children. It forbids the use of a particular kind of advertising considered to have a special appeal to children.

In my opinion this Regulation does not seek to regulate or to interfere with the operation of a broadcast undertaking. In relation to the facts of this case it seeks to prevent Kellogg from using a certain kind of advertising by any means. It aims at controlling the commercial activity of Kellogg. The fact that Kellogg is precluded from using televised advertising may, incidentally, affect the revenue of one or more television stations but it does not change the true nature of the Regulation. In this connection the case of *Carnation Co. Ltd. v. Quebec Agricultural Marketing Board* (1968), 67 D.L.R. (2d) 1, [1968] S.C.R. 238, is analogous.

Kellogg is not exempted from the application of restriction upon its advertising practices because it elects to advertise through a medium which is subject to federal control. A person who caused defamatory material to be published by means of a televised programme would not be exempted from liability under provincial law because the means of publication were subject to federal control. Further, he could be enjoined from repeating the publication. In my opinion the position of Kellogg in relation to this Regulation is analogous. It cannot justify conduct which has been rendered illegal because it is using the medium of television.

Throughout these reasons I have stressed the fact that it is Kellogg and not the television station which is sought to be enjoined. The question is whether Kellogg's conduct has been regulated by the provincial legislation. Whether the Regulation could be applied to the television station itself or whether an injunction against Kellogg would bind such station does not arise in this case and I prefer to express no opinion with respect to it.

In my opinion para. (*n*) is within the power of the Province to enact and applies to all persons who employ advertising as a means of selling their goods in the Province of Quebec.

Finally, it was contended that if the Regulation was, in other respects, *intra vires* of the Province, Parliament had already legislated in respect of the matter of broadcast advertising and, this being so, the federal legislation was paramount.

Section 16 of the *Broadcasting Act,* R.S.C. 1970, c. B-11, defines the powers of the Canadian Radio-Television Commission. Paragraph (*b*) of ss.(1) provides that, in furtherance of its objects the Commission, on the recommendation of its Executive Committee, may, *inter alia,*

> (*b*) make a regulations applicable to all persons holding broadcasting licenses...
>
> (ii) respecting the character of advertising and the amount of time that may be devoted to advertising,

In fact the Commission has not exercised this power, and so there is no federal legislation governing the character of broadcasting advertising. Consequently, this is not a case in which it becomes necessary to determine whether a conflict exists between federal and provincial legislation on similar subject-matters.

In my opinion both of the constitutional questions submitted for argument should be answered in the negative. I would allow the appeal, set aside the judgment of the Court of Appeal and restore the judgment at trial, with costs to the appellant as against the respondent throughout. There should be no costs payable by or to any of the intervenants.

Appeal allowed

1.3.6 *Gay Alliance Toward Equality* v. *Vancouver Sun* (1979), 97 D.L.R. (3d) 577 (S.C.C.)

APPEAL from a judgment of the British Columbia Court of Appeal, 77 D.L.R. (3d) 487, [1977] 5 W.W.R. 198, allowing an appeal from a judgment of MacDonald, J., [1976] W.W.D. 160, holding that a board of inquiry under the *Human Rights Code of British Columbia,* 1973 (B.C.) (2nd Sess.), c. 119, did not err in deciding that the respondent newspaper failed to show reasonable cause for refusing to print an advertisement submitted by the appellant.

MARTLAND, J.: The issues in this appeal arise in respect of the application of the provisions of s.3 [since am. 1974, c.114, s.6(a)] of the *Human Rights Code of British Columbia,* 1973 (B.C.) (2nd Sess.), c.119. That section appears under a heading "Discriminatory Practices" and it read at the relevant time as follows:

> 3(1) No person shall
> (a) deny to any person or class of persons any accommodation, service, or facility customarily available to the public; or
> (b) discriminate against any person or class of persons with respect to any accommodation, service, or facility customarily available to the public.
> unless reasonable cause exists for such denial or discrimination.
> (2) For the purposes of subsection (1),
> (a) the race, religion, colour, ancestry, or place of origin of any person or class of persons shall not constitute reasonable cause; and
> (b) the sex of any person shall not constitute reasonable cause unless it relates to the maintenance of public decency...

The Act established a commission, the British Columbia Human Rights Commission. It provided for the appointment of a director, who is the chief executive officer of the Commission. When the director receives a complaint alleging a contravention of the Act, he is required to investigate and endeavour to effect a settlement of the alleged contravention. If he is unable to settle an allegation, provision is made for the appointment of a board of inquiry which investigates the allegation. The board of inquiry, if it is of the opinion that an allegation is justified, may order a person who has contravened the Act to cease such contravention and may order such person to make available to the person discriminated against such rights, opportunities, or privileges as, in the opinion of the board, he was denied. The board is also empowered to direct the payment of compensation and to make orders as to costs.

An appeal is given from a decision of the board of inquiry to the Supreme Court on any question of law or jurisdiction or any finding of fact necessary to establish its jurisdiction that is manifestly incorrect. The rules under the *Summary Convictions Act*, R.S.B.C. 1960, c.373, governing appeals by way of stated case are made applicable.

A complaint was filed by an individual complainant on behalf of the appellant, the Gay Alliance Toward Equality, hereinafter referred to as "Alliance", alleging that the respondent, the Vancouver Sun, hereinafter referred to as "Sun", had refused to publish an advertisement promoting the sale of subscriptions to "Gay Tide" in the classified advertising section of the Sun newspaper in violation of s.3 of the Act. The Sun advised the Alliance by letter that the advertisement was "not acceptable for publication in this newspaper".

The Sun's refusal to print the advertisement was because it promoted subscriptions to "Gay Tide". "Gay Tide" is a publication which reflects the purposes of the Alliance, *i.e.*, to establish recognition for the thesis that homosexuality is a valid and legitimate form of human sexual and emotional expression in no way harmful to society or the individual and completely on a par with heterosexuality.

A board of inquiry was constituted to consider the complaint of the Alliance. After conducting a hearing, the board found that there had been a violation of s.3 of the *Human Rights Code*.

From this decision the Sun appealed. A case was stated by the board as required under the Act. The stated case referred to the facts previously mentioned. Paragraphs 10, 11 and 12 of the stated case are as follows:

> 10. The refusal by the Appellant to publish the advertisement in question was stated to be the result of a policy which the paper has in its advertising department (as distinct from its editorial department) to avoid any advertising material dealing with homosexuals or homosexuality, and the Appellant argued that this policy was justified on three grounds:
>
> (1) That homosexuality is offensive to public decency and that the advertisement would offend some of its subscribers;
>
> (2) That the Code of Advertising Standards, a Code of Advertising Ethics subscribed to by most of the daily newspapers in Canada includes the following section:
>
> > "Public decency — no advertisement shall be prepared, or be knowingly accepted which is vulgar, suggestive or in any way offensive to public decency."
>
> and that the advertisement in question did not conform to the standards therein set out; and
>
> (3) That the Appellant newspaper had a duty to protect the morals of the community.
>
> 11. This Board of Inquiry found that the central theme of the Appellant's argument was that the policy in question was predicated on a desire to protect a reasonable standard of decency and good taste.
>
> 12. Assessing all the evidence offered on the question of the cause or motivation behind the Appellant's refusal to publish the Respondent's advertisement, the majority of the Board of Inquiry found the inevitable conclusion to be that the real reason behind the policy was not a concern for any standard of public decency, but was, in fact, a personal bias against homosexuals and homosexuality on the part of various individuals within the management of the Appellant newspaper. Board Member Dr. Dorothy Smith dissented on this point and held that there was no evidence whatsoever on which the Board could make such a finding; and that, in particular there was no evidence to rebut the Appellant's repeated statements that its policy was predicated on a desire to protect a reasonable standard of decency and good taste.

The questions of law stated in the stated case are as follows:

> The appellant desires to question the finding that a violation did take place on the grounds that the said Judgment was erroneous in point of law or in excess of jurisdiction, the questions submitted being:

1. Was the Board of Inquiry correct in law in holding that pursuant to Section 3(1) of the Human Rights Code of British Columbia that classified advertising was a service or facility customarily available to the public.
2. Was the Board of Inquiry correct in law in holding that the Appellant herein denied to any person or class of persons any accommodation, service or facility customarily available to the public or discriminated against any person or class of persons with respect to any accommodation service or facility customarily available to the public pursuant to Section 3(1) of the Human Rights Code of British Columbia.
3. Was the Board of Inquiry correct in law in holding that pursuant to Section 3(1) of the Human Rights Code of British Columbia that the Appellant herein did not have reasonable cause for the alleged denial and did not have reasonable cause for the alleged discrimination.

Sun's appeal to a Judge of the Supreme Court of British Columbia was dismissed [[1976] W.W.D. 160], but its appeal to the Court of Appeal succeeded by a majority decision [77 D.L.R. (3d) 487, [1977] 5 W.W.R. 198]. It is from that judgment that the present appeal, with leave, has been brought to this Court.

The following excerpts from the judgments of Branca, J.A., and Robertson, J.A., who comprised the majority in the Court of Appeal, state the basis upon which they were of the opinion that Sun's appeal should be allowed.

Per Branca, J.A. [at p. 494]:

The Board concluded that having assessed all of the evidence that it was a personal bias on the part of various individuals, within the management of the advertising department of the newspaper, which was the real reason motivating the refusal to publish and not a genuine concern on the part of the newspaper for any standard of public decency. It seems to me that the real question for determination was not whether certain individuals within management had a bias against homosexuals or homosexuality which may have motivated the policy, but whether or not the resultant policy dealing with public decency even though motivated by a bias on the part of certain individuals constituted a reasonable cause for the refusal to publish. In other words, despite the fact that certain individuals may have had that bias and that bias might well have motivated the refusal, the vital question remained: did the resultant policy of the newspaper furnish reasonable cause within the meaning of those words as used in s.3 of the *Human Rights Code* which in the event might constitute a lawful ground for refusal.

Per Robertson, J.A. [at p. 496]:

It is my view that the words in s.3(1) of the Code, ''unless reasonable cause exists'' require the application of an objective test: Does such a cause exist? It is wrong in law to substitute for this the subjective test that the Board applied: What motivated the person who denied or discriminated and was this motivation reasonable cause for the denial or discrimination? To put it another way: If reasonable cause does in fact exist, the person discriminated against cannot claim the benefit of s.3, even though the other person did not know of the existence of the cause; conversely, if reasonable cause does not in fact exist, the other person cannot justify his act of discrimination by a genuine belief that a reasonable cause did exist.

Of course, in applying the Code the ''cause'' must be considered in relation to the person and the circumstances. Also, it must be borne in mind that the members of majorities have rights and sensibilities. I do not think that it is the intention of the Code that these are generally to be ignored for the benefit of those who are different. The words ''unless reasonable cause exists'' make this abundantly clear.

If the grounds upon which the Board reached its decision are to be gathered from the stated case alone, it appears from para. 12 that the Board went wrong, in that it applied the wrong test, that of motivation, and gave no effect to the evidence referred to in para. 10(1), that the advertisement would offend some of the newspaper's subscribers, which in addition would, of course, result in a loss of subscribers and afford reasonable cause for declining to accept the business.

The first two questions of law stated in the stated case raise a serious issue as to the extent to which the discretion of a newspaper publisher to determine what he wishes to publish in his newspaper has been curtailed by the *Human Rights Code*. Is his decision not to publish some item in his newspaper subject to review by a board of inquiry set up under the Act, with power, if it considers his decision unreasonable, to compel him to publish that which he does not wish to publish?

The Supreme Court of the United States, in 1974, in *Miami Herald Publishing Co. v. Tornillo,* 418 U.S. 241, had to consider whether a Florida statute violated the First Amendment's guarantee of freedom of the press. This statute granted to a political candidate the right to equal space in a newspaper to answer criticism and attacks on his record by a newspaper. This right is somewhat similar to that defined in s.3 of Bill No. 9 entitled "An Act to ensure the Publication of Accurate News and Information", which had been reserved by the Lieutenant-Governor of Alberta, and which was under consideration in this Court: see *Reference re Alberta Legislation,* [1938] 2 D.L.R. 81, [1938] S.C.R. 100 [affd [1938] 4 D.L.R. 433, [1939] A.C. 117 *sub nom. A.-G. Alta. v. A.-G. Can.,* [1938] 3 W.W.R. 337 (P.C.) (the *Alberta Press* case)].

The Supreme Court of the United States held that the statute under consideration was a violation of the First Amendment. In the course of his reasons for judgment, Chief Justice Burger, who delivered the opinion of the Court, said that the statute failed to clear the barriers of the First Amendment because of its intrusion into the function of editors. He went on to say at p. 258:

> A newspaper is more than a passive receptacle or conduit of news, comment, and advertising. The choice of material to go into a newspaper, and the decisions made as to limitations on the size and content of the paper, and treatment of public issues and public officials — whether fair or unfair — constitute the exercise of editorial control and judgment. It has yet to be demonstrated how governmental regulations of this crucial process can be exercised consistent with First Amendment guarantees of a free press as they have evolved at this time.

The *Canadian Bill of Rights,* s.1(*f*), recognizes freedom of the press as a fundamental freedom.

While there is no legislation in British Columbia in relation to freedom of the press, similar to the First Amendment or to the *Canadian Bill of Rights,* and while there is no attack made in this appeal on the constitutional validity of the *Human Rights Code,* I think that Chief Justice Burger's statement about editorial control and judgment in relation to a newspaper is of assistance in considering one of the essential ingredients of freedom of the press. The issue which arises in this appeal is as to whether s.3 of the Act is to be construed as purporting to limit that freedom.

Section 3 of the Act refers, in paras. (a) and (b), to "service... customarily available to the public". It forbids the denial of such a service to any person or class of persons and it forbids discrimination against any person or class of persons with respect to such a service, unless reasonable cause exists for such denial or discrimination.

In my opinion the general purpose of s. 3 was to prevent discrimination against individuals or groups of individuals in respect of the provision of certain things available generally to the public. The items dealt with are similar to those covered by legislation in the United States, both federal and state. "Accommodation" refers to such matters as accommodation in hotels, inns and motels. "Service" refers to such matters as restaurants, bars, taverns, service stations, public transportation and public utilities. "Facility" refers to such matters as public parks and recreational facilities. These are all items "customarily available to the public". It is matters such as these which have been dealt with in American case law on the subject of civil rights.

The case in question here deals with the refusal by a newspaper to publish a classified advertisement, but it raises larger issues, which would include the whole field of newspaper advertising and letters to the editor. A newspaper exists for the purpose of disseminating information and for the expression of its views on a wide variety of issues. Revenues are derived from the sale of its newspapers and from advertising. It is true that its advertising facilities are made available, at a price, to the general public. But Sun reserved to itself the right to revise, edit, classify or reject any advertisement submitted to it for publication and this reservation was displayed daily at the head of its classified advertisement section.

The law has recognized the freedom of the press to propagate its views and ideas on any issue and to select the material which it publishes. As a corollary to that, a newspaper also has the right to refuse to publish material which runs contrary to the views which it expresses. A newspaper published by a religious organization does not have to publish an advertisement advocating atheistic doctrine. A newspaper supporting certain political views does not have to publish an advertisement advancing contrary views. In fact, the judgments of Duff, C.J.C., Davis and Cannon, JJ., in the *Alberta Press* case, previously mentioned, suggest that provincial legislation to compel such publication may be unconstitutional.

In my opinion the service which is customarily available to the public in the case of a newspaper which accepts advertising is a service subject to the right of the newspaper to control the content of such advertising. In the present case, the Sun had adopted a position on the controversial subject of homosexuality. It did not wish to accept an advertisement seeking subscription to a publication which propagates the views of the Alliance. Such refusal was not based upon any personal characteristic of the person seeking to place that advertisement, but upon the content of the advertisement itself.

Section 3 of the Act does not purport to dictate the nature and scope of a service which must be offered to the public. In the case of a newspaper, the nature and scope of the service which it offers, including advertising service, is determined by the newspaper itself. What s.3 does is to provide that a service which is offered to the public is to be available to all persons seeking to use it, and the newspaper cannot deny the service which it offers to any particular member of the public unless reasonable cause exists for so doing.

In my opinion the Board erred in law in considering that s.3 was applicable in the circumstances of this case. I would dismiss the appeal with costs.

RITCHIE, SPENCE and PIGEON, JJ., concur with MARTLAND, J.

DICKSON, J. (dissenting): Counsel for the Vancouver Sun strongly contended for the traditional right of editorial control over newspaper content, including advertising. English law is remarkably bereft of guidance on the subject of editorial control over advertising. But in the United States, the common law is clear. Perhaps the best statement of the law is found in *Approved Personnel Inc. v. The Tribune Co.* (1965), 177 So. 2d 704 (Dist. C.A. Fla.) at p. 706:

> In the absence of any statutory provisions to the contrary, the law seems to be uniformly settled by the great weight of authority throughout the United States that the newspaper publishing business is a private enterprise and is neither a public utility nor affected with the public interest. The decisions appear to hold that even though a particular newspaper may enjoy a virtual monopoly in the area of its publication, this fact is neither unusual nor of important significance. The courts have consistently held that in the absence of statutory regulation on the subject, a newspaper may publish or reject commercial advertising tendered to it as its judgment best dictates without incurring liability for advertisements rejected by it.

In "Annotation — Right of Publisher of Newspaper or Magazine, in Absence of Contractual Obligation, to Refuse Publication of Advertisement", by E. L. Kellett, 18 A.L.R. 3d 1286 at pp. 1287-8, the following summary is provided:

> With the exception of one case, it has universally been held that in the absence of circumstances amounting to an illegal monopoly or conspiracy, the publisher of a newspaper or magazine is not required by law to accept and publish an advertisement, even where the advertisement is a proper one, and the regular fee for publication has been paid or tendered....
>
> The reasons for refusing to compel publication of an advertisement are that at common law a newspaper is strictly a private enterprise, is not a business clothed or affected with a public interest as is a public utility, innkeeper, or railroad, and that newspaper publishers are accordingly free to contract and deal with whom they please in conformity with the inherent right of every person to refuse to maintain trade relations with any individual.

In the British Royal Commission on the Press, 1947-49, Report (Cmd. 7700, 1949), there is a brief discussion of the "right of newspapers to reject advertisements" at p. 144:

> We have received evidence that some newspapers refuse all advertisements of a particular class. This is a different matter. We consider that a newspaper has a right to refuse advertisements of any kind which is contrary to its standards or may be objectionable to its readers. This right, however, should not be exercised arbitrarily.

I think it would be correct to state that a newspaper has a right to reject advertising at common law.

Apart from the common law position, counsel for the Vancouver Sun also cast his argument in terms of press freedom. This raises issues which have not been satisfactorily resolved, either in Canada, in Britain or in the United States. These issues which can be defined broadly as (1) the content of the term "freedom of the press"; (2) the distinction between "political" and "commercial" speech; and (3) the vexed issue of access to the press. The discussion which follows is not for the purpose of resolving any constitutional issue. There is no constitutional challenge to s.3(1) of the *Human Rights Code of British Columbia*. I wish merely to sketch the broad and important judicial background to the question posed in the case at bar.

As a starting point, I can do no better than quote from the British Royal Commission on the Press, Final Report (Cmd. 6810, 1977), pp. 8-9:

> Freedom of the press carries different meanings for different people. Some emphasise the freedom of proprietors to market their publications, others the freedom of individuals, whether professional journalists or not, to address the public through the press; still others stress the freedom of editors to decide what shall be published. These are all elements in the right to freedom of expression. But proprietors, contributors and editors must accept the limits to free expression set by the need to reconcile claims which may often conflict. The public,

> too, asserts a right to accurate information and fair comment which, in turn, has to be balanced against the claims both of national security and of individuals to safeguards for their reputation and privacy except when these are overridden by the public interest. But the public interest does not reside in whatever the public may happen to find interesting, and the press must be careful not to perpetrate abuses and call them freedom. Freedom of the press cannot be absolute. There must be boundaries to it and realistic discussion concerns where those boundaries ought to be set.
>
> We define freedom of the press as that degree of freedom from restraint which is essential to enable proprietors, editors and journalists to advance the public interest by publishing the facts and opinions without which a democratic electorate cannot make responsible judgments.

Later in their report, the Commissioners discuss legal constraints on the press and make the following general comment which, save for the freedom of the press assured by the *Canadian Bill of Rights,* is equally applicable to Canada (at p. 183):

> This country is unlike many others in having no laws which relate specifically to the press. There is no constitutional guarantee of the freedom of the press, as there is in the United States, and no judicial surveillance of the contents of the newspapers, as there is in Sweden. Nevertheless, there are areas of general law which relate predominantly, and in some cases almost exclusively, to the activities of the press. In important ways, legal provisions help to maintain the delicate balance between freedom of the press and the public interest.

In Canada, as in Britain, much of the protection of the freedom of the press must derive from the interpretation of the "general law" rather than from a constitutional guarantee, and from the interpretation of statutes such as the British Columbia *Human Rights Code* as they may affect the press. While admittedly the *Alberta Press* case, *Reference re Alberta Legislation,* [1938] 2 D.L.R. 81, [1938] S.C.R. 100 [affd [1938] 4 D.L.R. 433, [1939] A.C. 117 *sub nom. A.-G. Alta. v. A.-G. Can.*, [1938] 3 W.W.R. 337 (P.C.)], dealt with the constitutional validity of the "Alberta Press bill", as it was termed, the comments of Chief Justice Duff and Mr. Justice Cannon in that case are important in defining the notion of freedom of the press in the Canadian context.

In the United States, freedom of the press rests upon the First Amendment, which reads:

> Congress shall make no law respecting an establishment of religion, or prohibiting the free exercise thereof; or abridging the freedom of speech, or of the press, or the right of the people peaceably to assemble, and to petition the Government for redress of grievances.

The framers of the United States Constitution linked freedom of speech in the First Amendment to freedom of the press to provide an effective forum for such expression: "Conflict Within the First Amendment: A Right of Access to Newspapers", 48 N.Y.U.L.R. 1200 (1973). In the result, there would appear to be general agreement in Britain, Canada, and the United States, as to the "free public discussion" rationale for freedom of the press.

Within the First Amendment in the United States two issues have been much discussed: whether the First Amendment mandates equal protection for "commercial" as opposed to "political" speech, and whether the First Amendment not only protects expression once it comes to the fore, but also serves to ground an affirmative right of access to the media. In response to these issues two trends can be discerned in the American cases. The first is the obliteration of any meaningful distinction between "political" and "commercial" speech within the First Amendment. The second is the rejection of a right of access to the press based upon the First Amendment.

The so-called "commercial speech" doctrine finds its origin in the case of *Valentine v. Crestensen* (1942), 316 U.S. 52 at p. 54, where Mr. Justice Roberts, on behalf of the Court, stated unequivocally: "We are equally clear that the Constitution imposes no such restraint [the First Amendment] on government as respects purely commercial advertising." I do not intend any detailed canvas of the American authorities other than to say that the "commercial" exception appeared to retain its virility as recently as the case of *Pittsburgh Press Co. v. Pittsburgh Commission on Human Relations* (1973), 413 U.S. 376, but the ambit of that case was shortly thereafter cut down in *Bigelow v. Virginia* (1975) 421 U.S. 809, and further narrowed the following year in *Virginia State Board of Pharmacy v. Virginia Citizens Consumer Council Inc.* (1976) 425 U.S. 748, where the Court struck down the restrictions on prescription drug advertising found in Virginia law as violating the First Amendment. Nor has this wave receded: see *Bates v. State Bar of Arizona* (1977), 97 S. Ct. 2691, where State bar restrictions on advertising by lawyers were struck down.

A separate line of cases has upheld the view that the First Amendment serves no affirmative function, *i.e.*, it does not mandate any right of access, however limited, to the media: see *Chicago Joint Board, Amalgamated Clothing Workers of America A.F.L.-CLO v. Chicago Tribune Co.* (1969), 307 F. Supp. 422 (N.D. Ill); affd 435 F.2d 470 (7th Cir.); *certiorari* denied 402 U.S. 973. Any doubts, so far as the United States is concerned, as to a right of access to newspapers, would appear to be settled by the Supreme Court in *Miami Herald Publishing Co. v. Tornillo* (1974), 418 U.S. 241. The newspaper had refused to print Tornillo's replies to editorials critical of his candidacy for State office and Tornillo brought suit seeking injunctive and declaratory relief under Florida's "right of reply" statute. That statute provided that:

> ... if a candidate for nomination or election is assailed regarding his personal character or official record by any newspaper, the candidate has the right to demand that the newspaper print, free of cost to the candidate, any reply the candidate may make to the newspaper's charges. The reply must appear in as conspicuous a place and in the same kind of type as the charges which prompted the reply, provided it does not take up more space than the charges. Failure to comply with the statute constitutes a first-degree misdemeanour.

While the Circuit Court held the statute unconstitutional as an infringement on the freedom of the press under the First and Fourteenth Amendments, the Florida Supreme Court found no such violation, free speech being enhanced and not abridged by the statute, which furthered the "broad societal interest in the free flow of information to the public". This view was rejected by the Supreme Court on the ground that it constituted interference by the Government with the exercise of editorial control and judgment, and hence with First Amendment guarantees of a free press. See also *Columbia Broadcasting System Inc. v. Democratic National Committee* (1973), 412 U.S. 94.

Before leaving the American cases it is, I think, appropriate to note that these cases were decided in light of a strong First Amendment constitutional underpinning, and legislation such as that found in the British Columbia *Human Rights Code* was not in issue. Our limited jurisprudence, to which I will shortly refer, would appear to accept a greater degree of regulation in respect of newspaper advertising than is apparent in the United States.

VI

Although freedom of the press is one of our cherished freedoms, recognized in the *quasi*-constitutional *Canadian Bill of Rights,* the freedom is not absolute. Publishers of newspapers are amenable to civil and criminal laws which bear equally upon all businessmen and employers, generally, in the community, for example, those regulating labour relations, combines, or imposing non-discriminatory general taxation. False and misleading advertising may properly be proscribed. In *Cowen et al. v. A.-G. B.C. et al.,* [1941] 2 D.L.R. 687, [1941] S.C.R. 321, the central question was whether a 1939 amendment to the British Columbia *Dentistry Act,* which barred any person not registered under the Act from practising or offering to practise dentistry in the Province, was limited to acts within the Province, and press freedom was not raised. The result of the decision, however, was the maintenance of an injunction to prevent the publication of certain advertisements in a daily newspaper. In *Benson & Hedges (Canada) Ltd. et al. v. A.-G. B.C.* (1972), 27 D.L.R. (3d) 257, 6 C.P.R. (2d) 182, [1972] 5 W.W.R. 32, (B.C.S.C.), an Act, the effect of which was "to prohibit advertising by any person of tobacco products", was upheld, although press freedom does not appear to have been in issue or argued. In *R. v. Telegram Publishing Co. Ltd.* (1960) 25 D.L.R. (2d) 471, 129 C.C.C. 209, [1960] O.R. 518 *sub nom. R. v. Toronto Magistrates, Ex p. Telegram Publishing Co.* (Ont. H.C.), Mr. Justice Schatz held that a section of the *Liquor Control Act* of Ontario prohibiting the publication of any announcement concerning liquor was not an encroachment on the freedom of the press, or upon freedom of speech.

Newspapers occupy a unique place in western society. The press has been felicitously referred to by de Toqueville as "the chief democratic instrument of freedom". Blackstone wrote, "The liberty of the press is indeed essential to the nature of a free state." Jefferson went so far as to assert, "Were it left for me to decide whether we should have a government without newspapers, or newspapers without a government, I should not hesitate a moment to prefer the latter." There is a direct and vital relationship between a free press and a free society. The right to speak freely, publish freely, and worship freely, are fundamental and indigenous rights, but it is "freedom governed by law", as Lord Wright observed in *James v. Commonwealth of Australia,* [1936] A.C. 578 at p. 627. In the *Alberta Press* case, *supra,* we find these words of Sir Lyman P. Duff, C.J.C., at p. 108 D.L.R., p. 134 S.C.R.:

> Some degree of regulation of newspapers everybody would concede to the Provinces. Indeed, there is a very wide field in which the Provinces undoubtedly are invested with legislative authority over newspapers; but the limit, in our opinion, is reached when the legislation effects such a curtailment of the exercise of the right of public discussion as substantially to interfere with the working of the parliamentary institutions of Canada...

Governments in Canada have generally respected press independence and have followed a policy of non-intervention.

There is an important distinction to be made between legislation designed to control the editorial content of a newspaper, and legislation designed to control discriminatory practices in the offering of commercial services to the public. We are dealing in this case with the classified advertising section of a newspaper. The primary purpose of commercial advertising is to advance the economic welfare of the newspaper. That part of the paper is not concerned with freedom of speech on matters of public concern as a condition of democratic polity, but rather with the provision of a "service or facility customarily available to the public'' with a view to profit. As such, in British Columbia a newspaper is impressed with a statutory obligation not to deny space or discriminate with respect to classified advertising, unless for reasonable cause. It should be made clear that the right of access with which we are here concerned has nothing to do with those parts of the paper where one finds news or editorial content, parts which can in no way be characterized as a service customarily available to the public. The effect of s.3 of the British Columbia *Human Rights Code* is to require newspapers within the Province to adopt advertising policies which are not in violation of the principles set out in the *Code*.

VII

I turn now to the stated case, paras. 10, 11, and 12 of which read:

> 10. The refusal by the Appellant to publish the advertisement in question was stated to be the result of a policy which the paper has in its advertising department (as distinct from its editorial department) to avoid any advertising material dealing with homosexuals or homosexuality, and the Appellant argued that this policy was justified on three grounds:
>
> (1) That homosexuality is offensive to public decency and that the advertisement would offend some of its subscribers;
>
> (2) That the Code of Advertising Standards, a Code of Advertising Ethics subscribed to by most of the daily newspapers in Canada includes the following section:
>
> > ''Public decency — no advertisement shall be prepared or be knowingly accepted which is vulgar, suggestive or in any way offensive to public decency.''
>
> and that the advertisement in question did not conform to the standards therein set out; and
>
> (3) That the Appellant newspaper had a duty to protect the morals of the community:
>
> 11. This Board of Inquiry found that the central theme of the Appellant's argument was that the policy in question was predicated on a desire to protect a reasonable standard of decency and good taste.
>
> 12. Assessing all the evidence offered on the question of the cause or motivation behind the Appellant's refusal to publish the Respondent's advertisement, the majority of the Board of Inquiry found the inevitable conclusion to be that the real reason behind the policy was not a concern for any standard of public decency, but was, in fact, a personal bias against homosexuals and homosexuality on the part of various individuals within the management of the Appellant newspaper. Board Member Dr. Dorothy Smith dissented on this point and held that there was no evidence whatsoever on which the Board could make such a finding; and that, in particular there was no evidence to rebut the Appelant's repeated statements that its policy was predicated on a desire to protect a reasonable standard of decency and good taste.

It seems clear from the foregoing that the Vancouver Sun in its advertising department, as distinct from its editorial department, had a particular policy. That policy was to avoid any advertising material dealing with homosexuals or homosexuality. The paper advanced three grounds as constituting reasonable cause, the ''central theme'' of which was a ''desire to protect a reasonable standard for decency and good taste''.

In its main factum, the respondent newspaper contended that the board failed to address itself to the only question posed by the statute, ''did reasonable cause exist?'', and instead substituted a determination as to motive for refusing the advertisement. Although the stated case leaves something to be desired in terms of clarity, there does not seem to be any doubt that the board rejected the three grounds advanced on the part of the paper in justification of its refusal to publish the advertisement. A majority of the board also found that the real reason for the refusal to publish was a personal bias against homosexuals and homosexuality on the part of various individuals within the management of the newspaper. The paper, therefore, had failed to establish reasonable cause. Much was made of the word "motivation" and "the real reason behind the policy". These words do not give any particular trouble. We need not indulge in nice appraisal based upon casuistic distinctions between the meaning of "cause" and "motive", words which are virtually synonymous.

I have earlier adverted to the matter of reasonable cause. "Reasonableness" is normally a question of fact. The most recent authoritative affirmation of that statement is from Lord Hailsham, L.C., in *Re W. (An Infant),* [1971] A.C. 682 at p. 699:

> And, be it observed, "reasonableness," or "unreasonableness," where either word is employed in English law, is normally a question of fact and degree and not a question of law so long as there is evidence to support the finding of the court.

Whatever else it may have done, the board of inquiry in the case at bar found the fact of "reasonable cause" adversely to the respondent newspaper. From that finding, there is a very limited right of appeal provided by s.18 of the British Columbia *Human Rights Code*. The section reads in part:

> 18. An appeal lies from a decision of a board of inquiry to the Supreme Court upon
> (a) any point or question of law or jurisdiction; or
> (b) any finding of fact necessary to establish its jurisdiction that is manifestly incorrect,

The jurisdiction of the board of inquiry is not challenged. Insufficiency of evidence was not even argued in this Court or in the Courts below.

Counsel for the Sun argued that the *Human Rights Code* does not purport to be, and should not be employed as, an instrument to compel a newspaper to accept advertisements which it can reasonably be said will harm its reputation and standing. If the paper had taken that position before the board and had established adverse economic impact, the board's conclusions might well have been different. What counsel is really asking this Court to do is make new findings of fact. This we cannot undertake unless there is no evidence to support the board's findings or unless those findings are perverse. In my view, Mr. Justice MacDonald expressed the legal position correctly when he said:

> Whether particular circumstances amount to reasonable cause for denial or discrimination under s.3 is purely a question of fact. It must be decided as a matter of law, under a proper definition of the phrase "reasonable cause". The only restraints which the law places upon the triers of fact are the provisions of s.3(2). They may not find the race, religion, colour, ancestry, or place of origin of any person or class of persons reasonable cause unless it relates to the maintenance of public decency or to the determination of premiums or benefits under contracts of insurance. What the appellant's submission does is to take some elements — what it submits are the circumstances of its case — and ask the Court to find that, as a matter of law, they must constitute reasonable cause. But it is really an invasion of the area of fact. If the appellant's submission is sound, how long is the list of different plausible circumstances which the court would be bound to find constituted reasonable cause?

In an alternative argument, counsel submitted that, if the board did address itself to whether reasonable cause for the refusal existed on an objective basis, then the board erred in failing to construe the term "reasonable cause" solely in relation to the characteristics of the person tendering the advertisement. The argument, as I understand it, would limit the Code to unreasonable refusals based upon the characteristics of the persons seeking the public service. It was said the board erred in considering the text of the advertisement which gave rise to the denial of service. The paper, at most, discriminated against the idea of a thesis of homosexuality, and it is no offence to discriminate against ideas. A number of American authorities based on the First Amendment, to which I have earlier referred, were relied upon. The argument is an interesting one but, for the reasons given by the Chief Justice, whose judgment in draft I have had the advantage of reading, I would reject the argument.

I would only add in concluding that I do not think a newspaper, or any other institution or business providing a service to the public, can insulate itself from human rights legislation by relying upon "honest" bias, or upon a statement of policy which reserves to the proprietor the right to decide whom he shall serve.

I am unable to find in the stated case any convincing proof that the board of inquiry misunderstood the evidence or misdirected itself in law. I note again that there has been no constitutional challenge on the ground that interference with the right of a newspaper to control its content is an attempt to abrogate the rights of a free press and is, consequently, outside the legislative jurisdiction of the Province of British Columbia.

I would allow the appeal, set aside the judgment of the British Columbia Court of Appeal and restore the judgment of MacDonald, J., and the order of the board of inquiry, with costs throughout.

BEETZ, J., concurs with MARTLAND, J.
ESTEY, J., concurs with DICKSON, J.
PRATTE, J., concurs with MARTLAND, J.
[LASKIN, C.J.C. also dissented]

Appeal dismissed.

1.3.7 *Re Public Service Board, Dionne and Attorney-General of Canada* (1978), 83 D.L.R. (3d) 178. (S.C.C.)

LASKIN, C.J.C.: — This appeal raises a constitutional question which, by an order of March 16, 1977, was formulated as follows:

> Are section 23 of the *Public Service Board Act* (R.S.Q. 1964, c.229) and the ordinances rendered pursuant thereto unconstitutional, *ultra vires* or inoperative to the extent that they apply to a cabledistribution public service as defined in the regulation respecting cabledistribution public service (O.C. 3565-73 of the 25th of September, 1973) adopted pursuant to section 3a of the *Communications Department Act* (S.Q. 1969, c.65).

The Quebec Court of Appeal in dealing with the issues raised by this question concluded unanimously, in reasons delivered by Tremblay, C.J.Q., that it was beyond the competence of the Province of Quebec to regulate the operation of cable distribution systems through which television signals were captured and transmitted to subscribers. In the result, the Quebec Court of Appeal set aside three decisions of the Quebec Public Service Board which had authorized François Dionne, a respondent in this Court, and Raymond D'Auteuil, one of the appellants herein, to operate cable distribution enterprises in certain defined areas in the Province and which had settled certain questions touching the carrying out of the authorizations. Dionne alone challenged the validity of the decisions of the Board, a challenge which required a consideration of the statutory authority exercised by the Board, and leave, as required by Quebec law, was obtained to bring the challenge before the Quebec Court of Appeal.

In its judgment setting aside the decisions of the Quebec Public Service Board and assigning exclusive competence over the operation of cablevision to the Parliament of Canada, the learned Chief Justice referred to and relied on the judgment of the Federal Court of Appeal in *Re Capital Cities Communications Inc. et al. and Canadian Radio Television Com's* (1975), 52 D.L.R. (3d) 415, 19 C.P.R. (2d) 51, [1975] F.C. 18, as well as on the judgment of the Privy Council in *Re Regulation and Control of Radio Communication; A.-G. Que. v. A.-G. Can.*, [1932] 2 D.L.R. 81, [1932] A.C. 304, [1932] 1 W.W.R. 563, and the judgment of the British Columbia Court of Appeal in *Re Public Utilities Com'n and Victoria Cablevision Ltd. et al.* (1965), 51 D.L.R. (2d) 716, 52 W.W.R. 286. The *Capital Cities* case came before this Court in late January of this year, after the Quebec Court of Appeal had rendered judgment in the present case — the judgment of the Quebec Court of Appeal was also brought to the notice of this Court — and this Court had an opportunity in that appeal to consider issues similar to those raised here [81 D.L.R. (3d) 609, 18 N.R. 181]. Indeed, the Attorney-General of Quebec, the main appellant herein, was an intervenant before this Court in the *Capital Cities* case, and his factum and the oral argument presented by counsel on his behalf canvassed fully the same issues that are raised in the present case. This Court concluded, on the facts established in the *Capital Cities* case, that exclusive legislative authority in relation to the regulation of cablevision stations and their programming, at least where such programming involved the interception of television signals and their retransmission to cablevision subscribers, rested in the Parliament of Canada.

Since the matter was argued anew in the present case, and since other Provinces intervened in support of the Quebec Attorney-General's challenge to exclusive federal competence (they having also intervened in the *Capital Cities* case), I think it desirable that something more be said here, notwithstanding the extensive canvass that was made in the *Capital Cities* case. The two central strands of what I may call the provincial submissions wre that (1) two enterprises, having no necessary connection with each other, were involved in television operations and in cablevision operations, and (2) the fact that different controlling entities were involved in those operations emphasized the separateness of the enterprises, and since the cable distribution operation was locally situate and limited in its subscriber relations to persons in Quebec it was essentially a local work or undertaking within provincial competence under s.92(10) of the *British North America Act, 1867*.

The fundamental question is not whether the service involved in cable distribution is limited to intraprovincial subscribers or that it is operated by a local concern but rather what the service consists of. This is the very question that was faced by the Privy Council in the *Radio* case, *supra,* (in a different context, it is true) and which was also before that body in *A.-G. Ont. et al. v. Winner et al.*, [1954] 4 D.L.R. 657, [1954] A.C. 541, 13 W.W.R. (N.S.) 657. There is another element that must be noticed, and that is that where television broadcasting and receiving is concerned there can no more be a separation for constitutional purposes between the carrier system, the physical apparatus, and the signals that are received and carried over the system than there can be between railway tracks and the transportation service provided over them or between the roads and transport vehicles and the transportation service that they provide. In all these cases, the inquiry must be as to the service that is provided and not simply as to the means through which it is carried on. Divided constitutional control of what is functionally an interrelated system of transmitting and receiving television signals, whether directly through air waves or through intermediate cable line operations, not only invites confusion but is alien to the principle of exclusiveness of legislative authority, a principle which is as much fed by a sense of the constitution as a working and workable instrument as by a literal reading of its words. In the present case, both the relevant words and the view of the constitution as a pragmatic instrument come together to support the decision of the Quebec Court of Appeal.

I should emphasize that this is not a case where the cable distribution enterprises limit their operations to programmes locally produced by them for transmission over their lines to their local subscribers. Admittedly, they make use of television signals received at their antennae, both from within and without the Province; and the fact that they may make changes or deletions in transmitting the off-air programmes to their subscribers does not affect their liability to federal regulatory control. The suggested analogy with a local telephone system fails on the facts because the very technology employed by the cable distribution enterprises in the present case establishes clearly their reliance on television signals and on their ability to receive and transmit such signals to their subscribers. In short, they rely on broadcasting stations, and their operations are merely a link in a chain which extends to subscribers who receive the programmes through their private receiving sets. I do not think that any argument based on relative percentages of original programming and of programmes received from broadcasting stations can be of any more avail here than it was in *Re Tank Truck Transport Ltd.* (1960), 25 D.L.R. (2d) 161, [1960] O.R. 497 *sub nom. R. v. Toronto Magistrates, Ex p. Tank Trunk Transport Ltd.;* affirmed 36 D.L.R. (2d) 636, [1963] 1 O.R. 272.

For these reasons, as well as for those in the *Capital Cities* case, in which judgment is being given concurrently with the judgment herein, I would dismiss the appeal with costs. There will be no costs to the Attorney-General of Canada nor to or against any of the intervenors.

MARTLAND, RITCHIE, SPENCE and DICKSON, JJ., concur with Laskin, C.S.C. BEETZ and DE GRANDPRÉ, JJ. concur with PIGEON, J.

1.3.8 Notes on the Implied Bill of Rights; from Peter Hogg, *The Constitutional Law of Canada* (Toronto: Carswell, 1977)

For many of us any regulation by government of the expression of ideas, and especially the prior restraint involved in censorship, is abhorrent. But in the context of the federal distribution of powers "the constitutional issue ... is simply whether the particular suppression or enlargement is competent to the Dominion or to the Province, as the case may be". In the absence of a bill of rights, the issue is "which jurisdiction should have power to work the injustice not whether the injustice should be prohibited completely".

It is understandable that some writers and judges have wanted to confront directly the question whether any legislative body in Canada should have the power to impair fundamental civil liberties. It is, of course, the theory that there are some "injustices" which should be "prohibited completely" which is the impulse to adoption of a bill of rights. However, there have been some suggestions in the case law of an "implied bill of rights" in the B.N.A. Act. Duff C.J.'s opinion in *Alberta Press* (but not Cannon J.'s) can be read as suggesting that not only the provincial Legislatures, but also the federal Parliament, are incompetent to curtail political discussion in Canada. In *Saumur,* as we have seen, Rand, Kellock and Locke JJ. quoted with approval from Duff C.J.'s opinion in *Alberta Press,* and Kellock J. specifically pointed out that it was possible to read an implied bill of rights into Duff C.J.'s comments. In *Switzman,* Rand J. left open the possibility that Parliament as well as the Legislatures might not be competent to curtail freedom of discussion; but Abbott J. went further, saying explicitly that "Parliament itself could not abrogate this right of discussion and debate".

Abbott J.'s obiter dictum in *Switzman* is the only unequivocal expression of the implied bill of rights theory in the Supreme Court of Canada. It is of course opposed to the conventional wisdom that legislative powers in Canada are exhaustively distributed. The indications which have been suggested in favour of the implied bill of rights are the preamble to the B.N.A. Act, which refers to "a constitution similar in principle to that of the United Kingdom", and the establishment by the B.N.A. Act of representative parliamentary institutions. The reasoning is that the framers of the B.N.A. Act would not have contemplated the abrogation of free speech by either level of government when it has been traditionally enjoyed in the United Kingdom and when it is "the breath of life of parliamentary institutions". A difficulty with this line of reasoning is that the central feature of the constitution of the United Kingdom, and of its Parliament, was in 1867, and still is, parliamentary sovereignty. In the United Kingdom the tradition of respect for civil liberties is not reflected in the law of the constitution. Any of the civil liberties, including free speech, can be abolished by the Parliament at any time. Thus, when the B.N.A. Act established parliamentary institutions on the model of the United Kingdom, the plausible assumption would be, as the courts have so often emphasized, that the Canadian institutions would enjoy powers of the same order as those of the Parliament at Westminster. Any limitations on legislative power, such as those entailed by the federal system, could be expected to be expressed, or at least very clearly implied. This seems especially clear with respect to a bill of rights. The framers of the B.N.A. Act had the United States constitution before them — it was their only useful precedent. They followed its federal character, but they deliberately did not copy its bill of rights. It is the theory of exhaustive distribution, not the implied bill of rights, which is more faithful to both the history and the text of the B.N.A. Act.

1.3.9 The Canadian Bill of Rights (1960)

The Bill of Rights was enacted by Parliament in 1960 when John Diefenbaker's Progressive Conservatives controlled the government. The act anticipated many of the provisions of the Canadian Charter of Rights and Freedoms. It included provisions saying, for example, that freedom of the press is a fundamental right. However, the statute was not part of the Constitution. It was an ordinary statute subject to repeal like any other statute passed by Parliament. Its application was limited to the laws enacted by the Federal Parliament. As it turned out, no case in the Supreme Court relating to freedom of the press was adjudicated on the basis of this statute.

THE CANADIAN BILL OF RIGHTS
8-9 ELIZABETH II

CHAPTER 44

An Act for the Recognition
and Protection of Human Rights
and Fundamental Freedoms.

[Assented to 10th August, 1960.]

The Parliament of Canada, affirming that the Canadian Nation is founded upon principles that acknowledge the supremacy of God, the dignity and worth of the human person and the position of the family in a society of free men and free institutions;

Affirming also that men and institutions remain free only when freedom is founded upon respect for moral and spiritual values and the rule of law;

And being desirous of enshrining these principles and the human rights and fundamental freedoms derived from them, in a Bill of Rights which shall reflect the respect of Parliament for its constitutional authority and which shall ensure the protection of these rights and freedoms in Canada:

THEREFORE Her Majesty, by and with the advice and consent of the Senate and House of Commons of Canada, enacts as follows:

PART I

BILL OF RIGHTS

1. It is hereby recognized and declared that in Canada there have existed and shall continue to exist without discrimination by reason of race, national origin, colour, religion or sex, the following human rights and fundamental freedoms, namely,

(a) the right of the individual to life, liberty, security of the person and enjoyment of property, and the right not to be deprived thereof except by due process of law;

(b) the right of the individual to equality before the law and the protection of the law;

(c) freedom of religion;

(d) freedom of speech;

(e) freedom of assembly and association; and

(f) freedom of the press.

2. Every law of Canada shall, unless it is expressly declared by an Act of the Parliament of Canada that it shall operate notwithstanding the Canadian Bill of Rights, be so construed and applied as not to abrogate, abridge or infringe or to authorize the abrogation, abridgment or infringement of any of the rights or freedoms herein recognized and declared, and in particular no law of Canada shall be construed or applied so as to

(a) authorize or effect the arbitrary detention, imprisonment or exile of any person;

(b) impose or authorize the imposition of cruel and unusual treatment or punishment;

(c) deprive a person who has been arrested or detained

(i) of the right to be informed promptly of the reason for his arrest or detention,
(ii) of the right to retain and instruct counsel without delay, or
(iii) of the remedy by way of *habeas corpus* for the determination of the validity of his detention and for his release if the detention is not lawful;

(d) authorize a court, tribunal, commission, board or other authority to compel a person to give evidence if he is denied counsel, protection against self crimination or other constitutional safeguards;
(e) deprive a person of the right to a fair hearing in accordance with the principles of fundamental justice for the determination of his rights and obligations;
(f) deprive a person charged with a criminal offence of the right to be presumed innocent until proved guilty according to law in a fair and public hearing by an independent and impartial tribunal, or of the right to reasonable bail without just cause; or
(g) deprive a person of the right to the assistance of an interpreter in any proceedings in which he is involved or in which he is a party or a witness, before a court, commission, board or other tribunal, if he does not understand or speak the language in which such proceedings are conducted.

3. The Minister of Justice shall, in accordance with such regulations as may be prescribed by the Governor in Council examine every proposed regulation submitted in draft form to the Clerk of the Privy Council pursuant to the *Regulations Act* and every Bill introduced in or presented to the House of Commons, in order to ascertain whether any of the provisions thereof are inconsistent with the purposes and provisions of this Part and he shall report any such inconsistency to the House of Commons at the first convenient opportunity.

4. The provisions of this Part shall be known as the *Canadian Bill of Rights*.

1.4 The Canadian Charter of Rights and Freedoms, 1982 and Current Judicial Practice

1.4.1 A Note on the Structure of the Charter

The Charter combines ancient civil liberties such as those enshrined in writs of Habeas Corpus and the Magna Carta with modern notions of human rights.

As noted above, sections 1 and 2 are especially important to students of media law. Section 2(b) declares that "freedom of thought, belief, opinion and expression, including freedom of the press and other media of communication" are amongst the freedoms fundamental to the organization of Canadian society. Section 1 guarantees these freedoms and the other rights set out in the Charter subject to "such reasonable limits prescribed by law as can be demonstrably justified in a free and democratic society".

The rest of the Charter guarantees democratic rights (such as the right to vote) in sections 3-5; mobility rights in section 6; legal rights (such as the right to be tried for an offence within a reasonable length of time) in sections 7-14; equality rights (such as the right to the equal benefit of the law without discrimination) in section 15; and linguistic and educational rights in sections 23 and 24. Sections 25 to 31 add some important qualifiers — for example, section 31 says that nothing in the Charter "extends the legislative powers of any body or authority'', and section 32 describes the sphere within which the Charter operates by saying that it applies to all matters of government in Canada.

The Charter has substantially expanded the scope of judicial review in Canada. Under the Constitution Act, 1867, the courts were empowered to determine if Parliament or the legislatures were acting within their respective jurisdictions. A decision by a court that a statute passed by Parliament usurped the authority of a provincial legislature would mean that the statute was a nullity, of no force. By contrast, the Charter confers on the courts the additional and extraordinary power to examine whether contested legislation conforms to the values and declarations in the Charter. The autonomy and power of each level of government have been diminished to the extent that the legislation each passes must in the end conform to the substantive standards contained in the Charter. Section 52 of the Constitution Act, 1982 makes this clear by declaring that ''The Constitution of Canada is the supreme law of Canada, and any law that is inconsistent with the provisions of the Constitution is, to the extent of the inconsistency, of no force and effect.''

Section 52 means that judicial review now embraces the whole field of fundamental freedoms, civil liberties and human rights.

Since the Charter was proclaimed, the Supreme Court of Canada has made it clear that its provisions will be made to apply only to the state and its institutions. If, for example, a statute contains provisions which are deemed to be unjustifiable encroachments on freedom of expression, the Court will strike them down. If, on the other hand, a private individual, such as a publisher, interferes with a journalist's right to free expression, a court is unlikely to interfere. Similarly, in defamation cases involving private individuals, neither a journalist nor a private citizen is likely to benefit from the Charter.

Canada's Constitution acquired some of the characteristics of the U.S. Constitution when the scope of judicial review was expanded so drastically. The Supreme Court of Canada began to exercise powers long held by the Supreme Court of the United States, this despite the fact that Canada purports to be a parliamentary democracy rather than a republic. Parliamentary democracies are marked by an acceptance of a basic constitutional rule that Parliament is supreme. The Canadian version of that principle, until 1982, was that Parliament was supreme in its domain and the provincial legislatures were supreme in theirs. From another perspective, then, the Charter represents another step in the Americanization of our institutions.

The extent to which the notion of parliamentary supremacy survives in our constitution is found in section 33 of the Constitution Act, 1982, which says ''Parliament or the legislature of a province may expressly declare ... that (an) Act ... shall operate notwithstanding the provisions included in Section 2 (fundamental freedoms) or sections 7 to 15 (legal rights) ...'' If such an act is passed, the enabling declaration will lapse after five years. In other words, statutes which are in conflict with the terms of the Charter, but which rely upon the notwithstanding provision in section 33 will either disappear from the statute books in five years or be debated and renewed.

Finally, parts II to V of the Constitution Act, 1982, contain declarations of rights of the aboriginal people of Canada, principles governing the management of regional disparities and procedures for amending the Constitution. While these parts of the Constitution are important, they do not directly affect questions of freedom of expression or of the press.

1.4.2 Constitution Act, 1982

PART I

CANADIAN CHARTER OF RIGHTS AND FREEDOMS

Whereas Canada is founded upon principles that recognize the supremacy of God and the rule of law:

Guarantee of Rights and Freedoms

Rights and freedoms in Canada

1. The *Canadian Charter of Rights and Freedoms* guarantees the rights and freedoms set out in it subject only to such reasonable limits prescribed by law as can be demonstrably justified in a free and democratic society.

Fundamental Freedoms

Fundamental freedoms

2. Everyone has the following fundamental freedoms:
(*a*) freedom of conscience and religion;
(*b*) freedom of thought, belief, opinion and expression, including freedom of the press and other media of communication;
(*c*) freedom of peaceful assembly; and
(*d*) freedom of association.

Legal Rights

Life, liberty and security of person

7. Everyone has the right to life, liberty and security of the person and the right not to be deprived thereof except in accordance with the principles of fundamental justice.

Proceedings in criminal and penal matters

11. Any person charged with an offence has the right
(*a*) to be informed without unreasonable delay of the specific offence;
(*b*) to be tried within a reasonable time;
(*c*) not to be compelled to be a witness in proceedings against that person in respect of the offence;
(*d*) to be presumed innocent until proven guilty according to law in a fair and public hearing by an independent and impartial tribunal;

Enforcement

Enforcement of guaranteed rights and freedoms

24. (1) Anyone whose rights or freedoms, as guaranteed by this Charter, have been infringed or denied may apply to a court of competent jurisdiction to obtain such remedy as the court considers appropriate and just in the circumstances.

Application of Charter

Application of Charter

32. (1) This Charter applies
(*a*) to the Parliament and government of Canada in respect of all matters within the authority of Parliament including all matters relating to the Yukon Territory and Northwest Territories; and

(*b*) to the legislature and government of each province in respect of all matters within the authority of the legislature of each province.

Exception

(2) Notwithstanding subsection (1), section 15 shall not have effect until three years after this section comes into force.

Exception where express declaration

33. (1) Parliament or the legislature of a province may expressly declare in an Act of Parliament or of the legislature, as the case may be, that the Act or a provision thereof shall operate notwithstanding a provision included in section 2 or sections 7 to 15 of this Charter.

Operation of exception

(2) An Act or a provision of an Act in respect of which a declaration made under this section is in effect shall have such operation as it would have but for the provision of this Charter referred to in the declaration.

Five year limitation

(3) A declaration made under subsection (1) shall cease to have effect five years after it comes into force or on such earlier date as may be specified in the declaration.

Re-enactment

(4) Parliament or the legislature of a province may re-enact a declaration made under subsection (1).

Five year limitation

(5) Subsection (3) applies in respect of a re-enactment made under subsection (4).

Primacy of Constitution of Canada

52. (1) The Constitution of Canada is the supreme law of Canada, and any law that is inconsistent with the provisions of the Constitution is, to the extent of the inconsistency, of no force or effect.

Constitution of Canada

(2) The Constitution of Canada includes
(*a*) the *Canada Act 1982*, including this Act;
(*b*) the Acts and orders referred to in the schedule; and
(*c*) any amendment to any Act or order referred to in paragraph (*a*) or (*b*).

1.4.3 Section 2(b): The Scope and Meaning of Freedom of Expression

The starting point for an analysis of the Charter by students of media law is section 2(b). That section gives constitutional protection to freedom of expression. As with all charter cases, a court first must determine whether a right or freedom, such as a 2(b) freedom, has been invaded or limited or denied. In order to do this it must determine what the phrase ''freedom of expression'' means and the range of activities it embraces.

1.4.3.1 *Re Ontario Film and Video Appreciation Society and Ontario Board of Censors* (1983), 41 O.R. (2d) 583 (Ont. Div. Ct.)

J. HOLLAND, BOLAND and LINDEN JJ.: We are all of the view that ss.3(2)(*a*) and (*b*), 35 and 38 impose a limitation on the freedom of expression of the applicant as guaranteed by s.2(*b*) of the Charter. It is clear to us that all forms of expression, whether they be oral, written, pictorial, sculpture, music, dance or film, are equally protected by the Charter. The burden, therefore, falls upon the Attorney-General to satisfy us on the balance of probabilities that the requirements of s.1 of the Charter have been met, and "[t]he standard of persuasion to be applied by the court is a high one if the limitation in issue is to be upheld as valid": see Evans C.J.H.C. in *Rauca, supra* [at p. 716 O.R., p. 423 D.L.R.]. By placing such an onus on governments, the Charter inhibits the courts from permitting the dilution of the guaranteed fundamental freedoms. Hence, any limit placed on these freedoms must be shown to be *demonstrably justifiable in a free and democratic society;* it must be a *reasonable limit;* and it must be a limit that is *"prescribed by law"*.

1.4.3.2 *Koumoudouros* v. *Municipality of Metropolitan Toronto* (1984), 8 C.R.R. 179 (Ont. H.C.)

EBERLE J.: ...The applicants' submissions that nude burlesque dancing is an expression, even an artistic expression, that is guaranteed to them by the guarantee of "freedom of expression" in the Charter, raises what is to me a most interesting question: is the Charter dealing with "artistic" expression at all when it guarantees "freedom of expression"? The close linking in s.2(*b*) of the Charter of the freedoms of thought, belief, opinion and expression, suggests rather that freedom of expression refers to the freedom of communication of ideas and opinions among the citizens of Canada, so that, in broad terms, those citizens may continue to live in the free and democratic society referred to in s.1 of the Charter. Furthermore, s.2(*b*) goes on, after providing for "freedom of expression", with the following words "including freedom of the press and other media of communication"; these words reinforce the view that the thrust of s.2(*b*) is in the political and governmental domain, a domain in which the freedoms of thought, belief, opinion and expression are inseparable from a free and democratic society. Further, it must not be forgotten that the Charter is found in the *Constitution Act, 1982,* which is one of Canada's principal constitutional documents, concerned with the fundamental political and governmental structures of the nation.

Nevertheless, in these cases it is not necessary, and is indeed unwise, to attempt to determine the precise ambit of freedom of expression. It is preferable to decide them on the basis of evidence in the record. The sales figures found at pp. 100-104, when taken with the evidence already referred to, put the matter in perspective, and emphasize the intimate connection between exposed female pubic areas and the dollar volume of liquor sales in the applicants' premises.

Therefore, assuming, without deciding, that "expression", in the Charter includes "artistic" expression, the conclusion from the evidence is clear that the right claimed in these cases is not a right to freedom of artistic expression but the right to expose performers' pubic areas for the purpose of stimulating liquor sales. I find it difficult to accept that the framers of the Charters had any such right in mind and the whole tenor and effect of the language in the Charter belies such a right.

The question to be decided is a question of constitutionality, not of taste; and I am satisfied that the "freedom of expression" guaranteed by the Charter does not include the public exposure of female pubic areas for the primary purpose of selling larger quantities of liquor. Accordingly the requirement of opaque clothing in cl. 28(2) of the by-law does not infringe upon the "freedom of expression" guaranteed by s.2(*b*) of the Charter.

In the result, therefore, the applications fail upon all grounds and must be dismissed with costs.

SIROIS J. concurs with EBERLE J.

Applications dismissed.

1.4.3.3 *Re Information Retailers Association of Metropolitan Toronto Inc. and Municipality of Metropolitan Toronto* (1985), 52 O.R. (2d) 449 (C.A.)

HOULDEN, CORY and ROBINS JJ. A.: Freedom of expression is a fundamental freedom protected by s.2(*b*) of the Charter. The protection applies to all phases of expression from writer, artist and photographer through to distributor and retailer and on to reader and viewer: *R. v. Videoflicks Ltd. et al.* (1984), 48 O.R. (2d) 395 at p. 431, 14 D.L.R. (4th) 10 at p. 46, 15 C.C.C. (3d) 353 (C.A.); *Re Ontario Film & Video Appreciation Society and Ontario Board of Censors* (1984), 45 O.R. (2d) 80*n*, 5 D.L.R. (4th) 766*n*, 38 C.R. (3d) 271 (C.A.). The freedom to distribute and sell is as essential to the exercise of the freedom as the freedom to publish, for without the means of disseminating expression, the publication would be of little value. Non-obscene "adult books and magazines", no matter how tasteless or tawdry they may be, are entitled to no less protection than other forms of expression; the constitutional guarantee extends not only to that which is pleasing, but also to that which to many may be aesthetically distasteful or morally offensive; it is indeed often true that "one man's vulgarity is another's lyric".

1.4.3.4 *Re Klein and Law Society of Upper Canada; Re Dvorak and Law Society of Upper Canada* (1985), 50 O.R. (2d) 118 (Ont. Div. Ct.).

CALLAGHAN J. (EBERLE J. concurring):

Fee advertising and freedom of expression

The threshold problem in these two applications is the meaning of the word "expression" in s.2(*b*) of the Charter. The entirety of s.2 of the Charter reads as follows:

> *Fundamental freedoms*
> 2. Everyone has the following fundamental freedoms:
> (*a*) freedom of conscience and religion;
> (*b*) freedom of thought, belief, opinion and expression, including freedom of the press and other media of communication;
> (*c*) freedom of peaceful assembly; and
> (*d*) freedom of association.

It is submitted on behalf of the applicants that the words "freedom of expression" in s.2(*b*) should be given their ordinary meaning and should be read as protecting all forms of "expression", including commercial speech. Commercial speech includes truthful and non-misleading fee advertising, such as "I will sell you X at Y price". Such advertising is clearly an "expression". The question is whether it is an expression within the meaning of s.2(*b*) of the Charter.

Counsel on behalf of Klein argues that it is enough that the statement be found an expression to place it within the protection afforded by s.2(*b*) and that the court's attention should then be directed to s.1 of the Charter. I do not agree that such a literal and purposeless interpretation of the Charter is proper. The Charter is a "living tree" and is to be interpreted in a liberal and expansive way: *Law Society of Upper Canada v. Skapinker*, [1984] 1 S.C.R. 357 at p. 365, 9 D.L.R. (4th) 161 at p. 167, 11 C.C.C. (3d) 481 at p. 487. That does not mean, however, that the course urged by counsel for Klein is the proper one for the Court to follow. To call the Charter a "living tree" is to import some purpose and context into the interpretation of the Charter, if only, to extend the metaphor, because trees have roots and some direction in their growth. Indeed, Canadian decisions regarding the Charter have had recourse to previous law, if only to provide a context for interpreting the provisions of the Charter. For example, the Ontario Court of Appeal stated in *Re Federal Republic of Germany and Rauca* (1983), 41 O.R. (2d) 225 at p. 244, 145 D.L.R. (3d) 638 at p. 658, 4 C.C.C. (3d) 385, that: "...the Charter was not enacted in a vacuum and the rights set out therein must be interpreted rationally having regard to the then existing laws". And in *R. v. Antoine* (1983), 41 O.R. (2d) 607, 148 D.L.R. (3d) 149, 5 C.C.C. (3d) 97, Martin J.A., for the court, cited Lord Wilberforce in *Minister of Home Affairs v. Fisher et al.*, [1980] A.C. 319, a case involving the interpretation of the Constitution of Bermuda, at p. 329 (the citation appearing at p. 614 O.R., p. 156 D.L.R.):

> "A Constitution is a legal instrument giving rise, amongst other things, to individual rights capable of enforcement in a court of law. *Respect must be paid to the language which has been used and to the traditions and usages which have given meaning to that language*. It is quite consistent with this, and with the recognition that rules of interpretation may apply, to take as a point of departure for the process of interpretation a recognition of the character and *origin* of the instrument, and to be guided by the principle of giving full recognition and effect to those fundamental rights and freedoms with a statement of which the Constitution commences."

(Emphasis changed.)

The U.S. Supreme Court has taken the same approach to its own Constitution. In *Robertson v. Baldwin* (1897), 165 U.S. 275, the court said at p. 281:

> The law is perfectly well-settled that the first ten amendments to the Constitution, commonly known as the Bill of Rights, were not intended to lay down any novel principles of government, but simply to embody certain guarantees and immunities which we have inherited from our ancestors, and which had from time immemorial been subject to certain well-recognized exceptions arising from the necessities of the case.

And in *Dennis v. United States* (1950), 341 U.S. 494, Mr. Justice Frankfurter, concurring in the court's affirmation of the lower judgment, said at p. 521:

> Just as there are those who regard as invulnerable every measure for which the claim of national survival is invoked, there are those who find in the Constitution a wholly unfettered right of expression. Such literalness treats the words of the Constitution as though they were found on a piece of outworn parchment instead of being words that have called into being a nation with a past to be preserved for the future.

Turning then to the Canadian jurisprudence as it existed prior to the Charter, it seems clear that to the extent that there was a freedom of expression to be found, it was one that applied exclusively to matters of political (and possibly cultural) speech.

Such protection as existed was extended to such speech because of the vital role it played in a democratic State. As was said by Cannon J. in *Reference re Alberta Statutes,* [1938] S.C.R. 100 at pp. 145-6, [1938] 2 D.L.R. 81 at p. 119:

> Freedom of discussion is essential to enlighten public opinion in a democratic State; it cannot be curtailed without affecting the right of the people to be informed through sources independent of the government concerning matters of public interest. There must be an untrammelled publication of the news and political opinions of the political parties contending for ascendancy.... Democracy cannot be maintained without its foundation: free public opinion and free discussion throughout the nation of all matters affecting the State within the limits set by the criminal code and the common law.... The province may deal with [a citizen's] property and civil rights of a local and private nature within the province; but the province cannot interfere with his status as a Canadian citizen and his fundamental right to express freely his untrammelled opinion about government policies and discuss matters of public concern.

This freedom of expression and discussion, such as existed, did not extend to commercial advertising of the kind which is the subject of these two applications. For as was said by Dickson J., albeit in dissent, in *Gay Alliance Toward Equality v. Vancouver Sun,* [1979] 2 S.C.R. 435 at p. 469, 97 D.L.R. (3d) 577 at pp. 601-2, [1979] 4 W.W.R. 118:

> The primary purpose of commercial advertising is to advance the economical welfare of the newspaper. That part of the paper is not concerned with freedom of speech on matters of public concern as a condition of democratic policy, but rather with the provision of a ''service or facility customarily available to the public'' with a view to profit.

Simply because commercial speech involves an expression does not mean that it must, somehow, be accounted for under s.2(*b*). In my view, this is to confuse form with substance. Pure commercial speech mimics political speech in form (both involve an expression), but not in substance or function. Commercial speech flows from the realm of economic activity; political speech from that of politics and government. In a democratic society the economic realm must be subordinate to the political realm. The people may determine through their elected representatives and properly so, how to regulate their economic affairs and through that, their economic speech. In doing so, their only concern need be with the process which generates the regulation. For so long as the regulation is the result of the democratic process and so long as the well-springs of that process are kept pure, through the protections afforded it by a Constitution, then there can be no valid complaint by the regulated. Complex economies are possible only under the shelter afforded them by the State and its institutions. Political regulation of individuals, however, is a different matter. Even if such regulation flows from a pure democratic process, it may be struck down, for in regulating the political activities of individuals a government may fetter the democratic process itself and, hence, bring democracy into jeopardy. Political speech is related to and prevents the fettering of the democratic process. It, of necessity, must fall within s.2(*b*). The Charter, to a certain extent, inferentially recognizes a separation of the realms of economic and political activity and the subordination of the former to the latter. Nowhere does it speak expressly of economic rights. Section 6(2)(*b*), which provides for a right ''to pursue the gaining of a livelihood'', was interpreted in the Supreme Court of Canada in the *Skapinker* case to refer to mobility rights, rather than a pure economic right to work. Section 7, in speaking of a right ''to life, liberty and security of the person'' is placed under the heading ''Legal Rights'' and is grouped with those rights that deal with the rights of an accused person. The Charter reflects a concern with the political rights of the individual and does not, in my view, reflect a similar concern with the economic sphere nor with its incidents such as commercial speech.

Prima facie then, the freedom of expression guaranteed by s.2(*b*) of the Charter would appear to apply to the expression of ideas and opinions relating to the political and governmental domains of the country. (I leave aside the question of whether or not artistic expression falls within s.2(*b*)). Indeed, this is the interpretation suggested by my brother Eberle J. in this court, in *Re Koumoudouros et al. and Municipality of Metropolitan Toronto* (1984), 45 O.R. (2d) 426 at p. 435, 6 D.L.R. (4th) 523 at p. 533, 11 C.C.C. (3d) 364, where he said:

> The close linking in s.2(*b*) of the Charter of the freedoms of thought, belief, opinion and expression, suggests rather that freedom of expression refers to the freedom of communication of ideas and opinions among the citizens of Canada, so that, in broad terms, those citizens may continue to live in the free and democratic society referred to in s.1 of the Charter. Furthermore, s.2(*b*) goes on, after providing for ''freedom of expression'', with the following words ''including freedom of the press and other media of communication'', these words reinforce the view that the thrust of s.2(*b*) is in the political and governmental domain, a domain in which the freedoms of thought, belief, opinion and expression are inseparable from a free and democratic society. Further, it must not be forgotten that the Charter is found in the *Constitution Act, 1982,* which is one of Canada's principal constitutional documents, concerned with the fundamental political and governmental structures of the nation.

But, as already noted, the applicants urge upon the court a broader and more expansive interpretation of ''expression'', one broad enough to cover the words ''I will sell you X for Y price''. In doing so, they relied heavily on the United States Supreme Court decisions in *Virginia State Board of Pharmacy v. Virginia Citizens Consumer Council* (1976), 425 U.S. 748, and in *Bates v. State Bar of Arizona* (1977), 433 U.S. 350. In the *Virginia Citizens* case, the court held that truthful, non-misleading advertising of the prices for standardized, pre-packaged medical products and drugs was a protected form of speech under the First Amendment. In the *Bates* case, the court applied the *Virginia Citizens* case to lawyers and held that price advertising for ''routine'' legal services, such as uncontested divorces, was also a form of protected speech under the First Amendment.

The traditional view in the United States had been that pure commercial speech was not protected under the First Amendment. This view was best exemplified by the Supreme Court's decision in *Valentine v. Crestenson* (1942), 316 U.S. 52, where in a short four-page decision, Mr. Justice Roberts, on behalf of the court, stated unequivocally at p. 54:

> This court has unequivocally held that the streets are proper places for the exercise of the freedom of communicating information and disseminating opinion and that though the state and municipalities may appropriately regulate the privilege in the public interest, they may not unduly burden or prescribe its employment in these public thoroughfares. *We are equally clear that the Constitution imposes no such restraint on government as respects purely commercial advertising.*

(Emphasis added.)

The Supreme Court in the *Virginia Citizens* case disparaged *Crestenson* as ''casual, almost off-hand'': *Virginia Citizens, supra,* n. 16, p. 759. Mr. Justice Stewart, in his concurring judgment, stated at p. 776 that the court in reaching its decision was ending the ''anomalous situation'' that had been created by *Crestenson*.

It is to be noted, however, that *Crestenson* had been firmly rooted in the well-established First Amendment jurisprudence that had existed at that time and which had protected freedom of speech as the ''matrix, the indispensable condition of nearly every other form of freedom'': see *Talko v. Connecticut* (1937), 302 U.S. 319, Cardozo J. for the court, at p. 327. Its centrality flowed from its function in a democratic state, a function which both justified its constitutional protection and provided the criterion by which any ''speech'' or ''expression's'' claim to such protection was measured. In a long line of authority (*Republica v. Oswald* (1788), 1 Dall. 319, 1 Am. Dec. 246; *Commonwealth v. Blanding* (1825), 3 Pick. 304, 15 Am. Dec. 214; *Grosjean v. American Press Co.* (1936), 297 U.S. 233) it was established that the predominant purpose of the First Amendment freedoms was to preserve speech and press as a vital source of public information in relation to public matters and those entrusted with the public business.

Given such jurisprudence, it is not surprising that the Supreme Court came to the decision it did in *Crestenson*. If its decision seemed casual in its brevity, it was only because it stood four square within the *rationale* that underlay the First Amendment. Pure commercial speech says nothing about how people are governed, or how they should govern themselves. Indeed, it stands outside of public discourse: it could be said in a tyranny or a democracy, a monarchy or a society without a government at all. Providing no support to a democracy, it did not claim constitutional protection until *Bigelow v. Virginia* (1975), 421 U.S. 809, and then the *Virginia Citizens* case in 1976.

To justify its abrupt about-face in these cases, the Supreme Court offered two *rationales* for extending First Amendment protection to pure commercial speech. The first was to say that the nature of the information conveyed — and the strength of the public's interest in such information — justified its protection under the First Amendment: *Virginia Citizens, supra,* pp. 764-5 and 780. In the court's opinion, the value of the information conveyed, and what justified its constitutional protection, lay in its contribution to informed decision-making by the public: *ibid.*, and see *Bates, supra,* at p. 364.

The second *rationale* attempted to forge a link between commercial and non-commercial (*i.e.*, political) speech. It did this by creating a formula wherein price advertising supported a free market, which, in turn, supported a free or democratic society. Thus, in the *Virginia Citizens* case, *supra,* at p. 765, the court states:

> Moreover, there is another consideration that suggests no line between publicly ''interesting'' or ''important'' commercial advertising and the opposite kind could ever be drawn. Advertising, however tasteless and excessive it sometimes may seem, is nonetheless dissemination of information as to who is producing and selling what product, for what reason, and at what price. So long as we preserve a predominantly free enterprise economy, the allocation of our resources in large measure will be made through numerous private economic decisions. It is a matter of public interest that those decisions, in the aggregate, be intelligent and well-informed. To this end, the free flow of commercial information is indispensable.... And it is indispensable to the proper allocation of resources in a free enterprise system, it is also indispensable to the formation of intelligent opinions as to how that system ought to be regulated or altered. Therefore, even if the First Amendment were thought to be primarily an instrument to enlighten public decision-making in a democracy, we could not say that the free flow of information does not serve that goal.

It can be said that this second *rationale,* with respect, is not convincing on its face. First, as already suggested, commercial speech is independent of and stands outside of political discourse. Information about the price at which a seller will sell his goods, and the decisions to purchase those goods that are made on the basis of that information, have absolutely nothing to say about, and no impact on, political discourse. Second, the "free market" is itself only an idea, one particular idea, about how goods should be distributed in society. It being only an idea about how goods should be allocated among citizens, there is nothing to prevent society from deciding that some other method of allocation is better. As Rehnquist J. noted in dissent in the *Virginia Citizens* case, *supra,* at p. 784:

> While there is again much to be said for the court's observation as a matter of desirable public policy, there is certainly nothing in the United States Constitution which requires the Virginia Legislature to hew to the teachings of Adam Smith in its legislative decisions regulating the pharmacy profession.

Indeed, this *rationale* was not subsequently repeated by the court. Rather, the court came to rest its protection of commercial speech on its informational content alone. This came to be the sole *rationale*: see Mr. Justice Powell in *Central Hudson Gas & Electric Corp. v. Public Service Com'n of New York* (1980), 447 U.S. 557 at p. 563: "The First Amendment's concern for commercial speech is based on the informational function of advertising."

The court in *Virginia Citizens* attempted to downplay the novelty of this *rationale* by citing prior decisions which had characterized the First Amendment protections as extending to information. In particular, both Blackmun J., for the court, and Stewart J., in his concurring decision, cited *Bigelow v. Virginia, supra,* at pp. 762 and 780, respectively; Mr. Justice Blackmun (at p. 762) also cited *Thornhill v. Alabama* (1940), 310 U.S. 88. Yet close analysis of these cases supports the observations of Rehnquist J. in dissent, who argued that the information protected had always and only related to political discussion: *Virginia Citizens, supra,* at p. 787.

The major problem with the decision in the *Virginia Citizens* case, one ignored then but subsequently acknowledged, was that the *rationales* which justified the constitutional protection of non-commercial (political and cultural) speech on the one hand, and commercial speech on the other, were fundamentally different. Indeed, they were antagonistic. As Mr. Justice Powell, for the court, emphasized in *Ohralik v. Ohio State Bar Ass'n* (1978), 436 U.S. 447 at p. 456:

> To require a parity of constitutional protection for commercial and non-commercial speech alike could invite dilution, simply by a leveling process, of the force of the Amendment's guarantee with respect to the latter kind of speech. Rather than subject the First Amendment to such a devitalisation, we instead have afforded commercial speech a limited measure of protection, commensurate with its subordinate position in the scale of First Amendment values, while allowing modes of regulation that might be impermissible in the realm of non-commercial expression.

Indeed, commercial speech was afforded not just a "limited measure" of protection; it was provided "a lesser protection": *Central Hudson Gas & Electric Corp. v. Public Service Com'n of New York* (1980), 447 U.S. 557 at p. 563. The lesser protection that was afforded commercial speech was founded on the premise that such speech, "although meriting some protection, is of less constitutional moment than other forms of speech": *Central Hudson Gas, supra,* at n. 5, p. 563. It was this lack of identity in the natures of commercial and non-commercial speech, if not the outright antagonism between the two, which justified "less precision" in the regulation of commercial speech than of political speech by the government: *Re Primus* (1978), 436 U.S. 412 at pp. 434 and 438. As the court itself noted in *Friedman v. Rogers* (1979), 440 U.S. 1, the decision in *Virginia Citizens* represented "a substantial extension of traditional free-speech doctrine which poses special problems not presented by other forms of protected speech": n. 9, pp. 10-1. The court went on in the same note to say that because of the

> ...special character of commercial speech and the relative novelty of First Amendment protection of such speech, we act with caution in confronting First Amendment challenges to economic legislation that serves legitimate regulatory interests. Our decisions dealing with more traditional First Amendment problems do not extend automatically to this as yet uncharted area.

But if commercial speech serves a function completely different from that associated with non-commercial speech; if its too-close association with political speech threatens to devalue the latter and the First Amendment; if it is of less moment; if it is entitled to less protection, and to regulations formulated with less precision, than that to which non-commercial speech is entitled, then surely the question arises, why protect it at all? This question is all the more pertinent in Canada's case, where we are asked to embark on a voyage that the U.S. Supreme Court, with 200 years of experience in attempting to define the ambit of non-commercial speech has characterized as being on uncharted seas. As we are not bound to follow the decisions of that court there is, in my view, no sound reason for doing so in the present case.

Counsel for the applicant, Klein, suggests that some of this judicial hesitancy may be put down to the absence in the U.S. Constitution of any equivalent of the Charter's s.1. Lacking any recourse to an express constitutional limit, the Supreme Court must create its own, while, at the same time, defining the substantive nature of the rights to be protected. According to counsel's argument then, the court need not concern itself when interpreting s.2(*b*) with the "commonsense differences" (the words are those of the Supreme Court in the *Virginia Citizens* case, *supra,* at n. 24, p. 771) between commercial speech and non-commercial speech, or with the problem of how that difference should or should not be reflected in the regulation to which each form of speech is subject. Rather, the court can leave that issue to its s.1 analysis.

But, with respect, this argument misconstrues what the United States Supreme Court was doing. The court is not simply saying that a free and democratic society may tolerate more regulation of free speech when it takes the form of pure commercial speech. Rather, it was also saying, and emphasizing, that pure commercial speech was substantively different from political speech. Thus, the fact that it fell under the First Amendment did *not* justify the application of the same criteria and tests when judging the legitimacy of its regulation by the government. In other words, the Supreme Court developed a new set of criteria, unique to commercial speech, to evaluate such regulation. The Supreme Court can do that precisely because the reasonable limits that are built into the U.S. Constitution are judge-made limits. The Charter, on the other hand, with its express provision of a reasonable limits clause in s.1, must of necessity preclude such a course of action. The alternative is for the Canadian Courts to develop two separate and different interpretations of s.1, one to be used where political speech is involved, the other where commercial speech is involved. That approach surely invites chaos.

Such an approach would also draw Canadian courts into a case-by-case review of regulation of most forms of commercial expression, a task better left to the people's elected representatives. For it is clear from subsequent developments in the U.S. jurisprudence that the effect of the decision in *Virginia Citizens* was to throw open to doubt the vast regulatory system governing commercial speech that had developed over the years. As a result, the Supreme Court has, inexorably, been drawn into a continuous judicial review of regulatory policy. In spite of its protest that *Virginia Citizens* did not mean that commercial speech could not be regulated, the Supreme Court has been forced to evaluate a number of various regulatory schemes already. Since the nature of such schemes depends on the nature of the product or service or industry to be regulated, the purpose of the regulation, and the parties involved, each scheme has had to be the subject of judicial scrutiny.

The court has heard cases involving questions of whether or not it was permissible under the First Amendment to prohibit promotional advertising by an electrical utility (maybe): *Central Hudson, supra;* promotional advertising by chiropractors (yes): *Talsky v. Department of Registration & Education,* 370 N.E. 2d 173; *certiorari* denied 99 S. Ct. 84; the use of trade names by a practising optometrist (yes): *Friedman, supra;* solicitation of clients by mail, by a lawyer for a political cause (no): *Primus, supra;* solicitation of clients in person where the lawyer approaches the client for reasons of self-interest (yes): *Ohralik, supra;* solicitation of clients by a lawyer when the client approaches the lawyer (maybe): *Ohralik, supra;* commercial billboards (probably): *Metromedia, Inc. v. City of San Diego* (1981), 453 U.S. 490, and active, as opposed to passive, solicitation of former clients by a lawyer who has left his former firm (yes): *Adler, Barish, Daniels, Levin et al. v. Epstein* (1978), 393 A. 2d 1175; appeal dismissed, *certiorari* denied 442 U.S. 907.

This case-by-case review of all such regulatory legislation has led to no clear test as to the extent that commercial speech is protected. It also highlights the irony of the *Virginia Citizens* case, for it demonstrates that legal effect is still being given to a distinction — that between commercial and non-commercial speech — which was supposedly erased by that case. It is clear, however, that commercial speech is of less moment than political speech within the First Amendment. It would appear that its inclusion thereunder threatens to devalue the latter unless the court is eternally vigilant.

The present American situation is well-expressed by Mr. Justice Rehnquist in dissent in *Central Hudson, supra,* at pp. 598-9:

> I remain of the view that the Court unlocked a Pandora's Box when it "elevated" commercial speech to the level of traditional political speech by according it First Amendment protection in *Virginia Pharmacy Board v. Virginia Citizens Consumer Council* 425 U.S. 748 (1976). The line between "commercial speech", and the kind of speech that those who drafted the First Amendment had in mind, may not be a technically or intellectually easy one to draw, but it surely produced far fewer problems than has the development of judicial doctrine in this area since *Virginia Pharmacy Board*. For in the world of political advocacy and its market place of ideas, there is no such thing as a "fraudulent" idea: there may be useless proposals, totally unworkable schemes, as well as very sound proposals that will receive the imprimatur of the "marketplace of ideas" through our majoritarian system of election and representative government. The free flow of information is important in this context not because it will lead to the discovery of any objective "truth", but because it is essential to our system of self-government.
>
> The notion that more speech is the remedy to expose falsehood and fallacies is wholly out of place in the commercial bazaar, where if applied logically the remedy of one who was

> defrauded would be merely a statement available upon request, reciting the Latin maxim "*caveat emptor*". But since "fraudulent speech" in this area is to be remediable under *Virginia Pharmacy Board, supra,* the remedy of one defrauded is a lawsuit or an agency proceeding based on common-law notions of fraud that are separated by a world of difference from the realm of politics and government. What time, legal decisions, and common sense have so widely severed, I declined to join in *Virginia Pharmacy Board* and regret now to see the court reaping the seeds that it there sowed. *For in a democracy, the economic is subordinate to the political, a lesson that our ancestors learned long ago, and that our descendants will undoubtedly have to learn many years hence.*

(Emphasis added.)

I would conclude that there is no reason to expand the meaning of the word "expression" in s.2(*b*) of the Charter to cover pure commercial speech. Commercial speech contributes nothing to democratic government because it says nothing about how people are governed or how they should govern themselves. It does not relate to government policies or matters of public concern essential to a democratic process. It pertains to the economic realm and is a matter appropriate to regulation by the Legislature. Accordingly, the Rules of Professional Conduct, the commentaries thereunder and all decisions of Convocation as they relate to fee advertising, are within the jurisdiction of the Law Society. Having said this, I do not want to be taken as saying Klein could be disciplined for his brochures. The Law Society's power here is to discipline for professional misconduct or conduct unbecoming a barrister and solicitor. I do not see how Klein could be disciplined for doing in print that which he is under an obligation to do verbally: that is, inform his clients or potential clients fairly and in a non-misleading fashion what to expect regarding both his services and his prices. That, however, is a matter for the determination of the Law Society, as is the complaint in relation to advertising against Dvorak.

Conversations with the press — s.2(b) of the Charter

The applicant, Dvorak's, contacting of the press is entitled to the protection of s.2(*b*). I adopt, without repeating, my discussion of the purpose and function of s.2(*b*) of the Charter and of the jurisprudence in both Canada and the United States respecting freedom of expression. The applicant's expression here was precisely the kind intended to be protected by the Charter. It serves a social purpose and provides information on a matter of potential public interest and debate, namely, the manner of fee advertising for lawyers.

Rule 13, Commentary 18, provides as follows:

> RULE 13
>
> Lawyers should make legal services available to the public in an efficient and convenient manner which will command respect and confidence and by means which are compatible with the integrity, independence and effectiveness of the profession.
>
> *Commentary*
>
> 18.(a) A lawyer should not initiate contact with the news media on behalf of himself in respect of any cause or matter in which he is involved in his professional capacity. Furthermore, a lawyer should not, whether he initiates contacts with the news media or is contacted by them, use that opportunity to publicize himself. The lawyer may initiate contact with the media for the purpose of requesting a correction of any published error relating to his conduct, the conduct of his client or the cause or matter involved.

The lawyer should be careful not to make any statement to the media which would constitute contempt of court.

(b) A lawyer contacted by the media for a personal interview concerning his own career may grant such an interview provided that he conducts himself in such interview in a manner consistent with the Rules of Professional Conduct.

A lawyer has a moral, civic and professional duty to speak out where he sees an injustice. Furthermore, lawyers are, by virtue of their education, training and experience, particularly well-equipped to provide information and stimulate reason, discussion and debate on important current legal issues and professional practices: see Rule 12. Speech of this kind surely lies at the core of the constitutional right guaranteed by s.2(*b*). Rule 13, Commentary 18, restricts such right. Again, a client's interest in many situations and, more particularly, a client's freedom of expression may be legitimately served by having his lawyer initiate contact with the news media. The effect of this Rule is to prevent or impede the client through his lawyer from exercising his constitutionally-guaranteed right. In addition, the public has a constitutional right to receive information with respect to legal issues and matters pending in the courts and in relation to the profession and its practices. This right is substantially impaired by the said Rule in that it significantly restricts the right of the press and other media to offer — and the right of the public to receive and discuss — information of important public issues relating to the law and the operation of legal institutions. A threat of discipline by one's governing professional body is a grave and weighty one which will substantially restrict the willingness to speak out on matters of public interest.

1.4.3.5 A Note on Advertising and Free Expression

While the courts have in the past suggested that only Parliament may legislate so as to restrict freedom of expression, it has traditionally been accepted that the provinces may make laws about advertising. In *A.G. Canada* v. *Law Society of British Columbia* (1982) 137 D.L.R. (ed) 1, Estey, J., speaking for the Supreme Court of Canada, said:

> The freedom of expression with which the court is here concerned of course has nothing to do with the elective process and the operations of our democratic institutions, the House of Commons and the provincial legislature. We are indeed speaking about the right of economic free speech, the right to commercial advertising. It can hardly be contended that the province by proper legislation could not regulate the ethical, moral and financial aspects of a trade or profession within its boundaries. (p. 44-45)

[For similar statements, see *R.* v. *Telegram Publishing Co.* (1960), 25 D.L.R. (2d) 471; and *Benson and Hedges Ltd.* v. *A.G. British Columbia* (1972), 27 D.L.R. (3d) 257. Post-Charter cases have adopted a similar approach holding that "expression" in section 2(b) does not include advertising or commercial speech. See *Klein and Law Society of Upper Canada; Re Dvorak and Law Society of Upper Canada (1985),* 50 O.R. (2d) 118 (Div. Ct.); *Grier* v. *Alberta Optometric Association and Council of Management of Alberta Optometric Association,* [1985] 5 W.W.R. 436 (Alta. Q.B.); and *R.* v. *Prof. Technology of Canada Ltd.* (1986), 7 C.R.D. 525.100-01 (Alta. Prov. Ct.). Although not expressed in these terms, the distinction is similar in some respects to that made by U.S. courts between "political" or "core" speech and "commercial" speech. The effect of this distinction has been that commercial speech does not attract the same degree of protection under the First Amendment as does political speech. (See *Valentine* v. *Chrestensen* (1942) 316 U.S. 52.) Recent decisions have cast doubt on this distinction. (See *Virginia State Board of Pharmacy* v. *Virginia Citizens Consumer Council* (1976) 425 U.S. 748.)]

A recent Quebec decision has suggested that advertising may be included in "expression". See *Irwin Toy Ltd.* v. *A.G. of Quebec* (1986) 32 D.L.R. (4th) 641.

Advertising in Canada is regulated under both federal and provincial laws.

Federal law is extensive. The Combines Investigation Act (RSC 1970, c.C-23) seeks to limit false or misleading advertising. The Broadcasting Act (RSC 1970, c.B-11) imposes restrictions, not on advertisers, but on broadcasters.

Section 28 of the Broadcasting Act purports to limit broadcast advertising during federal election campaigns. This raises an interesting question. If we adopt the distinction noted above, is political advertising primarily "political" and therefore deserving of the protection afforded to "core" speech, or is it primarily "advertising" and therefore deserving only of the protection afforded to "commercial" speech?

The various sets of regulations made under the Broadcasting Act (see, for example, the Television Broadcasting Regulations, CRC 1978, c.381) lay down detailed rules concerning advertising. The Food and Drug Act (RSC 1970, c.F-27) deals with advertisements for food and drugs. The Trade Marks Act (RSC 1970, c.T-10) deals in part with comparative advertising.

The Textile Labelling Act (RSC 1970, c.46 (1st Supp.)) and the Consumer Packaging and Labelling Act (SC 1970-71, c.41) both seek to limit false or misleading labelling. The Criminal Code (RSC 1970, c.C-34) contains a number of provisions which affect advertising.

Provincial laws are similarly extensive. For example, in Ontario, the Business Practices Act (RSO 1980, c.55) and the Consumer Protection Act (RSO 1980, c.87) both deal with false or misleading advertising. The Election Finances Reform Act (RSO 1980, c.134), s.38 deals with broadcast advertising during provincial elections.

On 13 November 1891 the Carbolic Smoke Ball Company inserted the following advertisement in various English newspapers:

> £100 reward will be paid by the Carbolic Smoke Ball Company to any person who contracts the increasing epidemic of influenza, colds, or any disease caused by taking cold, after having used the ball three times daily for two weeks according to the printed directions supplied with each ball. £100 is deposited with the Alliance Bank, Regent Street, shewing our sincerity in the matter.

On the strength of this advertisement a woman bought a smoke ball and used it three times a day for a period of two months. She then contracted influenza. She was able to recover £100 from the company. (*Carlill* v. *Carbolic Smoke Ball Company* [1938] 1 Q.B. 256). Despite this decision, the tradition of the courts has been to regard advertising claims as "mere puffs" that is, as statements which do not give rise to contractual obligations.

The contemporary approach to the control of false and misleading advertising relies on regulation by the state rather than private litigation.

Comparative advertising seems popular today. The legal risk involved is that by saying nasty things about your competitors' products you may be laying yourself open to civil proceedings. The obscure tort in question is called "slander of goods". See *Frank Flaman Wholesale Ltd.* v. *Firman* (1982) 20 CCLT 246.

1.4.3.6 *National Citizens Coalition* v. *Attorney-General for Canada* (1984), 11 D.L.R. (4th) 481 (Alta. Q.B.)

MEDHURST J.: — On October 25, 1983, the Parliament of Canada enacted Bill C-169 (now 1980-81-82-83 (Can.), c.164) entitled "An Act to amend the Canada Elections Act (No. 3)".

Section 15 thereof provides:

> 15. Section 72 of the said Act is repealed and the following substituted therefor:
>
> "72(1) Every printed advertisement, handbill, placard, poster or dodger that promotes or opposes the election of a registered political party or candidate and that is displayed or distributed during an election by or on behalf of a registered party or a candidate shall indicate that it was authorized by the registered agent of the party or by the official agent of the candidate, as the case may be, and bear the registered agent's or official agent's name.
>
> "(2) Every one who prints, publishes, distributes or posts up, or who causes to be printed, published, distributed or posted up, any document referred to in subsection (1) is, unless it bears the name and authorization required under that subsection, guilty of an offence against this Act."

Section 70.1(1) of the *Canada Elections Act*, R.S.C. 1970, c.14 (1st Supp.), provides:

> 70.1(1) Every one, other than
>
> (*a*) a candidate, official agent or any other person acting on behalf of a candidate with the candidate's knowledge and consent, or
>
> (*b*) a registered agent of a registered party acting within the scope of his authority as such or other person acting on behalf of a registered party with the actual knowledge and consent of an officer thereof,
>
> who, between the date of the issue of the writ for an election and the day immediately following polling day, incurs election expenses is guilty of an offence against this Act.

It is submitted on behalf of the plaintiffs that these sections of the *Canada Elections Act* are in violation of ss. 2(*b*), and 3 of the *Canadian Charter of Rights and Freedoms* (herein called the Charter) which provide:

> 2. Everyone has the following fundamental freedoms:
>
> (*b*) freedom of thought, belief, opinion and expression, including freedom of the press and other media of communication;
>
> 3. Every citizen of Canada has the right to vote in an election of members of the House of Commons or of a legislative assembly and to be qualified for membership therein.

It is contended on behalf of the plaintiffs that the foregoing provisions of the *Canada Elections Act* are in breach of the democratic rights and fundamental freedoms provided by the Charter. Specifically it is argued that s. 70.1(1), which prohibits anyone, other than registered parties or candidates, from incurring election expenses as defined during an election campaign, is a prohibition or limitation on freedom of expression provided by s.2(*b*), of the Charter. Section 72 is stated to have the same effect. As well these sections are said to violate the democratic right to vote which, it is agreed, means the right to an informed vote as provided in s.3 of the Charter.

The defendant contends that the present provisions of the *Canada Elections Act* are the result of many years of legislative development which provides fairness and equality in the procedures governing the election of Members of Parliament. If these sections do provide a limitation of rights and freedoms, and it is argued that they do not, then they are reasonable limits and can be demonstrably justified in a free and democratic society.

The first question that arises is whether there has been a limitation or restriction on a guaranteed right or freedom under the Charter. The sections in question are said by the defendant to result in a greater exchange of opinions and ideas than would otherwise be the case as a result of protective measures and the result is a system with greater fairness and openness. I believe, however, that the sections on their face do limit the actions of anyone other than registered parties or candidates from incurring election expenses during the prescribed time and in this sense there is a restriction on freedom of expression. If such constraint is to be allowed then, in my view it must meet the tests set out in s.1 of the Charter.

1.4.3.7 *Re New Brunswick Broadcasting Co. Ltd. and CRTC* (1984), 13 D.L.R. (4th) 77 (F.C.A.)

THURLOW C.J.: In my opinion, the argument confuses the freedom guaranteed by the Charter with a right to the use of property and is not sustainable. The freedom guaranteed by the Charter is a freedom to express and communicate ideas without restraint, whether orally or in print or by other means of communication. It is not a freedom to use someone else's property to do so. It gives no right to anyone to use someone else's land or platform to make a speech, or someone else's printing press to publish his ideas. It gives no right to anyone to enter and use a public building for such purposes. And it gives no right to anyone to use the radio frequencies which, before the enactment of the Charter, had been declared by Parliament to be and had become public property and subject to the licensing and other provisions of the *Broadcasting Act*. The appellant's freedom to broadcast what it wishes to communicate would not be denied by the refusal of a licence to operate a broadcasting undertaking. It would have the same freedom as anyone else to air its information by purchasing time on a licensed station. Nor does the Charter confer on the rest of the public a right to a broadcasting service to be provided by the appellant.

1.4.3.8 *Irwin Toy Ltd.* v. *A.G. Que.* (1986) 32 D.L.R. (4th) 641 (Que. C.A.)

JACQUES J.A.: (translation) ...There are, however, no rules of interpretation which exclude commercial expression from freedom of expression.

The wording of s.2(*b*) does not limit freedom of expression to certain types of expression, for example, political, artistic, cultural and others.

"Freedom" is not just a value, it is a basic condition for the enjoyment and maintenance of all other values.

The meaning of the words "thought", "belief", "opinion" and "expression" is determinate and undefined but they do describe values. The section does not specify what thoughts, what beliefs nor what opinions are protected by the freedom guaranteed by the Charter. The same is true of the concept "expression"; its content is not restrictive, being such as "to make responsive by some sign" a thing, an idea, etc. It is not so much the word itself nor its context which limits the thing at issue, rather it is the way in which it is done.

This can be done through spoken or written language, cartoons or drawings, a film or an announcement which informs the public or any person.

The idea, or what is being communicated, can be anything legal, just as the means itself can be any legal medium.

It is not for the court to accord more prestige to political, artistic or cultural expression than to commercial expression, or to find that the nature and scope of one is greater than that of another since the Charter makes no such distinction. Artistic or cultural expression very often has a commercial purpose, for example, films, videos, records, etc., as do other activities of a purely commercial nature. Nor it is up to a government to decide what people should not know with respect to commerce, although a government can impose the obligation to disclose all facts pertinent to any commercial activity, *e.g.*, the composition of foodstuffs, etc.

The economic choices of the citizens are just as important, if not more important, than their artistic and cultural choices. These choices depend on what information is available and they cannot be enlightened choices unless such information circulates as freely as possible. Today everything is judged on the basis of freedom of expression; it has become a kind of universal standard.

I am, therefore, of the view that commercial expression, or "commercial speech", is included in freedom of expression as guaranteed by s.2(*b*) of the Charter, with the exception, of course, of "such reasonable limits prescribed by law as can be demonstrably justified in a free and democratic society".

1.4.3.9 *Committee for the Commonwealth of Canada* v. *The Queen in Right of Canada* (1986) 25 D.L.R. (4th) 460 (F.C.T.D.)

DUBE J.: — By this action the court is asked to declare that the areas open to the public at Montreal International Airport (Dorval) constitute a public forum where fundamental freedoms can be exercised.

The first plaintiff, the Committee for the Commonwealth of Canada, is a non-profit corporation established pursuant to the *Canada Corporations Act,* R.S.C. 1970, c.C-32. The other two plaintiffs are leading members of the committee. The last plaintiff, the Parti de la République du Canada, was duly registered in August, 1984 (after the action at bar was filed), as a political party pursuant to the provisions of s.13 of the *Canada Elections Act,* R.S.C. 1970, c.14 (1st Supp.), having nominated at least fifty candidates in the last federal election. At the request of counsel for the plaintiffs, the Parti pour la République du Canada was added as a plaintiff when the hearing of this matter began in Montreal on December 10, 1985.

The facts alleged in the statement of claim are not in dispute and can be very briefly stated. On March 22, 1984, the plaintiffs François Lepine and Christiane Deland went to the Dorval airport terminal "to communicate" to members of the public at that place, and discuss with them, the aims and objectives of the committee. After being questioned by a constable on duty, the two plaintiffs subsequently met with the assistant manager of the airport, who told them they had no right to engage in politics in the airport.

The defendant, for her part, alleges that the airport in question is the property of Her Majesty the Queen in right of Canada, represented by the Minister of Transport, which is admitted. In particular, she refers to the *Department of Transport Act,* R.S.C. 1970, c.T-15, which authorizes the Governor in Council to enact the regulations necessary to administer the airport, specifically the *Government Airport Concession Oper-*

ations Regulations, C.R.C. 1978, c.1565, and more precisely s.6, which prohibits anyone, without written authorization from the Minister, from "advertis[ing] or solicit[ing] anything at an airport on his own behalf or on behalf of any other person".

In my view these regulations deal with the control over the operation of taxis at airports and apply to that type of activity, not to the right of persons to express their philosophies or beliefs or their political ideas through direct communication with other persons who may be on the premises.

In the case at bar, the two plaintiffs were not carrying on a business in the airport. They were trying to disseminate their political ideas. They were carrying placards and distributing pamphlets in the open area on the first floor of the airport, the level open to the public for the purchase of tickets and for awaiting departures. Their purpose was not to hold public meetings on the premises or to make speeches from a podium or with a loudspeaker.

It was established at the hearing that the Dorval airport management have always uniformly and impartially prohibited all public activities of the kind, whether political, religious or otherwise. The only exception to this prohibition, as mentioned at the hearing, is the sale of poppies by veterans each November.

In his testimony, the Dorval operations manager explained that about 20,000 passengers use the airport daily, often accompanied by other persons. There may be some 2,000 arrivals an hour. There are about 3,800 employees in the building. The total area of the first floor is 170,000 square feet and the public has access to some 63,000 square feet. This floor also offers booths operated by airlines, shops, newsstands, drug stores, restaurants, hairdressing parlours, and so on, for the convenience and comfort of the travelling public. Space is distributed so as to expedite the movement of air traffic. The public areas are thronged with people in peak periods. Passengers waiting to depart are already sufficiently nervous. It is not in their interests to allow solicitation, the manager said.

On the other hand, the plaintiff François Lepine has travelled by air to the United States and testified that political activities are allowed in major U.S. airports. In particular, he recalled seeing there persons sitting at a table located in the public area of an airport distributing leaflets with political posters up on the wall.

Section 1 of the *Canadian Charter of Rights and Freedoms* guarantees certain rights and freedoms, subject only to such reasonable limits prescribed by law as can be demonstrably justified in a free and democratic society. One of the fundamental freedoms guaranteed in s.2 is the freedom of opinion and expression, including freedom of the press and other media of communication.

I was quoted no Canadian jurisprudence (and I was not able to find any) either under the Charter of the *Canadian Bill of Rights* dealing with the exercise of the freedom of expression in such public places as airports. American courts, however, have on several occasions applied the First and Fourteenth Amendments.

Freedom of speech in Canada was imported along with the common law from the United Kingdom and so enshrined in the Confederation Act. The provinces expressed therein their desire to be federally united into a Dominion "with a constitution similar in principle to that of the United Kingdom". A Dominion with a "Government resting ultimately on public opinion reached by discussion and the interplay of ideas. If that discussion is placed under licence, its basic condition is destroyed": see Rand J. in *Saumur v. City of Quebec,* [1953] 4 D.L.R. 641 at p. 671, [1953] 2 S.C.R. 299 at p. 330, 106 C.C.C. 289.

It seems plain and obvious to me that the public terminal concourses in our Canadian airports, as well as in American airports, have become contemporary extensions of the streets and public places of yesterday. They are indeed "modern crossroads" for the intercourse of the travelling public. In principle, freedom of expression and communication ought not to be abridged in those public forums. The absolute prohibition imposed by the Dorval authorities upon the rather benign and innocuous activities of the plaintiffs flies in the face of the *Canadian Charter of Rights and Freedoms.*

Of course, freedom of expression in a public forum is not unlimited. It may be circumscribed within reasonable limits for the general comfort and convenience of the travelling public. The proper authorities may draw regulations so as to safeguard the well-being and security of the passengers as well as the efficiency of the transportation functions of an airport. But the airport authorities may not impose a categorical interdiction so as to smother the fundamental freedom of persons to peacefully disseminate their political, religious, or other beliefs in a public place.

For those reasons, the declaration sought by the plaintiffs is granted with costs.

Judgment for plaintiffs.

1.4.3.10 *International Fund for Animal Welfare Inc.* v. *The Queen* (1986) 30 C.C.C. (3d) 80 (F.C.T.D.)

McNair J.: The regulations subjected to attack in the present lawsuit are the following provisions of the *Seal Protection Regulations,* C.R.C. 1978, c.833, *viz:*

> 11(2) No person shall use a helicopter or other aircraft in searching for seals unless he has an aircraft sealing license issued by the Minister.
>
> (3) An aircraft sealing license may be issued only in respect of an aircraft registered in Canada under Part II of the *Air Regulations* made pursuant to the *Aeronautics Act.*
>
> (5) Except with the permission of the Minister, no person shall
>
> (*a*) land a helicopter or other aircraft less than ½ nautical mile from any seal that is on the ice in the Gulf Area or Front Area; or
>
> (*b*) operate a helicopter or other aircraft over any seal on the ice at an altitude of less than 2,000 feet, except for commercial flights operating on scheduled flight plans.
>
> (6) No person shall, unless he is the holder of a license or a permit, approach within half a nautical mile of any area in which a seal hunt is being carried out [enacted SOR/78-167].

The first issue concerns the constitutional validity of the above mentioned provisions of the *Seal Protection Regulations,* which the plaintiffs have challenged in their action by invoking s.2(*b*) of the Charter. The question thus raised for determination is whether the regulations deny to the plaintiffs their guaranteed right of freedom of expression within the meaning of s.2(*b*) of the Charter. This right, it is contended, must be seen to include "freedom to seek, receive and impart information and ideas of all kinds", whether by the written or spoken word or photography or whatever other media of communication might be chosen. Although I.F.A.W. is unquestionably a redoubtable protester, the gist of the case is not concerned with the right to protest *per se*. The plaintiffs' evidence is that they have never deliberately interfered with the sealers. Their avowed objective is access to information rather than altercation and confrontation.

On the issue of constitutionality, it is the plaintiffs' contention that the impugned provisions of the *Seal Protection Regulations* violate their right of free access to information contrary to s.2(*b*) of the Charter. It is further contended that the regulatory prohibitions against landing or flying an aircraft in proximity to any seal on the ice have the effect of rendering meaningless any licence or permit to approach within half a nautical mile of an area where a seal hunt is being carried out. The plaintiffs also submit that I.F.A.W. is a member of the media. I cannot accept this last-mentioned submission. The defendants contend, on the other hand, that the right of freedom of expression is limited to the dissemination of ideas and beliefs in the expressible sense and does not comprehend the broader aspect of access to information as the fountainhead for the formulation and expression of those ideas and beliefs.

An expansive and purposive scrutiny of s.2(*b*) leads inevitably, in my judgment, to the conclusion that freedom of expression must include freedom of access to all information pertinent to the ideas or beliefs sought to be expressed, subject to such reasonable limitations as are necessary to national security, public order, public health or morals, or the fundamental rights and freedoms of others.

1.4.3.11 *Retail, Wholesale and Department Store Union, Local 580* v. *Dolphin Delivery Ltd.* (1986) 2 S.C.R. 573

McINTYRE J.: As has been noted above, the only basis on which the picketing in question was defended by the appellants was under the provisions of s.2(*b*) of the *Charter* which guarantees the freedom of expression as a fundamental freedom. Freedom of expression is not, however, a creature of the *Charter*. It is one of the fundamental concepts that has formed the basis for the historical development of the political, social and educational institutions of western society. Representative democracy, as we know it today, which is in great part the product of free expression and discussion of varying ideas, depends upon its maintenance and protection.

The importance of freedom of expression has been recognized since early times: see John Milton., *Areopagitica; A Speech for the Liberty of Unlicenc'd Printing, to the Parliament of England* (1644), and as well John Stuart Mill, "On Liberty" in *On Liberty and considerations on Representative Government* (Oxford 1946), at p. 14:

> If all mankind minus one were of one opinion, and only one person were of the contrary opinion, mankind would be no more justified in silencing that one person, than he, if he had the power, would be justified in silencing mankind.

And, after stating that "All silencing of discussion is an assumption of infallibility", he said, at p. 16:

> Yet it is as evident in itself, as any amount of argument can make it, that ages are no more infallible than individuals; every age having held many opinions which subsequent ages have deemed not only false but absurd; and it is as certain that many opinions now general will be rejected by future ages, as it is that many, once general, are rejected by the present.

Nothing in the vast literature on this subject reduces the importance of Mill's words. The principle of freedom of speech and expression has been firmly accepted as a necessary feature of modern democracy. The courts have recognized this fact. For an American example, see the words of Holmes J. in his dissent in *Abrams v. United States,* 250 U.S. 616 (1919), at p. 630:

> Persecution for the expression of opinions seems to me perfectly logical. If you have no doubt of your premises or your power and want a certain result with all your heart you naturally express your wishes in law and sweep away all opposition .... But when men have realized that time has upset many fighting faiths, they may come to believe even more than they believe the very foundations of their own conduct that the ultimate good desired is better reached by free trade in ideas — that the best test of truth is the power of the thought to get itself accepted in the competition of the market, and that truth is the only ground upon which their wishes safely can be carried out.

Prior to the adoption of the *Charter,* freedom of speech and expression had been recognized as an essential feature of Canadian parliamentary democracy. Indeed, this Court may be said to have given it constitutional status. In *Boucher v. The King,* [1951] S.C.R. 265, Rand J., who formed a part of the majority which narrowed the scope of the crime of sedition, said, at p. 288:

> There is no modern authority which holds that the mere effect of tending to create discontent or disaffection among His Majesty's subjects or ill-will or hostility between groups of them, but not tending to issue in illegal conduct, constitutes the crime, and this for obvious reasons. Freedom in thought and speech and disagreement in ideas and beliefs, on every conceivable subject, are of the essence of our life. The clash of critical discussion on political, social and religious subjects has too deeply become the stuff of daily experience to suggest that mere ill-will as a product of controversy can strike down the latter with illegality. A superficial examination of the word shows its insufficiency: what is the degree necessary to criminality? Can it ever, as mere subjective condition, be so? Controversial fury is aroused constantly by differences in abstract conceptions; heresy in some fields is again a mortal sin; there can be fanatical puritanism in ideas as well as in mortals; but our compact of free society accepts and absorbs these differences and they are exercised at large within the framework of freedom and order on broader and deeper uniformities as bases of social stability. Similarly in discontent, affection and hostility: as subjective incidents of controversy, they and the ideas which arouse them are part of our living which ultimately serve us in stimulation, in the clarification of thought and, as we believe, in the search for the constitution and truth of things generally.

In *Switzman v. Elbling,* [1957] S.C.R. 285, where this Court struck down Quebec's padlock law, Rand J. again spoke strongly on this issue. He said, at p. 306:

> But public opinion, in order to meet such a responsibility, demands the condition of a virtually unobstructed access to and diffusion of ideas. Parliamentary government postulates a capacity in men, acting freely and under self-restraints, to govern themselves; and that advance is best served in the degree achieved of individual liberation from subjective as well as objective shackles. Under that government, the freedom of discussion in Canada, as a subject-matter of legislation, has a unity of interest and significance extending equally to every part of the Dominion. With such dimensions it is *ipso facto* excluded from head 16 as a local matter.
>
> This constitutional fact is the political expression of the primary condition of social life, thought and its communication by language. Liberty in this is little less vital to man's mind and spirit than breathing is to his physical existence. As such an inherence in the individual it is embodied in his status of citizenship.

In the same case, Abbott J. said, at p. 326:

> The right of free expression of opinion and of criticism, upon matters of public policy and public administration, and the right to discuss and debate such matters, whether they be social, economic or political, are essential to the working of a parliamentary democracy such as ours.

He went on to make extensive reference to the words of Duff C.J. in *Reference re Alberta Statutes,* [1938] S.C.R. 100, at pp. 132-33, strongly supporting what could almost be described as a constitutional position for the concept of freedom of speech and expression in Canadian law, and then said, at p. 328:

> Although it is not necessary, of course, to determine this question for the purposes of the present appeal, the Canadian constitution being declared to be similar in principle to that of the United Kingdom, I am also of opinion that as our constitutional Act now stands, Parliament itself could not abrogate this right of discussion and debate. The power of Parliament to limit it is, in my view, restricted to such powers as may be exercisable under its exclusive legislative jurisdiction with respect to criminal law and to make laws for the peace, order and good government of the nation.

It will be seen at once that Professor Peter W. Hogg, at p. 713 in his text, *Constitutional Law of Canada* (2nd ed. 1985), is justified in his comment that:

> Canadian judges have always placed a high value on freedom of expression as an element of parliamentary democracy and have sought to protect it with the limited tools that were at their disposal before the adoption of the Charter of Rights.

The *Charter* has now in s.2(*b*) declared freedom of expression to be a fundamental freedom and any questions as to its constitutional status have therefore been settled.

The question now arises: Is freedom of expression involved in this case? In seeking an answer to this question, it must be observed at once that in any form of picketing there is involved at least some element of expression. The picketers would be conveying a message which at a very minimum would be classed as persuasion, aimed at deterring customers and prospective customers from doing business with the respondent. The question then arises. Does this expression in the circumstances of this case have *Charter* protection under the provisions of s.2(*b*), and if it does, then does the injunction abridge or infringe such freedom?

The appellants argue strongly that picketing is a form of expression fully entitled to *Charter* protection and rely on various authorities to support the proposition, including *Reference re Alberta Statutes, supra; Switzman v. Elbling, supra;* the American cases of *Thornhill v. Alabama,* 310 U.S. 88 (1940) (*per* Murphy J., at p. 95); *Milk Wagon Drivers Union v. Meadowmoor Dairies,* 312 U.S. 287 (1941), (*per* Black J., at p. 302), and various other Canadian authorities. They reject the American distinction between the concept of speech and that of conduct made in picketing cases, and they accept the view of Hutcheon J.A. in the Court of Appeal, in adopting the words of Freedman C.J.M. in *Channel Seven Television Ltd. v. National Association of Broadcast Employees and Technicians,* [1971] 5 W.W.R. 328, that "Peaceful picketing falls within freedom of speech".

The respondent contends for a narrower approach to the concept of freedom of expression. The position is summarized in the respondent's factum:

> 4. We submit that constitutional protection under section 2(b) should only be given to those forms of expression that warrant such protection. To do otherwise would trivialize freedom of expression generally and lead to a downgrading or dilution of this freedom.

Reliance is placed on the view of the majority in the Court of Appeal that picketing in a labour dispute is more than mere communication of information. It is also a signal to trade unionists not to cross the picket line. The respect accorded to picket lines by trade unionists is such that the result of the picketing would be to damage seriously the operation of the employer, not to communicate any information. Therefore, it is argued, since the picket line was not intended to promote dialogue or discourse (as would be the case where its purpose was the exercise of freedom of expression), it cannot qualify for protection under the *Charter*.

On the basis of the findings of fact that I have referred to above, it is evident that the purpose of the picketing in this case was to induce a breach of contract between the respondent and Supercourier and thus to exert economic pressure to force it to cease doing business with Supercourier. It is equally evident that, if successful, the picketing would have done serious injury to the respondent. There is nothing remarkable about this, however, because all picketing is designed to bring economic pressure on the person picketed and to cause economic loss for so long as the object of the picketing remains unfulfilled. There is, as I have earlier said, always some element of expression in picketing. The union is making a statement to the general public that it is involved in a dispute, that it is seeking to impose its will on the object of the picketing, and that it solicits the assistance of the public in honouring the picket line. Action on the part of the picketers will, of course, always accompany the expression, but not every action on the part of the picketers will be such as to alter the nature of the whole transaction and remove it from *Charter* protection for freedom of expression. That freedom, of course, would not extend to protect threats of violence or acts of violence. It would not protect the destruction of property, or assaults, or other clearly unlawful conduct. We need not, however, be concerned with such matters here because the picketing would have been peaceful. I am therefore of the view that the picketing sought to be restrained would have involved the exercise of the right of freedom of expression.

1.4.3.12 *R.* v. *Zundel* (1987) 35 D.L.R. (4th) 338 (Ont. C.A.)

THE COURT: When determining the limits of freedom of expression, a distinction must be drawn at the outset between "rights" and "freedoms". A "right" is defined positively as what one can do. A "freedom", on the other hand, is defined by determining first the area which is regulated. The freedom is then what exists in the unregulated area — a sphere of activity within which all acts are permissible. It is a residual area in which all acts are free of specific legal regulation and the individual is free to choose. The regulated area will include restrictions for purposes of decency and public order, and specifically with respect to the freedom of expression, prohibitions concerning criminal libel and sedition. It is what Rand J. described in *Saumur v. City of Quebec and A.-G. Que.* (1953), 106 C.C.C. 289 at p. 322, [1953] 4 D.L.R. 641 at p. 670, [1953] 2 S.C.R. 299 at p. 329, as "the residue inside the periphery". This is the approach to rights and freedoms which was taken in the McRuer Report of the Royal Commission Inquiry into Civil Rights, Report 2, vol. 4, pp. 1493-96 (1969), and was adopted by Bayda C.J.S. in *Re Retail, Wholesale & Department Store Union, Locals 544, 496, 635 & 955 et al. and Government of Saskatchewan et al.* (1985), 19 D.L.R. (4th) 609 at pp. 616-8, [1985] 5 W.W.R. 97 at pp. 105-8, 39 Sask. R. 193. It is also the approach recently adopted by the Court of Appeal of British Columbia in *Re Cromer and British Columbia Teachers' Federation et al.*, July 18, 1986 (unreported) at pp. 12-3 [since reported 29 D.L.R. (4th) 641 at pp. 649-50, [1986] 5 W.W.R. 638, 4 B.C.L.R. (2d) 273]. In our opinion it is the right approach.

1.4.3.13 *R.* v. *Kopyto* (1988) 24 O.A.C. 81 (Ont. C.A.)

CORY, J.A.: ... Considering now the purpose of s.2(b), it is difficult to imagine a more important guarantee of freedom to a democratic society than that of freedom of expression. A democracy cannot exist without the freedom to express new ideas and to put forward opinions about the functioning of public institutions. These opinions may be critical of existing practices in public institutions and of the institutions themselves. However, change for the better is dependent upon constructive criticism. Nor can it be expected that criticism will always be muted by restraint. Frustration with outmoded practices will often lead to vigorous and unpropitious complaints. Hyperbole and colourful, perhaps even disrespectful language, may be the necessary touchstone to fire the interest and imagination of the public, to the need for reform, and to suggest the manner in which that reform may be achieved.

[31] The concept of free and uninhibited speech permeates all truly democratic societies. Caustic and bitting debate is, for example, often the hallmark of election campaigns, parliamentary debates and campaigns for the establishment of new public institutions or the reform of existing practices and institutions. The exchange of ideas on important issues is often framed in colourful and vitriolic language. So long as comments made on matters of public interest are neither obscene nor contrary to the laws of criminal libel, citizens of a democratic state should not have to worry unduly about the framing of their expression of ideas. The very lifeblood of democracy is the free exchange of ideas and opinions. If these exchanges are stifled, democratic government itself is threatened.

[32] History has repeatedly demonstrated that the first step taken by totalitarian regimes is to muzzle the media and then the individual in order to prevent the dissemination of views and opinions that may be contrary to those of the government. The vital importance of freedom of expression cannot be overemphasized. It is important in this context to note that s.2(b) of the **Charter** is framed in absolute terms, which distinguishes it, for example, from s.8 of the **Charter,** which guarantees the qualified right to be secure from *unreasonable* search. The rights entrenched in s.2(b) should therefore only be restricted in the clearest of circumstances.

1.4.4 Applying Section 1

The second stage in the assessment of the constitutionality of a contested statute involves an analysis of the meaning of section 1 of the Charter which operates as a broad qualifier. The Charter guarantees the rights and freedoms it proclaims subject only to such reasonable limits prescribed by law as can be demonstrably justified in a free and democratic society.

There are three guideposts in section 1: (i) reasonable limits; (ii) prescribed by law; and (iii) demonstrably justified in a free and democratic society. The courts have made it the responsibility of the State to justify any limits on Charter guarantees. In other words, the courts have placed the responsibility of justifying the limits on a fundamental freedom on its authors — that is to say, the Crown.

1.4.4.1 Reasonable limit

1.4.4.1.1 *Re Klein and Law Society of Upper Canada; Re Dvorak and Law Society of Upper Canada* (1985) 50 O.R. 118 (Div. Ct.)

CALLAGHAN J. (EBERLE J. concurring): ... The effect of the Rule, in my view, is to impair the right of the lawyer, client and the public to disseminate and receive information to an extent which greatly exceeds any legitimate legislative or regulatory purpose of the respondent Law Society. This Rule, in my view, will have an unjustifiable chilling effect on the exercise of the freedom of expression. Even lawyers who do not "initiate" contact with the news media or who "initiate" contact for a purpose will be dissuaded from exercising their freedom of expression as the Law Society itself has taken the position that:

> ... any interview with the media about court proceedings invites the inference that it was given to publicize a lawyer and carries the danger of being a contempt of court. The Society intends to institute discipline proceedings where appropriate to ensure that the Rule is observed.

(See Law Society communiqué No. 145, March 22 and 23, 1984.)

It may be that to initiate contact with the press will, in some circumstances, invite the inference of self-aggrandizement, but such circumstances must, in my mind, be rare, if only because the press, in all likelihood, will be unwilling to print stories whose only relevance is to the lawyer's ego. It is true that in many cases public attention on the lawyer will flow from a story concerning his case or his client. Such attention is an inherent part of political and social discussion in this country: open debate will always result in someone being in the limelight. Indeed, that is how it should be, for someone who sparks a public debate must be there to take responsibility for any conflagration that results. On the other hand, a lawyer who contacts the media for the purpose of self-promotion or self-aggrandizement may be engaging in conduct which the Law Society may well find to constitute conduct unbecoming a barrister and solicitor and which conduct might well be the appropriate subject-matter of a precisely formulated Rule or commentary thereunder.

If the concern is that a lawyer may disparage the courts, the Law Society or a fellow lawyer, then adequate safeguards already exist. To contact the press and denigrate improperly a fellow lawyer or the Law Society would surely be conduct unbecoming a barrister and a solicitor and it would not be protected by the Charter since its purpose was one for which the Charter was not designed. And as to a contact made in contempt of court, that is a matter for the court, not the Law Society, to regulate (though such a judicial finding might be grounds for further discipline by the Society).

I can therefore see no valid regulatory purpose which justifies the broad restriction on freedom of expression contained in Rule 13, Commentary 18 and, accordingly, I would issue an order declaring Commentary 18 of Rule 13 of no force or effect and quash the complaint of the Law Society filed against the applicant, Dvorak, on January 16, 1984, in so far as it includes a charge that he initiated a contact with news media and used the opportunity to publicize himself. In all other respects the application will be dismissed. As this is a matter of some public importance, it is not a proper case for costs.

1.4.4.1.2 *Re Information Retailers Associations of Metropolitan Toronto Inc. and Municipality of Metropolitan Toronto* (1985), 52 O.R. (2d) 449 (C.A.)

HOULDEN, CORY and ROBINS JJ. A.: In March, 1983, the appellant passed By-law 41-83 which amended By-law 107-78 by adding provisions that required retail sellers of "adult books or magazines" to be licensed and to comply with specified display regulations. The amendment was enacted on the purported authority of s. 222 of the *Municipal Act*. Although By-law 107-78 contained regulations with respect to "adult entertainment parlours", prior to this amendment its definition of that term was limited to the provision of "services" and did not apply to "goods". Sellers of books and magazines, adult or otherwise, were not previously governed by this by-law and, it follows, were not required to be licensed. The March, 1983 amendments compelled the licensing of:

> 2(27a) Every person who provides in any premises or part thereof, in pursuance of a trade, calling, business or occupation, adult books or magazines, or who operates any premises or part thereof in which such books or magazines are so provided.

The corresponding definitions are set forth in ss.1(1a)(a) of By-law 107-78 as amended. The definition of "adult book or magazine" was further amended in May, 1983, but it may none the less be helpful to reproduce the original definition section in its entirety:

> 1. (1a)(a) "Adult book or magazine", means any book or magazine appealing to or designed to appeal to sexual or erotic appetites or inclinations.
>
> (b)(i) "Book or magazine appealing to or designed to appeal to sexual or erotic appetites or inclinations" means any book or magazine of which a feature or characteristic is the portrayal or depiction, by means of photographs, drawings, or otherwise, of the specified body areas of any person or persons, or of which a feature or characteristic of a substantial part thereof is such portrayal or depiction.
>
> (ii) Notwithstanding the generality of sub-paragraph (i), nothing contained therein shall be deemed to apply to any book or magazine other than those referred to in section 222 of the Municipal Act.
>
> (c) "To provide", when used in relation to any book or magazine, means to sell, offer to sell or display for sale by retail or otherwise such book or magazine, and "provider", "providing" and "provision" have corresponding meanings.
>
> (d) Specified body areas" means:
>
> (a) in the case of a female person, her breasts; and
>
> (b) in the case of all persons, the pubic, perineal and perianal areas and the buttocks.

Schedule 41 was also added to By-law 107-78. The regulations contained in this schedule demand that every operator who provides adult books or magazines in any premises or part thereof comply with certain display requirements. Operators of "adult entertainment parlour stores" are excepted, that term being defined to cover the relatively small number of stores in which the *principal* business is the provision of books or magazines or other goods or services appealing to or designed to appeal to sexual or erotic appetites or inclinations. The sections of the by-law applicable to operators of such stores are not in issue in this case. The relevant display restrictions are set forth in sch. 41 as follows:

> 3. (1) Every operator who provides adult books or magazines in any premises or part thereof other than an adult entertainment parlour store, or who operates such premises or part thereof, shall comply with the following regulations in respect of such premises or part:

(a) No adult book or magazine shall be displayed at a height of less than 1.5 metres above floor level, unless such book or magazine is in a part of the premises to which the public is not permitted physical access.

(b) All adult books or magazines offered for sale or displayed in such premises or part shall be placed behind an opaque barrier of a size and nature which shall ensure that the cover of every such book or magazine while so displayed, except for the name thereof, may not be seen by any member of the public.

Shortly following the enactment of the amending by-law in March, 1983, the municipality referred the by-law to the legislation and licensing committee requesting that it be given further consideration by the committee. This request was prompted by a concern that the definition of "adult book or magazine" was broad enough to bring legitimate works of art and photography within its purview and, as well, by a concern that, given the option of enforcement by prosecution, the licensing requirement and annual fee imposed by the by-law constituted unnecessary impositions on the small businesses effected by the by-law. On May 10, 1983, the appellant enacted By-law 82-83 which changed the definition of "adult book or magazine" but left the licensing requirement and other provisions of the March amendment in place. The amended definition of "adult book or magazine", and it is this definition that the Divisional Court declared void for vagueness, reads:

1(1a)(a) "Adult book or magazine" means any book or magazine:

(i) of which a principal feature or characteristic is the portrayal or depiction, by means of photographs, drawings or otherwise, of one or more of the specified body areas of any person or persons; and

(ii) which appeals to or is designed to appeal to erotic or sexual appetites or inclinations.

...

Books were included in the by-law notwithstanding the apprehension of some members of council that the by-law could have the effect of prohibiting the open display of legitimate works of art and photography. The May, 1983 revision of the definition of "adult book or magazine" did not, in my view, succeed in narrowing the then existing definition so as to avoid the likelihood of that consequence. There is no denying that many books sold in bookstores (and several have been filed in evidence to illustrate the point) contain as a principal feature or characteristic, nudity or partial nudity and, regardless of the dignity of presentation, can fairly be said to appeal to or be designed to appeal to sexual inclinations. On the wording of the definition, these books would fall within its purview requiring that they be displayed in the same manner as "skin" magazines, in this case behind an opaque barrier but potentially, as some similar by-laws require, in sealed packages or wrappings.

It is no answer for the municipality, having prescribed a definition broad enough to encompass these books, to say that booksellers would, as a matter of common understanding, be aware of the type of publication the by-law is designed to regulate or that the by-law can be subjected to a narrowing construction; nor is it any answer to say that the municipality can be relied on not to enforce the by-law with respect to "legitimate" books. Booksellers should not be left to guess whether or not it is intended that a particular book be within the purview of the by-law; nor should they be left to the vagaries of bureaucratic enforcement or, indeed, to the popular pressures that may arise to influence enforcement. "Bookselling", as Mr. Justice Fortas once observed, "should not be a hazardous profession": *Ginsberg v. State of New York,* 390 U.S. 629 at p. 674.

As the by-law stands, a bookseller is obliged by s.2(27a) to make important daily decisions as to whether he must have a licence for the sale of a particular book or whether a book must be placed behind a blinder. Without detailing the licensing scheme, which was amended shortly before this appeal, it confers a discretion on the licensing commission to refuse or revoke a licence on the basis of whether the applicant's conduct affords reasonable grounds for a belief that he will not carry on the business "in accordance with law and with integrity and honesty"; previously the licensing commission was empowered to take an applicant's "character" into account in determining whether his carrying-on of the business may be in any way adverse to the "public interest". Licensed booksellers are subject to municipal inspection. Contravention of the by-law can result in serious consequences including not only the imposition of a fine but, by virtue of s.329 of the *Municipal Act,* the premises may be ordered closed for a period not exceeding two years for failure to obtain a licence and, by virtue of the *Landlord and Tenant Act,* R.S.O. 1980, c.232, a tenant engaged in a business for which a licence is required under a by-law passed under s.222 may have his lease forfeited if the licence is not obtained.

It is to be noted that shortly before the by-law's enactment the mayor of Toronto, one of its leading proponents, in a memorandum to the metropolitan council expressed his reservations about both the inclusion of "books" and the proposed licensing requirement. With respect to the latter he wrote, with some clairvoyance:

> ... I feel very strongly that the proposed licensing mechanism is not necessary to achieve compliance, and that prosecution of violators of the by-law is a preferable route to take. *The licensing mechanism seems to me to be an over-regulation* which was not contemplated in my original proposal of September 14, 1982. Such a requirement might well result in a challenge to the by-law and frustrate my original intention of requiring *magazines* to be placed 1.5 metres (5 feet) above the floor and behind an opaque barrier.

(Emphasis added.)

It seems to me also that the licensing scheme is an "over-regulation" and, like the scope of the by-law, goes beyond the bounds required to achieve the objective. I am not persuaded that it can be justified on the basis that it provides "a simpler, more effective and speedier" means of enforcing the regulation than prosecution in the courts. Without questioning the good faith of the appellant, licensing schemes clearly can operate and historically have operated as a form of prior restraint on the free flow of expression. While the scheme here relates to what would seem to be a rather minor display restriction, concern about its potential effect has been voiced in these proceedings by the organized Canadian book publishing and book selling industries. Affidavits objecting to the by-law have been filed not only on behalf of the respondent, Retailers and Publishers, but also on behalf of the Canadian Book Publishers Council, the Book and Periodical Development Council and the Association of Canadian Publishers. They, in short, are apprehensive that, to avoid problems with licensing inspectors, booksellers will tend to assign books with erotic content which may conceivably be covered by the by-law's "unworkable definition" to a "ghetto" or special area in the store; that in the long run the number of such books carried in stock will be reduced; that experimental and non-traditional books will be the most affected; and that editorial selection of material will respond by seeking to ensure that material accepted for publication will be such, or presented as such, that it will not be subject to regulation.

In my opinion, these concerns are not without foundation and represent a risk which ought not to be run. Having regard to the broadly-phrased scope of the by-law, the consequences of non-compliance, the perception of at least some booksellers that a ''social stigma'' attaches to a licence issued pursuant to legislation designed to control ''adult entertainment parlours'', and the nuisance involved in satisfying the licensing and display requirements, there may be a tendency on the part of some booksellers to comply with the law by not selling books which by any stretch of the interpretive imagination can be said to fall within the ambit of the by-law. The resulting self-censorship would limit or impede the marketing of a protected form of expression and interfere with the public's right of access to non-obscene books with erotic pictorial content. Legal over-kill is ill-suited to the delicate sphere of free expression and, here, is fatal to the by-law.

Returning more specifically to magazines, as I have already indicated, so long as the regulation is sufficiently limited in its reach and sufficiently precise in its terms to enable retailers to know with reasonable certainty what magazines are covered, reasonable regulation as to manner and place of display will not infringe the protected freedom. In the case of this by-law, whether it be seen as overbroad or vague (and an element of vagueness is intrinsic in overbroad legislation) the vice is essentially the same: it lacks a definition proportionate to its aim which would give those governed by it and those who administer it a reasonable opportunity to know what is covered by it, and to act accordingly.

It would appear from the magazines tendered as representative of the type at which the display regulation is directed, that these publications are characterized by content featuring the depiction or portrayal of the nude human body, generally female, in such a pose or posture that the viewers' attention or concentration is focused on the breasts or genital areas or in which the breasts or genital areas are exposed and provocatively emphasized. If, under s.222, the municipality wishes to pass a by-law with respect to magazines ''appealing to or designed to appeal to erotic or sexual appetites or inclinations'', a form of words can doubtless be devised which will make abundantly clear the distinguishing characteristics of the publications meant to be included in the general words of the Act. I see no reason why a by-law cannot be drawn which will meet the required standards of specificity and at the same time not impinge on the constitutional guarantee of freedom of expression more than is necessary to achieve the legitimate end sought.

1.4.4.2 Prescribed by Law

1.4.4.2.1 *Re Ontario Film and Video Appreciation Society and Ontario Board of Censors* (1983), 41 O.R. (2d) 583 (Div. Ct.)

J. HOLLAND, BOLAND and LINDEN JJ: The next issue is whether the limits placed on the applicant's freedom of expression by the board of censors were ''prescribed by law''. It is clear that statutory law, regulations and even common law limitations may be permitted. But the limit, to be acceptable, must have legal force. This is to ensure that it has been established democratically through the legislative process or judicially through the operation of precedent over the years. This requirement underscores the seriousness with which courts will view any interference with the fundamental freedoms.

The Crown has argued that the board's authority to curtail freedom of expression is prescribed by law in the *Theatres Act,* ss.3, 35 and 38. In our view, although there has certainly been a legislative grant of power to the board to censor and prohibit certain films, the reasonable limits placed upon that freedom of expression of film-makers have not been legislatively authorized. The Charter requires reasonable limits that are prescribed by law; it is not enough to authorize a board to censor or prohibit the exhibition of any film of which it disapproves. That kind of authority is not legal for it depends on the discretion of an administrative tribunal. However dedicated, competent and well-meaning the board may be, that kind of regulation cannot be considered as ''law''. It is accepted that law cannot be vague, undefined, and totally discretionary; it must be ascertainable and understandable. Any limits placed on the freedom of expression cannot be left to the whim of an official; such limits must be articulated with some precision or they cannot be considered to be law.

There are no reasonable limits contained in the statute or the regulations. The standards and the pamphlets utilized by the Ontario Board of Censors do contain certain information upon which a film-maker may get some indication of how his film will be judged. However, the board is not bound by these standards. They have no legislative or legal force of any kind. Hence, since they do not qualify as law, they cannot be employed so as to justify any limitation on expression, pursuant to s.1 of the Charter. We draw comfort in this conclusion from the views of Professor Beckton, in *The Canadian Charter of Rights and Freedoms: Commentary* (1982), p. 107 (Tarnopolsky & Beaudoin, editors), where she wrote:

> Clearly statutes which create censorship boards without specific criteria would be contrary to the guarantees of free expression, since no line is drawn between objectionable and non-objectionable forms of expression. Now standards will have to be created to measure the limits to which obscene expressions may be regulated.

This does not mean that the censorship scheme set out in the *Theatres Act* is invalid. Clearly the classification scheme by itself does not offend the Charter. Nor do we find that ss.3, 35 and 38 are invalid, but the problem is that standing alone they cannot be used to censor or prohibit the exhibition of films because they are so general, and because the detailed criteria employed in the process are not prescribed by law. These sections, in so far as they purport to prohibit or to allow censorship of films, may be said to be ''of no force or effect'', but they may be rendered operable by the passage of regulations pursuant to the legislative authority or by the enactment of statutory amendments, imposing reasonable limits and standards.

1.4.4.2.2 *Re Ontario Film and Video Appreciation Society and Ontario Board of Censors* (1984), 45 O.R. (2d) 80 (C.A.)

MacKinnon A.C.J.O.: We would go further than the Divisional Court on this issue. In our view, s.3(2)(*a*), rather than being of ''no force or effect'', is *ultra vires* as it stands. The subsection allows for the complete denial or prohibition of the freedom of expression in this particular area and sets no limits on the Ontario Board of Censors. It clearly sets no limit, reasonable or otherwise, on which an argument can be mounted that it falls within the saving words of s.1 of the Charter: ''subject only to such reasonable limits prescribed by law''. Further, like the Divisional Court, we conclude that s.3(2)(*b*) and ss.35 and 38 cannot be interpreted and applied in their present form to support the censorship of film although they have a valid role to play otherwise. As pointed out by the Divisional Court, there is no challenge in these proceedings to the system of film classification, nor to the general regulation of theatres and projectionists and other matters dealt with in the statute and regulations.

Note: In response to the Ontario Court of Appeal decision the legislature amended the Theatres Act.

1.4.4.2.3 An Act to Amend the Theatres Act, 1984, S.O. 1984, c.56

APPROVAL OF FILMS AND ADVERTISING

Approval of film

35. (1) Before the exhibition or distribution in Ontario of a film, an application for approval to exhibit or distribute and for classification of the film shall be made to the Board.

Idem

(2) After viewing a film, the Board, in accordance with the criteria prescribed by the regulations, may refuse to approve the film for exhibition or distribution in Ontario.

Conditional

(3) The Board, having regard to the criteria prescribed by the regulations, may make an approval conditional upon the film being exhibited in designated locations and on specified dates only.

Quorum

(4) Except as otherwise provided, for the purpose of exercising a power under clause 3(5)(a) or (d), three members of the Board constitute a quorum.

Review of decision

(5) Where a film has been submitted for approval and classification under subsection (1), the person submitting the film, on payment of the prescribed fee, may appeal the Board's decision by submitting the film for reconsideration by a panel of the Board and that panel, after viewing the film, shall make a decision on its approval and classification.

Decision final

(6) A decision by a panel of the Board under subsection (5) as to classification is final.

Panel

(7) The panel referred to in subsection (5) shall be composed of at least five members, none of whom had participated in a previous decision on the film.

Appeal

(8) A person who has appealed under subsection (5) may appeal the Board's decision as to approval to the Divisional Court in accordance with the rules of court and, where there is an appeal, the Minister is entitled to be heard.

Powers of Court on appeal

(9) An appeal under subsection (8) may be made on question of law or fact or both and the Court may affirm or may rescind the decision of the Board and may direct the Board to take any action that the Board may take and as the Court considers proper.

Reconsideration of film by Board

35a. (1) Where the chairman of the Board is of the opinion that the criteria prescribed by regulation respecting subject-matter or content in films have changed since a film was originally approved and classified and that the film may not be entitled to the approval or classification determined at the time of the original decision, the chairman may require that the film be submitted for reconsideration by the Board.

Idem

(2) Where a film is submitted for reconsideration under subsection (1), the provisions of section 35 apply with necessary modifications except that no fees shall be charged.

Exhibition of film

38. (1) No person shall exhibit, distribute or offer to distribute or cause to be exhibited, distributed or offered for distribution in Ontario any film that has not been approved by the Board.

Idem

(2) No person shall exhibit or cause to be exhibited in Ontario any film that has been approved by the Board subject to any conditions except in accordance with those conditions.

Alteration of film

39. No person shall alter or cause to be altered, for the purpose of exhibition or distribution in Ontario, any film from its state as approved by the Board.

1.4.4.2.4 O. Reg. 56/85. Regulation to Amend Regulation 931 of Revised Regulations of Ontario, 1980, Made Under the Theatres Act

21. (1) In exercising its authority under sections 3 and 35 of the Act, the Board shall consider the film in its entirety and take into account the general character and integrity of the film.

(2) After viewing a film, the Board may refuse to approve a film for exhibition or distribution in Ontario where the film contains,

(*a*) a graphic or prolonged scene of violence, torture, crime, cruelty, horror or human degradation:

(*b*) the depiction of the physical abuse or humiliation of human beings for purposes of sexual gratification or as pleasing to the victim:

(*c*) a scene where a person who is or is intended to represent a person under the age of sixteen years appears,

(i) nude or partially nude in a sexually suggestive context, or

(ii) in a scene of explicit sexual activity;

(*d*) the explicit and gratuitous depiction of urination, defecation or vomiting;

(*e*) the explicit depiction of sexual activity;

(*f*) a scene depicting indignities to the human body in an explicit manner;

(*g*) a scene where there is undue emphasis on human genital organs; or

(*h*) a scene where an animal has been abused in the making of the film.

(3) In this section, "sexual activity" means acts, whether real or simulated, of intercourse or masturbation, and includes the depiction of genital, anal or oral-genital connection between human beings or human beings and animals, and anal or genital connection between human beings by means of objects. O. Reg. 56/85, s.2.

1.4.4.3 Demonstrably Justified in a Free and Democratic Society

1.4.4.3.1 *Re Ontario Film and Video Appreciation Society and Ontario Board of Censors* (1983), 41 O.R. (2d) 583 (Div. Ct.)

J. HOLLAND, BOLAND and LINDEN JJ: As for being demonstrably justifiable in a free and democratic society, it has been held that there must be a reasonable ground upon which a limitation can be based for it to be ''justifiable'': see Chief Justice Evans, *Rauca, supra*. Chief Justice Deschênes has suggested that we must focus on the ''validity'' of the ''objective'' of the legislation: *Quebec Ass'n of Protestant School Boards* case, *supra*. It is obvious that the *Theatres Act* (and its predecessors back to 1911) primarily seeks, among other things, to prevent socially offensive films from being publicly shown in Ontario. Eight other provinces and many other free and democratic countries have similar legislation: see *Report of the Committee on Obscenity and Film Censorship*, U.K. Cmnd. 7772 (1979). Moreover, the federal criminal prohibition against obscenity is evidence that there is and has been sufficient concern in this country about this problem to enact legislation to combat it. We are satisfied, therefore, that some prior censorship of film is demonstrably justifiable in a free and democratic society. (No one questioned that Canada and each of its constituent provinces and territories are free and democratic.)

1.4.4.3.2 *National Citizens Coalition* v. *Attorney-General for Canada* (1984), 11 D.L.R. (4th) 481 (Alta. Q.B.)

MEDHURST J.: This change in the law made in 1983 was considered by counsel for the defendant to have been necessary to protect the interest of the legislation which had imposed spending restrictions on candidates and parties for the purpose of providing a system of fairness and equality of opportunity in the election of Members of Parliament. This is said to be a rational and reasonable basis for the limitation imposed as required by s.1 of the Charter. The danger of mischief perceived was referred to by Professor Courtney in this way in p. 22 of his paper:

> Were special interest groups or individuals free to participate in the electoral process totally without constraints, they would enjoy advantages not otherwise available to the political parties. The fact is that the respective roles and responsibilities of political parties and special interest groups are different. Political parties are electorally accountable for their acts, which is one of the ways in which the term ''responsible government'' is given meaning in a parliamentary system. Generally every three or four years political parties are held to account by the electorate. By definition, special interest groups are necessarily different. They have more narrowly-defined interests, goals and memberships than political parties and, in the final analysis, they are not electorally responsible for their activities.

The means used are said to be justified as all third parties have the potential to jeopardize the stated objective of the legislation.

In determining the question of whether a fundamental freedom should be limited one must consider the value that such individual freedom is intended to serve.

The importance of the freedom to express oneself freely and without fear of reprisal is indicated by the fact that such freedom is now contained in the Charter. It is said by many to be one of the most significant of freedoms in a democratic society since the political structure depends on free debate of ideas and opinions. This is said to be of particular importance at election time. It is further suggested that freedom of expression concerning activities of government should be protected from limitations since this is essential to the functioning of a democracy.

Belzil J.A. in *Big M Drug Mart, supra,* noted at p. 147 D.L.R., p. 315 Alta. L.R., that President F. D. Roosevelt declared in an address to Congress on January 6, 1941, that:

> "In future days, which we seek to make secure, we look forward to a world founded upon four essential human freedoms:
> "The first is freedom of speech and expression — everywhere in the world."

In *Reference re Alberta Legislation,* [1938] 2 D.L.R. 81 at p. 119, [1938] S.C.R. 100 at pp. 145-6, Cannon J. stated:

> Under the British system, which is ours, no political party can erect a prohibitory barrier to prevent the electors from getting information concerning the policy of the Government. Freedom of discussion is essential to enlighten public opinion in a democratic State; it cannot be curtailed without affecting the right of the people to be informed through sources independent of the Government concerning matters of public interest. There must be an untrammelled publication of the news and political opinions of the political parties contending for ascendancy.

In this same decision, *Reference re Alberta Legislation,* Chief Justice Duff refers to a Parliament working "under the influence of public opinion and public discussion" and, on p. 107 D.L.R., p. 133 S.C.R., said:

> There can be no controversy that such institutions derive their efficacy from the free public discussion of affairs, from criticism and answer and counter-criticism, from attack upon policy and administration and defence and counter-attack; from the freest and fullest analysis and examination from every point of view of political proposals. This is signally true in respect of the discharge by Ministers of the Crown of their responsibility to Parliament, by members of Parliament of their duty to the electors, and by the electors themselves of their responsibilities in the election of their representatives.
>
> The right of public discussion is, of course, subject to legal restrictions; those based upon considerations of decency and public order, and others conceived for the protection of various private and public interests with which, for example, the laws of defamation and sedition are concerned. In a word, freedom of discussion means, to quote the words of Lord Wright in *James v. Commonwealth of Australia,* [1936] A.C. 578 at p. 627, "freedom governed by law."
>
> Even with its legal limits, it is liable to abuse and grave abuse, and such abuse is constantly exemplified before our eyes; but it is axiomatic that the practice of this right of free public discussion of public affairs, notwithstanding its incidental mischiefs, is the breath of life for parliamentary institutions.

McDonald J. considered the meaning of a reasonable limit in *Reich,* supra, and concluded after a review of the relevant authorities that it meant having a rational basis. At p. 709 he said:

> In my opinion, the words "reasonable limits" as used in s.1 mean "capable of being supported as a rational means of achieving a rational objective".

In *Re Southam Inc. and The Queen (No. 1)* (1983), 146 D.L.R. (3d) 408 at p. 424, 3 C.C.C. (3d) 515 at p. 531, 41 O.R. (2d) 113 (Ont. C.A.), McKinnon A.C.J.O. said:

> In determining the reasonableness of the limit in each particular case, the court must examine objectively its argued rational basis in light of what the court understands to be reasonable in a free and democratic society.

McDonald J. also stated in *Reich,* at p. 713:

> The yardstick by which the court should judge whether it has been shown that the limitation can be demonstrably justified in terms of the means chosen to achieve the legislative object,

are that the means and the object must be consistent with the existence of freedom and democracy.

The justification for the limitation is said to be the need to ensure a level of equality amongst all participants in federal elections. According to the statements of the Barbeau Committee and the later Chappell Committee as well as representatives of all three political parties, it is beneficial to the electoral system to have spending restrictions on the part of parties and candidates at election time. This benefit, it is said, would be lost if such restrictions were not extended to third parties during the same period. This is the justification of the value gained by society in limiting the freedom of expression as set out in the 1983 amendments to the *Election Expenses Act.*

In assessing the respective values the court is not able to consider whether there may have been other means available to achieve the same objective. It is not for the court to rewrite legislation so that it might conform with freedoms protected by the Charter. The requirement that such limitation on fundamental rights and freedoms be prescribed by law preserves the separation of legislative and judicial functions.

The tests must be applied on the basis of the likelihood that the mischief or the harm perceived would occur and that is therefore a reasonable limitation and demonstrably justified.

In my opinion the limitation must be considered for the protection of a real value to society and not simply to reduce or restrain criticism no matter how unfair such criticism may be. It has been said that the true test of free expression to a society is whether it can tolerate criticism of its fundamental values and institutions. A limitation to the fundamental freedom of expression should be assessed on the basis that if it is not permitted then harm will be caused to other values in society. This requires, as has been said, a balancing of the respective interests of society and of the individual.

Care must be taken to ensure that the freedom of expression, as guaranteed by s.2 of the Charter, is not arbitrarily or unjustifiably limited. Fears or concerns of mischief that may occur are not adequate reasons for imposing a limitation. There should be actual demonstration of harm or a real likelihood of harm to a society value before a limitation can be said to be justified.

In my view it has not been established to the degree required that the fundamental freedom of expression need be limited. The limitation has not been shown to be reasonable or demonstrably justified in a free and democratic society.

Accordingly, I hold that the laws under review, s.70.1(1) and s.72 of the *Canada Elections Act,* are inconsistent with s.2(*b*) of the Charter and to this extent are of no force or effect.

Counsel may speak to costs at their convenience.

1.4.4.3.3 Ronald G. Atkey, "Corporate Political Activity", (1985) *23 The University of Western Ontario Law Review*, 129

Note: The following observations taken from "Corporate Political Activity" help put this decision in context.

The National Citizens' Coalition (NCC) has started a political and legal debate with far reaching implications for corporate political activity and freedom of expression.

Starting with the Canadian Charter of Rights and Freedoms and several U.S. Supreme Court decisions striking down statutory limitations on political expenditures by corporations, the NCC laid the legal groundwork for a challenge to provisions in the Canada Elections Act (the Elections Act). These prohibited anyone other than nominated candidates and registered parties incurring election expenses or placing political advertisements during an election campaign. These provisions, the NCC claimed, had the effect of muzzling persons or groups who wanted to speak out on political issues independent of the established parties or candidates or who felt that these were not properly representing their views.

The NCC planned carefully. It incorporated a federal non-profit corporation without share capital called "National Citizens' Coalition Inc./Coalition Nationale des Citoyens Inc.". It then sought to determine the most suitable province in which to seek a declaration that these provisions of the Elections Act violated the Charter, and not surprisingly, chose Alberta. The NCC then waited for Parliament to accept the recommendation of the Chief Electoral Officer in his 1983 Annual Report that the defence under section 70.1(4) of the Elections Act be eliminated. This allowed a defence under section 70.1 if it could be established that the individual or organisation was "promoting an issue of public policy" or "advancing the aims of their organization" and that they were acting in good faith. The justification for this recommendation was that the defence had permitted certain persons to spend unlimited sums of money to promote or oppose a particular candidate or registered party which did not have to be accounted for. The recommendation passed quietly through the House of Commons supported by all parties.

Early in 1984, which was likely to be an election year, the NCC commenced its court action in Alberta claiming a remedy for an impending breach of its rights under sections 2(b) and 3 of the Charter. It claimed that it would not be able to take strong positions independent of the established political parties or candidates in the forthcoming election campaign due to the limitations in sections 70.1 and 72 of the Elections Act.

Mr. Justice Medhurst in the Alberta Court of Queen's Bench obliged the NCC with a decision on 25 June 1984, a few days before the official election call by Prime Minister Turner. He granted the plaintiff corporation standing to challenge the validity of the provisions on behalf of all who were affected by them and found that the impending breach of the plaintiff's Charter rights was "reasonably foreseeable in the near future" and that the matter could be heard at that time.

...

Faced with this decision in the midst of a difficult election campaign in the summer of 1984, the Turner government chose not to appeal. The new government under Prime Minister Mulroney could hardly have proceeded with the appeal in September. Mulroney having announced in opposition six months previously that he should not have supported the amendment in question. Thus, the *NCC* decision stands.

1.4.4.3.4 *International Fund for Animal Welfare* v. *The Queen* (1986) 30 C.C.C. (3d) 80 (F.C.T.D.)

MCNAIR J.: Much of the underpinning of the plaintiffs' case rests on a memorandum submitted by Donald D. Tansley, Deputy Minister, to the Honourable Romeo LeBlanc sometime during the latter part of 1978. The memorandum dealt with objectives and policies for controlling access to the sealing operations in 1979 and sets out a number of alternative policy options and conclusions. The stated objectives to which the plaintiffs take most exception are the following:

a. to reduce adverse national and international publicity on sealing;
b. an ostensible mechanism for reducing interference with the sealing operations.

The plaintiffs make much play of the word "ostensible". The face page of the memorandum indicated that the majority consensus of those involved with the *Seal Protection Regulations* favoured the view that a limited number of protesters should be permitted access to the 1979 sealing operations for observational purposes only. It is true that the memorandum dealt with the pros and cons of a number of policy alternatives but there is no compelling evidence that the underlying purpose was the suppression of freedom of opinion and expression. In my view, the Tansley memorandum is relatively innocuous and largely inconclusive.

More telling from the plaintiffs' standpoint is a news release from the Honourable Romeo LeBlanc dated February 28, 1978, wherein the Minister explained the regulations requiring a permit or licence for any person to visit the immediate area of the seal hunt. The Minister explained that the purpose of the amendments to the regulations was to prohibit unjustifiable interference in the lawful activities of the sealers rather than to prevent legitimate observation of the seal herds. He went on to make this further statement regarding the issuing of permits and licences: "We will not, however, allow persons or groups near the sealing operations whose announced intention is to interfere with the livelihood of authorized and licensed fishermen."

A departmental circular of February 16, 1982, respecting procedures and guidelines for visitors' permits repeated the admonition that permits would not be issued "to individuals or groups whose stated objective is to disrupt the hunt".

The question thus posed is this: were the regulations aimed at the conservation and protection of seals and the proper management and control of the seal fishery, having regard to the seal harvest in light of its historic and traditional origins and the rights of those who earned a living therefrom, or was the paramount purpose that of suppressing freedom of expression? In my opinion, the purpose behind the regulations was a perfectly valid one. None the less, the actual effect was to impinge on the plaintiffs' right of freedom of expression enshrined in the Charter in the broad connotation of freedom of access to information. *Prima facie,* their right has been violated and it becomes necessary to turn now to s.1 of the Charter to determine whether the limit is one that is "reasonable" and "demonstrably justified in a free and democratic society".

Hogg, *Constitutional Law of Canada,* 2nd ed. (1985), makes this significant statement in reference to s.1 consideration at p. 688:

> In the end, Charter cases will not be decided by a nice parsing of the words and phrases in s.1. What is called for is a weighing of three factors: (1) the importance of the Charter right that has been infringed; (2) the extent of the infringement; and (3) the importance of the governmental interest asserted in justification. The significance of the phrase "demonstrably justified" is that a court must be satisfied that factor (3) clearly outweighs the combined effect of factors (1) and (2). This is an ineluctably discretionary judgment by a court which cannot easily be captured in any verbal formula.

The burden of proof of justification rests on the defendants as the proponents of the impugned legislation. What kind of proof is required? The answer is far from clear. The prevailing view is that there should be sufficient cogent evidence to persuade the court as to the reasonableness of the limitation in terms of striking a balance between legitimate social interests and the rights of the individual, except in cases where this is obvious and self-evident: *per* Dickson C.J.C., in *R. v. Oakes, supra,* at p. 347

C.C.C., p. 138 S.C.R. In the latter situation, strong submissions would probably suffice to tip the scale. In other cases the evidence of justification could conceivably take the form of social science reports or studies. The modes of proof will undoubtedly vary according to the circumstances of the particular case.

The Prime Minister made a statement concerning the 1977 conviction of Brian Davies in which he stated that the purpose of the regulatory prohibitions against landing or flying an aircraft near any seal on the ice was to bring to an end the former unregulated and extremely hazardous practice of hunting seals by aircraft. Henceforth, hunters could only approach the site of the hunt by ship. There is other evidence to the same effect. There is no compelling evidence that the purpose of the regulations was to deny access to the news media. In fact, all indications point the other way. In 1982, there were 49 requests for observer permits to view the hunt of which eight were refused, including the three representatives of I.F.A.W. Of the 41 requests granted, the bulk were to members of the media. Similarly, in 1983, 19 requests for permits were made, of which 15 were granted and four were refused. Among those granted, nine were to media personnel.

What other justifications are there, if any, for the stringent prohibition against landing or flying aircraft close to any seal on the ice? I find on the evidence that the presence of low-flying aircraft would cause some dispersion of the seal herds. Dr. David Lavigne, the plaintiff's principal expert on seals, confirmed this during his testimony. Davies himself honestly admitted to it. The fact was also unequivocally corroborated by the evidence of Messrs. Renaud and Small, sealing captains of many years proven experience. The evidence also established that buzzing aircraft would disrupt the normal pattern of nursing behaviour between mother seal and whitecoat pup but the quantifiable extent of actual detriment was left to conjecture and inference. Conceivably, there would have to be some.

Was the governmental restriction against active protestors reasonable in the circumstances? There is something of a fine line between the activity of searching for information to mount an effective protest against a lawful commercial activity and the act of protesting that activity at the very scene of operations. The sealers were becoming sensitive to the fanfare and reluctant to have their photographs taken. The sealers were perceived by the government as an important social, economic and political constituency and the governmental objective was to recognize their right to pursue their livelihood free from the interference of protestors. The ice pans are no place to stage a protest. This was the firm conviction of senior fisheries protection officer, Stanley Dudka, born of long experience at the scene of many hunts. He alluded to five occasions over the years when he had to rescue Davies or some of his compatriots because of weather conditions or other adversities.

Dr. Lavigne related the eerie personal experience of having crossed an ice pan in the morning on his way to the hunt and retracing his steps in the afternoon to find that his footprints were obliterated because the ice pan which he had earlier traversed had afterwards done a complete flip-flop in the leads of open water. Safety alone would necessarily impose some restriction of free access.

Based on the totality of evidence, it is my opinion that the collective governmental interest of protecting both the seals and the fundamental right of the sealers to pursue their historical avocation clearly outweighs the plaintiffs' enshrined right of freedom of access to information. In the result, the limitations prescribed by the *Seal Protection Regulations* are reasonable in the circumstances and demonstrably justifiable by the normal, perceptive standards of a free and democratic society.

1.4.4.3.5 Constitution Act, 1982, s.52

If a restriction on freedom of expression fails the test of s.1 of the Charter, the judge, on the basis of s.52 of the Constitution Act, 1982, will declare the law which imposes the restriction to be invalid:

Primacy of Constitution of Canada

52. (1) The Constitution of Canada is the supreme law of Canada, and any law that is inconsistent with the provisions of the Constitution is, to the extent of the inconsistency, of no force or effect.

1.4.4.4 A General Approach to Section 1: *R.* v. *Oakes*, [1986] 1 S.C.R. 103

Oakes was charged with unlawful possession of a narcotic for the purpose of trafficking, contrary to s.4(2) of the Narcotic Control Act, R.S.C. 1970, c.N-1. After the trial judge found that Oakes was in possession of a narcotic and thereby guilty as charged, Oakes lawyer brought a motion challenging the constitutional validity of s.8 of the Act. That section provided that once the accused was found to be in possession of a narcotic, he was presumed to be in possession for the purpose of trafficking. Unless the accused could prove this was not his intent, he had to be convicted of trafficking. The trial judge and the Ontario Court of Appeal held that s.8 of the Act was a reverse onus clause which violated the presumption of innocence guaranteed by s.11(d) of the Charter. The Crown appealed to the Supreme Court of Canada. Excerpts of Chief Justice Dicksons's reasons for upholding the Ontario Court of Appeal decision are reproduced here. In this case, the Chief Justice laid down a general approach to be followed in applying section 1.

... To establish that a limit is reasonable and demonstrably justified in a free and democratic society, two central criteria must be satisfied. First, the objective, which the measures responsible for a limit on a *Charter* right or freedom are designed to serve, must be "of sufficient importance to warrant overriding a constitutionally protected right or freedom": *R. v. Big M Drug Mart Ltd., supra,* at p. 352. The standard must be high in order to ensure that objectives which are trivial or discordant with the principles integral to a free and democratic society do not gain s.1 protection. It is necessary, at a minimum, that an objective relate to concerns which are pressing and substantial in a free and democratic society before it can be characterized as sufficiently important.

Second, once a sufficiently significant objective is recognized, then the party invoking s.1 must show that the means chosen are reasonable and demonstrably justified. This involves "a form of proportionality test": *R. v. Big M Drug Mart Ltd., supra,* at p. 352. Although the nature of the proportionality test will vary depending on the circumstances, in each case courts will be required to balance the interests of society with those of individuals and groups. There are, in my view, three important components of a proportionality test. First, the measures adopted must be carefully designed to achieve the objective in question. They must not be arbitrary, unfair or based on irrational considerations. In short, they must be rationally connected to the objective. Second, the means, even if rationally connected to the objective in this first sense, should impair "as litte as possible" the right or freedom in question: *R. v. Big M Drug Mart Ltd., supra,* at p. 352. Third, there must be a proportionality between the *effects* of the measures which are responsible for limiting the *Charter* right or freedom, and the objective which has been identified as of "sufficient importance."

1.4.5 G. Stuart Adam. "Why Should the Press Be Free? A Journalist's Reflections on the Charter"

The title of my address is "Why Should the Press be Free?". It may not surprise you to learn that occasionally that question is on the exam in a course I teach in media law and ethics. It may also not surprise you to learn that some of the answers, regardless of how they are phrased, indicate that the respondents don't believe in the press's freedom, at least they are happier to justify restrictions on the press rather than to assert powerfully that there should be very few limitations. Today, regardless of the declarations in the Charter of Rights and Freedoms, and regardless of a longstanding affection for the phrase "freedom of the press", it seems that there are lobbies — some more powerful than others — putting pressure on politicians to extend law and regulation over the press and diminish the space within which it may freely operate. This is not new. There has always been and will continue to be a tension between the desire for freedom and the desire for order — or for contradictory privileges and rights. It's just that the current version of that tension is harder to address than it was when authoritarian politicians or religious bureaucracies were using their power to restrict and manage speech. There is, I think, a growing public affection for regulation and as necessary as it might be in other areas, it is dangerous in the area of speech.

The practical occasions for testing this hypothesis may be considered in the questions judges and policy makers are asked to answer these days. "Should journalists be allowed to name the victims in trials involving young offenders?" "Should the trials of young offenders be held *in camera?*" "Can a judge turn a court into an *in camera* proceeding to save the reputation of an accused?" "Can a journalist make disparaging remarks about an ethnic minority?" "Is Keegstra a criminal?" "Is pornography dangerous?" "Should hate propaganda be a matter of strict liability?" "Should the Broadcasting Act enable the cabinet to direct the CRTC on matters of content?" There are of course no easy answers to such questions and it is clearly up to wise legislators and judges to provide authoritative answers. All being well, they will be guided by a public which is attached to democratic values and can endure the degree of anarchy and responsibility that democracy requires. True democrats prefer persuasion to compulsion.

At the centre of these debates is the Charter of Rights and Freedoms. Annexed to the Canadian Constitution in 1982, the Charter's provisions are becoming well known as courts are required to judge its implications and secure the place of its principles.

No one should think that the Charter is without ambiguity. It encompasses fundamental freedoms in section 2 such as freedom of religion, assembly, association, belief and expression. In sections 7-15 it secures a set of due process or legal rights; sections 15, 16 and 35 proclaim in one way or another equality or human rights. And, finally, section 1 circumscribes the exercise of all of these rights and freedoms to reasonable limits prescribed by law as can be demonstrably justified in a free and democratic society.

Accordingly, it is not easy for a naive outsider or for an ambitious generalist to understand abstractly what will arise out of the operations of the Charter in our legal and cultural systems. Students of law will recognize that the problems and conflicts it promotes are not new. Students of journalism may be less aware and accordingly I refer them to the work of the American scholar, Thomas Emerson, who has written insightfully on the operations of the First Amendment to the American Constitution. The First Amendment, you will recall, says that Congress shall make no law that abridges freedom of the press. Its influence radiates strongly through American press law from contempt to espionage.

I think Emerson states the problem and speaks to the issues in an illuminating way. Here is what he says: ''In constructing and maintaining a system of freedom of expression, the principal problems and major controversies have arisen when the attempt is made to fit the affirmative theory — that is the affirmative functions served by the system [of free expression] — into a more comprehensive scheme of social values and social goals.'' He can be interpreted to mean in Canadian and in practical terms that although judicial proceedings must be protected, and although obscenity and hate propaganda statutes may be used to protect certain social values and groups, and, finally, although defamation statutes are legitimate, freedom of the press must be preserved. So the affirmative theory, which is the starting point for his analysis, is a comprehensive doctrine of freedom of the press. It is not naively formulated. Emerson knows perfectly well that there must be limits on freedom. But the challenge is to justify such freedom in a manner which will entail narrow limits. The challenge is to build a system of free expression, including the press, which, will operate vigorously within very limited boundaries. In other words, Emerson invites us to consider a powerful doctrine of freedom of expression or of the press and then to assimilate it — one could say almost reluctantly and only out of necessity — into other social, and particularly legal, goals of the society. So when I ask my students to answer the question, ''Why should the press be free?'', I am not asking them why should the press be absolutely free. I am asking rather — what doctrine and goals should we have in mind before we are asked to consider reasonable limitations? My address then is to answer the question I put occasionally to the students. I am not going to justify limitations so much as to justify freedom and thereby promote a cast of mind which celebrates freedom rather than authorizes limitations.

So what does freedom of the press mean? John Milton, in 1644 in his pamphlet ''Areopagitica'', asked for ''the liberty to know, to utter and to argue freely according to conscience above all liberties''. The subject of his pamphlet was the Licensing Act in Britain and the arguments he formulated were aimed at persuading the members of the Long Parliament to abandon licensing. What he wanted, therefore, was the right to know, to utter and to argue without prior restraint. Milton, like the eighteenth century judge Mansfield, would have said that the liberty of the press was the liberty to publish without prior restraint, subject to the consequences of law.

The question that follows the identification of these rights is, ''In whom do these rights inhere?'' They inhere obviously in individuals and, by virtue of that, I would say in journalists as in any ordinary citizen.

Finally, how are these rights justified? I have no pretensions as a philosopher or an interpreter of jurisprudence. But let me claim for the purposes of this presentation that there are two traditional grounds on which these rights are justified. The first is the ground of natural right. In this tradition it is asserted simply that there are certain rights that are inviolable and the state has no parallel right to deprive a citizen of them. The echoes of this tradition may be found in the words of the late Supreme Court Justice Ivan Rand who, in the Saumur case, remarked that ''freedom of speech, religion and the inviolability of the person are original freedoms which are at once the necessary attributes and modes of self expression of human beings and the primary conditions of their community life within a legal order''. A more literary expression of this position may be found in the writing of the British author George Orwell. For example, in his essay ''The Prevention of Literature'' which was published first in 1946 Orwell said:

> ...Literature is an attempt to influence the viewpoint of one's contemporaries by recording experience. And so far as freedom of expression is concerned, there is not much difference between a mere journalist and the most ''unpolitical'' imaginative writer. The journalist is unfree, and is conscious of unfreedom when he is forced to write lies or suppress what seems to him important news. The imaginative writer is unfree when he has to falsify his subjective feelings.... He may distort and caricature reality in order to make his meaning clear but he cannot misrepresent the scenery of his own mind: He cannot say with any conviction that he likes what he dislikes, or believes what he disbelieves. If he is forced to do so the only result is that his creative faculties dry up.

Orwell was saying in his own way what Rand was saying in his, namely, that there is a fundamental legitimacy to the recording of human thought and experience. It's like saying you can't really mess with the heads of individual citizens. Their rights to communicate with one another are sacred.

I do not want to carry this argument further than it ought to go. Orwell, like many literary figures, carries the anarchist position beyond a point acceptable to philosophers of law. Still, there is a point to the position he expresses which must be taken seriously. The point is that the record of human thought and expression, however it occurs, stands on its own as a starting point for social and political life. The natural rights position proclaims nothing more.

If one is uncomfortable with the implications of a natural rights philosophy, however it is argued, one can slip into a utilitarian position and, I suppose, that remains the dominant line amongst those who argue for freedom of expression. Emerson is among them. He formulates four functions or, to use the more classical language, utilities, which the system of free expression ought to serve. He says:

> Maintenance of a system of free expression is necessary (1) as a method of assuring individual self fulfillment, (2) as a means of attaining the truth, (3) as a method of securing participation by the members of society in social, including political decision making, and (4) as a means of maintaining the balance between stability and change in the society.

The philosopher of individuality is John Stuart Mill. His view of the individual was, of course, modern, secular and optimistic. For example, in his essay, *On Liberty* (1859), he said that ''the source of everything respectable in man either as an intellectual or moral being [is that] his errors are corrigible. He is capable of rectifying his mistakes, by discussion and experience. Not by experience alone. There must be discussion, to show how experience is to be interpreted''. His most important aim was to convince his fellow Britons that they should encourage, on a society-wide scale, opportunities for all individuals to grow intellectually. He went on to say:

> It really is of importance, not only what men do, but also what manner of men they are that do it. Among the works of man, which human life is rightly employed in perfecting and beautifying, is man himself.

So for Mill and for others, the right to know and to contemplate and to reflect and to choose was justified by the promise that any individual would become more accomplished, more thoughtful and more wise than he or she might have been if the field of information and truth was unduly restricted.

The philosophers of the attainment of truth, Emerson's second function, include all who champion science. There is a sense in which their godfather is John Milton. He said:

> ...our faith and knowledge thrives by exercise...Truth is a streaming fountain; if her waters flow not in perpetual progression, they sicken into a muddy pool of conformity and tradition.

Milton genuinely belleved that the removal of a censoring power and the emancipation of the intellect would produce wisdom and insight in all fields, particularly in the domains of religion and politics. His reflections are part and parcel of the theme in liberal thought which ties truth to social progress or, put differently, ties truth to the elevation of society as a whole. The promise was that individual insight would become collective knowledge or would produce collective benefits.

The philosophers of participatory decision making are the democratic theorists, and amongst them in the English-speaking world none is more important than the utilitarians including Jeremy Bentham and James Mill. For example, James Mill wrote:

> The point of greatest importance to [governments] is, to keep the people at large from complaining, or from knowing or thinking that they have any ground of complaint. If this object is fully attained, they may then, without anxiety, and without trouble, riot in the pleasures of misrule.

In James Mill's view the method of preventing governors from rioting in the pleasures of misrule would be to install a system of reporting and commenting on the activities of government. In his view these rights of reporting and commentary would be limited by very restricted notions of seditious libel and by the law of civil defamation. The rest would be free territory. He wrote:

> The end which is sought...by allowing anything to be said in censure of the government, is, to ensure the goodness of government... If the goodness of government could be ensured by any preferable means, it is evident that all censure of the government ought to be prohibited. All discontent with the government is only good, in so far as it is a means of removing real cause of discontent....

Accordingly, he said, ''the only means of removing the defects of vicious governments [is through] the freedom of the press'' or, as he put it later in this passage, the freedom of the press is ''the greatest safeguard of the interests of mankind''.

Many democratic theorists, including Mill, argued the case for freedom in the name of Emerson's fourth function, the maintenance of a balance between stability and change. The position is part and parcel of a simple theory of democracy and it says nothing more profound than if people have the freedom to know, to utter and to argue they will take their own voices seriously, believe that occasionally they will be heard and that their grievances can be redressed by a wise legislature. In other words, a recourse to violence is unnecessary. In sum, Emerson's functions or utilities can be used to justify the right of freedom of expression. But there is more to the argument than that.

I know that John Stuart Mill would be uncomfortable with the idea that he was a natural rights philosopher. I cannot be sure of this, but I imagine Mill would have shared Bentham's proposition that natural rights were ''anarchical fallacies'' or ''nonsence upon stilts''. However, Mill's declaration that the sacred democratic principle of majority rule should itself be limited is tantamount to a natural rights position. He said that majorities should not deprive minorities of their rights of free expression. He said the notion that "the people have no need to limit their power over themselves might seem axiomatic when popular government was a thing only dreamed about..." But in light of the serious aim of promoting individual human growth and the attendant benefits to all society, he said it is necessary to protect individuals, especially their thoughts, from the majority.

He went on to say:

> The limitation...of the power over individuals loses none of its importance when the holders of power are regularly accountable to the community...Protection...against the tyranny of the magistrate is not enough: there needs protection against the tyranny of the prevailing opinion and feeling; against the tendency of society to impose...its own ideas and practices as rules of conduct on those who dissent from them.

In other words, the system could not be democratic if a democratic principle could be used to usurp the individual rights on which the system was dependent. Not only that, the protections, while certainly necessary to protect individuals from the power of legislatures, were also necessary to protect individuals from the tyranny of convention and consensus in society at large.

Let me summarize then. What the liberal philosophers had in common, although they expressed it differently and with different goals in mind, is the belief that certain liberties or rights must be secure for a recognizably democratic system or process to occur. For example, there cannot be a democracy if the right to oppose is not secure; nor can there be a democracy if governments possess the power to define the meaning of events and values; nor can there be democracy if governments are not themselves governed by rules. Accordingly, a fundamental rule out of which democracies are constructed is the rule that says speech will be free. No government possesses the right to abrogate this fundamental freedom. Put a little differently, the act of governance in democracies is circumscribed by the notion of free expression. The limit on the power of governments is established by an understanding that the majorities they represent can, without violating other democratic rules, destroy the very rights on which the whole system turns. To give full license to the idea of majority rule without providing a limit to it would in the end be a denial of democracy itself.

The image or analogy that best suits this line of thinking comes more from architecture than from philosophy. This is not to deny that philosophical questions are important in the resolution of the puzzles of democratic theory, but rather to acknowledge that we build systems of politics and governance just as we build buildings. As a consequence, the fundamental freedoms may be seen as the foundations on which the democratic system rests. Since freedom of expression is a foundation, it may be seen as a means rather than as an end — as a starting point for democratic life rather than a goal or an end for which the political process or the regulatory machinery of the state can ordinarily be used.

The steps that make it possible for such liberals to advocate or approve freedom of expression include the reasons we have already reviewed, but most importantly and directly they include: 1) a distrust of the narrow and self-serving uses to which politicians can turn the machinery of state; 2) a belief that virtue and progress are more likely to come from acts of individual choice than from acts of compulsion; 3) a belief that the activities of state, conceived in the broadest political as well as in a narrow governmental sense, are the public's business; and 4) a belief that the public can be trusted. With respect to this last point, it does not follow that no judgment or sanction should be imposed on heresies or evil speech. Rather it is believed that in order for genuine freedom to occur, the court of public opinion rather than the courts of law should be used to censure and condemn. At the same time, there is a belief that certain interests must be protected against the abuses of free expression. For Canadian justices, such as Rand, consistent with the traditions of their intellectual forebears, this entailed an approval of the laws of defamation and contempt, probably official secrets and seditious libel in which palpable and immediate harms to the operations of state, the public order or private welfare could be measured. Thus Rand spoke of the "circumscription of...liberties" by civil and public law aimed at punishing "consequential incidents". The notions of incitement and the protection of the administration of justice and individuals have figured prominently in the justifications of these limitations.

Even if it sounds occasionally that absolute freedom is being advocated, the fact is that limitations have been explicitly defended in the very tradition that advocates the widest measure of freedom. However, the central feature of the tradition is the belief that limitations can only be imposed for the narrowest of reasons and then only in the face of a fundamental freedom on which the whole edifice of democracy rests.

*****

Now, before departing from this blueprint, it may be noted that in the late twentieth century it is not as easy as it once was to link it to the activities of journalists and journalism.

Journalistic activity has always been looked upon by some individuals or groups with suspicion and fear. In the nineteenth century, when James Mill wrote his essay on the press, the social and political elites wanted to limit and control the press, no doubt because they wanted "to riot in the pleasures of misrule". That James Mill thought so is no surprise. Nor is it a surprise that genuine democrats such as Mill would identify with the career and welfare of an upstart institution which was challenging those very elites. The faith in the press as an instrument for achieving good works began when the democratic spirit took hold in our culture and challenged established power.

But now, that phase of the democratic revolution is over. To some degree the press is an established institution or even part of an establishment and it has become, accordingly, harder to believe it possesses and acquits the same democratic mandate it once did. Members of our current reform movement are sometimes tempted to suspect that the press — especially in light of the scope of the Thomson and Southam empires — is not a genuinely democratic institution. So they sometimes join other groups in discrediting it.

Another reason which complicates the application of the blueprint to journalists is the word media. That word directs attention to institutions in which most journalists work rather than to journalists themselves. Such institutions may be very large and, notwithstanding the profound differences in function, they have some of the characteristics of major commercial and industrial enterprises.

Yet another reason is that journalists have their own agenda for covering society's stories and issues. The operations and practices of the news media probably confuse members of the public and seem to them sometimes remotely connected to the difficult chore of supporting the democratic edifice. Finally, journalists are not as able as other professional groups such as lawyers and doctors to camouflage their errors in judgment. Like the politicians whose work they so carefully monitor, their limitations and errors — and their courage and acumen — are public events.

Still, it is important to continue to recognize that there is much to be gained by conferring a wide measure of freedom on journalists to practise their craft as they see fit and it is no more absurd to connect their work to democracy than to connect the work of lawyers to notions of justice.

First, the right or the liberty is conferred on citizens. It is they who have the right to know that is going on about them and what the government is doing on their behalf. Equally, they have the right or liberty as citizens to utter and to argue freely. Secondly, if citizens have these liberties, then journalists possess them as well. It is hard to imagine it being otherwise. That some citizens exercise these rights and freedoms more vigorously than others is consistent with the division of labour in complex societies. This is not to make a virtue of the size and complexity of our society, but rather to recognize — perhaps even tragically — the inevitability of such divisions and specialization.

Put a little differently, the division of labour in a complex society makes it inevitable that specialists will emerge in the areas of communication and culture. In this respect, society's writers — including all who make their living as journalists — are on the receiving end of an act of delegation whereby, in a political sense especially, fundamental rights of freedom or expression are handled by journalists on behalf of the members of the public who are more distant from the centres of political and public action.

The exercise of these rights by journalists in a complex society is what brings the democratic process into being. Journalists and writers, not just those employed by the mass media, start the process of discussion and judgment by conveying and commenting on the news. They flood the air with stories and opinions covering an enormous range of political and social events. In a rough way, the notion that guides their work is that there is a public which is interested in what they say. That the law permits them a wide territory within which to practise their craft is consistent with the aims of democracy. The more freedom, the more discussion, the more democracy.

But to say the process begins with journalists and journalism is obviously different than saying it ends with them. Just as the conferral of these rights and liberties on citizens and journalists makes the quality and character of the process indeterminate, the exercise of them leads to outcomes that are themselves indeterminate. The public discussion begins where journalists sign off. Political, religious and moral discussion in society at large, along with the gossip of the trivial and the ephemeral, take some of what is contained in the media as points of reference. But for political and governmental discussion considered on its own and regardless of its venue, the relationship between the media and the public is both vital and profound.

To say that it could be arranged and done better and with better effects is obvious. To say that it is never done well is to fail to examine carefully what the best of our journalists are able to achieve under difficult circumstances. To say that journalists carry the full burden of responsibility for democracy is to miss the point. The key point is to recognize that in a developed society such as ours, we give a life to the notion of freedom of expression and, to some degree, to democracy by conferring rights on citizens and by encouraging journalists especially to enact them. This is how we Canadians do it.

Accordingly, the journalist's perspective on the Charter and the role of the media is that democracy is the issue. The ability of journalists to practise their craft turns on the manner in which the rights of freedom are secured in law or tradition. Put differently, citizens need these rights to be citizens of a democracy; creative people such as journalists need them in order to be genuinely and safely creative. These are not differences in kind so much as differences in degree. But they explain why journalists see themselves as being specially associated with the defence of these rights.

Paper delivered to the
School of Law, University of New Brunswick

February 1986 (revised)

CHAPTER TWO

Security, The Public Order and Democratic Institutions: Legal Limitations to Protect the State's Rights, Prerogatives and Responsibilities, Part I

2.1 A Note on Legitimacy and the Scope of State Power

The freedom of expression in the Constitution Act, 1982 is not, strictly speaking, the product of positive law. Although now sanctioned by the "supreme law of Canada", the fundamental freedoms have been understood historically as areas of human behaviour and action with which the State may not interfere. Put differently, there has been an historical understanding in liberal democracies that the State cannot enact statutes to create such freedoms; they are presumed to exist outside the domain of the legislated order. The State's responsibilities begin at the point where the exercise of such freedoms threatens an equally fundamental social interest. As will be seen in the cases, there is a practical notion in law of "balancing" the benefits of freedom against the benefits of protecting certain social or state interests with which the freedoms may be in conflict. As a consequence, the notion of "reasonable limits" expressed in section 1 of the Charter appears to legitimate an extensive range of restrictive laws. The limits may relate to the State's obligation to protect national security, prevent riots or the disruption of the legislative and legal processes; they may protect public morality by creating criminal penalties or administrative procedures to prevent the distribution of certain kinds of pornographic or violent material; they might protect minority groups from hate propagandists; or, finally, they might protect individuals from defamation.

The broad categories to which limitations are related — state rights, social values and groups, and individuals — are well established in the Canadian legal system, although the debate on the substance of the second set of restrictions remains vigorous.

But regardless of how some Canadians may regard obscenity or hate propaganda, few would challenge the notion that legislation can legitimately be used to protect certain interests — for example, bona fide state secrets. The Official Secrets Act is justified generally as an expression of the permission the Constitution grants through section 1 to Parliament to legislate a ''limit'' on freedom of expression. Whether the way in which the Act is written or applied is reasonable is another matter.

This chapter is concerned with the statutory limitations on freedom of expression which protect some of the State's rights, prerogatives and responsibilities. The items for analysis include national security, and public order and safety.

2.2 National Security

2.2.1 Emergencies Act, S.C., 1988, c.29, s.19(1), 38, 39, 40

The War Measures Act, which was invoked during both World Wars and again in October, 1970, during the so-called FLQ crisis, was repealed in 1988 and replaced by the Emergencies Act.

There are four levels of emergency distinguished in the new act: a Public Welfare Emergency caused by a natural disaster, disease, industrial accident or pollution; a Public Order Emergency caused by a ''serious'' threat to the security of Canada; an International Emergency caused by acts in which Canada is entangled ''of intimidation or coercion or the real or imminent use of serious force or violence''; and a War Emergency which ''means war or other armed conflict, real or imminent, involving Canada or any of its allies that is so serious as to be a national emergency''. The following provisions may be noted.

PART II PUBLIC ORDER EMERGENCY

19. (1) While a declaration of a public order emergency is in effect, the Governor in Council may make such orders or regulations with respect to the following matters as the Governor in Council believes, on reasonable grounds, are necessary for dealing with the emergency:

(a) the regulation or prohibition of

(i) any public assembly that may be expected to lead to a breach of the peace ...

PART IV WAR EMERGENCY

38. (1) When the Governor in Council believes on reasonable grounds, that a war emergency exists and necessitates the taking of special temporary measures for dealing with the emergency, the Governor in Council, after such consultation required by section 44, may, by proclamation, so declare.

(2) A declaration of a war emergency shall specify the state of affairs constituting the emergency to the extent that, in the opinion of the Governor in Council, it is possible to do so without jeopardizing any special temporary measures proposed to be taken for dealing with the emergency.

39. (1) A declaration of a war emergency is effective on the day on which it is issued, but a motion for confirmation of the declaration shall be laid before each House of Parliament and be considered in accordance with section 58.

40. (1) While a declaration of a war emergency is in effect, the Governor in Council may make such orders or regulations as the Governor in Council believes, on reasonable grounds, are necessary or advisable for dealing with the emergency.

(2) The Governor in Council may make regulations providing for the imposition

(a) on summary conviction, of a fine not exceeding five hundred dollars or imprisonment not exceeding six months or both that fine and imprisonment, or

(b) on indictment, of a fine not exceeding five thousand dollars or imprisonment not exceeding five years or both that fine and imprisonment

for contravention of any order or regulation made under subsection (1).

2.2.2 Section 33(1) of the Constitution Act, 1982

The regulations contemplated under s.40(1) of the Emergencies Act, could drastically limit freedom of expression. Could such regulations nonetheless survive Charter scrutiny? There are two possibilities. First, Parliament could rely on s.33 of the Charter to protect the Act and anything done under it from review. Section 33 says:

> 33(1) Parliament or the legislature of a province may expressly declare in an Act of Parliament or of the legislature, as the case may be, that the Act or a provision thereof shall operate notwithstanding a provision included in Section 2 or Sections 7 to 15 of this Charter.

Alternatively, a court could uphold censorship provisions under s.1 of the Charter of Rights and Freedoms.

2.2.3 A Note on the Application of the War Measures Act

In 1914, Parliament passed the first War Measures Act, which vested in the Governor-in-Council — the Cabinet in other words — substantial powers to enact binding regulations related to the security, defence, peace, order and welfare of Canada. War had been declared by King George V on behalf of the British Empire on Germany on 4 August 1914, and on Austro-Hungary on 12 August 1914.

Section 6 of the bill granted the Governor-in-Council the power to authorize,

> such acts and things, and to make from time to time such orders and regulations, as he may by reason of the existence of real or apprehended war, invasion, or insurrection deem necessary or advisable for the security, defense, peace, order, and welfare of Canada; and for greater certainty, but not so as to restrict the generality of the foregoing terms, it is hereby declared that the powers of the Governor in Council shall extend to all matters hereinafter enumerated...[1]

Six enumerated items included, first,

> (a) censorship and the control and suppression of publications, writings, maps, plans, photographs, communications and means of communication;[2]

The War Measures Act was given royal assent on August 22. The provisions of s.6, as well as other sections were, by s.3, to be in force only during a state of war, invasion, or insurrection, real or apprehended. Section 4 stated that a proclamation by His Majesty, or under the authority of the Governor-in-Council, would be conclusive evidence that war, invasion, or insurrection, real or apprehended, existed and had existed for any period of time stated. It was declared, accordingly, that war had existed since August 4, and that it would be deemed to exist until the Governor-in-Council by a proclamation published in *The Canada Gazette* declared that war no longer existed.

During the whole of the First World War, and for most of the year after it ended, the individual and communicative freedoms of many Canadians were limited by executive orders made pursuant to the War Measures Act. A large number of ethnic publications, some English-language publications, and, at the end of the war, many publications on the left of the political spectrum were banned.

On 12 September 1914 an Order-in-Council was issued, under the provisions of s.6 of the War Measures Act, prohibiting the publication or communication of military information, if the information was calculated to be, or might be directly or indirectly useful to the enemy. A criminal conviction was possible under the order whether or not the information was intended to be useful to the enemy. A test of *mens rea* was not required.

On September 24 an Order-in-Council was issued to provide for the censorship of telephone and telegraphic communication. The Secretary of State became responsible for enforcing this order on 1 November 1915.

The powers of censorship granted to the Postmaster General under the Act were enlarged by another Order-in-Council on 6 November 1914. This order granted the Postmaster General the authority to deny the privileges of the mails and to prevent the circulation or possession of any publication or material he believed,

> ...contains, has contained or is in the habit of containing articles...bearing directly or indirectly on the present state of war, or on the causes thereof, contrary to the actual facts, and tending directly or indirectly to influence the people of Canada against the cause of the United Kingdom...or in favour of the enemy...[3]

Seventy publications were prohibited by the terms of this order. They were predominantly German-language publications, although they included Russian, Hungarian, Ukrainian, Croatian, Finnish, Rutherian (a Ukrainian dialect), Yiddish, Syrian, and Hindu publications. Some English-language publications were also banned. The publications prohibited by warrant of the Postmaster General included:

1. Lincoln Freie Press, German-language weekly, Lincoln, Nebraska (withheld 26 June, 1915).
2. The Gaelic American, weekly newspaper, New York, N.Y. (withheld 11 September, 1915).
3. Abendpost, German-language daily, Chicago, Ill. (withheld 25 September, 1915).
4. The King, The Kaiser and Irish Freedom, a book by James McGuire (8 November, 1915).
5. Szabadsag (Liberty), Hungarian daily, Cleveland, Ohio (13 November, 1915).
6. American Independant, weekly, San Francisco (31 January, 1916).
7. Buffalo Volksfreund, German weekly, Buffalo, N.Y. (26 September, 1916).
8. Boston American, weekly, Boston, Mass. (11 November 1916).
9. Narodna Wola, Rutherian tri-weekly, Scanton, Pa. (18 December, 1916).
10. Der Wanderer, German weekly, St. Paul, Minn. (18 December, 1916).

Many of these publications belonged to the American Association of Foreign Language Newspapers, and it was widely believed that the Association was funded by the German and Austrian governments. English-language publications banned under this order included newspapers published by the Hearst syndicate. Some of the papers in the Hearst chain were critical of the British war effort and opposed to American involvement in the war.

In January, 1917, the several orders regarding censorship were collectively repealed and replaced by Consolidated Orders Respecting Censorship, 1917.[4] Besides reaffirming existing powers of censorship, the order further defined objectionable matter. The Chief Press Censor could withold from public consumption material which contained military or strategic information; material that commented unfavourably on the causes or operations of the war, or was intended or likely to cause disaffection to the Crown or to interfere with the success of the armed forces; material purporting to describe or actually describing any secret session of Parliament, or of any meeting of the Cabinet; and any matter dealing with a confidential government document. The writing, printing, publication, posting, circulation or possession of any material considered to belong to a prohibited category became a criminal offense punishable by imprisonment for up to five years and/or a fine of up to $5,000. Any copies of such publications, as well as printing presses, plant and machinery used in their printing, publication, or circulation would be seized.

Between February, 1917 and June, 1918, 81 publications were prohibited. The banning orders were largely directed towards non-English-speaking Canadians, although English-language publications were also seized. Some works prohibited under the consolidated orders included:

1. America's Relations to The Great War, a book by John Williams Burgess, formerly Dean of the Faculties of Political Science, Philosophy, and Pure Science, and professor of constitutional and international law, Columbia University, New York (withheld 7 February 1917).
2. The European War of 1914, Its Causes, Purposes and Probable Results, by John Williams Burgess (withheld 7 July 1917).
3. The Vampire of the Continent, a book by Count Ernest Zu Reventlow, translated from the German, published by The Jackson Press, New York, 1916 (7 February 1917).
4. The New World, a weekly published by The Fatherland Corporation, New York (20 February 1917).
5. The Jewish Morning Journal (The Morgan Journal), a daily newspaper published by the Jewish Press Pub. Co., New York (20 February 1917. Prohibition withdrawn 26 July 1917).
6. Oregon Deutches Zeitung, daily German-language newspaper, Portland, Oregon (20 February 1917).
7. The Minneapolis Freie Presse-Herold, weekly German-language newspaper, Minneapolis, Minn. (20 February 1917).
8. Velykoye Europayskaye Viny (The Great European War), Ukrainian magazine, New York (28 March, 1917).
9. Philadelphia Demokrat, German-language daily newspaper, Philadelphia, Penn. (28 March 1917).
10. Blaetter Und Bluten, a book in German, St. Louis, Mo. (18 April 1917).

One other supposed threat to the war effort was the Temperance Movement. The Censor's office, like all other branches of government, encouraged recruitment. Anything that could conceivably interfere with such efforts was subject to censorship and, as a consequence, a number of publications issued by the Temperance Movement were prohibited in the belief that they discouraged enlistment. The Temperance publications condemned the use of alcohol by Canadian troops and claimed that the liquor business was Britain's most dangerous enemy. Whether the purpose of these publications was to attack the Canadian forces or the drink trade was debated in the House of Commons and as a consequence Temperance literature was suppressed after September 1917.

However, the government's fear of information damaging to its recruiting efforts persisted. On 28 March 1918, a protest erupted in Quebec in opposition to the Military Service Act. As a consequence, an Order-in-Council was issued on April 16 saying it was illegal to publish, publicly express, or circulate information likely to have an objectionable effect. The effect of a publication rather than its subject matter determined whether an offense had been committed. Publishers could commit an offense without defying a specific prohibition order. A charge against a publication could be made at a local level by a Provincial Attorney General or Municipal Crown Attorney. These new regulations were never used to ban the Quebec nationalist press, although they were inspired by nationalist sentiment, and there was only one reported criminal case concerning a charge of breach of the order.[5]

Sedition charges were laid during the First World War under the Criminal Code. In *R.* v. *Trainor*[6] a man was convicted of sedition because while sitting in a drug store he said he approved of the sinking of the Lusitania. An appeal was allowed. The Alberta judge remarked that "(t)here had been more prosecutions for seditious words in Alberta in the past two years than in all the history of England for over one hundred years, and England has had numerous and critical wars in that time".

At the close of the war, Canada was confronted with a serious movement of anti-capitalist opinion. The Russian Revolution had made communism a world force, frightening the supporters of the existing system. The Consolidated Orders Respecting Censorship, 1918[7] was substantially the same as the 1917 consolidation except that it increased the emphasis on the prevention of undesirable information and opinion. An Order Respecting Enemy Publications[8] was also issued, followed by the Unlawful Associations order, 1918[9]. Under the terms of the Enemy Publications order, it became an offense to publish, import, or possess any publication printed in an enemy language unless the material was of a literary, scientific, religious or artistic character and did not contain objectionable matter. An enemy language was that of any country at war with Great Britain or in whole or in part occupied by a state at war with Great Britain. Enemy languages included German, Hungarian, Bulgarian, Turkish, Romanian, Russian, Ukrainian, Finnish, Srian, Croatian, Rutherian and Livonian (Latvian). Organizations outlawed by the Unlawful Associations order included:

The Industrial Workers of the World
The Russian Social Democratic Party
The Russian Revolutionary Group
The Russian Social Revolutions
The Russian Workers Union
The Ukrainian Revolutionary Group
The Ukrainian Social Democratic Party
The Social Democratic Party
The Social Labour Party
Group of Social Democrats of Bolsheviki
Group of Social Democrats of Anarchists
The Workers International Union
Chinese Nationalist League

Chinese Labour Association
The Finnish Social Democratic Party
The Revolutionary Socialist Party of North America

The government also directed its efforts against a perceived Bolshevik menace rather than the threat of enemy propaganda. Under the Consolidated Orders Respecting Censorship, 1918, examples of banned publications were:

1. The Morning messenger, English-language journal, Winnipeg, Manitoba (withheld 15 June 1918).
2. The Labour Defender, an English-language by-weekly pub. by the I.W.W. Defense Committee, New York (10 July 1918).
   All publications by the Industrial Workers of the World were prohibited by 2 October 1918.
3. To The Young Workers, a pamphlet in Russian by A. Karelyn, pub. by The Union of Russian Workmen, New York (21 September 1918).
4. Rabotchyj Narod (The Working People), newspaper, Winnipeg, Manitoba (21 September 1918).
5. The Canadian Forward, a monthly in English, edited by Isaac Bainbridge, Toronto, Ontario (2 October 1918).
6. The Western Clarion, a monthly in English, pub. by the Socialist Party of Canada, Vancouver, B.C. (5 October 1918).

The Unlawful Associations order was repealed in April of 1919 and replaced by s.99 of the Criminal Code.[10] The government's power to create such orders and regulations under the War Measures Act ceased with the issuance of the Treaty of Peace (Germany) Order, 1920.

*****

The 1914 War Measures Act was consolidated with little change in the Revised Statutes of 1927. By 1938, when hopes for peace had faded, an Interdepartmental Committee on Emergency Legislation was created to examine the legal capacity of the Ministry to take additional measures to protect the state in the event of war.[11] Some months later the committee announced:

> Pursuant to our terms of reference we have surveyed the position as regards the legislation which would be required in the event of grave emergency and we have reached the conclusion that little in the way of special legislation in Parliament will be required. Under the provisions of the War Measures Act, Chapter 206, Revised Statutes of Canada, 1927, the Governor in Council may do and authorize such acts and things, and make from time to time such orders and regulations as he may by reason of real or apprehended war, invasion or insurrection deem necessary or advisable for the security, defence, peace, order and welfare of Canada; ... It is clear, therefore, that this statute confers upon the Executive ample authority to take pretty well whatever action might be found to be necessary to meet the exigencies of war or other emergency.[12]

On 1 September 1939, the War Measures Act was renewed by proclamation and made retroactive to August 25. The legality of the Act had already been affirmed by the courts.[13] The Defence of Canada regulations were drawn up by an interdepartmental committee during the spring of 1939, and were approved by Cabinet. On September 3, under the War Measures Act, they were instituted.[14]

Despite the fact that Parliament met from September 7 through September 13 the regulations were not discussed. Parliament did not meet again for ordinary business until 16 May 1940. During the following winter and election campaign, the opposition parties attacked Mr. King and his colleagues as autocratic and dictatorial. A select committee on the Defence of Canada regulations was created on 13 June 1940. The regulations established new prohibitions enforceable by the courts and conferred extraordinary powers on the executive who were made immune from judicial review. New limits were imposed on freedom of speech and the press by regulation 39. The original rule stated:

> 39. No person shall by word of mouth: —
> a) spread reports or make statements, false or otherwise, intended or likely to cause disaffection to His Majesty or to interfere with the success of His Majesty's forces or of the forces of any allied or associated Powers or to prejudice His Majesty's relations with foreign powers, or
> b) spread reports or make statements, false or otherwise, intended or likely to prejudice the recruiting, training, discipline, or administration of any of His Majesty's forces.

Some weeks later, regulation 39A was included. It provided:

> 39A. No person shall print, make, publish, issue, circulate or distribute any book, card, letter, writing, print, publication or document of any kind containing any material, report or statement,
> a) intended or likely to cause disaffection to His Majesty or to interfere with the success of His Majesty's forces or of the forces of any allied or associated powers, or to prejudice His Majesty's relations with foreign powers;
> b) intended or likely to prejudice the recruiting, training, discipline or administration of any of His Majesty's troops; or
> c) intended or likely to be prejudicial to the safety of the State or the efficient prosecution of the war.[15]

It was later added that it would be a defence against such a prosecution to prove that the accused had intended not to aid or comfort the enemy, but merely to participate in the ordinary political processes.[16] Regulation 39B(2) provided that it was a defence to prove that the accused intended in good faith merely to criticize or point out errors or defects in the government, legislature, or administration of justice. However, the view of the court in one of the few reported cases under this regulation appeared to withdraw the protection afforded by the section.[17] The defendant was a high school teacher who, during a current events dicussion in his classroom, expressed pacifist opinions. The court examined his teaching technique and found that students were encouraged to accept no point of view at face value. There was no evidence to show that any student was influenced by the defendant's contributions to the discussion and that his statements were either intended or likely to interfere with the prosecution of the war. However, the court claimed that the intention of the regulations was to compel individuals to maintain silence or speak in the unconquerable spirit by which troops in action must be moved if they are to win.

The first restrictions on association were made by the execution of regulation 39C on 8 June 1940. Any association, society, group or organization which the Governor-in-Council declared to be illegal became so upon notice published in *The Canada Gazette*. Any person associated with such an organization became guilty of an offense. Guilty persons could be those who attended a meeting of an illegal organization, spoke publicly in advocacy of the organization, or distributed literature of an illegal organization. Outlawed groups were not just German or fascist. By 8 June 1940 the following societies had been declared illegal:

The Auslands Organization of the National Sozialistische Deutsche Arbeitpartei
The Deutsche Arbeitsfront
The Canadian Society for German Culture
The National Unity Party
The Canadian Union of Fascists
The Communist Party of Canada
The Young Communist League of Canada
The Canadian Labour Defence League
The League for Peace and Democracy
The Ukrainian Labour Farmer Temple Association
The Finnish Organization of Canada
The Russian Workers and Farmers Club
The Polish People's Association
The Canadian Ukrainian Youth Federation

The Ukrainian Labour Farmer Temple Association was declared illegal on the theory that it was being used for anti-war propaganda by the Communist Party. So far as the published expressions of the Association's periodicals go there appeared to be no basis for this belief. One hundred and eight pieces of property, mostly halls and meeting places in more Canadian cities, towns and villages, were seized by the R.C.M.P. under the authority of the Custodian of Alien Enemy Property Act and sold, many at fire sale prices and often to a rival Ukrainian society. On 12 June 1940, more groups were banned:

Italian Fascio Abroad
O.V.R.A., Opere Voluntere Repressione Anti-Fascisto (national Organization for the Repress of Anti-Fascism)
Dopolavoro (After Work Organization)
Associazione Combattenti Italiani (Italian War Veterans' Association)

The Jehovah's Witnesses were banned on 4 July 1940. In one case arising out of the ban, a Jehovah's Witness was convicted for making statements prejudicial to the safety of the State. He had complained about the expulsion of his children from school for refusing to salute the flag or sing the national anthem. His letter to the school administration explained why his religion quashed the conviction and held that what the accused wrote was neither intended or likely to affect the prosecution of the war, nor was it addressed to the general public.

The following groups were banned on 29 August 1940:

The Workers and Farmers Publishing Association
The Road Publishing Company
The Croatian Publishing Company
The Polish People's Press
The Serbian Publishing Association
The Finnish Society of Toronto

In further recognition of the ban on Jehovah's Witnesses, on 19 January 1941, the Watch Tower Bible and Tract Society and the International Bible Students' Association were also declared illegal.

Regulations 39 and 39A had a chilling effect on the ordinary complaints and grumblings of many Canadians. Between three to four hundred prosecutions had been initiated by the winter of 1941. The courts, who were often zealous in returning convictions, commonly sentenced offenders to six months imprisonment for prohibited oral utterances. The Minister of Justice explained in the House that,

> Some joyous friend may imbibe a little too much liquor in a tavern and think it smart, for instance, to say that the Germans are better soldiers than the British, or something like that. Such a man should not be treated as a real enemy who is plotting against the state. There the summary conviction (carrying a lighter maximum sentence) applies. But when a case is serious the prosecution should be by way of indictment, and I believe that the choice should be left to the Minister of Justice or the attorney general.[18]

Regulation 15 of the Defence of Canada regulations empowered the Secretary of State to make orders

> for preventing or restricting the publication in Canada of matters as to which he is satisfied that the publication, or, as the case may be, the unrestricted publication, thereof would or might be prejudicial to the safety of the State or the efficient prosecution of the war.

The suppression of material demmed to be hazardous to state security was widespread. By 27 March 1941, 325 periodicals had been suppressed or banned. The quantity of outlawed publications and some reported cases suggest that prosecution under these regulations was not limited to those reasonably understood to be a threat to the war effort. Most of the newspapers banned were foreign-language papers:

1. Gudok (The Canadian Whistle), Russian published in Winnipeg, Manitoba (withheld 28 March 1940).
2. Hlas L'Udu, Slovak, published by Hlas L'Udu Publishing Association, Toronto (withheld 6 July 1940).
3. Jiskra, Czech, published in Toronto (withheld 31 July 1940).
4. Glos Pracy, Polish, published by the Polish People's Press, Toronto (withheld 17 August 1940).
5. Der Zeg, Yiddish (withheld 17 August 1940).

Left-wing publications were outlawed. *The Clarion,* a Communist Party newspaper with a circulation of approximately 12,000 was banned along with nine other publications. The *Canadian Tribune* of Toronto, a successor to the banned *Clarion* was suspended for three weeks. The Communist Party of Canada was outlawed under regulation 39C. Regulation 21, which dealt with the internment of citizens of Canada to forestall acts of assistance to the enemy, was used to prosecute John A. (Pat) Sullivan, at the time considered to be the leading member of the Party.[19]

The House of Commons eventually decided to review the Defence of Canada regulations by selecting a committee composed of representatives from each party in proportion to their membership in the House. They were to inspect the provisions and operations of the regulations. Three years of meetings were held *in camera*. Criticism came chiefly from members of the C.C.F., who claimed that the regulations were too vague and contained inadequate safeguards against error. T.C. Douglas argued that newspapers could be suppressed without a hearing under regulation 15. He stated that organizations such as Jehovah's Witnesses and Technocracy Incorporated (banned 30 June 1941), whose subversive tendencies were not self-evident, had been outlawed under regulation 39C without any adequate explanation.[20] C.C.F. leader M.J. Coldwell said that the committee had two approaches to the regulations. "Some took the view that the regulations and final decisions should be administrative matters. Whilst the majority in both years took that view, a minority was of the opinion that the procedure should more nearly approximate a judicial procedure, and that at least the final decisions ought not be left to the minister and his advisers. Because what I may call the administrative view prevailed, to that extent I was not able to approve the report.[21]

The committee suggested the addition of the words "have knowingly in his possession in quantity" to regulation 39A. This was adopted by the Privy Council on 12 September 1940.[22]

In *R*. v. *Money* the possession of three or four copies of an illegal publication was ruled not sufficient for a conviction.[23] Furthermore, a bookstore or library which possessed works believed likely to be prejudicial to the safety of the state was not to be convicted if the number of copies was limited.[24]

The report of the committee concerning outlawed organizations was not welcomed by the government. Its main suggestion was that certain organizations cease to be illegal. These groups were the Communist Party of Canada, the Ukrainian Farmer Temple Association, the Finnish Organization of Canada, Technocracy Incorporated and the various Jehovah's Witnesses organizations. The recommendation that Jehovah's Witnesses and Technocracy Incorporated be dropped from the regulation 39C list was expressed unanimously by the committee. The Jehovah's Witnesses were viewed simply as an over-zealous religious organization and not a danger to the war effort. No member of the House moved the acceptance of the report when it was tabled and the government did not heed its advice. The Minister of Justice moved that the committee be appointed again in 1943. A member complained that "there is little use in setting up a committee of responsible members of this House to deal with questions of this kind if the government or Parliament is not going to give [more] consideration to its report than was given to the report made by the committee of last year".[25] The Minister was asked what harm would be done by removing the Communist Party from the 39C list. He replied that to propagate doctrines espoused by members of the Communist Party constituted sedition under the Criminal Code and the organization must remain outlawed.

In 1943, in spite of vigorous protests by the C.C.F., the new committee busied itself with matters concerned with naturalization and deportation and did not discuss the Defence of Canada regulations. On 14 October 1943, the Ukrainian Labour Farmer Temple Association, the Finnish Organization of Canada, Technocracy Incorporated and the Jehovah's Witnesses groups were once again legal. The emergency powers available during wartime were exercised for a certain time after the war for the sake of an orderly transition from war to peace. Regulations 15, 39, 39A, 39B and 39C were revoked on 16 August 1945.

The remarks of Mr. Coldwell in the House of Commons, 20 May 1940, may be cited as indicative of criticism against the extreme censorship powers contained in the Defence of Canada regulations: "We are prepared to support the struggle against aggression and for the preservation of democratic institutions, but we insist that democratic institutions be respected and safeguarded in our own country... Ever since the outbreak of war we have been governed by decree, largely in secrecy".[26]

Endnotes

1. An Act to confer certain powers upon the Governor-in-Council and to amend the Immigration Act (assented to 22 August 1914), s.6.
2. *Ibid.*, s.6(a).
3. P.C. 94, November 6, 1914, s.1.
4. P.C. 146, January 17, 1917.
5. *R.* v. *Watson* (1918) 15 O.W.N., 417 S.C.O., High Ct. Div.
6. [1917] 1 W.W.R., 415 (Alta. C.A.)
7. P.C. 1241, May 22, 1918.
8. P.C. 2381, September 25, 1918.
9. P.C. 2384, September 28, 1918.
10. *Statutes of Canada,* 1919.
11. Established by P.C. 531, March 14, 1938.
12. Report of the Interdepartmental Committee on Emergency Legislation, July, 1939.
13. *Fort Frances Pulp and Power Co.* v. *Manitoba Free Press Co.*, [1923] A.C. 695.
14. P.C. 2483, September 3, 1939.
15. P.C. 2891, September 27, 1939.
16. P.C. 146, January 14, 1940.
17. *R.* v. *Coffin,* [1940] 2 W.W.R. 592 (Alta. Pol. Ct.)
18. House of Commons Debates, Hansard, 1940 at p. 745.
19. *Ex parte Sullivan,* [1941] 1 D.L.R. 676.
20. Mr. T.C. Douglas 19:2, pp. 1188, 1189, March 3, 1941.
21. Mr. M.J. Coldwell 19:2, p. 3658, June 9, 1941.
22. P.C. 4750, September 12, 1940.
23. [1941] 1 W.W.R. 93 (B.C. Pol. Ct.).
24. *R.* v. *Ravenor,* [1941] 1 W.W.R. 191.
25. Mr. Angus MacInnis 9:4, p. 606, February 22, 1943.
26. Mr. M.J. Coldwell 9:1, p. 51, May 20, 1940.

2.2.4 Official Secrets Act, R.S.C. 1985, c.O-5

Spying

3. (1) Every person is guilty of an offence under this Act who, for any purpose prejudicial to the safety or interests of the State,

(*a*) approaches, inspects, passes over, or is in the neighbourhood of, or enters any prohibited place;

(*b*) makes any sketch, plan, model or note that is calculated to be or might be or is intended to be directly or indirectly useful to a foreign power; or

(*c*) obtains, collects, records, or publishes, or communicates to any other person any secret official code word, or pass word, or any sketch, plan, model, article, or note, or other document of information that is calculated to be or might be or is intended to be directly or indirectly useful to a foreign power.

If purpose prejudicial to safety of State

(2) On a prosecution under this section, it is not necessary to show that the accused person was guilty of any particular act tending to show a purpose prejudicial to the safety or interests of the State, and, notwithstanding that no such act is proved against him, he may be convicted if, from the circumstances of the case, or his conduct, or his known character as proved, it appears that his purpose was a purpose prejudicial to the safety or interests of the State; and if any sketch, plan, model, article, note, document or information relating to or used in any prohibited place, or anything in such a place, or any secret official code word or pass word is made, obtained, collected, recorded, published or communicated by any person other than a person acting under lawful authority, it shall be deemed to have been made, obtained, collected, recorded, published or communicated for a purpose prejudicial to the safety or interests of the State unless the contrary is proved.

Communication with agent of foreign power, etc.

(3) In any proceedings against a person for an offence under this section, the fact that he has been in communication with, or attempted to communicate with, an agent of a foreign power, whether within or outside Canada, is evidence that he has, for a purpose prejudicial to the safety or interests of the State, obtained or attempted to obtain information that is calculated to be or might be or is intended to be directly or indirectly useful to a foreign power.

When deemed to have been in communication

(4) For the purpose of this section, but without prejudice to the generality of the foregoing provision

(*a*) a person shall, unless he proves the contrary, be deemed to have been in communication with an agent of a foreign power if

(i) he has, either within or outside Canada, visited the address of an agent of a foreign power or consorted or associated with such agent, or

(ii) either within or outside Canada, the name or address of, or any other information regarding such an agent has been found in his possession, or has been supplied by him to any other person, or has been obtained by him from any other person;

(*b*) "an agent of a foreign power" includes any person who is or has been or is reasonably suspected of being or having been employed by a foreign power either directly or indirectly for the purpose of committing an act, either within or outside Canada, prejudicial to the safety or interests of the State, or who has or is reasonably suspected of having, either within or outside Canada, committed, or attempted to commit, such an act in the interests of a foreign power; and

(*c*) any address, whether within or outside Canada, reasonably suspected of being an address used for the receipt of communications intended for an agent of a foreign power, or any address at which such an agent resides, or to which he resorts for the purpose of giving or receiving communications, or at which he carries on any business, shall be deemed to be the address of an agent of a foreign power, and communications addressed to such an address to be communications with such an agent. R.S., c.198, s.3.

Wrongful communication, etc., of information

4. (1) Every person is guilty of an offence under this Act who, having in his possession or control any secret official code word, or pass word, or any sketch, plan, model, article, note, document or information that relates to or is used in a prohibited place or anything in such a place, or that has been made or obtained in contravention of this Act, or that has been entrusted in confidence to him by any person holding office under Her Majesty, or that he has obtained or to which he has had access while subject to the Code of Service Discipline within the meaning of the *National Defence Act* or owing to his position as a person who holds or has held office under Her Majesty, or as a person who holds or has held a contract made on behalf of Her Majesty, or a contract the performance of which in whole or in part is carried out in a prohibited place, or as a person who is or has been employed under a person who holds or has held such an office or contract,

(*a*) communicates the code word, pass word, sketch, plan, model, article, note, document or information to any person, other than a person to whom he is authorized to communicate with, or a person to whom it is in the interest of the State his duty to communicate it;

(*b*) uses the information in his possession for the benefit of any foreign power or in any other manner prejudicial to the safety or interests of the State;

(*c*) retains the sketch, plan, model, article, note, or document in his possession or control when he has no right to retain it or when it is contrary to his duty to retain it or fails to comply with all directions issued by lawful authority with regard to the return or disposal thereof; or

(*d*) fails to take reasonable care of, or so conducts himself as to endanger the safety of the sketch, plan, model, article, note, document, secret official code word or pass word or information.

Communication of sketch, plan, model, etc.

(2) Every person is guilty of an offence under this Act who, having in his possession or control any sketch, plan, model, article, note, document or information that relates to munitions of war, communicates it directly or indirectly to any foreign power, or in any other manner prejudicial to the safety or interests of the State.

Receiving code word, sketch, etc.

(3) Every person who receives any secret official code word, or pass word, or sketch, plan, model, article, note, document or information, knowing, or having reasonable ground to believe, at the time when he receives it, that the code word, pass word, sketch, plan, model, article, note, document or information is communicated to him in contravention of this Act, is guilty of an offence under this Act, unless he proves that the communication to him of the code word, pass word, sketch, plan, model, article, note, document or information was contrary to his desire.

Retaining or allowing possession of document, etc.

(4) Every person is guilty of an offence under this Act who

(*a*) retains for any purpose prejudicial to the safety or interests of the State any official document, whether or not completed or issued for use, when he has no right to retain it, or when it is contrary to his duty to retain it, or fails to comply with any directions issued by any Government department or any person authorized by such department with regard to the return or disposal thereof; or

(*b*) allows any other person to have possession of any official document issued for his use alone, or communicates any secret official code word or pass word so issued, or, without lawful authority or excuse, has in his possession any official document or secret official code word or pass word issued for the use of some person other than himself, or on obtaining possession of any official document by finding or otherwise, neglects or fails to restore it to the person or authority by whom or for whose use it was issued, or to a police constable. R.S., c.196, s.4.

Telegrams

7. (1) Where it appears to the Minister of Justice that such a course is expedient in the public interest, he may, by warrant under his hand, require any person who owns or controls any telegraphic cable or wire, or any apparatus for wireless telegraphy, used for the sending or receipt of telegrams to or from any place out of Canada, to produce to him, or to any person named in the warrant, the originals and transcripts, either of all telegrams, or of telegrams of any specified class or description, or of telegrams sent from or addressed to any specified person or place, sent to or received from any place out of Canada by means of any such cable, wire, or apparatus and all other papers relating to any such telegram as aforesaid.

Refusing or neglecting to produce

(2) Every person who, on being required to produce any such original or transcript or paper as aforesaid, refuses or neglects to do so is guilty of an offence under this Act, and is for each offence, liable on summary conviction to imprisonment, with or without hard labour, for a term not exceeding three months, or to a fine not exceeding two hundred dollars, or to both imprisonment and fine.

Harbouring spies

8. Every person who knowingly harbours any person whom he knows, or has reasonable grounds for supposing, to be a person who is about to commit or who has committed an offence under this Act, or knowingly permits to meet or assemble in any premises in his occupation or under his control any such persons, and every person who, having harboured any such person, or permitted any such persons to meet or assemble in any premises in his occupation or under his control, wilfully omits or refuses to disclose to a senior police officer any information that it is in his power to give in relation to any such person, is guilty of an offence under this Act. R.S., c.198, s.8.

Attempts, incitements, etc.

9. Every person who attempts to commit any offence under this Act, or solicits or incites or endeavours to persuade another person to commit an offence, or aids or abets and does any act preparatory to the commission of an offence under this Act, is guilty of an offence under this Act and is liable to the same punishment, and to be proceeded against in the same manner, as if he had committed the offence. R.S., c.198, s.9.

Power to arrest without warrant

10. Every person who is found committing an offence under this Act, or who is reasonably suspected of having committed, or having attempted to commit, or being about to commit, such an offence, may be arrested without, a warrant and detained by any constable or police officer. R.S., c.198, s.10.

Search warrants

11. (1) If a justice of the peace is satisfied by information on oath that there is reasonable ground for suspecting that an offence under this Act has been or is about to be committed, he may grant a search warrant authorizing any constable named therein, to enter at any time any premises or place named in the warrant, if necessary by force, and to search the premises or place and every person found therein, and to seize any sketch, plan, model, article, note or document, or anything that is evidence of an offence under this Act having been or being about to be committed, that he may find on the premises or place or on any such person, and with regard to or in connection with which he has reasonable ground for suspecting that an offence under this Act has been or is about to be committed.

In case of great emergency

(2) Where it appears to an officer of the Royal Canadian Mounted Police not below the rank of superintendent that the case is one of great emergency and that in the interest of the State immediate action is necessary, he may by a written order under his hand give to any constable the like authority as may be given by the warrant of a justice under this section. R.S., c.198, s.11.

Where offence deemed to have been committed

14. (1) For the purposes of the trial of a person for an offence under this Act, the offence shall be deemed to have been committed either at the place in which the offence actually was committed, or at any place in Canada in which the offender may be found

Public may be excluded from trial

(2) In addition and without prejudice to any powers that a court may possess to order the exclusion of the public from any proceedings

if, in the course of proceedings before a court against any person for an offence under this Act or the proceedings on appeal, application is made by the prosecution, on the ground that the publication of any evidence to be given or of any statement to be made in the course of the proceedings would be prejudicial to the interest of the State, that all or any portion of the public shall be excluded during any part of the hearing, the court may make an order to that effect, but the passing of sentence shall in any case take place in public.

Penalties

15. (1) Where no specific penalty is provided in this Act, any person who is guilty of an offence under this Act shall be deemed to be guilty of an indictable offence and is, on conviction, punishable by imprisonment for a term not exceeding fourteen years; but such person may, at the election of the Attorney General, be prosecuted summarily in the manner provided by the provisions of the *Criminal Code* relating to summary convictions, and, if so prosecuted, is punishable by a fine not exceeding five hundred dollars, or by imprisonment not exceeding twelve months, or by both.

2.2.5 Notes on the Official Secrets Act

2.2.5.1 Excerpts from Walter Tarnopolsky, "Freedom of the Press", in *Newspapers and the Law,* Ottawa, Minister of Supply and Services Canada, 1981, xi, 19-21

Official Secrets Act

Before discussing the Canadian Official Secrets Act, a consideration of the United Kingdom experience is enlightening. The first Official Secrets Act in the United Kingdom was enacted in 1889, apparently in reaction to a publication by a newspaper of the particulars of a secret treaty negotiated between England and Russia which was given to it by the government clerk whose job it was to copy the document. The government tried to prosecute the clerk for removing a state document, but was not successful because no document was stolen. An attempt was made to fill the gap by passing the Act, which made it a crime, *inter alia,* for a person wrongfully to communicate information which had been obtained while working as a civil servant. The Act used the standard criminal law approach of placing the burden of proof on the prosecution and defining the offences with considerable particularity.

Subsequently, in 1909, a German secret service officer came to London and openly admitted recruiting people for an espionage system for all of England. The government was advised that there was no offence for which he could be arrested. The result was the passing of a new Official Secrets Act in 1911, by which the onus of proof was shifted strongly against the accused. The Act made it a felony for any purpose prejudicial to the safety or interest of the state for anyone to approach any military or naval installation or other prohibited place, or to obtain or communicate information, or make a sketch or note, which might help an enemy. The Act also made it a misdemeanor for a person, having any information mentioned, or information entrusted in confidence by an officer of the Crown, or which was obtained as a Crown servant, to communicate that information to an unauthorized person, or to retain a sketch or other document, without any right to do so. Also, anyone receiving such document or information could be found guilty unless he proved that the communication to him was contrary to his desire. In the light of wartime experience, a new Act was enacted in 1920. Among other amendments, the new Act made it a felony to do any act preparatory to the commission of a felony under the Act.

It is particularly worthy of note that Official Secrets Acts are deliberately intended to cover more than just protection of national or state security; they are framed so widely as to cover all kinds of official information unrelated to security.

Soon after the enactment of the Official Secrets Act of 1911, the government of the United Kingdom sought means of clarifying the position of the press with respect to publication of sensitive information. The solution was to set up, in 1912, a committee (now known as the Services, Press and Broadcasting Committee) consisting of a majority of press and broadcasting members, along with the permanent secretaries (deputy ministers) of the various defence ministries. The object of the Committee is to let the press know unofficially when an offence could be committed under the Official Secrets Acts without risk of prosecution. What is involved are what are known as the "D" Notices.

The "D" Notice, which relates to defence matters "the publication of which would be prejudicial to the national interest", indicates what the government is willing to have the communications media publish or broadcast on security matters and what it does not wish the media to use, with the unofficial assurance that there will be no prosecution under the Acts as long as the press and broadcasting bodies comply. The system worked secretly and informally. On the one hand a minister could ignore the Committee; on the other, the press could ignore the "D" notice. It was not until 1961 when George Blake, an agent both for the British and the Russians, was convicted under the Official Secrets Acts that existence of the Committee first came to public notice.

In Canada we do not have "D" Notice arrangements, but we do have an Official Secrets Act. In fact, the first one was enacted in 1890, just a year after the United Kingdom Act. It was passed at the request of the United Kingdom and was an almost verbatim copy. Two years later, the provisions of the Canadian Act were transferred to the first Canadian Criminal Code, where they remained until the enactment of a new Official Secrets Act in 1939. However, both the 1889 and 1911 Official Secrets Acts of the United Kingdom had specifically applied not just to the United Kingdom, but to the overseas Dominions as well. Since the 1920 Act was specifically devised not to apply to the Dominions, and since Canada did not have an Official Secrets Act in the 20th century until 1939, the 1911 Act of the United Kingdom and the Canadian Criminal Code provisions were in force in this country. When the 1939 Act was drafted, it was in effect a combination of the 1911 and 1920 United Kingdom Acts.

The Official Secrets Act is somewhat difficult to read, in that the attempt has been to cast a wide enough net while not being too vague. Essentially it covers two distinct, if somewhat similar, activities: spying (Section 3), and wrongful communication of government information, or leakage (Section 4).

It is Section 4 which is of main concern to the press. Rather than quote its terms, which can be consulted in the statute books, it would be more instructive to quote the description of the "catch-all" nature of this section provided by the United Kingdom Franks Committee on the Official Secrets Act of 1911:

> The leading characteristic of this offence is its catch-all quality. It catches all official documents and information. It makes no distinctions of kind, and no distinctions of degree. All information which a Crown servant learns in the course of his duty is "official" for the purposes of section 2, whatever its nature, whatever its importance, whatever its original source. A blanket it thrown over everything; nothing escapes. The section catches all Crown servants as well as all official information. Again, it makes no distinctions according to the nature or importance of a Crown servant's duties. All are covered. Every Minister of the Crown, every civil servant, every member of the Armed Forces, every police officer, performs his duties subject to section 2.

What is equally important for the press is that Subsection (3) of Section 4 provides that:

> Every person who receives any...information, knowing, or having reasonable ground to believe, at the time when he receives it, that the...information is communicated to him in contravention of this Act, is guilty of an offence under this Act unless he proves that the communication to him of the...information was contrary to his desire.

Professor Friedland reports that of the 21 prosecutions under the 1939 Official Secrets Act, some 17 were concerned with the Gouzenko affair, just after the Second World War. Since then there have been only four. Two of these were concerned with Section 3, the espionage section, and so are not relevant to our topic. The third was the recent *Treu* case which, although under the leakage of information section (Section 4), is also not relevant since it concerned retaining classified documents and failing to take reasonable care of such documents. The fourth case is of direct concern because it involved the Toronto *Sun*. The *Sun* had published a document which had outlined suspected Russian spying activities in Canada, and which had been designated as "top secret". Charges were brought against both the publisher and the editor under Section 4 of the Act. However, at the preliminary inquiry stage, Judge Waisberg of the Ontario Provincial Court concluded that earlier disclosures had "brought the document, now 'shopworn' and no longer secret, into the public domain". He concluded that the document, even if it had ever been secret, was no longer so.

Although the approach taken by Judge Waisberg may be welcome to the press, there may be some question whether higher courts, if the case had been appealed, would have upheld such an interpretation; that is, it is not an offence to publish information, merely because some parts of it had been improperly leaked. It is interesting to note that the United Kingdom White Paper, in proposing amendments to the Act following the Franks Committee report, recommended that although the "mere receipt of protected information" should not be a criminal offence, communication by the recipient should be.

2.2.5.2 Law Reform Commission of Canada, *Crimes Against, the Stage,* Working Paper 49 (Ottawa, 1986) 30, 33-34

The worst examples of complexity and excess detail, however, are to be found in the *O.S.A.*, an Act which can fairly be condemned as one of the poorest examples of legislative drafting in the statute books. The Act only deals with leakage- and espionage-related offences: section 3, the spying offence proper, contains a long list of proscribed conduct; section 4 deals at length with wrongful communication or use of information, and then sets out three additional specific offences; sections 5, 6, 8 and 9 create further spying-related offences. All of these provisions are long-winded, some with sentences of over one hundred and fifty words in length, and many are incomprehensible. The *O.S.A.* devotes several pages and over a thousand words to espionage-related offences whereas the *Criminal Code* manages to say perhaps all that needs to be said about the offence of spying in one short paragraph (s.46(2)(*b*)). Despite all the detail and complexity, the *O.S.A.* espionage offences are no more precise than paragraph 46(2)(*b*) of the *Code;* indeed, their exact scope remains unclear.*

...

Finally there are specific problems of uncertainty that arise only in the *O.S.A.* Two examples will suffice. Foremost is the difficulty in ascertaining whether the Act is meant to apply only to secret and official information or to any kind of information. The statute itself offers conflicting possibilities. Legislative history suggests that the Act was not meant to be limited to secret and official information and that the words ''secret official'' were not meant to qualify the entire list of items protected, but only ''code word'' and ''password.'' On the other hand, the title of the Act and the fact these two words appear at the beginning of the list of items (''*secret official* code word, or password, or any sketch, plan, model, article, or note, or other document or information'') covered in the Act, suggest that only secret official information was meant to be protected by the Act. It is an indication of the uncertainty as to the intended meaning of the *O.S.A.* that the Québec Court of Appeal held that it applied to secret and official information only, whereas the Franks Committee concluded that the English Act had much wider application, with the words ''secret and official'' only qualifying ''code word or password,'' and not the other items listed. Clearly, this is a matter of such critical importance that it should only be settled by Parliament, not the courts.

The last (and equally unresolvable) example of the problem of uncertainty is found in section 8 of the *O.S.A.*, which rather cryptically makes it an offence to ''wilfully omit or refuse to disclose to a senior police officer'' certain information that one has about suspected spies. The phrase ''wilfully omit ... to disclose'' is ambiguous. Does it impose an affirmative duty to seek out and inform the senior police officer, or is one only bound to disclose information if one is actually being questioned? Clearly, such an exceptional duty to inform the police about suspected criminals should be worded in unequivocal language, so that people can know the extent of their criminal liability.

* See *infra,* pp. 33-4. The *O.S.A.* presented no serious impediments to the prosecution of Morrison (Long Knife) because of the strong evidence against him: he had confessed his crime in a television interview. On January 23, 1986, he pleaded guilty to violating *O.S.A.* paragraph 3(1)(*c*). See also *Re Regina and Morrison* (1984), 47 O.R. (2d) 185 (Ont. H.C.), appeal dismissed October 17, 1984.

2.3 Access to Information

2.3.1 Access to Information Act, R.S.C. 1985, c.A-1, ss.2, 4, 10, 13-27

PURPOSE OF ACT

2. (1) The purpose of this Act is to extend the present laws of Canada to provide a right of access to information in records under the control of a government institution in accordance with the principles that government information should be available to the public, that necessary exceptions to the right of access should be limited and specific and that decisions on the disclosure of government information should be reviewed independently of government.

(2) This Act is intended to complement and not replace existing procedures for access to government information and is not intended to limit in any way access to the type of government information that is normally available to the general public.

ACCESS TO GOVERNMENT RECORDS

Right of Access

4. (1) Subject to this Act, but notwithstanding any other Act of Parliament, every person who is

(*a*) a Canadian citizen, or

(*b*) a permanent resident within the meaning of the *Immigration Act, 1976,*

has a right to and shall, on request, be given access to any record under the control of a government institution.

(2) The Governor in Council may, by order, extend the right to be given access to records under subsection (1) to include persons not referred to in that subsection and may set such conditions as the Governor in Council deems appropriate.

(3) For the purposes of this Act, any record requested under this Act that does not exist but can, subject to such limitations as may be prescribed by regulation, be produced from a machine readable record under the control of a government institution using computer hardware and software and technical expertise normally used by the government institution shall be deemed to be a record under the control of the government institution.

10. (1) Where the head of a government institution refuses to give access to a record requested under this Act or a part thereof, the head of the institution shall state in the notice given under paragraph 7(*a*)

(*a*) that the record does not exist, or

(*b*) the specific provision of this Act on which the refusal was based or, where the head of the institution does not indicate whether a record exists, the provision on which a refusal could reasonably be expected to be based if the record existed,

and shall state in the notice that the person who made the request has a right to make a complaint to the Information Commissioner about the refusal.

EXEMPTIONS

Responsibilities of Government

13. (1) Subject to subsection (2), the head of a government institution shall refuse to disclose any record requested under this Act that contains information that was obtained in confidence from

(*a*) the government of a foreign state or an institution thereof;

(*b*) an international organization of states or an institution thereof;

(*c*) the government of a province or an institution thereof; or

(*d*) a municipal or regional government established by or pursuant to an Act of the legislature of a province or an institution of such a government.

(2) The head of a government institution may disclose any record requested under this Act that contains information described in subsection (1) if the government, organization or institution from which the information was obtained

(*a*) consents to the disclosure; or

(*b*) makes the information public.

14. The head of a government institution may refuse to disclose any record requested under this Act that contains information the disclosure of which could reasonably be expected to be injurious to the conduct by the Government of Canada of federal-provincial affairs, including, without restricting the generality of the foregoing, any such information

(*a*) on federal-provincial consultations or deliberations; or

(*b*) on strategy or tactics adopted or to be adopted by the Government of Canada relating to the conduct of federal-provincial affairs.

15. (1) The head of a government institution may refuse to disclose any record requested under this Act that contains information the disclosure of which could reasonably be expected to be injurious to the conduct of international affairs, the defence of Canada or any state allied or associated with Canada or the detection, prevention or suppression of subversive or hostile activities, including, without restricting the generality of the foregoing, any such information

(*a*) relating to military tactics or strategy, or relating to military exercises or operations undertaken in preparation for hostilities or in connection with the detection, prevention or suppression of subversive or hostile activities;

(*b*) relating to the quantity, characteristics, capabilities or deployment of weapons or other defence equipment or of anything being designed, developed, produced or considered for use as weapons or other defence equipment;

(*c*) relating to the characteristics, capabilities, performance, potential, deployment, functions or role of any defence establishment, of any military force, unit or personnel or of any organization or person responsible for the detection, prevention or suppression of subversive or hostile activities;

(*d*) obtained or prepared for the purpose of intelligence relating to

(i) the defence of Canada or any state allied or associated with Canada, or

(ii) the detection, prevention or suppression of subversive or hostile activities;

(*e*) obtained or prepared for the purpose of intelligence respecting foreign states, international organizations of states or citizens of foreign states used by the Government of Canada in the process of deliberation and consultation or in the conduct of international affairs;

(*f*) on methods of, and scientific or technical equipment for, collecting, assessing or handling information referred to in paragraph (*d*) or (*e*) or on sources of such information;

(*g*) on the positions adopted or to be adopted by the Government of Canada, governments of foreign states or international organizations of states for the purpose of present or future international negotiations;

(*h*) that constitutes diplomatic correspondence exchanged with foreign states or international organizations of states or official correspondence exchanged with Canadian diplomatic missions or consular posts abroad; or

(*i*) relating to the communications or cryptographic systems of Canada or foreign states used

(i) for the conduct of international affairs,
(ii) for the defence of Canada or any state allied or associated with Canada, or
(iii) in relation to the detection, prevention or suppression of subversive or hostile activities.

16. (1) The head of a government institution may refuse to disclose any record requested under this Act that contains

(*a*) information obtained or prepared by any government institution, or part of a government institution, that is an investigative body specified in the regulations in the course of lawful investigations pertaining to
(i) the detection, prevention or suppression of crime, or
(ii) the enforcement of any law of Canada or a province,
if the record came into existence less than twenty years prior to the request;

(*b*) information relating to investigative techniques or plans for specific lawful investigations;

(*c*) information the disclosure of which could reasonably be expected to be injurious to the enforcement of any law of Canada or a province or the conduct of lawful investigations, including, without restricting the generality of the foregoing, any such information
(i) relating to the existence or nature of a particular investigation,
(ii) that would reveal the identity of a confidential source of information, or
(iii) that was obtained or prepared in the course of an investigation; or

(*d*) information the disclosure of which could reasonably be expected to be injurious to the security of penal institutions.

(2) The head of a government institution may refuse to disclose any record requested under this Act that contains information that could reasonably be expected to facilitate the commission of an offence, including, without restricting the generality of the foregoing, any such information

(*a*) on criminal methods or techniques;

(*b*) that is technical information relating to weapons or potential weapons; or

(*c*) on the vulnerability of particular buildings or other structures or systems, including computer or communication systems, or methods employed to protect such buildings or other structures or systems.

(3) The head of a government institution shall refuse to disclose any record requested under this Act that contains information that was obtained or prepared by the Royal Canadian Mounted Police while performing policing services for a province or a municipality pursuant to an arrangement made under section 20 of the *Royal Canadian Mounted Police Act,* where the Government of Canada has, on the request of the province or the municipality agreed not to disclose such information.

(4) For the purposes of paragraphs (1)(*b*) and (*c*), ''investigation'' means an investigation that

(*a*) pertains to the administration or enforcement of an Act of Parliament;

(*b*) is authorized by or pursuant to an Act of Parliament; or

(*c*) is within a class of investigations specified in the regulations.

17. The head of a government institution may refuse to disclose any record requested under this Act that contains information the disclosure of which could reasonably be expected to threaten the safety of individuals.

18. The head of a government institution may refuse to disclose any record requested under this Act that contains

(*a*) trade secrets or financial, commercial, scientific or technical information that belongs to the Governement of Canada or a government institution and has substantial value or is reasonably likely to have substantial value;

(*b*) information the disclosure of which could reasonably be expected to prejudice the competitive position of a government institution;

(*c*) scientific or technical information obtained through research by an officer or employee of a government institution, the disclosure of which could reasonably be expected to deprive the officer or employee of priority of publication; or

(*d*) information the disclosure of which could reasonably be expected to be materially injurious to the financial interests of the Government of Canada or the ability of the Government of Canada to manage the economy of Canada or could reasonably be expected to result in an undue benefit to any person, including, without restricting the generality of the foregoing, any such information relating to

(i) the currency, coinage or legal tender of Canada,

(ii) a contemplated change in the rate of bank interest or in government borrowing,

(iii) a contemplated change in tariff rates, taxes, duties or any other revenue source,

(iv) a contemplated change in the conditions of operation of financial institutions,

(v) a contemplated sale or purchase of securities or of foreign or Canadian currency, or

(vi) a contemplated sale or acquisition of land or property.

Personal Information

19. (1) Subject to subsection (2), the head of a government institution shall refuse to disclose any record requested under this Act that contains personal information as defined in section 3 of the *Privacy Act*.

(2) The head of a government institution may disclose any record requested under this Act that contains personal information if

(*a*) the individual to whom it relates consents to the disclosure;

(*b*) the information is publicly available; or

(*c*) the disclosure is in accordance with section 8 of the *Privacy Act*.

Third Party Information

20. (1) Subject to this section, the head of a government institution shall refuse to disclose any record requested under this Act that contains

(*a*) trade secrets of a third party;

(*b*) financial, commercial, scientific or technical information that is confidential information supplied to a government institution by a third party and is treated consistently in a confidential manner by the third party;

(*c*) information the disclosure of which could reasonably be expected to result in material financial loss or gain to, or could reasonably be expected to prejudice the competitive position of, a third party; or (*d*) information the disclosure of which could reasonably be expected to interfere with contractual or other negotiations of a third party.

(2) The head of a government institution shall not, pursuant to subsection (1), refuse to disclose a part of a record if that part contains the results of product or environmental testing carried out by or on behalf of a government institution unless the testing was done as a service to a person, a group of persons or an organization other than a government institution and for a fee.

(3) Where the head of a government institution discloses a record requested under this Act, or a part thereof, that contains the results of product or environmental testing, the head of the institution shall at the same time as the record or part thereof is disclosed provide the person who requested the record with a written explanation of the methods used in conducting the tests.

(4) For the purposes of this section, the results of product or environmental testing do not include the results of preliminary testing conducted for the purpose of developing methods of testing.

(5) The head of a government institution may disclose any record that contains information described in subsection (1) with the consent of the third party to whom the information relates.

(6) The head of a government institution may disclose any record requested under this Act, or any part thereof, that contains information described in paragraph (1)(*b*), (*c*) or (*d*) if such disclosure would be in the public interest as it relates to public health, public safety or protection of the environment and, if such public interest in disclosure clearly outweighs in importance any financial loss or gain to, prejudice to the competitive position of or interference with contractual or other negotiations of a third party.

Operations of Government

21. (1) The head of a government institution may refuse to disclose any record requested under this Act that contains

(*a*) advice or recommendations developed by or for a government institution or a Minister of the Crown,

(*b*) an account of consultations or deliberations involving officials or employees of a government institution, a Minister of the Crown or the staff of a Minister of the Crown,

(*c*) positions or plans developed for the purpose of negotiations carried on or to be carried on by or on behalf of the Government of Canada and considerations relating thereto, or

(*d*) plans relating to the management of personnel or the administration of a government institution that have not yet been put into operation,

if the record came into existence less than twenty years prior to the request.

(2) Subsection (1) does not apply in respect of a record that contains

(*a*) an account of, or a statement of reasons for, a decision that is made in the exercise of a discretionary power or an adjudicative function and that affects the rights of a person; or (*b*) a report prepared by a consultant or adviser who was not, at the time the report was prepared, an officer or employee of a government institution or a member of the staff of a Minister of the Crown.

22. The head of a government institution may refuse to disclose any record requested under this Act that contains information relating to testing or auditing procedures or techniques or details of specific tests to be given or audits to be conducted if such disclosure would prejudice the use or results of particular tests or audits.

23. The head of a government institution may refuse to disclose any record requested under this Act that contains information that is subject to solicitor-client privilege.

Statutory Prohibitions

24. (1) The head of a government institution shall refuse to disclose any record requested under this Act that contains information the disclosure of which is restricted by or pursuant to any provision set out in Schedule II.

(2) Such committee as may be designated or established under section 75 shall review every provision set out in Schedule II and shall, within three years after the coming into force of this Act or, if Parliament is not then sitting, on any of the first fifteen days next thereafter that Parliament is sitting, cause a report to be laid before Parliament on whether and to what extent the provisions are necessary.

25. Notwithstanding any other provision of this Act, where a request is made to a government institution for access to a record that the head of the institution is authorized to refuse to disclose under this Act by reason of information or other material contained in the record, the head of the institution shall disclose any part of the record that does not contain, and can reasonably be severed from any part that contains, any such information or material.

General

26. The head of a government institution may refuse to disclose any record requested under this Act or any part thereof if the head of the institution believes on reasonable grounds that the material in the record or part thereof will be published by a government institution, agent of the Government of Canada or Minister of the Crown within ninety days after the request is made or within such further period of time as may be necessary for printing or translating the material for the purpose of printing it.

27. (1) The head of a government institution may refuse to disclose any record requested under this Act

(*a*) during the first year after the coming into force of this Act, in the case of a record that was in existence more than three years before the coming into force of this Act;

(*b*) during the second year after the coming into force of this Act, in the case of a record that was in existence more than five years before the coming into force of this Act; and

(*c*) during the third year after the coming into force of this Act, in the case of a record that was in existence more than five years before the coming into force of this Act where, in the opinion of the head of the institution, to comply with a request for the record would unreasonably interfere with the operations of the government institution.

(2) Subsection (1) does not apply in respect of any record that is available to the public at the Public Archives at the time this Act comes into force.

2.3.2 *The Information Commissioner* v. *The Minister of Employment and Immigration* (1986), 3 F.C. 63

JEROME A.C.J.: This application under paragraph 42(1)(*a*) of the *Access to Information Act* [S.C. 1980-81-82-83, c. 111, Schedule I] came on for hearing at Ottawa, Ontario, on November 27, 1985. The facts are not in dispute and are contained in a Statement of Agreed Facts dated July 15, 1985, which reads, in part:

1. On May 23, 1984, the Employment and Immigration Commission received a request pursuant to the *Privacy Act* from D.F., a Canadian Citizen, requesting as follows:

> "I request full access to and disclosure of the immigration file relating to my sponsorship of my wife's application for permanent residence status in Canada. The Canadian Immigration Commission file number at the Vancouver office for the part of this file held there is 5133-15-6763. The Canadian Consulate General, Immigration Affairs, file number for that part of this file held in Seattle is 6054-B0138-5657. My wife's name is P.F."

2. By letter dated July 13, 1984, the said D.F. was given all personal information relating to him. Personal information relating to P.F. was exempted from disclosure pursuant to section 26 of the *Privacy Act*.

3. On May 23, 1984, the Employment and Immigration Commission received a request pursuant to the *Privacy Act* from P.F. requesting as follows:

> "I request full access to and disclosure of the immigration file and record. The Canadian Immigration Commission file number at the Vancouver office for the part of this file held there is 5133-15-6763. The Canadian Consulate General, Immigration Affairs, file number for the part of this file held in Seattle is 6054-B0138-5657. Access is requested to the whole of the records and files at these offices, including all correspondence, memoranda, and all other documentary material relating to myself, my immigration matters, my application for permanent residence, and the issues of my marital status in Canada, and whether I have been previously married in the Philippines."

4. By letter dated July 13, 1984, P.F. was denied access to the personal information requested by her on the basis that she was not a Canadian Citizen or Permanent Resident as required by subsection 12(1) of the *Privacy Act*.

5. On May 23, 1984, the Employment and Immigration Commission received a request pursuant to the *Access to Information Act* from D.F. requesting as follows:

> "The record of which and to which access is requested is the immigration file relating to my sponsorship of the application for permanent residence by my wife, P.F. The Canadian Immigration Commission file number at the Vancouver office for the part of the record there is 5133-15-6763. The Canadian Consulate General, Immigration Affairs, file number for the part of the record being held by that office in Seattle is 6054-B0138-5657. Access is requested to the whole of the record at these offices, including all correspondence, memoranda, and all other documentary material relating to myself, my sponsorship of my wife's application, the related immigration matters, and the allegation being made by the Canadian Immigration Commission that my marriage to my wife is defective or void in some way due to her alleged previous marriage."

6. By letter dated July 13, 1984, the said D.F. was notified that the information he requested constituted personal information which should be accessed under the *Privacy Act*, and that,

> since he had submitted a request under the *Privacy Act,* he would receive all personal information to which he was entitled in response to his *Privacy Act* request.

It is not disputed that the record in issue contains personal information as defined in section 3 of the *Privacy Act* [S.C. 1980-81-82-83, c.111, Schedule II] nor that the individual to whom that information relates has consented to its disclosure. Nevertheless, counsel contends that since subsection 19(2) provides that the head of a government institution may disclose personal information, it establishes with equal force a discretion not to disclose even though the conditions of subsection 19(2) have been met.

I reject the argument for two reasons: first, as a question of law, it is contrary to principles of statutory interpretation; second, it represents an approach that runs directly against the very purpose for which this legislation was enacted, as stated in the express provisions of the statute and confirmed in jurisprudence.

In terms of statutory interpretation, when legislators intend to create an obligation to do something, they use the word "shall". When they intend instead to establish a discretion or a right to do it, they use the word "may". Had the legislators intended here to repose residual discretion in the head of the government institution not to disclose information, even though the conditions of section 19(2) had been met, that appropriate and precise language would have been used. Of course, the Act does not establish the discretion not to disclose in such circumstances (in which case the respondent's argument might have had merit). The language chosen expresses the intent to establish a discretion to release personal information under certain circumstances. Those conditions having been fulfilled, it becomes tantamount to an obligation upon the head of the government institution to do so, especially where the purpose for which the statute was enacted is, as here, to create a right of access in the public. In support of the argument to the contrary, counsel for the respondent relied upon the decision of the Supreme Court of Canada in *Maple Lodge Farms Ltd. v. Government of Canada,* [1982] 2 S.C.R. 2. However, in the judgment in the Federal Court of Appeal [[1981] 1 F.C. 500], delivered by Le Dain J., and affirmed in the Supreme Court of Canada, the following significant passage appears [at page 508]:

> 7. On May 23, 1984, the Employment and Immigration Commission received a request pursuant to the *Access to Information Act* from the Complainant, Gerald G. Goldstein. That request is the request referred to in the Affidavit of Douglas W. McGibbon.
>
> 8. The said Gerald G. Goldstein is a Barrister and Solicitor practicing in the Province of British Columbia who represents the said P.F.

Together with his request for access, the complainant submitted a document signed by P.F. consenting to the release to the complainant of documents and information relating to her immigration matters. On July 13, 1984 the respondent informed the complainant that the information which he sought could not be obtained under the *Access to Information Act* because it was personal information about another person. A complaint was lodged with the Information Commissioner who, following an investigation, recommended that the information be released. The respondent subsequently provided the complainant with access to documents consisting of 5 pages, but refused to disclose in excess of 200 pages of documents. The applicant seeks a review of that refusal under paragraph 42(1)(*a*) of the *Access to Information Act:*

42. (1) The Information Commissioner may
(*a*) apply to the Court, within the time limits prescribed by section 41, for a review of any refusal to disclose a record requested under this Act or a part thereof in respect of which an investigation has been carried out by the Information Commissioner, if the Commissioner has the consent of the person who requested access to the record;
(*b*) appear before the Court on behalf of any person who has applied for a review under section 41; or
(*c*) with leave of the Court, appear as a party to any review applied for under section 41 or 44.

Section 48 of the *Access to Information Act* places upon the respondent the burden of establishing that she is authorized to refuse to disclose the record requested:

48. In any proceedings before the Court arising from an application under section 41 or 42, the burden of establishing that the head of a government institution is authorized to refuse to disclose a record requested under this Act or a part thereof shall be on the government institution concerned.

Counsel for the respondent argues that such authority exists under section 19 of the Act:

19. (1) Subject to subsection (2), the head of a government institution shall refuse to disclose any record requested under this Act that contains personal information as defined in section 3 of the *Privacy Act*.

(2) The head of a government institution may disclose any record requested under this Act that contains personal information if
(*a*) the individual to whom it relates consents to the disclosure;
(*b*) the information is publicly available; or
(*c*) the disclosure is in accordance with section 8 of the *Privacy Act*.
This is not a case for application of the principle recognized in *Julius v. The Right Rev. the Lord Bishop of Oxford* (1879-80) 5 App. Cas. 214 and referred to in *The Labour Relations Board of Saskatchewan v. The Queen on the relation of F.W. Woolworth Co. Ltd.*, [1956] S.C.R. 82 at page 87, that permissive words may be construed as creating a duty where they confer a power the exercise of which is necessary to effectuate a right.

It is my view, of course, that the present matter is precisely such a case and I therefore turn to the following passages of the two decisions referred to above. In *Julius v. Oxford (Bishop of)* (1880), 5 App. Cas. 214 (H.L.), Lord Blackburn states at pages 242-243:

But there are cases in which the authority or power given is not to do a judicial act, and yet there is a duty on the donee to exercise the power if it appears to be given to the donee for the purpose of making good a right, and he is called upon by those who have that right to exercise the power for their benefit.

And in *Labour Relations Board v. The Queen ex rel. F.W. Woolworth Company Limited and Agnes Slabick and Saskatchewan Joint Board, Retail, Wholesale and Department Store Union,* [1956] S.C.R. 82, Locke J. states at page 86:

The language of s.5, in so far as it affects this aspect of the matter, reads: —
5. The board shall have power to make orders: —
....

(i) rescinding or amending any order or decision of the board.

While this language is permissive in form, it imposed, in my opinion, a duty upon the Board to exercise this power when called upon to do so by a party interested and having the right to make the application (*Drysdale v. Dominion Coal Company* ((1904) 34 Can. S.C.R. 328 at 336): Killam J.). Enabling words are always compulsory where they are words to effectuate a legal right (*Julius v. Lord Bishop of Oxford* ((1880) 5 A.C. 214 at 243): Lord Blackburn).

Turning then to the purpose of the legislation, it is perhaps appropriate to return once again to the language I used in *Maislin Industries Limited v. Minister for Industry, Trade and Commerce,* [1984] 1 F.C. 939 [at pages 942 and 943]:

It should be emphasized however, that since the basic principle of these statutes is to codify the right of public access to Government information two things follow: first, that such public access ought not be frustrated by the courts except upon the clearest grounds so that doubt ought to be resolved in favour of disclosure; second, the burden of persuasion must rest upon the party resisting disclosure whether, as in this case, it is the private corporation or citizen, or in other circumstances, the Government. It is appropriate to quote subsection 2(1):

4. (1) Subject to this Act, but notwithstanding any other Act of Parliament, every person who is

(*a*) a Canadian citizen, or

(*b*) a permanent resident within the meaning of the *Immigration Act, 1976,*

has a right to and shall, on request, be given access to any record under the control of a government institution.

To repeat, the purpose of the *Access to Information Act* is to codify the right of access to information held by the government. It is not to codify the government's right of refusal. Access should be the normal course. Exemptions should be exceptional and must be confined to those specifically set out in the statute. In the present case, the applicant was quite properly informed that the information sought could not be obtained except by a Canadian citizen or a resident and could not involve disclosure of personal information about another person without their consent. Once those conditions were met, and they were here, the information should have been disclosed.

The application must therefore succeed. An order will go pursuant to section 49 of the Act ordering the respondent to disclose the records in issue to the complainant, Gerald G. Goldstein. The applicant should have her costs of this application.

2.3.3 "What Newsrooms Need To Know", Canadian Daily Newspaper Publishers Association, September, 1984

Overview

Freedom of Information became law in Canada when the federal government passed the long-awaited and much-delayed Access to Information Act (Bill C-43) on June 28, 1982. It received Royal Assent in the Senate on July 7, 1982.

As established in C-43, Section 2.(1), its purpose is "...to extend the present laws of Canada to provide a right of access to information in records under the control of a government institution in accordance with the principles that government information should be available to the public, that necessary exceptions to the right of access should be limited and specific, and that decisions on the disclosure of government information should be reviewed independently of government."

As this guide notes, "necessary exceptions to the right of access" are neither all that limited nor all that specific. And, the independent review, a judicial review in federal court, does not extend to Cabinet documents. These remain exempt. In short, you now have the right to learn some government secrets, but not Cabinet's.

However, it is a start and a cornerstone act on which amendments can be built. The Act provides for parliamentary review in three years, to determine its strengths and weaknesses.

Only court decisions in the next few years will determine the exact meaning of many of the phrases and how they will free or inhibit information.

This legislation extends only to federal government departments, institutions and crown corporations.

...

How FOI works

1. Any Canadian citizen or landed immigrant can request information from a federal government body. Cabinet may extend the right to citizens of other lands.

2. The information cannot be a Cabinet document (see Cabinet System reference) and there are five mandatory exemptions and 12 discretionary exemptions (more on these later). The right exists to seek a judicial review of a request for the discretionary exemptions if the government refuses to disclose information sought.

3. The head of a government institution or his designate (access coordinator is the technical term) must, within 30 days after receiving a formal request, either produce the information sought, or give the reasons for denial in writing. The government can request an extension of 30 days if it decides a search is complicated, if long consultation is necessary or if a third party must be told of the request.

4. Anyone refused access to information has the right to appeal to the Information Commissioner to review and assess the request. He has power similar to an auditor-general, and can enter any government office, call any witness, and study all documents and information except those of Cabinet. He can recommend that the information be released or withheld.

5. If the government refuses to comply with an Information Commissioner recommendation for release of what is sought, or if he agrees with the refusal, the matter can be taken to the Federal court within 45 days after the commissioner reports. The court has the final say.

What's available

1. Under the act, the federal government must provide on a yearly basis, a publication or index containing:

(a) A description of the organization and responsibilities of each federal government institution, including federal crown corporations, embracing details on the programs and functions of each division or branch of the institutions;

(b) A detailed description of all classes of records under the control of each government institution;

(c) A description of all manuals used by employees of each government institution in administering or carrying out any of the programs or activities concerned with their jobs.
(d) Each government institution must furnish the address of the Access Coordinator to whom request for information should be sent.

2. The index also includes a citizen's guide outlining basic rights under the act, instructions on how to use the index and make requests (with sample entries and requests), guidance on existing information and channels of information, and descriptions of where to go to get it.

3. At least twice a year, an updating bulletin is to be posted.

4. According to the act, these indices and bulletins should be found in government buildings, libraries, and post offices.

How to Use FOI

1. Based on the experiences of users of FOI in the United States, which has a more liberal Act than in Canada (its law was passed in 1966), it would seem a reporter, researcher or scholar should first contact the government institution's press officer, who may readily agree to supply all or part of the documents requested.

In the face of refusal here, the government institution's Access Coordinator should be approached. He may be persuaded to provide the documents sought without the need to file a formal access-to-information request.

The right to an independent review should be borne in mind. (The government must prove why the information should not be disclosed and the head of the government institution may feel that this isn't worth the trouble or potential cost. If the government institution loses in court, it has to pay.)

2. If the informal approach doesn't work, consult the index posted at a government office, post office or library and fill out an application form. It asks for subject, title, author and date of the document sought and specific decisions, meetings, or whatever else you hope it contains.

3. Be reasonably specific. It's not essential to provide an exact description of document and its precise location but a request should have sufficient detail to ensure a government employee familiar with the subject can locate the record with a reasonable amount of effort.

It's wise to send formal requests to several government institutions if you are unsure which one has the information sought. However, the index should help narrow the search.

Costs for FOI

1. Each search request should cost no more than $25, the fee set to cover government costs. However, should the staff search time exceed five hours, or should the volume of photocopying exceed standards yet do be set, the rate may be higher.

2. The government may waive or refuse fees.

3. Appeal can be lodged with the information commissioner if it's felt the fees are too high. He can waive the fee or seek redress.

FOI does not apply to the Cabinet system

The price that was paid for freedom of information legislation in Canada was the federal government's insistence on total exemption of Cabinet documents from access. The government retains absolute privilege on Cabinet confidences.

Section 69.(1) of the Access to Information Act reads:

''This Act does not apply to confidences of the Queen's Privy Council for Canada, including, without restricting the generality of the foregoing....''

While you still may have access to Cabinet data through normal journalistic channels such as leaks, the ''confidences'' include: memoranda to Cabinet, discussion papers containing background explanations, analyses of problems or policy options, Cabinet agenda and minutes, communications between ministers, briefing papers and draft legislation.

The phrase ''without restricting the generality of...'' is, in critics' minds, a dangerous one which a Cabinet minister or Clerk of the Privy Council could apply to just about any document on the grounds that it is a Cabinet document.

The documents exempt from access are those of the Queen's Privy Council of Canada. In other words, anything to do with the Cabinet, Prime Minister's Office, and their committees and anyone who was a Cabinet minister.

The limits of this exemption will likely be settled in the courts. That is, a person can seek to determine in court if a document is indeed a Cabinet document.

Exemptions which may be subject to federal court review

Mandatory exemptions

There are five mandatory exemptions in the act, but there is nothing preventing the request for a judicial review to force disclosure of the information.

The following are summaries of the five sections of the Act which include the phrase ''shall refuse to disclose'', the operative phrase for the mandatory exemptions:

Section 12. (1) ...information obtained in confidence from a government of a foreign state or institution, a group of allied states such as NATO, and a provincial or municipal government.

Section 16. (2) ...information that was obtained or prepared by the RCMP while performing contract police duties for a province or municipality where the federal government has, on the request of the province or municipality, agreed not to disclose such information.

Section 19. (1) ...any record requested under the act that contains personal information as defined in Section 3 of the Privacy Act — i.e. race, ethnic origin, color, religion, age, marital status; education, medical, criminal or employment records; address, fingerprints, or blood type; personal opinions or views of the individual; and private correspondence by the individual to government.

Section 20. (1) ...any record requested that contains trade secrets of a third party; financial, scientific or technical information that is confidential information supplied by a third party; information that could ''reasonably'' be expected to interfere with contractural or other negotiations of a third party and which could be expected to result in material financial loss or gain to, or prejudice the competitive position of, a third party. In other words, a businessman could not steal a competitor's secret information that has to be filed with Ottawa because of some law.

Section 24. (1) ...any information which is already prohibited by statute against disclosure. There are sections of 33 other acts which override Bill C-43's provisions (e.g., sections 178.14 and 178.2 of the Criminal Code which relate to information in an affidavit sworn before a judge for permission to use a wiretap).

Discretionary Exemptions

There are 12 discretionary exemptions which contain the operative phrase "may refuse to disclose..." Many, no doubt, will be tested under judicial review. These are:

Section 14 ...information which could "reasonably" be expected to be injurious to federal-provincial relations such as disclosure of strategies, tactics, consultations, or deliberations.

Section 15. (1) ...information the disclosure of which could "reasonably" be expected to be injurious to the conduct of international affairs, the defence of Canada or any state allied or associated with Canada, various intelligence activities, defence equipment development or use, and diplomatic correspondence.

Section 16. (1) ...any record containing information that is part of law enforcement, including detection, prevention or suppression of a crime. Two examples are the identity of confidential source and information injurious to the security of penal institutions.

Section 16. (2) ...information that could "reasonably" facilitate the commission of a crime, such as a blueprint explaining how to break into a secure building.

Section 17 ...information that could "reasonably" be expected to threaten the safety of individuals.

Section 18 ...much economic information, including any trade secrets or other government financial, commercial, scientific or technical information of substantive value; information that could prejudice the competitive position of a government institution, scientific or technical information obtained through research by an officer or employee of a government institution; information that could be "materially injurious" to the financial interests of Canada such as information relating to Canada's currency; a contemplated change in the bank interest rate or in government borrowing; contemplated changes in tariff rates, duties or any other revenue source; contemplated changes in the conditions of operation of financial institutions; contemplated sale or acquisition of land or property.

Section 21. (1) ...is quite vague, but may preclude any account of internal discussions, advice, or negotiations within the past 20 years concerning government employees, their ministers and the ministers' staff, as well as plans that relate to new institutions.

Section 23 ...information subject to solicitor-client privilege.

Section 26 ...if the information is "reasonably" expected to be released within 90 days after request is made for access. Additional time may be allowed for translation or printing.

Section 27 ...during the transitionary period (see below) from the time the Act came into force dating back to the time the information being requested was first acquired by a government institution. The transitionary period is to allow the government institution to properly file and record older information. The three classifications of the transitionary period are:

(a) during the first year of the Act's existence, you can request information dating back only three years prior to the Act coming into force.
(b) during the second year of the Act's existence, you can request information dating back five years prior to the Act coming into force.
(c) during the third year of the Act's existence, the government may refuse to disclose information that was in existence more than five years prior to the act coming into force if such a request would ''unreasonably'' interfere with the operations of the government institution.

This section may act as a face-saver for government institutions whose files are in such shambles that attempting to find out what they have been doing might be next to impossible.

What you have access to as the act specifies

Excluding the the wall-to wall exemptions, the Act does say the public can obtain some information without going through the Information Commissioner's Office or judicial review — not much, but some.

1. Under discretionary exemptions, for example, Section 21 on advice developed by or for a government institution or a minister does not include information dating back more than 20 years prior to the request, if the information still exists.

2. Disclosure of personal information is also authorized under Section 19.(2) of the Act if the individual to whom the information relates consents to the disclosure; if the information is already publicly available; or in limited other circumstances as described in Section 8 of the Privacy Act.

3. The public is entitled to a written explanation of the method of testing plus results obtained from government consumer-product and environment testing. However, you can't get the information on environmental testing if it was done as a service to a person, a group of persons, or an organization other than a government institution and was done for a fee. You also cannot get the preliminary methods used to develop the approved method of testing.

4. Any third party information may be disclosed if the third party consents.

5. Any third party information may be disclosed if it's in the public interest as it relates to public health, safety, or protection of the environment and if such public interest in disclosure clearly outweighs in importance any financial loss or gain to a third party.

The Information Commissioner

The Information Commissioner will be a powerful civil servant who will have the same rank and powers as a departmental deputy head. In addition, he will have an assistant and a full staff to carry out his duties.

The Information Commissioner can summon and enforce the appearance of witnesses, administer oaths, compel witnesses to provide written and oral evidence under oath, and order them to produce all documents relevant to the investigation and consideration of any and all complaints.

He can enter any premises occupied by a government institution and can examine or obtain copies of extracts from books or other records found in any premises relevant to his investigation. No information is to be withheld from the Information Commissioner on any grounds. In fact, if someone attempts to obstruct the Information Commissioner or his delegate, the offender is guilty of an offence and on summary conviction is liable to a fine not exceeding $1,000. In theory, he has access to every scrap of paper produced by the federal government and should be allowed to look at Cabinet documents to determine if they are Cabinet documents. The Information Commissioner is appointed to a seven-year term which may be renewed for additional seven-year terms. He prepares a yearly report on his office's activities and presents it to Parliament.

2.3.4 John D. McCamus, ''Freedom of Information in Canada'', *Government Publications Review,* 1983, Vol. 10, p. 51

At first glance, Canada might be expected to be rather inhospitable terrain for freedom of information legislation. The federal Parliament and the legislatures of the ten provinces are Westminster-style parliamentary governments. Members of the cabinet normally are drawn from those sitting members of the legislature who belong to the political party controlling a majority of the house. Party discipline requires backbenchers to offer unstinting support to the cabinet. Members of cabinet are responsible for the operation of the various departments and agencies of the federal government. Thus, in sharp contrast to the divisions inherent in the American separation of powers model, the Canadian system of government places effective control over both the executive and legislative branches of government in the hands of the Prime Minister and Cabinet. If the enactment of freedom of information legislation in the United States is to be explained in part by the existence of tension between the executive and legislative branches of government, such tension normally is absent in the Canadian context. Moreover, at the federal level, and in some of the provinces, at least one or another of the major political parties has dominated electoral politics for much of our recent history. For most of this century, for example, the federal Parliament has been controlled by the Liberal Party, with infrequent interludes of governance by the Progressive Conservative Party. Thus, whatever motivation there might otherwise be for a party in power to enact public access laws in the expectation that they might be of considerable use once the party again finds itself in opposition, also is typically absent....

It is perhaps less surprising that the gestation of this legislation at both the federal and provincial levels has been rather lengthy, notwinthstanding the fact that the freedom of information concept has enjoyed reasonably energetic support from a broad cross-section of public opinion. No doubt influenced to a considerable extent by developments in the U.S., the idea has been vigorously advocated by members of opposition parties of whatever political stripe as well as by business and labour groups, the Canadian Bar Association. The Canadian Civil Liberties Association, and associations of academics and public interest groups of various kinds, including at least two that were created exclusively for the purpose of promoting access laws. Although government spokesmen at all levels have suggested from time to time that there is little public support for access legislation, it nonetheless remains true that this idea has enjoyed persistent support from a remarkably broad cross-section of groups and individuals. This fact, together with the special interest taken in the subject by the press, has kept the subject on the Canadian political agenda throughout the past decade.

HISTORICAL DEVELOPMENT

Although academic interest in access legislation can be traced back to the mid '60s, serious political discussion of this subject did not begin at the federal level until 1973. In February of that year, the Liberal Government tabled in the House a cabinet directive titled "Notices of Motion for the Production of Papers" in which the Government adopted a general policy concerning access to information by members of the House. Rather like the American Freedom of Information Act, the directive adopted the general principle of granting access to information unless the information came within one or more of the listed exemptions. Unlike the American Act, the directive imposed no binding obligation on the Government to disclose and made no provision for independent review of decisions to withhold information. Later that year, a Private Members' bill setting forth a freedom of information scheme which had been introduced by Gerald Baldwin, M.P., the leading Conservative spokesman on the information issue, together with the cabinet directive, was referred to a parliamentary committee for its consideration. Referral of a Private Members' bill to committee is an unusual step in Canadian parliamentary practice and, therefore, was seen as a signal of serious governmental interest in the subject. The committee conducted extensive public hearings. Interestingly, the Government tabled before the committee a document prepared by Mr. D.F. Wall, one of its senior officials, titled "The Provision of Government Information" which was a report originally prepared for internal purposes, recommending the adoption of policies favouring much greater public access to government records. This, too, suggested rowing support for the freedom of information idea in governmental ranks. In December 1975, the committee tabled its own report recommending the enactment of a freedom of information scheme.

The response of the Liberal Government to this recommendation was not immediate. In June 1977, the then Secretary of State, the Hon. John Roberts, tabled a Green Paper espousing the general principle that "assessment of government depends on full understanding of the context in which decisions are made" and exploring various areas of difficulty involved in the drafting of a freedom of information scheme. The Green Paper evidenced extreme sensitivity on the question of the review of decisions to deny access. The discussion in the Paper made a noble effort to undermine the suggestion offered by many others that the courts, as in the American scheme, should have the authority to overrule a governmental decision to refuse disclosure. The essence of the argument made on this point in the Green Paper and, indeed, by many federal and provincial spokesmen before and since, was that judicial review of decisions to deny access to government records would be inconsistent with the constitutional convention of ministerial responsibility. This was, and remains, an interesting exercise in political rhetoric. Although there appears to be no merit whatsoever in the claim of inconsistency, governments have attempted to defend their tradition of refusing inconvenient disclosures under the guise of preserving our Parliamentary heritage. The constitutional reality, however, is that the convention of ministerial responsibility has nothing to do with the tradition of non-disclosure. On the contrary, the convention asserts that Ministers of the Crown are responsible individually and collectively to the Legislature for the administration of the executive branch of government. The historical significance of a principle rendering the Ministers of the Crown accountable to the Legislature is obvious; it is also obvious, of course, that with the rise of political parties and acceptance of the principle of party solidarity, the accountability of the Cabinet to the Legislature is more a matter of form than substance. Thus, more cynical observers argue that "ministerial responsibility" is a shopworn constitutional myth and that one of the very compelling arguments in favour of freedom of information laws in parliamentary jurisdictions is that it would restore a measure of that very kind of accountability that was originally secured by the convention of ministerial responsibility. With the publication of the Green Paper, the question of judicial review came to dominate public discussion of the freedom of information issue. Ultimately, in December 1977, the Green Paper itself was referred back to the same parliamentary committee that had conducted the earlier hearings, for further study.

A related and very important development in July 1977 at the federal level was the enactment of The Canadian Human Rights Act. Which contained, in Part IV, a scheme conferring broad rights of access to government files containing personal information as part of a privacy protection scheme. Ironically, it appears that no explicit connection was drawn between this enactment and the general desirability of freedom of information laws. One of the most notable achievements of the 1966 American Act had been the granting of a right of access to information in government records concerning oneself. Consistent with the views stated in the Green Paper, Part IV did not grant a right to judicial review of decisions to deny access. Appeals could be taken by disappointed individuals to a Privacy Commissioner who was given the power only to investigate and recommend disclosure, the ultimate power to decide residing with the appropriate Minister. Nonetheless, the establishment of a functioning access scheme for personal records must be seen as an important step. Successful implementation of Part IV demonstrated that many of the most difficult administrative problems involved in an access scheme could be resolved without creating unbearable burdens on the various departments and agencies of the federal government.

ESTABLISHING A FEDERAL LAW

At the federal level, the leisurely pace of activity on this subject quickened during 1978 and 1979. The parliamentary committee, having again conducted extensive hearings, tabled a report in June of 1978 calling for the enactment of a freedom of information law. In the early months of 1979, The Law Reform Commission of Canada, a government advisory body then engaged in extensive review of the activities of federal administrative agencies, published a research paper recommending the enactment of an access scheme covering the activities of such agencies. Finally, in the spring of 1979, public statements were made by the Liberal Government that a freedom of information law would be introduced in the near future. The promised bill did not materialise prior to the fall of Prime Minister Trudeau's Liberal Government in the federal election of May 1979. The Conservative Leader, Mr. Clark, focussed considerable attention on the freedom of information issue during the election campaign and in October 1979, the newly-elected Conservative Government tabled its promised freedom of information legislation, together with a Privacy Protection Act which would have effected substantial revisions to Part IV of The Canadian Human Rights Act. The Conservative bill was similar in its essentials to American national freedom of information and privacy laws. It provided for a general principle of access subject to a more-or-less recognisable list of exemptions, together with access and correction rights relating to personal information. Most importantly, the Conservative bill provided for judicial review of government decisions to refuse access. Together with the proposed legislation, the Conservative Government tabled a series of cabinet discussion papers on which the bill was said to be based, and indicated that this kind of material would be routinely made available under the proposed legislation. Although the short-lived Conservative Government fell before this legislation was enacted, there can be little doubt that the popularity of this Conservative initiative added to the pressure for some action on this question on the reelected Liberal Government.

Federal freedom of information legislation was promised by the re-elected Trudeau government in the Speech From the Throne of April 14, 1980, and ultimately, on July 17, 1980, Bill C-43, a somewhat reworked version of the earlier Conservative bill, was given first reading. The passage of the bill through the House proved to be both prolonged and controversial. Committee hearings which began in March of 1981 continued on and off for more than a year and, in early 1982, it was widely rumoured that the government would not proceed with the bill. Ultimately, however, after revising some features of the bill, C-43 was enacted on June 28, 1982...

THE NEW LAW

In its essential features, the Canadian Act is similar to American national freedom of information and privacy laws. A broad right of public access, in the sense of allowing individuals an opportunity to examine a record or obtain a copy thereof, is conferred, subject to a list of exemptions. The government is under an obligation to make reasonable efforts to sever exempt from non-exempt material and to disclose the latter. Requests for access must receive a response within a statutory time limit. Requestors may be charged fees for the cost of reproduction and, in some cases, search time. Decisions to deny access are subject to initial review by an Information Commissioner, but ultimately may be appealed to the courts, although, as will be seen, this right is restricted with respect to certain of the exemptions.

In contrast to the American legislation, the drafting style of the Canadian statute is rather prolix. The Access to Information Act ultimately will occupy some fifty-odd pages of the federal statute book. Further, there are a number of respects in which the Canadian statute departs from the American model and offers some evidence of the nature of the political culture within which it was produced. Thus, access is to be granted in either of Canada's official languages in any case where a translation of the document exists or where it is deemed to be in the public interest that a translation be made. Perhaps the most important evidence of the Canadian flavour of the statute is to be found in the provisions exempting certain records from disclosure.

Although the Canadian Act contains exemptions pertaining to international affairs and defence, records containing advice or recommendations, material withheld under other statutes, trade secrets and other confidential commercial information, solicitor-client privilege, personal information, and law enforcement records, which are roughly analagous to the first seven exemptions of the American Act, the drafting of each provision is less biased in favour of disclosure than the equivalent provision of the American Act. In addition, the Canadian Act contains a substantial number of additional exemptions, some of which reflect the peculiar nature of Canadian political institutions and some others which appear to represent attempts to learn from and improve upon American experience with access legislation. It may be useful to illustrate some of these points.

Quite apart from the exemption for material containing advice or recommendations, the Canadian Act includes a comprehensive exemption of virtually all cabinet records, including "memoranda the purpose of which is to present proposals or recommendations" to the cabinet. If broadly construed, it is obvious that the exemption of these records effects a wholesale exclusion of material, whether or not factual in nature, related to policymaking processes. Although cabinet secrecy is often defended in parliamentary jurisdictions on grounds of high constitutional principle, it is obvious that this provision simply reflects the desire of the inner circle of the government to immunize itself completely from the inconvenience and potential embarrassment of disclosures under the access scheme. The provision of the statute stipulates that the Act does not "apply" to cabinet records. Accordingly, cabinet records are not subject to the severability rule. Further, under related legislation, the government has given itself an unreviewable right to refuse to disclose cabinet records to a court. Ironically, in the course of introducing its new freedom of information scheme, the Canadian government has enacted one of the most secretive executive privilege rules to be found in the western world.

The Canadian Act also has an explicit exemption for material the disclosure of which reasonably could be expected to be injurious to the federal government's ability to conduct federal-provincial affairs. As Canadian governments at both the federal and provincial levels have long-established practices of secrecy with respect to federal-provincial dealings, it is reasonable to anticipate that much information relating to intergovernmental contact will be withheld under this provision. Although federal relations in the Canadian polity are made more difficult by the presence of a small number of very large provincial units and, at the present time, by the fact that one of these provinces, Quebec, is governed by a party committed to the separation of that province from the federal state, it is difficult to defend so comprehensive an exemption. Obviously, if broadly construed, this provision will permit the withholding of a vast and important body of government information.

The Canadian Act also contains generous exemptions relating to government proprietary information which have no counterpart in the American legislation. This no doubt reflects, in part, the much more important role played in Canada by public enterprise. Even prior to the recent and substantial intervention of public enterprise in the resources sector, the total revenue of federal and provincial Crown corporations had been estimated at approximately 10% of Canada's gross national product. The most important of the federally-chartered commercial Crown corporations simply are exempted from the new Canadian access scheme. Those few covered by the scheme, however, will find that information which they would normally treat as confidential will be quite adequately protected by appropriate exemptions.

A number of the exempting provisions included in the statute evidently constitute attempts to learn from what public officials at least would view as deficiencies in the American scheme. Thus, the exemption for law enforcement material permits, in the American manner, the withholding of information the disclosure of which could reasonably be expected to be injurious to law enforcement activities. In addition, however, the Act confers upon the government the power to exempt by regulation the investigative records of any law enforcement body. It remains to be seen which bodies will be so exempted, but it may safely be assumed that the power to exempt by regulation is the Canadian response to the practical problems encountered under the American Act by federal law enforcement and security agencies.

The disclosure of personal data concerning identifiable individuals is an obvious point of difficulty under a freedom of information scheme. The American Act exempts such data where disclosure would amount to a "clearly unwarranted invasion of personal privacy" and thus requires a balancing of the disclosure and privacy interests arising in the context of each request. The Canadian scheme approaches this problem by simply exempting almost all personal data from the access scheme, and then by conferring on the government what is essentially an unreviewable discretion to disclose personal data in the context of the new privacy protection legislation. The Canadian Act thus has avoided the alleged uncertainties of the American balancing test, but does so at the cost of transporting another rather substantial percentage of government record holdings into the realm of discretionary disclosure.

Canadian officials often have been surprised to learn that information disclosed in confidence by Canadian agencies to their American counterparts might be disclosed under the American access scheme. No reciprocal difficulty will arise under the Canadian Act, however, as a broad exemption for confidential intergovernmental disclosures has been included in the statute. The provision protects international exchanges of information as well as exchanges between various levels of government within Canada. Again, this is a provision which is capable of shielding a vast body of information in a federal state. However, it will eliminate a practical problem inherent in the American scheme which, indeed, has surfaced in the American caselaw.

In its exemption for international affairs and defence, the Canadian Act departs from the American model by explicitly setting forth the criteria for exemption in the statute itself. The American Act, it will be recalled, simply exempts material which has been classified properly by executive order. The Canadian provision is thought to be an improvement inasmuch as disclosure under the statute will operate quite independently of any classification system put in place by the executive or any changes made to the system from time to time. This benefit may be an illusory one, however, in that the American system of classification and declassification of documents has been, and probably will remain, more conducive to disclosure than the Canadian statutory provision.

A number of other minor exemptions could be mentioned, but perhaps the case has been made that the Canadian scheme appears to have been drafted in a frame of mind which essentially was sympathetic to past practices of government secrecy and confidentiality. Accordingly, it may well be that the most important features of the scheme will be those which create informal pressures in favour of disclosure. From this point of view, the office of the Information Commissioner may prove to be instrumental in any success the new legislation achieves in promoting the disclosure of government information to the public. Individuals who have been denied access may request a review of this decision by the Commissioner, who must in turn investigate the complaint and make a recommendation as to whether or not the record should be disclosed. Although the Commissioner has no power to order disclosure, extensive investigatory powers are conferred by the statute, including the power to examine any record to which the Act applies.

The role of the Information Commissioner thus will be very similar to that of the Privacy Commissioner under Part IV of The Canadian Human Rights Act. The current incumbent of the latter position, Inger Hansen, attributes much of her success in promoting access to the fact that her incapacity to make binding orders has encouraged public officials to deal with her in a more open and cooperative fashion than might be expected. One may be encouraged to hope, therefore, that the Information Commissioner under the new scheme will be able to assist in the creation of an environment within which public officials will generously construe the rights of access created by the scheme.

If the Commissioner's investigation does not result in disclosure of the requested document, the disappointed individual may pursue further appeal to the Federal Court of Canada. The Court does have the power to order disclosure, but the scope of the Court's ability to review decisions to deny access is subject to two important restrictions. First, as has been mentioned above, the Court has no power to review a decision taken by a cabinet official to refuse to disclose cabinet records. The Act is said not to "apply" to cabinet records and this, together with the fact that collateral legislation permits a Minister to exercise a unilateral right to withhold cabinet records from judicial proceedings, means that the government has retained an unreviewable discretion to classify documents as cabinet records and thereby lift them out of the statutory scheme. With respect to records covered by the statute, however, a second limitation on judicial review is imposed. In the case of five exemptions — those relating to federal-provincial relations, international affairs and defence, law enforcement, the security of penal institutions, and the financial interests of the Government of Canada — the scope of review is limited to a determination of whether or not the head of the institution refusing disclosure had "reasonable grounds" on which to refuse disclosure of the record. Thus, in the context of law enforcement for example, the Court cannot make an independent judgment as to whether or not disclosure reasonably would be expected to be injurious to law enforcement, but must defer to the decision of the public official in question if satisfied that the official had reasonable grounds for the decision to deny access. With respect to other exemptions, however, the scope of judicial review is unrestricted and will operate, presumably, more or less in the fashion that it has under the American Act.

An interesting feature of the procedures for review is that the Canadian statute confers procedural and substantive rights on so-called third parties, i.e., private individuals whose personal information is contained in a government record which the government proposes to disclose, or commercial firms whose proprietary information is the subject of a proposed disclosure. Third parties are entitled to timely notice of a decision to disclose, and may intervene in or indeed initiate review procedures at the Information Commissioner or Federal Court level. The exemptions for personal information and commercially valuable information are mandatory in the sense that the government must refuse to disclose an exempt record and third parties, therefore, have a substantive right to seek to enjoin disclosure in the Federal Court. As has been indicated above, very little personal information potentially is accessible under the Act. Access will be given only to certain basic information concerning the status of public servants and consultants and the identity of recipients of government licences and other forms of largesse. Disputes concerning access to personal data, therefore, are not likely to produce much three party litigation. In the commercial context, however, the prospects for access are much greater and the likelihood of substantial third party litigation more real. No doubt, the Federal Court of Canada will be called upon with some frequency to determine the kinds of information which, if disclosed, "could reasonably be expected to result in material financial loss or gain to, or could reasonably be expected to prejudice the competitive position of, a third party".

Apart from the conferral of access rights, the Canadian Act does impose affirmative obligations to publish certain kinds of material or otherwise make information available to members of the public. Again, however, the Canadian scheme is more modest in these respects than its American counterpart. One of the great triumphs of the American scheme, as far as administrative lawyers are concerned, is that it requires the publication and indexing of the so-called "secret law" of the federal agencies. Under the Canadian scheme, agencies are required only to make available at their headquarters any manuals used by their employees in carrying out their programmes. The statute, however, does impose an affirmative obligation to publish certain other kinds of information which will be of assistance to individuals seeking access to information under the Canadian scheme. Indeed, the rather ambitious requirement that government institutions publish "a description of all classes of records under the control of each government institution in sufficient detail to facilitate the exercise of the right of access under this Act" will impose substantial burdens on the information systems personnel of the federal government.

OVERVIEW

There can be no doubt but that the new Canadian federal freedom of information scheme contains many features which will disappoint those who have advocated legislation of this kind. However, given the structural realities of Canadian politics and the deeply-entrenched traditions of government secrecy, it must be said that it is, to some extent, remarkable that legislation of this kind has been enacted at all. Some will attribute this limited degree of success to the power of a great idea, or to the continuing vitality of democratic ideals in the Canadian political culture. Others, I suspect, will see the Canadian flirtation with freedom of informations schemes at both federal and provincial levels as enduring evidence of the profound influence of American political fashion on Canadian political life. Whatever its political root, however, and despite the fact that the Canadian embrace of the freedom of information concept does seem rather tentative, the new Canadian statute, together with its provincial counterparts, constitute, in my view, important and hopefully irreversible steps in the direction of a more open and accountable set of political institutions in Canada.

2.3.5 Provincial Access to Information Laws

Provinces that have access to information legislation are Nova Scotia, New Brunswick, Newfoundland and Quebec. As well, Ontario's legislature passed Bill 34, An Act to provide for Freedom of Information and Protection of Individual Privacy which became effective 1 January 1988.[1]

Nova Scotia enacted the first access to information legislation in Canada. An Act respecting Access by the Public to Information on File with the Government[2] was proclaimed on 11 October 1977 and in force on 1 November 1977. In this act, "access" means either the opportunity to examine an original record or the provision of a copy, at the option of the government. Unlike most access to information legislation, the Nova Scotia act does not begin with the principle that all information is available. Section 3 states that certain listed categories of information are available upon request. This includes information concerning the organization of departments. A department is any board, commission, foundation, agency, or association whose members are appointed by the legislature or under an order-in-council. Access is also permitted to information respecting the administration, rules of procedure, forms, statements of general policy, decisions of administrative tribunals, personal information pertaining to the requestor, annual reports, regulations and any amendments, revisions, or repeals. Every person is given the right, not only residents of Nova Scotia. There is no separate Privacy Act and both access and privacy are covered in one document.

Section 3 is followed by a list of exceptions in s.4, where material which would be classified as public under the previous section can be withheld. Access is not permitted to information that might reveal personal information concerning another person, result in financial gain or loss to a person or department, or that might influence negotiations in progress leading to an agreement or contract.

Access is not permitted if releasing the information might jeopardize the ability of a department to function competitively, injure relations with another government, interfere with the administration of justice, or be detrimental to the proper custody of prisoners. Material such was obtained during an investigation into violations of a statute may also be withheld. No person may acquire information that would be likely to disclose legal opinions provided to a department, privileged communications between solicitor and client on departmental business, or information likely to disclose opinions or recommendations by public servants in matters of decision by a minister of the Executive Council. Any information that would be likely to disclose draft legislation or regulations or which would probably disclose confidential information protected by law may not be released.

The Nova Scotia act has been criticized as being too restrictive for several reasons.[3] The government does not have to provide a catalogue or index of documents on file. A requestor may then find it difficult to make a precise request. The Consumer Protection Act[4] allows the registrar to disseminate information on many subjects such as methods of granting credit and practices of lenders. But a specific request under the access legislation could be denied as not falling within the provisions of s.3 of the Act, as not being precise enough, or as being information regarding another person under s.4(a).

There is no procedure for appeals to an independent body. If an individual is denied access to information following the initial application, he or she may then make a written request for the information to the deputy head of the appropriate department. The deputy head then has 15 working days to grant or deny the request. If, after the passage of 15 days, no response is received by the applicant, the request is considered to have been denied. Otherwise, a denial of a request for information must be in writing and include the reasons for the denial and a statement informing the person that he or she has a right to further appeal. The requestor may then appeal directly to the responsible minister. The minister has 30 days to review the request and must either support or overrule the denial.

If an applicant is still not satisfied, the final mode of redress is an appeal to the House of Assembly. The final decision on the release of information is made by a majority vote. The individual concerned must obtain the assistance of a member of the House to present a motion. The procedure has been described as "fallacious and inadequate"[5] and is not subject to a time limit. An appeal remains on the order paper until called by the government and does not have to be heard. A politically sensitive appeal may be denied by the government with the support of the majority of the Assembly.[6]

The restrictiveness of the Nova Scotia act has been tested by lawyer K. R. Evans in his attempt to obtain consumer information from various government departments.[7]

The information sought was not particularly important to the government and all nine requests were similar in nature. The following requests were made:

1. Names and addresses of direct sellers whose licences had been revoked, cancelled, or suspended, and those presently being investigated, together with reasons therefore, under the *Direct Sellers Licensing and Regulation Act* S.N.S. 1975, c.9.
2. Reports of inspectors on completed investigations under the *Consumer Reporting Act* S.N.S. 1973, c.4.
3. Reports of inspections of canneries, fish plants, and packaged fish products under the *Meat and Canned Foods Act* R.S.C. 1970, c.M-6.
4. Names and addresses of any cannery or fish plant which has had its licence cancelled under the *Fisheries Act*.
5. Reports of inspectors and research results under the *Amusement Services Safety Act* S.N.S. 1975, c.2.
6. The regulations and conditions used by the Board of Commissioners of Public Utilities and results of investigations under the *Gasoline and Fuel Oil Licensing Act* R.S.N.S. 1967, c.11.
7. Reports regarding purchasing information, availability of supply parts, service, delivery, etc., on the purchase of automobiles under the *Government Purchases Act* R.S.N.S. 1967, c.120.
8. Reports regarding purchasing information, availability of supplies and services on the purchase of office equipment under the *Government Purchases Act* R.S.N.S. 1967, c.120.
9. Reports of inspectors under the *Day Care Services Act* S.N.S. 1970-71, c.13.

The requested material was denied, with a broad range of reasons given. Requests 5, 7 and 8 were not classifiable under s.3. No information was available on any files for requests 2, 3 and 4. Requests 1 and 9 could contain information which might reveal personal information concerning another person. Requests 1 and 6 might have included information which would be likely to disclose information obtained during an investigation concerning violations of an enactment or the administration of justice. Lastly, request 9 concerned information not identified precisely enough.

A new Freedom of Information Bill[8] was given first reading in the Nova Scotia legislature on 6 March 1981.

The New Brunswick Right to Information Act[9] originated in 1974 with the tabling of a White Paper containing a draft bill prepared by the Cabinet Secretariat. It was retabled in 1977 in almost identical form. An ad hoc committee was created to review the proposed legislation as well as to receive suggestions and comments from interested groups and individuals. The committee was composed of members of the Law Reform Division of the Provincial Department of Justice and the Cabinet Secretariat. As a result of the findings of the committee a revised Right to Information Act was passed in the legislature and assent to on 28 June 1978. It was proclaimed in force 1 January 1980 and consolidated 1 October 1985. The Act has been viewed as thoughtful and progressive legislation.[10] It gives every person the right to request and receive information relating to the public business of the province. It applies equally to residents and non-residents. Emphasis is placed on the responsibility of ministers for policies enunciated by their departments. When the Act was proclaimed in 1980, nine exemptions to the general right of access were listed. Three more were added in 1982.[11]

There is no right to information under the Act where its release,[12]

6(a) would disclose information the confidentiality of which is protected by law;

(b) would reveal personal information, given on a confidential basis, concerning another person;

(c) would cause financial loss or gain to a person or department, or would jeopardize negotiations leading to an agreement or contract;

(c1) would reveal financial, commercial, technical, or scientific information;

(i) given by an individual or a corporation that is a going concern in connection with financial assistance applied for or given under the authority of a statute or regulation of the province, or

(ii) given in or pursuant to an agreement entered into under the authority of a statute or regulation, if the information relates to the internal management or operations of a corporation that is a going concern;

(d) would violate the confidentiality of information obtained from another government;

(e) would be detrimental to the proper custody, control or supervision of persons under sentence;

(f) would disclose legal opinions or advice provided to a person or department by a law officer of the Crown, or privileged communications as between a solicitor and client in a matter of department business;

(g) would disclose opinions or recommendations by public servants for a minister or the Executive Council;

(h) would disclose the substance of proposed legislation or regulations;

(h1) would reveal information gathered by police, including the R.C.M.P., in the course of investigating any illegal activity or suspected illegal activity, or the source of such information;

(h2) would disclose any information reported to the Attorney General or his agent with respect to any illegal activity or suspected illegal activity, or the source of such information; or

(i) would impede an investigation, inquiry or the administration of justice.

Of particular interest in the legislation is the establishment of an independent appeal mechanism to review decisions taken by ministers who deny access to government records. Some Canadian observers have expressed concern that the adoption of binding independent review, especially by the judiciary, could erode the constitutional principle of ministerial responsibility. This was the analysis in a White Paper on the topic tabled in the New Brunswick Legislative Assembly in June 1977.[13] American and Swedish experience was dismissed in the White Paper with the contention that freedom of information schemes of those jurisdictions were at odds with the parliamentary system.

Two types of appeal are provided. An applicant may refer the matter to the Provincial Ombudsman or to a judge of the Court of Queen's Bench. The Provincial Ombudsman's power is limited to investigation and making recommendations.[14] This can be an inexpensive and relatively quick method of obtaining information. The New Brunswick courts, however, are empowered to inspect documents and order the disclosure of documents to applicants. Objections to judicial review may be that the cost and inconvenience to persons seeking access to government documents is likely to place this mechanism beyond the means of many. No further appellate review beyond the Court of Queen's Bench is allowed.

The Act defines "department" broadly and couples it with a provision that the Act shall only apply to the departments specifically listed in its regulations. Yet it may be difficult for a layperson to determine whether a particular public body requires a listing separate from a particular Ministry listing. For example, the Worker's Compensation Board is not listed in the current regulations. It could nonetheless be within the Act because the Department of Labour, whose Minister is responsible to the legislature for the Board's activities is listed. Some institutional coverage is uncertain and it is difficult to determine whether the government is being consciously difficult. Notable bodies missing in the regulations are the Human Rights Commission and the Industrial Relations Board.[15]

Problems are found in the provisions of the Act setting forth exemptions from the general principle of public access to government records. The exemptions are concise, but the terms and expressions employed are vague and can pose significant problems of interpretation.[16]

Another concern relates to commercial information (s.6(c)). If the exemption is interpreted to protect commercial organizations from any disclosure of government records which may result in unfavourable publicity, then the section would risk undermining the public accountability object of the statute. In *Re Daigle*[17] the leader of the official opposition in the New Brunswick legislature sought judicial review of a decision of the minister responsible for the administration of the New Brunswick Electric Power Commission denying his request for access to a "Work Sampling Study". The material filed before Stevenson, J. included an affidavit of a Commission official that alleged public disclosure of the study would cause financial gain or loss to contractors as the assessment would become available to owners and other contractors and so influence future contracts. The application of s.6(c) was rejected on the ground that a significant basis had not been established in the evidence for a conclusion that harm would result from disclosure. Judge Stevenson stated:[18]

> It is my view, however, that the application of paragraph 6(c) of the Act — so far as the question of financial loss or gain is concerned — must be determined on a narrower ground. In my opinion, to successfully rely on that exclusion, it must be established that the loss or gain would result directly from disclosure of the information. Here the Minister relies on what can only be characterized as a speculative future gain or loss to the contractor.

Newfoundland's Act Respecting Freedom of Information[19] received royal assent on 16 June 1981 and came into force 1 January 1982 along with a separate Privacy Act. The Act states its purpose is to provide a right of access by the public to information in records of departments and to subject that right only to specifically limited exceptions. Its Schedule lists all government departments and ministries as well as some 50 governmental agencies, institutions, boards and Crown corporations. School boards and municipalities excluded. However, the Municipalities Act deals with the public's right to inspect and receive documents and records held by municipal councils. One area not covered at all is the Newfoundland school system. This was a deliberate exclusion by the government, which felt that the denominational nature of the system made government interference inappropriate.[20]

In formulating the legislation, the justice ministry reviewed the legislation of Nova Scotia and New Brunswick as well as the proposed federal acts and sought the advice of bodies such as the Newfoundland branch of the Canadian Bar Association and Memorial University. The university was instrumental in expanding the categories of persons eligible to use the Act. A draft bill had limited the right of access to Canadian citizens living in Newfoundland and corporations carrying on business within the province. The faculty association at the university objected to the limitation claiming it would prevent non-Canadian scholars and researchers from gaining information. As a result, a third category of landed immigrants living in the province was included.

The Act contains 18 sections as well as a Schedule listing the government bodies to which it applies. Section 1 and 2 provide definitions of words used within the Act while sections 3 and 4 describe its purpose and define who has a right to access. A request for information must be in writing and addressed to the minister or head of the relevant department or governmental body. The request must specify the subject matter of the information sought with a particular emphasis on time, place and event to enable its identification. If identification is not possible with the information supplied the applicant is invited to supply further details. A written reply granting, denying or referring the request to another department must be made within 30 days of its receipt. Where a request is granted the information, upon payment of the necessary fees, must be reproduced and released. There is no provision for inspection prior to reproduction. If, however, the information has already been or will be published elsewhere the applicant will be advised of this. The Act permits severability, which means that parts of documents that cannot be released may be deleted and the remainder reproduced.

Categories of information exempt from access are classified under the three headings of non-discretionary exceptions, personal information and discretionary exceptions. Section 9 contains 6 sub-sections of non-discretionary exceptions, generally referring to Cabinet documents and intergovernmental relations, as well as documents required to be kept confidential by statute. The Premier of the province may authorize the release of non-discretionary information other than that which has been obtained in confidence from other governments or is protected from release by statute.

Section 10 prohibits access to personal information. Material pertaining to racial origin, ethnicity, colour, religion, marital status, education, medical, criminal or employment history, fingerprints or blood type, personal opinions or views, correspondence of a confidential nature and views or opinions of another person about the individual concerned may not be released. This protection does not extend to civil servants as it relates to their position or functions or to information where there is a right of access under another provincial act. The section allows people to obtain information about themselves or about individuals who have given permission for the release of this type of material. Such permission must be in writing, signed, witnessed and notarized.

Section 11 contains six discretionary exceptions permitting access to information to be refused. Access to information concerning federal-provincial negotiations, law enforcement investigations, economic interests of the province, legal opinions or advice given to the government, proposed legislation and financial, commercial, scientific or technical data as it relates to a third party's financial or competitive position may be denied by a governmental head.

Sections 12 to 14 set out an appeal procedure which may take as much as 90 days to complete. If a request for information is denied or there is no reply within the appropriate time from a governmental head, an applicant may appeal to the Ombudsman. The Ombudsman shall review and investigate the matter within 30 days of receiving the referral. The Ombudsman may recommend to the head to grant the request in whole or in part and the minister or head must, within 30 days of receiving this recommendation accept or reject its contents. If an appeal is rejected both the Ombudsman and the applicant are notified as well as any third party involved. Thirty days are allowed in which to appeal to the trial division of the Supreme Court of Newfoundland.

This is a court of final appeal and it may examine any documents in camera to determine the correctness of withholding the information.

While the request and appeal procedures are reasonably uncomplicated when two parties are involved, it is more complex when a third person or party is affected. If the information might harm a third party's interests, the minister or head is required to notify that party that it has received an information request. The notice includes a description of the information and informs the party it has 20 days to make representations as to why the information should not be disclosed. If the third party objects to the release of information the minister has a further 30 days to rule on the objection and then must give the third party a written decision. That decision must again include a notice that the party has another 20 days to ask for a review of the decision. If no request for a review is made the information is disclosed. Appeals to the Ombudsman or the court involving a third party must also be directed to the third party.

On 6 May 1982, Jean-François Bertrand, Minister of Communications tabled in the Quebec National Assembly An Act Respecting Access to Documents Held in Public Bodies and the Protection of Personal Information.[21] It was passed on 21 June 1982 with the unanimous assent of the Assembly. The Act provides for both access to information and the protection of personal information held by public bodies. It applies to all provincial public bodies and all recorded information, but not to government drafts, personal notes or working papers. Public bodies include government agencies, municipal and school boards, health and social service agencies as well as institutions of higher learning where more than half of the operating expenses are paid for by the provincial government. Public bodies must organize their documents in a manner conducive to their retrieval and maintain up-to-date classification schemes sufficiently precise to allow access. Every public body is required to name a person in charge of implementation of the Act. Access to information is free of charge, although a fee may be paid for costs of reproducing documents. Documents may be examined on the premises during working hours.

Limitations on access are mandatory and non-mandatory. Information regarding the administration of justice and public security cannot be released if likely to impede the progress of judicial proceedings, cause prejudice, reveal information, hamper an investigation, reveal an investigative method, endanger a person's safety, facilitate the escape of a prisoner or reveal a communications system used in law enforcement. Restrictions that are open to interpretation by a head may be regarding material received from a government other than that of Quebec, its agency or an international organization. If such information would likely be detrimental to any government or international organization its release may be restricted. A public body may refuse to release information if its disclosure would likely impede negotiations in progress with another public body in a field with their competitors. Information may also be withheld if it involves an industrial secret, if it concerns a transaction where disclosure would likely benefit or seriously harm a person, or have a serious adverse effect on the economic interests of the public body or persons under its jurisdiction. A public body may also refuse to release information it controls if disclosure of the information might hamper negotiation of a contract or result in financial loss for itself or gain for another person. Information can be withheld if its disclosure would likely reduce the competitive margin of a public body.

In some circumstances, a third party must consent to the release of information. A third party is entitled to receive notice by mail within 20 days of the request. This party is invited to submit written observations concerning the material requested.

The protection of privacy extends to the confidentiality of nominative information. Information in any document which allows a person to be identified is nominative. All nominative information is confidential unless the person the information concerns authorizes its disclosure. Exceptions to the rule include disclosures to the attorney of the public body if the information is required to prosecute someone for an offence against an act applicable in Quebec or to any law enforcement officers in the course of their duties. Confidential information may be released for urgent health or safety reasons. It may be released to the *archives nationales* and the *Bureau de la statistique du Québec* according to law.

Everyone who collects nominative information must state the name and address of the body on whose behalf it is being collected, the use to which the information is to be put and categories of persons who may have access to it. Persons have the right to access to their own nominative information, but there are some restrictions and a right of correction exists unless the public body can prove that the file does not warrant correction.

An Access Commission is established by the Act and consists of three members appointed to five-year terms by the National Assembly upon a motion by the Prime Minister and approved by at least a two-thirds vote. A similar vote is required for the dismissal of a member. The Commission has various duties and powers concerning the rights, issuing, standards, interpretation and investigation of complaints regarding access to information. It must also publish and distribute at least every two years an index of all files held by public bodies.

Public bodies must obtain a license for the collection of personal information and register with the Access Commission. Such licences are renewable and initially valid for five years. Every public body must ensure that personal information is kept as current, accurate and relevant as possible.

The government may by order authorize a public body to establish a confidential file. This is a different file and usually concerns law enforcement. Any order establishing, amending or cancelling a confidential file must be tabled in the National Assembly.

The Quebec act contains review and appeal provisions. Any person denied access may appeal in writing to the Access Commission for a review of the decision. Reviews may also be requested regarding the amount of time taken in a request for information search or a fee charged for processing the request. The Commission has a right of access to all information. It can order a public body to release a document, or correct, delete or discontinue the use or release of personal information. Both the public body and the applicant can appeal a decision of the Commission to the Provincial Court. Penalties for knowingly impeding or denying access to information where access is not to be denied include a maximum fine of $1,000 and anyone who knowingly releases material that was not permitted to be released may be fined up to $2,500. A person harmed by a decision of a public body to release information concerning him or her may seek compensation from the Superior Court.

In March of 1977, the Ontario government established a Commission on Freedom of Information and Individual Privacy. Its purpose was to study and report to the Attorney General of Ontario ways and means to improve public information policies. Public information practices of other jurisdictions were examined, as were right of access and appeal, ways of categorizing information, effectiveness of present procedures and the protection of individual privacy and the right of recourse in regard to the use of government records. The Commission released its final report titled *Public Government for Private People*[22] in September 1980. In the intervening period the Commission invited briefs from members of the public, conducted hearings in various centres of the province and mounted a substantial campaign of research and investigation.[23] The general legislation recommended by the Commission was to follow the American form of a broad right to access of information by the public subject to specified limitations. This included an appeal process where an independent arbiter could make a binding decision. The Commission concluded that some exceptions to access were in accord with constitutional traditions, but not inconsistent with the enactment of an access law. The commonly accepted rationales of access to information legislation — improving the mechanisms of public accountability and of government, encouraging informed debate and participation in decision-making, encouraging the fairness of decision-making affecting individuals and protecting privacy interests — were put forward.

Ontario enacted its Act to Provide for Freedom of Information and Protection of Individual Privacy in 1987.[24]

A request for information must be made in writing and should provide sufficient information about the document so that an experienced employee, with reasonable effort, can identify it. If the request has been forwarded to the wrong department or agency, the recipient must transfer the request and notify the applicant of the correct location of the document. Once a request is received, the institution must make a decision to grant or deny access within 30 days. This period can be extended in a narrow range of situations such as where the request involves a large number of records. The Lieutenant-Governor-in-Council must annually publish a compilation listing all institutions. The document must specify where a request for information should be made, where general indexes of institutions have been made available and whether an institution has a library or reading room available for public use. A head of an institution may delete restricted information but must include notice of the deletion.

The Act lists exemptions to the right of access. A head will refuse to disclose a record if it reveals Cabinet records which the Executive Council have not agreed to permit the release of. Some recommendations made to the government by public servants may be withheld. A head may deny access to material if its disclosure could reasonably be expected to interfere with law enforcement or an investigation. Law enforcement reports may also be withheld. If the disclosure of a document could reasonably prejudice relations with other governments or reveal confidential information from an international organization it may be withheld. Records which may, upon publication, prejudice the defence of Canada, disclose third-party information such as a trade secret, scientific, technical, commercial or financial information or disclose economic and other interests in Ontario may as well be withheld. A head can refuse to reveal information subject to solicitor-client privilege. A head shall not allow access to personal information to anyone other than the person to whom the information relates except under specific limited circumstances. A disclosure of personal information is presumed to constitute an invasion of privacy unless it refers to the classification, salary range and benefits or employment responsibilities of a public servant, discloses financial or other details of a contract for personal services between an individual and an institution or documents details of some licence, permit or similar financial benefit conferred on an individual by an institution. In this situation the individual must represent one per cent or more of all persons and organizations in Ontario receiving a similar benefit.

Part III of the Act concerns protection of individual privacy and the collection and retention of personal information. Part IV establishes an appeal process. The Commission had recommended establishment of review mechanisms pertaining to a department's or agency's granting or denial of access to records. Individuals denied access to information may appeal any decision. However, the exercise of the discretion of a head to disclose or refuse to disclose information found to be included under a listed exemption cannot be appealed. An appeal has to be made within 30 days after notice has been given to the requestor. Upon receiving a notice of appeal, the Commissioner must inform the head of the institution concerned and any affected parties. The Commissioner may authorize a mediator to investigate the circumstances of any appeal and try to effect a settlement. Should this be impossible, the Commissioner must conduct an inquiry to review the head's decision. This inquiry may be conducted in private. The onus in an inquiry is on the head to prove that a report falls within one of the specified exemptions. After all of the evidence has been received, the Commissioner must make an order disposing of the issues raised by the appeal. The order can contain any terms and conditions the Commissioner considers appropriate.

The Ontario Act contains specific offences. No person can wilfully disclose information in contravention of the Act, wilfully maintain a data bank that contravenes the Act, or obtain personal information under false pretences. Persons found guilty of any of these offences are liable to a fine not exceeding $2,000.

Endnotes

1. 2nd Session, 33 Legislature, Ontario, 35 Elizabeth II, 1986.
2. S.N.S., Ch. 10.
3. Maureen A. Mancuso, ''Nova Scotia's Freedom of Information Act of 1977 and the Bill of 1981'', *Canada's New Access Laws: Public and Personal Access to Government Documents,* ed., Donald C. Rowat, (Ottawa: Carleton University, 1983) pp. 57-75.
4. R.S.N.S. 1967, c.53, s.3(d).
5. ''Nova Scotia Freedom of Information Act of 1977 and the Bill of 1981'', p. 64.
6. Tom Riley, ''Freedom of Information: The Nova Scotia Law'', *Civil Service Review 50,* 3 September 1977, p. 29.
7. Evans, K.R., ''Nova Scotia Freedom of Information Act,'' (1979) 5 *Dal. L.J.* 494.
8. Bill 40, 3rd Session, 52 General Assembly, Nova Scotia 30 Elizabeth II, 1981.
9. S.N.B., 1978, c.R-10.3.
10. James B. Rule, ''Comment'', *Freedom of Information: Canadian Perspectives,* ed., John McCamus, (Toronto: Butterworths, 1981), p. 29.
11. S.6(c) as amended by S.N.B., 1982, c.58.
12. S.6, S.N.B. 1982, c.58.

13. New Brunswick, *Freedom of Information: Outline of Government Policy Pertaining to a Legislated Right of Access by the Public to Government Documents.* (Fredericton: Legislative Assembly of New Brunswick [the Premier]. Tabled June 1977).
14. R.S.N.B. 1973 Co. 5 as amended by S.N.B. 1976, c.43; 1979 c.41.
15. New Brunswick Regulations 1985, Vol. 11, 68-85.
16. James B. Rule, ''Comment''.
17. (1980) 30 N.B.R. (2nd) 209.
18. *In Re Daigle* (1980) 30 N.B.R. (2nd) 209 at p. 216.
19. 1981, Ch. 5.
20. Debates of the House of Assembly, Province of Newfoundland and Labrador, 19 March, 20 March, 9 April, 18 June, 1981, pp. 3099-3100.
21. 1982, ch. A21.
22. Toronto, Queen's Printer, 1980.
23. McCamus, John D., ''The Report of the Ontario Commission on Freedom of Information and Individual Privacy: A Synopsis'', *Freedom of Information: Canadian Perspectives,* (Toronto: Butterworths, 1981), p. 307.
24. S.O. 1987, c.25.

2.4 Public Order and Criminal Libel

2.4.1 A Note on Criminal Libel

Criminal libel embraces a range of offences against the state and the public order. Technically, it includes seditious libel, defamatory libel, blasphemous libel and obscene libel. The first two of these are included in this chapter because of the manner in which they might still be used to protect institutions of state such as the legislatures, Parliament or the courts.

Although each has played an important role in limiting freedom of expression, the law of seditious libel has played the most central role in the emergence of free political expression. As that law has declined in importance there has been a corresponding growth in toleration for political opposition.

The law of seditious libel used to have two functions. The first of these was to punish incitements to riot or incitements to commit acts which would disturb the public order. The current Canadian hate propaganda law expresses some of the spirit of the traditional law in the sections referring to advocating genocide or the killing of a group defined by ethnic, linguistic or racial characteristics.

The modern law of seditious libel continues to restrict speech which incites riots, but as will be seen in the *Boucher* case, the Supreme Court of Canada has interpreted the law so as to broaden free expression by requiring a disturbance or a crime against the state as a planned outcome of the seditious words.

The second function of the law of seditious libel, as with its civil counterpart, was to protect the reputation of state institutions. In its earlier incarnations, the law incorporated a belief that opinions — however calmly and deliberately expressed — which condemned the established political and social order were dangerous. The notions of treason and seditious libel were blurred for most of the seventeenth and eighteenth centuries. There was a belief, often expressed by eighteenth-century judges, that if the people were allowed to read material which would predispose them to dislike governing institutions, then the whole social and political order would eventually collapse.

That idea has not completely disappeared and if the vestiges of it are no longer serious parts of the modern law of seditious libel, expressions of it may be found here and there in twentieth-century Canadian history. For example, section 98 of the old Criminal Code prohibited membership in certain organizations including the Communist Party. A parallel sentiment was expressed in the case of *Switzman* v. *Elbling and the Attorney-General of Quebec* in which the Quebec Padlock law was at issue. That law prohibited the circulation of Communist material in Quebec from 1937 until 1957 when it was finally ruled *ultra vires* by the Supreme Court of Canada.

As will be seen below, the part of the law of contempt of court called "scandalizing the court" is equally a vestige of the old notion of seditious libel. That law renders criminal disrespectful and aggressively expressed condemnations of judges or the courts.

That the law of seditious libel has been central to the history of English and Canadian democracy can be seen by a consideration of the manner in which the law changed between the seventeenth century and the twentieth. During the seventeenth and eighteenth centuries in England it was a crime to promote disaffection against the Monarch and his or her heirs, the Government, Parliament, the administration of justice, the Constitution or the State. It was, for example, libellous in the eighteenth century to argue that the Glorious Revolution of 1688 and the end of the Stuart monarchy were unhappy events.

The law of seditious libel has gone through four distinctive phases. The first involved licensing. Printing came of age in the seventeenth century and for most of it there was a licensing act in place to prevent seditious (or blasphemous) libel from being committed. Those in power in England were so afraid of the effects of printing that they set up a licensing authority which empowered political and church authorities to examine all materials published for public circulation. These authorities exercised what the Americans now call 'prior restraint'. (We continue to examine films for obscene content in all Canadian provinces.) The end of licensing in 1695 marked the beginning of a second stage which lasted until 1792 when Fox's Libel Act was passed.

Stage two is a period during which the law was severely applied, but was constantly challenged and to some degree modified. The modifications came partly as a result of changes in attitude toward the importance and danger of seditious libel, but more so because the various oppositions to the ministries of the eighteenth century were able to challenge and eventually remove a set of legal instruments and devices associated with policing and prosecuting printers and writers.

When Fox's Libel Act was passed in 1792 the last trace of the special methods of applying the law, which had been conceived and elaborated during the licensing period, was removed. Until that act was passed, juries had very little to do in trials for libel. They could establish that the authorities had brought the right person to trial — that, for example, the accused actually wrote or published the material alleged to be criminal — and they could also rule on the meaning of the words. But it was the judge alone who decided whether the materials were libellous. Fox's Libel Act changed the role of juries and gave them the right to rule on the larger question of libel.

The third stage is marked by the absence of special legal instruments. From 1792 on, there was just a law — seriously and severely applied, but supported by conventional means of police and prosecution. It was sometimes harshly applied, especially in the period just before 1832. There was much radical publishing during that period and as a consequence many prosecutions. This stage of the law's evolution lasted through the nineteenth century and into the twentieth.

If rough measures are taken, the fourth stage is the period during the twentieth century when the law becomes relatively innocuous — when, for example, it becomes impossible to libel the State (with the exception of the courts). When the lawmakers had absorbed the idea that the State and its officials had to earn their reputations rather than compel them, the legal system expressed finally an idea which had had support in the eighteenth century. Still, it should be recognized that states are tempted occasionally to restore some of the ideas contained in the traditional law of seditious libel. They are sometimes tempted to criminalize political opinions, the purposes of which are to alter radically the political system or social order.

2.4.2 Criminal Code, ss.59-62 (seditious libel)

Sedition

Seditious words

59. (1) Seditious words are words that express a seditious intention.

Seditious libel

(2) A seditious libel is a libel that expresses a seditious intention.

Seditious conspiracy

(3) A seditious conspiracy is an agreement between two or more persons to carry out a seditious intention.

Seditious intention

(4) Without limiting the generality of the meaning of the expression "seditious intention", every one shall be presumed to have a seditious intention who

(*a*) teaches or advocates, or

(*b*) publishes or circulates any writing that advocates,

the use, without the authority of law, of force as a means of accomplishing a governmental change within Canada.

Exception

60. Notwithstanding subsection 59(4), no person shall be deemed to have a seditious intention by reason only that he intends, in good faith,

(*a*) to show that Her Majesty has been misled or mistaken in her measures;

(*b*) to point out errors or defects in

(i) the government or constitution of Canada or a province,

(ii) the Parliament of Canada or the legislature of a province, or

(iii) the administration of justice in Canada;

(*c*) to procure, by lawful means, the alteration of any matter of government in Canada; or

(*d*) to point out, for the purpose of removal, matters that produce or tend to produce feelings of hostility and ill-will between different classes of persons in Canada.

Punishment of seditious offences

61. Every one who

(*a*) speaks seditious words,

(*b*) publishes a seditious libel, or

(*c*) is a party to a seditious conspiracy,

is guilty of an indictable offence and is liable to imprisonment for fourteen years.

Offences in relation to military forces

62. (1) Every one who wilfully

(*a*) interferes with, impairs or influences the loyalty or discipline of a member of a force,

(*b*) publishes, edits, issues, circulates or distributes a writing that advises, counsels or urges insubordination, disloyalty, mutiny or refusal of duty by a member of a force, or

(*c*) advises, counsels, urges or in any manner causes insubordination, disloyalty, mutiny or refusal of duty by a member of a force,

is guilty of an indictable offence and is liable to imprisonment for five years.

"Member of a force"

(2) In this section, "member of a force" means a member of

(*a*) the Canadian Forces, or

(*b*) the naval, army or air forces of a state other than Canada that are lawfully present in Canada.

2.4.3 *Boucher* v. *The King* (1950) 1 D.L.R. 657 (S.C.C.)

KERWIN, J.: The question of seditious libel is always one of great delicacy, requiring from the trial Judge an instruction distinctly drawing to the attention of the jury the various elements that must be found before they may convict of the offence charged and applying the law to the evidence in the record. I agree with the Chief Justice that this was not done in the present case. The main element which it was necessary for the jury to find was an intention on the part of the accused to incite the people to violence or to create a public disturbance or disorder: *Reg.* v . *Burns, supra: Reg.* v. *Sullivan* (1868), 11 Cox C.C. 44; *R.* v. *Aldred* (1909), 22 Cox C.C. 1; *The King* v. *Caunt,* not reported but referred to in a note in 64 L.Q. Rev. 203. The use of strong words is not by itself sufficient nor is the likelihood that readers of the pamphlet in St. Joseph de Beauce would be annoyed or even angered, but the question is, was the language used calculated to promote public disorder or physical force or violence. In coming to a conclusion on this point, a jury is entitled to consider the state of society or, as it is put by Chief Justice Wilde in his charge to the jury in *The Queen* v. *Fussell* (1848), 6 St. Tr. (N.S.) 723 at p. 762:

"You cannot, as it seems to me, form a correct judgment of how far the evidence tends to establish the crime imputed to the defendant, without bringing into that box with you a knowledge of the present state of society, because the conduct of every individual in regard to the effect which that conduct is calculated to produce, must depend upon the state of the society in which he lives. That may be innocent in one state of society, because it may not tend to disturb the peace or to interfere with the right of the community, which at another time, and in a different state of society, in consequence of its different tendency, may be open to just censure."

This, it should be noted, was said at a trial at the Central Criminal Court before the Chief Justice, Baron Parke and Maule J. An instruction to the same effect was given in *Reg.* v. *Burns, supra,* by Cave J., of whose charge it is stated generally, at p. 88 of the 9th edition of Russell on Crime, that the present view of the law is best stated therein. Reference might also be made to the words of Coleridge J. in his charge to the jury in the later case of *R.* v. *Aldred,* 22 Cox C.C. 1 at p. 3: "You are entitled also to take into account the state of public feeling. Of course there are times when a spark will explode a powder magazine; the effect of language may be very different at one time from what it would be at another."

While the jury must consider the question of good faith in accordance with s.133A of our Code, it will be noticed that that section specifically states that no one shall be deemed to have a seditious intention *only* because he intends in good faith to show or point out the matters mentioned. The jury should be charged that if they find good faith on the part of the accused, and if in their opinion there is nothing more in the case, the accused is entitled to an acquittal; but, if in addition to that good faith, there was an intention on the part of the accused to create public disorder or promote physical force, or that notwithstanding the motives of the accused the natural tendency of the words (and therefore the intention) was to create such disturbances, then they would be entitled to find a verdict of guilty.

The decision of the Judicial Committee in *Wallace-Johnson* v. *The King,* [1940] A.C. 231, is not of assistance as there it was held merely that the provisions of the Gold Coast Criminal Code were clear and unambiguous and intended to contain as far as possible a full and complete statement of the law of sedition in the Colony, and that, therefore, the English common law as expounded in the *Burns* case was inapplicable. Nor are the quoted decisions in the Supreme and other Courts of the United States of any real help. Many of them deal with the "clear and present danger" doctrine in construing statutes with reference to the applicability of the First and Fourteenth Amendments to the Federal Constitution and all depend upon that Constitution and laws which are alleged to infringe its provisions. It is strictly unnecessary to consider Létourneau C.J.'s dissent that the trial Judge did not charge the jury sufficiently or properly on the question of reasonable doubt but even if the dissent be not well founded, the charge in this respect exhibits the very minimum that could be held to be sufficient and is not to be recommended.

There was evidence in the document itself, taken, as it must be, with all the other circumstances, upon which a jury after a proper charge as outlined above, could find the accused guilty, and the conviction should, therefore, be set aside and a new trial directed.

TASCHEREAU J.: — The appellant has been charged of seditious libel under s.133 of the *Code*. He was found guilty by a jury at St. Joseph de Beauce, P.Q. and sentenced to one month in jail. The Court of Appeal confirmed this verdict; Létourneau C.J. and Galipeault J., who dissented, would have ordered a new trial.

The appellant who is a Witness of Jehovah, resides at Ste. Germaine, County of Dorchester, P.Q. and it is not contested that during the month of December, 1946, at St. Joseph de Beauce, he distributed a pamphlet entitled "Quebec's burning hate for God and Christ and Freedom, is the shame of all Canada". The publishers are the "Watch Tower Bible and Tract Society of Toronto", and it is in evidence that over 1,500,000 copies were printed in English, French and Ukrainian.

Amongst other things, this pamphlet contains the following statements:

"Before the hot denials and protests and false countercharges boom out from the priestly keepers of Quebec Province and whip up an unreasonable frenzy, calmly and soberly and with clear mental faculties reason on the evidence presented in support of the above-headlined indictment...

"Did the parish priests that have stood by and approvingly witnessed such outrages show regard or disregard for Christian principles? And what about Quebec's law-making bodies that frame mischief by law to "get" those not favored by the ruling elements? and her police forces that allow mobsters to riot unchecked while they arrest the Christian victims, sometimes for no more than distributing Bibles or leaflets with Bible quotations... and what of her judges that impose heavy fines and prison sentences against them and heap abusive language upon them, and deliberately follow a malicious policy of again and again postponing cases to tie up tens of thousands of dollars in exorbitant bails and keep hundreds of cases pending?...

"In a torrential downpour all the foregoing violences and injustices rain down daily upon Jehovah's witnesses in Quebec province.... Such deeds are the outgrowth of burning hate, and cause the finger of shame to point to Canada... Not satisfied with throwing tomatoes and potatoes and rocks, this time the Catholic hoodlums added to the bombardment cucumbers, rotten eggs and *human excrement!*...

"All the French Canadian courts were so under priestly thumbs that they affirmed the infamous sentence, and it was not until the case reached the Supreme Court of Canada that judgment was reversed...

"All well informed persons in Canada grant that Quebec province with its 86-percent-Catholic population is under church-and-state rule. In the Quebec legislature the crucifix is placed above the Speaker's Chair, and in the Quebec Parliament buildings alongside the throne of the lieutenant-governor of Quebec is installed a throne for the cardinal. It was reportedly the cardinal who instigated the notorious Padlock Act, supposedly against a mere handful of Communists, but which Act left "Communist" undefined so that anyone not suiting the priests and their puppet politicians could be prosecuted. The Act was used against Jehovah's witnesses....

"All the facts unite to thunderously declare that the force behind Quebec's suicidal hate is priest domination. Thousands of Quebec Catholics are so blinded by the priests that they think they serve God's cause in mobbing Jehovah's witnesses...

"Quebec Catholics will show love for God and Christ and freedom not only by words but also by righteous deeds. They will join with the many thousands of other Quebec people, Catholic and Protestant and non-religious, that have vigorously protested the wicked treatment meted out to Jehovah's witnesses in that benighted, priest-ridden province....

"Quebec, Jehovah's witnesses are telling all Canada of the shame you have brought on the nation by your evil deeds. In English, French and Ukrainian languages this leaflet is broadcasting your delinquency to the nation. You claim to serve God; you claim to be for freedom. Yet if freedom is exercised by those who disagree with you, you crush freedom by mob rule and gestapo tactics.... Quebec, you have yielded yourself as an obedient servant of religious priests, and you have brought forth bumper crops of evil fruits."

The Crown contends that these statements were calculated to disturb the tranquillity of the State, by creating *ill-will* between different classes of the King's subjects. The main ground of dissent in the Court below, is that there has been misdirection and also non-direction by the trial Judge on such essential points, that the accused did not get a fair trial. Létourneau C.J. with whom Galipeault J. concurred, without further elaborating said in his dissenting judgment [p. 120]: "According to the usual procedure in every jury trial, the learned Judge had the duty of defining and explaining the offence that was charged, and particularly what was or might be a *seditious libel* and *seditious intention,* first in a general way and afterwards in view of the circumstances of the case: the meaning and the import of the sections of the *Criminal Code* relating to *seditious libel*."

The learned Chief Justice was obviously dissatisfied with the definition of seditious libel given at the trial by Savard J., who told the jury that a seditious libel was "the publication or distribution of a pamphlet, or of a harmful, injurious writing which may provoke hate and discord amongst the different classes of His Majesty's subjects." (translation)

Mr. Stein for the appellant strongly argued that this definition is quite insufficient, and that another essential element of the crime of seditious libel is that there should be an incitation to violence, disorder or the commission of unlawful acts, before there may be a seditious libel or a seditious intent.

The appellant does not seriously dispute that the definition given by Savard J. is in accordance with the law as it was formerly, but submits that in our modern times, it is quite antiquated. The freedom of speech and of press and of worship, which is secured to the people of this country would exclude, according to the appellant, from the offence of seditious libel any and all statements which merely stir up or tend to stir up "ill-will" or "hostility" between His Majesty's subjects.

The pertinent sections of the Criminal Code are ss.133 and 133A, which read as follows:

"133(1) Seditious words are words expressive of a seditious intention.

"(2) A seditious libel is a libel expressive of a seditious intention.

"(3) A seditious conspiracy is an agreement between two or more persons to carry into execution a seditious intention.

"(4) Without limiting the generality of the meaning of the expression 'seditious intention' everyone shall be presumed to have a seditious intention who publishes, or circulates any writing, printing or document in which it is advocated, or who teaches or advocates, the use, without the authority of law, of force, as a means of accomplishing any governmental change within Canada."

"133A. No one shall be deemed to have a seditious intention only because he intends in good faith, —

"(*a*) to show that His Majesty has been misled or mistaken in his measures; or

"(*b*) to point out errors or defects in the government or constitution of the United Kingdom, or of any part of it, or of Canada or any province thereof, or in either House of Parliament of the United Kingdom or of Canada, or in any legislature, or in the administration of justice; or to excite His Majesty's subjects to attempt to procure, by lawful means, the alteration of any matter in the state; or

"(*c*) to point out, in order to their removal, matters which are producing or have a tendency to produce feelings of hatred and ill-will between different classes of His Majesty's subjects."

These sections were undoubtedly inspired by arts. 114 and 115 of Stephen's Digest on Criminal Law, as they read at the time of the drafting of our Code in 1892. They were as follows:

Article 114

Seditious Intention Defined

"A seditious intention is an intention to bring into hatred or contempt, or to excite disaffection against the person of, His Majesty, his heirs or successors, or the government and constitution of the United Kingdom, as by law established, or either House of Parliament, or the administration of justice, or to excite His Majesty's subjects to attempt otherwise than by lawful means, the alteration of any matter in Church or State by law established, or to incite any person to commit any crime in disturbance of the peace, *or to raise discontent or disaffection amongst His Majesty's subjects, or to promote feelings of ill-will and hostility between different classes of such subjects.*

"An intention to show that His Majesty has been misled or mistaken in his measures, or to point out errors or defects in the government or constitution as by law established, with a view to their reformation, or to excite His Majesty's subjects to attempt by lawful means the alteration of any matter in Church or State by law established, or to point out, in order to their removal, matters which are producing, or have a tendency to produce, feelings of hatred and ill-will between classes of His Majesty's subjects, is not a seditious intention.

Article 115

Presumption as to Intention

"In determining whether the intention with which any words were spoken, any document was published, or any agreement was made, was or was not seditious, every person must be deemed to intend the consequences which would naturally follow from his conduct at the time and under the circumstances in which he so conducted himself.''

It seems clear that these definitions given by Stephen were, at the time his Digest was published, a complete statement of the law of England.

Russell on Crime, 9th ed., vol. 1, p. 87 defines sedition as follows:

''SEDITION consists in acts, words, or writings intended or calculated, under the circumstances of the time, to disturb the tranquillity of the State, by creating ill-will, discontent, disaffection, hatred, or contempt towards the person of the King, or towards the Constitution or Parliament or the Government, or the established institutions of the country, *or by exciting ill-will between different classes of the King's subjects,* or encouraging any class of them to endeavour to disobey, defy, or subvert the laws or resist their execution, or to create tumults or riots, or to do any act of violence or outrage or endangering the public peace.

''When the offence is committed by means of writing, or print, or pictures, it is termed seditious libel.''

If any further authority is needed, *vide:* Archbold's Criminal Pleading, Evidence and Practice, 28th ed., p. 1139; Harris, Criminal Law, 14th ed., p. 39.

Nowhere do we find that incitation to violence is a necessary element of the crime, as suggested by counsel for the appellant, and our Canadian Courts have always accepted that view as being the true meaning of ss.133 and 133A of the *Code*.

In *R.* v. *Felton* (1915), 28 D.L.R. 372, 25 Can. C.C. 207, 9 A.L.R. 238, the Supreme Court of Alberta decided that [D.L.R. and Can. C.C. headnote]: ''Under Cr. Code secs. 132 and 134, it is an indictable offence to speak seditious words, *i.e.*, words expressive of a seditious intention, and a conviction will be sustained if the words were a slander on the British Government and were uttered either with the intent of *raising disaffection and discontent among His Majesty's subjects,* or with intent to promote public disorder by insulting and annoying the hearers so that a breach of the peace is a probable consequence.''

In *R.* v. *Cohen* (1916), 28 D.L.R. 74 at p. 76, 25 Can. C.C. 302 at p. 305, 9 A.L.R. 329, Stuart J., with whom Scott and Beck JJ. concurred, speaking for the Supreme Court of Alberta, said: ''Therefore on the whole I think there was evidence presented to the jury from which they could, if they saw fit, infer that the words used were likely to cause disaffection among His Majesty's subjects *and to stir up ill-will and hostility between different classes of His Majesty's subjects.*''

It might also be useful to refer to *R.* v. *Trainut*, (1916), 33 D.L.R. 658 at pp. 664-5, 27 Can. C.C. 232 at pp. 239-40, 10 A.L.R. 164, where the majority of the same Court said:

''So with sedition, it is not the disloyalty of the heart that the law forbids. Neither is it the utterance of a word or two which merely reveal the existence of such disloyalty that the law can punish under the name of sedition. It is the utterance of words which are expressive of an intention to bring into hatred or contempt, or to excite disaffection against, the person of His Majesty or the government and constitution of the country, to excite people to attempt otherwise than by lawful means the alteration of any matter in the state by law established, *to raise discontent and disaffection among His Majesty's subjects, or to promote feelings of ill-will and hostility between different classes of His Majesty's subjects.'*

''These are the words of the English draft Code, and *the Commissioners said it was as near a definition of the law as they could make.*''

In the case of *Duval* v. *The King* (1938), 64 Que. K.B. 270, the Court of Appeal of the Province of Quebec decided that a conviction should not be disturbed, "if there is any evidence in the record which would justify the jury in coming to the conclusion that the words complained of in the pamphlets are seditious and that the natural consequence of the distribution of the pamphlets was to excite contempt for His Majesty's Government or to bring the administration of the law into contempt and impair its functions or to disturb the tranquillity of the state by *creating ill-will, discontent, disaffection, hatred or contempt towards the established institutions of the country.*" [headnote]

Many other judgments and authors could also be cited where the same definition of sedition would be found, and which would show that ss.133, 133A of the *Code* have been inspired by Stephen's Digest, and that the definition therein given is the one that has been accepted by the Courts of this country.

A case also decided in England is the case of *Reg*. v. *Burns and others,* who were indicted for unlawfully and maliciously uttering seditious words of and concerning Her Majesty's Government with an intent to incite to riot, and, in other counts, *with intent to stir up ill-will between Her Majesty's subjects* and for conspiring together to effect the said objects. This case was heard at the Central Criminal Court before Cave J., and it is reported in 16 Cox C.C. 355. At p. 363, Cave J. told the jury: "And, although as a judge I can tell you no more than that, that the intention to *incite ill-will amongst the different classes of Her Majesty's subjects may be seditious, and that is for you to decide.*"

Some recent judgments in England seem to go further, and support the appellant's view, but I do not think that they settle the law of this country. I am quite satisfied, there being no definition in our Code, of sedition and seditious libel, that it was clearly intended by Parliament to accept the English common law definition as it existed in 1892.

Of course, in Canada, the English criminal law applies in certain cases, but, it is easily understood that the English jurisprudence cannot be considered as the law of this land, if it does conflict with the text or the spirit of our Code.

In *Wallace-Johnson* v. *The King,* [1940] A.C. 231, which was an appeal from the West African Court of Appeal, the Judicial Committee of the Privy Council accepted the definition of sedition as found in the Code of that country, and as that definition was clear, their Lordships found that *incitement to violence was not a necessary ingredient of the crime of sedition,* and that the Criminal Code nowhere required proof from the words themselves of any intention to produce such a result. Speaking for the Committee, Viscount Caldecote L.C., after citing ss.(8) (para. 6) of s.330, which reads as follows: " 'A seditious intention' is an intention to promote feelings of ill-will and hostility between different classes of the population of the Gold Coast", said at pp. 239-40:

"The present case, however, arose in the Gold Coast Colony, and the law applicable is contained in the Criminal Code of the Colony. It was contended that the intention of the Code was to reproduce the law of sedition as expounded in the cases to which their Lordships' attention was called. Undoubtedly the language of the section under which the appellant was charged lends some colour to this suggestion. There is a close correspondence at some points between the terms of the section in the Code and the statement of the English law of sedition by Stephen J. in the Digest of Criminal Law, 7th ed., arts. 123-126, quoted with approval by Cave J. in his summing up on *Reg.*

v. *Burns and others* (1886), 16 Cox C.C. 355 at pp. 359-60. The fact remains, however, that it is in the Criminal Code of the Gold Coast Colony, and not in English or Scottish cases, that the law of sedition for the Colony is to be found. The Code was no doubt designed to suit the circumstances of the people of the Colony. The elaborate structure of s.330 suggests that it was intended to contain, as far as possible, a full and complete statement of the law of sedition in the Colony. It must, therefore be construed in its application to the facts of this case free from any glosses or interpolations derived from any expositions, however authoritative, of the law of England or of Scotland."

And further, at pp. 240-1. His Lordship proceeds: "Nowhere in the section is there anything to support the view that *incitement to violence* is a necessary ingredient of the crime of sedition."

I, of course, fully appreciate that these views may to a certain extent curtail the liberty of the press and the right to free speech, but the powers of this Court do not extend beyond the interpretation of the laws as enacted by Parliament. Here, of course, is not the proper forum where they may be amended.

Although I do not agree with what has been said on this question by my brother Kerwin, I fully concur with him on the other points he has raised, and I would therefore quash the conviction, and direct a new trial.

RAND J. (dissenting in part): — This appeal arises out of features of what, in substance, is religious controversy, and it is necessary that the facts be clearly appreciated. The appellant, a farmer, living near the Town of St. Joseph de Beauce, Quebec, was convicted of uttering a seditious libel. The libel was contained in a four-page document published apparently at Toronto by the Watch Tower Bible & Tract Society, which I take to be the name of the official publishers of the religious group known as the Witnesses of Jehovah. The document was headed "Quebec's Burning Hate for God and Christ and Freedom Is the Shame of all Canada": it consisted first of an invocation to calmness and reason in appraising the matters to be dealt with in support of the heading; then of general references to vindictive persecution accorded in Quebec to the Witnesses as brethren in Christ; a detailed narrative of specific incidents of persecution; and a concluding appeal to the people of the Province, in protest against mob rule and gestapo tactics, that through the study of God's Word and obedience to its commands, there might be brought about a "bounteous crop of the good fruits of love for Him and Christ and human freedom". At the foot of the document is an advertisement of two books entitled "Let God be True" and "Be Glad, Ye Nations", the former revealing, in the light of God's Word, the truth concerning the Trinity, Sabbath, prayer, etc., and the latter, the facts of the endurance of Witnesses in the crucible of "fiery persecution".

The incidents, as described, are of peaceable Canadians who seem not to be lacking in meekness, but who, for distributing, apparently without permits, Bibles and tracts on Christian doctrine; for conducting religious services in private homes or on private lands in Christian fellowship; for holding public lecture meetings to teach religious truth as they believe it of the Christian religion; who, for this exercise of what has been taken for granted to be the unchallengeable rights of Canadians, have been assaulted and beaten and their Bibles and publications torn up and destroyed, by individuals and by mobs; who have had their homes invaded and their property taken; and in hundreds have been charged with public offences and held to exorbitant bail. The police are declared to have exhibited an attitude of animosity toward them and to have treated them as the criminals in provoking by their action of Christian profession and teaching, the violence to which they have been subjected; and public officials and members of the Roman Catholic Clergy are said not only to have witnessed these outrages but to have been privy to some of the prosecutions. The document charged that the Roman Catholic Church in Quebec was in some objectionable relation to the administration of justice and that the force behind the prosecutions was that of the priests of that Church.

The conduct of the accused appears to have been unexceptionable; so far as disclosed, he is an exemplary citizen who is at least sympathetic to doctrines of the Christian religion which are, evidently, different from either the Protestant or the Roman Catholic versions: but the foundation in all is the same, Christ and his relation to God and humanity.

The crime of seditious libel is well known to the common law. Its history has been thoroughly examined and traced by Stephen, Holdsworth and other eminent legal scholars and they are in agreement both in what it originally consisted and in the social assumptions underlying it. Up to the end of the 18th century it was, in essence, a contempt in words of political authority or the actions of authority. If we conceive of the governors of society as superior beings, exercising a divine mandate, by whom laws, institutions and administrations are given to men to be obeyed, who are, in short, beyond criticism, reflection or censure upon them or what they do implies either an equality with them or an accountability by them, both equally offensive. In that lay sedition by words and the libel was its written form.

But constitutional conceptions of a different order making rapid progress in the 19th century have necessitated a modification of the legal view of public criticism; and the administrators of what we call democratic government have come to be looked upon as servants bound to carry out their duties accountably to the public. The basic nature of the common law lies in its flexible process of traditional reasoning upon significant social and political matter; and just as in the 17th century the crime of seditious libel was a deduction from fundamental conceptions of government, the substitution of new conceptions, under the same principle of reasoning called for new jural conclusions: *Bourne* v. *Keane*, [1919] A.C. 815.

As early as 1839 in *Reg*. v. *Collins*, 9 Car. & P. 456 at pp. 460-1, 173 E.R. 910, Littledale J., in his charge to the jury, laid it down that "you are to consider whether.... [they] meant to excite the people to take the power into their own hands, and meant to excite them to tumult and disorder.... the people have a right to discuss any grievances that they have to complain of, but they must not do it in a way to excite tumult,", which Stephen, in vol. 2 of his History of the Criminal Law at p. 375, sums up: "In one word, nothing short of direct incitement to disorder and violence is a seditious libel." Coleridge J. in *R*. v. *Aldred* (1909), 22 Cox C.C. 1, at p. 3, used these words: "The man who is accused may not plead the truth of the statements that he makes as a defence to the charge, nor may be plead the innocence of his motive; that is not a defence to the charge. The test is not either the truth of the language or the innocence of the motive with which he publishes it, but the test is this: was the language used calculated, or was it not, to promote public disorder or physical force:" ((1941), 85 Sol. Jo., 251). The language used must, obviously, be related to the particular matters in each case complained of.

This development is to be considered also in the light of the practice in administering the law of seditious words followed after *Fox's Libel Act* of 1792. The jury in such cases by its right under the statute to bring in a general verdict, must, in addition to the publication of the libel and its meaning, have found a seditious intention. That meant more than the issue of the writing knowing what it contained. The Act was interpreted as requiring the libel to have been published with an *illegal* intention. The word "intention" was not always clearly differentiated from indirect purpose or motive, but if the intention, as envisaging immediate or proximate response, regardless of a remote object of whatever nature, was illegal, the libel was seditious.

Stephen suggests a theoretical continuity of the law by taking that Act to have made material those consequential allegations such as of ill-will, disaffection, etc., with which the early indictments were liberally encumbered, but which were looked upon as formal or assumed as necessary effects of the libel otherwise seditious. But if that is sound, then we must have regard to the sense which they then bore; and it would seem to be clear that they signified feelings and attitudes toward established authority.

The definition of seditious intention as formulated by Stephen, summarized, is, (1) to bring into hatred or contempt, or to excite disaffection against, the King or the Government and Constitution of the United Kingdom, or either House of Parliament, or the administration of justice; or (2) to excite the King's subjects to attempt, otherwise than by lawful means, the alteration of any matter in Church or State by law established; or (3) to incite persons to commit any crime in general disturbance of the peace; or (4) to raise discontent or disaffection amongst His Majesty's subjects; or (5) to promote feelings of ill-will and hostility between different classes of such subjects. The only items of this definition that could be drawn into question here are that relating to the administration of justice in (1) and those of (4) and (5). It was the latter which were brought most prominently to the notice of the jury, and it is with an examination of what in these days their language must be taken to mean that I will chiefly concern myself.

There is no modern authority which holds that the mere effect of tending to create discontent or disaffection among His Majesty's subjects or ill-will or hostility between groups of them, but not tending to issue in illegal conduct, constitutes the crime, and this for obvious reasons. Freedom in thought and speech and disagreement in ideas and beliefs, on every conceivable subject, are of the essence of our life. The clash of critical discussion on political, social and religious subjects has too deeply become the stuff of daily experience to suggest that mere ill-will as a product of controversy can strike down the latter with illegality. A superficial examination of the word shows its insufficiency. What is the degree necessary to criminality? Can it ever, as mere subjective condition, be so? Controversial fury is aroused constantly by differences in abstract conceptions; heresy in some fields is again a mortal sin; there can be fanatical puritanism in ideas as well as in morals; but our compact of free society accepts and absorbs these differences and they are exercised at large within the framework of freedom and order on broader and deeper uniformities as bases of social stability. Similarly in discontent, disaffection and hostility: as subjective incidents of controversy, they and the ideas which arouse them are part of our living which ultimately serve us in stimulation, in the clarification of thought and, as we believe, in the search for the constitution and truth of things generally.

Although Stephen's definition was adopted substantially as it is by the Criminal Code Commission of England in 1880, the latter's report, in this respect, was not acted on by the Imperial Parliament, and the Criminal Code of this country, enacted in 1891, did not incorporate its provisions. The latter omits any reference to definition except in s.133 to declare that the intention includes the advocacy of the use of force as a means of bringing about a change of Government and by s.133A, that certain actions are not included. What the words in (4) and (5) must in the present day be taken to signify is the use of language which, by inflaming the minds of people into hatred, ill-will, discontent, disaffection, is intended, or is so likely to do so as to be deemed to be intended, to disorder community life, but directly or indirectly in relation to Government in the broadest sense: Phillimore J. in *R.* v. *Antonelli & Barberi* (1905), 70 J.P. 4 at p. 6, "seditious libels are such as tend to disturb the government of this country." That may be through tumult or violence, in resistance to public authority, in defiance of law. This conception lies behind the association which the word is given in C.S.L.C. 1861 c.10, s.1(1), dealing with illegal oaths: "To engage in any seditious, rebellious, or treasonable purpose"; and the corresponding s.131(*a*)(i) of the *Code:* "To engage in any mutinous or seditious purpose."

The baiting or denouncing of one group by another or others without an aim directly or indirectly at Government, is in the nature of public mischief: *R.* v. *Leese & Whitehead,* (The Times, September 22, 1936, cited in 85 Sol. Jo. 252); and incitement to unlawful acts is itself an offence.

This result must be distinguished from an undesired reaction provoked by the exercise of common rights, such as the violent opposition to the early services of the Salvation Army. In that situation it was the hoodlums who were held to be the lawless and not the members of the Army: *Beatty* v. *Gillbanks* (1882), 9 Q.B.D. 308. On the allegations in the document here, had the Salvationists been arrested for bringing about by unlawful assembly a breach of the peace and fined, had they then made an impassioned protest against such treatment of law-abiding citizens, and had they thereupon been charged with seditious words, their plight would have been that of the accused in this case.

These considerations are confirmed by s.133A of the *Code,* which is as follows:

"133A. No one shall be deemed to have a seditious intention only because he intends in good faith. —

"(*a*) to show that His Majesty has been misled or mistaken in his measures; or

"(*b*) to point out errors or defects in the government or constitution of the United Kingdom, or of any part of it, or of Canada or any province thereof, or in either House of Parliament of the United Kingdom or of Canada, or in any legislature, or in the administration of justice; or to excite His Majesty's subjects to attempt to procure, by lawful means, the alteration of any matter in the state; or,

"(*c*) to point out, in order to their removal, matters which are producing or have a tendency to produce feelings of hatred and ill-will between different classes of His Majesty's subjects."

This, as is seen, is a fundamental provision which, with its background of free criticism as a constituent of modern democratic Government, protects the widest range of public discussion and controversy, so long as it is done in good faith and for the purposes mentioned. Its effect is to eviscerate the older concept of its anachronistic elements. But a motive or ultimate purpose, whether good or believed to be good is unavailing if the means employed is bad; disturbance or corrosion may be ends in themselves, but whether means or ends, their character stamps them and intention behind them as illegal.

The condemned intention lies then in a residue of criticism of Government, the negative touchstone of which is the test of good faith by legitimate means toward legitimate ends. That claim was the real defence in the proceedings here but it was virtually ignored by the trial Judge. On that failure, as well as others, the Chief Justice of the King's Bench and Galipeault, J. have rested their dissent, and with them I am in agreement.

But a further question remains. In the circumstances, should the appellant be subjected to a second trial? Could a jury, properly instructed and acting judicially have found, beyond a reasonable doubt, a seditious intention in circulating the document? In the heading is the chief source of resentment but there are also statements, such as the insinuation of the part played by the Church in judicial administration and the role of some of the clergy in the prosecutions, which offend likewise. Now these allegations are inferences and conclusions drawn from the facts and incidents presented in detail which the accused was ready with evidence to prove, and it is obvious that they and the matters from which they are deduced, must be read together. When it is said that Quebec hates Christ, it is hate *sub modo;* it means that to persecute is to hate, and that to hate those who follow and love Him, *i.e.,* the Witnesses, for what they do in His service, is to hate Him. Only in that manner can the real intention evidenced by the document be appreciated.

The writing was undoubtedly made under an aroused sense of wrong to the Witnesses; but it is beyond dispute that its end and object was the removal of what they considered iniquitous treatment. Here are conscientious professing followers of Christ who claim to have been denied the right to worship in their own homes and their own manner and to have been jailed for obeying the injuction to "teach all nations". They are said to have been called "a bunch of crazy nuts" by one of the Magistrates. Whatever that means, it may from his standpoint be a correct description; I do not know; but it is not challenged that, as they allege, whatever they did was done peaceably, and, as they saw it, in the way of bringing the light and peace of the Christian religion to the souls of men and women. To say that is to say that their acts were lawful. Whether, in like circumstances, other groups of the Christian Church would show greater forebearance and earnestness in the appeal to Christian charity to have done with such abuses, may be doubtful. The Courts below have not, as, with the greatest respect, I think they should have, viewed the document as primarily a burning protest and as a result have lost sight of the fact that, expressive as it is of a deep indignation, its conclusion is an earnest petition to the public opinion of the Province to extend to the Witnesses of Jehovah, as a minority, the protection of impartial laws. No one would suggest that the document is intended to arouse French-speaking Roman Catholics to disorderly conduct against their own Government, and to treat it as directed, with the same purpose, towards the Witnesses themselves in the Province, would be quite absurd: in relation to Courts, it is, to use the language of s.133A, pointing out, "in order to their removal", what are believed to be "matters which are producing or have a tendency to produce feelings of hatred and ill-will between different classes of His Majesty's subjects". That some of the expressions, divorced from their context, may be extravagant and may arouse resentment, is not, in the circumstances, sufficient to take the intention of the writing as a whole beyond what is recognized by s.133A as lawful.

Where a conviction is set aside, this Court must dispose of the appeal as the justice of the case requires; and where the evidence offered could not, under a proper instruction, have supported a conviction, the accused must be discharged: *Schwartzenhauer* v. *The King,* [1935], 3 D.L.R. 711, S.C.R. 367, 64 Can. C.C. 1; *Manchuk* v. *The*

King, [1938], 3 D.L.R. 693, S.C.R. 341, 70 Can. C.C. 161; *Savard & Lizotte* v. *The King*, [1946], 3 D.L.R. 468, S.C.R. 20, 85 Can. C.C. 254.

I would therefore, allow the appeal, set aside the conviction, and order judgment of acquittal to be entered.

ESTEY J. (dissenting in part): — This is an appeal under s.1023 of the *Code* on questions of law raised in the dissenting opinions of the learned Judges in the Court of King's Bench (Appeal Side) of the Province of Quebec [95 Can. C.C. 119]. The appellant was convicted of seditious libel in that he did on or about December 11, 1946, at St. Joseph "dans le district de Beauce", distribute a pamphlet entitled "La haine ardente du Québec, pour Dieu, pour le Christ, et pour la liberté, est un sujet de honte pour tout le Canada". Upon appeal this conviction was affirmed, Létourneau C.J. and Galipeault J. dissenting.

The pamphlet consists of four pages entitled as aforesaid which the appellant admitted he had read and distributed. The main issue is, therefore, whether the appellant had a seditious intention in distributing and thereby publishing the pamphlet.

There were several points raised in the dissenting opinions but it will be sufficient to continue the discussion to two of them, namely, that the learned trial Judge in charging the jury (a) did not sufficiently define " seditious intention", (b) did not adequately explain to the jury the place and meaning of "reasonable doubt".

A "seditious libel" is defined in s.133 of the *Code*, the material part of which reads:

"133(1) Seditious words are words expressive of a seditious intention.

"(2) A seditious libel is a libel expressive of a seditious intention."

A "seditious intention" is not defined in either s.133 or in any other part of the Code and we must therefore look to the common law. It will there be found that the definition in Stephen's "Digest of the Criminal Law", 5th ed., p. 70, and described by the Commissioners who prepared the draft of the English Code to be "as accurate a statement of the existing law as we can make", is generally accepted.

This is set out in s.102 of the draft Code:

"A seditious intention is an intention to bring into hatred or contempt, or to excite disaffection against the person of Her Majesty, or the Government and Constitution of the United Kingdom or of any part of it as by law established, or either House of Parliament, or the administration of justice; or to excite Her Majesty's subjects to attempt to procure otherwise than by lawful means the alteration of any matter in Church or State by law established; or to raise discontent or disaffection amongst Her Majesty's subjects; or to promote feelings of ill-will and hostility between different classes of such subjects:

"Provided that no one shall be deemed to have a seditious intention only because he intends in good faith to show that Her Majesty has been misled or mistaken in her measures; or to point out errors or defects in the Government or Constitution of the United Kingdom or of any part of it as by law established, or in the administration of justice, with a view to the reformation of such alleged errors or defects; or to excite Her Majesty's subjects to attempt to procure by lawful means the alteration of any matter in Church or State by law established; or to point out in order to their removal matters which are producing or have a tendency to produce feelings of hatred and ill-will between different classes of Her Majesty's subjects.

"Seditious words are words expressive of or intended to carry into execution or to excite others to carry into execution a seditious intention."

While the foregoing definition has never been enacted as part of our Criminal Code, the proviso was enacted in our first Code in 1892 as part of s.123 (1892, c.29) and was deleted by an amendment in 1919 [c.46, s.4] and re-enacted in 1930 and is now s.133A (1930, c.11, s.2).

The learned trial Judge did not discuss a "seditious intention" in the terms of or in terms similar to those in the foregoing definition more than to say that a seditious intention is one "to provoke feelings of ill-will and hostility between different classes of His Majesty's Subjects," and expressed it in French as follows: "Le Libelle séditieux c'est la publication ou la distribution d'un pamphlet, ou d'un écrit injurieux, blessant, et qui peut provoquer de la haine et de la discorde parmi les différentes classes de sujets de Sa Majesté."

However vague and indefinite the words "ill-will and hostility" may be when read as part of the foregoing definition of sedition, they are certainly more so when, as in this case, they were stated to the jury as separate and apart therefrom.

Cave J. in *Reg.* v. *Burns* (1886), 16 Cox C.C. 355, referred to the foregoing definition as somewhat vague and general and particularly that portion reading "ill-will and hostility between different classes of Her Majesty's subjects". This vague and general character is further emphasized in Law of the Constitution, Dicey, 9th ed., p. 244, where, after pointing out that the law permits publication of statements indicating "the Crown has been misled, or that the government has committed errors... and, in short, sanctions criticism of public affairs which is *bona fide* intended to recommend the reform of existing institutions by legal methods", the learned author concludes: "But any one will see at once that the legal definition of a seditious libel might easily be so used as to check a great deal of what is ordinarily considered allowable discussion, and would if rigidly enforced be inconsistent with prevailing forms of political agitation."

The foregoing emphasizes the importance of intention and the necessity of a trial Judge explaining to a jury, in such a ease as here, the meaning of "intention to promote feelings of ill-will and hostility between different classes" of His Majesty's subjects as an essential in the offence of sedition.

In determining whether a seditious intention is present in a particular case, the language of Fitzgerald J. in *Reg.* v. *Sullivan* (1868), 11 Cox C.C. 44, at p. 45, adopted by Cave J. in *Reg.* v. *Burns*, 16 Cox C.C. at p. 361, is pertinent: "'Sedition has been described as disloyalty in action, and the law considers as seditious all those practices which have for their object to excite discontent or disaffection, to create public disturbances, or to lead to civil war; to bring into hatred or contempt the Sovereign or the Government, the laws or constitution of the Realm, and generally all endeavours to promote public disorder.' "

Stephen's History of the Criminal Law of England, vol. 2, p. 375: "In one word, nothing short of direct incitement to disorder and violence is a seditious libel."

Reg. v. *Burns, supra,* and other authorities rather indicate that an intention to incite something less than violence is sufficient, and that the offence of sedition is committed if it be established that the parties charged intentionally incited ill-will and hostility between different classes of citizens in such a manner as may be likely to cause public disorder or disturbance. It will be recognized that one may freely and forcefully express his views within the limits defined by the law. Those engaged in campaigns or controversies of a public nature may cause feelings of hatred and ill-will but it does not at all follow that those taking part therein and causing these feelings are acting with a seditious intention. The essential, without which there cannot be sedition, is the presence of a seditious intention as above defined and which is a fact to be determined on the evidence adduced in each case.

It is therefore important to determine whether there was any evidence which in law would support a verdict of guilty which in this case, would include a finding that the appellant in distributing this pamphlet acted with a seditious intention.

The Crown asked the jury to find the intention of the accused from the language of this four-page pamphlet. Nine excerpts from it were specifically embodied in the indictment. These, however, cannot be read separate and apart, but rather their meaning and effect must be determined by reading and construing them in relation to the statements in the pamphlet as a whole.

The pamphlet is entitled, as already stated, "La haine ardente du Québec, pour Dieu, pour le Christ, et pour la liberté, est un sujet de honte pour tout le Canada". In the first paragraph the reader is requested to "calmly and soberly and with clear mental faculties reason on the evidence presented in support of the above-headlined indictment". Then follows a recitation of facts and circumstances in support of the conclusions that the witnesses of Jehovah are ill-treated and their freedom to worship according to the tenets of their religion denied; and that this condition exists because members of the judiciary, police and groups of citizens are directed and controlled by the priests of the Roman Catholic Church. All of which the pamphlet declares to be contrary to the principles of Christianity and that "such blind course will lead to the ditch of destruction. To avoid it turn from following men and traditions, and study and follow the Bible's teaching; that was Jesus' advice". This is the appeal made to all who read this pamphlet. It does not disclose an intention, nor reading the pamphlet as a whole can it be concluded that it is calculated to incite persons or classes of persons to acts or conduct leading to public disorder or disturbance. On the contrary, the pamphlet stresses the view that if the plea therein contained is acted upon the existent ill-will and hatred will disappear and the interference complained of will no longer exist. In these circumstances it is difficult to conclude that the appellant in distributing and publishing this pamphlet was doing so with a seditious intention.

We are not, however, left in this case with respect to a seditious intention to the construction of the pamphlet alone. The appellant gave evidence on his own behalf. He explained that he was a minister of the Witnesses of Jehovah, that hatred and ill-will already existed against Jehovah's Witnesses and that he had read the pamphlet and distributed it, as he explained (translation):

"A. In the desire to make known the things contained in the pamphlet in order to have the persecutions undergone by the Witnesses of Jehovah changed so that men of good will may know the things.... not in order to stir up hatred or trouble as the Witnesses just said that there had been no stirring up... Q. When you distributed that, what was the object? A. With the object that people would see that the world after having come to know of what is in this pamphlet, might see to it that the Government and the authorities should take the means to correct these things and that there should be no more persecutions, it was truly with that object so that men of good-will might have the vision to preach peace and live in peace whereas you see them speak of hatred all the time."

The appellant specifically denied that he had any intention of creating public disorder; on the contrary he stated that he desired to establish peace between the Roman Catholics and the Witnesses of Jehovah. He stated: "I have studied it, read it and have seen the facts."

Apart from this general declaration, he deposed that it was his own child, eleven years of age, referred to in the pamphlet who, because of her religious views, was expelled from her school.

The learned trial Judge in the course of his charge suggested that the distribution of this pamphlet was a ludicrous or strange way to effect a reconciliation. The conduct of the appellant may not only, in the opinion of the learned trial Judge, but of many others, be ludicrous or strange. That, however, is quite apart from the question whether the appellant had, upon the whole of the evidence, a seditious intention.

The good faith of the appellant in distributing this pamphlet was directly in issue under s.133A(*c*). He, in the course of his evidence as above indicated, adopted as true the statements in the pamphlet. The truth of the pamphlet is not a defence to a charge of sedition but if the facts set out in the pamphlet are untrue, evidence to that effect would have gone far to have shown the appellant did not act in good faith. No such evidence was adduced.

The conduct on the part of any group in Canada which denies to or even interferes with the right of the members of any religious body to worship is a matter of public concern. The pamphlet, in the conception of the appellant as he deposed, discusses such an interference. He pledged his oath that it sets forth facts and circumstances which establish this interference with respect to the rights of the Witnesses of Jehovah to worship in the Province of Quebec and that hatred and ill-will exist toward them. He believed the plea set forth in the pamphlet would remove that hatred and ill-will and the interference would cease. He therefore, as he deposed, in good faith and for that purpose published and distributed the pamphlet. No evidence was introduced to contradict any of these factors and therefore the evidence here adduced brings this position of the appellant within the provisions of s.133A already quoted.

The facts as set forth in the pamphlet may be inaccurately stated, even incorrect and the comments unjustified. The statements in it may be objectionable, even repugnant to some and provoke ill-will and hatred. That, however, is not sufficient. It still remains to be proved as a fact that the accused acted with a seditious intention. Under s.133A that intention does not exist if the appellant's conduct was within that section and he was acting in good faith. The evidence of good faith on behalf of the defence is consistent with the intent and purpose of the pamphlet as therein expressed and no evidence has been adduced to the contrary. The onus rested upon the Crown throughout to prove beyond a reasonable doubt that the accused acted with a seditious intention and this record does not disclose any evidence that would properly sustain a verdict that the accused possessed such an intention.

The appeal should be allowed, the conviction quashed and a judgment and verdict of acquittal directed to be entered.

New trial ordered.

2.4.4 Law Reform Commission of Canada, *Crimes Against the State,* Working Paper 49 (Ottawa, 1986) 32, 35-36

The seditious offences in sections 60, 61 and 62 [now sections 59, 60 and 61] provide yet another example of uncertainty in the *Code*. For example, the three offences of speaking seditious words, publishing a seditious libel and being a party to a seditious conspiracy, each require that there be a "seditious intention," but this phrase is not defined. Subsection 60(4) tells us what will be presumed to be a seditious intention and section 61 tells us what will not be treated as a seditious intention, and yet nowhere in the *Code* is there a conclusive definition of what is in fact a seditious intention. Instead we have to turn to the common law to find its meaning, but the common law definition is also vague and uncertain.

...

The offence of sedition provides another example of an outdated and unprincipled law. The original aim of the crime of sedition was to forbid criticism and derision of political authority, and as Fitzjames Stephen pointed out, the offence was a natural concommitant of the once prevalent view that the governors of the State were wise and superior beings exercising a divine mandate and beyond the reproach of the common people. With the coming of age of parliamentary democracy in the nineteenth century, government could no longer be conceived as the infallible master of the people, but as their servant, and subjects were seen to have a perfect right to criticize and even dismiss their government. Indeed it is essential to the health of a parliamentary democracy such as Canada that citizens have the right to criticize, debate and discuss political, economic and social matters in the freest possible manner. This has already been recognized by our courts and now the *Canadian Charter of Rights and Freedoms* provides additional guarantees of political freedom of expression (see ss.2, 3). Is it not odd then that our *Criminal Code* still contains the offence of sedition which has as its very object the suppression of such freedom? In the *Boucher* case, the Supreme Court of Canada tries to deal with this inconsistency by taking a narrow view of the common law definition of a seditious intention. Applying their narrow definition, there no longer seems to be a need for a separate offence of sedition, because the only conduct that would be proscribed by it could just as well be dealt with as incitement ..., conspiracy ..., contempt of court, or hate propaganda ... . Clearly, *legislative* revision is in order as well.

2.4.5 Criminal Code, ss.297-317 (Defamatory libel)

297. In sections 303, 304 and 308, "newspaper" means any paper, magazine or periodical containing public news, intelligence or reports of events, or any remarks or observations thereon, printed for sale and published periodically or in parts or numbers, at intervals not exceeding thirty-one days between the publication of any two such papers, parts or numbers, and any paper, magazine or periodical printed in order to be dispersed and made public, weekly or more often, or at intervals not exceeding thirty-one days, that contains advertisements, exclusively or principally.

Definition

298. (1) A defamatory libel is matter published, without lawful justification or excuse, that is likely to injure the reputation of any person by exposing him to hatred, contempt or ridicule, or that is designed to insult the person of or concerning whom it is published.

Mode of expression

(2) A defamatory libel may be expressed directly or by insinuation or irony

(*a*) in words legibly marked upon any substance, or

(*b*) by any object signifying a defamatory libel otherwise than by words.

Publishing

299. A person publishes a libel when he

(*a*) exhibits it in public,

(*b*) causes it to be read or seen, or

(*c*) shows or delivers it, or causes it to be shown or delivered, with intent that it should be read or seen by the person whom it defames or by any other person.

Punishment of libel known to be false

300. Every one who publishes a defamatory libel that he knows is false is guilty of an indictable offence and is liable to imprisonment for five years.

Punishment for defamatory libel

301. Every one who publishes a defamatory libel is guilty of an indictable offence and is liable to imprisonment for two years.

Extortion by libel

302. (1) Every one commits an offence who, with intent

(*a*) to extort money from any person, or

(*b*) to induce a person to confer upon or procure for another person an appointment or office of profit or trust,

publishes or threatens to publish or offers to abstain from publishing or to prevent the publication of a defamatory libel.

Idem

(2) Every one commits an offence who, as the result of the refusal of any person to permit money to be extorted or to confer or procure an appointment or office of profit or trust, publishes or threatens to publish a defamatory libel.

Punishment

(3) Every one who commits an offence under this section is guilty of an indictable offence and is liable to imprisonment for five years.

Proprietor of newspaper presumed responsible

303. (1) The proprietor of a newspaper shall be deemed to publish defamatory matter that is inserted and published therein, unless he proves that the defamatory matter was inserted in the newspaper without his knowledge and without negligence on his part.

General authority to manager when negligence

(2) Where the proprietor of a newspaper gives to a person general authority to manage or conduct the newspaper as editor or otherwise, the insertion by that person of defamatory matter in the newspaper shall, for the purposes of subsection (1), be deemed not to be negligence on the part of the proprietor unless it is proved that

(*a*) he intended the general authority to include authority to insert defamatory matter in the newspaper, or

(*b*) he continued to confer general authority after he knew that it had been exercised by the insertion of defamatory matter in the newspaper.

Selling newspapers

(3) No person shall be deemed to publish a defamatory libel by reason only that he sells a number or part of a newspaper that contains a defamatory libel, unless he knows that the number or part contains defamatory matter or that defamatory matter is habitually contained in the newspaper.

Selling book containing defamatory libel

304. (1) No person shall be deemed to publish a defamatory libel by reason only that he sells a book, magazine, pamphlet or other thing, other than a newspaper that contains defamatory matter if, at the time of the sale, he does not know that it contains the defamatory matter.

Sale by servant

(2) Where a servant, in the course of his employment, sells a book, magazine, pamphlet or other thing, other than a newspaper, the employer shall be deemed not to publish any defamatory matter contained therein unless it is proved that the employer authorized the sale knowing that

(*a*) defamatory matter was contained therein, or

(*b*) defamatory matter was habitually contained therein, in the case of a periodical.

Publishing proceedings of courts of justice

305. No person shall be deemed to publish a defamatory libel by reason only that he publishes defamatory matter

(*a*) in a proceeding held before or under the authority of a court exercising judicial authority, or

(*b*) in an inquiry made under the authority of an Act or by order of Her Majesty, or under the authority of a public department or a department of the government of a province.

Parliamentary papers

306. No person shall be deemed to publish a defamatory libel by reason only that he

(*a*) publishes to the Senate or House of Commons or to a legislature, defamatory matter contained in a petition to the Senate or House of Commons or to the legislature, as the case may be,

(*b*) publishes by order or under the authority of the Senate or House of Commons or of a legislature, a paper containing defamatory matter, or

(*c*) publishes, in good faith and without ill will to the person defamed, an extract from or abstract of a petition or paper mentioned in paragraph (*a*) or (*b*).

Fair reports of parliamentary or judicial proceedings

307. (1) No person shall be deemed to publish a defamatory libel by reason only that he publishes in good faith, for the information of the public, a fair report of the proceedings of the Senate or House of Commons or a legislature, or a committee thereof, or of the public proceedings before a court exercising judicial authority, or publishes, in good faith, any fair comment upon any such proceedings.

Divorce proceedings an exception

(2) This section does not apply to a person who publishes a report of evidence taken or offered in any proceeding before the Senate or House of Commons or any committee thereof, upon a petition or bill relating to any matter of marriage or divorce, if the report is published without authority from or leave of the House in which the proceeding is held or is contrary to any rule, order or practice of that House.

Fair report of public meeting

308. No person shall be deemed to publish a defamatory libel by reason only that he publishes in good faith, in a newspaper, a fair report of the proceedings of any public meeting if

(*a*) the meeting is lawfully convened for a lawful purpose and is open to the public,

(*b*) the report is fair and accurate,

(*c*) the publication of the matter complained of is for the public benefit, and (*d*) he does not refuse to publish in a conspicuous place in the newspaper a reasonable explanation or contradiction by the person defamed in respect of the defamatory matter.

Public benefit

309. No person shall be deemed to publish a defamatory libel by reason only that he publishes defamatory matter that, on reasonable grounds, he believes is true, and that is relevant to any subject of public interest, the public discussion of which is for the public benefit.

Fair comment on public person or work of art

310. No person shall be deemed to publish a defamatory libel by reason only that he publishes fair comments

(*a*) upon the public conduct of a person who takes part in public affairs, or

(*b*) upon a published book or other literary production, or on any composition or work of art or performance publicly exhibited, or on any other communication made to the public on any subject,

if the comments are confined to criticism thereof.

When truth a defence

311. No person shall be deemed to publish a defamatory libel where he proves that the publication of the defamatory matter in the manner in which it was published was for the public benefit at the time when it was published and that the matter itself was true.

Publication invited or necessary

312. No person shall be deemed to publish a defamatory libel by reason only that he publishes defamatory matter

(*a*) on the invitation or challenge of the person in respect of whom it is published, or

(*b*) that it is necessary to publish in order to refute defamatory matter published in respect of him by another person,

if he believes that the defamatory matter is true and it is relevant to the invitation, challenge or necessary refutation, as the case may be, and does not in any respect exceed what is reasonably sufficient in the circumstances.

Answer to inquiries

313. No person shall be deemed to publish a defamatory libel by reason only that he publishes, in answer to inquiries made to him, defamatory matter relating to a subject-matter in respect of which the person by whom or on whose behalf the inquiries are made has an interest in knowing the truth or who, on reasonable grounds, the person who publishes the defamatory matter believes has such an interest, if

(*a*) the matter is published, in good faith, for the purpose of giving information in answer to the inquiries,

(*b*) the person who publishes the defamatory matter believes that it is true,

(*c*) the defamatory matter is relevant to the inquiries, and

(*d*) the defamatory matter does not in any respect exceed what is reasonably sufficient in the circumstances.

Giving information to person interested

314. No person shall be deemed to publish a defamatory libel by reason only that he publishes to another person defamatory matter for the purpose of giving information to that person with respect to a subject-matter in which the person to whom the information is given has, or is believed on reasonable grounds by the person who gives it to have, an interest in knowing the truth with respect to that subject-matter if

(*a*) the conduct of the person who gives the information is reasonable in the circumstances,

(*b*) the defamatory matter is relevant to the subject-matter, and

(*c*) the defamatory matter is true, or if it is not true, is made without ill-will toward the person who is defamed and is made in the belief, on reasonable grounds, that it is true.

Publication in good faith for redress of wrong

315. No person shall be deemed to publish a defamatory libel by reason only that he publishes defamatory matter in good faith for the purpose of seeking remedy or redress for a private or public wrong or grievance from a person who has, or who on reasonable grounds he believes has the right or is under an obligation to remedy or redress the wrong or grievance, if

(*a*) he believes that the defamatory matter is true,

(*b*) the defamatory matter is relevant to the remedy or redress that is sought, and

(*c*) the defamatory matter does not in any respect exceed what is reasonably sufficient in the circumstances.

Proving publication by order of legislature

316. (1) An accused who is alleged to have published a defamatory libel may, at any stage of the proceedings, adduce evidence to prove that the matter that is alleged to be defamatory was contained in a paper published by order or under the authority of the Senate or House of Commons or a legislature.

Directing verdict

(2) Where at any stage in proceedings referred to in subsection (1) the court, judge, justice or magistrate is satisfied that matter alleged to be defamatory was contained in a paper published by order or under the authority of the Senate or House of Commons or a legislature, he shall direct a verdict of not guilty to be entered and shall discharge the accused.

Certificate of order

(3) For the purpose of this section a certificate under the hand of the Speaker or clerk of the Senate or House of Commons or a legislature to the effect that the matter that is alleged to be defamatory was contained in a paper published by order or under the authority of the Senate, House of Commons or legislature, as the case may be, is conclusive evidence thereof.

Verdicts

Verdicts in cases of defamatory libel

317. Where, on the trial of an indictment for publishing a defamatory libel, a plea of not guilty is pleaded, the jury that is sworn to try the issue may give a general verdict of guilty or not guilty upon the whole matter put in issue upon the indictment, and shall not be required or directed by the judge to find the defendant guilty merely on proof of publication by the defendant of the alleged defamatory libel, and of the sense ascribed thereto in the indictment, but the judge may, in his discretion, give a direction or opinion to the jury on the matter in issue as in other criminal proceedings, and the jury may, on the issue, find a special verdict.

2.4.6 *R.* v. *Georgia Straight Publishing Ltd.* (1969) 4 D.L.R. (3d) 383 (B.C. Co. Ct.)

MORROW, CO. CT. J.: — The accused stand charged for

That they the said GEORGIA STRAIGHT PUBLISHING LTD., and DANIEL MCLEOD and ROBERT CUMMINGS at the City of Vancouver, County of Vancouver, Province of British Columbia, between the 10th day of July 1968 and the 10th day of August, 1968, unlawfully without lawful justification or excuse did publish a defamatory libel of and concerning Magistrate Lawrence Eckhardt on Page 6 of the Georgia Straight, Volume 2, dated July 26 — August 8 and numbered 23 in the words. "Eckhardt, Magistrate Lawrence — The Pontius Pilate Certificate of Justice — (Unfairly maligned by critics, Pilate upheld the highest traditions of a judge by placing law and order above human considerations and by helping to clear the streets of Jerusalem of degenerate non-conformists.) The Citation reads: "To Lawrence Eckhardt, who, by closing his mind to justice, his eyes to fairness, and his ears to equality, has encouraged the belief that the law is not only blind, but also deaf, dumb and stupid. Let history judge your actions — then appeal", designed to insult the said Magistrate Lawrence Eckardt, contrary to the form of the Statute in such case made and provided and against the peace of our Lady the Queen her Crown and Dignity.

The indictment was preferred under s.251 of the Canadian *Criminal Code* which reads:

251. Every one who publishes a defamatory libel is guilty of an indictable offence and is liable to imprisonment for two years.

When the hearing opened, counsel agreed on all of the facts with the exception of "publication" by Cummings; exs. 1 and 4 set out the admissions.

Exhibit 2 was the certificate of incorporation of Georgia Straight Publishing Limited.

Exhibit 3, being p. 6 of the Georgia Straight, contained the article complained of.

Exhibit 5 is a copy of the judgment of His Worship Magistrate Eckhardt wherein one Persky was convicted of "loitering" under Order in Council 104 being B.C. Reg. 10/63, which regulation was made pursuant to the provisions contained in s.49 of the *Department of Public Works Act,* R.S.B.C. 1960, c.109.

Exhibit 6 is an editorial taken from the Vancouver Province of April 10, 1968; it is entitled "Mr. Bonner End This Nonsense".

Exhibit 7 is the decision of Seaton, J., dismissing the appeal by way of stated case of the said Persky; therein, in effect, he ruled that the Magistrate had acted correctly in disposing of the matter as he did.

The prosecution relief on the admissions and the exhibits.

The defence called one witness, the accused, Robert Howard Cummings; he is a journalist employed by the accused Georgia Straight Publishing Limited and is the author of the article in question, the purpose of which, in his words was a "spoof, joke, satire or piece of humour along the lines of the 'City Town Fool Award' "; he was, he claimed, satirizing the Establishment; in ex. 3 he awarded the "Order of the Abundant Flatulence" to several individuals and specifically he awarded Magistrate

Eckhardt the "Pontius Pilate Certificate of Justice" using the words contained in the indictment.

In direct examination he outlined how the police had made selective arrests of non-conformists and stressed the fact that the regulation under which the authorities proceeded was discriminatory and that the Magistrate agreed it was; it was on the basis of that decision he made the award.

The said Cummings testified that the accused McLeod was the editor and publisher of the paper which is virtually a one-man company. In cross-examination he said he had been with the paper over a year and wrote articles steadily. As to the title, "Order of Abundant Flatulence", in his words, this meant "super abundance of gas in the intestinal tract or pomposity" and he was trying to take pomposity out of the Establishment. The defence argued along five lines:

(1) There is no evidence as to publication against the accused Cummings.
(2) There was no intent to insult.
(3) The words are not defamatory.
(4) If they are defamatory, the accused are entitled to the protection of s.259 of the *Cr. Code* which reads:

> No person shall be deemed to publish defamatory libel by reason only that he publishes defamatory matter that, on reasonable grounds, he believes is true, and that is relevant to any subject of public interest, the public discussion of which is for the public benefit.

(5) If the words are defamatory, the accused are entitled to the benefit of s.260 of the *Code* which reads:

> No person shall be deemed to publish a defamatory libel by reason only that he publishes fair comments
>
> (*a*) upon the public conduct of a person who takes part in public affairs...

25 — 4 D.L.R. (3d)

As to the first line of argument there can be no doubt there was publication under s.249(*b*); in his own evidence Cummings admitted he was the author of the article which appeared on p. 6 and the paper was distributed; he is a journalist and it would be odd, indeed, if he did not intend his writings to be read; he also falls within s.21 of the *Code* (Parties to Offence — Common Intent). As to the second defence, nowhere in s.248 does the word "intent" appear; the definition has two parts; the latter reads "or that is designed to insult the person of or concerning whom it is published". If it had been the decision of Parliament to use the word "intent" it would have done so as has been done in many other sections; instead of the word "intent" the section uses the word "designed"; this word simply means "to put together" or "purpose".

As regards the third, fourth and fifth defences, these seem to overlap and will be considered together. The defence emphasized that because the regulation or law was bad the words should be taken to mean criticism against the law rather than against the Magistrate. I disagree as the article is directed against the Magistrate, not the law.

A perusal of p. 6 of ex. 3 indicates how far the accused went; there is a sketch of the award in question which I consider to be in very bad taste, particularly the description of it; the "Order of the Abundant Flatulence" is described in detail in column one; in so far as Magistrate Eckhardt is concerned, he should have been praised for drawing the attention of the authorities to a law that he did not feel could be enforced generally; instead, he was accused of having "closed his mind to justice, his eyes to fairness and his ears to equality" which words are insulting.

I am grateful to counsel for giving me the many authorities they did. I have read them all; the following have been helpful: *Salmond on Torts,* 14th ed., dealing with privilege and privileged reports, at p. 198, the author has this to say:

> The statement is judged by the standard of an ordinary, right-thinking member of society. Hence the test is an objective one, and it is no defence to say that the statement was not intended to be defamatory, or uttered by way of a joke.

See *Capital and Counties Bank, Ltd. v. Henty & Sons* (1882), 7 App. Cas. 741; again, at p. 222, under the heading ''Privilege'' the author has this to say:

> The cases in which privilege exists are, generally speaking, those in which there is some just occasion for publishing defamatory matter in the public interest or in the furtherance or protection of the rights or lawful interests of individuals. In such cases the exigency of the occasion amounts to a lawful excuse for the attack so made upon the plaintiff's reputation. The right of free speech is allowed wholly or partially to prevail over the right of reputation.

In regard to this last quotation, the difficulty the accused find themselves in is the fact that they have defamed the Magistrate rather than making an attack on the law which they had a right to do.

Candler v. Crane Christmas & Co., [1951] 1 All E.R. 426 at pp. 431 and 442. This case was put forth by the defence to indicate the great conflict there has been in trying to resolve the issue at bar. It was contended one of the reasons the statements made were not defamatory was that it was directed against a bad law rather than against a bad Judge. The defence quoted from the judgment at p. 431 quoting Denning, L.J., but he was dissenting.

In addition the case is distinguishable from the case at bar as the accused were not commenting on the law but rather commenting on the fact that the Magistrate had acted improperly. The comments were not proved to be true and they were unfair and they could not be classed as a discussion for the public benefit; ss.259 and 260 do not help them.

The Queen v. Gray, [1900] 2 Q.B. 36 at p. 40. Here the headnote reads [paraphrased]:

> The publication in a newspaper of an article containing a scandalous abuse of a judge with reference to his conduct as a judge in a judicial proceeding which has terminated is contempt of court, punishable by the court on summary process.

Hoare v. Silverlock (1848), 12 Q.B. 624 at p. 632, 116 E.R. 1004. The headnote reads [paraphrased]:

> This case revolves around the fable of ''The Frozen Snake''; the verdict found the plaintiff entitled to judgment since the jury may have understood the words, ''frozen snake'' to charge the plaintiff with ingratitude to friends; it is no objection in arrest of judgment that the words are not explained by innuendo.

In the case at bar, innuendo is not involved as the words, taken in their ordinary meaning, are very clear.

Gatley on Libel and Slander, 6th ed., is authority for the proposition that innuendo must be pleaded but no innuendo is necessary in the case at bar as the words are defamatory in their common use.

''Pilate (Pontius Pilate)'': this word is defined in the Oxford Dictionary as a term of reproach.

R. v. Unwin, [1938] 1 D.L.R. 529 at pp. 530-1, 69 C.C.C. 197 at pp. 199-200, [1938] 1 W.W.R. 339. The accused was tried before Ives, J., and a jury on a charge in two counts:

(1) the publishing of a defamatory libel knowing it to be false;

(2) the publishing of a defamatory libel.

The writing complained of was a printed leaflet headed "Bankers' Toadies" followed by the words, *inter alia*, "God made Bankers' Toadies, just as He made snakes, slugs, snails and other creepy-crawly, treacherous and poisonous things. NEVER therefore, abuse them — just exterminate them!" On the reverse side, under the heading "Bankers' Toadies", were the names of nine citizens of Edmonton and the institutions with which they are associated and underneath their names were the words, in larger type, "Exterminate Them". The jury returned a verdict of guilty on the first count and the accused was sentenced to three months' imprisonment. On appeal, it was held the leaflet was beyond question defamatory of the persons named; this was a private prosecution and during the course of the judgment in the Appellate Division, Harvey, C.J.A., at pp. 532-3 D.L.R., pp. 201-2 C.C.C., had this to say:

> It is further objected that the jury should have been directed that if they considered that the private prosecutor who by the way in the notice of objection is described as "General Griesbach," was bringing the prosecution to vindicate his own private character, there should be no conviction and he should be left to his civil rights. It is stated in Russell on Crimes, 9th ed., p. 695, that the disposition of the Courts is to discourage criminal prosecutions launched merely to extract apologies or vindicate private character leaving the party libelled to civil remedies, and it is stated in the same work at p. 698 that: — "a scandal published of three or four persons is punishable on the complaint of one or more, or all of them." Of course there could have been nine separate civil actions for this libel but the purpose of the prosecution one gathers from the evidence was not so much for the regress of private wrongs as to punish for the wrong done the public. There certainly is nothing in the case that would warrant conclusion that civil proceedings would be an appropriate remedy.

The appeal and application for leave to appeal from the sentence was dismissed on all respects.

The penal provisions relating to criminal libel were, I believe, inserted in the *Code* to apply against people who make the type of statements made in the case at bar; I agree that public discussion should not be muzzled but invective does not advance the truth and I feel the accused have fallen within the definition following s.247. The defence contended that the paper was merely a college type of periodical but there was no evidence as to this.

There have been few cases of defamatory libel in our Courts but the words of Harvey, C.J.A., in *R. v. Unwin* seem to be apropos; it is unfortunate the accused did not apply their undoubted talents in a constructive sense.

I find all accused guilty as charged.

Accused convicted.

2.4.7 Robert Martin, "Law Reform Commission of Canada, Working Paper 35: Defamatory Libel", 1984, 22 *U.W.O. Law Review*, p. 249

The Criminal Code contains a number of unusual prohibitions. These are the result of particular historical circumstances which no longer obtain. Few Canadians today would, I imagine, regard the playing of three-card monte or the possession of crime comics as acts likely to undermine the social order. Yet both are crimes. Criminal libel is another of these anachronistic survivals.

The crime of libel originated in England in the 17th century. This was a time when the state was not sensitive to the importance of freedom of speech. Criminal libel was, pure and simple, an instrument of repression.

Canada inherited criminal libel along with the rest of the general English criminal law. The Criminal Code of Canada recognises three categories of criminal libel — seditious libel, blasphemous libel, and defamatory libel. None of these offences looms very large. The Supreme Court of Canada effectively disposed of sedition in 1950. Blasphemy seems moribund, although in England the House of Lords has recently attempted to revive it. Canadians — not many, it is true — continue to be prosecuted for defamatory libel and some are convicted.

The Law Reform Commission of Canada is in the process of carrying out a general review of our criminal law. As part of this exercise, the Commission has published a *Working Paper* on defamatory libel. It is unfortunate that the Commission did not study the whole field of criminal libel. That is, however, the only point where I wish to take issue. The *Working Paper* is a thorough, careful study. It is well documented, systematically organized, and clearly written. Its recommendations are straightforward and sensible. All of which is a convoluted way of saying that I like the *Working Paper* a lot and agree with it completely.

The purport of the Law Reform Commission's argument is that the offence of defamatory libel is neither necessary nor desirable in late 20th century Canada. I will attempt to summarise the argument.

The Court of Star Chamber created the offence of defamatory libel, in part at least, to discourage duelling. Since duelling is not widely perceived as a major social issue in Canada today, this fact alone would lead one to question the utility of maintaining the offence. But there is more.

The Commission believes that the tort of defamation provides both protection for reputation and a means of seeking redress against character assassins. The Commission thinks this should be enough. It is disturbed by the fact that statements or expressions which would not give rise to tortious liability might, nonetheless, be regarded as criminal. The *Working Paper* notes that mere insults can amount to defamatory libel, that publication to the victim alone is sufficient, and that truth is not a complete defence.

The Commission notes further that the offence of defamatory libel is badly expressed in the Criminal Code and that it is "... defective because it is not a full *mens rea* offence".

The effect of the Canadian Charter of Rights and Freedoms is addressed. Not only does the offence appear to deny the fundamental freedom of expression, it seems in a number of respects to be inconsistent with the presumption of innocence.

There is no social policy justification, the Law Reform Commission believes, for keeping defamatory libel in the Criminal Code. A number of dubious arguments in support of this are surveyed and quickly, and properly, dismissed. The lack of enthusiasm for the offence in a number of other Commonwealth states is mentioned.

At the end of its analysis, the Commission asks the right question, the only question:

> If there were no previously existing crime of libel, would it be necessary to create one now?

The answer, by this point, is obvious. And the *Working Paper's* main recommendation is equally clear and direct.

There should be no offence of defamation in the new *Criminal* Code or elsewhere.

Bravo!

The broader issue raised by this Working Paper is important. The issue is this. In a democratic society are there circumstances in which mere words, with nothing more, should properly be the subject of a criminal prosecution? The Commission was faced with this question in its *Report* on Contempt of Court and made a mess of it. The people who drafted the Criminal Law Reform Bill of 1984 had the good sense to pay no attention to the Commission's recommendations. But now that it seems to have got itself back on track, the Law Reform Commission of Canada might consider tackling the complicated and difficult issue of freedom of speech and the criminal law.

CHAPTER THREE

Judicial Proceedings: Legal Limitations to Protect the State's Rights, Prerogatives and Responsibilities, Part II

3.1 A Note on the Protection of Judicial Proceedings

The courts are public institutions. Their business is public business. Accordingly, there is a tradition in common law countries that the courts will remain open to the public and, subject to certain rules, what happens in them may be fully described in the media. The Constitution of Canada contains expressions of these principles. They are implied in the guarantees of freedom of the press in section 2(b) of the Charter, and explicit in section 11(d) which says that a person charged with an offence has the right "to be presumed innocent until proven guilty in a fair and public hearing by an independent and impartial tribunal". Those provisions speak to the public's right to know and to the rights of an accused person. The quality of justice is assumed to be related to the principle of openness.

However, there are a number of rules that apply to reporting the activities of courts and judges which journalists must know in detail. These rules have emerged from the courts themselves or have been legislated. They deliberately restrict freedom of expression. The justification for the rules is that they are supposed to provide a balance between free expression and the rights of individuals to fair trials. In fact, the rules are a haphazard and random collection of restrictions.

Technically, the law includes both statutory limitations on freedom of expression — the prohibitions on publishing the names of young offenders or victims of sexual crimes are examples — and the uncodified law of criminal contempt. The law of contempt can be considered alongside the several statutory rules since the latter serve the same purpose and are similarly inspired.

The purpose of the law of contempt is said to be the protection of the administration of justice. There are two types: *in facie* contempt, which means in the face of the court or in the courtroom itself; and *ex facie* contempt, or a contempt which occurs outside the court. A decision by a journalist to disobey an order by a judge to reveal the sources on which he or she based a story could lead to a citation for an *in facie* contempt. Some journalists have refused to obey such orders on the grounds that to do so would require breaking promises they made in order to gather the information in the first place.

Ex facie contempt includes ''scandalizing the court'' or criticising it or a judge by suggesting in vigorous language that justice has been thwarted or corrupted. Saying a judge is stupid or corrupt could earn a journalist a citation for contempt. Another *ex facie* contempt could occur if a judge ordered that certain materials or facts not be published during a proceeding and a journalist proceeded to do so anyway.

The law of contempt also empowers a judge to cite a journalist for breeching the sub-judice rule. When a charge has been laid and the matter is formally within the court's jurisdiction, public discussion is then restricted to contemporaneous and accurate reports of the facts or proceedings. Editorials which urge or predict a particular finding are viewed as usurping the court's authority. Publishing the criminal record of a defendant could prejudice the court's view of him or her, prevent a fair trial, and thereby be in contempt of court. It would be contrary to the *sub judice* rule to broadcast or publish an assumption that a defendant was guilty.

Technical breaches of the *sub judice* rule or other parts of the law of contempt will not lead inevitably to a prosecution. The timing and character of the breach, the size of the community, the place of publication or broadcast or whether the matter is to be decided by a judge or a judge and jury can all have a bearing. In the latter case, it is believed that juries are easier to prejudice than judges and that judges in the highest courts are the most difficult to prejudice.

3.2 The Principle of Openness

3.2.1 *Re Southam Inc. and the Queen* (1) (1983), 41 O.R. (2d) 113 (Ont. C.A.)

How the issue arose

On June 11th a reporter employed by the respondent Southam Inc. attended with counsel at the Provincial Court (Family Division) in Ottawa presided over by His Honour Judge Guzzo. They were advised that reporters or other members of the general public were not permitted to be present during the hearing of proceedings under the *Juvenile Delinquents Act*. Counsel for the respondent thereupon made an application to Judge Guzzo requesting that the public and, in particular, representatives of the media, be permitted to be present at such hearings.

After hearing submissions, Judge Guzzo was of the view that the Attorneys-General of Ontario and Canada should be served with notice of the respondent's application before he considered the submissions made. The application was, accordingly, adjourned to permit respondent's counsel time to research the matter further. The respondent did not renew this particular application but the same reporter once again, on June 15th, attempted to enter Judge Guzzo's court-room. Upon being advised that the reporter was not a witness in the proceedings involving a juvenile delinquent, Judge Guzzo directed her to leave the court-room.

The respondent then moved before the learned motions court judge for an order "in the nature of *mandamus* compelling His Honour Judge Guzzo of the Provincial Court (Family Division) to permit the applicants to be present during the hearings of proceedings held in Provincial Court (Family Division) in Ottawa pursuant to the *Juvenile Delinquents Act,* R.S.C. 1970, c.J-3". It was, we were advised, a general motion to "open the Juvenile Court" not related to any specific proceedings. The application was made pursuant to "the provisions of Sec. 24 of the *Constitution Act 1982*". Initially, in its appellant's statement, the Crown argued that the respondent did not have status to bring the application and that the Supreme Court of Ontario was not "a court of competent jurisdiction" within the meaning of that phrase found in s.24(1) of the Charter. However, as already noted that position was not pressed during the argument, the Crown agreeing that the application was properly before Mr. Justice Smith. Counsel also agreed that the Crown has a right of appeal in the instant case under s.28 of the *Judicature Act,* R.S.O. 1980, c.223. It is not necessary, accordingly, for me to consider these two questions further.

During the course of the argument in the court below the respondent altered its application in regard to the relief it sought and asked for a declaration that s.12(1) of the *Juvenile Delinquents Act* was ultra vires. The motions court judge granted the declaration requested.

The argument which was made before us and which found favour with the motions court judge was that the exclusion of the public from such trials offends "freedom of expression, including freedom of the press", guaranteed by the Charter.

The sections of the Charter to which we were referred are the following:

Rights and freedoms in Canada

1. The *Canadian Charter of Rights and Freedoms* guarantees the rights and freedoms set out in it subject only to such reasonable limits prescribed by law as can be demonstrably justified in a free and democratic society.

Fundamental freedoms

2. Everyone has the following fundamental freedoms:

...

(*b*) freedom of thought, belief, opinion and expression, including freedom of the press and other media of communications;

Other rights and freedoms not affected by Charter

26. The guarantee in this Charter of certain rights and freedoms shall not be construed as denying the existence of any other rights or freedoms that exist in Canada.

We were also referred to s.52 of the *Constitution Act, 1982* which establishes the supremacy of the Constitution of Canada, including the Charter, over other laws, and provides the basis for judicial review of legislation in Canada:

52(1) The Constitution of Canada is the supreme law of Canada, and any law that is inconsistent with the provisions of the Constitution is, to the extent of the inconsistency, of no force or effect.

This section gives to the court the necessary power to make the requested declaration if there is found to be the required inconsistency. The basic question is whether the trial of children *in camera* is a breach of freedom of "opinion and expression, including freedom of the press and other media communication". Following the wording in some American authorities the motions court judge held that freedom of expression and of the press are "adjuncts" to the concept of the openness of our judicial system and the right of access to the courts.

Is free access to the courts a fundamental right or freedom?
Section 2(b) of the Charter

There can be no doubt that the openness of the courts to the public is one of the hallmarks of a democratic society. Public accessibility to the courts was and is a felt necessity; it is a restraint on arbitrary action by those who govern and by the powerful. The most recent and comprehensive review of principle in this area of the law was made by Dickson J. in his reasons for the majority in *A.-G. N.S. et al. v. MacIntyre* (1982), 65 C.C.C. (2d) 129, 132 D.L.R. (3d) 385, 40 N.R. 181.

In this case, a television journalist applied for an order requiring a justice of the peace to make available to him for inspection, search warrants and informations in his possession. A Supreme Court Judge allowed the application and held that the journalist, as a member of the general public, was entitled to inspect executed search warrants and supporting informations. The Nova Scotia Court of Appeal dismissed the appeal from that judgment and did not restrict the right of access to only executed warrants. The Supreme Court dismissed the appeal but restricted the right of access, as had the Supreme Court Judge, to executed search warrants.

In the course of his reasons, Dickson J. said (pp. 144-5 C.C.C., pp. 400-1 D.L.R., pp. 188-9 N.R.):

> The question before us is limited to search warrants and informations. The response to that question, it seems to me, should be guided by several broad policy considerations, namely, respect for the privacy of the individual, protection of the administration of justice, implementation of the will of Parliament that a search warrant be an effective aid in the investigation of crime, and finally, a strong public policy in favour of "openness" in respect of judicial acts. The *rationale* of this last-mentioned consideration has been eloquently expressed by Bentham in these terms:
>
> > "In the darkness of secrecy, sinister interest, and evil in every shape have full swing. Only in proportion as publicity has place can any of the checks applicable to judicial injustice operate. Where there is no publicity there is no justice. Publicity is the very soul of justice. It is the keenest spur to exertion and surest of all guards against improbity. It keeps the judge himself while trying under trial."
>
> The concern for accountability is not diminished by the fact that the search warrants might be issued by a Justice *in camera*. On the contrary, this fact increases the policy argument in favour of accessibility. Initial secrecy surrounding the issuance of warrants may lead to abuse, and publicity is a strong deterrent to potential malversation.
>
> In short, what should be sought is maximum accountability and accessibility but not to the extent of harming the innocent or of impairing the efficiency of the search warrant as a weapon in society's never-ending fight against crime.

And, at pp. 145-6 C.C.C., pp. 401-2 D.L.R., p. 190 N.R.:

> It is now well established, however, that covertness is the exception and openness the rule. Public confidence in the integrity of the Court system and understanding of the administration of justice are thereby fostered. As a general rule the sensibilities of the individuals involved are no basis for exclusion of the public from judicial proceedings. The following comments

of Laurence J. in *R. v. Wright,* 8 T.L.R. 293, are apposite and were cited with approval by Duff J. in the *Gazette Printing Co. v. Shallow* (1909), 41 S.C.R. 339, at p. 359:

> " 'Though the publication of such proceedings may be to the disadvantage of the particular individual concerned, yet it is of vast importance to the public that the proceedings of courts of justice should be universally known. The general advantage to the country in having these proceedings made public more than counterbalances the inconveniences to the private persons whose conduct may be the subject of such proceedings.' "

The leading case is the decision of the House of Lords in *Scott v. Scott,* [1913] A.C. 417. In the later case of *McPherson v. McPherson,* [1936] A.C. 177 at p. 200, Lord Blanesburgh, delivering the judgment of the Privy Council, referred to "publicity" as the "authentic hall-mark of judicial as distinct from administrative procedure".

It is, of course, true that *Scott v. Scott* and *McPherson v. McPherson* were cases in which proceedings had reached the stage of trial whereas the issuance of a search warrant takes place at the pre-trial investigative stage. The cases mentioned, however, and many others which could be cited, establish the broad principle of "openness" in judicial proceedings, whatever their nature, and in the exercise of judicial powers. The same policy considerations upon which is predicated our reluctance to inhibit accessibility at the trial stage are still present and should be addressed at the pre-trial stage.

And, at pp. 146-7 C.C.C., pp. 402-3 D.L.R., p. 191 N.R.:

Ex parte applications for injunctions, interlocutory proceedings, or preliminary inquiries are not trial proceedings, and yet the "open court" rule applies in these cases. The authorities have held that subject to a few well-recognized exceptions, as in the case of infants, mentally disordered persons or secret processes, all judicial proceedings must be held in public. The editor of Halsbury's Laws of England, 4th ed., vol. 10, para. 705, p. 316, states the rule in these terms:

> "In general, all cases, both civil and criminal, must be heard in open court, but in certain exceptional cases, where the administration of justice would be rendered impracticable by the presence of the public, the court may sit in camera."

At every stage the rule should be one of public accessibility and concomitant judicial accountability; all with a view to ensuring there is no abuse in the issue of search warrants, that once issued they are executed according to law, and finally that any evidence seized is dealt with according to law. A decision by the Crown not to prosecute, notwithstanding the finding of evidence appearing to establish the commission of a crime may, in some circumstances, raise issues of public importance.

In my view, curtailment of public accessibility can only be justified where there is present the need to protect social values of superordinate importance. One of these is the protection of the innocent.

He concluded that the effective administration of justice would be frustrated if individuals were permitted to be present when the warrants were issued and that the exclusion of the public from the proceedings attending the actual issuance of the warrant was justified. However, once the warrant has been executed, the need for concealment virtually disappears and "The curtailment of the traditionally uninhibited accessibility of the public to the working of the Courts should be undertaken with the greatest reluctance" (pp. 148-9 C.C.C., pp. 404-5 D.L.R., p. 193 N.R.).

In the instant case, counsel for the Crown argued strenuously that public access to the courts was not a specific or fundamental right guaranteed by the Charter and therefore s.24(1) could not be invoked as it had no application to the question. Further, he argued, that being so, there was no need to resort to s.1 and determine whether s.12(1) imposed "reasonable limits... as can be demonstrably justified in a free and democratic society".

It is true that public accessibility to the courts is not spelled out in terms as part of the fundamental freedoms. Counsel argued that "freedom of the press" is limited by s.2(*b*) itself, in that it is but part of freedom of thought, belief, opinion and expression. I do not believe that it is appropriate to use the word "limited" in connection with s.2(*b*) although I do accept that freedom of the press refers to the dissemination of expression of thought, belief or opinion through the medium of the press. If anything, the words "freedom of expression" would seem to have a wider or larger connotation than the words "freedom of the press".

Counsel for the Crown pointed out that the wording in the Charter with regard to "freedom of the press" differs significantly from that in the First Amendment to the United States Constitution. The First Amendment reads, in part:

> Congress shall make no law... abridging the freedom of speech or of the press; or the right of the people peaceably to assemble...

It can be seen that the reference is to freedom of the press, *simpliciter,* unlike the Charter which includes freedom of the press in freedom of thought, belief, opinion and expression. However, whether the American case-law on freedom of the press is of persuasive authority is of small moment in the instant case as the respondent is relying on s.2(*b*) as guaranteeing to the general public free access to the courts as an integral part of the fundamental freedom of opinion and expression. It is not an issue of "freedom of the press" *per se.*

In *Richmond Newspapers, Inc. et al. v. Commonwealth of Virginia et al.* (1980), 100 S. Ct. 2814, 48 L.W. 5008, the Supreme Court of the United States considered for the first time the narrow question of whether the right of the public and the press to attend criminal trials was guaranteed under the United States Constitution. One Stevenson had been indicted for murder, three abortive trials had taken place and he was being tried in the same court for a fourth time. At the opening of that trial, counsel for the accused moved that it be closed to the public and the prosecutor stated that he had no objection. The trial judge thereupon ordered the court-room cleared. Richmond Newspapers subsequently moved to intervene and ultimately took the issue to appeal.

In delivering the lead judgment of the court, Chief Justice Burger reviewed at some length the Anglo-American history of criminal trials. This review emphasized that from time immemorial, judicial trials have been held in open court, to which the public have free access. He concluded that "from this unbroken, uncontradicted history, supported by reasons as valid today as in centuries past, we are bound to conclude that a presumption of openness inheres in the very nature of a criminal trial under our system of justice" (p. 2825). He went on to say (p. 2826):

> The First Amendment, in conjunction with the Fourteenth, prohibits governments from "abridging the freedom of speech or of the press; or the right of the people peaceably to assemble, and to petition the government for a redress of grievances". These expressly guaranteed freedoms share a common core purpose of assuring freedom of communication on matters relating to the functioning of government. Plainly it would be difficult to single out any aspect of government of higher concern and importance to the people than the manner in which criminal trials are conducted.

As stated, counsel for the Crown submits that the right of public access to the courts does not fall under the fundamental freedoms guaranteed by the Charter. I do not agree. The Charter as part of a constitutional document should be given a large and liberal construction. The spirit of this new "living tree" planted in friendly Canadian soil should not be stultified by narrow technical, literal interpretations without regard to its background and purpose; capability for growth must be recognized: *Re s.24 of B.N.A. Act; Edwards et al. v. A.-G. Can. et al.*, [1930] 1 D.L.R. 98 at pp. 107-8, [1930] A.C. 124 at p. 136, [1929] 3 W.W.R. 479. Although said in a very different connection, it is apposite here: "For the letter killeth but the spirit giveth life."

Trials of juveniles are not criminal trials as such and the enforcement process is "specially adapted to the age and impressibility of juveniles and fundamentally different, in pattern and purpose, from the one governing in the case of adults": *A.-G. B.C. v. Smith,* [1969] 1 C.C.C. 244 at p. 251, [1967] S.C.R. 702 at p. 710, 65 D.L.R. (2d) 82 at p. 88. Nevertheless, serious criminal matters are heard by juvenile courts, matters in which there is a public interest and concern, and in which in many cases, it is acknowledged by the Crown, no necessary interest of the juvenile is served by the exclusion of the public from such hearings.

It is true, as argued, that free access to the courts is not specifically enumerated under the heading of fundamental freedoms but, in my view, such access, having regard to its historic origin and necessary purpose already recited at length, is an integral and implicit part of the guarantee given to everyone of freedom of opinion and expression which, in terms, includes freedom of the press. However the rule may have had its origin, as Mr. Justice Dickson pointed out, the "openness" rule fosters the necessary public confidence in the integrity of the court system and an understanding of the administration of justice. The respondent has established that its right, as a member of the public, under s.2(*b*) of the Charter, has, *prima facie,* been infringed.

Is s.12(1) a reasonable limit as can be demonstrably justified in a free and democratic society?
Section 1 of the Charter

I turn now to the last question to be answered: is the exclusion of the public under s.12(1) a reasonable limit prescribed by law as can be demonstrably justified in a free and democratic society (to quote the relevant words of s.1 of the Charter)? As a subsidiary consideration, the standard as formed by Mr. Justice Dickson would have to be met, namely: "[C]urtailment of public accessibility can only be justified where there is present the need to protect social values of superordinate importance." A preliminary question which has to be determined is: upon whom is the burden of establishing that the limit in issue is a reasonable one demonstrably justifiable in a free and democratic society?

"Onus" or "burden" of proof under s.1

The Crown takes the initial position that the freedoms granted under s.2 of the Charter, guaranteed by s.1, are conditioned, qualified or limited rights by virtue of the wording of s.1 which qualifies the rights and freedoms by making them subject to reasonable limits on a particular basis. The onus or burden, the argument goes, is on him who is asserting that his particular freedom has been infringed or breached to establish that the limit imposed by the law being attacked, is an unreasonable limit which *cannot* be demonstrably justified in a free and democratic society.

It appears to me that that position and the reasoning supporting it is strained and inappropriate to the clear wording of the two sections. Section 2 states that everyone has the named fundamental freedoms. Section 1 guarantees those rights and, although the rights are not absolute or unrestricted, makes it clear that if there is a limit imposed on these fundamental rights by law, the limits must be reasonable and demonstrably justified in a free and democratic society. The wording imposes a positive obligation on those seeking to uphold the limit or limits to establish to the satisfaction of the court by evidence, by the terms and purpose of the limiting law, its economic, social and political background, and, if felt helpful, by references to comparable legislation of other acknowledged free and democratic societies, that such limit or limits are reasonable and demonstrably justified in a free and democratic society. I cannot accept the proposition urged upon us that, as the freedoms may be limited ones, the person who establishes that, *prima facie,* his freedom has been infringed or denied must then take the further step and establish, on the balance of probabilities, the negative, namely, that such infringement or limit is unreasonable and cannot be demonstrably justified in a free and democratic society. In some case, of course, the frivolous nature of the claim to protection of a freedom or right and of the submissions made in support will be immediately apparent and it will not take great effort to determine that the claim to a guaranteed freedom or right is not tenable under the Charter and under the circumstances. But that is not this case.

As part of his submission in connection with the alleged onus or burden on the respondent, counsel for the Crown pointed out that under s.24(1) the applicant initiates the proceeding and, accordingly, the usual rules should apply, namely, that if at the end of the hearing the court is undecided and matters are left in balance, then the application must fail. He argued that the onus has always been on an applicant claiming that a Legislature has exceeded in legislation or a portion thereof, its legislative jurisdiction or competence. He submitted that, under the "presumption of constitutionality", there is a clear evidentiary burden on the applicant which includes establishing that the limit is not a reasonable one and that it is not demonstrably justified in a free and democratic society. It does not appear to me that the so-called "presumption of constitutionality" assists in this type of case. There is no conflict here between two legislative bodies, federal and provincial, claiming jurisdiction over a particular legislative subject-matter. This rather is a determination whether a portion of a law is inconsistent with the provisions of the Constitution, the supreme law of Canada. This supreme law was enacted long after the *Juvenile Delinquents Act* and there can be no presumption that the legislators intended to act constitutionally in light of legislation that was not, at that time, a gleam in its progenitor's eye. In any event, like Chief Justice Deschênes, I am of the view that the complete burden of proving an exception under s.1 of the Charter rests on the party claiming the benefit of the exception or limitation: *Quebec Ass'n of Protestant School Boards et al. v. A.-G. Que. et al. (No. 2)* (1982), 140 D.L.R. (3d) 33 at p. 59.

Is the limit a "reasonable limit" as can be demonstrably justified in a free and democratic society?

It is agreed that the limit in the instant case is "prescribed by law".

The learned motions court judge, in the course of his reasons, stated [70 C.C.C. (2d) 257 at p. 262, 38 O.R. (2d) 748 at p. 754 *sub nom. Reference re Constitutional Validity of s.12 of Juvenile Delinquents Act,* 141 D.L.R. (3d) 341 at p. 347]: "That the courts possess an inherent jurisdiction to forbid access [to the courts] in certain narrow instances, is beyond dispute." If that were so I would have very little difficulty in giving effect to the respondent's position. However, a statutory court such as the provincial court (family division) has no inherent jurisdiction but has only that jurisdiction which is specifically conferred on it by statute. Both counsel before us agreed that the motions court judge was in error in this regard.

However, counsel for the respondent sought to support the position that a family court judge had a discretion under the *Juvenile Delinquents Act* to close his court by arguing that such a discretion was given under ss.12(2) and 36(1) of that Act. Section 12(2), quoted, beginning as it does with the words, "Such trials", refers back to s.12(1), the section under attack. That section directs that trials of children shall be held *in camera* and ss.(2) is a permissive section dealing with the location of the trials to be held *in camera*. Section 12(1) is absolute in its terms and s.12(2) was not intended to give and does not give an additional discretionary power to the judge to exclude the public which, in view of the wording of s.12(1), would be quite unnecessary.

Section 36(1) reads:

> 36(1) Every juvenile court has such and like powers and authority to preserve order in court during the sittings thereof and by the like ways and means as now by law are or may be exercised and used in like cases and for the like purposes by any court in Canada and by the judges thereof, during the sittings thereof.

The power given to the juvenile court to preserve order and cite for contempt of court has no relevance to a discretionary power to exclude the public in order to protect the interests of the child and advance the perceived purpose and object of juvenile hearings. A juvenile judge could not use this subsection to exclude the public (and the press as part of the public) at the beginning of a hearing when there is no prospect of nor concern for disorder.

We are accordingly left in the unhappy position of it being all or nothing. If s.12(1) is allowed to stand, so long as the present Act is in existence the public is excluded from every such hearing; if s.12(1) is struck down the public, until further amendment, can attend all such hearings without regard to any other interests. There is no half-way house such as now exists in similar legislation actual and contemplated, where the court is given a discretion to exclude the public in the best interests of the child and ultimately of the public. The choice, accordingly, at present has to be made between the two absolutes.

The purpose of the legislation under review is effectively set out in ss.3(2) and 38 of the Act:

> 3(2) Where a child is adjudged to have committed a delinquency he shall be dealt with, not as an offender, but as one in a condition of delinquency and therefore requiring help and guidance and proper supervision.
>
> ...
>
> 38. This Act shall be liberally construed in order that its purpose may be carried out, namely, that the care and custody and discipline of a juvenile delinquent shall approximate as nearly as may be that which should be given by his parents, and that as far as practicable every juvenile delinquent shall be treated, not as criminal, but as a misdirected and misguided child, and one needing aid, encouragement, help and assitance.

As the motions court judge pointed out, the *Young Offenders Act,* 1980-81-82 (Can.), c.110 (which will replace the *Juvenile Delinquents Act*), enacted but not yet proclaimed in force, is now based on the principle of responsibility and accountability (s.3(1)). Under that Act hearings are open to the public with the court having the power under certain conditions or circumstances to exclude any or all members of the public from the proceedings, with certain exceptions. It is not an automatic exclusion as under the present legislation.

Section 39 of the *Young Offenders Act* reads:

> 39(1) Subject to subsection (2), where a court or justice before whom proceedings are carried out under this Act is of the opinion
>
> (*a*) that any evidence or information presented to the court or justice would be seriously injurious or prejudicial to
>
> (i) the young person who is being dealt with in the proceedings,
>
> (ii) a child or young person who is a witness in the proceedings,
>
> (iii) a child or young person who is aggrieved by or the victim of the offence charged in the proceedings, or
>
> (*b*) that it would be in the interest of public morals, the maintenance of order or the proper administration of justice to exclude any or all members of the public from the court room,
>
> the court or justice may exclude any person from all or part of the proceedings if the court or justice deems that person's presence to be unnecessary to the conduct of the proceedings.
>
> (2) A court or justice may not, pursuant to subsection (1), exclude from proceedings under this Act
>
> (*a*) the prosecutor;
>
> (*b*) the young person who is being dealt with in the proceedings, his parent, his counsel or any adult assisting him pursuant to subsection 11(7);
>
> (*c*) the provincial director or his agent; or
>
> (*d*) the youth worker to whom the young person's case has been assigned.
>
> (3) The youth court, after it has found a young person guilty of an offence, or the youth court or the review board, during a review of a disposition under sections 28 to 33, may, in its discretion, exclude from the court or from a hearing of the review board, as the case may be, any person other than
>
> (*a*) the young person or his counsel,
>
> (*b*) the provincial director or his agent,
>
> (*c*) the youth worker to whom the young person's case has been assigned, and
>
> (*d*) the Attorney General or his agent,
>
> when any information is being presented to the court or the review board the knowledge of which might, in the opinion of the court or review board, be seriously injurious or seriously prejudicial to the young person.

When and if the *Young Offenders Act* in its present form will be proclaimed in force cannot be predicted.

Counsel for the appellant, although candidly acknowledging that not every hearing under the *Juvenile Delinquents Act* would call for the exclusion of the public, argued that to give effect to the declared purpose of the Act, it was necessary to close all juvenile court hearings to the public and this is a reasonable limit on the rights of the public to be present at trials. He pointed out that in smaller municipalities the presence of friends and curious neighbours could have a chilling and inhibiting effect on the evidence of the child and parents or guardian. The court might not have the necessary full information to be able to reach a proper understanding in order to give the necessary aid, encouragement and protection to the child. He, in substance, argued the grounds that give to the court under the proposed legislation (s.39) the discretionary power to exclude members of the public. The difference is that the reasoning is used to support the reasonableness of mandating the total exclusion of the public in all cases, not to support the use of a discretionary power.

Counsel submitted that the interests of the public are protected in that s.12(3) gives to the court the discretion to allow for the publication of the identity of the child. Further, it was suggested that the offensive aspects of a "private" trial are ameliorated by other parts of the governing Act. For example, there is no prohibition against speaking to those who were in attendance at the hearing nor against securing a transcript of the proceedings. The parents or guardians must be served with notice of any charge of delinquency and may be present and be heard (ss.10 and 22(4)). The child's probation officer must be present in the court in order to represent the interests of the child when the case is heard (s.31); the juvenile court committee, being a committee of citizens, may be present at any session of the juvenile court (ss.27 and 28). The child is entitled to be represented by counsel. All these are factors which, counsel for the appellant argues, establish that s.12(1), in the context of the Act, does not truly deprive the public of the right of access to the courts, and therefore it is a reasonable limit on s.2(*b*) of the Charter.

While the argument is superficially an attractive one, it does not meet the basic objection under the Charter respecting the arbitrary nature of the operation of the section. Further, the examples of public access to the proceedings recited above (some of which are indirect at best) raise with even greater clarity and emphasis the question of the necessity and reasonableness of an absolute bar in all cases. It can be seen that under the *Young Offenders Act* although the court is given the discretionary power to exclude all members of the public, it cannot exclude the young offender, his parents, his counsel or his youth worker (probation officer). Such representation of the public does not, in my view, satisfy the required fundamental freedom of expression as earlier reviewed, or reasonably qualify the arbitrary nature of the absolute effect of the present section.

Counsel for the appellant argued that, in any event, the limit imposed on the fundamental freedom was a *reasonable limit demonstrably justified in a free and democratic society* (emphasis added). In support of his position he pointed out that the section had been on the Canadian statute books since 1908 without objection, and that Canada was a free and democratic society. It seems to me that this reasoning, by itself, has little to do with the requirements of s.1 of the Charter. If the fact that an Act had been on our statute books without challenge for a period of years was determinative of the question an issue raised by s.1, no statute or section of a statute in existence prior to the Charter coming into force could be effectively challenged.

We are left, at present, to a certain extent wandering in unexplored terrain in which we have to set up our own guide-posts in interpreting the meaning and effect of the words of s.1 of the Charter. In determining the reasonableness of the limit in each particular case, the court must examine objectively its argued rational basis in light of what the court understands to be reasonable in a free and democratic society. Further, there is, it appears to me, a significant burden on the proponent of the limit or limits to demonstrate their justification to the satisfaction of the court. As I said earlier that may be easily done in a number of cases.

In determining whether the limit is justifiable, some help may be derived from considering the legislative approaches taken in similar fields by other acknowledged free and democratic societies. Presumably this may also assist in determining whether the limit is a reasonable one. It may be that some of the rights guaranteed by the Charter do not have their counterpart in other free and democratic societies and one is sent back immediately to the facts of our own society. In any event I believe the court must come back, ultimately, having derived whatever assistance can be secured from the experience of other free and democratic societies, to the facts of our own free and democratic society to answer the question whether the limit imposed on the particular guaranteed freedom has been demonstrably justified as a reasonable one, having balanced the perceived purpose and objectives of the limiting legislation, in light of all relevant considerations, against the freedom or right allegedly infringed.

...

In England, no person shall be present at any sitting of a juvenile court except, *inter alia,* "bonâ fide representatives of newspapers or news agencies" and "such other persons as the court may specially authorise to be present": see the *Children and Young Persons Act,* 1933 (U.K.), c.12, s.47.

I should note that in all the cases where the media is allowed to be present, there is, similar to s.12(3) of the *Juvenile Delinquents Act,* a ban on the publication of the name of the child or anything that might lead to his identification. The court, however, is given the discretion to lift the ban.

If any majority approach can be identified from the review of comparable legislation, it is that juvenile courts are given the discretion to exclude members of the public depending upon its view of the circumstances. There are comparatively few jurisdictions where the prohibition of access is absolute with no discretion left to the hearing judge to determine whether it is appropriate and necessary to exclude all or any of the public.

As I stated earlier, I think it is necessary to view the reasonableness of the absolute ban in light of the purpose of the ban as balanced against the fundamental right guaranteed by the Charter.

Although there is a rational basis for the exclusion of the public from hearings under the *Juvenile Delinquents Act,* I do not think an absolute ban in all cases is a reasonable limit on the right of access to the courts, subsumed under the guaranteed freedom of expression, including freedom of the press. The net which s.12(1) casts is too wide for the purpose which it serves. Society loses more than it protects by the all-embracing nature of the section. As stated earlier, counsel for the Attorney-General was quick to acknowledge (and very fairly so) that not every juvenile court proceeding would require the barring of public access. An amendment giving jurisdiction to the court to exclude the public from juvenile court proceedings where it concludes, under the circumstances, that it is in the best interests of the child or others concerned or in the best interests of the administration of justice to do so would meet any residual concern arising from the striking down of the section. As Mr. Justice Martin said in *R. v. Oakes* (released February 2, 1983, unreported) [since reported 2 C.C.C. (3d) 339, 40 O.R. (2d) 660] we are not entitled to rewrite the statute under attack when considering the applicability of the provisions of the Charter. Parliament can give the necessary discretion to the court to be exercised on a case-to-case basis which, in my view, would be a prospective reasonable limit on the guaranteed right and demonstrably justifiable. The protection of social values of "superordinate importance" referred to by Dickson J. in *A.-G. N.S. et al. v. MacIntyre* (1982), 65 C.C.C. (2d) 129, 132 D.L.R. (3d) 385, 26 C.R. (3d) 193, does not require, in my view, an absolute bar in all cases of the public, including the press, from juvenile court proceedings.

The appellant in the present case has not demonstrably justified the limit imposed by s.12(1) as a reasonable one in this free and democratic society and, accordingly, the appeal is dismissed.

Appeal dismissed.

Note: The Juvenile Delinquents Act is no longer law. See section 3.5.2.2 for relevant provisions of the Young Offenders Act.

3.2.2 *Edmonton Journal* v. *Attorney-General of Alberta and Attorney-General of Canada* (1983), 28 Atla. L.R. (2d) 369 (Q.B.)

D. C. McDonald J.: ... Counsel for all the applicants rely heavily upon the judgment of the Court of Appeal of Ontario in *Re Southam Inc. and R.* (1983), 41 O.R. (2d) 113, 34 C.R. (3d) 27, 33 R.F.L. (2d) 279, 3 C.C.C. (3d) 515. That case did not concern a fatality inquiry or a coroner's inquest. It concerned a trial of a juvenile in juvenile court on a charge of juvenile delinquency. The court held that s.12(1) of the Juvenile Delinquents Act, R.S.C. 1970, c.J-3 infringed s.2(*b*) of the Charter. Section 12(1) states:

> 12(1) The trials of children shall take place without publicity and separately and apart from the trials of other accused persons, at suitable times to be designated and appointed for that purpose.

The court held that although free access to the courts is not specifically enumerated in the Charter under the heading of fundamental freedoms:

> ... such access, having regard to its historic origin and necessary purpose... is an integral and implicit part of the guarantee given to everyone of... freedom of the press... The "openness" rule fosters the necessary public confidence in the integrity of the court system and in understanding of the administration of justice. (per MacKinnon A.C.J.O. at p. 525.)

The court upheld the declaration granted in the High Court of Justice that s.12(1) of the Juvenile Delinquents Act is ultra vires.

The order made by the Ontario Court of Appeal was different from that of Dea J. of this court, in *R. v. B. (G.),* 24 Alta. L.R. (2d) 226, [1983] 3 W.W.R. 141, (sub nom. *Edmonton Journal v. A.G. Alta.*) 4 C.C.C. (3d) 59, 146 D.L.R. (3d) 673, 4 C.R.R. 296, 42 A.R. 383. That case was decided on 7th January 1983, but was not referred to by the Ontario Court of Appeal in *Re Southam Inc. and R.*, supra, which was decided on 31st March 1983. The Ontario case is said to be now on appeal to the Supreme Court of Canada.

Dea J. denied that s.12(1) of the Juvenile Delinquents Act infringes s.2(*b*) of the Charter. He held that s.2(*b*) does not create a "right of access". At p. 232 he said:

> In my view, the freedom of expression guaranteed by the Charter does not include a right of access. In view of the wording of the Charter, a finding of a right of access incorporated into the guaranteed freedom of expression by necessary implication would be tantamount to writing into the Charter what Parliament chose to leave out.

However, he held that s.12(1) of the Act, if read as a blanket mandatory requirement of exclusion, is inconsistent with s.11(*d*) of the Charter in that it is inconsistent with the right to a public hearing. He held that there is no "superordinate importance" (to use the words of Dickson J. of the Supreme Court of Canada in the pre-Charter case of *MacIntyre v. A.G.N.S.*, [1982] 1 S.C.R. 175, 26 C.R. (3d) 193, 65 C.C.C. (2d) 129, 132 D.L.R. (3d) 385, 49 N.S.R. (2d) 609, 96 A.P.R. 609, 40 N.R. 181) in holding *all* juvenile trials in camera. In order to secure the rationale of protecting the child in a case where that is the appropriate result, he held that the word "shall" in s.12(1) should be "read down" so as to read "may". He also held that his order would have prospective effect only.

The decision of the Ontario Court of Appeal in *Re Southam Inc. and R.*, supra, should not be read as authority for a broad proposition that the "freedom of the press" protected by s.2(*b*) encompasses a general "right of access" to information generated in the process of government beyond the judicial process. In delivering the judgment of the court, MacKinnon A.C.J.O. (at p. 523) treated "freedom of the press" as referring to "the dissemination of expression of thought, belief or opinion through the medium of the press", and noted that "If anything, the words 'freedom of expression' would seem to have a wider or larger connotation than the words 'freedom of the press' ". He noted also, without expressing disapproval, that counsel for the respondent newspaper was

> ...relying on s.2(*b*) as guaranteeing to the general public free access to the courts as an integral part of the fundamental freedom of opinion and expression. It is not an issue of "freedom of the press" *per se*.

At p. 525 he noted that "serious criminal matters are heard by juvenile courts, matters in which there is a public interest and concern". He then concluded, as I have noted [also at p. 525], that

> free access to the courts... is an integral and implicit part of the guarantee given to everyone of freedom of opinion and expression which, in terms, includes freedom of the press

and that the "openness" rule "fosters the necessary public confidence in the integrity of the court system and an understanding of the administration of justice".

In *R. v. B. (G.)*, supra, Dea J. concluded, as did MacKinnon A.C.J.O., that "freedom of the press" is not a freedom that is "separate and independent" from "freedom of thought, belief opinion and expression". However, he also held that "freedom of expression" does not incorporate a "right of access". I need not here consider the reasoning which led him to that conclusion. I simply note the conclusion.

...

3.2.3 *R.* v. *Robinson* (1983), 41 O.R. (2d) 764 (Ont. H.C.)

BOLAND J. (orally): — This is an application pursuant to s.24(1) of the *Canadian Charter of Rights and Freedoms* to continue the temporary order prohibiting the broadcast and publication of the name, address and other information that would identify the applicant who has been charged with murder under s.218 of the *Criminal Code*.

Section 2(*b*) of the Charter provides everyone with specific fundamental freedoms including:

> (*b*) freedom of thought, belief, opinion and expression, including freedom of the press and other media of communication.

Section 11(*d*) provides that

> 11. Any person charged with an offence has the right
>
> ...
>
> (*d*) to be presumed innocent until proven guilty according to law in a fair and public hearing by an independent and impartial tribunal.

Section 1 guarantees these rights and freedoms "subject only to such reasonable limits prescribed by law as can be demonstrably justified in a free and democratic society".

Section 24(1) states:

> 24(1) Anyone whose rights or freedoms, as guaranteed by this Charter, have been infringed or denied may apply to a court of competent jurisdiction to obtain such remedy as the court considers appropriate and just in the circumstances.

The issue surfaced on March 27, 1983, when the applicant was charged with murder. The following afternoon his counsel obtained a temporary publication ban from Mr. Justice Osler, on the name, address and any other information that would identify the accused. The application was based on the premise that the right of the accused to be presumed innocent as guaranteed by the Charter would be infringed if his name and address were published or broadcast. The order was served on the media and Mr. Justice Osler arranged for his temporary order to be reviewed on the merits on April 5, 1983.

Counsel for the applicant contended there was a confrontation between the freedom of the press and the public's "right to know" *and* the individual's right to be presumed innocent until proven guilty, the right to a fair trial and the right to security of the person. He argued that free press and fair trial cannot coexist as absolutes.

Counsel for the media urged the court to find the temporary order infringes or denies the fundamental freedom of expression, including freedom of the press as guaranteed by the Charter and was not a reasonable limit prescribed by law as can be demonstrably justified in a free and democratic society.

Having reviewed the material, I would like to emphasize that there was no suggestion of contempt raised on the application and there is no evidence of irresponsible reporting on the part of the media. I am satisfied that the publication of the name of the applicant, who has been charged with murder, would not infringe or deny his right to be presumed innocent and his right to a fair trial.

The presumption of innocence referred to in s.11(*d*) of the Charter is a presumption in favour of an accused which operates at trial and gives rise to the burden of proof beyond a reasonable doubt which rests upon the Crown throughout the trial. That presumption does not create a right in an accused person to undermine the statutory power to secure fingerprint identification or affect the conduct of a bail hearing or remain anonymous until after trial. Such a right would have to be based on statutory or common law.

The right to a fair trial is fundamental to our system of justice. There is nothing new about this concept. Moreover there are numerous procedural safeguards to ensure the accused a fair trial in the face of pre-trial publicity such as the juror's oath, the trial judge's instructions to the jury with respect to the media, the rights of the accused in jury selection, the screening of jurors by the trial judge, the criminal standard of proof and possibly a change of venue.

Furthermore, the essential quality of the criminal process in a democracy is the absence of secrecy. From the information to the acquittal or conviction, our judicial process is characterized by public access. The public has the right to be informed and the media has a duty to advise the public what is happening in our courts. Openness prevents abuse of the judicial system and fosters public confidence in the fairness and integrity of our system of justice. The press is a positive influence in assuring fair trial.

Parliament is supreme as a lawmaking body and the traditional role of the judiciary is to interpret the law. Where Parliament has concluded that the public interest dictates that the names of persons involved in the judicial process be withheld from the public, Parliament has created specific statutory prohibitions. For example, the *Criminal Code* provides when the name of the complainant in cases of sexual assault is not to be published and provides similar prohibitions with respect to the names of children and wire-taps. Parliament has not seen fit to legislate such a right in favour of an adult accused and such a right is not supported by the Charter.

On the other hand, freedom of the press is a fundamental freedom guaranteed by the Charter. If a free press is to fulfil its function it requires access to information that should be public and it requires freedom to print without prior restraint. Prior restraint should only be imposed on the press in extraordinary circumstances. There are no extraordinary circumstances in this case and I find there is no right provided by the Charter that has been infringed or denied.

For these reasons I am not continuing the order and the application is dismissed.

Application dismissed.

3.2.4 *Re Regina and Unnamed Person* (1985), 22 C.C.C. (3d) 284 (Ont. C.A.)

ZUBER J.A.: — This is an appeal by Southam Inc. and the Brockville Recorder and Times Limited from an order made by Keith J. prohibiting the publication or broadcast of the identity of a female person. An appreciation of the issues requires only a brief outline of the facts.

On May 1, 1984, a 17-year-old woman was charged in the provincial court (criminal division) at Brockville with two offences: infanticide, contrary to s.216 of the *Criminal Code,* and neglect to obtain assistance in childbirth contrary to s.226 of the *Criminal Code*. While these charges generated some publicity, the 17-year-old woman was not identified.

On June 13, 1984, counsel for the young woman brought an application before Mr. Justice Keith in Motions Court in Ottawa seeking prohibition of the publication of the identity of the young woman. Both of the appellants were served with notice of the application and both appeared before the learned judge and made submissions.

The basis of the application was simply that the unnamed young woman would suffer embarrassment and possibly detrimental effects with respect to employment. It was also said that members of her family would also suffer embarrassment and detrimental effects with respect to employment.

On this basis the order was made:

(1) prohibiting the broadcast or publication of the identity of the young woman who was the subject of the charges;
(2) directing that the criminal proceedings be held *in camera* (excepting only representatives of the media), and
(3) providing that this order not be the subject of any time-limit.

...there is no statutory basis for the order in this case. The respondent and the Attorney-General argue that the authority to make the order in this case proceeds from the inherent jurisdiction of a judge of the High Court.

The term "inherent jurisdiction" is one that is commonly and not always accurately used when arguments are made with respect to the jurisdictional basis upon which a court is asked to make a particular order. The inherent jurisdiction of a superior court is derived not from any statute or rule of law but from the very nature of the court as a superior court: (see, generally, I. H. Jacob, "The Inherent Jurisdiction of the Court", Current Legal Problems 23 (1970). Utilizing this power, superior courts, to maintain their authority and to prevent their processes from being obstructed or abused, have amongst other things punished for contempt of court, stayed matters that are frivolous and vexations and regulated their own process. The limits of this power are difficult to define with precision but cannot extend to the creation of a new rule of substantive law.

In *R.* v. *McArthur* (1984), 13 C.C.C (3d) 152, 10 C.R.R. 220, Dupont J. made an order prohibiting the publication of the names of witnesses who were to testify at trial. Dupont J. was the trial judge. It was his view that if the identity of the witnesses were published, the witnesses (who were inmates of the penitentiary) might be deterred from testifying. With respect, I think that such an order was properly within the inherent jurisdiction of the court to protect the trial that was being conducted. In the case at hand, Keith J. was of course not protecting the integrity of any matter that was otherwise before him.

It appears, as well, that a superior court has power under its inherent jurisdiction to render assistance to inferior courts to enable them to administer justice fully and effectively: see *Jacob, supra,* p. 48. However, in the case at hand, there is nothing in the material to suggest that either the provincial court or the county court required assistance from the High Court in order that they might fully and effectively administer justice. The order in this case was made not to protect the process before the court but simply to protect the accused and her family from embarrassment and other potential losses that might flow from identification.

The respondents rely heavily upon the judgment of Linden J. in *R. v. P.* (1978), 41 C.C.C (2d) 377, 3 C.R. (3d) 59. In that case, the accused had been acquitted on a charge of soliciting for the purpose of prostitution. The Crown appealed to the High Court by way of stated case. The accused sought to avoid embarrassment to his wife and children and applied to Linden J. of the High Court for an order prohibiting the publication of his identity. Linden J. said at p. 378:

> It falls to this Court to determine whether the interests of the public is best served by protecting the identity of this individual or whether it would be preferable to permit the public to know not only the details of the offence, but also the name of the person involved. The Court is invited to make this order pursuant to its inherent jurisdiction and pursuant to s.768(1)(*d*) of the *Criminal Code* which reads as follows:
>
> "768(1) Where a case is stated under this Part, the superior court shall hear and determine the grounds of appeal and may
>
> ...
>
> make
>
> (*d*) any other order in relation to the matter that it considers proper, and..."

Linden J. then proceeded to deal with the merits of the matter and made the order asked for. Linden J., however, did not further discuss the issue of jurisdiction. Nor did he say whether he found power under s.768(1) or in his inherent jurisdiction. Later, Steele J. was asked to continue the order made by Linden J.: *R. v. P.* (1978), 43 C.C.C. (2d) 197, 3 C.R. (3d) 62. Steele J. held that he had the power to continue the order but declined to do so. In *Re Regina and Several Unnamed Persons* (1983), 8 C.C.C. (3d) 528, 4 D.L.R. (4th) 310, 44 O.R. (2d) 81, O'Brien J. was asked to prohibit publication of the identity of an accused person in a proceeding in a court other than the High Court. The basis of the application was similar to the basis of the application in the case at hand — embarrassment and possible loss of employment. O'Brien J. accepted the premise that he had inherent jurisdiction to make such an order but declined to do so.

To the extent that these cases support the premise that a High Court Judge can issue a non-publication order respecting matters pending before other courts where no case is made out to show that those other courts require the assistance of a superior court so that justice can be fully and effectively administered, I must respectfully disagree with them. Other than the decision by Linden J. and the approvals by way of *obiter* that followed, I have been unable to discover any principle or any case which supports the proposition that there is inherent jurisdiction in the High Court to make the order in the case at hand. In my respectful view, the order which is the subject of this appeal has little, if anything, to do with protecting the process of the court. What the respondents seek in this case is the creation of a discretionary right of privacy to be extended to those caught up in the criminal process. I conclude that Keith J. was without jurisdiction to make the order which is the subject of this appeal. In the result, the appeal is allowed and the order of Keith J. is set aside and the application for the non-publication order is dismissed.

Appeal allowed.

3.2.5 Criminal Code, s.487.2

Restriction on publicity

487.2 (1) Where a search warrant is issued under section 487 or 443.1 or a search is made under such a warrant, every one who publishes in any newspaper or broadcasts any information with respect to

(*a*) the location of the place searched or to be searched, or

(*b*) the identity of any person who is or appears to occupy or be in possession or control of that place or who is suspected of being involved in any offence in relation to which the warrant was issued,

without the consent of every person referred to in paragraph (*b*) is, unless a charge has been laid in respect of any offence in relation to which the warrant was issued, guilty of an offence punishable on summary conviction.

Can this provision be justified in a free and democratic society?

3.2.6 *Canadian Newspapers Co. Ltd.* v. *Attorney-General for Canada* (1986), 32 D.L.R. (4th) 293 (Ont. H.C.J.)

OSLER, J.: — ... Each of the substantive motions was for a declaration that s.443.2(1) [now s.487.2] of the *Criminal Code* of Canada is contrary to s.2(*b*) of the *Canadian Charter of Rights and Freedoms,* and hence void pursuant to s.52 of the *Constitution Act, 1982*.

Counsel for the Attorney-General of Canada, with whom counsel for the Attorney-General for Ontario agreed, conceded at the outset that there was a *prima facie* violation and that the onus of justifying the impugned section of the *Code* under s.1 of the Charter fell on the Crown and that he was prepared to argue first.

Counsel for the applicants agreed with the position taken by the Crown but asserted the right to state their case in full and, in the interests of completeness, I agreed to permit them to do so. ...

For the applicant, Canadian Newspapers Company Ltd., publisher of the Globe and Mail newspaper, it is admitted that it has published at least one story which is, on the face of it, in violation of s.443.2(1), and that it is now liable to punishment "for publishing truthful information that it is in the public interest to disclose".

Virtually the same position was taken by counsel for Southam Inc., on behalf of the Hamilton Spectator, which based at least one story on the same set of facts as formed the basis of the Globe and Mail account.

At the conclusion of the argument, I was advised that the same issue was before the Court of Queen's Bench in Manitoba and had been heard by Mr. Justice Barkman but had not then been decided. Subsequently, I have been provided with a transcript of the oral judgment delivered by Barkman J. on June 17, 1986 [since reported 28 C.C.C. (3d) 379]. I find myself in agreement with the result reached by him, but I shall state as shortly as possible my reasons for reaching that conclusion.

The law respecting access of the public to search warrants and their supporting documents was extensively reviewed by the Supreme Court of Canada in *A.-G. N.S. et al. v. MacIntyre* [1982] 1 S.C.R. 175, 132 D.L.R. (3d) 385, 65 C.C.C. (2d) 129, a case decided before the proclamation of the *Canadian Charter of Rights and Freedoms*. The Court divided five to four, the majority judgment being given by Dickson J., as he then was, with whom Laskin C.J.C., McIntyre, Chouinard and Lamer JJ. concurred, while Martland J. was joined by Ritchie, Beetz and Estey JJ. in dissent.

In that case, the applicant, who was a journalist, sought a declaration that he was entitled to inspect search warrants and the information used to obtain them, and took the position that his standing as a journalist was no higher than that of any member of the general public.

The Nova Scotia Supreme Court, Appeal Division, broadened the declaration made by the court of first instance and held that a member of the public was entitled to inspect informations upon which search warrants had been issued, and to be present in open court when search warrants are issued.

The majority in the Supreme Court of Canada dismissed the appeal but varied the declaration of the Appeal Division to provide that after a search warrant has been executed, and objects found as a result of the search brought before a justice of the peace under s.446 of the *Criminal Code,* a member of the public is entitled to inspect the warrant and the information upon which it has been issued, pursuant to s.443 of the *Code*.

The Appeal Division based its reasons partly upon its conclusion that the issuance of a search warrant was a judicial act, performed in open court, at which members of the public had a right to be present. Martland J., with whom Dickson J. does not disagree in this respect, was at pains to point out that, while the function of the justice in issuing a warrant may be considered to be a judicial function, there was no requirement in s.443 of the *Code* that the justice should perform his function in court and in fact what he does is not properly termed an adjudication but merely a grant of authority to the applicant in a proper case. No notice is required and there is no opposite party before the justice when he makes or refuses his order, and hence cases dealing with the requirement of court proceedings being carried on in public were really of no relevance.

Martland J. went on to find that there was no logical reason why documents not subject to public examination prior to the execution of search warrants should become subject to such examination thereafter, at least until any resulting case has come to trial.

Martland J. based himself largely upon the need to protect the secrecy of police proceedings and particularly, in many cases, the identity of informers, and also upon the need to ensure a fair trial of the person suspected and not to have that right prejudiced by the disclosure and publication of hearsay allegations prior to trial.

Martland J. also recognized that the release to the public of the contents of informations and search warrants may be harmful to a person who may have no personal connection with the commission of an alleged offence but whose premises are permitted by the warrant to be searched: ''Publication of the fact that such a warrant had been issued in respect of his premises would be highly prejudicial to him'' [pp. 200-1 S.C.R., p. 395 D.L.R., p. 139 C.C.C.].

Dickson J., for the majority, characterizes a search warrant as an instrument that, through the enactment of s.443 of the *Code,* has legalized what would otherwise be an illegal entry of premises and illegal seizure of property. He pointed out that the issuance of such a warrant is a judicial act on the part of a justice, although usually performed *ex parte* and *in camera* by the very nature of the proceedings.

The judgment pointed out that, in passing s.443, Parliament balanced two interests, one having to do with civil liberties and the protection of individuals from interference with the enjoyment of their property, and the other being the effective detection and proof of crime and the prompt apprehension and conviction of offenders. In balancing those interests, Parliament came down in favour of the detection and prosecution of crime and hence authorized the issue of warrants as an aid in the administration of justice and enforcement of the provisions of the *Code*.

Dickson J.'s brief review of the English practice indicated that there was no general right to inspect and copy judicial records and documents, but only a right exercisable when an applicant can demonstrate some direct and tangible interest or proprietary right in the documents.

At p. 183 S.C.R., p. 400 D.L.R., p. 144 C.C.C., it was pointed out that the question of access before the Court was limited to search warrants and informations:

> The response to that question, it seems to me, should be guided by several broad policy considerations, namely, respect for the privacy of the individual, protection of the administration of justice, implementation of the will of Parliament that a search warrant be an effective aid in the investigation of crime, and finally, a strong public policy in favour of ''openness'' in respect of judicial acts.

After some remarks on the policy of ''accountability'' generally, the judgment goes on, at p. 184 S.C.R., p. 401 D.L.R., p. 145 C.C.C., as follows:

> In short, what should be sought is maximum accountability and accessibility but not to the extent of harming the innocent or of impairing the efficiency of the search warrant as a weapon in society's never-ending fight against crime.

In dealing with the argument that the privacy of individuals was to be protected, Dickson J. reiterated that openness was to be the rule if public confidence in the integrity of the court system was to be fostered: ''As a general rule the sensibilities of the individuals involved are no basis for exclusion of the public from judicial proceedings'' [p. 185 S.C.R., p. 402 D.L.R., p. 146 C.C.C.]:

In view of some of the submissions made to me, what is said at pp. 186-7 S.C.R., p. 403 D.L.R., p. 147 C.C.C., is of importance to the present case:

> At every stage the rule should be one of public accessibility and concomitant judicial accountability; all with a view to ensuring there is no abuse in the issue of search warrants, that once issued they are executed according to law, and finally that any evidence seized is dealt with according to law. *A decision by the Crown not to prosecute, notwithstanding the finding of evidence appearing to establish the commission of a crime may, in some circumstances, raise issues of public importance.*
>
> In my view, curtailment of public accessibility can only be justified where there is present the need to protect social values of superordinate importance. One of these is the protection of the innocent.
>
> Many search warrants are issued and executed, and nothing is found. In these circumstances, does the interest served by giving access to the public outweigh that served in protecting those persons whose premises have been searched and nothing has been found? Must they endure the stigmatization to name and reputation which would follow publication of the search? Protection of the innocent from unnecessary harm is a valid and important policy consideration. In my view that consideration overrides the public access interest in those cases where a search is made and nothing is found. The public right to know must yield to the protection of the innocent. If the warrant is executed and something is seized, other considerations come to bear.

(Emphasis mine.)

Dickson J. then went on to consider the question of the effective administration of justice and, for much the same reasons as were outlined by Martland J. in his dissenting judgment, agreed that, for the effective administration of justice, the issuance of a search warrant must be the result of an *in camera* proceeding, and must be an exception to the open-court principle.

At p. 188 S.C.R., p. 404 D.L.R., p. 148 C.C.C., the learned judge pointed out that, once the warrant has been executed, the force of the "administration of justice" argument abates, and he went on to find that if the argument for inspection by an interested person is overwhelming, as he finds, there is no justification for distinguishing between such a person and the general public, and that the "curtailment of the traditionally uninhibited accessibility of the public to the working of the courts should be undertaken with the greatest reluctance".

Dickson J. went on to allow for the supervisory and protecting power of every court over its own records, and stated that access can be denied in a proper case but that the burden of proving that public access should not be allowed lies, in each case, upon the person who would deny the exercise of the right.

The formal declaration of the court therefore was [at p. 190 S.C.R., p. 405 D.L.R., p. 149 C.C.C.]:

> ... that after a search warrant has been executed, and objects found as a result of the search are brought before a justice pursuant to s.446 of the *Criminal Code,* a member of the public is entitled to inspect the warrant and the information upon which the warrant has been issued pursuant to s.443 of the *Code.*

Much was said in argument before me about the exception made by Dickson J. when nothing has been found as a result of the search, and his justification for not permitting access to the documents in such a case because of the need to protect the innocent. This need he considered to be a social value of "superordinate importance".

In common with, I think, all counsel who appeared before me, I have difficulty in equating the person upon whose premises nothing has been found in the execution of a search warrant with "the innocent".

Without further comment on that particular difficulty, I go on to point out that the Charter now intervenes and, on its broadest reading, appears, by s.2(*b*), to raise openness to a constitutional right. Everyone, including specifically the press and other media of communication, is guaranteed the freedom of expression. At first blush, this would appear to exclude the reservation made by Dickson J. in favour of "the innocent". Left alone, then, it might be said that the press and other media have absolute freedom to report whatever comes to their knowledge by virtue of the right to freedom of expression.

Section 1 of the Charter, however, as has now been emphasized in many decided cases, guarantees rights and freedoms subject only to "such reasonable limits prescribed by law as can be demonstrably justified in a free and democratic society".

The sequence, then, can roughly be said to be as follows. In *MacIntyre*, the principle of openness was declared but a reservation was made in favour of "the innocent", as described therein. The subsequent enactment of the Charter would, on its face, appear to eliminate the reservation and make "openness" and the right to express what is disclosed by openness an absolute. However, the Charter contains in itself a reservation in favour of reasonable limits as there described.

The onus has been declared to lie squarely on those advocating limits to justify them under the provisions of s.1 of the Charter and, while this need only be shown to the degree of probability required in civil litigation rather than beyond a reasonable doubt, the weight of conviction must nevertheless be commensurate with the importance of the matter at issue and the significance of the result.

While in my view the matter does not turn primarily upon the following consideration, it must nevertheless be pointed out that there is a discriminatory element present in s.443.2 by virtue of the definition of "newspaper" as found in s.261 of the *Criminal Code*. The word is there defined so as to include only papers, magazines and periodicals published at intervals not exceeding 31 days. What is forbidden to daily, weekly or monthly publications is permitted to bi-monthly, quarterly or annual publications. While there may be some practical reason for the distinction thus made, it is quite plain that s.443.2(1) is a *prima facie* violation of the Charter, which provides for freedom of the entire press. Even if s.1 of the Charter can be invoked to justify a curtailment of that freedom, no legal reason appears to exist that would authorize curtailment of the rights of part of the press while leaving the balance free to exercise all its rights.

The limits and application of s.1 of the Charter have recently been examined by the Supreme Court of Canada in *R. v. Oakes* [1986] 1 S.C.R. 103, 26 D.L.R. (4th) 200, 24 C.C.C. (3d) 321. That was a case in which an accused was charged with the possession of a narcotic for the purpose of trafficking contrary to s.4(2) of the *Narcotic Control Act*. The trial judge held that the provision of s.8 of that Act compelling an accused found in possession to establish that he did not have the narcotic for the purpose of trafficking, violated the guarantee of the presumption of innocence in s.11(*d*) of the Charter and that it was therefore invalid. An appeal by the Crown to the Ontario Court of Appeal was dismissed, as was a further appeal to the Supreme Court of Canada.

In the latter Court, Dickson C.J.C., for the majority, examined in detail the application of s.1 of the Charter. He adopted what was said by Wilson J. in *Re Singh and*

Minister of Employment & Immigration and 6 other appeals, [1985] 1 S.C.R. 177 at p. 218, 17 D.L.R. (4th) 422 at p. 468, 14 C.R.R. 13, that it "is important to remember that the courts are conducting this inquiry in light of a commitment to uphold the rights and freedoms set out in the other sections of the *Charter*." The judgment went on to state that the words "free and democratic society" compelled the Court to be guided by the values and principles essential to such a society, including "respect for the inherent dignity of the human person".

At pp. 138-9 S.C.R., p. 227 D.L.R., p. 348 C.C.C., of the judgment are set out the two central criteria which must be satisfied in meeting that standard.

> First, the objective, which the measures responsible for a limit on a *Charter* right or freedom are designed to serve, must be "of sufficient importance to warrant overriding a constitutionally protected right or freedom": *R. v. Big M Drug Mart Ltd.* [[1985] 1 S.C.R. 295 at p. 352, 18 D.L.R. (4th) 321, 18 C.C.C. (3d) 385].
>
> ...
>
> Second, once a sufficiently significant objective is recognized, then the party invoking s.1 must show that the means chosen are reasonable and demonstrably justified. This involves "a form of proportionality test": *R. v. Big M Drug Mart Ltd., supra,* at p. 352. Although the nature of the proportionality test will vary depending on the circumstances, in each case courts will be required to balance the interests of society with those of individuals and groups. There are, in my view, three important components of a proportionality test. First, the measures adopted must be carefully designed to achieve the objective in question. They must not be arbitrary, unfair or based on irrational considerations. In short, they must be rationally connected to the objective. Second, the means, even if rationally connected to the objective in the first sense, should impair "as little as possible" the right or freedom in question: *R. v. Big M Drug Mart Ltd., supra,* at p. 352. Third, there must be a proportionality between the effects of the measures which are responsible for limiting the *Charter* right or freedom, and the objective which has been identified as of "sufficient importance".

Applying these criteria to the present case, it is apparent that the principal objective of Parliament in enacting s.443.2 of the *Criminal Code* was to protect the privacy of the classes of persons enumerated in para. (*b*) of s-s. (1) and, as a possible secondary objective, to safeguard the rights of such persons to a fair trial.

A right to privacy is recognized in such cases as *Hunter et al. v. Southam Inc.,* [1984] 2 S.C.R. 145, 11 D.L.R. (4th) 641, 14 C.C.C. (3d) 97, and the right to a fair trial is declared by s.11(*d*) of the Charter itself.

In my view, both of these objectives are "of sufficient importance to warrant overriding a constitutionally protected right or freedom", namely, freedom of the press.

A much more difficult question is whether the means chosen are reasonable and demonstrably justified.

Before applying the three components of the proportionality test as determined in *R. v. Oakes,* in my opinion s.443.2(1)(*b*) of the impugned sections contains language of such vagueness and ambiguity as to render it entirely inappropriate as an indication of when it is justifiable to violate a constitutionally guaranteed right. Under the provisions of the section, it is necessary for anyone who proposes to publish the proscribed information in a newspaper to obtain the consent of "any person who is or appears to occupy or be in possession or control of" the place searched. Quite apart from difficulties of syntax, to whom must a person appear to occupy and at what time must that appearance be demonstrated? Even more difficult, how are persons "suspected of being involved in any offence in relation to which the warrant was issued" to be identified? By whom is such person to be suspected? Is the involvement to be limited to participation or does it include a victim? In my view, such language is highly unsatisfactory for the purpose sought to be achieved.

Turning then to the specific components of the proportionality test considered by Chief Justice Dickson, I find myself unable to conclude that some of the language of s-s. (1) is rationally connected to the objective sought to be achieved. If the objective is to protect the privacy rights of innocent parties, why is the prohibition to be maintained after a charge or charges are laid, provided such charges do not comprise "any offence in relation to which the warrant was issued"? If, as not infrequently happens, a warrant is issued to search premises in the belief that evidence pertaining to a robbery or to a case of break and enter will be found, and instead evidence pointing strongly to the illegal possession of narcotics is discovered, the privacy of the "person", whoever that may be, is to be protected even after the charge has been laid.

As to the second component, I am unable to find that the freedom of the press to publish is impaired as little as possible by the very broad language of this section. It appears to me, as it did to Barkman J. in the Court of Queen's Bench in Manitoba [see *Canadian Newspapers Co. Ltd. v. A.-G. Can.* (1986), 31 D.L.R. (4th) 601, 28 C.C.C. (3d) 377], that the prohibition against publishing the location of the place searched or the identity of any person coming within the description of the section until consents have been obtained or a relevant charge has been laid, applies to publication regardless of the source of the information. It was submitted, on behalf of the Attorney-General of Canada and the Attorney-General for Ontario, that in practice the courts would no doubt interpret the language to prohibit only publication of information obtained from inspection of the warrant or the supporting information. This technique of "reading down" so as to interpret language in favour of its constitutionality is one that has been discouraged by the Supreme Court of Canada in connection with Charter questions. In my view, to adopt that technique is to ignore the rule that the onus of supporting a restriction under s.1, and establishing that it goes no further than reasonably necessary to secure a worthy objective, lies upon the proponent of the legislation.

With respect to the third component, a necessary proportionality between the effects of the measure and the objective, it is my opinion that the effects are too far reaching and too injurious to the freedom at issue to be justified under s.1. It is easy to become impatient with the press and to criticize it for what may at times appear to be sensationalism. It is not necessary that the motives of the press be altruistic for the importance of press freedom to be apparent. As was stated in *Reference re Alberta Legislation*, [1938] S.C.R. 100 at pp. 145-6, [1938] 2 D.L.R. 81 at p. 119:

> Freedom of discussion is essential to enlighten public opinion in a democratic State; it cannot be curtailed without affecting the right of the people to be informed through sources independent of the government concerning matters of public interest. There must be an untrammelled publication of the news and political opinions of the political parties contending for ascendency.

There can be no discussion when there is no information. We are fortunate enough to live in a country where police abuse has not been a major concern. Nevertheless, overzealousness is not unknown and mistakes do occur. The execution of a search warrant is in itself a major invasion of someone's privacy. So long as the present section stands, the botched or illegal execution of a search warrant may never come to public notice without the consent of one or more private individuals. Such individuals, however sensitive their own feelings may be, should not be given the power to prevent the disclosure of police mistake or misconduct.

Additionally, the very fact that no charge is laid may in some circumstances properly merit criticism and, in my view, the failure to lay a charge, or even to lay a particular charge "in relation to which the warrant was issued", should not justify the prohibition of publication.

I am, therefore, of the opinion that the section offends against the Charter and cannot be justified by s.1, and the declaration asked for will therefore issue.

I shall be prepared to receive submissions on the matter of costs within 30 days from the publication of these reasons. Alternatively, if counsel prefer to make their submissions in person a date will be set for that purpose.

3.2.7 Courts of Justice Act, 1984, S.O. 1984, c.11, s.146

Prohibition against photography, etc., at court hearing

146. (1) Subject to subsections (2) and (3), no person shall,

(a) take or attempt to take a photograph, motion picture, audio recording or other record capable of producing visual or aural representations by electronic means or otherwise,

(i) at a court hearing,

(ii) of any person entering or leaving the room in which a court hearing is to be or has been convened, or

(iii) of any person in the building in which a court hearing is to be or has been convened where there is reasonable ground for believing that the person is there for the purpose of attending or leaving the hearing; or

(b) publish, broadcast, reproduce or otherwise disseminate a photograph, motion picture, audio recording or record taken in contravention of clause (a).

Exceptions

(2) Nothing in subsection (1),

(a) prohibits a person from unobtrusively making handwritten notes or sketches at a court hearing; or

(b) prohibits a solicitor or party acting in person from unobtrusively making an audio recording at a court hearing that is used only for the purposes of the litigation as a substitute for notes.

Exceptions

(3) Subsection (1) does not apply to a photograph, motion picture, audio recording or record made with authorization of the judge,

(a) where required for the presentation of evidence or the making of a record or for any other purpose of the court hearing;

(b) in connection with any investitive, naturalization, ceremonial or other similar proceeding; or

(c) with the consent of the parties and witnesses, for such educational or instructional purposes as the judge approves.

Offence

(4) Every person who contravenes this section is guilty of an offence and on conviction is liable to a fine of not more than $10,000 or to imprisonment for a term of not more than six months, or to both. R.S.O. 1980, c.223, s.67.

3.2.8 *R.* v. *Rowbotham* (No. 3) (1976), 2 C.R. (3d) 241 (Ont. Co. Ct.)

3rd November 1976. BORINS Co. Ct. J. (orally): — Gentlemen, I had occasion to speak to you briefly in chambers with respect to the situation that has caused me to reconvene the court in this case, and I think that for the purposes of the record, it would be appropriate if I briefly outlined what occurred.

On Monday, 1st November, at about 4:45 p.m. the sheriff came into my office to advise me that there was a photographer loitering in the vicinity of my car in the parking area to the west of the court house, and this person advised the sheriff that he was there to take a photograph of me. The sheriff accompanied me to my car at about 5:00 p.m. and there was a man there with a camera. The sheriff told him that he was not to take a photograph of me, and I told this person the same thing. After I had told him not to take a photograph of me, he did so, or appeared to do so. The camera made a clicking sound. The sheriff identified himself. He requested that this person accompany us into the court house, which he did. He came into my office and identified himself as Chris Rennie. He said that he had been instructed to take a photograph of the prosecutor in this case, and the two undercover officers involved in this case, and of the judge in this case. When I asked him who gave him these instructions, he said that he was working for a magazine in the United States called "High Times". However, he was unable to tell me who the editor of the magazine is, or he did not want to tell me who the editor of the magazine is, and I advised him that in my opinion he was acting in an irresponsible manner, doing what he did. I told him that a responsible journalist would have asked permission to take my photograph and presumably he would be governed by whatever my response to the request would have been. To say that this young man acted in a flippant, rude manner would be an understatement.

The sheriff asked him to surrender his camera to him. He was about to do so, then asked if it would be acceptable if he surrendered the film. He said that it would be. The film is now in the custody of the sheriff, and as stated to Chris Rennie, the film would not be destroyed. However, I indicated to him that he would have to apply to the court if he wished to have the film returned to him.

Yesterday, 2nd November, Maedel Co. Ct. J. advised me at about 2:30 p.m. that there were two people with cameras just outside of the south-west door, the judge's entrance to the court house, and that they had apparently taken a photograph of Gord Russell, one of the sheriff's officers. It was at that stage that I determined the court ought to be reconvened today so that I could advise you formally of what has occurred so that the matter could be placed on the record.

The legislature of this province has recently enacted a section of the Judicature Act, R.S.O. 1970, c.228, s.68*a* [en. 1974, c.81, s.3], which prohibits the taking of photographs, motion pictures, or other records capable of producing visual representations by electronic means at a judicial proceeding, or of a person entering or leaving the court room in which the judicial proceeding is to be or has been convened, or of any person in the precincts of the building in which the judicial proceeding is to be or has been convened. The legislature has provided rather severe penalties for anyone in contravention of this section. If he is convicted of the offence contrary to this section, a fine of not more than $10,000, or imprisonment for a term of not more than six months, or both, represent the penalties which the legislature, in its view, feels is appropriate. However, the section does not cover the taking of photographs outside the court house. The "precincts of the building" are defined in s.68*a*(1)(*c*) as being "the space enclosed by the walls of the building", so that it would appear that this section does not relate to what occurred on 1st November or 2nd November.

It is my view that a trial judge in any trial occupies a special role, and he is to be free of harassment both in and out of the court room. I should add that on Monday, 1st November, after Mr. Rennie gave the film to the sheriff, he left my office. I remained in the building for about ten minutes. When I left to go home, he was there outside the court house. He approached my car after I began entering it and began shouting at me from a distance of two or three feet away, that I was abusing the freedom of the press. Freedom of the press is certainly a relevant term, as I indicated earlier. The press has an obligation to be responsible. It has been my experience that the press in this jurisdiction and in Metropolitan Toronto have always conducted themselves in a responsible manner.

Whether the failure to comply with the request of a trial judge outside the court room constitutes a contempt of court is another matter upon which I do not care to express myself at the present time. There is certainly a matter of public interest involved. In my view, those persons who are responsible for the enforcement of law are entitled to do so free from harassment and interference which may fall short of a criminal offence as defined in the Criminal Code.

So that a similar situation such as I have described does not occur, I feel that I must make an order in this case, and I do so with considerable regret, because I do value the freedom of the press, and responsible reporting and responsible journalism. However, if it exceeds the bounds of responsible journalism, I feel that such an order as the one I am about to make is required.

ORDER

The following order is, therefore, made:

No person shall take, or attempt to take any photograph, motion picture, or other record capable of producing visual representations by electronic means or otherwise, of any person in any way involved in the case of Regina and Robert Wilson Rowbotham and others, either inside the Peel County Court House, or outside the Peel County Court House, or publish, broadcast, reproduce, or otherwise disseminate any photograph, motion picture, or record taken or made in contravention of this order.

This order is meant to complement the provisions of s.68*a* of the Judicature Act.

3.2.9 Patricia Chisholm "No Cameras in Court", *Ontario Lawyers Weekly,* 20 January 184, p. 1

The long campaign of broadcasters for the relaxation of Ontario's prohibition against electronic courtroom coverage has run up against a new roadblock.

Chief Justice William Howland, of the Ontario Court of Appeal, announced the shelving of a questionnaire on 'cameras-in-court' at a press conference prior to the annual opening of the courts, held here January 9.

The Special Committee on the Media, the subcommittee of the Bench and Bar Council studying the matter, had proposed such a questionnaire be completed by all Ontario lawyers, before the Committee responded to a January 1983 request by the Radio Television News Directors Association for an 18-month cameras-in-court experiment.

Amendments to s.67 of the *Judicature Act* would be required for such a project.

The consents of the parties and of the court are currently required for electronic coverage of trials. (See OLW report, August 12).

The sudden halt came after Chief Justice Laskin wrote to Justice Minister Mark MacGuigan November 3, 1983, stating the Canadian Judicial Council had recently concluded television should not be allowed in court proceedings.

The position of the Canadian Judicial Council was so "strong, definite, unqualified and final" that both the Attorney General and the Treasurer of the Law Society declined to support the questionnaire's circulation, Chief Justice Howland said.

"I don't want to give the impression that the issue of cameras-in-court is dead," he told reporters. "There is nothing to prevent anyone from expressing their views on the matter — I would be very surprised if the media allowed the issue to die."

The Chief Justice described a visit by the Special Committee to a televised trial in New Jersey earlier this year as an "unfortunate experience."

"There was a lot of moving around the court room — it was very disturbing."

The New Jersey judiciary had assured the Committee the commotion was unusual, he explained. "We asked for a special demonstration and that is what we got."

He added that he has heard no complaints about electronic coverage of the Grange Commission, permitted because those hearings are not 'judicial proceedings.'

Note: See also *R.* v. *Squires (No. 2)* (1986) 25 C.C.C. (3d) 44.

Note: On the question of television in the courtroom, see Daniel J. Henry, "Electronic Public Access to the Court" in Anisman and Linden (eds.), *The Media, The Courts and the Charter*, Toronto, 1986.

3.2.10 Law Reform Commission of Canada, *Public and Media Access to the Criminal Process*, Ottawa: Minister of Supply and Services Canada, 1987, (Working Paper, 56)

Electronic Media Coverage

23. (1) Electronic media coverage should be permitted in relation to appeals in criminal cases.

(2) Use of audio recorders should be permitted in criminal proceedings as a substitute for, or in addition to, handwritten notes.

(3) A national experiment with electronic media coverage of criminal trials should be conducted with a view to studying comprehensively the impact of the presence of video and still cameras and audio recorders on witnesses, counsel, judges and jurors.

Commentary

There is much speculation about whether the presence of television cameras affects the fact-finding process. There is no reason to suspect, in our opinion, that electronic media coverage of appeals would in any way interfere with those proceedings, so long as the court was able to maintain an atmosphere of decorum conducive to a proper hearing on the matters before it. Technology that is presently available would, we believe, allow appellate courts to proceed in a dignified fashion. Thus, in Recommendation 23(1), we suggest that there be no limit placed on electronic media coverage of criminal appeals. Where a publication ban is in force, the electronic media would, of course, be bound by it along with the other media.

Recommendation 23(2) suggests that use of audio recorders be permitted in criminal proceedings. Audio recorders constitute a means for ensuring the accuracy of statements and testimony made in legal proceedings. A recent study revealed "a high level of serious error" was discovered in an analysis of quotations published by the print media in relation to the trial of Colin Thatcher. Use of audio recorders was recommended by the study's author to improve this situation. Use of audio recorders in court by the media was also recommended by the New South Wales Law Reform Commission. It found that use of recorders did not constitute a nuisance or interfere with proceedings. That Commission recommended, however, that recordings be broadcast to the public only with leave of the court. Audio recordings may be made of legal proceedings in the United Kingdom again only with leave of the court. Recordings may not be broadcast. Our proposal would merely permit recorders to be used to obtain statements and testimony made in a criminal proceeding with complete accuracy. We do not recommend at this time that recordings be broadcast. Any recommendation regarding the broadcast of recorded proceedings should await the results of the experiment we propose in Recommendation 23(3). While it may seem incongruous to permit audio recorders to be used in criminal proceedings, but not to allow recordings to be broadcast, it is our view that any impact that the introduction of recorders would be likely to have on the process would relate to the participants' knowledge that their comments could ultimately be broadcast. This may result in nervousness or self-consciousness on their part which should be studied along with the impact of video recording and broadcasts.

Recommendation 23(3) reflects our hesitancy to make a definitive recommendation supporting or opposing blanket electronic media coverage. We believe that a meaningful decision on this issue can only follow a comprehensive study for a significant period of time in various parts of the country. The guidelines for the experiment would have to be generated in consultation with many groups, such as the Canadian Judicial Council, the Canadian Bar Association, provincial law societies, Crown attorneys, law professors, the police and social scientists. Guidelines for the media have already been proposed by the Radio Television News Directors Association and could form the basis for media activity during the experiment. Comparative studies of the effects of audio, as opposed to video, recording ought to form part of the experiment, as should a comparison of electronic with conventional media coverage. The data should be carefully analyzed by social science experts and the conclusions widely circulated. In the absence of clear evidence that electronic media coverage has a significantly greater impact on participants than present media activity, electronic media should be given access to criminal trials on the same footing as other media.

Technology now permits unobtrusive audio or video recording. No special lighting is required; sound can be transmitted through the courts' own sound recording system; only one video camera is necessary to serve all media outlets. The effectiveness of the present technology has been borne out in electronic media coverage of the Royal Commission of Inquiry into Certain Deaths at Hospital for Sick Children and Related Matters (the Grange Commission). Both the Commission's counsel and its Commissioner have been persuaded, after months of experience with intensive electronic media activity, that the media's presence had no adverse impact. Rather, according to Justice Grange, the introduction of television into courtrooms would perform a valuable public benefit:

> I do not want [television] in all courts at all times. I do, however, think it should be tried in some courts at some times under controlled conditions. The reason is simple. The public must know what goes on in our courts and the only way they can get a proper conception is the way they get their conception of all our institutions, i.e. through television. And the ignorance of the public of our system and the way it runs (as opposed to some other system or some totally imaginary systems) is appalling.

We concur with this opinion in principle. However, doubts about the impact of electronic media coverage on the trial process will always linger in the absence of a satisfactory empirical study. This study should, therefore, precede the introduction of electronic media on a scale beyond what is now permitted.

3.3 Contempt of Court Generally

3.3.1 *Attorney-General* v. *Leveller Magazine Ltd. and Others* [1979] A. C. 440 (H. L.)

February 1, 1979, Lord Diplock. My Lords, in November 1977 three defendants, two of whom were journalists, had been charged with offences under the Official Secrets Act. Committal proceedings against them were being heard before the Tottenham Magistrates' Court acting as examining justices. The proceedings extended over a considerable number of days. On the first day, on the application of counsel for the prosecution, some of the evidence was heard in camera pursuant to section 8 (4) of the Official Secrets Act 1920. On the third day, November 10, counsel for the prosecution made an application that the next witness whom he proposed to call should, for his own security and for reasons of national safety, be referred to as "Colonel A" and that his name should not be disclosed to anyone. The magistrates, upon the advice of their clerk, ruled, correctly but with expressed reluctance, that this would not be possible and that although the witness should be referred to as "Colonel A," his name would have to be written down and disclosed to the court and to the defendants and their counsel. The prosecution decided not to call that witness and the proceedings were adjourned.

The hearing was resumed four days later on November 14. The prosecution called, instead of "Colonel A," another witness. Counsel for the prosecution applied for him to be referred to as "Colonel B," and that his name be written down and shown only to the court, the defendants and their counsel. This was said to be necessary for reasons of national safety; risk to "Colonel B's" own security was not relied on. Counsel for the defendants raised no objection to the course proposed; the magistrates assented to it and the witness then gave evidence in open court. He was throughout referred to as "Colonel B"; his real name was never mentioned. For the purposes of the proceedings for contempt of court with which the Divisional Court and now your Lordships have been concerned, it must be taken, although initially there was conflicting evidence as to this, that the magistrates gave no express ruling or direction other than that the witness was to be referred to in court as "Colonel B" and not by his real name and that his real name was to be written down and disclosed only to the court, the defendants and their counsel.

In the course of the cross-examination of "Colonel B" questions were put the effect of which was to elicit from him (1) the official name and number of the army unit to which he belonged and (2) the fact that his posting to it was recorded in a particular issue of "Wire," the magazine of the Royal Corps of Signals which is obtainable by the public. These answers enabled his identity to be discovered by anyone who cared to follow up this simple clue. The line of questioning which elicited this information was pursued without objection from counsel for the prosecution, the witness or the magistrates; and the answers which made his identity so easy to discover were included in the colonel's deposition read out to him in open court before he signed it.

In the issue of "Peace News" for November 18 these two pieces of information about "Colonel B" elicited in open court were published; and in the issue for December 16, the name of "Colonel B" was disclosed and an account was given of his military career. In the January and March 1978 issues of another magazine, "The Leveller," the name of "Colonel B" was published. Finally, in the issues of the "Journalist" for March and April 1978 published by the National Union of Journalists, "Colonel B" was again identified by name.

All this occurred before the trial of the defendants at the Central Criminal Court began.

On March 22, 1978, the Attorney-General brought in the Divisional Court proceedings for contempt of court against Peace News Ltd. and Leveller Magazine Ltd. and persons responsible for the publication in those periodicals of the articles which published the real name of "Colonel B"; and on April 18, 1978, he brought similar proceedings against the National Union of Journalists in respect of the articles appearing in the "Journalist." In each of these proceedings the statement filed pursuant to R.S.C., Ord. 52, r.2 contained an allegation that at the committal proceedings in the Tottenham Magistrates' Court on November 14, 1978, not only had the magistrates permitted "Colonel B" not to disclose his identity but their chairman had also given an express direction in open court that no attempt should be made to disclose the identity of "Colonel B." Before the three motions, which were heard together, came on for hearing, an affidavit by the clerk to the Tottenham Magistrates' Court was filed, denying that any such explicit direction had been given by the chairman of the magistrates and stating that the reason why such a direction was not given was because he had advised the magistrates that they had no power to do so. In view of this evidence the hearing of the motions proceeded on the basis that no explicit direction had been given to those present at the hearing that no attempt should be made to disclose the identity of "Colonel B"; and that what had happened at the committal proceedings in relation to the witness being referred to only as "Colonel B" was as I have already stated it.

My Lords, it is not disputed that the disclosure of "Colonel B's" identity by the appellants was part of a campaign of protest against the Official Secrets Act. It was designed, no doubt, to ridicule the notion that national safety needed to be protected by suppression of the colonel's name. The only question for your Lordships is whether in doing what they did the appellants were guilty of contempt of court.

The Divisional Court found contempt of court established against all appellants but made orders only against the National Union of Journalists and the two companies. The National Union of Journalists was fined £200, Peace News Ltd. and Leveller Magazine Ltd. were each fined £500. Against these orders these appeals are now brought to this House.

In the judgment of the Divisional Court delivered by Lord Widgery C.J. it is pointed out that contempt of court can take many forms. The publication by the appellants of the witness's identity after the magistrates had ruled that he should be referred to in their court only as "Colonel B" was held by the Divisional Court to fall into a class said to be exemplified in *Attorney-General* v. *Butterworth* [1963] 1 Q.B. 696 and *Reg.* v. *Socialist Worker Printers and Publishers Ltd., Ex parte Attorney-General* [1975] Q.B. 637 and variously described in the course of the judgment as "a deliberate flouting of the court's authority," "a flouting or deliberate disregard outside the court [of the court's ruling]," a "deliberate intention of frustrating the arrangement which the court had made to preserve Colonel B's anonymity" and finally a "deliberate flouting of the court's intention." I do not think that any of these ways of describing what the appellants did is sufficiently precise to lead inexorably to the conclusion that what they did amounted to contempt of court. Closer analysis is needed.

The only "ruling" that the magistrates had in fact given was that the witness should be referred to *at the hearing in their court* as "Colonel B" and that his name must be written down and shown to the court, the defendants and their counsel but to no one else. That it was also the only ruling that they intended to give is apparent from the fact that they had been advised by their clerk that it was the only ruling that they had power to give, however much they might have preferred to give a wider one. None of the appellants committed any breach of this ruling. What they did, and did deliberately, outside the court and after the conclusion of "Colonel B's" evidence in the committal proceedings, was to take steps to ensure that this anonymity was not preserved.

My Lords, although criminal contempts of court make take a variety of forms they all share a common characteristic: they involve an interference with the due administration of justice either in a particular case or more generally as a continuing process. It is justice itself that is flouted by contempt of court, not the individual court or judge who is attempting to administer it.

Of those contempts that can be committed outside the courtroom the most familiar consist of publishing, in connection with legal proceedings that are pending or imminent, comment or information that has a tendency to pervert the course of justice, either in those proceedings or by deterring other people from having recourse to courts of justice in the future for the vindication of their lawful rights or for the enforcement of the criminal law. In determining whether what is published has such a tendency a distinction must be drawn between reporting what actually occurred at the hearing of the proceedings and publishing other kinds of comment or information; for prima facie the interests of justice are served by its being administered in the full light of publicity.

As a general rule the English system of administering justice does require that it be done in public: *Scott* v. *Scott* [1913] A.C. 417. If the way that courts behave cannot be hidden from the public ear and eye this provides a safeguard against judicial arbitrariness or idiosyncrasy and maintains the public confidence in the administration of justice. The application of this principle of open justice has two aspects: as respects proceedings in the court itself it requires that they should be held in open court to which the press and public are admitted and that, in criminal cases at any rate, all evidence communicated to the court is communicated publicly. As respects the publication to a wider public of fair and accurate reports of proceedings that have taken place in court the principle requires that nothing should be done to discourage this.

However, since the purpose of the general rule is to serve the ends of justice it may be necessary to depart from it where the nature or circumstances of the particular proceeding are such that the application of the general rule in its entirety would frustrate or render impracticable the administration of justice or would damage some other public interest for whose protection Parliament has made some statutory derogation from the rule. Apart from statutory exceptions, however, where a court in the exercise of its inherent power to control the conduct of proceedings before it departs in any way from the general rule, the departure is justified to the extent and to no more than the extent that the court reasonably believes it to be necessary in order to serve the ends of justice. A familiar instance of this is provided by the "trial within a trial" as to the admissibility of a confession in a criminal prosecution. The due administration of justice requires that the jury should be unaware of what was the evidence adduced at the "trial within a trial" until after they have reached their verdict; but no greater derogation from the general rule as to the public nature of all proceedings at a criminal trial is justified than is necessary to ensure this. So far as proceedings in the courtroom are concerned the trial within a trial is held in open court in the presence of the press and public but in the absence of the jury. So far as publishing those proceedings outside the court is concerned any report of them which might come to the knowledge of the jury must be withheld until after they have reached their verdict; but it may be published after that. Only premature publication would constitute contempt of court.

In the instant case the only statutory provisions that have any relevance are section 8(4) of the Official Secrets Act 1920 and section 12(1)(*c*) of the Administration of Justice Act 1960. Both deal with the giving of evidence before a court sitting in camera. They do not apply to the evidence given by "Colonel B" in the instant case. Their relevance is thus peripheral and I can dispose of them shortly.

Section 8(4) of the Act of 1920 applies to prosecutions under that Act and the Official Secrets Act 1911. It empowers but it does not compel a court to sit to hear evidence in private if the Crown applies for this on the ground that national safety would be prejudiced by its publication. Section 12(1) of the Act of 1960 defines and limits the circumstances in which the publication of information relating to proceedings before any court sitting in private is of itself contempt of court. The circumstance defined in section 12(1)(*c*) is

> "where the court sits in private for reasons of national security during that part of the proceedings about which the information in question is published;..."

So to report evidence in camera in a prosecution under the Official Secrets Act would be contempt of court.

In the instant case the magistrates would have had power to sit in camera to hear the whole or part of the evidence of "Colonel B" if this had been requested by the prosecution; and although they would not have been bound to accede to such a request it would naturally and properly have carried great weight with them. So would the absence of any such request. Without it the magistrates, in my opinion, would have had no reasonable ground for believing that so drastic a derogation from the general principle of open justice as is involved in hearing evidence in a criminal case in camera was necessary in the interests of the due administration of justice.

In substitution for hearing "Colonel B's" evidence in camera which it could have asked for the prosecution was content to treat a much less drastic derogation from the principle of open justice as adequate to protect the interests of national security. The witness's evidence was to be given in open court in the normal way except that he was to be referred to by the pseudonym of "Colonel B" and evidence as to his real name and address was to be written down and disclosed only to the court, the defendants and their legal representatives.

I do not doubt that, applying their minds to the matter that it was their duty to consider — the interests of the due administration of justice — the magistrates had power to accede to this proposal for the very reason that it would involve less derogation from the general principle of open justice than would result from the Crown being driven to have recourse to the statutory procedure for hearing evidence in camera under section 8(4) of the Official Secrets Act 1920; but in adopting this particular device which on the face of it related only to how proceedings within the courtroom were to be conducted it behoved the magistrates to make it clear what restrictions, if any, were intended by them to be imposed upon publishing outside the courtroom information relating to those proceedings and whether such restrictions were to be precatory only or enforceable by the sanction of proceedings for contempt of court.

My Lords, in the argument before this House little attempt was made to analyse the juristic basis on which a court can make a "ruling," "order" or "direction" — call it what you will — relating to proceedings taking place before it which has the effect in law of restricting what may be done outside the courtroom by members of the public who are not engaged in those proceedings as parties or their legal representatives or as witnesses. The Court of Appeal of New Zealand in *Taylor* v. *Attorney-General* [1975] 2 N.Z.L.R. 675 was clearly of opinion that a court had power to make an explicit order directed to and binding on the public ipso jure as to what might lawfully be published outside the courtroom in relation to proceedings held before it. For my part I am prepared to leave this as an open question in the instant case. It may be that a "ruling" by the court as to the conduct of proceedings can have binding effect as such within the courtroom only, so that breach of it is not ipso facto a contempt of court unless it is committed there. Nevertheless where (1) the reason for a ruling which involves departing in some measure from the general principle of open justice within the courtroom is that the departure is necessary in the interests of the due administration of justice and (2) it would be apparent to anyone who was aware of the ruling that the result which the ruling is designed to achieve would be frustrated by a particular kind of act done outside the courtroom, the doing of such an act with knowledge of the ruling and of its purpose may constitute a contempt of court, not because it is a breach of the ruling but because it interferes with the due administration of justice.

So it does not seem to me to matter greatly in the instant case whether or not the magistrates were rightly advised that they had in law no power to give directions which would be binding as such upon members of the public as to what information relating to the proceedings taking place before them might be published outside the courtroom. What was incumbent upon them was to make it clear to anyone present at, or reading an accurate report of, the proceedings what in the interests of the due administration of justice was the result that was intended by them to be achieved by the limited derogation from the principle of open justice within the courtroom which they had authorised, and what kind of information derived from what happened in the courtroom would if it were published frustrate that result.

There may be many cases in which the result intended to be achieved by a ruling by the court as to what is to be done in court is so obvious as to speak for itself; it calls for no explicit statement. Sending the jury out of court during a trial within a trial is an example of this; so may be the common ruling in prosecutions for blackmail that a victim called as a witness be referred to in court by a pseudonym (see *Reg.* v. *Socialist Worker Printers and Publishers Ltd., Ex parte Attorney-General* [1975] Q.B. 637); but, in the absence of any explicit statement by the Tottenham magistrates at the conclusion of the colonel's evidence that the purpose of their ruling would be frustrated if anything were published outside the courtroom that would be likely to lead to the identification of ''Colonel B'' as the person who had given evidence in the case, I do not think that the instant case falls into this class.

The ruling that the witness was to be referred to in court only as ''Colonel B'' was given before any of his evidence had been heard and at that stage of the proceedings it might be an obvious inference that the effect intended by the magistrates to be achieved by their ruling was to prevent his identity being publicly disclosed. As I have already pointed out however the evidence that he gave in open court in cross-examination did in effect disclose his identity to anyone prepared to take the trouble to consult a particular issue (specified in the evidence) of a magazine that was on sale to the public. This evidence was elicited without any protest from counsel for the prosecution; no application was made that this part of the evidence should be heard in camera; no suggestion, let alone request, was made to members of the press present in court that it should not be reported; and once it was reported the witness's anonymity was blown.

In these circumstances whatever may have been the effect intended to be achieved by the magistrates at the time of their initial ruling, this, as it seems to me, had been abandoned with the acquiescence of counsel for the Crown, by the time that ''Colonel B's'' evidence was over. I see no grounds on which a person present at or reading a report of the proceedings was bound to infer that to publish that part of the colonel's evidence in open court that disclosed his identity would interfere with the due administration of justice so as to constitute a contempt of court. Indeed the natural inference is to the contrary and it may not be without significance that no proceedings were brought against ''Peace News'' in respect of the issue of November 18 in which this evidence was published, without actually stating what would be found to be the colonel's name if the particular issue of ''Wire'' were consulted. But if there was no reason to suppose that publication of this evidence would interfere with the due administration of justice, how could it reasonably be supposed that to take the final step of publishing the name itself made all the difference?

My Lords, I would allow these appeals upon the ground that in the particular and peculiar circumstances of this case the disclosure of ''Colonel B's'' identity as a witness involved no interference with the due administration of justice and was not a contempt of court.

The difficulty that has arisen, as my noble and learned friends Viscount Dilhorne and Lord Edmund-Davies point out, is because the proceedings were launched upon the basis that at the conclusion of ''Colonel B's'' evidence the chairman of the examining magistrates had "stressed that no attempt should be made to disclose the identity of Colonel B." At the hearing, however, the proceedings, if persisted in, had to be conducted on the basis that no such explicit statement had been made. So everything was left to implication except the actual ruling as to how the witness was to be referred to in court and as to the persons to whom alone his real name and identity were to be disclosed.

My Lords, in cases where courts, in the interests of the due administration of justice, have departed in some measure from the general principle of open justice no one ought to be exposed to penal sanctions for criminal contempt of court for failing to draw an inference or recognise an implication as to what it is permissible to publish about those proceedings, unless the inference or implication is so obvious or so familiar that it may be said to speak for itself.

Difficulties such as those that have arisen in the instant case could be avoided in future if the court, whenever in the interests of due administration of justice it made a ruling which involved some departure from the ordinary mode of conduct of proceedings in open court, were to explain the result that the ruling was designed to achieve and what kind to information about the proceedings would, if published, tend to frustrate that result and would, accordingly, expose the publisher to risk of proceedings for contempt of court.

LORD EDMUND-DAVIES. My Lords, it is manifest that this appeal is of considerable public importance. The salient facts have been related in the speech of my noble and learned friend Lord Diplock and I shall not repeat them. Although I regard the proper outcome of these benighted proceedings as clear, the hearing in your Lordships' House has ranged over such a wide area that I do not propose to restrict myself simply to indicating how they should be disposed of. There has been much discussion of many aspects of the confused and confusing law relating to what, as Lord Cross of Chelsea complained in *Attorney-General* v. *Times Newspapers Ltd.* [1974] A.C. 273, 322, is still unfortunately called "contempt of court" which were not touched upon when that appeal was heard in your Lordships' House. Though not strictly necessary for present purposes, in these circumstances it would, as I believe, be unfortunate if we withheld such views as we have formed regarding them, and (like others of your Lordships) I do not propose to do so. This seems all the more desirable in view of the fact that it was only 18 years ago that, for the first time, a general right of appeal in cases of civil or criminal contempt of court was created (see Administration of Justice Act 1960, section 13) and there has been comparatively little judicial comment on the topic meanwhile.

> "The phrase ' contempt of court' does not in the least describe the true nature of the class of offence with which we are here concerned.... The offence consists in interfering with the administration of the law; in impeding and perverting the course of justice.... It is not the dignity of the court which is offended — a petty and misleading view of the issues involved — it is the fundamental supremacy of the law which is challenged." (*Johnson* v. *Grant,* 1923 S.C. 789, 790, *per* Lord President Clyde.)

When contempt is alleged the courts have for generations found themselves called upon to tread a judicial tightrope, for, as Phillimore J. put it in *Rex* v. *Blumenfeld, Ex parte Tupper* (1912) 28 T.L.R. 308, 311:

> "The court had to reconcile two things — namely, the right of free speech and the public advantage that a knave should be exposed, and the right of an individual suitor to have his

case fairly tried. The only way in which the court could save both was to refuse an unlimited extension of either right. It became, then, a question of degree."

This dilemma most frequently arises in relation to press and other reports of court proceedings, for the public interest inherent in their being fairly and accurately reported is of great constitutional importance and should never lead to punitive action unless, despite their factual accuracy, they nevertheless threaten or prejudice the due administration of justice.

It is of paramount importance to examine at the outset the statement filed pursuant to R.S.C., Ord. 52, r.2 in support of the present proceedings for contempt brought against Leveller Magazine Ltd., Peace News Ltd., the National Union of Journalists and various individuals. Taking as a typical example that filed on April 17, 1978, in relation to the "Journalist," we find the following assertions:

"(b) The said 'Colonel B' had properly been permitted not to disclose his identity when giving evidence by the said magistrates, the chairman directing in open court that no attempt should be made to disclose the identity of 'Colonel B.' (c) The said National Union of Journalists was at all material times well aware that the aforesaid direction had been given. (d) The said disclosure of the identity of 'Colonel B' tended and was calculated to prejudice the due administration of justice: it was intended to flout the aforesaid direction and make it difficult for witnesses in the position of 'Colonel B' to give evidence in open court."

The basis of these assertions unquestionably was the earlier affidavit of a Miss Butler, a member of the Director of Public Prosecutions' staff, that, the examining magistrates having ruled that "Colonel B's" name should be written down and shown only to the court, defence counsel and the defendants, on the Crown's contention that disclosure would not be in the interests of national security:

"At the conclusion of the proceedings on that day the chairman of the justices reminded the court of his earlier ruling *and stressed that no attempt should be made to disclose the identiy of 'Colonel B.'*"

The words which I have emphasised undoubtedly constituted the "direction" relied upon by the Attorney-General in his motion to commit. But before it was heard, Mr. Pratt, the clerk to the justices, swore an affidavit in which he said:

"The Official Secrets Act provides for exclusion of all or part of the public... but I am not aware of any other provision relevant to these proceedings enabling an order to be made such as is referred to or implied in Anne Butler's affidavit and that was the reason why the magistrates did not make any order such as she refers to — because I advised them that they had no power to do so."

Confronted by this latter affidavit, during the hearing of the motion counsel for the Attorney-General sought leave to amend his grounds by substituting the word "procedure" for the word "direction" in paragraphs (c) and (d) of the Attorney-General's statement. But the Divisional Court refused leave to amend. As I see it, it follows that the whole proceedings thereafter must be regarded as having taken place upon the basis that a committal was sought upon the single ground (a) that the magistrates had given a direction that no attempt must be made to disclose the identity of "Colonel B," and (b) that deliberate publication of his identity by the appellants sprang from their determination to disregard that direction. That, and that alone, was the case which the appellants were called upon to meet. And, whatever view one may hold of their behaviour generally, in my judgment it is irrefutable that the appellants destroyed that case. Or perhaps it would be more accurate to say that it had already been destroyed by affidavit, for at no time during the hearing did the Attorney-General contend that the magistrates had in fact given the direction deposed to by Miss Butler. Yet the Divisional Court seemingly attached no importance to this decisive fact. Lord Widgery C.J. said [1979] Q.B. 31, 43:

> "Central to all the [appellants'] arguments was the contention that this type of contempt requires a direction or mandatory order of a court and breach of that order, whereas here it is said that there was no order against disclosure, but merely a request."

After considering the challenge to Miss Butler's evidence, he continued:

> "In view of that conflict of evidence, counsel for the Attorney-General has not sought to rely on any disregard of such a statement, but relies on the earlier ruling in conformity with which it is said Colonel B gave his evidence. Indeed, if the chairman of the justices did say what Miss Butler says he said, its direct authority would only have gone to those within the court. The relevant ruling for present purposes was when the court gave permission for Colonel B to write down his name, in accordance with the same decision it had made for Colonel A. It is the authority of that rulin which is for consideration. If it was an effective ruling, a later so-called 'direction' would have added nothing to it, and consequently can be ignored."

A little later, dealing with the power of a court to allow a witness to write down his name, to order a witness to leave the court and so on, Lord Widgery C.J. added, at p. 44:

> "They are matters on which the court gives a ruling or a decision. The court may add something which can be called a formal direction, but no such formality is required. All such rulings are given, and only purported to be given, to those in court and not outside it. A flouting in court of the court's ruling will be a contempt. Equally, a flouting or deliberate disregard outside the court will be a contempt if it frustrates the court's ruling.... The fact that the justices' ruling had no direct effect outside the court does not prevent the publications here in question from being a contempt if they were made with the deliberate intention of frustrating the arrangement which the court had made to preserve Colonel B's anonymity. It is this element of flouting the court which is the real basis of the contempt here alleged. It can be sustained without proof that something like a direction or a specific order of the court has been breached."

Yet a little later, Lord Widgery C.J. added, at p. 45:

> "The contempt here relied upon is the deliberate flouting of the court's intention. The public has an interest in having the courts protected from such treatment and that is the public interest on which the Attorney-General relies."

My Lords, I have to repeat with the greatest respect that the Attorney-General had moved to commit the appellants upon an entirely different basis and upon that basis alone. The basis having in effect been abandoned by the Attorney-General, in my judgment it was not open to the Divisional Court (and particularly after refusing to allow him to amend his grounds of application) to entertain an entirely different case upon which to commit the appellants for criminal contempt.

This is no mere judicial quibble. Persons charged with criminal misconduct are entitled to know with reasonable precision the basis of the charge. If proceedings such as the present were tried on indictment and the statement of the charge "Criminal Contempt," it would be impermissible to present a case wholly different from that outlined in the particulars of the charge and then to urge that the departure was immaterial, since the new misconduct relied upon was, like the old, simply another variety of criminal contempt.

Nor, my Lords, would it be acceptable were the Attorney-General to urge, in effect, that no injustice has here been done, since the *wishes* of the court were clear and the determination of the appellants to flout or disregard those wishes equally clear. Mr. Sedley rightly observed that, if no direction was in fact given, thinking cannot have made it so, and the appellants were correct in thinking that by publishing they were breaching no ruling of the court. I have to say respectfully that I am uneasy about the view expressed by Lord Widgery C.J. that "the deliberate flouting of the court's *intention*" is sufficient to constitute criminal contempt, for as O'Connor J. said in *P. A. Thomas & Co.* v. *Mould* [1968] 2 Q.B. 913, 923:

> "...where parties seek to invoke the power of the court to commit people to prison and deprive them of their liberty, there has got to be quite clear certainty about it."

In the absence of any such ruling as that deposed to by Miss Butler, but denied by the clerk of the court, was it the unmistakable intention of the magistrates in the present case that no one should behave as these appellants later did, particularly when those magistrates were specifically advised by their clerk that they had no power to make any order restricting the publication outside their court of "Colonel B's" identity? In such circumstances "intention" and "preference" seem indistinguishable. The latter would have been manifested by the expression of a mere request that no such publication should take place, and when the magistrates elected to discontinue sitting in camera and thereafter did no more than rule that in their court the name of the witness should be written down, their "intention" regarding what must or must not be done outside court was, in my judgment, indeterminable. Indeed, it was ex hypothesi non-existent, since they had been advised that they could in no way control such conduct. They might well have *preferred* that no publication of "Colonel B's" name should take place anywhere or at any time, but it is going too far to say that they had manifested an intention to do all they could to guard against it by ruling as they did. "No man should be condemned by an implication," observed my noble and learned friend, Lord Diplock, in the course of counsel's submissions. Condemnation is even more objectionable when the implication underlying the court's conduct is simply a matter of conjecture, and I have already indicated why I consider that such omission was fatal in the circumstances and should lead to these appeals being allowed.

I should add that I am for a like reason not wholly satisfied about the ratio decidendi of the Divisional Court in *Reg.* v. *Socialist Worker Printers and Publishers Ltd., Ex parte Attorney-General* [1975] Q.B. 637 in contempt proceedings following upon a blackmail prosecution in which the trial judge had directed that the victims who gave evidence should be referred to in court by letters, notwithstanding which the defendants proceeded to publish their names. I have ascertained that the ipsissima verba of the statement filed by the Attorney-General pursuant to R.S.C., Ord. 52, r.2 were that:

> "...the said publication tended and was calculated to prejudice the due administration of justice by causing victims of blackmail to fear publicity and thus deter them from coming forward in aid of legal proceedings or from seeking the protection of the law and/or by holding up to public obloquy witnesses who had given evidence in criminal proceedings."

One of the two grounds upon which the Divisional Court granted the application to commit was (in the words of Lord Widgery C.J., at pp. 649-650):

> "...that by publishing the names of these two witnesses in defiance of the judge's directions the respondents were committing [a] blatant affront to the authority of the court...."

If there was any "direction" it was at best implicit. And it should be observed that no publication of the victims' names took place until the judge was about to sum up, and there was accordingly no question of the administration of justice in *that* case being prejudiced by their being deterred from giving evidence for the prosecution. So the basis of the decision seems to be that publication was objectionable on the *general* ground that in any and every blackmail case the administration of justice in future prosecutions will be interfered with if victims' names are published. But, while many (and perhaps most) would accept this, is it necessarily so? I certainly recall one eminent judge (now retired) who in such cases scrutinised with very great care counsel's request that the victims should remain anonymous and emphatically rejected the idea that in every such case the administration of justice would automatically be prejudiced by publication. Counsel for two of the appellants in the present case submitted that it does not follow that everything done which had the effect of deterring possible witnesses necessarily constitutes a contempt, the proper test being whether it is a *prohibited* act calculated to deter. The time may yet come when this House will be called upon to adjudicate upon the point.

Neither in *Reg.* v. *Socialist Worker Printers and Publishers Ltd., Ex parte Attorney-General* [1975] Q.B. 637 nor in the instant case did the court give any direction against publication purporting to operate outside the courtroom. It has to be said that hitherto the view seems to have been widely accepted that no such power exists. Thus, in the *Socialist Worker* case the present Attorney-General submitted, at p. 639:

> "The trial judge did not give any express direction about revealing the names of the witnesses in the press. Indeed, he had no power to make orders affecting the press or other media in their conduct outside the court."

He nevertheless added:

> "The direction could only protect the witnesses effectively if their names were not revealed subsequently. Hence the direction was concerned with publication outside as well as inside the court."

Defence counsel likewise submitted, at p. 640: "A trial judge has no power to order the press not to publish matters elicited at an open trial."

In the present appeals, again, appellants and respondents alike concurred in submitting that (as, indeed, Lord Widgery C.J. had himself observed: see [1979] Q.B. 31, 43) the magistrates' court had no power to direct that there should be no publication in the press or by any other means of the identity of the "Colonel B" who had given evidence before them. Lord Rawlinson Q.C. for the Attorney-General, told your Lordships in terms that the court could not direct the outside world, but added that its ruling nevertheless extended outside its walls. For myself I found this difficult to follow, particularly as no illustrations were forthcoming of what learned counsel had in mind. After considerable reflection I have come to the conclusion that a court has no power to pronounce to the public at large such a prohibition against publication that all disobedience to it would automatically constitute a contempt. It is beyond doubt that a court has a wide inherent jurisdiction to control its own procedure. In certain circumstances it may decide to sit wholly or in part in camera. Or witnesses may be ordered to withdraw, "lest they trim their evidence by hearing the evidence of others" (as

Earl Loreburn put it in *Scott* v. *Scott* [1913] A.C. 417, 446). Or part of a criminal trial may be ordered to take place in the absence of the jury, such as during the hearing of legal submissions or during a "trial within a trial" regarding the admissibility of an alleged confession. Or the court may direct that throughout the hearing in open court certain witnesses are to be referred to by letter or number only. But it does not follow that, were a person (and even one with knowledge of the procedure which had been adopted) thereafter to make public that which had been wholly or partially concealed, he would be ipso facto guilty of contempt. Nothing illustrates this more clearly than the hearing of evidence in camera,

> "...it [being] plain that inherent jurisdiction exists in any court which enables it to exclude the public where it becomes necessary in order to administer justice." (*Rex* v. *Governor of Lewes Prison, Ex parte Doyle* [1917] 2 K.B. 254, *per* Viscount Reading C.J., at p. 271).

It might be thought that disclosure of that which had been divulged only in secret would in all cases constitute the clearest example of contempt. Thus we find Oliver J. saying in *Rex* v. *Davies, Ex parte Delbert-Evans* [1945] K.B. 435, 446:

> "...everything the public has a right to know about a trial..., *that is to say, everything that has taken place in open court,* may be published, and beyond that there is no need or *right* to go." (The italics are mine.)

But *Scott* v. *Scott* [1913] A.C. 417 has long established that this is not so. And the Administration of Justice Act 1960 provides in terms by section 12(1):

> "The publication of information relating to proceedings before any court sitting in private shall not of itself be contempt of court except in the following cases..."

Five types of proceedings are then set out, ending with

> "(*e*) where the court (having power to do so) expressly prohibits the publication of all information relating to the proceedings or of information of the description which is published."

Section 12(4) provides:

> "Nothing in this section shall be construed as implying that any publication is punishable as contempt of court which would not be so punishable apart from this section."

I am in respectful agreement with Scarman L.J. who said in *In re F. (orse. A.) (A Minor) (Publication of Information)* [1977] Fam. 58, 99 that this last obscure subsection

> "...was enacted to ensure that no one would in future be found guilty of contempt who would not also under the pre-existing law have been found guilty."

And what appears certain is that at common law the fact that a court sat wholly or partly in camera (and even where in such circumstances the court gave a direction prohibiting publication of information relating to what had been said or done behind closed doors) did not of itself and in every case necessarily mean that publication thereafter constituted contempt of court.

For that to arise something more than disobedience of the court's direction needs to be established. That something more is that the publication must be of such a nature as to threaten the administration of justice either in the particular case in relation to which the prohibition was pronounced or in relation to cases which may be brought in the future. So the liability to be committed for contempt in relation to publication of the kind with which this House is presently concerned must depend upon all the circumstances in which the publication complained of took place.

It may be objected that, in an area where the boundaries of the law should be defined with precision, such a situation confronts those engaged in the public dissemination of information with perils which cannot always be foreseen or reasonably safeguarded against. To retort that this has always been so affords no comfort, but intelligent anticipation of what would be fair and what would be unfair can go a long way to ease the burden of the disseminators. They would themselves be in all probability the first to resist court "directions" as to what they may or may not publish, and I have already expressed my disbelief in their general validity. But the press and others could, as I believe, be helped were a court when sitting in public to draw express attention to any procedural decisions it had come to and implemented during the hearing, to explain that they were aimed at ensuring the due and fair administration of justice and to indicate that any who by publishing material or otherwise acting in a manner calculated to prejudice that aim would run the risk of contempt proceedings being instituted against them. Farther than that, in my judgment, the court cannot go. As far as that they could, as I believe, with advantage go. The public and the press would thereby be relieved of the burden of divining what was the court's "intention," for this would have been made clear and it would be up to them to decide whether they would respect it or frustrate it. Even so, ignoring the warning by disobedience or otherwise would not of itself necessarily establish a case of contempt. But the knowledge that the warning had been given should prove at least a guide to possible consequences and would render it impossible for the person responsible for publication to urge (as was done in *Reg.* v. *Socialist Worker Printers and Publishers Ltd., Ex parte Attorney-General* [1975] Q.B. 637, 646A-B) that he was under the impression that the court had merely *requested* that there be no disclosure of certain specified matters, or that, as the editor of the "Journalist" said in the present case:

> "...my understanding was that [Colonel B] had been permitted to write his name down rather than give it in evidence but that there was no direct [intimation] .... that his name should not be published."

Were such intimation as I have in mind given by the court, the possible plea of a publisher that he had no knowledge of it would be of little moment. In such cases as the instant one, we are concerned not with improper publication by a private individual (as to whom nothing presently arises) but with people controlling or connected with powerful organs of publicity who, for reasons of their own (one of which may be no more than the desire to boost sales), decide to take the course of defiant dissemination of matter which ought to be kept confidential. It is incumbent upon such people to ascertain what had happened in court. They have the means of doing this, and they cannot be heard to complain that they were ignorant of what had taken place. Perhaps the time has come when heed should be paid to the view expressed in the Phillimore Report on Contempt of Court (1974) (Cmnd. 5794), at p. 60, in reference to *Reg.* v. *Socialist Worker Printers and Publishers Ltd., Ex parte Attorney-General* [1975] Q.B. 637:

> "We incline to the view that the important question of what the press may publish concerning proceedings in open court should no longer be left to judicial requests (which may be disregarded) nor to judicial directions (which, if given, may have doubtful legal authority) but that legislation... should provide for these specific circumstances in which a court shall be

empowered to prohibit, in the public interest, the publication of names or of other matters arising at a trial.''

Although it should be unnecessary, perhaps I ought to add that nothing I have said should be regarded as implying that there can be no committal for contempt unless there has been some sort of warning against publication. While, for the reasons I have indicated, it would be wise to warn, the court is under no obligation to do so. And there will remain cases where a court could not reasonably have considered a warning even desirable, such as where the later conduct complained of should not have been contemplated as likely to occur. *Reg.* v. *Newcastle Chronicle and Journal Ltd., Ex parte Attorney-General* (unreported), January 17, 1978, is an example of such a case. There the Divisional Court rightly held contempt proved where, during the course of a trial on an indictment containing 20 counts for dishonesty, a newspaper reported that on arraignment on the first day the defendant had pleaded guilty to four of the counts and that the trial was proceeding only on the remaining 16. Lord Widgery C.J. rightly commented:

> ''It is to be observed that the learned trial judge gave no sort of warning to representatives of the press in his court that the evidence would contain matter which should not be reported. I do not think that there is any obligation on the judge to give a warning to the press, or indeed to anybody else, when the matter complained of and relied upon is so elementary and well understood as this one.... Certainly it does not seem to me to be an unfair burden on the newspaper reporter to say that he ought to know (and, knowing, ought to practise in his profession) that any reference to additional offences committed by the accused is something which ought to be kept out of the jury's ears *unless* there is some clear exception which covers the matter.''

My Lords, I said at the outset that I should digress, and I fear I have done so at some length, but I comfort myself by the reflection that I am not alone among your Lordships in this respect. Let me now return to the matter in hand and say that, for the reason earlier indicated, I hold that all these appeals should be allowed.

LORD RUSSELL OF KILLOWEN. My Lords, I propose to state briefly my conclusions on the questions relevant to this case. From what happened in connection with the deposition of ''Colonel B,'' and from the opening sentence of that deposition itself, it was clear that the examining magistrates decided that his identity should have strictly limited publication. Contempt of court in its essentials consists in interference with the due administration of justice. It is true that in this case the application by the Crown to which the magistrates acceded was based upon the suggestion that revelation of the witness's identity would be inimical to national safety, and no specific mention appears to have been made of the requirements of the due administration of justice. But this was a prosecution under the Official Secrets Act.

In my opinion it really goes without saying that behind the application (and the decision) lay considerations of the due administration of justice. In the first place an alternative to the via media adopted would be an application that ''Colonel B's'' evidence be taken in camera, and in principle the less that evidence is taken in camera the better for the due administration of justice, a point with which journalists certainly no less than others would agree. In the second place a decision on anonymity — the via media — would obviously, and for the same reasons, be highly desirable in the interest of the due administration of justice as a continuing process in future in such cases. In the third place it appears to me that the furtherance of the due administration of justice was the only ground to support the decision of the magistrates.

I arrive therefore at the conclusion that it should have been apparent to the appellants, from the very form of the deposition of "Colonel B," that the magistrates had arrived at a decision on his anonymity designed to promote not merely national safety but the due administration of justice. (Incidentally I reject entirely the specious suggestion that there was here merely a polite request to the press not to publish the identity.)

I do not, my Lords, regard as of any relevance the question whether the magistrates had any power or authority directly to forbid all publication of "Colonel B's" identity. The field in which contempt of court, or, as I prefer to describe it, improper interference with the due administration of justice, may be committed is not circumscribed by the terms of an order enforceable against the accused. I find no problem in the concept that a decision or direction may have no immediate aim and no direct enforceability beyond the deciding and directing court, but yet may have such effect in connection with contempt of court. Merely to state, as is the law, that in general contempt of court is the improper interference with the due administration of justice is to state that it need not involve disobedience to an order binding upon the alleged contemnor.

Where then, in the light of these principles, stands the present case? I dismiss at once the fact, which I am prepared to assume, that the *motive* which induced the appellants to publish the identity of "Colonel B" was that they considered the Crown's view that its revelation would endanger national safety to be nonsense. Their motive is irrelevant to guilt if they intended to do that which amounted in law to interference with the due administration of justice and therefore contempt.

It is at this stage that I feel great concern with this case. There can be no doubt that the publication in toto of "Colonel B's" deposition was permissible without contempt of court. In it was to be found a reference to a particular edition of the Royal Corps of Signals publication "Wire" in which "Colonel B" admitted in his deposition that his name in association with his stated then current posting was to be found. (I believe that the reference to the particular edition was due to a question by the clerk to the magistrates and not to cross-examining counsel.) This edition of "Wire" was available to the public, including anyone who read a report of the deposition, which of course was freely reportable; no doubt it was also deposited in the British Museum. No objection was raised by the prosecution to this part of the deposition, nor by the magistrates.

The position therefore was that, notwithstanding the decision of the magistrates designed to preserve the anonymity of "Colonel B," his deposition itself revealed at one simple remove his identity. Publication in full of his deposition, given as it was in open court, could not have been a contempt. It would have told the world (if interested) where to look for "Colonel B's" identity. Would it have transgressed the limits of the permissible if the publication of the deposition had been accompanied by a re-publication of the stated edition of "Wire," or the relevant extracts from it? I do not think so. The substance of the magistrates' decision would not have been breached. The gaff was already blown by the deposition, to the publication of which no objection could be taken.

For these reasons, which depend entirely upon the totally revealing content of "Colonel B's" deposition, I would allow these appeals. I see no sufficient justification for holding that the direct short cut to breach of the decided anonymity of "Colonel B" is to be regarded in the particular circumstances of this case as a contempt of court.

If, my Lords, I may summarise:

(1) The decision of the examining magistrates should have been recognised by the appellants as one designed to preserve the anonymity of "Colonel B."

(2) That decision should be taken as made in the interests of the due administration of justice, both in that case, and in the due administration of justice as a continuing process.

(3) No specific warning of a risk of contempt of court by ignoring the decision should be necessary to found such a charge, though it might be useful.

(4) There was no justification for thinking that this decision involved merely a request.

(5) But for the substantially self-identifying content of "Colonel B's" legitimately reportable deposition I would have been for dismissal of these appeals.

(6) Because, and only because, the properly reportable deposition of "Colonel B" really in itself revealed his identity, without protest from either magistrates or prosecution, I would allow these appeals, with costs here and below.

Lord Scarman. My Lords, when an application is made to commit for contempt of court a journalist or editor for the publication of information relating to the proceedings of a court, freedom of speech and the public nature of justice are at once put at risk. The general rule of our law is clear. No one shall be punished for publishing such information unless it can be established to the satisfaction of the court to whom the application is made that the publication constitutes an interference with the administration of justice either in the particular case to which the publication relates or generally. Parliament clearly had the general rule in mind when in 1960 it enacted that even the publication of information relating to proceedings before any court sitting in private shall not of itself be contempt of court save in specified exceptional cases: section 12(1) of the Administration of Justice Act 1960.

The law does not treat any, or every, interference with the course or administration of justice as a contempt. The common law rule which was affirmed by this House in *Scott* v. *Scott* [1913] A.C. 417 is that the interference must be such as to render impracticable the administration of justice or to frustrate the attainment of justice either in the particular case or generally.

Further, since such interference is a criminal offence, the court to whom the application to commit is made must be satisfied beyond reasonable doubt that the interference is of such a character. If the court is not sure, the application must be dismissed.

Three questions arise for consideration in this appeal. (1) Did the examining justices have power to sit in private to take the evidence of the witness described in court as "Colonel B"? (2) Did they have the power, without going into private session, to require evidence as to the identity of the witness to be written down and not to be mentioned in open court? (3) If either of the first two questions be answered in the affirmative, was it a contempt of court to publish information relating to the identity of the witness?...

Contempt of court — the third question

The law of contempt of court has been, throughout its history, bedevilled by technicalities. One of them was raised in this appeal. Can a court make an order, or give a ruling, which is binding on persons who are neither witnesses nor parties in the proceedings before the court? It is a misconception of the nature of the criminal offence of contempt to regard it as being an offence because it is the breach of a binding order.

The offence is interference, with knowlege of the court's proceedings, with the course of administration of justice: see *In re F. (orse. A.) (A Minor) (Publication of Information)* [1977] Fam. 58. It was for this reason, no doubt, that Lord Widgery C.J. in this case stressed the element of "flouting" the authority of the court. Though I would not have chosen the word, I think it does reflect the essence of the offence, namely that the conduct complained of, in this case the publication, must be a deliberate frustration of the effort of the court to protect justice from interference.

In the present case the examining justices took a course which was a substitute for sitting in private. If, as I think, the device is an acceptable extension of the common law power of a court to control its proceedings by sitting in private, where necessary, in the court's judgment, to protect the administration of justice from interference, section 12(1) of the Administration of Justice Act 1960 is relevant. For the principle governing contempt of court when a court sits in private must also govern the situation where the common law device is used in substitute for private session. The subsection is in these terms:

> "The publication of information relating to proceedings before any court sitting in private shall not of itself be contempt of court except in the following cases, that is to say — (*a*) where the proceedings relate to the wardship or adoption of an infant or wholly or mainly to the guardianship, custody, maintenance or upbringing of an infant, or rights of access to an infant; (*b*) where the proceedings are brought under Part VIII of the Mental Health Act 1959, or under any provision of that Act authorising an application or reference to be made to a Mental Health Review Tribunal or to a county court; (*c*) where the court sits in private for reasons of national security during that part of the proceedings about which the information in question is published; (*d*) where the information relates to a secret process, discovery or invention which is in issue in the proceedings; (*e*) where the court (having power to do so) expressly prohibits the publication of all information relating to the proceedings or of information of the description which is published."

The subsection confers no new powers upon the court. It leaves the common law and statutory powers of sitting in private exactly as they were. Paragraphs (*a*), (*b*), (*d*), and (*e*) add nothing to the common law. It would be strange if the exception stated in paragraph (*c*) should prove alone to have made a fundamental modification in the law. I do not so interpret it. It provides for the case where at common law or by statute the court may sit in private for reasons of national security. The statutory power which the justices had under section 8(4) of the Act of 1920 is not relevant, because the justices chose not to sit in private. The common law power is relevant, because the device employed was within the inherent power of the court at common law.

But since the common law power to sit in private arises only if the administration of justice be threatened, the third question becomes one of fact. What was the reason for the justices' ruling? If it was to avert an interference with the administration of justice, was there material upon which the ruling could reasonably be based? The third question cannot therefore be answered without considering the facts. Here I find myself in a state of doubt.

I do not think that the Attorney-General has discharged the burden of proof upon him. Uncertainty surrounds, and continues to surround, the ruling made by the justices and its object. First, one cannot be sure that they took into account all the matters to which it was their duty to have regard if they were giving notice in open court that to protect the administration of justice the name of the witness was not to be published. The justices clearly had regard to national security, but did they understand that, in exercising their common law power, the national security risk must be shown also to be a risk to the administration of justice and assess the degree of the latter risk? Did they address themselves to that question at all? It cannot be said with any certainty that they did, or that the Crown adduced any material, by way of evidence or otherwise, to show that the national security issue was such that publication of the colonel's name would endanger the due administration of justice.

Secondly, there was, and remains, considerable doubt as to the nature of the "ruling." Was it a decision, an indication, or only a request? As all know who have experience of the forensic process in this country, courts frequently allow a witness to write down his name or address or to give some other specified evidence (e.g., a medical or welfare report) in writing and make it clear that they do not wish the matter to be mentioned in open court. A court may do so only to save a witness or a party from distress or pain, e.g., in a personal injury or matrimonial case. On the other hand, a court may, as the Attorney-General contends in this case, have in mind that publication outside, as well as inside, the court is to be prevented as an interference with the administration of justice. Unless the ruling in this case is to be interpreted as a decision taken to prevent interference with the administration of justice, the publication of information as to "Colonel B's" identity would be no contempt. If, upon its proper intepretation, the "ruling" was no more than an indication or request, publication would be no contempt. It is only if the ruling must be read as a prohibition of publication in the interests of the administration of justice, i.e., as falling within paragraph (*e*) of section 12(1) of the Act of 1960, that the appellants can, in my judgment, be found guilty of contempt. After a careful study of the case and listening to full argument, I remain unsure as to the nature and object of the ruling.

I would summarise my conclusions thus. If a court is satisfied that for the protection of the administration of justice from interference it is necessary to order that evidence either be heard in private or be written down and not given in open court, it may so order. Such an order, or ruling, may be the foundation of contempt proceedings against any person who, with knowledge of the order, frustrates its purpose by publishing the evidence kept private or information leading to its exposure. The order or ruling must be clear and can be made only if it appears to the court reasonably necessary. There must be material (not necessarily evidence) made known to the court upon which it could reasonably reach its conclusion, and those who are alleged to be in contempt must be shown to have known, or to have had a proper opportunity of knowing, of the existence of the order (see *In re F. (orse. A.) (A Minor) (Publication of Information)* [1977] Fam. 58).

Neither the Crown nor the examining justices made clear what they were seeking to do or upon what grounds the court was being asked, and decided, to act. That certainty which the criminal law requires before a man can be convicted of a criminal offence is lacking. I would, therefore, allow the appeals.

Appeals allowed with costs.

3.3.2 Criminal Code, ss.9, 10

Contempt of court is unique in Canadian criminal law in that it is nowhere given a statutory definition.

9. Notwithstanding anything in this Act or any other Act, no person shall be convicted or discharged under section 736

(*a*) of an offence at common law,

(*b*) of an offence under an Act of the Parliament of England, or of Great Britain, or of the United Kingdom of Great Britain and Ireland, or

(*c*) of an offence under an Act or ordinance in force in any province, territory or place before that province, territory or place became a province of Canada,

but nothing in this section affects the power, jurisdiction or authority that a court, judge, justice or provincial court judge had, immediately before the 1st day of April 1955, to impose punishment for contempt of court.

10. (1) Where a court, judge, justice or magistrate summarily convicts a person for a contempt of court committed in the face of the court and imposes punishment in respect thereof, that person may appeal

(*a*) from the conviction, or

(*b*) against the punishment imposed.

(2) Where a court or judge summarily convicts a person for a contempt of court not committed in the face of the court and punishment is imposed in respect thereof, that person may appeal

(*a*) from the conviction, or

(*b*) against the punishment imposed.

(3) An appeal under this section lies to the court of appeal of the province in which the proceedings take place, and, for the purposes of this section, the provisions of Part XVIII apply, *mutatis mutandis*.

3.3.3 *R.* v. *Kopyto* (1988) 24 O.A.C. 81 (Ont. C.A.)

CORY, J.A.: The common law offence of contempt of court is thus preserved by s.8. There are two types of conduct which come within the scope of criminal contempt. Firstly, there is contempt in the face of the court. This type of offence encompasses any word spoken or act done in or in the precinct of the court which obstructs or interferes with the due administration of justice or is calculated to do so. It would include assaults committed in the court, insults to the court made in the presence of the court, interruption of court proceedings, a refusal of a witness to be sworn or, after being sworn, refusal to answer. Secondly, the offence may be committed by acts which are committed outside the court. Contempt not in the face of the court includes words spoken or published or acts done which are intended to interfere or are likely to interfere with the fair administration of justice. Examples of that type of contempt are publications which are intended or are likely to prejudice the fair trial or conduct of a criminal or civil proceeding or publications which scandalize or otherwise lower the authority of the court, and acts which would obstruct persons having duties to discharge in a court of justice.

3.4 Scandalizing the Court

How far can the media, and individuals, go in criticizing judges and the courts? Note the contrast between the liberal approach laid down in *Ambard* which is, in theory, also the Canadian law, and the actual results reached in the Canadian cases.

3.4.1 *Ambard* v. *Attorney-General of Trinidad and Tobago*, [1936] A.C. 322, Judicial Committee of the Privy Council

LORD ATKIN. This is an appeal, by special leave, from an order of the Supreme Court of Trinidad and Tobago ordering the appellant to pay a fine of 25*l*., or in default to be imprisoned for one month, for contempt of Court, and further ordering him to pay the costs of the proceedings as between solicitor and client.

In June, 1934, one, Joseph St. Clair, was charged at the Sessions, Port of Spain, before Gilchrist J. and a jury on an indictment containing two counts, one charging the accused with attempt to murder a superior officer, the second with shooting with intent to do grievous bodily harm. It appears that the accused fired his rifle at the officer but failed to hit him. He was found guilty on the second count, with a recommendation to mercy, and was sentenced on June 12 to eight years' hard labour. He did not appeal.

At the same sessions, one, John Sheriff, was charged before Robinson J. and a jury on an indictment containing three counts, (1) wounding with intent to murder a particular woman, (2) wounding with intent to murder generally, (3) wounding with intent to do grievous bodily harm. It appears that he attacked with a razor, and seriously mutilated, a woman who was not the person he had intended to attack. He was convicted on the third count, and was sentenced on June 14 to seven years' hard labour. After sentence he said: "I give notice of appeal," and on June 20 filed formal notice of appeal against his conviction. His appeal eventually succeeded, apparently on the ground of misdirection, and the conviction was quashed. Meanwhile, on June 29, the present appellant, who is the editor-manager and part proprietor of a daily newspaper called the Port of Spain Gazette, published the article which has been found to constitute a contempt of Court. He did not write it, but revised it editorially before publication, and undoubtedly is fully responsible for its publication. It is necessary for the purposes of this case to consider the whole article. It was as follows: —

THE HUMAN ELEMENT

"Many years ago, it used to be a rather interesting feature of one of the English publications to draw pointed attention, in parallel columns to the strangely anomalous differences between the sentences imposed by various magistrates and judges in cases which seemed, from the reports, to present a fair similarity of facts. In some quarters, the criticism — often unexpressed in actual words — was resented as taking no account of circumstances which a judge was fully entitled to give effect to, though they might not strike the ordinary reader of the press reports. But on the whole, it was felt that, in the majority of instances, useful public service was rendered by this showing up of the inequalities of legal punishments. In Trinidad it must often have occurred to readers of the proceedings in our criminal courts, both inferior and superior, how greatly the personal or human element seems to come into play in awarding punishment for offences. No question is here involved as to the justification for the convictions; it is assumed, and we believe it to be no unjustified assumption, that in the great majority of cases accused persons are seldom convicted except upon thoroughly satisfactory evidence; and a small number of appeals which succeed, when based upon the plea of the innocence of the prisoner of the offence charged, may be regarded as sufficient proof of that. It is the inequality of the sentences as fitting the circumstances of the offences that seems to often demand some comment. And if we here venture to draw attention to this, it is not by any means with the idea of confirming popular opinion as to the inherent severity or leniency of individual judges or magistrates, but simply with a view to inviting consideration of a matter that must, and in fact does, cause adverse comment amongst the masses as to the evenness of the administration of justice in Trinidad. In two recent cases has it been thought by the public that the sentences imposed by two different judges have been open to such criticism. In the one case, a man stood indicted for the seriously grave offence of shooting at his superior officer with intent to murder him. There seems no doubt that had it not been for the prisoner's failure to shoot straight — a thing at which he himself marvelled openly — he must have killed the officer. Not doubt, as was brought out in evidence (and perhaps to an even greater degree than was proved), the man was suffering under the effects of constant provocation; but in addition to all else, there was this to aggravate the crime, that the offender was a trained member of a military body, presumably well disciplined, and that to have used a lethal weapon to which his position gave him easy access and with it to have attempted the murder of his officer is a thing regarded in most quarters as peculiarly heinous. The sentence imposed on conviction was eight years, which, on the assumption of good conduct, means release at the end of six years. The other case was one in which a man stood charged with a peculiarly brutal act of wounding with a razor, his victim, a woman who was shortly to have become a mother, being so terribly injured that for a long time it seemed quite probable she would die. On conviction, the sentence imposed by another judge on this prisoner was seven years, which, on the assumption of good conduct, means release at the expiration of five years and a quarter. Had either of these two cases stood alone, it is quite likely that the sentences would have passed uncommented upon; for neither of them is, in itself, what might be described as a lenient one. But coming together as they did at the same sessions and within a day or two of each other, they have created in the public mind an impression that the former was as unduly severe as the latter was lenient. Both, it is true, were for attempted murder. In both cases a deadly weapon was used. And while some may think that, as we stated above, the military relationship between the prisoner and his intended victim in the first case rendered the matter graver from an official viewpoint, yet, on the other hand, in the shooting case, no one, providentially, was injured, and much provocation was proved, whereas in the razor slashing case, (assuming the facts proved by the Crown to be true), there does not appear to have been any provocation, while, on the contrary, the attack was made on a woman unknown to or by the accused, whom he mistook for someone else. Surely there might have been expected rather more effect to have been given to the recommendation from the jury to mercy in the first case; and surely, in the other, it would have been more in accord with public opinion as to the need for stern suppression of such attacks had the learned judge been able to see his way to impose a considerably more severe term of imprisonment; the more so in view of the fact that there was absolutely no intimation from the jury that they thought any leniency might properly be shown. We fully realise that the infliction of the sentence is entirely in the discretion of judge, who has a wide latitude, from a few days to life-long imprisonment for the crime of attempted murder. But equally is it usually expected that the fullest consideration will be given to the recommendation of a jury for mercy. Assuming, therefore, that eight years' hard labour in lieu of the 20 years which many persons fully expected would be passed, fairly represents an effectual concession to the jury's views, the opinion has been fully expressed that the seven years passed on the razor slasher was far too little for the crime he had committed. And we do not think we are wrong in saying that, as a rule, some weight is given by judges to the question of whether a prisoner succeeded or failed in committing the crime he stands charged with. As we have pointed out, though in both of these cases, the Crown alleged and the jury found, an attempt to murder, in the one case that attempt failed completely — through no fault of the prisoner, it is true: in the other the attempt, while providentially failing, resulted in terrible mutilation of the woman who was the victim. It is painful at all times to have to urge the insufficiency of a punishment inflicted; and we wish it to be distinctly appreciated that we dissociate ourselves from those who regard one judge as habitually severe or another as habitually lenient. Yet we do think that if some way could be devised for the greater equalisation of punishment with the crime committed, a great deal would have been achieved towards the removal of one frequent cause for criticism of the sentences passed in our various criminal courts."

On July 3 the Attorney-General gave notice of motion to the Registrar of the Supreme Court that he would move for an order nisi calling upon the appellant to show cause why a writ of attachment should not issue against him for his contempt in publishing the article in question, and on the same date an order nisi was made by the Court in the terms of the notice of motion. The notice and the order nisi were at first limited to contempt in publishing an article calculated to interfere with the due course of justice, the complaint being that it was improper having regard to Sheriff's pending appeal. Later, it was amended so as to include a complaint that the article contained "statements and comments which tend to bring the authority and administration of the law into disrepute and disregard." In this amended form the matter came before the full Court consisting of the Chief Justice and Gilchrist and Robinson JJ. It was heard on various days in July, and on September 5 the Chief Justice gave the judgment of the Court. He acquitted the appellant of contempt in respect of the pending appeal of Sheriff: and no more need be said on that point. But he found that the article was written with the direct object of bringing the administration of the criminal law by the judges into disfavour with the public, and desiring to impose a penalty which, if relatively light, would yet emphasize that, while the judges would place no obstruction in the way of fair criticism of their performance of their functions, untruths and malice would not be tolerated, he fined the respondent 25*l*., in default, one month's imprisonment, and ordered him to pay the costs of the proceedings to be taxed between solicitor and client. The formal judgment, slightly departing from the wording of the oral judgment, recited that the appellant had committed a contempt of Court, the article having been written "with the direct object of bringing the administration of the criminal law in this Colony by the judges into disrepute and disregard," so following the amended order nisi.

Their Lordships can find no evidence in the article, or in any facts placed before the Court, to justify the finding either that the article was written with the direct object mentioned, or that it could have that effect: and they will advise His Majesty that this appeal be allowed. It will be sufficient to apply the law as laid down in *Reg*. v. *Gray* (1) by Lord Russell of Killowen C.J. (2): "Any act done or writing published calculated to bring a Court or a judge of the Court into contempt, or to lower his authority, is a contempt of Court. That is one class of contempt. Further, any act done or writing published calculated to obstruct or interfere with the due course of justice or the lawful process of the Courts is a contempt of Court. The former class belongs to the category which Lord Hardwicke L.C. characterised as 'scandalising a Court or a judge.' (*In re Read and Huggonson* (1).) That description of that class of contempt is to be taken subject to one and an important qualification. Judges and Courts are alike open to criticism, and if reasonable argument or expostulation is offered against any judicial act as contrary to law or the public good, no Court could or would treat that as contempt of Court.''

And that, in applying the law, the Board will not lose sight of local conditions, is made clear in the judgment in *McLeod* v. *St. Aubyn* (2), where Lord Morris, after saying that committals for contempt of Court by scandalizing the Court itself had become obsolete in this country, an observation sadly disproved the next year in the case last cited, proceeds (3): ''Courts are satisfied to leave to public opinion attacks or comments derogatory or scandalous to them. But it must be considered that in small colonies, consisting principally of coloured populations, the enforcement in proper cases of committal for contempt of Court for attacks on the Court may be absolutely necessary to preserve in such a community the dignity of and respect for the Court.''

But whether the authority and position of an individual judge, or the due administration of justice, is concerned, no wrong is committed by any member of the public who exercises the ordinary right of criticising, in good faith, in private or public, the public act done in the seat of justice. The path of criticism is a public way: the wrong headed are permitted to err therein: provided that members of the public abstain from imputing improper motives to those taking part in the administration of justice, and are genuinely exercising a right of criticism, and not acting in malice or attempting to impair the administration of justice, they are immune. Justice is not a cloistered virtue: she must be allowed to suffer the scrutiny and respectful, even though outspoken, comments of ordinary men.

In the present case the writer had taken for his theme the parennial topic of inequality of sentences, under the text ''The Human Element,'' using as the occasion for his article the two sentences referred to. He expressly disclaimed the suggestion that one of the particular judges was habitually severe, the other habitually lenient. It is unnecessary to discuss whether his criticism of the sentences was well founded. It is very seldom that the observer has the means of ascertaining all the circumstances which weigh with an experienced judge in awarding sentence. Sentences are unequal because the conditions in which offences are committed are unequal. The writer is, however, perfectly justified in pointing out, what is obvious, that sentences do vary in apparently similar circumstances with the habit of mind of the particular judge. It is quite inevitable. Some very conscientious judges have thought it their duty to visit particular crimes with exemplary sentences; others equally conscientious have thought it their duty to view the same crimes with leniency. If to say that the human element enters into the awarding of punishment be contempt of Court it is to be feared that few in or out of the profession would escape. If the writer had, as journalist, said that St. Clair's sentence was, in his opinion, too severe: and on another occasion that Sheriff's sentence was too lenient, no complaint could possibly be made: and the offence does not become apparent when the two are contrasted. The writer in seeking his remedy, as has been remarked by the Supreme Court, has ignored the Court of Criminal Appeal: but he might reply that till such a Court has power, on the initiative of the prosecution, to increase too lenient sentences, its effect in standardising sentences is not completely adequate. It appears to their Lordships that the writer receives less than justice from the Supreme Court in having untruths imputed to him as a ground for finding the article to be in contempt of Court. He has correctly stated both offenders to have been charged with intent to murder; and though he has subsequently inaccurately stated that the conviction of both affirmed that intent, yet seeing that both were convicted of the same intent — namely, to do grievous bodily harm, the reasoning as to unevenness of sentence appears to have been unaffected. And it seems of little moment that the writer thought that this sentence might be for life instead of in fact being for 15 years. If criticism of decisions could only safely be made by persons who accurately knew the relevant law, who would be protected? There is no suggestion that the law was intentionally mis-stated.

Their Lordships have discussed this case at some length because, in one aspect, it concerns the liberty of the Press, which is no more than the liberty of any member of the public, to criticise temperately and fairly, but freely, any episode in the administration of justice. They have come to the conclusion that there is no evidence upon which the Court could find that the appellant has exceeded this right, or that he acted with untruth or malice, or with the direct object of bringing the administration of justice into disrepute. They are satisfied that the Supreme Court took the course they did with a desire to uphold the dignity and authority of the law as administered in Trinidad; there nevertheless seems to their Lordships to have been a misconception of the doctrine of contempt of Court as applied to public criticism. A jurisdiction of a very necessary and useful kind was applied in a case to which it was not properly applicable, and this, in the view of their Lordships, has resulted in a substantial miscarriage of justice. Acting, therefore, on the principles enumerated in the first part of this judgment as applicable to appeals from convictions for contempt of Court, their Lordships will humbly advise His Majesty that this appeal be allowed, and that the order of the Supreme Court, dated September 5, 1934, be set aside. The respondent must pay the costs here and in the Court below.

Solicitors for appellant: *Maples, Teesdale & Co.*
Solicitors for respondent: *Burchells.*

3.4.2 *Re Nicol* [1954] 3 D.L.R. 690 (B.C.S.C.)

CLYNE J.: — Two weeks ago the owners, proprietors and printers of the Vancouver Province, its publisher Mr. A. W. Moscarella, its editor-in-chief Mr. H. H. C. Anderson, and Mr. Eric Nicol appeared before me to answer a charge of contempt of Court and to show cause why they should not be committed for a contempt said to have been contained in an article written by Mr. Nicol which was published by the Province on the 20th of last month.

The contempt charged in this case is of an unusual character. It is not a contempt arising out of the disobedience to the orders of the Court, nor does it arise from interference with the fair trial of a cause which is pending before the Courts. The offence which is alleged consists in the publication, after the conclusion of a trial, of remarks which are said to be derogatory of the Court and calculated to bring the Court and the administration of justice into contempt and disrepute. As contempts of this nature are fortunately rare and as the jurisdiction to punish this type of contempt should be exercised with scrupulous care and only when the case is clear, I reserved the matter for consideration: see *R.* v. *Gray,* [1900] 2 Q.B. 36. Speaking for myself, I consider that it is a jurisdiction which should be exercised, not in vindication of the character of any individual, nor in retort to any personal affront, but only in the public interest when the Court then becomes bound to exercise it: *R.* v. *Davison* (1821), 4 B. & Ald. 329, 106 E.R. 958.

The facts are that on Thursday, March 18th, William Gash was found guilty by a jury of the murder of Frank Pitsch and was sentenced to be hanged on June 22nd next. On Saturday, March 20th, the Vancouver Province published an article written by Mr. Nicol in which he pictured himself as being tried after death before God for the murder of William Gash, the man convicted of the murder of Pitsch, and pleading guilty to killing him by hanging on June 22, 1954. In the second paragraph of the article he uses these words: "Although I did not myself spring the trap that caused my victim to be strangled in cold blood, I admit that the man who put the rope around his neck was in my employ. Also serving me were the 12 people who planned the murder, and the judge who chose the time and place and caused the victim to suffer the exquisite torture of anticipation." He then proceeds to elaborate his confession and addresses to his Maker a plea for mercy in his own behalf.

Counsel for the newspaper has urged that there was no intention to cast any slur upon the Court but that the article was written to express opposition to capital punishment and in particular to capital punishment by hanging. From the extravagant language used by the writer there can be no doubt that it was written in opposition to capital punishment. It is to be noted, however, that the article goes much further than a discussion of capital punishment and indicates that in the writer's opinion society is responsible for having caused William Gash to commit murder. It continues in this vein:

"And I know that the society to which I belong, and which has killed this man, may have provoked him and may provoke others to the same crime. Hunger, temptation, worldly desires — can I say that I am innocent of all responsibility for these incitements to kill?

"I know that I cannot. In a society where all of us enjoyed what most of us enjoy, no man would kill another. Society is what I, and my accomplices, have made it, and one of the things we have made it is a death-trap for William Gash. No, Your Honour, I never said that William Gash was paying his debt to society. What did he owe to us, that we should drive him to murder, then commit him to the hell of the death chamber?"

The facts of the case of *R.* v. *Gash* were fully reported in the press. At the time Gash committed the crime with which he was charged he was 19 years of age. He came from what appeared to be a respectable, hard-working family. He married when he was eighteen and has one child. He was not working at the time of the murder. His wife and child had been living with him at his father's home, but had gone to live with her people, his father having apparently been unwilling to continue to support his son and his son's family. There was no apparent reason why Gash should not have obtained work. He was strong and healthy and there was no suggestion at trial that he was not of average intelligence. He had enough skill in wood-working to have taught this subject as a voluntary worker at a recreational centre where he also had some reputation as a good boxer. He had done casual work from time to time but did not appear to be active in his search for employment and was spending his time frequenting a public golf course. There is no doubt that he wanted money, but apparently he was unwilling to work for it. About 6 weeks before the murder he told a friend that he intended to rob an acquaintance by the name of Pitsch who was known to carry a good deal of money upon his person, and several weeks later he communicated his intention to another friend. He invited them to join with him in the enterprise and described the weapon which he intended to use and eventually did use to render his victim unconscious. When asked by one of his friends what he would do if the unfortunate man recognized him, he explained he would have to kill him.

I have mentioned these facts because I conceive that, if the jury's verdict had been perverse, the newspaper would have had a perfect right to criticize it. The time for appeal has now expired and I feel free to comment upon the jury's finding. Under no stretch of imagination could the verdict be said to have been perverse and in fact defence counsel in his address made no attempt to offer a defence in law but confined himself to a plea for compassion, mainly on account of the offender's youth, to which the jury acceded by adding as a rider to its verdict a very strong recommendation for mercy. In these circumstances, and in spite of the fact that in order to obtain money Gash preferred to kill rather than to work, Mr. Nicol states that society had driven him to murder.

It is clear, therefore, that in writing the article Mr. Nicol not only was seeking to express his opposition to capital punishment but he was also presenting an argument against a man's individual responsibility for his acts. There is no doubt that in a great number of cases environment has much to do with causes of crime, but in the present case it does not appear that the accused was lacking in the ordinary advantages which are available to the youth of this country. He was not suffering from hunger as Mr. Nicol's article appears to indicate, nor was the crime committed in the heat of passion nor under the influence of any temptation other than the desire to steal money. The only thing suggested by his counsel in his plea to the jury for compassion was that the accused's father had been unnecessarily harsh to him in refusing to continue to support him with his wife and child. On the evidence it appears that the murder of Pitsch had been coldly premeditated by Gash for some time and robbery appears to have been the only motive for the killing. Under the circumstances it is difficult to understand why any blame should be attached to society for the actions of the accused, or why society should be accused of making "a death trap for William Gash".

Counsel for the Crown argues that in seeking to relieve the accused from any moral responsibility for the crime and in blaming society at large, the writer of the article and the Vancouver Province are attempting to undermine the administration of justice. He argues that the article tends to encourage individuals to do wrong with an easy conscience in the belief that it is the state and not the individual who is ultimately responsible and he suggests that in the case of a number of young people who happen to be familiar with the facts of this particular crime the article is likely to have very deleterious effects.

The philosophy underlying this article is very familiar. It denies the individual's responsibility for his actions and by the same token it denies the individual's freedom of choice and the exercise of free-will. It blames society for the wrongs committed by individuals because it says by reason of social or economic pressures the individual is unable to do otherwise. It affords the individual the means of escaping the moral consequences of any wrongful act by enabling him to say: "Because of the influences which have surrounded me from my birth I have become the sort of person that I am, and I am not responsible for those conditions which have moulded my character." It is the materialistic philosophy of determinism which is very popular in some quarters of the world-to-day and which emphasizes the importance of causes and minimizes the importance of the choice by the individual between good and evil. In its last result it elevates the importance of the state at the expense of the individual and leaves to the state the acceptance of responsibility for both good and evil.

Whatever opinion may be held as to the moral conceptions involved in this article, it is no part of the duty or function of the Court to deal with a question of ethics in an application of this kind. The newspaper is free to express its views upon questions of morality and it is for its readers to decide whether or not they agree with them. It is free to express its views upon the workings of our penal system and it is free to say whether or not it believes that men should be punished for their crimes or whether they should be excused by reason of some external or internal conditioning. Our Courts have been astute to protect the freedom of speech and, from the point of view of contempt proceedings, the morality of the article is irrelevant and it is for those who read to decide for themselves if the philosophy expressed therein is pernicious or not.

Whether or not contempt has been committed in this case must depend upon the construction to be put upon the paragraph in which the reference is made to the jury as being "the twelve people who planned the murder". Counsel for the newspaper has suggested rather faintly that the article should not be read with specific reference to the Gash trial or to the Gash jury. This contention must be definitely rejected. As counsel for the Crown has pointed out, the article consists of eleven paragraphs and in eight of those paragraphs the name of Gash appears. The murder of Pitsch by Gash received considerable publicity in the press and there can be no question that anyone reading the article would most certainly consider that the article had direct reference to the case of William Gash and to the jury who tried him. In pursuing his allegory Mr. Nicol has inextricably involved the facts of this case in the web of his fantasy.

Counsel for the newspaper states that the article was written in the form of an allegory, and, in a somewhat tepid apology printed the day before these proceedings came on for hearing the Vancouver Province stated that the object of the column was to express the opposition of Mr. Nicol to execution by hanging and that in order to dramatize the subject Mr. Nicol mentioned the Gash murder case. The writer of the apology overlooks the fact that the Gash case was "mentioned" in eight paragraphs out of eleven, and that the verb "to mention" hardly does justice to the exaggerated and heavy-handed use which Mr. Nicol made of the case. The tenor of the apology is to the effect that the article should not be construed as a contempt, but if it were capable of such interpretation it was to be regretted. It does not explain why it was necessary for Mr. Nicol, in order to adorn his allegory with a moral, to refer to the jurors as persons planning to commit murder. It does not explain why Mr. Nicol's ingenuity was insufficient to accomplish his ends without branding twelve innocent people as criminals.

It was not necessary for counsel to point out the particular literary form in which the article was written, in view of the fact that whatever type of symbolism a writer chooses to use is irrelevant to the issue in cases of this kind. Allegories have frequently been used as vehicles of criticism or abuse but the point to be decided here is whether the words are in fact abusive and whether they have been unjustifiably applied to the members of the jury while performing their functions as such.

The word "murderer" is a term of opprobrium and, even when it is used in circumstances where actual killing is not implied, it nevertheless carries a connotation of evil intent. To plan or conspire to commit murder is a criminal act. The use of words imputing a criminal offence is actionable *per se* because they expose to public shame the person against whom they are directed and a newspaper has no greater licence to defame than any ordinary member of the public. The fact that a public issue is involved such as the question of capital punishment does not justify or excuse the application of defamatory words to those discharging public duties. Long ago Sir James Mansfield C.J. held that to call a man a murderer and an assassin was not to be excused merely by the fact that he was a candidate for Parliament: *Harwood* v. *Astley* (1804), 1 Bos. & P.N.R. 47, 127 E.R. 375; see also *Pankhurst* v. *Hamilton* (1887), 3 T.L.R. 500. Regardless of the purpose which Mr. Nicol had in mind when he wrote the article, his reference to the members of the Gash jury as being ''the twelve persons who planned the murder'' amounts in my view to a gratuitous insult. It would have been quite easy for Mr. Nicol to have accomplished his purpose without making remarks of this kind.

I have considered whether it might be sufficient to leave the individual members of the jury to assert whatever rights which they may have against Mr. Nicol and the publishers of the Province in the civil Courts, but I have reached the conclusion, upon the strength of the authorities cited to me by Crown counsel, that the Court cannot permit juries to be accorded this sort of treatment during the course of an Assize. The men and women who serve upon our juries are performing one of the most onerous and important functions in the life of a free society. It is a duty which is far from pleasant, especially in a murder case. It is quite possible that members of the jury sitting upon the Gash case may have held similar views to those of Mr. Nicol in regard to capital punishment. However, it is no part of the jury's duty to decide the punishment which is to be meted out to a convicted person. All the jury is required to do is to reach a decision upon the facts. Each juror is sworn to bring in a true verdict upon the facts, and if the facts are such that the crime is proved beyond reasonable doubt and the members of the jury are unanimous in that opinion then they have no other course upon their oaths but to bring in a verdict of guilty. This is often a most painful duty and the distress in having to find a youth of 19 years of age guilty of murder was apparent upon the faces of some of the jurors who tried the Gash case. However, these men discharged their duty honestly as do other men and women who serve upon juries in Canada and the Court would be derelict in its duty if it did not protect them from the degradation of being referred to as criminals. I have no hesitation in finding that the remarks concerning the jury as published in the Province were insulting and contemptuous in the sense of that word as used by Lord Russell of Killowen C.J. in *R.* v. *Gray,* [1900] 2 Q.B. 36, as approved in *Ambard* v. *A.-G. Trinidad,* [1936] A.C. 322, and in *Perera* v. *The King,* [1951] A.C. 482.

There is another aspect of the article which must also be taken into consideration, and that is the effect which it may have upon future juries. The last Assize at Vancouver continued for 3 months and the next Assize is starting in a few weeks. Members of the community serve upon juries at these long Assizes at a good deal of inconvenience to themselves and it would not be surprising if they should express unwillingness to serve if they are to be exposed to undeservedly shameful epithets cast upon them by a newspaper. No doubt members of juries at following Assizes who are called upon to sit in murder cases will have in mind that if they bring in verdicts of guilty they will run the risk of being described as persons who have planned a murder or worse and for that reason this type of newspaper comment must be stopped. It may well be that Mr. Nicol, in his anxiety to assert his own opinions in regard to punishment for crime, hoped that by writing this article he would discourage juries from bringing in verdicts of guilty in capital cases, and it is quite conceivable that the article might have that result. Counsel for the Vancouver Province stated that in his opinion the words of the article would have no effect upon jurors, but he might have come to a different conclusion if he had heard the vigorous protests addressed to me through the Sheriff of the county by members of the jury at the Assize which has just been finished. There could have been no possible objection to Mr. Nicol raising in his column a strenuous objection to capital punishment and urging that clemency be extended to William Gash, and this he could have done effectively without descending to vilification of the Gash jury. To say that he did not intend to cast any slur upon the Court or jury begs the question, as what must be considered on this phase of the matter is the effect of the article upon the minds of the public and of future juries. From this aspect, the article can be said to obstruct the administration of justice in that it is calculated to interfere with future juries and to deter them from carrying out their duties in reaching true verdicts upon the facts as presented to them. I cannot escape the conclusion that the effect of the writing and publishing of the article is such as "to bring a Court.... into contempt, or.... to obstruct or interfere with the due course of justice or the lawful process of the Courts": *R.* v. *Gray*, [1900] 2 Q.B. at p. 40; *Izuora* v. *The Queen,* [1953] A.C. 327 at p. 334.

It is also necessary for me to deal with the reference to "the judge who chose the time and place and caused the victim to suffer the exquisite torture of anticipation". If these words could be construed in the light of a personal affront. I should pay no attention to them. The test which should be applied is whether or not they discredit the Court as such and bring the administration of justice into disrepute. They clearly have reference to the interval of 3 months between the date of sentence, March 18th, and the date set for execution, June 22nd, which is mentioned in the opening paragraph of the article. The mischief here is the inference, to one unfamiliar with the processes of the law, that the Judge in fixing the date of execution caused and intended to cause the convicted man "the exquisite torture of anticipation". Few people are aware of the fact that in sentencing a man to death the Court always postpones the date of execution in order to give the convicted man time to appeal to the Court of Appeal, and then, if his appeal is rejected, time to appeal to the Supreme Court of Canada, and then, if both appeals fail, still to leave ample time for an application for clemency to the Governor-General in Council, when the most careful consideration is always given to the circumstances of the case by the Governor-General and his advisers before it is decided whether the death penalty should be exacted or clemency exercised. It is important that the mind of the public should not be affected by any insidious idea that the Judge who presided at the Gash trial exercised his choice of an execution date for the purpose of causing the convicted man additional suffering by having to wait in anticipation of the sentence being carried out. Nothing of course, could be further from the truth. It is discreditable to the administration of justice that any false suggestion should be made to the public that the sentences of the Court involve any idea of torture and the words are contemptuous in that they carry with them an imputation of improper motives on the part of the Judge who imposed the sentence: see *Ambard* v. *A.-G. Trinidad,* [1936] A.C. at p. 335.

Mr. Nicol and the publishers of the Vancouver Province have every right in the world to express their views on capital punishment, but in denouncing capital punishment they have chosen to include in their denunciation those who are charged with the duty of carrying out the law as it exists. If Mr. Nicol and his employers wish to change the law their broadsides should be directed to Parliament, and they have in their possession a powerful medium for expressing their opinions. But they should not, and must not, seek to inflame public opinion against the Courts, and the article read as whole is undoubtedly inflammatory. There is no question of freedom of the press involved here. The press can and should criticize a law which it believes to be wrong. The press is at liberty to criticize a Judge or a jury if a Judge or jury should act improperly, for, as Lord Atkin said in the *Ambard* case [p. 335], "Justice is not a cloistered virtue". The business of the Courts is transacted in public and it is important that what goes on in the Courts should be reported by the press so that the public should know and should be able to judge whether its system of justice is being administered fairly and properly. No wrong is committed by anyone who criticizes the Courts or a Judge in good faith, but it is of vital importance to the public that the authority and dignity of the Courts should be maintained and that when criticism is offered it should be legitimate. To refer to the jurors in this case as criminals and to describe the Judge as causing exquisite torture is calculated to lower the dignity of the Court and to destroy public confidence in the administration of justice, and a practice of this kind must be stopped and stopped immediately in the public interest. I find the parties guilty of contempt and if it were not for the fact that the Vancouver Province possesses a long and respected background in this community and that an apology, even though inept, has been made, I would impose severe penalties. Taking those factors into consideration, I impose a fine of $250 upon the author of the article and a fine of $2,500 upon the publishers and proprietors of the Vancouver Province and they must pay the costs of these proceedings.

Note: Several members of the jury in the Gash case sued Nicol and his newspaper civilly for libel and were successful. See *MacKay* v. *Southam Co. Ltd.* (1955), 1 D.L.R. (2d) 1 (B.C.C.A.).

3.4.3 *Re Oullett* (1976), 72 D.L.R. (3d) 95 (Que. C.A.)

TREMBLAY, C.J.Q. (translation): — The appellant is appealing a judgment of the Superior Court of the District of Montreal, dated January 23, 1976, finding him guilty of contempt of Court and sentencing him on the same day in the following terms:

> I hereby suspend the passing of sentence on the Respondent for a period of three (3) months, subject to the terms of a Probation Order which, in addition to the usual condition to keep the peace and be of good behaviour, will contain the condition that the Respondent shall, within ten (10) days from this day, make publicly and in writing a full, complete and unreserved apology to Mr. Justice MacKay, to this Court and to the people of Canada for the contempt committed by him on December nineteenth, nineteen seventy-five, and shall reaffirm therein unreservedly his confidence in the Judicial System of his Country. If this condition of the Probation Order is not complied with, then, in accordance with the Law, the Respondent will be brought back before me to be dealt with according to Law.
> I further order the Respondent to pay the costs of the present proceedings, which costs are hereby fixed in the amount of five hundred dollars ($500.00), which sum is to be paid within thirty (30) days from this date, to the Clerk of the Crown at Montreal, and to be paid by the said Clerk to R. C. Holden, Q.C., Special Prosecutor ad hoc.
> In default of payment of the said sum, execution may issue in the ordinary way.

On December 19, 1975, Mr. Justice MacKay of the Superior Court rendered judgment in the present case acquitting the accused companies of the offences they were charged with. In the afternoon of the same day, the appellant, then a Member of the

Parliament of Canada and Minister of Consumer and Corporate Affairs, made a statement to a journalist regarding this acquittal. Claiming that this statement constituted a contempt of Court, Mr. Justice MacKay summoned the appellant to appear before him on January 8, 1976. The appearance took place and the case was referred to the Associate Chief Justice of the Superior Court who passed judgment and imposed the sentence being appealed.

The appellant argues three grounds which he states as follows:

(1) the summary procedure used in this case was totally unjustified;

(2) the statement which the appellant is alleged to have made, if it was really made, was a privileged statement;

(3) the text of the journalist Freeman does not faithfully report the words of the appellant and the learned trial Judge did not have a valid reason to set aside the true statement made by the appellant and which he reported during his testimony.

I shall examine each of his grounds, but in a different order.

First, let me question if the trial Judge was correct in holding that the statement attributed to the appellant constituted a contempt of Court. Here is the text of this statement:

> I will ask Ron Basford to launch an appeal. I find this judgment completely unacceptable. I think it is a silly decision. I just cannot understand how a judge who is sane could give such a verdict. It is a complete shock and I find it a complete disgrace.

I entirely agree with the trial Judge in his finding that this statement, if it was made, constitutes a contempt of Court. When a Minister of the Crown finds that he cannot understand how a sane Judge could give a silly decision, such a Minister is not qualified to render justice and is not qualified to state that a Judge rendering such a decision is likely to hamper him in the exercise of his functions and also hamper the Courts in general in the exercise of their functions. Certainly, the decisions of Judges are subject to criticism as are the decisions of all other public men. But criticism of a decision is not stating that the person who gave it is an imbecile, which is contempt of Court "by scandalizing the Court" and this kind of contempt of Court is always prohibited. This proposition seems to me so evident that I do not think it necessary to cite a long list of authorities. However, since certain people for the last few years, with more persistency than good faith, insist and repeat that contempt of Court has fallen into disuse in England, permit me to refer to the judgment of the House of Lords of July 18, 1973, in the case of *Attorney-General v. Times Newspapers Ltd.*, [1973] 3 All E.R. 54, and in particular to the following excerpt from the opinion of Lord Diplock (p. 71):

> ... in any civilised society it is a function of government to maintain courts of law to which its citizens can have access for the impartial decision of disputes as to their legal rights and obligations towards one another individually and towards the state as representing society as a whole. The provision of such a system for the administration of justice by courts of law and the maintenance of public confidence in it are essential if citizens are to live together in peaceful association with one another. "Contempt of court" is a generic term descriptive of conduct in relation to particular proceedings in a court of law which tends to undermine that system or to inhibit citizens from availing themselves of it for the settlement of their disputes.

On the particular point which interests us, the following excerpt from Lord Simon is also revealing (p. 82):

But once the proceedings are concluded, the remit is withdrawn, and the balance of public interest shifts. It is true that the pan holding the administration of justice is not entirely cleared. The judge must go on to try other cases, so the court must not be scandalised.

But, the appellant says that the statement he was alleged to have made is incomplete and does not have the meaning attributed to it. Here is how he expressed himself (D.C., p. 343):

Q. Would you mind going to the next sentence please?
A. "I just cannot understand how a Judge who is sane could give such a verdict."
Q. What are your comments on this subject?
A. I must say that upon the reading of this sentence, there is something missing. I spoke to Mr. Freeman to tell him that I did not understand this decision. "I cannot understand" how a Judge as sane as Judge MacKay could arrive at such a verdict. I must say that for a long time after, I noticed this sentence had been given an interpretation which was radically the opposite of what I could have told Mr. Freeman. On its face, it seems clear to me that it is not a complete sentence. It is not a sentence which conveys properly the thought I had and which I told Mr. Freeman. I saw later that my words had been given a sanity aspect by hinting that I wondered about the Judge's sanity. I must say categorically that I never made such comments, that I never said that to Mr. Freeman and that I never intended the meaning that was later given to this sentence. On the contrary! On its face, it seems to me that I could not understand that a Judge with such sensible competence as Judge MacKay could give such a verdict. It is exactly the contrary of what I was imputed to have said.

As I remarked at the hearing, I do not see how the interpretation suggested here by the appellant might help him. If a Crown Minister cannot understand how a sensible Judge could have passed such a judgment, the conclusion is that this judgment rests on unwarranted reasons, which in no way could inspire confidence in this Judge and in justice in general.

The appellant also invokes his inaccurate knowledge of the English language which brought him to translate the French word "sense" by the word "sane", and that the prosecution now gives it the meaning of "mentally sane". I do not think that the appellant's claim makes his position any better. I have earlier translated the adjective "sane" by the word "sense".

It is therefore my opinion that the trial Judge was correct in holding that the statement proferred by the appellant on December 19, 1975, constituted a contempt of Court and that this ground of appeal is not well-founded.

Let me examine then the trial Judge's decision that the summary procedure used in this case was justified.

Without hesitation I answer affirmatively. I have already said that the appellant's statement was of a nature so as to hinder the Courts in the performance of their function. Furthermore, this statement was not made by just anybody. It is a statement made by a Minister of the federal Crown which necessarily enjoys considerable credit and authority. This statement was advertised all over the country. It was urgent that a strong disapproval be pronounced in order to stop the harm done to the administration of justice in our country from spreading.

The appellant relies on our judgment in *Hébert v. Procureur Général de la Province de Québec*, [1966] Que. Q.B. 197. This case can in no way be compared to the present case. In the case of *Hébert*, the murder of which Coffin was found guilty was committed in June, 1953, the verdict was pronounced on August 5, 1954. The book which was claimed to constitute a contempt of Court was published in December, 1963. It was followed by a public inquiry which showed the assertions found in the book had no basis and that the author had not examined the trial record. Finally, the request for contempt was filed over a year after the publication of the book. That is why I felt justified in writing that the conduct of the Attorney-General was an admission to the effect "that there was no emergency and that the Court must not proceed summarily, since he thought he could wait a year before coming before the Courts" (at p. 220). In the present case on the contrary, the judgment was passed on December 19, 1975, the contempt of Court was committed the same day and the appellant was summoned to appear on January 8, 1976. Furthermore, the public knew that the appellant knew about the procedures of which he was speaking and the credibility of his statement was enhanced. It was important to act quickly in order to destroy, if possible, in the mind of the public the disastrous effect of this statement on the administration of justice in our country.

It is my opinion that the trial Judge was correct in concluding that the summary procedure used in this case was justified.

I now have to consider whether the trial Judge was right in concluding that the statement made by the appellant was not privileged.

We must recall that the statement in question was uttered in an antechamber of the Commons where journalists are admitted to interview Ministers and deputies. The appellant was not then participating in any of the proceedings of the Commons or its committees. He was not speaking on behalf of the Government or his ministry. He was giving a journalist his opinion with respect to a judgment which had just been passed by the Superior Court of the District of Montreal.

This circumstance is very different from the one in the case of *Roman Corp. Ltd. et al. v. Hudson's Bay Oil & Gas Co. Ltd. et al.* (1973), 36 D.L.R. (3d) 413, [1973] S.C.R. 820; affirming 23 D.L.R. (3d) 292, [1972] 1 O.R. 444, affirming 18 D.L.R. (3d) 134, [1971] 2 O.R. 418, which was decided by the Courts of Ontario and the Supreme Court of Canada. In that case, the plaintiff was appealing statements made by the Prime Minister of Canada and another Minister of the Crown in the Chamber, announcing the intention of the Government to propose legislation for the purpose of stopping the completion of a transaction between the representatives of two commercial societies as well as a telegram sent repeating this statement. The Courts of Ontario decided that the statements and the telegram were privileged, but the Supreme Court of Canada simply said that the actions of Ministers could not give rise to criminal complaints.

In the present case, I have already expressed the opinion that the statement of the appellant constitutes a contempt of Court and I cannot admit that this statement uttered outside of the Chambers constitutes "proceedings in Parliament".

It is therefore my opinion that the trial Judge was right in concluding that the appellant's statement was not privileged and the last ground of the appellant has no basis.

Therefore, I would dismiss the appeal against conviction.

As to the sentence, the order of probation includes the obligation by the appellant to present apologies. It is evident that if he does it, the appellant will not do it willingly. With respect to the contrary opinion, I am not at all convinced that it is useful to impose this obligation on the appellant. Forced apologies are humiliating for the person uttering them. Moreover, in the present case, they would not mean anything to persons concerned, except maybe to tickle their ego and they would not in any way better the administration of justice in Canada. Finally, if the appellant persisted in refusing to apologize, the Superior Court and, maybe the Court of Appeal, would have to devote to this case time which would be better employed for more important cases for the people of Canada. I would therefore strike out the order of probation forcing him to apologize.

Regarding the pecuniary sentence imposed as costs, I would also modify it. I think that I can take judicial notice of the fact that counsel for the prosecution estimates the value of his services at a more considerable sum than $500. In the circumstances, I would maintain the obligation to pay this amount of $500, but as a fine and not as costs.

I would therefore allow the appeal against the sentence and I would modify this sentence by striking out from the probation order the obligation to apologize and the joint sanction by declaring that the sum of $500 shall be paid by the appellant as a fine and not as costs.

MONTGOMERY, J.A.: — I have had the advantage of reading the notes of the Chief Justice. I am in full agreement with him that appellant was properly found guilty of contempt of Court. I have some reservations regarding the sentence.

Regarding the appeal against conviction, I wish to comment further on the point raised in the first chapter of appellant's factum: that Associate Chief Justice Hugessen erred in proceeding against appellant in a summary manner, in view of the fact that the contempt with which appellant was charged was not committed in the face of the Court [28 C.C.C. (2d) 338, 67 D.L.R. (3d) 73, 34 C.R.N.S. 234]. It is suggested, on the authority of *Hébert v. Procureur Général de la Province de Québec,* [1966] Que. Q.B. 197, that the proceedings should rather have been by indictment, even though it is acknowledged that they were conducted in such a way that appellant had detailed knowledge of the charge in advance, that he retained the presumption of innocence in his favour, that he was not forced to testify and that he had every opportunity to defend himself. I cannot take seriously the argument that he was deprived of a right to trial by jury. Our *Criminal Code* contains numerous examples of offences where the accused has no right to a jury trial (*v.* for example s.483).

Counsel for appellant in fact reproaches those responsible for the prosecution of the charge with having innovated, suggesting that it was not in their power to do so and that they had to choose between the traditional summary proceedings and indictment. I do not agree. There is nothing in the *Criminal Code* to lay down any specific procedure for contempt of Court proceedings. It has always been recognized that the Courts have a wide discretion in this field, and I would not limit this discretion where it is exercised in such a way as to give greater protection to an accused person.

I share the doubts expressed by Hugessen, A.C.J. (at pp. 484-5), as to whether contempt of Court is now an indictable offence in Canada, in view of s.8 of the *Criminal Code*. Even if legally justifiable, proceedings by indictment for contempt of Court have seldom been taken, either in this country or in England. Hugessen, A.C.J., refers to *R. v. Tibbits and Windust,* [1902] 1 K.B. 77, as having been cited as the last indictment for contempt of Court in England, but the charge there was rather one of obstruction of justice. (This was a case of publication during a trial of newspaper articles prejudicial to the accused.) Mr. Justice MacKay might, of course, have taken a civil action in damages for libel, but in that case he would probably have been restricted to claiming the damages to his own feelings, it being unlikely that he could have proved any material damages. In contempt of Court proceedings, it is not the outrage to an individual Judge that is punished; it is the affront to the authority and dignity of the Courts as a whole.

As pointed out by our Chief Justice, who formed one of the majority in the *Hébert* case, the facts in that case were altogether different, there having been a double lapse of time, between the trial the conduct of which Hébert had attacked and the alleged contempt, and again between the contempt and the proceedings taken to rebuke it. There was no such lapse in the present case. The offending words were uttered immediately after a statement, perfectly proper in itself, that appellant would seek to have the case taken to appeal, and in fact an appeal is now pending.

I fully agree that the Courts should use sparingly the power to punish summarily for contempt, but the present case has convinced me that it is idle to hope for help from the Executive Branch of Government, particularly in that most serious class of cases where the offender is himself a Member of the Executive. At the beginning of his address to our Court, the attorney who appeared to represent the Attorney-General of this Province (the only attorney before us, apart from counsel for appellant) informed us that he had no mandate to adopt a partisan attitude, and in the introduction to his factum he quotes from the instructions given to him by the Department of Justice in the following terms [translation]:

> Your mandate will consist of putting yourself at the disposal of the Court of Appeal, in answering all the questions which the judges of the Court of Appeal will deem useful to ask. Moreover, you will not have to be on the side of the defence or the prosecution in this case, but you will have to make certain that the administration of justice unfolds in accordance with the rules of the applicable law.

It is to his credit that, despite these limitations placed upon him, he was able to be of some assistance to the Court.

In the Court below, the prosecution was represented by an attorney appointed *ad hoc* by MacKay, J., Hugessen, A.C.J. (D.C., at p. 478), expressly approved this practice, but with all respect, I think it would have been preferable had counsel been selected by some Judge other than MacKay, J., himself. Subject to this one qualification, I am satisfied that both MacKay, J., and Hugessen, A.C.J., took the measures that were not only proper but the best possible to rebuke promptly this outrageous contempt without depriving the offender of any reasonable opportunity to defend himself.

Regarding this sentence, I agree with our Chief Justice that it would be futile at this stage to expect appellant to make excuses in a satisfactory form. I sympathize with the desire of Hugessen, A.C.J., to give to appellant one last chance to make an *amende honorable,* but appellant has amply demonstrated that he is a man incapable of admitting that he may have been wrong. I recognize that the offending words were spoken in haste and without opportunity for reflection. They display a lack of restraint and judgment deplorable in a Minister of the Crown, but we are all human, and there are few of us who have not at some time uttered in haste words that we have afterwards had cause to regret.

It is appellant's subsequent conduct that I find impossible to condone. His half-apologies, attempting to place the blame upon the press, I regard as an aggravation rather than as an extenuation, and still more so his technical defences, such as his unwarranted attempts to take shelter behind his immunity as a Member of Parliament.

The bringing of the present appeal I regard as a further aggravation. His counsel had the good sense to drop some of the least plausible of his technical defences, but there is still this insistence on parliamentary immunity. Hugessen, A.C.J., mentions a number of aggravating factors, but there is one that he very properly chose to suppress. This has since, unfortunately, come to light and has been the subject of a report by the Chief Justice of the Superior Court to the Minister of Justice. It is now notorious that appellant sought to bring pressure to bear on Hugessen, A.C.J., while these proceedings were pending, through a Cabinet colleague whom he thus risked involving in his own disgrace.

I agree with our Chief Justice that it would be contrary to the public interest to send appellant back to the Court below for sentencing. As an alternative, we might ourselves impose an additional penalty, *e.g.*, a nominal term of imprisonment. While this might not be undeserved, I prefer to take into account the fact that, for a man in appellant's position, the mere fact of being condemned for contempt of Court is in itself a severe punishment, particularly where it involves a finding that the explanations given by him are entirely unacceptable (*v.* the comments of Hugessen, A.C.J., D.C., at p. 508).

Hugessen, A.C.J., has condemned appellant to pay $500, to be deposited in Court and remitted to the prosecuting counsel. With all respect for the contrary opinion, I cannot agree that this was an unwarranted exercise of his discretion or that we should be influenced by knowledge that this attorney has subsequently claimed a much larger sum. I agree with Hugessen, A.C.J., that it is desirable that a special prosecutor be appointed in cases such as this. This necessarily gives rise to the question of how such counsel should be remunerated. I would have thought that a member of the Bar might consider it an honour to be given the opportunity of acting to uphold the dignity of the Courts. Still, it is but reasonable that such counsel should receive some nominal honorarium to compensate him for his loss of time.

In view of the complexity of the technical objections presented by appellant, I might have been disposed to award more than $500, but Hugessen, A.C.J., had counsel before him and was in a better position than I am to estimate a reasonable fee. One point has, however, been overlooked. Because of appellant's technical objections to the jurisdiction of the Courts of this Province, the prosecution had a survey plan prepared (ex. P-11), and Hugessen, A.C.J., appears (at p. 495) to have found this useful. It may be reasonable to expect a member of the Bar to offer his services in a case such as this for a purely nominal fee, but the same cannot be said of a land surveyor. Someone must pay him, and it seems to me only fair that this should be appellant. With all respect for the contrary opinion, I would not condemn appellant to pay a fine but would add to the condemnation already pronounced one to pay the cost of the prosecution's exhibits.

In summary, I would dismiss the appeal against conviction but would maintain the appeal against sentence and vary the sentence by quashing that part of it relating to further excuses and adding a condemnation to pay the cost of the prosecution's exhibits.

BERNIER, J.A. (translation): — I share the opinion of my brothers that the appeal against conviction should be dismissed. I would dispose of the sentence as suggested by the Chief Justice, but adding however the obligation by the appellant to pay for the costs of the land surveyor J. F. Goltz for the reasons expressed by my brother Montgomery.

3.4.4 *R.* v. *Kopyto* (1988) 24 O.A.C. 81 (Ont. C.A.)

CORY, J.A.: Harry Kopyto was convicted of contempt of court by scandalizing the court. This appeal is brought from that conviction.

FACTUAL BACKGROUND

For a number of years the appellant acted as the lawyer for his friend, Mr. Dowson. Mr. Dowson was from 1961 to 1972 the Executive Secretary and subsequently Chairman of the League for Socialist Action. Allegations have been made that the R.C.M.P. had investigated the activities of the League and Mr. Dowson in an improper manner.

The appellant on behalf of Dowson, brought an action for defamation. The alleged defamation was contained in a summary of the R.C.M.P. investigation of the League that was read by the Attorney General in the Legislature. The claim was struck down by the Federal Court of Appeal...

The appellant, again on behalf of Dowson, also sought to have criminal charges brought against members of the R.C.M.P. for purportedly forging letters during their investigation of the League. The legal proceedings involving these charges also had a long and unsuccessful history.

On May 11, 1982 the appellant, still acting for Dowson, instituted civil proceedings in the Small Claims Court against members of the R.C.M.P. The allegation was made that the defendants had conspired to injure Dowson and had made injurious false statements about him. This action too gave rise to a number of well-publicized proceedings. Eventually a truncated version of the case came before Judge Zuker. The decision was reserved. On December 12, 1985, carefully considered reasons were delivered by Judge Zuker. He dismissed the plaintiff's claim, in part on the grounds that the action was not brought within the statutorily prescribed limitation period.

Following the release of the reasons a reporter from the Globe and Mail called the appellant seeking his comments on the judgment. The appellant indicated that he would call the reporter back after he had read the reasons. On the next day, December 17, 1985, the appellant called the reporter. He gave a long statement, portions of which were included in an article published in the Globe and Mail on December 18, 1985, and which form the subject matter of the charge against him.

The appellant admitted that the Globe and Mail quoted him correctly. The quotations read as follows:

This decision is a mockery of justice. It stinks to high hell. It says it is okay to break the law and you are immune so long as someone above you said to do it.

Mr. Dowson and I have lost faith in the judicial system to render justice.

We're wondering what is the point of appealing and continuing this charade of the courts in this country which are warped in favour of protecting the police. The courts and the RCMP are sticking so close together you'd think they were put together with Krazy Glue.

THE DECISION AT TRIAL ON THE CHARGE OF CONTEMPT OF COURT

The learned trial judge gave careful, complete and detailed reasons for his conclusion that the appellant was guilty of the offence of contempt of court by scandalizing the court. He observed that there was no doubt about the appellant's sincerity or the bona fides of his desire to correct what the appellant perceived to be a social injustice.

He rejected the appellant's contention that the remarks had referred to "systemic bias" and that they had not been intended to malign Judge Zuker. He found the appellant's statements to be "a vitriolic unmitigated attack on the trial judge" and, as well, "a blatant attack on all judges of all courts". The appellant's words, he observed, went far beyond criticism and demonstrated an intention to vilify.

The trial judge also concluded that the offence of scandalizing the court did not constitute an infringement of s.2(b) of the **Canadian Charter of Rights and Freedoms** which guarantees freedom of expression. Furthermore, he determined that even if the offence did constitute an infringement of s.2(b), it was a justifiable limitation under s.1 of the **Charter.**

...

The courts play an important role in any democratic society. They are the forum not only for the resolution of disputes between citizens but also for the resolution of disputes between the citizen and the state in all its manifestations. The more complex society becomes the greater is the resultant frustration imposed on citizens by that complexity and the more important becomes the function of the courts. As a result of their importance the courts are bound to be the subject of comment and criticism. Not all will be sweetly reasoned. An unsuccessful litigant may well make comments after the decision is rendered that are not felicitously worded. Some criticism may be well founded, some suggestions for change worth adopting. But the courts are not fragile flowers that will wither in the hot heat of controversy. Rules of evidence, methods of procedure and means of review and appeal exist that go far to establishing a fair and equitable rule of law. The courts have functioned well and effectively in difficult times. They are well-regarded in the community because they merit respect. They need not fear criticism nor need they seek to sustain unnecessary barriers to complaints about their operations or decisions.

...

In my view, statements of a sincerely held belief on a matter of public interest, even if intemperately worded, so long as they are not obscene or criminally libelous, should, as a general rule, come within the protection afforded by s.2(b) of the **Charter.** It would, I think, be unfortunate if freedom of expression on matters of public interest so vital to a free and democratic society was to be unduly restricted. The constitutional guarantee should be given a broad and liberal interpretation. The comment of the appellant came within the ambit of that protection. This, I believe, must be the conclusion, whether the two step procedure described in **R. v. Oakes** is followed or the approach to s.2(b) set forth in **R. v. Zundel** is adopted.

It remains to be determined whether the offence of contempt by scandalizing the court is a constitutionally permissible limit on the protection afforded the appellant's words.

3. *If the Words are "Protected" by s.2(b) of the* ***Charter*** *does the Offence of Contempt by Scandalizing the Court Constitute a Constitutionally Permissible Limit on that Protection?*

It is incumbent upon the Crown to establish, on a balance of probabilities, that the limitation on freedom of expression imposed by the offence of scandalizing the court meets the requirement of s.1 of the **Charter.** That section reads:

> "1. The **Canadian Charter of Rights and Freedoms** guarantees the rights and freedoms set out in it subject only to such reasonable limits prescribed by law as can be demonstrably justified in a free and democratic society."

A s.1 analysis can usefully be divided into three parts: first, is the limit a reasonable limit? Second, is the limit prescribed by law? Third, can the limit be demonstrably justified in a free and democratic society?

. . .

It was conceded by counsel for the intervenant and I am satisfied that the first criterion was met in that the objective of protecting the administration of justice was of sufficient importance to warrant overriding a constitutionally protected right or freedom. However, in my view, the second criterion has not been satisfied. Without requiring any proof of the matter the offence *assumes* that the words which are the subject-matter of the charge will bring the court into contempt or lower its authority. This I take to be an unwarranted and questionable assumption, and leads me to conclude that the offence has not been "carefully designed to achieve the objective in question". By undertaking the proceedings the prosecution must be taken as alleging that the words spoken by the accused which were "calculated to bring the administration of justice into disrepute" will in fact have such an effect. If this is not the basis of the charge then the measure adopted is arbitrary, unfair or based upon irrational considerations. If the essence of the charge is, as it must be, that the words spoken do, bring the court into contempt, then it would not be unreasonable to require the prosecution to prove that this is in fact the effect of those words. This requirement is lacking in the offence of scandalizing the court as it is presently known.

It may be helpful in considering this issue to recall that when dealing with contempt cases arising out of statements made pertaining to cases that are pending or under consideration, the courts have *always* required proof that the statements constituted a serious danger to the administration of justice. That is to say that the Crown must show that such statements put the function of the courts in serious question. In **Attorney General v. Times Newspaper Ltd.,** Lord Denning, M.R., in the Court of Appeal (reversed in the result by the House of Lords) stated:

> I regard it as of the first importance that the law which I have just stated should be maintained in its full integrity. We must not allow 'trial by newspaper' or 'trial by television' or trial by any medium other than the courts of law. But, in so stating the law, I would emphasise that it applies only 'when litigation is pending and is actively in suit before the court'. To which I would add that there must appear to be *'a real and substantial danger of prejudice'* to the trial of the case or to the settlement of it.
>
> (emphasis added)

This was essentially the test laid down by the European Court later in that same case. That requirement should also be an essential condition of the offence of scandalizing the court, as it would go some distance towards ensuring that the offence "impairs 'as little as possible' the right or freedom in question". In the absence of such a requirement the limitation imposed by the offence cannot meet the proportionality test as it is both arbitrary and irrational, based as it is on the unproved assumption that the comment will lower the authority of the court. I am confident that the public, if not the media, will take into account the source of the comment before deciding that the court should be regarded with contempt or its authority lowered.

Furthermore, there is some question as to what mens rea is required to prove the offence of scandalizing the court. It has been said that the words themselves can constitute the offence. Yet it would seem reasonable to require the Crown to prove that the accused either intended to cause disrepute to the administration of justice or was reckless as to whether that disrepute would follow in spite of the reasonable foreseeability of that result from the words used. Anything less would also seem to be contrary to the proportionality test as it applies too arbitrary a standard.

In light of the conclusion that the offence of scandalizing the court is not a reasonable limitation on freedom of expression it is not necessary to consider whether the offence is prescribed by law as required by s.1 of the **Charter.** If it had been I would have concluded that **R. v. Cohn,** supra, makes it clear that it is.

CONCLUSION

I am of the view that the offence of contempt by scandalizing the court does not constitute or impose a reasonable limitation upon the guaranteed right of freedom of expression provided by s.2(b) of the **Charter.** As the words spoken by the appellant are protected by s.2(b) and the offence of scandalizing the court is not a constitutionally permissible limit on that protection, the conviction must be set aside.

HOULDEN, J.A.: Montgomery, J., found that the appellant's statements constituted a vitriolic, unmitigated attack upon Judge Zuker. He also found that they were made with intent to vilify, that they were a blatant attack on all judges of all courts in Canada, and that they implied bias on the part of all judges. Notwithstanding these findings, there is no doubt that what was said by the appellant was an "expression" within the meaning of s.2(b).

In **R. v. Zundel,** we held that freedom of expression is not absolute. In determining the limits of the freedom, the court observed that it is necessary to first determine the regulated area; the freedom is then what exists in the unregulated area. The court did not find it necessary to define the limits of the unregulated area where freedom of expression is supreme. It held that the offence created by s.177 of the **Code** of spreading falsehoods knowingly was the antithesis of seeking truth through the free exchange of ideas. In finding that the conduct covered by s.177 did not fall within the unregulated area, the court said:

> It would appear to have no social or moral value which would merit constitutional protection. Nor would it aid the working of parliamentary democracy or further self-fulfilment. In our opinion an offence falling within the ambit of s.177 lies within the permissibly regulated area which is not constitutionally protected. It does not come within the residue which comprises freedom of expression guaranteed by s.2(b) of the **Charter.**

The determination of whether statements that may constitute contempt by scandalizing the court fall within the regulated or unregulated area is a difficult one. As the Supreme Court of Canada pointed out in **Retail, Wholesale and Department Store Union, Local 580 et al. v. Dolphin Delivery Ltd.:**

> The principle of freedom of speech and expression has been firmly accepted as a necessary feature of modern democracy.

Before conduct is placed in the regulated area, I believe that a court should be satisfied that it is clearly antithetical to the freedom conferred by s.2(b); the regulated area must, if freedom of expression is to have meaning, be very narrow in scope. Expression of opinion about the conduct of judges or courts after a case has been decided, no matter how vitriolic, scurrilous or vilifying are not, in my judgment, antithetical to the freedom of expression conferred by s.2(b) of the **Charter,** and hence, should not be placed in the regulated area. I am not to be taken as suggesting that "freedom of expression" would preclude a civil action for defamation by the judge, but only that it would preclude proceedings for committal for contempt of court.

...

The inclusion of contempt by scandalizing the court in the regulated area could lead to orthodoxy, and orthodoxy, in my opinion, is neither essential nor desirable for the proper functioning of our judicial system. Courts and judges should be subject to criticism, no matter how extreme; they will function better as a result of it.

Since the statements made by the appellant are protected by s.2(b) of the **Charter,** it is necessary to turn to s.1 of the **Charter** to see if the law proscribing contempt by scandalizing the court is a reasonable limit demonstrably justifiable in a free and democratic society. For s.1 to be applicable, the limit must be "prescribed by law". Ms. Codina argued that the law as to scandalizing the court was too vague and uncertain to be such a limit. With respect, I do not agree. This branch of the law has been clearly defined by both English and Canadian courts. A person would have no difficulty in ascertaining the law and regulating his conduct accordingly. The law of contempt of court by scandalizing the court is, therefore, a limit prescribed by law.

The onus of proving that the law of contempt by scandalizing the court is a reasonable limit under s.1 is, of course, upon the Crown. This is not a case, however, where evidence is required, the elements of the s.1 analysis being "obvious or self-evident": **R. v. Oakes.**

The criteria for the application of s.1 have been clearly defined by Dickson, C.J.C., in **R. v. Oakes.** First, the objective of the prescribed law must relate to concerns which are pressing and substantial and which are of sufficient importance to warrant overriding the constitutionally protected freedom. The objective of this branch of the law is perhaps best summed up in Borrie & Lowe's **Law of Contempt.**

> The necessity for this branch of contempt lies in the idea that without well-regulated laws a civilised community cannot survive. It is therefore thought important to maintain the respect and dignity of the court and its officers, whose task it is to uphold and enforce the law, because without such respect, public faith in the administration of justice would be undermined and the law itself would fall into disrepute.

In my opinion, this objective is of sufficient importance to satisfy the first condition of **R. v. Oakes** for the application of s.1.

Second, once a sufficiently significant objective has been identified, the party having the onus must show that the means chosen to protect that objective are reasonable and demonstrably justified. This involves a "proportionality test". There are three components of this test: (a) the means adopted must be rationally connected to the objective; (b) the means adopted should go no further than is required to achieve the objective; and (c) there must be a proportionality between the effect of the means adopted and the objective.

It is the second component of the proportionality test which causes me concern in this case. The present law assumes that if any act is done or writing is published calculated to bring the court or a judge of a court into contempt or to lower his authority, then it is necessary to curtail freedom of expression and to penalize the offender. Mr. Doherty submitted that this went a great deal further than was required to achieve the objective of the prescribed law. With respect, I agree with this submission.

Freedom of speech and expression were well recognized rights in Canada prior to the **Charter.** In **Retail, Wholesale and Department Store Union, Local 580 v.**

Dolphin Delivery Ltd., McIntyre, J., quoted with approval the following passage from Hogg, **Constitutional Law of Canada** (2nd Ed. 1985):

> Canadian judges have always placed a high value on freedom of expression as an element of parliamentary democracy and have sought to protect it with the limited tools that were at their disposal before the adoption of the **Charter of Rights.**

The freedom guaranteed by s.2(b) of the **Charter** should not be limited to any greater extent than is absolutely essential. As Lord Morris of Borth-Y-Gest said in **Attorney General v. Times Newspapers Ltd.:**

> But as the purpose and existence of courts of laws is to preserve freedom within the law for all well disposed members of the community, it is manifest that the courts must never impose any limitations on free speech or free discussion or free criticism beyond those which are absolutely necessary.

In my judgment, the restraint imposed by the existing law of contempt by scandalizing the court is not proportionate to the objective sought to be attained.

GOODMAN, J.A.: ... In my opinion the application of the **Charter** to the common law now places a limitation on freedom of expression and opinion as they relate to the administration of justice from utterances or statements which consist of assertions of facts which are false and are known to be false by the person making the assertion or are recklessly made by such person. It also places such limitation on those freedoms where the utterances consist of an expression of an opinion which is not honestly and sincerely held. That limitation and consequently the offence of contempt is constitutionally valid, however, only where the utterance or statement is found to result in a clear, significant and imminent or present danger to the fair and effective administration of justice. In that case it meets the test of proportionality and becomes a reasonable limitation prescribed by law which can be demonstrably justified in a free and democratic society. The limitation and consequently the offence of contempt will not be constitutionally valid where such utterances are calculated to bring the administration of justice into disrepute even if it is proven that they in fact do unless the clear and present danger test is also met.

I agree with the statement of my brother Houlden that our judiciary and courts are strong enough to withstand criticism after a case has been decided no matter how outrageous or scurrilous that criticism may be. That reflects the present state of affairs having regard to the circumstances which exist in Canada today. It would require an extreme combination of unusual circumstances at the present time to suffice to convince a court that utterances or statements constitute a real, significant and imminent or present danger to the fair and effective administration of justice. The utterances with which the court is concerned in the present case, having regard to all the circumstances, fall far short of meeting the test. Nevertheless, in my opinion, the offence of contempt for utterances and statements made outside of the court remains a constitutionally valid offence subject to strict proof of the fulfillment of the prescribed conditions necessary for the commission thereof.

Note: The Court of Appeal overturned Kopyto's conviction by a majority of three to two. The dissenting judgments have been omitted.

3.4.5 Robert Martin, "Criticising the Judges", 28 *McGill Law Journal* 1, pp. 13-20

1. Scandalising the Court

Having established a general context, I will turn now to an analysis of a specific aspect or branch of the law of contempt of court — scandalising the court. Scandalising the court is that portion of the criminal law which is brought to bear to punish individuals who say nasty things about courts or judges. This form of contempt is now unknown in England; there has not, it appears, been a successful prosecution for fifty years. It is unfortunately, alive and well in Canada.

The law of contempt generally is supposed to protect against interference with the due administration of justice. Scandalising the court seeks to sanction, in the classic definition, "any act done or writing published calculated to bring a court or a judge of the court into contempt or lower his authority". Such statements may involve either (a) scurrilous abuse of a judge or court, or (b) imputing improper motives to a judge or court. We have on the highest judicial authority that scandalising the court is not intended to prevent criticism of judges or the courts. Thus Lord Atkin stated in *Ambard* v. *A.-G. Trinidad and Tobago:*

> But whether the authority and position of an individual judge, or the due administration of justice, is concerned, no wrong is committed by any member of the public who exercises the ordinary right of criticising, in good faith, in private or public, the public act done in the seat of justice. The path of criticism is a public way: the wrong headed are permitted to err therein: provided that members of the public abstain from imputing improper motives to those taking part in the administration of justice, and are genuinely exercising a right of criticism, and not acting in malice or attempting to impair the administration of justice, they are immune. Justice is not a cloistered virtue: she must be allowed to suffer the scrutiny and respectful, even though outspoken, comments of ordinary men.

What I propose to do now is to look at the Canadian cases, sort them, more or less, into the two recognised categories of scandalising the court, assess the results of the decisions, and note some technical problems.

a. *Scurrilous Abuse*

It is not easy to define scurrilous abuse. Canadians have been found guilty under this rubric for: describing the judge and jury at a murder trial as being themselves murderers and, to boot, torturers; saying that a judicial decision was "silly" and could not have been made by a sane judge, calling a court a "mockery of justice"; writing of a particular proceeding that "the whole thing stinks from the word go"; accusing a court of "intimidation" and "iron curtain" tactics; and vowing with respect to a particular magistrate, "if that bastard hears the case I will see to it that he is defrocked and debarred". The people who made these statements were: a columnist in a major urban daily newspaper; a federal cabinet minister; the editor of a university student newspaper; a municipal politician; a reporter for an urban daily; and a provincial cabinet minister. On the other hand, a columnist for a large urban daily who described a coroner's inquiest as "one of the worst examples of idiocy by public officials that I've ever seen" was acquitted. The cases do not suggest any clear standard for determining what is or is not scurrilous abuse. Courts have convicted on the basis of language which they found "vulgar, abusive, and threatening" or which exceeded the "bounds of temperate and fair criticism''. The New Brunswick Court of Queen's Bench recently advanced the extraordinary assertion that criticism which was ''ungentlemanly'' was contemptuous. In order to amount to scurrilous abuse it appears that the statement in question must identify a particular judge or court. Beyond that, the crucial factor seems to be the literary taste of the presiding judge. If the judge finds the words used excessive then there will likely be a conviction.

b. *Imputing Improper Motives*

Imputing improper motives is a concept that should be susceptible to more precise definition. What appears to be involved here is an allegation of partiality, bias or prejudice. The cause or origin of the alleged improper motive is irrelevant. The allegation may be directed at the judiciary as a whole, at a particular court or group of judges, at a specific, named judge, or at a jury. Contempts of this nature are viewed with considerable disfavour by the Canadian judiciary. Such statements are seen as undermining the reputation for integrity and fairness upon which, it is claimed, the independence of the judiciary is based. The extreme sensitivity of the judges in such matters is illustrated in *Re Duncan*. Lewis Duncan was a lawyer, a Q.C. in fact, arguing an appeal before the Supreme Court of Canada in 1957. Duncan suspected that one member of the Court was prejudiced against him. It was Duncan's belief that this prejudice originated with a personal incident thirty years earlier and that it had been demonstrated in two previous cases before the Supreme Court of Canada in which he had been involved. There was some dispute as to what Duncan actually said to the court, but the essence was that he did not want Locke J. to be a member of the panel hearing his client's appeal and that he did not believe the administration of justice would be served if Locke J. remained on the panel. Accordingly, he requested that Locke J. withdraw. Kerwin C.J.C., speaking for himself and six other judges (not including Locke J.) had no hesitation in holding that Duncan's remarks were contemptuous. Duncan was ordered to pay a fine of $2,000 or, failing that, to serve sixty days in jail. This fine was one of the largest ever imposed in a Canadian contempt case.

c. *General Considerations*

Some general questions remain to be answered with respect to scandalising the court. First, is truth a defence? This issue is unlikely to arise where the statements in question amount to scurrilous abuse, since truth or falsity has little to do with a statement being abusive or not. However, where improper motives on the part of a judge have been suggested, can the accused contemnor seek to prove the truth of such allegations? If I have written that judge X accepts bribes, can I escape punishment by proving that judge X is on the take? The answer is an equivocal *no*. There is no Canadian case directly on point, but all the commentators, having made appropriate disclaimers, agree that truth is not a defence. Secondly, is *mens rea* required? The question should be rephrased since, it will be remembered, the burden of proof is on the accused. Can the accused escape liability by establishing the absence of *mens rea*, that is to say, by showing that the statement in question was not intended to interfere with the due administration of justice? The answer here is clear. It is — *no*.

Finally, what is the range of punishment that is awarded in such cases? The most common punishment is a fine. In 1963, the publisher of *The Division Court Reporter*, a periodical which alleged partiality and corruption on the Division Court bench, was fined $4,000, or about $12,000 in 1982 dollars. This is the largest fine in a reported case. In 1969, the writer of an article in a student newspaper which described the courts as "simply the instruments of the corporate elite" was sentenced to ten days imprisonment without the option of paying a fine. Occasionally, the contemnor may be ordered to apologise to the court. This may be imposed either in conjunction with, or independently of, a fine.

3.5 The Sub Judice Rule

The following statutory and case materials explore the *sub judice* rule. What may, and may not, be reported with respect to proceedings that are actually before the courts?

3.5.1 Robert Martin, "Contempt of Court: The Effect of the Charter", in Anisman and Linden (eds.), *The Media, The Courts and The Charter* (Toronto: Carswell, 1986), pp. 208-210

The *sub judice* rule seeks to control the publication of information which might affect the outcome of judicial proceedings. It has been said that the *sub judice* rule merely postpones, but does not prevent, the publication of certain information. This distinction would not be accepted by a journalist, since the newsworthiness of information is often a function of its timeliness.

Both the ambit of the *sub judice* rule and the justification for it were enunciated by Lord Reid in *A.G. v. Times Newspapers:*

> The law on this subject is and must be founded entirely on public policy. It is not there to protect the private rights of parties to a litigation or prosecution. It is there to prevent interference with the administration of justice and it should in my judgment be limited to what is reasonably necessary for that purpose. Public policy generally requires a balancing of interests which may conflict. Freedom of speech should not be limited to any greater extent than is necessary but it cannot be allowed where there would be real prejudice to the administration of justice.

As a definition of the rule this is elegant, but not very precise. What information will, if published, cause real prejudice to the administration of justice? The honest answer is that no one really knows for sure. Similarly, at what point does the *sub judice* rule begin to apply and at what point does it cease to? Here again there is uncertainty. After careful analysis, for example, Stuart Robertson can only state that "the closer the publication time of the offensive communications is to the time of the trial, the greater is the risk of interfering with the legal proceeding".

This vagueness has an unfortunate effect on journalists, an effect which seriously inhibits freedom of expression. Contempt of court is a crime. People, generally, prefer to avoid being convicted of crimes. This natural desire is reinforced when the definition of the crime is vague. And the circumspection thereby induced is further reinforced by the caution of lawyers. The result is stories of which the following is a not unduly exaggerated example:

> Stout balding Mr. John Jones, cashier to a firm of textile converters, was missing yesterday from his home in Cemetery Avenue, Openshaw.
>
> Round the corner in Funeral Street, Mr. Henry Brown said he had not seen his blonde attractive wife Mamie since the weekend.

A director of the firm which employs Mr. Jones said yesterday that the firm's books would have been due for audit next week. Mr. Jones was also the treasurer of the local Working Men's Holiday Fund.

Neighbours described Mrs. Brown as a gay girl. It is understood that she and Mr. Jones were close friends.

At a flat in Southpool, stout balding Mr. Arthur Smith said he had never heard of Mr. Jones of Openshaw. Blonde attractive Mrs. Dolly Smith said she had never been known as Mamie Brown. Early yesterday police were seeking to interview a stout, bald-headed man who they believed could be of assistance to them in their inquiries into a case of fraudulent conversion.

A man accompanied police to Southpool police station. Blows were exchanged in Southpool's High Street after a man ran at high speed along the street. Police ran at high speed along the street after a man.

Later a man was detained. A man will appear in court today.

If we turn to the justification for the rule we realize that we are being asked to accept it as a matter of faith. There is no empirical basis upon which it can be determined that the publication of a particular piece of information does or does not constitute an interference with the administration of justice. The concerns that are usually expressed with respect to pre-trial publicity tend to focus on the effect such publicity may have on the reputations of individuals, in particular the accused in a criminal proceeding, and on questions of good taste. These may both be significant matters, but neither has anything to do with whether there will or will not be a fair trial.

Does pre-trial publicity actually influence anybody? The following statement of Quigley J. in the Alberta Court of Queen's Bench is interesting. He was replying to the argument advanced by counsel for James Keegstra that the publicity surrounding the case had been such that it might be impossible to find a panel of impartial jurors.

> You know, I don't buy that argument. I don't buy the argument that people in high places or the newspapers or television necessarily have the influence that you're ready to give them. As a matter of fact, you know, there's another school of thought that they used to teach us when I was younger, that you — you only believed about 10 percent of what you read but, you know, I don't think the general public in the populace of Alberta are such that they're led by the nose by any particular politician or any person in so-called high places or led by people in low places, or that those with less education, more education, lack the ordinary good will that most people have. So, you know, to assume that that is a conclusion, is not one that this Court would — would take. I've been sitting in these courts now for 27 years. So I've seen juries act and I've seen many things happen that shores up the fact that I'm not so quick to draw the conclusion that because people in high places say something, or [a] newspaper writes an editorial for or against something, that ordinary people don't just use that as one factor when they come to a conclusion of how they're going to view a certain matter.

Or take the view which Monnin C.J.M. expressed recently with respect to a highly publicized murder trial.

> The mere fact that a previous trial, ending in no verdict, has been reported at length in the media should not ordinarily provide a case of probable bias or prejudice on the part of the jurors at the second trial for the same offence. It is most unfair to prospective jurors and contrary to the jury system to assume that since these prospective jurors may have some prior knowledge of the case by virtue of the media they are probably biased or prejudiced.

If these judges are right and in the absence of any evidence to the contrary, I am inclined to believe they are, much of the justification for the *sub judice* rule falls away. But the matter becomes even stranger when we consider the application of the rule to proceedings before appellate courts. It is clear that the rule does not apply to appellate proceedings with equal rigour. The reason for this is straightforward. Many trials take place before juries. Juries are composed of ordinary human beings who are, presumably, susceptible to being swayed by what they read or hear or see in the media. But there are no juries in appellate courts, only judges, and judges can be relied upon to be sufficiently detached not to be caught up in media-inflamed public passions. I raise the point here to draw attention to the judicial presumptuousness which underlies much of the law of contempt of court.

Finally, one should note that certain aspects of the *sub judice* rule have been codified. Thus, we find in the Criminal Code, for example, prohibitions on reporting certain information with respect to preliminary inquiries, bail hearings, sexual offence proceedings and so on. These statutory prohibitions have the virtue of being reasonably clear and precise.

3.5.2 Statutory Sub Judice

3.5.2.1 Sexual Offences

3.5.2.1.1 Criminal Code, ss.166, 271, 272, 273, 276, 486

166. (1) A proprietor, editor, master printer or publisher commits an offence who prints or publishes

(*a*) in relation to any judicial proceedings any indecent matter or indecent medical, surgical or physiological details, being matter or details that, if published, are calculated to injure public morals;

(*b*) in relation to any judicial proceedings for dissolution of marriage, nullity of marriage, judicial separation or restitution of conjugal rights, any particulars other than

(i) the names, addresses and occupations of the parties and witnesses,

(ii) a concise statement of the charges, defences and countercharges in support of which evidence has been given,

(iii) submissions on a point of law arising in the course of the proceedings, and the decision of the court in connection therewith, and

(iv) the summing up of the judge, the finding of the jury and the judgment of the court and the observations that are made by the judge in giving judgment.

(2) Nothing in paragraph (1)(*b*) affects the operation of paragraph (1)(*a*).

(3) No proceedings for an offence under this section shall be commenced without the consent of the Attorney General.

(4) This section does not apply to a person who

(*a*) prints or publishes any matter for use in connection with any judicial proceedings or communicates it to persons who are concerned in the proceedings;

(*b*) prints or publishes a notice or report pursuant to directions of a court; or

(*c*) prints or publishes any matter

(i) in a volume or part of a genuine series of law reports that does not form part of any other publication and consists solely of reports of proceedings in courts of law, or

(ii) in a publication of a technical character that is *bona fide* intended for circulation among members of the legal or medical professions.

Sexual assault

271. (1) Every one who commits a sexual assault is guilty of

(*a*) an indictable offence and is liable to imprisonment for ten years; or

(*b*) an offence punishable on summary conviction.

Sexual assault with a weapon, threats to a third party or causing bodily harm

272. Every one who, in committing a sexual assault,

(*a*) carries, uses or threatens to use a weapon or an imitation thereof,

(*b*) threatens to cause bodily harm to a person other than the complainant,

(*c*) causes bodily harm to the complainant, or

(*d*) is a party to the offence with any other person,

is guilty of an indictable offence and is liable to imprisonment for fourteen years.

Aggravated sexual assault

273.(1) Every one commits an aggravated sexual assault who, in committing a sexual assault, wounds, maims, disfigures or endangers the life of the complainant.

Punishment

(2) Every one who commits an aggravated sexual assault is guilty of an indictable offence and is liable to imprisonment for life.

No evidence concerning sexual activity

276. (1) In proceedings in respect of an offence under sections [271, 272, 273], no evidence shall be adduced by or on behalf of the accused concerning the sexual activity of the complainant with any person other than the accused unless

(*a*) it is evidence that rebuts evidence of the complainant's sexual activity or absence thereof that was previously adduced by the prosecution;

(*b*) it is evidence of specific instances of the complainant's sexual activity tending to establish the identity of the person who had sexual contact with the complainant on the occasion set out in the charge; or

(*c*) it is evidence of sexual activity that took place on the same occasion as the sexual activity that forms the subject-matter of the charge, where that evidence relates to the consent that the accused alleges he believed was given by the complainant.

Notice

(2) No evidence is admissible under paragraph (1)(*c*) unless

(*a*) reasonable notice in writing has been given to the prosecutor by or on behalf of the accused of his intention to adduce the evidence together with particulars of the evidence sought to be adduced; and

(*b*) a copy of the notice has been filed with the clerk of the court.

Hearing

(3) No evidence is admissible under subsection (1) unless the judge, magistrate or justice, after holding a hearing in which the jury and

the members of the public are excluded and in which the complainant is not a compellable witness, is satisfied that the requirements of this section are met.

Publication prohibited

(4) The notice given under subsection (2) and the evidence taken, the information given or the representations made at a hearing referred to in subsection (3) shall not be published in any newspaper or broadcast.

Offence

(5) Every one who, without lawful excuse the proof of which lies upon him, contravenes subsection (4) is guilty of an offence punishable on summary conviction. ...

486. (1) Any proceedings against an accused shall be held in open court, but where the presiding judge, provincial court judge or justice, as the case may be, is of the opinion that it is in the interest of public morals, the maintenance of order or the proper administration of justice to exclude all or any members of the public from the court room for all or part of the proceedings, he may so order.

Reasons to be stated

(2) Where an accused is charged with an offence mentioned in section 274 and the prosecutor or the accused makes an application for an order under subsection (1), the presiding judge, Provincial Court judge or justice, as the case may be, shall, if no such order is made, state, by reference to the circumstances of the case, the reason for not making an order.

Order restricting publication

(3) Where an accused is charged with an offence mentioned in section 274, the presiding judge, Provincial Court judge or justice may, or if application is made by the complainant or prosecutor, shall, make an order directing that the identity of the complainant and any information that could disclose the identity of the complainant shall not be published in any newspaper or broadcast.

3.5.2.1.2 *Canadian Newspapers Co. Ltd.* v. *Attorney-General for Canada* (1985), 49 O.R. (2d) 557 (C.A.). Leave to appeal to the Supreme Court of Canada granted April 24, 1985

HOWLAND C.J.O.: ... The sensibilities of an adult person, whether he or she is the accused or a witness, is not a valid basis for limiting the publication of criminal proceedings or excluding the public from the court-room: *A.-G. N.S. et al. v. MacIntyre, supra,* at p. 185 S.C.R., p. 146 C.C.C., p. 402 D.L.R.; *Re Regina and Several Unnamed Persons* (1983), 44 O.R. (2d) 81 at pp. 84-5, 8 C.C.C. (3d) 528 at pp. 531-2, 4 D.L.R. (4th) 310 at pp. 313-4.

I am in agreement with Osborne J. that s.442(3) of the *Code* in providing for an order prohibiting the publication of the identity of the complainant and of any information that could disclose her identity *prima facie* infringed the freedom of the press under s.2(*b*) of the Charter to report what transpired at a public trial.

...

What is the social value to be protected by s.442(3) [now, s.486(3)]? It is to facilitate the prosecution of persons charged with serious sexual offences within s.246.4

of the *Code,* and for that purpose to encourage the victims to come forward and complain, and to be prepared to testify at the trial of the accused. In satisfying the onus which lies upon it the Attorney-General for Canada is entitled to tender extrinsic evidence.

...

I consider that it has been clearly established that the social value to be protected, namely, the bringing of those who commit such sexual offences to justice, is of superordinate importance and can merit a prohibition against publication of the victims' identity or of any information that could disclose it. It is a reasonable limitation on the freedom of the press. The representatives of the media still have the right of access to the court-room and to publish everything that transpires, with the exception only of the identity of the complainant and information which could disclose that identity. The Attorney-General for Canada has demonstrably justified the reasonableness of such a limitation on a balance of probabilities, subject only to the question whether such a prohibition order should be mandatory on the application of the complainant or of the prosecutor.

...

I am not persuaded that the Attorney-General for Canada has demonstrably justified that the mandatory prohibition order under s.442(3) upon the application of the complainant or the prosecutor is a reasonable limitation. It is not required as it was in the *Global Communications* case to ensure that the accused received a fair trial. There is no evidence that the needs of Canada for such legislation are greater than the needs of other free and democratic societies to whose legislation I have referred. The administration of justice is dependent on public confidence in the judiciary. The discretion given to the trial judge under s.442(3) to make a prohibition order is a sufficient safeguard for the protection of the identity of the complainant. In most cases it will no doubt be made as a matter of course. However, in an exceptional case where it is not merited the presiding judge should have an opportunity to refuse to make it.

Under s.52(1) of the *Constitution Act, 1982,* s.442(3) of the *Code* is, to the extent that it requires the making of a mandatory order, inconsistent with the Charter and of no force and effect. This does not result in s.442(3) being declared invalid in its entirety. The offending portion of s.442(3) can be severed.

...

I would allow the appeal in the civil proceeding and vary the order of Osborne J. by declaring that s.442(3) is valid with the exception of the words ''or if application is made by the complainant or prosecutor, shall''.

3.5.2.2 Young Offenders

3.5.2.2.1 Young Offenders Act, R.S.C. 1985, c.Y-1

Transfer to ordinary court

16. (1) At any time after an information is laid against a young person alleged to have, after attaining the age of fourteen years, committed an indictable offence referred to in section 553 of the *Criminal Code* but prior to adjudication, a youth court may, on application of the young person or his counsel, or the Attorney General or his agent, after affording both parties and the parents of the young person an opportunity to be heard, if the court is of the opinion that, in the interest of society and having regard to the needs of the young person, the young person should be proceeded against in ordinary court, order that the young person be so proceeded against in accordance with the law ordinarily applicable to an adult charged with the offence.

Order restricting publication of information presented at transfer hearing

17. (1) Where a youth court hears an application for a transfer to ordinary court under section 16, it shall

(a) where the young person is not represented by counsel, or

(b) an application made by or on behalf of the young person or the prosecutor, where the young person is represented by counsel,

make an order directing that any information respecting the offence presented at the hearing shall not be published in any newspaper or broadcast before such time as,

(c) an order for a transfer is refused or set aside on review and the time for all reviews against the decision has expired or all proceedings in respect of any such review have been completed; or

(d) the trial is ended, if the case is transferred to ordinary court.

Offence

(2) Every one who fails to comply with an order made pursuant to subsection (1) is guilty of an offence punishable on summary conviction.

Meaning of "newspaper"

(3) In this section, "newspaper" has the meaning set out in section 297 of the *Criminal Code*.

Protection of Privacy of Young Persons

Identity not to be published

38. (1) Subject to this section, no person shall publish by any means any report,

(a) of an offence committed or alleged to have been committed by a young person unless an order has been made under s.16 with respect thereto, or

(b) of a hearing, adjudication, disposition or appeal concerning a young person who committed or is alleged to have committed an offence

in which the name of the young person, a child or a young person who is a victim of the offence or a child or a young person who appeared as a witness in connection with the offence, or in which any information serving to identify such person or child, is disclosed.

Limitation

(1.1) Subsection (1) does not apply in respect of the disclosure of information in the course of the administration of justice where it is not the purpose of the disclosure to make the information known in the community.

Ex parte application for leave to publish

(1.2) A youth court judge shall, on the ex parte application of a peace officer, make an order permitting any person to publish a report described in subsection (1) that contains the name of a young person, or information serving to identify a young person, who has committed or is alleged to have committed an indictable offence, if the judge is satisfied that

(a) there is reason to believe that the young person is dangerous to others; and
(b) publication of the report is necessary to assist in apprehending the young person.

Order ceases to have effect

(1.3) An order made under subsection (1.2) shall cease to have effect two days after it is made.

Application for leave to publish

(1.4) The youth court may, on the application of any person referred to in subsection (1), make an order permitting any person to publish a report in which the name of that person, or information serving to identify that person, would be disclosed, if the court is satisfied that the publication of the report would not be contrary to the best interests of that person.

Contravention

(2) Every one who contravenes subsection (1)(a) is guilty of an indictable offence and is liable to inprisonment for not more than two years; or
(b) is guilty of an offence punishable on summary conviction.

Provincial judge has absolute jurisdiction on indictment

(3) Where an accused is charged with an offence under paragraph (2)(a), a provincial court judge has absolute jurisdiction to try the case and his jurisdiction does not depend on the consent of the accused.

Exclusion from hearing

39. (1) Subject to subsection (2), where a court or justice before whom proceedings are carried out under this Act is of the opinion
(a) that any evidence or information presented to the court or justice would be seriously injurious or seriously prejudicial to
(i) the young person who is being dealt with in the proceedings,
(ii) a child or young person who is a witness in the proceedings,
(iii) a child or young person who is aggrieved by or the victim of the offence charged in the proceedings, or
(b) that it would be in the interest of public morals, the maintenance of order or the proper administration of justice to exclude any or all members of the public from the court room, the court or justice may exclude any person from all or part of the proceedings if the court or justice deems that person's presence to be unnecessary to the conduct of the proceedings.

Exception

(2) Subject to section 650 of the *Criminal Code* and except where it is necessary for the purposes of subsection 13(6) of this Act, a court or justice may not, pursuant to subsection (1), exclude from proceedings under this Act
(a) the prosecutor;
(b) the young person who is being dealt with in the proceedings, his parent, his counsel or any adult assisting him pursuant to subsection 11(7);
(c) the provincial director or his agent; or
(d) the youth worker to whom the young person's case has been assigned.

Exclusion after adjudication or during review

(3) The youth court, after it has found a young person guilty of an offence, or the youth court or the review board, during a review of a disposition under sections 28 to 32, may, in its discretion, exclude from the court or from a hearing of the review board, as the case may be, any person other than

(a) the young person or his counsel,

(b) the provincial director or his agent,

(c) the youth worker to whom the young person's case has been assigned, and

(d) the Attorney General or his agent, when any information is being presented to the court or the review board the knowledge of which might, in the opinion of the court or review board, be seriously injurious or seriously prejudicial to the young person.

Exception

(4) The exception set out in paragraph (3)(a) is subject to subsection 13(6) of this Act and section 577 of the *Criminal Code*.

3.5.2.2.2 *Southam* v. *R.* (1984), 42 C.R. (3d) 336, at 354-360 (Ont. H.C.)

HOLLAND J.:

Reasonable Limit

Counsel for the applicant placed great emphasis on the fact that the expert witnesses agreed that the absolute ban provided for in s.38(1) was not "necessary", and he argued that the limit could therefore not be considered "reasonable and demonstrably justifiable". Counsel for the Attorney General of Canada countered this by arguing that he did not have to prove that the legislation was necessary or perfect or even the best answer to the problem. He said he only had to prove that the legislation has a "rational basis" and is "in furtherance of a reasonable state object", and relied on the following cases:

In *Re Southam Inc.*, supra, MacKinnon A.C.J.O. said at p. 424:

"We are left, at present, to a certain extent wandering in unexplored terrain in which we have to set up our own guideposts in interpreting the meaning and effect of the words of s.1 of the Charter. In determining the reasonableness of the limit in each particular case, the court must examine objectively its argued rational basis in light of what the court understands to be reasonable in a free and democratic society."

In *R. v. T.R.* (1984), 10 C.C.C. (3d) 481, 7 D.L.R. (4th) 205, 52 A.R. 149 at 156 (Q.B.):

"Section 12(3) [of the Juvenile Delinquents Act], to a moderate extent, is inconsistent with s.2(*b*) of the *Charter*. But in my view the limit upon freedom of the press which is imposed by s.12(3) is a reasonable one and is demonstrably justified in a free and democratic society. This is one of those cases in which, without any evidence or very much in the way of information as to what is done in other free and democratic societies, the court can conclude as a matter of reasoning that such a limit is 'reasonable' in the sense that it is in furtherance of a reasonable state object (already referred to) and that it is demonstrably justified."

In *Nat. Citizens' Coalition Inc. — Coalition Nat. des Citoyens Inc. v. A.G. Can.*, [1984] 5 W.W.R. 436 at 449-50, 32 Alta. L.R. (2d) 249 (Q.B.), Medhurst J., speaking for the court, said:

"McDonald J. considered the meaning of reasonable limit in *Reich* [*Reich v. Alta. College of Physicians & Surgeons* (1984), 31 Alta. L.R. (2d) 205 (Q.B.)] and concluded after a review of the relevant authorities that it meant having a rational basis. At p. 18 he said:

" 'In my opinion, the words "reasonable limits" as used in s.1 mean "capable of being supported as a rational means of achieving a rational objective".' "

In *R. v. D.*, Ont. H.C., 12th June 1984 (not yet reported), Osborne J. put it in the following way:

"There is, however, one somewhat dominant, analytical common demoninator emerging from those cases. In *Global* [*Re Global Communications Ltd. and A.G. Can.* (1984), 44 O.R. (2d) 609, 38 C.R. (3d) 209 (sub nom. *Re Smith; Global Communications Ltd. v. California*), 10 C.C.C. (3d) 97, 5 D.L.R. (4th) 634, 2 O.A.C. 21 (C.A.)], Thorson J.A. put it this way at p. 614:

> " 'I think the time has come when the issue ought to be decided from the broader perspective of the presumed policy object of the legislation here in question, standing back if need be from what the cases have said on the subject.'

"McKinnon A.C.J.O. said in *Southam* [supra] at p. 134:

> " 'The net which s.12(1) casts is too wide for the purpose which it serves. Society loses more than it protects by the all-embracing nature of the section.'

"It is quite apparent that in both *Global* and *Southam* emphasis was placed upon the policy objectives of the legislation alleged to infringe the Charter right in issue."

A consideration of whether a limit on a guaranteed freedom is reasonable involves a balancing of the competing interests, so that what is lost by the limitation can be compared with what is gained by the legislation.

As the Court of Appeal said in *Rauca*, supra, at p. 241:

"In approaching the question objectively, it is recognized that the listed rights and freedoms are never absolute and that there are always qualifications and limitations to allow for the protection of other competing interests in a democratic society. A readily demonstrable example of this is 'freedom of speech' which is limited or qualified by the laws of defamation, obscenity, sedition, etc. Lord Reid pointed out in *Attorney-General v. Times Newspapers Ltd.*, [1974] A.C. 273 at p. 294:

> " 'Public policy generally requires a balancing of interests which may conflict. Freedom of speech should not be limited to any greater extent than is necessary but it cannot be allowed where there would be real prejudice to the administration of justice.' "

The freedom at issue here is the freedom of expression, including freedom of the press. In the context of s.38(1) this involves the freedom to publish, and in the context of s.39(1)(*a*) it involves access to the courts. To be balanced against the value of that freedom is the value to society and to involved youths of protecting young people involved in youth court proceedings from the damaging effects of publicity.

Freedom of the Press

In *Gay Alliance Toward Equality v. Vancouver Sun; B.C. Human Rights Comm. v. Vancouver Sun*, [1979] 2 S.C.R. 435, [1979] 4 W.W.R. 118, 10 B.C.L.R. 257,

97 D.L.R. (3d) 577, Dickson J. in dissent enunciated the following definition of "freedom of the press" at p. 598 [quoting from the British Royal Commission on the Press, Final Report (1977), p. 9]:

"We define freedom of the press as that degree of freedom from restraint which is essential to enable proprietors, editors and journalists to advance the public interest by publishing the facts and opinions without which a democratic electorate cannot make responsible judgments."

The value of access to the courts has been held by the Supreme Court of Canada to be so important to society that its curtailment "can only be justified where there is present the need to protect social values of *superordinate importance*": *MacIntyre v. A.G. N.S.*, [1982] 1 S.C.R. 175, 26 C.R. (3d) 193 at 213, 65 C.C.C. (2d) 129, 132 D.L.R. (3d) 385, 49 N.S.R. (2d) 609, 96 A.P.R. 609, 40 N.R. 181.

In *Re Southam Inc. and R.*, supra, MacKinnon A.C.J.O. for the Ontario Court of Appeal said the following about free access to the courts at p. 418:

> "...in my view, such access, having regard to its historic origin and necessary purpose already recited at length, is an integral and implicit part of the guarantee given to everyone of freedom of opinion and expression which, in terms, includes freedom of the press. However the rule may have had its origin, as Mr. Justice Dickson pointed out, the 'openness' rule fosters the necessary public confidence in the integrity of the court system and an understanding of the administration of justice."

The aim of s.38(1) and s.39(1)(*a*) is the protection of young people from harmful effects which publicity may have on them. A corollary to this is the protection of society, since, on the evidence of the experts, most young offenders are one-time offenders only and the less harm on them from their experience with the criminal justice system the less likely they are to commit further criminal acts. Thus it can be said that the legislation is also aimed at rehabilitation of the young person.

The declaration of principles in s.3 of the YOA helps in ascertaining the aim of the legislation and points to the importance of special treatment for young people. While I have previously set these out, it is well worth mentioning them again. Section 3(1)(*a*) declares that young persons must bear responsibility for their actions, although they should not in all circumstances be held accountable or suffer the same consequences for their behaviour as adults, and s.3(1)(*b*) recognizes that society must be afforded protection from illegal behaviour. Section 3(1)(*c*) is particularly important:

"(*c*) young persons who commit offences require supervision, discipline and control, but, because of their state of dependency and level of development and maturity, they also have special needs and require guidance and assistance".

This was essentially the thrust of the evidence from the expert witnesses, with the obvious result that children should be treated differently from adults and that the criminal justice system should, in some ways, operate differently for children than for adults. Where there is good reason for a young person to be tried in adult court, the trial may be transferred under s.16 of the YOA.

The introduction to the YOA, 1982 — Highlights booklet describes the YOA [at p. 1] as "one of the most significant pieces of social policy legislation to have been passed in recent years". While this may well be indisputable, the good to be gained by having the legislation in place must be weighed against the loss to the press in particular and society in general from the limited denial of a freedom. In examining this question, it is necessary to look at s.38(1) and s.39(1)(*a*) separately.

Section 38(1)

Section 38(1) of the YOA is absolute and, in the words of MacKinnon A.C.J.O. in *Re Southam Inc. and R.*, supra [p. 421]: "We are accordingly left in the unhappy position of it being all or nothing." In *Re Southam,* the Court of Appeal was considering s.12(1) of the JDA, which provided that trials of all juveniles were to be held in camera. In striking down s.12(1) as not being a reasonable limit on the rights of access to the courts, MacKinnon A.C.J.O. said at p. 429:

> "The net which s.12(1) casts is too wide for the purpose which it serves. Society loses more than it protects by the all-embracing nature of the section. As stated earlier, counsel for the Attorney-General was quick to acknowledge (and very fairly so) that not every juvenile court proceeding would require the barring of public access."

Counsel for the applicant relied on this decision and I must say that at first blush it does seem to deny the validity of a total ban, particularly where it has been conceded that the total ban is not necessary. However, on closer examination I believe that the differences between s.12(1) of the JDA and s.38(1) of the YOA are important. In s.12(1) of the JDA, the effect of the total ban reached further than mere accessibility to the courts, since it also resulted in an effective ban on the publication of *any* details of the court proceedings. If the press is not allowed to be present, it can hardly report on what happened at the proceeding.

Section 38(1) does not contain an absolute ban, and consequent denial of freedom of the press, in the same way. The press is entitled to be present (subject to s.39(1)(*a*)) and can publish everything except the identity of a young person involved. Admittedly, there may be other information which the press cannot publish because it may tend to reveal the identity of a young person, but the essence of the provision is that the press is entitled to publish all details except one. Counsel for the Attorney General of Canada termed the identification of the young person a "sliver of information", and submitted that this is not an essential detail for the making of responsible judgment by a democratic electorate (to meet the test in *Gay Alliance,* supra).

In my view, based on the evidence which I heard from expert witnesses, the protection and rehabilitation of young people involved in the criminal justice system is a social value of the "superordinate importance" which justifies the abrogation of fundamental freedom of expression, including freedom of the press, to the extent effected by s.38(1) of the YOA. Section 38(1) is, in my view, a reasonable limitation on that freedom.

Section 39(1)(a)

This provision gives to the youth court judge the discretion to exclude any member of the public if, in his or her opinion, any of the criteria set out in the section are met. Thus, the section does not impose an absolute ban, as did s.12(1) of the JDA.

When the Court of Appeal decided *Re Southam Inc. and R.*, supra, the YOA had been enacted but not yet proclaimed. Section 39(1)(*a*) was proclaimed at it was set out in *Re Southam,* with the addition of the word "seriously" before the word "prejudicial". At pp. 429-30 MacKinnon A.C.J.O. said:

"An amendment giving jurisdiction to the court to exclude the public from juvenile court proceedings where it concludes under the circumstances, that it is in the best interests of the child or others concerned or in the best interests of the administration of justice to do so would meet any residual concern arising from the striking down of the section. As Mr. Justice Martin said in *R. v. Oakes* (released February 2, 1983, unreported) (since reported, 145 D.L.R. (3d) 123, 2 C.C.C. (3d) 339, 409 O.R. (2d) 660), we are not entitled to rewrite the statute under attack when considering the applicability of the provisions of the Charter. Parliament can give the necessary discretion to the court to be exercised on a case-to-case basis which, in my view, would be a prospective reasonable limit on the guaranteed right and demonstrably justifiable.''

While these statements by MacKinnon A.C.J.O. were clearly obiter and therefore not strictly binding upon me, I feel that I must given them great weight and that they are indicative of the view that the Court of Appeal would take on the constitutionality of s.39(1)(*a*). Admittedly, the Court of Appeal did not hear evidence and full argument on s.39(1)(*a*), but it is my opinion that the evidence I have heard strengthens the view expressed by the Court of Appeal.

Again, I hold that the interests of society in the protection and rehabilitation of young people involved in youth court proceedings is a value of such superordinate importance that it justifies the discretion given to a youth court judge under s.39(1)(*a*). Section 39(1)(*a*) is, in my view, a reasonable limitation on freedom of expression, including freedom of the press.

Having made those decisions, I am aware that I have not referred to legislation of other free and democratic societies. I have considered the legislation for the United Kingdom, the United States and the Commonwealth which were put before me, and they indicate that there is a range of legislation acceptable in other free and democratic societies. In my view, ss.38(1) and 39(1)(*a*) are within the acceptable range.

In any event, I do not need to rely on legislation in other jurisdictions. While I accept that in some circumstances it may be helpful, I adopt the words of Osborne, J. in *R. v. D.*, supra:

``The fact that this legislation is not mirrored in other free and democratic societies may cause one to pause, but, it seems to me, not stop. This is a Canadian solution to a problem that I am sure exists in all jurisdictions. The Canadian solution is not to be rejected because others have seen fit not to follow the path chosen by Parliament in order to better protect the victims of alleged sexual assault.''

Note: For further restrictions on the publication of family proceedings, see ss.57(7), 71(2) of the Child Welfare Act, R.S.O. 1980, c.66. Also, for contempt proceedings in coroner's inquests see s.51 of The Coroner's Act, 1972, R.S.O. 1980, c.93.

3.5.2.3 Preliminary Inquiries

3.5.2.3.1 Criminal Code, ss.537(1)(h), 539, 542

Powers of Justice

POWERS OF JUSTICE — Remand for observation — Direct issue to be tried — Section 615 applicable.

537. (1) A justice acting under this Part may

(*h*) order that no person other than the prosecutor, the accused and their counsel shall have access to or remain in the room in which the inquiry is held, where it appears to him that the ends of justice will be best served by so doing;

Taking Evidence of Witnesses

ORDER RESTRICTING PUBLICATION OF EVIDENCE TAKEN AT PRELIMINARY INQUIRY — Accused to be informed of right to apply for order — Failure to comply with order — "Newspaper".

"539. (1) Prior to the commencement of the taking of evidence at a preliminary inquiry, the justice holding the inquiry

(*a*) may, if application therefor is made by the prosecutor, and

(*b*) shall, if application therefor is made by any of the accused,

make an order directing that the evidence taken at the inquiry shall not be published in any newspaper or broadcast before such time as, in respect of each of the accused,

(*c*) he is discharged; or

(*d*) if he is ordered to stand trial, the trial is ended."

(2) Where an accused is not represented by counsel at a preliminary inquiry, the justice holding the inquiry shall, prior to the commencement of the taking of evidence at the inquiry, inform the accused of his right to make application under subsection (1).

(3) Every one who fails to comply with an order made pursuant to subsection (1) is guilty of an offence punishable on summary conviction.

(4) In this section, "newspaper" has the same meaning as it has in section 297.

542. (1) Nothing in this Act prevents a prosecutor giving evidence at a preliminary inquiry any admission, confession or statement made at any time by the accused that by law is admissible against him.

(2) Everyone who publishes in any newspaper, or broadcasts, a report that any admission or confession was tendered in evidence at a preliminary inquiry or a report of the nature of such admission or confession so tendered in evidence unless

(a) the accused has been discharged, or

(b) if the accused has been ordered to trial, the trial has ended,

is guilty of an offence punishable on summary conviction.

3.5.2.3.2 *R.* v. *Banville* (1983) 45 N.B.R. (2d) 134 (Q.B.)

[1] HOYT, J. [orally]: This is an appeal from both the conviction entered against and sentence imposed upon Beurmond Banville by Provincial Court Judge James D. Harper for not complying with an order made by another Provincial Court Judge in which he prohibited the publication of evidence at a preliminary inquiry contrary to s.467(3) of the *Criminal Code of Canada*.

[2] Judge Harper's decision is reported in (1982), 41 N.B.R. (2d) 114; 107 A.P.R. 114. The facts are given in detail by him and I do not propose to repeat them here in such detail.

[3] Briefly, Mr. Banville, a reporter for the Bangor Daily News, a daily newspaper printed in Bangor, Maine with general circulation in eastern and northern Maine, attended a preliminary inquiry which was held on February the 15th, 1982, in the Provincial Court in Edmundston, Madawaska County, New Brunswick. The presiding judge, upon the request of defence counsel and using the provisions of s.467(1) of the *Criminal Code,* made an order prohibiting the publication of evidence taken at the preliminary inquiry in the following terms:

Be the order of this court that all of the evidence advanced in this preliminary hearing be banned from being published in any mode of media until the conclusion of this particular matter.

[4] That order was made in open court with Mr. Banville present and in addition he was personally warned by the presiding judge and counsel for the Crown and the defence.

[5] Mr. Banville filed a story which included some of the prohibited material. The story was published in the February 16th, 1982 issue of the Bangor Daily News. In all some 56 or 57 copies of that issue of the paper were distributed in Canada with 17 of those copies being distributed in Edmundston where the trial of the accused eventually occurred. Also some of the papers were delivered to Clair, which like Edmundston, is in the County of Madawaska from which county the jury was selected.

[6] Mr. Banville, as I said, was charged under s.467(3) of the *Criminal Code* and upon conviction by Judge Harper was fined $200.00. In Mr. Banville's appeal from his conviction he presses some 8 grounds of appeal. They are:

(a) The learned trial judge erred in law in finding that the *Constitution Act,* 1981, which proclaimed as law, a *Canadian Charter of Rights and Freedoms,* is not retroactive in its aspects and has no bearing on the present case.

(b) The learned trial judge erred in law in finding that s.1 of the *Charter* fully justifies the existence of s.467 of the *Criminal Code of Canada,* R.S.C. 1970, c.C-34.

(c) The learned trial judge erred in law in failing to consider the applicability of s.1(f) of the *Canadian Bill of Rights (1960)* to the present case.

(d) The learned trial judge erred in law in holding that "the actual geographical area of publication is of no legal import" when s.5(2) of the *Criminal Code* prohibits a conviction in Canada for an offence committed outside of Canada.

(e) The learned trial judge erred in law in finding the appellant guilty of the offence charged on the basis of s.21 of the *Criminal Code* when there was no proof of the commission of the principal offence within Canada.

(f) The learned trial judge erred in law in finding that the appellant "published" in his capacity as reporter.

(g) The learned trial judge erred in law in finding that the court had jurisdiction over the offence when there was no evidence of the commission of the offence in Canada.

(h) The learned trial judge erred in law in his application of the legal principle "de minimis non curat lex."

[7] The first 3 grounds of appeal deal with the *Canadian Charter of Rights and Freedoms* which came into force on April the 17th, 1982, as part of the *Constitution Act* of 1982.

[8] Briefly, the appellant contends that s.2(b) of the *Charter* has retrospective effect and strikes down s.467(1) of the *Criminal Code* as it places a restriction on the freedom of the press. To support this argument, he says that s.1(f) of the *Bill of Rights* codified this previously although unwritten freedom.

[9] My view is that, in some applications, the *Charter* does have retrospective application. In *R. v. Davidson* (1982), 40 N.B.R. (2d) 702; 105 A.P.R. 702, I held that articles seized as a result of a police search before April 17th, 1982, could be rejected at a trial held after that date if their seizure brought the administration of justice into disrepute. I might say that to date this appears to be a minority view. *R. v. Potma,* 7 W.C.B. 365, appears to be the more generally accepted view. Here, however, there is nothing of a continuing nature, as there was in both *Davidson* and *Potma,* which stretches over April 17th, 1982. There was no evidence tainted by the *Charter*. Thus, the *Charter* has no application. The offence, if there was one, was complete on February the 16th, 1982.

[10] However, should I have found that the *Charter* did have application, I must think that s.467(1) of the *Criminal Code* is not a restraint on freedom of the press, which cannot be demonstrably justified in a free and democratic society.

[11] First of all, the section does not prevent an open trial, one which may be attended by reporters and the general public, nor does it prohibit the publication of evidence given at the preliminary inquiry. It only defers its publication until the accused is either discharged or his trial is ended. If the media wish to publish or broadcast evidence given at the preliminary inquiry, at that time there is no sanction. It may not be as newsworthy but the public's right to know is preserved and protected.

[12] Secondly, the mere fact that Parliament enacts a procedure which is apparently contrary to the *Charter* does not mean that such enactment is thus demonstrably justified in a free and democratic society. As Mr. Justice Smith said in *Re S.12 of the Juvenile Delinquents Act,* 8 W.C.B. 206:

> In my view, sovereignty of Parliament has been dealt a mild blow.

[13] There he struck down s.12(1) of the *Juvenile Delinquents Act,* R.S.C. 1970, c.J-3, which provides for the trials of children to take place without publicity.

[14] Here freedom of the press is said to be interfered with by s.467(1) because the publication of evidence given at a preliminary inquiry is delayed. The purpose of the section is to insure that the accused receive the fairest possible trial or as is said in s.11(d) of the *Charter of Rights:*

> Any person charged with an offence has the right to be presumed innocent until proven guilty according to law in a fair and public hearing by an independent and impartial tribunal.

[15] Thus, we appear to have 2 competing interests, freedom of the press and a fair and public trial before an independent and impartial tribunal. If there is such a conflict, and I am not certain that delay in reporting evidence of a preliminary inquiry is essential to the maintenance of a well-informed public opinion, then the concept of freedom of the press must, in my view, give way to the overriding obligation to insure that an individual have a fair trial before an independent and impartial tribunal. I find it difficult to accept that our democratic institutions are threatened if the public, including potential jurors, are delayed, not denied, but delayed in finding out that, for example,

> ...hairs found at the scene are consistent with a standard said to come from the accused's body.

[16] In *Re C.B.R.,* 8 W.C.B. 206, Mr. Justice Smith dealt with an application to quash the order of a judge prohibiting the publication of a motion for a change of venue in a criminal trial. He dismissed the application, and although I have not had the benefit of reading his reasons, the report that I have just cited says:

> ...the Charter did not contemplate that an accused's rights should be whittled down in the name of a general concept of freedom of the press, a weighing process being required with the right to a fair trial being paramount — In the circumstances, the court was not persuaded that a temporary ban in the circumstances of the case was an unreasonable exercise of the trial judge's discretion.

[17] I realize that there is a danger that each individual case can be rationalized on its merits, thus losing sight of the general principle. If s.467(1) was permissive rather than mandatory, the section would perhaps be easier to justify, as was the last case that I mentioned. The judge was exercising a discretion in prohibiting the publication of a motion for a change of venue and he made the order, which was upheld by Mr. Justice Smith, after hearing arguments of counsel. In dealing with blanket proscriptions, such as s.467(1), as I said, there is a danger that each case can be rationalized on its own merits and thus losing sight of the general principle. However, if there is a conflict between the two competing concepts, and I am not sure that there is, but if there is, the individual's right to a fair trial before an independent and impartial tribunal must prevail. Thus, I reject the argument that the *Charter of Rights and Freedoms,* even if it had retrospective effect, strikes down s.467(1) of the *Criminal Code.*

[18] Grounds 4 to 7 of the appellant relate to the jurisdiction of Canadian Courts over this offense. Judge Harper carefully considered this argument, as well as the *Charter* argument, and I do not disagree with his finding. Mr. Hanson suggested that Judge Harper may have found Mr. Banville guilty as an accessory in aiding in the offense which occurred in the United States... I do not understand that to be Judge Harper's decision. At pages 121 and 122 of the report he says, after quoting s.21 of the *Criminal Code:*

> It is beyond argument that publication of the evidence complained of would have been impossible if it had been reported by the defendant in the first instance. It follows, therefore, that if an offense occurred he is a party to it and, therefore, guilty of it.

[19] Mr. Banville wrote the story on February 15th, after he had knowledge of the order. Thus, he was the person who actually committed the offense. The publication was complete, in my view, when the story was made available to the public in Edmundston, to be precise, the following day.

[20] Mr. Hanson argues that a reporter does not publish a newspaper. That is so. But s.467(1) does not prohibit the publication of a newspaper. It prohibits the evidence taken at the preliminary inquiry from being published in a newspaper. The reporter, particularly one who knows of the ban, becomes guilty when his story is printed and circulated in Canada — if it contains evidence taken at the inquiry. I distinguish between publication and printing.

[21] The final ground of appeal against the conviction is that the offense is so trivial as not to be worthy of notice. I agree with Judge Harper whom after reviewing the authorities, said at page 127:

> The degree of such breach is of no consequences in coming to a decision upon whether or not the defendant is guilty of the charge, nor is his notice of any import. Once the breach

of the court order is established by the prosecution the probable or improbable results of the failure of the defendant to abide the order are of no significance only insofar as sentence is concerned.

[22] Initially I was not disposed to tinker with the sentence imposed by Judge Harper. If I may say so, he approached the task of sentencing with great sensitivity. Little harm was done and Mr. Banville voluntarily returned to Canada to face his trial. His defense was conducted with dignity. However, he was aware of the possible consequences should the story be published.

[23] However, I am of the view that this is an appropriate situation for a discharge. I feel that it would be clearly in the best interests of the accused, having regard to the nature and place of his employment, and not contrary to the public interest by ordering a discharge.

[24] I allow the appeal against the sentence and direct that the accused be discharged absolutely. In the result, the appeal against conviction is dismissed and the appeal against sentence is allowed with the substitution of an absolute discharge.

Appeal against conviction dismissed; appeal against sentence allowed.

3.5.2.3.3 Criminal Code, s.542

CONFESSION OR ADMISSION OF ACCUSED — Restriction of publication of reports of preliminary inquiry — "Newspaper".

542. (1) Nothing in this Act prevents a prosecutor giving in evidence at a preliminary inquiry any admission, confession or statement made at any time by the accused that by law is admissible against him.

(2) Every one who publishes in any newspaper, or broadcasts, a report that any admission or confession was tendered in evidence at a preliminary inquiry or a report of the nature of such admission or confession so tendered in evidence unless

(*a*) the accused has been discharged, or

(*b*) if the accused has been ordered to stand trial, the trial has ended (as am. S.C. 1985, c.19, s.101(2)).

is guilty of an offence punishable on summary conviction.

(3) In this section "newspaper" has the same meaning that it has in section 297.

3.5.2.4 Bail Hearings

3.5.2.4.1 Criminal Code, s.515

Judicial Interim Release

ORDER OF RELEASE — Release on undertaking with conditions, etc. — Idem — Conditions authorized — Detention in custody — Order of detention — Order of release — Idem — Sufficiency of record — Justification for detention in custody — Detention in custody for offence mentioned in s.469.

515. (1) Subject to this section, where an accused who is charged with an offence other than an offence listed in section 427 is taken before a justice, the justice shall, unless a plea of guilty by the accused is accepted, order, in respect of that offence, that the accused be released upon his giving an undertaking without conditions, unless the prosecutor, having been given a reasonable opportunity to do so, shows cause, in respect of that offence, why the detention of the accused in custody is justified or why an order under any other provision of this section should be made and where the justice makes an order under any other provision of this section, the order shall refer only to the particular offence for which the accused was taken before the justice.

(10) For the purposes of this section, the detention of an accused in custody is justified only on either of the following grounds, namely:

(*a*) on the primary ground that his detention is necessary to ensure his attendance in court in order to be dealt with according to law; and

(*b*) on the secondary ground (the applicability of which shall be determined only in the event that and after it is determined that his detention is not justified on the primary ground referred to in paragraph (*a*)) that his detention is necessary in the public interest or for the protection or safety of the public, having regard to all the circumstances including any substantial likelihood that the accused will, if he is released from custody, commit a criminal offence or an interference with the administration of justice.

ORDER DIRECTING MATTERS NOT TO BE PUBLISHED FOR SPECIFIED PERIOD — Failure to comply — ''Newspaper''.

517. (1) Where the prosecutor or the accused intends to show cause under section 515, he shall so state to the justice and the justice may, and shall upon application by the accused, before or at any time during the course of the proceedings under that section, make an order directing that the evidence taken, the information given or the representations made and the reasons, if any, given or to be given by the justice shall not be published in any newspaper or broadcast before such time as

(*a*) if a preliminary inquiry is held, the accused in respect of whom the proceedings are held is discharged, or

(*b*) if the accused in respect of whom the proceedings are held is tried or ordered to stand trial, the trial is ended.

(2) Every one who fails without lawful excuse, the proof of which lies upon him, to comply with an order made under subsection (1) is guilty of an offence punishable on summary conviction.

(3) In this section, ''newspaper'' has the same meaning as it has in section 297.

Note: The validity of this provision was upheld by the Ontario Court of Appeal in *Re Smith* (1984), 38 C.R. (3d) 209.

THORSON, J.A. observed at p. 228:

...The right to a fair trial is a fragile right. It is quite capable of being shattered by the kind of publicity that can attend a bail hearing and, once shattered, it may, like Humpty Dumpty, be quite impossible to put back together again. Often the proceedings at a bail hearing do not attract any particular media notice, but when they do, as they have in this case, the risk of prejudice to the accused in the matter of his or her subsequent trial can be severe, in the absence of a mechanism such as that provided in s.457.2(1) for minimizing that prejudice by means of a time-limited restraint on what can be published or broadcast about the hearing. In my opinion it is no answer at all that the need for such a mechanism might be avoided if only our legal system were otherwise and adopted a different approach altogether to the safeguarding of a fair trial for the accused. As has been said in other words elsewhere by this court, ultimately our courts must come back to our own free and democratic society in applying the test in this regard which s.1 of the Charter requires us to apply.

3.5.2.5 Jury Trials

3.5.2.5.1 Criminal Code, ss.648, 649

RESTRICTION ON PUBLICATION — Offence — "Newspaper".

648. (1) Where permission to separate is given to members of a jury under subsection 647(1), no information regarding any portion of the trial at which the jury is not present shall be published, after the permission is granted, in any newspaper or broadcast before the jury retires to consider its verdict.

(2) Every one who fails to comply with subsection (1) is guilty of an offence punishable on summary conviction.

(3) In this section, "newspaper" has the same meaning as it has in section 297.

Note: See *Toronto Sun* v. *A.G. Alberta* (1985), 39 Alta. L.R. 97, where a ban on publishing evidence given in a voir dire was held, because of the special circumstances of the case to extend beyond the completion of the trial.

DISCLOSURE OF JURY PROCEEDINGS.

649. Every member of a jury who, except for the purpose of

(*a*) an investigation of an alleged offence under subsection 127(2) in relation to a juror, or

(*b*) giving evidence in criminal proceedings in relation to such an offence,

discloses any information relating to the proceedings of the jury when it was absent from the courtroom that was not subsequently disclosed in open court is guilty of an offence punishable on summary conviction. 1972, c.13, s.49.

Note: The main source for reporters covering a trial is the lawyers involved. In its *Communique* dated March 22 and 23, 1984, the Law Society of Upper Canada stated that : "The Society has received complaints from the judiciary and others concerning the growing frequency of press interviews by counsel involved in court proceedings and shares this concern. The profession is reminded of the language of Commentary 18(a) to Rule 13 of the Rules of Professional Conduct and should be aware that any interview with the media about court proceedings invites the inference that it was given to publicize the lawyer and carries the danger of being a contempt of court. The Society intends to institute discipline proceedings where appropriate to ensure that the rule is observed." The Supreme Court of Ontario invalidated this restriction in *Re Klein and Law Society of Upper Canada; Re Dvorak and Law Society of Upper Canada* (1985), 50 O.R. (2d) 118.

3.5.3 Common Law Sub Judice

3.5.3.1 *Attorney-General* v. *Times Newspapers Ltd.* [1973] 3 All E.R. 54 (H.L.)

LORD REID. My Lords, in 1958 Distillers Co. (Biochemicals) Ltd. began to make and sell in this country a sedative which contained a drug thalidomide which had been invented and used in Germany. This product was available on prescription and was consumed by many pregnant women having been said to be quite safe for them. But soon there were cases of babies being born with terrible deformities. As such deformities do occasionally occur naturally, it took a little time to prove that these deformities were caused by the action of thalidomide in the unborn child at a certain stage of pregnancy. As soon as this was realised Distillers withdrew their product in 1961.

The matter attracted some publicity and the question arose whether Distillers were legally liable to pay damages in respect of these deformed children. Distillers denied liability and the first action against them was begun in 1962. Further publicity resulted in some 70 actions having been raised before 1968.

Claimants were faced by two difficulties. First there was a highly debatable legal question whether a person can sue for damage done to him before his birth. And secondly, an attempt to prove negligence by Distillers in putting this drug on the market would require long and expensive enquiries. The claimants combined to negotiate with Distillers and early in 1968 a settlement was reached by which Distillers agreed to pay to each claimant 40 per cent of the damages which he or she would recover if successful in establishing liability. Regarded from a purely legal point of view this appears to have been a very reasonable compromise.

Two cases were then tried by agreement to establish the proper measure of damages and ultimately 65 cases were settled, Distillers paying about a million pounds in all. But more cases gradually came to light. Leave to serve writs was now necessary and the first orders granting leave were made in July 1968. By February 1969, 248 writs had been served. A few more followed. And there were many cases where claims had been made but no writs served. It may be that there are still some cases where claims will be made. In all there appear to be more than 400 outstanding claims not covered by the 1968 settlement.

Distillers proposed to settle these claims by setting up a trust fund of over £3 million. But they made it a condition of any settlement that all claimants should agree to accept it. The great majority agreed but five refused to do so. One parent at least refused because payments out of the trust fund were to be based on need, and his financial position was such that his child would get no benefit from such a settlement.

An attempt was made to compel these five to agree by having the Official Solicitor appointed to look after the interests of their children. But the Court of Appeal, in April 1972, reinstated these five parents *(Re Taylor's Application)*. In June 1972 Distillers made some new proposals but they were not accepted. There were then 389 claims outstanding and there seemed little prospect of an early settlement.

The editor of the Sunday Times took a keen interest in this matter. He collected a great deal of material and on 24th September 1972 that newspaper published a long and powerful article. Two general propositions were argued at some length: first whether those who put such drugs on the market ought to be absolutely liable for damage done by them, and secondly that in such cases the currently accepted method of assessing damages is inadequate. But the sting of the article lay in the following paragraph:

> 'Thirdly, the thalidomide children shame Distillers. It is appreciated that Distillers have always denied negligence and that if the cases were pursued, the children might end up with nothing. It is appreciated that Distillers' lawyers have a professional duty to secure the best terms for their clients. But at the end of the day what is to be paid in settlement is the decision of Distillers, and they should offer much, much more to every one of the thalidomide victims. It may be argued that Distillers have a duty to their shareholders and that, having taken

account of skilled legal advice, the terms are just. But the law is not always the same as justice. There are times when to insist on the letter of the law is as exposed to criticism as infringement of another's legal rights. The figure in the proposed settlement is to be £3.25m., spread over 10 years. This does not shine as a beacon against pre-tax profits last year of £64.8 million and company assets worth £421 million. Without in any way surrendering on negligence, Distillers could and should think again.'

Distillers immediately brought this to the attention of the Attorney-General maintaining that it was in contempt of court. The Attorney-General decided to take no action. But this did not in any way prevent Distillers from bringing the matter before the court if they chose to do so. However they took no action.

I agree with your Lordships that the Attorney-General has a right to bring before the court any matter which he thinks may amount to contempt of court and which he considers should in the public interest be brought before the court. The party aggrieved has the right to bring before the court any matter which he alleges amounts to contempt but he has no duty to do so. So if the party aggrieved failed to take action either because of expense or because he thought it better not to do so, very serious contempt might escape punishment if the Attorney-General had no right to act. But the Attorney-General is not obliged to bring before the court every prima facie case of contempt reported to him. It is entirely for him to judge whether it is in the public interest that he should act.

The editor of the Sunday Times had in mind to publish a further article of a different character. As a result of communications between him and the Attorney-General regarding the article of 24th September, he sent the material for the further article to the learned attorney and this time the Attorney-General took the view that he should intervene. By a writ of 12th October 1972 he claimed an injunction against the respondents, who own the Sunday Times, restraining them from publishing the proposed article. The Divisional Court granted an injunction but the Court of Appeal on 16th February 1973 discharged the injunction. The Attorney-General now appeals to this House.

Before dealing with the arguments submitted to your Lordships I find it necessary to set out some general considerations which must govern the whole subject of contempt of court. It appears never to have come before this House; there is no recent review of the subject in the Court of Appeal; and the circumstances of cases which arise in practice are generally not such as to require any detailed analysis of the law. I cannot disagree with a statement in a recent report of Justice on the Law and the Press that the main objection to the existing law of contempt is its uncertainty. I think that we must try to remove that reproach at least with regard to those parts of the law with which the present case is concerned.

The law on this subject is and must be founded entirely on public policy. It is not there to protect the private rights of parties to a litigation or prosecution. It is there to prevent interference with the administration of justice and it should in my judgment be limited to what is reasonably necessary for that purpose. Public policy generally requires a balancing of interests which may conflict. Freedom of speech should not be limited to any greater extent than is necessary but it cannot be allowed where there would be real prejudice to the administration of justice.

In *Ambard v. Attorney-General for Trinidad and Tobago* Lord Atkin said:

'But whether the authority and position of an individual judge or the due administration of justice is concerned, no wrong is committed by any member of the public who exercises

> the ordinary right of criticising in good faith in private or public, the public act done in the seat of justice. The path of criticism is a public way: the wrong headed are permitted to err therein: provided that members of the public abstain from imputing improper motives to those taking part in the administration of justice, and are genuinely exercising a right of criticism and not acting in malice or attempting to impair the administration of justice, they are immune. Justice is not a cloistered virtue: she must be allowed to suffer the scrutiny and respectful even though outspoken comments of ordinary men.'

I think that these words have an application beyond the particular type of contempt in that case.

Discussion of questions of contempt generally begin with the observations of Lord Hardwicke L.C. in *The St. James's Evening Post Case*. Dealing with a case where there had been gross abuse of litigants he said:

> 'Nothing is more incumbent upon courts of justice, than to preserve their proceedings from being misrepresented; nor is there any thing of more pernicious consequence, than to prejudice the minds of the publick against persons concerned as parties in causes, before the cause is finally heard.'

And later:

> 'There are three different sorts of contempt. One kind of contempt is, scandalizing the court itself. There may be likewise a contempt of this court, in abusing parties who are concerned in causes here. There may be also a contempt of this court, in prejudicing mankind against persons before the cause is heard. There cannot be any thing of greater consequence, than to keep the streams of justice clear and pure, that parties may proceed with safety both to themselves and their characters.'

I do not think that Lord Hardwicke L.C. intended this to be a universally applicable definition, although it has too often been treated as if it were. It is a good guide but it must be supplemented in cases of a type which he did not have in mind.

We are particularly concerned here with 'abusing parties' and 'prejudicing mankind' against them. Of course parties must be protected from scurrilous abuse; otherwise many litigants would fear to bring their cases to court. But the argument of the Attorney-General goes far beyond that. His argument was based on a passage in the judgment of Buckley J. in *Vine Products Ltd. v. Mackenzie & Co. Ltd.*:

> 'It is a contempt of this court for any newspaper to comment on pending legal proceedings in any way which is likely to prejudice the fair trial of the action. That may arise in various ways. It may be that the comment is likely in some way or other to bring pressure to bear on one or other of the parties to the action, so as to prevent that party from prosecuting or from defending the action, or encourage him to submit to terms of compromise which he otherwise might not have been prepared to entertain, or influence him in some other way in his conduct in the action, which he ought to be free to prosecute or to defend, as he is advised, without being subject to such pressure.'

I think that this is much too widely stated. It is true that there is some authority for it but it does not in the least follow from the observations of Lord Hardwicke L.C. and it does not seem to me to be in accord with sound public policy. Why would it be contrary to public policy to seek by fair comment to dissuade Shylock from proceeding with his action? Surely it could not be wrong for the officious bystander to draw his attention to the risk that, if he goes on, decent people will cease to trade with him. Or suppose that his best customer ceased to trade with him when he heard of his lawsuit. That could not be contempt of court. Would it become contempt if, when asked by Shylock why he was sending no more business his way, he told him the reason? Nothing would be more likely to influence Shylock to discontinue his action. It might become widely known that such pressure was being brought to bear. Would that make any difference? And though widely known must the local press keep silent about it? There must be some limitation of this general statement of the law.

And then suppose that there is in the press and elsewhere active discussion of some question of wide public interest, such as the propriety of local authorities or other landlords ejecting squatters from empty premises due for demolition. Then legal proceedings are begun against some squatters, it may be by some authority which had already been criticised in the press. The controversy could hardly be continued without likelihood that it might influence the authority in its conduct of the action. Must there then be silence until that case is decided? And there may be a series of actions by the same or different landlords. Surely public policy does not require that a system of stop and go shall apply to public discussion.

I think that there is a difference between direct interference with the fair trial of an action and words or conduct which may affect the minds of a litigant. Comment likely to affect the minds of witnesses and of the tribunal must be stopped for otherwise the trial may well be unfair. But the fact that a party refrains from seeking to enforce his full legal rights in no way prejudices a fair trial whether the decision is or is not influenced by some third party. There are other weighty reasons for preventing improper influence being brought to bear on litigants, but they have little to do with interference with the fairness of a trial. There must be absolute prohibition of interference with a fair trial but beyond that there must be a balancing of relevant considerations.

I know of no better statement of the law than that contained in the judgment of Jordan C.J. in *Re Truth and Sportsman Ltd., ex parte Bread Manufacturers Ltd.*:

> 'It is of extreme public interest that no conduct should be permitted which is likely to prevent a litigant in a court of justice from having his case tried free from all matter of prejudice. But the administration of justice, important though it undoubtedly is, is not the only matter in which the public is vitally interested; and if in the course of the ventilation of a question of public concern matter is published which may prejudice a party in the conduct of a law suit, it does not follow that a contempt has been committed. The case may be one in which as between competing matters of public interest the possibility of prejudice to a litigant may be required to yield to other and superior considerations. The discussion of public affairs and the denunciation of public abuses, actual or supposed, cannot be required to be suspended merely because the discussion or the denunciation may, as an incidental but not intended by-product, cause some likelihood of prejudice to a person who happens at the time to be a litigant. It is well settled that a person cannot be prevented by process of contempt from continuing to discuss publicly a matter which may fairly be regarded as one of public interest, by reason merely of the fact that the matter in question has become the subject of litigation, or that person whose conduct is being publicly criticised has become a party to litigation either as plaintiff or as defendant, and whether in relation to the matter which is under discussion or with respect to some other matter.'

Guidance with regard to the dividing line between comment about a litigant which is permissible and that which involves contempt, is to be found in the judgment of Maugham J. in *Re William Thomas Shipping Co. Ltd.* The company had suffered severely from the prevailing depression and debenture holders sought liquidation. Sir Robert Thomas, the governing director, gave a statement to a Liverpool newspaper which it published. The debenture holders sought an order on the ground that the statement was in contempt of court. Maugham J. rejected an argument that the statement might influence the judge dealing with the proceedings for liquidation. But he went on to consider whether it is a contempt 'to abuse the parties concerned in a pending case or matter by injurious misrepresentations'. He held that there was contempt for that reason but added:

> 'I am not saying that if Sir Robert Thomas had fairly stated the result of the evidence on which the Court made the order for the appointment of a receiver and manager, and had in a temperate manner expressed his opinion that another course ought to have been taken by the plaintiff, the Court would have thought fit to interfere or could properly have interfered.'

So the dividing line there drawn was between comment containing injurious misrepresentation which was contempt and fair and temperate criticism which would not have been. That is emphasised by the last paragraph of his judgment where he deals with the newspaper. Their fault was that they were in too much of a hurry and published a statement of a most misleading character. I must follow that Maugham J. thought that if a newspaper published fair and temperate criticism of a litigant, it is in general entitled to do so.

I would compare with that case the decision of Talbot and Macnaghten JJ. in *Re South Shields (Thames Street) Clearance Order 1931*. The corporation had made a clearance order and the owners of property affected by it had taken the matter before the court. An article was published suggesting that the owners by their appeal were keeping the tenants out of new houses and hindering the progress of housing in the borough. The owners contended that this was contempt of court as tending to deter them and others from coming before the court. They relied on the *William Thomas Shipping Co.* case. But it was held that this would be an extension of the law of contempt beyond anything that could justify it. No reasons are given in the very brief report of the case but I think that the ground of judgment must have been that the article complained of did not go beyond fair and temperate comment on the owners' action. If the argument of the Attorney-General in the present case were right, I think that the case would have been wrongly decided. But it appears to me to have been rightly decided.

So I would hold that as a general rule where the only matter to be considered is pressure put on a litigant, fair and temperate criticism is legitimate, but anything which goes beyond that may well involve contempt of court. But in a case involving witnesses, jury or magistrates, other considerations are involved: there even fair and temperate criticism might be likely to affect the minds of some of them so as to involve contempt. But it can be assumed that it would not affect the mind of a professional judge.

In some recent cases about influencing litigants the court has accepted the law as stated in the passage from the judgment of Buckley J. in the *Vine Products* case, but has held that there is no contempt unless there is a serious risk that the litigant will be influenced. Perhaps this was an attempt to mitigate the extreme consequences of that view of the law, but I think this test is most unsatisfactory. First, when considering whether the risk is serious do you consider the particular litigant so that what would be contempt if he is easily influenced would not be contempt if the particular litigant is so strong minded as not to be easily influenced? That would not seem right but if you have to imagine a reasonable man in the shoes of that litigant the test becomes rather unreal. And then are you to take that one comment alone or are you to consider the cumulative effect if others are free to say and probably will say the same kind of thing?

I think that this view of the law caused the court to give wrong reasons for reaching a correct decision in *Attorney-General v. London Weekend Television*. The respondent company had produced a television programme about the thalidomide tragedy on 8th October 1972. So far as I can judge from the report it seems to have had much the same object and character as the Sunday Times article of 24th September. If the view which I take about that article is correct then I think that for similar reasons the television programme was not in contempt of court.

But the court, following the judgment of the Divisional Court in the present case, held that the programme 'bore many of the badges of contempt' and only dismissed the application on the ground that they were unable to say that the programme 'would result in the creation of a *serious* [their italics] risk' that the course of justice would be interfered with. They had said earlier 'We find that the spoken words on this programme did not have that impact which the producer might have hoped that they would have had on the viewers'. So the company only escaped because of their inefficiency. I cannot believe that the law could be left in such an unsatisfactory state.

I think, agreeing with Cotton L.J. in his judgment in *Hunt v. Clarke,* that there must be two questions: first, was there any contempt at all? and, secondly, was it sufficiently serious to require or justify the court in making an order against the respondent? The question whether there was a serious risk of influencing the litigant is certainly a factor to be considered in what course to take by way of punishment, as is the intention with which the comment was made. But it is I think confusing to import this into the question whether there was any contempt at all or into the definition of contempt.

I think the true view is that expressed by Lord Parker C.J. in *R. v. Duffy, ex parte Nash,* that there must be 'a real risk as opposed to a remote possibility'. That is an application of the ordinary de minimis principle. There is no contempt if the possibility of influence is remote. If there is some but only a small likelihood, that may influence the court to refrain from inflicting any punishment. If there is a serious risk some action may be necessary. And I think that the particular comment cannot be considered in isolation when considering its probable effect. If others are to be free and are likely to make similar comments that must be taken into account.

The crucial question on this point of the case is whether it can ever be permissible to urge a party to a litigation to forego his legal rights in whole or in part. The Attorney-General argues that it cannot and I think that the Divisional Court has accepted that view. In my view it is permissible so long as it is done in a fair and temperate way and without any oblique motive. The Sunday Times article of 24th September 1972 affords a good illustration of the difference between the two views. It is plainly intended to bring pressure to bear on Distillers. It was likely to attract support from others and it did so. It was outspoken. It said 'There are times when to insist on the letter of the law is as exposed to criticism as infringement of another's legal rights' and clearly implied that that was such a time. If the view maintained by the Attorney-General were right I could hardly imagine a clearer case of contempt of court. It could be no excuse that the passage which I quoted earlier was combined with a great deal of other totally unobjectionable material. And it could not be said that it created no serious risk of causing Distillers to do what they did not want to do. On the facts submitted to your Lordships in argument it seems to me to have played a large part in causing

Distillers to offer far more money than they had in mind at that time. But I am quite unable to subscribe to the view that it ought never to have been published because it was in contempt of court. I see no offence against public policy and no pollution of the stream of justice by its publication.

Now I must turn to the material to which the injunction applied. If it is not to be published at this time it would not be proper to refer to it in any detail. But I can say that it consists in the main of detailed evidence and argument intended to show that Distillers did not exercise due care to see that thalidomide was safe before they put it on the market.

If we regard this material solely from the point of view of its likely effect on Distillers I do not think that its publication in 1972 would have added much to the pressure on them created, or at least begun, by the earlier article of 24th September. From Distillers' point of view the damage had already been done. I doubt whether the subsequent course of events would have been very different in their effect on Distillers if the matter had been published.

But to my mind there is another consideration even more important than the effect of publication on the mind of the litigant. The controversy about the tragedy of the thalidomide children has ranged widely but as yet there seems to have been little, if any, detailed discussion of the issues which the court may have to determine if the outstanding claims are not settled. The question whether Distillers were negligent has been frequently referred to but so far as I am aware there has been no attempt to assess the evidence. If this material were released now it appears to me to be almost inevitable that detailed answers would be published and there would be expressed various public prejudgments of this issue. That I would regard as very much against the public interest.

There has long been and there still is in this country a strong and generally held feeling that trial by newspaper is wrong and should be prevented. I find for example in the report of Lord Salmon's committee dealing with the law of contempt with regard to Tribunals of Inquiry a reference to the 'horror' in such a thing. What I think is regarded as most objectionable is that a newspaper or television programme should seek to persuade the public, by discussing the issues and evidence in a case before the court, whether civil or criminal, that one side is right and the other wrong. If we were to ask the ordinary man or even a lawyer in his leisure moments why he has that feeling, I suspect that the first reply would be — well look at what happens in some other countries where that is permitted. As in so many other matters, strong feelings are based on one's general experience rather than on specific reasons, and it often requires an effort to marshall one's reasons. But public policy is generally the result of strong feelings, commonly held, rather than of cold argument.

If the law is to be developed in accord with public policy we must not be too legalistic in our general approach. No doubt public policy is an unruly horse to ride but in a chapter of the law so intimately associated with public policy as contempt of court we must not be too pedestrian. It is hardly sufficient to ask what Lord Hardwicke L.C. meant in 1742 when he referred to prejudicing mankind against parties before a cause is heard.

There is ample authority for the proposition that issues must not be prejudged in a manner likely to affect the mind of those who may later be witnesses or jurors. But very little has been said about the wider proposition that trial by newspaper is intrinsically objectionable. That may be because if one can find more limited and familiar grounds adequate for the decision of a case it is rash to venture on uncharted seas.

I think that anything in the nature of prejudgment of a case or of specific issues in it is objectionable not only because of its possible effect on that particular case but also because of its side effects which may be far reaching. Responsible 'mass media' will do their best to be fair, but there will also be ill-informed, slapdash or prejudiced attempts to influence the public. If people are led to think that it is easy to find the truth disrespect for the processes of the law could follow and, if mass media are allowed to judge, unpopular people and unpopular causes will fare very badly. Most cases of prejudging of issues fall within the existing authorities on contempt. I do not think that the freedom of the press would suffer, and I think that the law would be clearer and easier to apply in practice if it is made a general rule that it is not permissible to prejudge issues in pending cases.

In my opinion the law was rather too narrowly stated in *Vine Products Ltd. v. Mackenzie & Co. Ltd.* There the question was what wines could properly be called sherry and a newspaper published an article which clearly prejudged the issue. In my view that was technically in contempt of court. But the fault was so venial and the possible consequences so trifling that it would have been quite wrong to impose punishment or I think even to require the newspaper to pay the costs of the applicant. But the newspaper ought to have withheld its judgment until the case had been decided.

There is no magic in the issue of a writ or in a charge being made against an accused person. Comment on a case which is imminent may be as objectionable as comment after it has begun. And a 'gagging' writ ought to have no effect. But I must add to prevent misunderstanding that comment where a case is under appeal is a very different matter. For one thing it is scarcely possible to imagine a case where comment could influence judges in the Court of Appeal or noble and learned Lords in this House. And it would be wrong and contrary to existing practice to limit proper criticism of judgments already given but under appeal.

Now I must deal with the reasons which induced the Court of Appeal to discharge the injunction. It was said that the actions had been dormant or asleep for several years. Nothing appears to have been done in court but active negotiations for a settlement were going on all the time. No one denies that it would be contempt of court to use improper pressure to induce a litigant to settle a case on terms to which he did not wish to agree. So if there is no undue procrastination in the negotiations for a settlement I do not see how in this context action can be said to be dormant.

Then it was said that there is here a public interest which counterbalances the private interests of the litigants. But contempt of court has nothing to do with the private interests of the litigants. I have already indicated the way in which I think that a balance must be struck between the public interest in freedom of speech and the public interest in protecting the administration of justice from interference. I do not see why there should be any difference in principle between a case which is thought to have news value and one which is not. Protection of the administration of justice is equally important whether or not the case involves important general issues.

Some reference was made to the debate in the House of Commons. It was not extensively referred to in argument. But so far as I have noticed there was little said in the House which could not have been said outside if my view of the law is right.

If we were only concerned with the effect which publication of the new material might now have on the mind of Distillers I might be able to agree with the decision of the Court of Appeal though for different reasons. But I have already stated my view that wider considerations are involved. The purpose of the law is not to prevent publication of such material but to postpone it. The information set before us gives us hope that the general lines of a settlement of the whole of this unfortunate controversy may soon emerge. It should then be possible to permit this material to be published. But if things drag on indefinitely so that there is no early prospect either of a settlement or of a trial in court then I think that there will have to be a wakenment of the public interest in a unique situation.

As matters stand at present I think that this appeal must be allowed.

3.5.3.2 *Zehr* v. *McIsaac et al.* (1982) 39 O.R. (2d) 237 (Ont. H.C.)

O'DRISCOLL J.: —

I Type of application

The applicant seeks a conviction and committal against each person named as a respondent and a conviction and fine as against the corporate respondent as the result of an article published on p. 5 of the newspaper *The Globe and Mail* on Tuesday, February 9, 1982. It is alleged that McIsaac was the author of the contemptuous statements which were reported by Makin and his editor-in-chief, Doyle, and published by the corporate respondent.

The application fails as against all respondents.

II History

1. Steven Wayne Zehr, the applicant, was charged with raping a female "X" at the City of Barrie on November 14, 1978. He was tried at the Barrie Assizes by Callon J. and a jury and convicted.

2. Zehr launched an appeal from his conviction to the Ontario Court of Appeal. On June 23, 1980, that court (Howland C.J.O., Brooke and Thorson JJ.A.), quashed the conviction and ordered a new trial: 54 C.C.C. (2d) 65.

3. On March 2, 1981, the Attorney-General for Ontario preferred a two count indictment against Zehr:

(1) that Zehr raped a female "X" at the City of Barrie on November 14, 1978, and
(2) that Zehr raped a female "Y" at the City of Barrie on October 6, 1980.

4. On March 24, 1981, Labrosse J. ordered that Zehr be tried separately on each count and traversed the trial to the next sittings at Barrie, Ontario.

5. On May 25, 1981, at the new trial at the Barrie Assizes conducted by Grange J. with a jury, Zehr was arraigned on count No. 1 — that he did rape the female "X" at the City of Barrie on November 14, 1978; Zehr pleaded not guilty; the trial proceeded and on June 11, 1981, the jury rendered a verdict of "not guilty" on count No. 1. The Crown did not appeal the verdict of not guilty rendered at the new trial of count

On June 11, 1981, Grange J. ordered that count No. 2 (the charge of rape with regard to female "Y") be traversed to the September Assizes at Barrie, Ontario.

6. On July 13, 1981, Griffiths J. granted Zehr judicial interim release.

7. An order was made for a change of venue from Barrie to Toronto.

8. On September 17, 1981, on consent, a trial date was set for November 30, 1981, with regard to count No. 2.

9. At Toronto, on December 1, 1981, before Craig J. and a jury, Zehr was arraigned on count No. 2 — that he did rape the female "Y" at the City of Barrie on October 6, 1980; Zehr pleaded not guilty and the trial proceeded.

On December 14, 1981, the jury returned a verdict of "guilty as charged" on count No. 2. Zehr was remanded in custody to February 8, 1982, to await sentence.

10. On January 12, 1982, Zehr filed a notice of appeal from his conviction for rape on count No. 2, which appeal is still pending.

11. Prior to February 8, 1982, the Crown had served Zehr with notice that it would proceed against him as a dangerous offender under Part XXI of the *Criminal Code,* R.S.C. 1970, c.C-34 (s.688(*b*)).

12. On February 8, 1982, Craig J. heard submissions concerning psychiatric assessments of Zehr; at that time Crown counsel John McIsaac, advised Craig J.:

> You'd also be hearing about a circumstance involving a female by the name of "X". There will be a lengthy argument by my friend in relation to the admissibility of this testimony.

On the same day, February 8, 1982, Craig J., after hearing evidence from Dr. Russell Fleming, further remanded Zehr in custody until March 22, 1982.

13. On February 9, 1982, the article in question appeared in *The Globe and Mail* on p. 5:

FED UP WITH DECIDING ON CONFINING CRIMINALS INDEFINITELY, MD SAYS

by KIRK MAKIN

A director at the Penetanguishene Mental Health Centre says he is fed up with being asked to decide whether criminals should be designated dangerous offenders and thus incarcerated indefinitely.

The courts should stop foisting the question on psychiatrists and instead make the dangerous offender designation automatic if a crime is repeated a certain number of times, said Russell Fleming, director of the centre's forensic science unit.

The designation is seldom used but carries serious consequences. If a person is designated a dangerous offender, he is incarcerated indefinitely in a penal or mental institution and is on mandatory supervision for the rest of his life if he is released.

"It's like a life sentence," Dr. Fleming said in an interview yesterday. "Potentially, they can be kept forever."

He said his unit is asked to assess four or five candidates for dangerous offender status every year. The National Parole Board first reviews dangerous offenders after three years and every two years after that.

The courts "shouldn't ask us to get involved in this adversarial nonsense where a Crown attorney shops around for a right-wing psychiatrist to say the man should go (to an institution), while the defence shops around for a left-wing psychiatrist to say he shouldn't," Dr. Fleming said.

"I've never said this in court, but frankly I feel it's never a palatable experience," he said. "You have to make a decision on whether someone is or is not going to do it again. It makes much more sense to hinge it on something reasonable, like the number of previous convictions.

"You could devise a system where you get one free rape with a sentence of two years less a day at the most, a five-year penitentiary term for the second rape and dangerous offender status after the third."

Robert Ash, a Crown attorney in the Judicial District of York, said in an interview that he "can appreciate Dr. Fleming's frustration," but his office must retain psychiatrists to testify about the sanity of accused people in order to get a neutral opinion.

"There are psychiatrists who can be retained by defence counsel who will pretty well say whatever the defence wants them to say. We have to check to see exactly what's happening."

Jerry Cooper, a psychiatrist who often appears as a defence witness, said Dr. Fleming's reference to shopping around for psychiatrists is silly.

"I don't know of any psychiatrist so desperate he has to hire out.... If a defence lawyer gets an opinion adverse to his case, why should he just take my opinion?

"We just give out opinions and the lawyer decides. If a neurosurgeon said he had to open your head up, wouldn't you get a second opinion? I can be wrong, you know. Dr. Fleming can be wrong, too. We're not gods."

He said it would be destructive to justice if psychiatrists could not testify in dangerous-offender applications. "It's a sentence that's worse than life imprisonment. There are guys who were put there 15 years ago who are still there."

Dr. Fleming's remarks came after he testified in the Supreme Court of Ontario concerning a Crown application to have a convicted rapist designated a dangerous offender.

A 24-year-old man with a long record of breaking and entering was convicted in December of raping a woman while holding a knife to her throat.

He had one previous rape conviction, but the Ontario Court of Appeal ordered another trial at which the man was found not guilty.

"We and the police are satisfied he has done it twice anyway," John McIsaac, the Crown attorney handling the case, said in an interview. Persuading the judge hearing the dangerous-offender application that the man could commit another rape will be tough because of the successful appeal, he said. "But I'm going to try and revive it.

"Fortunately for the victims, they went along with him when he produced the knife. But if the next lady panics, we'll be investigating a murder, not a rape."

Dr. Fleming testified that his unit could not conduct a psychiatric assessment of the man now because it is filled to capacity. "There's simply too much at stake to do it in a hurry."

14. On March 22, 1982, Zehr was further remanded to May 10, 1982, on the dangerous offender application.

15. On May 10, 1982, at Toronto, the dangerous offender application commenced before Craig J. Crown counsel filed what was marked before me as ex. No. 3 (Crown submission on the admissibility of evidence) and submitted that on the Part XXI application, the Crown should be allowed to introduce the evidence it called at the trial of Zehr when it alleged that he raped the female "X" although the jury had acquitted Zehr of that offence (count No. 1).

16. On May 11, 1982, Craig J. ruled that the proposed evidence regarding female "X" on Count No. 1 was inadmissible (ex. No. 4).

17. On May 17, 1982, Craig J. dismissed the Crown's application under Part XXI, s.688(*b*) of the *Criminal Code;* on the same date Craig J. sentenced Zehr to five years on the conviction of rape on count No. 2 of the indictment and ordered a five-year prohibition under s.98(1) [rep. & sub. 1976-77, c.53, s.3] of the *Criminal Code*.

IV The case against Makin, Doyle and the publisher, the corporate defendant

Counsel for these respondents admits that Makin was the newspaper reporter, Doyle the editor-in-chief of "The Globe and Mail" and that the corporate defendant was the publisher of the article.

At the request of counsel for the Attorney-General and over the objections of counsel for the applicant, I permitted four exhibits to be filed by counsel for the Attorney General:

(a) Exhibit No. 1 — a certified copy of the two count indictment against Zehr preferred by the Attorney-General of Ontario;

(b) Exhibit No. 2 — a partial transcript of submissions made to Craig J. on February 8, 1982;
(c) Exhibit No. 3 — Crown submissions filed before Craig J. on May 10, 1982;
(d) Exhibit No. 4 — Craig J.'s ruling regarding the proposed evidence on the dangerous offender application that concerned count No. 1 in the indictment.

Counsel for the newspaper respondents submits that the article in question is not a contempt of court because:

1. the article in question does not name Zehr either directly or indirectly;
2. the article was published on February 9, 1982; the dangerous offender hearing was held on May 10, 1982, some three months later;
3. the *Criminal Code* required that Craig J., and he alone, be the judge to hear the Part XXI, s.688(*b*) application because Craig J. had been the trial judge on the trial of count No. 2.
4. The most appropriate forum for this motion was before Craig J. at the opening of the Part XXI, s.688(*b*) application. No such application was made to Craig J., the only person who could possibly have been prejudiced by the article in question.
5. On May 10, 1982, Craig J. heard the Crown's allegations that Zehr raped the female "X" — indeed the Crown's written submissions, ex. No. 3, deal exclusively with those allegations.
6. The article in question appeared on p. 5 of *The Globe and Mail;* the portions of the article that are attacked are the 16th, 17th, 18th and 19th paras. of a 20-para. article.
7. There is no allegation that any of these respondents intended to subvert the course of justice.

V. What is the test, what are the rules against which the impugned article is to be measured?

(i) *R. v. Payne and Cooper,* [1896] 1 Q.B. 577, 74 L.T. 351 at 352, *per* Lord Russell C.J.:

> That this summary power is most salutary no one can doubt, and it is a power which the court will not hesitate to use where there is any attempt to interfere with the administration of justice. But it is an arbitrary power, and, therefore, it ought to be used only in cases where the needs of justice call for its exercise. The learned counsel seems to think that every libel upon a person under trial is a contempt, but this is not necessarily so. To justify the exercise of this summary power something must have been published which was intended or clearly calculated to prejudice the fair trial of the charge or action.

per Wright J. [at p. 353 L.T.]:

> I agree entirely in what the Lord Chief Justice has said. As is pointed out by Cotton, L.J., in *Re O'Malley, Hunt v. Clarke* (1889), 61 L.T. 343, in all cases of this kind there are two questions involved. The first is: Is the publication of such a nature as to be calculated to interfere with a fair trial? If it is not so calculated, we have nothing to do with it. But even if it is calculated to interfere with a fair trial there is a second question. Is it a proper case for such an application? The rule laid down in *Re O'Malley, Hunt v. Clarke* (supra) for answering this is that such an application should not be made except in serious cases.

(ii) *R. v. Duffy et al.; Ex parte Nash,* [1960] 2 Q.B. 188, [1960] 2 All E.R. 891, Lord Parker C.J. at p. 896 All E.R.:

The question always is whether a judge would be so influenced by the article that his impartiality might well be consciously, or even unconsciously, affected. In other words, was there a real risk, as opposed to a remote possibility, that the article was calculated to prejudice a fair hearing?

(iii) *A.-G. v. Times Newspapers Ltd.*, [1974] A.C. 273, [1973] 3 All E.R. 54 at 63-64 (H.L.) *per* Lord Reid:

I think agreeing with Cotton L.J. in his judgment in *Hunt v. Clarke* (1889), 58 L.J.Q.B. 490, that there must be two questions: first, was there any contempt at all? and secondly, was it sufficiently serious to require or justify the court in making an order against the respondent? The question whether there was a serious risk of influencing the litigant is certainly a factor to be considered in what course to take by way of punishment, as is the intention with which the comment was made. But it is I think confusing to import this into the question whether there was any contempt at all or into the definition of contempt.

I think the true view is that expressed by Lord Parker C.J. in *R. v. Duffy, ex parte Nash,* [1960] 2 All E.R. 891 at 896, [1960] 2 Q.B. 188 at 200, that there must be "a real risk as opposed to a remote possibility". That is an application of the ordinary de minimis principle. There is no contempt if the possibility of influence is remote. If there is some but only a small likelihood, that may influence the court to refrain from inflicting any punishment. If there is a serious risk some action may be necessary. And I think that the particular comment cannot be considered in isolation when considering its probable effect. If others are to be free and are likely to make similar comments that must be taken into account.

(iv) *Meriden Britannia Co. Ltd. v. Walters* (1915), 34 O.L.R. 518 at 521, 25 D.L.R. 167, 24 C.C.C. 364, *per* Boyd C.:

The apprehension of detriment must be of a tangible character, plainly tending to obstruct or prejudice the due administration of justice in the particular case pending. Regard must be had to all the surrounding circumstances: the manner of trial, the time of publication, the causes leading to the publication, and the tenour of what is published.

(v) *R. v. Duffy, per* Lord Parker C.J. pp. 894-95 All E.R.:

In the present case there is no suggestion of any such intention, and the sole question is whether the article when published on May 10 was in all the circumstances calculated to interfere or calculated really to interfere with the hearing of the appeal, should one be brought. Looking at it in that way and in the absence of authority, we should have thought that the answer was plainly: "No". Even if a judge who eventually sat on the appeal had seen the article in question and had remembered its contents, it is inconceivable that he would be influenced consciously or unconsciously by it. A judge is in a very different position to a juryman. Though in no sense superhuman, he has by his training no difficulty in putting out of his mind matters which are not evidence in the case. This indeed happens daily to judges on Assize. This is all the more so in the case of a member of the Court of Criminal Appeal...

(vi) *Re Depoe et al. and Lamport et al.*, [1968] 1 O.R. 185, 66 D.L.R. (2d) 46, [1968] 2 C.C.C. 209 at 213, (H.C.J.).

The defendant Lamport was then a controller of the City of Toronto; on the day after the arrest of certain "hippies" he expressed his hope to the press that the courts would treat those people seriously on their charges of disturbing the peace.

Per Donohue J. at p. 189 O.R.:

The statements taken at their worst imply an assumption of the guilt of the accused and an attempt on the part of Mr. Lamport to prescribe a certain punishment for the offence.

It is to be remembered that the alleged offences will be tried not by juries but necessarily by a Magistrate. The Magistrates are professional Judges and I cannot conceive that any of them would be affected by Mr. Lamport's opinion as to the guilt of the accused. Likewise, in the matter of punishment for the offence it is inconceivable that Mr. Lamport's views would exert the slightest influence.

VI Conclusions

When I consider the type and tenor of the article, the lead on the article, the position of the article in the newspaper (p. 5), the absence of Zehr's name from the article, the absence of any sensationalism in connection with the article, the date of the article in relation to the date of the hearing, the fact that only one person, Craig J., was qualified to hear the proposed application under s.688(*b*) of the *Criminal Code,* that in court on May 10, 1982, Craig J. heard that Zehr had been charged, convicted and on a new trial had been found not guilty of the rape of the female "X", and considering the fact that Craig J. would have seen the two-count indictment as of the date of arraignment on December 1, 1981, I am led to the inevitable conclusion that "no judge would be so influenced by the article that his impartiality might be consciously or even unconsciously affected"; there was no real risk that the article was calculated to prejudice a fair hearing.

VII Result

The application is dismissed as against Makin, Doyle and the corporate defendant.

3.5.3.3 *Regina* v. *CHEK TV Ltd.* (1985) 23 C.C.C. (3d) 395 (B.C.S.C.)

McKenzie J.: — The Attorney-General, on behalf of Her Majesty the Queen, asks that the respondent television station be found guilty of criminal contempt of the court for broadcasting a news segment at 5:30 p.m. and repeating it at 11:20 p.m. on March 7, 1985. On that date I was presiding at Nanaimo with a jury over a first-degree murder trial of three accused, one of whom was Rodney Camphaug. Nanaimo is a "prime target audience" of the station which transmits from Victoria.

I heard the contempt petition at the specific request of both counsel because of my knowledge of the full circumstances.

The trial ran from January 14, 1985, with minor adjournments to April 26, 1985, when the jury found all three guilty as charged and each was sentenced to life imprisonment without eligibility for parole for 25 years. It lasted longer than any other British Columbia murder trial, so far as anyone can recall, and it was of a sensational kind involving underworld figures inhabiting a bizarre world of drugs and violence. Security measures at the courthouse were extraordinary with armed police standing inside and out, with questions asked at the court-room door and a metal detector used before spectators were allowed in. The three accused were brought each day from a prison in Victoria by a convoy of police vehicles and returned there each night.

The press in Nanaimo, Victoria and Vancouver gave the trial extensive coverage as did radio and television stations.

On March 7, 1985, the respondent station reported the trial happenings of the day in which Camphaug played a prominent role. His usual conduct in court was often highly aggressive and abusive of the judge, Crown counsel and the witnesses testifying for the Crown which included a number of men and women of disreputable character who had associated in one way or another, in and out of jail, with one or more of the accused. Many of these witnesses, for their own protection, were secreted away by the R.C.M.P. in unrevealed locations.

After giving its account of the day's trial happenings through a narrator who attended the trial the segment went on to display archival tape made five months before at the Victoria prison where at that time Camphaug had taken three guards hostage and had wounded one with a pistol shot. Camphaug was shown in a coloured sketch with pistol in hand and the wounded guard on the floor.

When the original broadcast about the hostage-taking was made in early October, 1984, the narrator said Camphaug "shot one prison guard and took two others hostage". When the film was run again on March 7, 1985, this statement was adjusted to "one of the guards was shot". This retreat to the passive was consciously made to avoid direct identification of Camphaug as the perpetrator. Despite this device the context of the episode as depicted and described left no doubt as to whose finger was on the trigger.

Also interwoven into the news segment on March 7, 1985, was an update on the condition of the injured guard who was recovering from his wound. He was reported as harbouring no resentment toward "the man who shot him". No viewer could possibly nominate anyone but Camphaug as that man.

On March 8, 1985, the day after the three-stories-in-one news broadcast Camphaug moved for a mistrial on the ground that its effect upon the jurors would be so prejudicial to him as to render a fair trial impossible.

The respondent immediately complied with Crown counsel's request for the tape of the impugned broadcast and counsel for the respondent appeared that afternoon when the tape was played and argument heard on the mistrial motion. Next day I delivered reasons for judgment dismissing the motion as follows:

> THE COURT: Well, I do not propose to delay delivering reasons for judgment because there have been mistrials recent or otherwise in Vancouver. Various grounds for mistrials occur all the time, but I have got to decide this motion on its merits.
>
> The accused Camphaug, now defending himself after dismissing his counsel on Thursday, March 7, 1985, the 36th day of the trial, applies on the 38th day of the trial for a mistrial because of a television news broadcast which was transmitted by channel 6, Victoria, CHEK TV, as Vancouver Island News at 5:30 p.m. preceding the CTV Evening News from Vancouver between 6:00 p.m. and 7:00 p.m., and repeated at 11:30 p.m. the same night following the CTV National News.
>
> Reasons for judgment have been given earlier on multiple motions for severance or mistrial from all three accused who are charged jointly with first degree murder.
>
> The impugned broadcast had two segments; the first of which covered the trial events of that day as introduced by the news anchorman and as narrated by a reporter attending this trial. The report was quite extensive and comprehensive, and was accompanied by several colour renderings of various of the trial participants including the jury. The first segment mentions all three of the accused by name.
>
> The court and all participants in the trial have seen the videotape which reproduced both segments of the broadcast; it having been supplied promptly by channel 6 following my request for it as relayed through Crown counsel.

As for the first segment, I thought it superior in its accurate recapitulation of some of the day's events at trial, and Camphaug and counsel for the other two accused have expressed no criticism of the first segment as such.

However, much criticism is levelled by Camphaug and the other two defence counsel at the second segment which immediately followed the first segment, and which deals with conduct attributed to Camphaug five months ago on October 5, 1984, when he was incarcerated at Wilkinson Road Gaol near Victoria awaiting trial on this charge.

The second segment is introduced by the anchorman who defers to a newsman who provides a voice-over for the rest of the segment, which showed some video camera shots combined with renderings of an artist's conception of interior prison scenes.

The following transcript contains the voice-over comments, but does not reproduce the words of the anchorman which were additional to the transcript.

> "Roderick Camphaug is also facing charges stemming from a hostage taking incident at the Wilkinson Road Gaol last fall. One of the guards was shot and seriously injured during the incident. Dan Kroffit has been recuperating from his wounds for the past five months and plans to go back to work as a guard at the prison as soon as he can. Howard Markson reports."

Then Markson's words follow:

> "October 5, 1984, Wilkinson Road Gaol. It's the early morning of October 5, 1984. Inmate Roderick Camphaug facing charges of murder in desperation takes three guards hostage. One of them is shot in the arm and lies bleeding for hours. The next day, guard Dan Kroffit is recovering in hospital and tells the News Hour of his frightening experience."

Then there is a brief clip showing the injured guard as of October 6, 1984. Then the voice-over continues and begins to relate contemporary events this way:

> "The bandages are gone now but some of the after effects remain. Kroffit is still under physiotherapy for the gunshot wound, though he is progressing well. He says everyone's been helpful since the incident including his employer. He's been off work the past 5 months but hopes to return soon."

It continues:

> "While the pain is mostly gone now, there are still reminders of those hours of terror. Kroffit was the first guard ever wounded at Wilkinson Road. He says he hopes he's the last, but only time which heals all wounds will tell."

In one of the artist's renderings displayed during the second segment three figures are shown in a barred room. One figure is seated with legs crossed on a sort of kitchen chair. He is apparently talking on a telephone which he holds in one hand and to his ear, and at the same time he is holding a revolver in the other pointing it at the two nearby guards. One guard is lying on the floor apparently wounded, and the other is kneeling over him apparently tending him.

In argument before me, Mr. Smith for Pawliw suggested that the seated figure has a "maniacal" look. This is not apparent to me. He appears to have a half smile on his face, and overall has a nonchalant posture.

In the second segment, after the short introductory narrative by the anchorman, there is a mixture of prison scenes with the newsman's voice-over narrative. The injured guard is shown as photographed by video camera the day after the incident, and again shown as photographed and recorded at sometime immediately prior to the Friday broadcast. In that second segment he displayed his arm where the bullet had entered and left, and he explained the physical effects and after effects of the injury. He does that in my opinion, in quite a restrained way.

The accused Camphaug, supported by the other two accused, takes particular exception to the following aspects of the second segment.

1. The voice-over speaks of "Camphaug facing charges of murder in desperation takes three guards hostage." The fact is, there is only one joint charge against the three accused. The defence says that the jury might be left with the false impression that other murder charges await Camphaug apart from this one.

2. The use of the word ''desperation'' suggest that Camphaug saw himself as so guilty at that time that the taking of hostages appeared to him to be the only escape.
3. The use of the word ''terror'' would recall to the jury the evidence of the pathologist called by the Crown who described how Diana Van Dooren must have been shot twice at close range, and her evidence would evoke Diana Van Dooren's final moments.
4. The segment might convince the jury that Camphaug is a man capable of shooting someone else and, therefore, it is more likely that he shot Diana Van Dooren or participated in that killing.
5. The fact that the segments were broadcast twice during the same evening would tend to drive the message more explicitly home in the minds of the jurors.

The three accused assert that the broadcast has created such prejudice to them that it would be impossible for them to receive a fair trial before this jury. They say that this is particularly true because this broadcast is just one of several prejudice-creating occurrences during this trial, and they combine to have the cumulative effect of rendering a fair trial impossible. They say that the prejudice created is beyond cure.

I must compare the present situation to that which existed in *R. v. Bengert et al. (No. 5),* 53 C.C.C. 481, 15 C.R. (3d) 114 *sub nom. R. v. Bengert et al.,* wherein the British Columbia Court of Appeal upheld Berger J. in refusing to declare a mistrial. I canvassed that authority extensively in the 19-page judgment dated February 7, 1985, when I denied a motion for a mistrial made by all three accused based on the impact on this jury of an article appearing in the Vancouver Sun which mentioned one of the present accused in connection with another murder trial then going forward in Vancouver. I will not canvass the principles of Bengert here again. The essential question to be answered is: ''Can these accused get a fair trial before this jury?'' (Berger J., p. 530).

The Crown's answer to that question is ''Yes.'' The Crown's main contention is the hostage taking at Wilkinson Road five months ago was a considerable media event and one that could not possibly escape the attention of the British Columbia public at large. Each juror coming forward two months ago for selection in this trial would inevitably be aware of the hostage-taking incident, and despite that awareness was sworn as a juror. If, at the time of swearing, the juror did not recall Camphaug's name and associate him with the incident, he or she shortly would have made the connection because of the evidence presented in this trial. Crown counsel deplores the impugned broadcast and wishes it had not been made. He conceded that it was inflammatory and prejudicial, but says it is markedly less so than the impugned broadcast in Bengert.

The accused take the opposite view and say this is a more blatant case than Bengert, taken in the light of other matters that have preceded it at this trial.

My view is the broadcast is less inflammatory and less prejudicial than the Bengert broadcast is. I am not going to detail the several differences. On the whole I do not believe that any great revelation was made to the present jurors by this broadcast. I assume when saying that, that all saw or at least heard about the broadcast. The broadcast did not suggest that the other two accused, Pawliw and Schnob, participated in the hostage-taking, and evidence has been earlier presented to the jury that they did not. I do not agree that there is a spill-over effect on the other two accused because of Camphaug's involvement.

In due course when charging the jury I must tell the jury of many things which they must disregard in reaching a verdict. I must, like Berger J., have confidence in the ability of present-day jurors to disregard what they may have heard outside the court-room, and I will tell them emphatically to do so. In this day of instant and wide-spread communication of sensational events it is impossible to put a cloak of silence about such incidents as a hostage-taking at Wilkinson Road during which a guard is shot. The freedom of the press is at stake and that freedom cannot be suppressed. No trial was in progress when the events occurred and were originally reported upon. By partly recapitulating those events during this trial, what CHEK TV has done is to remind the jurors of information — whether true or false information — which was already in their possession.

The trial will proceed as presently constituted and the motion for a mistrial is denied.

How the March 8th broadcast came about

The anchorman on the whole broadcast also serves as the assistant news director of the station and as chief editor of the 5:30 p.m. news. He is highly regarded by his superiors. In the normal course he asks the news director to review the script, if he feels any concern about it, before broadcast but on this day the news director was away. The anchorman had no one to whom he could readily turn. In giving evidence he admitted that "in retrospect" he had made the wrong decision but at the time "alarm bells did not go off".

On the morning of the impugned broadcast a tape had been made of an interview with the injured prison guard, Dan Krofitt. The anchorman thought it would be a good idea to link the two stories in the 5:30 news. In evidence he gave this account:

> When I came to work that morning, as I did every morning, I took a look at the stories that we are working on for the day and I noted that we had a crew in Nanaimo to cover the Van Dooren trial, and I also noted we had Howard Markson who was out talking to Dan Krofitt. I immediately recognized the two stories were linked because of Mr. Camphaug being a prime player in both of them, so it was my decision to run the second story immediately following the Van Dooren murder trial story. In retrospect, it was the wrong decision to make. But at the time alarm bells did not go off. I did not see that we had a problem. I know you can't bring a man's record up while he is on trial for another trial, but I did not think we had a problem because he had not been convicted on the hostage-taking incident. In fact, he was only facing charges. I didn't recognize the danger I was walking into, and then just proceeded to put the stories together, as you saw.

By his failure to appreciate that jurors take their oath to decide each case "according to the evidence", without any consideration of other evil doing by the accused unrelated to the charge, this broadcaster betrayed a fundamental ignorance of the rules governing a fair trial. Revelations going to bad character which are not directly related to the charge as a rule should not be made in court and the judge must assure that they are not made. Jurors, however, are not always in court. In the normal course, nowadays, jurors are not sequestered until they enter upon their deliberations. They are free after court to go out into the world where people talk, where newspapers are read, radio is heard and television is seen and heard. Because of the danger of jurors being contaminated from outside sources judges caution them at the outset of each trial not to talk to anyone about the case or to allow anyone to talk to them about it. Judges warn jurors not to be influenced by media accounts as they must decide the case only upon the evidence. Jurors are given credit for heeding these cautions but in high-profile cases the onslaught of pre-trial coverage is all-pervasive, unrelentingly detailed and endlessly repeated so the act of exclusion makes extraordinary demands upon a juror's mentality. People do not forget things because they are told to forget them. The best one can do is put extraneous knowledge to one side and decide strictly according to the evidence. The less the jurors are called upon to perform this feat the better it will be for justice.

The law will not allow publication of matters canvassed in court in the absence of jury. Proceedings at preliminary hearings are usually banned by judge's order. Such prohibitions are necessary limitations on press freedom because they serve the higher purpose of assuring a fair trial.

In the present case I find that the broadcaster was not alert to the danger of repeating, during a trial, an earlier broadcast of repellant conduct by one of the accused which was unrelated to the murder charge. I cannot ascribe to the broadcaster any intention to influence the course of justice or to cause prejudice to the accused man. It is obvious that his only desire was to improve his news story of the day's events at trial by linking those events, to make them more newsworthy, to earlier deplorable activities of the accused and to the human interest story of the injured guard recovering from his wound.

The news director gave evidence in these proceedings saying that had he been available he probably would have taken the intelligence of the jury into consideration and would have assumed they would have been fully aware of the hostage incident at the time of its occurrence and would have remembered it. He took it for granted they would also know that Camphaug had been charged but not convicted of any offence in connection with it. When the news director is in any doubt about the propriety of a script he refers it to legal counsel, who has the final say but in the present case he does not think he would have referred it had he seen it. He said he probably would have done exactly what the anchorman did.

The question to be determined here is whether the resurrection of the hostage-taking story so the jurors could view it again within the context of the murder trial is so offensive to the administration of justice as to constitute a contempt of court.

The law

Counsel cited 17 cases with varying degrees of applicability, but these three answered all the questions raised here.

Case A

R. v. Froese and British Columbia Television Broadcasting System Ltd. (No. 3) (1979), 50 C.C.C. (2d) 119, 15 C.R. (3d) 215 *sub nom. R. v. Bengert et al. (No. 18),* 12 C.P.C. 79, a decision of McEachern C.J.S.C.

Case B

R. v. Froese and British Columbia Television Broadcasting System Ltd. (No. 3), a decision of the British Columbia Court of Appeal, dismissing an appeal from Case A, by Nemetz C.J.B.C. [reported 54 C.C.C. (2d) 315, 18 C.R. (3d) 75, 23 B.C.L.R. 181].

Case C

R. v. Vairo and C.F.C.F. Incorporated (1982), 4 C.C.C. (3d) 274, 147 D.L.R. (3d) 547, a decision of Greenberg J. of the Quebec Superior Court (Criminal Jurisdiction) which considered and applied Cases A and B.

In Case A, McEachern C.J.S.C., accepted as a correct statement of the law of British Columbia what was said by Lord Denning in *Attorney-General v. British Broadcasting Corp.,* [1979] 3 All E.R. 45 at p. 54 [at p. 120]:

> "So far as criminal proceedings are concerned, when a person is charged with a criminal offence, the courts have always been anxious to prevent any newspaper or the like from publishing any matter which may prejudice the fair trial of the accused person. This was introduced at a time when most criminal cases were tried by jury; and it was thought they might be prejudiced if they had read beforehand in the newspapers of matters which were inadmissible in evidence at the trial, such as his previous convictions or his bad character; or statements made by witnesses not subject to cross-examination and the like. The courts intervened strongly so as to prevent anything in the nature of 'trial by newspaper' or 'trial by television' ".

He noted four principles which are basic to all criminal trials [at pp. 120-1]:

> [1] ...every person arraigned in a Canadian Court of criminal justice, whatever his antecedents, is protected throughout his trial by a presumption of innocence.
> [2] ...the burden of displacing the presumption of innocence rests upon the Crown and that such burden can only be discharged by placing before the jury a body of admissible evidence which establishes guilt beyond a reasonable doubt.
> [3] ...an indictment is decided only on admissible evidence...
> [4] ...evidence tending to establish bad character on the part of an accused cannot be placed before a jury except under very limited circumstances.

Following this he made these general comments:

> It is therefore a grave contempt for anyone, particularly the members of what is now called the media, to publish, before or during a trial, any statements, comments, or information which reflect adversely upon the conduct or character of an accused person, or to suggest directly or indirectly that he has been previously convicted of any offence, or to comment adversely or at all upon the strength or weakness of his defence. The harm that may be done is incalculable because in most cases it is impossible to determine what effect, if any, such statements or comments may have upon the jury. It will be most unfortunate and inconvenient, and not in the interests of the proper administration of justice, if it becomes necessary to resume the practice of separating juries from the rest of society during trials because a few irresponsible members of the media are unthinking enough to fail to follow the simple rules which must attend the conduct of every criminal trial.

In Case B, Nemetz C.J.B.C. concluded his judgment with these words [at p. 324]:

> I turn now to the second ground of appeal. Did the learned Chief Justice err in finding that the guilt of the appellants was proved beyond a reasonable doubt? In my opinion, he did not.
>
> As Lord Hardwicke, L.C., pointed out in *Roach v. Garvan (or Hall)* (1748), 2 Atk. 469 at p. 471, 26 E.R. 683 at p. 685:
>
> > "There cannot be anything of greater consequence, than to keep the streams of justice clear and pure, that parties may proceed with safety both to themselves and their characters."
>
> This *rationale* was echoed by Wills, J., in *R. v. Parke,* [1903] 2 K.B. 432 at pp. 436-7, as follows:
>
> > "The reason why the publication of articles like those with which we have to deal is treated as a contempt of Court is because their tendency and sometimes their object is to deprive the Court of the power of doing that which is the end for which it exists — namely, to administer justice duly, impartially, and with reference solely to the facts judicially brought before it."
>
> This latter passage demonstrates, in my view, the significance of the test to be applied in cases of this kind: whether the words spoken and broadcast were *calculated* to interfere with the course of justice. In order to make a finding of guilt, it is not necessary to find either that the words were intended to interfere, or that they did in fact interfere with the course of justice — for it will often be impossible to discover the effect of any statement upon a jury. It is only necessary to be satisfied beyond a reasonable doubt that the words were *calculated* to interfere in the sense of being *apt,* or having a *tendency,* to do so: see *R. v. Parke, supra,* and the judgments of this Court in *R. v. Hill* (1976), 33 C.C.C. (2d) 60, 73 D.L.R. (3d) 621, 37 C.R.N.S. 380, and *R. v. Perkins* (1980), C.A. 790656 (as yet unreported) [since reported 51 C.C.C. (2d) 369, [1980] 4 W.W.R. 763]. This was the test that the learned Chief Justice applied in arriving at his conclusion of guilt. It is my view that there was ample evidence before him to support that conclusion. I would, therefore, dismiss the appeal.

In Case C, Greenberg J. described in a clear way the special kind of intention required to support a finding of criminal contempt [at p. 276]:

> Criminal contempt is a criminal offence; it is an indictable offence, but it is an offence *sui generis*. That is to say, it is different from other indictable offences in that the accused contemner has no right to a trial by jury; his trial is before judge alone. This results from jurisprudence established over the centuries and which came down to us from the common law of England.
>
> However, as in any criminal offence, for conviction the weight of the proof required against the contemner is that beyond a reasonable doubt; that is to say of both the *actus reus* and the mens rea, subject to a qualification in respect to the latter which I will elaborate upon in a moment.
>
> Here, all the facts alleged are admitted. Also, both the corporate respondent and Mr. Vairo, through their attorney, have expressed to the court their unqualified and unreserved apologies and regrets. As to the *actus reus,* the facts are admitted; that is to say that the publication, by way of broadcast, took place as alleged in the petitions. As to the *mens rea,* in this instance it does not refer to an intention to commit a criminal contempt but rather to the intention to publish. That is to say, to knowingly and intentionally publish the material, irrespective of the absence of an intention or bad faith with respect to the question of criminal contempt itself.
>
> The question of the quality of the material and as to whether or not it constitutes a criminal contempt is decided objectively, that is to say without reference to the contemner's intention in that respect. The court must decide whether the material is objectively to be considered as such as is likely to, may tend to, or has the potential to obstruct; in this case obstruct the due administration of justice.

He spoke of the ''opposing fundamental rights'' of free speech, on the one hand, within which is encompassed the right of freedom of the press, and ''the other side of the coin, the public's right to know''.

In opposition to those rights, he said, ''we have the right of an accused to a fair trial by an impartial and independent tribunal'' and he followed with this passage [at pp. 277-8]:

> In cases of the kind with which this court is now seized we have the results of a collision between those respective fundamental rights. It can be described in one sense as the ''irresistible force'' of freedom of the press colliding with the ''immoveable object'' of the right of an accused to a fair trial by an independent and impartial tribunal. One must yield. Our law has decided, probably most wisely, that in such cases the freedom of the press must yield to the rights of the accused. This does not prevent, as Oswald said in his celebrated volume *Contempt of Court,* Canadian edition (1911), at p. 98:
>
> ''There is, of course, no objection to a fair and impartial report of proceedings at the hearing.''
>
> However, this does not give any of the media the right to conduct what has been referred to by Oswald and others as a ''trial by newspaper'' or, to bring us more up to date, we can equally say a ''trial by television''.

He found no malicious intention and no bad faith on the part of the broadcaster or his supervisors but said that ''both should have known better''. I make the same findings.

As in Case C, the words and sketches used in the impugned broadcast about Camphaug's part in the hostage-taking had the same effect in that they clearly tended [at p. 279]

> to convey to the minds of your average, reasonable listener or viewer the fact that this person is of a bad character and therefore, by one further step of deduction, likely to have committed the crime... of which he stands charged.

These further observations of Greenberg J. have equal application to the present case [at pp. 279-80]:

> The court has also considered the actual consequences of the acts of the contemners in the present instance. No mistrial was ordered. However, there was a risk, and I add a serious risk, of a mistrial. In any event, two days of the court's time were spent on the mistrial motions, their argument and the judgment thereon. There was therefore time wasted in respect of the progress of the trial, for during those two days no progress whatsoever was made with respect to the trial *per se*. As well, as far as the jurors were concerned, in the final analysis they were kept on duty in respect of that trial for two days longer than would have otherwise been necessary.
>
> I might add that I do not take into account the possibility of a new trial being ordered by the Court of Appeal. As yet we do not know if there has been an appeal or will be an appeal lodged with respect to the verdicts. In such event we have no way of knowing whether the appeal court will, on the basis of the incident here referred to or on the basis of this incident cumulated as to its effect with other subsequent, similar incidents during the trial, decide that in the over-all picture the accused did not have a fair trial and a new trial must be held.
>
> We have no way of knowing whether there will be such an appeal, or in the event of such an appeal what will be its outcome. I therefore must take the *status quo* as it now exists. Hence, no mistrial took place and I cannot and do not take into account the possibility of a new trial in the event of an appeal.

On the basis of the criteria derived from these authorities I find the respondent liable and guilty of contempt of court. I have done so in full awareness that the jurisdiction of the court to find a person or corporation guilty of contempt is discretionary and that the finding should only be made where there are serious grounds for its exercise and that it "is a weapon to be used sparingly, and always with reference to the interests of the administration of justice". *Re Murphy and Southam Press Ltd.* (1972), 9 C.C.C. (2d) 330, 30 D.L.R. (3d) 355, [1972] 6 W.W.R. 331 *sub nom. Brown v. Murphy et al.* a decision of Anderson J. (as he then was). He took the quoted word from Lord Morris, speaking for the Judicial Committee, in *McLeod v. St. Aubyn,* [1899] A.C. 549, at p. 362.

Counsel have not spoken to the matter of penalty and consideration of it was deferred pending a determination of the contempt issue. I ask that counsel arrange through the trial co-ordination office for a mutually convenient time for a hearing concerning penalty.

Judgment accordingly.

3.5.3.4 *Bellitti* v. *Canadian Broadcasting Corp.* (1973) 2 O.R. (2d) 232 (Ont. H.C.)

ZUBER, J. (orally): — This is an application to continue an injunction issued by Mr. Justice Fraser on November 6th, 1973.

Earlier this year, Mr. Bellitti, the applicant, was arrested and charged with three narcotic offences and was tried together with others before His Honour Judge Honsberger and a jury in the City of Toronto. The applicant Bellitti was convicted of conspiracy to import heroin and was acquitted on the other two charges. He is to be sentenced on November 12, 1973. He has appealed his conviction and it is said that he may independently also appeal the sentence.

On November 6th of this year, Mr. Fay, counsel for Mr. Bellitti, became aware that the Canadian Broadcasting Corporation was, in his words, "about to televise a documentary concerning the trial". On that basis an application was made to Mr. Justice Fraser who issued the order now before me. The order restrains the CBC from "communicating to the public in any form any of the proceedings before His Honour Judge Honsberger and the jury".

Clearly, the CBC has the right to freedom of the press, which is a variation of the liberty enjoyed by all of us as freedom of speech. It is obvious as well that this right is not an absolute right, but ends where such things as defamation, sedition, obscenity and contempt of Court begin. The problem in discerning the border, however, is frequently a difficult one and involves the balancing of competing public interests such as the freedom of speech and of the press and the public interest in the proper administration of justice. In this case, it is argued that the broadcast of this programme would constitute a contempt of Court. Contempt can take many forms, but in this case the point in issue is that this broadcast would constitute an interference with the administration of justice or, in other words, would prejudice a fair trial.

In my view, the argument to continue the injunction in its present form is completely untenable. Justice is administered in public and it is in the public interest that the proceedings be freely reported, save only those specific instances where prohibition of publicity is provided by statute. It is only when publication or broadcast departs from factual reporting and expresses comments or opinions and those comments or opinions interfere with the administration of justice or prejudice a fair trial that the broadcast or publication will constitute contempt of Court. The injunction, as it presently stands, would prohibit simple reporting and it seems to me obvious that this injunction cannot stand. The more particular question that faces us is whether an injunction in more modified terms should stand, that is, should the CBC be enjoined from broadcasting the specific programme which is the subject of this application on the grounds that it will interfere with the administration of justice or prejudice a fair trial.

In the affidavit material filed, the programme is simply described as "a documentary concerning the trial of the applicant". That bald assertion is not helpful. So, with the consent of counsel and in the presence of all of us, the film was shown. The film was entitled "Flour of the Poppy". It purported to show the facts disclosed at trial. This was done pictorially by showing places, vehicles, houses and so forth; the movements of people were depicted pictorially by the utilization of actors, but I pause to observe that with the exception of one or two minor instances there was no dialogue between the actors. A narrator described the events. It is said by counsel that this pictorial portrayal represents nothing more than the evidence that was given at trial. There is no material before me that suggests anything to the contrary. This pictorial representation related the facts upon which the prosecution was based. Later there was disclosure of the fact of arrest and trial and pictures were shown of the Metropolitan Toronto Court House, the empty interior of a court-room in that building and so forth. The narrator announced the length of the trial, I believe the name of the presiding Judge and the verdict of the jury and perhaps the length of time that it took them to reach a verdict.

The film also showed in another segment the process of growing poppies and producing heroin and the profits to be made. The film also showed a police officer who commented upon the shortage of police and there was some speculation as to whether or not activity of a similar sort was still going on undetected, but this was of a general nature. Specifically, there was no comment made or opinion expressed as to whether or not the verdict of the jury was right or wrong. There was no comment or opinion expressed, as I saw and heard the film, as to the sentence that should be given. In my opinion, there was no undue dramatization or emphasis of the matter which would indirectly operate on the mind of whoever pronounces sentence.

Since the jury has already reached a verdict of guilty, the question of the interference with the administration of justice or the issue of prejudice, as I understand the argument of the applicant, relates to three areas. Obviously the exhibition of this film can hardly prejudice the minds of the jurors who have now been discharged.

The first issue to be looked at is whether or not the exhibition of this film will interfere with the administration of justice in so far as it concerns the duty yet to be performed by Judge Honsberger in the pronouncing of sentence. As I have already stated, there is no comment in the film by way of directly or indirectly urging a high sentence or a low sentence. There is nothing in the film, as I saw it and heard it, that attempts to characterize the accused as a person who might deserve either a high or a low sentence. The maximum view that can be taken of this film is that simply because it is a pictorial representation rather than a printed account, it might have some extra impact. I cannot believe that this would make any difference to the mind of a professional Judge.

The second point raised by the applicant is the effect of the film on the pending appeal. As I have mentioned, I found nothing in the nature of comment in the film. However, even if any of the statements in the programme could be construed as comments, there is no prejudice to the appeal.

In *Attorney-General v. Times Newspapers Ltd.,* [1973] 3 All E.R. 54 at p. 65. Lord Reid said: "...it is scarcely possible to imagine a case where comment could influence judges in the Court of Appeal...", and Lord Simon stated at p. 83: "...any comment on pending appellate proceedings could only rarely be intrinsically an interference with the due course of law."

I subscribe to those views.

The third argument raised by the applicant relates to the effect of this film on jurors selected in a new trial, if that situation should arise. It is clear at once that all of this is largely speculative, hinged on the success of the appeal and on the fact that there may be a new trial, which is not the inevitable result of a successful appeal. This argument that a subsequent jury would accept this pictorial representation as fact and would thereby in some way be prejudiced in their assessment of the evidence at the subsequent trial, taken to its logical conclusion would lead to the prohibition of reporting any trial. A second trial always creates the possibility that the jurors in the second trial may be prejudiced by knowing something of the first one, either by having been present at the trial or having simply read the newspaper accounts. This problem is simply met and sorted out in the jury selection process. It seems to me that anyone seeing this programme would be in no different position with respect to service on a subsequent jury, if that eventuality arises, than would anyone who had either been at the trial or read newspaper accounts of it.

The fact that a new trial is only a possibility, and the fact that a person who watches this programme is really in no different position than those who either saw the trial or read about it, lead me to the conclusion that there is no real risk of prejudicing a fair trial or interfering with the administration of justice.

The application to continue the injunction is dismissed and the injunction dissolved.

A number of procedural arguments were raised by the CBC, upon which I express no opinion. It is not necessary for me to deal with them in view of the disposition that I have made of the matter on the merits.

Note: Recent decisions suggest that sub-judice may have some application to proceedings before appellate courts. See, for example, *Lortie* v. *R.* (1985), 46 C.R. (3d) 322.

3.5.3.5 *Bielek* v. *Ristimaki* Ontario High Court, 1979 Reported in S. Robertson, *Courts and the Media,* pp. 287-292

HENRY, J.: Now, this matter now comes before me at the end of an aborted trial in the action Hendrick R. Bielek v. Albert J. Ristimaki, which commenced on Monday last, June 18th, and has continued in one form or another until today, June 21st. Yesterday, after hearing an application by counsel for the defendant arising out of the publication of a press report in the Timmins Daily Press of June 19th, which included a specific reference to the amount of $500,000 being claimed by the plaintiff for libel and slander, which information was not conveyed to the jury and was therefore not mentioned in their presence in the court. The application was that I should proceed without a jury and discharge the jury. As I found, I am not authorized to do that in the absence of a waiver of the right to a trial by jury in a defamation action, which is prescribed by the Judicature Act [R.S.O. 1970, c.228, as am.]. On the basis of the facts before me and as I indicate in my reasons, because the publication in the press of the amount of the damages claimed must be assumed to find its way in one form or another to one or more members of the jury, I made the decision at what was an early stage of the trial which had proceeded to the point where only the plaintiff had been examined in chief, to abort the trial, declare a mistrial, and discharge the jury.

Because this matter arose out of the press report that I have mentioned, I called for the attendance of representatives and counsel for the newspaper, and for the attendance of the reporter who wrote the report. All are now before me with their counsel, Mr. G.C. Evans, Q.C., who acts on behalf of the newspaper, Thomson Publications, and who is also acting for Mr. Peter Black, the reporter, and Mr. Gregory Reynolds, the editor of the Timmins Daily Press. I have heard evidence called by Mr. Evans from both Mr. Black and from Mr. Reynolds, and I have heard the submissions of Mr. Evans on my request that he now show cause why one or more of those persons should not be found in contempt of this court. I may say that I have had great assistance from Mr. Evans, as well as from other counsel, although other counsel did not take part in this particular proceeding.

I find that the press report in question was published in the June 19th issue of the Timmins Daily Press, and that it contained the offending information about the amount of $500,000 claimed by the plaintiff in his pleadings against the defendant. There is no doubt, as Mr. Evans has quite properly conceded, that publication of this information in the circumstances was wrong. It is in evidence, and it was submitted to me by counsel, that this publication was primarily the result of inexperience on the part of a young reporter. I might say that the reporter, Mr. Black, acknowledges that. The information in question concerning the amount of damages claimed was not placed in evidence before the jury and is in no way before them to his knowledge. It is also in evidence that he was asked by his editor, Mr. Reynolds, whether the information in the report was all placed before the court in the presence of the jury, and that he assured his editor that this was so. In this of course, he was quite wrong, but I do not think that in telling his editor that he was actuated in any way by malice, or an attempt to say something which to his knowledge was not true. The amount of damages claimed was published contrary to the well-known rule in the conduct of trials before juries that information of any kind whatever that takes place in the courtroom in the absence of the jury ought not to be published in the news media during the currency of the trial. There is, of course, no obstacle to its publication at a later stage, and I emphasize that, because this is not a muzzle on the press — it is not to keep the public from knowing what happened; it is merely a rule of fairness and convenience to assure that the jury will not read for example of matters that are discussed on a voir dire which ought not to be brought to the attention of the jury and for which purpose the jury are excluded. As I say, that rule is well-known to reporters and editors generally in my experience, and there is no doubt about that before me. I find that the reporting of that figure so far as the reporter, Mr. Black is concerned, was deliberate although mistaken. The editor, Mr. Reynolds, has made an apology to the court orally when in the witness box for the course that was taken. The result of what happened is a mistrial and if I may put the matter bluntly, is, in this particular case, a subversion of the system of justice. The parties and the public have been put to considerable expense for the period of the trial which turned out to be abortive, and therefore that expense, and the time of those concerned, both of the parties, and witnesses, and counsel, has been to no avail. I might describe those costs and expenses perhaps in well-known terms as "costs thrown away."

In my opinion, it is the obligation of press reporters and their editors who control the publication of news in the media, whether the press or the electronic media, to ensure that what is published are matters that may be revealed, and also to ensure that they know the rules governing trials which specify what matters ought not to be published in the course of a trial. I emphasize that the responsibility is on a free but responsible press to be informed about those matters as part of their professional expertise. They are, after all, professionals and are, in my judgment, to be held accountable as such. In short they must know what they are doing when what they do may affect the rights of other people. This is only another way of saying that in a democratic regime, characterized by, among other things, a free press, the freedom conferred on the press (to use the well-known phrase appearing in Canada at least in the Alberta Press case) is freedom governed by law. The press is not free to invade the rights of others, and the liberties of others without being held to account in accordance with law. So, I say that surely it is incumbent upon those who publish, certainly professionally, to exercise a duty to inform themselves fully as professional people, as to what they may and may not publish, and particularly the time at which publication may be made. I accordingly find, and I do so beyond a reasonable doubt, that the newspaper, the Timmins Daily Press, as a corporation, is in contempt of this court for the action which has been taken. There can be no question that in our democratic society a free press is a fundamental pillar of our polity. It is also fundamental to the fair and impartial administration of justice by an independent judiciary. That a free press be at liberty to comment on and to publish proceedings in the courts, both the right of the public to know and the duty of in this case the professional press to report what is going on in a court, as well as in other parts of society, is so fundamental that it need not be further restated. Equally fundamental is the right of the citizen to bring his complaints before the courts to have a fair and impartial adjudication of his dispute with another citizen carried out and resolved in accordance with the principles which have been laid down over many many years in the common law courts to ensure the proper enforcement of those rights and to give the citizen his day in court. The right of free speech, and the right of the citizen that I have described, to a fair and impartial trial has been won at great cost and with great pain over the years and over, at times apparently, insurmountable odds against the executive and against powerful agencies in the state, whether public or private. The courts have, in our democratic society, been the organs which have established and maintained those rights. It is the right of every citizen to a trial by a jury in criminal and civil cases, and particularly in a defamation action, but that right, so far, from being supported and maintained by a free press, can be impaired and subverted by untutored or irresponsible exercise of the right to publish. The most important role of the press in respect of trials in our courts is to inform the public of what is happening and to monitor the system by close and informed scrutiny, and fair and responsible comment and criticism. It is not the role of the press to conduct itself in a way which will impair the effective and fair work of the judicial system, but the line must be drawn as here, where the right of the parties to a fair trial by jury is impaired or destroyed by an improper disclosure; indeed a disclosure at an inopportune time. The information may be published; that is it is not to be withheld from the public, but it ought not to be published at a time when justice may be impaired. In other words it's a question of timing, and one of the problems the press faces in these days is the timing of its news releases, which I think experience has shown, sometimes takes priority over the fairness of the publication at that particular time. Except in rare cases the public may ultimately be told all the information that is available. The question arises that the statement of claim from which the offending information was taken, is a public document. It is true that any press reporter is at liberty to go to the registrar's office and be shown the file which is a public document, except to the extent that portions of it may be, for good and sufficient reason by order of the court, sealed. That is not the case here, and those cases are indeed rare. Moreover there has been much publicity at an earlier stage concerning the damages asked of one-half million dollars in this case, but that publicity occurred some time ago, in November, 1977. Generally speaking there is no inhibition on the press reporting factual information at an early stage, although that is a matter which must be dealt with with caution, but if that information were still fresh in the minds of the public the court might feel it necessary to change the venue, but as is well known, the passage of time tends to make memories dim, and it frequently occurs that even where there has been wide publicity at a much earlier stage, a court does not consider that a fair trial will be impaired, for the very simple reason that it is not freshly brought into the minds of a jury panel, or the jury themselves if the press conducts itself properly. I should add that neither the judge nor the counsel could put the offending information about the amount of damages claimed to the jury in the court room without giving rise to a mistrial, and the press cannot be above that. The parties and the public in this case have been put to the expense of this abortive trial. In my opinion the press, who caused this situation, ought to be held accountable to the parties at least for the consequences of the improper report.

There is already an apology on behalf of the corporation involved, but I think it necessary to go beyond that. The contempt of the corporation, Thomson Newspapers, may in this case, be purged by payment to the two parties of their costs thrown away by the declaration of the mistrial arising out of the conduct of the press. The amount in question I am prepared to fix at $2500 to each party. The contempt will be purged if payment is made by Thomson Newspapers, or the Timmins Daily Press of the amount of $2500 to the solicitor for each party. That payment, in order to purge the contempt, is to be made on or before June 30th, 1979. In default of such payment being made I impose a fine upon the corporate newspaper of $7500, which fine shall be paid by cheque into the office of the Registrar of this Court in Toronto.

I turn now to the case of the reporter, Mr. Black. For the above reasons I find with some regret, that Mr. Black is in contempt of this court as is his employer, but he may purge that contempt by filing a written apology with this court. This apology may be made by letter addressed to The Registrar of the Supreme Court of Ontario, in Cochrane, to be forwarded to Toronto. No other penalty will be imposed.

I have also considered the position of the editor, Mr. Reynolds, and I do not propose to find him in contempt in view of the circumstances. He was given an incorrect assurance by his reporter that the facts were all facts placed before the jury, and that matter is therefore closed.

I add, in a general way, that in my opinion the course of responsible journalism (if I may use that phrase) is to know and inform the reporting staff of what matters, even those contained in public documents or in previous media reports, must not be published in circumstances that may come to the knowledge of the jury, or of a jury panel summoned for the assize at which a trial will take place. I give by way of example of such information only, and it's clearly not exhaustive, the one before me; namely general damages claimed, which, as is well known, can be quite misleading; payment of money into court by a defendant as part of the conduct of the pre-trial proceedings; and the fact that an insurance company, or some other indemnifier is going to pay any damages assessed against a defendant. Those, as I say, are not exhaustive, but they are examples we will find. Pleadings generally, unless they have been read to the jury, or proved by evidence at the trial, if published may not necessarily be fatal, but their publication does create the grave risk of alleging what a reporter may think are facts that are never in fact proved before the jury. In other words I think I should make it plain that public documents such as pleadings, that may come into the hands of a reporter, should be treated with the greatest caution because they may contain allegations which ought not to be known to the jury, whose task it is to decide the case only on the evidence placed before them as all jurors are firmly told by the trial judge. Usually the general facts upon which the case will be tried are disclosed in the opening address of counsel for the plaintiff to the jury. That, being made in open court is the source of the information from which press reports may properly be derived in most circumstances.

Those are my reasons gentlemen. I don't think there is anything I need to add. I will endorse on the record what I have just said, and perhaps I can do that in the lunch hour and read it to you gentlemen.

Gentlemen I believe I can now dispose of the matter of the change of venue. I intend to change the venue because if nothing else the publicity that has been during this week given to the issue that is being raised will be in people's minds in this community of some knowledge it might be difficult for them to have forgotten. I wouldn't say that it would not be possible to get a jury who hadn't heard of it, but in view of the nature of the question that gave rise to the mistrial, which is an extremely simple one, a simple fact might very well remain in people's minds over the course of the summer, so in the result therefore I have decided that I should change the venue to Bracebridge. I have looked at not only the state of the list there, but the state of the list in the other centres as well and I may simply say to you that although that assize will not start until the beginning of October, that the list is extremely short and there are only about two days' work ahead of you; and indeed the trial judge may be able to bring you on right away; that's up to him, so the venue will be changed then to the Fall Assize in Bracebridge. It starts October the 9th. There are two civil jury cases on the list which are forecast for two days total, and I think that probably it's up to counsel to speak to the trial judge and he of course will have to tell you whether he can bring you on at once, or wait for those two.

Now, gentlemen I endorse the following:

> Venue is changed to Bracebridge. Set down for trial at the assize commencing October 9th, 1979. The case is peremptory for the defendant. Any preliminary motions at the outset of trial to be on proper notice to the other party and the costs of this motion I would propose gentlemen, to reserve for the trial judge.

...

I think I would be remiss gentlemen, if I didn't say, when leaving the courtroom, to Mr. Black's superior, Mr. Reynolds, who is here, Mr. Reynolds I have put a considerable amount of blame on Mr. Black because he was the reporter on the firing line. I tried to make it plain to him that I thought he was not properly instructed and I think in that sense, in the instruction of reporters who go out to report a sophisticated thing like a jury trial, it isn't sufficient to send them out and give them one rule of thumb. I wouldn't like it to be thought that I was criticizing Mr. Black in the carrying out of his job. I think if he did anything wrong it was because he was not properly instructed.

Finding of contempt made; change of venue ordered.

3.5.3.6 *Re Church of Scientology of Toronto* v. *The Queen (No. 6)* (1986) 27 C.C.C. (3d) 193 (Ont. H.C.)

WATT J.: It would plainly appear that simple fear of embarrassment, whether of a witness or an accused person, is not a sufficient basis upon which to found a blanket prohibition enjoining in perpetuity publication of the identity of an accused or of the identity or evidence of a witness, actual or proposed. It would seem clear that the purpose of any order prohibiting publication, of whatever length and in whatever terms, is to protect the integrity of the court's process not merely to minimize the embarrassment of those charged with or giving evidence of crime.

It is, indeed, almost a commonplace where several accused jointly indicted are together presented for trial at a jury sittings that, upon a plea of guilty being entered by one or more accused upon arraignment before the presiding judge, to direct that there be no publication of the fact of such plea, the "facts" tendered in support of it, representations made and reasons given at the conclusion of the plea proceedings until the conclusion of the proceedings pending against the co-accused. Such orders are made and equally salutary whether the offence charged is listed in s.427 of the

Criminal Code or otherwise and whether the plea is preceded by re-election for trial by judge alone or consent to trial by judge alone by the accused who enters the plea of guilty. It would generally not seem to be thought that an order suspending publication is necessary in the event that all remaining accused are to be tried by judge alone or provincial court judge. It is assumed that in such cases the presiding judge is less likely to be affected by the publication of such information. For jurisdictional purposes, in my view, it matters not whether the judge to whom the application is made is, in circumstances like the present, sitting under Part XVI of the *Criminal Code* or whether he or she is presiding at a jury sittings whose procedure is regulated by Part XVII of the *Criminal Code*. The court is none the less a court of record and the fairness of the pending trials ought equally to be their concern. It is absolutely critical that if an order for non-publication is to be made that it be made in the plea of guilty proceedings, for in the event that it should not there be made it will be of no avail if left to the judge presiding in the jury trial thereafter taking place as the damage occasioned by such publicity may well, by then, have been done.

III CONCLUSION

It is, accordingly, my respectful view that, as a court of record, a provincial court judge, acting under Part XVI in receiving a plea of guilty tendered by one of several accused jointly charged has authority to entertain an application, on behalf of another or other accused jointly charged, for an order suspending publication of such matters disclosed in the proceedings upon the plea of guilty as may reasonably be said, if published, to impair the appearance of fairness in subsequent proceedings taken against such co-accused.

3.5.3.7 Aide-memoire on the *sub judice* rule in Stuart Robertson, *Courts and the Media*, (Toronto, Butterworths, 1981), p. 25

(1) Methods of Breaching the Rule

Members of the media breach the *sub judice* rule when they interfere, or potentially interfere, with the court's handling of a legal proceeding. The following is a list of the ways the media have been found to have interfered with the courts' processes.

(a) reporting that the accused has given a confession or admission before it is entered as evidence in open court;
(b) prejudging or urging a particular result in the legal proceeding;
(c) advising parties involved in a legal proceeding, thereby discouraging them from pursuing their interests;
(d) reporting that the accused in a criminal proceeding has a criminal record, or that the accused engages in criminal activities or consorts with criminals;
(e) reporting the identity of the accused when the identity is an issue in the proceeding;
(f) reporting the contents of court documents;
(g) reporting on one proceeding in such a way as to prejudice another action;
(h) breaching court orders;
(i) carrying on a media investigation while a related criminal matter is proceeding.

3.5.3.8 Criminal Records Act, R.S.C. 1985, c. C-47

6. (1) The Minister may by order in writing addressed to any person having the custody or control of any judicial record of a conviction in respect of which a pardon has been granted, require that person to deliver such record into the custody of the Commissioner.

(2) Any record of a conviction in respect of which a pardon has been granted that is in the custody of the Commissioner or of any department or agency of the Government of Canada shall be kept separate and apart from other criminal records, and no such record shall be disclosed to any person, nor shall the existence of the record or the fact of the conviction be disclosed to any person, without the prior approval of the Minister.

(3) The Minister shall, before granting the approval for disclosure referred to in subsection (2), satisfy himself that the disclosure is desirable in the interests of the administration of justice or for any purpose related to the safety or security of Canada or any state allied or associated with Canada. R.S., c.12 (1st Supp.), s.6.

3.6 Disobeying a Court Order

If a journalist is subpoenaed as a witness at a judicial proceeding and refuses to answer a question properly put, the refusal can amount to that form of contempt known as disobeying an order of the court. The refusal to reveal such information will be dealt with either summarily as a contempt or as an offence under a specific section of the Criminal Code, such as s.472.

3.6.1 Criminal Code, s.545

Procedure Where Witness Refuses to Testify

WITNESS REFUSING TO BE EXAMINED — Further commitment — Saving.

545. (1) Where a person, being present at a preliminary inquiry and being required by the justice to give evidence,

(*a*) refuses to be sworn,

(*b*) having been sworn, refuses to answer the questions that are put to him,

(*c*) fails to produce any writings that he is required to produce, or

(*d*) refuses to sign his deposition,

without offering a reasonable excuse for his failure or refusal, the justice may adjourn the inquiry and may, by warrant in Form 16, commit the person to prison for a period not exceeding eight clear days or for the period during which the inquiry is adjourned, whichever is the lesser period.

(2) Where a person to whom subsection (1) applies is brought before the justice upon the resumption of the adjourned inquiry and again refuses to do what is required of him, the justice may again adjourn the inquiry for a period not exceeding eight clear days and commit him to prison for the period of adjournment or any part thereof, and may adjourn the inquiry and commit the person to prison from time to time until the person consents to do what is required of him.

(3) Nothing in this section shall be deemed to prevent the justice from sending the case for trial upon any other sufficient evidence taken by him.

Note: There have been instances, although perhaps fewer than one might imagine, where Canadian journalists have been faced with judicial demands to reveal information.

3.6.2 Wilfred H. Kesterton, *The Law and the Press in Canada,* (Toronto, 1976), pp. 32-39

Probably no incident in recent times has aroused so much Canadian debate on the subject of confidentiality of sources as a 1969 event. Early that year the CBC public affairs show, "The Way It Is," prepared a film report on the city of Montreal. As part of this offering, John Smith, a member of the CBC unit, interviewed a man who claimed to be an FLQ terrorist. The man told Smith that it was his job to teach others how to make and set off bombs. Feeling that this sort of information was important to authorities concerned with protecting life and property, the CBC told the police. But the corporation did not name the man who had been interviewed because Smith had promised not to disclose his identity.

Smith was soon summoned to appear before the Montreal Fire Commission, the body chosen to investigate the bombings which had been taking place. By now Smith had come to believe the interview had been a hoax. Believing also that it was necessary to protect his sources, Smith refused to be sworn before the Fire Commission. Lawyers Marcel Beauchemin and Marcel Côté asked Fire Commissioner John McDougall to cite the CBC reporter-researcher for contempt of the hearing.

Summoned again, Smith again refused to be sworn. In doing so he read from a prepared text which said, "I know full well that the law obliges me to answer the questions of this Commission... but nevertheless I will not testify." He contended that "it is the job of the journalist to inform his public of the state of society" and that he "is continuously privy to confidential information." He maintained that giving assurances that information divulged confidentially will be so treated was as much a part of the journalist's function as it was a lawyer's. "If my refusal to testify is illegal," he said, "then it is illegal to have a free press and an informed public, because a press cannot be free and a public cannot be informed if journalists cannot give assurances... confidentiality will be kept confidential."

Reaction to the Smith incident was sharp and categorical. Predictably, many journalists condemned the sentencing and imprisonment of the CBC reporter-interviewer. Some editors and commentators demanded shield laws to protect journalists from having to divulge the sources of the stories they write or broadcast. Some claimed that denial of confidentiality might lead to the state of affairs existing in South Africa. They were afraid that an insistence on disclosure might help to bring about a situation in which papers could not print anything detrimental to the government. Others, believing that Canada should follow the example of the American shield law states, raised the question of whether courts should not be required to show that a matter was in the public interest before they could compel a journalist to reveal his sources.

The Toronto *Globe and Mail* editorialized about Bill 79, the Fire Investigations Act under which Smith had been summoned to the Commission hearing. The editorial said, "Bill 79 has... harshly bruised the legitimate rights of John Smith." It contended that "Bill 79 springs, not just from the dark waters through which Quebec is now passing, but from the style in which Canadian law, both inside and outside Quebec, has evolved." It also quoted approvingly — and attempted to apply to the Smith case — the words of Justice Oliver Wendell Holmes, in reference to another, American court: "To declare that the government may commit crimes in order to secure the arrest of private individuals — this would bring terrible retribution. Against that pernicious doctrine, this court should resolutely set its face.''

Was the John Smith case as significant as such commentators seemed to think? Was it a *cause célèbre?* Did it pose a real threat to the freedom of Canada's mass media? Should the journalist be given the blanket right to preserve the anonymity of the sources of his reports? Attempts made by many media professionals to answer such questions were not reassuring. Many editorial writers made errors in their assessment of the John Smith affair. Many were singularly uninformed about the law of the press in the area of contempt of court and the revealing of sources. Many seemed unaware of any underlying philosophy designed to reconcile the interests of the journalist with the interests of the society he serves.

Some critics of the Smith imprisonment made the issue of revealing of sources unnecessarily confusing by coupling it with an account of what the police were reported to have done to the prisoner. As Warren Davis described it, on the CBC television program, ''The Way It Is,'' ''[Smith] is then shackled, chained at the ankle, handcuffed to a guard and taken to Bordeaux jail, where, before a group of watching guards, he is stripped, given forms to sign, and in prison clothes put in a solitary cell in the punishment block, the hole.'' With similar emphasis Doug Collins asked whether the Oliver Wendell Holmes stricture previously quoted did not apply ''if, under the Fire Investigation Act, they can hold people... without right of consulting counsel.'' On the same program, other panelists hastened to point out that they too did not approve of any denial of the right of an arrested person to receive the advice of his solicitor at any time. But they were equally firm in pointing out that the iniquitous things which were alleged to have happened to Smith were an issue quite separate from his refusal to testify. Quite clearly it is possible to condemn the rather high-handed treatment which Smith was reported to have received and still favor the requirement that the journalist name his sources in appropriate situations.

Some critics made the mistake of regarding the Montreal incident as introducing a new threat, one perhaps unique to Quebec. In doing so they showed ignorance of Canadian contempt citation precedents. The fact is, of course, that Wigmore's four canons, discussed earlier in this chapter, apply equally throughout Canada. People knowledgeable in the law thought it a mistake to regard the Quebec contretemps as unique. The Quebec legislation was not a piece of isolated legislation, they said, since there were a similar act at the federal level and an Inquiry Act in each of the provinces. They called attention to the fact that any Supreme Court judge could commit reporters for refusal to disclose. Indeed, some felt that any Supreme Court judge in Canada might have imposed a longer sentence than the Montreal Five Investigation Commission did.

Many journalists, in a spontaneous reaction to a situation about which they were not too knowledgeable, seemed to regard the controversy as a contest between an all embracing requirement of disclosure under all circumstances and a complete and absolute protection of journalists under all circumstances. As a result they conceived the defencelessness of the journalist to be far greater than it actually is; and they called for an absolute protection which could not, under the free press-fair trial philosophy which prevails in Canada, be justified. The fact is that the media enjoy a degree of protection far greater than generally realized. As has been indicated earlier, it is also true that to grant the media the absolute privilege of keeping their sources secret might produce injustices that would outweigh any hardships imposed on the press by the requirement to name sources.

Related to the average journalist's ignorance about his obligation to disclose was a comparable ignorance about the previously discussed privileges of others involved with the law: husband and wife; solicitor and client; penitent and priest; doctor and patient. Such faulty knowledge was typified by John Smith when he claimed for the journalist the lawyer's privilege of confidentiality on the grounds that such confidentiality was as essential to the journalist's function as it was to the lawyer's. In doing so he showed no awareness of the difference between the lawyer-client and journalist-informant relationships — a difference which has already been examined.

There was still another facet of the John Smith affair about which commentators and editorialists were not too clear. Many discussed the CBC journalist's citation for contempt as though he had been punished for refusing to name sources, when, in point of fact, his offence had been to decline to answer any questions put to him by the Commission. Both Hyliard Chappell and Bruce Phillips on the "Something Else" program commented more knowledgeably. They were exceptional in realizing, as not too many journalist commentators did, that what Smith had done was, in fact, to say, "I refuse to give any evidence whatsoever;" they felt that Smith should have accepted the summons and then decided what answers to give after the questions were put. As Bruce Phillips commented, "It's pretty hard for him to defend not turning up at the hearing at all. If, on the other hand, he went and they demanded discolosure of sources he would have been on an entirely different wicket. He doesn't even know... for sure... what questions were going to be put to him. I think it's better to go to court and make a case there.

In his statement to justify his refusal to testify before the Montreal Fire Commission, John Smith protested that he was being required to reveal sources *even though he had not been charged with a criminal offence*. In doing so he implied that the requirement of disclosure was an exceptional one. The *Globe and Mail* editorial previously cited and Doug Collins in the program already referred to also gave the impression that they thought it remarkable that Smith should be so dealt with even though he was not arraigned under criminal proceedings. Yet there was nothing abnormal in what the Fire Commissioner had done, as was illustrated by the previously considered Blair Fraser, Jacqueline Sirois and Marie Torre cases, three earlier precedents which did not involve criminal prosecutions.

Perhaps the most influential journalist to speak out against the treatment of the CBC staffer and in favor of protection of sources was Gérard Pelletier. Interviewed by Patrick Watson, the Secretary of State took the view that under appropriate conditions, the most notable being that the privileged reporter be a *bona fide* journalist investigating stories in the performance of his professional duties, "the public interest will be best served" by granting him immunity. Mr. Pelletier made it clear that he felt that the decision for or against disclosure should be in the hands of the press rather than of the judiciary. The decisiveness of his answer was perhaps partially accounted for by the form used by Watson in one of his questions. After describing a hypothetical situation in which, through interview, a newspaper had learned that someone had been responsible for separatist violence, the CBC interviewer asked, "You would not feel obligated to go to the police and say, 'Here's how we got this story'?" Naturally enough, perhaps, Pelletier remarked in the course of his answer, "...we are not police informers, we are informers of the public..." Yet the picture thus conjured up hardly represents the disclosure vs. anonymity issue. There is a world of difference between (on the one hand) running to the police every time the press gets information that might conceivably affect public security, and (on the other) writing news stories based on such information and being willing to divulge sources on those rare occasions when the journalist is summoned to appear before a properly constituted court or commission.

An objection to the Pelletier assessment of the disclosure question is that it leaves it to the journalist exclusively to weigh the countervailing considerations of public and press interest, and to decide whether sources are to be divulged. Part of the argument against the granting of such a privilege arises out of the uncertainty of the status of journalism. It is not a profession, has no code of ethics, is not subject to self-regulation as is the case with law or medicine, and in Canada is just beginning to face the gentle and by no means ubiquitous scrutiny of press councils. Both its failure to achieve professional status and the unwisdom of setting up press councils with anything more than the power to admonish derives from the nature of the freedom it claims. It is a platitude that freedom of the press is no different in kind or degree than the freedom to which any citizen in the country is entitled. It might be argued that both the working journalist and the casual "man in the street" correspondent should be subject to the same type of Press Council supervision. The same line of reasoning suggests that if the press were granted the privilege of unvarying confidentiality so too should any member of the public be granted that privilege.

Mr. Chappell stated an opinion widely held by thoughtful students of the question when he said that he could not see how the privilege of confidentiality could be granted to the journalist without granting the same privilege to doctors, psychiatrists, social workers, probation officers and religious people. To extend the privilege that far, he thought, would seriously impair the ability of the courts to function. Others have made the same point about stockbrokers, accountants, detectives and officials of banks and trust companies, for which the right of confidentiality has sometimes been claimed.

Several commentators have expressed scepticism of the press in claiming privilege. They contend that if the journalist can repeat stories but conceal their source, he can invent stories and use privilege to conceal the pretense. They feel that the real motive for privilege is not zeal for the public good, but the desire for prestige or readership attention. Mr. Chappell felt that under the guise of confidentiality the newspaper might perpetrate a simple hoax. Desmond Morton, Osgoode Hall law school professor, considered the public interest not to be served by keeping confidentiality. He called attention to the fact that newspapers publish for a wide variety of reasons, one of which is to sell copies and make money, and that many journals, while speaking of the public interest at a high level of abstraction, were really concerned with their own private interest of trying to get a headline. While conceding that there might be occasions when such headlines might incidentally serve the public interest where a creative piece of journalism was involved, he felt that all too often such stories were only marginal to the public interest. Thus he did not believe journalism was justified in asking for a *generalized* (italics mine) protection when the value of non-disclosure was by no means proved.

All four legal authorities interviewed by Patrick Watson on the program, "The Way It Is," (Morton ; Maxwell Cohen, dean of the McGill Law School; Michel Côté, legal adviser to the Montreal Police Department; and Joseph Sedgwick, a distinguished practising lawyer with 46 years' experience) refused to accept Watson's suggestion that the law should require the court to show that it was in the public interest before it could compel a journalist to reveal his sources. Even Maxwell Cohen, who seemed most aware of the journalist's watch-dog role in exposing public acts to public scrutiny, felt that, in terms of Wigmore's fourth canon, "...the onus is really on the journalists to prove that they are on balance hampered in their job by the general duty to disclose."

When Watson persisted and questioned what public interest would be served by putting Smith in jail, Morton replied readily that Smith's punishment fulfilled the *pour encourager les autres* principle. He felt that what was done to Smith would encourage reporters not to rely on their unnamed sources but to go out and verify their information with evidence they could expose to public scrutiny.

Mr. Sedgwick supplemented the Morton answer by saying that, unless contumacious journalists were to be punished for defiance of the courts, the courts would be effectively amending the law, and that they would be implying that journalists have a protection which they do not, in fact, have.

All four legal authorities were at pains to point out that the law lays no heavy hand on the press through indiscriminate contempt citations. They firmly rejected Watson's implications that the fact that two *La Presse* reporters had just been excused from testifying in a Montreal trial indicated that the treatment of John Smith had somehow gone beyond what was right and proper. Mr. Sedgwick felt that "In the case of Mr. Smith it was thought that the public interest demanded that he should disclose [his source]. In the case of the two *La Presse* reporters it was thought that it didn't." He took this to show that the law as it stands is able to settle such questions with wisdom and discretion.

While there seemed to be a consensus that the power to punish contempt was needed to check irresponsibility and to protect the private and public interest, Professor Cohen at least showed an awareness of journalism's praiseworthy role in combatting government secrecy. He said, "Where you are dealing with an enormously complex series of relationships of the state to the individual, and where the state is still in many respects highly secrecy-oriented... journalism becomes a kind of countervailing power to unloosen the congealed secrecies that don't make the democratic process perhaps as loose-limbed as it ought to be." He believed that one of the prices society should be prepared to pay might be an increase in the area of insecurity resulting from an increased confidentiality of sources. But he felt that any changes in this direction should be made with "a certain sense of the other price we're paying for it, namely that you may be providing new privileges, the total consequences of which you cannot foresee." It is less a matter of irony and more an illustration of the intricacy of the revealing of sources question that journalists should claim the privilege of secrecy in order to help them thwart government secrecy.

Canadian journalists seem aware that the laws of contempt hold hazards. Bruce Phillips perhaps typified such a viewpoint when he said, speaking of the John Smith case, "I'm quite prepared to live with [the] situation and refuse to divulge sources and take the consequences. My view is that Smith and any other newspaperman worth his salt would behave that way. If he is given information in confidence he has his own bond upon it, and unless it is something affecting the security of the country or a matter of that character, he has no choice if he wishes to go on being a journalist except to defend the confidence that he has been given... I think the press is able to take care of itself in cases like this. I think that we've got to accept the fact there are going to be situations where the court's requirement for information is going to directly conflict with the reporter's obligation to his source of information... Sometimes [journalists] are going to land in jail because of it, but it wouldn't be the first time a journalist went to jail."

Journalists who did go to jail under the conditions described by Mr. Phillips would at least have been dealt with under the well-understood concept of "due process" of law, with the requirement to divulge being exacted only by a properly constituted court or commission. If the Alberta Press Act of 1937 had not been ruled *ultra vires* the government itself would have been empowered to compel disclosure without the journalist enjoying any of the protections built into the procedures which make up "due process." One of its harsh terms was that it would have required any newspaper "to name within twenty-four hours sources of any statement" made by that paper "within sixty days of the making of an order so to do." Failure to comply would have brought dire punishments. Journalists all across Canada recognized in the Bill a genuine threat to freedom and reacted with anger. Both the principles involved in the successful fight against the enactment and the public reaction to the measure made the affair a true Canadian *cause célèbre*.

By the Alberta Press Bill yardstick, the John Smith affair was not a *cause célèbre*.

3.6.3 John Sawatsky, "John Sawatsky Stakes Out The High Ground", (1986) 29 *Bulletin of the Centre for Investigative Journalism* 11

I didn't think the Crown would go through with it — use the media to prosecute a former Mountie for espionage.

But it did happen. I was subpoenaed to testify in the Long Knife case.

For years I had vaguely expected to experience something like this: sooner or later the needs of the media to expose events for the public good would collide with the desires of the courts. The Long Knife story happened to be the case.

Back in the 1950s the KGB slipped into Canada an Intelligence Officer who, posing as a Canadian photographer in Montreal named David Soboloff, fell in love with a Canadian woman (the wife of a Canadian soldier, just to make things a little more interesting.) Soboloff defected and the RCMP turned him into a double agent.

At the same time a Mountie, later given the codename Long Knife, fell deeply and unmanageably into debt, and sold the Soboloff secret to the Russians for an envelope full of cash. Soboloff soon returned to Moscow not knowing he had been betrayed. Soboloff never came back and the RCMP couldn't figure out how it had lost its number one agent.

Long Knife was eventually discovered and in January 1958 confessed to his Mountie superiors, who prosecuted him not for treason but for passing bad cheques. He was convicted and dismissed from the force. The RCMP never told its minister. Everything was covered up.

Publication of *For Services Rendered* in November 1982 exposed the whole affair but identified the treacherous Mountie only by the name Long Knife. At the same time CBC-TV's *The Fifth Estate* with Eric Malling filmed an interview of Long Knife in disguise. About a week later the *Winnipeg Free Press* published a story identifying Long Knife as former RCMP Corporal James Morrison and quoted Morrison acknowledging his role.

Mounties finally act

The RCMP, too embarrassed to prosecute Long Knife in 1958, was now too embarrassed *not* to prosecute. They raided my house, the CBC, Doubleday Canada Ltd., the *Winnipeg Free Press* as well as Morrison's home, arrested him and charged him with three counts of treason under the Official Secrets Act.

Malling and I were subpoenaed at the preliminary hearing in November 1983. I refused to answer a number of questions. Malling answered but skillfully avoided betraying Long Knife's identity.

Legal challenges delayed the trial until this year. One of the first things Justice Coulter Osborne did when the trial finally did start on Monday morning, last January 20, was to dismiss the jury until Wednesday while the defence and prosecution argued about which evidence was admissible. On Tuesday, with the jury still absent and with the press barred from publishing the proceedings, I was called.

Sources not revealed

I tried to be as helpful as possible until the questions required me to identify sources. At that point I replied frequently: ''I object to answering that question. The answer to that question is privileged. If I were to answer that question I would breach an express undertaking of confidentiality and violate and undermine an historical and ethical standard of my profession.''

I felt it important to state my position without apology. I wanted the court to know that I was not asking for mercy but claiming a right. Whether the judge would accept this claim or find me in contempt would have to await the return of the jury when I would testify all over again.

The jury returned the next morning and the Crown put me on notice for 2 P.M. Thursday.

My lawyer and I were busily lining up witnesses to help fight the expected contempt citation. Pierre Berton, Barbara Frum, Jock Ferguson and Walter Stewart waited in the wings. So did Nick Hills, June Callwood, Michael Enright and Peter Calamai. Some of these people contorted their schedules to clear time for a flight to Ottawa.

Pleaded guilty

Just before noon Thursday, as I was leaving for the Parliamentary Press Gallery en route to court, a phone call came in. Earlier that morning. Morrison surprised the court by pleading guilty to one of the three espionage counts. (In return the Crown dropped the other two). The case had suddenly ended just hours before the showdown.

In one sense I was disappointed. Freedom of the press under the Charter of Rights and Freedoms has yet to be interpreted and this case represented an excellent opportunity for a ruling favorable to the media. Clearly the Crown had abused its authority, having in the name of RCMP first covered up the story and then, when finally forced to act, compelled journalists to be *de facto* agents of the prosecution when virtually all the journalists' information originated from RCMP filing cabinets. The press had acted in the public interest and, on balance, the Crown had acted against it. It is hard to think of a better opportunity to have entrenched the media's privilege to protect sources.

...

At the moment, the media does not have the protection it deserves. Until that time arrives, those who cannot stand the heat of honoring commitments should not become involved with them in the first place.

3.6.4 Sawatsky's Notes

While John Sawatsky still believed that he would be asked to divulge his sources and thereby cited for contempt in the Long Knife trial, he prepared the following notes to be read into the court record. They express carefully the perspective of many thoughtful journalists on the exercise of the law of contempt when journalists refuse to comply with a court order to betray confidences and reveal the names of sources. The information in this case was covered up and Sawatsky stated persuasively that he had acted honourably and in the interests of justice when he researched and then published the facts. A justification for escaping the sanctions of the law of contempt in this case is that he performed a very important public duty relating directly to the standards of justice in Canada.

As noted earlier, the accused changed his plea and Sawatsky was not asked by the Court to testify.

Reasons for Refusing to Divulge Sources

John Sawatsky

I would like to explain my position to the court. I want to make it clear that my position in no ways suggests lack of respect for the court or anybody appearing before this court. I believe the court has a vital responsibility in seeing that justice is done.

Society must assist the court in carrying out its duties and I do not seek an unqualified exemption. If, as a citizen, I witness an accident and the court issues me a subpoena I would see it as my duty to give conscientious testimony and generally do what I reasonably can to assist the legal process. I would do so even in my role as a journalist when I have been a third-party witness. In fact my cooperation goes further as it clearly has here already today. I have made a genuine effort to answer questions as fully as I can. However I cannot provide source-sensitive information when the sources have been promised anonymity.

My role as a journalist is to put information on the public record. I have specialized in areas where little documentary material has been available to the public. Consequently most of my information comes from oral sources — who sometimes need to be convinced into talking — and this from time to time puts me into a position of being responsible for their anonymity. Such undertakings have enabled me to reveal stories that have served the public interest and would otherwise never have been revealed. Non-attribution is the basis on which some people talk to me and my ability to serve the public interest hinges directly on this trust.

The court's probing causes me two major concerns.

First, the court wants me to breach an express undertaking of confidentiality and violate and undermine an historic ethical practice of my profession. I believe it is wrong for the court to make this demand. Some people have entrusted their careers in my hands. If I discard this commitment I break my personal word and dishonour a fundamental rule of journalism, a rule that is virtually an oath. I feel I simply have no discretion here.

That is the ethical side. There is also a practical side. In reality the court is requiring me to sacrifice my livelihood. If I betray sources I cannot continue to function as a journalist. This is no philosophical issue. It is a continual reality for me. I conduct several long, probing interviews a week and I am only as good as the respect and confidence I receive. If I fail this responsibility here today, people will stop trusting me and my effectivenes will evaporate. Trust is hard to earn and easy to lose and I've spent years earning the trust of others. The court is asking me not only to answer a question but to forsake a career of 15 years.

As I said earlier, I see a duty to cooperate with the court. But ethically and practically the consequences of betraying sources are worse than any penalty the court is likely to impose. I cannot comply with the court's demand. I want to make it clear I feel obligated to stand firm to the end.

I was able to write *For Services Rendered* and only because people trusted me. I first learned of the Long Knife case in October or November of 1977 while researching my first book, *Men in the Shadows*. I tried but could not flesh out the story. So I dropped it. As far as I was concerned the Long Knife investigation was over and dead. Unexpectantly, my career changed course and I found myself writing a second RCMP book, which turned out to be *For Services Rendered*. By this time *Men in the Shadows* was published and some key people saw how carefully I protected sources. THAT was when the Long Knife investigation got back on track. I mention this to illustrate the direct correlation between the level of trust in me and my ability to reveal the Long Knife story. The Long Knife case is only one example.

This trust has carried over into my current research into lobbying. One lobbyist volunteered [that] he was talking to me because of the way I had obviously treated sources in my RCMP books.

Let me provide a hypothetical example of how an overreaching court can harm the public interest. If an influence peddler told me he was bribing the government I think everybody agrees the practice should be exposed and halted. No influence peddler will describe his activities if he believes I will become the Crown's star witness against him. Otherwise he might as well confess to the police. I would be a de facto policeman. The press would be crippled because, not surprisingly, sources would treat us as policemen rather than journalists. Everybody would suffer, including the court. Without an effective press, criminal cases that otherwise would have been exposed would never reach the court. The court cannot act on cases it never hears. So in the end our system of justice and — all society — would be damaged.

My role, which I take very seriously, is to inform the public so that the public can make independent and enlightened decisions for better or for worse. I'm not so much interested in what decision the public makes so long as it has access to as many facts as possible. Once I become an agent of the court, the police, or any other institution my role is compromised.

I take this stand not only for myself. I have given this matter considerable thought recently and have discussed it with colleagues. They agree I have no alternative. One colleague said: "John, you're doing this for all of us. Otherwise we couldn't function either."

It is impossible for a free society to operate without a free press. The role of the press must be respected and allowed to flourish. I realize the court has a job to do. I hope the court acknowledges that the media also have a crucial job to do.

Statement given when being cited for contempt of court

John Sawatsky

I'm being cited for being in contempt of court. I take issue with that allegation. Let's step back and take a broader look at my so-called "contempt". I agree that the administration of justice in society is fundamentally important and that the court system must be able to work and, furthermore, that people who set out to frustrate the working of the court are in contempt. But even a narrow view — one that gives no weight to my responsibility to uphold the ability of a free press to perform its duty — must conclude that my actions, in total, have not inhibited the administration of justice but, in fact, have assisted it.

The trial that is being heard here today is based on events that occurred more than 25 years ago. Most of the facts known today were known by officials in positions of appropriate authority shortly after they happened and yet the evidence was not referred to the Department of Justice or to the courts. This was not the result of oversight. The decision to withhold information was a conscious decision taken by the top officers of the RCMP. In my opinion, this decision to withhold evidence is an osbtruction of justice amounting to contempt.

In contrast, my actions have been consistent and clear and all directed toward exposing the events — to break the cover-up that prior to 1982 had blocked the case from reaching court. The court would not be hearing this case if the knowledge of events had continued to rest solely in the hands of the RCMP. That is why I say when you look at the whole context — and look at it fairly — my involvement has served to help the court to see that justice is done in society. Frankly, I don't see how you can justly find contempt against someone who uncovered the facts in the first place. It seems to me that the court's right to cite contempt should be reserved for those who originally conspired to frustrate the legal process.

Also, I think you have to look at motive. I think all sides agree that my position is not a device to hide skeletons or escape unethical behaviour. I have acted honourably both as journalist and citizen. In fact if I was less honourable — if I was a defendant who had performed some heinous crime I could exercise my right not to take the stand. That, in my layman's view, is contempt: frustrating the administration of justice by withholding information for selfish reasons. If I acted in that manner my position would be contemptuous and immoral but entirely lawful. I now find myself being very moral but seemingly not lawful. I realize this is not an easy matter for the court because other issues are involved. But it demonstrates the need for the court to look at motive and if the court examines motive it will conclude that my motive has been to correct injustice and not cause it.

There is good reason not to challenge somebody in my circumstances. Courts recognize the role of the press. A court will not allow witnesses in the same trial to sit in the courtroom for the very good reason that they should not hear what other witnesses say. But witnesses can read a newspaper and learn who said what. If the court pursued its interests narrowly it would prohibit press coverage of multi-day trials. But the court realizes that society has many interests to protect in addition to supporting the administration of justice. In this instance the court has concluded that freedom of the press takes precedence over the needs of the justice system.

It works the other way as well. The press may be barred from reporting evidence in preliminary hearings and in some kinds of trials the press must withhold names of victims. In these instances other interests are put ahead of the public's need to know. So neither the court nor the press always has everything it would ideally like. Both institutions acknowledge each other's interest and attach public good to it. So we're not talking about absolutes here. The court and the press have conflicting interests and try to accommodate each other. Yet both institutions have certain boundaries the other must not cross. For me — and I believe for the rest of the press as well — source protection is one of these inviolate boundaries. At this stage I must stop compromising and start defending my territory.

The court itself recognizes cases where confidences must remain sacred. The most notable example is the lawyer-client relationship. Why are lawyers not required to reveal everything about their clients? This would open a tremendous source of information for the court's benefit. Chances are that all kinds of unsavoury criminals who now get off would be convicted. This avenue, nevertheless, has been put off limits — and for good reason. Merely the threat of a subpoena to a defence lawyer would — for reasons that need no explaining — sabotage the lawyer's ability to defend the client. In very practical terms, the system would not work. The court, in its wisdom, recognizes the principle that a trial must exempt certain sources of information.

Court probing into journalistic sources — if successful — would also undermine a journalist's ability to function. In the same way that clients would stop confiding in their lawyers, sources would stop talking to reporters.

Why are lawyers exempted and not journalists? The legal profession — be they the Canadian Bar Association, the lawyers in the Department of Justice or judges — molds the law with a vested interest. The legal community is saying: "We'll exempt ourselves but not you." It is discriminatory and unfair.

There is one other issue I feel needs to be raised and that has to do with conflict of interest. I raise it only because I believe it touches directly on the ability of justice to prevail. With respect, your honour, I don't think you should be even presiding when adjudicating between two institutions when one of the institutions happens to be your own. On issues such as these you cannot possibly be an independent arbitrator no matter how good a judge you are nor how hard you attempt to be impartial. I am a traditionalist who believes that reporters should report and not advocate and I go to considerable lengths to practice this philosophy. Yet when it comes to freedom of the press, I acknowledge myself to be an advocate. Furthermore, I don't think I would be a good person to adjudicate a dispute between a newspaper and someone who complained of unfair coverage. I could probably do a fair analysis of the issues — but whose issues? Between my views on the need for public disclosure and the complainant's concern about the dangers of defamation, the complainant and I probably would not agree on what the appropriate issues were. I am an advocate for an effective and diligent press. I think judges are advocates for judicial authority. In fact I believe judges would be remiss if they were not because judges must protect their ability to carry out their responsibilities. The problem is that when judicial interests come into conflict with press interests a judge is no longer a disinterested party. A judge's ability to be unbiased is in question just as a journalist's bias must be questioned on a press complaint.

I am raising a fundamental issue — one so fundamental that its resolution should be left to society. When the legitimate needs of the press come into conflict with the legitimate needs of the court, the decision should rest with a jury. Not a jury of experts — because this is more a fundamental issue than a technical one — but a jury of citizens from all walks of life. By citing me for contempt you are de facto acting as a plaintiff. I do not think one gets fair process when the plaintiff and the judge are the same person.

I know what the law says. You have the lawful right to find me in contempt of court for not answering specific questions but you have no moral right to do so. In fact you would be abusing your moral authority. Society has entrusted a lot of authority in you and society expects you to handle this responsibility not only lawfully but wisely. Society also gives broad powers to the police. A police officer is able to stop a car and for no good reason cause the operator considerable distress while remaining entirely within the law. Customs inspectors at border points possess awesome powers which can be employed at any time. But these powers are reserved for critical situations. Society extends broad powers to certain agents but they were never meant to be blank cheques.

The case is even more compelling with judges. If the police overstep their moral authority the victim can appeal to a body of non-policemen. But when judges overstep their moral authority I must appeal to another judge. Given the fact that you have tremendous authority, and that there are fundamental rights involved, and that realistically there is no appeal, I believe the best public service the court could perform is by proceeding only with extraordinary caution. And, I believe, when all factors are taken into consideration, extraordinary caution in this case compels the court not to proceed with a contempt citation.

3.6.5 *Re Legislative Privilege* (1978) 83 D.L.R. (3d) 161 (Ont. C.A.)

LACOURCIERE, J.A.: — The Lieutenant-Governor in Council by O.C. 1899/77, dated July 6, 1977, approved by His Honour the Administrator of the Government of the Province of Ontario, referred to this Court for hearing and consideration certain questions pursuant to the *Constitutional Questions Act,* R.S.O. 1970, c.79. A copy of the Order in Council is annexed hereto as App. "A" [not printed]. The Court, being of the opinion that the questions posed were properly referable under the Act, gave directions for the publication of notice of the hearing. This notice, which was published in two Toronto newspapers, invited any interested parties to file submissions in writing before September 2, 1977. A copy of the notice is annexed hereto as App. "B" [not printed].

As a result of the said publications, notices of intention to make submissions were filed with the Court (1) on behalf of the Attorney-General for the Province of Ontario representing the Government of Ontario, (2) on behalf of the Liberal Caucus of the Ontario Legislature, (3) on behalf of the Leader of the New Democratic Party of Ontario and Patrick D. Lawlor, Q.C., member of the Legislative Assembly for Lakeshore, (4) on behalf of the Canadian Civil Liberties Association, and (5) on behalf of ABKO Medical Laboratories Limited. Subsequently, statements of the points intended to be submitted and the authorities upon which it was intended to rely were filed by counsel for the respective parties who appeared at the commencement of the hearing on November 14, 1977. No lay members of the public appeared in person or expressed any intention to present their personal views on the questions included in this reference.

The hearing commenced on November 14th and concluded in the afternoon of November 15, 1977. At the conclusion of the hearing the opinion of the Court was reserved.

For convenience of reference, the questions referred to the Court for its consideration are as follows:

> 1. Is it open to a court in a criminal proceeding to refrain from compelling a member of the Legislative Assembly to disclose the existence, source or content of a communication made to him by an informant (where such evidence would otherwise be relevant and admissible) on the ground that it is not in the public interest to disclose the existence, source or content of the communication, or on any other ground?
>
> 2. If so, and if on the basis of public interest, what principles and interest should the court consider in determining whether it is in the public interest to compel or to refrain from compelling such disclosure?
>
> 3. Does the Legislative Assembly of Ontario have the power to enact legislation protecting its members from being compelled by a court in a criminal case to disclose the existence, source or content of a communication from an informant?

General powers

This Court, in view of the narrow scope of the questions, does not have a mandate to report at large on the general concept of parliamentary privilege or, indeed, on the ordinary role and jurisdiction of the Court in determining the nature and extent of parliamentary privilege. It is sufficient to say that the Court has an undoubted right to consider the matters raised in the reference and argued at the hearing, and a duty to certify to the Lieutenant-Governor in Council its opinion on the matters referred, accompanied by a statement of its reasons.

Question 1

> 1. Is it open to a court in a criminal proceeding to refrain from compelling a member of the Legislative Assembly to disclose the existence, source or content of a communication made to him by an informant (where such evidence would otherwise be relevant and admissible) on the ground that it is not in the public interest to disclose the existence, source or content of the communication, or on any other ground?

The answer to this question involved an investigation of statute law and the common law with respect to the privileges granted to a member of the Legislative Assembly. The members of the Legislative Assembly of the Province of Ontario, the summoning of which was authorized by s.82 of the *British North America Act,* 1867 (U.K.), c.3, were not by that statute invested with any privileges, immunities and powers. The Legislature, in the exercise of its powers and to secure for its members the freedom to exercise their legislative functions, enacted what is now the *Legislative Assembly Act,* R.S.O. 1970, c.240.

The essential origins of this Act were enacted in 1876 by c.9, which was consolidated along with various provisions from several other statutes in R.S.O. 1877, c.12, and appeared subject to certain further amendments in R.S.O. 1887, c.11, and R.S.O. 1897, c.12. It was re-enacted in 1908 by c.5, and as so re-enacted has appeared subject to amendment, from time to time, in successive revisions to the present time.

The relevant sections of the Act with respect to the privileges, freedoms and exemptions of the members of the Legislature are as follows:

> 37. A member of the Assembly is not liable to any civil action or prosecution, arrest, imprisonment or damages, by reason of any matter or thing brought by him by petition, bill, resolution, motion or otherwise, or said by him before the Assembly or a committee thereof.

38. Except for a contravention of this Act, a member of the Assembly is not liable to arrest, detention or molestation for any cause or matter whatever of a civil nature during a session of the Legislature or during the twenty days preceding or the twenty days following a session.

39. During the periods mentioned in section 38, members, officers and employees of the Assembly and witnesses summoned to attend before the Assembly or a committee thereof are exempt from serving or attending as jurors in any court of justice in Ontario.

...

52. Except so far as is provided by section 40, nothing in this Act shall be construed to deprive the Assembly or a committee or member thereof of any right, immunity, privilege or power that the Assembly, committee or member might otherwise have been entitled to exercise or enjoy.

One would not expect to find in the *Legislative Assembly Act,* for reasons which we make clear in our answer to Q. 3, any statutory protection relieving a member of the Legislative Assembly from his ordinary testimonial duty when called as a witness in a criminal proceeding, because of the limits on the constitutional competence of the Legislature.

Section 37, dealing with a member's privilege of speech, is only applicable "by reason of any matter or thing brought by him by petition, bill, resolution, motion or otherwise, or said by him before the Assembly or a committee thereof". The fact that a member discusses an issue in the Assembly may not prevent a Court from compelling a member to disclose the source or content of a communication made to him by an informant. The intent of s.37 was to enact the common law rule of freedom of speech so as to allow members to express their views in the Assembly or a committee thereof without fear of an action for slander or libel.

Section 38 deals with freedom from arrest, but it is limited to matters of a "civil nature" and hence is inapplicable to criminal proceedings.

Section 52 makes it clear that the *Legislative Assembly Act* does not exhaustively declare all the privileges enjoyed by the members of the Legislative Assembly. It is for that reason that we have been referred to legal decisions to determine whether any privilege exists at common law which would justify the refusal of a member to disclose the source or content of a communication made to him by an informant.

The function of a Court of law being to arrive at the truth of the matter in dispute, all evidence relevant to the issue ought to be heard, unless the matters to be proved are so remote that it is not worthwhile to let them be proved, or, in a criminal case, the prejudicial effect so far outweighs the probative value that it would be unfair to the accused, and so detract from the search for the truth. And it follows from this that "Every person in the kingdom except the sovereign may be called upon and is bound to give evidence to the best of his knowledge upon any question of fact material and relevant to an issue tried in any of the Queen's courts, unless he can shew some exception in his favour...": *Ex. p. Fernandez* (1861), 10 C.B.(N.S.) 3 at p. 39, 142 E.R. 349. All this is implicit in the "rule of law".

Generally, in a criminal proceeding, a witness has an obligation and may be compelled to answer any and all relevant questions. The *Criminal Code* of Canada, R.S.C. 1970, c.C-34, as amended, has provisions for compelling the attendance of witnesses by way of subpoena. Part XIX of the *Criminal Code* deals with procuring the attendance of witnesses, with appropriate punishment for persons failing without lawful excuse to perform their obligation. The testimonial obligation of witnesses at trial is so fundamental to our system of criminal justice, that Courts are given a summary power to deal with defaulting witnesses by way of punishment for contempt of Court: s.636.

At a preliminary inquiry where a person is charged with an indictable offence, the provisions of s.472 of the *Criminal Code* of Canada apply, and provide as follows:

> 472(1) Where a person, being present at a preliminary inquiry and being required by the justice to give evidence,
>
> (*a*) refuses to be sworn,
>
> (*b*) having been sworn, refuses to answer the questions that are put to him,
>
> (*c*) fails to produce any writings that he is required to produce or
>
> (*d*) refuses to sign his deposition,
>
> without offering a reasonable excuse for his failure or refusal, the justice may adjourn the inquiry and may, by warrant in Form 16, commit the person to prison for a period not exceeding eight clear days or for the period during which the inquiry is adjourned, whichever is the lesser period.
>
> (2) Where a person to whom subsection (1) applies is brought before the justice upon the resumption of the adjourned inquiry and again refuses to do what is required of him, the justice may again adjourn the inquiry for a period not exceeding eight clear days and commit him to prison for the period of adjournment or any part thereof, and may adjourn the inquiry and commit the person to prison from time to time until the person consents to do what is required of him.
>
> (3) Nothing in this section shall be deemed to prevent the justice from sending the case for trial upon any other sufficient evidence taken by him.

There is an assumption in Q. 1 which has caused us some difficulty. The assumption is that the evidence, the disclosure of which is sought to be compelled from a member of the Legislative Assembly, ''would otherwise be relevant and admissible''. We find it difficult to visualize a case in which the existence or the source, and particularly the content of a communication made to a member of the Legislative Assembly would, in the normal course of events, become relevant and admissible. We are of the opinion that the existence or source of a communication would generally be irrelevant (and hence inadmissible) to the issues raised in a criminal case. The content of a communication, even if relevant, would normally be excluded as inadmissible to prove the truth of its content by the ordinary exclusionary rule regarding hearsay evidence. When pressed to give an example of when the content of such information would qualify as an exception, counsel could only think of a far-fetched example operating as an exception to the hearsay rule. Generally speaking, therefore, the disclosure of the content of an informant's communication to prove the truth of the facts contained therein would, in the absence of special circumstances, offend against the rules prohibiting the introduction of hearsay evidence.

In considering Q. 1, a clear distinction must be drawn between a *privilege,* on the part of a member of the Legislative Assembly and the *discretion of the Court* in criminal proceedings to refrain from exercising its power to compel a disclosure by the member, of the communication made to him.

We are of the view that the member of the Legislative Assembly does not have an absolute privilege, in a criminal proceeding, which would allow him to refuse to disclose the source or content of a communication made to him by an informer. No such privilege is granted, or could properly be granted, by the *Legislative Assembly Act:* see answer to Q. 3. According to principles of the common law, a provincial Legislature has ''every power reasonably necessary for the proper exercise of their functions and duties'': *Kielley v. Carson* (1841), 4 Moo. P.C. 63 at p. 92, 13 E.R. 225. As stated by Baron Parke in this leading case before the Privy Council at p. 88:

> The Statute Law on this subject [the power of a Legislature committing for contempt] being silent, the Common Law is to govern it; and what is the Common Law, depends upon principle and precedent.
>
> Their Lordships see no reason to think, that in the principle of the Common Law, any other powers are given them, than such as are necessary to the existence of such a body, and the proper exercise of the functions which it is intended to execute.

It is our opinion, therefore, that members of the Legislative Assembly do not possess any statutory or common law privilege founded on their status exempting them from their obligation to testify. They receive no special immunity in that respect.

Common law privilege

The common law has recognized certain types of communications which are privileged, subject to certain exceptions, and not subject to judicially enforced disclosure. The exempted classes include communications between solicitor and client; communications between husband and wife; communications concerning the deliberations of a jury; and, finally, communications with Government and Government officials. We are not concerned with the first three classes, which respectively rest upon social policy to promote freedom of consultation with legal advisers in the defence of legal rights, the need to preserve mutual trust and confidence in domestic relations and the obvious necessity in the administration of justice of preserving the secrecy of jury deliberations. The privilege respecting Government documents creates an exclusion which is limited to the requirements of the public interest in maintaining the confidentiality of its internal communications. We adopt the apt words of Lord Simon of Glaisdale in *D. v. National Society for Prevention of Cruelty to Children,* [1977] 2 W.L.R. 201 at pp. 221-2:

> The various classes of excluded relevant evidence may for ease of exposition be presented under different colours. But in reality they constitute a spectrum, refractions of the single light of a public interest which may outshine that of the desirability that all relevant evidence should be adduced to a court of law.

An extension of the so-called Crown privilege has been accorded, in the public interest, to protect from disclosure the identity of police informers. The *rationale* for this extension was clearly the importance to the public of the detection of crimes, and the necessity of preserving the anonymity of police informers to maintain the sources of information. This necessity has generally outweighed the public interest of full disclosure of relevant facts to the adjudicating tribunal. This privilege, however, is not absolute and is subject to one important exception, stated by Lord Diplock in *D. v. N.S.P.C.C., supra,* at p. 207:

> By the uniform practice of the judges which by the time of *Marks v. Beyfus,* 25 Q.B.D. 494 had already hardened into a rule of law, the balance has fallen upon the side of non-disclosure except where upon the trial of a defendant for a criminal offence disclosure of the identity of the informer could help to show that the defendant was innocent of the offence. In that case, and it that case only, the balance falls upon the side of disclosure.

The House of Lords in *D. v. N.S.P.C.C., supra,* extended the protection for the non-disclosure of police informants to protect the identity of an informant to the National Society for the Prevention of Cruelty to Children.

It is clear that the classes of evidence which give rise to privileged communications have foundations in social policy in which the general liability of every person to give testimony upon all facts inquired of in a Court gives way to more important social considerations: *Wigmore on Evidence,* McNaughton Revision (1961), vol. 8, p. 531, states:

> Looking back upon the principle of Privilege... four fundamental conditions may be predicated as necessary to the establishment of a privilege against the disclosure of communications between persons standing in a given relation:
>
> (1) The communications must originate in a *confidence* that they will not be disclosed;
>
> (2) This element of *confidentiality must be essential* to the full and satisfactory maintenance of the relation between the parties;
>
> (3) The *relation* must be one which in the opinion of the community ought to be sedulously *fostered;* and
>
> (4) The *injury* that would inure to the relation by the disclosure of the communications must be *greater than the benefit* thereby gained for the correct disposal of litigation.
>
> These four conditions being present, a privilege should be recognized; and not otherwise.

This passage was quoted and adopted by Spence, J., in *Slavutych v. Baker et al.* (1975), 55 D.L.R. (3d) 224 at p. 229, [1976] 1 S.C.R. 254 at p. 261, 38 C.R.N.S. 306, where he referred to it as "the doctrine of privilege as so ably considered in Wigmore".

The argument put forward to this Court in a most forceful and persuasive manner by Mr. Greenspan on behalf of the Civil Liberties Association is based on the analogy between a member of the Legislative Assembly and a police or local authority. It is argued that the member has a special status in the community, historically recognized by statute and common law: that he cannot effectively perform his legislative function without privileged access to protected sources of information. Placed at its highest, the argument in favour of non-disclosure is based on the necessity for a well informed member of the Assembly to gather information to enhance the value of this participation in the legislative process. The argument has to go so far as to state that a member of the Legislature cannot effectively perform his function unless the Court has a discretion to refuse to compel him, in a criminal proceeding, to disclose the identity of an imformant. We are of opinion that this argument fails. It is based on a confusion between the function and duty of the police in relation to law enforcement and the function and duty of a member of the Assembly which is in the area of law-making.

The member function, for which he receives privilege, is to participate in the Legislative Assembly or in committees thereof; and to bring matters by way of petition, bill, resolution, motion or otherwise. His major responsibility is in the field of legislation. He has no responsibility in the field of law enforcement, which is properly left to the Courts, upon the prosecution by the law enforcement officials. In brief, there is no reason under the third condition propounded by Wigmore for the recognition of a privilege, to say that the relation between members of the Assembly and informants "ought to be sedulously fostered". On the contrary, we believe the opinion of the community would be that informers with relevant information of criminal wrongdoings should be encouraged to go to the police, who are charged with the responsibility of investigating suspected crimes and breaches of statute law. The informer is then, regardless of his motive, acting in the public interest, to protect society from wrongdoers. However, if the informer chooses to impart his knowledge to a member of the

Assembly, his motives may be political in a partisan way, to embarrass the Government, or perhaps to help a party in opposition. The law may protect him in a defamation action, in the absence of malice (qualified privilege), or in civil litigation at the suit of a private party, on some extended view of public interest which we are not called upon to decide in this reference.

In our view, however, the discretionary exclusion of evidence as to the identity of informants in criminal proceedings should be *prima facie* limited to public enforcement officers. We can find no appropriate analogy between the function of a member and the police or public law enforcement officers which would justify a departure from the established rule that all relevant evidence is subject to forensic investigation.

Having regard to the totality of the public interest, we are unable to say that the injury which may be caused to the relation between the member of the Assembly and his potential informants would be greater than the benefit to be gained by the community by the proper and unimpaired disposition of criminal cases. Thus, the fourth condition of Wigmore is not satisfied, and no privilege should be recognized at common law.

Overriding exclusionary discretion

It was at one time thought that a trial Judge had, in criminal cases, an overriding discretion to exclude evidence even if such evidence was in law admissible: *Rumping v. Director of Public Prosecutions* (1962), 46 Cr.App.R. 398 at p. 403. In *R. v. Wray,* [1970] 4 C.C.C. 1, 11 D.L.R. (3) 673, [1971] S.C.R. 272, the Supreme Court of Canada made it clear that "under our law, the function of the Court is to determine the issue before it, on the evidence admissible in law, and it does not extend to the exclusion of admissible evidence" for any reason other than "to ensure that the accused has a fair trial" (*per* Martland, J., at p. 13 C.C.C., pp. 685-6 D.L.R., p. 288 S.C.R.).

In the *Wray* case, after reviewing the unwarranted extension of Lord du Parcq's statement in *Noor Mohamed,* [1949] A.C. 182, Martland, J., said at p. 17 C.C.C., pp. 689-90 D.L.R., p. 293 S.C.R.:

> This development of the idea of a general discretion to exclude admissible evidence is not warranted by the authority on which it purports to be based. The dictum of Lord Goddard, in the *Kuruma* case [[1955] A.C. 197] appears to be founded on *Noor Mohamed,* and it has, I think, been unduly extended in some of the subsequent cases. It recognized a discretion to disallow evidence if the strict rules of admissibility would operate unfairly against the accused. Even if this statement be accepted, in the way in which it is phrased, the exercise of a discretion by the trial Judge arises only if the admission of the evidence would operate unfairly. The allowance of admissible evidence relevant to the issue before the Court and of substantial probative value may operate unfortunately for the accused, but not unfairly. It is only the allowance of evidence gravely prejudicial to the accused, the admissibility of which is tenuous, and whose probative force in relation to the main issue before the Court is trifling, which can be said to operate unfairly.

We are of the view that the discretion so described and circumscribed, may in criminal proceedings only permit a Court to disallow a certain type of evidence operating unfairly against the accused. If Q. 1 is read in this light, the Court has a discretion to disallow certain admissible evidence. However, that is not how we read Q. 1, which is limited to the power of the Court to refrain from compelling a member to make certain stated disclosures "on the ground that it is not in the *public interest to disclose* the existence, source or content'' of an informant's communication to him (emphasis added).

The question so phrased can therefore refer only to a rule of exclusion based on public policy. In this respect, we have stated that in our view the exclusionary rule which obtains in respect of public prosecutions, ought not to be extended to persons whose main function is legislative.

The discretion — re otherwise admissible confidential information

In his statement Mr. Breithaupt referred to the general practice in Ontario whereby the Court has refused to order priests to answer questions involving confidential communications, although no legal basis exists for any objection to answer. In Ontario, the Judge's suggestion that such questions not be pressed has generally been accepted: *Cronkwright v. Cronkwright* (1970), 14 D.L.R. (3d) 168, [1970] 3 O.R. 784, 2 R.F.L. 241. There are also cases where the presiding Judge has not enforced the disclosure of communications made by a patient to his physician although they are not privileged: see *Dembie v. Dembie,* April, 1963, Ont. S.C. (not reported but discussed in 7 *Crim. L.Q*. 305 at p. 317 (1964-65)) [reported 21 R.F.L. 46]. These cases are not particularly helpful in answering Q. 1. This refusal to enforce the production of evidence otherwise admissible is not based on any overriding discretion known to the law. We must assume that these rulings have been based on what Lord Simon described as the ''moral authority'' of the presiding Judge, in the following passage of his speech in *D. v. National Society of Prevention of Cruelty to Children,* [1977] 2 W.L.R. 201 at p. 227:

> ...I think that the true position is that the judge may not only rule as a matter of law or practice on the admissibility of evidence, but can also exercise a considerable moral authority on the course of a trial. For example, in the situations envisaged the judge is likely to say to counsel: ''You see that the witness feels that he ought not in conscience to answer that question. Do you really press it in the circumstances?'' Such moral pressure will vary according to the circumstances on the one hand, the relevance of the evidence; on the other, the nature of the ethical or professional inhibition. Often indeed such a witness will merely require a little gentle guidance from the judge to overcome his reluctance. I have never myself known this procedure to fail to resolve the situations acceptably. But it is far from the exercise of a formal discretion. And if it comes to the forensic crunch, as it did in many of the cases I have referred to... it must be law, not discretion, which is in command. It may be that the members of the Law Reform Committee considered that a consistent use of moral suasion had resulted in a rule of practice emerging; cf. *Povey v. Povey* [1972] Fam. 40, 48-49 (although I am not convinced myself that it has). Lastly, many of the practical objections voiced by my noble and learned friend. Lord Hailsham of St. Marylebone, to the main and wider proposition advanced on behalf of the appellants seem to me to apply equally to the proposition of the Law Reform Committee. But it may be that some of the relationships will need re-examination as matters of practice or law; and it is to be borne in mind that it has been found expedient in some jurisdictions to modify the common law rule of disclosure by giving statutory immunity to, for example, doctors or priests.

We therefore conclude that there is no recognized discretion to exclude relevant and admissible evidence based on confidentiality alone.

Finally, the severity of the measure taken by the Court to compel disclosure by a member of the Legislative Assembly is a matter of discretion, to be exercised judicially so that justice will be done to the prosecution as well as to the defence case.

In summary, in answer to Q. 1, it is our considered view that, with the exception coming within the rule in *R. v. Wray,* it is not open to a Court in a criminal proceeding to refrain from compelling a member of the Legislative Assembly to disclose the existence, source or content of a communication made to him by an informant (where such evidence would otherwise be relevant and admissible) on the ground that it is not in the public interest to disclose the existence, source or content of the communication. The means taken by the Court to compel disclosure are not within the framework of this reference. No other ground has been advanced or argued before us to alter our view of Q. 1.

For the above reasons, we therefore certify to the Lieutenant-Governor in Council our opinion on this first question. By reason of our opinion in Q. 1, Q. 2 does not have to be answered. We also agree with the answer to Q. 3 propounded in the separate reasons of Houlden, J.A., and do hereby certify accordingly.

HOULDEN, J.A.: — I agree with the answers to Qq. 1 and 2 that have been given by Weatherston, J.A. Question 3 reads as follows:

> Does the Legislative Assembly of Ontario have the power to enact legislation protecting its members from being compelled by a court in a criminal case to disclose the existence, source or content of a communication from an informant?

In answering this question, it is necessary to turn, first, to s.92(1) of the *British North America Act,* 1867 (U.K.), c.3, which provides:

> 92. In each Province the Legislature may exclusively make Laws in relation to Matters coming within the Classes of Subjects next herein-after enumerated; that is to say, —
>
> 1. The Amendment from Time to Time, notwithstanding anything in this Act, of the Constitution of the Province, except as regards the Office of Lieutenant Governor.

In *Fielding et al. v. Thomas,* [1896] A.C. 600, the Judicial Committee of the Privy Council held that s.92(1) conferred authority on a provincial Legislature to pass Acts defining its powers and privileges. In delivering the reasons of the Board, Lord Halsbury, L.C., said (at pp. 610-1):

> It surely cannot be contended that the independence of the provincial legislatures from outside interference, its protection, and the protection of its members from insult while in the discharge of their duties, are not matters which may be classed as part of the constitution of the province, or that legislation on such matters would not be aptly and properly described as part of the constitutional law of the province.

I think it is clear, therefore, that by virtue of s.92(1) of the *British North America Act, 1867,* the Legislative Assembly of the Province of Ontario, in respect of proceedings over which it has legislative jurisdiction, has the power to enact legislation to protect its members from being compelled to disclose the existence, source or content of a communication from an informant.

Criminal law and procedure in criminal matters are not, however, within the legislative jurisdiction of a provincial Legislature. By s.91(27) of the *British North America Act, 1867,* exclusive legislative authority with respect to these subjects is given to the Parliament of Canada. The Legislative Assembly could not, therefore, enact legislation which would protect its members from being compelled to make disclosure in criminal proceedings: *Klein et al. v. Bell et al.,* [1955] 2 D.L.R. 513, [1955] S.C.R. 309; *Marshall v. The Queen* (1960), 129 C.C.C. 232, 26 D.L.R. (2d) 459, [1961] S.C.R.

123. Provincial legislation must be confined to proceedings over which the Legislative Assembly has legislative authority: *Klein v. Bell, supra,* at p. 518 D.L.R., p . 315 S.C.R.

In his submissions to the Court, Mr. Lawlor called to our attention s.37 of the *Canada Evidence Act,* R.S.C. 1970, c.E-10, as amended, which states:

> 37. In all proceedings over which the Parliament of Canada has legislative authority, the laws of evidence in force in the province in which such proceedings are taken, including the laws of proof of service of any warrant, summons, subpoena or other document, subject to this and other Acts of the Parliament of Canada, apply to such proceedings.

Mr. Lawlor contended that, if valid provincial legislation were enacted, it would, as a result of s.37, be applicable to criminal proceedings. This interpretation of s.37 was, however, conclusively rejected by the Supreme Court of Canada in *Marshall v. The Queen, supra.*

There is one other point, raised by Mr. Watt, which should be noted. Section 472(1)(*b*) of the *Criminal Code,* R.S.C. 1970, c.C-34, as amended, provides:

> 472(1) Where a person, being present at a preliminary inquiry and being required by the justice to give evidence,
>
> ...
>
> (*b*) having been sworn, refuses to answer the questions that are put to him,
>
> ...
>
> without offering a reasonable excuse for his failure or refusal, the justice may adjourn the inquiry and may, by warrant in Form 16, commit the person to prison for a period not exceeding eight clear days or for the period during which the inquiry is adjourned, whichever is the lesser period.

Mr. Watt submitted that if the Legislative Assembly were to pass valid legislation protecting its members from being compelled to disclose communications from informants, a Court might hold that this constituted "reasonable excuse" for refusing to answer questions on that subject at a preliminary inquiry. In the circumstances, I need express no firm opinion on this point, except to say that I think there is considerable strength in Mr. Watt's submission.

For the foregoing reasons, I am of the opinion that the answer to Q. 3 is that the Legislative Assembly of Ontario does not have the power to enact legislation protecting its members from being compelled by a Court in a criminal case to disclose the existence, source or content of a communication from an informant, and I so certify.

WEATHERSTON, J.A.: —

Question 1

I have had the privilege of reading the opinion of Mr. Justice Lacourciere, and agree with him that members of the Legislative Assembly do not possess any statutory or common law privilege founded on their status exempting them from their obligation to testify. Nevertheless, it is my opinion that a Judge does have a discretion to refrain from compelling any witness to disclose the existence, source or content of a communication made to him by an informant.

It is, of course, a fundamental rule that a witness may be compelled to testify as to any relevant fact within his knowledge "unless he can show some exception in his favour". This is essential if the truth is to be arrived at. But exceptions have been made when the public interest against disclosure outweighs the public interest in favour of full disclosure. Some of these exceptions have hardened into rules of law; others are left to the discretion of the Court as depending on the circumstances of the case.

Some exceptions that have hardened into rules of law have been mentioned by Mr. Justice Lacourciere in his opinion, under the heading "Common law privilege". All of these so-called privileges came into being in the first place by decisions of the Courts in the evolution of the common law. The reason why they came into being, and continue to exist, is the recognition by the Courts of some public policy that is of greater importance than the desirability that all relevant evidence should be heard.

In England, the Courts have continued to exercise a discretionary power to control the admissibility of evidence that would operate unfairly against an accused. The decision of the Supreme Court of Canada in *R. v. Wray,* [1970] 4 C.C.C. 1, 11 D.L.R. (3d) 673, [1971] S.C.R. 272, has limited the discretion of Canadian Judges to exclude relevant evidence which is tendered to the Court. But that is a different thing than saying that a Judge has no discretion to refrain from compelling a witness to testify against his will.

It is clearly for the Judge to say what, if any, penalty is to be imposed for refusal to testify; and surely if a Judge has the right to say he will impose no penalty, he has the right to tell a witness that he need not testify at all as to a particular matter. In my opinion, this question should be answered "yes".

Question 2

This question can be answered only in general terms. The public interest for or against disclosure of relevant information may vary from time to time and always depends on the particular circumstances of the case. Lord Hailsham acknowledged in his speech in *D. v. National Society for Prevention of Cruelty to Children,* [1977] 1 All E.R. 589 at p. 602, that the law had developed in this field during his own lifetime. His views are all the more valuable because of his long experience in Parliament. So it is not possible to lay down precise rules as to what principles and interests the Court should consider in determining whether it is in the public interest to compel or refrain from compelling disclosure of a confidential communication.

To begin with, one should start as Lord Hailsham did in *D. v. National Society for Prevention of Cruelty to Children, supra,* at p. 599:

> I start with the assumption that every court of law must begin with a determination not as a general rule to permit either party deliberately to withhold relevant and admissible evidence about the matters in dispute. Every exception to this rule must run the risk that because of the withholding of relevant facts, justice between the parties may not be achieved. Any attempt to withhold relevant evidence therefore must be justified and requires to be jealously scrutinised.

This assumption applies to all witnesses, and is, of course, of more importance in a criminal case, when the liberty of a subject is at stake than in a civil action, since the consequence of a failure to achieve justice is greater.

Secondly, the Court must be satisfied that the evidence sought to be withheld is truly relevant. If it is not, it is simply not admissible. But there may be cases where such evidence is marginally relevant, and in such cases, when balancing the scales of public interest, the Court should consider its probative value. If the probative value is slight, and the harm to be caused by disclosure considerable, then the public interest is in favour of non-disclosure. On the other hand, if it is shown that disclosure is necessary to establish the innocence of an accused, then disclosure must be compelled.

The mere fact that a communication has been made in confidence does not give either party a privilege against disclosure. ''But'', said Lord Denning, M.R., in *D. v. National Society for Prevention of Cruelty to Children,* [1976] 2 All E.R. 993 at p. 999:

> ...it is a very material consideration when deciding whether to compel disclosure. In holding the scales of justice, the courts should not allow confidences to be lightly broken. When information has been imparted in confidence, and particularly where there is a pledge to keep it confidential, the courts should respect that confidence. They should in no way compel a breach of it, save where the public interest clearly demands it, and there only to the extent that the public interest requires.

Thus, although the law does not recognize a privilege to refuse to disclose confidential communications between priest and penitent, or doctor and patient, it has for many years been the practice of Judges to ask counsel not to press the question, and such request has always, or almost always, been acceded to. The same concern would be had for communications made to social workers or others in efforts towards marriage reconciliation, or in proceedings involving the welfare of children. In all these cases the Court should give great weight to the fact of confidentiality, and, if the evidence is not vital to the due administration of justice, decline to compel disclosure.

I do not think that a member of Parliament, or of the Legislative Assembly, is limited to a legislative function. It has long been a major part of his responsibilities to intercede on behalf of his constituents who claim to be oppressed by governmental bureaucracy, and to bring to the notice of the Government cases where legislation is thought to be working unfairly. It must also be acknowledged now that members have assumed the responsibility of bringing alleged scandals in public administration to public attention. In all these cases the member may rely on information given to him in confidence. His effectiveness as a member may depend on confidences given and received, and the Court should respect those confidences unless the public interest clearly compels a breach of them.

A member of Parliament, or of the Legislative Assembly, who is in possession of relevant and material information given to him in confidence, and who seeks to respect that confidence, is in a position of conflict between these two public interests. As a loyal citizen, and a representative of the public, it is his first duty to see that justice be done. He should seek to withhold the source of his information only if he is satisfied in his own mind that in the long run, a breach of confidence would be more inimical to the public interest than a failure to achieve justice. His opinion should not be disregarded lightly by the Judge, but it is the Judge who must make the decision. In the final analysis, especially in a criminal case, if it is shown that justice cannot be achieved unless the source of information is divulged, then the scales should normally come down in favour of disclosure.

These than are, in general, the principles and interests which the Court should consider in determining whether it is in the public interest to compel or to refrain from compelling the disclosure of the existence, source or content of a communication made to a member of the Legislative Assembly by an informant.

Question 3

I agree with the opinion of Mr. Justice Houlden.

Judgment accordingly.

3.6.6 *Attorney-General* v. *Mulholland; Attorney-General* v. *Foster;* [1963] 2 W.L.R. 658 (C.A.), England

Lord Denning M.R. These are appeals by two journalists, Brendan Joseph Mulholland and Reginald William Foster, against sentences which have been passed upon them by Gorman J. A tribunal of inquiry was inquiring into matters which Parliament had required to be investigated. The chairman of the tribunal in pursuance of the statute, certified to the High Court that they had refused to answer the questions to which the tribunal had legally required an answer. After hearing the case and a claim of privilege which the journalists had put forward, the judge found each of them guilty as if he had been guilty of a contempt of court and passed sentence accordingly.

I need not go into the statute or the facts in great detail. It appears that allegations were made in some newspapers which reflected gravely on persons in high places and on naval officers and civil servants in the Admiralty. The articles clearly imported that there had been neglect of duty on their part in not discovering a spy who was in their midst. In making these allegations the newspapers were exercising the undoubted freedom which belongs to them. They are entitled to expose wrongdoing and to criticise the Government and anyone else, no matter how high and powerful he may be. But these were allegations which could not be overlooked. Coming from newspapers with such great influence for good or ill, they demanded investigation. If well founded, the security arrangements at the Admiralty needed complete overhaul and those at fault would have to pay the penalty for their neglect. So Parliament decided that there should be an investigation. It set up a tribunal to inquire into the matter as of urgent public importance. In the course of the inquiry the journalists responsible for these articles were asked to give the source of their information and they refused to answer.

Now, was this a question which they could legally be required to answer? That depends on two questions. First, was it relevant and necessary in this sense, that it was a question that ought to be answered to enable proper investigation to be made? Secondly, if it was, have the journalists a privilege in point of law to refuse to answer? Under the statute any witness before the tribunal is entitled to the same immunities and privileges as if he were a witness before the High Court. I turn to consider these two points in order, remembering that the certificate of the tribunal is not binding on the courts. The judge before whom it comes must inquire into the matters afresh to see if an offence has been committed.

So far as Mr. Mulholland is concerned, these were the three passages in the newspaper as to which he was asked his source. One was a passage in an article which asserted that "colleagues of his in the Admiralty called Vassall 'Auntie' to his face." Another passage in another article was this, that "a girl typist "in the Admiralty office where he worked and decided that no "£15-a-week clerk could possibly live the way he did honestly," and the third passage was that "it was the sponsorship of two "high ranking officials which led to Vassall avoiding the strictest "part of the Admiralty's security vetting." Mr. Mulholland was asked what were the sources of that information and he declined to give the source. He said he would not inquire from the source as to whether he was willing that it should be divulged. The chairman of the tribunal, Lord Radcliffe, directed him to answer and he declined.

Was the question relevant to the inquiry? Was it one that the journalist ought to answer? It seems to me that if the inquiry was to be as thorough as the circumstances demanded, it was incumbent on Mr. Mulholland to disclose to the tribunal the source of his information. The newspapers had made these allegations. If they made them with a due sense of responsibility (as befits a press which enjoys such freedom as ours) then they must have based them on a trustworthy source. Heaven forbid that they should invent them! And if they did get them from a trustworthy source, then the tribunal must be told of it. How otherwise can the tribunal discover whether the allegations are well founded or not? The tribunal cannot tell unless they see for themselves this trustworthy source, this witness who is the foundation of it all. The tribunal must, therefore, be entitled to ask what was the source from which the information came.

It is said that the tribunal had access to other sources of information which might make it unnecessary for the newspapers to disclose their source: and that the newspapers do not know of these other sources because so much of the proceedings were held in camera. I am not in the least impressed by this argument. Even if the tribunal did have access to other sources of information, nevertheless it is still necessary for the tribunal to know whence the newspapers got their information so as to confirm, contradict or complete these other sources. The root cause of the whole inquiry was the information which the newspapers published, and it is their sources which must be tracked down so as to see whether they are trustworthy or not. Once the source of the information is ascertained, the tribunal are better able to see whether it is such as to implicate or exculpate those concerned at the Admiralty.

I hold, therefore, that so far as Mulholland is concerned, these questions were both relevant and necessary to the inquiry which the tribunal had in hand.

So far as Foster is concerned, the case is rather different. We were invited by Mr. Cusack to take a special course with him on the ground that the questions were not relevant. The part of the article on which he was questioned was this: "Why did the "spy-catchers fail to notice Vassall, who sometimes wore women's clothes on West End trips?" When Foster was asked on that matter, he said he was not responsible for the word "wore." He said: "I was informed that Vassall was known to have "bought women's clothing in the West End." Then he was further asked whether he could remember the source of the information and he said he could not remember the particular source, the particular person; there were a number of people to be considered in these inquiries. But then he was asked: "If you cannot remember the names of your informants, can you remember the type of source from which your information came, and I added the specific question, did it come from a shop? (A.) It did not come from a shop. (Q.) How do you know it did not come from a shop? He was pressed on that question: did he know the type of source? He refused to answer as a matter of principle questions as to the type of source from which it came."

It was said by Mr. Cusack on his behalf that his case is different from Mr. Mulholland's. Here is a case of a man who did not remember the actual source. All he refused to give was the type of source. It was said that later Vassall himself gave evidence to the tribunal that he bought women's clothes in the West End. Why then was it necessary for this question to be pressed, at all events at this stage, when the later evidence has been given? I seems to me that the answer is simply this: the fact that Vassall bought women's clothes is not the whole point. The point is: did those about him in the Admiralty know it before he was arrested, and ought they to have reported it? Were they guilty of a neglect of duty? On that point the type of source is a relevant question which could be asked and was asked. It could and might have led to further inquiries which would have more nearly pinpointed the actual source so that it could be tracked down by the tribunal.

I feel that in Foster's case also the answer must be that the question was relevant and one that ought to be answered for the proper purposes of the inquiry.

But then it is said (and this is the second point) that however relevant these questions were and however proper to be answered for the purpose of the inquiry, a journalist has a privilege by law entitling him to refuse to give his sources of information. The journalist puts forward as his justification the pursuit of truth. It is in the public interest, he says, that he should obtain information in confidence and publish it to the world at large, for by so doing he brings to the public notice that which they should know. He can expose wrongdoing and neglect of duty which would otherwise go unremedied. He cannot get this information, he says, unless he keeps the source of it secret. The mouths of his informants will be closed to him if it is known that their identity will be disclosed. So he claims to be entitled to publish all his information without ever being under any obligation, even when directed by the court or a judge, to disclose whence he got it. It seems to me that the journalists put the matter much too high. The only profession that I know which is given a privilege from disclosing information to a court of law is the legal profession, and then it is not the privilege of the lawyer but of his client. Take the clergyman, the banker or the medical man. None of these is entitled to refuse to answer when directed to by a judge. Let me not be mistaken. The judge will respect the confidences which each member of these honourable professions receives in the course of it, and will not direct him to answer unless not only it is relevant but also it is a proper and, indeed, necessary question in the course of justice to be put and answered. A judge is the person entrusted, on behalf of the community, to weigh these conflicting interests — to weigh on the one hand the respect due to confidence in the profession and on the other hand the ultimate interest of the community in justice being done or, in the case of a tribunal such as this, in a proper investigation being made into these serious allegations. If the judge determines that the journalist must answer, then no privilege will avail him to refuse.

This seems to me the explanation of the cases on interrogatories to which we have been referred. The courts will not as a rule compel a newspaper in a libel action to disclose before the trial the source of its information. The reason is because, on weighing the considerations involved, the balance is in favour of exempting the newspaper from disclosure. The person who is defamed has his remedy against the newspaper and that is enough, without letting him delve round to see who else he can sue. It may rightly be said, as Buckley L.J. said in *Adam* v. *Fisher,* that the public has an interest to see that the newspapers are not compelled to disclose their source of information; unless, I would add, the interests of justice so demand. But that rule is not a rule of law; it is only a rule of practice which applies in those particular cases. It is made more general now and applies not only to newspapers but to other persons in the particular circumstances covered by R.S.C., Ord. 31, r.1A. It seems to me that whenever a case arises when the interests of justice or of the public require that there should be disclosure and the judge so rules, the newspapers must disclose the source of their information; they have no privilege in law to refuse.

I need not go through the authorities on this matter; they are few enough. The only cases that I have discovered where a journalist raised this question in our common law jurisdictions are three. The first was in the Parnell Inquiry Commission. On February 20, 1889, Mr. McDonald, the managing editor of The Times, was asked by Mr. Asquith: "(Q.) Do you not know who the writer of the article was? (A.) I do indirectly, not directly." (Q.) Who was it then? (A.) I do not know that I am bound to tell you. (Q.) I ask you a question? (A.) The conductors and the editor of The Times would be responsible for the statements contained in the paper, and I consider that that being so, counsel are not entitled to demand or to force from the conductors of The Times the names of the contributors. (Mr. Asquith, of counsel:) I know of no such privilege. (Sir Charles Russell, leading him:) The question is whether there is any such privilege as is claimed. (The President, Sir James Hannen, with whom sat Day J. and A. L. Smith J.:) There is no such privilege as that suggested by the witness. (Sir Charles Russell:) Then we are entitled to an answer to our question.'' Then after further discussion there was the ruling by the President. He said to Mr. Asquith: ''You are entitled to ask him as to specific statements which are made in some of these articles and to ascertain from him who is the writer, if he knows it. If he does not, you must take it that you have exhausted all the information you can get from this source.'' That is reported in The Times newspaper of Wednesday, February 20, 1889.

The next case in our common law jurisdictions is an Irish case: *O'Brennan* v. *Tully*. In that case the editor of a newspaper was called as a witness and was asked about the name of a writer of an anonymous letter. He was asked: ''Who was the writer of the letter? (A.) I promised the writer of the letter that I would refuse to disclose his name.'' Hanna J. said: You must disclose it in this court. (The witness:) I am sorry, sir, I promised I would not disclose it. (Hanna J.:) You are sworn to tell the truth; you must disclose it,'' and he ordered him to do it and the editor refused. The judge found him guilty of contempt of court and fined him £25.

The remaining case is a decision of the High Court of Australia in 1941, *McGuinness* v. *Attorney-General of Victoria,* where a Royal Commission was appointed to inquire into a question whether there had been bribery of members of the Victorian Parliament. A journalist was asked what was the source of his information. He refused to give it and he was held guilty of an offence against the Act and he was fined the sum of £15. The question whether a journalist was privileged or not was fully argued and considered by the High Court of Australia and it was unanimously held that there was no such privilege. The judgments of the court, particularly of Rich J. and Dixon J., are well worthy of study.

It seems to me, therefore, that the authorities are all one way. There is no privilege known to the law by which a journalist can refuse to answer a question which is relevant to the inquiry and is one which, in the opinion of the judge, it is proper for him to be asked. I think it plain that in this particular case it is in the public interest for the tribunal to inquire as to the sources of information. How is anyone to know that this story was not a pure invention, if the journalist will not tell the tribunal its source? Even if it was not invention, how is anyone to know it was not the gossip of some idler seeking to impress? It may be mere rumour unless the journalist shows he got it from a trustworthy source. And if he has got it from a trustworthy source (as I take it on his statement he has, which I fully accept), then however much he may desire to keep it secret, he must remember that he has been directed by the tribunal to disclose it as a matter of public duty, and that is justification enough.

I have no doubt that the journalist ought to have answered the questions put to them. These were questions they were legally required to answer and they have no privilege to refuse.

I would dismiss the appeal on the points of principle accordingly.

DONOVAN L.J. I agree. I add a few words only about the need for some residual discretion in the court of trial in case where a journalist is asked in the course of the trial for the source of his information. While the journalist has no privilege entitling him as of right to refuse to disclose the source, so I think the interrogator has no absolute right to require such disclosure. In the first place the question has to be relevant to be admissible at all: in the second place it ought to be one the answer to which will serve a useful purpose in relation to the proceedings in hand — I prefer that expression to the term "necessary." Both these matters are for the consideration and, if need be, the decision of the judge. And over and above these two requirements, there may be other considerations, impossible to define in advance, but arising out of the infinite variety of fact and circumstance which a court encounters, which may lead a judge to conclude that more harm than good would result from compelling a disclosure or punishing a refusal to answer.

For these reasons I think it would be wrong to hold that a judge is tied hand and foot in such a case as the present and must always order an answer or punish a refusal to give the answer once it is shown that the question is technically admissible. Indeed, I understood the Attorney-General to concur in this view, namely, that the judge should always keep an ultimate discretion. This would apply not only in the case of journalists but in other cases where information is given and received under the seal of confidence, for example, information given by a patient to his doctor and arising out of that relationship. In the present case, where the ultimate matter at stake is the safety of the community, I agree that no such consideration as I have mentioned, calling for the exercise of a discretion in favour of the appellants, arises, and that accordingly their appeals fail and must be dismissed.

DANCKWERTS L.J. I agree and I am bound to say that I thought the law was perfectly clear on the principal point which has been argued in these appeals.

LORD DENNING M.R. That is the argument on the point of principle. We still have the question as to the punishment.

Argument was then heard on the terms of imprisonment imposed.

LORD DENNING M.R. We feel that this is a case where the law was clearly declared by Gorman J. He gave Mr. Mulholland and Mr. Foster an opportunity to reveal their source of information and they have not done so. We have anxiously considered the sentences of six months and three months respectively which he passed on Mr. Mulholland and Mr. Foster, and after full consideration we have felt unable to adopt the view that the sentences are disproportionate to the serious nature of the offence.

3.6.7 *Re Canada Post Corporation and Canadian Union of Postal Workers (Varma)* (1985), 19 L.A.C. (3d) 361 (Can. Arb. Bd.)

KENNETH P. SWAN: ...Finally, I turn to the most important question, the substantive issue of the effect of both the common law and the *Canadian Charter of Rights and Freedoms,* in so far as they protect and preserve a freedom of the press, upon the validity of the particular subpoenas issued in this case.

I think it is undoubted that the freedom of the press has an important place in our common law, in the unwritten glosses on our constitution prior to the *Canadian Charter of Rights and Freedoms,* in the *Canadian Bill of Rights,* and in the *Canadian Charter of Rights and Freedoms* itself. It is an extremely important right, and one to which the courts have rightly afforded the widest possible protection. On the other hand, when one reviews the jurisprudence in this country, in the United Kingdom and, perhaps more relevant to the situation in Canada after the *Canadian Charter of Rights and Freedoms,* in the United States, whatever may be the dicta in specific cases there is simply no general privilege for journalists, no right for members of the journalistic profession to decline either to attend as a witness in a particular proceeding or to refuse to answer a particular question simply by reason of their employment as journalists. Where privilege, or something like privilege has been recognized, it has been very specific in nature, and it has been recognized either to protect public policy, or to protect a specific issue relating to the freedom of the press.

...

I turn to the leading American case, *Democratic National Committee et al. v. McCord et al.* (1973), 356 F. Supp. 1394. I shall return below to the other aspects of this case, and the extent to which it is persuasive. For the moment, the following comment from p. 1397 will suffice to demonstrate that the American courts have also rejected, despite a constitutional protection of freedom of the press, any general privilege for journalists, *qua* journalists, to refuse to testify in judicial proceedings:

> The Court is well aware that other courts in "civil" and "criminal" cases, and the Supreme Court of the United States in a landmark case involving a newsman's testimony before a Grand Jury, have been reluctant in the absence of a statute to recognize even a qualified newsman's privilege from disclosure of confidential news sources.

The U.S. Supreme Court decision referred to is *Branzburg v. Hayes* (1972), 408 U.S. 665, 92 S.Ct. 2646, 33 L. Ed. 2d 626. Later in the *Democratic National Committee v. McCord* decision, the court refers to the *Branzburg* decision as rendering improper "the implicit recognition of an absolute privilege for newsmen".

These cases, in my view, support the conclusion set out above that there is no general privilege for journalists. The questions which arise, either under the British or the American judicial system, are only questions of whether a journalist may refuse to answer a specific question, or may refuse to produce specific documentation. The cases, in my opinion, adequately indicate that the reasons given for permitting such a refusal have always been very specific to the material requested or to the question asked, and have not been general in nature.

To digress, it seems to me that there are good policy reasons for taking this approach. The protections being sought are protections for the press as an institution, rather than protections for individuals who may have made statements or comments to the press. The protections are quite different from those involved in the solicitor-client privilege, where it is the confidence of the client which is sought to be protected, rather than the freedom of action of the legal profession.

For this reason, it is a sound approach for the privilege to be specific rather than general in nature, based upon the identification of an issue of public policy arising from the existence of a constitutionally protected freedom of the press, rather than upon the general assertion that every journalist should be protected from giving evidence except in special circumstances.

Section 2 of the *Canadian Charter of Rights and Freedoms* is in the following terms:

> 2. Everyone has the following fundamental freedoms:

> ...
> (*b*) freedom of thought, belief, opinion and expression, including freedom of the press and other media of communication;

Given the way in which s.2(*b*) is written, I am of the view that it should be seen as a broad right to intellectual freedom, and not as a special concession to any class of individuals. Nor do I see that broad proposition in any way cast in doubt by any of the important cases which have dealt with the freedom of the press since the inception of the Charter. I think that all of those cases have treated press freedom as a part of a much broader freedom belonging to everyone: a freedom to be informed, a freedom to inquire, and a freedom to express the outcome of that information and that inquiry.

The specific issue to be addressed, therefore, is whether the mere fact of a subpoena to a journalist in relation to information learned in the course of journalistic activity constitutes a breach of the freedom of the press, as set out in s.2(*b*), so as to shift the onus to the person requesting the subpoena to justify that infringement in the terms of s.1. The practice under the Charter so far has been to define the freedoms quite broadly, and then to use s.1 as a balancing section, placing the onus firmly on the person asserting the right to infringe a fundamental freedom to justify that infringement. Even on a broad interpretation, however, I think it is carrying the freedom of the press too far to say that any subpoena to a journalist constitutes a breach of that freedom. In context, the freedom of the press must be seen as an institutional freedom: not a freedom for individuals employed in the institution but for the institution itself. As a consequence, in order to satisfy the threshold requirement that a breach of the fundamental freedom has been established by a particular course of conduct, the person asserting the breach must demonstrate some interference with the press as an institution, and not merely an inconvenience for the individuals who happen to ply their profession within that institution.

In *Democratic National Committee v. McCord,* the court was dealing with an attempt to require a large number of journalists and managing personnel of certain newspapers to appear for the taking of depositions, and to bring with them literally every piece of documentary evidence prepared in the course of investigating or reporting the notorious Watergate break-in. The process of taking depositions is not unlike discovery in Canadian courts, except that persons who are not parties may be required to be examined for depositions in wider circumstances than those in which discovery is available in the rules of civil procedure of Canadian provinces. In dealing with this attempt to examine journalists, the court made the following observation:

> This Court cannot blind itself to the possible ''chilling effect'' the enforcement of these broad subpoenas would have on the flow of information to the press, and so to the public. This court stands convinced that if it allows the discouragement of investigative reporting into the highest levels of government no amount of legal theorizing could lay the public suspicions engendered by its actions and by the matters alleged in these law suits.

The court observed that there had been no showing by any of the parties that alternative sources of evidence had been exhausted, or even approached, prior to issuing these broad subpoenas to these journalists. Moreover, there had been no positive showing of the materiality of the documents sought to be summoned. In short, the court appears to have decided that, prior to issuing a subpoena to a third party for discovery in a action in these circumstances, it would require a demonstration by the party seeking the subpoena very similar to the demonstration required in *Pacific Press Ltd.* before the issuance of a search warrant by a justice of the peace under Canadian law.

As I read these cases, it is an appropriate interpretation of s.2(*b*) of the Charter that before a subpoena issued to journalist *qua* journalist can constitute a *prima facie* breach of the freedom of the press, there must be a demonstration of some affirmative harm or danger to the institutional interests of the press, rather than merely inconvenience or annoyance to individual journalists. It may well be that a chilling effect, such as that created by the incredible breadth of discovery attempted in *Democratic National Committee v. McCord,* or by the judicially authorized raid on the premises of a newspaper to carry out a broad search for evidence from the data collected by the newspaper in carrying out the functions of the free press in *Pacific Press,* could constitute such a demonstration. Absent something to raise the issuance of a particular subpoena to an institutional threat to the freedom of the press, however, I would be of the view that the initial onus to demonstrate a breach of s.2(*b*) of the Charter could not be made out merely by the fact of the issuance of a subpoena to a journalist.

...

Note: The so-called "newspaper rule" holds that a media defendant in a libel action may refuse to reveal, *prior to trial,* sources of information forming the basis of the alleged libel. See *Reid* v. *Telegram Publishing* (1961), 28 D.L.R. (2d) 6; *Drabinsky* v. *Maclean-Hunter Ltd.* (1980), 108 D.L.R. (3d) 390; *Hatfield* v. *Globe and Mail* (1983), 41 O.R. (2d) 218; and *McInnes* v. *University Students' Council of the University of Western Ontario et al.* (1985), 48 O.R. (2d) 542.

Note: An excellent review of the law is Sidney N. Lederman, Patrick O'Kelly, and Margaret Grottenhaller, "Confidentiality of News Sources" in Anisman and Linden, (eds.), *The Media, The Courts, and The Charter.*

3.6.8 *Moysa* v. *Labour Relations Board and Attorney-General of Alberta* (1987), 52 Alta. L.R. (2d) 193, (Alta. C.A.)

APPEAL from decision of MacCallum J., 45 Alta. L.R. (2d) 37, 28 D.L.R. (4th) 140, 25 C.R.R. 346, 71 A.R. 70, dismissing appeal from order of Labour Relations Board requiring journalist to answer question.

A.H. Lefever and *T. Hurlburt,* for appellant.

W. Henkel, Q.C., for intervener, Attorney General of Alberta.

No one contra.

(Edmonton Appeal No. 8603-0713-AC)

May 6, 1987. Memorandum of judgment delivered from the bench by

MCCLUNG J.A. (for the court): — The appellant is a labour reporter for the Edmonton Journal. She seeks a form of testimonial immunity against revealing communications with a source whose information contributed to one of her commentaries in an ongoing labour dispute. She was ordered by the Labour Relations Board to answer a question relevant to the dispute and which involved her source. The order was confirmed by the Court of Queen's Bench following appeal [45 Alta. L.R. (2d) 37, 28 D.L.R. (4th) 140, 25 C.R.R. 346, 71 A.R. 70].

We agree with the reasoning and conclusion of the chambers judge that there is here no common law privilege, qualified or absolute, marking the relationship of journalist and source which would excuse the appellant from providing relevant evidence and which might involve source disclosure. That is the conclusion shared by the Commonwealth appellate authorities to which we have been referred.

We are of the view that the creation of any new category of privilege for reporters and their sources must be of legislative origin. Such provision has been made in the United Kingdom.

Section 2(*b*) of the Canadian Charter of Rights and Freedoms is raised by Mr. Lefever. It provides:

> 2. Every one has the following fundamental freedoms...
> (*b*) freedom of thought, belief, opinion and expression, including freedom of the press and other media of communication.

The declaration does not advance the appellant's claimed immunity to testimonial compulsion here. The freedom expressed has been held to protect and guarantee expression of thought, belief and opinion for all Canadians, including the press and other media. Beyond that we think that even the most liberal and purposive application of the wording in s.2(*b*) could not, even by necessary intendment, create the exclusionary enclave pursued by the appellant in this case.

We dismiss the appeal, affirm the order and return the case to the Labour Relations Board for completion.

Appeal dismissed.

3.7 Procedure in Contempt Cases

3.7.1 "Contempt of Court: The Effect of the Charter" by Robert Martin in Anisman and Linden, *The Media, The Courts and the Charter* (Toronto: Carswell, 1986)

The procedure followed in contempt cases is unusual. It denies many of the rights which we assume to be associated with criminal procedure. One can do no better than to quote the observation which Harold Laski made in 1928:

> A procedure stands self-condemned when it applies methods and ideas against which the whole of Anglo-American constitutional history has been a considered and masterful protest.

As is typical of the law of contempt of court generally, there exists substantial confusion as to precisely the procedure to be followed. I am not so foolhardy as to imagine I could resolve this confusion. Some general observations will suffice.

Contempt proceedings, regardless of the technical rubric under which we seek to subsume them, are show cause proceedings. This means that the person imagined to have committed the contempt is required to establish his innocence. The task is not made easier by the fact that in certain contempt cases the accused may not be able to call witnesses. Furthermore, it is implicit in the nature of show cause proceedings that the accused, if he is to have any hope of escaping conviction, will be compelled to testify.

There is no legal rule to prevent the judge before whom a contempt is supposed to have occurred or at whom apparently contemptuous remarks were directed from hearing the proceeding. Questions of *mens rea* are tangential. If, for example, the alleged contempt consists in a breach of the sub-judice rule, the accused will not be permitted to adduce evidence that he did not intend any interference with the due administration of justice. The court is concerned with whether the material is apt to, or has a tendency to, interfere with the administration of justice, and not with the actual intention of the accused. It has, however, been held that the presiding judge must be satisfied beyond a reasonable doubt of the guilt of the accused before convicting.

A particularly odious provision of the current law is that a person who is accused of having scandalized the court by imputing improper motives to a judge is not allowed to attempt to prove the truth of his allegations. There is no provision for a jury trial in contempt prosecutions. Since contempt is a common law crime there is no stipulated maximum punishment which may be awarded. The punishment for a common law crime is a matter within the discretion of the presiding judge.

3.8 Reforming the Law

3.8.1 Robert Martin, "An Open Legal System" (1985) 23 *U.W.O. Law Rev.* 169

The immediate prospects for reform are not good.

Since the Canadian Charter of Rights and Freedoms guarantees, in section 2(b), "freedom of ... expression, including freedom of the press and other media of communication" and since it seems beyond argument that the existing law of contempt substantially interferes with freedom of expression, one might have thought that the courts would use the Charter as a basis for effecting change. One would have been wrong.

The courts have heard cases dealing with those elements of the law of contempt which have been codified and those which have not.

In *R. v. Banville* an American reporter was charged with breaching an order made under s.467(3) of the Criminal Code prohibiting the publication of evidence given at a preliminary injury. The judge who heard the appeal before the New Brunswick Court of Queen's Bench was not sure that the section did involve an infringement of the Charter guarantee of freedom of expression, but concluded that even if it did, that freedom had to give way and that "... the individual's right to a fair trial before an independent and impartial tribunal must prevail". The judge did not specify how the publication of the information in question would prejudice the individual's right to a fair trial.

Re Smith had to do with the attempt of the U.S. government to extradite Catherine Smith to stand trial on a charge of murder. At a bail hearing the presiding judge issued an order under s.457.2(1) of the Criminal Code forbidding the publication of information given at the hearing. Global Communications Limited attacked the validity of s.457.2(1). Thorson, J.A. in the Ontario Court of Appeal accepted that the section imposed a limitation on freedom of expression; he was also willing to accept that the limitation could be justified under s.1 of the Charter. To Thorson the paramount consideration was that an individual receive a fair trial and he had no doubt that the unrestricted publication of the proceedings of a bail hearing created the risk of prejudicing that right. Parliament, in enacting s.457.2(1), made a deliberate choice between the claims of the media to report freely on matters before the courts and the right of the individual to a fair trial. The court accepted that choice as justified. The court explained the difference between the U.S. and Canadian versions of *sub-judice* on the basis of differences between both the methods of jury selection and the period during which juries are sequestered in the two countries.

Canadian Newspapers Ltd. v. A.G. Canada was a decision of the Ontario Court of Appeal which took a different approach. This case involved s. 442(3) of the Criminal

Code which required the judge presiding at a sexual offence prosecution to make an order prohibiting the identification of the victim if either the victim or the Crown applied for such an order. The court thought this provision infringed freedom of expression. The court further stated that only a social value of "superordinate importance" could justify such an infringement. And while the court believed that bringing sexual offenders to justice was such a value, it refused to give its imprimatur to the mandatory nature of s.442(3). In the result, the court redrafted the section so as to give a trial judge a discretionary authority to ban publication of the victim's identity.

There are two cases which deal with the uncodified aspects of contempt. In *A.G. Québec v. Laurendeau* an individual before a court on a summary motion to have him cited for contempt requested trial by jury on the basis of section 11(f) of the Charter. The court accepted that there was no maximum punishment for contempt. But it denied trial by jury on the ground that the rights specified in section 11 of the Charter were to be enjoyed only by "any person charged with an offence". In the view of the court, contempt was not an "offence", at least not in "the ordinary sense of the word". This approach did not subsequently find favour with the Ontario Court of Appeal. While not expressly rejecting the view of the Québec Court, Goodman, J.A. said in *R. v. Cohn:* "... a person cited for contempt is charged with an offence within the meaning of s.11".

R. v. Cohn is, in fact, the most careful judicial analysis yet produced of the Charter and contempt. The case did not deal with *sub judice* or scandalising, but rather with the refusal of a witness to testify when required to do so by a trial judge. Nonetheless, a number of Charter issues were canvassed by the court. In each instance the constitutional attack on the law of contempt was rejected.

It was argued that contempt is not given a statutory definition. "... The common law has provided a satisfactory definition", said the Court.

Of the summary procedure used in contempt cases the Court observed generally that

> ... the common law principles enunciated in the more recent cases in this jurisdiction are consistent with and do not conflict with or infringe upon the rights guaranteed by the Charter.

Of the argument that the judge before whom the contempt was alleged to have occurred presided over the contempt proceedings, the Court said, "There is no basis for a finding that the presiding judge in the present case was other than independent and impartial". Of the fact that this was a show cause proceeding, the Court held that there was no denial of the presumption of innocence. The court said that a show cause proceeding "...merely shifts the burden of adducing evidence as distinct from shifting the burden of persuasion to the accused". Finally, the court rejected a claim to trial by jury on the ground that the law had evolved in Canada to the point where the maximum punishment which could be imposed was imprisonment for a period less than five years.

If judicial reform is unlikely, what are the prospects for legislative reform? Again, the answer is not encouraging.

In 1982 the Law Reform Commission of Canada produced a *Report* on contempt of court. This *Report* was a disaster. The only useful portions of the *Report* were those dealing with procedure in contempt cases. The Commission advocated that the law of contempt be codified. It recommended that, except for two special instances, proceedings in contempt matters should be by way of indictment. An accused contemnor would, therefore, have all the procedural rights associated with ordinary criminal proceedings. Further, where a contempt was directed at a named judge, that judge was not to be permitted to hear the subsequent prosecution. And, fourthly, the maximum punishment for the various offences suggested by the Commission's draft bill was to be two years imprisonment.

The effect of the substantive recommendations in the *Report* would have been to make the law even more restrictive than it now is.

Scandalising was to be replaced by "affront to judicial authority", defined as follows: Everyone commits an offence who "(a) affronts judicial authority by any conduct calculated to insult a court, or (b) attacks the independence, impartiality or integrity of a court". While the existing scurrilous abuse is a nebulous standard, "conduct calculated to insult a court" is hardly an improvement. Indeed, the Law Reform Commission itself had no idea what this phrase meant. The only example vouchsafed was that under this definition "slurring a judge *qua* judge" would be an offence. Attacking the independence, impartiality or integrity of a court, which the Commission grandly characterised as "self-explanatory", is vastly broader than imputing improper motives. The Commission rejected the notion that truth should be a defence to this charge.

The only justification advanced in support of this continued sheltering of judges from public criticism was the tired and inaccurate statement that judges may not reply publicly to criticism directed to them.

Turning to the *sub judice* rule, one can say in the Commission's favour that it attempted once again to introduce a degree of precision into a dangerously vague area of the law.

When does the *sub judice* rule begin to operate? The Law Reform Commission itself noted the problem in its 1977 Working Paper on contempt. The draft bill in the *Report* stated that the proposed new offence of interfering with judicial proceedings would apply to proceedings which were "pending". "Pending" was defined in civil matters as the period beginning when a matter is set down for trial and ending when the trial is terminated; in criminal matters the period would run from the laying of an information or the proffering of an indictment until a verdict, order, or sentence is pronounced. One effect of this is that *sub judice* would not apply to appellate proceedings.

The substantive re-definition of the *sub judice* rule was the disturbing element. The new offence would be committed by anyone who "publishes or causes to be published anything he knows or ought to know may interfere with [pending judicial] proceedings". The English decision in *A.G. v. Times Newspapers Ltd* was much criticised as unduly limiting freedom of the press. The European Court of Human Rights strongly disapproved of the view taken by the House of Lords, and, indeed, the European Court's decision is one of the few instances when a national law that infringed a right guaranteed by the European Convention on Human Rights was held not to be "necessary in a democratic society". The standard that the House of Lords thought to be appropriate was rejected by the European Court as an undue restriction on freedom of expression. But that standard is substantially less restrictive than the one proposed by the Law Reform Commission of Canada. There is a significant difference between interfering with freedom of speech only where there is "real prejudice to the administration of justice" and attempting to prevent publication of material that one ought to know may interfere with judicial proceedings. Fortunately, the *Report* seems to have been rejected by the Government of Canada.

The omnibus Criminal Law Reform Bill which was introduced in Parliament in 1984 contained provisions for reform of the law of contempt of court. These were more encouraging. The existing common law was to be supplanted by statutorily-defined offences, all of which, presumably, would have attracted the procedural protections of both the Charter and the Criminal Code. Maximum penalties were specified. A judge was not to be able to preside at the trial of an offence which related to him or to a proceeding over which he had presided.

The *sub judice* rule was to be re-defined as follows:

> Every one who knowingly makes or causes to be made any publication that creates a substantial risk that the course of justice in any particular civil or criminal proceeding pending at the time of the publication will be seriously impeded or prejudiced is guilty of ...

This was something of an improvement. It seems that *means rea* was required. More important, the language, "substantial risk" that a "particular" proceeding will be "seriously impeded or prejudiced", suggests that some concrete evidence, rather than mere supposition, of impeding or prejudicing would be required. "Pending" was defined. The defences of "fair and accurate report", borrowed from libel law, and "discussion in good faith of public affairs" were created.

Scandalising the court was to involve:

> Every one who without lawful justification or excuse, wilfully makes or causes to be made any publication of a false, scandalous or scurrilous statement calculated to bring into disrepute a court or judge in his official capacity.

This provision could have gone much farther. Still, it did make clear that *mens rea* was required and that the offence did not embrace statements made about judges in their non-official capacities. More important, a defence of truth and public benefit was created.

The Bill died with the government that introduced it. The current Government of Canada has introduced proposals for criminal law reform, but these proposals do not touch contempt of court.

My own views on the directions reform should take are as follows.

The offence of scandalising the court has no place in the law of a democratic state and should be abolished. With respect to *sub judice,* there should be specific provisions in the Criminal Code which state precisely the sorts of information which may not be published about judicial proceedings and the time period within which such information is not to be published. A number of prohibitions of this nature now appear in the Code. In drafting such provisions there should be a bias in favour of openness.

3.9 Dealing With Material That Might Become Evidence in a Judicial Proceeding

Note: The material in this sub-section is not, strictly speaking, part of the law of contempt. It raises questions about the rights and duties of journalists with respect to material in their possession which the State may seek to use as evidence in proceedings before the courts.

3.9.1 Criminal Code, ss.139, 487

139. (1) Every one who wilfully attempts in any manner to obstruct, pervert or defeat the course of justice in a judicial proceeding,

(*a*) by indemnifying or agreeing to indemnify a surety, in any way and either in whole or in part, or
(*b*) where he is a surety, by accepting or agreeing to accept a fee or any form of indemnity whether in whole or in part from or in respect of a person who is released or is to be released from custody,

is guilty of

(*c*) an indictable offence and is liable to imprisonment for two years, or
(*d*) an offence punishable on summary conviction.

(2) Every one who wilfully attempts in any manner other than a manner described in subsection (1) to obstruct, pervert or defeat the course of justice is guilty of an indictable offence and is liable to imprisonment for ten years.

(3) Without restricting the generality of subsection (2), every one shall be deemed wilfully to attempt to obstruct, pervert or defeat the course of justice who in a judicial proceeding, existing or proposed,

(*a*) dissuades or attempts to dissuade a person by threats, bribes or other corrupt means from giving evidence;
(*b*) influences or attempts to influence by threats, bribes or other corrupt means, a person in his conduct as a juror; or
(*c*) accepts or obtains, agrees to accept or attempts to obtain a bribe or other corrupt consideration to abstain from giving evidence, or to do or to refrain from doing anything as a juror.

487. (1) A justice who is satisfied by information upon oath in Form 1, that there is reasonable ground to believe that there is in a building, receptacle or place

(*a*) anything on or in respect of which any offence against this Act or any other Act of Parliament has been or is suspected to have been committed,
(*b*) anything that there is reasonable ground to believe will afford evidence with respect to the commission of an offence against this Act or any other Act of Parliament, or
(*c*) anything that there is reasonable ground to believe is intended to be used for the purpose of committing any offence against the person for which a person may be arrested without warrant,

may at any time issue a warrant under his hand authorizing a person named therein or a peace officer

(*d*) to search the building, receptacle or place for any such thing and to seize it, and
(*e*) subject to any other Act of Parliament, to, as soon as practicable, bring the thing seized before, or make a report in respect thereof to, the justice or some other justice for the same territorial division in accordance with section 489.1.

(2) Where the building, receptacle, or place in which anything mentioned in subsection (1) is believed to be is in some other territorial division, the justice may issue his warrant in like form modified according to the circumstances, and the warrant may be executed in the other territorial division after it has been endorsed, in Form 25, by a justice having jurisdiction in that territorial division.

(3) A search warrant issued under this section may be in the form set out as Form 5 in Part XXV, varied to suit the case.

(4) An endorsement that is made on a warrant as provided for in subsection (2) is sufficient authority to the peace officers or such persons to whom it was originally directed and to all peace officers within the jurisdiction of the justice by whom it is endorsed to execute the warrant and to deal with the things seized in accordance with section 489.1 or as otherwise provided by law.

TELEWARRANTS — Information on oath and record — Administration of oath — Contents of information — Issuing warrant — Formalities respecting warrant and facsimiles — Providing facsimile — Affixing facsimile — Report of peace officer — Bringing before justice — Proof of authorization

487.1 (1) Where a peace officer believes that an indictable offence has been committed and that it would be impracticable to appear personally before a justice to make application for a warrant in accordance with section 258 or 487, the peace officer may submit an information on oath by telephone or other means of telecommunication to a justice designated for the purpose by the chief judge of the provincial court having jurisdiction in the matter.

(2) An information submitted by telephone or other means of telecommunication shall be on oath and shall be recorded verbatim by the justice who shall, as soon as practicable, cause to be filed with the clerk of the court for the territorial division in which the warrant is intended for execution the record or a transcription thereof, certified by the justice as to time, date and contents.

(3) For the purposes of subsection (2), an oath may be administered by telephone or others means of telecommunication.

(4) An information on oath submitted by telephone or other means of telecommunication shall include

(*a*) a statement of the circumstances that make it impracticable for the peace officer to appear personally before a justice;

(*b*) a statement of the indictable offence alleged, the place or premises to be searched and the items alleged to be liable to seizure;

(*c*) a statement of the peace officer's grounds for believing that items liable to seizure in respect of the offence alleged will be found in the place of premises to be searched; and

(*d*) a statement as to any prior application for a warrant under this section or any other search warrant, in respect of the same matter, of which the peace officer has knowledge.

(5) A justice referred to in subsection (1) who is satisfied that an information on oath submitted by telephone or other means of telecommunication

(*a*) is in respect of an indictable offence and conforms to the requirements of subsection (4),

(*b*) discloses reasonable grounds for dispensing with an information presented personally and in writing, and

(*c*) discloses reasonable grounds, in accordance with paragraph 443(1)(*a*), (*b*) or (*c*) or subsection 240(1), as the case may be, for the issuance of a warrant in respect of an indictable offence,

may issue a warrant to a peace officer conferring the same authority respecting search and seizure as may be conferred by a warrant issued by a justice before whom the peace officer appears personally pursuant to subsection 240(1) or 443(1), as the case may be, and may require that the warrant be executed within such time period as the justice may order.

(6) Where a justice issues a warrant by telephone or other means of telecommunication,

(*a*) the justice shall complete and sign the warrant in Form 5.1, noting on its face the time, date and place of issuance;

(*b*) the peace officer, on the direction of the justice, shall complete, in duplicate, a facsimile of the warrant in Form 5.1, noting on its face the name of the issuing justice and the time, date and place of issuance; and

(*c*) the justice shall, as soon as practicable after the warrant has been issued, cause the warrant to be field with the clerk of the court for the territorial division in which the warrant is intended for execution.

(7) A peace officer who executes a warrant issued by telephone or other means of telecommunication, other than a warrant issued pursuant to subsection 240(1), shall, before entering the place or premises to be searched or as soon as practicable thereafter, give a facsimile of the warrant to any person present and ostensibly in control of the place or premises.

(8) A peace officer who, in any unoccupied place or premises, executes a warrant issued by telephone or other means of telecommunication, other than a warrant issued pursuant to subsection 240(1), shall, on entering the place or premises or as soon as practicable thereafter, cause a facsimile of the warrant to be suitably affixed in a prominent place within the place or premises.

(9) A peace officer to whom a warrant is issued by telephone or other means of telecommunication shall file a written report with the clerk of the court for the territorial division in which the warrant was intended for execution as soon as practicable but within a period not exceeding seven days after the warrant has been executed, which report shall include

(*a*) a statement of the time and date the warrant was executed or, if the warrant was not executed, a statement of the reasons why it was not executed;

(*b*) a statement of the things, if any, that were seized pursuant to the warrant and the location where they are being held; and

(*c*) a statement of the things, if any, that were seized in addition to the things mentioned in the warrant and the location where they are being held, together with a statement of the peace officer's grounds for believing that those additional things had been obtained by, or used in, the commission of an offence.

(10) The clerk of the court with whom a written report is filed pursuant to subsection (9) shall, as soon as practicable, cause the report, together with the information on oath and the warrant to which it pertains, to be brought before a justice to be dealt with, in respect of the things seized referred to in the report, in the same manner as if the things were seized pursuant to a warrant issued, on an information presented personally by a peace officer, by that justice or another justice for the same territorial division.

(11) In any proceeding in which it is material for a court to be satisfied that a search or seizure was authorized by a warrant issued by telephone or other means of

telecommunication, the absence of the information on oath, transcribed and certified by the justice as to time, date and contents, or of the original warrant, signed by the justice and carrying on its face a notation of the time, date and place of issuance, is, in the absence of evidence to the contrary, proof that the search or seizure was not authorized by a warrant issued by telephone or other means of telecommunication.

RESTRICTIONS ON PUBLICITY — Definition of ''newspaper''.

487.2 (1) Where a search warrant is issued under section 487 or 487.1 or a search is made under such a warrant, every one who publishes in any newspaper or broadcasts any information with respect to

(*a*) the location of the place searched or to be searched, or

(*b*) the identity of any person who is or appears to occupy or be in possession or control of that place or who is suspected of being involved in any offence in relation to which the warrant was issued,

without the consent of every person referred to in paragraph (*b*) is, unless a charge has been laid in respect of any offence in relation to which the warrant was issued, guilty of an offence punishable on summary conviction.

3.9.2 Harold Levy, ''What Should We Do When the Cops Arrive?'' (1979) *Content* 95

FREEDOM OF EXPRESSION in Canada is being subverted on many fronts. Nowhere is the trend more evident than in the area of freedom of the press, both print and broadcast.

In the United States, a similar tendency toward subversion of a free press has occasioned an intense, concerned and often acrimonious debate.

But in Canada all is peaceful. True, the press is agonizing, but more over the latest Margaret Trudeau escapade or Joe Clark gaffe than over its own freedom.

And Canadians blithely coast along, apparently unconcerned or unaware that Canadian journalists have never had those rights which their U.S. counterparts are so distraught about losing.

FACT: Canadian journalists have always been compellable witnesses. No legal privilege has ever been recognized between journalists and their sources, just as no legal privilege attaches to communications between members of Parliament and their constituents, doctors and their patients, or even priests and their parishioners. And that's always been the law.

FACT: Parliament has not built into the search warrant process special protections to be applied when a news service is the object of the search.

The same provisions of the Criminal Code apply, whether the place sought to be searched is a newspaper or an outhouse.

Unfortunately, under Canadian law, all that stands between the government and the confidential sources of the reporter is a justice of the peace issuing a search warrant — and that's not much protection at all.

The only concern of the justice of the peace who issues the warrant is whether there is reasonable ground to believe that the search will yield evidence with respect to the commission of an offence.

Those experienced with the system suspect that the justice of the peace often acts as a "rubber stamp" for the police, issuing warrants in a routine fashion on the skimpiest of evidence and without a hearing.

FACTS: There is no requirement in law whatsoever, where the object of the search is a newspaper or a newsroom, that prior notice and a hearing be given in connection with the issuance of search warrants. Nor is there any requirement, where the newspaper is not suspected of a crime, that the state restrict itself to the subpoena process.

Such requirements would eliminate raids by the police on the offices of the media and would allow the courts to make the decision on the relevance and admissibility of the materials desired.

FACT: Police and government officials can legally tap journalists' telephones.

They are not limited to searching for or subpoenaing the long-distance telephone records of reporters and news organizations. In Canada's wire-tap legislation, The Protection of Privacy Act — better described as The Invasion of Privacy Act — there are no special provisions protecting the press. And under the Official Secrets Act, the federal solicitor-general can entirely by-pass the judicial process and on his own unreviewable authority order the interception of a journalist's communications. Although the number of interceptions carried out under the act must be disclosed, there is no way to know whether the communications of journalists has been intercepted by executive order.

FACT: The federal government is expected to reintroduce legislation, which died with the last session of Parliament, giving its solicitor-general the power to intercept anyone's mail, including mail to or from journalists, on his own order and without application to the court.

IN SUM, by failing to recognize the very special role of the press in a democratic society, successive Canadian governments have given their own investigators and law enforcement officials vast powers which make it easy to investigate, inhibit, discourage and disrupt the press, while at the same time, by intimidating sources and creating an "iron curtain" of secrecy under the Official Secrets Act, making it difficult for the press to investigate the government.

If you think that these powers have not been widely used or are not being used more and more frequently or likely will not be used against you, they have a look at our Dossier Noir on page 38 and keep in mind that this is just a partial list of offences against the press.

If you're still not convinced, then ask somebody with the Fredericton *Daily Gleaner* or Montreal's *Québec-Presse* or *Radio-Canada* or *The Toronto Sun* or the *CBC* or *Global* television or *The London Free Press* or *The Vancouver Sun* or the Trail, B.C. *Times*. They've all experienced police raids.

With such raids becoming ever more frequent, you might well ask what you can do to protect your independence. If so, turn to the next two pages and find out what you can do when the police arrive in your newsroom.

1. Ask to see the warrant.

BEFORE THE POLICE come to your door, they will have obtained a search warrant from a justice of the peace, authorizing a search of the specified documents, to be conducted within a particular time period.

The officers are obligated by law to produce the warrant upon request and may only execute it by day unless the justice authorizes execution by night.

2. Check the warrant for defects.

IT IS DIFFICULT for a layperson to make a decision on whether a search warrant is legally valid — and it is risky as well. Even an experienced lawyer might well be unable to predict whether a court would, at a subsequent date, declare a warrant to be valid in law or not.

In an interview for this article, *The Vancouver Sun's* Allan Fotheringham, whose newspaper is very experienced in such matters, said that, when the police arrive, they should be told to "get the hell out" until a lawyer can be summoned to determine the validity of the warrant.

He recognizes, however, that not all publications have the services of a lawyer at hand and that employees of the paper might find themselves in a dilemma if the police politely refuse and insist on entering to conduct their search.

Nonetheless it can be worthwhile to examine the warrant for obvious defects. If the warrant appears patently defective in that (1) it does not name or describe the premises to be searched or (2) does not contain a time limit within which the search is to be conducted or (3) does not detail the offence which the search is expected to reveal or (4) does not give details of the grounds on which the warrant was sought, you can stall the police by threatening to expose the defectiveness of the warrant to legal counsel and to instruct counsel to take steps against the police.

3. Let them search.

IF THE WARRANT appears a lawful one, those on the premises are obliged to stand aside and permit the search.

If you do not permit the police to enter in a voluntary manner, they are authorized to use reasonable force to effect an entry in order to conduct the search.

If you use force to impede their entry, you could be charged with obstructing the police.

Although the Criminal Code contains a procedure which requires the prosecution to make available copies of the material seized, it may well be advisable to seek permission to list the various items being removed or to photocopy on the premises prior to removal.

4. Say as little as possible.

THERE IS NO obligation whatsoever on any person in the premises to speak to the police or answer any questions put by the police during the course of the search. This was well understood by *Toronto Sun* editor Peter Worthington when RCMP officers visited him in search of a letter known to be in his possession and addressed to a high-ranking officer of the Security Service.

Worthington's comments, made in an interview for *Content,* are most instructive in regards to handling the police when they are searching for a single item.

The Mounties initially asked me to co-operate by voluntarily furnishing the letter to them, so that they would not have to obtain a search warrant. I refused to co-operate and, in fact, they had a search warrant with them all the time...It is well-known that newspaper offices are not the neatest places in the world. They looked everywhere — under pictures and behind desks. Finally, four or five hours later, they got around to the top drawer of my desk and almost missed the letter. It was a very confusing scene. I think it was Bob Johnson, then with the CBC, who said, ''I don't know if they will find a letter in this mess — but they may lose a Mountie.''

5. Protect sensitive material.

WHERE THE POLICE have in fact entered the premises and are intent on seizing an easily locatable item which may contain names or information of a confidential nature, an effective technique is to insist that the item be placed in an envelope which is then to be sealed and marked for the attention of either the justice of the peace who issued the warrant or the sheriff of the county in which the premises are located.

The value of this tactic is that the information must be kept confidential, beyond the scrutiny of the police, until a hearing can be held as to its admissibility in evidence at a future date.

6. Use cooperation to your own advantage:

ACCORDING TO Toronto lawyer Clayton C. Ruby, who is counsel to a television network, it is quite common for the police to request the co-operation of the station being searched.

In his view, there is little to lose in co-operating with regard to film which has been aired.

He has, however, advised his network to refuse to co-operate with regard to the outs. To co-operate puts the station in the position of acting as agents of the state in enforcing the law, a role inconsistent with the independence of a free press.

In Ruby's experience, the purpose of the police in obtaining the outs is usually to assist in identifying individuals who participated in a particular demonstration or disturbance.

Needless to state, where the network co-operates by turning over film that has been aired, it should be duplicated so that the police will not have the only copy.

Clayton Ruby cautions that, although there is no obligation imposed upon anyone to answer questions posed by the police or to assist in any way, this is not to say that total non-cooperation is advisable — only that it is important that the media should make their own decisions about co-operating.

What to do *before* the police arrive

Safeguard notes and outs.

EVERY JOURNALIST must have a personal solution for safeguarding crucial notes.

Clayton Ruby cautions that it is necessary to retain outs and reporters' notes in case of libel suits or allegations of inaccuracy and, therefore, does not advise his clients to destroy these materials. He cautions as well that, if you destroy material which you have been notified may be evidence in legal proceedings, you may be committing the crime of obstructing the course of justice.

However, in Ruby's view,

''It is foolish for the TV stations and the newspapers to keep their ''outs'' and reporters' notes in such a way that any fool with a search warrant can walk in and find them. Such material should be filed in ways which suit the convenience of the newspapers or TV stations, as opposed to the police.''

In the long run, however, prudence and common sense rather than paranoia is called for.

Learn about the law.

RUBY ALSO RECOMMENDS that the press and other media should retain counsel to hold meetings with staff on the subject of the rights and obligations of journalists so that they can evaluate situations as they arise and can react in an informed way.

Protect your subscribers.

ONE OF THE WORST features of the 1977 raid conducted by the police on the offices of the Pink Triangle Press was the seizure of a list of subscribers to *The Body Politic*.

Such evidence could have little value in a prosecution for mailing indecent matter, since all that is required to evidence the mailing of a periodical is a standard form from Canada Post and a copy of the issue in question. And, in fact, none of the material seized in the raid was introduced at trial.

The police could find pretexts for conducting raids on all sorts of publications expressing views different from those of the majority, thus exposing the subscribers to political harassment.

An effective method of protecting the subscription list involved the keeping of circulation documents off the premises with the use of a "fulfillment" house which utilizes computers equipped with magnetic tapes.

According the Rolf Brauch, the president of Brauch-Neville Associates Ltd., a fulfillment house is not a Japanese brothel — it is rather a service which assists the publisher by maintaining the circulation list and preparing the labels which are usually then affixed at the printers and mailed. The two principle concerns identified by Brauch are those of continuity and confidentiality.

Continuity is easily assured by maintaining a back-up tape containing the names of the subscribers. Thus, even if the police raided the fulfillment house and were able to identify a tape or a portion of a tape and seize it, the publisher would be left with a back-up tape and would thus be assured that the next issue could be readily mailed.

In order to ensure confidentiality, Brauch suggests that the customer be recorded in the firm's records under a pseudonym such as *Garden-Club News*.

The police would be confronted by a forest of racks containing hundreds of magnetic reels each containing between 300,000 and 600,000 names.

This method works because there is no obligation in law requiring anyone to assist the police by telling them where the original circulation documents are located or on which tape the subscription list is to be found.

An advantage of the system suggested by Brauch, is that not only are continuity and security preserved, but there is no extra cost to the customer.

What really boggles the mind is that it should be necessary in a free society for the media to have to indulge in such subterfuge in order to counter the unwarranted and unjustifiable intrusion of the state.

Fight fire with fire.

THE MEDIA HAVE a great advantage in that they can use their own facilities to report incidents of harassment by the police.

Back in 1972, when the Times of Trail, B.C. was visited by RCMP officers who questioned company employees about a series of articles describing routine activities of the local RCMP detachment, ME Herb Legg called upon the federal solicitor-general and provincial attorney-general to investigate whether members of the RCMP would return and highlighted the harassment on the front page.

There are numerous examples of such selective police harassment, but few are as odious as the actions of former Kitchener police chief Sidney Brown, who denied reporters with the Kitchener-Waterloo Record access to the Waterloo Regional Police Headquarters and access to further investigation information after photographs were published in the newspaper showing members of the force's tactical squad standing guard over a group of Henchmen Motorcycle Club members after a raid on their clubhouse. One of the pictures showed cyclists kneeling with their hands cuffed behind their backs under the waiting fangs of an angry-looking German shepherd.

Because of the intensive public pressure generated by the newspaper and the support of other media, the police chief had to retreat and the threatened criminal charges against employees of the paper in connection with the photographs were not pursued.

The lesson stemming from all of these incidents and so many others, is that the media must make the facts known whenever such harassment occurs.

3.9.3 *Pacific Press* v. *The Queen,* (1977), 38 C.R.N.S. 295 (B.C.S.C.)

28th June 1977. NEMETZ C.J.S.C.: — On Monday, 10th January 1977 B. Harrison, a British Columbia justice of the peace, affixed his signature to two documents, each entitled "Warrant to Search". Both documents were directed to the respondents Simon Wapniarski and Clare Savage (combines investigation officers with the Canada Department of Consumer and Corporate Affairs) and "To the Peace Officers in the said province". The first document purported to authorize and require the search of the premises of "The Vancouver Province" [sic] and the second "The Vancouver Sun". The Province and The Vancouver Sun are daily newspapers published in Vancouver. Both are printed by the petitioner, Pacific Press Ltd. The object of these searches was to obtain from the two newspapers written notes and tape recordings of interviews and journalists' photographs made and taken by the press at an abortive inquiry in Vancouver of the Restrictive Trade Practices Commission (the "commission").

The inquiry hearings had been scheduled for the week of 6th December 1976. The commission was to investigate certain matters relating to the operation of the fishing industry in this province. The trade union under investigation and other persons had objected to the commission conducting the inquiry in private and had demanded a public hearing. The commission refused. Apparently, on the morning of 6th December, to demonstrate their displeasure with the decision to conduct the inquiry in private, a number of persons picketed and occupied the premises in which the hearing was to be held and so prevented the opening of the inquiry. These tactics were repeated on 7th and 8th December with the result that the inquiry was adjourned sine die.

The respondents Wapniarski and Savage were present during the picketing and occupation. They had observed various persons, including newspapermen and photographers, conducting interviews and taking photographs of several of the people who had obstructed the inquiry. The Department of Consumer and Corporate Affairs, through its agents, decided to seek information regarding the identity of the picketers by soliciting the assistance of the various organs of the news media which had covered the events to which I have referred. This information, apparently, was sought to assist in bringing a prosecution under s.41 of the Combines Investigation Act, R.S.C. 1970, c.C-23, which makes it an offence for any person to impede an inquiry held under the provisions of that Act.

On 10th January 1977 Wapniarski telephoned the city editor of The Vancouver Sun and asked for information as to the identity of the persons engaged in the fracas of 6th to 8th December. The editor refused to give any information beyond that which had already been published by the paper. Wapniarski then told the editor that his department would apply for the issuance of a search warrant in order to obtain the information sought.

On the same day (10th January) Savage made a similar request of The Province. The warrants were granted by the justice of the peace on 10th January. The following day Wapniarski and Savage entered the Pacific Press building, served the warrants and proceeded to search those parts of the premises where the newspapers were being prepared for publication. In the course of the two searches the respondents seized 77 pieces of paper, a number of handwritten notes and 69 frames of negative film. They also seized a reporter's private "contact book", which contained a compilation of names and addresses of persons who acted as sources of information for the newspapers. There is little doubt that the search disrupted the operation of the newspapers and delayed the preparation and publication of both newspapers that day.

In addition to Wapniarski and Savage, Her Majesty the Queen in right of this province, the Attorney General for British Columbia and Mr. Harrison, the justice of the peace, are respondents. Counsel for the petitioner consented to abandon any claims the petitioner might have for damages against either of the combines investigation officers and Harrison, in the event of the success of the petition. The petitioner now applies for an order quashing the warrants. It also seeks an order that the documents and materials seized be returned.

The submissions made by counsel for the petitioner may be categorized under three general headings. They are:

1. The warrants were issued without statutory authority.

2. There was insufficient information before the justice on which he could act judicially in issuing the warrants as required by s.443(1)(*b*) of the Criminal Code, R.S.C. 1970, c.C-34.

3. The warrants themselves fail to comply with the requirements of the law.

Before considering these submissions, I will examine some general principles of law applicable to the use of search warrants in Canada. The search warrant is a tool in the administration of criminal law, allowing officers of the law to undertake the search of a man's house or other building with a view to discovering, amongst other things, evidence which might be used in the prosecution of a criminal offence. From time immemorial common law courts have been zealous in protecting citizens from the unwarranted use of this extraordinary remedy. As the four English judges who sat declared more than three centuries ago, "the house of everyone is to him as his castle and fortress, as well for his defence against injury and violence as for his repose": *Semayne's Case* (1604), 5 Co. Rep. 91a, 77 E.R. 195.

In 1948 former Farris C.J.S.C. of this court, in a decision in which he stated that "I have had the opportunity of discussing the case with my brother Judges presently available, who are in agreement with my findings" (*Re United Distillers Ltd.*, 88 C.C.C. 338 at 344, [1947] 3 D.L.R. 900) said [p. 341]:

"The law seems to be well established that in granting a warrant to search, the information before the Magistrate must be of such a nature as to permit him to grant the warrant judicially.

"It has been recognized that a warrant to search is the result of a statutory enactment and is repugnant to the old common law that a man's home or premises is his castle. That such a warrant should not be lightly granted seems to be recognized by all of the leading authorities and properly so, and that *the Magistrate in granting such warrant should have reasonable information before him to entitle him to judicially decide whether such warrant should issue or not*." (The italics are mine.)

As will be seen, infra, I have reached my conclusion in respect of The Province because of defects in the information. Because of the conclusions I have reached under the second heading of the petitioner's submission. I do not find it necessary to decide either the first or third points as they affect The Vancouver Sun. I will assume, without deciding, that the necessary statutory authority for the issuance of a search warrant in respect of a suspected offence under s.41 of the Combines Investigation Act, R.S.C. 1970, c.C-23, is to be found in s.443(1)(*b*) of the Criminal Code which provides:

"443.(1) A justice who is satisfied by information upon oath in Form 1, that there is reasonable ground to believe that there is in a building, receptacle or place...

"(*b*) anything that there is reasonable ground to believe will afford evidence with respect to the commission of an offence against this Act,...

"may at any time issue a warrant under his hand authorizing a person named therein or a peace officer to search the building, receptacle or place for any such thing, and to seize and carry it before the justice who issued the warrant or some other justice for the same territorial division to be dealt with by him according to law."

The law is settled that the justice of the peace, in exercising his discretionary jurisdiction under s.443(1), must act judicially: see *Regina v. Solloway and Mills*, 65 O.L.R. 303, 53 C.C.C. 271, [1930] 3 D.L.R. 770 at 774 (C.A.). In that case Riddell J.A. said in part:

"It will be seen that s.629 [the predecessor section to s.433(1)] provides that 'Any justice who is satisfied by information upon oath in form 1, that there is reasonable ground for believing that there is in any building...' may issue a search warrant. This, literally interpreted, would mean that whenever a justice is in fact so satisfied, whether he should have been so satisfied or not, he may issue the warrant. *But the issue of the warrant is a judicial act, and, as such, in the absence of statutory prohibition, its propriety may be examined by competent authority, which competent authority we are; and it is our duty to examine not into whether the justice was in fact satisfied but into whether he should have been satisfied*." (The italics are mine.)

(See also *Schumiatcher v. A.G. Sask.* (1960), 34 C.R. 152, 33 W.W.R. 132, 129 C.C.C. 267 (Sask.); and *Regency Realties Inc. v. Loranger* (1961), 36 C.R. 291 (Que.).)

Should he have been satisfied in the case at bar? In my respectful opinion he should not have been satisfied and I will delineate my reasons for coming to that conclusion. In the first place, it is manifest that the authorizing justice must be "satisfied by information upon oath in Form 1" that sufficient circumstances exist for him judicially to exercise his power. The words of McRuer C.J.H.C. in *Re Bell Telephone Co. of Can.*, 4 C.R. 162, [1947] O.W.N. 651, 89 C.C.C. 196 at 198, are particularly opposite. He said:

"Before a Justice *may* issue a search warrant, it is necessary that there be a sworn information that contains such a statement of facts as satisfies the Justice that there are reasonable grounds for believing any of the things set out in s.629. It is not sufficient that the Justice should be satisfied — he *must* be satisfied on reasonable grounds; *that is, the grounds of belief set out in the information must be such as would satisfy a reasonable man*. If there are not such grounds shown the Justice cannot be taken to have been satisfied on reasonable grounds." (The italics are mine.)

(See also the decision of Seaton J.A. in *B.X. Development Ltd. v. The Queen,* [1976] 4 W.W.R. 364, 31 C.C.C. (2d) 14 at 22, 70 D.L.R. (3d) 366 (B.C.C.A.).)

Counsel for the petitioner submits that the grounds set out in the information should not and could not have satisfied a reasonable man to authorize the warrants to issue against the two newspapers, and particularly against The Province. At this point I think it useful to reproduce the information upon which both warrants were issued:

"INFORMATION TO OBTAIN A SEARCH WARRANT

"CANADA:
PROVINCE OF BRITISH COLUMBIA,
CITY OF VANCOUVER.

Simon Wapniarski, Combines Investigation Officer, Bureau of Competition Policy, Canada Department of Consumer and Corporate Affairs

"This information of of Ottawa, Ontario , in the said City of Vancouver, hereinafter called the 'informant', taken before me, the undersigned Justice of the Peace in and for the Province of British Columbia.

"The informant says that he has reasonable and probable grounds to believe and does believe that there are certain things, namely notes of interviews, taped recordings of interviews, photographs and photographic film which will afford evidence of the commission of an offence against the Combines Investigation Act, namely that section 41 of the said Act has been violated by impeding, preventing or attempting to impede or prevent an inquiry and examination pursuant to section 17 of the said Act, and that his grounds for so believing are that the informant witnessed news reporters and newspaper photographers interviewing, photographing and filming persons involved in disrupting, impeding, preventing or attempting to impede or prevent the said inquiry and examination.

"In conversation with executives of both the Vancouver Sun and the Vancouver Province, the informant was told that the evidence sought and pertaining to the said offence (this offence occurring on the 6th, 7th, 8th and 9th days of December A.D. 1976) is held on the premises of both the Vancouver Sun and the Vancouver Province.

" and that he has reasonable grounds for believing that the said things or some part of them are in the premises of the building of The Vancouver Sun and the Vancouver Province, the informant was told that the said City of Vancouver.

"Wherefore the informant prays that a search warrant may be granted to search the said premises of the building of The Vancouver Sun for said things.

"SWORN before me this 10th day of January, A.D. 1977 at City of Vancouver.
" 'B. Harrison'

"[Illegible]

"A Justice of the Peace in and for the Province of British Columbia. "(Signature of informant.)"

Counsel for the petitioner first points to the fact that no separate information was sworn in support of The Province warrant. Assuming for a moment that such a procedure is proper, then Mr. Giles directs my attention to the prayer where the informant seeks a warrant only for the search of the premises of The Vancouver Sun. Leaving aside defects in grammar and detail (see McFarlane J.A. in *Re B.X. Development Ltd.,* supra, what can be said of the granting of a search warrant not prayed for under Form 1? I agree with Mr. Giles that this omission is fatal to the issuance of the warrant against The Province.

I turn now to consider the petitioner's second point that there was insufficient information before the justice on which he could act judicially in issuing the search warrant against The Vancouver Sun. Counsel for the petitioner submits that when a search warrant is sought against an organ of the free press of this country, the issuing justice, before exercising his judicial discretion, should weigh the competing interests of the free press on the one hand and the administration of justice on the other. As I understand Mr. Giles, he is not submitting that the press is exempted from the search provisions of the Criminal Code. What he says is that the justice, in exercising his judicial discretion, is obliged to consider, inter alia, before issuing the warrant, the special position of an organ of the free press set out in the Canadian Bill of Rights, R.S.C. 1970, App. III, and amendments thereto, ss.1(*f*) and 2:

"1. It is hereby recognized and declared that in Canada there have existed and shall continue to exist without discrimination by reason of race, colour, religion or sex, the following human rights and fundamental freedoms, namely...

"(*f*) freedom of the press.

"2. Every law of Canada shall, unless it is expressly declared by an Act of the Parliament of Canada that it shall operate notwithstanding the *Canadian Bill of Rights,* be so construed and applied as not to... abridge... any of the rights or freedoms herein recognized and declared".

Recently the Court of Appeal of England has again considered the difficult problem of setting down rules in the particular instance of the press (and its reporters) within the framework of the rules of evidence governing the giving of testimony and the issuance of subpoenas in trials: *Senior v. Holdsworth; Ex parte Independent Television News Ltd.,* [1976] 1 Q.B. 23. In that case a cameraman employed by Independent Television News ("I.T.N.") had taken certain lengths of film at a "Pop" festival which had been broken up by police. The plaintiff sued for damages for injuries he received and applied for a summons to obtain the film (transmitted or not) taken by the I.T.N. cameraman. The judge ordered it produced, but on appeal he was reversed and it was held that the order to produce the film was so wide as to be oppressive and therefore was set aside.

The judgments delivered by Lord Denning M.R., Orr and Scarman L.JJ. lend valuable assistance in the difficult problem of dealing with the rights of the free press in the courts. I quote a passage from Lord Denning M.R.'s judgment at p. 34 with which I am in respectful agreement:

"Next there is the special position of the journalist or reporter who gathers news of public concern. The courts respect his work and will not hamper it more than is necessary. They will seek to achieve a balance between these two matters. On the one hand there is the public interest which demands that the course of justice should not be impeded by the withholding of evidence. See *Rogers v. Home Secretary; Gaming Bd. for Great Britain v. Rogers,* [1973] A.C. 388 at 401, [1972] 2 All E.R. 1057, by Lord Reid. On the other hand, there is the public interest in seeing that confidences are respected and that newsmen are not hampered by fear of being compelled to disclose all the information which comes their way: see *Democratic National Committee v. McCord* (1973), 356 F. Supp. 1394, in the United States. As we said in this court as to oral testimony of a newsman:

" 'The judge... will not direct [him] to answer unless not only it is relevant but also it is a proper and, indeed, necessary question in the course of justice to be put and answered': See *A.G. v. Mulholland; A.G. v. Foster,* [1963] 2 Q.B. 477 at 489, [1963] 1 All E.R. 767.' "

Lord Denning M.R. went on to say that the courts had the power to order I.T.N. to produce and show the untransmitted film but that [pp. 34-35] "the court should exercise this power only when it is likely that the film will have a direct and important place in the determination of the issues before the court. The mere assertion that the film may have some bearing will not be enough. If the judge considers that request is irrelevant, or fishing, or speculative, or oppressive, he should refuse it." Scarman L.J. thought that a summons to produce should be set aside where what is sought is irrelevant, oppressive or *an abuse of the process of the court* or recognized by the law as privileged from production. Orr L.J. was of the view that there was a "degree of residual discretion in the court of trial or the tribunal" which should also "consider carefully any special hardship or difficulties that may be involved": pp. 37 and 38.

It is to be remembered that these views were given in the context of the laws of England where there is no statute analogous to our Bill of Rights.

In his judgment Lord Denning M.R. referred to *Democratic National Committee v. McCord,* supra, in which the First Amendment of the United States Constitution was held to extend to journalists a qualified privilege in respect of their obligation to testify in response to subpoena. In *McCord* it was held that a reporter could not be compelled to testify unless the judge was satisfied that all alternative sources of information had been exhausted and that the requirement of the administration of justice outweighed freedom of the press. I keep in mind what was said by the majority, per Ritchie J., at p. 345 in *Miller and Cockriell v. The Queen,* 33 C.R.N.S. 139, [1976] 5 W.W.R. 711, 31 C.C.C. (2d) 177, 70 D.L.R. (3d) 324, in considering the effect of American cases decided under the United States Constitution. However, the principle laid down in *McCord* was germane to Lord Denning M.R.'s reasoning in *Senior,* supra, and was supported by the Court of Appeal decision in *A.G. v. Mulholland,* supra, notwithstanding the constitutional differences between the two countries.

Where, then, does the matter stand in Canada? Counsel for the petitioner submits that Parliament has accorded the free press a special place under the Canadian Bill of Rights. Accordingly, he argues, ss.1(*f*) and 2 must be taken into consideration and weighed by the justice of the peace before he exercises his judicial discretion to grant the issuance of a search warrant against an organ of the free press of this country. A fortiori, he says, this fact is to be weighed in cases where the premises of the newspaper are not the premises of those persons accused of the crime. I agree with this submission. Furthermore, he submits, it was wrong in the circumstances to attempt to render the press an investigative arm of the state when other means of obtaining the names of the persons involved in the melee at the combines hearing may have been available. In particular, counsel points to the fact that many persons other than the newspaper people were in attendance at the combines office on the days in question and the material does not show whether these other people were approached to establish the identity of the participants in the fracas.

The issuing of any search warrant is a serious matter, especially when its issuance against a newspaper may have, as it did, the effect of impeding its publication. To use the words of my distinguished predecessor in *United Distiller Ltd.*, supra, the justice of the peace "should have reasonable information before him to entitle him to judicially decide whether such warrant should issue or not". In my opinion, no such reasonable information was before him since there was no material to show: 1. whether a reasonable alternative source of obtaining the information was or was not available; and 2. if available, that reasonable steps had been taken to obtain it from that alternative source.

In my opinion, the bringing of an application for a search warrant in these circumstances was an abuse of the process of the court. I therefore quash the warrants.

Note: See also *Descoteaux* v. *Mierzwinski* [1982], 1 S.C.R. 860.

3.9.4 A Note on Taking Photographs Against Instructions of the Police

Although photographers have a right to take photographs, such activity may become criminal if done against instructions of the police. Under s.129(a) of the Criminal Code it is an offence to resist or wilfully obstruct "a public officer or peace officer in the execution of his duty or any person lawfully acting in aid of such an officer." The offence of obstructing a police officer in the execution of his duty consists of three essential elements:

(1) there was an obstruction of the police officer;
(2) the obstruction affected the police officer in the execution of the duty he was then executing; and
(3) the person obstructing did so wilfully in the sense of intentionally and without lawful excuse.

(*R.* v. *Westlie* (1971), 2 C.C.C. (2d) 315 (B.C.C.A.); *R.* v. *Tortolano, Kelly and Cadwell* (1975), 28 C.C.C. (2d) 562 (Ont. C.A.); *R.* v. *Kalnins* (1978), 41 C.C.C. (2d) 524 (Ont. Co. Ct.); and *R.* v. *Sandford* (1980), 62 C.C.C. (2d) 89 (Ont. Prov. Ct.).)

In discussing the first two elements, the court in *Tortolano, Kelly and Cadwell* said that it is the purpose of the obstruction, not its result, that goes to the offence under s.129(a). Accordingly, an officer's duty need not be completely frustrated for a s.129(a) charge to made out. The fact that the obstruction did not prevent the officer from executing his duty is, therefore, no defence to a charge of obstructing a peace officer in the execution of his duty. Further, at the time of the obstruction, the officer need not be engaged in the performance of a specific duty in order to support a conviction under s.118(a) *(Westlie)*. And in determining whether the obstruction was "wilful", as required by the third element of the offence, it has been suggested that the court must take all the circumstances of the matter into consideration *(Sandford)*.

Press photographers have been convicted pursuant to s.129(a) in a couple of cases. In *Knowlton* v. *R.* (1973), 10 C.C.C. (2d) 377, the Supreme Court of Canada upheld the conviction of a photographer who tried to enter an area which had been cordoned off as a security measure during a visit to Vancouver by a foreign dignitary. A peace officer warned the photographer that he could not enter the area, but the photographer forcefully insisted on his right to do so and attempted to enter notwithstanding the warning. And in *Kalnins,* the Ontario County Court held that a charge under s.129(a) was made out against a press photographer who attempted to take pictures of a psychiatric patient being taken to the hospital by police. Although asked by the officer not to take any pictures, the accused insisted that it was his right to do so. The presence of the photographer greatly upset the patient, making it impossible initially for the ambulance attendants to remove the patient's stretcher from the ambulance.

In *Sandford,* however, a press photographer was found not guilty of a s.129(a) offence when he continued to take pictures of an accident scene although repeatedly told by police officers to get off the roadway to make way for the emergency crew still working at the scene. The charge was dismissed in that case because the judge was not satisfied that the obstruction was "wilfull".

Note: The law in this area has not yet been clearly defined. Neither the courts nor any of the legislatures in Canada recognize the right of the press to gather information. Accordingly, the rights of press photographers and media reporters to record on film items which they consider to be newsworthy must be seen as subordinate to the rights of police officers to conduct themselves in a reasonable manner in the execution of their duties.

CHAPTER FOUR

Legal Limitations Protecting Social Values and Social Groups

4.1 A Note on the Law and the Protection of Beliefs, Morals and Minorities

The laws protecting religious belief, minority groups and morality belong conceptually to criminal libel. Just as the law of seditious libel was used historically to protect the legitimacy (or the reputation) of the State and its institutions, the law of blasphemous libel has been used to protect the name of the Divine. Just as the law of seditious libel was used to prohibit incitements to riot, modern hate propaganda law is intended to prevent incitements which could harm racial or ethnic groups. The laws relating to obscene libel exist partly to promote standards of conduct and belief, but also to protect women and children from exploitation and harm.

However, debate continues about the content and rigour of such laws. This is, in part, because the social harms which the prohibited acts cause are not always easy to establish and, in part, because our social perceptions seem to be constantly changing. For example, advocates of liberalizing the practices governing the production and showing of explicit erotic material made substantial gains in the sixties. But this has been challenged by Bill C-54, the Conservative government's 1987 proposal to tighten the criminal code provisions about pornography.

One part of this trinity of moral prohibition may have been put to rest. Although the Criminal Code of Canada continues to prohibit blasphemous libel, there have been no reported cases since 1935. That blasphemy has ceased to be regarded as a crime reflects the process of secularization in which a substantial percentage of Canada's population profess neither a belief in God nor an attachment to a particular doctrinal tradition. It also reflects the norm, now rarely challenged, that regardless of the desirability or extent of such beliefs, the law in a pluralistic state cannot be legitimately used to enforce them. In other words, an idea that John Milton promoted in the seventeenth century has taken hold — namely, that individuals should be persuaded rather than compelled to believe one doctrine or another.

The idea that persuasion rather than compulsion is the best remedy to harms caused by words has haunted the career of the law prohibiting expressions of race hatred. That law, which dates from the early sixties, makes it a crime to advocate genocide or to promote hatred towards an identifiable group. But neither offence may be prosecuted without the consent of the Attorney-General of a province and the part of the law that applies to statements promoting race hatred includes provisions which establish defences to the charge and make it difficult to secure a conviction. As a consequence, there have been few charges brought under these sections of the Criminal Code.

To avoid the restrictions in the hate propaganda sections of the Criminal Code which make it difficult both to bring a charge and secure a conviction, the Crown proceeded against Ernst Zundel in 1985 under section 177 (now s.181). This makes it a crime to publish a statement which is known to be false and which can cause injury or mischief to a public interest. Zundel had published pamphlets that said the Holocaust, the murder of European Jews by the Nazis during the Second World War, did not occur and that the statement that six million Jews died in death camps was a lie promulgated by Zionists. It should be noted that the resort to s.177 suggests great reluctance on the part of the State to enforce the hate propaganda prohibitions.

If there has been hesitation in the area of hate propaganda, there has been confusion and continued debate in the areas of obscenity and pornography. As recently as 1962, the Supreme Court of Canada was asked to determine if "Lady Chatterley's Lover", was obscene. The Court determined that it was not and followed the wording of the 1959 amendments to the Criminal Code, rather than the classical common-law test of obscenity.

The new wording in the code allowed for a defence that countenanced both literary or artistic merits and community standards. However, the law has been subject to a debate because it has been variously interpreted across Canada and, in the opinion of some, has allowed for the circulation of films and videos which promote violence against women and children. The proposed 1987 amendments were intended to respond to these concerns and further specify the sorts of material which the law may legitimately render criminal. In the meantime, the judges have devoted themselves to redefining the law to bring it into line with contemporary concerns. The courts have both modernized and clarified the law — something Parliament has significantly failed to achieve.

Although these elements of the law affect freedom of expression in a fundamental way, they are not centrally important to the operations of newspapers and other news agencies. It is fair to say that producers of films and authors of fiction are more likely to face problems than are the news media.

4.2 Blasphemy

4.2.1 Criminal Code, s.296

Blasphemous Libel

OFFENCE — Question of fact — Saving.

296. (1) Every one who publishes a blasphemous libel is guilty of an indictable offence and is liable to imprisonment for two years.

(2) It is a question of fact whether or not any matter that is published is a blasphemous libel.

(3) No person shall be convicted of an offence under this section for expressing in good faith and in decent language, or attempting to establish by argument used in good faith and conveyed in decent language, an opinion upon a religious subject.

4.2.2 *Rex* v. *Rahard* (1935) 65 C.C.C. at 344

Libel II — What constitutes criminal libel.

The expression in writing of an opinion upon a religious question in bad faith and in language offensive and injurious to the religious convictions of those who do not share those convictions and of such a nature that it may lead to a disturbance of the public peace, constitutes blasphemous libel.

TRIAL on a charge of blasphemous libel.
G. Fauteaux, for the Crown; *A. H. Tanner,* for the accused.

PERRAULT, C.J.S.P.: — The indictment based upon s.198 of the Criminal Code states that the accused the Rev. Victor Rahard, while a minister of the Anglican Church situated at the Corner of Cartier & Sherbrooke Sts., in Montreal, published upon posters, a writing constituting blasphemous libel.

This case raises a very difficult and important question. Furthermore, I believe this is the first time that the question of blasphemous libel has been brought before our Canadian Courts under such circumstances.

Moreover, it must be understood that this does not involve a question of religious doctrine, but solely a legal question, that is, the application of s.198 of the Cr. Code. This section must be interpreted and it must be decided whether the writing published constitutes blasphemous libel.

In all justice to the defence and in order to better place the dispute before you I will reproduce the entire writing from which the present action arose.

"The Canadian Catholic Church, Anglican rite.

"Sermon by an old monk.

"The seven commandments of the Church of Rome.

"If Christ returned to visit all His churches, He could still chase the merchants from the temple crying: 'My house is a house of prayer and you have made it a den of thieves.' (St. Matthew, c.xxi, v.13.)

"Judas and the Roman priest.... The Mass.

"So Christ is sold. Judas sold Christ but did not kill Him, the priests attempt to sell Him and immolate Him. Judas sold Christ for a large sum of money; the Roman priests sell Him every day and even three times.

"Judas repented and threw his money away; the Roman priests do not repent and keep the money. Now what do you think of the papist religion?

"Christ has condemned the commandments of men whatever they may be when He said to the Pharisees: 'It is in vain that they honour Me teaching maxims and human ordinances; (Matthew, c.xv, v.3.)

"The Roman Church is not content with the commandments of God. She wished to have her own commandments for the satisfaction of her ambition and the prosperity of her shop."

"First of all it should be observed that these commandments bear a false name. It is not the commandments of the Church that they should have been called but commandments of the Roman clergy.

"These human commandments are not of God nor of universal morality nor of the conscience. They bind no one and their transgression may be considered as an act of enfranchisement in regard to usurped authority."

The indictment reproduced is in writing; the accused, the Rev. Victor Rahard assumes full and complete responsibility for the writing and its publication. He admits having on August 12, 1933, affixed it to the property of his church, the length of Sherbrooke St. in the eastern part of the City of Montreal in full view of passersby and especially of Roman Catholics and French Canadians who compose at least three-quarters of the population of the City of Montreal.

The facts are therefore established and are admitted by the parties; only a question of law remains. In his admission (ex. Da.) the Rev. Victor Rahard declares that he is a priest of the Anglican Church in Canada, that his ecclesiastical superiors have conferred upon him the charge of the church known by the name of Church of the Redeemer, situated upon Sherbrooke St. East where he has the right to preach the doctrine of his church.

Upon the argument the Crown maintained the following proposition; s.198 of the Cr. Code interpreted literally as well as in spirit gives every freedom of opinion upon any religious subject whatever; as it gives every latitude to the expression of this opinion in writing or otherwise, provided that this publication is made in good faith and in agreeable language, in such a manner as not to offend either by its terms or expressions the feelings of others who are not of the same opinion or point of view and finally to keep from disturbing the public peace through offensive or injurious terms.

In short to insure the public peace among His Majesty's subjects is the object of all the provisions of the Cr. Code.

On the other hand the defence maintains the following proposition: —

1. Blasphemy is a crime by English common law which exists only in an attack against the Divinity or Christianity in general; and the writing attacks neither the Divinity or Christianity.

2. By believing that the writing was directed against the Divinity or Christianity in general, the accused would be protected by s.198 of the Cr. Code because he attempted to establish in good faith and in decent language an opinion upon the question of religious doctrine.

3. That more particularly the statement he made regarding the Mass was part of the teaching of the Church of England; that in his capacity of priest he has the right to teach, just as he has the right to discuss, the question of whether belief in the Mass is well founded or not; for it is a question of controversy between the Roman and the Protestant Church.

4. That considering the place and the circumstances of the publication of this writing, criminal intent on the part of the accused could not be inferred.

At the outset I declared that this was not a question of doctrine but solely a question of law. Besides this Court is not called upon to determine the right of the accused to preach in his own church the religious doctrine which he deems fit, which right is not debated any more than his liberty of opinion. But could he, without contravening s.198 of the Cr. Code, publish the writing reproduced above in the terms and expressions used? That is the question which the Court has to decide.

This s.198 of the Cr. Code placed under Part V, under the rubrics "offences against religion, morals and public convenience" does not define blasphemous libel but contains the simple statement that blasphemous libel constitutes an offence and is a question of fact. Nevertheless the section contains the following provision: — "Provided that no one is guilty of a blasphemous libel for expressing in good faith and in decent language, or attempting to establish by arguments in good faith and conveyed in decent language, any opinion whatever upon any religious subject."

Hence it is to be noted that our Code speaks of a religious subject and not only of Divinity or of Christianity in general, but in order to understand and know the essential elements constituting the offence of criminal libel the common law must be resorted to. It is a principle of our Criminal law (s.16) that the English common law is applicable in our country although the subject is not specially mentioned in our Code. See Annotation, 48 Can. C.C., at p. 4.

"The common law jurisdiction as to crime is still operative notwithstanding the Criminal Code, but subject to the latter prevailing where there is a repugnancy between the common law and the Code" (*Rex v. Cole* (1902), 5 Can. C.C. 330).

The Supreme Court of Canada accepted this interpretation in *Brousseau v. The King* (1917), 29 Can. C.C. 207, at p. 209, 39 D.L.R. 114, at p. 115: — "The criminal common law of England is still in force in Canada, except in so far as repealed either expressly or by implication."

But the English common law in regard to a blasphemous libel has been varied with the ages. With the times and a new understanding of freedom of opinion, the doctrine and jurisprudence has attached significance to the intention of the author, to the terms used by him and to the circumstances rather than to the subject treated.

In Odgers on Libel and Slander, 5th ed., p. 498, it is said: — "It is the malicious intent to insult the religious feelings of others by profanely scoffing at all they hold sacred, which deserves and receives punishment."

And at p. 467: — "It is sufficient to prove a publication to the prosecutor himself, provided the obvious tendency of the words be to provoke the prosecutor and excite him to break the peace."

Blasphemy which otherwise was under the jurisdiction of the Ecclesiastical Courts, has come under the jurisdiction of the Civil Courts in order, the authors say, to prevent a disturbance of the peace. In the year 1676 in *Taylor's Case*, 1 Vent. 293, 86 E.R. 189, the English Courts sanctioned the axiom which, since that time, has often been invoked: "Christianity is parcel of the laws of England," and the following syllogism arose: "To disparage any part of the law of England is a crime. Christianity is a part of the law of England, therefore to disparage Christianity is a crime."

But later Lord Coleridge in the case of *Reg. v. Ramsay* (1883), 15 Cox C.C. 231, at p. 235, declared: — "I think that these old cases can no longer be taken to be a statement of the law at the present day. It is no longer true in the sense in which it was true when these *dicta* were uttered, that 'Christianity is part of the law of the land.'"

And further on he adds — "The principles of law remain, and it is the great advantage of the common law that its principles do remain; but then they have to be applied to the changing circumstances of the times. This may be called by some retrogression, but I should rather say it is progression — the progress of human opinion."

This case was decided in 1883 and established the following principle: — "The mere denial of the truth of the Christian religion, or of the Scriptures, is not enough, per se, to constitute a writing and blasphemous libel, so as to render the writer or publisher indictable. But indecent and offensive attacks on Christianity or the Scriptures, or sacred persons or objects, calculated to outrage the feelings of the general body of the community, do constitute the offence of blasphemy, and render writers or publishers liable at common law to criminal prosecution.''

This doctrine was maintained in the more recent decision of *Rex* v. *Gott* (1922), 16 Cr. App. R. 86. It decided as follows: —

''The essence of the crime consists in the publication of words concerning the Christian religion so scurrilous and offensive as to pass the limits of decent controversy and to be calculated to outrage the feelings of any sympathiser with Christianity. In considering whether these limits have been passed the circumstances in which the words are published should be taken into account. The limits of decent controversy would certainly be passed if the circumstances in which the words were published were such that the publication was likely to lead to a breach of the peace.''

Folkard in his Law of Slander and Libel, 7th ed., p. 361, interpreting the case of *Rex* v. *Woolston* (1729), 1 Barn. K.B. 162, 94 E.R. 112, declares: — ''It may be observed, that all the recorded instances of prosecution for blasphemy, subsequent to *Woolston's case,* have been for publication of indecent, scoffing, and opprobrious language against natural or revealed religion; and that in most of such cases, the jury have been directed to look both to the matter and manner of the publication in order to decide on its blasphemous quality; and in those cases where the defendants have been convicted, the judges, in the remarks they have made upon the mischievous tendency of the offence, have, usually, founded their reasons for the punishment awarded, more upon the offensive manner of the publication in the particular instances, than upon the matter itself; and all have cautiously avoided laying down any general prohibitory rule.''

It may be noted that the English jurisprudence attaches more importance to the intention of the author and the terms in which he expresses his opinion than to the subject treated and because of the danger of disturbing the public peace. This doctrine was expressed by Starkie in his work on the Law of Slander and Libel, 3rd ed., p. 590: — ''It is the mischievous abuse of this state of intellectual liberty which calls for penal censure. The law visits not the honest errors, but the malice of mankind. A wilful intention to pervert, insult, and mislead others, by means of licentious and contumelious abuse applied to sacred subjects, or by wilful misrepresentations or wilful sophistry, calculated to mislead the ignorant and unwary, is the criterion and test of guilt. A malicious and mischievous intention, or what is equivalent to such an intention, in law, as well as in morals, — a state of apathy and indifference to the interests of society, — is the broad boundary between right and wrong. If it can be collected from the circumstances of the publication, from a display of offensive levity, from contumelious and abusive expressions applied to sacred persons or subjects, that the design of the author as to occasion that mischief to which the matter which he publishes immediately tends, to destroy or even to weaken men's sense of religious or moral obligations, to insult those who believe by casting contumelious abuse and ridicule upon their doctrines, or to bring the established religion and form of worship into disgrace and contempt, the offence against society is complete.''

And in regard to this doctrine of Starkie, Lord Coleridge in *Reg* v. *Ramsay,* 15 Cox C.C., at p. 236, states: — ''It is my duty to lay down the law on the subject as I find it laid down in the best books of authority, and in 'Starkie on Libel,' it is there laid down as, I believe, correctly.''

Odgers, *ubi supra,* p. 498, says: — "This view of our law against blasphemy was strongly advocated by that eminent lawyer, the late Mr. Starkie... This is the view adopted by the Judges in the House of Lords in *Shore* v. *Wilson,* 9 Cl. & Fin. 355 [8 E.R. 450]. This is the view expressed in the admirable address of the late Chief Justice Coleridge to the jury in the case of *R.* v. *Ramsey and Foote.*"

See Odgers, 5th ed., p. 478. This author expresses the same doctrine as Starkie: —

"The intent to shock and insult believers, or to pervert or mislead the ignorant and unwary, is an essential element in the crime. *Actus non facit reum nisi mens sit rea.* The existence of such an intent is a question of fact for the jury, and the *onus* of proving it lies on the prosecution. The best evidence of such an intention is usually to be found in the work itself. If it is full of scurrilous and opprobrious language, if sacred subjects are treated with offensive levity, if indiscriminate abuse is employed instead of argument, then a malicious design to wound the religious feelings of others may be readily inferred.... This would tend to show that he did not write from conscientious conviction, but desired to pervert and mislead the ignorant; or at all events that he was criminally indifferent to the distinctions between right and wrong."

Our s.198 of the Cr. Code has been interpreted in a profound article by E. J. Murphy, K.C., representing the Crown in the case of *Rex* v. *Sterry.* He states as follows (48 Can. C.C., at p. 22): — "The question is, is the language used calculated and intended to insult the feelings and the deepest religious convictions of the great majority of the persons amongst whom we live? If so, they are not to be tolerated.... We must not do things that are outrageous to the general feeling of propriety among the persons amongst whom we live."

Rex v. *Pilon* (unreported) June 15, 1934, judgment of Wilson, J.; *Rex* v. *St. Martin* (1933), 40 Rev. de Jur. 411, Lacroix, J.S.P.; *Reg.* v. *Pelletier* (1900), 6 Rev. Leg. 116.

Hence it follows that s.198 of the Cr. Code must be interpreted to mean that it is permitted to express any opinion whatever upon a religious subject in a public document if this opinion is expressed in good faith and in decent language since anyone may support his opinion by arguments expressed in good faith and in decent language.

I believe it has been shown that that is not only our Canadian law but the most recent English doctrine and jurisprudence as well.

Let us apply these principles to the present case. It is certain that the document published August 12, 1933, deals with a religious subject.

Has the Rev. Victor Rahard expressed his opinion upon this religious question in good faith and in decent language? He wrote and published that the Roman Church is not satisfied with the commandments of God; that it wished to have its own commandments for the satisfaction of its own ambition and the prosperity of its shop. In other words the church to which a Roman Catholic goes to pray, where he has been baptized, where he fulfils his religious duties and where at the end of his life his body will be taken before its final rest in the cemetery, is a place of commerce. And what kind of trade?

And in order that there might be no mistake as to the meaning which the accused attaches to the word shop, he declares as follows: — "If Christ should return to visit all His churches He could still chase the merchants from the temples by crying 'My house is a house of prayer and you have made it a den of thieves.'"

Furthermore he compares the Roman priest to Judas saying: — "Although Judas sold Christ he did not kill Him while the priests attempt to sell Him and immolate

Him; the Roman priests sell Him for a few cents and do not repent but keep the money.'' And he concludes by saying: — ''Now what do you think of the papist religion?''

I maintain that these terms are offensive and injurious to the Roman Catholics and of such a nature that they may lead to a disturbance of the public peace.

Where in the above quoted words can be found an argument expressed in good faith or in decent language to sustain the opinion of the accused. The bad faith of the accused is more than manifest. This writing is posted the length of Sherbrooke St. in a place frequented above all by the Roman Catholic and French Canadian population, and in order to give more force and authority to the statements which he made in this writing, he places at its head the words ''Sermon by an old monk.''

What could be the impression upon a Catholic population of these words ''Sermon by an old monk'' may easily be understood.

If we apply the English doctrine which I have cited above, that is to say, taking into account the circumstances of the publication as well as the terms and expressions used by the accused, we have evidence of bad faith on the part of the accused.

I will repeat what was said by Mr. Murphy in his article in 48 Can. C.C., at p. 22: — ''The question is, is the language used calculated and intended to insult the feelings and the deepest religious convictions of the great majority of the persons amongst whom we live? If so, they are not to be tolerated.... We must not do things that are outrageous to the general feeling of propriety among the persons amongst whom we live.''

At the hearing of the case the accused, by this counsel, made a motion to quash on the ground of the nullity of the indictment because no intent was alleged therein. I do not believe that it is necessary to allege specially the intent in the indictment. Intent results from facts. Furthermore the indictment declares that the Rev. Victor Rahard published a blasphemous writing on August 12, 1933. And s.198 of the Cr. Code states that a blasphemous writing constitutes a criminal offence.

Hence it follows that the fact that the indictment alleges that the accused published a blasphemous writing was sufficient to include all the elements of the offence.

What is it which constitutes a blasphemous writing? That is a question of fact left to the appreciation either of the Judge or jury. That is the import of s.198 of the Cr. Code. As a result the motion to quash is dismissed and the accused is declared guilty.

4.2.3 *R.* v. *Gay News Ltd.* [1979] 1 All ER 898

R v Lemon
R v Gay News Ltd

HOUSE OF LORDS
LORD DIPLOCK, VISCOUNT DILHORNE, LORD EDMUND-DAVIES, LORD RUSSELL OF KILLOWEN AND LORD SCARMAN
20th, 21st, 22nd, 23rd, 27th NOVEMBER 1978, 21st FEBRUARY 1979

Criminal law — Blasphemy — Blasphemous libel — Ingredients of offence — Intent — Attack on Christianity — Poem describing acts of sodomy and fellatio with body of Christ — Whether subjective intent to attack Christianity required to be proved.

The appellants, the editor and publishers of a newspaper for homosexuals, published in the newspaper a poem accompanied by a drawing illustrating its subject-matter which purported to describe in explicit detail acts of sodomy and fellatio with the body of Christ immediately after His death and to ascribe to Him during His lifetime promiscuous homosexual practices with the Apostles and with other men. The appellants were charged with the offence of blasphemous libel. The particulars of the offence alleged that the appellants unlawfully and wickedly published or caused to be published a blasphemous libel concerning the Christian religion, namely 'an obscene poem and illustration vilifying Christ in His life and in His crucifixion'. The trial judge directed the jury that in order to secure the conviction of the appellants for publishing a blasphemous libel it was sufficient if they took the view that the publication complained of vilified Christ in His life and crucifixion and that it was not necessary for the Crown to prove an intention other than an intention to publish that which in the jury's view was a blasphemous libel. The appellants were convicted. They appealed to the Court of Appeal contending that a subjective intent on the part of the appellants to shock and arouse resentment among Christians had to be proved by the prosecution and that the judge had misdirected the jury. The Court of Appeal dismissed their appeal and they appealed to the House of Lords.

Held (Lord Diplock and Lord Edmund-Davies dissenting) — In order to secure a conviction for the offence of publishing a blasphemous libel it was sufficient, for the purpose of establishing mens rea, for the prosecution to prove an intention to publish material which was in fact blasphemous and it was not necessary for them to prove further that the defendants intended to blaspheme. Accordingly the appeals would be dismissed (see p 911 *d* to *g*, p 921 *d* to *f* and p 927 *f* to p 928 *a*, post).

R v Shipley (1784) 21 St Tr 847, *R v Hetherington* (1841) 4 St Tr NS 563, *R v Bradlaugh* (1883) 15 Cox CC 217 and *R v Ramsay and Foote* (1883) 15 Cox CC 231 considered.

Per Curiam. A blasphemous libel is material calculated to outrage and insult a Christian's religious feelings (see p 900 *g h*, p 906 *f g*, p 912 *d e*, p 920 *g h*, p 922 *b c*, p 924 *a* to p 925 *b* and p 927 *f* to p 928 *a*, post).

Per Lord Edmund-Davies and Lord Scarman. It was not an essential ingredient of the crime of blasphemy that the publication must tend to lead to a breach of the peace (see p 920 *f* and p 925 *b c*, post).

Decision of the Court of Appeal, Criminal Division [1978] 3 All ER 175 affirmed.

Appeals

On 11th July 1977 at the Central Criminal Court, before his Honour Judge Alan King-Hamilton QC and a jury, the appellants, Denis Lemon and Gay News Ltd, were convicted of blashemous libel, in a private criminal prosecution brought by the respondent, Mary Whitehouse. On 12th July Mr Lemon was sentenced to nine months' imprisonment suspended for 18 months, fined £500 and ordered to pay one-fifth of the costs of the prosecution and was also ordered to contribute a maximum of £434 towards his legal aid costs. Gay News Ltd were fined £1,000, to be paid within three months, and ordered to pay four-fifths of the prosecution costs. Both appellants appealed against conviction on the grounds, inter alia, that the trial judge erred in law (1) in ruling that intention, ie an intention to attack the Christian religion and/or to insult or outrage Christian sympathisers and/or believers, and/or to provoke a breach of the peace, was not a necessary element of the offence of blasphemous libel and (2) in ruling that an attack on Christ or the Christian religion was not a necessary element of the offence of blasphemy. Both appellants also applied for leave to appeal against sentence. On

17th March 1978 the Court of Appeal, Criminal Division (Roskill, Eveleigh LJJ and Stocker J) dismissed their appeals, refused them leave to appeal but certified that a point of law of general public importance was involved in the decision. The appellants appealed to the House of Lords pursuant to leave of the House granted on 17th May 1978. On 24th May the appeals were consolidated. The facts are set out in the opinion of Lord Diplock.

Louis Blom-Cooper QC and *Geoffrey Robertson* for the appellant Lemon.
Geoffrey Robertson for the appellant Gay News Ltd.
John Smyth and *Jeremy Maurice* for the Crown.

Their Lordships took time for consideration.

21st February. The following opinions were delivered.

LORD DIPLOCK. My Lords, the appellants are the editor and publishers of a newspaper called Gay News. As its name suggests its readership consists mainly of homosexuals though it is on sale to the general public at some bookstalls. In an issue of Gay News published in June 1976 there appeared a poem by a Professor James Kirkup entitled 'The Love that Dares to Speak its Name' and accompanied by a drawing illustrating its subject-matter. The poem purports to describe in explicit detail acts of sodomy and fellatio with the body of Christ immediately after His death and to ascribe to Him during His lifetime promiscuous homosexual practices with the Apostles and with other men.

The issue in this appeal is not whether the words and drawing are blasphemous. The jury, though only by a majority of ten to two, have found them to be so. As expressed in the charge against them they 'vilify Christ in His life and in His crucifixion', and do so in terms that are likely to arouse a sense of outrage amoung those who believe in or respect the Christian faith and are not homosexuals and probably among many of them that are. The only question in this appeal is whether in 1976 the mental element or mens rea in the common law offence of blasphemy is satisfied by proof only of an intention to publish material which in the opinion of the jury is likely to shock and arouse resentment among believing Christians or whether the prosecution must go further and prove that the accused in publishing the material in fact intended to produce that effect on believers, or (what comes to the same thing in criminal law) although aware of the likelihood that such effect might be produced, did not care whether it was or not, so long as the publication achieved some other purpose that constituted his motive for publishing it. Wherever I speak hereafter of 'intention' I use the expression as a term of art in that extended sense.

At the trial the judge in a carefully considered ruling given after lengthy argument held that the offence was one of strict liability. The ruling made irrelevant (and therefore inadmissible) any evidence by Mr Lemon, the editor of Gay News, about his own intentions in publishing the poem and drawing; accordingly he did not go into the witness box and no other evidence was called on behalf of the accused. The judge summed up to the jury in masterly fashion and in accordance with his ruling; the jury by a majority verdict convicted both appellants.

The convictions were upheld by the Court of Appeal, who certified that the following point of law of general public importance was involved in their decision to dismiss the appeals:

> 'Was the learned trial judge correct (as the Court of Appeal held) first in ruling and then in directing the jury that in order to secure the conviction of the appellants for publishing a blasphemous libel (1) it was sufficient if the jury took the view that the publication complained of vilified Christ in His life and crucifixion and (2), it was not necessary for the Crown to establish any further intention on the part of the appellants beyond an intention to publish that which in the jury's view was a blasphemous libel?'

My Lords, the offence of publishing a blasphemous libel has a long and at times inglorious history in the common law. For more than 50 years before the prosecution in the instant case was launched the offence seemed to have become obsolete, the last previous trial for it having taken place in 1922. Originally the offence was cognisable only in the ecclesiastical courts. Its history from the 17th century when jurisdiction over it was first assumed by the courts of common law until its apparent disappearance from the criminal calendar after 1922 is traced in fascinating detail in G.D. Nokes's work, A History of the Crime of Blasphemy, published in 1928 and now out of print. A shorter historical account is to be found in Lord Sumner's famous speech in *Bowman* v. *Secular Society Ltd,* but none of the speeches in that case touches at all on the question of intention. The judgment of the Court of Appeal in the instant case contains a valuable historical survey of most of the relevant cases with special reference to the intention of the publisher in publishing the blasphemous matter. In this House, too, the speeches to be delivered by my noble and learned friends, Viscount Dilhorne and Lord Edmund-Davies, will each incorporate a critical analysis of the varying terms in which judicial pronouncements on mens rea in blasphemous and seditious libel were expressed as the 19th century progressed. My own complete agreement with Lord Edmund-Davies's analysis relieves me of the task of attempting what would be no more than a paraphrase of it; but, since it leads to a conclusion as to the state of the law on this topic by the time the century ended which is diametrically opposed to that reached by Viscount Dilhorne (with which my noble and learned friend, Lord Scarman, also concurs) I feel bound to concede that by the beginning of the present century the law as to the mental elements in the offence of blasphemous libel was still uncertain. The task of this House in the instant appeal is to give to it certainty now, and to do so in a form that will not be inconsistent with the way in which the general law as to the mental element in criminal offences has developed since then.

Two things emerge clearly from the earlier history. First that between the 17th century and the last quarter of the 19th, when Sir James Fitzjames Stephen published his History of the Criminal Law of England the characteristics of the substantive offence of blasphemous libel had undergone progressive changes; and secondly, that, as Stephen reluctantly acknowledges in his chapter on seditious offences, those changes (which he personally regretted) were largely shaped by the procedural changes in the trial of prosecutions for all forms of criminal libel resulting from Fox's Libel Act 1792 and by the passing of Lord Campbell's Libel Act 1843.

In the post-Restoration politics of 17th and 18th century England, Church and state were thought to stand or fall together. To cast doubt on the doctrines of the established church or to deny the truth of the Christian faith on which it was founded was to attack the fabric of society itself; so blasphemous and seditious libel were criminal offences that went hand in hand. Both were originally what would now be described as offences of strict liability. To constitute the offence of blasphemous libel it was enough for the prosecution to prove that the accused, or someone for whose acts the law of libel held him to be criminally responsible, had published matter which (in trials held before Fox's Libel Act) the judge ruled, or (in trials held after that) the jury found, to be blasphemous, whether the accused knew it to be so or not. Furthermore, criminal libel in its four manifestations, seditious, blasphemous, obscene and defamatory, was unique among common law offences, in imputing to any person who carried on the business of publisher or bookseller, vicarious criminal liability for acts of publication done by persons in his employment even though these were done without his authority, consent or knowledge. Since in practice prosecutions were brought against publishers and booksellers rather than against authors, so long as this remained the law, as it did until the passing of s.7 of Lord Campbell's Libel Act in 1843, it could not logically be reconciled with the notion that the accused's own actual intention was a relevant element in the offence.

The severity of the law of blasphemous libel had, however, been somewhat mitigated before 1843 by judicial rulings not as to the mens rea but as to the actus reus of the offence. To publish opinions denying the truth of doctrines of the established Church or even of Christianity itself was no longer held to amount to the offence of blasphemous libel so long as such opinions were expressed in temperate language and not in terms of offence, insult or ridicule: see *R. v. Hetherington*. This introduces into the concept of the actus reus, in addition to the act of publication itself, the effect that the material published is likely to have on the minds of those to whom it is published.

At a period when an accused could not give evidence in his own defence and his intention to produce a particular result by his acts, where this was an ingredient of the offence, was ascertained by applying the presumption that a man intends the natural consequences of his acts, the distinction was often blurred between the *tendency* of the published words to produce a particular effect on those to whom they were published and the *intention* of the publisher to produce that effect. So that one finds F. L. Holt in his textbook on The Law of Libel published in 1816 defining blasphemous libel as requiring the publication to be made 'with an *intent* to subvert man's faith in God, or to impair his reverence of him' and during the 20 years before Lord Campbell's Libel Act in 1843 one also finds in reported summings-up of various judges occasional references to the *intention* of the accused.

The abolition in 1843 of vicarious criminal liability for blasphemous libel and the growing influence of Starkie's textbook on the law of criminal libel opened the way for a further development in the definition of the crime of blasphemous libel; but this time in its mental element or mens rea which was brought into closer harmony with the changed concept of the actus reus. Starkie was one of the Criminal Law Commissioners during the 1840s and became Downing Professor of Law at Cambridge. He adopted F. L. Holt's definition and elaborated it in a paragraph later to be adopted as an accurate statement of the law by Lord Coleridge C.J. in *R. v. Ramsay and Foote:*

> 'The law visits not the honest errors, but the malice of mankind. A wilful intention to pervert, insult, and mislead others, by means of licentious and contumelious abuse applied to sacred subjects, or by wilful misrepresentations or wilful sophistry, calculated to mislead the ignorant and unwary is the criterion and test of guilt. A malicious and mischievous intention, or what is equivalent to such an intention, in law, as well as morals — a state of apathy and indifference to the interests of society — is the broad boundary between right and wrong.'

The language in which this statement is expressed is perhaps more that of the advocate of law reform than of the draftsman of a criminal code. The reference to misleading others is probably outdated in this more sceptical and agnostic age unless what misleads is couched in terms that are likely to shock and arouse resentment among believing Christians. Nevertheless, the statement clearly requires intent on the part of the accused himself to produce the described effect on those to whom the blasphemous matter is published and so removes blasphemous libel from the special category of offences in which mens rea as to one of the elements of the actus reus is *not* a necessary constituent of the offence.

Although Stephen continued to resist in his writings what he described as this 'milder view of the law' accepted by Lord Coleridge C.J., it appears to have been adopted by judges in summing up in subsequent prosecutions for blasphemous libel which, after 1883, became very rare. The industry of G. D. Nokes enabled him to identify only five between 1883 and 1922. In the only one in which the summing-up is reported in a legal journal, *R. v. Boulter,* Phillimore J. read to the jury the first part of the passage from Starkie referring to wilful intention that I have cited above. In *R. v. Gott* the summing-up is reported only in The Freethinker for 8th January 1922. Avory J. is there recorded as being less specific in his citation from Lord Coleridge C.J., but refers to the necessity for the words to be 'calculated and *intended* to insult the feelings and the deepest religious convictions... of persons amongst whom we live'.

I accept that, on the state of the authorities, it is still open to this House to approve the stricter view of the law preferred by Stephen to the milder view adopted by Lord Coleridge C.J. in his summing-up in *R. v. Ramsay and Foote;* but there are, as it seems to me, compelling reasons why we should not. The paucity of subsequent prosecutions for blasphemous libel does not enable one to point to any judicial developments in the legal concept of the mens rea required in this particular offence; but this does not necessarily mean that the law of blasphemous libel, now the offence has been revived after a lapse of fifty years, should be treated as having been immune from those significant changes in the general concept of mens rea in criminal law that have occurred in the last hundred years. All of these in my opinion point to the propriety of your Lordships adopting the milder view that the offence today is no longer one of strict liability, but is one requiring proof of what was called in *Director of Public Prosecutions v. Beard,* a 'specific intention', namely, to shock and arouse resentment among those who believe in or respect the Christian faith.

The first great change that influenced the general concept of mens rea after 1883 was procedural, the passing of the Criminal Evidence Act 1898, which enabled the accused to testify as a witness in his own defence. Prior to this his actual intention could only be ascertained as a matter of inference from what he was proved to have done and the circumstances in which he did it; and juries were instructed to apply what was referred to as the 'presumption' that a man intends the natural consequence of his own acts. In the case of blasphemous libel if the jury found that words published by the accused, looked at objectively, had the tendency to produce the effect that it was the policy of the law to prevent, e.g. to shock and arouse resentment among believing Christians, then the application of the presumption was sufficient to convert this objective tendency into the actual intention of the accused. So the milder view of the law adopted by Lord Coleridge C.J. in 1883 might have had little practical effect if there had been any further prosecutions before the passing of the Criminal Evidence Act 1898.

Although this Act enabled the accused to give direct evidence of his own intention and thus added to the available material on which the jury's finding as to the accused's intention could be based, the presumption that a man intends the natural consequences of his own acts survived as a true presumption at least until the decision of this House in *Woolmington v. Director of Public Prosecutions,* that is to say, it was an inference that the jury was bound to draw unless the accused overcame the evidential burden of proving facts of a kind regarded by the law as being sufficient to rebut it.

This presumption, which was of general application to offences in which the intention of the accused to produce a particular proscribed result formed an essential element in the mens rea, has had a chequered history since 1898, both before and after *Woolmington*. Discussion of it is mainly to be found in cases of homicide. There were two schools of thought among the judges as to how the presumption could be rebutted. The stricter school applied what has come to be known as the 'objective test'. It took the view that if the result proscribed were foreseeable by a reasonable man as being a likely consequence of his act, the presumption that the accused intended that result could only be rebutted by proof that he was insane or, in charges of murder brought after the passing of the Homicide Act 1957, that he suffered from some abnormality of mind. The onus of proving insanity or abnormality of mind lay on the accused. The milder school which predominated 20 years ago, when I myself was trying criminal cases, applied the 'subjective test'. It treated the presumption, prior to *Woolmington,* as having the effect of casting on the accused the evidential burden of proving that he had *not* intended the natural consequences of his act. After *Woolmington* the evidential burden cast on the accused was the lesser one of inducing doubt in the jury's mind as to whether such was his intention. These competing views as to the nature and effect of the presumption and the authorities in support of each of them, are cited in the judgments of the Court of Criminal Appeal and of this House in *Director of Public Prosecutions v. Smith*. In the Court of Criminal Appeal the milder 'subjective test' prevailed; in this House the sticter 'objective test' triumphed.

If the law as expounded by this House in *Smith* had remained unchanged and had been treated as applicable beyond the field of homicide to other crimes which required a specific intention, which during the next six years, trial judges showed a uniform reluctance to do, blasphemous libel might well have reverted to what in effect would be an offence of strict liability. But Parliament stepped in to reinstate the milder view of the presumption by enacting s.8 of the Criminal Justice Act 1967:

> 'A court or jury, in determining whether a person has committed an offence, — (*a*) shall not be bound in law to infer that he intended or foresaw a result of his actions by reason only of its being a natural and probable consequence of those actions; but (*b*) shall decide whether he did intend or foresee that result by reference to all the evidence, drawing such inferences from the evidence as appear proper in the circumstances.'

This is now the law that your Lordships must apply. It throws no light on the question whether an intention to produce a particular effect on those to whom the blasphemous matter is published is an essential element in the offence of blasphemous libel; but, if it is, the section makes the 'subjective test' of the accused's intention applicable, and the evidence of the actual publisher as to what he intended or foresaw as the result of the publication becomes relevant and admissible to rebut the inference as to his intention that the jury might otherwise draw from what they themselves, as representing the reasonable man, considered would be the likely effect of what was published on those who saw and read it.

My Lords, if your Lordships were to hold that Lord Coleridge C.J. and those judges who preceded and followed him in directing juries that the accused's intention to shock and arouse resentment among believing Christians was a necessary element in the offence of blasphemous libel were wrong in doing so, this would effectively exclude that particular offence from the benefit of Parliament's general substitution of the subjective for the objective test in applying the presumption that a man intends the natural consequences of his acts; and blasphemous libel would revert to the exceptional category of crimes of strict liability from which, on what is, to say the least, a plausible analysis of the contemporaneous authorities, it appeared to have escaped nearly a century ago. This would, in my view, be a retrograde step which could not be justified by any considerations of public policy.

The usual justification for creating by statute a criminal offence of strict liability, in which the prosecution need not prove mens rea as to one of the elements of the actus reus, is the threat that the actus reus of the offence poses to public health, public safety, public morals or public order. The very fact that there have been no prosecutions for blasphemous libel for more than fifty years is sufficient to dispose of any suggestion that in modern times a judicial decision to include this common law offence in this exceptional class of offences of strict liability could be justified on grounds of public morals or public order.

The fear that, by retaining as a necessary element of the mens rea of the offence the intention of the publisher to shock and arouse resentment among believing Christians, those who are morally blameworthy will be unjustly acquitted appears to me to manifest a judicial distrust of the jury's capability of appreciating the meaning which in English criminal law is ascribed to the expression 'intention' of the accused. When Stephen was writing in 1883, he did not then regard it as settled law that, where intention to produce a particular result was a necessary element of an offence, no distinction is to be drawn in law between the state of mind of one who does an act because he desires it to produce that particular result and the state of mind of one who, when he does the act, is aware that it is likely to produce that result but is prepared to take the risk that it may do so, in order to achieve some other purpose which provided his motive for doing what he did. It is by now well-settled law that both states of mind constitute 'intention' in the sense in which that expression is used in the definition of a crime whether at common law or in a statute. Any doubts on this matter were finally laid to rest by the decision of this House in *Hyam v. Director of Public Prosecutions*.

Stephen, who deprecated this development of the criminal law as leading to a legal fiction, did not hesitate to express his own distrust of the jury's ability or willingness to distinguish between intention and motive. In writing of seditious libel he says:

> 'A jury can hardly be expected to convict a man whose motives they approve and sympathize with, merely because they regard his intention with disapproval. An intention to produce disaffection is illegal, but the motive for such an intention may be one with which the jury would strongly sympathize, and in such a case it would be hard even to make them understand that an acquittal would be against their oath.'

It had been just such judicial distrust of the reliability of juries that had led to the rule of procedure in the 18th century that was eventually abolished by Fox's Libel Act. Dare I suggest that it was just such distrust that led to the decision of this House in *Director of Public Prosecutions v. Smith* as to the legal nature of the presumption that a man intends the natural consequences of his acts that was reversed by the Criminal Justice Act 1967? If juries through sympathy do occasionally acquit a defendant whom the judge, applying the law strictly, would have convicted, it may be that that is one of the things that juries are for.

My own feeling of outrage at the blasphemous material with which the instant appeal is concerned makes it seem to me improbable that if Mr. Lemon had been permitted to give evidence of his intentions the jury would have been left in any doubt that whatever his motives in publishing them may have been he knew full well that the poem and accompanying drawing were likely to shock and arouse resentment among believing Christians and indeed many unbelievers. Nevertheless, Mr. Lemon was entitled to his opportunity of sowing the seeds of doubt in the jury's mind. By the judge's ruling he was denied this opportunity. For this reason, if the decision had lain with me, I would have allowed the appeal.

VISCOUNT DILHORNE. My Lords, the appellants, Denis Lemon and Gay News Ltd., were tried at the Central Criminal Court on an indictment which contained the following count:

> *'Statement of Offence*
> 'Blasphemous Libel.
>
> *'Particulars of Offence*
> 'Gay News Limited and Denis Lemon on a day or days unknown between the 1st day of May and 30th day of June 1976 unlawfully and wickedly published or caused to be published in a newspaper called Gay News No. 96 a blasphemous libel concerning the Christian religion namely an obscene poem and illustration vilifying Christ in His life and in His crucifixion.'

After a trial which lasted for seven days they were found guilty by a majority verdict of ten to two. They appealed to the Court of Appeal (Criminal Division) on a number of grounds. Their appeal against conviction was dismissed and they now appeal with the leave of this House, the Court of Appeal having certified that a point of law of general public importance was involved, namely the question:

> 'Was the learned trial Judge correct (as the Court of Appeal held) first in ruling and then in directing the jury that in order to secure the conviction of the appellants for publishing a blasphemous libel (1) it was sufficient if the jury took the view that the publication complained of vilified Christ in His life and crucifixion and (2) it was not necessary for the Crown to establish any further intention on the part of the appellants beyond an intention to publish that which in the jury's view was a blasphemous libel?

By their verdict the jury showed that they were satisfied that the publication complained of, a poem by a Professor James Kirkup and a drawing published alongside it, vilified Christ in His life and crucifixion and were blasphemous. That finding has not been challenged in this appeal, nor could it have been with the slightest prospect of success.

Gay News Ltd. publishes a newspaper for homosexuals called Gay News of which Denis Lemon is the editor. He holds the majority of the shares in that company. The jury's conclusion that they published the poem and the drawing was not challenged.

The only question to be decided in this appeal is what mens rea has to be established to justify conviction of the offence of publishing a blasphemous libel. The choice does not, in my opinion, lie between regarding the offence as one of strict liability or as one involving mens rea, for, as was said by Stephen in 1883 in his History of the Criminal Law of England:

> 'It is undoubtedly true that the definition of libel, like the definitions of nearly all other crimes, contains a mental element the existence of which must be found by a jury before a

defendant can be convicted, but the important question is, What is that mental element? What is the intention which makes the act of publishing criminal? Is it the mere intention to publish written blame, or is it an intention to produce by such a publication some particular evil effect?'

He said that he knew of no authority for saying that the presence of any specific intention other than the intent to publish was necessary before Fox's Libel Act 1792. During the course of the proceedings in Parliament on the Bill which became that Act, a number of questions were put to the judges. In their answer to one of them they said:

> 'The crime consists in publishing a libel. A criminal intention in the writer is no part of the definition of libel at the common law. "He who scattereth firebrands, arrows, and death," which, if not a definition, is a very intelligible description of a libel, is *eâ ratione* criminal; it is not incumbent on the prosecutor to prove his intent, and on his part he shall not be heard to say, "Am I not in sport?"'

In the *Dean of St. Asaph* case Erskine had argued that it had to be proved that the dean had had a seditious intent. That argument was rejected in that case as it was by the judges in their answer to Parliament. Prior to 1792 on a charge of publishing a seditious libel, the only questions left to the jury were (1) did the matter published bear the meaning ascribed to it in the indictment or information and (2) was it published by the defendant? It was for the judges to rule whether the matter published, bearing the sense ascribed to it, was seditious, that being regarded as a question of law (see *R. v. Shipley*). I do not doubt that the same procedure was followed when the charge was of publishing any other form of criminal libel.

It thus appears that prior to 1792 the specific intent of the accused was not an ingredient of the offence. Why was that? It is, I think, only explicable on the ground that the evil sought to be prevented by treating the publication of a libel as a criminal offence was the dissemination of libels. The mischief lay in the scattering of firebrands in the form of libels, and, if what was published was held to be seditious, the person who published it or was responsible for its publication was guilty. It mattered not, if what had been published was seditious, that he had no seditious intent (see *R. v. Shipley*).

The next question for consideration is, was the definition of a criminal libel altered later, either by Fox's Libel Act 1792 or in the course of the development of the common law, so that on a charge of publishing a seditious or a blasphemous libel proof that the defendant had a seditious or blasphemous intent, as the case might be, was essential to establish guilt?

Fox's Libel Act was 'An Act to remove Doubts respecting the Functions of Juries in Cases of Libel'. Its preamble stated that doubts had arisen whether on a trial 'for the making or publishing any libel' the jury could give their verdict 'upon the whole matter put in issue' and its first section provided that they might do so and that they should not be directed to find a defendant guilty merely on proof of publication by him and of the sense ascribed to the matter published in the indictment or information.

Parke B. in *Parmiter v. Coupland* said that the Act was declaratory and put prosecutions for libel on the same footing as other criminal cases. While the Act allowed a trial judge to tell the jury his opinion of the publication, after 1792 it was for the jury to decide what its character was.

I can see nothing in this Act 'to remove Doubts respecting the Functions of Juries' to justify the conclusion that it made a change in the definition of the offence of publishing a criminal libel. It does not mention intent, and if it had been the desire of Parliament to give statutory authority to the argument of Erskine in *R. v. Shipley* and to reject the opinion of the judges as to the ingredients of the offence, I regard it as inconceivable that the Act would have taken the form it did. Stephen, however, regarded it as having enlarged 'the old definition of a seditious libel by the addition of a reference to the specific intentions of the libeller — to the purpose for which he wrote', and said that the Act assumed that the specific intentions of the defendant were material. I must confess my inability to find in the Act any basis for either conclusion. Professor Holdsworth in his History of English Law recognised that the view that 'the crime was not so much the intentional publication of matter bearing the seditious or defamatory meaning... as its publication with a seditious or malicious intent' began to appear in the 18th century. He did not attribute this to Fox's Libel Act but to the practice of filling indictments 'with averments of every sort of bad intention on the part of the defendant', averments which in Stephen's opinion were surplusage.

The conclusion to which I come is that if any change in the definition of the offence occurred after 1792 it did not result from Fox's Libel Act.

Stephen also asserted that since that Act the law had ever since been administered on the supposition that the specific intentions of the defendant were material. My examination of the cases since 1792 leads me to think that that is not so and Professor Holdsworth said that the view that the publication had to be with a seditious or malicious intent was 'not finally got rid of till the nineteenth century'. I infer from what he said that he thought that that view was erroneous.

It was not until 1967 by the Criminal Justice Act, s.8, that it was enacted that a court or jury should not be bound in law to infer that an accused intended or foresaw a result of his actions by reason only of its being a natural and probable result of those actions but that whether he intended or foresaw that result had to be decided by reference to all the evidence drawing such inferences from the evidence as appeared proper. If the conclusion was reached that a particular publication was blasphemous and it was proved that the defendant had published it, it could be presumed under the old law that he had done so with intent to blaspheme. In many cases it may be that the existence of such an intent was undeniable but the fact that a man might be presumed to have such an intent or had that intent does not in my opinion lead to the conclusion that the existence of such an intent was an essential element in the crime, though it may account for a reference being made in some cases in the course of a summing-up to the accused's intent (see, for instance, *R. v. Hone, R. v. Richard Carlile, R. v. Moxon, R. v. Holyoake*).

In this appeal we are not, as I see it, concerned with how such an intent is to be established or its existence rebutted but whether it is an element in the offence. So with great respect to my noble and learned friend, Lord Diplock, I do not think that the terms of the Criminal Evidence Act 1898 and of s.8 of the Criminal Justice Act 1967 have any relevance to the question to be decided. If in a prosecution for the publication of a blasphemous libel the accused's intent to blaspheme has to be proved, the 1898 Act enables him to give evidence that he had no such intent and the 1967 Act gives guidance as to the proof of such an intent.

What I regard as of great significance is that in none of what I regard as the leading cases on the publication of a blasphemous libel is there to be found any direction to the jury telling them that it had to be proved that the defendant intended to blaspheme, and I have not found in any decided case any criticism of the omission to do so.

In *R. v. Mary Ann Carlile,* in an intervention, Best J. told the defendant that he would be happy to hear anything that she might urge to show that the publication was not a blasphemous libel and that she was not the publisher. It is not without significance that he said nothing about her intent particularly in view of the fact that in *R. v. Richard Carlile,* tried only a short time before, the direction to the jury had referred to the accused's intent.

A case of more importance is *R. v. Hetherington.* Hetherington was prosecuted for publishing a blasphemous libel, it being alleged that such a libel had been sold from his shop by his employee. He was convicted. It was not suggested that it had to be shown that he had any blasphemous intent, nor, it is to be noted, that the employee had any such intent. It sufficed to show that what was published was a blasphemous libel and that he was responsible for its publication. This vicarious criminal liability is wholly inconsistent with an intent to engage in blasphemy being regarded at that time as an ingredient of the offence.

Two years later Parliament changed the law, not by enacting that proof of such an intent was necessary for a conviction but by s.7 of Lord Campbell's Libel Act 1843 providing that, on a trial for the publication of a libel where the publication was by the act of a person other than the defendant but with his authority, it was competent for the defendant to prove that the publication was made without his authority, consent or knowledge, and that the publication did not arise from want of care or caution on his part. As Stephen observes by virtue of this Act the 'negligent publication of a libel by a bookseller who is ignorant of its contents' suffices to render him guilty and the fact that he may be found guilty if negligent is wholly inconsistent with the existence of any necessity to show that he intended to blaspheme. Again it may be noted that the intention of the person actually responsible for the publication was not relevant. If proof of such an intent was and is necessary, this Act did not serve any useful purpose.

I now come to the first of the two cases which I regard as the leading cases in this field. Prior to *R. v. Bradlaugh* there had been very considerable controversy about what constituted blasphemy. In the 18th century and before it appears to have been thought that any attack or criticism, no matter how reasonably expressed, on the fundamental principles of the Christian religion and any discussion hostile to the inspiration and perfect purity of the Scriptures was against the law. That was Stephen's view but in this case it was rejected by Lord Coleridge C.J. who told the jury that he thought the law had been accurately stated in Starkie on Slander and Libel in the following terms:

> 'The wilful intention to insult and mislead others by means of licentious and contumelious abuse offered to sacred subjects, or by wilful misrepresentations or wilful sophistry, calculated to mislead the ignorant and unwary, is the criterion and test of guilt. A malicious and mischievous intention, or what is equivalent to such an intention, in law, as well as morals — a state of apathy and indifference to the interests of society — is the broad boundary between right and wrong.'

At first sight the citation of this passage by Lord Coleridge C.J. might appear to give support to the view that such an intent on the part of the accused had to be proved but it is to be noted that Lord Coleridge C.J. began his summing-up by telling the jury that there were two questions to be considered, first, whether the publications in question were blasphemous libels and, secondly, whether, assuming them to be so, Mr. Bradlaugh was guilty of publishing them. He did not at any time tell the jury that they had to consider Mr. Bradlaugh's intent, an atonishing omission if he regarded it necessary to prove that he had a blasphemous intent, and the passage he cited from Starkie was cited by him as providing the test for determining whether or not the publication itself was blasphemous.

This, to my mind, is shown beyond doubt by the fact that, after citing Starkie, he said:

> 'That I apprehend to be a correct statement of the law, and if you think the broad boundary between right and wrong that is laid down in the passage, has been overpast in the articles which are the subject-matter of this indictment, then it will be your duty to answer the first question... against the defendant.'

And by his saying at the end of his summing-up:

> 'It is a question, first of all, whether these things are not in any point of view blasphemous libels, whether they are not calculated and intended to insult the feelings and the deepest religious convictions of the great majority of the persons amongst whom we live; and if so they are not to be tolerated any more than any other nuisance is tolerated. We must not do things that are outrages to the general feeling of propriety among the persons amongst whom we live. That is the first thing. Then the second thing is: Is Mr. Bradlaugh made out to have joined in the publication of these?'

'To say that the crime lies in the manner and not in the matter appears to me an attempt to evade and explain away a law which has no doubt ceased to be in harmony with the temper of the times' was Stephen's views, but since 1883 it has been accepted that it is the manner in which they are expressed that may constitute views expressed in a publication a blasphemous libel and this passage from Starkie has been relied on as providing the test for determining whether the publication exceeds that which is permissible. It is the intention revealed by the publication that may lead to its being held to be blasphemous. There was nothing in Lord Coleridge C.J.'s summing-up to support the view that there was a third question for the jury to consider, namely the intent of the accused.

This case was followed by *R. v. Ramsay and Foote,* a case greatly relied on by the appellants, a case of great importance and also tried by Lord Coleridge C.J. Again he told the jury that there were two questions for them to consider:

> 'First, are these publications in themselves blasphemous libels? Secondly, if they are so, is the publication of them traced home to the defendants so that you can find them guilty?'

He went on to say: 'The great point still remains, are these articles within the meaning of the law blasphemous libels?'

Again he cited the passage from Starkie, not as indicating that it must be shown that the accused had an intention to blaspheme but as providing the test for determining whether the articles exceeded the permissible bounds. Again Lord Coleridge C.J. gave no direction to the jury as to the intent of the accused, an omission which I regard as of great significance.

Lord Coleridge C.J.'s approach in this case was followed by Phillimore J. in *R. v. Boulter*.

While it may be that the development of the law as to seditious libel has now taken a different course, in *R. v. Aldred,* in the course of his summing-up on a charge of publishing a seditious libel, Coleridge J. told the jury that the accused could not plead the innocence of his motive as a defence to the charge, telling them that —

> 'The test is not either the truth of the language or the innocence of the motive with which he published it, but the test is this: was the language used calculated, or was it not, to promote public disorder or physical force or violence in a matter of State?'

and if the language was calculated to promote public disorder —

> 'then, whatever his motives, whatever his intentions, there would be evidence on which a jury might, on which I should think a jury ought, and on which a jury would decide that he was guilty of a seditious publication.'

This direction was not followed in *R. v. Caunt* a seditious libel case tried in 1947. The transcript of that case shows that counsel agreed that a man published a seditious libel if he did so with a seditious intent and Birkett J. so directed the jury.

It is not necessary in this appeal to decide whether Birkett J.'s direction was right or unduly favourable to the accused and whether *R. v. Aldred* was rightly decided for we are only concerned with blasphemous libel.

The last case to which I need refer is *R. v. Gott,* Avory J. in his summing-up cited the passage I have cited from the end of Lord Coleridge C.J.'s summing-up in *R. v. Bradlaugh*. He did not tell the jury that it was necessary to prove that the defendant had a blasphemous intent. He said nothing about the accused's intent. The case went to appeal but his omission to do so was not a ground of appeal or the subject of adverse comment by the Court of Criminal Appeal.

In the light of the authorities to which I have referred and for the reasons I have stated, I am unable to reach the conclusion that the ingredients of the offence of publishing a blasphemous libel have changed since 1792. Indeed, it would, I think, be surprising if they had. If it be accepted, as I think it must, that that which it is sought to prevent is the publication of blasphemous libels, the harm is done by their intentional publication, whether or not the publisher intended to blaspheme. To hold that it must be proved that he had that intent appears to me to be going some way to making the accused judge in his own cause. If Mr. Lemn had testified that he did not regard the poem and drawing as blasphemous, that he had no intention to blaspheme, and it might be, that his intention was to promote the love and affection of some homosexuals for Our Lord, the jury properly directed would surely have been told that unless satisfied beyond reasonable doubt that he intended to blaspheme they should acquit, no matter how blasphemous they thought the publication. Whether or not they would have done so on such evidence is a matter of speculation on which views may differ.

The question we have to decide is a pure question of law and my conclusions thereon do not, I hope, evince any distrust of juries. The question here is what is the proper direction to give to them, not how they might act on such a direction; and distrust, which I do not have, of the way a jury might act, does not enter into it.

My Lords, for the reasons I have stated in my opinion the question certified should be answered in the affirmative. Guilt of the offence of publishing a blasphemous libel does not depend on the accused having an intent to blaspheme but on proof that the publication was intentional (or, in the case of a bookseller, negligent (Lord Campbell's Libel Act 1843)) and that the matter published was blasphemous.

I would dismiss these appeals.

4.3 Expressions of Racism

4.3.1. Criminal Code ss.318, 319, 320 (formerly 281.1-281.3)

ADVOCATING GENOCIDE

318. (1) Every one who advocates or promotes genocide is guilty of an indictable offence and is liable to imprisonment for five years.

(2) In this section ''genocide'' means any of the following acts committed with intent to destroy in whole or in part any identifiable group, namely:
(*a*) killing members of the group, or
(*b*) deliberately inflicting on the group conditions of life calculated to bring about its physical destruction.

(3) No proceeding for an offence under this section shall be instituted without the consent of the Attorney General.

(4) In this section ''identifiable group'' means any section of the public distinguished by colour, race, religion or ethnic origin.

PUBLIC INCITEMENT OF HATRED —

319. (1) Every one who, by communicating statements in any public place, incites hatred against any identifiable group where such incitement is likely to lead to a breach of the peace, is guilty of
(*a*) an indictable offence and is liable to imprisonment for two years; or
(*b*) an offence punishable on summary conviction.

(2) Every one who, by communicating statements, other than in private conversation, wilfully promotes hatred against any identifiable group is guilty of
(*a*) an indictable offence and is liable to imprisonment for two years; or
(*b*) an offence punishable on summary conviction.

(3) No person shall be convicted of an offence under subsection (2)
(*a*) if he establishes that the statements communicated were true;
(*b*) if, in good faith, he expressed or attempted to establish by argument an opinion upon a religious subject;
(*c*) if the statements were relevant to any subject of public interest, the discussion of which was for the public benefit, and if on reasonable grounds he believed them to be true; or
(*d*) if, in good faith, he intended to point out, for the purpose of removal, matters producing or tending to produce feelings of hatred towards an identifiable group in Canada.

(4) Where a person is convicted of an offence under section 318 or subsection (1) or (2) of this section, anything by means of or in relation to which the offence was committed, upon such conviction, may, in addition to any other punishment imposed, be ordered by the presiding magistrate or judge to be forfeited to Her Majesty in right of the province in which that person is convicted, for disposal as the Attorney General may direct.

(5) Subsections 199(6) and (7) apply *mutatis mutandis* to section 318 or subsection (1) or (2) of this section.

(6) No proceeding for an offence under subsection (2) shall be instituted without the consent of the Attorney General.

(7) In this section

"communicating" includes communicating by telephone, broadcasting or other audible or visible means;

"identifiable group" has the same meaning as it has in section 318;

"public place" includes any place to which the public have access as of right or by invitation, express or implied;

"statements" includes words spoken or written or recorded electronically or electromagnetically or otherwise, and gestures, signs or other visible representations.

WARRANT OF SEIZURE —

320. (1) A judge who is satisfied by information upon oath that there are reasonable grounds for believing that any publication, copies of which are kept for sale or distribution in premises within the jurisdiction of the court, is hate propaganda, shall issue a warrant under his hand authorizing seizure of the copies.

(2) Within seven days of the issue of the warrant, the judge shall issue a summons to the occupier of the premises requiring him to appear before the court and show cause why the matter seized should not be forfeited to Her Majesty.

(3) The owner and the author of the matter seized and alleged to be hate propaganda may appear and be represented in the proceedings in order to oppose the making of an order for the forfeiture of the said matter.

(4) If the court is satisfied that the publication is hate propaganda, it shall make an order declaring the matter forfeited to Her Majesty in right of the province in which the proceedings take place, for disposal as the Attorney General may direct.

(5) If the court is not satisfied that the publication is hate propaganda, it shall order that the matter be restored to the person from whom it was seized forthwith after the time for final appeal has expired.

4.3.2 *R.* v. *Buzzanga and Durocher* (1979) 101 D.L.R. (3d) 488 (Ont. C.A.)

MARTIN, J.A.: — The appellants, Robert Buzzanga and Jean Wilfred Durocher, after a trial at Windsor before His Honour Judge J. P. McMahon, sitting without a jury, were convicted on an indictement charging them with wilfully promoting hatred against an identifiable group, namely, the French Canadian public in Essex County by communicating on or about January 12, 1977, at Windsor, statements contained in copies of a handbill entitled "Wake Up Canadians Your Future Is At Stake!", contrary to s.281.2(2) [enacted R.S.C. 1970, c.11 (1st Supp.), s.1] of the *Criminal Code*. [The relevant section is now 319-ed.]

Following the conviction of the appellants, the learned trial Judge suspended the passing of sentence and directed that they be released on probation for a period of two years. The appellants now appeal against their convictions and the appellant Durocher also appeals, in the alternative, against the sentence imposed upon him, on the ground that the learned trial Judge erred in not granting him a conditional or absolute discharge.

This case is somewhat incongruous in that the appellants identify with French-speaking Canadians against whom they are alleged to have wilfully promoted hatred.

The factual background

The appellant Durocher was born in Windsor, and is bilingual. His early education was received in a French-language public school, a bilingual high school and a French oblate seminary. He attended the University of Windsor for three years where he formed a bilingual theatre group which produced plays designed to show the harmony between the official languages of Canada. He was subsequently employed by the Essex County Board of Education and taught French. In August, 1976, he commenced to work for the Association Canadian Français de L'Ontario (hereafter, LACFO), an organization funded by the Secretary of State. His role in that organization, as he perceived it, was to stimulate and assist the French-speaking community of Essex County with respect to political, social and cultural matters, and in particular, in relation to the issue of the construction of a French-language secondary school.

The appellant Buzzanga was born of Italian parents in Egypt where he learned the French language. He said he went to France, but did not "fit in" and immigrated to Canada where he felt that he could achieve a sense of personal identity. He testified that he embraced the culture of the French Canadian people and identified himself with their aspirations for preserving their culture. He completed his education in Quebec and took courses at Laval University leading to a degree in French literature, but did not obtain a degree. He was employed for a time by the Canadian Broadcasting Corporation, and afterwards as a teacher at St. Bernard's school in Amherstberg. He became a director of LACFO in 1972.

There had been a movement for some time for the construction in Essex County of a French-language high school. The appellant Durocher testified that there had been an agreement between the Ministry of Education and the Essex County School Board for the construction of a French-language high school, under the terms of which the Essex County Board of Education received a grant of $500,000 to renovate two English-language schools and the Ministry of Education agreed to pay 95% of the cost of constructing a French-language high school. He testified that the Ministry subsequently reduced the grant rate from 95% to 77% of the cost of the proposed French-language high school, and the board decided not to build the school, although it had received and spent the grant to renovate the two English-language schools.

Eventually, the Essex County Board of Education was required by the *Essex County French-language Secondary School Act,* 1977 (Ont.), c.5, to construct the school. In the meantime, however, the French-speaking community, according to the testimony of the appellant Durocher, was "quite upset" by the position taken by the board of education.

There was a great deal of opposition, not entirely confined to the English-speaking community of Essex County, to the construction of the French-language high school. One of the strongest opponents of the construction of the high school was the Essex County Ratepayers Association, the chairman of which was Wilfred Fortowsky.

There was to be an election in the month of December, 1976, of members of the Essex County Board of Education. An action committee was formed by LACFO which set up an election office to inform the Francophone community of the stand taken by school-board candidates on the high school issue. The action committee compiled a list of the candidates whom they endorsed, but most of the candidates rejected the endorsement.

The list itself became an issue in the election and the appellant Durocher was accused of being an outside agitator sent in to stir up trouble in the francophone community of Essex County. The appellants were angered by the issue created by the action committee's endorsement of a list of candidates, and by the candidates' rejection of the endorsement. They were, of course, disappointed when the majority of candidates elected to the school board were persons who opposed the construction of the French-language high school.

After the election, the appellant Durocher began to organize a dinner-dance that "was designed as a political evening to engender protest against the treatment of Francophones and to put pressure on the government and the school board to react favourably to the school issue".

On January 5, 1977, Durocher issued a press release which read:

The Essex County Action Committee for a French-language high school

On January 29, 1977, approximately 1000 French-speaking ratepayers of Essex County and the Province of Ontario will assemble at 6 PM at Windsor's Cleary auditorium for a festive dinner-dance. What have we to celebrate? It was 65 years ago that the Provincial Government passed the infamous "Regulation 17" which forbade the teaching of the French language in Ontario. Today the same principle holds true in Essex County re the teaching of that language on the secondary level. We will celebrate 65 years of injustice. It was 8 years ago that the Francophones of Essex County actively began to fight for a French-language high school. We will celebrate 8 years of struggle. It has been 2 years since the Provincial Government has guaranteed the grants to cover construction of said school. We will celebrate 2 years of promises. It has been 1 year since the Essex Board of Education broke its promise to build said school after having spent the ½ million dollar "conditional grant" given them by the Provincial Government to secure that promise. We will celebrate 1 year of treachery. It was Lord Durham who said that the French-Canadians were a people without history & without culture and that they should & would be assimilated. It was a local Essex County politician who said last year that the Francophones of Essex County should accept assimilation and that our tax dollars should not be spent to prevent it. We will celebrate the perpetuation of racism and bigotry in Canadian history. But we will also act. On January 29, 1977, the Action Committee For A French-Language High School will exhort its fellow compatriots to take action, to no longer tolerate their status of second-class citizens, to openly and publicly condemn those "Canadians" who deny us our rights and thereby undermine the very foundations of our country and place its future in jeopardy. We invite all English-speaking medias of Ontario and Canada to come and cover this event at the Cleary Auditorium, to learn something of Canadian history and to witness the celebration of people who will not accept cultural and linguistic genocide.

Jean W. Durocher
Spokesman,
Essex County Action Committee
For A French-Language High School.

At about the same time, the appellants began preparing for dissemination the following document, the distribution of which is the subject of the charge:

WAKE UP CANADIANS
YOUR FUTURE IS AT STAKE!

IT IS YOUR TAX DOLLARS THAT SUBSIDIZE THE ACTIVITIES OF THE FRENCH MINORITY OF ESSEX COUNTY.

DID YOU KNOW THAT THE ASSOCIATION CANADIAN FRANÇAIS DE L'ONTARIO HAS INVESTED SEVERAL HUNDREDS OF THOUSANDS OF DOLLARS OF YOUR TAX MONEY IN QUEBEC?

AND THAT NOW THEY ARE STILL DEMANDING 5 MILLION MORE OF YOUR TAX DOLLARS TO BUILD A FRENCH LANGUAGE HIGH SCHOOL?

YOU ARE SUBSIDIZING SEPARATISM WHETHER IN QUEBEC OR ESSEX COUNTY.

DID YOU KNOW THAT THOSE OF THE FRENCH MINORITY WHO SUPPORT THE BUILDING OF THE FRENCH LANGUAGE HIGH SCHOOL ARE IN FACT A SUBVERSIVE GROUP AND THAT MOST FRENCH CANADIANS OF ESSEX COUNTY ARE OPPOSED TO THE BUILDING OF THAT SCHOOL?

WHO WILL RID US OF THIS SUBVERSIVE GROUP IF NOT OURSELVES?

IF WE GIVE THEM A SCHOOL, WHAT WILL THEY DEMAND NEXT... INDEPENDENT CITY STATES? CONSIDER THE ETHNIC PROBLEM OF THE UNITED STATES AND TAKE HEED.

WE MUST STAMP OUT THE SUBVERSIVE ELEMENT WHICH USES HISTORY TO JUSTIFY ITS FREELOADING ON THE TAXPAYERS OF CANADA, NOW.

THE BRITISH SOLVED THIS PROBLEM ONCE BEFORE WITH THE ACADIANS, WHAT ARE WE WAITING FOR...?

The statement was composed by the appellant Durocher whose facility with the English language was greater than that of Buzzanga.

The appellant Durocher testified that the francophone community seemed to be "fed up" with the issue of the French-language high school and was becoming apathetic. He said that although economics was the stated reason for not building the school, this was merely an excuse and the real reason was prejudice. The appellant Buzzanga shared Durocher's feeling in this respect.

Both appellants testified as to their purpose in preparing and distributing the pamphlets. The appellant Durocher testified that his purpose was to show the prejudice directed towards French Canadians and expose the truth about the real problem that existed with respect to the French-language school. He said that the statement was largely composed from written material he had seen and from experiences he had had, although the paragraph: "WHO WILL RID US OF THIS SUBVERSIVE GROUP, IF NOT OURSELVES?" was pure theatrics and has its origin in the quotation "Who will rid me of this meddlesome priest", attributed to Henry II. He testified in some detail as to the origin of various parts of the document and endeavoured to show that it reflected statements contained in such sources as letters to the editor of the Windsor Star, a document alleged to have been circulated by a member of the Essex County Ratepayers Association, a paid advertisement published in several newspapers, a book entitled "Bilingual Today, French Tomorrow", and the like. He said that he thought the pamphlet would be a catalyst that would bring a quick solution to the problem of the French-language school by provoking a Government reaction and thereby put pressure on the school board. He thought that by stating these things people would say: "This is ridiculous." A fair reading of his evidence is that he did not want to promote hatred against the "French people", for to do so would be to promote hatred against himself.

The appellant Buzzanga, too, said that he wanted to expose the situation, to show the things that were being said so that intelligent people could see how ridiculous they were. The pamphlet was intended as a satire. He wanted to create a furor that would reach the "House of Commons" and compel the Government to do something what would compel the opposing factions on the school question to reopen communications. He said it was not his intention "to raise hatred towards anyone".

The appellant Buzzanga arranged for the printing and distribution of the document. He placed the order for the printing of the document in the name of Wilfred Fortowsky, the president of the Essex County Ratepayers Association, but asked the printer to delete the name of Mr. Fortowsky when he picked up the material, leaving, however, the name of the Essex County Ratepayers Association on the order form. Neither Mr. Fortowsky nor the Essex County Ratepayers Association were, of course, aware that their names had been so used.

The appellant Buzzanga procured two 16-year-old boys, Martin Foley and Kevin Seguin, to distribute the handbills. Martin Foley testified that the appellants picked up Seguin and him in Buzzanga's car and drove them around while he and Seguin distributed the handbills. The appellants told them not to say anything about it and not to let anyone see them delivering the handbills. The handbills were distributed in apartment buildings, office buildings, a church and at the University of Windsor; the remainder were thrown in a snow bank at the Essex County Education Centre.

Apparently, the two youths were later questioned by Kevin Seguin's mother about their involvement and, a day or two later, Martin Foley called the appellant Buzzanga and asked him if the papers that he and Kevin Seguin had distributed were "French hate literature papers". He testified that the appellant Buzzanga said: "Don't say anything or I'll kill you, and tell Kevin that too." He later met both the appellants who were angry because they thought Kevin had told his mother, and he testified that the appellant Buzzanga said that if Kevin were there he would "run him over". The appellant Buzzanga denied making these statements but, in any event, it is clear that these extravagant statements, if made by the appellant Buzzanga, were neither intended nor understood by Foley to be serious threats to harm him or Kevin Seguin. The appellants then obtained some other documents for Foley to give to Mrs. Seguin to convince her that the youths were not involved in the distribution of the pamphlets which form the basis of the charge. Foley gave the papers, with which he had been supplied by the appellants, to Mr. Seguin but afterwards told him the truth.

The appellants testified that it had been their intention to come forward and acknowledge the authorship of the pamphlet but when the police investigation commenced they remained silent as a result of legal advice.

Father Claude Vincent of the Department of Sociology of the University of Windsor, a witness of eminent qualifications, testified that all persons belong to an ethnic group. He said that the Canadian Government Census assumes the existence of ethnic groups and that for census purposes a person's ethnic group is traced through the father. He testified that the term French Canadian represents the type of ethnic group. It has a distinct sense of identity, distinct sense of history, a common culture, a continuing tradition and, above all else, a consciousness of kind. He said that there is an identifiable French Canadian culture or community in Essex County. Within the term "culture" are subsumed the ideas of language, religion and history. He said that the more opposition there is to a particular group, the stronger the "in-group" solidarity becomes. It is, I think, clear that one of the purposes of the appellants in preparing and distributing the pamphlet was to "rally" the French-speaking community on the French-language secondary school issue.

Grounds of appeal

Although additional grounds of appeal were advanced, only the following grounds of appeal require discussion. The first and principal ground of appeal was that the learned trial Judge misdirected himself with respect to the meaning of the word "wilfully" in the expression "wilfully promotes hatred" in s.281.2(2) of the *Code* by holding that "wilfully" meant intentionally as opposed to accidentally....

The threshold question to be determined is the meaning of "wilfully" in the term "wilfully promotes hatred" in s.281.2(2) of the *Criminal Code*. It will, of course, be observed that the word "wilfully" modifies the words "promotes hatred", rather than the words "communicating statements".

The word "wilfully" has not been uniformly interpreted and its meaning to some extent depends upon the context in which it is used. Its primary meaning is "intentionally", but it is also used to mean "recklessly": see Glanville Williams, *Criminal Law, The General Part,* 2nd ed. (1961), pp. 51-2; Glanville Williams, *Textbook of Criminal Law* (1978), p. 87; Smith and Hogan, *Criminal Law,* 4th ed. (1978), pp. 104-5. The term "recklessly" is here used to denote the subjective state of mind of a person who foresees that his conduct may cause the prohibited result but, nevertheless, takes a deliberate and unjustifiable risk of bringing it about: see Glanville Williams, *Textbook of Criminal Law,* pp. 70 and 76; Smith and Hogan, *Criminal Law,* 4th ed., pp. 52-3.

The word "wilfully" has, however, also been held to mean no more than that the accused's act is done intentionally and not accidentally. In *R. v. Senior,* [1899] 1 Q.B. 283, Lord Russell of Killowen, C.J., in interpreting the meaning of the words "wilfully neglects" in s.1 of the *Prevention of Cruelty to Children Act,* 1894 (U.K.), c.41, said at pp. 290-1: "'Wilfully' means that the act is done deliberately and intentionally, not by accident or inadvertence, but so that the mind of the person who does the act goes with it."

On the other hand, in *Rice v. Connolly,* [1966] 2 Q.B. 414, where the accused was charged with wilfully obstructing a constable in the execution of his duty, Lord Parker, L.C.J., said at p. 419: "'Wilful' in this context not only in my judgment means 'intentional' but something which is done without lawful excuse...".

In *Willmott v. Atack,* [1976] 3 All E.R. 794, the appellant was convicted on a charge of wilfully obstructing a peace officer in the execution of his duty. A police officer, acting in the execution of his duty, arrested a motorist who struggled and resisted. The appellant, who knew the motorist, intervened with the intention of assisting the officer but, in fact, his conduct obstructed the officer. The Queen's Bench Divisional Court quashed the conviction and held that it was not sufficient to prove the appellant intended to do what he did, and which resulted in an obstruction, but that the prosecution must prove that the appellant intended to obstruct the officer.

The judgment of the Court of Criminal Appeal of Queensland in *R. v. Burnell,* [1966] Qd. R. 348, also illustrates that, depending on its context, the word "wilfully" may connote an intention to bring about a proscribed consequence. In that case the appellant was charged with arson in having set fire to a shed. Section 461 of the Queensland *Criminal Code* provides that "...any person who wilfully and unlawfully sets fire to... any building or structure is guilty of a crime...". The accused had deliberately set fire to some mattresses in a shed whereby the shed was set on fire. The trial Judge instructed the jury that "wilfully" connoted no more than a willed and voluntary act as distinguished from the result of an accident or mere negligence.

The Queensland Court of Criminal Appeal, in setting aside the conviction, held that in the context of the section "wilfully" required proof that the accused did an act which resulted in setting fire to the building with the intention of bringing about that result. Gibbs, J. (with whom Douglas, J., concurred), said at p. 356:

> Under s.461 it is not enough that the accused did the act which resulted in setting fire to the building foreseeing that his act might have that effect but recklessly taking the risk; it is necessary that the accused did the act which resulted in setting fire to the building with the intention of bringing about that result.

Mr. Manning conceded that in some cases the element of wilfulness is supplied by recklessness but he contended that in its context in s.281.2(2) of the *Criminal Code* "wilfully" means with the intention of promoting hatred. In the course of his argument, Mr. Manning stressed the definition of "wilfully" contained in s.386(1) of the *Code*, which reads:

> 386(1) Every one who causes the occurrence of an event by doing an act or by omitting to do an act that it is his duty to do, knowing that the act or omission will probably cause the occurrence of the event and being reckless whether the event occurs or not, shall be deemed, for the purposes of this Part, wilfully to have caused the occurrence of the event.

Mr. Manning emphasized that s.386(1) provides that wilfully is to have the meaning specified in that section for the purposes of Part IX of the *Code*. He argued with much force that the state of mind specified in s.386(1) is recklessness and that where Parliament intends to extend the meaning of wilfully to include recklessness it does so expressly. In *R. v. Rese*, [1968] 1 C.C.C. 363 at p. 366, [1967] 2 O.R. 451 at p. 454, 2 C.R.N.S. 99, Laskin J.A. (as he then was), referred to the definition now contained in s.386(1) as an extended meaning of "wilfully".

As previously indicated, the word "wilfully" does not have a fixed meaning, but I am satisfied that in the context of s.281.2(2) it means with the intention of promoting hatred, and does not include recklessness. The arrangement of the legislation proscribing the incitement of hatred, in my view, leads to that conclusion.

Section 281.2(1), unlike s.281.2(2), is restricted to the incitement of hatred by communicating statements *in a public place* where such incitement is likely to lead to a breach of the peace. Although no mental element is expressly mentioned in s.281.2(1), where the communication poses an immediate threat to public order, *mens rea* is, none the less, required since the inclusion of an offence in the *Criminal Code* must be taken to import *mens rea* in the absence of a clear intention to dispense with it: see *R. v. Prue; R. v. Baril* (1979), 46 C.C.C. (2d) 257 at pp. 260-1, 96 D.L.R. 577 at pp. 580-1, 8 C.R. (3d) 68 at p. 73. The general *mens rea* which is required and which suffices for most crimes where no mental element is mentioned in the definition of the crime, is either the intentional or reckless bringing about of the result which the law, in creating the offence, seeks to prevent and, hence, under s.281.2(1) is either the intentional or reckless inciting of hatred in the specified circumstances.

The insertion of the word "wilfully" in s.281.2(2) was not necessary to import *mens rea* since that requirement would be implied in any event because of the serious nature of the offence: see *R. v. Prue, supra*. The statements, the communication of which are proscribed by s.281.2(2), are not confined to statements communicated in a public place in circumstances likely to lead to a breach of the peace and they, consequently, do not pose such an immediate threat to public order as those falling under s.281.2(1); it is reasonable to assume, therefore, that Parliament intended to limit the offence under s.281.2(2) to the intentional promotion of hatred. It is evident that the use of the word "wilfully" in s.281.2(2), and not in s.281.2(1), reflects Parliament's policy to strike a balance in protecting the competing social interests of freedom of expression on the one hand, and public order and group reputation on the other hand....

I conclude, therefore, that the appellants "wilfully" (intentionally) promoted hatred against the French Canadian community of Essex County only if: (a) their conscious purpose in distributing the document was to promote hatred against that group, or (b) they foresaw that the promotion of hatred against that group was certain or morally certain to result from the distribution of the pamphlet, but distributed it as a means of achieving their purpose of obtaining the French-language high school.

Whether the trial Judge misdirected himself as to the meaning of wilfully?

The learned trial Judge in comprehensive reasons first considered whether the document objectively promoted hatred and concluded that the cumulative effect of the document rendered it a communication that promoted hatred against the French-speaking community of Essex County. He then said:

> It is, however, encumbent upon the Crown to prove beyond a reasonable doubt that the two accused wilfully promoted such hatred. In other words, has the Crown established the necessary element of *mens rea*. In considering the meaning to be given to the word "wilfully" in this section the Court must distinguish between what has been described by learned writers as primary and secondary intent: or to phrase it in a more understanding way, the distinction between intent and motive. I have earlier discussed the purpose or motive as explained by the accused themselves. They wished to create a situation that would require the intervention of senior levels of Government and result in the construction of the high school. It is in evidence that the handbill was, in fact, shown to a mediator representing the Minister of Education who was in this area attempting to resolve the school issue. It is, of course, a matter of judicial notice that the Province did pass special legislation requiring the construction of the school. It is extremely doubtful, however, that this document played any part in the formulation of that decision. It was also their desire to unify the French Canadian community. As Father Vincent stated, opposition from outside often cements an ethnic group and tends to strengthen people rather than weaken them.
>
> This is what the Court would refer to as the purpose or motive of the accused.
>
> Wilful in this section, however, means intentional as opposed to accidental. Miss Susan Moylan who testified for the accused was involved in the early discussions between the accused in the preparation of the handbill. She testified that the document was not to create strong feelings but to create strong actions and strong reactions. How one can do the latter without the former is beyond the comprehension of this Court. The accused themselves testified they wished to create controversy, furor and an uproar. What better way of describing active dislike, detestation, enmity or ill will. The motives of the accused may or may not be laudable. The means chosen by the accused was the wilful promotion of hatred.

Mr. Manning contended before us that the learned trial Judge erred in his interpretation of the meaning of "wilfully". He said that the trial Judge, in concluding that the document, viewed objectively, promoted hatred, separated the word "wilfully" from the words "promotes hatred" and, consequently, fell into error in only considering the question whether the document was distributed intentionally as opposed to accidentally, when the offence charged was committed only if the appellants' purpose in distributing the document was to promote hatred. Mr. Manning said that the trial

Judge was concerned only with the effect of the document, whereas if he had "looked for" an intention to promote hatred, he would have come to a different conclusion with respect to the appellants' guilt. Mr. Hunt for the Crown did not dispute that the central issue in the case is whether the appellants, when they distributed the pamphlet, intended to promote hatred. He contended, however, that the trial Judge found that the appellants intended to promote hatred as a means of accomplishing their purpose.

Despite Mr. Manning's able argument I am not persuaded that the learned trial Judge fell into the error of detaching the word "wilfully" from the words "promotes hatred" and applied it only to the distribution of the pamphlet. I am of the view, however, that the learned trial Judge erred in holding that "wilfully" means only "intentional as opposed to accidental". Although, as previously indicated, "wilfully" has sometimes been used to mean that the accused's act, as distinct from its consequences, must be intended and not accidental (as in *R. v. Senior,* [1899] 1 Q.B. 283), it does not have that meaning in the provisions under consideration.

The learned trial Judge's view of the meaning of "wilfully" inevitably caused him to focus attention on the intentional nature of the appellants' conduct, rather than on the question whether they actually intended to produce the consequence of promoting hatred. I observe that even if, contrary to the view which I have expressed, recklessness satisfies the mental element denoted by the word "wilfully", recklessness when used to denote the mental element attitude which suffices for the ordinary *mens rea,* requires actual foresight on the part of the accused that his conduct may bring about the prohibited consequence, although I am not unmindful that for some purposes recklessness may denote only a marked departure from objective standards. Where the prosecution, in order to establish the accused's guilt of the offence charged, is required to prove that he intended to bring about a particular consequence or foresaw a particular consequence, the question to be determined is what was in the mind of this particular accused, and the necessary intent or foresight must be brought home to him subjectively: see *R. v. Mulligan* (1974), 18 C.C.C. (2d) 270 at pp. 274-5, 26 C.R.N.S. 179; affirmed 28 C.C.C. (2d) 266, [1977] 1 S.C.R. 612, 66 D.L.R. (3d) 627.

What the accused intended or foresaw must be determined on a consideration of all the circumstances, as well as from his own evidence, if he testifies, as to what his state of mind or intention was.

Since people are usually able to foresee the consequences of their acts, if a person does an act likely to produce certain consequences it is, in general, reasonable to assume that the accused also foresaw the probable consequences of his act and if he, nevertheless, acted so as to produce those consequences, that he intended them. The greater the likelihood of the relevant consequences ensuing from the accused's act, the easier it is to draw the inference that he intended those consequences. The purpose of this process, however, is to determine what the particular accused intended, not to fix him with the intention that a reasonable person might be assumed to have in the circumstances, where doubt exists as to the actual intention of the accused. The accused's testimony, if he gives evidence as to what was in his mind, is important material to be weighed with the other evidence in determining whether the necessary intent has been established. Indeed, Mr. Justice Devlin, in his charge to the jury in *R. v. Adams* (The Times, April 10, 1957), said that where the accused testified as to what was in his mind and the jury "thought he might be telling the truth", they would "have the best evidence available on what was in his own mind". The background of the appellants and their commitment to preserving the French Canadian culture was, of course, relevant to the credibility of their denial that they intended to promote hatred against the French-speaking community of Essex County. The appellants' evidence as to their state of mind or intention is not, of course, conclusive.

In some cases the inference from the circumstances that the necessary intent existed may be so strong as to compel the rejection of the accused's evidence that he did not intend to bring about the prohibited consequence. The learned trial Judge did not, however, state that he disbelieved the appellants' evidence that they did not intend to promote hatred. He appears to have treated the appellants' testimony that they wished to create "controversy, furor and an uproar" as a virtual admission that they had the state of mind requisite for guilt.

I am, with deference to the learned trial Judge, of the view that an intention to create "controversy, furor and an uproar" is not the same thing as an intention to promote hatred, and it was an error to equate them. I would, of course, agree that if the appellants intentionally promoted hatred against the French-speaking community of Essex County as a means of obtaining the French-language high school, they committed the offence charged. The appellants' evidence, if believed, does not, however, as the learned trial Judge appears to have thought, inevitably lead to that conclusion. The learned trial Judge, not having disbelieved the appellants' evidence, failed to give appropriate consideration to their evidence on the issue of intent and, in the circumstances, his failure so to do constituted self-misdirection.

In view of the conclusion which I have reached it is necessary to refer only briefly to the other grounds of appeal which we regard as requiring discussion.

The exemption under s.281.2(3)(d)

Mr. Rosenberg contended that there was an evidentiary base for the application of the exemption under s.281.2(3)(*d*) of the *Criminal Code* and that the learned trial Judge erred in holding that it was not available to the appellants.

The learned trial Judge said:

> Counsel have submitted, however, that the accused are entitled to the statutory exemption in para. (*d*). An accused cannot be found guilty "if, in good faith, he intended to point out, for the purpose of removal, matters producing or tending to produce feelings of hatred towards an identifiable group in Canada".
>
> If the accused had produced a document, for example, which pointed out, that in their view, these statements were being made in Essex County and that the public should be aware of it then clearly they would be within the exemption. The exemption also works for the protection of the media, who in the course of editorial comment would be required for the purpose of removal to repeat such statements. The Parliament, in enacting this section, included the words "in good faith". Were the accused acting in good faith when Mr. Buzzanga used the name of Mr. Fortowsky in placing the order with the printer? Were the accused acting in good faith when they instructed young Foley and Seguin to deceive their parents? Were the accused acting in good faith when their stated objective was to deceive elected Members of Parliament and Ministers of the Crown? Surely not.

Mr. Rosenberg submitted that the requirement in s.281.2(3)(*d*) of "good faith" means no more than the accused "honestly" or "genuinely" intended to point out for the purpose of removal, matters producing or tending to produce feelings of hatred towards an identifiable group. He argued that if the appellants otherwise came within it, the exemption was available to them, notwithstanding that they did not act in an open and "above-board" manner. I accept Mr. Rosenberg's submission that the appellants' devious conduct did not, as a matter of law, exclude them from the exemption under s.281.2(3)(*d*). I also accept that the exemption under s.281.2(3)(*d*) is not, as a matter of law, limited to cases where the communication on its face expressly states that the matters producing or tending to produce feelings of hatred are pointed out for the purpose of removing them. The appellants' devious conduct and the character of the pamphlet were, however, relevant items of evidence to be weighed in determining whether the appellants came within the exemption. If the appellants were properly found to have wilfully promoted hatred as alleged, I would not readily have interfered with a finding that they had not brought themselves within the exemption.

The exemption contained in s.281.2(3)(*d*) is, in my view, provided out of abundant caution, and where a person has ''wilfully'' promoted hatred, the cases in which the exemption may successfully be invoked must be comparatively rare.

The persons referred to in the pamphlet

Dr. Bernhard Harder, who has a doctorate in English literature and linguistics, testified on behalf of the defence. The substance of his testimony was that from the point of view of linguistics the ''subversive'' group or element referred to in the pamphlet is the French minority who support the building of the French-language high school and not the French Canadian community in Essex County.

Counsel for the appellants, on the basis of the evidence, argued that even if the pamphlet promoted hatred, it promoted hatred only against the French minority who supported the building of the high school and not the French Canadian public in Essex County as alleged in the indictment, and the charge, as laid, was not proved.

I have serious reservations as to the admissibility of this evidence: see *Phipson on Evidence,* 12th ed. (1976), pp. 504-5. In any event, I agree with the trial Judge that the meaning of the document is to be gathered from its entirety, and the construction that would be placed upon it by the average person into whose hands it fell. I would not give effect to this ground of appeal.

Conclusion

I have concluded that the self-misdirection with respect to the meaning of the word ''wilfully'', and the failure to appreciate the significance of the appellants' evidence on the issue of intent requires a new trial. The outrageous conduct of the appellants in preparing and distributing this deplorable document was evidence to be weighed in determining their intent, but in the peculiar circumstances of this case I am not satisfied that the inferences to be drawn from it are such as to inevitably lead to a conclusion that they had the requisite intent or that the trial Judge would inevitably have reached that conclusion but for his self-misdirection.

In the result, I would allow the appeal, set aside the convictions and order new trials.

Appeal allowed; new trial ordered.

Note: It seems to be generally recognized that this decision has effectively eviscerated s.281.2. See, for example, the comments in Patrick D. Lawlor, *Group Defamation, Submissions to the Ontario Attorney General 1984*. The House of Commons Special Committee on Participation of Visible Minorities in Canadian Society made the following recommendations in 1984:

35. Justice Canada should prepare amendments to section 281.2(2) of the Criminal Code so that it is no longer necessary to show that an accused specifically intended to promote hatred, in order to obtain a conviction.
36. Justice Canada should prepare amendments to s.281.2(6) of the Criminal Code so that the consent of the provincial Attorneys General is no longer required for a prosecution in cases of public incitement of hatred.
37. Justice Canada should prepare amendments to the Criminal Code so that it is clear that the burden of raising special defences is on the accused.

4.3.3 Law Reform Commission of Canada, *Hate Propaganda* (Ottawa, 1986), 1. Working Paper, 50, pp. 39-41

In the 1986 working paper *Hate Propaganda,* the Law Reform Commission made the following conclusion and recommendations:

There is no easy solution to the problem of spreading hatred. Even among civil libertarians who believe strongly in protecting freedom of speech, opinion is divided as to whether these crimes are necessary.

These proposals may not meet with overwhelming approval from the public. On the one hand, visible minorities may regard with dismay the decision to retain, for the revised offence of fomenting hatred, the *mens rea* requirement of intent or purpose and all the existing defences. On the other hand, civil libertarians may be disappointed that we did not advocate abolition of the offence of wilfully promoting hatred, and indeed may shudder at the proposal to expand the definition of "identifiable group" to protect those groups enumerated specifically in subsection 15(1) of the Charter. Both sides may argue that the Commission has failed to act boldly and imaginatively on an important social issue.

Nonetheless, the proposals made here are entirely consistent with our view that, while the criminal law should uphold fundamental values, it should nonetheless be applied with restraint.

Admittedly, the very existence of these crimes of fomenting hatred is open to two fundamental objections. First, they encroach upon freedom of expression in an unjustifiable manner. In other words, restricting freedom of expression for some restricts freedom of expression for all. Second, they may not do what they are expected to do. After all, the Weimar Republic had crimes of hate propaganda; yet Hitler still came to power.

The crimes proposed in this Paper, however, infringe upon freedom of expression in a justifiable manner by ensuring that only the most serious kinds of hatred are caught by the criminal law. Moreover, these crimes will do what they are expected to do, in two ways: first, by underlining the fundamental values of equality and dignity; second, by deterring others from engaging in such activity.

Admittedly, too, the restricted definition of these crimes is open to the fundamental objection that they do not propose adequate legal controls on the propagation of hatred.

The issue here, however, is to what extent the *criminal law* must be used to combat fomenting hatred against identifiable groups. Given its coercive and brutal nature, criminal law must be used with restraint. It should be used as the last resort, not the first. Of course, our society can use other means to deal with the spreading of hatred. The work of human rights commissions is all-important in helping to eliminate attitudes which support discrimination. Perhaps a more effective way to deal with fomenting hatred would be to ensure that these commissions play a stronger role in combatting such attitudes. But the role of the criminal law must be limited to preventing the most harmful hatreds being aimed at clearly socially important groups. Otherwise, in the name of fighting hatred, our society runs the risk of creating unjustifiable repression.

The crimes dealing with hate propaganda should be amended or altered in the following manner.

Recommendations

General

Groups

1. All these crimes should protect those groups identifiable on the basis of race, national or ethnic origin, colour, religion, sex, age or mental or physical disability.

Placement

2. The definition of "identifiable group" should be removed from the offence of advocating genocide and put into a separate definition section.

3. These crimes should be placed in our new Code in a chapter on Offences against Society.

Specific Offences

Genocide

4. (1) Whether there should be a crime of genocide in our new Code should not be resolved by this Paper, but should be deferred for future consideration.

(2) The crime of advocating or promoting genocide should be retained. However, the crime should be modified to catch "advocating, promoting, or urging" genocide. Also, any recommendation concerning the requirement of the Attorney General's consent should await the results of a forthcoming Commission Working Paper on the Powers of the Attorney General.

Publishing False News

5. Section 177, the crime of publishing false news, should be abolished. Any new offence designed to deal with causing public alarm should be defined in a precise enough manner to prevent its being used to prosecute hatemongers.

Crimes of Promoting or Inciting Hatred in Section 281.2

6. (1) Both crimes should be amended to catch clearly any means by which hatred is fomented.

(2) The crime of inciting hatred in a public place where such incitement is likely to lead to a breach of the peace should be redefined in the following manner:

> Any person who intentionally [purposely] and publicly foments hatred in a public place where it is likely to cause harm to a person or damage to property commits a crime. ["Public place" would continue to be defined as including any place to which the public have access as of right or by invitation, express or implied.]

(3) The crime of wilfully promoting hatred, other than in private conversation, against any identifiable group, should be redefined in the following manner:

(a) Any person who intentionally [purposely] and publicly foments hatred against any identifiable group commits a crime.

(b) No person shall be convicted if he or she

(i) uses the truth and proves such truth;

(ii) in good faith, expresses an opinion upon a religious subject;

(iii) uses anything which, on reasonable grounds, he or she believes to be true and which was relevant to any subject of public interest, the discussion of which was for the public benefit; or

(iv) in good faith, intended to point out, for the purpose of removal, matters producing or tending to produce feelings of hatred towards an identifiable group in Canada.

(c) Any recommendation concerning the requirement of the Attorney General's consent should await the results of a forthcoming Commission Working Paper on the Powers of the Attorney General.

Forfeiture Provisions

7. In accordance with a recommendation made in our Report on *Search and Seizure*, section 281.3, dealing with *in rem* proceedings for seizure and forfeiture of hate propaganda, should be taken out of the *Code* and put into federal regulatory legislation.

It is open to question whether subsections 281.2 [now s.320] (4) and (5), which govern the forfeiture of material after conviction for a hate propaganda offence, belong among these crimes or among provisions dealing with sentencing.

4.3.4 *R.* v. *Keegstra* (1988) 60 Alta. L.R. (2d) 1 (Alta. C.A.)

June 6, 1988. The judgment of the court was delivered by

KERANS J.A.: — This is an appeal from conviction after trial by judge and jury on the charge that:

The accused, JAMES KEEGSTRA, between the 1st day of September, A.D. 1978 and the 31st day of December, A.D. 1982, inclusive at or near the Town of Eckville in the Province of Alberta, did unlawfully promote hatred against an identifiable group, to wit: the Jewish people, by communicating statements while teaching to students at Eckville High School contrary to the provisions of the Criminal Code.

The relevant parts of s.281.2 provide:

(2) Every one who, by communicating statements, other than in private conversation, wilfully promotes hatred against any identifiable group is guilty...

(3) No person shall be convicted of an offence under subsection (2)

(*a*) if he establishes that the statements communicated were true;

(*b*) if, in good faith, he expressed or attempted to establish by argument an opinion upon a religious subject;

(*c*) if the statements were relevant to any subject of public interest, the discussion of which was for the public benefit, and if on reasonable grounds he believed them to be true; or

(*d*) if, in good faith, he intended to point out, for the purpose of removal, matters producing or tending to produce feelings of hatred towards an identifiable group in Canada.

(6) No proceeding for an offence under subsection (2) shall be instituted without the consent of the Attorney General.

(7) In this section

"communicating" includes communicating by telephone, broadcasting or other audible or visible means;

"identifiable group" has the same meaning as it has in section 281.1;

"public place" includes any place to which the public have access as of right or by invitation, express or implied;

"statements" includes words spoken or written or recorded electronically or electromagnetically or otherwise, and gestures, signs or other visible representations.

Long before his trial, Keegstra asked a judge of the Court of Queen's Bench of Alberta to quash the charge against him on the ground that s.281.2 is an unconstitutional interference with the freedom of speech of Canadians generally. That was rejected by Quigley J. for reasons now reported: see *R. v. Keegstra* (1984), 19 C.C.C. (3d) 254.

The attack was renewed before us on appeal.

Our first task, then, is to pronounce not upon the Crown's case against Keegstra but rather his case against Parliament. In my view, that case has been made. Parliament has created the crime of promotion of hatred against the members of the named groups. That law goes on to require a jury to *convict* an accused despite the fact that the jury thinks that what was said might be true. That law also requires a jury to convict even though they are convinced that not one person in all of Canada actually came to hate any member of any group as a result of what an accused said, or indeed that there was any likelihood of that. The law thus fails to respect adequately the constitutional right of all Canadians to be convicted only when the crime is *established* beyond a reasonable doubt. It also fails adequately to respect free speech. For these two reasons, it has no force and effect. Therefore, there is no point to my dealing with the facts of this case, or what happened at trial, and I will not do so.

What follows, then, is an analysis of the Charter rules to explain these conclusions. In sum, I say this:

1. Section 281.2(3)(*a*) provides that no person shall be convicted if what he said is true. But, it also provides that an accused must prove that what he said was probably true before he can successfully invoke the defence. This obligation of proof raises the possibility that he might be convicted by a jury who have a doubt on the point, a possibility inconsistent with s.11(*d*) of the Charter, which provides that every person accused of a crime must be presumed innocent.

2. Also, s.281.2 is inconsistent with the protection of freedom of expression in s.2 of the Charter because mistakes of fact by speakers — even by speakers who have no reasonable grounds for the mistake — are protected by the Charter.

3. Moreover, s.281.2 is not a "demonstrably justifiable" limit on free speech. Several justifications were offered, not all of which I accept. Section 281.2 fails, however, the last test under s.1. It is not demonstrably justifiable because its sweep is too broad. It does not require that anybody actually come to hate a member of a protected group as a result of the promotion of hatred by the offender. The only protection offered by the law from that is that we should place our trust in prosecutorial discretion, and this is an inappropriate and an inadequate protection of a Charter right.

4. When an accused shows that the law under which he was charged is inconsistent with the Charter, s.52 of the Charter provides that the law "is of no force and effect", a result denied only in circumstances not present here. Accordingly, the charge against

Keegstra must be quashed — even though it is possible that he could have been convicted by a jury under a valid law that does not contain the imperfections in s.281.2.

I

I will first deal with the reverse onus issue. Section 281.2(3)(*a*) provides that an accused cannot be convicted "if he establishes that the statements communicated were true".

The Supreme Court of Canada has said that "establishes", in the context of the Criminal Code, means "proves on the balance of probabilities": see *R. v. Appleby,* [1972] S.C.R. 303, [1971] 4 W.W.R. 601, 16 C.R.N.S. 35, 3 C.C.C. (2d) 354, 21 D.L.R. (3d) 325 [B.C.]; *R. v. Shelley,* [1981] 2 S.C.R. 196, [1981] 5 W.W.R. 481, 21 C.R. (3d) 354, 26 C.R. (3d) 150, 59 C.C.C. (2d) 292, 123 D.L.R. (3d) 748, 3 C.E.R. 217, 9 Sask. R. 338, 37 N.R. 320.

The issue is whether this provision, so interpreted, offends s. 11(*d*) of the Charter, which provides:

> 11. Any person charged with an offence has the right...
> (*d*) to be presumed innocent until proven guilty according to law in a fair and public hearing by an independent and impartial tribunal.
> 11. Tout inculpé a le droit...
> (*d*) d'être présumé innocent tant qu'il n'est pas déclaré coupable, conformément à la loi, par un tribunal indépendant et impartial à l'issue d'un procès public et équitable.

The Supreme Court of Canada, in *R. v. Oakes,* [1986] 1 S.C.R. 103, 50 C.R. (3d) 1, 24 C.C.C. (3d) 321, 26 D.L.R. (4th) 200, 19 C.R.R. 308, 14 O.A.C. 335, 65 N.R. 87, decided that s.11(*d*) is breached if a law requires an accused to disprove "the existence of a presumed fact which is an important element in the offence" (p. 25). See also *R. v. Driscoll,* 54 Alta. L.R. (2d) 251, [1987] 6 W.W.R. 748, 60 C.R. (3d) 88, 38 C.C.C. (3d) 28, 79 A.R. 298 (C.A.), and *R. v. Singh,* Alta. C.A., Calgary Appeal No. 18108, 1st December 1987 [now reported 56 Alta. L.R. (2d) 177, 61 C.R. (3d) 353, 83 A.R. 69].

At first sight, the conclusion of a Charter breach seems inescapable. The Crown, however, argues that the rule in *Oakes* has no application in this case because s.281.2(3)(*a*) raises a *defence* in distinction to an *element of the offence:* see, for example, *R. v. Holmes* (1983), 41 O.R. (2d) 250, 32 C.R. (3d) 322, 4 C.C.C. (3d) 400, 145 D.L.R. (3d) 689, 4 C.R.R. 222 (C.A.) (affirmed by the Supreme Court of Canada, [1988] F.C.J. No. 39, published 26th May 1988, upholding the result but on different grounds). It is *Holmes* in the Ontario Court of Appeal upon which the Crown relied. That case dealt with the offence of possession of tools suitable for housebreaking. The opening words of the charging section, s.309(1), C.C.C., are "Every one who, without lawful excuse, the proof of which lies upon him, has in his possession..." The accused's argument that this reverse onus displaced the presumption of innocence was rejected. Lacourcière J.A., for a unanimous court, held (at pp. 330-31 C.R.) that these words do not

> ... raise any presumption or create any reverse onus in the true sense. The Crown must establish the... essential ingredients by proof beyond a reasonable doubt. Only then can the evidentiary *onus* be shifted to the accused... [emphasis added]

In my view, the law offers a defence, any defence, as an answer to a charge because the lawmaker judges that the condemnation of the accused would not be just in the face of its existence. Section 11(*d*) adds that it would not be just for an accused to be condemned if a doubt exists as to its existence. The problem with a defence that must be proven on the balance of probabilities is, of course, that it is possible that an accused might not quite meet it. As a result, a jury would be bound to convict even if the accused did succeed in leaving them in doubt about the defence. Telling the accused he must persuade the jury on the balance of probabilities is also telling the jury to ignore its doubts about a relevant issue. If s.11(*d*) does not forbid that, it has no meaning. See Mahoney, "The Presumption of Innocence: A New Era" (1988), 67 Can. Bar Rev. 1, which makes the same point after an extensive review of the cases. I reject the distinction made in *Holmes*.

The analysis in that case, following an approach traditional to the criminal law, distinguishes between elements of the offence essential to guilt and "defences". The classification of matters in this way can be of great assistance, because a "defence", unlike other elements of an offence, does not necessarily arise in every case. As a result, it is simpler, in a textbook or a jury charge or in the Criminal Code, to discuss and describe common defences separately from the definition of specific crimes. But I cannot comprehend why a practical tool becomes a Charter exception. The plain fact is that a "defence" in this sense remains the absence of the proof of guilt, and when relevant must be negatived beyond a reasonable doubt. *Holmes* does not dispute this.

The difficulty is that defences are *sometimes* called defences precisely *because* the law has placed an onus on the accused. See, for example, Glanville Williams, in Criminal Law: The General Part, 2nd ed. (1961), pp. 909-10: "In strictness", he says, "the word 'defence' should mean something in respect of which the persuasive or at least the evidential burden rests on the accused". To emphasize this difference, and avoid confusion, the Evidence Project, "Evidence: Burdens of Proof and Presumptions" (Law Reform Commission of Canada), suggested changing the label for this category from "defence" to "affirmative defence".

If the injunction in s.11(*d*) against a reverse onus does not apply to "defences", and a "defence" is to be defined as the creation of a reverse onus, what remains of the constitutional protection? Parliament can step around this most fundamental protection by eliminating an element from the express definition of any crime and stating its converse as a defence open to the accused if he can prove it. Murder, then, would become any killing, but the defence of no intention would be available to the accused if he can prove it. Section 8 of the Charter might give the accused the right to insist on some sort of standards for elements essential to a crime. But, by itself, s.11(*d*) does not give the accused a Charter right to complain when an expected element in an offence has suddenly gone missing. In my view, a reverse onus defence *must* be caught by it if it is to retain efficacy.

Long after supplementary argument in this case, and after the preparation of these reasons, the decision of the Supreme Court of Canada in *Holmes* was published. The ratio decidendi of the majority of the court was that the quoted words in s.309(1), C.C.C., which appeared to the Ontario Court of Appeal to have created a reverse onus, have become "superfluous" as a result of a curiously worded 1972 amendment to the section. All five judges on the court in *Holmes* agreed that this amendment added, as an additional element of the offence to be proven beyond a reasonable doubt by the Crown, that the accused must intend to use the tools for housebreaking, or have already used them for that purpose. As a result, as La Forest J. observed in his brief concurring reasons: "So interpreted, the section does not conflict with s.11(*d*) of the Charter."

Both Dickson C.J.C. (Lamer J. concurring) and McIntyre J. (Le Dain J. concurring) did make reference to the s.11(*d*) issue now before us. McIntyre J. said:

> Where, then, as in the case at bar, proof of guilt beyond a reasonable doubt is required without the benefit of any presumption before any need for a defence arises, s.11(*d*) of the Charter has not been offended. There has been no denial of the presumption of innocence. It has been overcome by proof according to law or by admissions of the accused, and the defence or excuse which is sought to be raised depends upon that fact. If he is convicted in the face of such a defence, it is not because he has been presumed guilty or because the commission of the crime has not been shown, but because his excuse was rejected after proof of the commission of the offence. An accused raising such a defence or excuse is not seeking relief because of an absence of guilt. He seeks relief despite his commission of the offence.

The Chief Justice responded:

> To limit s.11(*d*) to determinations whether an element is integral or extraneous to an offence, however, would lose sight of the fact that because of the grave social and personal consequences engendered by a finding of criminal liability, the law requires proof thereof beyond a reasonable doubt. Any burden on an accused which has the effect of dictating a conviction despite the presence of reasonable doubt, whether that burden relates to proof of an essential element of the offence or some element extraneous to the offence but nonetheless essential to verdict, contravenes s.11(*d*) of the Charter. An accused must not be placed in the position of being required to do more than raise a reasonable doubt as to his or her guilt, regardless of whether that doubt arises from uncertainty as to the sufficiency of Crown evidence supporting the constituent elements of the offence or from uncertainty as to criminal culpability in general.

These comments unfortunately do not spare us the obligation to decide whether a reverse onus defence offends s.11(*d*). As stated, I prefer the view that Parliament should not be permitted so easily to snip the golden thread.

I emphasize that it is not the proposing of a presumption that is unconstitutional, it is the refusal to give effect to doubt about it. A statutory presumption is only bad if it instructs a jury to draw an inference in the face of a doubt about its reasonableness. Thus, the Charter does not prevent the Crown from relying upon an inference, nor does it prevent Parliament from suggesting a tentative inference, which is the effect of imposing an evidentiary burden on the accused (as opposed to a burden of persuasion). Section 11(*d*) does not prevent a jury saying to itself: if that's all there is, we can only infer guilt. Such a reaction, or fear of it, effectively challenges an accused to do something because, unless he offers them something to justify a doubt, the jury will infer guilt. This does not impose any new or improper burden on the accused except the "burden" he has in every trial of guiding the trier of fact to see some reasonable grounds to have a doubt as to his guilt. The Crown, in turn, remains unable to call for a conviction if it has not removed any doubts in the minds of the jurors.

We accordingly turn to s.1. Is the possibility that an accused might be convicted under s.281.2 in the face of a doubt about the truth of his remarks a demonstrably justifiable limit on his right to be presumed innocent? The answer is that the impugned section does not pass the challenge to offer a valid competing claim. The admitted purpose of the reverse onus is to avoid the necessity for the Crown to prove a negative. This justifies a shift in evidentiary burden but not the burden of proof. I adopt the words of the Law Reform Commission, Evidence Project, p. 62:

> We think that any purpose achieved by casting on the accused a burden of persuasion can be equally accomplished by casting upon him a burden of producing evidence... Reverse

onus clauses are created for reasons of social policy — the need for strict law enforcement, fairness — the accused has greater access to the evidence, or probability — the non-existence of the element of the crime is so improbable that it would be a waste of time to require the Crown to disprove it in every case. All of these purposes can be accomplished by the creation of a presumption that shifts only the burden of producing evidence.

The model for this reverse onus is the civil law on defamation, as Mr. Fraser says. In the civil law, the *maxim ei incumbit probatio, qui dicit, non qui negat*, of which this is but an example, governs the law generally on the burden of persuasion. That is precisely the difficulty. Over the past 200 years, the criminal rule has diverged from the general rule. Because we recognize the huge difference in the resources and influence of the two adversaries in a criminal case, and because of the consequences of a conviction, the golden thread of the criminal law is that the Crown always has the burden, and a heavy one. The office of s.11(*d*) is to guarantee that tradition. To resort now to the rationale for the civil law is to forget that divergence, and the reasons for it: see D. Finley, "The Presumption of Innocence and Guilt: Why *Carroll* Should Prevail Over *Oakes*" (1984), 39 C.R. (3d) 115; A.W. MacKay and T.A. Cromwell, "*Oakes:* A Bold Initiative Impeded by Old Ghosts" (1983), 32 C.R. (3d) 221; T.A. Cromwell and A.W. MacKay, "*Oakes* in the Supreme Court: A Cautious Initiative Unimpeded by Old Ghosts" (1986), 50 C.R. (3d) 34; and J.C. Levy, "Reverse Onus Clauses in Canadian Criminal Law — An Overview" (1970), 35 Sask. L. Rev. 40.

Only one real possibility for an exception, it seems to me, can rationally exist: where the inference commanded by the statutory presumption is so persuasive that only a perverse jury would have a doubt. This might be so in the case of the presumption of sanity, but I do not need to explore that issue in this case. What about this case? Is the idea that some *truthful* remark might lead to hatred of somebody on account of his race, creed, colour or ethnic origin so preposterous as to be beyond concern? Mr. Fraser argues that "it is rational to conclude that there is no reason to hate people only on the basis of race, religion, colour or ethnic origin". He must go further. He must assert that no jury could rationally have a doubt on the point — in any case — in the absence of some additional evidence. The difficulty with "never", as always, is that it admits of no exceptions. When Winston Churchill said, in 1940, that the long, dark night of barbarism had descended over Europe, it is fair to say that his words both promoted hatred of members of a target group defined by s.281.2, and yet were true. I would like to think that the occasions where this might be said are rare, but we cannot deny that they exist.

Quigley J., on the preliminary motion, said that the Charter effectively provides in s.15 that no person should suffer in Canada on account of membership in the named groups. Can it be said as a result that the lack of any truthful basis for hatred of those groups is thereby asserted as utterly impossible, and thus a "constitutional truth"? Robert Bork, for example, has opposed toleration of even ineffectual talk about violent overthrow of democratic institutions because, he wrote, "It is not political speech because it violates constitutional truths": see Bork, "Neutral Principles and Some First Amendment Problems" (1971), 47 Ind. L.J. 1 at p. 31. The idea of a "constitutional truth", something to be taken as a fundamental truth in our society and not to be gainsaid by anybody, runs, however, squarely into the idea that tolerance of dissent is part of a free and democratic society. The Canadian Charter, unlike the European Convention on Human Rights (1950), 213 U.N.T.S. 222, in art. 17, does not contain an express term refusing to protect any "act aimed at the destruction of any of the rights and freedoms set forth herein ..." I think that Canadians are free, by the Charter, to hate and despise the Charter. In any event, even if constitutional truth is an exception to the rule of tolerance, I do not accept that the Charter declares unconditionally that discrimination on the named grounds is *never* valid, because that would deny the office of s.1.

No valid s.1 consideration justifies this breach of s.11(*d*).

II

I now turn to the attack based upon s.2(*b*) of the Canadian Charter of Rights and Freedoms, which provides:

> 2. Everyone has the following fundamental freedoms...
>
> (*b*) freedom of thought, belief, opinion and expression, including freedom of the press and other media of communication.
>
> 2. Chacun a les libertés fondamentales suivantes...
>
> (*b*) liberté de pensée, de croyance, d'opinion et d'expression, y compris la liberté de la presse et des autres moyens de communication.

Quigley J. held that the freedom of expression protected by these words did not include wilful promotion of hatred of groups identifiable in terms of colour, race, religion or ethnic origin. In any event, he said, the law was a demonstrably justifiable limit of the protected freedom. With respect, I do not agree with either conclusion. In my view, imprudent promotion of hatred falls within the definition of freedom of expression. Moreover, this legislation fails the proportionality test in s.1 of the Charter.

The learned chambers judge offered two reasons for his view. The first was that this sort of speech offended the principle, which he found enshrined in the Charter, that Canadians are all to be treated with equal dignity and respect. More precisely, members of the "target" groups defined in s.281.2 were named for special protection in both s.15 and s.27 of the Charter. His second reason was that legislation of this sort enhanced rather than limited free speech because hatemongering intimidates the victims, and this law "tends to banish the apprehension which might otherwise inhibit certain segments of our society from freely expressing themselves" (p. 268).

This court, since the decision under appeal, has said that the curtailment of a Charter right in order to give effect to a competing claim, including another Charter right, is best considered as part of the office of s.1 of the Charter, because that provision offers mechanics for the balancing that is inevitable when two valid claims are in conflict: see *Edmonton Journal v. Alta. (A.G.),* 53 Alta. L.R. (2d) 193, [1987] 5 W.W.R. 385, 41 D.L.R. (4th) 502, 78 A.R. 375 (C.A.) (leave to appeal to the Supreme Court of Canada granted [56 Alta. L.R. (2d) lviii, [1988] 2 W.W.R. lxvi, 83 A.R. 160]). This is not to say that there are no internal limits to the protection offered by s.2(*b*). Those limits must, however, spring from the nature and purpose of the right itself, and not from competing claims: see *Grier v. Alta. Optometric Assn.*, 53 Alta. L.R. (2d) 289, [1987] 5 W.W.R. 539 at 543-44, 42 D.L.R. (4th) 327, 79 A.R. 36 (C.A.). Insofar as the chambers judge's concern about harmful speech raises ideas about the need to balance free speech against other claims, such as the right of others to protection from harm, that is a s.1 consideration. The same should be said of his argument that laws against hatemongering produce a more fruitful climate for free speech. I therefore will return to these topics under that heading.

There is, nevertheless, an argument that the constitutional guarantee of free expression does not, having regard to nature and purpose of that right properly understood, extend to all speech. For example, one can say that calculated falsehood is not protected. This was accepted by the Ontario Court of Appeal in *R. v. Zundel* (1987), 58 O.R. (2d) 129, 56 C.R. (3d) 1, 31 C.C.C. (3d) 97, 35 D.L.R. (4th) 338, 29 C.R.R. 349, 18 O.A.C. 161 (C.A.), leave to appeal, S.C.C., denied 4th June 1987 [61 O.R. (2d) 588n, 56 C.R. (3d) xxviii, 23 O.A.C. 317]. That court rejected the suggestion that s.177 of the Criminal Code offends s.2(*b*) of the Charter. Unlike s.281.2, s.177 provides that it is a crime to knowingly spread false news. The court held that nothing about the idea of free speech justifies the protection of lies. This court in *Grier* reviewed several ideas underlying and justifying our tradition of free speech but none readily justify any protection for lies.

Lies, however, involve both untruth and knowledge of that by the speaker. Does s.2 also apply if just one or the other of these factors is present? The Crown argument invites consideration of a third factor: harm to others. I reject consideration of it at this stage. It raises competing claims, and is a s.1 issue. The Crown's remaining argument is that, even without harm, some untrue speech, though not a conscious lie, is not protected.

Mr. Fraser accepted that some false speech is protected (without the presence also of knowledge or harm) at least in the realm of public debate and exchange of political ideas. Indeed, it would be a hollow right if, to assert it, we first had to demonstrate that what we had to say was correct. The toleration of at least some error is part of our tradition and has been justified on both practical and philosophical grounds.

Of course, as he concedes, if some error is protected, all truth is protected. To avoid Charter offence, the crime cannot be committed by statements that promote hatred but that happen to be true. This concession causes some difficulty for the Crown in this case because s.281.2 does not expressly make untruth an element of the crime. Truth is, however, a defence by virtue of s.281.2(3)(*a*). Mr. Fraser argued that some hatemongering is neither true nor false but instead can be mere gestures or signs or "...derogatory remarks or name calling that is not capable of a determination of truth or falsity..." If the remark happens to be factually true, he argues, that affords a defence to the charge: nobody can be convicted for telling the truth but the untruth of the hateful remarks is not an element. We do not, for the purpose of this case, need to agree or disagree with his suggestion that some hatemongering does not in some way purport to tell a truthful thing about the victim. I accept that the section does not make it a crime to tell the truth, and thus does not offend s.2(*b*) in that way. The remaining issue has to do with the onus of proof, and that I have dealt with.

The argument of Mr. Fraser is that a combination of untruth and "objective awareness" falls outside protection of s.2 just like actual lies. Certainly, between the calculated falsehood on the one hand and innocent error on the other lies the middle ground of what one might call imprudent speech. By this I mean that the speaker is innocent of knowledge of the falsehood but is blameworthy in that he has not taken reasonable steps to discover if what he says is true or not. This seems to be the standard required by the law under review. Section 281.2(3)(*c*) provides that no person shall be convicted

> if the statements were relevant to any subject of public interest, the discussion of which was for the public benefit, and if *on reasonable grounds* he believed them to be true...

The question, then, is whether imprudent speech is protected by the Charter. On invocation of the "marketplace of ideas" justification for protected expression, one of the purposes reviewed in *Grier,* it is not just correct and careful comment that is protected. Mill said this of imprudent expression:

> ... all this, even to the most aggravated degree, is so continually done in perfect good faith, by persons who are not considered, and in many other respects may not deserve to be considered, ignorant or incompetent, that it is rarely possible, on adequate grounds, conscientiously to stamp the misrepresentation as morally culpable; and still less could law presume to interfere with this kind of controversial misconduct.
>
> [J.S. Mill, On Liberty, ed. C.V. Shields
> (New York: Bobbs-Merrill, 1956), p. 65.]

It is possible, of course, to exchange ideas prudently. Nevertheless, if too many obstacles are placed in the way of the exchange of ideas, obstacles that too little heed human weakness, prudent people will never say a word. Like Lord Porter in the Report of the Committee on the Law of Defamation (London, 1948), "I... cannot fail to be impressed by the danger of curtailing free and frank — albeit, hot and hasty — political discussion and criticism." In order to encourage people to speak up, an effort essential for the safe working of a democracy, it is necessary to offer some protection to at least the more ordinary forms of human weakness.

In sum, s.2(*b*) should be understood as protecting both innocent error and imprudent speech. Section 281.2 makes a crime of imprudent speech. In the result, I accept the contention of the accused that s.2(*b*) is engaged. The section limits the free expression guaranteed to Canadians by the Charter, and we must turn to consideration whether it is a demonstrably justifiable limit.

III

I shall use the method of analysis described in *Edmonton Journal v. Alta. (A.G.),* supra, at p. 201, and consider this law from four aspects.

(1) *Rationality:* Does s.281.2 have a rational relationship to a valid legislative object?

I acknowledge the assistance of counsel in supplying a very complete record of the legislative history of s.281.2, of the state of the law in other countries, and of Canada's international commitments. Mr. McKillop did argue that foreign law must be proven by expert testimony. With respect, that rule applies only when the court seeks to discover foreign law in order to apply it. In the Charter context, these materials are most often offered for the analysis of principles contained in the judgments, and not for a statement of foreign law. In this respect, they have the same status before us as academic opinion. Sometimes, they are offered as an indication of what other societies are doing, in support of an argument about what is appropriate for a free and democratic society. As such, they are always secondary materials and need not be subject to the evidentiary rule relied upon. This does not, of course, prevent the calling of expert evidence if thought appropriate.

The genesis of this law is clear; it springs from the recommendations of a Special Committee named by the Minister of Justice in January 1965 to assess "the dissemination of varieties of 'hate propaganda' in Canada": Report of the Special Committee on Hate Propaganda in Canada, 1965 (Ottawa: Queen's Printer, 1966), p. 1. (Later, two members of the committee also wrote in defence of its conclusions. See: Maxwell Cohen, "The Hate Propaganda Amendments: Reflections on a Controversy" (1970), 9 Alta. L. Rev. 103; and Mark MacGuigan, "Proposed Anti-hate Legislation: Bill S-5 and The Cohen Report", 15 Chitty's L.J., November 1967, 302). Its report suggested legislation very much like s.281.2, which was then introduced before Parliament in 1970.

The report identified four claims to justify a law: (a) the risk of civil disorder when victims react with anger; (b) the risk of a breakdown of traditional values if the hatred spreads; (c) the risk of the damage to the reputation of the victims; and (d) the risk of psychological stress suffered by victims. Unlike the analysis for most s.1 claims, where the social value of the competing claims is accepted, all four claims here stimulate controversy in terms of democratic theory and practice, and must be carefully weighed.

In my view, items (c) and (d), the protection of reputation and bodily harm, raise obviously valid competing claims. I must pass on to the next s.1 tests for them. This conclusion also is a complete answer to the alternative argument of the accused, which is that s.281.2 contradicts the Canadian Bill of Rights: see *R. v. Rocher,* [1984] N.W.T.R. 288, 16 C.C.C. (3d) 89, 14 D.L.R. (4th) 210, [1985] C.N.L.R. 151, 55 A.R. 387 (N.W.T.C.A.).

In the name of clarity, however, I must observe that some claims made by the committee, the Crown, and Quigley J. do not meet this branch of the test. Before proceeding to the next step, then, I will first deal with them.

The Cohen Committee underlined the impact of hatemongering on the members of the target group: a member can react by fighting back, by denying membership, or by ignoring the insult. The first threatens public order because of the temptation to fight back in kind: see pp. 30-31. This claim has been called the heckler's veto: if you say that, I will be furious and very likely will burn down the town; therefore, you should not say it. The traditional answer of the defenders of the marketplace approach to free speech is that this argument is not a competing claim to the claims of free speech but rather a contradiction of them. I agree. The marketplace theory assumes a relatively stable society of responsible truth searchers. This claim, like the claim for seditious libel, assumes the opposite, and is the antithesis of the marketplace approach: see *Black v. Law Soc. of Alta.,* 44 Alta. L.R. (2d) 1, [1986] 3 W.W.R. 590, 20 Admin. L.R. 140, 27 D.L.R. (4th) 527, 20 C.R.R. 117, 68 A.R. 259 (C.A.). See also: Notes, "Group Libel Laws: Abortive Efforts to Combat Hate Propaganda", infra, at p. 258. A valid s.1 claim cannot be merely a denial of the protected right: see *A.G. Que. v. Que. Assn. of Protestant Sch. Bd.,* [1984] 2 S.C.R. 66, 10 D.L.R. (4th) 321, 9 C.R.R. 133, 54 N.R. 196.

The only exception may be when the threat of widespread civil disorder is so imminent and real the very existence of our society is at threat. This is the "clear and present danger" rule.

After a review of the evidence of the existence of hate propaganda in Canada to 1964, the report said (pp. 27-28):

> The committee has received sufficient evidence to indicate that there exists in Canada a *comparatively small number* of individuals whose attitude to others is irrational and antisocial, and who direct their hostility at specific (usually minority) groups. [emphasis added]

A very recent study places verified current membership in racist organizations in Canada at 586 persons, mostly in Ontario. See Barrett, Is God a Racist? The Right Wing in Canada (University of Toronto Press, Toronto, 1987), pp. 30-40. The committee and Professor Barrett argue that this evidence is only the tip of the iceberg in terms of the extent of racist sentiment in Canada.

I do not deny the existence of race hatred in Canada today.

The Cohen Report, however, concedes that a general breakdown of law and order attributable to hatemongering is anything but imminent. Parliament cannot therefore invoke this exception.

Another concern of the committee was the breakdown of traditional values from "spread of the poison". Again, the marketplace approach assumes that a well-informed people need not be protected from making the wrong choice. Again, perhaps an exception can be made in a "time of stress" but, again, no crisis was asserted by the Cohen Report or by the Crown before us. Quite the contrary. The committee only argued that, despite the size and characteristics of the small group just described, the psychological process involved in the creation of prejudice is such that in some degree "many normally sensible and decent people are susceptible to it" (p. 27). Therefore, the *risk* of the hatred spreading exists. After a reference to recent history in western Europe, the report warned that the spread of hatred *could,* in a time of stress, "...mushroom into a real and monstrous threat to our way of life" (p. 24). In my view, before this concern can pass to the sufficiency test, the danger asserted must be more than the possibility of a possibility.

Additionally, Mr. Fraser for the Crown invokes Canada's international obligations. Canada has ratified the International Convention on the Elimination of All Forms of Racial Discrimination (1963), Yearbook of the United Nations 330, 3 I.L.M. 164, 58 A.J.I.L. 1081, 660 U.N.T.S. 195. Article 4(a) of that provides that the signatories "Shall declare an offence punishable by law *all* dissemination of ideas based on racial superiority or hatred..." (emphasis added). Mr. McKillop for the accused correctly argued that the signatories are required to balance that commitment against the need to protect free speech, an issue that has been the subject of discussion, and disagreement, at subsequent international meetings. It may be that an international commitment in contradiction of a Charter term can be validated under s.1, but we do not need to address that difficult issue in this case because this law goes beyond the condemnation of ideas based on *racial* hatred.

Additionally, Quigley J. made reference to s.15 and s.27 of the Charter, and made this point (p.268):

> In my view, the wilful promotion of hatred under circumstances which fall within s.281.2(2) of the *Criminal Code* of Canada clearly contradicts the principles which recognize the dignity and worth of the members of identifiable groups, singly and collectively; it contradicts the recognition of moral and spiritual values which impels us to assert and protect the dignity of each member of society; and it negates or limits the rights and freedoms of such target groups, and in particular denies them the right to the equal protection and benefit of the law without discrimination.

I agree with him that the promotion of hatred against the target groups can do violence to their Charter rights, and can cause them real injury. As I have already said, I cannot agree that the existence of s.15 and s.27 forbids Canadians from disagreeing with the ideas contained in those sections. I say again therefore that to forbid the expression of an idea merely because the idea is bad is a contradiction of s.2, and not a valid object for the purposes of s.1.

His statement also hints at yet another competing claim, the prevention of non-governmental discrimination in violation of s.15 and s.27. The Supreme Court of Canada, in *R.W.D.S.U. v. Dolphin Delivery Ltd.*, [1986] 2 S.C.R. 573, [1987] 1 W.W.R. 577, 9 B.C.L.R. (2d) 273, 38 C.C.L.T. 184, 33 D.L.R. (4th) 174, 87 C.L.L.C. 14,002, 25 C.R.R. 321, 71 N.R. 83, has since held, however, that private citizens are not bound by the Charter in the way that governments are. This is not quite, then, a case of the resolution of a conflict between two Charter-based claims.

(2) *Sufficiency:* Is the social need for s.281.2 sufficient to displace a protected right? To answer that question, we must first assess the importance of the valid claims (damage to reputation and physical harm) this statute seeks to serve.

Damage to reputation warrants some form of interference with free speech. The present law of defamation in most provinces prevents suit unless the claimant can show that he personally was in the likely contemplation of a reasonable reader or listener: see *Dowding v. Ockerby,* [1962] W.A.R. 110 (W. Aus. S.C.). This offers no remedy against generalized hatemongering. Nevertheless, the damage to reputation from that sort of thing is just as real as from actionable defamation: see Stephen Cohen, "Hate Propaganda — The Amendments to the Criminal Code" (1971), 17 McGill L.J. 740; and E.T. Marcus, "Group Defamation and Individual Actions: a New Look at an Old Rule" (1983), 71 Cal. L.R. 1532.

The Cohen Report also stresses the personal non-bodily injury that comes from verbal assault. This is not the same injury as damage to reputation, it is more like the injury from a broken leg. It is pain and suffering itself. Neither party before us sought to persuade us that the reality of this pain does not exist. Mr. Christie, on the contrary, protested not just once during oral argument that the accused in this case suffers great anguish because, on account of this charge, he faces public condemnation and vilification simply for his opinions. The accused no doubt therefore would readily acknowledge the reality and importance of the pain if its source was nothing other than, say, abuse based upon the colour of his skin. Every member of a target group can, like Shylock, say of his abuser,

> He hath disgraced me and hindered me half a million; laughed at my losses, mocked at my gains, scorned my nation, thwarted my bargains, cooled my friends, heated mine enemies. And what's his reason? I am a Jew. Hath not a Jew eyes? Hath not a Jew hands, organs, dimensions, senses, affections, passions, fed with the same food, hurt with the same weapons, subject to the same diseases, healed by the same means, warmed and cooled by the same winter and summer as a Christian is? If you prick us, do we not bleed? If you tickle us, do we not laugh? If you poison us, do we not die? [Merchant of Venice, Act 3, scene 1]

I accept the reality of the pain suffered by the vilified, and that it can do serious injury. It may even be that this sort of injury is one idea underlying s.15 and s.27 of the Charter, as Quigley J. claimed. The making of unjust or capricious distinctions is an attack on the dignity of the victim, and can result in a debilitating sense of alienation from society.

Nevertheless, a distinction can be made between the pain suffered by the target of isolated abuse and the crushing effect of the systemic discrimination of which Shakespeare's Shylock accuses the larger society of his time. Nobody enjoys being the target of name-calling, but the sense of outrage and frustration may be bearable if that abuse is rejected by the community as a whole. Then, the pain can be just a psychological pinprick. It becomes unbearable when it indeed cools one's friends and heats one's enemies. The degree of possible injury, then, falls across a broad spectrum. At the one end lies the response of annoyance or frustration, at the other the sense of total alienation, of being a social outcast or a "second-class citizen". This distinction is the source of great difficulty in terms of a sufficient justification for limits on free speech. I read the Cohen Report as recognizing this distinction, and seeking to justify limits only on the more extreme forms of hatemongering. The difficulty is to draw a line.

I think that it can be drawn clearly at one point: does anybody actually hate me as a result of this abuse? If the hatemonger begins to gain an audience, if a significant number of people actually accept his message or if that is a serious risk, then I begin to suffer significant harm because my reputational integrity is at stake. Professor D.A. Richards in Toleration and the Constitution (Oxford Press, 1986) (p. 197) describes the injury:

> Persons, who can robustly endure deprivation of such general goods as wealth or even health, experience a suicidal despair in the degradation of self worked by an unjust social contempt for their reputational integrity. For them, such an insult may mean the death of what is most intimately personal, most meaningful in their ambitions for their lives.

What significant harm does it do me, on the other hand, if my abuser is in turn ridiculed and perhaps ostracized by all my fellow citizens? Their rejection affirms my dignity and confirms to me that I am deserving of equal respect. I conclude that it is only when my abuser gains an audience that I am at serious risk. The argument of the learned chambers judge about a good climate for debate must be viewed in the light of this distinction. That climate is not clouded by ineffectual abuse.

Indeed, some argue that all that is required in response to hatemongering is condemnation by non-legal sanctions, like criticism and ostracism: see the discussion by Professor L.C. Bollinger in The Tolerant Society (Oxford: Clarendon Press, 1986). I share his view that it is paradoxical that some defenders of free speech insist that its abusers should be condemned by non-legal means, which can be grossly unfair, and not by legal means, which while they bite hard should also bite fairly. In any event, at the very least it must be said that, sometimes, the hatemonger will gain a following sufficiently large that formal and legal condemnation is appropriate.

It is now clear that the competing claim is based on the concern that somebody will believe what is said, and come to hate members of the target groups. Is this concern antithetical to the basic assumption of democracy, just asserted, that the people will make the right choice if all sides are heard in open debate? I think not. The idea of democracy might well require a belief that the majority will never succumb; it certainly does not require the foolish hope that nobody in our society will hate — even after open debate. In this sense, laws against group defamation are no more undemocratic than laws against individual defamation.

In my view, the need to protect the target groups specifically mentioned in s.281.2 from serious non-physical injury or reputational injury is a sufficient reason to limit imprudent speech. In other words, I accept that, sometimes, the harm is great enough to justify limits on the abuse. If I am right, the real issue is to gauge the proportionality of the intrusion, not to inveigh against all intrusions.

Even this cautious approval is, I appreciate, controversial. Counsel for the accused has marshalled a formidable and respectable army of opposition to this view. Those who dispute with me do not dispute the harm that comes from hatemongering. They argue rather that the cure may be worse than the ill. They suggest that the suffering of the target groups must be endured for democracy's sake; they worry that group libel laws trench upon the forbidden territory of private conscience; they say also that it is a small step from this sort of law to a major incursion; a few say that laws that require the pursuit of the truth are futile. Some of these arguments I challenge, most I would simply deflect by saying that they are really arguments about proportionality. I will deal with them in turn.

(a) The concern about a bad precedent: it is often said, in argument against restrictions on errant speech, that they might be the first step down the slippery path to the destruction of a free society. For example, the United States Circuit Court of Appeals, in *Collin v. Smith*, 578 F. 2d 1197 (1978) (*Village of Skokie v. Nat. Socialist Party of Amer.*, 69 Ill. 2d 605, 373 N.E. 2d 21, 14 Ill. Dec. 890 (Ill. S.C., 1978) (leave to appeal to the United States Supreme Court denied)), would not validate a ban on a neo-Nazi march because of

> ... the fundamental proposition that if these civil rights are to remain vital for all, they must protect not only those society deems acceptable, but also those whose ideas it quite justifiably rejects and despises.

This argument offers what Professor Bollinger, op. cit., has called the "fortress" model for protected free speech. It is an in terrorem argument that assumes that the courts cannot hold to rational limits, and therefore must hold to irrational ones. A similar argument was raised by Professor H.W. Arthurs in respect of the law under review: see Arthurs, "Hate Propaganda — An argument against Attempts to stop it by Legislation" (1970), 18 Chitty's L.J. 1 at p. 4, where he protests that it creates "...a precedent for repression, should an unhappy day ever arrive when less benevolent and liberal legislators occupy the benches of Parliament."

The fortress model leans toward a nearly absolute right of free speech on the ground that, if one fails to protect against even the more virulent forms of human weakness, one opens the door for further erosion of the right. I do not accept the fortress model for Canada: to accept it would be to fail our duty under s.1 of the Charter. Those who would argue against a particular limit on free speech must say something more than that the next one might be worse. They must argue that this one goes too far. That in turn is an argument about proportionality, not sufficiency.

(b) The concern about condemnation of opinion: it is vigorously argued for the accused that the law under review forbids him to express his own opinions on political and historical subjects. It is said that the "fundamental freedoms... are the *sine qua non* of a democratic society, and include the right to challenge accepted beliefs..." Richards, in the work cited, also argues that group libel laws typically condemn remarks that contain "evaluative conceptions", and require the state to make "abstract evaluative judgments". He complains (p. 191):

> Inevitably, such laws impose state restrictions in the core area of evaluative conceptions appealing to the moral powers of speakers and audiences on the basis of state judgments of the worth of such conceptions, thus usurping the sovereign moral judgment of the people.

I accept that, in general, the democratic ideal does not permit of any established opinion about the rightness or wrongness of any idea, excepting of course this one, and am not unmindful of the close connection of speech to matters of conscience and the possibility that somehow, if the expression of an opinion is limited, so also might be the right to hold that opinion. Nevertheless, as Richards elsewhere asserts, the claim to autonomy and freedom for one person sometimes must be curtailed — at the level of expression if not thought — to assure the same thing for others. My autonomy is limited when I cannot defame others; similarly the autonomy of those who would libel a group can be limited when otherwise the autonomy of the victims is at risk. It is all a question of how debilitating the injury is. The kind of injury described by Richards himself, and earlier quoted by me, and relied upon by the Cohen Report, does impair the equality and autonomy of the victim. In the end, there also is a concern about proportionality.

In passing, I should not be taken as accepting that laws of this sort "inevitably" trench upon opinion rather than fact. Indeed, I do not necessarily accept that this can be said of the law under review. That would depend upon the scope of the "religious subject" exception, something not explored in this case because Mr. Keegstra claimed to base his opinions upon empirical analysis of historical fact, and not upon religious conviction.

(c) The need for tolerance in a democratic society: Mr. McKillop adopts the words of the European Court of Justice in *Handyside v. U.K.* (1976), 1 E.H.R.R. 737 at 754, uttered in the context of a review of laws against the promotion of obscenity:

> Freedom of expression... is applicable... to... "ideas"... that offend, shock or disturb the State or any sector of the population. Such are the demands of that pluralism, tolerance and broadmindedness without which there is no "democratic society".

Respectable judicial and political opinion holds that citizens in a democratic society must show a courage and stoicism in the face of abusive exercise of freedom of expression. In *Skokie,* it was suggested that Jews who would be offended by a provocative neo-Nazi march should simply not attend: see 578 F. 2d 1207, 69 Ill. 2d 618-19. See also Aryeh Neier, Defending My Enemy: American Nazis, the Skokie case, and the Risks of Freedom (New York: Dutton, 1979).

I accept that the assumption behind the idea of toleration, an idea essential to a democracy, is that we must learn not to react badly to what we hear. No doubt hearing the promotion of race hatred, for example, affords us all an opportunity to be tolerant and wise, to permit it to be said and yet reject it, and thus demonstrate again that the citizens can be trusted to govern well in a democratic society. The question is whether we should conduct these dangerous little exercises on a playing field where somebody might get hurt. Should we say that all forms of non-physical injury are a price we all must pay in every circumstance for the advantages of a democratic society? With respect, I cannot. That reasoning may well apply to demand heroic stoicism from holders of public office or groups in society that hold special privileges. It no doubt also applies where the only offence is to aesthetic sensibilities, or the sense of frustration one has in the face of absurdity or stubborn stupidity. I do not understand why one must tolerate the debilitating injury that is possible from hatemongering. Again, what remains is an issue about proportionality: if the injury is serious enough, a limit is justifiable.

(d) The futility of the search for truth: I refer not to evidentiary problems but to a skepticism that, in the realm of ideas, is always uncertain about what is true and what is false — and which, as a result, is ironically itself intolerant, although only of certitude. I respond only that this law has not made any value-laden assertion other than that the risk of serious injury that target groups suffer is worthy of protection.

In conclusion, I accept that the test of sufficiency is met by the claim of the need to protect the member of the target group from hatemongering that creates a significant risk that enough Canadians will hate them that they might feel alienated from our society. That risk can arise if the message of the hatemonger is believed. The evidence is that it sometimes is. Therefore, a law against hatemongering might be justified. The remaining questions ask whether the form it has taken, s.281.2, C.C.C., is justifiable.

(3) *Clarity:* Does s.281.2 limit free speech in a way that is not prescribed by law? It is argued for the accused that this sub-test encompasses a "void for vagueness" doctrine, and it has been breached by the loose language in the section. Any difficulty with the section is susceptible to solution by judicial interpretation, and this test is met: see *R. v. Jahelka,* 54 Alta. L.R. (2d) 1, 58 C.R. (3d) 164, 36 C.C.C. (3d) 105 (sub nom. *R. v. Jahelka; R. v. Stagnitta*), 43 D.L.R. (4th) 111, 79 A.R. 44 (leave to appeal to the Supreme Court of Canada granted 2nd October 1987) [54 Alta. L.R. (2d) xxxix, 59 C.R. (3d) xxxiii, 84 A.R. 240].

(4) *Proportionality:* This test, in the words of Chief Justice Dickson in *R. v. Oakes,* supra, asks three questions: Is s.281.2 rationally connected to the objective? Does it impair the right as little as possible? Does it so severely trench on individual or group rights that the legislative objective, albeit important, is nevertheless outweighed by the abridgment?

As to the first, this law has been criticized as ill-considered. It has been said that it is unwise to attempt in the courtroom to decide historical fact, by which I mean the truth about events not in the ken of living witnesses, and that the law will fail to lessen the spread of hate: see, for example, the comment in Martin's, The Criminal Code of Canada (Toronto: Cartwright and Sons Ltd., 1955), p. 305. It is also said that the law will have the opposite of the intended effect on hatemongers because a trial will afford them a platform from which to repeat their message to an audience often otherwise unavailable: see Notes, "Group Libel Laws: Abortive Efforts to Combat Hate Propaganda" (1952), 61 Yale L.J. 252, at abuses of it.

I am unable to comprehend how an accused can be heard to attack a law as destructive of his liberties on the ground that it will not succeed. I do not view the "rational connection" part of the proportionality test as going so far as to permit me to judge whether this law will achieve its ends. It permits me only to ask whether there is any logical connection between the sufficient purpose and the means chosen. In this case, obviously, there is.

A valid question arises whether it is appropriate, in order to deal with non-physical injury, to invoke a criminal sanction. The Cohen Report rests its recommendation on its didactic effect. The choice is between the social advantages of a lesson in tolerance as against those of a lesson about abusive exercise of Charter rights. Parliament has decided that Canadians will be better democrats for being taught, by the criminal sanction, that some speech is an abuse of the right to free expression. Once the decision is taken to condemn a course of behaviour so that Canadians learn a lesson in democratic responsibility, it is difficult to gainsay the use of the criminal sanction the very purpose of which is to isolate and condemn anti-social behaviour. I cannot say that the use of the criminal law to discourage at least serious non-physical injury is clearly inappropriate. Whether some less drastic measure is sufficient to protect reputational integrity alone was not adequately explored before us.

As to the second and third questions, the Cohen Committee appreciated, even before the Charter, the need to make no major or unnecessary intrusion into free expression. They said (p. 61):

> It is our opinion that the Canadian people already have made the decision that as among conflicting values, preference must always be given to freedom of expression rather than to legal prohibitions directed at abuses of it. This is not to say that freedom of expression is regarded as an absolute, but only to insist that it will be esteemed more highly and weighted

more significantly in the legislative scales, so that legal markings of the borderline areas will always be such as to permit liberty even at the cost of occasional license.

A considerable effort at restraint was then made. The charging section is hedged around with a series of exceptions and defences. Ironically, most of the criticism of the section since its enactment is that it is *too* restrictive in its application: see, for example, "Hatred and the Law", the Canadian Bar Association, Report of the Special Committee on Racial and Religious Hatred (1984); "Equality Now", A Report of the Special Committee on Participation of Visible Minorities in Canadian Society (Ottawa, 1984); and Law Reform Commission of Canada, Hate Propaganda, Working Paper 50 (Ottawa: Supply and Services, 1984).

The accused nervertheless argued that the law is overly broad, and cited the *Skokie* case in support. Few illustrations of specific problems with this law were offered, but we have ourselves addressed those that have occurred to us. In that regard, the first question is why this law, whose claim is to protect reputational integrity and non-physical injury, can apply in cases where neither occurs. Section 281.2 requires only the promotion of hatred, it does not require successful promotion. It does not require, for guilt, the slightest degree of communal acceptance of the hatemonger's message notwithstanding that, as I have said, the key to serious harm is precisely that. Nor does it require any serious risk of that event. An accused can be convicted even though *nobody* believes him, or is likely to believe him.

All this arose because the Cohen Committee suggested, and Parliament accepted, civil libel as a model for this law. In a libel case, injury need not be proven, it is assumed. I have already questioned the aptness of one aspect of the model. (The elimination of the defence of honest mistake invites yet another, not raised by counsel in this case.) What of the presumption of harm? In the context of civil law, a presumption of damage to reputation simplifies proceedings, and a review of actual harm arises on assessment of damages. The transfer of that approach to the criminal law produces the impossible result that an accused cannot escape condemnation even by proving that he in fact caused injury to no person and no reputation.

In my opinion, this rule is overly broad. In several recent cases, the Supreme Court of Canada held that "broad-brush" legislation offends the proportionality test: see *Re B.C. Motor Vehicle Act*, [1985] 2 S.C.R. 486, [1986] 1 W.W.R. 481 (sub nom. *Ref re S. 94(2) of Motor Vehicle Act*), 69 B.C.L.R. 145, 48 C.R. (3d) 289, 36 M.V.R. 240, 23 C.C.C. (3d) 289, 24 D.L.R. (4th) 536, 18 C.R.R. 30, 63 N.R. 266; *R. v. Smith*, [1987] 1 S.C.R. 1045, [1987] 5 W.W.R. 1, 15 B.C.L.R. (2d) 273, 58 C.R. (3d) 193, 34 C.C.C. (3d) 97, 40 D.L.R. (4th) 435, 75 N.R. 321; and *R. v. Vaillancourt*, judgment rendered 3rd December 1987 [now reported [1987] 2 S.C.R. 636, 60 C.R. (3d) 289, 39 C.C.C. (3d) 118, 68 Nfld. & P.E.I.R. 281, 209 A.P.R. 281, 10 Q.A.C. 161, 81 N.R. 115 [Que.]]. In each case, the court accepted the sufficiency of the competing claim but struck the legislation down because, in service of that claim, it refused to distinguish between cases where condemnation served that claim and where it did not. In the first case, the competing claim was the need to discourage suspended drivers from reoffending, but mandatory conviction and jailing of those who innocently reoffend was too broad a brush. In the second, the competing claim was to discourage the drug traffic, but the mandatory minimal jail sentence for importation caught those who were not involved in the traffic, and was overly broad. In the third, the claim was the discouragement of the use by criminals of firearms, but a definition of murder went too far when it included a killing by the associate of the accused, who believed on reasonable grounds that the gun was not loaded.

Similarly, the competing claim here is to deter serious harm from hatemongering, but s.281.2 permits the conviction of a person who causes no serious harm or risk of harm. Therefore, it is disproportionate and cannot be affirmed.

It might be said that s.281.2 merely makes it a crime to *attempt* to do that which can justifiably be regulated — the spread of hatred against the target groups in our community. In this sensitive area, a law against mere attempts, particularly when honest mistake is not generally available as a defence, extends the law dangerously. It does not even limit itself to an attempt where a risk of serious harm is reasonably foreseeable.

It might be said that it would be impossible for the Crown to prove that the promotion has succeeded. I do not accept that. If the accused offers any real threat to the target groups, the Crown should be able to prove it.

It might be said that the requirement in s.281.2(6), C.C.C., for a fiat for prosecution is a sufficient protection from prosecution in cases where no real harm has been done. Certainly, during the 17 years since s.281.2 was enacted, there have been few prosecutions and little apparent intimidation. Canada has not, so far as I can judge, been cursed by a level of public debate so circumspect as to have lost vitality and frankness. On the other hand, it might be that the likelihood of a fiat is in inverse proportion to the harm done. The easiest fiat is in a case where the abuser has no public support, the hardest where he has much support. There is a risk that prosecutions under this law, which is designed to promote tolerance, might become a weapon of intolerance.

In any event, my problem with this solution is that the granting of a fiat is not subject to judicial review. The Supreme Court of Canada in *R. v. Jones,* [1986] 2 S.C.R. 284, 47 Alta. L.R. (2d) 97, [1986] 6 W.W.R. 577, 28 C.C.C. (3d) 513, 31 D.L.R. (4th) 569, 25 C.R.R. 163, 75 A.R. 133, 69 N.R. 241, said that one cannot successfully attack a law merely because the power potentially to offend the Charter is delegated to an official; one rather brings the official to account when he does. My difficulty is that, by tradition, the very purpose of the ministerial fiat is to place the decision in the political arena and beyond judicial review: see *Gouriet v. Union of Postal Wkrs.,* [1978] A.C. 445, [1977] 3 W.L.R. 300, [1970] 3 All E.R. 70 (H.L.). As such, I cannot accept it as a satisfactory solution to a Charter problem. On the authority of the *Smith* case, trust in prosecution discretion is not a defensible s.1 position.

It might be said that the mere utterance of, say, racial slurs, is offensive. Of course it is, but, as I took some pains to say earlier, free speech cannot be equated to polite speech. The justifiable limit relates to seriously harmful speech, and that must involve more than mere utterance. Nor, obviously, can the victim be the judge.

It might be said that the target groups are in a special category, selected precisely because they have already suffered enough. I agree that the specific mention in s.15 of the need to protect Canadians from invidious discrimination on the basis of race, creed, colour, and ethnic origin, as well as the mention in s.27 of the need to respect our multi-cultural heritage, tells us that no Canadian should be asked to suffer simply because of this heritage. I can only repeat in reply that this law catches more than that.

IV

It remains only to consider the question of remedy. Section 52 of the Charter provides, of course, that laws inconsistent with the Charter are "of no force and effect". Nevertheless, the courts have held that the remedy of a declaration to that effect, vital to the success of the accused here, can be withheld in some cases. See the discussion in *Edmonton Journal* and *R. v. Jahelka.*

The question that arises here is whether a prosecution under s.281.2 that would actually impair Charter rights is not remote and speculative. In many cases, for example, the existence of audience acceptance of the hatred promoted may be clear. Indeed, perhaps the reason why the decisive point about overbreadth was not explicitly made for Mr. Keegstra before us is that, while he had many defences, ineffectiveness was not one of them. He admitted at trial that he placed his controversial and idiosyncratic views before his students in a high school classroom. He did not utter them in the heat of passion, he expressed them dispassionately over many years. It appears from the evidence at trial that sometimes he succeeded in persuading the students.

Sometimes, however, the promoter of hatred may not be believed, and that possibility is not divorced from reality. I offer two examples, the harmless crank and the heated hyperbole. First, we all know somebody, often a relative or a colleague, whose views on some questions are embarrassingly prejudiced, and who seems unable to overcome the temptation to repeat them every time chance permits. He promotes hatred but has yet to win a convert. No doubt Parliament had him in mind when it enacted the "private conversation" exception. Every now and then, however, he will speak at a luncheon or a wedding. Shall there be no Hyde Park corners in Canada? This section exposes the harmless crank to prosecution.

The other example is far more important: in the excitement of public debate on the great issues of the day in a democracy like ours, emotions are stirred and people often are guilty of embarrassing overstatement and terrible ad hominem argument. One need only reflect on some of the current debates in Canadian society: about abortion, language rights, the claims of original peoples, expanded trade with the United States of America — even constitutional law. Does a week pass when some person does not utter an unfortunate remark — never, of course, overlooked by the media — that arguably might excite hatred upon religious, linguistic, national or ethnic lines? The Cohen Committee acknowledged all this (p. 65):

> Because so much of legitimate public debate is admittedly persuasive in intention and often cast in negative statements as well as in positive ones, and also because stereotyping seems to be an inevitable method of generalizing about groups, we realize that to recommend legislation against group defamation, without providing adequate safeguards for proper public discussion, could raise in question our very commitment to the essential democratic value of free expression... the test as to whether our recommendations about group defamation adequately safeguard free expression will be whether the exemptions we suggest leave sufficient latitude for the fullest legitimate public discussion however rough and tumble it may be.

The committee acknowledges that there should be no prosecution in those cases, but the safeguards against that risk are not good enough.

It might be said that the promotion of hatred is bound to get some audience. The Cohen Report says that a significant minority of Canadians are susceptible, and offers some psychological analysis to explain that susceptibility. That may be so, but it does not follow that every attempt to promote hatred will catch the ear of these people. It remains a question of fact in each case whether there was success. Can we say, for example, that Buzzanga was at all successful? See *R. v. Buzzanga* (1979), 25 O.R. (2d) 705, 49 C.C.C. (2d) 369, 101 D.L.R. (3d) 488 (C.A.).

In my view, this is not a case where a constitutional exemption or straightforward reading down can resolve the problem. Accordingly s.281.2 must be declared of no force and effect.

V

In the result, I respectfully disagree with Quigley J. and would consequently say that he erred in failing to quash the indictment.

I would allow the appeal, set aside conviction, and quash the charge.

In the result, we need not deal with the several dozen other grounds of appeal raised by Mr. Christie in his several factums. It should be noted that none had the slightest merit except those relating to the failure of the learned trial judge to charge that recklessness whether hatred might result was not sufficient for conviction, in compliance with the rule in *Buzzanga,* and his failure to permit a challenge for cause because of the inordinate pre-trial publicity, a previously unclear point settled since the trial by *Zundel*.

Appeal allowed.

4.3.5 Criminal Code s.181 (formerly s.177)

SPREADING FALSE NEWS.

181. Every one who wilfully publishes a statement, tale or news that he knows is false and that causes or is likely to cause injury or mischief to a public interest is guilty of an indictable offence and is liable to imprisonment for two years.

Note: In the case of *R.* v. *Kirby* (1970) 1 C.C.C. (2d) 286, the Quebec Court of Appeal quashed a conviction under this section. In this case the accused had published and distributed a parody of the Montreal Gazette. The headline story was entitled "Mayor Shot by Dope-enraged Hippie" and was accompanied by a photo of Jean Drapeau. The Court stated that while the statement was knowingly false, as well as being "stupid, pointless and in bad taste", it could not be said to be likely to cause injury or mischief to the public interest. The reasons given for this conclusion included that satire and parody have a long tradition ranging from Chaucer and Swift to Punch and the New Yorker, that the parody could be readily distinguished from the Gazette upon inspection, and that Mayor Drapeau himself appeared unconcerned.

4.3.6 H.R.S. Ryan, "The Trial of Zundel, Freedom of Expression and the Criminal Law", (1985) 44 C.R. (3d) 334

I

What we usually call "freedom of speech" is guaranteed in s.2 of the Canadian Charter of Rights and Freedoms, Constitution Act, 1982, Pt. I, in the words "freedom of thought, belief, opinion and expression, including freedom of the press and other media of communication". By s.1 of the Charter, that guarantee is made subject only to such reasonable limits prescribed by law as can be demonstrably justified in a free and democratic society. The recent trial, conviction and sentence of Ernst Zundel for publishing a statement that he knew to be false and that was likely to cause social or racial intolerance, contrary to s.177 of the Criminal Code of Canada, R.S.C. 1970, c.C-34, affords an excellent context for a discussion of the meaning of the concept of the freedom of expression, as it is understood in this country, and of the wisdom of the use of the criminal sanction against hateful words.

Zundel is a citizen of the Federal Republic of (West) Germany who has resided and successfully carried on business in Canada as a landed immigrant for about 20 years. He is also an active and apparently important member of what seems to be an unstructured international network of individuals and organizations one of whose professed goals is to convince the peoples of the world that the Nazi government of Germany did not, before and during World War II, undertake and come close to success in an almost incredibly massive effort to exterminate the Jews of Europe, in what is appropriately called "the Holocaust". He has been a publisher, in several countries, of anti-Semitic literature of various kinds on a large scale.

He recently published two pamphlets which became the subject matters of two criminal charges against him. The first, as reported in the press, was entitled, "The West, War and Islam", and asserted the existence of a gigantic international conspiracy of Jews, Freemasons, bankers and communists, to unite the nations of the west to make war on Islamic states, and otherwise to promote Zionism and to dominate world affairs. As so reported, the second was entitled "Did Six Million Really Die?", and described the well-known reports of the massacre of about 6,000,000 Jews and thousands of others in the Holocaust as a hoax perpetrated by the Jews of the world with the principal object of extorting vast sums of money from the German people for Zionist objects.

The international conspiracy that is reported as the subject of the first pamphlet is merely a new variation of an old canard that has been in circulation on and off during this century, and no doubt earlier, having ancient roots in persistent anti-Semitic prejudice. It has entered into plots of works of fiction by several authors, including the late John Buchan. This latest, equally fictitious, version brings together so unlikely a gang of fellow conspirators that the mere list of them virtually destroys the credibility of the pamphlet.

One would have thought that, if any historical event is irrefutably proved to have occurred, the Holocaust is such an event. Yet the second pamphlet is only one of several similar publications, of which more than one claim to be works of scholarship, written with the object of proving that the Holocaust did not occur. The unintended deaths of some hundreds of thousands of Jews in Germany and German-controlled countries during World War II are admitted, but the deliberate slaughter of millions is denied. In the second pamphlet, denial is based on attacks on the honour and veracity of survivors of the death camps, and indeed of those who died in them, and of the surviving Jews of the world, who are accused of inventing the story as a device for extortion.

Many Jews, particularly survivors of the Holocaust, believed that they could not ignore the claim that they had invented the story of the slaughter. A survivor of a death camp, Mrs. Sabina Citron, a leader of an organization called the Holocaust Remembrance Association, therefore appeared before a justice of the peace and charged Zundel with two offences under s.177 of the Criminal Code, above described, one for publishing each of the two pamphlets.

II

Sabina Citron charged Zundel with offences under s.177 of the Criminal Code in publishing statements that he knew to be false and that were likely to cause social or racial intolerance because she was advised that she had no other means of bringing Zundel to answer before the law for his publication of the two pamphlets.

Under the Customs Tariff, importation into Canada of written, printed or pictorial matter that is of treasonable or seditious character is prohibited. The recent rejection by the Federal Court of Apeal of this power as directed against matter of an indecent or immoral character, based on the vagueness and uncertainty in meaning of these adjectives, may have been overcome by a later legislative changes. In any event, treason and sedition are probably clear and certain enough in definition to support enforcement of the prohibition on these grounds. Obviously, this power does not apply to publication in Canada, and it was therefore of no use to Mrs. Citron.

Postal authorities have authority to deny use of the mails for the purpose of committing criminal offences, such as dissemination of hate propaganda or scurrilous matter below mentioned. This ban had been previously imposed on Zundel as a result of earlier publications, but had been removed. It appears that an application to have it re-imposed had been refused.

Publication of false defamatory matter is a civil wrong giving rise to an action by the wronged individual for damages and, in appropriate cases, for an injunction forbidding future publication.

> Publication of a defamatory libel can also be a criminal offence. However, in Canadian provinces whose law is based on the law of England, except in Manitoba, the civil action and criminal offence do not extend to defamation of a large group of people. If the group is so small and clearly-defined that the defamation can affect the reputation of its individual members, each member can sue or prosecute for the wrong done to him or her personally. Zundel's pamphlets attacked groups so large that individual members were not personally identified and therefore could not bring a civil action or lay a criminal information.

In Manitoba alone, under a provincial statute, a member of a racial or religious group of no matter what size can sue for an injunction forbidding publication of defamatory matter directed against the group. A Manitoba court could not restrain publication in Ontario, where Zundel operated.

There is a criminal offence of using the mails to deliver scurrilous matter, that is to say, matter that is grossly offensive or abusive in language. It does not appear that Zundel's pamphlets were expressed in such language, and words more than subject matter seem to constitute the offence.

There was at common law a criminal offence of publishing a seditious libel. Although this offence has been incorporated in the Criminal Code, it has not been defined there, and the common law definition of the offence continues in effect. The relevant variety of seditious libel is publication of a false statement with intent to promote feelings of ill will and hostility between different classes of citizens. At first glance, Zundel's pamphlets would seem to come within that definition, but in the famous *Boucher* case the Supreme Court of Canada defined another form of the offence very narrowly. The publication in question there was a Jehovah's Witness pamphlet entitled "Quebec's Burning Hate Against Christ and His Church", expressing violently-worded complaints about treatment of members of the movement by provincial authorities. It was clearly likely to promote ill will and hostility between Jehovah's Witnesses and the Quebec government. However, four of the judges of the Supreme Court of Canada held that the intention of the accused, Boucher, was not seditious unless he meant to incite members of the public, including members of the movement, to violence against constituted authority or to create a public disturbance or disorder against public authority. Applying the test of that decision to Zundel, it does not appear that he could be proved to have intended to foment directly violent attacks on Jews or disorder threatening Jews or a similar result, although his pamphlets might have been used by persons who had such an intention to support their incitements.

In 1966, carrying out a recommendation of the Special Committee on Hate Propaganda, Parliament created several offences, one of which Zundel may have committed. Under it, everyone who by communicating statements, other than in private conversation, wilfully promotes hatred against any identifiable group, defined as any group distinguished by colour, race, religion or ethnic origin, is guilty of an offence, punishable on indictment or summary conviction at the option of the prosecutor. This offence is hedged about with exceptions. The publisher is not guilty if the statements are true, or are relevant to a subject of public interest the discussion of which is for the public benefit and on reasonable grounds he believes them to be true, or if he intends in good faith to point out, for the purpose of removal, matter tending to produce feelings of hatred towards an identifiable group in Canada. The word "wilfully" is ambiguous in legal terminology. It can mean "wantonly or recklessly". Here, it may mean "deliberately". No prosecution on a charge of this offence can be commenced without the consent of the provincial Attorney General. The only conviction for an offence under this section of the Code was set aside on appeal. Many critics believed that nobody could be convicted under it.

Mrs. Citron applied to Attorney General McMurtry for consent to prosecution of Zundel on charges of commission of this offence in publication of each pamphlet. The Attorney General refused consent, apparently because he believed that a conviction could not be obtained. He may have been concerned about Zundel's professed purpose of clearing the German people, including German-Canadians, from a false accusation of being responsible for a horrible crime which he asserted had not been committed. The Attorney General might also have been in doubt about the interpretation of the phrase "promotion of hatred" and the meaning of "wilfully". The verdict in the actual trial, in which the jury apparently found that Zundel knew his statements on this subject to be false, suggests that he might have been convicted of this offence, but without the Attorney General's consent Mrs. Citron could not charge Zundel with it.

For these reasons she was advised that, unless Zundel could be convicted of the offence of publishing statements that he knew to be false and that were likely to cause injury or mischief to a public interest, there was no legal process by which she could successfully challenge his veracity and good faith. She therefore undertook to persuade, and succeeded in persuading, a justice of the peace that he should act on her charges of that offence and issue a summons or warrant by which Zundel could be brought before a criminal court to answer for his publications.

Mrs. Citron's action created a dilemma for the Attorney General. He could have stayed the prosecution, but that step would have been politically dangerous. He could have let Mrs. Citron continue as a private prosecutor, but that course was no doubt unattractive. He chose a third course and took over the conduct of the prosecution and designated counsel to manage it and conduct the trial.

III

Zundel did not deny that he had published the pamphlets. He claimed that the statements were true and that his purpose in publication was to reveal that truth to the world for the public good. The course of the trial therefore imposed on the prosecution the task of proving beyond a reasonable doubt that his pamphlets contained false statements, that he knew them to be false and that their publication was likely to cause injury or mischief to a public interest by causing racial or religious intolerance. In the eyes of many observers there was a great risk that such proof could not be attained. Counsel for the prosecution later acknowledged that he had not at first realized how demanding his task would be.

I will not discuss the issues of fact relating to the alleged international conspiracy of Jews, Freemasons, bankers and communists. The jury acquitted Zundel of the charge based on that pamphlet. They could reasonably have been convinced that the story was false to Zundel's knowledge but that it was not important enough to be likely to have the harmful effect claimed by the prosecution. They may have decided that Zundel could have believed it to be true. It is unlikely that the jurors believed in its truth. We are not allowed to do more than speculate about the reasons for their verdict, and they are not allowed to disclose them.

In any event, that pamphlet was of decidedly secondary importance compared with the other pamphlet, denying the occurrence of the Holocaust and accusing the Jews of the world of perpetrating a gigantic lie. Nevertheless, the evidence relating to it, showing Zundel's strongly anti-Semitic frame of mind, may have influenced the jurors in their deliberations on the subject of the Holocaust pamphlet.

How could one prove in court the gigantic operation required for the slaughter of 6,000,000 Jews in a process that extended over several countries and several years? Our law of evidence relies heavily on oral testimony of participants and eyewitnesses. The millions of the dead could not testify. Counsel for the prosecution, which we call "the Crown", produced several survivors of death camps, whose evidence was impressive. They were subjected to merciless cross-examination, during which they were directly or by inference accused of lying. Obviously, their combined experience, even though they were believed, as they ultimately were, could refer only to small fragments of the whole.

To complete the proof, Crown counsel introduced opinion evidence of several scholars whose studies and writings qualified them to be accepted as experts on the subject of the Holocaust. Their opinions based on those studies, subjected also to severe cross-examination, were admitted as evidence, which the jurors could accept in whole or in part or reject, of the occurrence of the Holocaust as a whole. The jurors must have accepted their opinions that the Holocaust occurred as reported.

Judges "take judicial notice" of facts or occurrences so well-known and beyond dispute that testimony concerning them is not required. Crown counsel tried twice during the trial to persuade the trial judge to "take judicial notice of the Holocaust", as the press reported his attempts. The judge did not do so. Of course, the occurrence of the Holocaust was a principal issue of fact and defence counsel naturally objected to the proposal. My view is that judicial notice could have been taken of the evidence and findings of fact on the subject in the proceedings of the International Military Tribunal by which a number of Nazi leaders and organizations were tried after World War II. Although the legal foundation for the tribunal in international law has been questioned by some critics, evidence before it on this subject included detailed testimony by German officials who took part in it, supported by their contemporary official records. The judgment was affirmed by the General Assembly of the United Nations in December 1946. The evidence in the later trial of Eichmann in Israel and other trials could have been added, although the legal basis for Eichmann's trial has been questioned. Technical problems would have had to be solved in putting evidence of this kind before the jury, but it would have been impressive and could have been used in cross-examination of Zundel and his witnesses.

Zundel's defence was based in part on attempts to discredit witnesses for the prosecution, in part on opinion evidence by several persons whose studies and publications denying the occurrence of the Holocaust gained for them acceptance as expert witnesses, and in part on Zundel's own evidence. His testimony was directed towards proving his authority for and his belief in the truth of his statements and the legitimacy of his purpose in publishing them. This, he said, was to show that the German people had been falsely accused and maligned, and had suffered and were suffering unjustly in consequence. It would have been enough to justify an acquittal if the jurors had been led to doubt the occurrence of the Holocaust, or to think that Zundel may have believed that his statements were true, or to doubt that the publication was likely to cause racial or religious intolerance. His counsel also laid stress on freedom of expression.

We may assume that the jurors believed beyond a reasonable doubt that the pamphlet about the Holocaust contained false statements, that Zundel knew they were false and that their publication was likely to cause racial or religious intolerance. Such findings, except on the relatively inscrutable question of Zundel's knowledge, are consistent with general understanding.

IV

The trial judge imposed a sentence of imprisonment for 15 months, to be followed by probation for three years, during which time Zundel is forbidden to discuss the Holocaust in any public communication. In his reasons for sentence, the trial judge expressed his personal condemnation of Zundel as an exponent of the "big lie" after the example of his acknowledged hero, Adolph Hitler. He based the sentence in part on the feeling of outrage at Zundel's conduct which he believed he sensed among members of the community.

An expression of the outrage of the community caused by an offence is accepted in our theory of judicial punishment as a justification for and one of the criteria for admeasurement of punishment. It is also commended by the Law Reform Commission of Canada. If justified, in any case, it is of doubtful value or authority in a case such as this. It is by no means clear that the prevailing sentiment of the community is outrage at Zundel's conduct. A commonly-expressed feeling is one of uncertainty about the propriety of the proceedings, overshadowing condemnation of Zundel. This uneasy feeling does not relate in the minds of many people to the conduct of the trial or the verdict. The concern is with the question whether there should have been a trial at all. The legitimacy of the prosecution is questioned by some critics, and more question its wisdom. Many say that Zundel has been given unwarranted publicity and an undue impression of his importance has been created. There is a common belief that he has been given an undeserved opportunity to claim the status of martyr. Some think that a sentence as severe as that which has been imposed may add plausibility to such a claim. Editorials and letters to the press continue to express concern over the process as a threat to freedom of expression.

These opinions illustrate an unhappy feeling shared by many people that in such proceedings the scope of criminal law is being extended too far. We have a general tendency to create too many crimes. It may be useful to have a process by which our authorized tribunals express rejection and condemnation of conduct such as Zundel's. The trouble is that when the offender has been convicted of a criminal offence he must, in our theory, be punished. In cases such as this the kind of punishment our penal law provides does not seem to be an appropriate response. The judge's words in imposing sentence on Zundel have no doubt rolled off his back like water from the back of the proverbial duck. Imprisonment will merely further convince him that he has been made a martyr. The following probation will extend the duration of that sensation. He will join his battery of defence witnesses in making a continual public display of his claim of martyrdom, which will gain him sympathy among certain segments of society where such a claim can create a favourable impression. Meanwhile, members of the general public have been more interested in the drama of the trial and verdict than in the sentence, while many continue to be uneasy about the whole process. He is now exploiting the propaganda value of the consequential order for his deportation.

Yet a trial conducted under the rules of our judicial process before a professedly and apparently in fact reasonably impartial tribunal established by the state, in which opponents strive on relatively equal terms to influence that result, is in many respects an appropriate method of resolving questions such as Zundel's pamphlets raised. With all its limitations and faults, our legal process is usually as capable of eliciting truth in a limited and clearly-defined two-sided inquiry as any other procedure we know of. The verdict of acquittal on the charge relating to the imaginary conspiracy reveals a sense of fairness, balance and restraint on the part of the jury. There must be in the minds of members of the public a general sense that the jury's verdict on the other charge was based on conclusive proof of the truth of previously-published reports of the Holocaust and the falsehood of Zundel's pamphlet.

On one element essential to guilt of this charge doubts have been expressed. What if Zundel was convicted of publishing what he believed to be true? If that were what occurred, our criminal law would seem to have been used for an oppressive and unjustifiable purpose. There is always a residue of uncertainty when a court finds that a person has lied as a witness or in a published statement. In criminal cases, we demand proof of guilt to such a high degree of probability that the triers of fact have no reasonable doubt of guilt. For practical purposes, we say that it is impossible to demand more convincing proof. Our judicial process requires us to rely on our official triers of fact to conform in good faith to the prescribed standard of persuasive force of the evidence they receive. In Zundel's case, there are many good reasons for believing that they did so and no reason known for believing or suspecting that they did not. In the past we have hanged men and women found guilty by the same test, and today we send them to prison for life. It seems beyond the limits of practicality of proof to demand a higher standard.

V

I come finally to the question whether, and if so to what extent, the Zundel trial, conviction and sentence have been consistent with our Canadian understanding of the principle of freedom of expression.

Among many attacks on the whole proceedings as an infringement of that freedom have been several editorial comments in the Toronto Globe and Mail. The leading editorial in the 18th March issue of that paper was based largely on criticism of s.177 of the Criminal Code, under which Zundel was convicted, where it was said:

"This amazing law hardly erects any barriers against those who would attack free speech... Section 177 makes it a criminal offence simply to knowingly publish a false statement that causes or is likely to cause injury or mischief to a public interest. There is no definition of public interest. There is no proof required that any injury or mischief actually occurred. Here is a criminal law against an indefinite probability that might amount only to an aggravation. The existence of such an arbitrary catch-all is inconsistent with a free society. Section 177 ought to be repealed."

These are substantial and serious criticisms, although the exact language of the criticism has been carefully selected for effect. To "knowingly publish a false statement" is not as clear an expression as to publish a statement that one knows to be false. No charge under the section could be sustained unless the public interest in question was identified, as it was in the charges against Zundel. Nevertheless, an element of vagueness and uncertainty is inherent in the words of the section and the identification of the public interest in the charges against Zundel was very general in terms. The issue of uncertainty in the meaning of "tendency" is validly raised.

One of the standards by which the reasonableness and justification of limits imposed by our laws on freedom of expression is clarity and certainty of definition. Section 177 may be vulnerable to attack on those grounds as infringing on the freedom of expression guaranteed by s.2 of the Charter of Rights and Freedoms. This defence was raised during the trial and will no doubt be raised again on appeal. If an appeal is successful on any ground, a new trial would be very difficult and expensive; the government might not pursue it. If s.177 were held to be inoperative, there could not be a new trial. Zundel would claim to have been vindicated and would no doubt continue his publications with triumphant fanfares.

There are, however, broader questions, not related directly to s.177 or the Zundel trial itself, with relation to our understanding of freedom of expression:

1. Should freedom of expression be guaranteed only for true statements or should it extend to those the publisher believes to be true?

2. If freedom to publish lies is not guaranteed, should every published lie constitute a criminal offence?

3. If some but not all published lies should constitute criminal offences, what kinds of lies should be criminal?

4. Should there be any non-criminal restraints on publishing lies?

5. What are reasonable and justifiable limits on freedom of expression where it exists?

The quoted Globe and Mail editorial suggests that its writer believes that there can be a justifiable criminal offence of publishing a statement one knows to be false, if the offence is sufficiently restricted in scope and clearly defined and its harmful value is clearly expressed and great enough to justify invocations of criminal sanctions. The language of s.2 of the Charter, which guarantees freedom of thought, belief, opinion and expression, suggests that freedom is guaranteed for expression of genuine belief or opinion. Reasoning from that association, it is arguable that the guaranteed freedom does not extend to publishing a statement one knows to be false. Common sense seems to support that proposition. If we were completely free to publish lies about one another, life in society would be intolerable.

Common sense seems also to suggest that not all published lies should be punished criminally. The criminal law enlists the whole power of the state to proscribe by solemn Parliamentary declaration defined conduct as sufficiently reprehensible to merit the description of "criminal", to compel the presence of an accused person before a solemnly-created court to be tried on criminal charges, to prove guilt by a solemn judicial process, to denounce guilt in a solemn judgment, and to punish the guilty by solemnly-imposed afflictive sanctions that may extend to loss of freedom and degrading treatment in prison. So great an exercise of public force and public condemnation and so severe a public reaction should not be expended on conduct that merits only slight or moderate disapproval or correction. The harm or danger caused by or harmful tendency of conduct should be severe to justify public intervention on such a scale. There are lies and lies, harms and harms, dangers and dangers, and tendencies and tendencies. Society can tolerate a considerable amount of lying and a considerable degree of harm or danger without invoking the criminal law.

That being so, how should criminal lies be recognized and defined? Present offences may afford examples. A seditious libel, as defined by the Supreme Court of Canada, if it consists of a statement known by the publisher to be false, published with intent to incite violence or disorder threatening the peace of society, may, it is suggested, reasonably be criminal. A statement known by the publisher to be false, published with intent to incite hatred or contempt directed against an individual or identifiable group, also seems reasonably punished criminally. What about Zundel's offence? Is it enough that the publisher is aware of the falsehood of a publication that causes or is likely to cause injury or mischief to a public interest? Here the attempt of definition becomes fuzzy. The relative importance of the public interest and the severity of the harm or political harm seem to require clarification. The test in sedition is related to the "clear and present danger" enunciated by the Supreme Court of the United States. The farther we move from that proximity, the more difficult it is to justify invoking the criminal law. Similarly, the distance from hatred to intolerance is considerable. In a society in which anti-Semitism is never far below the surface and in which certain fringe elements are easily incited to violence against Jews and synagogues, racial and religious intolerance directed against Jews is always dangerous. The same may be said of certain other "visible minorities", including some distinguished by colour. Larger, well-established racial or social groups are not as easily threatened. Discrimination in recognizing and defining the groups potentially at risk and the degree of harm or threatened harm would be difficult. The greater the particularity of definition, the greater the risk of over- or under-inclusion. The same risks, however, are present in broad and general terms. Section 177 is of doubtful justification. If it is to be retained, it requires clarification in definition and limitation in scope. In particular, the present section does not require that the publisher intend or be aware of the probable harm or tendency of the publication. It is suggested that guilt should require either such intention or awareness.

Voices are being raised to demand that the hate propaganada offence be broadened by deleting the word "wilfully" from the definition. Such a measure would be dangerous. At the least, an element of intention or awareness of the effect of the publication should be essential. When this offence was introduced, it was vigorously opposed by the late Frank Scott and other advocates of freedom of expression. The present definition is probably wide enough, or perhaps too wide.

The definition of "criminal libel" is too broad. If it is retained, it should require knowledge of the falsehood and intention or awareness of the severely adverse effect or a tendency to affect the reputation of the victim.

If, as I think, a trial is an appropriate process for ascertaining truth in such issues, and if the criminal law is an inappropriate weapon for the purpose of combatting falsehood, is there a better way of dealing with the problem? It seems that the civil law of defamation could be revised to good effect. The Manitoba statute could furnish an example. A member of an identifiable group, whether racial or religious or perhaps of another character, could sue in the civil court for an injunction to forbid publication of properly-defined defamatory statements about the group. In cases of deliberate and gross defamation, punitive damages of a reasonable amount might be added and made payable to a charitable organization, although this could come perhaps too close to a criminal sanction.

Should the publisher's belief in the truth of a published falsehood bring the publication within the gauranteed freedom of expression? I would say "Yes" in criminal law, but reckless ignorance might justify punishment of the publication of matter with intent to incite violence or public disorder, and particularly where the publisher is aware that it is likely to promote violence against members of an identifiable group.

4.3.7 *R.* v. *Zundel* (1987), 35 D.L.R. (4th) 338 (Ont. C.A.)

THE COURT: It is not necessary for the purpose of this appeal to define the limits of the unregulated areas where freedom of expression is supreme. The pertinent question is whether s.177 of the *Criminal Code* properly forms part of the permissibly regulated area. If it does, then it is not necessary to consider s.1 of the Charter. The nub of the offence in s.177 is the wilful publication of assertions of a fact or facts which are false to the knowledge of the person who publishes them, and which cause or are likely to cause injury or mischief to a public interest. It is difficult to see how such conduct would fall within any of the previously expressed *rationales* for guaranteeing freedom of expression. Spreading falsehoods knowingly is the antithesis of seeking truth through the free exchange of ideas. It would appear to have no social or moral value which would merit constitutional protection. Nor would it aid the working of parliamentary democracy or further self-fulfilment. In our opinion an offence falling within the ambit of s.177 lies within the permissibly regulated area which is not constitutionally protected. It does not come within the residue which comprises freedom of expression guaranteed by s.2(*b*) of the Charter.

...

Section 177 would appear to be a reasonable means of achieving the objective of prohibiting the spread of false news which a person knows to be false, and which causes or is likely to cause injury or mischief to a public interest. It impairs freedom of expression as little as is possible, and any impairment is proportionate to the objective to be achieved. Accordingly, we have concluded that if s.1 of the Charter is applicable, s.177 is a reasonable limit prescribed by law which can be demonstrably justified in a free and democratic society.

4.3.8 Canadian Human Rights Act R.S.C. 1985, c.H-6

Hate mongers

13. (1) It is a discriminatory practice for a person or a group of persons acting in concert to communicate telephonically or to cause to be so communicated, repeatedly, in whole or in part by means of the facilities of a telecommunication undertaking within the legislative authority of Parliament, any matter that is likely to expose a person or persons to hatred or contempt by reason of the fact that that person or those persons are identifiable on the basis of a prohibited ground of discrimination.

Exception

(2) Subsection (1) does not apply in respect of any matter that is communicated in whole or in part by means of the facilities of a broadcasting undertaking.

Interpretation

(3) For the purposes of this section, no owner or operator of a telecommunication undertaking communicates or causes to be communicated any matter described in subsection (1) by reason only that the facilities of a telecommunication undertaking owned or operated by that person are used by other persons for the transmission of such matter.

4.3.9 J. P. Boyer, *Political Rights: The Legal Framework of Elections in Canada* (Toronto: Buttersworth, 1981) pp. 308-9

...

These lessons appear to have been learned by governments and courts which have been called on to deal with the Western Guard Party in Canada. The Western Guard is a neo-fascist political organization with very few members but which, through its occasional public rallies and its taped telephone messages, made an impact on the public. Instead of seeking a law to make the Western Guard an unlawful organization generally, specific charges were brought against the leader and the party for identifiable breaches of the existing and adequate law. Thus, John Ross Taylor and the Western Guard Party were taken to court by the Canadian Human Rights Commission, on the grounds that the Party's telephone messages in Toronto in 1979 were violations of s.13(1) of the Canadian Human Rights Act.

Taylor and the Western Guard were brought before the Federal Court of Canada for having disobeyed the order of the Canadian Human Rights Commission to cease their discriminatory practice of using the telephone to communicate repeatedly tape-recorded messages. The order, dated July 20, 1979, was entered in the judgment book of the Federal Court of Canada, and was founded on the provisions of s.13(1) of the Canadian Human Rights Act.

The section makes it a "discriminatory practice" for a person or group of persons acting in concert to communicate telephonicly or to cause to be communicated, repeatedly, any matter that is likely to expose a person or persons to hatred or contempt "by reason of the fact that that person or those persons are identifiable on the basis of a prohibited ground of discrimination". The basis for the order was that a Human Rights Tribunal, appointed by the Commission to inquire into complaints against the recorded telephone messages of the Western Guard, had looked at transcriptions of the telephone messages and found that they exposed persons to hatred or contempt merely on the basis that those persons were Jewish. It ordered the respondents to cease this discriminatory practice.

The Federal Court observed that the Canadian Human Rights Commission was a relatively new institution created by Parliament to extend the present laws in Canada that proscribe discrimination and that protect the privacy of individuals, and that its mandate is strong and significant. "It is therefore very important, at this early stage", stated the Court, "that its mission be taken seriously by all, including would-be merchants of racial discrimination."

The Court found that John Ross Taylor had shown no intention to obey the Commission's order and no repentance for his violations of the law, and sentenced him to one year imprisonment, although the sentence was suspended "as long as he, or the Western Guard Party of which he is the Leader, do not use telephone communications for the dissemination of hate messages, or any messages the subject matter of which has been dealt with in the judgment of the Human Rights Tribunal". The Western Guard Party itself was fined $5,000, a sentence which was also suspended and would only take effect if the order of the Commission was further disobeyed. The order was disobeyed, and in June 1980 Mr. Justice Alan Walsh of the Federal Court of Canada ordered Taylor imprisoned and the Party fined. The appel by Taylor against this order was dismissed.

4.3.10 Ontario Human Rights Code S.O. 1981, c.53, ss.1-8, 12

PART I

FREEDOM FROM DISCRIMINATION

Services

1. Every person has a right to equal treatment with respect to services, goods and facilities, without discrimination because of race, ancestry, place of origin, colour, ethnic origin, citizenship, creed, sex, age, marital status, family status or handicap.

Accommodation

2. (1) Every person has a right to equal treatment with respect to the occupancy of accommodation, without discrimination because of race, ancestry, place of origin, colour, ethnic origin, citizenship, creed, sex, age, marital status, family status, handicap or the receipt of public assistance.

Harassment in accommodation

(2) Every person who occupies accommodation has a right to freedom from harassment by the landlord or agent of the landlord or by an occupant of the same building because of race, ancestry, place of origin, colour, ethnic origin, citizenship, creed, age, marital status, family status, handicap or the receipt of public assistance.

Contracts

3. Every person having legal capacity has a right to contract on equal terms without discrimination because of race, ancestry, place of origin, colour, ethnic origin, citizenship, creed, sex, age, marital status, family status or handicap.

Employment

4. (1) Every person has a right to equal treatment with respect to employment without discrimination because of race, ancestry, place of origin, colour, ethnic origin, citizenship, creed, sex, age, record of offences, marital status, family status or handicap.

Harassment in employment

(2) Every person who is an employee has a right to freedom from harassment in the workplace by the employer or agent of the employer or by another employee because of race, ancestry, place of origin, colour, ethnic origin, citizenship, creed, age, record of offences, marital status, family status or handicap.

Vocational associations

5. Every person has a right to equal treatment with respect to membership in any trade union, trade or occupational association or self-governing profession without discrimination because of race, ancestry, place of origin, colour, ethnic origin, citizenship, creed, sex, age, marital status, family status or handicap.

Harassment because of sex in accommodation

6. (1) Every person who occupies accommodation has a right to freedom from harassment because of sex by the landlord or agent of the landlord or by an occupant of the same building.

Harassment because of sex in workplaces

(2) Every person who is an employee has a right to freedom from harassment in the workplace because of sex by his or her employer or agent of the employer or by another employee.

Sexual solicitation by a person in position to confer benefit, etc.

(3) Every person has a right to be free from,

(*a*) a sexual solicitation or advance made by a person in a position to confer, grant or deny a benefit or advancement to the person where the person making the solicitation or advance knows or ought reasonably to know that it is unwelcome; or

(*b*) a reprisal or a threat of reprisal for the rejection of a sexual solicitation or advance where the reprisal is made or threatened by a person in a position to confer, grant or deny a benefit or advancement to the person.

Reprisals

7. Every person has a right to claim and enforce his or her rights under his Act, to institute and participate in proceedings under this Act and to refuse to infringe a right of another person under this Act, without reprisal or threat of reprisal for so doing.

Infringement prohibited

8. No person shall infringe or do, directly or indirectly, anything that infringes a right under this Part.

...

Announced intention to discriminate

12. (1) A right under Part I is infringed by a person who publishes or displays before the public or causes the publication or display before the public of any notice, sign, symbol, emblem, or other similar representation that indicates the intention of the person to infringe a right under Part I or that is intended by the person to incite the infringement of a right under Part I.

Opinion

(2) Subsection (1) shall not interfere with freedom of expression of opinion.

Note: A Manitoba prohibition similar to s.12 has been held not to apply to the editorial comment of a newspaper. See *Re Warren and Chapman* (1985), 11 D.L.R. (4th) 474. In Saskatchewan a similar provision has been held to apply to an advertising display outside a commercial establishment. See *Re Iwasyk* (1977), 80 D.L.R. (3d) 1 (Sask. Q.B.).

4.3.11 *Regina* v. *Buffalo Broadcasting Co. Ltd.* (1977), 36 C.P.R. (2d) 170 (Sask. Magistrates' Ct.)

BENCE, J.M.C.: — The defendant company is charged that on or about November 18, 1976, at Regina, in the Province of Saskatchewan, it did broadcast an abusive comment on a race contrary to s.29(1) of the *Broadcasting Act,* R.S.C. 1970, c.B-11, and the Regulations thereto. To this charge a plea of not guilty was entered and on the day fixed for trial counsel for the defendant company made a preliminary objection to the wording of the charge. As s.732(1) of the *Criminal Code* provides that such objection can only be made with leave once a plea has been entered that leave was granted: there being no objection on the part of the prosecutor. Mr. Gerein pointed out that there were no particulars as to the abusive comment, as to what race and as to the Regulation offended. Mr. Merchant then specified the following particulars:

> Between 9:05 a.m. on the date alleged in a poem and comments on a poem about the Pakistani race contrary to Regulation 5(1)(b).

The trial proceeded on the basis that the charge contained these particulars.

Defence counsel admitted that the letters CKRM constituted the call sign of Buffalo Broadcasting Company Ltd. There was testimony from a radio monitor analyst with the Canadian Radio-Television Commission that the Commission received a letter of complaint from a citizen living in Saskatchewan with respect to the broadcast in question and CKRM was required to send to the Commission an air check of all programming broadcast on November 18th from 9:00 a.m. to 12:00 noon. CKRM sent a cassette tape which was received by this witness and it was played in Court for the period mentioned in the charge. A typewritten transcript of that portion was entered in evidence. Mr. Gerein agreed that the tape, as played, was accurate. The citizen who made the complaint was called and testified that the tape played in Court was verbatim as he recalled the incident. No defence evidence was adduced and this constituted the evidence except for the filing of some documents including a certified true copy of the certificate of incorporation of the defendant company and of the licence granted to the defendant on June 13, 1975, for the call sign CKRM.

The portion of the broadcast giving rise to this was as follows:

ANNOUNCER #1: I don't know if I should read this poem or not. See what you think of the first verse of it.

ANNOUNCER #2: I'll let you know if it's offensive or not.

ANNOUNCER #1: I come to Canada poor and broke, Get on bus, see Manpower bloke, Kind man treat me really swell there Send me down to see the Welfare, Welfare say: come down no more We send the cash out to your door Norman Levy make you wealthy Medical Plan will make you healthy

How's that sound?

ANNOUNCER #2: I see that yeah, I'll go with that

ANNOUNCER #1: Six months on dole get plenty money Thanks to working man, real dummy Write to friends in Pakistan Tell them to come as fast as can They all come in rags and turbans I buy big house in suburbans They come with me, we live together Only one thing bad — the weather Fourteen families living in, Neighbours' patience wearing thin. Finally whites must move away I buy their house too, I say: Find more Pakis, house I rent More in garden, live in tent.

Is that good?

ANNOUNCER #2: Remember friends, smoke a pack a day

ANNOUNCER #1: Send for family, they all trash They all draw more welfare cash Everything is going good Soon we own the neighbourhood Now on quiet summer nights Go to temple, watch the fights. We have hobby, it called breeding Baby bonus keep us feeding

How we doing so far?

ANNOUNCER #2: Pretty good. (unintelligible)

ANNOUNCER #1: Two years later, big bank roll Still go to Manpower, still draw dole Kids need dentist, wife needs pills We get free, we got no bills White man good, he pay all year To keep the welfare running here Bless all white men, big and small For paying tax to keep us all.

(Laughter) This is good

ANNOUNCER #2: Did you write this?

ANNOUNCER #1: We thank Canada, damn good place Too damn good for white man race If they don't like coloured man, Plenty room, back in Pakistan.

(Laughter) that's not all

ANNOUNCER #2: Oh, you're kidding

ANNOUNCER #1: That's it yeah

ANNOUNCER #1: That's good.

ANNOUNCER #2: Did you write that? Or is it...

ANNOUNCER #1: No... Canada damn good place Too darn good for white man race If they no like colored man

ANNOUNCER #2: Drive a cab in Pakistan

ANNOUNCER #1: Hey, that's cute. Do you like that?

ANNOUNCER #2: That's good... if Mary wrote that

ANNOUNCER #1: I don't know if she wrote it or not but

ANNOUNCER #2: Certainly is funny

ANNOUNCER #1:	That's good. Good morning
LADY CALLER:	Good morning
ANNOUNCER #1:	How are ya?
LADY CALLER:	Pretty good.
ANNOUNCER #1:	That's good. What's your name?
LADY CALLER:	Carol Campbell
ANNOUNCER #1:	Carol Campbell
LADY CALLER:	Yeah
ANNOUNCER #2:	Carol the Barrel, they call her
LADY CALLER:	(laughs) Thanks
ANNOUNCER #1:	Did you hear the poem, Carol?
LADY CALLER:	Yes, I did. I thought that was really good.
ANNOUNCER #1:	Kind of funny, isn't it, eh?
LADY CALLER:	Uh, huh, that's for sure.

The Broadcasting Act provides:

Broadcasting Policy for Canada

3. It is hereby declared that

(*a*) broadcasting undertakings in Canada make use of radio frequencies that are public property and such undertakings constitute a single system, herein referred to as the Canadian broadcasting system, comprising public and private elements.

(*b*) the Canadian broadcasting system should be effectively owned and controlled by Canadians so as to safeguard, enrich and strengthen the cultural, political, social and economic fabric of Canada;

(*c*) all persons licensed to carry on broadcasting undertakings have a responsibility for programs they broadcast but the right to freedom of expression and the right of persons to receive programs, subject only to generally applicable statutes and regulations, is unquestioned;

(*d*) the programming provided by the Canadian broadcasting system should be varied and comprehensive and should provide reasonable, balanced opportunity for the expression of differing views on matters of public concern, and the programming provided by each broadcaster should be of high standard, using predominantly Canadian creative and other resources;

(*e*) all Canadians are entitled to broadcasting service in English and French as public funds become available;

(*f*) there should be provided, through a corporation established by Parliament for the purpose, a national broadcasting service that is predominantly Canadian in content and character;

(*g*) the national broadcasting service should

(i) be a balanced service of information, enlightenment and entertainment for people of different ages, interests and tastes covering the whole range of programming in fair proportion,

(ii) be extended to all parts of Canada, as public funds become available,

(iii) be in English and French, serving the special needs of geographic regions, and actively contributing to the flow and exchange of cultural and regional information and entertainment, and

(iv) contribute to the development of national unity and provide for a continuing expression of Canadian identity;

(*h*) where any conflict arises between the objectives of the national broadcasting service and the interests of the private element of the Canadian broadcasting system, it shall be resolved in the public interest but paramount consideration shall be given to the objectives of the national broadcasting service;

(*i*) facilities should be provided within the Canadian broadcasting system for educational broadcasting; and

(*j*) the regulation and supervision of the Canadian broadcasting system should be flexible and readily adaptable to scientific and technical advances;

and that the objectives of the broadcasting policy for Canada enunciated in this section can best be achieved by providing for the regulation and supervision of the Canadian broadcasting system by a single independent public authority.

...

Objects of the Commission

15. Subject to this Act and the *Radio Act* and any directions to the Commission issued from time to time by the Governor in Council under the authority of this Act, the Commission shall regulate and supervise all aspects of the Canadian Broadcasting system with a view to implementing the broadcasting policy enunciated in section 3 of this Act.

Powers of the Commission

16(1) In furtherance of its objects, the Commission, on the recommendation of the Executive Committee, may

(*a*) prescribe classes of broadcasting licences;

(*b*) make regulations applicable to all persons holding broadcasting licences, or to all persons holding broadcasting licences of one or more classes.

- (i) respecting standards of programs, and the allocation of broadcasting time for the purpose of giving effect to paragraph 3(*d*),
- (ii) respecting the character of advertising and the amount of time that may be devoted to advertising,
- (iii) respecting the proportion of time that may be devoted to the broadcasting of programs, advertisements or announcements of a partisan political character and the assignment of such time on an equitable basis to political parties and candidates,
- (iv) respecting the use of dramatization in programs, advertisements or announcements of a partisan political character,
- (v) respecting the broadcasting times to be reserved for network programs by any broadcasting station operated as part of a network,
- (vi) prescribing the conditions for the operation of broadcasting stations as part of a network and the conditions for the broadcasting of network programs,
- (vii) with the approval of the Treasury Board, fixing the schedules of fees to be paid by licensees and providing for the payment thereof,
- (viii) requiring licensees to submit to the Commission such information regarding their programs and financial affairs or otherwise relating to the conduct and management of their affairs as the regulations may specify, and
- (ix) respecting such other matters as it deems necessary for the furtherance of its objects; and

(*c*) subject to this Part, revoke any broadcasting licence other than a broadcasting licence issued to the Corporation.

(2) A copy of each regulation or amendment to a regulation that the Commission proposes to make under this section shall be published in the *Canada Gazette* and a reasonable opportunity shall be afforded to licensees and other interested persons to make representations with respect thereto.

29(1) Every licensee who violates the provisions of any regulation applicable to him made under this Part is guilty of an offence and is liable on summary conviction to a fine not exceeding twenty-five thousand dollars for a first offence and not exceeding fifty thousand dollars for each subsequent offence.

(2) Every licensee who violates the provisions of section 28 is guilty of an offence and is liable on summary conviction to a fine not exceeding five thousand dollars.

(3) Every person who carries on a broadcasting undertaking without a valid and subsisting broadcasting licence therefor, or who, being the holder of a broadcasting licence, operates a broadcasting undertaking as part of a network other than in accordance with the conditions of such licence, is guilty of an offence and is liable on summary conviction to a fine not exceeding one thousand dollars for each day that the offence continues.

The *Radio (A.M.) Broadcasting Regulations,* SOR/64-49, provide:

Broadcasting Generally

5(1) No station or network operator shall broadcast
- (*a*) anything contrary to law;
- (*b*) any abusive comment on any race or religion;
- (*c*) any obscene, indecent or profane language;
- (*d*) any false or misleading news;
- (*e*) any program on the subject of birth control unless that program is presented in a manner appropriate to the medium of broadcasting;
- (*f*) any program on the subject of venereal diseases unless that program is presented in a manner appropriate to the medium of broadcasting;
- (*g*) any advertising content in the body of a news broadcast and for the purpose of this section, a summary is deemed to be a part of the body of the broadcast;
- (*h*) except with the consent in writing of a representative of the Commission, any appeal for donations or subscriptions in money or kind on behalf of any person or organization other than
  - (i) a church or religious body permanently established in Canada and serving the area covered by the station,
  - (ii) a recognized charitable institution or organization,
  - (iii) a university, or
  - (iv) a musical or artistic organization whose principal aim or object is not that of monetary gain;
- (*i*) any programme involving a lottery or similar scheme that is prohibited by the *Criminal Code;* [rep. & sub. SOR/70-286]
- (*j*) any program reconstructing or simulating the direct description of any sport or other event through a description prepared from wired reports or other indirect source of information unless assurance has been given in writing to a representative of the Commission that source material will not be obtained directly or indirectly from a broadcast of the event, and
  - (i) a reconstructed broadcast shall not be broadcast until after the conclusion of the event if an actuality broadcast of the event is available in the area,
  - (ii) a reconstructed broadcast shall be identified at the beginning and end thereof as having been so prepared, and if it is more than fifteen minutes in length, it shall be identified at the end of each fifteen-minute period, and
  - (iii) the form of such announcement shall be:

    "This program is a reconstructed broadcast of .... (name of event) ....",

    "This program has been a reconstructed broadcast of .... (name of event) ....",

    or some suitable variation of these forms; or [am. SOR/65-519, s.1(1)]
- (*k*) any telephone interview or conversation, or any part thereof, with any person unless

(i) the person's oral or written consent to the interview or conversation being broadcast was obtained prior to such broadcast, or

(ii) the person telephoned the station for the purpose of participating in a broadcast. [rep. & sub. SOR/70-256, s.3]

(1) (*a*) [Revoked SOR/70-256, s.3; effective January 18, 1971]

(2) The value of articles or money to be awarded in any single contest sponsored in whole or in part by or on behalf of the station shall not exceed five thousand dollars, and no station shall broadcast more than one such contest per month.

(3) Subsection (2) does not apply to a contest

(*a*) in which the value of articles or money to be awarded is one hundred dollars or less; or

(*b*) which are wholly sponsored by or wholly paid for by any advertiser or group of advertisers.

Mr. Gerein raised several points in his defence of the company. Firstly, he submitted that the word ''abusive'' is not applicable to this particular type of situation; that to abuse a thing is to misuse it or to take something and use it for a wrong purpose. Secondly, that a comment is a statement about something else; to read off a literary work (and I do not think Mr. Gerein was intending to class this as such) is not comment. He suggested that if a person criticizes something he comments on it. Further, he submitted that the poem in question was not a statement about the Pakistani people in general but about only one person and it was a statement of fact not a comment. He referred to the fact that only one person testified that it was offensive and according to the transcript in evidence one person thought it was good. He pointed out that there was no evidence of a Pakistani finding it abusive. Then he dealt with the matter of proof that a race was involved. He suggested that there was no proof that Pakistani are a race and no judicial notice of that can be taken. He said the United Nations (Charter) does not acknowledge the existence of a race and suggested race is a scientific myth. He argued that the race is Indian and there is nothing in texts or otherwise to suggest that Pakistani make up a race. Mr. Gerein submitted that the CRTC did not have jurisdiction to pass s.5(1)(*b*); that it exceeds any of the powers given in s.16 of the *Broadcasting Act* and nothing in the Act gives the CRTC the right to censor any particular programme. He cited *National Indian Brotherhood et al. v. Juneau et al. (No. 3)*, [1971] F.C. 498, and *R. v. CKOY Ltd.* (1976), 28 C.P.R. (2d) 1, 70 D.L.R. (3d) 662, 30 C.C.C. (2d) 314 (Ont. C.A.) [reversing 19 C.P.R. (2d) 1, 25 C.C.C. (2d) 333, 9 O.R. (2d) 549 (Ont. H.C.J.)]. His final point was that s.29 creates the offence for breach of the Regulations. He submitted that there was no evidence that on November 18, 1976, the defendant company was a licensee. He cited *R. v. Empire Hotel Co. Ltd.* (1971), 4 C.C.C. (2d) 97, [1971] 5 W.W.R. 106, where Disbery, J., held that a certificate that the company had been granted a licence for the current year did not prove that on the date in question the hotel was licensed.

On the merits of this charge I would have no hesitation in holding that the broadcasting of this poem was an abusive comment about the Pakistani race and within the mischief aimed at by s.5(1)(*b*). I went to a rather old dictionary that I have — Cassells New English Dictionary published in 1946. The three words — abuse, comment and race — which Mr. Gerein felt were inappropriate to the present situation — were defined as follows:

> *Abuse* — (verb) to put to an improper use, misuse, to reproach coursely, to use in an illegitimate sense, to pervert the meaning of, to maltreat, act cruelly to; to violate, to deflower; to deceive.
>
> (noun) improper treatment or employment; misuse; a corrupt practice or custom; insulting or scurrilous language; perversion from the proper meaning; violation.

There seems to me little doubt that the content of this poem was insulting and scurrilous and to use it was to maltreat and act cruelly to another.

> *Comment* — (noun) A remark, a criticism; a note interpreting or illustrating a work or portion of a work.

I do not think that either of these words — abuse or comment — can be interpreted as narrowly as Mr. Gerein would have me do. In my opinion the poem itself may be described as a comment. In addition, there were clearly comments in the poem.

> *Race* — a group or division of persons, animals or plants sprung from a common stock; a particular ethnical stock (as the Caucasian, mongolian, etc.); a subdivision of this, a tribe, nation or group of people, distinguished by less important differences; a clan, a family, a house; a genus, species, stock strain or variety, of plants or animals, persisting through several generations; lineage, pedigree, descent; a class of persons or animals differentiated from others by some common characteristic; a peculiar quality, a strong flavour, as of wine; natural disposition.

I did not think that the definition of the words — comment or abuse — would change much over the years but being a bit in doubt as to the word ''race'' I checked it with a more modern dictionary — the Shorter Oxford English Dictionary (1973) and I could find little difference. Again, the word ''race'' is wider than the interpretation sought by Mr. Gerein and would, on this definition, in my opinion, clearly include the term ''Pakistani''. In Howitt's Dictionary of English Law under Pakistan the following appears:

> The Indian Independence Act, 1947, set up two independent Dominions in India known respectively as India and Pakistan. Both were independent republics which accepted the Crown as the symbol of the free association of the independent nations who are members of the Commonwealth. This did not, however, imply allegiance to the Crown or affect the sovereignty of the republic. Pakistan is no longer a member of the Commonwealth. See Pakistan Act, 1973; Pakistan Act 1974. See Gledhill, Pakistan.

Under s.11 of the *Interpretation Act,* R.S.C. 1970, c.I-23:

> 11. Every enactment shall be deemed remedial, and shall be given such fair, large and liberal construction and interpretation as best ensures the attainment of its objects.

At the same time, this Regulation being a penal provision must be strictly interpreted and any doubt must be resolved in favour of the accused. These apparently contradictory propositions have to be nicely balanced but I have no hesitation in saying that on common sense interpretation of s.5(1)(*b*) the defendant company broadcast an abusive comment in the sense of an insulting or scurrilous remark about the Pakistani race. While the poem purports to speak of an individual it is clearly aimed, in my opinion, at all members of the Pakistani race or the Pakistani people generally.

I turn now to the two technical objections raised by Mr. Gerein. First, that there was no proof that the defendant is a licensee and that s.29 makes it an offence for a licensee to broadcast and contravene the Regulations. The situation is very similar to that facing the Crown in *R. v. Empire Hotel Co. Ltd., supra,* cited by Mr. Gerein. There the company was charged that it on June 6, 1970, at Elrose in the Province of Saskatchewan permitted a person under the age of 19 years to be in an outlet contrary to the *Liquor Licensing Act,* R.S.S. 1965, c.383. Section 138(4) [am. 1970, c.8, s.32(13)(*d*)] thereof reads:

> 138(4) No licensee or any employee of a licensee shall suffer or permit a person apparently or to the knowledge of the licensee, or of the employee, under the age of nineteen years to enter, be in or remain in the outlet.

The Crown filed a certificate that declared that the defendant had been licensed under the *Liquor Licensing Act* in March, 1970, and unless sooner cancelled or revoked it would continue to be licensed for a period of one year from the date of issue. Disbery, J., held there was no admissible evidence that the defendant was a licensee on the material date and the conviction was quashed on appeal. I note that the charge in that case did not allege that the defendant was a licensee as is the case here. If it is not alleged then does the Crown have to prove it? No objection was taken to the charge prior to the plea nor was any objection taken on this point when leave was granted to object to the charge on other grounds after the plea of not guilty was entered. In my opinion, the Crown was under no obligation to prove that the defendant company was a licensee. See *R. v. Cote,* judgment dated February 7, 1977 — Supreme Court of Canada [reported 73 D.L.R. (3d) 752, 33 C.C.C. (2d) 353, [1978] 1 S.C.R. 8] reversing the Saskatchewan Court of Appeal [reported 21 C.C.C. (2d) 474, [1975] W.W.D. 59] — a decision in which it was held that a charge which omitted an essential ingredient was valid as no objection was taken before the plea. In any event I would hold that there was some evidence before me that the defendant company was licensed — certainly the defendant company was carrying on the broadcasting business on the date alleged with the knowledge and consent of the CRTC as if it did hold a licence — the Latin phrase — *Omnia praessumuntur legitime facta donec probetim in contrarium* — all things are presumed to have been legitimately done, until the contrary is proved — would appear to apply and common sense would dictate that I so hold on the basis that it is a reasonable inference from the evidence adduced that the defendant did hold such a licence at the time and it would be unreasonable to permit the defendant to plead as a defence that it might have been committing another offence. The objection that the CRTC did not have the authority to pass s.5(1)(*b*) presents, in my opinion, a greater problem. In *R. v. CKOY Ltd., supra,* the accused radio station was charged with breach of s.5(1)(*k*) of the *Radio (A.M.) Broadcasting Regulations* of the *Broadcasting Act* which prohibits the broadcasting of any telephone interview unless the person interviewed has called the station for the purpose of participating in the broadcast or has consented to the interview being broadcast. At trial the charge was dismissed on the basis that the Regulation was outside the regulatory powers granted by the CRTC. An appeal by the Crown was dismissed but on further appeal to the Court of Appeal of the Province of Ontario the appeal was allowed and the case was remitted to the trial Judge to enter a conviction.

In considering the question of whether or not there was power to make the particular Regulation in that case, Mr. Justice Evans said [at pp. 5-6 C.P.R., p. 667 D.L.R.]:

> I do not conceive it to be the function of the Court to evaluate and balance the competing factors, favourable or unfavourable, which the implementation of the particular Regulation may create; that, in my view, is the responsibility cast upon the Commission. The Court looks at the Regulation in an objective manner and asks whether the Commission in promul-

gating this Regulation exceeded the statutory authority vested in it. This does not mean that the Commisison has unlimited power to pass Regulations. Section 15 provides the restriction, "...the Commission shall *regulate* and *supervise* all aspects of the Canadian broadcasting system with a view to implementing the *broadcasting policy enunciated* in section 3 of this Act". If s.5(1)(*k*) reasonably falls within s.3 then it is *intra vires* the Commission.

It is obvious from the broad language of the Act that Parliament intended to give to the Commission a wide latitude with respect to the making of Regulations to implement the policies and objects for which the Commission was created.

Both Mr. Justice Evans and Mr. Justice Brooke referred to s.16(1)(*b*)(i) of the *Broadcasting Act* and held that that section allows the Commission to regulate "respecting standards of programs..." while s.3(*d*) requires that "the programming provided... should be of high standard..." and then held that the impugned Regulation is to prohibit an undesirable broadcasting technique, one which does not reflect the high standard of programming which the Commission must by regulation of licensees, endeavour to maintain. Reference was made to freedom of speech and freedom of the press being curtailed but the two Judges held that the Regulation protects the freedom of speech by protecting the privacy of the individual and is consistent with the other freedom. Mr. Justice Brooke added [at p. 10 C.P.R., p. 672 D.L.R.]:

The purpose of the section of the Regulation cannot be attacked on that basis and so long as it is the maintenance of the high standard of broadcasting in accordance with its objects, the Commission has the power to enact it.

The difficulty of this question is apparent in that the Court of Appeal members split two to one and there is now an appeal pending in the Supreme Court of Canada. Mr. Justice Dubin, who dissented, referred to *National Indian Brotherhood et al. v. Juneau et al. (No. 3)*. This case was also cited by Mr. Gerein as I have indicated above. The facts of that case were that some time in March, 1970, the CTV Network screened the film entitled "The Taming of the Canadian West" which according to the National Indian Brotherhood and others is blatantly racist, historically inaccurate and slanderous to the Indian race and culture. Various avenues were explored including a request that the CRTC conduct a formal investigation. Eventually this was denied and this ruling came on an application for an order forcing the CRTC to hold and conduct a public inquiry. The application was dismissed by Walsh, J., and he made certain observations with respect to the *Broadcasting Act* which Dubin, J.A., referred to in his dissenting judgment and Mr. Gerein used in his argument. These, in part, were as follows [at p. 12 C.P.R., p. 675 D.L.R.]:

"Reading the Act as a whole and in particular the sections to which I have referred, I find it difficult to conclude that Parliament intended to or did give the Commission the authority to act as a censor of programmes to be broadcast or televised. If this had been intended, surely provision would have been made somewhere in the Act giving the Commission authority to order an individual station or a network, as the case may be, to make changes in a programme deemed by the Commission, after an inquiry, to be offensive or to refrain from broadcasting same. Instead of that, it appears that its only control over the nature of programmes is by use of its power to revoke, suspend or fail to renew the licence of the offending station."

and at p. 13 C.P.R., p. 676 D.L.R.:

"This seems to impose a sort of self-censorship on the individual licensees which is, in practice, not very effective and does not prevent them from producing from time to time programmes which are in poor taste or offensive to a substantial number of viewers. So long as they do not infringe on laws relating to slander, libel or obscenity, they are apparently on safe ground as there is nothing in the Act which gives the CRTC the right to act as censor of the contents of any individual programme.''

And at p. 10 C.P.R., p. 673 D.L.R., Dubin, J.A., said:

I have had the advantage of reading the judgments of my learned brothers, both of whom have concluded that the above-cited Regulation has been validly enacted by the Commission. With deference, I do not agree. It is trite to say that there must be a clear grant of legislative authority before a Commission such as the Canadian Radio-Television Commission like the one in issue here, particularly where a breach of the Regulation is, by the Act, created an offence. [I think something is missing from the statement such as the words ''make a Regulation'' following the word ''Commission''.]

And he added [at p. 12 C.P.R., pp. 674-5 D.L.R.]:

As my brothers have observed, the Regulation in issue purports to strike down an undesirable broadcasting technique. The fact that the object of the Regulation may very well be a laudatory one is quite irrelevant. The broadcast in issue in this case may have been one of considerable public interest, or may have been one which was quite offensive, but the Regulation in question here would prohibit it, whatever quality it may have, if no consent is obtained to it being broadcast. It is only one step removed to contemplate the Regulation reading that no such interview could be broadcast without the consent of the Commission itself. It could then equally be said that the Commission was thereby seeking to establish a high standard of programming, but looked at in that way it cannot be anything other than a form of censorship.

As was the case in *R. v. CKOY Ltd.*, the only provisions of s.16(1)(*b*) which set out the power of the Commission to make regulations of this nature, are subpara. (i) respecting standards of programmes and subpara. (ix) respecting such other matters as it deems necessary for the furtherance of its objects. One would have thought Parliament would have been more specific if it intended to give the power in question. The whole of subpara. 16(1)(*b*)(i) must be considered. It reads:

(i) respecting standards of programs and the allocation of broadcasting time for the purpose of giving effect to paragraph 3(*d*),

Section 3(*d*) reads:

(*d*) the programming provided by the Canadian broadcasting system should be varied and comprehensive and should provide reasonable, balanced opportunity for the expression of differing views on matters of public concern, and the programming provided by each broadcaster should be of high standard, using predominantly Canadian creative and other resources;

The Commission side-stepped the responsibility in the *National Indian Brotherhood* case and I cannot help thinking that Walsh, J., and Dubin, J.A., are correct when they say that there is nothing in the *Broadcasting Act* which gives the CRTC the right to act as censor of the contents of any individual programme. I quote from the judgment of Walsh, J., at pp. 515-6 of the report cited, *supra:*

Section 3(*c*) of the Act, under the heading ''Broadcasting Policy for Canada'' sets forth:

3. It is hereby declared that

...

> (*c*) all persons licensed to carry on broadcasting undertakings have a responsibility for programs they broadcast but the right to freedom of expression and the right of persons to receive programs, subject only to generally applicable statutes and regulations, is unquestioned;
>
> This seems to impose a sort of self-censorship on the individual licensees which is, in practice, not very effective and does not prevent them from producing from time to time programmes which are in poor taste or offensive to a substantial number of viewers. So long as they do not infringe on laws relating to slander, libel or obscenity, they are apparently on safe ground as there is nothing in the Act which gives the CRTC the right to act as censor of the contents of any individual programme. It is apparent in the manner in which the Commission handled this complaint that it does not intend to act as such. The revocation, suspension or failure to renew a licence is such a serious matter that it is not a course the Commission is likely to adopt save for grave and repeated offences, and it would appear that it is reluctant to use this power as a threat to compel the individual licensees or, in the present case, a broadcasting chain, to alter or withhold a programme with respect to which complaints have been received. The most it was prepared to do in the present case was to attempt to bring the parties together in the hope that they, themselves, might find a satisfactory solution to their controversy. I therefore find that under the existing law the decision of the Executive Committee that it would not be in the public interest to hold a public hearing was an administrative one which it was entitled to make. It is not for the Court to comment on whether or not the CRTC should be given more powers of control over the subject-matter of programmes broadcast or televised by its licensees as this is a decision which Parliament alone can make but, at present, it is evident that the powers given to it in this field are very limited and ineffective.

In *R. v. CKOY Ltd.* the Court of Appeal of Ontario was dealing with a much different regulatory power. Mr. Justice Evans, however, appears to agree with Walsh, J., and Dubin J.A., with respect to the power of censorship because he said, at p. 6 C.P.R., p. 668 D.L.R., of the report cited above:

> The right of prohibition in s.5(*k*)(i) is not to be confused with censorship. The Commission does not attempt to censor the content of the conversation or to deny the right of freedom of expression.

Mr. Justice Evans applied this test [at p. 6 C.P.R., p. 667 D.L.R.]: "If s.5(1)(*k*) reasonably falls within s.3 then it is *intra vires* the Commission." In my view s.5(1)(*b*) of the Regulations does not reasonably fall within ss.3 and 16 of the Act so that it is *ultra vires* and this prosecution cannot be maintained.

While the programme or portion of it we are concerned with here was in jocular vein and while there have been many races and nationalities that have been made the butt of jokes, in my view, this "poem" went far beyond those we have been accustomed to hearing. But if there is to be this regulatory provision where is the line to be drawn? It is much like trying to draw lines as to what is obscene and what is not and one can visualize the difficulties that would be encountered. If the broadcaster is not prepared to impose a sort of self-censorship as suggested by Mr. Justice Walsh then the CRTC can refuse to renew its licence or appropriate statutory provisions can give it power to do so. The charge is dismissed.

Charge dismissed.

Note: The decision of the Supreme Court of Canada in *CKOY Ltd.* v. *Her Majesty The Queen,* [1979] 1 S.C.R. 2 casts doubt on this decision.

4.3.12 Regulations Respecting Radio Broadcasting, s.3.

PART I

Broadcasting Content

A licensee shall not broadcast
(a) anything in contravention of the law;
(b) any abusive comment that, when taken in context, tends or is likely to expose an individual or a group or class of individuals to hatred or contempt on the basis of race, national or ethnic origin, colour, religion, sex, age or mental or physical disability;
(c) any obscene or profane language;
(d) any false or misleading news; or
(e) any telephone interview or conversation, or any part thereof, with any person unless
(i) the person's oral or written consent to the interview or conversation being broadcast was obtained prior to the broadcast, or
(ii) the person telephoned the station for the purpose of participating in a broadcast.

4.4 Obscenity

4.4.1 Criminal Code ss.163-169 (formerly ss.159-165)

Offences Tending to Corrupt Morals

Corrupting morals

163. (1) Every one commits an offence who
(*a*) makes, prints, publishes, distributes, circulates, or has in his possession for the purpose of publication, distribution or circulation any obscene written matter, picture, model, phonograph record or other thing whatsoever, or
(*b*) makes, prints, publishes, distributes, sells or has in his possession for the purpose of publication, distribution or circulation, a crime comic.

Idem

(2) Every one commits an offence who knowingly, without lawful justification or excuse,
(*a*) sells, exposes to public view or has in his possession for such a purpose any obscene written matter, picture, model, phonograph record or other thing whatsoever,
(*b*) publicly exhibits a disgusting object or an indecent show,
(*c*) offers to sell, advertises, publishes an advertisement of, or has for sale or disposal any means, instructions, medicine, drug or article intended or represented as a method of causing abortion or miscarriage, or
(*d*) advertises or publishes an advertisement of any means, instructions, medicine, drug or article intended or represented as a method for restoring sexual virility or curing venereal diseases or diseases of the generative organs.

Defence of public good

(3) No person shall be convicted of an offence under this section if he establishes that the public good was served by the acts that are alleged to constitute the offence and that the acts alleged did not extend beyond what served the public good.

Question of law and question of fact

(4) For the purposes of this section it is a question of law whether an act served the public good and whether there is evidence that the act alleged went beyond what served the public good, but it is a question of fact whether the acts did or did not extend beyond what served the public good.

Motives irrelevant

(5) For the purposes of this section the motives of an accused are irrelevant.

Ignorance of nature no defence

(6) Where an accused is charged with an offence under subsection (1) the fact that the accused was ignorant of the nature or presence of the matter, picture, model, phonograph record, crime comic or other thing by means of or in relation to which the offence was committed is not a defence to the charge.

"Crime comic"

(7) In this section, "crime comic" means a magazine, periodical or book that exclusively or substantially comprises matter depicting pictorially

(*a*) the commission of crimes, real or fictitious, or

(*b*) events connected with the commission of crimes, real or fictitious, whether occurring before or after the commission of the crime.

"Obscene"

(8) For the purposes of this Act, any publication a dominant characteristic of which is the undue exploitation of sex, or of sex and any one or more of the following subjects, namely, crime, horror, cruelty and violence, shall be deemed to be obscene.

Warrant of seizure

164. (1) A judge who is satisfied by information upon oath that there are reasonable grounds for believing that any publication, copies of which are kept for sale or distribution in premises within the jurisdiction of the court, is obscene or a crime comic, shall issue a warrant under his hand authorizing seizure of the copies.

Summons to occupier

(2) Within seven days of the issue of the warrant, the judge shall issue a summons to the occupier of the premises requiring him to appear before the court and show cause why the matter seized should not be forfeited to Her Majesty.

Owner and author may appear

(3) The owner and the author of the matter seized and alleged to be obscene or a crime comic may appear and be represented in the proceedings in order to oppose the making of an order for the forfeiture of the said matter.

Order of forfeiture

(4) If the court is satisfied that the publication is obscene or a crime comic, it shall make an order declaring the matter forfeited to Her Majesty in right of the province in which the proceedings take place, for disposal as the Attorney General may direct.

Disposal of matter

(5) If the court is not satisfied that the publication is obscene or a crime comic, it shall order that the matter be restored to the person from whom it was seized forthwith after the time for final appeal has expired.

Appeal

(6) An appeal lies from an order made under subsection (4) or (5) by any person who appeared in the proceedings

(*a*) on any ground of appeal that involves a question of law alone,

(*b*) on any ground of appeal that involves a question of fact alone, or

(*c*) on any ground of appeal that involves a question of mixed law and fact,

as if it were an appeal against conviction or against a judgment or verdict of acquittal, as the case may be, on a question of law alone under Part XXI and sections 673 to 696 apply *mutatis mutandis*.

Comment

(7) Where an order has been made under this section by a judge in a province with respect to one or more copies of a publication, no proceedings shall be instituted or continued in that province under section 163 with respect to those or other copies of the same publication without the consent of the Attorney General.

Definitions "court"

(8) In this section "court" means a county or district court or, in the Province of Quebec, the provincial court, the court of the sessions of the peace, the municipal court of Montreal and the municipal court of Quebec;

"(*a*.1) in the Provinces of New Brunswick, Manitoba, Alberta and Saskatchewan, the Court of Queen's Bench;"

"crime comic

"crime comic" has the same meaning as it has in section 163;

"judge"

"judge" means a judge of a court.

Tied sale

165. Every one commits an offence who refuses to sell or supply to any other person copies of any publication for the reason only that such other person refuses to purchase or acquire from him copies of any other publication that such other person is apprehensive may be obscene or a crime comic.

Restriction on publication of reports of judicial proceedings

166. (1) A proprietor, editor, master printer or publisher commits an offence who prints or publishes

(*a*) in relation to any judicial proceedings any indecent matter or indecent medical, surgical or physiological details, being matter or details that, if published, are calculated to injure public morals;

(*b*) in relation to any judicial proceedings for dissolution of marriage, nullity of marriage, judicial separation or restitution of conjugal rights, any particulars other than

(i) the names, addresses and occupations of the parties and witnesses,

(ii) a concise statement of the charges, defences and counter-charges in support of which evidence has been given,

(iii) submissions on a point of law arising in the course of the proceedings, and the decision of the court in connection therewith, and

(iv) the summing up of the judge, the finding of the jury and the judgment of the court and the observations that are made by the judge in giving judgment.

Saving

(2) Nothing in paragraph (1)(*b*) affects the operation of paragraph (1)(*a*).

Consent of Attorney General

(3) No proceedings for an offence under this section shall be commenced without the consent of the Attorney General.

Exceptions

(4) This section does not apply to a person who

(*a*) prints or publishes any matter for use in connection with any judicial proceedings or communicates it to persons who are concerned in the proceedings;

(*b*) prints or publishes a notice or report pursuant to directions of a court; or

(*c*) prints or publishes any matter

(i) in a volume or part of a *bona fide* series of law reports that does not form part of any other publication and consists solely of reports of proceedings in courts of law, or

(ii) in a publication of a technical character that is *bona fide* intended for circulation among members of the legal or medical professions.

Immoral theatrical performance

167. (1) Every one commits an offence who, being the lessee, manager, agent or person in charge of a theatre, presents or gives or allows to be presented or given therein an immoral, indecent or obscene performance, entertainment or representation.

Person taking part

(2) Every one commits an offence who takes part or appears as an actor, performer, or assistant in any capacity, in an immoral, indecent or obscene performance, entertainment or representation in a theatre.

Mailing obscene matter

168. Every one commits an offence who makes use of the mails for the purpose of transmitting or delivering anything that is obscene, indecent, immoral or scurrilous, but this section does not apply to a person who makes use of the mails for the purpose of transmitting or delivering anything mentioned in subsection 166(4).

Punishment

165. Every one who commits an offence under section 163, 165, 166, 167 or 168 is guilty of

(*a*) an indictable offence and is liable to imprisonment for two years, or

(*b*) an offence punishable on summary conviction.

4.4.2 Law Reform Commission of Canada, *Limits of Criminal Law; Obscenity: A Test Case* (Ottawa: Information Canada, 1975) (Working Paper, 10) pp. 39-49

...In practical terms, however, how far does it make sense to use the criminal law against any act causing harm or running counter to our values? Take for example our test case of obscenity. How far should we use criminal law against obscenity? Even if obscenity offends, results in harm and threatens some of our values, do we really need to bring in the whole machinery of the criminal law?

The use of criminal law, we pointed out, imposes a cost. The convicted offender who is punished and the citizen who is forbidden to do the act prohibited both suffer a cost. One cost is a reduction of their freedom. Of course if the act in question is quite obviously a serious wrong, like murder, we are not worried by this loss of liberty. With Justice Holmes we reply: "your freedom to shake your fist ends where my chin begins". On the other hand, the less serious the act, the more concern for freedom — one reason among others why acts in no way wrong shouldn't be prohibited by criminal law and perhaps why even some immoral acts aren't in fact prohibited by it.

After all, in Canada as in many countries, an act can be wrong without being criminal. Here attention always focusses on fornication, homosexuality and lesbianism. But these are poor examples. We don't all agree that such things are wrong. Besides we can find much better examples of non-criminal wrongful acts. Two spring to mind: *lying and breaking promises*.

To tell a serious lie is clearly wrong. By this we mean a serious lie where there are no justifying or excusing circumstances. It is wrong because it militates against the truth-telling value, a value which we saw was necessary to society. Why hasn't lying, then, been made a crime? It has been, but only in certain circumstances: (1) Where the lie amounts to fraud and (2) where it amounts to perjury. Short of cases where there is a danger of pecuniary loss or miscarriage of justice, liars are left to the informal sanctions of social intercourse.

The same with breaking promises. Again, breaking one's promise is clearly wrong. And here again by this we mean breaking a serious promise where there are no justifying or excusing factors. It is wrong because it militates against the highly useful social practice of promising. All the same, it hasn't generally been made a crime. At most the promise-breaker, may be liable for breach of contract. And where he isn't even liable in contract, he too is left to the more informal sanctions of society.

One reason for not invoking criminal law in both these cases is the loss of liberty involved. This might well be too high a price to pay. All the more so, because of two extra factors. One is that lies and breaking promises range from very serious conduct down to relatively trivial behaviour and we wouldn't want every item of such trivial behaviour to set in motion the whole panoply of police, prosecutors, courts and prison officers. The other factor is that criminal law isn't the only way of bolstering truth and promising — there are other informal and possibly more effective social sanctions in reserve.

Another reason for not involving criminal law in such matters is the financial cost. We simply can't afford to take the criminal justice sledgehammer to every nut. Criminal law is a blunt and costly instrument best reserved for large targets — for targets constituting "clear and present danger" — which justify the monetary expense involved. Prosecute every simple lie or breach of promise and the game isn't worth the candle. How does this apply to obscenity?

Is it worth using criminal law against obscenity? Quite obviously obscenity itself won't ever be as significant a target for the criminal law as murder, say, or rape or robbery. Equally obviously, however, it isn't utterly without significance. Public obscenity clearly has significance — it annoys, disgusts, offends. As such it merits just as much and just as little place within the criminal law as other species of nuisance. Loud noises, nauseating smells and so on aren't anything like as serious as murder. But still they do make life less tolerable and so we use the criminal law against them to a limited degree. Society thinks the cost is worth it. So may it be with public, or involuntary, obscenity.

But what about private, or voluntary, obscenity? "A problem left to itself", said the playwright N. F. Simpson, "dries up or goes wrong. Fertilize it with a solution and you'll hatch dozens". What problems might we hatch by trying to fertilize voluntary obscenity with a criminal law solution?

First, in order to prevent a person's private voluntary enjoyment of obscenity, we should be calling in law enforcement agents to invade his privacy and freedom. By this we should ourselves be contravening some of those very values which we are trying to protect by preventing obscenity. In order to foster freedom, privacy and human dignity, we should in fact be invading the offender's own privacy, dignity, and freedom — his freedom of speech, of expression and of living his life in his own way, as well as his freedom to be secure in his own home from the interventions of the authorities.

Of course there's nothing self-contradictory about this. It could be argued that the threat obscenity poses to these values and to the value regarding violence is such as to justify this invasion. Some indeed will say that the danger that voluntary consumption of obscenity will lead to Manson murders is sufficient justification. But is it? How clear and obvious is the danger? Obvious enough for us to want to deal with it by risking another danger — the danger of all our homes being open to entry, search and seizure on mere suspicion of obscenity? Obvious enough for us to want to divert law enforcement resources on to this potential harm and away from actual harms such as murder, rape and robbery? Is that the sort of society we want?

The art of politics, however, — and law is ultimately a branch of politics — is the art of the possible, the art of the practical. And is it really practical to use the criminal law against voluntary obscenity simply on account of the conflict between obscenity and our taboo on violence? Not that there may not be other and better reasons for using the law against voluntary obscenity. After all, mightn't it be in the voluntary consumer's own best interest to use the law against him? Mightn't we be justified in using the law to protect him from himself?

But is it ever right to save a person from himself? Of course it is. A person might harm himself through ignorance, error or mistake: to stop him drinking something which, unknown to him, is poison is obviously justifiable — he would want us to. Or again, a person might harm himself through weakness of will or loss of selfcontrol: to stop him drinking himself blind on wood alcohol is clearly justifiable — he'd surely thank us afterwards. In both these cases the person we protect against himself will in general — though not at the moment of being protected — put his long-term welfare before his short-term preference.

But what if he prefers a moment of bliss to a lifetime's welfare? Of course he might not fully appreciate what is involved: he may have got his priorities wrong just now, but later come to see things as we do. But suppose, despite maturity, he just orders his priorities a different way. Suppose he really sets more store on a moment's ecstacy than on a long and healthy life. He's merely out of step with us, that's all. "If a man doesn't keep pace with his companions", said Thoreau, "perhaps it is because he hears a different drummer: let him step to the music which he hears, however measured or far away". Different people, different preferences. In the ultimate analysis each man must choose his own priorities: no one can choose them for him.

This isn't so with children. Children are a special case. We rightly stop toddlers playing with fire for their own good. Why can't we say the same about obscenity? For even though ultimately people should choose their own priorities and make their own commitments, they need maturity to do so. Children don't yet have this maturity, and exposure to obscenity could possibly prevent them reaching it. Free choice requires protection against influences militating against it: early brain-washing into some creed could rule out a full and free religious commitment later: early exposure to addictive drugs could preclude a freer choice of lifestyle in maturity; and early exposure to obscenity could possibly foreclose a person's options afterwards. So a limited paternalism is not at odds with liberty; in fact it serves to buttress it.

Unlimited paternalism is a different matter. Treating children as children is one thing, treating adults as children quite another. On this point we agree with John Stuart Mill that a man's own good, either physical or moral, is not a sufficient warrant for exercising power over him against his will. With Montesquieu we hold that, "changing people's manners and morals mustn't be done by changing the law".

But may there not still be a reason for using the criminal law against voluntary obscenity? May it not be justifiable in order to prevent overall decline in values?

As we saw earlier, it isn't impossible that widespread obscenity could cause decline in general values. This helps to make it justifiable to use the law to prohibit involuntary public obscenity and exposure of children to obscenity. Would it also make it justifiable to go further and outlaw private, voluntary, obscenity?

This brings us back to the notion of shared values and morality as the cement that binds society together. So important are these values that they have to be protected. Indeed Devlin once suggested that acts contravening and therefore threatening such values are acts akin to treason.

At the root of the analogy is the claim that a society is entitled to protect itself against change and dissolution. Yet is a society entitled to use the criminal law to resist change? If it's entitled to use it to combat treason, why shouldn't it be similarly entitled to use it to combat change due to declining values?

But why is society entitled to use the force of criminal law against treason? A paradigm case of treason is the use of force to overthrow the government or constitution. Why is this a crime? After all the new government or constitution might be an improvement. Even in Canada the constitution can't be perfect, otherwise why hold conferences to try and alter it? On the other hand, the new one might be worse. Or lots of people might consider it worse. And they of course would never have been consulted.

There is an obvious moral difference, then, between forcibly changing the government or constitution and doing this by peaceful means — by persuading society itself to change its institutions. Violent attack on these institutions, then, is rightly a crime, while non-violent attempts to bring about political changes are not. "Like may be repelled with like", says common law principle. Violent attacks can justifiably be met with force — the force of the criminal law. Non-violent advocacy of change can justifiably be met only with counter-argument in favour of the status quo. Society can justifiably use the criminal law to stop itself *being changed* but not to stop itself *changing*.

What light does this throw on society's right to use the criminal law to stop decline in moral values? If obscenity brings about decline by changing moral values, are society and its values simply changing or are they being changed? In one sense neither, in another both. Our moral values aren't being changed by force — indeed it is hard to imagine how they could be. And yet we're not just being asked to change them. Public obscenity, after all, tramples on values many hold and forces us, unless we yield our right to frequent public places, to see and become used to seeing obscenity; and this may lessen our sensitivity and may undermine our present values. To this extent society is entitled to use the criminal law against obscenity. But if the spectator has an option and consumes it willingly, society has less right to use the criminal law, for here the victim of obscenity is changing his values himself — another aspect of the argument that adults should be free to choose obscenity if they want.

But what if their voluntary consumption of obscenity weakens the values of society as a whole? Now is society entitled to use the criminal law against this risk? It depends how great the risk is to essential values. Suppose we could prove indubitably that individual consumption of pornography would thoroughly undermine the principle against violence. In that event it would be time to use the criminal law against such individual consumption. But that time hasn't arrived. The threat to the anti-violence principle — and we don't deny that there may be one — is uncertain, hard to assess and still a matter for speculation. A wholly clear and present danger hasn't been proved.

A further objection to using the criminal law against private consumption of obscenity by adults is the risk of increasing its profitability. Forbidden fruit, if not sweeter, is always dearer. Illegalising it adds an extra cost. It could be that those with most to lose from the legalising of obscenity may be the dealers who supply it. Certainly there is some evidence of this from Denmark.

Lastly, one final snag. Use criminal law against obscenity and perhaps we obscure the real problem. To take an analogy, our criminal law has concerned itself with non-medical use of drugs, but may not the real problem be the overall use of drugs in the modern "chemical" society? So with obscenity. The law concerns itself with "undue exploitation of sex", but may not the real problem be something else — our society's reluctance to be open and direct in dealing with sexual matters? Sex is a basic human drive but also something calling for maturity.

Obscenity, however, is immaturity. Obscenity is at odds with personal growth. At best, as in a dirty joke or filthy postcard, it is, as Orwell pointed out, a sort of mental rebellion against a conspiracy to pretend that human nature has no baser side. At worse, it is, as D. H. Lawrence said, an attempt "to insult sex, to do dirt on sex". Neither obscenity nor the law relating to it helps towards a maturer view of sex.

...So should obscenity be against the criminal law? In our view, yes, and no. Public obscenity — like other nuisances that give offence — can rightly be the subject of the criminal law. Private obscenity — which causes little, if any, harm and which doesn't threaten significantly — on the whole cannot. That's not to say that it can't be the subject of other types of law.

Criminal law, after all, is only one weapon in the arsenal of the law. Others are administrative regulation, customs laws, planning laws and finally tax laws. What may and what may not be published might best be dealt with by administrative control

— a technique that is particularly appropriate perhaps to television and radio. Again, in so far as the pornography industry isn't homegrown, customs regulation is an obvious method of dealing with the problem. Or, if we accept that some obscenity is here to stay, mightn't a sensible approach be to use city planning to mark out certain areas for obscenity and to keep the rest obscenity-free? Or finally, if obscenity, like alcohol, is going to be always with us, why not use our tax laws to do two things — to siphon off some of the excess profit from the industry and at the same time to apply a measure of discouragement to the trade?

These questions, however, are outside the scope of this Working Paper. How far our objectives are best achieved by criminal or civil law techniques, how far criminal law enforcement against obscenity should allow for local varying standards, how far the present legal definition of obscenity should remain or be replaced by something else and where precisely the line between public and private should be drawn — all these are matters calling for more detailed legal and empirical research than is called for by this inquiry which, though focussing on obscenity, does so primarily as a test case to illuminate the general question of the proper scope and ambit of the criminal law. Such an inquiry rather serves to indicate the proper goals or objectives of criminal law in connexion with the specific problem of obscenity, and so to indicate in general the reaches and the limits of the criminal law.

What, therefore, are our justified objectives with obscenity? As we have said public obscenity can rightly be a crime. Public obscenity then should remain an offence. In practical terms this means continued prohibition against lurid posters, advertisements, magazines and so on being shown in public. It also means restricting what can be broadcast and televised.

Private obscenity too can rightly be a crime, as we have said, when it comes to children. In practice this means that things like the Ottawa peep-show discussed earlier remain against the law. It doesn't mean of course that children won't ever get obscenity. They will — just as they get cigarettes and alcohol and other things we try to guard them from. But retaining the criminal law may still have effect. In effect it will serve at least to keep obscenity out of the classroom and restrict it to the playground — and this can have two results: it may help to limit the amount of obscenity that children are exposed to, and it will give underlining support to the general view that obscenity is not for public consumption.

Apart from this, however, private obscenity in our view should no longer be a crime. In this context the criminal law can't properly be used either to save the individual or society from itself. Individuals should be free to choose their own life-style and society should be free to change. In practical terms this would mean considerable change. It would mean decriminalizing much obscenity. In detail it would mean that pornography stores, pictures and so on carefully restricted to "adults only" would be allowed.

On the other hand decriminalizing — "legalizing", as it is sometimes called — would not imply condoning. Chamfort spoke truly when he said: "It is easier to make things legal than legitimate". In any case, voluntary consumption of obscenity could still be wrong in the civil law: contracts, for instance, to put on obscene displays for private consumption could still be contrary to public policy and so illegal. Besides, voluntary obscenity could still be dealt with, and surely better dealt with, by less formal sanctions, which after all are cheaper, and not only in monetary terms. The formal sanctions of the criminal law are in many ways too expensive.

In short, we must always bear in mind the price we pay for using criminal law. That price — in terms of suffering, loss of liberty and financial cost — sets limits to the proper use of criminal law. Acts of violence, acts of terror and acts causing serious distress can justifiably fall within that law. So too, occasionally, can obscenity when it gives serious offence and causes real annoyance by threatening fundamental values. This after all is what the criminal law is for — dealing with acts that threaten or infringe essential or important values.

Restrict the criminal law to these kinds of acts and we may hope that even in a world where we get nothing for nothing, at least we won't get nothing for our penny too.

4.4.3 Ian A. Hunter, "Obscenity, Pornography and Law Reform", (1975) 2 *Dalhousie Law Journal*, pp. 482-483, 498-504

One of the greatest obstacles to discussion of obscenity and pornography is definitional imprecision: people seldom agree on what the terms mean. If one cannot define what it is one is talking about, it is difficult to know what, if anything, should be done about it. Throughout this paper, I distinguish between obscenity and pornography. My working distinction is this: obscenity is material depicting, however explicitly, sexual activities between adult consenting human beings. Pornography is material whose principal theme is sexual activity between other than consenting adults: primarily depicting violence, bondage or torture of unwilling victims for sexual gratification; or sexual activity involving other than consenting adults (necrophilia, sexual activity with children, bestiality, etc.). The distinction is based on the type of sexual activity depicted. This is a distinction, not a definition. Even as a distinction, it has conceptual flaws. It is not always capable of exact application. But it has one saving virtue: it classifies questionable material into two categories in rought accord with actual practice in the trade. By and large, only obscenity (as distinguished above) is available over-the-counter even in "adults only" bookstores in Canada. Pornography is available under-the-counter or by mail importation. The practical utility of a definition or distinction is as important as its conceptual clarity. Professor Samek has pointed out that the search for a satisfactory definition of obscenity is futile: it has led to "...a wild goose chase after the true essence of the concept. 'What is (the essence of) obscenity?' does not lend itself to a true or false answer any more than the question 'What is (the essence of) time?' Legal concepts do not have one true essence which can be found..." The introduction to the Fox study paper illustrates our present definitional confusion and validates Samek's observation. Rather than the multiplication of equally vague synonyms (which is what happens when people set out to define obscenity) I have chosen to adopt a working distinction which when applied to questionable material yields the same rough and ready classification which the trade itself follows. The distinction works and that is its value. In part its application must remain intuitive, but this is probably inevitable in dealing with obscenity. In *Jacobellis* v. *Ohio* Stewart J. held that criminal prohibitions apply only to "hard-core pornography" and continued: "I shall not today attempt further to define the kinds of material I understand to be embraced within that shorthand description; and perhaps I could never succeed in intelligibly doing so. But I know it when I see it."...

4. Law Reform: A Proposal

Whatever the offensive characteristics of pornography, the central question is: Ought the criminal law to concern itself with censorship? Is the social cost worth it? And if so, how best can it be done?

Pornography is, I submit, utterly without redeeming social value; it is offensive and potentially dangerous and ought to be prohibited. But that is easier said than done. Most pornography available in Canada is imported by mail either by the recipient himself, or by an adult bookstore for "under the counter" retail. To be effective, criminal prohibitions would require a more consistent pattern of enforcement than the present random forays of local morality squads.

Obscenity is of dubious social value and shares, in part, the offensive and dangerous characteristics of pornography. Nevertheless, there are two important differences. Published obscenity usually makes some pretensions, however threadbare, to "serious" art or literature. For example, men's magazines will intersperse articles among their photographs; even pulp novels will attempt to organize the sexual encounters around some meagre plot. Human fallibility and censorships' inherent potential for abuse demand great caution. No civilized person wants to see contemporary authors again hounded by the zealous descendants of Bowdler and Comstock. Censorship of anything with even a tenuous claim to art or literature must be guarded against. Also, obscenity (as I have defined it) limits itself to sexual acts between consenting human beings. As such, it is entitled to greater tolerance than pornography. An ideal criminal law system would reflect these differences between obscenity and pornography.

But, first questions first: should the criminal law be concerned at all? Or is this unjustifiable paternalism? An attempt to save people from themselves? The simplicity of the question unfortunately defies an equally simple answer. I could envision circumstances in which censorship of pornography would be paternalistic. For example, if a majority, or even a substantial minority of Canadians, determined to practise necrophilia, and amuse themselves by looking at books and magazines about it, continuing the criminal prohibition (presently contained in section 178 of the Criminal Code) could be justified only by a kind of moral paternalism. That is, although physically harmless, such conduct was so immoral that, whatever one's inclinations, one ought to be prohibited from engaging in it. In such a society, criminal prohibitions, however well-intentioned, would be ineffective. There is simply no use legislating in the teeth of fundamental community practices. It could be argued that a society given over to necrophilia would not deserve saving. But in any event, law could not save it. What Justice Learned Hand wrote about the spirit of liberty applies also to the spirit of public morality: "...it lies in the hearts of men and women; when it dies there, no constitution, no law, no court can save it; no constitution, no law, no court can even do much to help it, and while it is alive it needs no constitution, no law, no court to save it." But it seems highly unlikely that we have reached this stage with pornography. And, however objectionable to some, paternalism in the criminal law is here to stay. Objections to criminal prohibitions on pornography as paternalistic deserve the same credence as objections to criminal prohibitions on polygamy. Indeed, the latter have more cogency, Polygamy may accord with genuinely held religious beliefs, and criminal prohibitions may effectively require believers to choose between conformity to law or conformity to religious precepts. So far as I am aware, no group has yet made a sacrament of pornography.

Obscenity is a different matter. Playboy magazine and its imitators circulate freely and without undue public protest. Any supermarket bookrack will today contain paperbacks exploiting sex in ways that even Fanny Hill's vivid imagination did not conceive. Society has tacitly condoned obscenity. The courts have attempted to set limits to it. Outright prohibitions on obscenity might be regarded as unduly paternalistic.

There are four primary objectives which any reform of obscenity law should strive to achieve. First, the law should distinguish between obscenity and pornography. Second, people should not be exposed involuntarily to either. Third, some more adequate method of gauging "contemporary community standards" must be sought. Finally, the social cost of enforcement ought not to be disproportionate to the benefits expected.

I suggest a new obscenity section of the Criminal Code making it an offence to make, print, publish, distribute, sell, or circulate for profit any "offensive publication". "Offensive publication" would be defined in two subsections as follows (these are, at best, rough definitions requiring greater polishing):

(a) "Obscenity: any publication shall be deemed to be obscene if a jury, properly instructed, finds that its effect, considered as a whole, is to unduly exploit sex."

(b) "Pornography: any publication shall be deemed to be pornographic if a jury, properly instructed, finds that its effect, considered as a whole, is to debase or degrade human beings, or to outrage contemporary standards of decency or humanity currently accepted in the community."

(c) "It is a question of fact for the jury whether a publication is an "offensive publication" within the meaning of this section." The following section of the Code should provide:

"No person shall be convicted of an offence under this section if he establishes that he took sufficient effective precautions to ensure that the availability of any publication found to be obscene was confined to adult persons."

What is proposed, then, is a statutory distinction between obscenity and pornography. Criminal sanctions, including fines, imprisonment, and forfeiture of offending material, would follow upon conviction, after a jury trial, of publishing or distributing pornography. Section 159(3) (i.e. the defence of public good) would theoretically be available to the accused; but it must be exceedingly rare that it would be successful given the proposed definition of pornography.

Obscenity prosecutions, on the other hand, would involve a two-stage jury trial. First, the jury would have to determine whether the publication in question "unduly" exploited sex. The onus of proof would be on the Crown and expert evidence would (as now) be admissible. If the jury found that the publication was "obscene" the second stage would occur. Here the accused has the onus of establishing that he took "...sufficient, effective precautions" to ensure that minors were not exposed to this material. This is a deliberately heavy onus. It seeks to make the person who profits from trading in obscenity the effective insurer against the risks of malfunctioning. Such a scheme could shift the cost of policing from the taxpayer to those who reap profit from obscenity. It provides a great incentive to those in the obscenity business because it gives them criminal immunity so long as they police their operation to ensure that access to obscenity is limited to adults. By requiring that the precautions taken are both "sufficient" and "effective" the scheme requires the jury to see that the accused's policing system is adequate in practice and not just in theory.

This statutory defense and reverse onus of proof partially resolves the problem of involuntary access: i.e. those who object to having obscenity thrust upon them. Obviously, no proprietor who chose to openly display obscenity in his store window to random passers-by could claim to have restricted its availability solely to adults. I doubt that criminal law can go much beyond that. There are, of course, other statutes that deal with obscenity; the *Post Office Act,* in particular, can aid in prohibiting the mailing of unsolicited obscenity. However, further protection against involuntary access must come through the law of nuisance.

There are precedents for a two-stage trial process. The English *Prevention of Crimes Act* of 1908 required the jury to first try the accused on the charge presented then, on conviction, to have a separate trial to determine whether he was an ''habitual criminal'' and deserving of preventive detention. Our own Criminal Code provisions on preventive detention require two separate proceedings, although applications under section 690 are heard without a jury. Another precedent is the English *Sentence of Death (Expectant Mothers) Act* of 1931 which required that on conviction for murder of a woman who alleged to be pregnant, the jury should conduct a second trial, in advance of sentencing, to determine the authenticity of her allegation.

A jury trial is the only honest procedure if we are to continue to pay lip service to judging offensive literature by a ''contemporary community standards'' test. Nothing in the judicial process is as futile or as derisory as a Judge setting for himself the task of deciding whether ''...the exploitation of sex... is undue in the sense that it exceeds that limit of acceptability or tolerance which is to be tested by the contempory Canadian community.'' Apart from the difficulty of finding a consensus in the ''contemporary Canadian community'' on the least controversial of topics (witness any Gallup poll) who could be less qualified than Judges, uniformly drawn as they are from the same background, education and career, to discern it? The farce becomes unsustainable when two judges in the same city, with the same background and training, themselves disagree about whether the work in question violates these perceived standards.

Of course juries may also come to inconsistent conclusions. But the jury is a great deal more representative than a judge, more in touch with community mores, and (no disrespect intended) more likely to be practical and sensible in such matters than a judge. Also, twelve heads are better than one even if the one is legally-trained to determine a question that essentially requires a representative cross-section of normative opinion. Also, the jury ensures that the test of obscenity is local rather than national. At present, the standard applied is supposed to be national although, of course, the actual standard applied (if any) must inevitably be local. An acknowledged local standard is preferable on the merits — after all, why should the literary choices of Torontonians be circumscribed by the residents of Rosewater, Saskatchewan or vice versa — but also as a small contribution to public honesty, and a large contribution to the demythologization of the legal system. To those who mistrust juries (after all, what if a Mississippi jury decided that pictures of blacks and whites together are obscene?) there are several rejoinders, none alone satisfactory, but collectively reassuring. First, (unless I can handpick my judge, which is unfair) I prefer the collective good sense of the jury to that of a single judge. Secondly, the jury's power here is not absolute. It is constrained in three ways: (1) by the ordinary power of a trial judge to refuse to allow a case to go to the jury on the basis that there is no evidence; (2) by the judge's responsibility to sum up the evidence and direct the jury on the law; (3) by the supervisory jurisdiction of appeal courts.

The moral judgments of a society must ultimately be decided by its citizens. But it is not feasible to put every question involving moral judgment to popular referendum so that each citizen has his say. Some decisions are delegated to a representative cross-section of citizenry: the jury. Of course, with the benefit of hindsight, the jury may make wrong or perverse decisions. So may any other person or institution. But wrong decisions are not immutable. They can be changed by new laws. I do not subscribe to Blackstone's view that juries are "the glory of English law". In most civil cases, and many criminal cases, the jury trial is disappearing and good riddance to it. As a method of fact determination, it is poor. The American historian, Carl Becker, has written: "Trial by jury, as a method of determining facts, is antiquated... and inherently absurd — so much so that no lawyer, judge, scholar, prescription-clerk, cook or mechanic in a garage would ever think for a moment of employing that method for determining the facts in any situation that concerned him." But for sensing and applying the shifting moral standards of a community, we have no better alternative.

Obscenity originated with sedition and blasphemy. Over time, it has come to mean "undue exploitation of sex". I suggest that this should no longer be the concern of the criminal law, so long as (a) "legalizing" obscenity does not automatically mean legalizing pornography along with it; and (b) if an effective, inexpensive policing system to guard against corruption of children can be devised. It is submitted that the scheme proposed does this. It also provides a more sensible method of gauging the moral judgments of the community. If adults choose to indulge in obscenity and are somehow "corrupted" by it, they are the authors of their own misfortune. Their "injuries" are self-inflicted, and they, not society, bear responsibility.

4.4.4 Bill C-239. An Act to Amend the Criminal Code. First Reading, 31 October 1977

1. Subsection 159(8) of the *Criminal Code* is repealed and the following substituted therefor:

"(8) In this Act,

"obscene thing" includes any explicit representation or detailed description of a sexual act and any pictorial representation tending to solicit partners for a sexual act;

"sexual act" means

(*a*) masturbation,

(*b*) any act of sado-masochism, and

(*c*) any act of anal, oral or vaginal intercourse;

whether alone or with or upon another person, animal, dead body or inanimate object, and includes an attempted or simulated sexual act."

2. The said Act is further amended by adding thereto, immediately after section 166 thereof, the following new section:

"166.1 (1) Every one commits an offence who photographs, produces, publishes, imports, exports, distributes, sells, advertises or displays in a public place anything that depicts a child performing a sexual act or assuming a sexually suggestive pose while in a state of undress.

(2) Every one who commits an offence under this section is guilty of

(*a*) an indictable offence and is liable to imprisonment for two years, or

(*b*) an offence punishable on summary conviction and is liable to a fine in the discretion of the court.

(3) Every one convicted of an offence under this section is liable to forfeit to the Crown any matter or thing, or part thereof, to which the offence relates.

(4) In this section,
"child" means a person who is or appears to be under the age of sixteen years."

Note: Bill C-239 was withdrawn after first reading and the subject-matter was referred to the Standing Committee on Justice and Legal Affairs.

4.4.5 Standing Committee on Justice and Legal Affairs, "The Third Report to the House (Report on Pornography)," 22 March 1978. pp. 7-10

The present definition of obscenity is vague and imprecise. It has led to confusion and dismay in the minds of the public, retailers, distributors, police officers, Crown prosecutors, defence lawyers, judges, and juries. This uncertainty in the law of obscenity is one of the factors causing the character of the sexually explicit material to change drastically in the past ten years. It has become more widely-disseminated and more easily available throughout the country.

Obscenity must be redefined in the Criminal Code to deal with the current situation. Much of this sexually explicit material depicts, describes, and advocates acts and simulated acts of violence, exploitation, subjugation, and humiliation. It promotes values and behaviour which are unacceptable in a society committed to egalitarian, consensual, mutual and non-violent human relationships. Most troubling of all has been the recent influx and availability of sexually explicit material involving children in suggestive situations either alone or with other children, adults, animals or objects. This kind of material is unacceptable in a civilized society and should be denounced and prohibited. Since the effective enforcement of the obscenity provisions of the Criminal Code is dependent upon a clear definition, it is essential that S.159(8) Cr.C. be amended to make it evident what type of sexually explicit material will not be tolerated in this country.

Recommendation 4: Section 159(8) of the Criminal Code should be amended to define obscenity more clearly and to include sexually explicit material involving children within that definition in the following or similar terms:

"159. (8) For the purposes of this Act, a matter or thing shall be deemed to be obscene where

(*a*) a dominant characteristic of the matter or thing is the undue exploitation of sex, crime, horror, cruelty or violence, or the undue degradation of the human person; or

(*b*) the matter or thing depicts or describes a child

(i) engaged or participating in an act or simulated act of masturbation, sexual intercourse, gross indecency, buggery or bestiality, or

(ii) displaying any portion of its body in a sexually suggestive manner.

159. (9) In this section,
"child" means a person who is or appears to be under the age of sixteen years."

The community standards controversy is one that has raged throughout this country since 1959 when the present definition of obscenity was adopted. Canada is a country whose strength is in its diversity — many values and concerns differ from one place to another. The appreciation and acceptance of sexually explicit materials is no exception to this general principle. One of the most common complaints heard about the present idea of community standards in the case law is that although they may express some vague country-wide level of tolerance or acceptance they are not necessarily reflective of local or regional feeling. Since it appears that real community standards are local in nature, they should be determined by the inhabitants of the region, township, city, town, or village where an obscenity prosecution is undertaken. This is best done by trying obscenity cases before a judge and jury. As was seen earlier, the role of experts in obscenity trials has led to undesirable results, and in our view they should not be permitted to testify in such cases. The purpose of having a jury is to let a representative group of the community itself express the standards of the community as the jurors see and feel them, and the use of expert witnesses is inconsistent with such a purpose.

Recommendation 5: Section 498 of the Criminal Code should be amended to permit the Attorney General to override an accused's option for mode of trial, and request a trial by jury in cases where the prosecution is taken under S.159 in the following or similar terms:

> "498. The Attorney General may, nothwithstanding that an accused elects under sections 464, 484, 491 or 492 to be tried by a judge or magistrate, as the case may be, require the accused to be tried by a court composed of a judge and jury, unless the alleged offence is one that is punishable with imprisonment for less than five years, and where the Attorney General so requires, a judge or magistrate has no jurisdiction to try the accused under this Part and a magistrate shall hold a preliminary inquiry unless a preliminary inquiry has been held prior to the requirement by the Attorney General that the accused be tried by a court composed of a judge and jury."

Recommendation 6: The testimony or evidence of expert witnesses as to community standards should under no circumstances be permitted during the trial of a person who has been charged with a criminal offence under S.159. This should be done by adding Ss.10 to S.159 in the following or similar terms:

> "159. (10) Where an accused is tried for an offence under this section, no opinion evidence is admissible with respect to community standards in order to prove that any matter or thing is or is not obscene, any law or practice to the contrary notwithstanding."

The most unacceptable of the sexually explicit material so easily available is that involving infants and children. Many of these young people are what are commonly called "runaways" who have fled from troubled family situations and who have been enticed into the worlds of prostitution and drug abuse. Their participation in the production of this type of sexually explicit material is frequently incidental to these other parts of their lives. The consequence of the exploitation of children in such ways is often tragic both for these young people themselves and for their families. It is therefore necessary to deal severely with those who procure and entice children and young people for the purposes of prostitution and the production of sexually explicit material.

Recommendation 7: Section 166 of the Criminal Code should be amended to make the procurement of children for the purposes of prostitution or to participate in the production of sexually explicit materials criminal offences punishable by ten years imprisonment in the following or similar terms:

> "166. (1) Every one commits an offence who
>
> (*a*) procures a child to engage in or to assist any person to engage in a sexually explicit act, or
>
> (*b*) orders, is party to, or knowingly receives the avails of the defilement, seduction or prostitution of a child.

(2) Every one who commits an offence under this section is guilty of an indictable offence and is liable to imprisonment for ten years.

(3) In this section,
''child'' means a person who is under the age of sixteen years; and
''sexually explicit act'' includes any act or simulated act of masturbation, sexual intercourse, gross indecency, buggery or bestiality, or the display of any portion of one's body in a sexually suggestive manner.''

The easy accessibility of both acceptable and unacceptable sexually explicit material was vividly brought to the attention of the Committee during its hearing of evidence. This often takes the form of theatrical advertising, as well as book or magazine displays in neighbourhood retail outlets. Many members of the community where this type of material is publicly displayed find it offensive and have expressed the wish to have it controlled. The Committee has been impressed by the evidence presented to it showing the easy availability of sexually explicit material to young people. Where sexually explicit material is available to the adult members of Canadian society, this should be done through the adoption of discreet advertising, display and sales policies. Under no circumstances should such material be made visible or available to those who are not adults.

Recommendation 8: Provincial, regional, municipal and local authorities should adopt the necessary licensing, zoning, and child protection legislation, regulations, and by-laws to ensure that acceptable sexually explicit material is advertised, displayed, and sold discreetly to adults and under no circumstances to children or young people.

4.4.6 Bill C-19 An Act to Amend the Criminal Code, ss.159(8), 163.1

In 1984 a Criminal Reform Bill was introduced in Parliament. This Bill would have replaced s.159(8) of the Criminal Code with the following:

> ''(8) For the purposes of this Act, any matter or thing is obscene where a dominant characteristic of the matter or thing is the undue exploitation of any one or more of the following subjects, namely, sex, violence, crime, horror or cruelty, through degrading representations of a male or female person or in any other manner.
>
> (9) Where a court convicts a person of an offence under this section, it shall make an order declaring the matter or thing by means of or in relation to which the offence was committed forfeited to Her Majesty in right of the province in which the proceedings took place, for disposal as the Attorney General may direct.''

It would also have added a new s.163.1:

> **''163.1** Where any film or videotape is presented, published or shown in accordance with a classification or rating established for films or videotapes pursuant to the law of the province in which the film or videotape is presented, published or shown, no proceedings shall be instituted under section 159 or 163 in respect of such presentation, publication or showing or in respect of the possession of the film or videotape for any such purpose without the personal consent of the Attorney General.''

4.4.7 Canada, Special Committee on Pornography and Prostitution, *Report* (1985) (Fraser Report)

1. Criminal Code

Recommendation 1

The term ''obscenity'' should no longer be used in the Criminal Code, and the heading ''Offences Tending to Corrupt Morals'' should also be removed.

Recommendation 2

New criminal offences relating to "pornography" should be created, with care being exercised to ensure that the definition of the prohibited conduct, material or thing is very precise.

Recommendation 3

The federal government should give immediate consideration to studying carefully the introduction of criminal sanctions against the production or sale or distribution of material containing representations of violence without sex.

Recommendation 4

There should be no sanctions introduced respecting material that is 'disgusting' even though our proposed repeal of section 159 would remove the existing offence related to a disgusting object.

Recommendation 5

Controls on pornographic material should be organized on the basis of a three-tier system. The most serious criminal sanctions would apply to material in the first tier, including a visual representation of a person under 18 years of age, participating in explicit sexual conduct, which is defined as any conduct in which vaginal, oral or anal intercourse, bestiality, necrophilia, masturbation, sexually violent behaviour, lewd touching of the breasts or the genital parts of the body, or the lewd exhibition of the genitals is depicted. Also included in tier one is material which advocates, encourages, condones, or presents as normal the sexual abuse of children, and material which was made or produced in such a way that actual physical harm was caused to the person or persons depicted.

Less onerous criminal sanctions would apply to material in the second tier. Defences of artistic merit and educational or scientific purpose would be available. The second tier consists of any matter which depicts or describes sexually violent behaviour, bestiality, incest or necrophilia. Sexually violent behaviour includes sexual assault, and physical harm depicted for the apparent purpose of causing sexual gratification or stimulation to the viewer, including murder, assault or bondage of another person or persons, or self-infliction of physical harm.

Material in the third tier would attract criminal sanctions only when it is displayed to the public without a warning as to its nature or sold or made accessible to people under 18. In tier three is visual pornographic material in which is depicted vaginal, oral, or anal intercourse, masturbation, lewd touching of the breasts or the genital parts of the body or the lewd exhibition of the genitals, but no portrayal of a person under 18 or sexually violent pornography is included.

Recommendation 6

The provinces and the municipalities should play a major role in regulation of the visual pornographic representations that are not prohibited by the Criminal Code through film classification, display by-laws and other similar means. The provinces should not, however, attempt to control such representations by means of prior restraint.

Recommendation 7

Section 159 of the Criminal Code should be repealed, and replaced with the following provision:

PORNOGRAPHY CAUSING PHYSICAL HARM

159(1)(a) Everyone who makes, prints, publishes, distributes, or has in his possession for the purposes of publication or distribution, any visual pornographic material which was made or produced in such a way that actual physical harm was caused to the person or persons depicted, is guilty of an indictable offence and liable to imprisonment for five years.

(b) Everyone who sells, rents, offers to sell or rent, receives for sale or rent or has in his possession for the purpose of sale or rent any visual pornographic material which was made or produced in such a way that actual physical harm was caused to the person or persons depicted is guilty

(i) of an indictable offence and is liable to imprisonment for two years, or

(ii) of an offence punishable on summary conviction and is liable to a fine of not less than $500 and not more than $2,000 or to imprisonment for six months or to both.

(c) ''visual pornographic material'' includes any matter or thing in or on which is depicted vaginal, oral or anal intercourse, sexually violent behaviour, bestiality, incest, necrophilia, masturbation, lewd touching of the breasts or the genital parts of the body, or the lewd exhibition of the genitals.

SEXUALLY VIOLENT AND DEGRADING PORNOGRAPHY

159(2)(a) Everyone who makes, prints, publishes, distributes or has in his possession for the purposes of publication or distribution any matter or thing which depicts or describes:

(i) sexually violent behaviour;
(ii) bestiality;
(iii) incest, or
(iv) necrophilia

is guilty of an indictable offence and liable to imprisonment for five years.

(b) Everyone who sells, rents, offers to sell or rent, receives for sale or has in his possession for the purpose of sale or rent any matter or thing which depicts or describes:

(i) sexually violent behaviour;
(ii) bestiality;
(iii) incest, or
(iv) necrophilia

is guilty

(i) of an indictable offence and is liable to imprisonment for two years, or

(ii) of an offence punishable on summary conviction and is liable to a fine of not less than $500 and not more than $1,000 or to imprisonment for six months or to both.

(c) Everyone who displays any matter or thing which depicts

(i) sexually violent behaviour;
(ii) bestiality;
(iii) incest; or
(iv) necrophilia

in such a way that it is visible to members of the public in a place to which the public has access by right or by express or implied invitation is guilty of

(i) an indictable offence and is liable to imprisonment for two years, or

(ii) an offence punishable on summary conviction and is liable to a fine of not less than $500 and not more than $1000 or to imprisonment for six months or to both.

(d) Nobody shall be convicted of the offence in subsection (2)(a) who can demonstrate that the matter or thing has a genuine educational or scientific purpose.

(e) Nobody shall be convicted of the offence in subsection (2)(b) who can demonstrate that the matter or thing has a genuine educational or scientific purpose, and that he sold, rented, offered to sell or rent or had in his possession for the purpose of sale of rent the matter or thing for a genuine education or scientific purpose.

(f) Nobody shall be convicted of the offences in subsections (2)(a) and (2)(b) who can demonstrate that the matter or thing is or is part of a work of artistic merit.

(g) Nobody shall be convicted of the offence in subsection (2)(c) who can demonstrate that the matter or thing

(i) has a genuine educational or scientific purpose; or

(ii) is or is part of a work of artistic merit,

and

(iii) was displayed in a place or premises or a part of premises to which access is possible only by passing a prominent warning notice advising of the nature of the display therein,

(h) In determining whether a matter or thing is or is not part of a work of artistic merit the court shall consider the impugned material in the context of the whole work of which it is a part in the case of a book, film, video recording or broadcast which presents a discrete story. In the case of a magazine or any other composite or segmented work the court shall consider the impugned material in the context of the specific feature of which it is a part.

DISPLAY OF VISUAL PORNOGRAPHIC MATERIAL

159(3)(a) Everyone who displays visual pornographic material so that it is visible to members of the public in a place to which the public has access by right or by express or implied invitation is guilty of an offence punishable on summary conviction.

(b) No one shall be convicted of an offence under subsection (1) who can demonstrate that the visual pornographic material was displayed in a place or premises or a part of premises to which access is possible only by passing a prominent warning notice advising of the display therein of visual pornographic material.

(c) For purposes of this section "visual pornographic material" includes any matter or thing in or on which is depicted vaginal, oral or anal intercourse, masturbation, lewd touching of the breasts or the genital parts of the body, or the lewd exhibition of the genitals, but does not include any matter or thing prohibited by subsections (1) and (2) of this section.

FORFEITURE OF MATERIAL

159(4) In any proceedings under section 159(1)(a) and (b), 159(2)(a) and (b), and 164, where an accused is found guilty of the offence the court shall order the offending matter or thing or copies thereof forfeited to Her Majesty in the Right of the Province in which proceedings took place, for disposal as the Attorney General may direct.

ABSENCE OF DEFENCE

159(5) It shall not be a defence to a charge under sections 159(1)(a) and 159(2)(a) that the accused was ignorant of the character of matter or thing in respect of which the charge was laid.

DUE DILIGENCE DEFENCE

159(6) Nobody shall be convicted of the offences in sections 159(1)(b) and 159(2)(b) who can demonstrate that he used due diligence to ensure that there were no representations in the matter or thing which he sold, rented, offered for sale or rent, or had in his possession for purposes of sale or rent, which offended the section.

DIRECTORS

159(7) Where an offence under this section committed by a body corporate is proved to have been committed with the consent or connivance of, or to be attributable to any neglect on the part of, any director, manager, secretary or other similar officer of the body corporate, or any person who was purporting to act in any such capacity, he as well as the body corporate shall be guilty of the offence and shall be liable to be proceeded against and punished accordingly.

DEFINITIONS

159(8) For purposes of this section, "sexually violent behaviour" includes
(i) sexual assault,
(ii) physical harm, including murder, assault or bondage of another person or persons, or self-infliction of physical harm, depicted for the apparent purpose of causing sexual gratification to or stimulation of the viewer.

Recommendation 8

Section 160 of the Code, allowing forfeiture proceedings to be brought, as an alternative to a criminal charge, should be retained in the Code but its application should be limited to tier one and tier two material.

Recommendation 9

To clarify the law on this point, section 160 should be amended to make it clear that the onus rests on the Crown under this section to prove beyond a reasonable doubt that the material comes within either tier one or tier two.

Recommendation 10

Section 161 of the Code should be amended as follows:

161. Everyone who refuses to sell or supply to any other person copies of any publication for the reason only that such other person refuses to purchase or acquire from him copies of any other publication that such other person is apprehensive may offend section 159(1) or section 159(2) of the Code is guilty of an indictable offence and is liable to imprisonment for two years.

Recommendation 11

Section 162 of the Code should be repealed.

Recommendation 12

Section 164 of the Code should be repealed and replaced by:

MAILING PORNOGRAPHIC MATERIAL

164(1) Everyone who makes use of the mails for the purpose of transmitting or delivering any matter or thing which:
(a) depicts or describes a person or persons under the age of 18 years engaging in sexual conduct,
(b) advocates, encourages, condones, or presents as normal the sexual abuse of children
is guilty of an indictable offence and liable to imprisonment for ten years.

(2) Everyone who makes use of the mails for the purpose of transmitting or delivering any matter or thing which:
(a) by virtue of its character gives reason to believe that actual physical harm was caused to the person or persons depicted, or
(b) depicts or describes:
(i) sexually violent behaviour,
(ii) bestiality,
(iii) incest, or
(iv) necrophilia
is guilty of an indictable offence and liable to imprisonment for five years.

(3) Everyone who makes use of the mails for the purpose of transmitting or delivering unsolicited visual pornographic material to members of the public is guilty of an offence punishable on summary conviction.

(4) Nobody shall be convicted of the offence in subsection (2)(b) who can demonstrate that the matter or thing mailed

(i) has and is being transmitted or delivered for a genuine educational or scientific purpose, or

(ii) is or is part of a work of artistic merit.

(5) It shall not be a defence to a charge under subsections (1) and (2) of this section that the accused was ignorant of the character of the matter or thing in respect of which the charge was laid.

(6) For purposes of this section ''visual pornographic material'' includes any matter or thing in or on which is depicted vaginal, oral or anal intercourse, masturbation, sexually violent behaviour, incest, bestiality, necrophilia, lewd touching of the breasts or the genital parts of the body, or the lewd exhibition of the genitals.

Recommendation 13

Section 165 of the Criminal Code should be repealed.

Recommendation 14

Section 163 of the code should be repealed and replaced by:

LIVE SHOWS

163(1) Everyone who, being the owner, operator, lessee, or manager, agent or person in charge of a theatre or any other place in which live shows are presented, presents or gives or allows to be presented or given therein a performance which advocates, encourages, condones or presents as normal the sexual abuse of children is guilty of an indictable offence and liable to imprisonment for ten years.

(2) Everyone who, being the owner, operator, lessee, manager, agent or person in charge of a theatre or any other place in which live shows are presented, presents or gives or allows to be presented or given therein a performance which

(a) involves actual physical harm is being caused to a person participating in the performance, or

(b) represents:

(i) sexually violent behaviour;

(ii) bestiality;

(iii) incest; or

(iv) necrophilia

is guilty of an indictable offence and liable to imprisonment for five years.

(3) Everyone who, being the owner, operator, lessee, manager, agent or person in charge of a theatre or any other place in which live shows are presented, presents or gives, or allows to be presented or given therein without appropriate warning a performance in which explicit sexual conduct is depicted

is guilty of an offence punishable on summary conviction.

(4) It shall not be a defence to a charge under subsections (1) and (2) that the accused was ignorant of the character of the production.

(5) Nobody shall be convicted of the offence under subsection (2)(b) who can demonstrate that

(i) the performance is or is part of work of artistic merit; and

(ii) the performance was presented or given in a place or premises or a part of premises to which access is possible only by passing a prominent warning notice advising of the nature of the performance.

(6) For purposes of subsection 3 it shall be sufficient to establish that an appropriate warning was given that the performance was presented or given in a place or premises or a

part of premises to which access is possible only by passing a prominent warning notice advising of the nature of the performance.

(7) For purposes of subsection 3 "explicit sexual conduct" includes vaginal, oral or anal intercourse, masturbation, lewd touching of the breasts or the genital parts of the body, or the lewd exhibition of the genitals.

Recommendation 15

The provinces and the municipalities should play a major role in regulation of live performances involving sexual activity that are not prohibited by the Criminal Code, through licensing, zoning and other similar means.

Recommendation 16

Section 170 of the Criminal Code should be amended to add the following provision:

This section has no application to a theatre or other place licensed to present live shows.

4.4.8 Bill C-114, An Act to Amend the Criminal Code, s.138, 1986

In 1986, Bill C-114 was the result of further amendments made to the legislation concerning obscenity and pornography. The following excerpt from that bill focusses on the attempt to re-define the offence of pornography.

1. Section 138 of the *Criminal Code* is amended by adding thereto, in alphabetical order within the section, the following definitions:

"degrading pornography"

""degrading pornography" means any pornography that shows defecation, urination, ejaculation or expectoration by one person onto another, lactation, menstruation, penetration of a bodily orifice with an object, one person treating himself or another as an animal or object, an act of bondage or any act in which one person attempts to degrade himself or another;

"pornography"

"pornography" means any visual matter showing vaginal, anal or oral intercourse, ejaculation, sexually violent behaviour, bestiality, incest, necrophilia, masturbation or other sexual activity;

"pornography that shows physical harm"

"pornography that shows physical harm" means any pornography that shows a person in the act of causing or attempting to cause actual or simulated permanent or extended impairment of the body of any person or of its functions;

"sexually violent behaviour"

"sexually violent behaviour" includes sexual assault and any behaviour shown for the apparent purpose of causing sexual gratification to or stimulation of the viewer, in which physical pain is inflicted or apparently inflicted on a person by another person or by the person himself."

4.4.9 Bill C-54, An Act to Amend the Criminal Code, ss.1 and 2, 1987

In 1987, Bill C-54 was introduced in Parliament in a further effort to amend Criminal Code legislation dealing with pornography.

1. Section 138 of the *Criminal Code* is amended by adding thereto, in alphabetical order within the section, the following definitions:

"erotica" ""erotica" means any visual matter a dominant characteristic of which is the depiction, in a sexual context or for the purpose of the sexual stimulation of the viewer, of a human sexual organ, a female breast or the human anal region;

"pornography" "pornography" means

(*a*) any visual matter that shows

(i) sexual conduct that is referred to in any of subparagraphs (ii) to (vi) and that involves or is conducted in the presence of a person who is, or is depicted as being or appears to be, under the age of eighteen years, or the exhibition, for a sexual purpose, of a human sexual organ, a female breast or the human anal region of, or in the presence of, a person who is, or is depicted as being or appears to be, under the age of eighteen years,

(ii) a person causing, attempting to cause or appearing to cause, in a sexual context, permanent or extended impairment of the body or bodily functions of that person or any other person,

(iii) sexually violent conduct, including sexual assault and any conduct in which physical pain is inflicted or apparently inflicted on a person by that person or any other person in a sexual context,

(iv) a degrading act in a sexual context, including an act by which one person treats that person or any other person as an animal or object, engages in an act of bondage, penetrates with an object the vagina or the anus of that person or any other person or defecates, urinates or ejaculates onto another person, whether or not the other person appears to be consenting to any such degrading act, or lactation or menstruation in a sexual context,

(v) bestiality, incest or necrophilia, or

(vi) masturbation or ejaculation not referred to in subparagraph (iv), or vaginal, anal or oral intercourse, or

(*b*) any matter or commercial communication that incites, promotes, encourages or advocates any conduct referred to in any of subparagraphs (*a*)(i) to (v);"

1974-75-76, c.48, s.25; 1984, c.41, s.2

2. Sections 159 to 165 of the said Act are repealed and the following substituted therefor:

Dealing in pornography

"159. (1) Every person who deals in pornography is guilty of an offence.

Definition of "deals"

(2) For the purposes of this section, a person deals in pornography if the person imports, makes, prints, publishes, broadcasts, distributes, possesses for the purpose of distribution, sells, rents, offers to sell or rent, receives for sale or rental, possesses for the purpose of sale or rental or displays, in a way that is visible to a member of the public in a public place, the pornography.

Punishment

(3) Every person who commits the offence referred to in subsection (1) with respect to any matter referred to in subparagraph (*a*)(i)

or (ii) of the definition "pornography" in section 138 or any matter or communication referred to in paragraph (*b*) of that definition, if the matter or communication is in relation to conduct referred to in either of those subparagraphs, is guilty of an indictable offence and is liable to imprisonment for a term not exceeding ten years.

Idem

(4) Every person who commits the offence referred to in subsection (1) with respect to any matter referred to in any of subparagraphs (*a*)(iii) to (v) of the definition "pornography" in section 138 or any matter or communication referred to in paragraph (*b*) of that definition, if the matter or communication is in relation to conduct referred to in any of those subparagraphs, is guilty

(*a*) of an indictable offence and is liable to imprisonment for a term not exceeding five years; or

(*b*) of an offence punishable on summary conviction.

Idem

(5) Every person who commits the offence referred to in subsection (1) with respect to any matter referred to in subparagraph (*a*)(vi) of the definition "pornography" in section 138 is guilty

(*a*) of an indictable offence and is liable to imprisonment for a term not exceeding two years; or

(*b*) of an offence punishable on summary conviction.

Defences

159.1 (1) Where an accused is charged with an offence under section 159, other than an offence that is in relation to conduct referred to in subparagraph (*a*)(i) or (ii) of the definition "pornography" in section 138 or any matter or communication referred to in paragraph (*b*) of that definition, if the matter or communication is in relation to conduct referred to in either of those subparagraphs, the court shall find the accused not guilty if the accused establishes, on a balance of probabilities, that the matter or communication in question has artistic merit or an educational, scientific or medical purpose.

Declaration of court

(2) Where a court finds an accused not guilty by reason of the defence of artistic merit set out in subsection (1), the court shall declare that the matter or communication that formed the subject-matter of the alleged offence is not pornography.

Children in pornography

159.2 (1) Every person who

(*a*) uses, induces, incites, coerces or agrees to use a person who is under the age of eighteen years to participate in the production of any matter referred to in subparagraph (*a*)(i) of the definition "pornography" in section 138 or any matter or communication referred to in paragraph (*b*) of that definition and that involves a person referred to in subparagraph (*a*)(i) of that definition, or

(*b*) depicts a person as being under the age of eighteen years in such matter or communication

is guilty of an indictable offence and is liable to imprisonment for a term not exceeding ten years.

Possession

(2) Every person who, knowingly, without lawful justification or excuse, possesses any matter referred to in subparagraph (*a*)(i) of the

> definition "pornography" in section 138 or any matter or communication referred to in paragraph (*b*) of that definition and that involves a person referred to in subparagraph (*a*)(i) of that definition is guilty of an offence punishable on summary conviction.

4.4.10 *Brodie* v. *The Queen,* [1962] (S.C.C.) 681

APPEALS from a judgment of the Court of Queen's Bench, Appeal Side, Province of Quebec, affirming a judgment of Fontaine J. Appeals allowed, Kerwin C.J. and Taschereau, Locke and Fauteux JJ. dissenting.

F. B. Scott, Q.C., and *M. Shacter,* for the appellants.

C. Wagner, André Tessier, Q.C., and *Gabriel Houde, Q.C.*, for the respondents.

THE CHIEF JUSTICE *(dissenting):* — By leave of this Court Brodie, Dansky and Rubin appeal from judgments of the Court of Queen's Bench of the Province of Quebec[1] dismissing their appeals from judgments of the Court of Sessions of the Peace for the District of Montreal declaring a certain book "Lady Chatterley's Lover", by D. H. Lawrence, to be obscene and forfeited to Her Majesty in accordance with the provisions of s.150A of the *Criminal Code* of Canada. The three appeals raise the same question and it is sufficient to deal with the case of Brodie.

Section 150 of the *Criminal Code* including subs. 8 which was enacted July 18, 1959, by 7-8 Eliz. II, c.41, and s.150A of the Code enacted at the same time by the same chapter read as follows:

150. (1) Every one commits an offence who

(*a*) makes, prints, publishes, distributes, circulates, or has in his possession for the purpose of publication, distribution or circulation any obscene written matter, picture, model, phonograph record or other thing whatsoever, or

(*b*) makes, prints, publishes, distributes, sells or has in his possession for the purpose of publication, distribution or circulation, a crime comic.

(2) Every one commits an offence who knowingly, without lawful justification or excuse,

(*a*) sells, exposes to public view or has in his possession for such a purpose any obscene written matter, picture, model, phonograph record or other thing whatsoever,

(*b*) publicly exhibits a disgusting object or an indecent show,

(*c*) offers to sell, advertises, publishes an advertisement of, or has for sale or disposal any means, instructions, medicine, drug or article intended or represented as a method of preventing conception or causing abortion or miscarriage, or

(*d*) advertises or publishes an advertisement of any means, instructions, medicine, drug or article intended or represented as a method for restoring sexual virility or curing venereal diseases or diseases of the generative organs.

[1] [1961] Que. Q.B. 610, 36 C.R. 200.

(3) No person shall be convicted of an offence under this section if he establishes that the public good was served by the acts that are alleged to constitute the offence and that the acts alleged did not extend beyond what served the public good.

(4) For the purposes of this section it is a question of law whether an act served the public good and whether there is evidence that the act alleged went beyond what

served the public good, but it is a question of fact whether the acts did or did not extend beyond what served the public good.

(5) For the purposes of this section the motives of an accused are irrelevant.

(6) Where an accused is charged with an offence under subsection (1) the fact that the accused was ignorant of the nature or presence of the matter, picture, model, phonograph record, crime comic or other thing by means of or in relation to which the offence was committed is not a defence to the charge.

(7) In this section, ''crime comic'' means a magazine, periodical or book that exclusively or substantially comprises matter depicting pictorially

(*a*) the commission of crimes, real or fictitious, or

(*b*) events connected with the commission of crimes, real or fictitious, whether occurring before or after the commission of the crime.

(8) For the purposes of this Act, any publication a dominant characteristic of which is the undue exploitation of sex, or of sex and any one or more of the following subjects, namely, crime, horror, cruelty and violence, shall be deemed to be obscene.

150A. (1) A judge who is satisfied by information upon oath that there are reasonable grounds for believing that any publication, copies of which are kept for sale or distribution in premises within the jurisdiction of the court, is obscene or a crime comic, shall issue a warrant under his hand authorizing seizure of the copies.

(2) Within seven days of the issue of the warrant, the judge shall issue a summons to the occupier of the premises requiring him to appear before the court and show cause why the matter seized should not be forfeited to Her Majesty.

(3) The owner and the author of the matter seized and alleged to be obscene or a crime comic may appear and be represented in the proceedings in order to oppose the making of an order for the forfeiture of the said matter.

(4) If the court is satisfied that the publication is obscene or a crime comic, it shall make an order declaring the matter forfeited to Her Majesty in right of the province in which the proceedings take place, for disposal as the Attorney General may direct.

(5) If the court is not satisfied that the publication is obscene or a crime comic, it shall order that the matter be restored to the person from whom it was seized forthwith after the time for final appeal has expired.

(6) An appeal lies from an order made under subsection (4) or (5) by any person who appeared in the proceedings

(*a*) on any ground of appeal that involves a question of law alone,

(*b*) on any ground of appeal that involves a question of fact alone, or

(*c*) on any ground of appeal that involves a question of mixed law and fact,

as if it were an appeal against conviction or against a judgment or verdict of acquittal, as the case may be, on a question of law alone under Part XVIII and sections 581 to 601 apply *mutatis mutandis*.

(7) Where an order has been made under this section by a judge in a province with respect to one or more copies of a publication, no proceedings shall be instituted or continued in that province under section 150 with respect to those or other copies of the same publication without the consent of the Attorney General.

(8) In this section,

(*a*) "court" means a county or district court or, in the Province of Quebec

(i) the court of the sessions of the peace, or

(ii) where an application has been made to a district magistrate for a warrant under subsection (1), that district magistrate,

(*b*) "crime comic" has the same meaning as it has in section 150, and

(*c*) "judge" means a judge of a court or, in the Province of Quebec, a district magistrate.

It was under the provisions of s.150A that an information was laid and a summons issued to Brodie as the occupant of premises within the jurisdiction of the Court of the Sessions of the Peace. A copy of the book seized was put in evidence. Under reserve by the judge of counsel's right so to do, witnesses were called on behalf of Brodie and were cross-examined to some extent. It has been contended on behalf of the appellant that having cross-examined the witnesses the Crown cannot now be heard to say that their evidence was inadmissible. There is a good deal to be said for this argument but it is unnecessary to deal with the point because, in my view, by subs. 8 of s.150 Parliament has prescribed that an objective test be applied. Before the enactment of subs. 8 the rule laid down by Chief Justice Cockburn in *R. v. Hicklin* had been applied in England and in various Courts in Canada. This was to the effect that the test of obscenity was whether the tendency of the matter charged is "to deprave and corrupt those whose minds are open to such immoral influences, and into whose hands a publication of this sort may fall". I agree with counsel for the appellant that this is not the rule to be followed in applying the amendment and that the judge of first instance was in error in so doing. It was argued that notwithstanding statements of intention to the contrary the judges in the Court of Queen's Bench applied the *Hicklin* rule. I am unable so to read their reasons, but, in any event, I desire to make it clear that I do not apply it.

So far as relevant to this appeal, under subs. 8 of s.150 of the Code, a publication is to be deemed obscene if (a) a dominant characteristic of the publication is (b) the undue exploitation (c) of sex. The witnesses called on behalf of the appellant and some, if not all, of the judgments in Courts in England and the United States, put in by his counsel, claim that the dominant characteristic of the book is to show the evils of industrialism in England and the damage it does to the human soul. A careful reading of the book satisfies me that this is not so. This view is based not merely on the comparatively short space allotted to any such thing as compared with that taken up with sex, but on a comprehensive view of the publication. Another matter relied on is the alleged preeminence of "blood knowledge" over "mind knowledge" in the lives of human beings. These terms were invented by Lawrence, it is said, to show that the animal state of man's nature should be in better balance with mind knowledge.

The use of "four-letter words" by itself might or might not make a book one in which sex was exploited unduly so as to make that feature a dominant characteristic, but they cannot be treated in isolation from the scenes depicted in which they are used. The witnesses called on behalf of the appellant have not succeeded in showing that this is a work of art in which there is no undue exploitation of sex and that that is not the dominant characteristic of the book. I pay no attention to the price charged for the book but it is not without significance that on the cover above the title "Lady Chatterley's Lover — D. H. Lawrence" appears: "Complete Unexpurgated Authentic Authorized Edition" and that below the title appears the following: "'This Signet

Edition is the only complete unexpurgated version of LADY CHATTERLEY'S LOVER authorized by the estate of Frieda Lawrence for United States publication''... By themselves these matters might appear insignificant but notwithstanding the protestations of the representative of the publishers they lend weight to the conclusion arrived at.

By reason of war wounds, the husband of Lady Chatterley was rendered impotent and, in order, as in substance the author puts it, that the wife should not be frustrated, she approached Mellors, her husband's gamekeeper, who was separated from his wife. In fact, she led him to the relationship that is afterwards set out in such great detail. There is not merely a description of one episode only, but of several, and it is sufficient to state that all of them are set forth in great detail that might have been expected in the Greece and Rome of ancient times.

The evidence for the defence was competent in order to give the opinion of the witnesses as to the merits of the book as a work of art, but in some parts it is made clear that opinions may differ. That would entail a comparison of any evidence that might be adduced in any particular instance and even then the answers on the point would not determine whether a dominant characteristic of the publication was the undue exploitation of sex. That would still have to be determined by the tribunals before which the matter came and in the present case the answers must be in the affirmative.

The appeals should be dismissed.

TASCHEREAU J. *(dissenting)* — ...

The question which is to be solved is the following: Do we find that there is in this publication a *dominant characteristic* which is the *undue exploitation of sex?* If so, the book is *deemed to be obscene*. I find it unnecessary to determine whether s.150(8) is exhaustive or not. It is sufficient, I think, to say that if we find in the book a dominant characteristic which is the undue exploitation of sex, it must be banned. The law says *a* dominant and not *the* dominant characteristic. Moreover I believe that, without deciding as to its legality or illegality, too much weight has been attached to the expert evidence which has been adduced. The lawful or unlawful circulation of a book cannot be conditioned by the subjective tastes or propensities of witnesses, whatever may be their literary aptitudes. A more objective legal aspect of the question has to be considered.

This book is the story of an upper class Englishman who came back paralyzed from the first world war. He operated his coal mines and occasionally wrote novels particularly noteworthy for their mediocrity. His wife, Constance, is dissatisfied and frustrated. After having refused the suggestion of her husband to have a child with one of his friends, which he would recognize as his own, she meets Mellors, the game keeper, who, in Lawrence's mind, is the archetype of the ''natural man''. He is an offspring of the labour class and is quite intellectually independent. Constance and Mellors then start an intimate relationship, and when she becomes pregnant, she decides to divorce Chatterley and marry the game keeper.

The author then minutely describes with unholy satisfaction more than fifteen adulterous scenes in the hen-house, the brush wood of the nearby fields, or the living quarters of the game keeper. Nothing is left even to the most vivid imagination. All the episodes are brutally described, and the conversation between the two lovers is of a low and vulgar character. Words are used that no decent person would dare speak without, in my view, offending the moral sense of anyone who believes in the ordinary standards of decency, self-respect and dignity.

It is said on behalf of the book that there are three principal characteristics which distinguish this novel:

1. That it is an attack on industrialism and its evils in England;
2. The emphasis on "blood knowledge" rather than "mind knowledge";
3. The redeeming power of love when sex is treated as something beautiful and holy.

It has also been argued that this novel is placed in a setting which emphasizes its literary qualities and it is praised as a significant work of a major English novelist. I must say that I believe that this book has been over-glorified. Lawrence may have given many fine contributions to English literature; he may have been stamped as a classic of our modern times, but all the beautiful things that he may have written cannot legalize what the law forbids. He has, of course, a great gift for description, for setting forth in words what is the product of his fertile imagination, but all the art he unfolds does not change the nature of "Lady Chatterley's Lover". I never thought that the frame could make the picture.

Even if, as argued, this book were a work of art, I think that art can co-exist with obscenity and does not exclude it. A nudity is not an obscenity. The great museums of the world are filled with paintings of the human body, and it would be a nonsense to hold the view that Rembrandt, Leonardo de Vinci, Michel-Ange, Raphaël or Renoir have painted obscenities. There is nothing in those masterpieces which is offensive to modesty or decency, or that expresses or suggests lewd thoughts, as "Lady Chatterley's Lover" does.

It is my view, that if any industrial ills have existed or do exist now in England, and that if there are conflicts between capital and labour, the solution of the problem cannot be found in Lawrence's book. The evidence does not reveal the results obtained by the publication of the book, and there is nothing to indicate that this so-called palliative has even momentarily relieved the ills that Lawrence thought affected the British Isles. In order to improve the social conditions in England, if they have to be improved, I have more faith and hope in sound legislation enacted by Parliament, than in the adulterous scenes described by Lawrence in his book.

Whether the emphasis should be placed on "blood knowledge" or "mind knowledge", in order to purify the social atmosphere of England, or whether sex should be treated as something beautiful and holy in order to become the redeeming power of love, are ideologies that may possibly be the guides of future generations. The diffusion of these patriotic ideas, cherished by Lawrence, are surely not forbidden by law. What in my view is objectionable, is not the aim pursued by the author, although I find it an illusory promise of future happiness, but the means employed for the demonstration of his thesis.

He relies on sex and adultery to dissolve the clouds of social evils that he believes are hanging over the skies of England. In doing so, he violates, I think, s.150(8) of the *Criminal Code,* and I am convinced that we must necessarily find in the book "an undue exploitation of sex", which is "*a dominant*" characteristic of the work. "Undue" in the ordinary English language means of course "unreasonable", "unjustifiable". It conveys the idea that what is said goes beyond what is appropriate or necessary to prove the proposition that one endeavours to demonstrate to the public. I know of no one capable of finding words or imagining scenes that could be added to this publication to make it more obscene. Over three-quarters of the book, or 250 pages deal with filthy, obscene descriptions that are offensive to decency, and entirely unnecessary for what we have been told is the purpose of the book. Nobody would seriously think that this novel could be shown on television or that any respectable publisher would make available to the public in a newspaper or a magazine the complete story of "Lady Chatterley's Lover", without shocking the feelings of normal citizens. I am not aware that obscenity is, under the law, the exclusive prerogative of novelists, whatever may be their outstanding talent.

I have no hesitation in reaching the conclusion that the book comes clearly within the ban of the Act, and that the three appeals should be dismissed....

JUDSON J.: — The proceedings against this book, Lady Chatterley's Lover, by D. H. Lawrence, were taken under s.150A of the *Criminal Code* enacted in 1959. A Judge, on an information laid by a police officer, issued a warrant of seizure for copies of the book on certain premises and then issued a summons to the occupiers requiring them to appear before the Court and show cause why the matter seized should not be forfeited to Her Majesty. The owners of the premises appeared at the trial to show cause in the Court of Sessions of the Peace for the District of Montreal. This Court, on June 10, 1960, declared that the publication was obscene and made an order directing the forfeiture of the seized copies in accordance with s.150A, subs. (4), of the Code. This judgment was unanimously affirmed on appeal to the Court of Queen's Bench on April 7, 1961. On May 29, 1961, this Court granted leave to appeal and declared that the leave was granted at large.

In 1959 a new definition of "obscenity" was introduced into the *Criminal Code* of Canada by the enactment of subs. (8) of s.150. This reads:

> For the purposes of this Act, any publication a dominant characteristic of which is the undue exploitation of sex, or of sex and any one or more of the following subjects, namely, crime, horror, cruelty, and violence, shall be deemed to be obscene.

This section is before this Court for the first time. It is enacted for the purposes of the Act not merely for the purposes of the section in which it appears, which is s.150. It applies to proceedings for the seizure of a book under s.150A and, in my opinion, in which I am in agreement with Casey J. in the Court of Queen's Bench, it precludes the application of any other test and specifically the one that had been applied in *R. v. Hicklin,* and followed in *R. v. American News; R. v. National News;* and *R. v. Stroll*. The *Hicklin* test was "whether the tendency of the matter charged as obscenity is to deprave and corrupt those whose minds are open to such immoral influences and into whose hands a publication of this sort may fall." All the jurisprudence under the *Hicklin* definition is rendered obsolete by the enactment of the new and exclusive definition of obscenity contained in subs. (8) of s.150. Under this definition it must be found that all four elements of obscenity are present before there can be a condemnation of the book. There must be a characteristic which is dominant and this dominant characteristic must amount to an exploitation of sex which is undue. If any of these elements is missing, the charge fails.

The matter is, of course, one of great importance. A writer who faces a charge of obscenity is entitled to know by what standard his work is to be judged and what defence, if any, he is called upon to make. Under the *Criminal Code*, as amended in 1959, there is no double standard, that is to say (1) the statutory definition intended to strike down the obvious, and (2), the *Hicklin* test still in the background, although unstated in the Code, for those works that are not within the statutory definition. If there is to be a double standard, it must be expressly set out in the Code and I would disapprove of *R. v. Munster*, where, in sending the case back for a new trial, the Supreme Court of Nova Scotia *in banco* held that there was error when the magistrate directed himself exclusively according to s.158(8) on the ground that the subsection does not purport to be a definition of what is obscene and because matter not included with its provisions may be obscene under the *Hicklin* test.

If a result such as this is to be brought about the legislation must define the two standards of obscenity and tell the Court that the charge is proved if the work offends either standard. I note that this is the way that the New Zealand legislation is framed, *Re Lolita,* and also the Australian legislation, although not so clearly, as considered in *Wavish v. Associated Newspapers Ltd.; MacKay v. Gordon & Gotch (Australasia) Ltd.;* and *Kyte-Powell v. Heinemann Ltd.* Otherwise, why define obscenity for the purposes of the Act, if it is still permissible for the Court to take a definition of the crime formulated 100 years ago and one that has proved to be vague, difficult and unsatisfactory to apply?

In contrast, I think that the new statutory definition does give the Court an opportunity to apply tests which have some certainty of meaning and are capable of objective application and which do not so much depend as before upon the idiosyncrasies and sensitivities of the tribunal of fact, whether judge or jury. We are now concerned with a Canadian statute which is exclusive of all others.

The inquiry then must begin with a search for a dominant characteristic of the book. The book may have other dominant characteristics. It is only necessary to prove that the undue exploitation of sex is a dominant characteristic. Such an inquiry necessarily involves a reading of the whole book with the passages and words to which objection is taken read in the context of the whole book. Of that now there can be no doubt. No reader can find a dominant characteristic on a consideration of isolated passages and isolated words. Under this definition the book now must be taken as a whole. It is not the particular passages and words in a certain context that are before the Court for judgment but the book as a complete work. The question is whether the book as a whole is obscene not whether certain passages and certain words, part of a larger work, are obscene.

A search for a dominant characteristic of the book also involves an inquiry into the purpose of the author. What was he trying to do, actually doing, and intending to do? Had he a serious literary purpose or was his purpose one of base exploitation? There is no doubt that English jurisprudence has rejected under the *Hicklin* test any evidence that the author or others may wish to give of a book's literary or artistic merit as distinct from scientific value. One cannot ascertain a dominant characteristic of a book without an examination of its literary or artistic merit and this, in my opinion, renders admissible the evidence of the author and others on this point. Evidence concerning literary and artistic merit has been excluded in England on the ground of irrelevancy and a supposed rule excluding evidence of opinion on the very fact which is before the Court for decision. Wigmore's opinion is that there never was any basis for such a general rule (3rd ed., s.1921).

The test of the admissibility of this kind of opinion evidence under the present definition in the Code must be whether it is relevant to the determination of a dominant characteristic in the book. I can well understand that some judges and juries might think that such evidence would not help them to a decision and that others might be of the opposite opinion. I would join the second group. I can read and understand but at the same time I recognize that my training and experience have been, not in literature, but in law and I readily acknowledge that the evidence of the witnesses who gave evidence in this case is of real assistance to me in reaching a conclusion.

The evidence in this case is all one way. The Crown rested its case on the mere production of the book. Oral evidence was given by Mr. Hugh MacLennan and Mr. Morley Callaghan on the literary and artistic merit of the book and the position of Lawrence in the world of English literature. A third witness who gave oral evidence was Mr. Harry T. Moore, a teacher and critic. Many reviews were also filed written by outstanding literary critics in the United States. There is real unanimity in their opinions that the book is a true and sincere representation of an aspect of life as it appeared to the author. No objection was taken to the admissibility of this evidence. The Crown asked for two or three adjournments for the purpose of refuting it but produced no such evidence. It was then that objection was taken to its admissibility. Even if objection had been taken at the time of its tender, I would hold that it was admissible for the purposes that I have stated.

Lawrence had certain opinions about the organization of modern industrial society and its effect upon the relations between man and woman. He chose to express these opinions in a work of imagination, written about an adulterous relationship between the wife of an impotent man of property and that man's servant. Whether his choice of medium was a good choice for the preaching of his ideas and whether the ideas themselves were foolish and wrong-headed are matters upon which there may be a difference of opinion. But a theme of adultery, and what to some readers — and there must be many of these — appears to be a stilted assertion that there exists an important connection between the organization of an industrial society and the sexual relations between man and woman, do not, in themselves, give the book a dominant characteristic condemned by the section of the Code.

This novel is a complex piece of writing. It is, in part, but only in part, the story of the development of the relationship between the man and the woman and an outspoken description of their sexual relations. This could be described as a dominant characteristic of the book although such a description could be criticized as an over-simplification. The objectionable characteristic is, of course, to be found in the explicit description and the four letter words. With these qualities, the question is, as I have already stated, whether the book as a whole as a dominant characteristic of undue exploitation of sex.

The phrase "undue exploitation" suggests, at first sight, an element of tautology but I do not think that this is a sound view. There is a difference between a statute which condemns a book a dominant characteristic of which is the exploitation of sex and one which condemns the undue exploitation of the theme. The use of the word "undue" recognizes that some exploitation of the theme is of common occurrence. What I think is aimed at is excessive emphasis on the theme for a base purpose. But I do not think that there is undue exploitation if there is no more emphasis on the theme than is required in the serious treatment of the theme of a novel with honesty and uprightness. That the work under attack is a serious work of fiction is to me beyond question. It has none of the characteristics that are often described in judgments dealing with obscenity — dirt for dirt's sake, the leer of the sensualist, depravity in the mind of an author with an obsession for dirt, pornography, an appeal to a prurient interest, etc. The section recognizes that the serious-minded author must have freedom in the production of a work of genuine artistic and literary merit and the quality of the work, as the witnesses point out and common sense indicates, must have real relevance in determining not only a dominant characteristic but also whether there is undue exploitation. I agree with the submission of counsel for the appellant that measured by the internal necessities of the novel itself, there is no undue exploitation.

Counsel for the appellant also submits that if ''undueness'' is to be measured by the usages of contemporary novelists and writers, then this book cannot be condemned. Mr. Callaghan and Mr. MacLennan both gave evidence on this point, which is really directed to standards of acceptance prevailing in the community. No matter what form of words may be used. I doubt whether any tribunal, whether judge or jury, can get very far in an obscenity case without being influenced, either consciously or unconsciously, by considerations such as these. The only judicial examination of ''undue exploitation'' or ''undue emphasis'' that I have found is in Australia and New Zealand. As I have already stated the New Zealand legislation begins by telling the court what matters are to be taken into consideration in determining whether a publication is indecent. Then four standards are set out, some of which undoubtedly suggest the *Hicklin* test. Finally, the next section says: ''Subject to the provisions of the last preceding section any document or matter which unduly emphasizes matters of sex, horror, crime, cruelty or violence shall be deemed to be indecent within the meaning of this Act.''

The first consideration of ''undue emphasis'' appears in the judgment of Fullagar J. in *R. v. Close*. To me it is very impressive. He said at p. 465:

> There does exist in any community at all times — however the standard may vary from time to time — a general instinctive sense of what is decent and what is indecent, of what is clean and what is dirty, and when the distinction has to be drawn, I do not know that today there is any better tribunal than a jury to draw it.... I am very far from attempting to lay down a model direction, but a judge might perhaps, in the case of a novel, say something like this: ''It would not be true to say that any publication dealing with sexual relations is obscene. The relations of the sexes are, of course, legitimate matters for discussion everywhere.... There are certain standards of decency which prevail in the community, and you are really called upon to try this case because you are regarded as representing, and capable of justly applying, those standards. What is obscene is something which offends against those standards.''

Offence against the standards of the community as a test of ''undueness'' as outlined by Fullagar J. seems to have been accepted in subsequent cases in Australia and New Zealand although it has not been considered by the High Court of Australia. The principle has not escaped criticism as judicial legislation (24 Mod. L.R. 768). I am not satisfied that the criticism is altogether valid. Surely the choice of courses is clear-cut. Either the judge instructs himself or the jury that undueness is to be measured by his or their personal opinion — and even that must be subject to some influence from contemporary standards — or the instruction must be that the tribunal of fact should consciously attempt to apply these standards. Of the two, I think that the second is the better choice.

But no matter whether the question of ''undue exploitation'' is to be measured by the internal necessities of the novel itself or by offence against community standards, my opinion is firm that this novel does not offend. I would allow the appeals and dismiss the charge and direct that the seized copies of the book be returned to their owners.

RITCHIE J.: — The course of these proceedings in the Courts below is set out in the reasons of other members of the Court and the relevant sections of the *Criminal Code* are reproduced in full in the reasons of the Chief Justice so that it would be superfluous for me to reiterate them.

While I agree that this appeal should be disposed of in the manner proposed by my brother Judson, I do not share his opinion that the language of s.150(8) constitutes an exclusive definition of "obscenity" for the purposes of the *Criminal Code* and in spite of the fact that Crown counsel argued the appeal on this basis I find it necessary to express the contrary view.

In finding this publication to be obscene, the learned trial judge did not consider himself to be confined to the test of obscenity provided by s.150(8) and felt free to consider also the standard set by Cockburn C.J. in *R. v. Hicklin* when he said:

> ...the test of obscenity is this, whether the tendency of the matter charged as obscenity is to deprave and corrupt those whose minds are open to such immoral influences, and into whose hands a publication of this sort may fall.

While affirming the decision at trial, Mr. Justice Casey in the Court of Queen's Bench stated himself to be convinced of the soundness of the appellants' argument to the effect that the provisions of s.150(8) exclude all other tests of obscenity formerly used, and, as has been indicated, it was on this basis that the present appeal was argued by counsel for both parties before this Court.

Section 150(8) provides that:

> For the purposes of this Act, any publication a dominant characteristic of which is the undue exploitation of sex, or of sex and any one or more of the following subjects, namely, crime, horror, cruelty and violence, shall be deemed to be obscene.

With the greatest respect for those who hold a different view, I am unable to construe the language of this section as meaning that no publication can be obscene for the purpose of the *Criminal Code* unless it has undue exploitation of sex as a dominant characteristic. On the contrary, I share the opinion expressed by Ilsley C.J. in *R. v. Munster,* when he said of this section at p. 159: "It does not purport to be a definition of 'obscene'. Matter not included in its provisions may be obscene."

The words "shall be deemed" have a variable meaning depending upon the context in which they occur, but although they are employed in more than thirty separate instances in the *Criminal Code* and are used in many other statutes, I have been unable to find any case holding that when it is provided that a given set of circumstances "shall be deemed" for the purposes of the Act in question to fall into a certain category, Parliament is to be taken to have intended to exclude from that category all circumstances which would otherwise have been included in it.

In the *Criminal Code* the expression "shall be deemed" is frequently used to extend the meaning of a word or phrase so that it is to be treated for the purposes of the Act or a section of the Act as connoting matters which would not otherwise necessarily be considered as coming within its ordinary and accepted meaning (e.g., ss.3(2), 5A(4), 38(2), 41(2), 42(3), 269(5), 294(b) and 371(1) and as to the extension of territorial jurisdiction, s.419). In my view, it is in this sense that the expression is used in s.150(8).

Sections 150 and 150A are found in Part IV of the *Criminal Code* which bears the heading *"SEXUAL OFFENCES, PUBLIC MORALS AND DISORDERLY CONDUCT"* and the sub-heading directly preceding s.150 reads *"OFFENCES TENDING TO CORRUPT MORALS"*. These headings afford some indication of the fact that this legislation was initially enacted for the purpose of protecting society against the corruption of public morals by the publication of obscene material, and before the enactment of s.150(8) the *Hicklin* test was widely accepted as the only yardstick by which obscenity was to be measured. But corruption of morals is only one harmful aspect of the publication of obscene material, and the *Hicklin* test leaves out of account publications which are obscene in the sense of being offensive and shocking to the community standards of decency unless they can also be said to have a tendency to deprave and corrupt. Under that test Stable J. in my opinion correctly instructed the jury in *R. v. Martin Secker Warburg, Limited,* when he said:

> The charge is not that the tendency of the book is either to shock or to disgust. That is not a criminal offence. The charge is that the tendency of the book is to corrupt and deprave.

In my opinion the enactment of s.150(8) had the effect of expanding the meaning of "obscene" for the purposes of the *Criminal Code* to include all publications which have undue exploitation of sex as a dominant characteristic whether or not they can be shown to have a tendency to corrupt and deprave and thus of protecting the public against the shocking and disgusting in addition to the depraving and corrupting aspects of obscenity. In my view it is in this sense that the word "undue" is employed in s.150(8) and it carries the meaning of "undue having regard to the existing standards of decency in the community."

I do not think that this Court is bound by, nor would I follow, those authorities which have tended to construe the *Hicklin* definition as meaning that literature available to the community is to be limited by the standard of what is considered to be suitable reading material for adolescents, but I do think that in discharging his duty under s.150A if a judge is satisfied that the publication before him is likely to have a lowering effect on the moral fibre of adolescent boys and girls or of any other significant segment of the community he would be justified in declaring such a publication to be "obscene" even if it did not contain all the ingredients specified in s.150(8). On the other hand, if the judge is satisfied that the publication contains all those ingredients, that is an end of the matter as far as he is concerned and he must make an order "declaring it to be forfeited to Her Majesty in the Right of the Province in which the proceedings take place." (s.150A(4)).

Under s.150A the burden of deciding whether the publication is likely to corrupt a significant segment of the population and the burden of determining what is or what is not "undue" so as to offend community standards is placed upon the judge before whom the publication is brought, and while it is true that his decision in either case must be a subjective one and will of necessity be coloured in some degree by his own predispositions on such questions, this is not a unique position for a judge under our system of law, and under the *Criminal Code* it is he and he alone who must be "satisfied that the publication is obscene...." if it is to be forfeited. It should be remembered, however, that these sections of the *Criminal Code* are enacted for the protection of the public and obscenity is not to be determined by the fact that a publication may offend the prude or excite the frustrated; it must be offensive to community standards or be likely to deprave or corrupt a recognizable segment of the public.

I agree with Mr. Justice Judson that this inquiry necessarily involves the reading and consideration of the publication as a whole and that it is not only relevant but desirable to consider evidence of the opinions of qualified experts as to the artistic and literary qualities of the publication.

Having read the publication which is now before us as a whole and having considered the evidence of the experts called for the defence and the extensive, critical and other material having to do with the book which has been filed, I have little doubt that D. H. Lawrence deliberately selected sex as a dominant characteristic of ''Lady Chatterley's Lover'' and that one of the chief messages which he sought to convey was that there is nothing shameful or dirty about the natural functions of the body and that the ultimate physical fulfilment of love between the sexes is a thing of tenderness and beauty having no aspects of obscenity or pornography. It may be said with justice that the author has, in several isolated passages, employed language and depicted scenes which, standing alone, unduly exploit sex, but the opinion is widely held by men of high literary qualifications that this book as a whole constitutes an outstanding contribution to 20th-century English literature and the passages to which I refer must be regarded as an integral part of the wider theme. Although sex is a dominant characteristic of the book and although there are isolated passages which, when read alone, unduly exploit sex, it does not appear to me to follow that these passages, read as a part of the whole book, have the effect of making the undue exploitation which they contain a dominant characteristic of the publication so as to bring it within the provisions of s.150(8) of the *Criminal Code*. Nor do I think that any significant segment of the population is likely to be depraved or corrupted by reading the book as a whole.

I agree with counsel for the appellant that the defence of the public good is available under s.150A and while we are not required to pass judgment on the literary or artistic qualities of the book or its author, it nevertheless seems to me that any harmful effect which these objectionable passages might have upon those who seek them out for separate reading is counterbalanced by the desirability of preserving intact the work of a writer who, according to the only evidence before us, is regarded as a great artist by teachers, authors and critics whose opinion is entitled to respect.

I would allow these appeals.

[Kerwin, C.J. and Taschereau, Locke and Fauteux, JJ. dissenting; Judson, Ritchie, Abbott and Cartwright, JJ. in the majority].

4.4.11 *R.* v. *Red Hot Video Ltd.* (1985), 45 C.R. (3d) 36 (B.C.C.A.)

18th March 1985. Nemetz C.J.B.C. (Hinkson J.A. concurring): — After a trial before Collins Prov. J. in the Provincial Court at Victoria, Red Hot Video Limited (the appellant) was convicted of three counts of possession for the purpose of distribution of three obscene videotapes, ''Bad Girls'', ''The Filthy Rich'', and ''Candy Stripers'' [[1983] B.C.W.L.D. 1626]. The convictions were appealed to Melvin Co. Ct. J. of the County Court of Vancouver Island, who on 6th March 1984 dismissed the appeal and affirmed the convictions [38 C.R. (3d) 275, [1984] B.C.W.L.D. 1226, [1984] W.C.D. 116, 11 C.C.C. (3d) 389, 10 C.R.R. 377]. The appellant now seeks leave to appeal to this court.

The Criminal Code provides in part:

> 159. (1) Every one commits an offence who
> (*a*) makes, prints, publishes, distributes, circulates, or has in his possession for the purpose of publication, distribution or circulation any obscene written matter, picture, model, phonograph record or other thing whatsoever, or
> (*b*) makes, prints, publishes, distributes, sells or has in his possession for the purpose of publication, distribution or circulation, a crime comic...
> (8) For the purposes of this Act, any publication a dominant characteristic of which is the undue exploitation of sex, or of sex and any one or more of the following subjects, namely, crime, horror, cruelty and violence, shall be deemed to be obscene.

Counsel for the appellant concedes that Parliament is entitled to legislate against obscenity or pornography. He further concedes that all three films are obscene. He acknowledges that "Bad Girls" and "The Filthy Rich" are concerned solely with sex and violence, and that "Candy Stripers" is concerned solely with sex sans violence.

However, it is submitted that:

1. Section 159 is so "vague and overbroad" that it violates the principles of fundamental justice guaranteed by s.7 of the Canadian Charter of Rights and Freedoms, i.e., that "Everyone has the right to life, liberty and security of the person and the right not to be deprived thereof except in accordance with the principles of fundamental justice."

2. Section 159 is not a "reasonable limit" upon freedom of expression within the meaning of s.1 and s.2(*b*):

> 1. The *Canadian Charter of Rights and Freedoms* guarantees the rights and freedoms set out in it subject only to such reasonable limits prescribed by law as can be demonstrably justified in a free and democratic society.
> 2. Everyone has the following fundamental freedoms:...
> (*b*) freedom of thought, belief, opinion and expression, including freedom of the press and other media of communication.

By way of preface, it is to be noted that historically Canadian courts have been disinclined to act as censors of depictions or writings which allegedly are obscene. To the contrary, it is only if it is shown that such writings or depictions are clearly obscene that the courts will act: *R. v. Dom. News & Gifts (1962) Ltd.*, 40 C.R. 109, 42 W.W.R. 65, [1963] 2 C.C.C. 103, reversed [1964] S.C.R. 251, 42 C.R. 209, [1964] 3 C.C.C. 1 (accepting the dissent of Freedman J.A. in its entirety). Eroticism contained in a written or visual artistic matrix is one thing, obscenity is another.

Here, we are not faced with having to determine whether the films before us are obscene. They are conceded to be obscene. For centuries democratic societies have set certain limits to freedom of expression. Libel and slander are two such limitations. Obscenity is also a limitation. As Dickson J.A. (now C.J.C.) said in *R. v. Great West News Ltd.*, 10 C.R.N.S. 42, 72 W.W.R. 354, [1970] 4 C.C.C. 307 at 309 (Man. C.A.):

> ...all organized societies have sought in one manner or another to suppress obscenity. The right of the state to legislate to protect its moral fibre and well-being has long been recognized, with roots deep in history. It is within this frame that the courts and judges must work.

Again, in *R. v. Prairie Schooner News Ltd.* (1970), 75 W.W.R. 585, 12 Cr. L.Q. 462, 1 C.C.C. (2d) 251 at 271 (Man. C.A.), the learned Chief Justice considered the scope of free speech under the old Canadian Bill of Rights and said this in part:

> Freedom of speech is not unfettered either in criminal law or civil law. The *Canadian Bill of Rights* was intended to protect, and does protect, basic freedoms of vital importance to all Canadians. It does not serve as a shield behind which obscene matter may be disseminated without concern for criminal consequences. *The interdiction of the publications which are the subject of the present charges in no way trenches upon the freedom of expression which the Canadian Bill of Rights assures.* [The italics are mine.]

It is my view that these words apply equally to the new Charter of Rights and Freedoms, s.2(*b*) and s.7. If we look at American decisions one must take care to consider the basic difference between their Bill of Rights and our Charter. Section 1 of the Canadian Charter provides that the rights and freedoms set out in the Charter are guaranteed "subject only to such reasonable limits prescribed by law as can be demonstrably justified in a free and democratic society". The American Bill of Rights does not have such a limitation. This Canadian proviso is of paramount importance when one examines American case law for assistance in interpreting our Charter. Even with the lack of such limitation, the Supreme Court of the United States, in considering their First Amendment, has held that "obscenity is not within the area of protected speech or press": *Ginsberg v. New York,* 390 U.S. 629 at 635, 20 L. Ed. 2d 195, 88 S. Ct. 1274, rehearing denied 391 U.S. 971, 20 L. Ed. 2d 887, 88 S. Ct. 2029 (1968), per Brennan J. Also see *New York v. Ferber,* 484 U.S. 747, 73 L. Ed. 2d 1113 at 1120-21, 102 S. Ct. 3348 (1982), where White J. adopted this tenet from *Chaplinsky v. New Hampshire,* 315 U.S. 568 at 571-72, 86 L. Ed. 1031, 62 S. Ct. 766 (1942):

> There are certain well-defined and narrowly limited classes of speech, the prevention and punishment of which have never been thought to raise any Constitutional problem. These include the lewd and obscene... It has been well observed that such utterances are no essential part of any exposition of ideas, and are of such slight social value as a step to truth that any benefit that may be derived from them is clearly outweighed by the social interest and morality...

Accordingly, the first question is whether the definition of obscenity contained in s.159(8) is so "vague and overbroad" that persons of ordinary intelligence are unable to ascertain its meaning and thus have their rights under s.7 of the Charter negated.

I agree with counsel for the appellant that the laws must not be vague. In particular, a criminal statute must delineate with certitude an understandable and ascertainable standard. I turn, therefore, as a guide for the citizen, to examine s.159. Subsection (8) was first enacted in 1959 [by 1959 (Can.), c.41, s.11]. It was considered by the Supreme Court of Canada in *Brodie v. R.; Dansky v. R.; Rubin v. R.*, [1962] S.C.R. 681, 37 C.R. 120, 132 C.C.C. 161, 32 D.L.R. (3d) 507. Speaking of s.159(8) [then s.150(8) of the Criminal Code, 1953-54 (Can.), c.51], Judson J., speaking for himself and Cartwright, Abbott and Martland JJ., said [at p. 702]:

> ...I think that the new statutory definition does give the Court an opportunity to apply tests which have some certainty of meaning and are capable of objective application and which do not so much depend *as before* upon the idiosyncrasies and sensitivities of the tribunal of fact, whether judge or jury. [The italics are mine.]

Of course, "as before" referred to the old *Hicklin* test (*R. v. Hicklin* (1868), L.R. 3 Q.B. 360), which the learned justice considered "vague, difficult and unsatisfactory to apply" [p. 702]. This statement of Judson J. was referred to with approval 16 years later by Laskin C.J.C. and Spence and Dickson JJ. in *Dechow v. R.*, [1978] 1 S.C.R. 951, 40 C.R.N.S. 129, 35 C.C.C. (2d) 22, 76 D.L.R. (3d) 1, 16 N.R. 204.

Mr. Henderson, for the appellant, submits that the vagueness in s.159 lies in the use of the "community standard" test to determine what is obscene under s.159(8). That proviso states that a publication is obscene if a dominant characteristic of it is the "undue exploitation" of sex or sex with other elements stated therein such as violence. The Supreme Court of Canada has held that there is undue exploitation when the accepted standards of tolerance in the contemporary Canadian community have been exceeded: *Brodie v. R.*, supra. First it is argued that the community tolerance standard is such a difficult and elusive concept that it leaves citizens unable to predict with any certainty whether they are partaking in proscribed activity.

I cannot accept this submission. The fact of the matter is that in all the cases cited to us by both counsel the courts found no difficulty in applying the community standards rule. As was pointed out by Dickson J.A. in *R. v. Great West News Ltd.*, supra, at p. 315:

> If any inference can be drawn from *Brodie* it is that the Judge must, in the final analysis, endeavour to apply what he, in the light of his experience, regards as contemporary standards of the Canadian community. In so doing he must be at pains to avoid having his decision simply reflect or project his own notions of what is tolerable.

What, then, are the standards to be considered? These standards were eloquently articulated by Freedman J.A. (as he then was) in *Dom. News,* supra, and I quote him in part [p. 116]:

> Those standards are not set by those of lowest taste or interest. Nor are they set exclusively by those of rigid, austere, conservative, or puritan taste and habit of mind. Something approaching a general average of community thinking and feeling has to be discovered.

He went on to state that the standards must be of the Canadian contemporary community, since the mores of society change.

Having these tenets in mind, what can be said of the films under consideration? Of "Bad Girls" there is nothing that can be said to have it escape the sanction set out in the understandable and certain language of s.159(8), which states that any publication a dominant characteristic of which is the undue exploitation of sex *or of sex and* any one or more of the following subjects, namely, crime, horror, *cruelty and violence,* shall be deemed to be obscene. A reading of Collins Prov. J.'s description leaves me in no doubt whatsoever that "Bad Girls" is wholly destitute of a literary plot, but consists in not only repetitive depictions of a sexual orgy including cunnilingus, fellatio and buggery, but also a belt beating of a naked woman. It portrays dehumanizing and degrading sexual behaviour accompanied with violence, behaviour unacceptable by any Canadian community standard.

As for "Filthy Rich", the film falls into the same category as "Bad Girls", since the scenes depicted include violence (rape), and cunnilingus, fellatio, buggery and group sex. I see very little difference in "Candy Stripers". While the sexual behaviour may not be as overtly violent as in the other two films, we have here a visual depiction of the undue exploitation of sex together with cruelty.

As Shannon J. noted [at p. 331 (C.R.)] in *R. v. Wagner,* Alta. Q.B., 18th January 1985 (not yet reported) [now reported 43 C.R. (3d) 318, 36 Alta. L.R. (2d) 301], such unduly exploitative films, even if devoid of acts of violence, degrade men and women by portraying them as having animal characteristics. "Women, particularly, are deprived of unique human character or identity and are depicted as sexual playthings, hysterically and instantly responsive to male sexual demands.'' I agree and add that this type of degrading vilification of women is unacceptable by any reasonable Canadian community standard.

Accordingly, it is my opinion that s.159 and the use of the community standard test in its interpretation is not so ''vague and overbroad'' as to impinge on the right set out in s.7 of the Charter.

If s.159 is a limitation upon the rights set out in s.7 and s.2, is it a reasonable limitation that can be demonstrably justified in a free and democratic society? In my opinion it is. Judges are not so insulated from observing community standards that they have failed to notice the growing concern expressed by the Canadian community at large that the undue sexual exploitation of women and children depicted in certain publications and films can, in certain circumstances, lead to abject and servile victimization. To protect these classes of our society, Parliament has enacted s.159, a precise and understandable standard for the guidance of those who would contravene contemporary Canadian community standards.

Melvin Co. Ct. J. was right in upholding the decision of the learned trial judge. I would dismiss this appeal.

ANDERSON J.A.: — After a trial before Collins Prov. J. the appellant was convicted pursuant to s.159(1)(*a*) of the Code of three counts of possession of obscene videotapes for the purpose of distribution [[1983] B.C.W.L.D. 1626]. An appeal was taken to Melvin Co. Ct. J., who affirmed the convictions [38 C.R. (3d) 275, [1984] B.C.W.L.D. 1226, [1984] W.C.D. 116, 11 C.C.C. (3d) 389, 10 C.R.R. 377], and the appellant now seeks leave to appeal from the judgment of Melvin Co. Ct. J.

The videotapes in question were described by the learned trial judge as follows:

> I viewed the three videotapes in court. ''Bad Girls'' contains scenes showing close-up and explicit views of female and male genitalia, erection, cunnilingus, sexual intercourse, fellatio and buggery. There are scenes of women masturbating, of a man ejaculating in the face of a woman, of lesbian love-making, again showing close-up and explicit views of female genitalia. A naked woman in chains is ordered to urinate on a man. Women are made to watch acts of fellatio and ejaculation on the naked body of a woman. An act of cunnilingus is performed on a woman while she is bound. A naked woman, while in chains, is beaten with a belt and asked if she wants the assailant's penis. When she agrees, she is required to commit fellatio while other persons watch. This conduct arouses the others and soon there is a sex orgy with lesbian love-making, cunnilingus, fellatio, sexual intercourse and ejaculation. The film from beginning to end portrays prolonged and close-up scenes of sexual activity in the most explicit manner. Nothing is left to one's imagination and the sexual activity is not simulated.
>
> ''The Filthy Rich'' opens with scenes of cunnilingus by two couples. Then both couples engage in sexual intercourse. In each case there are prolonged and vivid close-up views of male and female genitalia. The film, like ''Bad Girls'', continues with almost unending scenes of cunnilingus, both male and female masturbation, sexual intercourse in various positions, male ejaculation, fellatio, fellatio and cunnilingus together, erections, rape, buggery and group sex. As in ''Bad Girls'', the sex acts are not simulated.
>
> ''Candy Stripers'' opens with a vivid and explicit scene of sexual intercourse, culminating in the man ejaculating in the woman's face. Thereafter the film for the most part has an almost continuous string of scenes depicting explicit acts of lesbianism, with women performing what might best be described as ''female cunnilingus'' on one another and inserting fingers in one another's anus. In all cases there are prolonged close-up views of female genitalia. In several scenes a woman is shown masturbating with a banana. In other scenes

a man places a finger in a women's vagina, then two fingers, then three fingers and eventually his whole hand up to his wrist. When he withdraws his hand a woman takes over and eventually places both of her hands in the vagina of the same woman. These scenes are prolonged and extremely explicit. There are scenes showing acts of cunnilingus, sexual intercourse, buggery, ejaculation in the face of women, and fellatio. Towards the end of the film a party deteriorates into what can best be described as a sex orgy. As in the other films, the acts I have described are not simulated.

It is conceded by counsel for the appellant that all three videotapes are "obscene". It is agreed that "Bad Girls" and "Filthy Rich" are concerned solely with sex and elements of violence. It is also agreed that "Candy Stripers" is concerned solely with sex not involving violence. The grounds upon which the application for leave to appeal is founded are:

(1) that s.159(8) of the Criminal Code is so vague, uncertain, overbroad and incapable of definition that it violates the principles of fundamental justice guaranteed by s.7 of the Charter; and

(2) that s.159(8) of the Criminal Code is not a "reasonable limit" upon freedom of expression within the meaning of s.1 and 2(*b*) of the Charter.

Section 159(8) of the Criminal Code reads as follows:

> (8) For the purposes of this Act, any publication a dominant characteristic of which is the undue exploitation of sex, or of sex and any one or more of the following subjects, namely, crime, horror, cruelty and violence, shall be deemed to be obscene.

The relevant sections of the Charter are:

> 1. The Canadian Charter of Rights and Freedoms guarantees the rights and freedoms set out in it subject only to such reasonable limits prescribed by law as can be demonstrably justified in a free and democratic society.
>
> 2. Everyone has the following fundamental freedoms:...
>
> (*b*) freedom of thought, belief, opinion and expression, including freedom of the press and other media of communication...
>
> 7. Everyone has the right to life, liberty and security of the person and the right not to be deprived thereof except in accordance with the principles of fundamental justice.

In his factum, counsel for the Crown makes the following concession:

> The respondent agrees that:
>
> "It is accepted that law cannot be vague, undefined, and totally discretionary; it must be ascertainable and understandable. Any limits placed on the freedom of expression cannot be left to the whim of an official; such limits must be articulated with some precision or they cannot be considered to be law."
>
> *Re Ontario Film & Video Appreciation Society and Ontario Board of Censors*, supra 41 O.R. (2d) at p. 592, 147 D.L.R. (3d) at p. 67.

In view of the concession made by counsel for the Crown, the major issue in this appeal is whether or not s.159(8) of the Criminal Code is so vague "that men of common intelligence must necessarily guess at its meaning and differ as to its application": see *Hamilton Independent Variety & Confectionery Stores Inc. v. Hamilton* (1983), 20 M.P.L.R. 241, 143 D.L.R. (3d) 499 at 507, 4 C.R.R. 230 (Ont. C.A.).

The argument of counsel for the appellant with respect to this issue may be summarized as follows:

(a) The courts have encountered great difficulty in defining national standards of "undueness".

(b) Section 159(8) of the Code does not describe the sexual acts the depiction of which constitutes an offence.

(c) Section 159(8) does not contain any definition of the words "exploitation", "undueness" or "sex".

(d) While the courts have held that "undueness" is to be determined by national community standards, such standards do not enable a citizen to ascertain what may or may not be depicted.

(e) National community standards are virtually impossible to ascertain or define.

(f) Community standards vary from time to time.

(g) It is much more difficult to ascertain the national level of tolerance than the national level of approval.

(h) The expert evidence adduced in this case shows that there can be no true national standard.

(i) There is no mechanism by which a citizen can obtain "prior approval" of material which he desires to publish.

(j) The decision as to whether or not to prosecute depends on the arbitrary determination by police and prosecutors that published material does or does not offend against national community standards.

The argument of counsel for the appellant has considerable merit but must, in my opinion, fail for the following reasons:

(1) The fact that the terms of a statute are not capable of precise definition is not in itself a reason for holding that the statute does not disclose an offence known to the law.

(2) The standards fixed by the courts are not so lacking in precision as not to enable a citizen "to foresee, to a degree that is reasonable in the circumstances, the consequences which a given action may entail".

(3) The standards fixed by the courts are rendered more precise by the constitutional limitations on Parliament set out in s.2 of the Charter of Rights because all limitations on freedom of expression must, in accordance with s.1 of the Charter, be "reasonable" and "demonstrably justified in a free and democratic society".

...

The principles enunciated in the above authorities may be summarized as follows:

1. The test to be applied in determining what is undue exploitation within s.159(8) is whether the accepted standards of tolerance in the contemporary Canadian scene have been exceeded.

2. The standard is a national standard.

3. While expert evidence may be helpful, it is for the judge, in the final analysis, to endeavour to apply what he, in the light of his experience, regards as contemporary standards of the Canadian community.

4. Something approaching a general average of community thinking has to be discovered.

5. The manner and circumstances of distribution are relevant in determining whether or not a publication is obscene (distribution to a private adult audience or otherwise).

6. In determining "undueness" the artistic and literary purposes of the author must be considered.

7. No material will be condemned unless it is clearly "undue".

8. "Undueness" is to be measured by the "tolerance" of the average Canadian and not by the "tastes" of the average Canadian.

"Men of common intelligence" would also know that the words "undue exploitation of sex" will be construed in the context of "obscenity". The word "obscene" is defined in the Shorter Oxford English Dictionary, 3rd ed. (1944), as follows:

> (-Fr. *obscène* or L. *obscenus, obscaenus* ill-omened, abominable, disgusting, indecent, orig. a term of augury.) 1. Offensive to modesty or decency: expressing or suggesting lewd thoughts 1598: 2. Offensive to the senses or the mind; disgusting, filthy, *arch*.

The word "obscenity" is defined as follows:

> Obscene quality or character: a. Indecency, lewdness (esp. of language); in *pl*. obscene words or matters; b. Foulness, loathsomeness; in *pl*. foul acts, dirty work — 1807.

It will be seen, therefore, that material will not be classed as obscene unless the material falls within the above definitions. The material must be so "filthy or disgusting" as not to be tolerated by the average Canadian.

The words "undue exploitation of sex" are also used in a pejorative sense. Thus there must be an excessive emphasis on sex for a base or selfish purpose.

It is said, however, that it is impossible for "men of common intelligence" to ascertain contemporary national standards of tolerance. This argument cannot, in my opinion, prevail. "Men of common intelligence" can seek guidance as to the "national standard of tolerance" from the decided cases. While the decided cases do deal with questions of fact, which differ to some degree in each case, these cases do offer, when viewed as a whole, a national consensus as to the "Canadian standard of tolerance".

...

In my view, having regard to the guidelines spelled out by the courts and to the contemporary Canadian standards held to apply by the learned judges in the above cases, it cannot be said that "men of common intelligence" cannot ascertain the prevailing "national standard of tolerance". To summarize, while difficulties may arise from time to time in rare cases, making it difficult for a prosecutor, a policeman or a citizen to ascertain whether certain material does or does not offend against s.159(8), the definition of "obscenity" enunciated by the Supreme Court of Canada, when read together with the decided cases, makes it possible for any person to ascertain with reasonable certainty whether the material proposed to be published is or is not within the purview of s.159(8). To give a precise definition is impossible. The law is not perfect. We cannot do perfect justice. The courts have, however, devised a reasonable, workable standard in this area of the law.

While, as I have said, it is not wise or possible to give a precise definition of "obscenity", it is possible to illustrate the type of material that does not fall within contemporary Canadian standards of tolerance.

Material lacking serious literary, artistic, political or scientific value dealing to an excessive degree with explicit sex involving violence will be prohibited. Likewise, similar material dealing with explicit sex involving the participation of children will be prohibited. Similar sexually explicit material portraying men and women as having animal characteristics will also be prohibited, even though there is an absence of physical violence. This type of material was described by Shannon J. in *R. v. Wagner*, supra, as follows [at p. 331]:

> In sexually explicit pornography that is free of violence, but is degrading or dehumanizing, men and women are often verbally abused and portrayed as having animal characteristics. Women, particularly, are deprived of unique human character or identity and are depicted

as sexual playthings, hysterically and instantly responsive to male sexual demands. They worship male genitals and their own value depends upon the quality of their genitals and breasts.

I wish to emphasize that the word "undue" denotes excessive emphasis on sex and that the presence of isolated depictions of explicit sex will not be prohibited. I would also emphasize that "sex" must be a dominant characteristic and that even if, for example, the material dealt to a substantial degree with explicit sex and violence if the material was of serious literary, artistic, political or scientific value it would not, except in rare cases, be subject to condemnation. It is my view that, while the material might be devoted almost entirely to explicit sex, explicit sex could not be said to be a dominant characteristic if the theme, plot or purpose had serious literary, artistic, political or scientific merit. The only dominant characteristic would be the theme, plot or purpose and all other characteristics, including explicit sex, would be subservient to the theme, plot or purpose. It will be observed that the videotapes condemned by the judges in the *Doug Rankine, Ramsingh* and *Wagner* cases, all supra, were all without merit of any kind, literary, artistic or otherwise. "Men of common intelligence" could easily ascertain that they were entirely without merit and were clearly contrary to "national standards of tolerance."

It will also be observed that s.2(*b*) of the Charter narrows the scope of s.159(8) of the Code. Any limitation on freedom of expression must meet the strict requirements of s.1 of the Charter, namely, that the limitation is reasonable and such "as can be demonstrably justified in a free and democratic society". We must be careful, therefore, not to prohibit the publication of materials for the sole reason that the materials do not meet with popular approval or do not appeal to pupular tastes. In my view, a restriction on freedom of expression can be "demonstrably justified" only if it can be shown that the material sought to be banned from publication causes or threatens to cause real and substantial harm to the community. In this respect it is my opinion that publication of material placing excessive emphasis on explicit sex with violence, explicit sex involving children and explicit sex portraying human beings as having animal characteristics results in substantial harm to the community and we are thus justified in prohibiting the publication of such material.

It has been said that videotapes of the type condemned by the courts are not a threat to society because they are seen only in private by a consenting adult audience. Quite apart from the risk that these videotapes may fall into the hands of children, it is my opinion that such materials are clearly a threat to society. They constitute a threat to society because they have a tendency to create indifference to violence insofar as women are concerned. They tend to dehumanize and degrade both men and women in an excessive and revolting way. They exalt the concept that in some perverted way domination of women by men is accepted in our society.

I would add that, in determining whether or not the requirements of s.1 of the Charter have been satisfied, it seems to me that we should not decide these matters in a vacuum but should have regard to the provisions of the Charter as a whole, including s.28, reading as follows:

> 28. Notwithstanding anything in this Charter, the rights and freedoms referred to in it are guaranteed equally to male and female persons.

If true equality between male and female persons is to be achieved it would be quite wrong in my opinion to ignore the threat to equality resulting from the exposure to male audiences of the violent and degrading material described above. As I have said, such material has a tendency to make men more tolerant of violence to women and creates a social climate encouraging men to act in a callous and discriminatory way towards women.

Apart from such harmful and offensive material involving the subject of sex, we are not justified in restricting free expression in this area in any way. It must be remembered that freedom of expression includes the freedom to receive all material which is not harmful to others. It follows that in the privacy of his home every citizen is entitled to read, see or hear all material involving the subject of sex which is not harmful to others.

In conclusion, I would stress that we must be careful not to restrict freedom of expression beyond what is clearly required for the protection of society. We cannot ban the publication of all harmful or offensive material involving the subject of sex. At the expense of repetition, the only material that can be banned is material which is clearly offensive, explicit, excessive and substantially harmful, in the manner described above.

I adopt the remarks of Clare Beckton in "Freedom of Expression (S.2(b))", c.5 of Tarnopolsky and Beaudoin (eds.), Canadian Charter of Rights and Freedoms: Commentary (1982), at p. 107:

> With the entrenchment of s.2(b) of the Charter the Supreme Court will have to face squarely the limits of censorship. Clearly statutes which create censorship boards without specific criteria would be contrary to the guarantees of free expression, since no line is drawn between objectionable and non-objectionable forms of expression. Now standards will have to be created to measure the limits to which obscene expression may be regulated.
>
> Although the American approach does not offer much assistance for Canadian courts, it is submitted that the overbreadth approach or even a test similar to the clear and present danger standard should be used. It is not enough to say merely that moral standards are offended by the proliferation of obscene material, without demonstrating that harm is caused by the dissemination of objectionable material. If freedom of expression is to be a valuable right, a moral sense of indignity is not a sufficient reason for prohibiting access to allegedly obscene material. Any censorship which is not clearly justifiable interferes with the right of free expression. Clearly there are legitimate interests to be protected, particularly as they pertain to access by minors to material described as obscene or pornographic, but the danger is ever present from legislation that is overbroad, and from the lack of clear standards against which to measure the material.

To apply the points made in the above-quoted passage to the case on appeal:

1. Section 2(*b*) of the Charter prevents Parliament from enacting legislation to prohibit the publication of any materials unless it can be demonstrably justified that the publication of such materials will clearly cause substantial harm to the community.

2. As exemplified in these reasons, clear standards have been established in respect of s.159(8) and "men of common intelligence" can ascertain whether or not the material sought to be published comes within the prohibited area.

The materials in question offend against the standard enunciated in s.159(8) because they constitute a threat of real and substantial harm to the community. They have no literary or artistic merit and in a revolting and excessive way create an attitude of indifference to violence insofar as women are concerned and tend to dehumanize both men and women. They approve the domination of women by men as an acceptable social philosophy.

For the above reasons, I would dismiss the appeal.

Appeal dismissed.

4.4.12 S. Noonan, "Annotation to *R.* v. *Wagner*", (1985) 43 C.R. (3d) 318-320

Feminists will undoubtedly applaud the *Wagner* decision as heralding an enlightened approach to an area in which the law has long been unresponsive to, and unaffected by, the feminist critique of pornography. Shannon J. rules that the degree of sexual explicitness per se does not determine whether materials are obscene within the meaning of s.159(8) of the Criminal Code, R.S.C. 1970, c.C-34. For the first time, a Canadian court has recognized that there exists a separate category of depictions, namely, erotica, within which any amount of graphicness is permissible. Instead the focus is on the manner in which sexual activities are presented; the degree of explicitness assumes relevance only within a context in which there is violence, lack of consent, or inherent inequality between the parties. This holding, with the concomitant assertion that exploitation of sex will be "undue" where the participants are depicted "in a manner that is degrading or dehumanizing", serves to substantially align the Code's obscenity provisions with the feminist conception of pornography.

The distinction between obscenity and pornography has been the subject of considerable academic attention. Many writers allege that the history of obscenity legislation is steeped in notions of preserving public morals or enforcing basic standards of decency; it is a "morality" which posits that explicit sexual depictions, particularly outside the sanctioned contexts of marriage and procreation, threaten the morals or fabric of society itself: see, for example, *R. v. Hicklin* (1868), L.R. 3 Q.B. 360, which established the common law test for obscenity of "tendency to deprave". Arguably, the same moralistic flavour underlies s.159, found in Pt. IV of the Code under the heading "Offences Tending to Corrupt Morals". Moreover, despite the fact that materials are deemed obscene where there is undue exploitation of sex, or one of the "sex-plus" categories (crime, violence, horror, etc.), judicial attention has largely focused on sexual explicitness simpliciter: see K. Mahoney, "Obscenity, Morals, and the Law" (1985), p. 41, to be published in the Ottawa Law Review. Furthermore, the equation of undue sexual exploitation with undue sexual explicitness is seen as misapprehending the nature of the harm to be addressed.

Feminist theory resoundingly rejects the proposition that materials which are sexually explicit or arouse the prurient interest are intrinsically problematic. Rather, from this perspective, it is the manner in which sexuality and sexual encounters are depicted that is determinative. Thus, MacKinnon and Dworkin define pornography as the "sexually explicit subordination of women graphically depicted": see Draft Ordinance, city of Minneapolis (1983). The feminist discourse speaks of pornography not only in terms of its tendency to endorse violence against women but in terms of its false representation of female sexuality: women are frequently depicted as desiring humiliation, degradation or subordination. Another concern is that pornography tends to objectify or dehumanize the persons portrayed, so that the participants are stripped of all individuality and all persons as a "gender class" are thereby reduced to their genitalia. In short, the harm of pornography as perceived by feminists is its tendency to sanction force, coercion, degradation and dehumanization within sexual relationships.

The assertion that the existing obscenity legislation is an ineffectual and misconceived tool for dealing with feminist concerns must be re-examined. The *Wagner* decision is not the first in which judges have adopted the discourse of degradation and dehumanization. In *R. v. Doug Rankine Co.* (1983), 36 C.R. (3d) 154 at 173, 9 C.C.C.

(2d) 53 (Ont. Co. Ct.), Borins Co. Ct. J. held that the community level of tolerance would be exceeded by "films which consist substantially or partially of scenes which portray violence and cruelty in conjunction with sex, particularly where the performance of indignities degrades and dehumanizes the people upon whom they are performed". A similar approach was also adopted by Ferg J. in *R. v. Ramsingh* (1984), 14 C.C.C. (3d) 230, 29 Man. R. (2d) 110 (Q.B.), and Harrison Prov. J. in *R. v. Chin,* Ont. Prov. Ct., 22nd February 1983 (not yet reported).

While these decisions contextualize sexual explicitness by acknowledging that the questions of degradation and dehumanization must also be analyzed, they nonetheless (in the absence of violence, or other "sex-plus" requirements) revert to the view that explicitness can be determinative of the issue of undue exploitation. The virtue of the *Wagner* decision is that it does not.

By removing erotica, which portrays "positive and affectionate human sexual interaction, between consenting individuals participating on the basis of equality" (p. 331), from the ambit of s.159, the decision establishes that the method of portrayal of sexual activities will distinguish unacceptable from permissible forms of representation.

Another interesting development in this area is the growing judicial disenchantment with use of the "community standards of tolerance" test in assessing whether the standard of "undue" sexual exploitation has been transgressed. Strong criticisms were expressed by Borins Co. Ct. J. in *R. v. Nicols* (1985), 43 C.R. (3d) 54 (Ont. Co. Ct.), although he considered himself bound to it by precedent. In *R. v. Pereira-Vasquez,* post, p. 336, Millward Co. Ct. J. holds that the "community standards of tolerance" test is inapplicable where the issue of artistic integrity does not arise. In such cases sexual exploitation is to be determined in accordance with the plain, ordinary meaning of the word "undue", i.e., "going beyond what is appropriate, warranted or natural; excessive". In *R. v. Neil's Ventures Ltd.*, N.B. Prov. Ct., 8th February 1985 (not yet reported), and *R. v. Lynne's Sound Ltd.*, N.B. Prov. Ct., 4th March 1985 (not yet reported), Harper Prov. J. squarely rejects the community standards of tolerance test, holding that there is no binding precedent for it in the Supreme Court or in New Brunswick.

This development seems regrettable. On the one hand, the test of "community standards of tolerance" has largely been applied in a liberal manner, so as to license the proliferation of pornographic materials. On occasion the test has become circuitous, in that evidence of availability of the materials on the market has become indicative of tolerance. However, one must not lightly dismiss the view that the determination of community standards is a process through which the feminist perspective may be heard. This process is empowering, insofar as the court allows the community to define what is pornographic and the nature of the harm produced by it. In both the *Rankine* and *Wagner* decisions, the court heard expert evidence which assisted in its determination of whether the films in issue were obscene. In light of these cases, would a return to pure judicial subjectivity be a progressive step?

4.4.13 *Towne Cinema Theatres Ltd.* v. *R.* (1985), 45 C.R. (3d) 1 (S.C.C.)

9th May 1985. DICKSON C.J.C. (LAMER and LE DAIN JJ. concurring): — The question is whether the trial judge applied the proper test in finding Towne Cinema Theatres Ltd. guilty of presenting an obscene entertainment. The indictment reads:

> That The Towne Cinema Theatres Ltd., at Edmonton, in the Judicial District of Edmonton, Alberta, on or about the 27th day of January, A.D. 1980, being the person in charge of a theatre, namely: Jasper Cinema (Blue) at 10120 — 156 Street, did unlawfully present to an audience an entertainment, namely: a motion picture entitled ''Dracula Sucks'' which entertainment was immoral, indecent or obscene, contrary to the Criminal Code.

...

The accused company was convicted and fined $1500.

II *On Appeal*

In a brief judgment, the Court of Appeal of Alberta dismissed the appeal. The court noted it was not its function to judge the merits of the film, and it had not found it necessary to see the film; its sole function was to review the propriety of the trial. The judgment continued:

> We have reviewed the reasons for judgment given in support of this conviction. Those reasons are blunt and impactive. The trial judge, sitting as a jury, was obliged to determine in an objective way what was tolerable in accordance with the con-temporary standards of the Canadian community. As a trier of fact he was entitled to draw on his experience in the community. He had to consider the expert evidence but was entitled to reject it and obviously did. In this we are paraphrasing the remarks of Howland C.J.O. in *R. v. Sudbury News Service* (1978), 18 O.R. (2d) 428, 39 C.C.C. (2d) 1 at 7 (C.A.).

The judgment concluded thus:

> The reasons of the trial judge challenged in this appeal must be considered in the context of his whole judgment and the argument which immediately preceded it. The trial judge found that the only theme of the film ''Dracula Sucks'' was sex and violence, extreme and explicit. He found no plot. He asked himself what are contemporary community standards and considered all the evidence led. He cautioned himself on the dangers of slipping into subjective standards and concluded that the film did not meet the objective test. We see no grounds, in law, to disturb this conviction and dismiss the appeal.

III *Issues*

In his factum, counsel for Towne Cinema raised five grounds of appeal. At the hearing oral argument was presented on only two of these grounds, both alleging errors in the trial judge's determination of the community standard of tolerance.

In view of the importance of the issues raised in this appeal, the court felt that it would be proper to request a rehearing before a full bench.

The court requested counsel to address the following four questions:

> 1. Assuming that for purposes of s.159, undue exploitation of sex is to be assessed on the basis of community standards, do these standards refer to what one would find acceptable for oneself to see or read, or to what one would tolerate others seeing or reading?
>
> 2. How is this standard to be ascertained by the trier of fact?
>
> 3. How is an impugned film to be measured against it?
>
> 4. What is the relevance, if any, of the audience to which a film is geared in determining whether it is obscene under s.159(8)?

In my view the following issues arise from the two grounds argued on the appeal and the four questions addressed at the rehearing:

1. What is the proper interpretation of the word ''undue'' in s.159(8) of the Criminal Code?
2. Must the Crown adduce evidence to establish undueness?

IV *Undueness and the Community Standards Test*

In 1959 Parliament amended the provisions of s.150 (now s.159) of the Criminal Code dealing with obscenity by adding subs. (8) [en. 1959 (Can.), c.41, s.11], which reads:

> (8) For the purposes of this Act, any publication a dominant characteristic of which is the undue exploitation of sex, or of sex and any one or more of the following subjects, namely, crime, horror, cruelty and violence, shall be deemed to be obscene.

Any doubt that might previously have existed on the question of whether s.159(8) embodied the proper or the exclusive test for obscenity in relation to a film was implicitly resolved by this court in *Dechow v. R.*, [1978] 1 S.C.R. 951, 40 C.R.N.S. 129, 35 C.C.C. (2d) 22, 76 D.L.R. (3d) 1, 16 N.R. 204. A number of decisions in various jurisdictions had previously concluded that films were ''publications'' and therefore properly dealt with under s.159(8): see *R. v. Fraser*, 52 W.W.R. 712, [1966] 1 C.C.C. 110, 51 D.L.R. (2d) 408 (B.C.C.A.); *R. v. Goldberg*, [1971] 3 O.R. 323, 4 C.C.C. (2d) 187 (C.A.); and *Daylight Theatre Co. v. R.*, [1973] 6 W.W.R. 717, 24 C.R.N.S. 368, 17 C.C.C. (2d) 451 (Sask. Dist. Ct.).

Dechow dealt with an allegation of obscenity with regard to an exhibition of sex stimulators. Using language and reasoning easily extendible to motion pictures, Ritchie J., writing for the majority, held that the objects in question, accompanied as they were by printed instructions for their use, were ''publications'' within the meaning of that term in s.159. They were therefore to be judged by the standard laid down in s.159(8), which was the sole test of obscenity in relation to publications. Laskin C.J.C., speaking for a minority of the court, preferred the view that the articles in question were not publications. He was, however, of the opinion that the court should apply exclusively the test in s.159(8) in respect of allegations of obscenity whether such allegations are made under s.159 (which deals with publications) or one of the other sections of the Code, such as s.163 (under which the charge against Towne Cinema was laid) or s.164.

The practical effect of the two judgments, though they differ widely in approach, is, for present purposes, the same: s.159(8) embodies the sole test of obscenity in relation to motion pictures. It supersedes rather than supplements the much-criticized test enunciated by Cockburn C.J. in *R. v. Hicklin* (1868), L.R. 3 Q.B. 360.

In Canada, the notion of ''community standards'', as relevant to the determination of obscenity, has its origins in the judgment of Judson J. (speaking also for Abbott and Martland JJ.) in *Brodie v. R.; Dansky v. R.; Rubin v. R.*, [1962] S.C.R. 681, 37 C.R. 120, 132 C.C.C. 161, 32 D.L.R. (2d) 507, the ''Lady Chatterley's Lover'' case. *Brodie* was the first obscenity appeal to come before this court following the introduction of s.159(8) and Judson J.'s explication of this section reveals a very clear awareness of the criticism that had been leveled against the *Hicklin* test and an intention to avoid its pitfalls in the future. In *Hicklin* Cockburn C.J. had said:

> ...I think the test for obscenity is this, whether the tendency of the matter charged as obscenity is to deprave and corrupt those whose minds are open to such immoral influences, and into whose hands a publication of this sort may fall.

This definition had been criticized for its focus on the reactions of the weakest and least capable members of society, for its disregard of serious purpose or artistic merit in the impugned material and for its excessive dependence on subjective conjecture on the part of the trier of fact. In *Brodie,* Judson J. expressed the view [at p. 701] that by the enactment of s.159(8) ''All the jurisprudence under the *Hicklin* definition is rendered obsolete'' and [at p. 702] that the new definition gave the court ''an opportunity to apply tests which have some certainty of meaning and are capable of objective application and which do not so much depend as before upon the idiosyncrasies and sensitivities of the tribunal of fact, whether judge or jury''. Henceforth, the standard for obscenity would be an ''undue exploitation of sex'' and Judson J. proposed two tests which he regarded as capable of objective application to determine such ''undueness''.

The first test focused on the ''internal necessities'' of the work in question. In the American case of *U.S. v. Kennerley,* N.Y. Dist. Ct., 209 F. 119 (1913), Learned Hand J. had reluctantly felt bound to apply the *Hicklin* test, but said, at pp. 120-21: ''I question whether in the end men will regard that as obscene which is honestly relevant to the adequate expression of innocent ideas.''

In *Brodie,* at pp. 704-705, Judson J. applied this principle to the newly-enacted statutory definition:

> ...I do not think that there is undue exploitation if there is no more emphasis on the theme than is required in the serious treatment of the theme of a novel with honesty and uprightness... The section recognizes that the serious-minded author must have freedom in the production of a work of genuine artistic and literary merit and the quality of the work, as the witnesses point out and common sense indicates, must have real relevance in determining not only a dominant characteristic but also whether there is undue exploitation.

Judson J.'s second test for ''undueness'' looked to the standards of the community. The concept of ''community standards'' had previously been applied by courts in Australia and New Zealand as a measure of whether a work exhibited an ''undue emphasis'' on sex. Judson J. regarded this reading of undue as meaning ''what the community regards as excessive'' to be preferable to what he saw as the only alternative (p. 706):

> Surely the choice of courses is clear-cut. Either the judge instructs himself or the jury that undueness is to be measured by his or their personal opinion — and even that must be subject to some influence from contemporary standards — or the instruction must be that the tribunal of fact should consciously attempt to apply these standards. Of the two, I think that the second is the better choice.

Judson J. made no attempt to harmonize or integrate his two tests. He simply concluded that, whether the question was approached on the basis of the internal necessities of the novel itself or on the basis of an offence against community standards, undue exploitation of sex was not a dominant characteristic of ''Lady Chatterley's Lover''.

In the present case, no argument was addressed to the ''artistic merit'' or ''serious purpose'' of ''Dracula Sucks'' — nor, I should think, could such an argument plausibly be made. This court is not, therefore, called upon to expound the relationship between Judson J.'s two tests. We need only consider the issue of obscenity from the point of view of community standards.

Nevertheless, as will presently appear, it is important to remember that from the very beginning of this court's consideration of s.159(8) ''community standards'' have been viewed as *one* measure of ''undueness'' in the exploitation of sex. They have never been seen as the *only* measure of such undueness; still less has a breach of community standards been treated as in itself a criminal offence.

There are other ways in which exploitation of sex might be "undue". Ours is not a perfect society and it is unfortunate but true that the community may tolerate publications that cause harm to members of society and therefore to society as a whole. Even if, at certain times, there is a coincidence between what is not tolerated and what is harmful to society, there is no necessary connection between these two concepts. Thus, a legal definition of "undue" must also encompass publications harmful to members of society and, therefore, to society as a whole.

Sex-related publications which portray persons in a degrading manner as objects of violence, cruelty or other forms of dehumanizing treatment may be "undue" for the purpose of s.159(8). No one should be subject to the degradation and humiliation inherent in publications which link sex with violence, cruelty, and other forms of dehumanizing treatment. It is not likely that at a given moment in a society's history such publications will be tolerated: see *R. v. Doug Rankine Co.* (1983), 36 C.R. (3d) 154 at 173, 9 C.C.C. (3d) 53 (Ont. Co. Ct.); *R. v. Wagner,* Alta. Q.B., 16th January 1985 (not yet reported) [now reported 43 C.R. (3d) 318, 36 Alta. L.R. (2d) 301]; *R. v. Chin,* Ont. Prov. Ct., 22nd February 1983 (not yet reported).

However, as I have noted above, there is no *necessary* coincidence between the undueness of publications which degrade people by linking violence, cruelty or other forms of dehumanizing treatment with sex, and the community standard of tolerance. Even if certain sex-related materials were found to be within the standard of tolerance of the community, it would still be necessary to ensure that they were not "undue" in some other sense, for example, in the sense that they portray persons in a degrading manner as objects of violence, cruelty, or other forms of dehumanizing treatment.

In the present case, however, only the community standard of tolerance is directly in issue. The rest of this decision will be concerned with the community standard of tolerance.

Two years after the *Brodie* case this court, in *Dom. News & Gifts Ltd. v. R.*, [1964] S.C.R. 251, 42 C.R. 209, [1964] 3 C.C.C. 1, adopted in toto the dissenting reasons delivered in the Court of Appeal of Manitoba by Freedman J.A., 42 W.W.R. 65, 40 C.R. 109, [1963] 2 C.C.C. 103. In that case, as in this, the allegedly obscene material had no discernible serious purpose or artistic merit. Freedman J.A.'s discussion of whether or not it unduly exploited sex was therefore focused on its relationship to community standards. Applying Judson J.'s observation in *Brodie* about the need to test undueness by objective criteria, Freedman J.A. elaborated on several requisite characteristics of the community standards to be applied. He held that the standards must be *Canadian* standards, not those prevailing elsewhere, and that they must be *contemporary* standards reflecting the current level of candour with regard to sexual matters, not the level of the past. On the question of which contemporary Canadians are to be the touchstone of "community standards" Freedman J.A. said at p. 116:

> Those standards are not set by those of lowest taste or interest. Nor are they set exclusively by those of rigid, austere, conservative, or puritan taste and habit of mind. Something approaching a general average of community thinking and feeling has to be discovered. Obviously, this is no easy task, for we are seeking a quantity that is elusive. Yet the effort must be made if we are to have a fair objective standard in relation to which a publication can be tested as to whether it is obscene or not. The alternative would mean a subjective approach, with the result dependent upon an varying with the personal tastes and predilections of the particular Judge who happens to be trying the case.

In 1974, in *R. v. Odeon Morton Theatres Ltd.*, [1974] 3 W.W.R. 304, 16 C.C.C. (2d) 185, 45 D.L.R. (3d) 224 (Man. C.A.), Freedman C.J.M. had much the same to say with regard to the appropriate community standard to apply in determining whether the film "Last Tango in Paris" was obscene at p. 188:

> The learned trial Judge made it abundantly clear that his obligation was to consider the film not according to his own subjective views but according to the objective test furnished by contemporary community standards in Canada. Indeed he expressly stated in his reasons for judgment that his personal views were adverse to the acceptability of the film but that he was setting aside those views. That of course was the correct and judicial thing to do.

I said earlier that the undue exploitation of sex is the touchstone of obscenity under s.159(8), and that a breach of community standards is simply one measure of such undueness. It is harm to society from undue exploitation that is aimed at by the section, not simply lapses in propriety or good taste. In *R. v. Prairie Schooner News Ltd.* (1970), 75 W.W.R. 585, 12 Cr. L.Q. 462, 1 C.C.C. (2d) 251 (Man. C.A.), Monnin J.A. and I considered this point at p. 269:

> The court was urged to define "community standards" as community standards of acceptance, *i.e.*, tolerance. I would accept this definition. In the *Brodie* case Judson, J., referred, p. 181, to "standards of acceptance prevailing in the community". In the *Great West News* case, we referred to contemporary standards of tolerance. I have no doubt, as Dr. Rich testified, and as the Judge agreed, a distinction can be made between private taste and standard of tolerance. It can hardly be questioned that many people would find personally offensive, material which they would permit others to read. Parliament, through its legislation on obscenity, could hardly have wished to proscribe as criminal that which was acceptable or tolerable according to current standards of the Canadian community.

A similar point was made by Weatherston J.A., delivering the judgment of the Ontario Court of Appeal in *R. v. Penthouse Int. Ltd.* (1979), 23 O.R. (2d) 786, 46 C.C.C. (2d) 111 at 114-15, 96 D.L.R. (3d) 735 (leave to appeal refused [1979] 1 S.C.R. xi, 23 O.R. (2d) 786n, 46 C.C.C. (2d) 111n):

> Is is neither helpful nor accurate to say that the standard of tolerance is synonymous with the moral standards of the community... The words "moral standards of the community" mean no more than a consensus of what is right and what is wrong...
> The question, in any event, is not whether the content of the publication goes beyond what the contemporary Canadian community thinks is right, but rather whether it goes beyond what the contemporary Canadian community is prepared to tolerate.

R. v. Sudbury News Service Ltd. (1978), 18 O.R. (2d) 428, 39 C.C.C. (2d) 1 (C.A.), was concerned with the distribution to certain confectionery stores of magazines alleged to be obscene, including "Penthouse" and "Oui". Howland C.J.O., speaking for the Ontario Court of Appeal, reviewed the relevant authorities and then, in a number of propositions distilled from those authorities, expressed, in my view admirably, the present state of Canadian law as applied to the question presently before the court.

I have taken the liberty of extracting the following propositions from various places in the judgment: (i) in determining what is undue exploitation within s.159(8), one of the tests to be applied is whether the accepted standards of tolerance in the contemporary Canadian community have been exceeded; (ii) the standards must be contemporary as times change and ideas change with them, one manifestation being the relative freedom with which the whole question of sex is discussed; (iii) it is the standards of the community as a whole which must be considered and not the standards of a small segment of that community such as the university community where a film was shown; (iv) the decision whether the publication is tolerable according to Canadian community standards rests with the court; (v) the task is to determine in an objective way what is tolerable in accordance with the contemporary standards of the Canadian community, and not merely to project one's own personal ideas of what is tolerable.

The cases all emphasize that it is a standard of *tolerance,* not taste, that is relevant. What matters is not what Canadians think is right for themselves to see. What matters is what Canadians would not abide other Canadians seeing because it would be beyond the contemporary Canadian standard of tolerance to allow them to see it.

Since the standard is tolerance, I think the audience to which the allegedly obscene material is targeted must be relevant. The operative standards are those of the Canadian community as a whole, but since what matters is what other people may see it is quite conceivable that the Canadian community would tolerate varying degrees of explicitness depending upon the audience and the circumstances. I would adopt the following passage of Howland C.J.O. in *Sudbury News Service,* supra, at p. 8:

> The next question which arises is the extent to which the manner and circumstances of distribution are relevant in determining whether or not a publication is obscene. There are some publications which are so blatantly indecent that they would not be tolerable by the Canadian community under any circumstances. Some pictures are offensive to the majority of people to the point that the Canadian community would not tolerate them on a billboard, or on the cover of a magazine, or on a television screen where persons of all ages and sensibilities would be exposed to them, but would be prepared to tolerate them being viewed by persons who wished to view them. Some pictures would not be acceptable by Canadian community standards in a children's bedtime story-book or primer but would be in a magazine for general distribution. The Canadian community might be prepared to tolerate the exhibition of a motion picture to an adult audience, but would consider the exhibition of the same motion picture to a general audience, which included children, to be an undue exploitation of sex. Similarly, the general distribution of certain magazines to a neighbourhood store accessible to all ages would not be tolerable, whereas the distribution of such magazines to "adult" book-stores to which children under a certain age were not admitted might not be objectionable. The packaging and pricing of a publication may also be relevant in considering whether Canadian community standards have been exceeded. The distribution of magazines in plastic covers marked "adult" in some respects might act as an attraction rather than a deterrent unless the price was high enough to place it beyond the reach of most children.

In endorsing this view I am modifying the position I had adopted in the Manitoba Court of Appeal in *R. v. Great West News Ltd.,* 72 W.W.R. 354, 10 C.R.N.S. 42, [1970] 4 C.C.C. 307 at 317 (leave to appeal denied [1970] S.C.R. ix).

With that review of the cases, I turn now to the trial judgment in the present case. The appellant submits that the trial judge misdirected himself in holding that his assessment of the local community's feeling of "revulsion" was determinative of the Canadian community standard of tolerance, and in thereby employing a subjective and regional rather than an objective and national test. According to the appellant the Crown must prove beyond a reasonable doubt that the film would not be tolerated by the Canadian community in the sense that those who do not wish to view it will not accept or tolerate the fact that others do and will see it.

In delivering judgment the trial judge said:

> I do not have the benefit of a jury. In making the remarks I have made, I do not feel that I am imposing my own standards completely, although how can one help but be subjective

> in a case like this? None of us live on an island; we all live in a world which, as evidence has suggested today, is becoming more tolerant of explicit sex in films and more tolerant of violence. Somebody has got to draw the line and I do not know how far community standards are prepared to be stretched before somebody does draw the line on the type of garbage that I saw this morning.
>
> I am satisfied that this film is a long way from meeting the contemporary community standards. It may satisfy a certain element of a community, it may gratify them, but I am prepared to say that the majority of the community would feel the same revulsion for this show that I felt when I left there this morning.
>
> When I say the dominant theme of this film was sex and violence, I am not being entirely correct: it is the only theme. There is no plot, there is no story whatsoever, unless it is hidden in such a way that I could not find it. I was making notes at the time the show was on, but I was able to watch it in its entirety.

In the present case I think, with respect, that the trial judge applied a standard of taste, not tolerance, as reflected in these words:

> ...I am prepared to say that the majority of the community would feel the same revulsion for this show that I felt when I left there this morning.

In my view this statement can only be interpreted as saying that most people would be personally offended. The judge did not direct his mind to the question whether most people would tolerate others seeing the film in question. In that I think he erred.

It should also be noted that the trial judge gave no consideration to the fact that ''Dracula Sucks'' was restricted to adults only, and that only those who chose to see it would be exposed to it. As I have said, these factors are important considerations in applying a test of tolerance.

The appellant argues, as I have indicated, that the trial judge applied a subjective and local standard rather than a national objective test. In *Brodie,* supra, Judson J. makes it clear that the trier of fact is not supposed simply to apply his own subjective standard but rather to assess the community standard. The statement of the trial judge, ''I do not feel that I am imposing my own standards completely'', seems to imply that he is imposing his own standards primarily and lends support to the submission of the appellant that the test applied was subjective and not objective. In particular, the sentence reading: ''Somebody has got to draw the line and I don't know how far community standards are prepared to be stretched before somebody does draw the line on the type of garbage that I saw this morning,'' suggests that the judge is imposing his own standard — somebody has to draw the line and he is going to be the one to do it.

Reading his comments as a whole, I can reach no conclusion other than the trial judge applied his own subjective standards of taste and not community standards of tolerance.

V *The Evidentiary Issue*

The appellant's second ground is that the judge failed to have regard to the unrebutted evidence of the chairman of the censor board that the film did not fall below contemporary community standards. Counsel for the appellant does not contend that censor board approval is a bar to a criminal prosecution. He readily concedes that it is for the courts to decide whether a publication is obscene: *Daylight Theatre Co. v. R.,* supra; *R. v. McFall* (1975), 26 C.C.C. (2d) 181 (B.C.C.A.).

Counsel does, however, take the point that in light of the evidence, not disputed, of the approval of the allegedly obscene film by all of the censor boards or classification boards across the country there was an additional onus on the Crown to adduce evidence to establish beyond a reasonable doubt that the film went beyond what the contemporary Canadian community is prepared to tolerate. In support of this argument counsel cited several passages on the subject of expert evidence from the dissenting judgment of Laskin J.A. (as he then was) in *R. v. Cameron,* [1966] 2 O.R. 777, 49 C.R. 49, [1966] 4 C.C.C. 273, 58 D.L.R. (2d) 486 (Ont. C.A.), and urged us to accept them as correct statements of the evidentiary requirements in obscenity cases.

The issue of who must place evidence of what before the trier of fact in obscenity cases is a vexing and recurring problem. Under the *Hicklin* rule expert evidence was in general held to be irrelevant. As Laidlaw J.A. explained in *R. v. Amer. News Co.*, [1957] O.R. 145, 25 C.R. 374, 118 C.C.C. 152 at 157 (C.A.), since, under the *Hicklin* test, the gravamen of the offence was a tendency to deprave or corrupt, evidence as to artistic merit — no matter how reliable — was held to be irrelevant to the issue of obscenity. And as for evidence tending to show that the material in question had no tendency to deprave or corrupt, Laidlaw J.A.'s discussion, at p. 161, illustrates that the prevailing rules of evidence held such testimony to be inadmissible opinion evidence going to the very question to be determined by the trier of fact.

With the inception of the new statutory definition in s.159(8) this rigid inflexibility was considerably relaxed. In *Brodie,* supra, at p. 703, Judson J. made it clear that expert evidence as to the seriousness of the artist's purpose and the artistic merit of the material in question was certainly admissible, and, in his view, very helpful:

> I can read and understand but at the same time I recognize that my training and experience have been, not in literature, but in law and I readily acknowledge that the evidence of the witnesses who gave evidence in this case is of real assistance to me in reaching a conclusion.

In the *Prairie Schooner* case, supra, one issue was the admissibility of expert evidence (in the form of public opinion polls) on the question of the actual state of contemporary community standards. At p. 266 of the report of that case there appears the following passage in the judgment of Monnin J.A. and myself:

> ... it would seem to me that when it becomes necessary to determine the true nature of community opinion and to find a single normative standard, the Court should not be denied the benefit of evidence, scientifically obtained in accordance with accepted sampling procedure, by those who are expert in the field of opinion research. Such evidence can properly be accorded the status of *expert* testimony. The state of mind or attitude of a community is as much a fact as the state of one's health; it would seem therefore as proper to admit the opinion of experts on the one subject as on the other. [The italics are mine.]

To hold expert evidence *admissible* with regard to the factual underpinnings of the community standard test for "undueness" is, of course, not the same as holding such evidence to be *mandatory*. In *R. v. Great West News Ltd.*, supra, the appellants attempted to impose precisely that obligation on the Crown. It was argued that the Crown must fail because no evidence had been put before the court from which the court could objectively determine prevailing community standards. Counsel submitted that the court must determine from evidence placed before it by the Crown: (i) What is the community standard, that is to say, what is the standard of tolerance of Canadians as a whole to material of the nature of that impugned? (ii) Does the material impugned so far transcend that standard as to be branded as criminal? After a review of the cases, and speaking also for Smith C.J.M., I had occasion to say, at pp. 314-15:

> The authorities would seem to ascribe to the Judge a much more important role in the assessment of contemporary community standards than counsel for the appellants would accord him. I do not find in *Brodie*, or elsewhere in the Commonwealth, any majority opinion that expert evidence of community standards is an essential ingredient to a finding of guilt. If any inference can be drawn from *Brodie* it is that the Judge must, in the final analysis, endeavour to apply what he, in the light of his experience, regards as contemporary standards of the Canadian community. In so doing he must be at pains to avoid having his decision simply reflect or project his own notions of what is tolerable.

I am unaware of any majority opinion, since the *Great West News* judgment, in Canada or elsewhere in the Commonwealth, which has made expert evidence of community standards mandatory. To impose on the Crown a positive requirement to adduce expert evidence as to community standards would be unrealistic. Expert evidence is always expensive, sometimes simply not available and frequently unreliable. The American experience — based, to be sure on a somewhat different test for obscenity — has been summarized in *Paris Adult Theatre I v. Slaton*, 413 U.S. 49 at 56, 37 L.Ed. 2d 446, 93 S.Ct. 2628 (1973), note 6. Obscenity, it is said:

> ... is not a subject that lends itself to the traditional use of expert testimony... indeed the "expert witness" practices employed in these cases have often made a mockery out of the otherwise sound concept of expert testimony.

U.S. v. Various Articles of Obscene Merchandise, U.S.C.A., 2nd Circ., 709 F. 2d 132 at 135 (1983), a recently reported American obscenity decision, confirms that, although the government bears the burden of proving each element of obscenity (including a breach of community standards) to the satisfaction of the trier of fact, expert evidence of community standards is not constitutionally required, and that absent (or even in the face of) such evidence the impugned materials may "speak for themselves" so as to ground a conviction for obscenity.

This is essentially the situation that obtains in Canada. In *R. v. Cameron*, supra, in the judgment cited by the appellant, Laskin J.A. distills from the case law five propositions regarding the law of obscenity. The fifth, at p. 513, is:

> 5. Expert evidence is admissible on the issue of 'undueness' but it must be weighed by the Court even when it is all one way and stands uncontradicted.

With respect, I agree that this is an accurate statement of the law. If later passages in Laskin J.A.'s dissent do in fact retreat from this position, so as to suggest that expert evidence, whether in chief or in rebuttal, is a legal prerequisite for a finding of obscenity, then with great respect I cannot agree. I consider as accurate the following statement of evidentiary requirements enunciated in the recent decision of Borins Co. Ct. J. in *R. v. Doug Rankine Co.*, supra, at pp. 171-72:

> It is well established that, if the material itself is introduced into evidence, expert evidence as to obscenity or community standards is not required. Indeed, even if it is presented, the trier of fact is not bound to accept it. There is no necessity for the judge or jury to rely on evidence introduced in court as the basis for identifying community standards. Therefore, the trier of fact may determine for himself or herself (or themselves, in cases tried by a jury) the content of the community standard which is to be applied in determining whether the material in issue exceeds that standard. It is an objective test which applies. The test is not

> based on the level of tolerance of the judge or the jury. It is what the judge or jury believe the national level of tolerance to be.

Although, with great respect, I would not subscribe to any suggestion in Laskin J.A.'s dissent in *R. v. Cameron,* supra, that expert evidence is mandatory, I would nonetheless adopt his comment at p. 515 of that judgment:

> Of course, that ultimate issue was for him [the judge], but even the most knowledgeable adjudicator should hesitate to rely on his own taste, his subjective appreciation, to condemn art. He does not advance the situation by invoking his right to apply the law and satisfying it by a formulary advertence to the factors which must be canvassed in order to register a conviction.

What is essential to a determination of undueness by means of the community standards test is that the trier of fact formulate an opinion of what the contemporary Canadian community will tolerate. In forming this opinion, the trier of fact must assess the community consensus. This assessment will inevitably involve judgments about values since it is one that touches the very fundamental mores and viewpoints of the Canadian community.

I would repeat, however, that this inquiry, though involving judgments about values, must be distinguished from the application of the trier of fact's subjective opinions about the tastelessness or impropriety of certain publications. The decision must focus on an objective determination of the community's level of tolerance and whether the publication exceeds such level of tolerance, not the trier of fact's personal views regarding the impugned publication. Thus, the role of an appellate court on an appeal from a determination of the community standard is to ensure that the trier of fact's decision is based on an opinion of the community standard of tolerance, not on his or her opinion about the tastelessness or impropriety of the impugned publication.

Evidence of the community's standard of tolerance may well be useful and indeed desirable in many cases. Nonetheless, I do not consider that there must be evidence, expert or otherwise, which the trier of fact accepts before a particular publication can be determined to violate the community standard. It is the opinion of the trier of fact on the community standard of tolerance with which we are concerned. It ought not to be stated as a matter of law that the trier of fact must have evidence, expert or otherwise, to be able to form an opinion on the community standard of tolerance.

As I have indicated, the defence did lead evidence of Mr. Hooper, the Chairman of the Alberta Censor Board, for the purpose of showing that the film did not fall below contemporary community standards. The trial judge made only one reference to this evidence:

> Now, whether or not the film was approved by the censor board, as far as I am concerned, has nothing whatsoever to do with whether or not the Crown can prefer an indictment against it for providing an immoral, indecent or obscene performance. The court is the one that has to decide that.

The law is clear that a trier of fact does not have to accept testimony, whether expert or otherwise. He can reject it, in whole or in part. He cannot, however, reject it without good reason. In this case, it was incumbent on the trial judger to consider and assess the weight, if any, to be given to the evidence, indicative of community standards of tolerance, afforded by the approval of the film by censor boards or classification boards as well as the fact that no complaints had been received by the board in Alberta although more than 8500 people had viewed the film. He might, for instance, have considered the following assessment of similar evidence with regard to "Last Tango in Paris" by Freedman J.A. in *R. v. Odeon Morton Theatres Ltd.*, supra, at p. 196:

> [The issue of obscenity] must be determined according to contemporary community standards in Canada. Relevant to that determination are many factors. One is the testimony of the experts, to be judicially assessed and weighed. Another is the circumstance that the film is adult fare only, as it has been given the classification "Restricted Adult", thereby becoming unavailable to persons under 18 years of age. A third is the fact that the film is being shown in New Brunswick, Quebec, Ontario, and British Columbia, in all of which Provinces it was given clearance by censor boards who made no deletions in it. (The film is of course being shown in many other countries in the world as well.) The record does not disclose a single Province that has banned "Last Tango". I am loath to believe that Manitobans are less tolerant, less sophisticated, or more in need of protective shelter than other Canadians.

In the present case the trial judge should certainly not have rejected the evidence before him without explanation.

It must also be kept in mind that the Crown must prove its case beyond a reasonable doubt. If at the end of the case the trial judge, whether on the basis of the defence evidence or otherwise, has a reasonable doubt that the material falls below community standards, he must acquit. There is no onus on the accused to show that community standards have been met.

In my view the trial judge erred in failing to have regard to the unrebutted evidence of the Chairman of the Censor Board of Alberta.

Both the points advanced by the appellant are well taken. I would therefore allow the appeal, set aside the judgments at trial and on appeal, and order a new trial.

...

WILSON J.: — I concur in the result reached by the Chief Justice. I wish, however, to express my own view as to what the trial judge did in this case that constituted error in law. In so doing I have found it necessary to some extent to revert to first principles. I start with the wording of s.159(8) of the Criminal Code, which reads:

> (8) For the purposes of this Act, any publication a dominant characteristic of which is the undue exploitation of sex, or of sex and any one or more of the following subjects, namely, crime, horror, cruelty and violence, shall be deemed to be obscene.

It seems to me that the question which the section poses is: is the undue exploitation of sex a dominant characteristic of this movie? The narrower question is: is the exploitation of sex in this movie "undue"? If the exploitation of sex in the movie is not "undue", then it matters not that the exploitation of sex is a dominant characteristic of the movie; it cannot be obscene under the section. The primary question, then, to which all others are subordinate, is: is the exploitation of sex in the movie "undue"?

I turn to the test of "undueness". How is "undueness" to be measured? Clearly it postulates a standard which cannot be exceeded and that standard has been stated by the courts to be an objective one, the contemporary community standard in Canada. The problem then becomes one of how to identify that contemporary community standard in order to decide whether or not it has been exceeded.

The standard we are concerned with, it seems to me, is the degree of exploitation of sex which the Canadian community at any given point of time is prepared to accept in its movies. This is sometimes referred to as the Canadian standard of tolerance. I take no issue with the word tolerance. In my view there is no difference in meaning between acceptance by the community and tolerance by the community. I do not find it helpful, however, to refine further on that standard by identifying it as the degree of exploitation of sex to which Canadians are prepared to have other Canadians exposed. I think this is a different standard, a much more difficult one to identify and one not mandated by the section.

The test by which the trier of fact must assess the community standard is an objective one. The community standard itself, however, necessarily contains an element of subjectivity, since what must be objectified are the subjective views of the entire community as to what degree of exploitation of sex is acceptable. To identify the community standard in terms of the degree of exploitation of sex to which Canadians are prepared to have other Canadians exposed has the effect, however, of introducing an even greater degree of subjectivity into the community standard. I believe this is so because what Canadians consider to be acceptable for other Canadians is likely to depend heavily on which other Canadians they have in mind. The community may feel that the degree of exploitation of sex in a particular film would be unacceptable if the film were shown to an audience of young people or senior citizens but nevertheless feel that it would be acceptable if the film were shown to a university group. In determining this community standard the trier of fact would be forced to speculate not only on what the community considers to be acceptable but on which particular constituency the community has in mind in setting the standard of acceptability.

I think we have to approach the question more directly and ask: do Canadians today accept this degree of exploitation of sex in their movies? If they do, then the movie is not obscene. If they do not, then the exploitation is "undue" and, if it is a dominant characteristic of the movie, the movie is deemed to be obscene under the section. It is not, in my opinion, open to the courts under s.159(8) of the Criminal Code to characterize a movie as obscene if shown to one constituency but not if shown to another. I do not doubt that it is desirable to regulate the movies that can be shown to different constituencies. A movie which is not obscene within the meaning of the Criminal Code may still not be desirable viewing material for persons under the age of 18. Such regulation, as will be mentioned later in these reasons, is authorized in various provincial jurisdictions but it is the regulation of material which is not obscene under the Code. I do not think the court would, by segregating the community into different groups for purposes of ascertaining the standard of tolerance the community would adopt for each group, inject into s.159(8) of the Criminal Code a series of different tests of obscenity. In my view, a movie is either obscene under the Code based on a national community standard of tolerance or it is not. If it is not, it may still be the subject of provincial regulatory control.

"Undueness", however, is not purely a matter of degree. It must have reference to the total context of the movie. As Judson J. said in *Brodie v. R.; Dansky v. R.; Rubin v. R.*, [1962] S.C.R. 681 at 702, 37 C.R. 120, 132 C.C.C. 161, 32 D.L.R. (2d) 507, in discussing obscenity in literature:

> It is not the particular passages and words in a certain context that are before the Court for judgment but the book as a complete work. The question is whether the book as a whole is obscene not whether certain passages and certain words, parts of a larger work, are obscene.

The same point was made by Freedman C.J.M. in *R. v. Odeon Morton Theatres Ltd.*, [1974] 3 W.W.R. 304, 16 C.C.C. (2d) 185 at 193, 45 D.L.R. (3d) 224 (Man. C.A.), when, in speaking of the film "Last Tango in Paris," he said:

> It must be judged as a whole. It should not be condemned as obscene merely by reference to its sexual episodes or to its occasional gross and earthy language. Both the episodes and the language must be assessed in the context of and in their relationship to the entire film.

Coming back, then, to the determination of the community standard in the terms I have described, namely, the standard the community at any given time is prepared to accept or tolerate, how is this moral consensus to be ascertained? I describe it as a "moral" consensus because I agree with the Chief Justice that we are not concerned here with matters of "taste". To use the standard accepted by members of the community for themselves does not, in my view, substitute "taste" for moral acceptability. I think it is incorrect to say that when I am deciding whether or not I myself am prepared to be shown a certain type of movie I am making a decision merely on the basis of *taste* but when I am deciding whether or not I am prepared to have that same movie shown to others I am making a decision on the basis of *tolerance*. This, in my view, is a false distinction. In either case tolerance in the sense of moral acceptability is the issue — in the former case moral acceptability to myself and in the latter moral acceptability to others. People may, of course, refuse to patronize certain movies on grounds of taste but this is not at all what we are concerned with under the Criminal Code.

The Shorter Oxford English Dictionary, 3rd ed. (1944), defines "toleration" as "the action or practice of tolerating or allowing what is not actually approved". It is apparent from this definition that there is a distinction between that which is not approved and that which is not to be tolerated. In *R. v. Doug Rankine Co.* (1983), 36 C.R. (3d) 154 at 173, 9 C.C.C. (3d) 53 (Ont. Co. Ct.), Borins Co. Ct. J. made the following assessment of community standards of tolerance in relation to what may be described as "sex films":

> In my opinion, contemporary community standards would tolerate the distribution of films which consist substantially of scenes of people engaged in sexual intercourse. Contemporary community standards would also tolerate the distribution of films which consist of scenes of group sex, lesbianism, fellatio, cunnilingus, and anal sex. However, films which consist substantially or partially of scenes which portray violence and cruelty in conjunction with sex, particularly where the performance of indignities degrades and dehumanizes the people upon whom they are performed, exceed the level of community tolerance.

In drawing this distinction I do not think that Borins Co. Ct. J. was suggesting that the average Canadian finds the former type of film to his or her taste or that such films are inoffensive to most Canadians. Rather, I think that Borins Co. Ct. J. recognized that, whether or not Canadians found the former type of films distasteful, they were prepared to tolerate their being shown.

It seems to me that the undue exploitation of sex at which s.159(8) is aimed is the treatment of sex which in some fundamental way dehumanizes the persons portrayed and, as a consequence, the viewers themselves. There is nothing wrong in the treatment of sex per se but there may be something wrong in the manner of its treatment. It may be presented brutally, salaciously and in a degrading manner, and would thus be dehumanizing and intolerable not only to the individuals or groups who are victimized by it but to society at large. On the other hand, it may be presented in a way which harms no one, in that it depicts nothing more than non-violent sexual activity in a manner which neither degrades nor dehumanizes any particular individuals or groups. It is this line between the mere portrayal of human sexual acts and the dehumanization of people that must be reflected in the definition of ''undueness''.

How is the court to determine where the line is drawn? By guidelines read into the definition as a matter of interpretation of the word ''undue''? By consideration of the presumed social ills sought to be avoided by restrictions on freedom of publication? By statistics showing what people are prepared to look at and what they are not? The courts have said that the test is an objective one and clearly that must be so. But objectivity requires criteria and the courts have not been too successful in evolving them. Yet this is a criminal offence and it is basic to our system of criminal justice that the public know what conduct is criminal and what is not.

This, it seems to me, militates very strongly against a community standard test of undueness which varies with ''the targeted group''. I believe it is important to the publishing industry to have some degree of certainty as to when they may be exposing themselves to a criminal charge. The only way to provide that degree of certainty is, in my opinion, to have a uniform community standard test of ''undueness'' under the Code. With great respect to those who think otherwise, I see nothing in s.159(8) which would permit something to be obscene under the section when shown to X but not obscene when shown to Y. Moreover, it seems to me that this approach would inevitably lead to problems where a publication targeted to one group by the accused fell into the hands of others.

As I see it, the essential difficulty with the definition of obscenity is that ''undueness'' must presumably be assessed in relation to consequences. It is implicit in the definition that at some point the exploitation of sex becomes harmful to the public or at least the public believes that to be so. It is therefore necessary for the protection of the public to put limits on the degree of exploitation and, through the application of the community standard test, the public is made the arbiter of what is harmful to it and what is not. The problem is that we know so little of the consequences we are seeking to avoid. Do obscene movies spawn immoral conduct? Do they degrade women? Do they promote violence? The most that can be said, I think, is that the public has concluded that exposure to material which degrades the human dimensions of life to a subhuman or merely physical dimension and thereby contributes to a process of moral desensitization must be harmful in some way. It must therefore be controlled when it gets out of hand, when it becomes ''undue''.

Addressing the problem of ''undueness'' in the context of agreements which ''prevent or lessen, unduly, competition'' in a product, Idington J. said in *Weidman v. Shragge* (1912), 46 S.C.R. 1 at 20-21, 2 W.W.R. 330, 20 C.C.C. 117, 2 D.L.R. 734:

> This being a criminal statute we must try to find the vicious purpose aimed at in order to bring parties within its prohibitions...
>
> Crimes usually imply something all right-minded men condemn...
>
> The test must in each case be the true purpose and its relation to the activities specified in and by the words of the statute and a finding of an evil or vice answering to the descriptive word ''unduly''.

He found the vicious purpose in the context of combines legislation to be the destruction of all competition. What is the vicious purpose aimed at in the case of obscenity legislation? The statutory definition does not provide an answer nor, with respect, does the existing jurisprudence.

The test of the community standard is helpful to the extent that it provides a norm against which impugned material may be assessed but it does little to elucidate the underlying question as to why some exploitation of sex falls on the permitted side of the line under s.159(8) and some on the prohibited side. No doubt this question will have to be addressed when the validity of the obscenity provisions of the Code are subjected to attack as an infringement on freedom of speech and the infringement is sought to be justified as reasonable. Suffice it to say that clearly some fairly basic values are designed to be protected by the obscenity provisions and the community standards test is premised on the assumption that these values are held in common by the contemporary Canadian community.

The community standard test in Canada, I believe, had its origin in *Brodie,* supra, the "Lady Chatterley's Lover" case, in which four members of this court concluded that the definition of obscenity introduced into the Code in 1957 made the test in *R. v. Hicklin* (1868), L.R. 3 Q.B. 360, obsolete. In their view it was no longer necessary to show a tendency to corrupt and deprave if the dominant characteristic of the publication was an exploitation of sex which was "undue". The test of "undueness", said Fauteux J. at p. 697, was whether the exploitation was shocking and disgusting "having regard to the existing standards of decency in the community..." Judson J. agreed at pp. 705-706 that the standards of acceptance prevailing in the community provided the test of "undueness" for purposes of the definition. The statutory definition, he felt, could not be superimposed upon the *Hicklin* test without leaving the citizen in the position of not knowing whether he was committing a criminal act or not.

The community standard test was applied the same year (1962) in Manitoba by Freedman J.A. (as he then was) dissenting in *R. v. Dom. News & Gifts Ltd.,* 42 W.W.R. 65, 40 C.R. 109, [1963] 2 C.C.C. 103. The learned justice said he would have judged the magazines by the standards of the community and this court, in reversing the decision of the Manitoba Court of Appeal ([1964] S.C.R. 251, 42 C.R. 209, [1964] 3 C.C.C. 1), unanimously approved and adopted his reasons. I quote the relevant passage in full from pp. 116-17 of Freedman J.A.'s reasons:

> The case for the Crown stands or falls on the applicability or otherwise of the first part of the definition — namely, that a dominant characteristic of these magazines was "the undue exploitation of sex".
>
> Can it fairly be said that this was a dominant characteristic of either Dude or Escapade? I have examined them both with care. That they do not qualify as reading matter which I would personally select for myself even in an idle hour is undoubtedly the case. But that does not make them obscene. In this area of the law one must be especially vigilant against erecting personal tastes or prejudices into legal principles. Many persons quite evidently desire to read these magazines, even though I do not. I recognize, of course, that the mere numerical support which a publication is able to attract is not determinative of the issue whether it is obscene or not. Let a publication be sufficiently pornographic and it will be bound to appeal, in the hundreds or thousands, to the prurient, the lascivious, the ignorant, the simple, or even the merely curious. Admitting, therefore, that a large readership is not the test, I must yet add that it is not always an entirely irrelevant factor. For it may have to be taken into account when one seeks to ascertain or identify the standards of the community in these matters. Those standards are not set by those of lowest taste or interest. Nor are they set exclusively by those of rigid, austere, conservative, or puritan taste and habit of mind. Something approaching a general average of community thinking and feeling has to be discovered.

> Obviously, this is no easy task, for we are seeking a quantity that is elusive. Yet the effort must be made if we are to have a fair objective standard in relation to which a publication can be tested as to whether it is obscene or not. The alternative would mean a subjective approach, with the result dependent upon and varying with the personal tastes and predilections of the particular Judge who happens to be trying the case.
>
> Community standards must be contemporary. Times change, and ideas change with them. Compared to the Victorian era this is a liberal age in which we live. One manifestation of it is the relative freedom with which the whole question of sex is discussed. In books, magazines, movies, television, and sometimes even in parlour conversation, various aspects of sex are made the subject of comment, with a candour that in an earlier day would have been regarded as indecent and intolerable. We cannot and should not ignore these present-day attitudes when we face the question whether Dude and Escapade are obscene according to our criminal law.
>
> Community standards must also be local. In other words, they must be Canadian. In applying the definition in the *Criminal Code* we must determine what is obscene by Canadian standards, regardless of attitudes which may prevail elsewhere, be they more liberal or less so.
>
> I think I should add my view that, in cases close to the border line, tolerance is to be preferred to proscription. To strike at a publication which is not clearly obscene may have repercussions and implications beyond what is immediately visible. To suppress the bad is one thing: to suppress the not so bad, or even the possibly good is quite another. Unless it is confined to clear cases, suppression may tend to inhibit those creative impulses and endeavours which ought to be encouraged in a free society.

In reversing the Manitoba Court of Appeal Taschereau C.J.C. said at p. 251:

> We are all of opinion that the appeals should be allowed. We agree with the reasons given by Freedman J.A. in the Court of Appeal for Manitoba. We wish to adopt those reasons in their entirety and do not find it necessary to add anything to them.

I would respectfully adopt "the Freedman approach" as the law applicable to this case.

If I am correct as to how the community standard in Canada is to be identified, namely, with reference to what Canadians at any given point of time will accept in their movies, then what is the significance of the evidence of the unanimous approval of this film by the censor boards of all the provinces having such boards?

I believe that there is an onus on the Crown to put evidence before the court on the issue of "undueness". I cannot see how the community standard against which the allegedly obscene matter has to be measured can be identified without it. In *R. v. Cameron,* [1966] 2 O.R. 777, 49 C.R. 49, [1966] 4 C.C.C. 273, 58 D.L.R. (2d) 486 (C.A.), Laskin J.A. (as he then was) pointed out in dissent that because a judge or jury may be limited in the geographical range of his exposure, which in turn might result in "a limitation of opportunity of appreciation and understanding" of the particular subject matter — in that case artists' drawings — expert evidence was indispensable. He said at p. 515:

> I think that such evidence would always be necessary to support the case for the Crown as well as to support the defence, especially where, as here, pictures by artists of repute are seized from a reputable gallery. Holding this view, I cannot but be surprised that the Crown in the case at bar produced no expert evidence and relied on the pictures themselves to convey obscenity to the Magistrate. Of course, that ultimate issue was for him, but even the most knowledgeable adjudicator should hesitate to rely on his own taste, his subjective appreciation, to condemn art. He does not advance the situation by invoking his right to apply the law and

satisfying it by a formulary advertence to the factors which must be canvassed in order to register a conviction.

Laskin J.A. was, of course, speaking of expert evidence in the context of that case but it seems to me that the point is well made with respect to non-expert evidence as well. Having regard to the fact that the onus is on the Crown to establish obscenity beyond a reasonable doubt, it seems to me that the onus is on it to establish both what the community standard of acceptability is and that the accused has gone beyond it. The accused may counter the Crown's evidence of the community standard with evidence of its own and the judge may reach his decision on the evidence in the usual way. In my view it is naive to think that a judge, drawing on his own experience alone, can determine the objective standard against which impugned conduct is to be measured. As Borins Co. Ct. J. said in *R. v. Doug Rankine Co.*, supra, the legislature cannot credibly expect a trier of fact to have his finger on the "'pornographic pulse' of the nation" [p. 172]. Moreover, it is wrong in principle. It leaves the accused with no way of knowing the case it has to meet, at what level of acceptability the line will be drawn by any particular judge. There is no certainty. It is the length of the Chancellor's foot imported into the criminal law.

The result feared by Laskin J.A. when no evidence is presented to the trial judge is precisely what happened here. The trial judge made "a formulary advertence to the factors that had to be canvassed". He indicated that he knew that the test of "undueness" was an objective one, that he had to decide whether or not the film exceeded the standard of acceptability to the community as a whole, but he then proceeded to attribute the sense of revulsion which he experienced on viewing the film to the community as a whole. He gave no indication of the basis on which he felt able to make that leap and there is no suggestion that he took into consideration the evidence of censor board approval which was before him. That evidence was not contested and, having regard to the statutory purpose for which these boards were created, I think it was relevant evidence and evidence which he was obliged to consider.

The legislation creating these boards varies from province to province but the role of the boards, generally speaking, is to approve, prohibit or regulate the exhibition of films within their respective provinces. The boards are not empowered only to approve or disapprove films in toto. In some provinces the legislation also authorizes the boards to "remove by cutting or otherwise" parts of films. Most provinces have a film classification system, the classes, generally speaking, being "general", "adult" and "restricted".

Since the business of these boards is to assess films on an ongoing basis for the very purpose of determining their acceptability for viewing by the community as a whole or a segment of the community depending upon classification, they must be regarded as tribunals with expertise at least on the community standard within their own province. It is hard to think that a judge, or even a jury, sitting in or drawn from a local area would be better informed as to what was acceptable to Canadians across the country. Moreover, in this case at least, the boards' assessments disclose a remarkable degree of uniformity. I do not see how the learned trial judge, applying an objective test and giving proper consideration to that evidence, could have reached the result he did. I believe it is clear from his reasons that he saw his role, not as applying the community standard, but as raising the standard if he personally thought it was too low. I think he was clearly in error in this regard.

The Court of Appeal on this aspect of the case stated:

> The trial judge, sitting as a jury, was obliged to determine in an objective way what was tolerable in accordance with the contemporary standards of the Canadian community. As a trier of fact he was entitled to draw on his experience in the community. He had to consider the expert evidence but was entitled to reject it and obviously did.

With respect, I think it is far from obvious that the trial judge rejected the expert evidence. The only comment he made on it was:

> Now, whether or not the film was approved by the censor board, as far as I am concerned, has nothing whatsoever to do with whether or not the Crown can prefer an indictment against it for providing an immoral, indecent or obscene performance. The court is the one that has to decide that.

There is no question that the approval of the censor board does not preclude the preferring of an indictment. The issue the judge had to decide was the significance of the approvals as evidence of the community standard of acceptance. It seems to me that he never addressed his mind to that issue.

In my view, the practice of allowing the trier of fact to rely exclusively on his or her personal experience of community standards of tolerance (see *R. v. Great West News Ltd.*, 72 W.W.R. 354, 10 C.R.N.S. 42, [1970] 4 C.C.C. 307 at 314-15 (Man. C.A.)) is an invitation to the type of error committed by the trial judge in this case. The problem can be readily avoided by requiring the Crown to adduce evidence of the community standard. The trier of fact would then determine the community standard on the basis of the evidence before him in the same way as he determines the factual issues in any other kind of criminal case.

I cannot see how such a requirement would, as has been suggested, frustrate the Crown's ability to secure a conviction in a meritorious case. At present the trier of fact in an obscenity case can be faced with the unenviable task of deciding the level of tolerance of a community of 24,000,000 people on the basis of nothing more than his or her own personal experience. In effect, what the trier of fact does in the absence of evidence is attribute by inference his or her own perception to the entire Canadian community. I would think that requiring the trier of fact to make the determination on the basis of evidence adduced would render the task easier rather than more difficult. It would also, in my view, inspire greater public confidence in the result. Moreover, it might well have the very desirable effect of enhancing uniformity in the application of the law of obscenity since evidence of community standards which is relevant to one prosecution will commonly be relevant to others.

I agree with the Chief Justice that the appeal must be allowed, the judgment at trial and on appeal set aside and a new trial ordered.

Appeal allowed; new trial ordered.

Note: As to whether s.159 of the Criminal Code infringes or denies "freedom of expression", see *R.* v. *Wagner* (1985), 43 C.R. (3d) 318 (Alta. Q.B.); *R.* v. *Pereira-Vasquez (Martinez)* (1985), 43 C.R. (3d) 336 (B.C. Co. Ct.); *R.* v. *St. John News Co.* (1985), 64 N.B.R. (2d) 318 (Q.B.); *Germain* v. *R.* (1985), 21 D.L.R. (4th) 296 (S.C.C.); *R.* v. *Lynnco Sound Ltd.* (1985), 61 N.B.R. (2d) 301 (Q.B.); *R.* v. *Neil's Ventures Ltd.* (1985), 61 N.B.R. (2d) 42 (Q.B.); and *R.* v. *Video World Ltd.* (1985), 32 Man. R. (2d) 41 (Prov. Ct.).

4.4.14 *Popert et al.* v. *R.* (1981), 19 C.R. (3d) 393 (Ont. C.A.)

ZUBER J.A.: — The appellants were charged that in 1977 they made use of the mails for the purpose of transmitting indecent, immoral or scurrilous matter contrary to s.164 of the Criminal Code, R.S.C. 1970, c.C-34. The case was tried in the Provincial Court before Harris Prov. J., who acquitted the appellants [45 C.C.C. (2d) 385].

The Crown appealed to Ferguson Co. Ct. J., who disagreed with Harris Prov. J. on a number of legal issues. He set aside the acquittal and ordered a new trial [51 C.C.C. (2d) 485]. The appellants appeal to this court seeking a reversal of Ferguson Co. Ct. J.'s order and a restoration of the verdict of acquittal.

The Facts

The facts in this case are disarmingly simple. The appellants Popert, Jackson and Hannon are all officers of the corporate appellant, Pink Triangle Press, which publishes a newspaper entitled "The Body Politic". The December 1977-January 1978 issue of this publication (Ex. 1), which is the subject of this prosection, was sent through the mails to subscribers in Canada and the United States. The subscribers, it is conceded, are homosexuals. The publication addresses itself to that readership.

Exhibit 1 contains an article entitled "Men Loving Boys Loving Men". The central figures of this article are apparently fictional characters named Peter, Barry and Simon. The article describes the relationship of these men with young boys, and particularly acts of buggery and gross indecency, and concludes that "they... deserve our praise, our admiration and our support".

It is appropriate to mention at this point that no issue is taken in this court as to whether the personal appellants were insulated from criminal responsibility by the corporate appellant.

While the facts are not complicated, they have spawned a number of troublesome legal issues. Both of the learned judges who have thus far dealt with this case have responded to the problems by the delivery of detailed written reasons.

Harris Prov. J. placed the acquittal of the appellants on four grounds. These grounds are:

(a) Section 164 is not aimed at the distribution by mail of magazines or journals to subscribers;

(b) There is insufficient evidence to establish a community standard;

(c) The word "immoral" in s.164, being undefined, does not establish an acceptable area for a lawful action; and

(d) Exhibit 1, as a whole or in part, is not indecent.

On the hearing of this appeal, Mr. Ruby argued (and I agree) that it was not necessary that Harris Prov. J. be right on every issue. A single valid reason for acquittal is sufficient and if one can be found the acquittal should be restored. I propose to deal in turn with each of the four reasons for acquittal.

(a) The purpose of s.164

Section 164 of the Criminal Code is as follows:

"164. Every one commits an offence who makes use of the mails for the purpose of transmitting or delivering anything that is obscene, indecent, immoral or scurrilous, but this section does not apply to a person who makes use of the mails for the purpose of transmitting or delivering anything mentioned in subsection 162(4).''

Harris Prov. J. was of the view that this section was not designed to catch the kind of distribution of mailed material that occurred in this case, but was designed to catch the sick individual who, rather than indulging in obscene telephone calls, indulges in obscene, indecent, immoral or scurrilous mailing.

I find no basis for such a restriction on this section. By its own plain words, it applies to *everyone* who makes use of the mails in the manner prohibited by the section.

(b) Community standards

It is apparent that the real issue in this case is whether the article ''Men Loving Boys Loving Men'' published in The Body Politic is immoral or indecent. (I leave aside the term ''scurrilous'' as having no application to the facts of this case.)

The determination of what is immoral or indecent is to be determined by a judge, not by reference to his own standards of indecency or immorality but by reference to a community standard. I defer, for the moment, the exact nature of the community standards test. The learned trial judge, however, was of the opinion that there rested on the Crown an obligation to produce evidence and prove a community standard. In his reasons for judgment he said at p. 400:

''... in this case the trial Judge must determine *on the evidence* what is the community standard of acceptance of material that is or may be indecent, immoral or scurrilous.''

And, at p. 403:

''I am of the opinion that all in all the evidence adduced from the majority of both Crown and Defence witnesses establishes nothing which really assists the Court in ascertaining the limits of community tolerance...''

And at p. 411:

''In the result, therefore, I, having found... that there is insufficient evidence to establish a community standard... it follows that each of the accused is not guilty of this charge...''

In my view, the learned trial judge was in error. The referrence to a community standard imports an objective test into the ascertainment of indecency and immorality and, while evidence with respect to community standards is admissible and sometimes helpful, it is not a fact which the Crown is obliged to prove as a part of its case: see *R. v. Prairie Schooner News Ltd.* (1970), 75 W.W.R. 585, 12 Cr. L.Q. 462, 1 C.C.C. (2d) 251 (Man. C.A.); *R. v. Great West News Ltd.*, 10 C.R.N.S. 42, 72 W.W.R. 354, [1970] 4 C.C.C. 307 (Man. C.A.).

(c) Immoral

In turning his attention to the word ''immoral'' as used in s.164, Harris Prov. J. expressed the view that he could find no legally enforceable meaning in the term ''immoral'' and, as a result, Ex. 1 could not be legally immoral. I concede that the term ''immoral'' is a word of imprecise meaning and that it may be difficult to apply. However, the problem is not unique. Often the law, whether a product of case law or statute, expresses itself in imprecise terms such as ''reasonable'', ''undue'', and ''dangerous''. It is through such words that the values of the community find expression in the courtroom. It is the function of the courts to work as best as they can with the tools in hand. In my view, the learned trial judge was wrong in simply finding no meaning in this word.

(d) Indecent

As his final reason for acquittal, Harris Prov. J. held that using the "ordinary meaning" of the word "indecent" he could not find that Ex. 1 was indecent. It is at this point that Mr. Ruby presents his most forceful argument. It is his position that if Harris Prov. J. was right in finding that the material was not indecent then, in the circumstances of this case, neither could the impugned material be immoral. Further, the errors with respect to other issues then become unimportant and the Crown's case must fail.

I begin by observing that Ferguson Co. Ct. J. did not, as he might have done, simply disagree with Harris Prov. J. as to the assessment of the publication. Instead, he dealt with certain matters of law involved in the determination of whether or not Ex. 1 was indecent.

In his approach to the issue of indecency, Harris Prov. J. began by dealing with the publication as a whole. This was an error. It was the specific article that was the focus of this case. In some instances an otherwise indecent part of a single work, such as a novel, may be redeemed by the artistic necessity to maintain the integrity of a plot or story line. Exhibit 1 is not a single work. It is a newspaper containing a variety of material that has no connection with the impugned article. In *R. v. Penthouse Internat. Ltd.* (1979), 46 C.C.C. (2d) 111 (Ont. C.A.), Weatherston J.A. dealt with a magazine and said at p. 117:

"Each page must be looked at more or less in isolation from the others, for it is but rarely that a reader of a magazine will start at the beginning and read through to the end. Offensive passages or pictorial presentations in a magazine cannot be saved merely by surrounding them with profound articles on foreign policy."

That principle applies here.

In his concluding paragraph, however, the trial judge stated that he found that the term "indecent" did not apply either to Ex. 1 as a whole or *the article therein primarily objected to by the Crown*. In this conclusion, as well, there was error in law. In dealing with the term "indecent", he purported to apply "the ordinary meaning" of the term. He had earlier found insufficient evidence to establish a community standard and, as a result, discarded that concept. I agree with Ferguson Co. Ct. J. that the trial judge's conclusion, reached upon a test which ignored the community standards test, must be open to doubt. I further agree with Ferguson Co. Ct. J. that, as a result of the legal errors which occurred, the verdict of acquittal is vitiated and, as a result, the order directing a new trial must stand.

There remains, however, one further issue. In directing a new trial, Ferguson Co. Ct. J. directed his attention to the community standards test to be applied in determining whether the impugned material is either indecent or immoral. He came to the conclusion that the appropriate measure of the terms "immoral" or "indecent" was the community standard of immorality or indecency. He rejected the community standard of tolerance as the appropriate test in determining the application of these terms.

In cases dealing with obscenity, it is now accepted that the appropriate test is the community standard of tolerance: see *R. v. Penthouse Internat. Ltd.*, supra; *R. v.*

Sudbury News Service Ltd. (1978), 18 O.R. (2d) 428, 39 C.C.C. (2d) 1 (C.A.); and *R. v. Prairie Schooner News Ltd.*, supra. In my respectful view, the same test should be applied in determining whether material is immoral or indecent. In *R. v. Prairie Schooner News Ltd.*, Dickson J.A. (as he then was) said at p. 269:

> "In the *Great West News* case, we referred to contemporary standards of tolerance. I have no doubt, as Dr. Rich testified, and as the Judge agreed, a distinction can be made between private taste and standard of tolerance. It can hardly be questioned that many people would find personally offensive, material which they would permit others to read. Parliament, through its legislation on obscenity, could hardly have wished to proscribe as criminal that which was acceptable or tolerable according to current standards of the Canadian community."

Although those words were written within the context of the case dealing with obscenity, in my view they apply with equal validity to the terms "indecent" and "immoral" in this case. Further, the advantage of a consistent test in the application of these various terms is not insignificant.

For the foregoing reasons this appeal is dismissed.

Appeal dismissed.

Note: A new trial was held, as ordered. At this trial the accused were acquitted again. The Crown again appealed to the County Court which ordered another new trial. The accused appealed this ruling to the Court of Appeal, which again upheld the County Court. The third trial has yet to be held.

4.4.15 Canada Post Corporation Act, R.S.C. 1985, c.D-5, s.43

USE OF MAILS FOR UNLAWFUL PURPOSES

Unlawful use of mails

43. (1) Where the Minister believes on reasonable grounds that any person

(*a*) is, by means of the mails,

(i) committing or attempting to commit an offence, or

(ii) aiding, counselling or procuring any person to commit an offence, or

(*b*) with intent to commit an offence, is using the mails for the purpose of accomplishing his object,

the Minister may make an order (in this section... called an "interim prohibitory order") prohibiting the delivery, without the consent of the Minister, of mail addressed to or posted by that person (in this section... called the "person affected").

4.4.16 *Luscher* v. *Deputy Minister, Revenue Canada, Customs and Excise* (1985), 45 C.R. (3d) 81 (F.C.A.)

Annotation

Before the advent of the Charter, void for uncertainty was a well-recognized ground of challenge to by-law offences (see, for example, *Harrison v. Toronto* (1982), 39 O.R. (2d) 721, 31 C.R. (3d) 244, 19 M.P.L.R. 310, 140 D.L.R. (3d) 309 (H.C.)), but our courts had recoiled from its availability in the case of other types of criminal sanction. In *R. v. Pink Triangle Press* (1979), 45 C.C.C. (2d) 385 (Ont. Prov. Ct.), Harris Prov. J. held that the undefined term "immoral" in s.164 of the Criminal Code was so "ambiguous and indefinite" (p. 407) that it had "no legally enforceable meaning" (p. 408). This decision was, however, soon reversed (51 C.C.C. (2d) 485 (Co. Ct.)) and on further appeal the Ontario Court of Appeal (19 C.R. (3d) 393 (sub nom. *Popert v. R.*), 58 C.C.C. (2d) 505) confirmed that the trial judge had erred. On behalf of the court Zuber J.A. agreed that the meaning of "immoral" *was* imprecise but, observing that the courts often had to interpret imprecise terms such as "reasonable", "undue" and "dangerous", held at p. 398 that the courts had "to work as best they can with the tools in hand".

Now various Courts of Appeal have held that a Charter right or freedom cannot be subject to a reasonable limit prescribed by law under s.1 if that law is too vague. In adopting in this context the complex United States doctrine of "void for vagueness", our courts have now opened a "Pandora's box of constitutional concepts": see Mansell's annotation to *Ont. Film & Video Appreciation Soc. v. Ont. Bd. of Censors* (1983), 34 C.R. (3d) 74, at p. 74. The ruling of the Divisional Court of the Ontario Supreme Court in *Ont. Film & Video Appreciation Soc. v. Ont. Bd. of Censors* (1983), 41 O.R. (2d) 583, 34 C.R. (3d) 73 at 83, 147 D.L.R. (3d) 58, 5 C.R.R. 373, was obiter — as it was held that a non-binding set of guidelines promulgated by pamphlet were not capable of being law, a decision that was confirmed by the Ontario Court of Appeal, 45 O.R. (2d) 80, 38 C.R. (3d) 271, 5 D.L.R. (4th) 766, 7 C.R.R. 120, 2 O.A.C. 388. Now, however, there is express authority for the void for vagueness approach to the concept of reasonable limits in the decisions of the British Columbia Court of Appeal in *R. v. Red Hot Video Ltd.*, ante, p. 36, and *R. v. Robson,* ante, p. 68, also 31 M.V.R. 220, and by the Federal Court of Appeal in *Luscher*. The rulings that our existing obscenity laws are not too vague — express in *Red Hot Video* and obiter in *Luscher* — now seem ironic in view of the level of complexity characterizing the Supreme Court of Canada judgments in *Towne Cinema Theatres Ltd. v. R.*, ante, p. 1, also [1984] 4 W.W.R. 1.

Don Stuart

HUGESSEN J.: The principal thrust of the appeal to this court is not against the decision of the deputy minister, which was confirmed by Anderson Co. Ct. J., but against the legislation under which that decision was reached. The appellant argues that tariff item 99201-1 is an infringement upon the freedoms protected by s.2(*b*) of the Canadian Charter of Rights and Freedoms and, as such, inoperative as not being saved by the excepting words of s.1. The appellant does not argue that Parliament could not prohibit or regulate the importation of material of this sort, commonly described as "smut", but rather that the prohibition as drawn in the legislation is invalid. I am in agreement with that submission.

Tariff item 99201-1, read the conjunction with s.14 of the Custums Tariff, prohibits the importation of:

> Books, printed paper, drawings, paintings, prints, photographs or representations of any kind of a treasonable or seditious, or of an immoral or indecent character.

Section 2(*b*) of the Charter enshrines and protects as "fundamental" freedoms:

> (*b*) freedom of thought, belief, opinion and expression, including freedom of the press and other media of communication.

That a prohibition whose first object is "books" is prima facie an infringement of the freedoms protected by s.2(*b*) appears to me to be a proposition not requiring demonstration.

No freedom however, can be absolute and those guaranteed by the Charter are no exception. They are, by s.1, subject to:

> 1. ...such reasonable limits prescribed by law as can be demonstrably justified in a free and democratic society.

That text, in its turn, makes it clear enough that the task of demonstrating the justification for a limitation of a protected freedom falls upon government: see *Re Southam Inc. and R.* (1983), 41 O.R. (2d) 113, 34 C.R. (3d) 27, 33 R.F.L. (2d) 279, 3 C.C.C. (3d) 515, 146 D.L.R. (3d) 408, 6 C.R.R. 1 (C.A.); *Re Germany (Fed. Republic) and Rauca* (1983), 41 O.R. (2d) 225, 34 C.R. (3d) 97 (sub nom. *R. v. Rauca*), 4 C.C.C. (3d) 385, 145 D.L.R. (3d) 638, 4 C.R.R. 42 (C.A.).

...

What has to be determined today is whether the words of tariff item 99201-1, together with any judicial gloss which has been placed on them, are sufficiently clear to constitute a "reasonable limit prescribed by law".

The first observation to be made in this regard is that the words "immoral" and "indecent" are nowhere defined in the legislation. This at once serves to distinguish the provisions of tariff item 99201-1 from the obscenity provisions of the Criminal Code, which contains in s.159(8) words which might be thought to give to those provisions sufficient certainty and particularity.

Secondly, the words "immoral" and "indecent" are highly subjective and emotional in their content. Opinions honestly held by reasonable people will vary widely. The current public debate on abortion has its eloquent and persuasive adherents on both sides arguing that their view alone is moral, that of their opponents immoral. Standards of decency also vary even (or perhaps especially) amongst judges. The case of *R. v. P.*, 3 C.R.N.S. 302, 63 W.W.R. 222, [1968] 3 C.C.C. 129 (Man. C.A.), provides an interesting example of a learned and articulate debate between the present Chief Justices of Canada and Manitoba respectively as to whether an act of heterosexual fellatio performed in private (such as Ex. 1 herein depicts, amongst other things) was grossly indecent. (The case was, of course, decided prior to the enactment of the present s.158 of the Criminal Code, by which Parliament legislated an end to the controversy.)

While obscenity under the Criminal Code is, by statutory definition, limited to matters predominantly sexual, there is no such limitation upon the concepts of immorality or indecency, and this is so notwithstanding the judicial gloss which has carried over into the test for immorality or indecency the test of community standards of tolerance. As stated by Lord Reid in *Knuller v. D.P.P.*, [1973] A.C. 435 at 458, [1972] 3 W.L.R. 143, 56 Cr. App. R. 633 (H.L.):

> Indecency is not confined to sexual indecency: indeed it is difficult to find any limit short of saying that it includes anything which an ordinary decent man or woman would find to be shocking, disgusting and revolting.

While it is, of course, true that the judicial overlay of the community standards of tolerance test has done something to reduce the inherent subjectivity of the words "immoral" and "indecent", this has, if anything, had the effect of increasing their uncertainty. Community standards themselves are in a constant state of flux and vary widely from place to place within the country. Yet the courts are obliged to apply a contemporary and nationwide standard.

...

I would add that it is, of course, no answer to the argument that a limitation on freedom is so vague as to be unreasonable to say that this publication or that is so immoral or indecent that it clearly falls afoul of the prohibition. One might as well argue that the Tale of Peter Rabbit was clearly not immoral or indecent and could therefore be admitted. Even the most defective provision is unlikely to be so vague as not to permit the placing of some cases on one side of the line or the other. What is significant is the size and importance of the grey area between the two extremes. Vagueness or uncertainty, like unreasonableness, are not themselves absolutes but tests by which the courts must measure the acceptability of limits upon Charter-protected freedoms.

Finally, let it be quite clear that what the Charter protects in s.2(*b*) is not acts or deeds but thought, expression and depiction. While the activities shown in the subject magazine are probably, as far as one can determine, legal, it would make no difference if they were crimes. The depiction of murder, real or imagined, is protected by s.2(*b*), but that does not mean that the Charter has declared open season for assassination.

I conclude that, insofar as it prohibits the importation of matters of immoral or indecent character, tariff item 99201-1 is not a reasonable limitation upon the freedoms guaranteed by s.2(*b*) of the Charter and is of no force or effect.

4.4.17 Customs Tariff, R.S.C. 1970, c.C-41 as am. 1984-85, c.12, ss.1 and 2

1. Tariff item 99201-1 of Schedule C to the *Customs Tariff* is repealed and the following substituted therefor:

"99201-1 Books, printed paper, drawings, paintings, prints, photographs or representations of any kind

(*a*) of a treasonable or seditious character;

(*b*) that are deemed to be obscene under subsection 159(8) of the *Criminal Code;* or

(*c*) that constitute hate propaganda within the meaning of subsection 281.3(8) of the *Criminal Code*."

2. Tariff item 99201-1, as enacted by section 1, shall cease to have effect on June 30, 1986.

4.4.18 Broadcasting Act, Radio (A.M.) Broadcasting Regulations, C.R.C. 1970, c.379, r.5(1) as am. SOR/84-786

Broadcasting Generally

5. (1) No station or network operator shall broadcast

(*a*) anything contrary to law;

"(*b*) any abusive comment that, when taken in context, tends or is likely to expose an individual or a group or class of individuals to hatred or contempt on the basis

of race, national or ethnic origin, colour, religion, sex, age or mental or physical disability;''
(*c*) any obscene, indecent or profane language;
(*d*) any false or misleading news;
(*e*) any program on the subject of birth control unless that program is presented in a manner appropriate to the medium of broadcasting;
(*f*) any program on the subject of venereal diseases unless that program is presented in a manner appropriate to the medium of broadcasting;

4.4.19 A Note on Film Censorship Laws in Canada

All of the provinces and the territories have passed legislation dealing with the exhibition of films. See the following: Amusements Act, R.S.A. 1980, c.A-41; Motion Picture Act, R.S.B.C. 1979, c.284; Amusements Act,R.S.M. 1970, c.A-70; Theatres, Cinematographs and Amusements Act, R.S.N.B. 1973, c.T-5; The Censoring of Moving Pictures Act, R.S.N. 1970, c.30; Theatres and Amusements Act, R.S.N.S. 1967, c.304 (C.S.N.S. c.T-10); Theatres Act, R.S.O. 1980, c.498; Entertainments Act, R.S.P.E.I. 1974, c.E-7; Cinema Act, S.Q. 1983, c.37; Theatres and Cinematographs Act, R.S.S. 1978, c.T-11; Motion Pictures Ordinance, C.O.Y.Y. 1978, c.M-10. The provisions of the above Acts that deal specifically with censorship of films will be highlighted in the following note.

1. *Alberta*

The Amusements Act, R.S.A. 1980, c.A-41 is typical of the other provincial film censorship laws. A censor, or board of censors of up to three persons, with the power to ''permit or prohibit the exhibition of any film in Alberta'' may be appointed by the Lieutenant Governor in Council (sections 9 and 10(1)). Any film which the censor permits to be exhibited must bear his/or her stamp of approval (s.12). A film not bearing such a stamp may be seized and confiscated (s.16). Under s.15(1), ''any film to be exhibited by or on behalf of an educational organization'' may be exempt from censorship. And an appeal from the censor's decision is provided for in s.10(2).

The Lieutenant Governor in Council may make various regulations including ''prescribing that all or any of the advertising or other matter be submitted to the censor and not be used within Alberta except with his or their approval'' (s.23(m)(iii)).

Anyone who contravenes ''the Act or regulations is guilty of an offence and liable to a fine of not more than $200 and in default of payment to imprisonment for a term not exceeding 6 months'' (s.22).

2. *British Columbia*

Pursuant to s.2 of the Motion Picture Act, R.S.B.C. 1979, c.284, a ''film classification director, together with other employees required for the administration of this Act, may be appointed under the Public Service Act''. Of the various powers given to the director in s.4, he may:

(b) review film, and, when authorized by the person submitting film to him for approval, and as a condition of approval, remove by cutting or otherwise a portion that he/or she does not approve of for exhibition or display;

(c) subject to this Act, approve, prohibit or regulate exhibiting or displaying of a film in the Province;
(d) review advertising matter for an exhibition or display of film;
(e) subject to this Act, approve, prohibit or regulate advertising in connection with a film or the exhibiting or displaying of film...

Before any film is publicly exhibited or displayed in a movie theatre in British Columbia it must first be submitted to the director for approval, unless the director otherwise orders (s.6(1)) or the film is exempt under s.6(2). Section 6(2) provides that the director's approval is not required for films owned, produced, sponsored, exhibited or displayed by,

(a) Canada or the Province or by their ministries, departments or agencies;
(b) a university;
(c) a film society; or
(d) an educational institution approved by the Minister of Education where that institution uses the film for educational purposes; or
(e) films exempted by the Lieutenant Governor in Council.

Where the director approves a film, he/or she is to affix a stamp or attach a certificate to it signifying approval (s.6(3)). Further, a sample of advertising matter in connection with a film, its exhibition or display must be approved by the director before the ad may be used or displayed (s.7(1)). Any "decision or order of the director regulating or prohibiting the exhibiting of a film in the Province" may be appealed (s.5(1))(a) as amended by S.B.C. 1983, c.10, Sch. 2).

Under s.13 the Lieutenant Governor in Council may make various "regulations and orders including those

(c) respecting the use, classification, exhibition and display of films;
(d) respecting the use and display of advertising matter in connection with a film or its exhibition,
...
(g) exempting a motion picture theatre, film exchange or film from this Act.

Section 12(2):

> A person who contravenes this Act or the regulations or an order of the director made under this Act or the regulations commits an offence and is liable on conviction to a fine not exceeding $300 or to imprisonment for not more than 6 months, or to both a fine and imprisonment, and every day the contravention continues constitutes a separate offence.

In addition, the director may suspend or cancel the licence held by a person convicted for any offence under s.12 (s.12(4)).

3. *Manitoba*

The Lieutenant Governor in Council may appoint a film classification board of up to fifteen people under s.22(1) of the Amusements Act, R.S.M. 1970, c.A-70 (as amended by S.M. 1972, c.74; 1974, c.14, s.4). The board is empowered to classify all films prior to their exhibition in the province and to control and regulate the advertising of films (s.22(3)) as amended by S.M. 1984-85, c.17, c.1(3)). Before they are exhibited, all films must be inspected and classified by the board (s.23(1) as amended by S.M. 1972, c.74) and stamped to so certify (s.26(1) as amended by S.M. 1972, c.74; 1974, c.14, s.5). Under s.26(3) the board may review any film at any time, cancel the original certificate of classification and issue a new one. Any film exhibited or brought into Manitoba for exhibition that does not bear the board's stamp certifying classification or does not comply with the Act or regulations in some other way may be seized and confiscated (s.28(1) as amended by S.M. 1972, c.74; 1974, c.14, s.7). Purusant to s.24(1) as amended by S.M. 1972, c.74, certain advertising matter may be removed if it is "of an immoral, obscene, or indecent nature, or depicts any murder, robbery, or criminal assault, or the killing of any person". An appeal lies from any ruling or decision of the board (s.22(T) as amended by S.M. 1972, c.74).

Interestingly, Manitoba is the only province to:

> If deemed desirable the Lieutantant Governor in Council may cooperate with the governments of other provinces in Canada in appointing a joint film classification board, composed of not more than fifteen persons nominated by the provincial governments for the purpose of classifying any film or slide to be used or exhibited in any of the provinces represented by the members of the joint film classification board in accordance with this Act. (s.22(4) as amended by S.M. 1972, c.74).

The Lieutenant Governor in Council may make regulations under s.35(1),

> (d) prohibiting or regulating the display of advertisements at or in respect of any place of amusement; and
>
> (e) respecting all such matters, acts, and things as are necessary and any matters, acts and things in which express provision is not made in this Act, or in which only partial provision is made.

Section 32 (as amended by S.M. 1972, c.74) lays out the general penalty for contravention of the Act or regulations:

> Except where otherwise specifically provided in this Act, and except for a violation of subsection (3) of section 28.1 [penalty to minor], every person who is guilty of a violation of this Act or any of the regulations, is liable on summary conviction to a fine of not less than two hundred dollars or more than two thousand dollars.

4. *New Brunswick*

The New Brunswick Film Classification Board, consisting of three or more persons, is to be set up pursuant to s.9(1) of the Theatres, Cinematographers and Amusements Act, R.S.N.B. 1973, c.T-5. Section 9(2) (as amended by S.N.B. 1985, c.69, s.3):

> (a) to classify films and videofilms for use or exhibition in the Province; and
>
> (b) to permit or prohibit any performance in a theatre or any amusement in a place of amusement for participation in which by the public fees are charged.

A film not classified by the Board in accordance with the regulations is not to be exhibited to the public (s.12.1, S.N.B. 1985, c.69, s.6). Section 10 (as amended by S.N.B. 1985, c.69, s.4) provides for an appeal from a decision of the Board under s.9(2)(b).

The Lieutenant Governor in Council may make regulations for or in relation to the following matters under s.32:

> (b) licensing and regulating or prohibiting any performance in a theatre, and any amusement or recreation in a place of amusement, and any amusement or recreation for participating or indulging in which by the public or some of them, fees are charged by an amusement owner;

...

(g) prohibiting or regulating the exhibiting and exchange of film;

(g.1) prescribing the classifications that may be applied to films and videofilms and the classes of persons to whom films and videofilms of particular classifications may be exhibited and made available;

(g.2) prescribing the factors to be considered by the Board in applying a particular classification to a film or videofilm;

(g.3) respecting the manner in which videofilms may be displayed to the public in a video exchange;

((g.1) to (g.3) added in S.N.B. 1981, C.69, s.9)

...

(m) any other matter that appears to the Lieutenant Governor in Council necessary or expedient for the purpose of giving full effect to the provisions of this Act or to any of said provisions;

...

(o) respecting the seizure, forfeiture and disposal of films and videofilms that are exhibited or made available to the public in contravention of the Act or regulations;

(added S.N.B. 1985, C.69, s.9)

The general penalties provisions of the Act state:

31(2) A person who violates any of the other provisions of this Act, or the regulations made hereunder, is liable to a penalty of not less than twenty-five dollars nor more than two hundred dollars.

31(3) A person in default of payment of a fine imposed in respect of an offence under this Act is liable to imprisonment in accordance with subsection 31(3) of the Summary Convictions Act.

5. *Newfoundland*

In its entirety, the Censoring of Moving Pictures Act, R.S.N. 1970, C.30 provides:

1. This Act may be cited as The Censoring of Moving Pictures Act.
2. The Lieutenant Governor in Council may appoint a board consisting of three persons, to be called the Board of Censors, and hereinafter called the Censors, a majority of which Board shall be a quorum.
3. The Censors, or any of them may at any time enter any building or place where any exhibition of moving pictures is carried on, for the purpose of inspecting and passing upon the fitness for public exhibition of any moving or stationary picture, films or slides used or displayed in such building or place; and any person hindering or obstructing any of the Censors in the performance of such duty shall be subject to a penalty not exceeding one hundred dollars, or, in default of payment, to imprisonment for a period not exceeding two months.
4. A quorum of the Board of Censors present at any such exhibition may, by oral or written notification to the proprietor of such exhibition or to the person operating the projection machine thereat, summarily prohibit the exhibition of any moving or stationary picture, film or slide which they may consider to be injurious to the morals of the public, or against the public welfare, or offensive to the public, and any such proprietor or operator exhibiting such film or slide after the receipt of such notification, shall be guilty of an offence against this Act, and shall be subject, for each such offence, to a penalty not exceeding one hundred dollars, or, in default of payment, to imprisonment for a period not exceeding two months.

6. *Nova Scotia*

Pursuant to s.3(1) of the Theatres and Amusements Act, R.S.N.S. 1967, c.304 (C.S.N.S. c.T-10) the Governor in Council may set up an Amusements Regulation Board, consisting of one or more people. The Board

> may, in accordance with the criteria prescribed by the regulations, permit or prohibit ... the use or exhibition in Nova Scotia or in any part or parts thereof for public entertainment of any film (s.3(2)(a) as amended by S.N.S. 1985, c.2T, s.4(1))

and

> classify a film (s.3(2A)(a) added by S.N.S. 1985, c.2T, s.4(2)).

Regulations may be made by the Governor in Council under s.2(1):

> (b) regulating and licensing or prohibiting any performance or performances in a theatre or theatres, and any amusement or amusements, recreation or recreations for participating or indulging in which by the public or, some of them, fees are charged by an amusement owner;
> (g) prohibiting and regulating the exhibition, sale, lease and exchanging of films;
> (h) any other matters that appear to the Governor in Council necessary or expedient for the purpose of giving full effect to the provisions of this Act or to any of said provisions;
> (ba) prescribing criteria in accordance with which the Board may exercise its powers. (Added S.N.S. 1985, c.25, s.3).

General penalties for contraventions of the Act are provided for in s.20(1).

> Where the Board is satisfied after due inquiry that any film exchange or theatre owner has violated this Act or any regulations made hereunder the Board may:
>
> (a) revoke or cancel any licence of such film exchange; or
> (b) revoke or cancel any licence of such theatre owner; or
> (c) attach to any of such licences such terms, conditions or restrictions as it deems advisable.

And an additional penalty of up to one year in prison will be imposed where a violation of the Act or the regulations causes "either directly or indirectly to any person either bodily injury or loss of life" (s.10).

Section 8 (as amended by S.N.S. 1983, c.4T, s.1) also provides that it is a summary conviction offence, punishable as an offence under the Consumer Protection Act, to violate or fail to comply with any provision of the Act, the regulations, or an order or direction given under the Act or the regulations.

7. *Ontario*

Major amendments were made to the Theatres Act, R.S.O. 1980, c.498 in 1984 (S.O. 1984, c.56). Pursuant to s.3(1) of the 1984 amendment, the "Board of Censors" became the "Ontario Film Review Board", consisting of such persons "as the Lieutenant Governor in Council may appoint". The Board is given power, under s.3(T) of the amended Act:

> (a) subject to the regulations, to approve, prohibit and regulate the exhibition and distribution of film in Ontario;
> (b) when authorized by the person submitting film for approval, to remove from the film any portion that it does not approve of for exhibition or distribution;

(c) subject to the regulations, to approve, prohibit or regulate advertising in Ontario in connection with any film or the exhibition or distribution thereof;

Before a film may be exhibited in Ontario, an application for approval to exhibit and for classification of the film must be made to the Board (s.35, S.O. 1984, c.56). The Board, after viewing a film, may, "in accordance with the criteria prescribed by the regulations", refuse to approve the film for exhibition in Ontario (s.3T(2), S.O. 1984, c.56) or "make an approval conditional upon the film being exhibited in designated locations and on specified dates only" (s.35(3), S.O. 1984, c.56). Any film not approved by the Board is not to be exhibited (s.38, S.O. 1984, c.56) and once approved, a film is not to be altered. (s.39, S.O. 1984, C.56). The Board's approval of a film is to be indicated "in the manner prescribed by the regulations" (s.36, S.O. 1984, C.56). A sample of advertising matter intended for public display in connection with a film or its exhibition must first be approved by the Board (s.40(1), S.O. 1984, C.56) and so stamped (s.40(6), S.O. 1984, C.56). The Board's decision on approval and classification may be reviewed (s.35(5), S.O. 1984, C.56) or appealed (s.57). Section 35a of the 1984 amendment also provides:

(1) Where the chairman of the Board is of the opinion that the criteria prescribed by regulation respecting subject-matter or content in films have changed since a film was originally approved and classified and that the film may not be entitled to the approval or classification determined at the time of the original decision, the chairman may require that the film be submitted for reconsideration by the Board.
(2) Where a film is submitted for reconsideration under sub-section (1), the provisions of section 35 apply with necessary modifications except that no fees shall be charged.

Regulations may be made under s.63(1):

9. prohibiting and regulating the use, distribution or exhibition of film or any type or class thereof; (S.O. 1984, c.56, s.22)
10. prohibiting and regulating the use and display of any advertising matter in connection with any film or exhibition thereof;
30. exempting any theatre, film exchange, projector, film or person or any class or type thereof from any provision of this Act or the regulations;
31. prescribing criteria on which the Board may exercise its powers under sections 3, 35 and 40 including prescribing the film or advertising content or subject matter that the Board may refuse to approve; (S.O. 1984, C.56)

...

Every person who "knowingly fails to comply with any order, direction or other requirement made under" the Theatres Act, or contravenes any of its provisions or regulations is guilty of an offence and may be fined up to $2,000, or in default of payment, required to serve up to one year in jail, or both (s.61(1)).

8. *Prince Edward Island*

The Entertainments Act, R.S.P.E.I. 1974, c.E-7, does not establish a film censorship, review or classification board. The Act primarily concerns entertainment taxes and licensing. The only sections which deal with the censorship of films are ss.2(b), 2(p) and 17. Pursuant to s.2(b), the Lieutenant Governor in Council is empowered to make regulations "licensing, regulating or prohibiting any entertainment in any place of entertainment". Section 2(p) provides that the Lieutenant Governor in Council may make regulations "respecting any other matter for the purpose of giving full effect to this Act and the regulations". And under s.17:

> Except as otherwise provided in this Act or the regulations, a person contravening or failing to comply with this Act or the regulations is guilty of an offence and is liable, on summary conviction, to a fine of not more than five hundred dollars in respect to each offence and in default of payment, to imprisonment for a term not exceeding ninety days.

9. *Quebec*

The "Regie du Cinéma" is established under s.123 of the Cinema Act, S.Q. 1983, c.37, to be composed of three members (s.124). The functions of the Regie include classifying films "according to the segments of the total audience to which they are directed" (s.135(1)). Every print of every film intended for exhibition to the public must be stamped by the Regie showing the classification assigned to the film (s.82) before it may be exhibited (s.76). Any film not stamped or any print of a film used in contravention of the Act or any of the regulations may be seized (s.176). The Regie's decisions may be reviewed or appealed pursuant to ss.149-166.

Of the several regulations the Regie may make, s.167(2) empowers it to "establish standards and conditions for the exhibition of a stamp, the posting up and the exhibition of the classification of a film, including any information or warning that must appear thereon".

The general offences and penalties provision (s.178) states:

> Any person who infringes section 76, 86, 87, 90, 92, 98, 99, 100, 102, 111, 114, 118, 120, 121, 122 or 177 or a regulation made under this chapter is guilty of an offence and liable, in addition to costs, to a fine of not less than $100 nor more than $1,000 in the case of an individual and not less than $500 nor more than $2,000 in the case of a corporation or partnership and, for a subsequent offence within five years, to a fine or not less than $200 nor more than $5,000 in the case of an individual and not less than $1,000 nor more than $10,000 in the case of a corporation or partnership.

10. *Saskatchewan*

The Theatres and Cinematographs Act, R.S.S. 1978, c.T-11 provides for the continuation of the one — to four — member Saskatchewan Film Classification Board (s.7(1)). The board is empowered, under s.7(3):

> (a) to approve or disapprove films that are intended for exhibition in Saskatchewan;
> (b) when authorized by the person who submits film to the board for approval, to remove by cutting or otherwise from the film any portion thereof that it does not approve for exhibition in Saskatchewan.

All films intended for public exhibition in Saskatchewan must first be submitted to the Board which is to examine them and pass upon their fitness for public exhibition (s.8(1)), unless they are exempted under s.8(2). Pursuant to s.8(2), the Board need not examine the following films:

> (a) films owned or sponsored by the Government of Canada or the Government of Saskatchewan;
> (b) films owned or sponsored by a university, film society or other educational institution approved by the Minister of Education; or
> (c) films designated for the purpose of advertising, demonstrating or instructing in the use of commercial or industrial products, and where a dispute arises as to whether or not a

film is designed for such purpose the question may be referred to the minister and his decision thereon is final.

All films passed or permitted by the Board to be exhibited must be so stamped (s.8(3)). Advertising material intended to be used in connection with a film to be exhibited in Saskatchewan must first be submitted to the Board to ensure that it is fit for public exhibition or display (s.12). Newspaper advertisements are dealt with separately. Section 13 provides:

(1) No person shall insert or cause to be inserted in a newspaper or other periodical an advertisement describing or in any way dealing with a film, that:
(a) gives details of a criminal action or depicts criminals as admirable or heroic characters;
(b) is immoral or obscene or suggests lewdness or indecency;
(c) offers evil suggestions to the minds of young people or children; or
(d) is for any other reason injurious to public morals or opposed to the public welfare.

(2) The board may require any person to submit before publication, for its approval or rejection, the proofs of proposed advertisements.

(3) Any person who fails to comply with subsection (2) is guilty of an offence.

A film not bearing the board's stamp may be seized and confiscated (s.14). And (s.9(1) sets up an appeal committee to consider and determine appeals from the board's decisions.

The Lieutenant Governor in Council may make the following regulations "for the purpose of carrying out the provisions of this Act according to their intent (s.18):

...

(d) prescribing the terms and conditions under which films may be sold, leased, exchanged or exhibited;

(i) respecting any other matter or thing that may be necessary for the carrying out of the provisions of this Act.

The general penal provision (s.16) states:

A person who violates any provisions of this Act or the regulations, for which no penalty is provided, is guilty of an offence and liable on summary conviction to a fine not exceeding $500 with costs, and to a further fine of $25 for every day after conviction during which the offence continues, and in default of payment to imprisonment for a period not exceeding three months.

11. *Northwest Territories*

No specific film censorship, review or classification board exists in the Northwest Territories. Rather, under s.9(2)(e) of the Motion Pictures Ordinance, R.O.N.W.T. 1974, c.M-14, officers appointed by the Commissioner are given the "power and duties to examine, censor or report on films". Only those films which the Commissioner chooses must be submitted to an officer for approval before they are exhibited (s.20(1)). And it is the Commissioner, or an officer, who, in his discretion, makes the decision to "prohibit the exhibition of a film or slide to prevent the use of dialogues and pictures depicting criminal or immoral scenes or that are otherwise injurious to public morals or opposed to public welfare". (s.20(2)).

The Commissioner may also make regulations (s.21), including those "(d) governing the classification and censorship of films".

The general penalty for violation of any provision of the ordinance or regulations is up to $200, three months in jail, or both (s.22).

12. *Yukon Territory*

The Motion Pictures Ordinance, C.O.Y.T. 1978, c.M-10 does not contain any specific provisions on the censorship of films.

CHAPTER FIVE

Legal Limitations... Private

5.1 A Note on the Law, Reputation and Privacy

While many of the limitations on freedom of expression are found in the criminal law, some are also found in the civil law of the provinces.

The most important part of the provincial law affecting freedom of expression and, more particularly, the freedom of journalists is the law of civil defamation. The common law and provincial defamation statutes confer on individuals a right to sue journalists or others who publish or broadcast material which unjustifiably damages their reputation.

Defamation encompasses the two sub-categories of libel and slander. Since libel is the part of the law which directly affects journalists, the materials on defamation in this chapter will focus entirely on it. There is, in addition, a short section on the right to privacy which, like defamation, reflects a respect for individual rights that may limit the right to publish information.

Libel is a part of the law of torts. Just as individuals can sue for damages when someone's negligence has led to an injury to their person, they may sue for injury to their reputation. A libel is an unjustified statement, published or broadcast, that subjects a person to hatred, ridicule or contempt or, put differently, it is a false statement to a person's discredit. It is a strict liability tort. Whether or not the injury to reputation was intended, the injuring party is held responsible. The law is complex and journalists must understand its complexity. Much that they write or broadcast pertains to reputation.

A defamation suit begins when a person notifies an alleged defamer that he or she is going to sue. There are a number of stages in the procedure, but if the matter gets to court, the plaintiff must prove that the matter is defamatory, that it refers to the plaintiff, and that it has been published.

The defendant must defend the allegedly libellous statement. The defendant can choose one or a combination of four lines of defence. The first of these is justification. The defendant argues that the statement about the plaintiff is true. If the truth of the statement can be proved, there is a complete defence. This defence should demonstrate to journalists that their standards for publishing material related to reputation should be the same as the standards of evidence recognized by a court.

A second defence is consent. A journalist may publish a defamatory statement if the person defamed consents to its publication. Thirdly, a journalist may plead that the matter is privileged. There are provisions in most libel and slander acts which provide a guide to occasions of privilege.

Finally, the law provides for the defence of fair comment in which the defendant demonstrates that the defamatory statements are not allegations of fact, but honestly expressed opinions based on facts that are true.

Journalists should recognize that they and their editors and publishers may be responsible for damaging an individual's reputation and could pay a healthy sum in damages to that person. In 1982, the Canadian Broadcasting Corporation was required to pay the Deputy Attorney-General of the Province of British Columbia $125,000, plus costs, for declaring that he had used his position improperly to interfere in the judicial process on behalf of friends.

The law also embraces a notion of privacy, although it is very limited and so far cautiously interpreted. It is still generally the law in Canada that you can publish anything you like about another person as long as it is true.

5.2 Defamation

5.2.1 Anne Skarsgard, ''Freedom of the Press'', (1980-81) 45 *Saskatchewan Law Review* pp. 296-99

A. What Is Defamation?

In *Parmiter* v. *Coupland* Parke J. defined defamation as ''a publication, without justification or lawful excuse, which is calculated to injure the reputation of another by exposing him to hatred, contempt or ridicule.'' This classical formulation of the tort is misleading in two respects. Firstly, it does not make clear the fact that defamation is a *false* statement about the plaintiff. Secondly, the words ''calculated to injure'' convey the impression that defendant's intention is relevant. Defamation is a strict liability tort and good faith is no defence. Said Scrutton L.J. in *Tourner* v. *National Provincial and Union Bank of England:*

> I do not myself think this ancient formula is sufficient in all cases, for words may damage the reputation of a man as a business man, which no one would connect with hatred, ridicule or contempt.

In *Youssoupoff* v. *Metro-Goldwyn Mayer Pictures Ltd.* he quoted with approval Cave J. in *Scott* v. *Sampson:*

> The law recognizes in every man a right to have the estimation in which he stands in the opinion of others unaffected by false statements to his discredit.

And in *Slim* v. *Stretch* Lord Atkin formulated the modern test for determining whether a statement is defamatory: Would the words tend to lower the plaintiff in the estimation of right-thinking members of society generally?

Fleming agrees that feelings of disapprobation are not necessary to the tort provided that the words cause the plaintiff to be shunned and avoided. This definition takes into account the fact that an attribution of misfortune such as an allegation that a man is insane or that a woman had been raped has a tendency to lower a person's standing in the community even though it does not arouse feelings of animosity in the minds of decent people.

The interest protected by the tort is an individual's reputation described as "perhaps the most dearly prized attribute of civilized man." What is the meaning of the word "reputation"? In popular parlance a person's reputation is what other peoples say or think of him, maybe what image they hold of him. But does a person actually have a public image or is this "image" only a statistical conclusion drawn from numerous individual images? No doubt a person's wife, employer, subordinate and friends all have different images of him. In other words, "reputation" is a legal fiction used by the courts to describe a variety of interpersonal relations that have been damaged as a result of the defamatory statement.

The idea that a person's reputation is valuable and should not be harmed with impunity has been recognized for a very long time. The law of Moses forbade slandering anyone, especially a person in authority, and in Ancient Rome, by the law of the Twelve Tables, anybody who slandered another "by words or defamatory verses" was to be beaten with a club.

Roman law distinguished written defamation (*malum carmen* and *famous libellus*) from oral defamation *(injuria verbalis),* which was a less serious tort. This distinction was not made in the common law until the end of the eighteenth century. Until that time in our law both libel and slander could involve either spoken or written statements, but they were entertained in different courts, slander at first only in ecclesiastical courts and later also in civil courts, whereas libel was primarily a criminal action of sedition and was entertained in the Star Chamber.

The Church tried slander actions because of its jurisdiction over sin. If a person's reputation was sufficiently evil, he was put "on his trial". If he was acquitted, it was those who had defamed him who had committed a sin and were put on trial in their turn. If convicted, the defamers were required to do penance and were sometimes even excommunicated.

As civil courts gained influence, the doctrine developed that the ecclesiastical courts could not try sin if there was also a civil cause of action. By the sixteenth century this doctrine was applied to slander imputing a common law crime. Because most common law crimes involved trespass to the person which is actionable *per se* without proof of damages, the false allegation that someone had committed such a crime became actionable *per se* also, and general damages could be recovered. Later the class of slander actionable per se was increased to include not just slander imputing a common law crime, but also imputations of a "hideous disease" and injury to business reputation. The former was probably included because the Church, by administering the last rites to those who were about to enter a leper colony, relinquished its jurisdiction over lepers, while an injury to one's reputation in one's trade or calling was deemed temporal in nature and therefore removed from the Church's jurisdiction.

The Star Chamber had jurisdiction over libel until its abolition in 1641, at which time libel actions were transferred to the same common law courts which had previously taken over slander jurisdiction from the church courts. Unfortunately the consolidation of defamation actions in one court did not result in a more unified body of law. The Roman distinction between spoken defamations actionable as slander and written defamations actionable as libel was revived, an accident of history that has contributed towards making our present day law of defamation needlessly complicated, irrational and often unfair.

The distinction between libel and slander is an important one. Libel is a crime as well as a tort, whereas slander is a tort only. Of more practical importance, as criminal prosecution for libel is rare, is the fact that only libel is actionable without proof of special damage, because damage is presumed. Special damage is harm flowing directly from the act which is either economic loss or is capable of pecuniary assessment. Normally slander, a less serious tort, is not actionable without proof of special damage. However, there are four exceptions to this rule. Slander accusing the plaintiff of being charged with a crime, an imputation that the plaintiff is, at present, infected with a "loathsome disease", slandering the plaintiff with respect to his trade or profession, and attacks on the plaintiff's chastity are actionable per se, without proof of damage.

Said Lord Mansfield in *Thorley* v. *Lord Kerry:*

> An action for a libel may be brought on words written, when the words, if spoken, would not sustain it.

Although the distinction between the spoken and the written word is important, there is a further test for distinguishing libel from slander, and that is the test of performance. Libel is published in a "permanent" form. For example, a statue, a cartoon, an effigy, even chalk marks on a wall are observed through the sense of sight and published in a permanent form and are therefore libels if defamatory. In this context "permanent" does not mean that the form will endure for a long time, but that it is not transient like the spoken word or a gesture.

This distinction was easy enough to make two hundred years ago, but the advent of the electronic media of communication, has posed many problems. How does one classify defamatory statements broadcast over the radio or television? Would a spontaneous defamatory statement broadcast live and untaped over radio or television be classified as slander, and would the same statement become libel if read or memorized from a script or if it was taped and thus available in permanent form? But if the rationale behind the distinction between permanent and transitory forms is the fact that the former is capable of wider circulation, should defamation on radio and television be treated as libel? Or should we distinguish between broadcasts for general reception and those for only a limited audience, such as broadcasts on amateur shortwave radio frequencies, police, fire or taxi radio frequencies, or closed-circuit television?

There are no uniform answers to these questions. Legislation providing that defamatory words in a broadcast constitute libel has been introduced in Ontario, England and Australia, whereas the Canadian *Uniform Defamation Act* enacted so far only in Alberta, Manitoba and the Yukon abolishes the distinction between libel and slander and makes all defamation actionable without proof of damage.

Such legislation, if introduced in the other Canadian provinces, would remedy the unwarranted preferred position of the electronic media over the press under the strict common law rule. In the remainder of this paper we shall assume that the defamation, whether published in the press or on the radio or television, is libelous. (Such an assumption is supported by the facts. In many cases of radio or television defamation either there is a script or else the program has been taped.)

Note: For a full and careful statement of the law, see Raymond E. Brown, *The Law of Defamation in Canada*, (Toronto, 1987), 2 vols.

5.2.2 The Plaintiff's Case

5.2.2.1 *Brannigan* v. *S.I.U.*, (1964), 42 D.L.R. (2d) 249 (B.C.S.C.)

HUTCHESON, J.: — In this action the plaintiff seeks to recover damages for libel.

The plaintiff is a seaman living in the City of Vancouver, in the Province of British Columbia and is a member of the union known as the Canadian Brotherhood of Railway Transport and General Workers. This union is generally referred to as the C.B.R.T. and I will use that designation.

The defendant is a union known as the Seafarers' International Union of Canada. I will refer to it as the S.I.U.

The plaintiff has been a seaman since 1937. At that time he became a member of the Canadian Seamen's Union. That union was outlawed and, according to the evidence, by reason of its being Communist-dominated. The plaintiff came to British Columbia in 1952 and at that time became a member of the West Coast Canadian Seamen's Union. Later the West Coast Canadian Seamen's Union was merged with the S.I.U. and, on that taking place, the plaintiff became a member of the latter union. In 1959 he left the S.I.U. The circumstances of his leaving, as I understand it, were that there was a strike by the Marine Workers' Union, who had established a picket line, and the plaintiff received instructions from a dispatcher of the S.I.U. to remain at his work which involved his crossing the picket line. The plaintiff did not believe that he should cross the picket line and he refused to carry out his instructions. This resulted in his being expelled from the S.I.U. Following his expulsion from the S.I.U. he was instrumental in forming in the City of Vancouver the C.B.R.T. Local 400. Upon the formation of that local he held for a time the post of financial secretary but, finding that he did not have the necessary educational qualifications, he ceased to hold that office. As I have already mentioned, he is presently a member of the C.B.R.T.

The defendant publishes and distributes what is referred to in the pleadings as a newspaper and which is known as the "Canadian Sailor". This paper is distributed among the members of the S.I.U. and is sent to other unions and to companies and, generally speaking, to any person or corporation who may ask to be placed upon the mailing list. The circulation of this publication on August 23, 1961, was at least 15,000, according to the evidence.

In the issue of the Canadian Sailor of August 23, 1961, under the heading "C.B.R.T. Official Waves Red Flag" there is a photograph of a parade and particularly of two men in that parade carrying between them a banner upon which are the words "Communist Party of Canada". Below that picture appear these words: "Positive proof that the C.B.R.T. is Commie tinged is the picture shown here. It is a picture of the May Day parade in Vancouver in 1961, and the Commie pictured on right is none other than the Financial Secretary of the Vancouver local of the C.B.R.T. WILLIAM BRANNIGAN."

Roderick B. Heinekey, the vice-president of the S.I.U. in charge of the Pacific Coast, was examined for discovery and upon his examination agreed that the word "Commie" in the caption under the photograph means "Communist" and that the William Brannigan referred to therein is the plaintiff.

It is not disputed that the person pictured on the right is the plaintiff nor is it disputed that it was erroneously stated that (a) it is a picture of the May Day parade in Vancouver in 1961, and (b) that William Brannigan was the financial secretary of the Vancouver local of the C.B.R.T. The picture is a picture of the May Day parade in Vancouver in the year 1960 at which time William Brannigan had ceased to be the financial secretary of the Vancouver local of the C.B.R.T.

In his evidence the plaintiff stated that the placard he was carrying did have words upon it. While he cannot remember the exact wording of the placard, which was not composed by him but was given to him to carry, he thinks it was to the effect, "Canada Needs More Ships" or "Canada Needs More Jobs" but he is definite in his sworn testimony that the wording on the sign had nothing to do with Red countries or Communist countries and that he was not nor to his knowledge was any one in his group giving support to the Communist party.

Other than denials of publication and circulation, the defences pleaded on behalf of the defendant may be summarized as follows:

(a) neither the words nor the photograph were reasonably capable of causing injury to the plaintiff or his character, credit or reputation or capable of bringing him into public scandal, odium or contempt;

(b) the issue of Canadian Sailor of December 13, 1961, contained a public apology intended to correct any errors contained in the issue of the Canadian Sailor of which the plaintiff complains;

(c) The words complained of are true in substance and in fact, and

(d) that the plaintiff marched in the May Day parade at some distance behind a banner bearing the words "Communist Party of Canada" and in so far as the words referring to the plaintiff and of which the plaintiff complains consist of expressions of opinion, they are fair comment on a matter of public interest.

I find that the article published on August 23, 1961, taken as a whole, both the picture and the accompanying printed statements, is clearly a statement that the plaintiff was, as of the date of the publication, a Communist.

While noting the difficulty of giving an exhaustive definition of libel, the learned authors of *Gatley on Libel & Slander,* 5th ed., p. 16 state:

> Any written or printed words which tend to lower a person in the estimation of right-thinking men, or cause him to be shunned or avoided, or expose him to hatred, contempt, or ridicule, constitute a libel.

This statement is, in my view, supported by the decided cases.

Having in mind, as I must, the time, place and circumstances under which the statement was made, I am of the opinion that it was defamatory of the plaintiff to publish of him that he was a Communist. With respect, I find confirmation of this view in the words of O'Halloran, J.A., who stated at pp. 178-9 of his judgment in *Martin v. Law Society of B.C.,* [1950] 3 D.L.R. 173:

> Labour Unions, Universities, and other public bodies have publicly sought and are still seeking to rid themselves of men and women professing Communist beliefs. It has come to be univer-

sally accepted in the Western nations that it is dangerous to our way of life to allow a known Communist or Communist sympathizer to remain in a position of trust or influence.

And those of Robertson, J.A., at p. 192:

> Every one knows that many Trade Unions are expelling Communists from their organizations. I think that neither the Government of Canada, nor that of the United States, nor that of England knowingly would employ a Communist.

See also *Burns et al. v. Associated Newspapers, Ltd.* (1925), 42 T.L.R. 37; *Dennison et al. v. Sanderson,* [1946] 4 D.L.R. 314, [1946] O.R. 601.

The plaintiff was a member of a trade union and had been active in the organization of the local to which he belongs.

5.2.2.2 *Thomas* v. *CBC* [1981] 4 W.W.R. 289 (N.W.T.S.C.)

DISBERY, J.: The defendant Sanders prepared and assisted other CBC employees in the preparation of four news stories concerning the drilling operations at K 91 and an explosion that occurred on the drillship Explorer I, for broadcasting over the radio facilities of CBC. Such were all broadcast within a period of approximately 19 hours. The plaintiff alleges that the said broadcasts defamed him. Transcripts of the four broadcasts, admitted by the defendants to be true and correct transcripts thereof, were filed as part of Ex. P75 and are pleaded verbatim in para. 7 of the amended statement of defence. I will now set forth these broadcasts seriatim and, inter alia, the extent of the defendant Sanders' participation in them.

The First Broadcast.

The first broadcast was made on 3rd February 1977 about 5:30 p.m. as part of CBC's regular daily news program "CBC Mackenzie News" for reception by the public in the Northwest Territories and other nearby northern areas. The broadcast was as follows:

"(CBC) CBC News has learned that Dome Petroleum required a substantial amendment to its drilling authority at the Explorer I site last summer. The amendment authorized by lower level officials in the Department of Indian Affairs and Northern Development resulted in the company having unexpected problems from the gas pressure from the bottom of the well. These pressure problems could have led to the explosion of Explorer I which killed one drill worker. Larry Sanders has the story.

"(Sanders) The original drilling authority approved by the federal cabinet last April required Dome to secure its drill pipe and casing with cement before it entered any high pressure zones that might contain oil. Because they did not start drilling until early August, to meet this requirement would have meant Dome would not have been able to reach any substantial depth since securing the casing with cement all the way down takes much more time. By the end of August Explorer I had drilled to 4,000 feet and had secured the casing with cement. Dome wanted to drill down to 10,000 feet right away so they applied for an amendment to the drilling authority to stop the cementing at the 4,000 foot level. The amendment was approved without any long examination by Maurice Thomas the supervisor of the Oil and Gas Division in Yellowknife. Mr. Thomas says he approved the amendments because Dome did not expect any high pressure gas or oil until at least 12,000 feet. But by September 10th they had reached just below 10,000 feet and unexpectedly hit water and gas at very high pressure. Because they did not expect to hit pressure at that depth they had great difficulty controlling the well from that point on. Gas and water flowed continually from the bottom and Mr. Thomas says Dome tried plugging it at different depths for four weeks without any success. Mr. Thomas says after the explosion of October 12th they finally sealed off the well at the top and left it for the winter. If the amendment to the drilling authority had not been approved they would not have had any of these problems. Securing the casing with cement all the way down to 10,000 feet would also likely have prevented the gas problems which led to the explosion that killed data engineer, George Ross MacKay. None of these facts were presented to the inquest jury last month which found that Mr. MacKay's death was an industrial accident. More information will likely come to light when the federal advisory committee on offshore drilling makes it [sic] preliminary report public in a tour of the North starting February 14th. Until then government officials here will not say whether they will allow such an amendment to Dome's drilling authority in next summer's operations. But the government officials do admit that if Dome had encountered oil instead of gas, the environmental catastrophe for the Beaufort Sea would have been public long before now. Larry Sanders, CBC News, Ottawa.

"(CBC) The reaction to the new information about Dome's drilling operation last summer is already coming in. The Committee for Original People's Entitlement has called again on the federal government to hold a public inquiry into the whole operation. Bob Delury, a biologist for COPE, says the additional information proves that the government is not able to regulate Dome effectively, nor is the company able to regulate itself. Wally Firth says the amendment is a betrayal of public faith since Dome was able to change the rules for drilling once they were in operation. Mr. Firth says he supports COPE's call for an independent inquiry before Dome can proceed this summer with more drilling. Vince Steen the vice president of ITC said the credibility of government monitors should be questioned. Mr. Steen says independent inspectors who are not so close to Dome should be authorized to keep track of the operations from the ship."

The defendant Sanders, hereinafter referred to as "Sanders" for brevity's sake, was the author of the first two paragraphs. The first or lead-in paragraph was spoken by the program's newscaster. Sanders himself spoke the second paragraph. The final paragraph was spoken by the newscaster. The initials "ITC" appearing in the third paragraph designate the Inuit Tapirisat Canada or Eskimo Brotherhood. This third paragraph was not written by Sanders but he provided the information therefor to the newsroom....

The Statement of Claim.

The Defamation Ordinance (hereafter referred to as "the Ordinance") by s.4 enacts as follows:

"4. In an action for defamation the plaintiff may allege that the matter complained of was used in a defamatory sense, specifying the defamatory sense without alleging how the matter was used in that sense, and the pleading shall be put in issue by the denial of the alleged defamation; and, where the matters set forth, with or without the alleged meaning, show a cause of action, the pleading is sufficient."

By this salutary enactment this court is no longer plagued by many former precedents as to the sufficiency of statements of claim where an innuendo is raised together with the pleading of extrinsic facts in support thereof. Several such precedents were considered by the court in *Grubb v. Bristol United Press,* [1963] 1 Q.B. 309, [1962] 2 All E.R. 380 (C.A.).

After identifying the parties in its first three paragraphs, the plaintiff's statement of claim in paras. 4 and 5 alleges the making of the said four broadcasts by the defendants. Paragraph 6 alleges that the broadcasts referred to the plaintiff either "by name or by reference as the government official who was responsible for the issuing of a Drilling Authority and amendments to the Drilling Authority to Dome Petroleums Ltd." to drill K 91.

Paragraph 7 alleges that certain of the statements that the plaintiff complains of as defamatory were made by the defendants in each and every one of the four broadcasts.

Paragraphs 8 to 11 inclusive, give particulars, broadcast by broadcast, of specific words, phrases, clauses and sentences which were included in and form part of such broadcasts considered separately and which the plaintiff complains, directly or by innuendos naturally arising therefrom, defamed him.

Paragraphs 12 to 16, inclusive, of the statement of claim read as follows:

"12. By the use of the words in the four preceding paragraphs the Defendants meant, and were understood to mean:

"(a) that the Plaintiff permitted the amendment to the Drilling Authority without careful consideration and sufficient examination of the facts, and was thereby negligent and incompetent in the performance of his duties as Regional Oil and Gas Conservation Engineer;

"(b) that the Plaintiff permitted the amendment without regard to the safety of the drilling operation and to the consequences to the environment, and was thereby negligent and incompetent in the performance of his duties as Regional Oil and Gas Conservation Engineer;

"(c) that the amendment authorized by the Plaintiff caused the subsequent problems in the drilling operations;

"(d) that the amendment authorized by the Plaintiff caused the explosion which resulted in the death of George Ross MacKay;

"(e) that the Plaintiff improperly authorized the amendment;

"(f) that the amendment authorized by the Plaintiff was contrary to government regulations;

"(g) that the Plaintiff was under the control and influence of the Operator, and failed to perform his duties as Regional Oil and Gas Conservation Engineer in an independent and impartial manner;

"(h) that the Plaintiff engaged in an improper scheme to withhold or suppress evidence from the coroner's inquest;

"13. The Plaintiff says that the defamatory meanings alleged in the immediately preceding paragraph are the natural and ordinary meanings of the words in paragraphs 8, 9, 10 and 11, or alternatively, that taken in the context of the whole of each of the said radio broadcasts, and by reason of the other statements published on the said radio broadcasts, that the words in paragraphs 8, 9, 10 and 11 have the meanings, and were understood to have the meanings alleged in the immediately preceding paragraph.

"14. The words published on the said radio broadcasts were calculated to have and had the effect of disparaging the Plaintiff and exposing him to public scandal and contempt.

"15. By the use and publication of the said words the Defendants have imputed to the Plaintiff a lack of fitness, incompetence, negligence and impropriety in the conduct of his duties as a government official.

"16. The Plaintiff says that the amendment authorized by the Plaintiff did not cause the subsequent 'problems' in the drilling operations, nor did the said amendment cause the explosion which resulted in the death of George Ross MacKay."

The defendants in their joint statement of defence denied the defamations alleged by the plaintiff, and by virtue of s.4 of the Ordinance such allegations were put in issue in this action.

It is common ground that in the area served by the regional program "CBC Mackenzie News" on 3rd and 4th February there were approximately 24,700 persons resident. It is also common ground that on said 4th February the national program, "The World at Eight", had an actual audience of approximately 540,000 listeners, including, of course, listeners in the Territories.

The First Broadcast.

I now turn to a consideration of the first broadcast made at 5:30 p.m. on 3rd February, and as to whether the plaintiff was defamed therein and thereby. I have adopted and applied the following authorities and statements as to what constitutes a defamatory imputation.

Gatley on Libel and Slander, 7th ed. (1974), pp. 13-14, para. 31, states as follows:

"The gist of the torts of libel and slander is the publication of matter (usually words) conveying a defamatory imputation. A defamatory imputation is one to a man's discredit, or which tends to lower him in the estimation of others, or to expose him to hatred, contempt or ridicule, or to injure his reputation in his office, trade or profession, or to injure his financial credit. The standard of opinion is that of right-thinking persons generally. To be defamatory an imputation need have no actual effect on a person's reputation; the law looks only to its tendency. A true imputation may still be defamatory, although its truth may be a defence to an action brought on it; conversely untruth alone does not render an imputation defamatory."

Tallis J., adopted and applied this excerpt in *England v. C.B.C.*, [1979] 3 W.W.R. 193 at 206, 97 D.L.R. (3d) 472 (N.W.T.S.C.).

In *Cherneskey v. Armadale Publishers Ltd.* supra, Ritchie J. with Laskin C.J.C., Pigeon and Pratte JJ. concurring, at p. 623, approved the following excerpt from Gatley, 7th ed., pp. 4-5, para. 4, where the learned author said:

"Any imputation which may tend 'to lower the plaintiff in the estimation of right-thinking members of society generally,' ... or 'to expose him to hatred, contempt or ridicule,' is defamatory of him."

This excerpt was applied by Tallis J. in *England v. C.B.C.*, supra, at p. 207 together with the immediately following sentence, namely:

"An imputation may be defamatory whether or not it is believed by those to whom it is published."

I have also adopted and applied the following authorities as to what constitutes a defamatory imputation made with respect to a person's profession, trade or occupation, or with respect to the carrying out by the holder of a public or private office of the duties and responsibilities pertaining thereto.

In *England* v. *C.B.C.* Tallis J. said at p. 208:

"Learned counsel for the defendants cited the following excerpt from Gatley on Libel and Slander, 7th ed., pp. 31-32, paras. 57 and 58, where he said:

"'Any imputation which may tend to injure a man's reputation in a business, employment, trade, profession, calling or office carried on or held by him is defamatory. To be actionable, words must impute to the plaintiff some quality which would be detrimental, or the absence of some quality which is essential, to the successful carrying on of his office, profession or trade. The mere fact that words tend to injure the plaintiff in the way of his office, profession or trade is insufficient. If they do not involve any reflection upon the personal character, or official, professional or trading reputation of the plaintiff, they are not defamatory.

"'It is defamatory to impute to a man in any office any corrupt, dishonest or fraudulent conduct or other misconduct or inefficiency in it, or any unfitness or want of ability to discharge his duties, and this is so whether the office be public or private, or whether it be one of profit, honour or trust. Thus, it has been held defamatory to charge a parish overseer with oppressive conduct towards the poor of the parish, or a vestry clerk with having misappropriated or misapplied the parish moneys, or a mayor of a borough, though retired from office, with ignorance of his duties, partiality and corruption.'"

Learned counsel for the defendants cited the following excerpts from Odgers on Libel and Slander, 6th ed. (1929), to be found at pp. 25 and 46 respectively:

"It is libellous to impute to a member of any profession, that he does not possess the skill or technical knowledge necessary for the proper practice of such profession, or that he had been guilty of any discreditable conduct in his profession...

"...they must be shown to have been spoken of the plaintiff in relation thereto, and to be such as would prejudice him therein... They must impeach either his skill or knowledge or attach his conduct therein. His special office or profession need not be expressly named or referred to, if the charge made be such as must necessarily affect him in it. And in determining whether the words used would necessarily so affect the plaintiff, regard must be had to the mental and moral requirements of the office he holds or the profession or trade he carries on. Where integrity and ability are essential to the due conduct of the plaintiff's office or profession, words impugning his integrity or ability are clearly actionable for they then imply if he is unfit to continue therein."

The first of the main facts that the plaintiff must prove to succeed in this action so far as the first broadcast is concerned is that he was identified to the listeners as the person whose conduct was attacked in the course of the broadcast in a defamatory way. As Ritchie J. in *Skyes* v. *Fraser,* [1974] S.C.R. 526, [1973] 5 W.W.R. 484 at 495, 39 D.L.R. (3d) 321, affirming [1971] 3 W.W.R. 161, which affirmed [1971] 1 W.W.R. 246, said:

"...there are two questions to be determined at the outset. The first is a question of law as to whether the statement complained of can, having regard to its language, be regarded as capable of referring to the respondent."

The transcript, ante, proves that the plaintiff was named four times in the course of the broadcast. He was further identified during the broadcast as being the supervisor in Yellowknife of the oil and gas division of the federal Department of Indian Affairs and Northern Development and a low level official of that department. Not only were the words used "capable of referring to the plaintiff" but they specifically designated him by name.

The plaintiff's next task is to satisfy the court that the words that were used in the said broadcast were themselves, per se, capable of conveying a meaning tending to defame the plaintiff, either by forthrightly saying so or by a reasonable inference flowing therefrom. The alleged slander must be found in what is so said or inferred therefrom.

In *Grubb v. Bristol United Press Ltd.*, supra, Holroyd Pearce L.J. said, at p. 390:

"Thus, there is one cause of action for the libel itself, based on whatever imputations or implications can reasonably be derived from the words themselves, and there is another different cause of action, namely, the innuendo, based not merely on the libel itself but on an extended meaning created by a conjunction of the words with something outside them. The latter cause of action cannot come into existence unless there is some extrinsic fact to create the extended meaning. This view is simple and accords with common sense."

In *England v. C.B.C.*, supra, Tallis J. [p. 205] approved the following excerpt from Gatley on Libel and Slander, 6th ed., p. 68, para. 120, where the learned author said:

"It is well settled that the question whether words which are complained of are capable of conveying a defamatory meaning is a question of law, and is therefore one calling for the decision of the court. If the words are so capable, then it is a question for the jury whether the words do, in fact, convey a defamatory meaning."

The law has long settled upon and established the touchstone to be used by Her Majesty's judges in determining whether or not words used by a defendant and alleged to be libellous or slanderous were capable of conveying to the persons to whom they were published a meaning defamatory of the plaintiff.

In *Rubber Improvement v. Daily Telegraph,* supra, Lord Reid said, at p. 259:

"The leading case is *Capital & Counties Bank v. Henty* (1882), 7 App. Cas. 741 at 745 (H.L.). In that case Lord Selborne L.C. said: "The test, according to the authorities, is, whether under the circumstances in which the writing was published, reasonable men, to whom the publication was made, would be likely to understand it in a libellous sense."

And Lord Devlin in the same case, said, at p. 277:

"My Lords, the natural and ordinary meaning of words ought in theory to be the same for the lawyer as for the layman, because the lawyer's first rule of construction is that words are to be given their natural and ordinary meaning as popularly understood. The proposition that ordinary words are the same for the lawyer as for the layman is as a matter of pure construction undoubtedly true. But it is very difficult to draw the line between pure construction and implication, and the layman's capacity for implication is much greater than the lawyer's. The lawyer's rule is that the implication must be necessary as well as reasonable. The layman reads in an implication much more freely; and unfortunately, as the law of defamation has to take into account, is especially prone to do so when it is derogatory."

It therefore becomes my duty to determine if the words that were spoken in the first broadcast, upon being given their natural and ordinary meaning as understood by average, right-thinking and reasonable persons, *could* convey to such persons who heard the broadcast a derogatory meaning tending to defame the plaintiff.

In *Rubber Improvement v. Daily Telegraph,* at p. 258, Lord Reid said:

"What the ordinary man would infer without special knowledge has generally been called the natural and ordinary meaning of the words."

And at p. 259:

"In *Nevill v. Fine Arts & Gen. Ins. Co.,* [1897] A.C. 68 at 72, 73 (H.L.), Lord Halsbury said: '...what is the sense in which any ordinary reasonable man would understand the words of the communication so as to expose the plaintiff to hatred, or contempt or ridicule... it is not enough to say that by some person or another the words *might* be understood in a defamatory sense.' These statements of the law appear to have been generally accepted and I would not attempt to restate the general principle.

"In this case it is, I think, sufficient to put the test in this way. Ordinary men and women have different temperaments and outlooks. Some are unusually suspicious and some are unusually naive. One must try to envisage people between these two extremes and see what is the most damaging meaning they would put on the words in question."

See also *Jones v. Bennett* (1967), 59 W.W.R. 449 at 454-55, reversed 63 W.W.R. 1, which was reversed [1969] S.C.R. 277, 66 W.W.R. 419, 2 D.L.R. (3d) 291; and *Lawson v. Burns,* [1975] 1 W.W.R. 171, 56 D.L.R. (3d) 240 (B.C.).

Divesting myself of such professional legal knowledge and skill in the interpretation of words and the application of legal rules pertaining thereto that I have acquired over the years, and summoning to my aid such common sense as I possess, I have figuratively replayed the broadcast by reading the transcript thereof. Average, ordinary, right-thinking reasonable men and women, hereafter referred to as "average ordinary persons", who listened to this broadcast heard, inter alia, that the plaintiff was the supervisor of the oil and gas division in Yellowknife; and that he had "approved without any long examination" "a substantial amendment" to the drilling authority held by Dome Petroleum for the drilling of K 91. The listeners further heard the amendment described as a "betrayal of public faith" and that the government is not able to regulate Dome effectively". The listeners further heard that the drilling operations, as authorized by the amendment approved by the plaintiff, resulted in the company encountering gas pressure problems from the bottom of the well; and that such problems "could have led to the explosion of Explorer I which killed one drill worker", and that if the amendment had not been approved by the plaintiff the company would not have had the pressure problems or the explosion that killed the drill worker.

Read as a whole, the broad and general import of the words spoken in this broadcast were capable, per se, of conveying to an average ordinary person hearing it a defamatory imputation that the plaintiff had improperly performed the duties of his public office of supervisor of the federal oil and gas division of the department by approving a "substantial amendment" without giving proper consideration to the potential dangers such might engender, and that as a result of his misconduct the explosion that killed MacKay later occurred. Furthermore in carrying on his office as such supervisor, the plaintiff was not able to "regulate Dome effectively" and thus was unfit to hold that office. I have no difficulty in finding that the words spoken in the first broadcast were capable of defamatory meanings with reference to the plaintiff.

The plaintiff pleads and his counsel submits that, in addition to the two defamatory meanings I have just mentioned and found the broadcast to be capable of, the broadcast is also capable of additional other defamatory meanings. Be that as it may, nothing would be gained by my cataloguing such additions to a broadcast already found by me to be pregnant with such capabilities, other than to be able to say that the broadcast was a little more pregnant by reason of such additional capabilities.

Sitting without a jury as the trier of the facts, it becomes my duty at this point to decide if, under the circumstances in which the words were spoken, the words used in the broadcast, upon being given their natural and ordinary meanings as understood by average ordinary persons, conveyed to such persons who heard them derogatory imputations that were not only capable of but did, *in fact*, defame the plaintiff.

The broadcast identified the plaintiff by name four times. The average ordinary person would, in my opinion, infer from the broadcast, not merely that the plaintiff had failed to carry out his duties as such supervisor in a competent manner, but that his conduct had been so wrong that it had amounted to "a betrayal of public faith". It was said in the broadcast that the attacked amendment and the plaintiff's approval of it were not disclosed to the coroner's jury at the inquest into MacKay's death, thereby implying that the plaintiff had participated in a "cover up" of the amendment and his approval. The broadcast also said that the plaintiff had participated in the breaking of drilling regulations by Dome Petroleum. I repeat the grounds and reasons that I have given above in finding this broadcast to have been capable of conveying defamatory imputations to the persons who heard it. In this broadcast what had been called "the sting" of the slander by some judges was the tying together of the plaintiff's conduct with the explosion and death of MacKay, thereby imputing that the death resulted from the plaintiff's wrongful conduct. The authorities are clear that all these derogatory imputations must be viewed cumulatively in order to determine what the real impact of the broadcast would have been upon the average ordinary listener. In my opinion, the cumulative impact of these derogatory imputations did defame the plaintiff both in his professional occupation as a petroleum engineer and also in his office as regional conservation engineer, one of whose duties was to supervise the drilling operations of K 91. The effect of hearing the "sting" might well lower the plaintiff in the estimation of average ordinary persons and even expose him to their hatred, contempt or ridicule.

5.2.2.3 *Murphy* v. *LaMarsh,* (1970), 73 W.W.R. 114 (B.S.S.C.)

WILSON, C.J.S.C — The plaintiff Murphy was formerly employed as a radio newsman in the press gallery at Ottawa reporting for his radio station the doings of Parliament and the Government of Canada and general political news, including the public and private actions of politicians who were in the public eye.

The defendant Julia (more usually called Judy) LaMarsh is the author of, and the defendant McClelland and Stewart Limited is the publisher of, a book of political reminiscences called *Memoirs of a Bird in a Gilded Cage,* first published in 1968.

The first edition of this book, 10,000 copies, contained statements about the plaintiff which he says are defamatory and upon which this lawsuit is based. It is necessary to cite the impugned passage in full, from pp. 151, 152 and 153:

"A brash young radio reporter, named Ed Murphy (heartily detested by most of the Press Gallery and the members), had somehow learned that Maurice Lamontagne (then Secretary of State, and a long-time friend and adviser of the Prime Minister) had purchased furniture but had not paid for it. It sounded like an odd enough situation but what made it appear sinister was the fact that the furniture had been purchased from Futurama Galleries, a Montreal firm which was owned by a couple of gamblers, named Sefkind, who had disappeared in the wake of the Quebec Government's inquiry into bankruptcy. Futurama Galleries had gone into bankruptcy with Lamontagne's debt still showing on its books, and no payments had been made for furniture nor interest in over two years. Again, the hue and cry was raised over what might be — or might have been. A minister might have so compromised himself by being party to such an unusual 'credit' arrangement that he could be pressured into paying off the debt by trading some special treatment from the Government for his debtors or their associates. What that 'special treatment' might be was never specified, but it must be granted that it isn't inconceivable that there could be some.

"Maurice Lamontagne has a very lively, young-seeming wife, who likes nice things. As a university economist, I doubt that he had ever earned much money. He certainly had not while he was a full-time adviser to Pearson, in Opposition, when he began to buy his furniture. As a minister, his salary was, of course, much improved, but there were many demands upon it (although not so many as upon most Quebec ministers, who were expected to be pretty lavish with constituents' wedding presents and other similar gifts at Christmas or graduations; his wealthy predecessor in the riding of Outremont-St. John, now Senator Romuald Bourque, continued to look after the riding as though he were still its member, leaving Lamontagne free of those usual financial commitments). However, Maurice and his wife, Jeannette, liked to live comfortably and to entertain their friends well. He furnished a home in Ottawa for them, buying all his furniture from Futurama, then noted for the type and quality of furniture they sold. It would not, I think, be unusual for any firm to extend credit, even in such large amounts, for any reasonable period of time. After all, a minister's income is fairly assured, and fairly substantial (although unlike a private business arrangement, everyone knows what a minister is paid), and no minister could permit word to get around that he wasn't paying his bills, so men in public life are normally fairly good credit risks. (That is the way I bought my own furniture for my Ottawa apartment, entirely on credit, even as a private member of Parliament, and I paid it off without any difficulty to myself or worry to my Ottawa suppliers. The difference in Lamontagne's case, of course, is that most people pay regularly until their balance is paid, and the public, which buys furniture most often upon credit arrangements, knows that heavy interest is ordinarily charged.) In Lamontagne's case, when the firm went bankrupt and the matter became public, over two years after his first purchases, he had not paid anything. The exposure of the matter was, of course, acutely embarrassing, because it drew attention to his personal financial situation (completely, when he gave a statement of the whole sorry deal to the press and the House), and no one likes to have to do that. But Lamontagne considered that there was not much else to be concerned about, and he felt, and I think still feels, that he was hounded out of office for doing something that was not reprehensible. For he was indeed hounded out. Although the Prime Minister appeared to stand by him for nearly a year, until he had run again and been re-elected in late 1965, gaining some personal vindication, Pearson had been trying to force his resignation during much of that period. René Tremblay was caught in the furniture scandal too, although perfectly innocently. He had also bought furniture from Futurama in November, 1963, but he had not received full delivery at first and refused to pay the balance until full delivery might be made. He did pay the whole account only three months later, in February 1964. There could be no supportable suggestion that he had compromised himself."

In subsequent editions (25,000 copies) the words "heartily detested by most of the Press Gallery and the members" were deleted and they are also omitted from a paper-back edition of which 50,000 copies are being circulated by another publisher.

The passage just cited ("heartily detested by most of the Press Gallery and the members") is alleged to be libellous. The plaintiff also claims that the latter part of the extract cited, considered in its context, imputes to the plaintiff a disreputable action, the hounding of Mr. Lamontagne out of office, and is therefore libellous.

Miss LaMarsh was Member of Parliament for Niagara Falls from 1960 to 1968 and was, from 1963 to 1968, a Minister in a Government headed by Mr. Lester Pearson as Prime Minister and consisting of members of the Liberal political party.

Miss LaMarsh's memoirs were; her publisher tells me, expected to be a lively and colourful account of her political career. A good deal of the book fits readily into that definition and if Mr. Murphy's head is left bloody it is not the only one.

The first question is whether or not it is libel to say of a man in Mr. Murphy's occupation that he was "heartily detested" by most of his colleagues and by most Members of Parliament.

Plaintiff's counsel has not argued that the word "brash" is defamatory. I have given some thought to this conception — that the word "brash" is the governing word in the sentence and that the words "heartily detested by most of the Press Gallery and the members" are only inserted to reflect the reaction of those persons to Mr. Murphy's brashness. I have come to the conclusion that this interpretation of what Miss LaMarsh has said will not stand analysis — the statement, in parenthesis, that Mr. Murphy was heartily detested is an independent clause, emphasized by the parenthesis, and not clearly related to the quality of brashness. I do not say that brashness cannot arouse detestation. "Brash", in Canada bears, I think, more the American meaning stated in *Webster's Dictionary,* 1966 of "bumptious", "tactless", "loudly assertive", rather than the English meaning given in the *Oxford Dictionary* of "bold", "rash" or "impudent". But I do not think Miss LaMarsh has asserted that Mr. Murphy is detested because of his brashness; I think she has merely said he is detested by majorities of two groups of people.

These are the people best placed to know and value him, his associates in the press gallery and the Members of Parliament with whom he must associate and about whom he writes.

Ordinarily a libel is more specific than the one alleged here. A shameful action is attributed to a man (he stole my purse), a shameful character (he is dishonest), a shameful course of action (he lives on the avails of prostitution), a shameful condition (he has the pox). Such words are considered defamatory because they tend to bring the man named, according to the classic definition, into hatred, contempt or ridicule. The more modern definition, given by Lord Atkin, in *Sim v. Stretch* 52 TLR 669, 80 Sol J 703, [1936] 2 All ER 1237, at 1240, is words tending "to lower the plaintiff in the estimation of right-thinking members of society generally." Perhaps words likely to cause a man to be detested" might also, although not an all-inclusive definition, fit into the class of defamatory words.

The difference between this and other cases I have read or tried is that no shameful action or characteristic or condition is directly attributed to Mr. Murphy. It is only said of him that he is heartily detested. A fairly careful search of authority has revealed to me no case in which the libel alleged has been couched in such terms — an allegation of bad repute without some direct supporting charge of wrongdoing or bad character.

It is obvious that any decision as to whether or not such words as were used here are libellous must be approached with care. Under proper circumstances I think it must generally be open to writers to express of certain persons opinions as to their popularity or unpopularity, perhaps to say they are by some classes of people liked or disliked. The words used, the circumstances, the person who comments, the person upon whom the comment is made, must all be considered. It may be permissible, for instance, in certain circumstances, to say of a politician that he is losing his popularity, even though such words will certainly not help him in his career and may well hurt him.

The first thing to consider is the nature of the operative word "detested" and this was much discussed at the trial. The *Oxford Dictionary* gives to the word "detests" the meanings "hate", "abominate", "abhor", "dislike intensely". *Webster's Dictionary,* I think, is more up to date in its definitions when it says, "Detest indicates very strong aversion but may lack the actively hostile malevolence associated with hate."

I would say, for instance, that Hamlet hated, or thought he ought to hate Claudius, the murderer of his father and the defiler, as Hamlet thought, of his mother but that he detested Polonius as a sycophant and a tedious moralizing bore ("These tedious old fools": Act II scene 2).

But "detest" remains a strong word. While it may express the feeling one has toward a boor, a bore or a braggart, it may also express the feeling one has toward an unscrupulous reporter, a reporter whose actions have displayed bad character. I do not think that the reasoning in *Capital & Counties Bank v. Henty* (1882) 7 App. Cas. 741, 52 L.J.Q.B. 232, applies here. The words used are not, as in that case, capable of a harmless meaning and alternatively and rather vaguely of a bad meaning, so that the harmless meaning should be preferred. They are disparaging in any sense, more disparaging in one sense than the other and it seems to me that in those circumstances, where it is clear that right-thinking persons can and probably will properly interpret them as defamatory, there must be liability. The tendency to defame is there.

No wrong or evil is directly attributed to Mr. Murphy but it is said of him that most men who have most to do with him in his occupation heartily detest him. I have no doubt that the ordinary reader, who is not perhaps inclined to such an analysis of words as I have here attempted would, after reading this, think "There must be something wrong or bad about this man Murphy to make these people detest him." Since I think this is the test to be applied, I think the words are defamatory. The effect is the same as would have resulted if it had been said, "He bears a bad reputation among his associates."

The witnesses Charles Lynch and John Webster, speaking as reporters, think otherwise. I am basing my opinion on my conception of what the legendary "right-thinking man" would take the words to mean and I would not want to exclude either witness from that class. I have no reason to doubt the honesty or the correctness of their evidence as reflecting their own opinions. But I must remember that neither Mr. Lynch nor Mr. Webster is an ordinary everyday reader of books attaching to the words in question their conventional effect. Mr. Lynch says that he would, as an employer of newsmen, be interested in a man described as heartily detested by most of the press gallery (which he calls a competitive jungle) and the House, because detestation is a price, a mark of success in press gallery writing, and political approval a warning of failure. Mr. Webster says that to be disliked by a politician may be a badge of honour to a reporter. This evidence has a considerable bearing on the question of damages, which I shall come to later. But the esoteric meaning attached by these initiates to the effect of detestation is not one that would spring to the mind of the ordinary citizen who reads the book, and it is from that level that I must form my opinion.

I should deal with one case relied on by the defendant. *Robinson v. Jermyn* (1814) 1 Price 11, 145 ER 1314. The defendants were proprietors of or subscribers to a room called "the Cassino" which they frequented, presumably for social purposes. They posted a regulation of the Cassino reading thus, "The Rev. John Robinson, and Mr. James Robinson, inhabitants of this town, not being persons that the proprietors and annual subscribers think it proper to associate with, are excluded this room." They were sued by the Rev. Robinson for libel. Thomson, C.B. said at p. 16:

> "The demurrer to these pleas involves the material question, whether the publication of the words laid in the declaration are properly the subject matter of an action, and whether, under the circumstances, they amount to a libel. The words are, 'The Rev. John Robinson and Mr. James Robinson, not being persons that the proprietors or annual subscribers think it proper to associate with, are excluded this room.' It seems to me to be a material allegation in this declaration that the plaintiff was officiating minister, but there is certainly nothing affecting him in his clerical character in these words. It then goes on to state, that the words were published in one of the written regulations of the room. Now the principal ground on which this action can be supported is, that it does in substance contain an averment, that these plaintiffs were not fit for common association — that they were not proper persons for general society; and nothing will help this declaration, unless it can be collected from it, that such an insinuation was the object of the words. Now it does not seem to me, that such an imputation can be inferred. It seems merely that these defendants did not think that the plaintiffs were proper persons to be associated with by them; but that may proceed from other causes than such as must appear on the face of the declaration, to have been insinuated, to constitute a libel. There might be reasons assigned not at all affecting the moral character of the plaintiffs; for the defendants may not have thought them agreeable or sociable. They may have considered them troublesome and officious; or, for some other such reasons, improper for their society."

I think this case is clearly distinguishable. The defendants were, in the first place, stating their own opinion, not purporting to report that of other persons. The words were not defamatory. They merely indicated a disinclination by the subscribers to associate with certain persons. It is true that here, as there, the opinion in question was that of a certain body of people, not of society generally. But it seems to me that the mild assertion by persons directly interested of a disinclination to associate with certain other persons is a far cry from a bold statement that a man is heartily detested by most of his associates. If, in this case, Miss LaMarsh had expressed her own detestation of the plaintiff I would have thought little of it but it is a different matter when she attributes, without foundation, detestation of Mr. Murphy to his associates.

5.2.2.4. *Vogel* v. *CBC* (1982), 21 C.C.L.T. 105

ESSON, J.: ...I have made many references to the impression conveyed to viewers. That is a matter which must be considered in assessing television programmes which, by reason of their transitory nature, tend to leave the audience with an impression rather than a firm understanding of what was said. Images, facial expressions, tones of voice, symbols and the dramatic effect which can be achieved by juxtaposition of segments may be more important than the meaning derived from careful reading of the words of the script. Television is different from the printed word. The interested reader can reread and analyze. The emphasis in considering the defamatory impact of, say, a newspaper story must therefore be upon the words used. Libel by television is, in this respect, more like slander. In slander cases, regard may be had to such things as gestures and intonations: see Gatley on Libel and Slander (7th ed., 1974), p. 500, para. 1225. Here, regard must be had to the devices used to create an impression that what was being reported was a serious scandal.

5.2.2.5 *E. Hulton and Co.* v. *Jones*, [1910] A.C. 22 (House of Lords)

The plaintiff, Mr. Thomas Artemus Jones, a barrister practising on the North Wales Circuit, brought the action to recover damages for the publication of an alleged libel concerning him contained in an article in the *Sunday Chronicle,* a newspaper of which the defendants were the printers, proprietors, and publishers. The article, which was written by the Paris correspondent of the paper, purported to describe a motor festival at Dieppe, and the parts chiefly complained of ran thus: "Upon the terrace marches the world, attracted by the motor races — a world immensely pleased with itself, and minded to draw a wealth of inspiration — and, incidentally, of golden cocktails — from any scheme to speed the passing hour.... 'Whist! there is Artemus Jones with a woman who is not his wife, who must be, you know — the other thing!' whispers a fair neighbour of mine excitedly into her bosom friend's ear. Really, is it not surprising how certain of our fellow-countrymen behave when they come abroad? Who would suppose, by his goings on, that he was a churchwarden at Peckham? No one, indeed, would assume that Jones in the atmosphere of London would take on so austere a job as the duties of a churchwarden. Here, in the atmosphere of Dieppe, on the French side of the Channel, he is the life and soul of a gay little band that haunts the Casino and turns night into day, besides betraying a most unholy delight in the society of female butterflies." The plaintiff had in fact received the baptismal name of Thomas only, but in his boyhood he had taken or had been given, the additional name of Artemus, and from that time he had always used, and had been universally known by, the name of Thomas Artemus Jones or Artemus Jones. He had, up to the year 1901, contributed signed articles to the defendants' newspaper. The plaintiff was not a church warden, nor did he reside at Peckham. Upon complaint being made by the plaintiff of the publication of the defamatory statements in the article, the defendants published the following in the next issue of their paper: "It seems hardly necessary for us to state that the imaginary Mr. Artemus Jones referred to in our article was not Mr. Thomas Artemus Jones, barrister, but, as he has complained to us, we gladly publish this paragraph in order to remove any possible misunderstanding and to satisfy Mr. Thomas Artemus Jones we had no intention whatsoever of referring to him." The defendants alleged that the name chosen for the purpose of the article was a fictitious one, having no reference to the plaintiff, and chosen as unlikely to be the name of a real person, and they denied that any officer or member of their staff who wrote or printed or published or said before publication the words complained of knew the plaintiff or his name or his profession, or his association with the journal or with the defendants, or that there was any existing person bearing the name of or known as Artemus Jones. They admitted publication, but denied that the words were published of or concerning the plaintiff. On the part of the plaintiff the evidence of the writer of the article and of the editor of the paper that they knew nothing of the plaintiff, and that the article was not intended by them to refer to him, was accepted as true. At the trial witnesses were called for the plaintiff, who said that they had read the article and thought that it referred to the plaintiff.

LORD LOREBURN L.C. My Lords, I think this appeal must be dismissed. A question in regard to the law of libel has been raised which does not seem to me to be entitled to the support of your Lordships. Libel is a tortious act. What does the tort consist in? It consists in using language which others knowing the circumstances would reasonably think to be defamatory of the person complaining of and injured by it. A person charged with libel cannot defend himself by shewing that he intended in his own breast not to defame, or that he intended not to defame the plaintiff, if in fact he did both. He has none the less imputed something disgraceful and has none the less injured the plaintiff. A man in good faith may publish a libel believing it to be true, and it may be found by the jury that he acted in good faith believing it to be true, and reasonably believing it to be true, but that in fact the statement was false. Under those circumstances he has no defence to the action, however excellent his intention. If the intention of the writer be immaterial in considering whether the matter written is defamatory, I do not see why it need be relevant in considering whether it is defamatory of the plaintiff. The writing, according to the old form, must be malicious, and it must be of and concerning the plaintiff. Just as the defendant could not excuse himself from malice by proving that he wrote it in the most benevolent spirit, so he cannot shew that the libel was not of and concerning the plaintiff by proving that he never heard of the plaintiff. His intention in both respects equally is inferred from what he did. His remedy is to abstain from defamatory words.

It is suggested that there was a misdirection by the learned judge in this case. I see none. He lays down in his summing up the law as follows: "The real point upon which your verdict must turn is, ought or ought not sensible and reasonable people reading this article to think that it was a mere imaginary person such as I have said — Tom Jones, Mr. Pecksniff as a humbug, Mr. Stiggins, or any of that sort of names that one reads of in literature used as types? If you think any reasonable person would think that, it is not actionable at all. If, on the other hand, you do not think that, but think that people would suppose it to mean some real person — those who did not know the plaintiff of course would not know who the real person was, but those who did know of the existence of the plaintiff would think that it was the plaintiff — then the action is maintainable, subject to such damages as you think under all the circumstances are fair and right to give to the plaintiff."

I see no objection in law to that passage. The damages are certainly heavy, but I think your Lordships ought to remember two things. The first is that the jury were entitled to think, in the absence of proof satisfactory to them (and they were the judges of it), that some ingredient of recklessness, or more than recklessness, entered into the writing and the publication of this article, especially as Mr. Jones, the plaintiff, had been employed on this very newspaper, and his name was well known in the paper and also well known in the district in which the paper circulated. In the second place the jury were entitled to say this kind of article is to be condemned. There is no tribunal more fitted to decide in regard to publications, especially publications in the newspaper Press, whether they bear a stamp and character which ought to enlist sympathy and to secure protection. If they think that the licence is not fairly used and that the tone and style of the libel is reprehensible and ought to be checked, it is for the jury to say so; and for my part, although I think the damages are certainly high, I am not prepared to advise your Lordships to interfere, especially as the Court of Appeal have not thought it right to interfere, with the verdict.

LORD ATKINSON. My Lords, I concur with the judgment which has been delivered by my noble and learned friend on the woolsack, and I also concur substantially with the judgment delivered by Farwell L.J. in the Court of Appeal. I think he has put the case upon its true ground, and I should be quite willing to adopt in the main the conclusions at which he has arrived.

LORD GORELL. My Lords, I concur also with the judgment which has been pronounced by the Lord Chancellor. I also wish to express my concurrence with the observations which my noble and learned friend Lord Atkinson has made upon the judgment of Farwell L.J.

LORD SHAW OF DUNFERMLINE. My Lords, I concur in the observations which have been made by the Lord Chancellor, but for my own part I should desire in terms to adopt certain language which I will now read from the judgment of the Lord Chief Justice: "The question, if it be disputed whether the article is a libel upon the plaintiff, is a question of fact for the jury, and in my judgment this question of fact involves not only whether the language used of a person in its fair and ordinary meaning is libellous or defamatory, but whether the person referred to in the libel would be understood by persons who knew him to refer to the plaintiff."

My Lords, with regard to this whole matter I should put my propositions in a threefold form, and, as I am not acquainted by training with a system of jurisprudence in which criminal libel has any share, I desire my observations to be confined to the question of civil responsibility.

In the publication of matter of a libellous character, that is matter which would be libellous if applying to an actual person, the responsibility is as follows: In the first place there is responsibility for the words used being taken to signify that which readers would reasonably understand by them; in the second place there is responsibility also for the names used being taken to signify those whom the readers would reasonably understand by those names; and in the third place the same principle is applicable to persons unnamed but sufficiently indicated by designation or description.

My Lords, I demur to the observation so frequently made in the argument that these principles are novel. Sufficient expression is given to the same principles by Abbott C.J. in *Bourke* v. *Warren* (1) (cited in the proceedings), in which that learned judge says: "The question for your consideration is whether you think the libel designates the plaintiff in such a way as to let those who knew him understand that he was the person meant. It is not necessary that all the world should understand the libel; it is sufficient if those who know the plaintiff can make out that he is the person meant." I think it is out of the question to suggest that that means "meant in the mind of the writer" or of the publisher; it must mean "meant by the words employed." The late Lord Chief Justice Coleridge dealt similarly with the point in *Gibson* v. *Evans* (2), when in the course of the argument he remarked: "It does not signify what the writer meant; the question is whether the alleged libel was so published by the defendant that the world would apply it to the plaintiff."

5.2.2.6 *Booth et al.* v. *BCTV* (1983) 139 D.L.R. (3d) 88 (B.C.C.A.)

LAMBERT J.A.: — It is not necessary to call upon you, Mr. Alexander, in reply on the cross-appeal.

This is a defamation case. The words were spoken in 1972. They were recorded on tape and broadcast on television and published all in 1972. The trial took place in 1975 and this appeal is from the trial judgment at that time [summarized [1976] W.W.D. 78].

In 1972, there was a change in the law affecting prostitution and the defendant television system or one of its employees conceived the idea of interviewing a prostitute. The defendant, Margo Wong, was interviewed by the defendant, David Rinn, on television in a programme produced by the defendant, Clapp, and broadcast by the defendant British Columbia Television Broadcasting System Limited.

The words that are in issue in the case are set out in the reasons of Mr. Justice Hinkson, the trial judge, and they are these:

Q. What are policemen like in Vancouver?

A. Some of them are O.K. and some of them are not. There's good ones and crooked ones.

Q. Are there any payoffs in Vancouver?

A. Yeah there's about — in one night maybe twelve cops get paid off from different squads.

Q. You've paid them off?

A. I've paid them off quite a few times.

Q. How much?

A. Ummm — if it goes Vag "C" charge usually you have to pay them maybe half a bill — fifty dollars. If it's for narcotics you usually up a hundred — two-hundred dollars.

Q. Could you name individuals involved?

A. Oh I could — yeah — but I'm not gonna name them — cause that would just get me up a creek without a paddle — but there is, I'd say three on the Morality Squad that are quite high for payoffs and I know two on the Narc Squad that are high up — right up on top that take payoffs, and there's a few other ones on — like Traffic — you know they're special squads that take some.

The interview was broadcast by the defendant, British Columbia Television Broadcasting System Limited, at least twice, I understand on the same day, and then had a wider dissemination after that, but the scope of any wider dissemination was not in issue at the trial or before us.

The plaintiffs are 11 members of the Vancouver City Police Force, or they were in 1972. They are all members of the narcotics squad. There was in 1972 a vice department in the Vancouver City Police Force, and within that department four separate squads: the narcotics squad, the liquor squad, the morality squad and gambling squad.

Organization of the narcotics squad was that a staff sergeant was in charge, Staff Sergeant Devries. His second in command at that time was Sergeant Grierson, who had only been appointed a week at the time of the utterance of the defamatory words. Staff Sergeant Devries and Sergeant Grierson worked predominately on the administrative aspects of the squad and did not do much, if any, street work. There were eleven other members of the narcotics squad. There were at least two, and perhaps three, separate subgroups. One was comprised of Detective Booth as the senior detective in length of service and senior in that he exercised some supervision over the work of the other members of that undercover subgroup. That group dealt with street dealings in drugs, as they are called.

Another subgroup dealt with dealings in drugs at a higher level and it was referred to as the trafficking subgroup because of the nature of the work they were engaged in, the trafficking in drugs at a higher level than street dealings. Detective Donald was the senior man in that grouping, and working with him were Detectives Simmons and Larke, but they again were working under his overall control as they worked together. So, the senior man in the undercover street group was Detective Booth, and in the trafficking group, Detective Donald.

The pleadings described the plaintiffs and defendants, but the substance of the allegations is set out in paras. 18 and 19 which follow the statement of the words alleged to be defamatory and I will set out paras. 18 and 19:

> 18. In the said interview the words "...and there's a few other ones on — like Traffic — you know they're special squads that take some", were interpreted by the respective families, friends, acquaintances and colleagues of the Plaintiffs, WILLIAM DONALD, STANLEY SIMMONS and KENNETH LARKE, respectively, as referring to the aforementioned three Plaintiffs who were and were known to be members of a unit within the Narcotics Squad at that particular time which unit was generally referred to as "the Traffic Squad" and was organized specifically to investigate the illegal movement of, and dealing or trafficking in narcotic drugs and substances. Furthermore, each of the other Plaintiffs herein have worked as members of "the Traffic Squad" from time to time throughout their association with the drug division of the Vancouver City Police Department and likewise were considered by their families, friends, acquaintances and colleagues as members of "the Traffic Squad".
>
> 19. By the words mentioned in Paragraph 16 hereof, the Defendants and each of them meant and were understood, by the Plaintiffs and each of them, and their respective families, friends, acquaintances and colleagues to apply to and mean that the Plaintiffs and each of them were dishonest, corrupt and unfit to act in connection with their respective professions as policemen and members of the Police Narcotics Squad.

Counsel on the appeal referred very largely to the same leading authorities in relation to defamation that consists of statements referring to more than one person without naming particular persons, and those leading cases are *Knupffer v. London Express Newspaper, Ltd.*, [1944] 1 All E.R. 495; *Morgan v. Odhams Press Ltd. et al.*, [1971] 2 All E.R. 1156. Counsel referred to other cases but those are the principal cases relied on and those were the principal cases relied on by the trial judge. There is no significant dispute between counsel as to the broad legal concepts that are applicable and, as I understand their arguments, neither counsel takes objection to the statements of law by the trial judge but rather take objections both on the appeal and the cross-appeal to the application of that law to the particular words in this case and the circumstances in this case.

The overriding issue in cases of this kind where the words are clearly defamatory in themselves is whether the words were published of and concerning the particular plaintiff who is claiming, and in addressing that question Viscount Simon says in the *Knupffer* case at p. 497:

> There are two questions involved in the attempt to identify the appellant as the person defamed. The first question is a question of law — can the article, having regard to its

> language, be regarded as capable of referring to the appellant? The second question is a question of fact, namely, does the article in fact lead reasonable people, who know the appellant, to the conclusion that it does refer to him? Unless the first question can be answered in favour of the appellant, the second question does not arise, and where the trial judge went wrong was in treating evidence to support the identification in fact as governing the matter, when the first question is necessarily, as a matter of law, to be answered in the negative.

In the *Morgan* case we were particularly referred to the judgment of Lord Morris of Borth-y-Gest which indicates that the dual nature of the test grows out of the practice in charging juries in cases of defamation.

The trial judge deals more extensively than I have with the law, but I do not think that it is necessary to go further than I have done. He adopts the test set out by Viscount Simon and he applies it to eliminate all of the 11 plaintiffs except two, Booth and Donald. As I understand his reasons, he is saying that the words referring to "two on the Narc Squad that are high up — right up on top", are capable when considered in relation to the facts of this case of being considered as being published of and concerning only Booth and Donald.

The trial judge also considers that the remainder of the words are, as a matter of law, not capable of being considered as published of and concerning any of the other plaintiffs other than Booth and Donald.

The trial judge then goes on and considers the evidence of 12 or 14 witnesses who gave the view that they took when they heard the defamatory statements or heard about the defamatory statements, and he concludes that a reasonable person on hearing these statements would think that they were said of and concerning Booth and Donald, and on that basis the trial judge finds liability of the defendants to Booth and Donald.

In his assessment of damages he awarded $7,500 to each of those plaintiffs as compensation and $5,000 to each of those plaintiffs by way of exemplary damages. The exemplary damages, therefore, totalled $10,000 and were awarded after careful consideration and a listing of those factors that justified such an award, particularly the prospect of profits being made by the broadcasting defendant from the excitement generated by a story of this nature, and the assistance of all of the defendants in publishing the defamatory statement after being requested not to do so until an opportunity had been given to the police departments to investigate the truth of what was alleged.

An appeal has been brought by the defendants British Columbia Television Broadcasting and Clapp, the only two defendants who were represented at the trial. Their appeal is as to liability.

A cross-appeal has been brought by the plaintiff, Donald, and by the nine other plaintiffs, other than Booth, who did not recover on their claim.

In relation to the appellant Donald, the cross-appeal asks for a higher award of exemplary damages. In relation to the other cross-appellants the cross-appeal asks for a finding that the defendants are liable to them and then asks for damages, both compensatory damages and exemplary damages.

I turn first to the appeal. Three points were argued.

The first was whether the words were capable of being considered as being published of and concerning the plaintiffs Booth and Donald.

The submission of counsel for the appellant was that they are only capable of referring to the staff sergeant who was in charge of the narcotics squad and the sergeant who was his second in command.

As I have said, the actual phrase was: "two on the Narc Squad that are high up — right up on top". In my opinion, we are not concerned with what the speaker subjectively meant to say; we are concerned with the meaning that reasonable men would take from what was said. But words, of course, are merely a mode of communication and all the circumstances of the communication must be considered as well as the mode that was used. The kind of person that the speaker was, and the kind of knowledge that people would anticipate that the speaker would have are relevant factors in determining the content of the communication. The circumstances in which the words are used are also relevant. So is the general audience to which the statements might be considered to be directed, and the special audience with special knowledge of the organization of the Vancouver Police Department. These too are relevant factors in deciding whether reasonable people generally, or whether reasonable people with special and particular knowledge, would find that the defamatory statement was published of and concerning the particular plaintiff.

The speaker was Margaret Wong, a prostitute with some knowledge but clearly not any detailed knowledge of the organization of the drug squad. There is no reason to believe that she would know of the transfer or personality of the second in command a week before she spoke. There is no reason to believe that when she says that she is referring to someone right on the top that she was referring to an inside administrator of the department who has overall supervision.

The trial judge found that those words were capable of referring to Booth and Donald. He found that those words were not capable of referring to the junior members in seniority and in work of the squad and, indeed, he found that the words were only capable of referring to Booth and Donald. He reached that conclusion on the basis of the words themselves, but also on the evidence that had been led and, of course, where the trier of fact and decider of law are the same there is no reason for any precise separation of the functions or decision of the two questions that have been raised by Viscount Simon. The ultimate question remains whether the words were published of and concerning the plaintiff. After considering all the evidence the trial judge decided that they were capable of being considered as published of and concerning Booth and Donald and that they were not capable of being considered as published of and concerning anyone other than Booth and Donald. I agree.

The second point in the appeal raised by counsel for the appellant relates then to Booth and Donald and is that even if the words were capable of being considered as published of and concerning them that reasonable men would not have concluded that they were published of Booth and Donald and that even on the basis of the evidence that particular people did consider them published of Booth and Donald that, on the whole of the evidence, it should not have been concluded that a reasonable man would consider them as published of Booth and Donald.

Counsel for the appellant took us through the relevant parts of the evidence of 12 or even 14 witnesses on this point, and indeed there were considerable variations in their reactions to the story. However, counsel for the appellant concedes that he is not asking us to reassess on the balance of probabilities the conclusion reached by the trial judge on the question of fact, whether a reasonable person would be led to the conclusion that reference was to Booth and Donald. He said on the basis of the evidence the trial judge was clearly wrong in his conclusion.

In my opinion, on the basis of the evidence that was read to us, the trial judge was not clearly wrong. He reached a conclusion on a question of fact and, in my opinion, there was ample evidence to support that conclusion, that a reasonable person who knew Booth and Donald might well conclude that the defamatory words were uttered of and concerning them.

The third point related to the pleadings. In my opinion, para. 19 of the statement of claim was an ample pleading to support the conclusion of the trial judge, notwithstanding that the judgment of the trial judge did not come within the more particular pleading in para. 18 that I have recited and, indeed, as I understood his argument, counsel for the appellant did not press this third point.

For those reasons I would dismiss the appeal.

I turn now to the cross-appeal. It comes essentially to two points.

The first is that the defamatory words were uttered of and concerning all 11 of the plaintiffs and not just Booth and Donald. The major ground on which this is put is that all were members of the narcotics squad, that the words should not be construed as if they were a statute, but should be considered as a communication made orally and that in considering that communication the true question is what would reasonable people take from the words as an impression, as well as or coupled with the more precise content of the words, but not limited to the precise grammatical content of the words.

I do not disagree with counsel for the plaintiffs on the cross-appeal with his view as to the proper way of considering the words spoken. It is the impression that they convey that is crucial. But, in my opinion, the words "two on the Narc Squad that are high up — right on top" and the other words that surround them do not, in law, have a link with the other nine plaintiffs. It is true that the evidence indicates that there was immediate suspicion of all of the members of the narcotics squad and indeed there may well have been suspicion beyond that into the morality squad, into the vice squad as a whole, but that suspicion is more a matter of the mind of the person who heard the statement and his or her association with particular members of the police force. A neighbour who knows only one police officer, for example, and hears something about the police force would think immediately of that police officer, whether the words that are used have any real link to that police officer or not. So, an immediate suspicion is not necessarily an indication that the words are capable of being considered as published of and concerning the particular plaintiff. I think a good deal of the evidence was in that category.

After considering the evidence to which we were referred and considering both the precise words that I have quoted and the surrounding words, I agree with the trial judge that the other nine plaintiffs were not included and not capable of being included as being referred to in the words that were uttered.

A second point was made in relation to the members of the trafficking subgroup of the narcotics squad.

The trial judge dealt carefully with the evidence of how traffic and trafficking were used by the police witnesses and by other witnesses and he reached the conclusion that, again, the words were not capable of being considered as referring to the two plaintiffs, Simmons and Larke, who worked in the trafficking subgroup. On the basis of the evidence I agree with the trial judge.

The second point on the cross-appeal related to damages. Very fairly, counsel for the plaintiffs on the cross-appeal said that he was not asking us to reassess in 1982 and by 1982 standards the award that had been made by the trial judge in 1975 with respect to defamatory words uttered in 1972. His submission was that by 1975 standards the award of a total of $10,000 as exemplary damages was inordinately low. He did not refer us specifically to any cases decided in this jurisdiction and, indeed, my recollection of those cases indicates that they would not support a submission that $10,000 was inordinately low for a case such as this. The case was clearly an appropriate one, in my view, for an award of exemplary damages but, in my opinion, an award of $10,000 in total was a fit award and it was appropriate to divide it as to $5,000 to each of the two plaintiffs in whose favour judgment on liability had been made.

For those reasons I would dismiss the cross-appeal.

ANDERSON J.A.: — I agree.
MACFARLANE J.A.: — I agree.
LAMBERT J.A.: — The appeal and the cross-appeal are dismissed.

Appeal and cross-appeal dismissed.

5.2.2.7 *Planned Parenthood Federation* v. *Fedorik* (1982) 135 D.L.R. (3d) 714, at 718 (Nfld. Sup. Ct., Trial Div.)

NOEL J.: The law recognizes in every company a right to have the estimation in which it stands in the opinion of other persons unaffected by false statements to its discredit. The wrong of defamation is committed when a person publishes to a third person an untrue imputation against the reputation of another. In this regard, a company is treated as a person. Any imputation which may tend to lower the plaintiff in the estimation of right-thinking members of society generally, or to cut it off from society, or to expose it to hatred, contempt or ridicule is defamatory of it.

5.2.2.8 *Whitaker* v. *Huntington* (1981), 15 C.C.L.T. 19, at 21-22 (B.C.S.C.)

December 10, 1980. VERCHERE J.: — This is an action for damages for libel. The defendant is a Member of Parliament and, on December 6th, 1977, after having attended on the day before a meeting of the Standing Committee on Transport and Communications, where the estimates of the Post Office were under consideration, he spoke by telephone from Ottawa to the host of a "talk show" broadcast by radio in Vancouver about the Post Office and its employees. In the course of his remarks, he offended members of the plaintiff local, including then president, Mr. Whitaker, and its vice-president, Mr. Ingram, particularly when he said:

> "Mr. Huntington: Yeah, now who marched down to the Fishermen's Hall to take a vote, the information I get within the Union, is that about 50 to 51 per cent of the membership, 55 per cent of the membership at meetings get to vote, and the other 45 per cent have no voice at all, and that's why I...
> Mr. Murphy: They have no voice...?
> Mr. Huntington: Well, they are quiet people. They aren't people that can group together or who want to group together in muscle-bound units and stand up and fight this imposed leadership and it's about a 55 to 45 proposition I believe in the Vancouver workers' union. The point I was trying to get across to Mr. Blais the Postmaster General yesterday was, why he doesn't use his initiative in this very key position and important position he has, use his initiative in the Cabinet to put in a law that orders democracy in union affairs where there

is a government supervision of the vote, wording in the unions to do with federal activities and where there is a government supervised ballot to protect the rank and file worker in that union. That whole organization is not there for the benefit of people who want to tear down the system, Ed, and unless somebody in J.J. Blais' position is going to start to put some pressure on, the government isn't going to move, they're going to allow this process of disintegration to continue. I'm simply not down here to watch it happen.''

Upon the telephone lines being opened for public participation in the show, Mr. Ingram promptly spoke to the defendant and after a long conversation about what he had said, a meeting was sought to be arranged. None was held, but in the result, on May 16th following, the defendant appeared in person at the radio station and after the union's secretary had broadcast a ''press release'' attributed to Mr. Whitaker, the defendant commented on it and added:

> ''I can defend the democratic freedom that I want to see survive in this country as strongly as he can destroy it though, and that's what I am out to do.''

Apparently aggrieved at what had been said, the plaintiffs started this action on July 26th following. Then about eight months later a statement of claim was filed and there, after asserting that all the above-quoted words had been falsely and maliciously broadcast and that the last-quoted words, in particular, referred and were intended to refer to Mr. Whitaker, the plaintiffs attributed the following meaning to them, namely:

> ''8. The natural and ordinary meaning of the said words was that the Plaintiff, Peter Whitaker, and the Plaintiff, The Canadian Union of Postal Workers, prevented the full participation of the members of the Vancouver Local of the Canadian Union of Postal Workers, in the affairs of the Union; that the Vancouver Local of the Canadian Union of Postal Workers was an undemocratic union and was not responsive to the majority wishes of the membership; that the membership did not have full opportunity of participating in all the affairs, activities and committees of the union; and that because of this, Mr. Whitaker, the Plaintiff and The Canadian Union of Postal Workers, was trying to destroy democratic freedom in Canada.''

I agree that that interpretation is reasonable.

5.2.2.9 *Stark* v. *Toronto Sun* (1983) 42 O.R. (2d) 791, at 794-795 (Ont. H.C.)

The *Odhams Press* case, *supra,* is relied upon as denying a claim in libel to the individual plaintiffs by reason of the lack of sufficient particulars pleaded in the statement of claim from which it might be inferred that the words were published of the individual plaintiffs. This principle was applied in *Seafarers, Int'l Union of Canada et al.* v. *Lawrence* (1979), 24 O.R. (2d) 257, 97 D.L.R. (3d) 324, 13 C.P.C. 281, in the course of proceedings and prior to it reaching the Court of Appeal. I take cognizance of the fact that this case differs from *Seafarers* in that there, the words complained of were not directed to all members of the union. They referred to ''some'' as being thugs. The action in defamation being a personal one, each plaintiff was obligated to plead facts that gave him or her a cause of action. Having read the two articles in this case with great care, my conclusion is that the individual plaintiffs have failed to establish the necessary link between themselves and the words used. They have pleaded membership in Operation Dismantle but they must go further. They must bring their personal reputations into play and they must as a minimum rely on pertinent facts in the pleadings that will raise the question of the tendency which the words have of lowering them in the estimation of others. This they have failed to do. There is nothing in the pleadings to indicate an identification on the part of these plaintiffs in the minds of the public with the organization. It is particularly imperative in libel actions that individual plaintiffs set out fully their individual causes of action when the class which was allegedly defamed is as wide and as ideological as Operation Dismantle is.

I turn now to Rule 75 and to its applicability to the circumstances of this case. Operation Dismantle is a non-incorporated association and cannot be sued. Can a representative action be maintained by one or more on behalf of all the members as a class? It would seem that *prima facie* the rule applies and a class action ought to be permitted. If it can be said that the members of Operation Dismantle were libelled, they all have the same interest in the result of the action.

What must be kept firmly in mind, however, is that the unincorporated body "Operation Dismantle" cannot be defamed. Only its members can. The distinction is important because the danger is forever lurking in the background of actions being prosecuted superficially on behalf of members of a class when in reality they are suing for and on behalf of the unincorporated association or entity. It will be a difficult judgment call to make in each case. When defamatory words are spoken of the members of a small association comprising 10 members for instance, a representative action would lie, as long as the pleadings were satisfactory, even absent specific names in the offensive article. Indeed a representative action would be encouraged in the interest of avoiding multiplicity of proceedings. But an opposite pole exists.

From the other extreme in my view may be taken a case like the present one. The line of demarcation may on occasion be fuzzy. In my opinion it is not so here. The members of a specific union as an instance may be defamed. Speaking generally, the members of the "union movement" in the country cannot be. The nature and size of the class must be studied, its composition scrutinized and its object defined. When it casts too wide and too philosophical or ideological a net on most or all acocunts, then Rule 75 ought not to be resorted to.

In the result the statement of claim is struck and the action dismissed *in toto*. Costs to the defendants.

Application allowed.

5.2.2.10 The Defamation Act, Manitoba R.S.M. 1970, c.60, s.19

Libel of race or creed.

19(1) The publication of a libel against a race or religious creed likely to expose persons belonging to the race, or professing the religious creed, to hatred, contempt or ridicule, and tending to raise unrest or disorder among the people, entitles a person belonging to the race, or professing the religious creed, to sue for an injunction to prevent the continuation and circulation of the libel; and the Court of Queen's Bench may entertain the action.

Am.

Persons liable.

19(2) The action may be taken against the person responsible for the authorship, publication, or circulation, of the libel.

Meaning of "publication".

19(3) The word "publication" used in this section means any words legibly marked upon any substance or any object signifying the matter otherwise than by words, exhibited in public or caused to be seen or shown or circulated or delivered with a view to its being seen by any person.
Am.

One action only.

19(4) No more than one action shall be brought under subsection (1) in respect of the same libel.
R.S.M., c.60, s.20; am.

5.2.2.11 An Act to Amend the Defamation Act S.M. 1980, c.30, ss.2, 7

Cl. 2(f) added.

2 Section 2 of the Act is further amended by adding thereto, at the end thereof, the following clause:

(f) "publish" includes transmission, emission, dissemination or the making public of writings, signs, signals, symbols, pictures and sounds of all kinds, from or by a newspaper or from or by broadcasting and "publication" has a corresponding meaning.

Subsec. 19(3) am.

7 Subsection 19(3) of the Act is amended by striking out the words "publication" used in this section means" in the 1st thereof and substituting therefor the words, figure and letter "in this section, "publication" in addition to the meaning set out in clause 2(f), includes".

Note: A court has suggested that this section is *ultra vires,* first, because it deals with "what is, in essence, criminal libel" and secondly, because matters "tending to raise unrest or disorder among the people" have been dealt with by Parliament in the Criminal Code. See *Courchene* v. *Marlborough Hotel* (1971) 20 D.L.R. (3d) 109. No other province has such a provision.

5.2.2.12 Ontario Libel and Slander Act, R.S.O. 1980, c.237, ss.1, 2

INTERPRETATION

Intrepretation

1. (1) In this Act,

(*a*) "broadcasting" means the dissemination of writing, signs, signals, pictures and sounds of all kinds, intended to be received by the public either directly or through the medium of relay stations, by means of,

(i) any form of wireless radioelectric communication utilizing Hertzian waves, including radiotelegraph and radiotelephone, or

(ii) cables, wires, fibre-optic linkages or laser beams,

and ''broadcast'' has a corresponding meaning.

(*b*) ''newspaper'' means a paper containing public news, intelligence, or occurrences or remarks or observations thereon, or containing only, or principally, advertisements, printed for distribution to the public and published periodically, or in parts or numbers, at least twelve times a year. R.S.O. 1970, c.243, s.1(1); 1980, c.35, s.1.

Meaning of words extended

(2) Any reference to words in this Act shall be construed as including a reference to pictures, visual images, gestures and other methods of signifying meaning. R.S.O. 1970, c.243, s.1(2).

LIBEL

What constitutes libel

2. Defamatory words in a newspaper or in a broadcast shall be deemed to be published and to constitute libel. R.S.O. 1970, c.243, s.2.

Note: Similar definitions of ''broadcasting'' appear in the Defamation Act of Manitoba (S.N. 1980, c.30, s.2(a) and Newfoundland's Defamation Act (S.N. 1983, c.63, s.2(a)). In the majority of the provinces, however, ''broadcasting'' is to be interpreted as follows:

> ''broadcasting means the dissemination of any form of radioelectric communication, including radiotelegraph, radiotelephone and the wireless transmission of writing, signs, signals, pictures and sounds of all kinds by means of Hertzian waves.

(Uniform Defamation Act, s.1(a). See also Defamation Act, R.S.P.E.I. 1974, c.D-3, s.1(a); Defamation Ordinance, R.O.N.W.T. 1974, c.D-1, s.2(a); Defamation Ordinance, R.O.Y.T. 1975, c.D-1, s.2(1); and Defamation Act, C.S.N.S. 1979, c.D-3, s.1(a) which adds the words ''intended to be received by the public either directly or through the medium of relay stations''.) Both Alberta's Defamation Act and British Columbia's Libel and Slander Act offer more specific definitions. Section 1(a) of the Alberta Act (R.S.A. 1980, C.D-6) reads:

> ''broadcasting'' means a transmission, emission or reception to the general public of signs, signals, writing, images, sounds or intelligence of any nature by means of electromagnetic waves of frequencies lower than 3000 gigahertz.

And s.1 of the British Columbia Act (as amended by S.B.C. 1985, c.10, s.9) states:

> ''broadcasting'' means the dissemination of writing, signs, signals, pictures, sounds of intelligence of any nature intended for direct reception by, or which is available on subscription, to the general public
>
> (a) by means of a device utilizing electromagnetic waves of frequencies lower than 3000 GHZ propogated in space without artificial guide, or
>
> (b) through a community antenna television system operated by a person licensed under the Broadcasting Act (Canada) to carry on a broadcasting receiving undertaking and ''broadcast'' has a corresponding meaning.

Newfoundland is the only province which shares Ontario's definition of ''newspaper'' (Defamation Act, S.N. 1983, c.63, s.2(a)). Most of the other provinces have adopted the wording of s.1(c) of the Uniform Defamation Act:

> 1(c) ''newspaper'' means a paper, (i) containing news, intelligence, occurrences, pictures or illustrations, or remarks or observations thereon,
>
> (ii) printed for sale, and

(iii) published periodically, or in parts or numbers, at intervals not exceeding thirty-one days between the publication of any two of such papers, parts or numbers.

(See Defamation Act, R.S.A. 1980, c.D-6, s.1(c); The Defamation Act, R.S.M. 1970, c.D-20, s.2(c); Defamation Act, R.S.N.B. 1973, c.D-5, s.1(c); Defamation Act, C.S.N.S. 1979, c.D-3, s.1(c); Defamation Act, R.S.P.E.I. 1974, c.D-3, s.1(c); Defamation Ordinance R.O.N.W.T. 1974, c.D-1, s.2(c); and Defamation Ordinance, R.O.Y.T. 1975, c.D-1, s.2(1))

''Newspaper'' under the British Columbia Libel and Slander Act, R.S.B.C. 1979, c.234, s.1, and the Saskatchewan Libel and Slander Act, R.S.S. 1978, c.L-14, s.2(a), includes a paper containing public news, intelligence or occurrences, or any remarks or observations in it printed for sale and published periodically, or in parts or numbers at intervals not exceeding thirty-one days between the publication of any two papers, parts or numbers; and also a paper printed in order to be dispersed and made public weekly or more often, or at intervals not exceeding thirty-one days, and containing only, or principally, advertisements.

And s.1 of Quebec's Press Act, R.S.O. 1977, c.P-19 provides:

> For the purposes of this act, the word ''newspaper'' means every newspaper or periodical writing the publication whereof for sale and distribution is made at successive and determined periods, appearing on a fixed day or by irregular issues, but more than once a month and whose object is to give news, opinions, comments or advertisements.

A provision similar to Ontario's s.1(2) is to be found only in Nova Scotia's Defamation Act (s.1(2)). And s.2 of the British Columbia Libel and Slander Act stands alone in resembling s.2 of the Ontario Libel and Slander Act. Almost all of the other provinces' Acts, along with the Uniform Defamation Act, state that,

> ''defamation'' means libel or slander (Uniform Defamation Act, s.1(b); Alberta Defamation Act, s.1(b); Manitoba Defamation Act, s.2(b); New Brunswick Defamation Act, s.1; Newfoundland Defamation Act, s.2(b); Nova Scotia Defamation Act, s.1(b); Prince Edward Island Defamation Act, s.1(b); Northwest Territories Defamation Ordinance, s.2(b); and Yukon Territory Defamation Ordinance, s.2(1)).

5.2.2.13 *Basse* v. *Toronto Star Newspapers Ltd. et al.* (1984) 37 C.P.C. 213, at 216-17 (Ont. H.C.)

MONTGOMERY J.:

The Facts

Sydney Brown made allegedly defamatory statements to the defendant newspapers about the plaintiff in his capacity as acting Chief of Police for the Waterloo Regional Police Force.

The Toronto Star published some of these allegedly defamatory statements. The words were then repeated by other communications media throughout the country which caused the plaintiff further injury.

The offending paragraphs follow:

14. ''The libel of the plaintiff was further aggravated by the fact that communications media throughout the country reported the words published by the defendants as aforesaid which reporting of such words repeated and perpetuated the libel complained of, causing further and irreparable harm and damage to the reputation of the plaintiff.

15. The plaintiff further complains that in publishing the words complained of the corporate defendants and their agents or employees knew or ought to have known that statements made to them by the defendant, Sydney Brown, were defamatory and libellous and, further, that such words would have been repeated by other communications media throughout the Dominion of Canada.''

The law

The objectionable paragraphs constitute a separate cause of action and a separate head of damages which, under these circumstances, may not be imputed to the original publisher of an alleged libel.

''Every republication of a libel is a new libel and each publisher is answerable for his act''. (Gatley on Libel and Slander (8th ed. 1981), paras. 261, 266).

Speight v. Gosnay (1891), 60 L.J.Q.B. 231 (C.A.), a case involving slander, laid down four situations in which he who uttered a slander might by held responsible for the subsequent repetition of the words. The third point is the only one relevant here — that is, where the repetition is the natural and probable consequence of the original publication.

In my view, the repetition of the words orignally published by the Toronto Star was not a natural and probable consequence of the initial publication. There is no liability upon the original publisher of the libel when the repetition is the voluntary act of a free agent, over whom the original publisher had no control and for whose acts he is not responsible: see Ward v. Weeks (1830), 7 Bing. 211 at 215, 131 E.R. 81, approved in Weld-Blundell v. Stephens, [1920] A.C. 956 at 999; Eyre v. New Zealand Press Assn. Ltd., [1968] N.Z.L.R. 736 at 744 (S.C.); Macy v. New York World-Telegram Corp. (1957), 161 N.Y.S. 2d 55 at 60 (C.A.).

The Master was also wrong in holding that the paragraphs under attack could be relevant to aggravation of damages. A jury should not take into account in assessing damages against the original publisher any damage done to the plaintiff by any defamatory matter for which the original publisher was not responsible: see Gatley on Libel and Slander (8th ed., 1981), para. 1451; Harrison v. Pearce (1858), 1 F. & F. 567 at 569, 175 E.R. 855 at 856; Assoc. Newspapers v. Dingle, [1964] A.C. 371 at 397-398, 410, 417 (H.L.).

The offending paragraphs are, therefore, struck out. Costs before the Master and of this appeal to the appellant in the cause.

Appeal allowed.

5.2.2.14 *Farrell* v. *St. John's Publishing Co.* (1986) 58 Nfld. & P.E.I.R. 66 (Nfld. C.A.)

MORGAN, J.A.: A plaintiff's cause of action in libel does not crystallize at the time the writ is served. The wrong has continuing effect and the defendant may, by subsequent conduct, further injure the plaintiff's reputation by 'rubbing salt in the wound'. The whole behaviour of the defendant toward the plaintiff is relevant to the issue of damages and his whole conduct ''before action, after action and in court during the trial'' may properly be considered. (See **Praed v. Graham** (1889), 24 Q.B.D. 53). Thus repeated publications of the same libel by the same defendant may be treated as aggravation of the original injury and be the basis of a higher award than would otherwise be given. They ought not to be treated, however, as giving rise to a separate and independent right to damages.

5.2.3 The Defendant's Case

5.2.3.1 Anne Skarsgard, "Freedom of the Press", pp. 302-03

a) Outline of the law:

Once the plaintiff proves the three elements of a libel action, he has a prima facie case. The defendant then has three possible defences: justification, privilege and fair comment. We shall now discuss these defences and their usefulness to the media by comparing the respective positions in England, the United States and Canada.

If the allegedly defamatory statement turns out to be true, that is, if the defence of "justification" is successful, there is no cause of action in the tort of defamation, as the law of defamation protects a person's reputation only insofar as he deserves it. Due to a presumption of falsity of all defamatory statements, the plaintiff does not have to prove the falsity of the words. Truth is treated, in England and Canada at least, as an affirmative defence that must be raised by the defendant and on which he has the burden of proof. In the United States the position is different. In *New York Times* v. *Sullivan* the court held that a plaintiff who is a public person must show knowledge or reckless disregard of the falsity of the statement, and in *Gertz* v. *Robert Welch, Inc.* it held that a plaintiff who is a private person must, for all practical purposes, show falsity as well. It is unclear whether this amounts to a formal shift in the United States from defendant having to prove the truth of the statement to plaintiff having to prove its falsity. In any event, this development in the law puts the media in the United States in a much better position than they enjoy in England or in Canada.

The defence of justification can be criticized on several grounds. First of all, it denies a remedy to a plaintiff who has suffered a very real loss, even if disclosure of the facts about him serves no useful purpose. For example, if a rehabilitated ex-convict has his criminal record maliciously broadcast, he has no action in defamation. To quote Paul Weiler:

> If society has no sufficient interest to render desirable the destruction of a person's reputation, truth should no longer legally justify a harmful statement, whether this is accomplished by internal reform of the law of defamation or the development of a right to privacy.

Although Saskatchewan is one of a handful of provinces that have privacy acts, privacy suits have been so far practically non-existent.

Another criticism of the defence of justification is that it seems to go against all the principles of justice. Someone who maliciously spreads rumours which he believes to be false with the intention of harming someone else does not have to compensate his victim for the loss of his reputation if the gossip turns out to be true. On the other hand, if a paper prints a story which it non-negligently and on reasonable grounds believes to be true and it turns out to be false, or if a true statement in the story is capable of an innuendo meaning in light of extrinsic facts not known to the writer, the paper is liable. Absurd laws such as this one do a great deal of harm by contributing to public mistrust of legal institutions.

b) The usefulness of justification to the press:

Justification is of little practical importance as it is not often pleaded by the press. The onus of proving the substantial truth of every statement claimed to be defamatory is a heavy one. This is especially so since the court determines what the truth is and the outcome of its determination is uncertain at best. Furthermore, should the plea of justification fail, it will seriously aggravate the damages.

Since justification is not a very useful defence, let us see whether the press can rely on the defences of qualified privilege and fair comment.

There is a fundamental difference between the defence of justification on one hand and the defences of qualified privilege and fair comment on the other. If a defendant relies on justification, he claims that he did not defame the plaintiff at all as defamation consists of the publication of a *false* statement. If he pleads qualified privilege or fair comment he concedes that he had made an untrue defamatory statement about the plaintiff, but he claims immunity from the duty of compensating the plaintiff for his loss because it was in society's interest that he should make the statement. These two defences have been devised to enable the court to strike a balance between the interest of the defamed individual in tort compensation and the interest of society in freedom of expression.

5.2.3.1.1 Justification

5.2.3.1.1.1 *Brannigan* v. *S.I.U.* (1964), 42 D.L.R. (2d) 249 (B.C.S.C.)

HUTCHESON, J.: I turn to the defence of justification, that is the allegation that the words complained of are true in substance and in fact.

The defendant called no evidence in support of that allegation but relied solely on inferences it submitted should be drawn from the plaintiff's activities and associations in the past as admitted by him. The facts and associations from which I am asked to draw the inference that the plaintiff is a Communist are, as I understand counsel's submissions, the following:

1. That one Thompson was formerly the vice-president of the C.S.U. and while the plaintiff was a member of that union.
2. That the C.S.U. was outlawed because it was Communist-dominated.
3. That Thompson formed the W.C.S.U. and became president thereof and that the plaintiff joined that union.

From these facts I am asked to infer that the plaintiff was a Communist. To reach that conclusion one would first have to infer from the fact that Thompson was vice-president of the C.S.U. that he was a Communist and that the plaintiff when he joined the W.C.S.U., was aware that he was. I am not prepared to draw that inference but, even if I were, it would not then follow from the fact that the plaintiff joined the W.C.S.U., which Thompson had formed and of which he became president, that the plaintiff was himself a Communist. A man may well be required by the nature and circumstances of his employment to join a certain union and the fact that he does so knowing that others in that union, even in executive positions, are Communists does not of itself brand him as a Communist.

4. That the W.C.S.U. merged with the S.I.U. and the plaintiff became a member of the latter union but was later expelled. It is not suggested that he was expelled because of any Communistic leanings on his part.
5. That the plaintiff was then active in the formation of the C.B.R.T., Local 400, and associated with him in forming that local were William Mozdir, Dave West and one Cox.

The plaintiff identified as William Mozdir the man shown in the picture published August 23, 1961, carrying the banner bearing the words "Communist Party of Canada" and who had been erroneously stated to be the plaintiff, and from this it is submitted that he, Mozdir, is a Communist and by reason of his association with Mozdir it should be inferred that the plaintiff is a Communist.

Even assuming that it can be inferred that Mozdir was a Communist, again it does not follow that the plaintiff knew that he was nor does it follow, even if he did know and associated with him in the formation of Local 400 of the C.B.R.T. following his expulsion from the S.I.U., that he, the plaintiff, shared the Communistic views of Mozdir and was himself a Communist.

The only evidence in respect to Dave West was that the plaintiff had heard other members of the union refer to him as a Communist and had never heard Dave West deny it. Such evidence would not justify the inference that West was a Communist or that the plaintiff associated with him knowing him to be a Communist, or shared any of his views in that respect. There was no evidence as to Cox other than that he was one of those who formed Local 400 of the C.B.R.T.

6. That following the formation of Local 400 of C.B.R.T. and the plaintiff becoming a member of that local, Thompson, who was an organizer of C.B.R.T. paid by National headquarters, joined that local and eventually became president thereof. Again even if it were assumed that Thompson was a Communist by reason of his earlier association with the C.S.U., the fact that a Communist joined a local and even became the president thereof does not of itself justify the inference that the members of that local, and particularly the plaintiff, knew he was a Communist or were themselves Communists.

7. That the plaintiff took part in the May Day parade in the City of Vancouver in the year 1960. The plaintiff admitted that he was asked by a friend to join in that parade and that he did so in a group that represented what was spoken of as "an unemployed union". The so-called "unemployed union" is not what is commonly thought of as a union but is a group supported by a number of unions and made up by members of those unions who are unemployed. The activities of this group are described by the plaintiff as follows: "We had parades and demanded jobs and keeping the boys together so they wouldn't cross picket lines... more or less a propaganda organization." This group of unemployed men in the parade each carried separate placards.

The alleged apology published by the defendant while ambiguous does bear an interpretation suggesting that the placard carried by the plaintiff supported the policies of the Communist party. The defendant called no evidence as to what the wording on that placard was and, as I have already pointed out, the wording on that particular placard is illegible in the printed picture. The plaintiff has sworn that while he cannot remember the exact wording it had nothing to do with Red or Communistic countries. He did not compose the placard but, as I mentioned above, his recollection is that it was to the effect, "Canada Needs More Ships" or "Canada Needs More Jobs".

The plaintiff admitted that he had marched in a May Day parade on one other occasion, namely in 1930, when he had marched in the May Day parade in Montreal. He also agreed with the suggestion by counsel for the defendant that the May Day parade in Vancouver was sponsored by the Communist Party of Canada and was of that general tenor. He said however, in effect, that his reason for marching in the parade was because he felt that it might result in some benefit to himself.

There were, according to the plaintiff's evidence, 1,000 or 1,500 men in the parade which extended for fifteen or sixteen city blocks. It was contended on behalf of the defendant that, assuming that the May Day parade is Communist-sponsored, it must be inferred that all persons, in this case all of the 1,000 or 1,500 taking part in that parade, are Communists. This contention I do not accept. It is clear from the photograph that the Communist Party of Canada had a contingent in that parade but there were also other contingents representing unions and other labour groups such as the ''unemployed union'' and I am not prepared to hold by reason of the fact that a person takes part in a May Day parade, which includes a contingent representing the Communist Party of Canada and even if that party has been instrumental in sponsoring the parade, that that person is a Communist.

The facts upon which the defendant relies, considered *seriatim* or together, do not lead me to the conclusion that the plaintiff is a Communist and I find that the defendant has failed to satisfy the onus that was upon it to uphold its plea of justification and to prove that the words complained of to the effect that the plaintiff was a Communist are true in substance and in fact.

The plaintiff swears that he is not a Communist and never has been and that he is not now and never was a member of the Communist Party of Canada nor had any connection with that party. That evidence stands unrebutted.

5.2.3.1.1.2 *Baxter* v. *CBC* (1974), 30 N.B.R. (2d) 102, at 113-118 (N.B.C.A.)

RYAN, J.A.: A report referred to as the Clarkson, Gordon Report commissioned by Premier Richard Hatfield disclosed certain irregularities within the operation of the New Brunswick Department of Tourism. In December, 1972, the report was turned over to Mr. Baxter as Minister of Justice for consideration. In January, 1973, Mr. Baxter instructed Chief Superintendent William Hurlow to investigate the irregularities to determine if there was any evidence of criminality involved. Sergeants K. E. Taylor and R. C. Wolsey were assigned to carry out the investigation. In the course of doing so, a number of persons were interviewed by the officers including one Mr. J. K. Matchett. He apparently was closely associated politically with the former Minister of Tourism, Mr. J. C. VanHorne, and was concerned with the construction of certain tourism facilities in the Province by one of Matchett's companies. According to an internal report dated September 27, 1973, written by Sgt. Taylor, Matchett explained generally about his financial contributions to the Progressive Conservative Party and percentages paid by him by way of ''kickbacks'' on profits made by his companies on contracts awarded to him. According to the report, Matchett told the officers that, if payments were not made further contracts would not be awarded, or at least it would be difficult to obtain future contracts.

On October 3, 1973, Mr. Horace B. Smith, a Cabinet Minister in the Progressive Conservative Government of Premier Hatfield complained to Mr. Baxter to the effect that the R.C.M.P. were investigating party bank accounts and questioning Mr. Larry Machum, one of the individuals who looked after financial matters for the party. Mr. Baxter told Mr. Smith he was not aware of such an investigation, but he would make inquiries, which he instituted by calling C/S William Hurlow the same day.

As a result of Mr. Baxter's call to C/S Hurlow, Hurlow contacted Superintendent J. G. Giroux and a meeting was arranged for the afternoon of the following day which was attended by Mr. Baxter, C/S Hurlow, S/ Giroux and the Deputy Minister of Justice Mr. Gordon Gregory. At the meeting, which was held at Mr. Baxter's office, Mr. Baxter initiated discussions by asserting that he had been told that members of the R.C.M.P. were investigating political contributions to the Progressive Conservative Party, checking party bank accounts and interviewing Mr. Machum which Mr. Baxter said was beyond the scope of the investigation he had instructed the police to make. S/ Giroux told Mr. Baxter that he had met with the investigating officers that morning and instructed them that they were not to investigate legitimate contributions to the Progressive Conservative Party. The substance of S/ Giroux's reply to Mr. Baxter is contained in a memo to file dictated October 9, 1973, which is reproduced in its entirety at pp. 132 and 133 of the Report. The introductory paragraph relates to the meeting and the subject matter discussed at it. Paragraph 2 relates to the concern of Mr. Baxter as related above. Paragraph 3 reads as follows:

> 3. I told the Minister, and the others, that I had reviewed the investigation that morning with the investigators, and I had already instructed the members that the matter of political contributions and the secret bank account that a Party could have had nothing to do with the investigation we are conducting, and we are not going to investigate that angle. Furthermore, I told the Minister that I didn't think we had interviewed Mr. Macklin (Mr. Machum) but we had obtained this information about political contributions and the number of the bank account in Moncton by accident and not by asking for it specifically. I added that from the information I had from the investigators, I could only conclude that political contributions made by individuals or Corporations to a political Party did not have any connection with our investigation and that the investigators had been instructed accordingly. The Minister was satisfied.

A final report of the investigation into the Department of Tourism dated November 28, 1973, was written by Sgt. Wolsey. It refers to the instructions given by S/ Giroux to Taylor and himself to the effect that no investigation was to be conducted into party contributions and that, under no circumstances, was the matter relating to the bank account in Moncton to be pursued.

Further letters were written by S/ Giroux confirming the fact that he had instructed Sgts. Taylor and Wolsey not to investigate legitimate contributions to the Progressive Conservative Party. (see pages 134 to 138 of the Report.)

The alleged defamatory words were spoken by Mr. Malling in a documentary telecast broadcast, as mentioned above, on April 20, 1977. The script is reproduced at pages 117 to 131 of the Report. I quote in part from it; the portion alleged to contain the defamation is underlined:

> Reporter: Higgins covery-up (sic) charge is a challenge to the basic integrity of Hatfield's government. It could not be allowed to stand so Hatfield set up a judicial inquiry which will investigate the charge later this month. The judge's findings could well force either Higgins or Hatfield out of politics. Higgins is holding his evidence for the inquiry but in our own investigation in New Brunswick, we acquired secret documents which do suggest political interference aimed at stopping an investigation of Conservative Party fund raising. In an internal police memo written *in September, 1973, an RCMP sergeant reported that a man under investigation for another matter makes many references to kickbacks to a Conservative Party fund. The police wanted to follow that lead, but then a week later they were stopped by the then Minister of Justice, John Baxter, and their own superiors.* In a note to file, J. B. Giroux, a senior RCMP officer in New Brunswick, describes a meeting with New Brunswick Justice Minister Baxter and his deputy on October 4th. 'The

> Minister said he is concerned about the scope and direction the investigation has taken, specifically, political contributions to the Conservative Party. He feels this has nothing to do with the investigations and we should not inquire into this field'. But the minister didn't have to worry. The senior policeman reported that he had already stifled the investigation. So, although the police had information suggesting that illegal kickbacks had or were being paid, they did not pursue the matter. In another memo, November 8th, 1973, the investigating officer reports accidentally finding what appeared to him to be suspicious payments apparently destined for the Conservative Party, but following his superior's instruction, they ignored them. 'On instruction Giroux, we made it clear that we were not interested in political contributions to the party. We were careful to avoid reference to, or show undue interest in this aspect'.

The trial judge after quoting excerpts from several judgments and textbooks on the law of libel and slander concluded that the words complained of were defamatory, and that the defence of fair comment was not available to the defendants in that, in his opinion, the impugned words were "not comments at all but incorrect statements of facts". I agree with these findings.

Although the trial judge canvassed and summarized the evidence in detail in his judgment as it relates to the defendant's plea of justification or truth, I will refer briefly to it.

The program, according to the testimony of Mr. Malling and Mr. Robin Taylor, a senior producer of the Fifth Estate, was based on a speech delivered in the Legislative Assembly by Mr. Robert J. Higgins, then Leader of the Opposition, on March 3, 1977, and on certain documents obtained by one Philip Mathias, referred to at times as "the secret documents". The documents referred to are Sgt. Taylor's internal report dated September 27, 1973, and S/ Giroux's memo to file dated October 9, 1973 (supra).

In his speech Mr. Higgins referred to a meeting held in 1972 attended by the Premier, Mr. Richard Hatfield, some senior cabinet ministers and members of the committee of the Progressive Conservative Party at which the system used to collect money for the party was discussed. The speech is reproduced in its entirety at pages 139-142 of the Report. I quote in part from it:

> The RCMP in this province became aware of these activities. Mr. Speaker, I am informed and I believe that as early as 1973 the Department of Justice of this province of New Brunswick attempted to thwart investigation into the financing of the Progressive Conservative Party. I am informed that a meeting took place in October 1973 between the Department of Justice and senior officials of the Royal Canadian Mounted Police. As a result of this meeting, the investigating officers were instructed by their superior not to pursue investigation into Progressive Conservative Party financing.

It is to be noted that Mr. Higgins did not say that the investigation into "kickbacks" had been stopped by Mr. Baxter as stated by Mr. Malling, but he did say that the investigating officers had been instructed not to pursue the investigation into Progressive Conservative party financing. No doubt Mr. Higgins had in his possession, or at least had read S/ Giroux's memo to file when he spoke of Mr. Baxter's instructions to S/ Giroux and C/S Hurlow at the meeting of October 4, 1973. S/ Giroux in his testimony said he explained to Sgts. Taylor and Wolsey that they were not to investigate legitimate party contributions, but they could investigate "kickbacks" to the party if criminality was suspected. In addition, as mentioned by the trial judge, neither Sgts. Taylor nor Wolsey were called to verify their written reports.

Mr. Matchett called as a witness by counsel for the defendants testified that any monies he had given to the party had been given voluntarily, and not by way of "kickbacks" as reported by Sgt. Taylor.

S/ Giroux in his testimony categorically denied that Mr. Baxter interfered with the investigation into the Department of Tourism and that it was the investigation into "Political contributions" and not "kickbacks" that Mr. Baxter wanted restricted.

In my opinion, the trial judge's findings, and I refer particularly to his finding "that the originator of the instruction to restrict the investigation into the Department of Tourism and the activities of Mr. VanHorne, its dismissed Minister, was S/ Giroux and not Mr. Baxter and that it was the investigation into *political contributions,* not *kickbacks* which was to be restricted", are supported by the evidence as the trial judge's finding that the defendants failed to establish their defence of justification or truth.

5.2.3.1.1.3 *Munro* v. *Toronto Sun* (1982), 21 C.C.L.T. 261, at 292 (Ont. H.C.)

HOLLAND J.:

(a) The great power and influence possessed by the media is an important factor in moulding public opinion and its exercise requires great care to be taken as otherwise great harm can result.
(b) There *must* be a separation of functions between the reporter and the editor, it being the responsibility of the editor to confirm the accuracy of the contents of a story before publication.
(c) Where important documentation has been obtained it is good practice to put it in a safe place and to thereafter work from a copy.
(d) There must be constant supervision maintained by the editor over the reporter, with a regular reporting requirement.
(e) It is the editor's responsibility to know in detail before publication, the documentation to support the story and the reliability of the sources and so ensure its accuracy.
(f) When the story is prepared — and the paper has the "goods" on the person targetted in the story — it is basic and necessary that that person be confronted with the story so that his reaction be obtained. This could cause the story to be discarded *and* could also enable the newspaper to add those comments should publication take place. A sound reason (there are others) for this to be established practice, is that it prevents the newspaper from publishing an incorrect story with all the attendant problems which that would generate.

Much of this was non-contentious. Only Worthington, as I recall, commented that the process, while technically correct, was practically not feasible. His view that a newspaper must place trust in its reporter or else no story would ever be published does not impress me as conforming to sound journalistic practice and I do not agree with it. There must be a marked difference in the function and responsibilities of the reporter and investigative reporter and those of senior management of a newspaper prior to publication of any article or news story. Newspapers or other forms of news communication media which do not clearly recognize and follow the careful course above, designed to ensure the taking of all reasonable safeguards to establish the accuracy of news story content and sources, act at their peril should these be found to be absent.

Freedom of the press has long been recognized in democratic society as a vital necessary. Given that freedom, in my opinion the work of the *investigative* reporter must meet the test of *absolute reliability,* and those who may be responsible for that reporter's efforts *must* take steps to ensure that this is accomplished. This was not done here.

5.2.3.1.1.4 *Gordon* v. *Caswell* (1984), 33 Sask. R. 202 (Q.B.)

On January 7, 1982, the defendant wrote a letter to Saskatoon City Council in which she sought to influence Council's decision against funding the Family Service Bureau, which was then intending to bring to Saskatoon the plaintiff for the purpose of delivering a public lecture. The plaintiff is a tenured professor attached to the Department of Child and Family Studies of the College of Human Development at Syracuse University in the State of New York. I accept his statement that he accepts invitations to deliver lectures and does indeed lecture in many parts of the United States of America, in Canada, and in other countries of the Free World.

The plaintiff particularizes his complaint by alleging that the following words of the plaintiff's letter are untrue and therefore defamatory of him, and I quote: "Sol Gordon is opposed because he condones any type of sexual expression, condones wholesale contraceptive and abortion availability, and opposes parental responsibility and Judeo-Christian morality." Gordon categorically denies what is imputed to him by the defendant's words.

Also complained of were certain excerpts attached to the defendant's letter. Concerning these, I want to note at this point that it is agreed by counsel that the excerpts are photocopies of a pro-life newspaper and not quotations from the writings of the plaintiff.

The defence has assembled in evidence certain of the plaintiff's writings and emphasizes particularly the comics on sex and the film shown here, and argues that these are publications which bear out what the defendant says of the plaintiff in her letter to Council. I have examined that literature. The issue, I repeat, is not the rightness or the wrongness of what the plaintiff expresses in that literature. Rather, the nub of the matter is whether the defendant has portrayed his views incorrectly to City Council.

May I restate the issue by putting it this way, — would that right thinking member of society, having read the literature in evidence, and viewed the film, — would that person misrepresent the plaintiff's view on responsible sexual education, if he or she said of it what the defendant said. I recall the film; it does not speak of marriage or sexual intercourse in marriage. It addresses itself, as I conclude from the action portrayed, to young people, to teenagers, and presumably highschool boys and girls. I believe it assumes that they are sexually active, and that they are not married. Birth control devices and their purpose and use are discussed. The film does not advocate intercourse, nor does it advocate the use of birth control, but neither does it issue any condemnation or prohibition in respect of either intercourse or birth control. I could add, the same is true of masturbation. It is silent on any moral view. The question which arises in my view is this, can that right thinking person, as I defined that person earlier, impute to it a moral message? What kind or which message is not significant or relevant to what I must decide in this case? It is not significant here to determine whether there is a right message or a wrong message, the point is whether a right thinking person could legitimately, — with common sense, I suggest, extract from the film or the literature, the sex comics, the same message which the plaintiff did, and express it in the language she used when writing to City Council. On that question, I conclude affirmatively that she could.

I return to a further consideration of the defendant's statement to City Council and I quote: "Sol Gordon is opposed because he condones any type of sexual expression, condones wholesale contraceptive and abortion availability, and opposes parental responsibility and Judeo-Christian morality." I have already said that a right minded person reading the plaintiff's sex comics, and viewing the film which he endorses, could have come to the same conclusion as did the defendant. But I say this with one qualification. The literature I have examined does not, I believe, admit the conclusion that the plaintiff approves any or all forms of sexual expression. In so concluding, I do not disregard the defence argument based upon the comic strip about the cowboy and the horse. I base my opinion rather upon the general thrust of the literature, and the film, and conclude that the defendant's expression approaches the extreme.

Nevertheless, the fact is that the defendant was addressing a public body on a highly controversial matter, and in truth she could have used less extreme language. But there is case law cited in the defendant's brief upon which I found my conclusion that the terminology used does not destroy the general thrust of the message which she, as a right minded citizen of Saskatoon, had a right to extrapolate from what she saw and read from the plaintiff's work.

Because I have concluded that the burden imposed by the rule pertaining to the law of justification has been met by the defendant, I will not discuss the defence of qualified privilege which she has raised. Nor do I believe that malice is in issue. To the contrary, I am satisfied to say, after hearing her testimony, that the defendant was motivated by a sincerity to serve her fellow citizens by defending a tradition which she holds, and which she expressed in her evidence, that sexual conduct should be portrayed in a framework, a tradition which defends chastity before marriage, and fidelity after.

As I said when I began, a democratic society will be maintained if freedom of speech on matters touching the well being of society is guaranteed. In the ongoing debate, defamation is of course excluded. Here, the plaintiff chose a particular vehicle of communication, and in doing so exposed himself to the risk of the interpretation placed upon his work by the defendant.

In the result, he has not proved that he was defamed. The plaintiff's action is for the foregoing reasons dismissed, with costs.

Action dismissed.

5.2.3.1.1.5 Ontario Libel and Slander Act, R.S.O. 1980, c.237, s.23

23. In an action for libel or slander for words containing two or more distinct charges against the plaintiff, a defence of justification shall not fail by reason only that the truth of every charge is not proved if the words not proved to be true do not materially injure the plaintiff's reputation having regard to the truth of the remaining charges. R.S.O. 1970, c.243, s.23.

5.2.3.1.1.6 A Note on the Law in Nova Scotia

The only other province with such a provision is Nova Scotia (see Defamation Act, C.S.N.S. 1979, c.D-3, s.8)

5.2.3.1.2 Fair Comment

5.2.3.1.2.1 Alexander Stark, *Dangerous Words* (Toronto, Ryerson Institute of Technology 1985, p. 15

IN THIS FIELD of fair comment, the music critic, the literary reviewer, the editorial writer, and the newspaper columnist have gone at times to amazing lengths and still enjoyed the protection which the law gives. Take, for example, such a case as that of the Cherry sisters, brought against the Des Moines *Leader* in the State of Iowa in 1901. At one time the Cherry sisters had been the toast of the vaudeville stage. But the years had crept up on them and the toast had become cold and uninteresting. Unwisely they planned a comeback, and the dramatic critic of the Des Moines paper had this to say about their appearance; "Effie is an old jade of fifty summers, Jess is a frisky filly of forty, and Addie, the flower of the family, a capering monstrosity of thirty-five. Their long skinny arms equipped with talons at the extremities, swung mechanically, and anon waved frantically at the suffering audience. The mouths of their rancid features opened like caverns and sounds like the wailing of damned souls issued therefrom. They pranced around the stage with a motion that suggested a cross between the *danse du ventre* and a fox trot — strange creatures with painted faces and hideous mien. Effie is spavined, Addie has stringhalt and Jessie, the only one who showed her stockings, has legs with calves as classic in their outline as the curves of a broom handle." But the court held that the statement was not libellous and said, "One who goes upon the stage to exhibit himself to the public, or who gives any kind of performance to which the public is invited, may be freely criticized." And it added further, "Surely, if one makes himself ridiculous in his public performances, he may be ridiculed by those whose duty or right it is to inform the public regarding the character of the performance."

5.2.3.1.2.2 *Pearlman* v. *CBC* (1982), Man. L.R. (2d) 1, at 21 (Man. Q.B.)

MORSE J.: It is stated in the text on *Defamation* by Duncan and Neill (1978), at p. 68, para. 12.14:

> The general rule is that, in order to qualify as fair comment, an expression of opinion must satisfy the following objective test: could any man honestly express that opinion on the proved facts?...

In my view, the defendants have met this objective test. I think the defendants could honestly describe a landlord such as the plaintiff, who acted as he did with respect to his properties and his tenants, as a person who had "no morals, principles, or conscience". These are, of course, strong words. But the defendants were entitled to express themselves strongly provided they honestly believed in the opinion which they expressed. I have no doubt that they did honestly believe in what they said.

5.2.3.1.2.3 Anne Skarsgard, "Freedom of the Press", pp. 307-316

a) Outline of the law:

The rationale of the defence of fair comment is to protect the defendant's right of freedom of speech and the public's right to find out what is happening in matters of legitimate public interest. A successful plea of the defence means that even if the plaintiff proves all the ingredients of a prima facie case of defamation, the defendant will not have to compensate him.

To succeed in this defence, the defendant must prove
1) that the comment was on a matter of public interest;
2) that the comment was fair;
3) that the words complained of were comment and not statement of fact. The defence is defeated if plaintiff can show express malice.

1) The defendant has to prove that the matter was of public interest. The best definition as to what constitutes a matter of public interest is found in Lord Denning's judgement in *London Artists* v. *Littler:*

> Whenever a matter is such as to affect people at large, so that they may be legitimately interested in, or concerned at, what is going on, or what may happen to them or others; then it is a matter of public interest on which everyone is entitled to make fair comment.

Thus the scope of matters of public interest is very wide. However, public interest must be legitimate. Gossip-mongering and gratuitous attacks on character are not protected by the defence, although it is often hard to draw the line between aspects of a public official's character which are strictly his own business and those which affect his fitness for office.

2) The comment must be fair. The word ''fair'' is misleading because it suggests that the comment must be reasonable. Actually the limits of fair comment are very wide and include comments which to many people would appear both unfair and unreasonable. For this reason the Faulks Committee in Britain recommended that the word ''fair'' be dropped and the defence renamed ''comment''.

Comment, to be ''fair'' in the technical sense of this defence, must be based on true facts. However, where the facts are protected by an occasion of qualified privilege, the defendant does not have to prove their truth.

Another component of the requirement of fairness is a source of some confusion, and was the main issue in the *Cherneskey* case. Many courts and commentators have stated that comment, to be fair, had to represent an honestly held opinion, that is, it must satisfy the subjective test: ''Did the defendant honestly believe the comment?'' Duncan and Neill, on the other hand, propose an objective test: ''Could any man honestly express that opinion on the proved facts?'' Whichever test is used, the honestly held opinion need not be reasonable. In the words of Lord Esher in *Merivale* v. *Carson:*

> Every latitude must be given to opinion and to prejudice... Mere exaggeration, or even gross exaggeration, would not make the comment unfair. However wrong the opinion expressed may be in point of truth, or however prejudiced the writer, it may still be within the prescribed limits... When you come to a question of fair comment you ought to be extremely liberal...

Similarly, Diplock J. said in *Silkin* v. *Beaverbrook Newspapers Ltd.*,

> So in considering this case, members of the jury, do not apply the test of whether you agree with it. If juries did that, freedom of speech, the right of the crank to say what he likes, would go. Would a fair-minded man holding strong views, obstinate views, prejudiced views, have been capable of making this comment? If the answer to that is yes, then your verdict in this case should be a verdict for the defendants.

3) Finally, the words complained of must be comment, not statement of fact. The facts on which the statement is based should be either set out clearly or indicated by

the commentator with sufficient clarity so that his audience is aware of the facts that form the basis of the comment. (However, setting out the facts on which the opinion is based is not an absolute requirement as long as the subject matter commented on is in the common knowledge of both the commentator and his audience.) This is how Lord Porter explained the principle in *Kemsley* v. *Foot:*

> If the defendant accurately states what some public man has really done, and then asserts that 'such conduct is disgraceful' this is merely an expression of his opinion, his comment on the plaintiff's conduct. So, if without setting it out, he identifies the conduct on which he comments by clear reference. In either case, the defendant enables his readers to judge for themselves how far his opinion is well founded; and therefore, what would otherwise be an allegation of fact becomes merely comment. But if he asserts that the plaintiff has been guilty of disgraceful conduct, and does not state what that conduct was, this is an allegation of fact for which there is no defence but privilege or truth.

Furthermore, the comment must be separated from statements of fact to be recognized as comment. Wrote Fletcher Moulton L.J. in *Hunt* v. *Star Newspaper Co. Ltd.,*

> Comment in order to be justifiable as fair comment must appear as comment and must not be so mixed up with facts that the reader cannot distinguish between what is report and what is comment.

Although the comment can include inferences of fact, it must be recognized as comment. It if often extremely difficult, if not impossible, to distinguish between assertions of fact and statements which represent inferences drawn by the commentator. However, the distinction is a crucial one, as the defence of fair comment is available to protect an untrue defamatory inference, but not to protect a statement of fact, even though proved true, unless the defence of justification is also pleaded.

This point was elucidated by Field J. in *O'Brien* v. *Marquis of Salisbury:*

> It seems to me... that comment may sometimes consist in the statement of a fact, and may be held to be comment if the fact so stated appears to be a deduction or conclusion come to by the speaker from the facts stated or referred to by him, or in the common knowledge of the person speaking and those to whom the words are addressed and from which his conclusions may reasonably be inferred.

It should be pointed out that the above excerpts have all been culled from English decisions. The last one, saying that even a statement of fact may be held to be comment under certain circumstances, is an especially good example of the latitude English courts have traditionally given to the defence.

Since the distinction between fact and comment is often murky at best, the same principles of interpretation can lead one to diametrically opposed results. In Britain, because of this liberal interpretation given to the defence of fair comment by the courts, it has been a useful tool for safeguarding freedom of expression in the press. In the United States the defence has become unnecessary since both untrue statements of fact and of comment are protected by the extremely wide scope afforded to qualified privilege under the *New York Times* rule. In Canada, however, a number of recent decisions seem to have eroded the defence of fair comment to the point where one wonders whether it still serves a useful purpose.

b) The usefulness of fair comment to the press:

The best-known recent case on the defence of fair comment is *Cherneskey* v. *Armadale Publishers Ltd.,* the case of the Saskatoon alderman and lawyer who sued the Saskatoon Star-Phoenix for libel. The paper published a defamatory letter accusing Alderman Cherneskey of racism because of the stand he took at a City Council meeting (accurately reported in the paper) concerning the continuing existence of a native alcoholic rehabilitation centre in a residential neighbourhood. The letter writers were out of the jurisdiction and were not called as witnesses, consequently there was no evidence before the court whether they honestly believed what they had written. The newspaper management gave evidence that no one at the paper believed the alleged libel against the plaintiff.

The newspaper pleaded the defence of fair comment. The trial judge refused to put the defence before the jury, saying that a comment to be fair had to be an honestly held opinion, and there was no evidence that anybody held the opinion expressed in the letter. The decision was overturned by the Saskatchewan Court of Appeal. The two majority judges held that the requirement of honestly held opinion was satisfied in the case of a newspaper publishing the opinion of others, if the management honestly believed that the letter expressed the honestly held opinion of the writer. The plaintiff appealed to the Supreme Court of Canada which allowed the appeal and restored the trial decision, with Dickson, Spence and Estey JJ. dissenting.

The Supreme Court did not decide whether the defence would have been available had the writers believed the statement and the newspaper did not, or had the newspaper believed it, but there was no evidence whether the writers did. (In *Lyon and Lyon* v. *Daily Telegraph Ltd.* the defence of fair comment succeeded in connection with a letter to the editor where there was no evidence as to the writer's state of mind, but dicta suggested that the newspaper agreed with the opinion expressed.)

According to the majority in the Supreme Court if the belief is not shown to be honestly held, the comment cannot be fair. Honesty of belief is an essential ingredient of the defence and one that the defendant has to prove.

Dickson J. in his powerful dissent relied on Duncan and Neill's formulation of the defence, according to which the defendant has to establish that the statement is comment, that it is based on substantially true facts on a matter of public interest, and that the comment is *objectively* fair, that is, it satisfies the following objective test: ''Could any man honestly express that opinion on the proved facts?'' According to this view the defendant's subjective state of mind is only relevant as evidence of express malice which, if proven, would defeat the defence. The onus of proving express malice is on the plaintiff.

This interpretation of the law is also supported by Lord Denning in *Adams* v. *Sunday Pictorial Newspapers (1920) Ltd.*:

> The truth is that the burden on the defendant who pleads fair comment is already heavy enough. If he proves that the facts are true and that the comments, objectively considered, were fair, that is, if they were fair when considered without regard to the state of mind of the writer, I should not have thought that the plaintiff had much to complain about; nevertheless it has been held that the plaintiff can still succeed if he can prove that the comments, subjectively considered, were unfair because the writer was actuated by malice.

Dickson J.'s argument in favour of an objective test in the first stage of this inquiry is very persuasive. Why have the second test of express malice if the first stage already includes the ingredients of the subjective test? Where the defendant is the writer himself, the two stages can be telescoped into one, but if he is not, this short-cut becomes unworkable.

The majority decision is an excellent example of conceptualism. It was arrived at through the mechanical application of a formula that obviously does not fit the facts of the case. The result is an absurdity that runs counter the rationale behind the defence. The purpose of the defence of fair comment is to encourage freedom of expression. As Mr. Justice Dickson eloquently pointed out, if we make the defence available to newspapers only if they print opinions with which they agree, they would be engaged in a sort of self-censorship antithetical to a free press.

The decision was wrong for yet another reason. It singled out the publisher of the statement for harsher treatment than the commentator himself. Had the two letter writers been made defendants they could have relied on the defence, while the paper was held liable.

The press was not slow in reacting to the decision handed down on November 21, 1978. Within two days a commentary by Joan Cohen appeared in the Ottawa Citizen, followed by another commentary on November 28 by Maurice Western, which was reprinted in other newspapers. The commentary explored the decision with all its implications for the press and for freedom of speech. On January 20, 1979 yet another article appeared, this time in the Financial Post, by William Monopoli. Said Mr. Monopoli:

> Most Canadians probably believe that they have freedom of speech and that such freedom is a fundamental right in a democratic society.
>
> But a recent decision of the Supreme Court of Canada suggests that the right may be severely limited...
>
> *Unless the effects of the judgement are changed by legislative action,* or unless the court modifies its opinion in another case — neither of which is a reasonable near-term possibility — the decision may well intimidate publishers and editors and deter them from printing any letter dealing with a controversial subject, lest they be sued for libel. (emphasis added)

Monopoli underestimated the clout of the media. Less than a month later, on February 12, an editorial in the Toronto Globe and Mail called on the attorney-general of each province to revise its libel and slander statutes to nullify the ruling. In early April the Canadian Press reported that Ontario Attorney-General Roy McMurtry said in an interview that the Uniform Law Conference which was to meet in August in Saskatoon should study the *Cherneskey* decision. Mr. McMurtry was further reported to favour an amendment to the Ontario *Libel and Slander Act.* By early June another Canadian Press story reported that Ontario would introduce the new legislation in the fall. Said Mr. McMurtry:

> As attorney-general I have a constitutional role as guardian of the community's civil liberties and in relation to this matter I have no doubt that to violate the right to communicate is to eviscerate democracy.

The following day a story in the Saskatoon Star-Phoenix indicated that Saskatchewan Attorney-General Roy Romanow also favoured an amendment to Saskatchewan's *Libel and Slander Act* to restore the law to what it was prior to the *Cherneskey* decision.

In August 1979 the Uniform Law Commissioners amended the uniform statute to deal with the problem, and urged the provinces to adopt it. According to the amended *Uniform Defamation Act* the publisher of an opinion may rely on the defence of fair comment if a person could objectively hold the opinion. Alberta has already amended its *Libel and Slander Act* along these lines. The Saskatchewan Government introduced a similar bill in the legislature, but it was tabled at the end of the last session.

Thus, our laws can change surprisingly quickly when a powerful and influential lobby like the Canadian Daily Newspaper Publishers Association is affected. One must remember, however, that the amendment, if passed, will provide relief in only a small area of the law of defamation. The defence of fair comment will be available to the press when publishing opinions with which they do not agree, as long as the opinion is objectively fair. The amendment will not alter their position when they publish their own opinions. Furthermore, if courts continue to characterize comments as statements of fact, or as comment based on implied false facts, or if they use the wrong test to determine whether the comment is fair, the press will have a long, hard road ahead.

Let us look at some recent decisions and at the way the courts handled the defence of fair comment.

In the 1978 case of *Baltrop* v. *Canadian Broadcasting Corporation* a Nova Scotia trial court dismissed a libel charge against the CBC laid by a Dr. Donald Baltrop, who was a paid consultant to Canadian Metals Co. in Toronto. Dr. Baltrop was interviewed in a program called "Dying of Lead" on *As It Happens,* then his statements were discredited by another interviewee, an American doctor who said:

> I regret to say that my personal experience, and the experience of many of my colleagues in the States, with so-called experts on behalf of industry, has been very unfortunate. I've come to the belated conclusion that it is possible to buy the data you want. I've tested this particular viewpoint with relation to a very wide range of consumer and occupational problems in which I have been involved and I would be happy to substantiate for you the thesis that it is possible to buy any information you want, to substantiate any viewpoint. Dr. Baltrop is a paid consultant to the lead industry. He is paid to say what he has just said.

Everybody would agree that the second-last sentence is a statement of fact. The crux is the characterization of the last sentence. Taken by itself, it could be taken as a statement of fact. However, when considered in context, it becomes clearly an inference drawn by the American doctor from his opinion that "it is possible to buy any information you want", and from the true fact that Dr. Baltrop was a paid consultant, and is therefore comment. This was the position taken by the trial judge. However, the Nova Scotia Supreme Court did not agree. In its view the defence of fair comment could not be raised as the statement was not comment at all but an implied factual assertion that Dr. Baltrop was dishonest. The CBC could have won under this characterization only by the defence of justification by proving that Dr. Baltrop was indeed dishonest in saying what he said.

In *Vander Zalm* v. *Times Publishers* the British Columbia Minister of Human Resources sued for libel the publishers and editors of the Victoria Times as well as the free-lance cartoonist who depicted him pulling the wings off flies. On the Minister's lapel were inscribed the words: Human Resources. Said the trial judge:

> Literally, upon its face, the cartoon depicts the plaintiff as a person with a love of cruelty who enjoys causing suffering to defenceless creatures. That was a false misrepresentation of the character of the plaintiff as a person or in his role as Minister.

The paper pleaded the defence of fair comment, but failed. Munroe J. agreed with counsel for the plaintiff that the cartoon conveyed a statement of fact rather than a comment as no grounds for the opinion were set out. (Quaere whether it would have made a difference if the cartoon had been accompanied by a caption). However, the court did not find it necessary to decide whether the cartoon conveyed a statement of fact or of comment as, in its view, the defence failed on other grounds.

With respect, a political cartoon is, by definition, comment. The facts on which the comment is based need not be set out by the commentator as long as these facts are familiar to his audience. Said Field J. in *O'Brien* v. *Salisbury:*

> If a statement in words of a fact stands by itself naked, without reference, either expressed or understood, to other antecedent or surrounding circumstances notorious to the speaker and to those to whom the words were addressed, there would be little, if any, room for the inference that it was understood otherwise as a bare statement of fact, and then if untrue, there would be no answer to the action.

It follows that, if the statement is understood with reference to antecedent or surrounding circumstances familiar to the speaker and to his audience, then it qualifies as comment.

The ratio of Munroe J.'s decision was that, even assuming that there was comment, it was based on untrue facts and therefore it was not fair. What are these untrue facts? We are not told. The court merely says that, although the Minister's statements and decisions were controversial, they "could not fairly lead an ordinary person to conclude that the plaintiff acted in a cruel, sadistic or thoughtless manner when performing his duties." It seems that the court equates "untrue facts" with "unfair comment". And why is the comment unfair? Because the ordinary person (i.e. the judge) would not draw this conclusion from the Minister's record.

As we have already seen, under the general test of fair comment, "fair" is not equated with "reasonable". As long as a person might honestly hold a view on the facts, the comment is fair, however obstinate or exaggerated it may be. In the words of Lord Esher in *Merivale* v. *Carson,* "However wrong the opinion expressed may be in point of truth, or however prejudiced the writer, it may still be within the prescribed limits."

Could it be that Mr. Justice Munroe thought that the comment imputed dishonourable conduct or base motives to the plaintiff? Under those circumstances the test as to fairness is uncertain. There are three possibilities:

1) The defence of fair comment is not applicable and the only way to defend such a comment is to show that it is the only possible inference from the primary facts, that is, by a defence of justification;

2) The defence of fair comment is applicable but the defendant must satisfy the judge or jury that the comment was a reasonable inference from the facts commented on;

3) The general test of fair comment applies. According to Duncan and Neill this is the better view, as "a test based on reasonableness runs counter to the whole concept of the defence of fair comment. Furthermore, it is difficult in practice to draw an accurate dividing-line between cases which involve an imputation of dishonourable conduct and those which do not."

In *Vander Zalm* the trial judge seems to have applied the intermediate test of reasonableness to determine whether the comment was fair. However, if this was his intention, he should have pointed out that he was applying the special test because, in his view, there was imputation of dishonourable conduct.

It is unlikely, however, that Munroe J. intended to apply the special test as he had applied this same "reasonableness" test in an earlier decision and, as we shall see shortly, there could have been no imputation of dishonourable conduct in *Holt* v. *Sun Publishing Co*. Furthermore, when *Vander Zalm* was appealed, the appeal was allowed, all five judges agreeing that Munroe J. had erred by applying the wrong test.

There was no agreement in the British Columbia Court of Appeal on whether the cartoon was, in fact, defamatory. Aikins J.A. held that it was not, thereby overruling Munroe J. on a question of fact. Hinkson J.A. agreed with the trial judge that the cartoon was defamatory. Craig J. did not think that the cartoon was defamatory, but was not prepared to say that the trial judge was clearly wrong, while Nemetz and Seaton JJ.A. were not sure whether the cartoon was defamatory or not. All five agreed, however, that the defendants were not liable in any event because the defence of fair comment was available to them.

Nemetz J.A. held, with Aikins and Hinkson JJ.A. concurring, that Munroe J. erred in applying the test of reasonableness to decide whether the comment was fair. In other words, the question should not have been whether the facts pleaded would fairly lead to the conclusion that the plaintiff was cruel, but whether the comment represented the honest opinion of the commentator.

Craig J.A. held that Munroe J. erred in saying that the comment was based on untrue facts. The ''fact'' forming the basis of the comment was not, as implied by Munroe J., that the minister was depicted as cruel. The facts were set out in the particulars by the defendants, and consisted of sixteen highly controversial public statements or acts of the minister, all but one of which were conceded by him to be true. Craig J.A. agreed with Nemetz and Hinkson JJ.A. that the true test of fairness was whether the defendant honestly held the view expressed, thereby following the subjective test that carried the day in the *Cherneskey* decision. Justice was done under the particular circumstances of this case, because the cartoonist was available to give evidence and because the editors happened to agree with the opinion expressed in the cartoon. Either one of these circumstances would probably have been sufficient to satisfy the subjective test requiring that the opinion be honestly held. The fact remains that *Cherneskey* being the law in every province except Alberta, the press is not protected when publishing opinions which are fair, but with which they do not agree, unless the commentator is available to testify about his state of mind.

But let us go back to *Holt* v. *Sun Publishing* to see what treatment Mr. Justice Munroe gave to the defence of fair comment in that case. M.P. Simma Holt sued the Vancouver Sun for printing an editorial criticizing her for interviewing Charles Manson groupie Lynette ''Squeaky'' Fromme and planning to ask permission to carry a message from her to Charles Manson. Holt was touring California prisons as a member of the Commons committee on prisons. The editorial stated:

> But interviewing or carrying messages for such as mass murderer Charles Manson and his groupies in U.S. jails is not what Mrs. Holt and Mr. Reynolds are paid to be doing as members of the Commons committee on prisons. What they are supposed to be doing is concentrating on finding ways of improving Canada's chaotic prison system. As someone who knows prisoners and prison conditions, Mrs. Holt is eminently qualified to offer solutions if she can keep her mind on the task at hand...

Holt sued and the paper unsuccessfully pleaded fair comment. Munroe J. said in his decision:

> The defence of fair comment depends upon the comment having been made upon true facts. Were the words used true in substance and in fact? I think not. Upon the evidence I find that there is no basis upon which it can reasonably be said that interviewing Fromme or any prison inmate was beyond the scope of what the plaintiff was being paid to do as a member of the subcommittee on prisons, nor is there any basis for saying that she failed or neglected in her

duty to concentrate on finding ways to improve Canada's prison system, or that she interviewed Charles Manson or carried messages for him and his groupies in U.S. jails, or that she failed to keep her mind on the task at hand.

Just as he did in *Vander Zalm,* Munroe J. does not say explicitly which are the untrue facts forming the basis of the comment. He does not say whether the enumerated statements fall into the category of untrue fact or comment based on untrue fact. In *Vander Zalm* the court found it unnecessary to determine the threshold question of whether the cartoon was statement of fact or comment; in *Holt* it did not bother to separate fact from comment. In both instances it applied the same test of "reasonableness" to what one assumes it considered comment. In essence, the judge dismissed the defence because he disagreed with what was said, something Diplock J. cautioned the jury against in *Silkin* v. *Beaverbrook Newspapers Ltd.*

Mr. Justice Munroe heard yet another defamation case in 1978. In *Masters* v. *Fox* a newspaper imputed corrupt or dishonest motives to candidates running for municipal office. It should come as no surprise that the defence of fair comment failed here too. The court held that the imputation was not one that a fair-minded person could reasonably draw from the facts. In this case it was appropriate to choose the test of reasonableness, as there was an imputation of dishonourable conduct or base motives but again, the determination of whether the comment was reasonable should have been left to the jury.

All these decisions in favour of defamed plaintiffs reflect the low priority accorded to freedom of speech in our society. This could be due partly to a certain paternalism, a mistrust of the irrational, cranky element which is the hallmark of an immature society. Contrast this with the England of Pope and Swift where biting, even violent satire was not only tolerated but enjoyed because society was basically assured, stable and content. The decisions also reflect the low esteem in which our society holds the media. There is a general feeling today, a feeling no doubt shared by the judiciary, that the "paperazzi", although not elected and often not even very knowledgeable, wield enormous and unwarranted power and need to be curbed. Journalists, so the theory goes, look for scandal to sell copy, they snoop and are, in the words of a columnist, "anti-capitalist left-wing bleeding hearts who... wouldn't know privacy from a privet hedge." Although there may be some truth in these contentions and the press is not always as responsible as one would expect, surely the answer is not to muzzle it. Courts should ask themselves whether, in denying the defence of fair comment to the media, they are not indulging in overkill. There may be better ways of curbing the power of the press than by confining it to the role of dispenser of bland information. There is talk in Saskatchewan of creating a press council along the British model with the purpose of upgrading the press from within. However, the British experience in this area has not been too successful. Maybe government action to prevent concentration of ownership would do more to help present a wider and better balanced spectrum of opinion to the public.

Note: Fair comment is defined as an expression of opinion made in good faith and without malice on a matter of public interest. In order to succeed in the defence of fair comment the defendant must:

a. show that the statements which are claimed to be defamatory are expressions of opinion, not allegations of fact;
b. show that some factual basis is stated upon which the opinion expressed could plausibly be based, unless the facts are notorious;

c. show that, to the extent the material in question contains both allegations of fact and expressions of opinion, the allegations of fact are true, that the expressions of opinion are plausibly based upon or derived from them, and that the allegations of fact and the expressions of opinion are clearly distinguished from each other.
d. show that the matter with respect to which the statements in question were made is one of public interest;
e. show that the statements in question are an honest expression of his real opinion, or, to put it slightly differently, that he honestly believes in the opinion expressed.

The defendant is not required to show that the statements were made without malice. The plaintiff may attempt to negative the defence of fair comment by establishing that the defendant was actuated by malice in making the statements.

5.2.3.1.2.4 *Vander Zalm* v. *Times Publishers* (1980), 18 B.C.L.R. 210 (B.C.C.A.)

15th February 1980. NEMETZ C.J.B.C.: — On 22nd June 1978 there appeared on the editorial page of the Victoria Times, one of the city of Victoria's leading daily newspapers, a cartoon depicting the plaintiff, William N. Vander Zalm, a cabinet minister then holding the office of Minister of Human Resources in the government of British Columbia. It was drawn by the defendant Robert Bierman, a freelance political cartoonist who had contributed cartoons to the newspaper for many years. Alongside the cartoon there appeared an actual photograph of the minister, as part of a reprinted editorial criticizing Mr. Vander Zalm's statements and policies. It is apparent that the cartoon exaggerated the facial features of the plaintiff. It depicted Mr. Vander Zalm smiling, seated at a table, and engaged in plucking the wings from a fly. Other flies, without wings, were shown moving on the table. On the plaintiff's lapel were inscribed the words "Human Resources".

The minister sued for damages, claiming that the cartoon libelled him. He pleaded that the newspaper, its editor, its publisher and Mr. Bierman alleged by the cartoon that he was "a person of cruel and sadistic nature who enjoys inflicting suffering and torture on helpless beings who cannot protect themselves". The action was heard by Munroe J., sitting without a jury. The defendants pleaded that the cartoon was not defamatory, and that in any event it was fair comment. The learned trial judge rejected these contentions and found for the plaintiff, awarding damages of $3,500 against the defendants. This is an appeal from that judgment [[1979] 2 W.W.R. 673, 8 C.C.L.T. 144, 96 D.L.R. (3d) 172].

Before addressing myself to the issues, I should like to make some prefatory observations as to political cartoons in general. Counsel were agreed that there was a paucity of decided cases concerning libel arising from political caricatures or cartoons — despite the fact that such cartoons have had a long history of publication in Canada as well as in most of the Western world. As a result, as noted by the learned editors of Gatley on Libel and Slander, 7th ed. (1974), p. 15, n. 23: "the limits of what is permissible in the way of cartoons... are undefined". I have examined definitions of the word "cartoon" in its modern use (coined, it is suggested, by the editors of Punch) and would adopt the one set out by the scholar Winslow Ames in the Encyclopaedia Britannica (1961):

> "...a pictorial parody... which by the devices of caricature, analogy and ludicrous juxtaposition sharpens the public view of a contemporary event, folkway, or political or social trend. It is normally humorous but may be positively savage."

Now the well-known test for whether a statement or allegation is defamatory is set out in Salmond on Torts, 17th ed. (1977), pp. 139-40, from which I quote as follows:

"A defamatory statement is one which has a tendency to injure the reputation of the person to whom it refers; which tends, that is to say, to lower him in the estimation of right-thinking members of society generally and in particular to cause him to be regarded with feelings of hatred, contempt, ridicule, fear, dislike or disesteem."

I have placed these two quotations in juxtaposition because it becomes obvious that most political cartoons have, inherent in their satire, a tendency to lower their subject in the estimation of the public. Nevertheless, it has been said that persons accepting public office can expect attack and criticism on the grounds that "the public interest requires that a man's public conduct shall be open to the most searching criticism", per Bain J. in *Martin v. Man. Free Press Co.* (1892), 8 Man. R. 50 at 72. However, the question of what constitutes valid "searching criticism" and what constitutes libel must be examined in the context of all the surrounding circumstances.

I turn now to the consideration of the cartoon. The defendants denied that the cartoon defamed the plaintiff and pleaded that in any event the cartoon was fair comment on a matter of public interest and that accordingly there was no libel. I have had the privilege of reading the reasons for judgment prepared by each of my brothers Seaton, Hinkson and Craig JJ.A., and agree with them that, even if the cartoon was prima facie defamatory, the defence of fair comment was available in the circumstances. However, I should like to advance my own view of why that defence was available here.

The three elements of the defence of fair comment are well known. First, the matter must be recognizable to the ordinary reasonable man as a comment upon true facts, and not as a bare statement of fact. Secondly, the matter commented upon must be one of public interest. There must, in short, be a public nexus between the matter and the person caricatured. In a case such as this, the cartoonist may not intrude upon the private life of a public man, no matter how interesting such an intrusion may be to the public, nor may he expose a private person to unsought publicity. Finally, as explained by Diplock J. (as he then was) in *Silkin v. Beaverbrook Newspapers,* [1958] 1 W.L.R. 743 at 747, [1958] 2 All E.R. 516, and by the Supreme Court of Canada in *Cherneskey v. Armadale Publishers Ltd.,* [1979] 1 S.C.R. 1067, 24 N.R. 271, the comment must be "fair" in that it must, to quote Martland J. in *Cherneskey* at p. 1073, "represent an honest expression of the real view of the person making the comment". At the trial of this action, the availability of the defence turned on this last element. Munroe J. specifically left open the question of whether the matter was comment or not, and did not find it necessary to consider the question of public interest. The learned judge held that the defence failed because the facts pleaded as the basis for the alleged comment "could not... fairly lead to the imputation arising from the cartoon" (p. 675).

I agree with my brother Hinkson that in making this finding the learned judge applied the wrong test. It is to be remembered that the questions of whether the matter complained of is fact or comment, and if it is comment whether it is "fair", are questions of fact: see *Jones v. Skelton,* [1963] 1 W.L.R. 1362, [1963] 3 All E.R. 952 (P.C.). Consequently in a libel action such as this, heard by a judge sitting without a jury, whether the defence of fair comment succeeds or not rests upon the trial judge drawing proper inferences from proven facts. The question of credibility does not necessarily arise. Certainly it did not arise in this case. Accordingly, an appellate tribunal is in as good a position as the trial judge to draw the proper inferences.

Now as I have already noted, the act of putting oneself in the public arena tends to invite appraisal of one's public conduct. The evidence clearly shows that the minister was not unaware of the widespread publicity attending his public conduct over the period in question. The learned trial judge in his reasons for judgment put it succinctly and I quote him in part [p. 675]:

> "During the 14 years that the plaintiff has been engaged in public life he has been a controversial figure, not adverse to expressing publicly his opinion upon contentious matters."

Sixteen instances of controversial statements and acts attributed to the minister were pleaded by the defendants as particulars of facts upon which the cartoon was said to comment. Each of them had received considerable publicity. These particulars are set out in the judgment of my brother Craig, and I note that only one, para. (h), was categorically denied by the plaintiff. All of the other 15 were either entirely acknowledged or substantially conceded after qualification. I refer by way of example only to those matters arising in paras. (a), (b), (e), (l), (m), (n) and (p):

"a. That the Plaintiff, within hours of being appointed Human Resources Minister in December, 1975, stated that he would develop ways of dealing with welfare recipients who refused to 'pick up their shovels.'

"b. That the Plaintiff, since assuming the role of Minister of Human Resources, has cut off funding for a number of community groups that had been providing valuable services for those in need....

"e. That in March, 1976, the Plaintiff tightened regulations so that fewer people in British Columbia would be classified as handicapped and so be eligible for handicapped benefits....

"l. That in October, 1977, the Plaintiff stated that young people should be denied assistance because they have more mobility to find jobs.

"m. That in January, 1978, the Plaintiff ordered that even emergency welfare aid be refused to persons in areas where the picking of hallucinogenic mushrooms is common.

"n. That in March, 1978, the Plaintiff suggested that the current level of unemployment insurance payments to single people should be reduced....

"p. That in June, 1978, the Plaintiff commented that native Indians in Vancouver should return to their reserves because there was 'more opportunity' there for them."

Now, one can approve or disapprove of these ministerial concerns, but there is little doubt that these statements were provocative. It should not, therefore, have come to the minister as a surprise that these statements would become well known to the public and that someone would respond to them. One such person was the defendant cartoonist. In giving evidence at the trial, Mr. Bierman was questioned as to the meaning of the cartoon. I quote his testimony in part:

"MR. BIERMAN: This particular cartoon — I tried to say with it that the Minister of Human Resources had a cruel attitude to the underprivileged position and defenceless people under his ministry where, in particular, I was referring to the Indians.

"MR. FARQUHAR: Now, could you describe, please, the significance of the various components of the cartoon?

"MR. BIERMAN: Oh, I could describe it by what I would say that I used the body which I labelled as Human Resources, the ministry, the head on it as a caricature of Mr. Vander Zalm who at that time was the Minister of Human Resources, and the fly depicts the helpless Indians that were in his words, 'Attracted to the big lights'. And what he is doing there, he is more or less clipping their wings. However, he is pulling them out which is different from clipping, but he's clipping their wings so they can't roam around any longer or fly around to the bright lights, not realizing the pain that he causes.

"MR. FARQUHAR: Was there any particular reason why you did that cartoon at that time?

"MR. BIERMAN: Yes, that was in relation to a statement that the Indians were attracted to the bright lights and excitement of the big city and, I take it, it was Vancouver and should return to their reserves if they still wanted to qualify for welfare. And that they had better opportunity there on the reserves.

"MR. FARQUHAR: Now, in addition to that statement by the minister, at the time that you prepared the cartoon, did you have in mind any other actions of the Minister of Human Resources?

"MR. BIERMAN: Yes sir."

In my view, these statements and actions of the minister, including the statement concerning Indians which was publicized only a few days before the publication of the cartoon, provided the necessary substratum of sufficiently publicized facts to enable the ordinary reader to recognize the nexus of the cartoon and the statements. Ordinary and reasonable persons in this country are well acquainted with the allegorical nature of political cartoons and, in my opinion, would have little difficulty in recognizing this cartoon as a comment upon such facts; a comment, indeed, of the very sort which Mr. Bierman testified he intended to make. Nor can it be doubted that the facts commented upon were matters of considerable public interest and concerned the minister in his public rather than his personal capacity.

The next question that arises is whether the comment was "fair". In charging the jury in the *Silkin* case, supra, Lord Diplock explained the test in this way [p. 747]:

"I have been referring, and counsel in their speeches to you have been referring, to fair comment, because that is the technical name which is given to this defence, or, as I should prefer to say, which is given to the right of every citizen to comment on matters of public interest. But the expression 'fair comment' is a little misleading. It may give you the impression that you, the jury, have to decide whether you agree with the comment, whether you think it is fair. If that were the question you had to decide, you realize that the limits of freedom which the law allows would be greatly curtailed. People are entitled to hold and to express freely on matters of public interest strong views, views which some of you, or indeed all of you, may think are exaggerated, obstinate or prejudiced, provided — and this is the important thing — that they are views which they honestly hold. The basis of our public life is that the crank, the enthusiast, may say what he honestly thinks just as much as the reasonable man or woman who sits on a jury, and it would be a sad day for freedom of speech in this country if a jury were to apply the test of whether it agrees with the comment instead of applying the true test: was this an opinion, however exaggerated, obstinate or prejudiced, which was honestly held by the writer?"

The question, then, is this: Did the comment made by the cartoon represent the honest opinion of Mr. Bierman? At the end of the cartoonist's examination-in-chief, the following exchange took place:

"MR. FARQUHAR: Now, you have testified as to what you intended the cartoon to say about the Minister of Human Resources, did that represent your honest opinion of the Minister of Human Resources at the time you prepared the cartoon?

"MR. BIERMAN: Yes, sir."

Now, as I have already stated, what the cartoonist intended the cartoon to say, as quoted above, coincides, in my opinion, with what the ordinary and reasonable person would take the cartoon as saying; namely, it is a comment of the nature Mr. Bierman described, concerned solely with the plaintiff in his ministerial capacity. I conclude from the whole of Mr. Bierman's testimony that that indeed represents an honest expression of his real view. No question arises as to credibility since it is obvious that the learned trial judge did not disbelieve the cartoonist, and no issue arose in this regard. Having these factors before us, is the defence of fair comment available? I think it is. As, in the circumstances of this case, it is my respectful view that the cartoon represents fair comment on a matter of public interest, I would, therefore, allow the appeal and dismiss the action.

HINKSON J.A.: — ...In these circumstances it is necessary then to turn to the other defence raised by the appellants, namely, fair comment. At trial the appellants relied upon the statements made and decisions taken by the respondent as minister as constituting the facts upon which the comment was made. The learned trial judge said in discussing this aspect of the matter [p. 675]:

> "During the 14 years that the plaintiff has been engaged in public life he has been a controversial figure, not adverse to expressing publicly his opinion upon contentious matters. Nevertheless, upon the evidence I find that the controversial statements made by the plaintiff and relied upon by the defendants were such that he was entitled to hold and to express, and the decisions made by him as minister were made in good faith pursuant to his duty and responsibility as such minister, and could not fairly lead an ordinary person to conclude that the plaintiff acted in a cruel, sadistic or thoughtless manner when performing his duties. His statements and acts, as one would expect, were approved by some and disapproved by others, but could not in my opinion fairly lead to the imputation arising from the cartoon."
> In my view the learned trial judge erred in disposing of the defence of fair comment in that way.

In *Cherneskey v. Armadale Publishers Ltd.*, [1978] 6 W.W.R. 618, 7 C.C.L.T. 69, 90 D.L.R. (3d) 321, Martland J. at p. 636 said:

"A clear statement of the nature of the defence of fair comment is found in the summing up to the jury of Diplock J. (as he then was) in the case of *Silkin v. Beaverbrook Newspapers,* [1958] 1 W.L.R. 743 at 747, [1958] 2 All E.R. 516:

" 'I have been referring, and counsel in their speeches to you have been referring, to fair comment, because that is the technical name which is given to this defence, or, as I should prefer to say, which is given to the right of every citizen to comment on matters of public interest. But the expression 'fair comment' is a little misleading. I may give you the impression that you, the jury, have to decide whether you agree with the comment, whether you think it is fair. If that were the question you had to decide, you realize that the limits of freedom which the law allows would be greatly curtailed. People are entitled to hold and to express freely on matters of public interest strong views, views which some of you, or indeed all of you, may think are exaggerated, obstinate or prejudiced, provided — and this is the important thing — that they are views which they honestly hold. The basis of our public life is that the crank, the enthusiast, may say what he honestly thinks just as much as the reasonable man or woman who sits on a jury, and it would be a sad day for freedom of speech in this country if a jury were to apply the test of whether it agrees with the comment instead of applying the true test: was this an opinion, however exaggerated, obstinate or prejudiced, which was honestly held by the writer?' "

The Supreme Court of Canada decided in the *Cherneskey* case, in respect of the defence of fair comment, that it is dependent upon the fact that the words used must represent an honest expression of the real view of the person making the comment.

In response to that proposition, counsel for the respondent advanced a number of submissions. First, he contended that the message in the cartoon was a statement of fact rather than an expression of opinion. In my view there is no merit in that submission. It is not contended by the respondent that the cartoon was to be interpreted literally and as I have already indicated, having regard to the fact that the respondent was well known in public life and that he was being described in his capacity as Minister of Human Resources, a moment's reflection by the reader of the newspaper would indicate that the cartoon referred to the statements and policies of the respondent as Minister of Human Resources and that the message in the cartoon was a comment on those statements and policies. Approached in that way it seems to me that there were facts before the reader which formed the basis for the comment.

Second, it was contended that the appellant Bierman who drew the cartoon, had no honest belief in the opinion being expressed. In giving his evidence in chief this witness testified:

Q. And what, if anything, were you intending the cartoon to say? A. This particular cartoon I tried to say with it that the Minister of Human Resources had a cruel attitude to the underprivileged position and defenceless people under his ministry where, in particular, I was referring to the Indians."

At the conclusion of his evidence in chief the witness testified that the cartoon represented his honest opinion of the Minister of Human Resources at the time the cartoon was prepared.

In cross-examination it was suggested that the witness had portrayed the respondent as a cruel and sadistic person. A discussion took place as to the meaning of sadistic at which point the trial judge intervened as follows:

"THE COURT: Let us assume for the purpose of this question that a person that pulls the wings off a fly is a sadistic person in the sense that he enjoys seeing other creatures suffering. It may be a poor definition, adopting that stand, you say your cartoon shows him as a sadistic person or otherwise?

"THE WITNESS: Otherwise, sir.

"THE COURT: Why do you say that? A. Because it is an assumption that anybody that pulls wings off flies is a sadistic person and I don't agree with that. If a child pulls wings off of a fly, is the child sadistic or if a person that is evil-minded, is that person sadistic? Any person that doesn't know picking wings off flies causes pain and suffering and nevertheless does it —

"THE COURT: You don't suggest that the minister depicted in your cartoon is either a child nor evil-minded? A. In the cartoon, the minister is evil-minded.

"Q. You're not suggesting that you had an honest opinion at the time that you drew that cartoon that Mr. Vander Zalm was evil-minded? A. Not an honest opinion, I knew better, but in my cartoon I drew him as being a feeble-minded person, thoughtless and cruel."

In my view, the witness was adhering to his evidence in chief as to the opinion he had formed and that such was his honest belief.

The defence also called Miss B. J. McLintock, the editor of the Victoria Times newspaper. She had seen the cartoon in the page proof on the morning of 22nd June 1978 and had permitted it to be published. Her evidence disclosed that she considered that the statements and policies of the respondent while he was Minister of Human Resources marked him as performing his duties in a cruel manner and that this was an opinion honestly held by her at the time that she approved the publication of the cartoon.

The learned trial judge appeared to consider that the statements and policies of the respondent could not fairly lead an ordinary reasonable person to conclude that he acted in a cruel manner in performing his duties. But it seems to me that does not apply the proper test. If the appellants Bierman and McLintock honestly held that view then, because the subject matter was a matter of public interest, they were entitled to express that opinion without becoming liable to the respondent.

I conclude that the defence of fair comment should prevail. In the result I would allow the appeal and dismiss the action.

CRAIG J.A.: — This conclusion, therefore, requires a consideration of the defence of fair comment. What is "fair comment"? It must be "the expression of an opinion based on true facts, *i.e.*, facts admitted or proved to be true" — Gatley on Libel and Slander, 6th ed. (1967), p. 325 — but the "true facts" need not be stated at the time of the expression of the opinion. They may be implied and specified as particulars in the defence: *Kemsley v. Foot,* [1952] A.C. 345, [1952] 1 All E.R. 501 (C.A.). If the commentator sets out the facts in the comment he may rely on the defence of fair comment only if he proves every fact to be true. On the other hand, if he merely implies the fact, or facts, in the comment and gives the facts in the form of particulars he need establish only the truth of one of the facts: see *Kemsely v. Foot,* supra.

The word "fair" in the phrase "fair comment" is a misnomer because it conveys the concept that comment must be "reasonable". This is not the case as pointed out by Diplock J. in addressing the jury in *Silkin v. Beaverbrook Newspapers,* [1958] 1 W.L.R. 743, [1958] 2 All E.R. 516 at 520, when he said:

"So in considering this case, members of the jury, do not apply the test of whether you agree with it. If juries did that, freedom of speech, the right of the crank to say what he likes, would go. Would a fair-minded man holding strong views, obstinate views, prejudiced views, have been capable of making this comment? If the answer to that is yes, then your verdict in this case should be a verdict for the defendants. Such a verdict does not mean that you agree with the comment. All it means is that you think that a man might honestly hold those views on those facts."

Counsel for the respondent submitted to the trial judge, and to this court, that the plea of "fair comment" was unavailable because there were "no facts stated" at the time of the publication of the cartoon from which there could be an inference that the cartoon was a fair comment. He submitted that the cartoon was not a comment on a matter of public interest but, solely, a statement of fact vilifying the respondent. In a portion of the reasons of the trial judge which I have quoted, he said that while he thought there was "merit" in the submission he did not find it necessary to decide that issue because he felt that the defence of fair comment failed "in any event".

The statement of defence contains a number of facts upon which the appellants rely in support of the defence of fair comment. In his cross-examination the respondent conceded, frankly, that he had said or done some of the things set out in the particulars in the statement of defence. The nature of the cartoon indicates that the cartoonist is commenting, unfavourably, on the conduct of the appellant as Minister of Human Resources. The nature of the conduct is set out in the particulars in the statement of defence. I think that the publisher could not be expected to accompany the cartoon with a statement of facts upon which the cartoon was based, nor could the cartoonist be expected to incorporate all these facts in the cartoon.

In his reasons for judgment, the trial judge said [p. 674]: "The defence of fair comment cannot prevail if the facts on which comment is made are untrue and defamatory. No comment can be fair which is built upon facts which are invented or misstated". I infer from his judgment that he considered that the depiction of the respondent as a "cruel" man was false and that this was, therefore, an untrue allegation. However, that is not the fact upon which the appellants were relying. The facts upon which the cartoonist was relying to make his comment were set out in the particulars. The respondent conceded that some of the particulars, at least, were true. The test was, therefore — did the appellants honestly hold the views which they purported to express in the cartoon on the facts, or any of them, set out in the particulars?

The tenor of Bierman's testimony and the appellant McLintock's testimony was that they honestly felt that in some of his actions as Minister of Human Resources the minister acted in a cruel and thoughtless way.

I infer from the reasons for judgment that the trial judge did not disbelieve the testimony of the appellants, or find that they did not honestly hold the opinions which they expressed, but that rather the facts upon which they based the statement were untrue. Yet, as I have pointed out, some of the facts, at least, upon which the appellants relied in expressing their opinion were admitted by the respondent.

Many would regard the cartoon as anything but "fair" comment. On the other hand, I think that there was a basis upon which the appellants could properly rely upon the defence of fair comment. I think that the trial judge applied the wrong test in rejecting it.

The problem is, should the action be dismissed or should the appeal simply be allowed and a new trial directed? If the trial judge had disbelieved the testimony of the appellant Bierman and the appellant McLintock that they honestly held the view which was expressed by the cartoon the defence of fair comment would have failed. As I have already said, I think that the trial judge did not disbelieve the appellants' testimony and that, therefore, the appropriate disposition of the case would be to allow the appeal and to dismiss the action.

5.2.3.1.2.5 *Farrell* v. *St. John's Publishing Co.* (1986) 58 Nfld. & P.E.I.R. 66 (Nfld. C.A.)

MORGAN, J.A.: For the defence of fair comment to succeed it must be based upon the truth of the facts upon which the comment is made. A writer cannot adopt as true the untrue statement of facts made by others, and then comment on them on the assumption that they are true. "In order to give room for the plea of fair comment the facts must be truly stated."

5.2.3.1.2.6 *Pound* v. *Scott* (1973), 4 W.W.R. 403 (B.C.S.C.)

22nd March 1973. WOOTTON J.: — Action for damages for libel.

The alleged libellous article is one authored by the defendant Scott and published by the defendant Victoria Press Limited in one issue of its newspaper, the Victoria Daily Times.

The defendant Scott is a well-known columnist, and the column in question, accompanied by a photograph of the defendant Scott, was published on 13th August 1971 (Ex. 1). It reads as follows:

"Old Refrain

"Come Now, Doctor
Watch The Facts

"Death is inevitable. Taxes are inevitable. Inevitable, too, is the British immigrant doctor preaching to Canadians on the evils of 'socialized medicine.' Heigh-ho. That's life.

"Even so, I was astonished at the incredible yardage of newsprint gratuitously provided earlier this week on our good Page Five to a British immigrant doctor whose information was somewhat tired (five years out of date), whose prejudices were even narrower than others of his kind and whose motivation for breaking into the usually shunned glare of public opinion seems to have been a kind of outright blackmail.

"What 33-year-old Dr. Brian S. Pound, of our town, is telling us, gentle reader, is that if the British Columbia government goes any further toward 'socialized medicine' he will take off for other parts where things are done more to his liking. It cannot be considered an idle threat, either. That's just what Dr. Pound did when he pulled out of Britain. 'If we don't like it,' he told our Don Vipond, 'then it's up to us to get out,' a contingency that does not appear to be included in the Hippocratic Oath.

"Dr. Pound is not unusual since thousands of British doctors have been doing that in the 25 years since Britain's National Health Service assumed a world leadership in humanitarian medicine, but he does seem rather young and inexperienced to have made such a bold decision.

"Indeed, most of his time in England appears to have been in training, for which the British taxpayer shelled out $22,500. (Dr. Pound told Vipond that it cost the state a mere $6,000 to give him the education that's earned him such rich rewards in British Columbia, but the official 1967 figure on state subsidies for doctor training in the United Kingdom was $22,500 per doctor: if that's what it cost to license Dr. Pound they sure as shootin' got a small return on the investment.)

"It was a matter of conscience, Dr. Pound told Vipond, to rebel against Britain's 'second rate' medicine and certainly one must agree that there is nothing 'second rate' about his subsequent career as a general practitioner in Victoria. His listed income under B.C. Medicare was $41,452 two years ago, $53,291 last year. (Just once I'd like to meet a British doctor who left as a matter of conscience without instantly doubling or tripling his income.)

"Apart from the background of his brief practice, Dr. Pound is in the classic tradition of such immigrants who so often justify the desertion of their nation and their patients by a paranoic attack on the British system and issue the warning that It Can Happen Here. To that, all I can say is (1) we should be so lucky and (2) isn't it just a teeny-weeny bit cheeky for this Johnny-Come-Lately to be threatening us if our elected representatives displease him?

"Dr. Pound's main beef against the National Health Service is the familiar lament that the general practitioner is not given hospital privileges, that, as he told Vipond, 'if you can't treat the patient with an aspirin you've got to refer him.'

"Even in those days when the young doctor was on the scene, that was patently untrue, as he surely knows. Then, and now, 90 per cent of all the nation's ills are treated in the British family doctor's surgery. Under the system the general practitioner is just exactly the primary diagnostician that he is in Canada, the difference being that the referral is made to a specialist when there is an operation to be performed in hospital.

"There are two schools of thought on this. My own doctor in London was one of those who thought it the best system, hadn't used a knife in 20 years except for an occasional circumcision, and considered it only sensible logic that, whether it be a tonsillectomy or a lobotomy, surgery was for the specializing technician. The point is that it is an arguable question. To let Dr. Pound get away with his one-sided, sweeping generalization can hardly be said to be objective reporting.

"It must be said, as well, that Dr. Pound is either unaware of recent efforts to widen the function of the general practitioner in Britain or that he chose not to inform Vipond of this trend.

"This has been the great story in Britain over the past few years, under both the Labor and Conservative governments. The aim has been to set up clinics and group practices, often in conjunction with local authority public health centres. Its success goes a long way to wiping out Dr. Pound's 'aspirin' argument.

"This polyclinic idea, demonstrably effective in the Soviet Union and recommended in the first blueprint of the National Health Service, means that doctors may combine various specialties in obstetrics, pediatrics, geriatrics, chiropody and other fields, rent offices on the premises of health centres and use the centre's nursing and secretarial staff and diagnostic equipment.

"In other cases, with the encouragement and financial assistance of the Ministry of Health, group practices, involving from three to 12 doctors, are replacing the old one-man operations.

"When the service began in 1948 three of every four practices were single-handed. Now three of every four are group arrangements. There are new challenges, new rewards, including higher incomes. What Dr. Pound describes as 'tremendous apathy' is simply not true.

"What I am saying is that Dr. Pound, to my knowledge, was not at all fair in his presentation of these facts. As for his opinion, I find it equally suspect. Any man who describes health as 'a commodity' and the doctor's role as 'free trade with his customers,' is hardly qualified to judge a national medical scheme based on the philosophy that good health is every citizen's right. For all its faults, Britain's National Health Service is dedicated to that security — womb-to-tomb, as the saying goes — and may still serve as a model for a comprehensive plan in these climes.

"If that means the disappearance of Dr. Pound to new climes — where? Hawaii, perhaps? — then so be it."

The cause and source of that criticism by the defendant Scott is an article published three days earlier, namely, 10th August 1971 (Ex. 2) by a reporter, Donald Vipond, of the defendant Victoria Press Limited. That article was one following an interview sought by the plaintiff of the said Vipond in order that his, the plaintiff's, views concerning the practice of medicine and in particular his view of "state medicine in Britain", otherwise known as the National Health Service, might be published. The cause and source of that activity on the part of the plaintiff, I conclude, were two Orders in Council passed by the Lieutenant-Governor of British Columbia in Council. Copies of these Orders in Council are exhibits in this case. They deal with the use of medical laboratories, etc.

The views of the plaintiff were published on 10th August 1971 in the article entitled "Do People Realy Want Second-Rate Medicine?" and the preface to the article is in the following words:

"The doctors, traditionally silent as a group are angry again. Last year it was over government publication of their earnings under Medicare. Now they are aroused over arbitrary decisions by the provincial cabinet affecting how they practise.

"Here are the views of one of them, a city physician who fled state medicine in Britain and fears that the same conditions that made him move are now threatened in B.C.

"Dr. Pound believes that medicine is a commodity which he has to sell, with the right of free trade with his customers.

"He speaks for himself in this interview with Times reporter Don Vipond. Whether his views represent most of the doctors in the community is uncertain; only the reaction of his colleagues can determine that."

The views of the plaintiff were freely expressed to the reporter Vipond. The latter quoted words of the plaintiff throughout the article as well as summarizing others. As to that article the plaintiff swore that he took no exception, but he did say that he felt that Vipond had not stressed the "thrust" of some of his views in adequate fashion.

It is therefore in the light of the article of 10th August that the Court must view the article or column of the defendant Scott. This is not a case of a deliberate act of defamatory insult. It is rather a case of criticism by one person, having knowledge and experience in an area covered by the writing of another person, in an area of public interest.

I observe that in the statement of claim the plaintiff says that he was, at all times material to this action, a physician and surgeon carrying on practice in Victoria, British Columbia.

The fact of the matter is, in my respectful opinion, that the plaintiff on his own motion entered into the forum of public discussion, pitting his knowledge as an observer of the National Health Service in Great Britain and the Health Service in British Columbia against other opinion. It was as such an observer that he was being criticized by the defendant Scott in his article. The plaintiff could not complain that, because references were made to him, the column of the defendant Scott in fact printed and published certain words "of the plaintiff and of him in the way of his said profession and in relation to his conduct therein". Like a boxer, having entered the ring, he must accept the blows given him provided always that none is "below the belt". He must participate as a boxer, viz., as a commentator against contrary views and will have no privilege in the contest because he is in fact a doctor of medicine unless it appear that a deliberate and improper attack be made upon him in his capacity as a doctor of medicine or such an attack may properly be implied or inferred.

A fair reading of the article expressing the plaintiff's views as published on 10th August indicates a novel idea of the professional doctor of medicine in relation to his profession. In addition to that, the plaintiff professed to be knowledgeable as of the date of his article of the conditions existing in Great Britain. He also gave evidence as to his own experiences in the practice of the profession of medicine in Great Britain and his own participation therein. In one particular matter and one of considerable importance, when dealing with his own knowledge, I comment that he had given to the reporter Vipond particulars. Although the item in the Vipond article of 10th August is a summary by the man Vipond, the plaintiff swore that he took no exception to that article. The said Vipond noted the following:

"Pound recalls seeing 60 to 70 patients between 10 in the morning and noon, another 30 or 40 between 6 and 10 in the evening. Then house calls."

Then I quote words used by him:

"I was too busy to be able to stop and think... Nobody's getting a fair deal, least of all the patient."

As to those numbers, I do not believe the plaintiff. I observed him during the course of cross-examination and I observed that, when he was dealing with those figures, he was extremely nervous and had lost the composure that was otherwise displayed throughout the time when he was the witness before the Court. In addition, the witness Anderson, a man called as a person having special knowledge in the medical field in Great Britain, gave evidence of his appreciation of the numbers of patients who could be seen per diem and would be seen per diem. The plaintiff was asked as to estimates of time per patient. All this evidence when assessed, along with the discomfiture displayed by the plaintiff, convinced me that the plaintiff was not being truthful in that particular. Consequently I am of the opinion that his opinions expressed to the reporter Vipond were not entirely truthful. In addition, his appreciation of the position of the doctor of medicine was unorthodox and likely to have encouraged comment.

As to the defendant Scott, I conclude that he had had considerable opportunity to observe the National Health Service. He had not only been a patient thereunder, as had members of his family, but he had written a series of articles upon the subject which had been published, four in number, in the Toronto Daily Star. He had been a resident of Britain for a number of years. I concluded, in the light of experience, that he was informed. The witness Anderson confirmed the knowledge that the witness Scott had demonstrated.

It is true, as he swore, that he was annoyed by what he considered an unfair and unjust criticism on the part of the plaintiff of the National Health Service. He therefore wrote his article willingly, and particularly because the manager of the defendant considered there should be some reply made to the article, Ex. 2.

My first duty is to determine if the words complained of are capable of being defamatory.

Having in mind Ex. 1 and para. 7 of the statement of claim, I conclude that some of the words in the article may be defamatory. If some are defamatory, such defamatory meaning not being excused, the plaintiff must succeed and there must be an assessment of damages.

The plaintiff has chosen the words he considers defamatory and he indicates the inference that may be drawn, viz., the inference that would be drawn by the public reading the article, the ordinary man in the street. All this is set out in para. 7, supra.

The defences raised here were briefly:

1. No libel.
2. Qualified privilege.
3. Justification and fair comment in a rolled-up plea.
4. Justification (by amendment at trial).

Had there been a jury before me I would have had to explain to the jury that there was a case to be considered by them as to whether or not there was in fact a libel of the plaintiff. I would have directed the jury on the law as I direct myself now on the law in relation to the matter of fair comment by reference to relevant authorities. I quote from Gatley on Libel and Slander, 6th ed., p. 750:

"It is for the jury to decide, subject to the direction of the judge, whether the words complained of are allegations of fact or comments, and, if expressions of opinion, whether such comments are fair comment or not. But in every case it is first of all the duty of the judge to determine whether the words are capable of being comment and whether there is any evidence of unfairness to go to the jury. '*The jury if the Court is of opinion that there is some evidence* that the comment is unfair, finds whether it is so or not.' The question whether the comment is fair or not is eminently a question for the jury, *provided there is any evidence* of unfairness."

In that work there follow the observations of Collins M.R. in *McQuire v. Western Morning News,* [1903] 2 K.B. 100 at 110:

"No doubt in most cases of this class there are expressions in the impugned document capable of being interpreted as falling outside the limit of honest criticism, and, therefore, it is proper to leave the question to the jury, and in all cases where there may be a doubt it may be convenient to take the opinion of a jury. But it is always for the judge to say whether the document is capable in law of being a libel. It is, however, for the plaintiff, who rests his claim upon a document which on his own statement purports to be a criticism of a matter of public interest, to show that it is a libel — i.e., that it travels beyond the limit of fair criticism; and therefore it must be for the judge to say whether it is reasonably capable of being so interpreted."

It was contended by the defendants that there was qualified privilege available to the defendants in this matter. I am of the opinion that that defence was not available to them. I refer again to Gatley, supra, at p. 702, where para. 703 reads as follows:

"703. Fair comment distinguished from qualified privilege. The defence of fair comment must also be distinguished from that of qualified privilege. In the defence of fair comment the right exercised by the defendant is shared by every member of the public. 'Who is entitled to comment? The answer to that is "everyone". A newspaper reporter or a newspaper editor has exactly the same rights, neither more nor less, than every other citizen.' Per Diplock J. in *Silkin v. Beaverbrook Newspapers,* [1958] 1 W.L.R. 743 at 746, [1958] 2 All E.R. 516. In that of qualified privilege the right is not shared by every member of the public, but is limited to an individual who stands in such relation to the circumstances that he is entitled to say or write what would be libellous or slanderous on the part of anyone else. 'For instance, if a master is asked as to the character of a servant, and he says that the servant is a thief, he has a privilege which no one else would have.' 'A privileged occasion is one on which the privileged person is entitled to do something which no one who is not within the privilege is entitled to do on that occasion. A person in such a position may say or write about another person things which no other person in the kingdom can be allowed to say or write. But, in the case of a criticism upon [a matter of public interest whether it be the conduct of a public man or] a published work, every person in the kingdom is entitled to do, and is forbidden to do exactly the same things, and therefore the occasion is not privileged."

Fair comment is well explained at p. 731 of Gatley, supra, in the following paragraph:

"732. *The latitude of fair comment.* In the following passage from his summing-up in *Stopes v. Sutherland,* [1925] A.C. 47, Lord Hewart C.J. points out the latitude of fair comment:

"'What is it that fair comment means? It means this — and I prefer to put it in words which are not my own; I refer to the famous judgment of Lord Esher M.R. in *Merivale v. Carson* (1887), 20 Q.B.D. 275 at 280-81: "Every latitude," said Lord Esher, "must be given to opinion and to prejudice, and then an ordinary set of men with ordinary judgment must say [not whether they agree with it, but] whether any fair man would have made such a comment... Mere exaggeration, or even gross exaggeration, would not make the comment unfair. However wrong the opinion expressed may be in point of truth, or however prejudiced the writer, it may still be within the prescribed limit. The question which the jury must consider is this — would any fair man, however prejudiced he may be, however exaggerated or obstinate his views, have said that which this criticism has said?" Again, as Bray J. said in *Rex v. Russell; Ex parte Morris* (1905), 93 L.T. 407: "When you come to a question of fair comment you ought to be extremely liberal, and in a matter of this kind — a matter relating to the administration of the licensing laws — you ought to be extremely liberal, because it is a matter on which men's minds are moved, in which people who do know, entertain very, very strong opinions, and if they use strong language every allowance should be made in their favour. They must believe what they say, but the question whether they honestly believe it is a question for you to say. If they do believe it, and they are within anything like reasonable bounds, they come within the meaning of fair comment. If comments were made which would appear to you to have been exaggerated, it does not follow that they are not perfectly honest comments." That is the kind of maxim which you may apply in considering whether that part of this matter which is comment is fair. Could a fairminded man, holding a strong view, holding perhaps an obstinate view, holding perhaps a prejudiced view — could a fair-minded man have been capable of writing this? — which, you observe, is a totally different question from the question. Do you agree with what he has said?' "...

I have dealt with the matter, as the trial indicated I should do, on the basis of justification and fair comment.. I conclude that what the writer and defendant Jack Scott did was to robustly criticize the plaintiff upon the article which was published at his behest and contained his views based upon his reported knowledge. I have considered the claim of the plaintiff and, in particular, the claims particularized in para. 7 of the statement of claim. I base my judgment upon the alternatives 1 to 8 above, which I adopt as my conclusions. Those conclusions, together with my study of the whole words of the text of Ex. 1, the alleged libellous article, convince me that there has been fair comment made in a matter of public interest and that necessarily includes justification of the article and a finding of no malice. The action of the plaintiff must therefore be dismissed with costs.

5.2.3.1.2.7 *Mack* v. *North Hill News Ltd.*, (1964), 44 D.L.R. (2d) 147 (Alta. S.C.)

...The defence of fair comment pleaded in these actions has become known as the "rolled-up plea" and is distinguished from the plea of justification in *Sutherland et al. v. Stopes*, [1925] A.C. 47, the headnote of which states:

> The plea in an action for libel that in so far as the words complained of consist of allegations of fact they are true in substance and in fact and in so far as they consist of expressions of opinion they are fair comments made in good faith and without malice on a matter of public interest is not a plea partly of justification and partly of fair comment, but is a plea of fair comment only.

Viscount Finlay, in distinguishing the defence of fair comment from that of justification, says at pp. 62-3:

> It is clear that the truth of a libel affords a complete answer to civil proceedings. This defence is raised by plea of justification on the ground that the words are true in substance and in fact. Such a plea in justification means that the libel is true not only in its allegations of fact but also in any comments made therein.
>
> The defence of fair comment on matters of public interest is totally different. The defendant who raises this defence does not take upon himself the burden of showing that the comments are true. If the facts are truly stated with regard to a matter of public interest, the defendant will succeed in his defence to an action of libel if the jury are satisfied that the comments are fairly and honestly made. To raise this defence there must, of course, be a basis of fact on which the comment is made.
>
> For a good many years past a practice has prevailed of raising this defence by what has been called the "rolled up plea," but it will be found that this term is a misnomer based on a misconception of the nature of the plea. Such a plea states that the allegations of fact in the libel are true, that they are of public interest, and that the comments upon them contained in the libel were fair. The allegation of truth is confined to the facts averred, and the averment as to the comments is not that they are true but only that they were made in good faith, and that they are fair and do not exceed the proper standard of comment upon such matters.
>
> There has been a good deal of misconception as to the nature of this plea. It has been sometimes treated as containing two separate defences rolled into one, but it in fact raises only one defence, that being the defence of fair comment on matters of public interest. The averment that the facts were truly stated is merely to lay the necessary basis for the defence on the ground of fair comment. This averment is quite different from a plea of justification of a libel on the ground of truth, under which the defendant has to prove not only that the facts are truly stated but also that any comments upon them are correct.

And

> Such a defence on the ground of fair comment will fail if the jury are satisfied that the libel was malicious or that it exceeded the bounds of fair comment.
>
> On the question of fair comment, the law is in my opinion correctly stated by the Master of the Rolls (afterwards Lord Collins) in the case of *McQuire* v. *Western Morning News Co.*, [1903] 2 K.B. 100, 111: "It is, however, for the plaintiff, who rests his claim upon a document which on his own statement purports to be a criticism of a matter of public interest, to shew that it is a libel — i.e., that it travels beyond the limit of fair criticism; and therefore it must be for the judge to say whether it is reasonably capable of being so interpreted."

There are three essentials to such a defence enumerated by Fletcher Moulton, L.J., in *Hunt v. Star Newspaper Co.*, [1908] 2 K.B. 309 at pp. 319-20 in these words:

> The law as to fair comment, so far as is material to the present case, stands as follows: In the first place, comment in order to be justifiable as fair comment must appear as comment and must not be so mixed up with the facts that the reader cannot distinguish between what is report and what is comment: see *Andrews* v. *Chapman* (1853), 3 C. & K. 286.... In the next place, in order to give room for the plea of fair comment the facts must be truly stated. If the facts upon which the comment purports to be made do not exist the foundation of the plea fails....
>
> Finally, comment must not convey imputations of an evil sort except so far as the facts truly stated warrant the imputation.

The nature of the plea is concisely summed up by Riddell, J., in *Augustine Automatic Rotary Engine Co. v. Saturday Night Ltd.*, (1917), 34 D.L.R. 439 at p. 447, 38 O.L.R. 609 at p. 619 in these words: "... it means that all allegations of fact concerning the plaintiff are true and that the remainder of the comments on the plaintiff are fair as justified by facts."

This statement of the rolled-up plea was cited and applied by the Ontario Appellate Division in *Boys v. Star Printing & Publishing Co.*, [1927] 3 D.L.R. 847, 60 O.L.R. 592...

5.2.3.1.2.8 Ontario Libel and Slander Act R.S.O. 1980, c.237, s.24

Fair comment

24. In an action for libel or slander for words consisting partly of allegations of fact and partly of expression of opinion, a defence of fair comment shall not fail by reason only that the truth of every allegation of fact is not proved if the expression of opinion is fair comment having regard to such of the facts alleged or referred to in the words complained of as are proved. R.S.O. 1970, c.243, s.24.

5.2.3.1.2.9 *Cherneskey* v. *Armadale Publishers* (1979), 90 D.L.R. (3d) 321 (S.C.C.)

MARTLAND, J.: — The facts which give rise to the present appeal are stated in the reasons of my brothers Ritchie and Dickson. I agree with the disposition of the appeal proposed by the former. I wish to comment on one of the grounds which he adopts for allowing the appeal which I consider to be sufficient to dispose of the matter.

The issue before this Court is as to whether the Judge at trial erred in taking away from the jury the defence of fair comment. Before doing so, the trial Judge discussed the matter with counsel and stated his reasons for taking this course. They are as follows, and I agree with them:

> It is, of course, the burden of the defendant to prove this defence and it does not arise until after the jury has found the words complained of to apply to the plaintiff and that they are defamatory of him.
>
> I shall not try to decide whether if the opinion of the writers of the letter is honest and sincere that this fact absolves the publisher or the editor of the paper from a similar opinion. In the present trial that is not necessary because here there is no evidence that the offending words, if they are in fact defamatory of the plaintiff, which is a matter for the jury — there is no evidence that those words express the honest opinion of anyone, either the writers of the letter or of anyone on the editorial staff of the Star-Phoenix or its publisher. The evidence seems to be that the defendants had a contrary opinion or none at all. Without such honest opinion I cannot tell the jury that the defence of fair comment is available to the defendant.

> I thought I had better put that on the record, gentlemen, so that my position is clear and the reason for my ruling is clear....

In the present case, the corporate defendant is the owner and publisher of The Star-Phoenix, a Saskatoon newspaper in which the words complained of were published, and the respondent, King, is the editor of that newspaper. The evidence of the officer produced for examination for discovery by the respondent company, and that of the respondent, King, make it clear that the letter complained of did not represent the honest expression of their real views.

The writers of the letter were not called to give evidence,and so there is no evidence to prove that the letter was an honest expression of their views. The only evidence we have is that the respondent, King, said, with reference to the writers of the letter, ''we figured that was their opinion or their view or their observations''.

This is not a sufficient basis to enable the respondents to rely upon the defence of fair comment. There is no evidence to show that the material published, which the jury found to be defamatory, represented the honest opinion of the writers of the letter, or that of the officers of the newspaper which published it. In these circumstances the trial Judge was properly entitled to decide not to put the defence of fair comment to the jury.

RITCHIE, J.: — This is an appeal brought pursuant to leave granted by the Court of Appeal of Saskatchewan from a judgment of that Court setting aside a judgment rendered at trial by Mr. Justice MacPherson, sitting with a jury, and ordering a new trial of this libel action which was brought by the appellant, a practising lawyer and alderman of the Saskatoon City Council, as a result of a letter published in the correspondence column of The Star-Phoenix, a newspaper published in Saskatoon, of which the respondent Armadale Publishers Limited (hereinafter referred to as ''Armadale'') is the owner and publisher and the respondent Sterling King is the editor.

The facts giving rise to this litigation are accurately and fully stated in the dissenting judgment of Mr. Justice Brownridge in the Court of Appeal which is now conveniently reported at 79 D.L.R. (3d) 180 (hereinafter referred to as the ''report'') at p. 183 *et seq.* [also reported in [1977] 5 W.W.R. 155], but in order to fully understand the questions to which this appeal gives rise it will be necessary for me to summarize them briefly.

The alleged libel of which the appellant complains is contained in a letter written to The Star-Phoenix by two law students concerning a petition which was presented to the Saskatoon City Council and which was apparently drafted with the assistance of the appellant. The petition presented on behalf of fifty-four citizens was directed against the establishment of an Alcoholic Rehabilitation Centre in what was alleged to be a residential section of Saskatoon and the report of its presentation to Council as published in The Star-Phoenix referred in particular to Indians and Metis, whose use of the centre was alleged to be detrimental to the area. In this regard Mr. Yaworski, who presented the petition, was reported as saying that the establishment of the centre was going to turn the area into ''an Indian and Metis ghetto''.

The only express reference made to the appellant in this report was contained in the last paragraph reading:

> Alderman Morris Cherneskey told Council he did not think the zoning by-laws of the area envisioned 15 people living in one place, and until it is fully clarified it should not operate as an alcoholic rehabilitation centre when the citizens of the neighbourhood are concerned.

Having read this article, the two law students proceeded to write a letter to The Star-Phoenix which was published in a column headed "Editor's Letter Box", at the foot of which the following statement was printed:

> Letter writers are requested to provide addresses and phone numbers to allow checking for authenticity and accuracy. Letters must be signed — no pseudonyms will be published. *All are subject to editing for* length, *general interest,* grammar, style *and good taste*. Letters under 250 words are preferred.

(The italics are mine.)

In his charge to the jury, the learned trial Judge touched on this phase of the matter, saying:

> The Star-Phoenix, as the evidence indicates, has a right to decline to publish. They chose to publish and they, as they indicated, have a right to insist upon their right to edit. That's their privilege, naturally.

The letter complained of was itself headed "Racist Attitude", and it is reproduced in full at pp. 183-4 of the D.L.R. report, but the real sting of the language complained of is contained in the last three paragraphs which read:

> As a law student and an articling law student, we are appalled by the stance adopted by Alderman Cherneskey, himself a lawyer. We appreciate his sympathy with the concerns of certain members of the white community; however, we thoroughly disagree with his contention the centre should cease its operation until such time as the application of the relevant zoning bylaw has been clarified. We feel this situation is not unlike that of a man charged with a criminal offence. Such a man is deemed innocent until proven guilty.
>
> That Alderman Cherneskey should imply the onus is upon those operating the centre to establish their right to remain in the neighborhood until further clarification, is abhorrent to all concepts of the law. At the very least, it flies flagrantly in the face of the principles of natural justice. It is unbecoming a member of the legal profession to adopt such an approach.
>
> Although we do not reside in the particular neighborhood in question, we would have no objection whatsoever to such a centre operating in our neighborhood. We entirely support the project initiated by Clarence Trotchie and hope the racist resistance exhibited will be replaced by the support and encouragement which the project deserves.

In the course of his reasons for judgment in the Court of Appeal, Mr. Justice Brownridge points out that [at pp. 184-5]:

> Prior to the trial the defendants sought leave to join as third parties the two authors of the offending letter but this application was refused on appeal... *At the trial it was agreed by counsel that both letter writers were out of the jurisdiction and neither was called as a witness.*

(The italics are mine.)

By his statement of claim the appellant claimed damages for defamation of his personal character in relation to his profession and in his office as an alderman, and by para. 8 made the following general claim:

> The plaintiff further says that the said heading and letter as a whole would tend to lower the plaintiff in the estimation of right-thinking members of society generally and the citizens of Saskatoon in particular and that the words are defamatory.

By their joint defence the defendants pleaded:

8. In so far as the said letter, exclusive of the said heading, set out in paragraph 3 of the Statement of Claim consists of statements of fact they are true in substance and in fact and in so far as the said words consist of expressions of opinion, they are fair and bona fide comment made without malice upon the said facts which are a matter of public interest.

9. The publication of the said letter was an occasion of qualified privilege.

The plaintiff's reply is phrased in the following terms.

REPLY

In answer to the Defendant's Statement of Defence wherein they plead fair comment and qualified privilege, which is not admitted but denied, the Plaintiff says that the heading and the letter were published with express malice and joins issue.

The questions put to the jury by the learned trial Judge and their answers are as follows:

1. Would a reasonably minded reader imply that the words "racist attitude" in the heading over the letter refer to the plaintiff?
   Answer: "No".
2. If your answer to question number 1 is yes, then are those words defamatory?
   Answer: "Not applicable".
3. Would a reasonably minded reader imply that the words "racist resistance" in the last sentence of the letter refer to the plaintiff?
   Answer: "Yes".
4. If your answer to number 3 is yes, then are those words defamatory?
   Answer: "Yes".
5. Do the words in the fourth and fifth paragraphs of the letter directly or by innuendo defame the plaintiff as Alderman?
   Answer: "Yes".
6. Do the words is the fourth and fifth paragraphs of the letter directly or by innuendo defame the plaintiff as a lawyer?
   Answer: "Yes".
7. If you have answered yes to questions 2, 4, 5 and 6 or any one or more of them, what damages do you award the plaintiff?
   Answer: "$25,000. & costs".

I think it convenient at this stage to say that I am in agreement with Mr. Justice Brownridge, for the reasons which he has stated at p. 187 of the report, that the defence of qualified privilege is not available to the defendants in the present case. This view was adopted by Mr. Justice Bayda who observed at p. 196:

> I have read the reasons for judgment of my brother Brownridge, and respectfully agree that for reasons similar to those expressed by the Supreme Court of Canada, in *Douglas v. Tucker,* [1952] 1 D.L.R. 657, [1952] 1 S.C.R. 275; *Globe and Mail Ltd. v. Boland* (1960), 22 D.L.R. (2d) 277, [1960] S.C.R. 203, and *Jones v. Bennett* (1968), 2 D.L.R. (3d) 291, [1969] S.C.R. 277, 66 W.W.R. 419, the defence of qualified privilege is not available to the defendants in the present case. I also agree with the conclusions reached by him in respect of the other grounds of appeal, save the ground involving the plea of fair comment. In that regard, I have reached the opposite conclusion, namely, that the learned trial Judge should not have taken away from the jury the defence of fair comment.

Mr. Justice Brownridge found no merit in ''the other grounds of appeal'', and Mr. Justice Hall stated at the opening of his reasons for judgment [at p. 193]:

> The significant ground of appeal is that which alleges error by the trial Judge in refusing to put to the jury the defence of fair comment.

It is thus apparent that all members of the Court of Appeal were concerned only with the complaint that the trial Judge had erred in taking the defence of fair comment away from the jury and this was the main issue presented in this Court.

In the present case the plaintiff's (appellant's) plea that the words used in the letter are defamatory is couched in language which has long been accepted as giving rise, upon publication, to an action for defamation by the person to whom it refers. In this regard I refer to the following excerpt from *Gatley on Libel and Slander,* 7th ed. (1974), p. 5, para. 4, where he said:

> Any imputation which may tend ''to lower the plaintiff in the estimation of right-thinking members of society generally'' ... or ''to expose him to hatred, contempt or ridicule'' is defamatory of him.

This language was in large measure adopted by the trial Judge in addressing the jury.

Accordingly, as I agree with the trial Judge that the words used are capable of being construed as tending to lower the plaintiff in the estimation of right-thinking members of society generally, a *prima facie* cause of action arises, and in my view a plea of fair comment by way of defence does not of itself have the effect of saddling the plaintiff with the burden of proving that the comment was unfair. This plea constitutes a vital part of the case for the defendants and in my view the burden of proving each ingredient of the defence so pleaded should rest upon the party asserting it. One of these ingredients is that the person writing the material complained of must be shown to have had an honest belief in the opinions expressed and it will be seen that, in my view, the same considerations apply to each publisher of that material.

The question of burden of proof in such cases was considered by Lord Morris of Borth-y-Gest in *Jones v. Skelton,* [1963] 1 W.L.R. 1362 at p. 1379, where he said:

> ...if a defendant publishes of a plaintiff words which a jury might on the one hand hold to be fact or might on the other hand hold to be comment, and if a plaintiff does not accept that any of the words are true or does not accept that any of them are comment and if a defendant chooses to assert that some of the words are fair comment (made in good faith and without malice) on facts truly stated it must (assuming that the judge rules in regard to the public interest) be for the defendant to prove that which he asserts. If a plaintiff does not acknowledge that there are any words of comment and if the words are reasonably capable of being held by a jury to be statements of fact the plaintiff's overall burden of proving his case does not involve a duty of proving that comment (the existence of which he denies) is unfair.

In commenting on this statement, Mr. Justice Bayda observed at p. 200 of the report:

> It is plain from these remarks (which I adopt as a correct statement of the law) that where the pleadings, as in the present case, disclose that the plaintiff does not acknowledge the words complained of are comments or opinions, but the defendants, in their pleadings, raise the issue of comment and of fairness of the comment, the onus is on the defendants to prove fair comment. The normal principle that he who asserts, must prove, applies. In such event (assuming the words complained of are capable of being a comment and further assuming that condition (b) mentioned above is not applicable as is the situation here), it is for the

Judge to determine, as a matter of law, (1) whether there is any evidence of (a), that is, any evidence entitling the jury to find that the statements upon which the comments are based are true; and (2) whether there is any evidence of condition (c), *viz.*, the requirement of honesty. If he finds there is some evidence to support the finding that those conditions are met, he must place the defence of fair comment before the jury for their consideration (assuming that he has previously ruled that the element of public interest was proved). If, on the other hand, the trial Judge finds as a matter of law, that there is no evidence to support the presence of either of these two conditions, he should not put the defence of fair comment to the jury.

In cases where the essential ingredients of either the plea of "qualified privilege" or that of "fair comment have been established by the defence, then if it can be proved that the statements complained of were made or written maliciously, the plea must fail; but in my view no burden lies upon the complainant to prove malice unless and until either plea has been shown to be supported by the evidence.

Here the plea of "express malice" was added midway through the evidence called on behalf of the plaintiff (appellant) and it is, in my view, important to appreciate that this allegation forms no part of the main case but is inserted entirely by way of answer to the respondents' claim of "qualified privilege" and "fair comment". As I have indicated, the defence of qualified privilege is not available to the defendants, and the question of malice could only arise in the present case if there were some evidence to indicate that the comment complained of was otherwise fair, and this cannot be said unless the opinions expressed are honestly held.

As I have already observed, it is an essential ingredient to the defence of fair comment that it must be the honest expression of the writer's opinion and in this regard I refer to the following statement made by Lord Porter in *Turner (orse. Robertson) v. Metro-Goldwyn-Mayer Pictures, Ltd.*, [1950] 1 All E.R. 449 at pp. 462-3, where he said, commenting on the charge to the jury in that case where the defence was qualified privilege:

> Its early words on this part of the case express exactly what the authorities convey. "Fair comment" (in effect the learned judge says) "has to be an honest expression of the real opinion of the defendants when they wrote it..." "Did they honestly and really think that she" (the appellant) "was completely out of touch with the tastes and entertainment requirements of the picture-going millions who are also radio listeners and that her criticisms are on the whole unnecessarily harmful to the film industry? Did they honestly hold that opinion and really believe it? If they did — then they were not abusing the occasion." Such a direction is, I think, entirely accurate and could not be attacked, and similar language is to be found in other parts of the summing-up. On the other hand, language of this kind is frequently interspersed with words which suggest that the criterion is whether fairminded men could hold that view. Let me take one example only. It runs:
>
> > "First of all... do you think that a fair-minded man capable of impartial judgment of the plaintiff's [appellant's] talks... could come to that conclusion. Was there anything in them or in her conduct which would lead a fair man honestly to entertain the opinion that the defendants expressed in this letter?"
>
> Similar observations appear throughout the summing-up and, undoubtedly, if they were found alone there would have been clear misdirection. It is said, however, in the first place, that, in his cross-examination and address, leading counsel for the respondents used the phrase and accepted the burden that fair-mindedness was required. I do not think that the record justifies this allegation, but if it did I should think it immaterial. Secondly, it is argued with more force that, when the summing-up is regarded as a whole, a jury would not be misled, but would rightly apprehend that honesty, not reasonableness, was the state of mind required.

> My Lords, I cannot take this view. I have read the summing-up as a whole more than once and I think a jury might well have come to the conclusion that both honesty and reasonableness were necessary and that the defendants were unreasonable and therefore malicious. It is, I think, difficult for the uninstructed mind to guard against such a misconception, and to my mind the clearest direction is necessary to the effect that irrationality, stupidity or obstinacy do not constitute malice, though in an extreme case there may be some evidence of it. The defendant, indeed, must honestly hold the opinion he expresses but no more is required of him.

In the same case Lord Oaksey stated at p. 475:

> In the absence of any evidence that the respondents did not honestly hold the opinions expressed in their letter, I see no grounds on which they could be held to have exceeded the limits of fair comment.

After having heard lengthy argument as to whether or not this defence should be left to the jury in the present case, the trial Judge made the following ruling:

> I shall not try to decide whether if the opinion of the writers of the letter is honest and sincere that this fact absolves the publisher or the editor of the paper from a similar opinion. In the present trial that is not necessary because here there is no evidence that the offending words, if they are in fact defamatory of the plaintiff, which is a matter for the jury — there is no evidence that those words express the honest opinion of anyone, either the writers of the letter or of anyone on the editorial staff of The Star-Phoenix or its publisher. The evidence seems to be that the defendants had a contrary opinion or none at all. Without such honest opinion I cannot tell the jury that the defence of fair comment is available to the defendant.

Honesty of belief has been characterized by Lord Denning, M.R., in *Slim et al. v. Daily Telegraph, Ltd. et al.*, [1968] 1 All E.R. 497 at p. 503, as "the cardinal test" of the defence of fair comment, and in the context of the present case this must mean honesty of belief in the opinions expressed in the letter complained of.

It has long been established that the state of mind of the publisher of the alleged libel is directly in issue where there is a plea of fair comment. This is illustrated in the case of *Plymouth Mutual Co-operative & Industrial Society, Ltd. v. Traders' Publishing Ass'n, Ltd.*, [1906] 1 K.B. 403, where the question was whether an interrogatory addressed to the state of mind of the defendant, who had pleaded fair comment, was admissible and, after referring to the case of *White & Co. v. Credit Reform Ass'n & Credit Index, Ltd.* [1905] 1 K.B. 653, Vaughan Williams, L.J., said, at pp. 413-4:

> It seems to me that that case shews that an interrogatory of this kind is just as relevant and admissible in a case where the defence is fair comment as in one where it is privilege. In either case the question raised is really as to the state of mind of the defendant when he published the alleged libel, the question being in the one case whether he published it in the spirit of malice, in the other whether he published it in the spirit of unfairness. In either case I think such an interrogatory as the one now in question is admissible.

And later at p. 418 of the same report, Fletcher Moulton, L.J., said:

> ...I am clear that, both in cases in which the defence of privilege and in those in which the defence of fair comment is set up, the state of mind of the defendant when he published the alleged libel is a matter directly in issue...

Perhaps the most singular feature of the present case is that the state of mind of the defendants is established by their own evidence to the effect that they did not honestly hold the opinions expressed in the letter. This is illustrated by the following excerpt from the evidence of the defendants in relation to the comments complained of. Mr. R. Struthers, who was the executive vice-president of the defendant Armadale, stated in the course of cross-examination as follows:

> Q. But of course there is no question but what you do not believe Morris Cherneskey to be a racist?
> A. No, I do not.
> Q. You do not believe Morris Cherneskey to be a person with a racist attitude?
> A. I do not believe him to be so.
> Q. And in any capacity, as a lawyer, you don't believe him to be a lawyer with a racist attitude?
> A. No.
> Q. Or an alderman with a racist attitude?
> A. No.

The same witness had given the same answers when speaking as the officer examined for discovery on behalf of the defendant Armadale.

The second defendant, Sterling King, who was the editor of The Star-Phoenix, stated that he had no opinion as to the approach of Cherneskey in relation to the white community in the area in question but it was his honest opinion that Cherneskey had a reputation for honesty and integrity as a lawyer and alderman.

It will be remembered that Mr. Justice Bayda adopted the passage from the reasons for judgment of Lord Morris of Borth-y-Gest in *Jones v. Skelton,* which I have already quoted, and the reasons for judgment of Mr. Justice Brownridge and Mr. Justice Bayda both satisfy me that, if the writers of the letter here in question had been the defendants in this action and had entered a plea of fair comment, both these Judges would have found that the burden of proving honest belief in the opinions expressed rested upon the defence.

Mr. Justice Bayda, however, allowed this appeal on the ground that a newspaper, in republishing defamatory opinions which do not reflect its honest opinion, is nevertheless entitled to rely on the defence of fair comment on the ground that it honestly believed that those who wrote the letter were honestly expressing their true views. In this regard reliance is placed on the case of *Lyon et al. v. Daily Telegraph, Ltd.,* [1943] 2 All E.R. 316. In that case the author, who had used a *nom de plume* and given a fictitious address, was never discovered and the newspaper therefore had no means of determining whether the views expressed were honestly held by the writer or not, but the defence of fair comment was upheld in the Court of Appeal where Scott, L.J., said at p. 318:

> There is no question but that the comment contained in the letter represented the honest opinion of the "Daily Telegraph"; and at the trial no doubt was cast upon the complete belief of the newspaper that they were publishing a letter in which the writer was making a fair comment on a matter of public interest.

The obvious distinction between that case and the present one is that the letter complained of here did not express the honest opinion of The Star-Phoenix, and there is no evidence that the views therein expressed were honestly held by the writers, but Scott, L.J., later in the same judgment, said at p. 319:

> Although there is no direct authority, I think that the question of law is really implicit in the well-established rule that the publishers of a newspaper, when defendants in an action

for libel, cannot, on the issue of fair comment, be required to disclose the source of their information. If the innocent state of mind of the writer of a letter published in the newspaper was a relevant fact, which had to be proved by him before his plea of fair comment could be established, it would go far towards justifying counsel's argument; but the very existence of the exceptional rule about interogatories and discovery in the case of newspaper defendants seems to me to presuppose a rule of law that, at least in the absence of special circumstances (on the possibility of which I express no opinion), there is no such presumption or onus, and that fairness of the comment contained in the newspaper's correspondence columns must be judged by its tenor, subject only to the proviso that the statements of fact upon which the comment is based are not untrue.

This latter passage is primarily concerned with the rule that the publishers of a newspaper cannot be required to disclose their source of information, but the language employed in the last sentence might be construed as meaning that the fairness of the letter complained of is to be judged by its tenor, which I construe as a suggestion that the language used in correspondence columns of a newspaper is to be judged according to whether there is anything in the letter in question which would lead a fair man honestly to share the opinion which the language conveyed. It is to be remembered that the judgment of the Court of Appeal in the *Lyon* case was rendered some seven years before the House of Lords decided the case of *Turner, supra,* and I do not think there is anything in the views expressed by Scott, L.J., which can be taken as fixing any standard except honesty as the touchstone of the defence of fair comment. It is to be noted also that Scott, L.J., limited his opinion to cases where there was "an absence of special circumstances" as to which he expressed no opinion. The opinion expressed, therefore, cannot be treated as including the special circumstances of the publisher and editor of the newspaper having stated affirmatively that the letter does not express their honest opinion.

Mr. Justice Bayda, however, expressed the following opinion [at p. 201]:

Where, however, the defendant is a publisher of the impugned words and in particular is a newspaper which publishes in its letters-to-the-editor column a letter capable of being defamatory, what is the acceptable standard? It is indisputable that if such a newspaper honestly holds the opinions expressed in the impugned writing, and was not actuated by malice then as in the case of the writer, condition (c) [honesty] would be satisfied (*Slim v. Daily Telegraph, Ltd., supra; Lyon and Lyon v. Daily Telegraph, Ltd. [supra]*. But is a different (I hesitate to say "lower") standard acceptable? Suppose the newspaper cannot be said to hold the opinions expressed in the impugned writing but honestly believes that they represent the real opinions of the writer (in other words, an honest belief that they were publishing a letter in which the writer was making a fair comment upon a matter of public interest) and, in addition, is not actuated by malice in publishing the letter, is that an acceptable state of mind for a plea of fair comment to succeed? I have concluded that it is.

This conclusion which lies at the very heart of this case, is based on an *obiter dictum* of Lord Denning, M.R., in the case of *Slim v. Daily Telegraph, supra,* where, as in the *Lyon* case, it was found that the newspaper honestly held the views expressed, and Lord Denning observed at p. 503:

...the right of fair comment is one of the essential elements which go to make up our freedom of speech. We must ever maintain this right intact. It must not be whittled down by legal refinements. When a citizen is troubled by things going wrong, he should be free to "write to the newspaper": and the newspaper should be free to publish his letter. It is often the only way to get things put right. The matter must, of course, be one of public interest. The writer

> must get his facts right: and he must honestly state his real opinion. But that being done, both he and the newspaper should be clear of any liability. They should not be deterred by fear of libel actions.

In the penultimate paragraph of the same judgment, Lord Denning stated:

> On the face of these letters, I think that the comments made by Mr. Herbert and the Daily Telegraph were fair comments on a matter of public interest. *They* honestly said what *they* thought.

(The italics are mine.)

It must be apparent, as it seems to me, that the sentence last above quoted refers to the honesty of both the writer and the newspaper so that this case, in my opinion, affords no authority for the proposition that comments published in a newspaper need not be honest expressions of the newspaper's opinion in order to support a defence of fair comment so long as the newspaper can show its belief that the comments were an honest expression of the real opinion of the writer.

If the publication of the libel had been confined to the letter and the writers had been sued or, alternately, if it had originated with the newspaper and its publisher, it would in either case have been necessary to show honest belief in order to sustain the defence of fair comment. The same considerations would thus in my opinion apply to the newspaper and the writers.

In my opinion each publisher in relying on the defence of fair comment is in exactly the same position as the original writer. In this latter regard, I refer to the opinion delivered by Lord Denning in the Privy Council in *"Truth" (N.Z.) Ltd. v. Holloway,* [1960] 1 W.L.R. 997, where a newspaper published an article calling for an inquiry concerning import licences, in which it stated that a Mr. Judd had told a man who was inquiring about import licences to "See Phil and Phil would fix it". The newspaper's comment on this was: "By Phil his caller understood him to mean the Honourable Philip North Holloway, the Minister of Industry and Commerce." Holloway brought an action for libel against the newspaper and in commenting on the trial Judge's charge to the jury, Lord Denning had this to say at pp. 1002-3:

> The words actually used by the judge to the jury were these: "If you accept that those words were spoken by Judd, it is not a defence at all that a statement that might be defamatory is put forward by way of report only. It does not help the defendant that the way that it is put is that Judd said 'See Phil and Phil would fix it.' The case is properly to be dealt with as if the defendant itself said 'See Phil and Phil and Phil would fix it.'"
>
> Their Lordships see nothing wrong in this direction. It is nothing more nor less than a statement of settled law put cogently to the jury. Gatley opens his chapter on Republication and Repetition with the quotation: "Every publication of a libel is a new libel, and each publisher is answerable for his act to the same extent as if the calumny originated with him," see Gatley on Libel and Slander, 4th ed., p. 106. This case is a good instance of the justice of this rule. If Judd did use the words attributed to him, it might be a slander by Judd of Mr. Holloway in the way of his office as a Minister of the Crown. But if the words had not been repeated by the newspaper, the damage done by Judd would be as nothing compared to the damage done by this newspaper when it repeated it. It broadcast the statement to the people at large: and it made it worse by making it one of the grounds on which it called for an inquiry, for thereby it suggested that some credence was to be given to it.

It appears to me to follow from this that where, as here, there is no evidence as to the honest belief of the writers of the letter, and the newspaper and its publisher have disavowed any such belief on their part, the defence of fair comment cannot be sustained.

In this regard the language employed by Lord Shaw in *Arnold v. The King-Emperor* (1914), 83 L.J.P.C. 299 at p. 300, is appropriate. He there said:

> Their Lordships regret to find that there appeared on the one side of this case the time-worn fallacy that some kind of privilege attaches to the profession of the Press as distinguished from the members of the public. The freedom of the journalist is an ordinary part of the freedom of the subject, and to whatever lengths the subject in general may go, so also may the journalist, but, apart from statute law, his privilege is no other and no higher. The responsibilities which attach to his power in the dissemination of printed matter may, and in the case of a conscientious journalist do, make him more careful; but the range of his assertions, his criticisms, or his comments is as wide as, and no wider than, that of any other subject. No privilege attaches to his position.

These views were adopted in this Court in *Globe and Mail Ltd. v. Boland* (1960), 22 D.L.R. (2d) 277 at p. 281, [1960] S.C.R. 203 at p. 208.

These authorities satisfy me that the newspaper and its editor cannot sustain a defence of fair comment when it has been proved that the words used in the letter are not an honest expression of their opinion and there is no evidence as to the honest belief of the writers. In view of this finding, I do not consider it necessary to deal with the other submissions made on behalf of the appellant.

I cannot leave this question without reference to the reasons for judgment of Mr. Justice Hall wherein he expressed the view, which was not shared by the two other Judges sitting in the appeal, that, where the defence of fair comment is pleaded the burden of disproving "honesty of belief" lies upon the plaintiff. In so deciding Mr. Justice Hall equates lack of "honest belief" with "malice", saying at p. 194 of the report:

> It is apparent that saying that there must be an honest belief is the same as saying that the comment cannot be made maliciously. We are, therefore, in the instant case really dealing with the reply of malice.

This statement appears to me to overlook the distinction between the defence of "privilege", which can only be defeated by proof of malice and the defence of "fair comment", which presupposes honest belief on the part of the author or publisher. This distinction is recognized in the case of *Plymouth Mutual Cooperative & Industrial Society v. Trader's Publishing Ass'n, supra*. Speaking of the different considerations affecting the defence of "privilege" on the one hand and "fair comment" on the other, Vaughan Williams, L.J., said at pp. 413-4:

> In either case the question raised is really as to the state of mind of the defendant when he published the alleged libel, the question being in the one case whether he published it in the spirit of *malice*, in the other whether he published it in the spirit of *unfairness*.

(The italics are mine.) As honesty of belief is an essential component of the defence of fair comment, that defence involves at least some evidence that the material complained of was published in a spirit of fairness.

I cannot accept the proposition apparently adopted by Hall, J.A., that where, as here, the words are capable of a defamatory meaning they are presumed to give expression to an opinion honestly held until the contrary is shown.

Mr. Justice Hall appears to find some support for his views in the decision of Lord Denning, M.R., in *Egger v. Viscount Chelmsford et al.*, [1965] 1 Q.B. 248 at p. 265, from which I extract the following excerpt.

> If the plaintiff seeks to rely on malice to aggravate damages, or to rebut a defence of qualified privilege, or to cause a comment, otherwise fair, to become unfair, then he must prove malice...

I read this statement as meaning that, where the defendant has shown that the comment is ''otherwise fair'', the burden rests upon the plaintiff to prove malice. Here, as I have said, the defence of ''qualified privilege'' is not available to the defendants and the defence of fair comment can only be sustained if the comment made is ''otherwise fair''.

In the present case, as I have said, there is no allegation of malice in the statement of claim, but if there had been any evidence to sustain a plea of fair comment, it would have been for the jury to say whether malice had been established.

On the pleadings here it was for the Judge to determine whether the words used were capable of a defamatory meaning and for the jury to decide whether they were in fact defamatory. The question of whether they constituted fair comment would also be for the jury if there were any evidence whatever to support it; but in the absence of such evidence, and in face of the defendants' evidence as to lack of honest belief, no question of malice arises.

It will have been seen, however, that in the absence of any proof of the honest belief of the writers, and having regard to the denial of honest belief by the defendants themselves, the defence of fair comment cannot, in my view, prevail.

This does not mean that freedom of the press to publish its views is in any way affected, nor does it mean that a newspaper cannot publish letters expressing views with which it may strongly disagree. Moreover, nothing that is here said should be construed as meaning that a newspaper is in any way restricted in publishing two diametrically opposite views of the opinion and conduct of a public figure. On the contrary, I adopt as descriptive of the conclusion which I have reached, the language used by Brownridge, J.A., in the following excerpt from his reasons for judgment in the Court of Appeal, where he said at p. 192 of the report:

> What it does mean is that a newspaper cannot publish a *libellous* letter and then disclaim any responsibility by saying that it was published as fair comment on a matter of public interest but it does not represent the honest opinion of the newspaper.

For all these reasons I would allow this appeal and restore the judgment at trial. The appellant is entitled to his costs throughout.

5.2.3.1.2.10 Robert Martin, ''Libel and Letters to the Editor'', (1983) *Queen's Law Journal* 188

COMMENT ON THE CHERNESKEY DECISION

A. *Legal Doctrine*

Cherneskey is an illustration of the notion that hard cases make bad law. The more one studies the opinions, the more paradoxical they appear. On its face the dissenting judgment of Dickson, J. appears to uphold freedom of speech. Examined more carefully, its implications are disturbing. Conversely, the majority judgment of Ritchie, J., while clearly unfortunate as between the parties actually before the court, is based on principles which are conducive, in their broad application, to the protection of freedom of speech.

The doctrinal question at issue was the content of the fair comment defence. For Ritchie, J. the essence of fair comment was honest belief. If, assuming the other requirements noted above had been met, the opinions in question constituted an expression of the defendant's honest belief, then the defence of fair comment was established. Where Ritchie, J. got into serious trouble was in his application of this principle to the facts of the case. It was his view that since these defendants did not honestly hold the opinions in question they could not raise fair comment. This is an absurd conclusion and one which, as will be pointed out below, could easily have been avoided.

Dickson, J. sought to escape the doctrinal shoal on which Ritchie, J. foundered. Mr. Justice Dickson argued, basing his views largely on those put forward by the English writers Duncan and Neill in their treatise on defamation, that a two stage analysis must be adopted in determining whether a comment is fair. First, one must apply an *objective* standard: "is the comment one that an honest, albeit prejudiced, person might make in the circumstances?" If the answer to this question is no, the comment is not fair. If the answer is yes, a further, *subjective* question may arise. The plaintiff may seek to show that the defendant was "actuated by malice". The presence of malice will render the comment unfair. Applying this analysis, Dickson, J. was able to conclude that Armadale Publishers could properly raise the defence of fair comment.

Now the approach described is effective to avoid the difficulty that led the majority of the Supreme Court of Canada to find for Cherneskey. All the commentators seem to agree that the result reached by Dickson, J. would have been more desirable and just. Unfortunately, Dickson, J.'s analysis has some unpleasant ramifications. Since the English decision of *Merivale* v. *Carson* it has been accepted that notions of reasonableness have no place in the application of fair comment. That is, a defendant is not required, in order to discharge the onus of satisfying the court that a comment is fair, to prove that it is reasonable. To put it as simply as possible, a jury does not have to agree with a comment in order to find that it is fair.

Both the Faulks Committee in the U.K. and the Committee on Defamation in New Zealand anticipated the issue in *Cherneskey*. They each recommended that when the opinion in question was the opinion of some person other than the defendant, fair comment might be relied upon if the defendant honestly believed that the opinion was genuinely held by the other person. Had this reasoning been followed in *Cherneskey,* the defendants would have succeeded by satisfying the court that they believed the writers of the letter were expressing their honest opinion. Such an approach both preserves the essence of the defence of fair comment and is a logical extension of it.

The approach I have advocated has so far been put forward only in where the plaintiff has sought to use evidence that one co-defendant was actuated by malice in order to negative the defences of fair comment or qualified privilege raised by another co-defendant. It is submitted that there is no objection in principle to applying this analysis to the facts of *Cherneskey*.

In sum, good sense and a concern for freedom of speech both argue against the result reached in *Cherneskey*. Dickson, J. sought to avoid this result, but in doing so suggested that the standard to be used in determining whether a comment was fair might be an objective one. This might be taken as suggesting a criterion of reasonableness, a development which is exceedingly undesirable. A better approach would have been to accept the existing basis of fair comment and ask: ''did the defendants honestly believe that the two law students were stating their honest opinion?'' This analysis also precludes, as will be evident below, many of the unfortunate consequences of the various statutory responses to *Cherneskey*.

B. Effect on Newspapers

The Court's application of the fair comment defence was highly technical and highly abstract. It was also based on a fundamental misunderstanding of the way newspapers work. Apart from the editorial pages, a newspaper is not, and should not be, a collection of the opinions of its editor and publisher. And even if a newsroom did exhibit an unnaturally high degree of internal control and centralization, it would still print wire stories, syndicated columns, and material written by freelancers. The monolithic notion of the organization of Canadian newspapers which is implicit in the Supreme Court's decision in *Cherneskey* does not accord with reality. Nonetheless, it was the decision of the Supreme Court of Canada and must, until amended or overruled by competent legislation, be followed in the courts of the common law provinces.

There were many in the newspaper industry who regarded the decision as unsatisfactory and, indeed, as dangerous to freedom of the press. The obvious fear was that newspapers would run a risk in printing letters to the editor containing opinions with which editors or publishers did not agree. As a result, newspapers would become more cautious about printing letters to the editor which expressed strong opinions. And this was precisely what happened. A survey conducted by the Ontario Press Council in 1979 revealed that, of 28 Ontario daily newspapers contacted, 19 had been influenced in the way they handled letters to the editor by the *Cherneskey* decision. Without repeating the findings of the survey, the most common response was that newspapers had become more cautious in dealing with letters.

While the Supreme Court of Canada's decision constituted a binding precedent with respect to courts in the nine common law provinces, the rule which had been enunciated in *Cherneskey* could only be altered by provincial legislation. That is, the jurisdiction to legislate with respect to defamation rests exclusively with the provinces. The paradox, then, is that while the application of the Supreme Court's ruling was national, that ruling could only be dispensed with on a province by province basis.

Critical views about the *Cherneskey* decision were expressed in the Ottawa *Citizen*, the *Financial Post* and the *Globe and Mail*. These newspapers called for legislative action. The Ontario Press Council and the Attorneys-General of Ontario and Saskatchewan advocated reform. The Uniform Law Conference discussed the matter at its meeting in Saskatoon in August, 1979. In the result, four provinces — Alberta, Manitoba, New Brunswick, Ontario — and the two territories amended their defamation statutes in 1980.

THE CHERNESKEY AMENDMENTS

Generally, all the amendments go far beyond what would have been necessary to overcome the precise problem created by the *Cherneskey* decision. First, none of the amendments confines itself to letters to the editor. Each addresses itself to ''opinion'', which means, presumably, all opinion whether expressed in a letter or in any other form. Secondly, the amendments are not restricted to newspapers and extend to any opinion which is "published". Finally, as will be argued in more detail below, the amendments are, assuming that their original purpose was to overcome the *Cherneskey* decision, drafted unnecessarily broadly. They may well amount, under the right circumstances, to licences to defame.

Each of the amendments will be commented on below.

A. *Manitoba, Yukon Territory, and the Northwest Territories*

On 29 July 1980 Manitoba adopted a new s.9.1 of its Defamation Act.

> 9.1(1) Where the defendant published allegedly defamatory matter that is an opinion expressed by another person, a defence of fair comment shall not fail for the reason only that the defendant did not hold the opinion, if
> (a) the defendant did not know that the person expressing the opinion did not hold the opinion; and
> (b) a person could honestly hold the opinion.
> (2) For the purpose of this section, the defendant is not under a duty to inquire into whether the person expressing the opinion holds the opinion.

The form of words is that adopted by the Uniform Law Conference of Canada in 1979. Identical wording was adopted in the Yukon and the Northwest Territories. The wording appeared also in the relevant clause of a bill introduced in the Saskatchewan legislature in 1980, but not enacted.

The general effect of the amendment is that an editor or publisher who is the defendant in a libel action is not precluded from raising the defence of fair comment with respect to opinions expressed by other people in letters to the editor (or in any other form) with which he does not agree. The section is only to apply to opinions which "a person could honestly hold". For reasons already suggested, this form of words, clearly derived, via Dickson, J. in *Cherneskey,* from Duncan and Neill, is undesirable. Either it suggests a standard of reasonableness in fair comment, or it is meaningless. That is, if the words do not ask a court to objectively assess the content of an opinion, they ask it to determine if it is merely an opinion which someone might hold. Given the apparently limitless range of human thought, it is difficult to imagine an opinion which someone might not subscribe to. The defendant is further protected by subsection (2) which absolves him from any duty of enquiring whether people who write letters to the editor actually believe in the opinions they are expressing. Subsection (1)(a) is confusing. Read literally, it appears to require that in order for a defendant to take advantage of the section he must show that he did *not* know that the writer of a letter to the editor did *not* hold the opinion expressed in the letter. It would follow logically that, if the defendant *did* know that the writer of a letter *did* hold the opinion expressed in the letter, he would not be able to rely on the section. Interpreted in this fashion, the amendment would fail to achieve its ostensible purpose of avoiding the application of the *Cherneskey* rule. It would appear that the point of the subsection is to prevent the defence being raised when the defendant *did* know that the letter writer *did not* hold the opinion. But this is unnecessary. Such a fact situation would quite properly be regarded by any court as evidence of malice, thus negativing the defence of fair comment. The fact that such a convoluted form of words was used to make a point that should be obvious only adds to the general impression that the amendment was not carefully thought out.

B. New Brunswick

New Brunswick changed its law on 4 July 1980. The new section 8.1 of its Defamation Act is, with one slight variation, identical to s.9.1 of the Manitoba Act quoted above. The variation is an addition to subsection (1).

> 8.1(1)(c) The person expressing the opinion was identified in the publication.

This section simply provides that a defendant may not use the section to make out a defence of fair comment with respect to an anonymous letter to the editor. It is not clear what would happen if a letter were published under a pseudonym.

C. Alberta

Alberta and Ontario adopted different approaches, each derived from a wording which they suggested to the Uniform Law Conference, but which was rejected by that body. The Alberta statute, which became law on 22 May 1980, amended that province's Defamation Act by adding a new s.9.1.

> 9.1(1) If a defendant published an opinion expressed by another person, other than an employee or agent of the defendant, that is alleged to be defamatory, a defence of fair comment shall not fail by reason only that the defendant did not hold that opinion.
>
> (2) Notwithstanding subsection (1), the defence of fair comment is not available to a defendant if it is proved that he acted maliciously in making the publication.

Alberta's amendment is the most carefully drafted of the six. The phrase "other than an employee or agent of the defendant" confronts a real problem that could arise with respect to the Manitoba, Ontario, New Brunswick, and territories' amendments if those amendments were to be interpreted literally by a court. Assume that a newspaper publishes an ostensibly defamatory opinion *not* in a letter to the editor but, for example, in a news story. Assume further that the story in question is written by a reporter on the staff of the newspaper and has a by-line that indicates this. If the person defamed brings an action against only the corporation which publishes the newspaper and does not join the writer of the story as a co-defendant, the Manitoba, New Brunswick, Ontario, and territories' amendments would afford a very broad defence. The corporate defendant would only need show that the opinion in question was that of another person and that it was an opinion which some person could hold. It would not then matter whether the actual writer of the story held the opinion expressed or not.

Subsection (2) simply makes clear that, as has been the position under common law, evidence of malice can be used to negative the defence of fair comment. There is no reason to imagine that a court would interpret the Manitoba, New Brunswick, Ontario or territorial amendments differently from this.

D. Ontario

Ontario amended its Libel and Slander Act on 19 June 1980 by the addition of a new section 25.

> 25. Where the defendant published defamatory matter that is an opinion expressed by another person, a defence of fair comment by the defendant shall not fail for the reason only that the defendant or the person who expressed the opinion, or both, did not hold the opinion, if a person could honestly hold the opinion.

For the same general reasons as indicated with respect to the other amendments, the Ontario amendment is a substantial boon to media defendants. It has, as do all the amendments, a potential application which goes far beyond letters to the editor. Even if we confine ourselves to letters to the editor, the rule embodied in the Ontario amendment is a substantial and, it is suggested, an undesirable departure from principle. It says that a newspaper can successfully raise the defence of fair comment with respect to an opinion contained in a letter to the editor even if neither the publisher, editor, nor the writer of the letter honestly believes in the opinion. This is unnecessary.

The flaw in all the amendments is that they proceed from an acceptance of Mr. Justice Dickson's analysis. A much simpler form of words would have achieved the objective of avoiding the result in *Cherneskey* and yet not at the same time have created so many new and unnecessary difficulties:

> Where the defendant published allegedly defamatory matter that is an opinion expressed by another person, a defence of fair comment shall not fail for the reason only that the defendant did not hold the opinion if the defendant honestly believed that the person expressing the opinion did hold the opinion.
>
> Note: See also s.11 of the Newfoundland Defamation Act, S.N. 1983, c.63

5.2.3.1.2.11 *Masters* v. *Fox* (1978), 85 D.L.R. (3d) 64, (B.C.S.C.)

MacFarlane, J.: — The plaintiffs, who were unsuccessful candidates in a municipal election, claim damages for an alleged libel upon them during the course of the election campaign.

The plaintiffs plead, in paras. 6-13 inclusive of the statement of claim, as follows:

6. The Plaintiffs are and were members of Community Planning Action Committee, which is a community group devoted to Civic and Regional Planning and which has printed and published pamphlets advocating Civic and Regional Planning.
7. The Plaintiffs, as Community Planning Action Committee members, were electoral candidates for the office of civic alderman for the Municipality of Courtenay in the Province of British Columbia, in an election held on the 20th day of November, A.D. 1976.
8. The Plaintiff, Richard Von Fuchs, has held a number of employments, including a position with the British Columbia Civil Liberties Association.
9. The Plaintiff, Ruth Masters, is unmarried, an environmentalist, and has made her concerns for the environment known both in the newspaper and in public meetings.
10. On or about the 12th day of November, A.D. 1976, the Defendants, William Mathis, as editor of the Forum section of the *Comox District Free Press,* and the Defendant, E. W. Bickle Ltd., as owner and publisher of the *Comox District Free Press,* published in the *Comox District Free Press* and circulated to members of the general public of the Comox Valley and various other parts of Vancouver Island, in the Province of British Columbia, a statement of the Defendant, A. E. Fox, which read:

    ''Election time is here again with some of the same old types trying to get in on the action. During the past year the Communist Party Action Committee has managed to belch a lot of bile and in the process make every effort to con the people into believing they are concerned with local issues and the orderly progress of the community — when in point of fact they are much more interested in spreading their particular brand of political venom — all of it under the guise of community interest (witness Oct. 14, at the Civic Centre).

"I would not think that the voter has much of a problem in selecting a suitable and worthwhile candidate. With a full time career lay about and an old maid would appear (at a glance) to be an excellent recipe for a loser — but in spite of all some of these loud mouth windbags are going to tell and show everyone how to be winners and whatever the problem — you name it and they will cure it. Not one of them could run a peanut stand without a grant or subsidy and I would even suggest that one of them should be careful that the natural vegetation doesn't slowly take over and immobilize all activity.

"It would be unfortunate if the voter was misled by some of their published rubbish which might permit (by accident) a few to get their grubby bands onto the tail end of a few more tax dollars."

11. This statement of the Defendant, A. E. Fox, referred to above was captioned, either at the request of the aforesaid Defendant, or by the Defendant, William Mathis, "It's Election Time."
12. The said statements contained in paragraph 10 are defamatory in their natural and ordinary meaning and in the innuendoes contained therein in that they mean and were understood to mean the following:
    (a) that the Plaintiffs as members of the Community Planning Action Committee are members of the Communist Party.
    (b) that the Plaintiffs as Community Planning Action Committee's electoral candidates for civic aldermen for the Municipality of Courtenay in the Province of British Columbia are members of the Communist Party.
    (c) that the Plaintiffs as members of Community Planning Action Committee were attempting to deceive the electors of Courtenay in the Province of British Columbia and the public, generally, and, particularly, by using issues of community interest as a means of popularizing the theories and plans of the Communist Party.
    (d) that the Plaintiffs as Community Planning Action Committee's aldermanic candidates for civic aldermen for the Municipality of Courtenay in the Province of British Columbia were attempting to deceive the electors of Courtenay in the Province of British Columbia, and the public, generally and particularly, by using issues of community interest as a means of popularizing the theories and plans of the Communist Party.
    (e) that the Plaintiffs were not worthwhile or suitable candidates due to their inability to support themselves or manage financial affairs.
    (f) that the Plaintiff, Richard Von Fuchs, did not have employment or had not had employment and was accordingly shiftless, lazy, and a loser and, therefore, unable to suitably manage civic affairs if elected.
    (g) that the Plaintiff, Ruth J. Masters, was unmarried and a loser and accordingly was unable to manage financial affairs or manage other people's affairs, and therefore, was not suitable for public office.
    (h) that the Plaintiff, Ruth J. Masters, was senile and/or as an environmentalist was likely to be immobilized by the environment and/or her environmental concerns.
    (i) that the Plaintiffs' election material was misleading the public in order that the Plaintiffs could misappropriate the public's money if elected.
    (j) that the Plaintiffs were guilty of improper and/or illegal and/or criminal use of the public's money.
13. The statements were false and malicious at the time of their being made and remain wholly false in substance and in fact and are defamatory and concerning the Plaintiffs.

The defendants deny the allegations of fact contained in paras. 6-9 inclusive, and in paras. 12-13, but are silent as to paras. 10 and 11. The defendants plead that the words complained of were not published of and concerning the plaintiffs, were not defamatory of the plaintiffs, and raise a defence of fair comment as follows:

In further answer to the whole of the Statement of Claim these Defendants say that the words complained of are expressions of opinion and are fair comment made in good faith and without malice on a matter of public interest, namely the conduct of an election for public office in the community and the qualifications of the candidates therein.

The plaintiffs sought and obtained particulars of facts upon which the opinion referred to in the foregoing paragraph of the statement of defence is based, which are as follows:

(a) that it was election time;
(b) that the Plaintiffs were running for office;
(c) that the Community Planning Action Committee had at least one card carrying Communist on its executive committee, and that this person had not remained silent as to his political views during the time he was on the executive of the Community Planning Action Committee;
(d) that the Plaintiffs were members of the Community Planning Action Committee and had both expressed left wing views;
(e) that the Plaintiff Von Fuchs was at times a ''social democrat'', at times a member of the New Democratic Party, and was an American who had left the United States for political reasons and was a draft dodger;
(f) that the Plaintiff Von Fuchs, in letters to the editor and in political speeches had expressed views opposed to the free enterprise system, or some aspects thereof;
(g) that the Plaintiff Von Fuchs frequently changed his employment and was unemployed from time to time;
(h) that the Plaintiff Masters is 57 years of age and a spinster;
(i) that the Plaintiff Masters is a Socialist and a member of New Democratic Party and has actively promoted natural vegetation;
(j) that the likelihood was that both Plaintiffs would lose the election;
(k) that in their campaign and in several public utterances, the Plaintiffs proposed the solutions to a number of problems;
(l) that the Plaintiffs did not have any known record of success of running an independent private business of their own in the community;
(m) that the Plaintiffs were attempting to be elected to public office and thereby reach a position from which they would have some responsibility in the management of public funds, viz., tax dollars.

There is no real issue as to the substantial truth of those allegations of fact, except as to (g) which relates to the employment record of the plaintiff Von Fuchs.

...Counsel for the plaintiffs concedes that the words complained of were written upon a matter of public interest, namely, the conduct of an election for public office in the community and the qualifications of the candidates therein.

The first question of substance is whether the words complained of were published of and concerning the plaintiffs. Several witnesses have been called by the plaintiffs who have said that, upon reading the letter soon after its publication, they understood it to refer to the plaintiffs. I accept their evidence. It is clear from reading the article that a reasonable person in the community in which it was published would identify the plaintiffs as the objects of the criticism. The letter was published on November 12, 1976, about eight days before the municipal election. It obviously refers to the candidates of a particular organization, which is described in the letter as the Communist Party Action Committee. There was not any committee of that name in the community and the reference, obviously a play on words, was to the only organization which was sponsoring candidates in that election campaign, namely, the Community Planning

Action Committee (CPAC), a group concerned with planning and environmental matters. There were three candidates sponsored by the organization, and they were described on a one-sheet brochure as "Your CPAC Aldermanic Candidates for Courtenay". The names, photographs and description of the candidates were displayed prominently on one side of the sheet and the aims and objectives of CPAC, the Community Planning Action Committee, were set forth on the other side. The brochure had been distributed to households in the community. The candidates had been prominently identified in lawn signs and by the media, and were well-known in the community as candidates for CPAC. It is suggested by the defendants that reference in the letter may have been to other candidates running in the election. I do not think so. The letter, as a whole, appears to relate to the one organization and its candidates. There were two female candidates, one of whom was a relatively young married woman. Miss Masters is 57 years of age, unmarried and an environmentalist, who was described in the brochure as belonging "to over 20 environment organizations". She was the only one of the three candidates who could be described as an "old maid" and as one who "should be careful that the natural vegetation doesn't take over and immobilize all activity" (a reference to her well-known concern to preserve natural vegetation in the area). Mr. Von Fuchs, having been a candidate previously, was the only one of the three who fitted the description "some of the same old types". The statement, "witness Oct. 14, at the Civic Center", was a reference to him because he was the only one of the three candidates who had been prominent in the local "Day of Protest". His participation on October 14th had been prominently publicized in the local press. Although the description of him as a "full time career lay about" was inaccurate, it obviously was not a reference to Miss Masters or the third candidate and, by elimination, could be taken, and was taken, to refer to him. I will say more about the characterization when I turn to discuss the question of defamation. I find that the letter was published of and concerning the plaintiffs.

In what sense do the plaintiffs contend that the words complained of are defamatory? Counsel for the plaintiffs has cited what I said in *Gill v. Garcha and Dhillon* (unreported, but dated November 8, 1976), at pp. 7-8, as follows:

> The author of *Gatley on Libel and Slander*, 7th ed., while recognizing that there is no wholly satisfactory definition of defamatory imputation, has this to say in para. 31 of the text:
>
> "31. The defamatory imputation.
>
> "The gist of the torts of libel and slander is the publication of matter (usually words) conveying a defamatory imputation. A defamatory imputation is one to a man's discredit, or which tends to lower him in the estimation of others, or to expose him to hatred, contempt or ridicule, or to injure his reputation in his office, trade or profession, or to injure his financial credit. The standard of opinion is that of right-thinking persons generally. To be defamatory an imputation need have no actual effect on a person's reputation; the law looks only to its tendency."
>
> I have no hesitation in finding that the imputations contained in the *Lok Awaz* editorial, when read in context and in the light of the whole editorial, are such that tend to lower the plaintiff in the estimation of right-thinking members of society generally.

The contention of counsel for the plaintiffs is that (although the false implication that the plaintiffs are members of a communist organization could be said to be defamatory) the real bite of the alleged libel is the imputation of dishonourable or dishonest motives to the plaintiffs. It is contended that the clear inference arising from the letter was that CPAC and, in the context of the letter, its candidates, had been making "every effort to con" (that is, deceive) the electorate, and that their true motives were not honest concern and interest in the community in which they lived and in which they sought office, but rather that their real reason for running for office, which they sought to conceal, was to spread "their particular brand of political venom", namely, communism. It should be stated immediately that neither plaintiff was or is a member of the Communist Party. Each was, in fact, a member of the New Democratic Party but there is no evidence whatsoever that either was using or attempting to use CPAC to spread or advance the aims of any political party. CPAC was a non-political organization which had amongst its members one known Communist, three Liberals, some Conservatives, probably some Social Crediters and about a dozen New Democratic Party members. Total membership of the group ran, at times, between 100-200 members.

Both plaintiffs were involved in numerous community organizations of a non-political nature, and had been very active and concerned with issues of a planning and environmental nature. There is no evidence that, as candidates in 1976, they had any motive other than a desire to serve their community. Their interests and their "leanings" were well-known, and there was no evidence of any deception or concealment by them as to their aims and objectives, if elected.

It is contended on behalf of the defendants that such imputation, if there be one, was concerning the organization, not its individual members, and not these plaintiffs. The plaintiffs cite *Knupffer v. London Express Newspaper Ltd.,* [1944] A.C. 116 (House of Lords) at p. 123, where it was said that if a defamatory statement made of a class or group can reasonably be understood to refer to every member of it, each one has a cause of action. I am satisfied here that the first paragraph of the letter in question was intended to refer to each active member of the committee and, by reference to those running in the election, was intended, in particular, to refer to the plaintiffs who, as candidates, were then advancing the aims and objectives of the committee.

The second paragraph of the letter is devoted largely to personal abuse of the candidates, to which I will return later. The last and concluding paragraph picks up the introductory theme by again appearing to question the motives of the candidates and, in particular, by warning the voters that if they were "misled" by the "published rubbish" of the candidates, then a few (presumably the CPAC candidates) might "get their grubby hands onto the tail end of a few more tax dollars". The use of the word "grubby" (defined in the Shorter Oxford English Dictionary as "dirty, grimy") is not applicable to the plaintiffs in any proper sense and appears to me, when read in context and in the light of the opening paragraph, to imply not only that the election of such candidates would be undesirable, but that public funds would not be safe in their hands. Again, in my opinion, the author has left a defamatory imputation with the reader.

Returning to the second paragraph of the letter the plaintiff Masters is characterized as an "old maid" and as one "who should be careful that the natural vegetation doesn't slowly take over and immobilize all activity". The descriptions are in poor taste, are insulting, and are an attempt to ridicule the candidate, but I do not think that any reasonable person would think any less of Miss Masters, having regard to the fact that the characterization, albeit crude, was obviously the word of an extremist carried away in the heat of an election campaign. The final insult, referable to Miss Masters' interest in environmental matters, was linked with the hackneyed allegation, which is habitually levelled in this Province by the right wing at the left wing, that the latter could not "run a peanut stand without a grant or subsidy". Again, I do not think, that such a remark in those circumstances would tend to lower the plaintiffs in the estimation of right-thinking members of society generally.

One cannot, however, dismiss the description of the plaintiff Von Fuchs as being a "full time career lay about" with such ease. That is clearly an imputation that he did not work, that he made a career of avoiding work, and that he was shiftless and lazy. Even counsel for the defendants conceded that the evidence at trial shows Mr. Von Fuchs to have been an energetic and very active person in many organizations in the Comox Valley, and a regular (although described as "auxiliary") worker on the ferry, "Sechelt Queen", from May, 1976, to the date of trial. To those who did not know Mr. Von Fuchs, the writer sought to convey a very different, false and damaging impression.

Turning then to the defence that the words complained of are expressions of opinion and are fair comment made in good faith on a matter of public interest: Mr. Harvey, counsel for the editor Mathis and the defendant newspaper company, has cited many authorities which deal with the defence of fair comment, but is content to say that the position of the defendants here can be best summed up by adopting the language of Lord Denning, M.R., in *Slim v. Daily Telegraph Ltd.*, [1968] 2 Q.B. 157 at p. 170, as follows:

> These comments are capable of various meanings. They may strike some readers in one way and others in another way. One person may read into them imputations of dishonesty, insincerity and hypocrisy (as the judge did). Another person may only read into them imputations of inconsistency and want of candour (as I would). But in considering a plea of fair comment, it is not correct to canvass all the various imputations which different readers may put upon the words. The important thing is to determine whether or not the writer was actuated by malice. If he was an honest man expressing his genuine opinion on a subject of public interest, then no matter that his words conveyed derogatory imputations; no matter that his opinion was wrong or exaggerated or prejudiced; and no matter that it was badly expressed so that other people read all sorts of innuendoes into it; nevertheless, he has a good defence of fair comment. His honesty is the cardinal test. He must honestly express his real view. So long as he does this, he has nothing to fear, even though other people may read more into it, see *per* Lord Porter in *Turner v. M.G.M. Pictures Ltd.*, [1950] 1 All E.R. 449, H.L. and *per* Diplock J. in *Silkin v. Beaverbrook Newspapers Ltd.*, [1958] 2 All E.R. 516. I stress this because the right of fair comment is one of the essential elements which go to make up our freedom of speech. We must ever maintain this right intact. It must not be whittled down by legal refinements. When a citizen is troubled by things going wrong, he should be free to "write to the newspaper": and the newspaper should be free to publish his letter. It is often the only way to get things put right. The matter must, of course, be one of public interest. The writer must get his facts right: and he must honestly state his real opinion. But that being done, both he and the newspaper should be clear of any liability. They should not be deterred by fear of libel actions.

The words of Lord Denning, M.R., reported at p. 170 aforesaid, were, in part, adopted by Bayda, J.A., in *Cherneskey v. Armadale Publishers Ltd. et al.* (1977), 79 D.L.R. (3d) 180 at p. 202, [1977] 5 W.W.R. 155 at pp. 180-81. He also referred to *Silkin v. Beaverbrook Newspapers Ltd.*, [1958] 2 All E.R. 516, although he did not quote from it. In that case Diplock, J., in summing up to a jury had this to say, at p. 520:

> So in considering this case, members of the jury, do not apply the test of whether you agree with it. If juries did that, freedom of speech, the right of the crank to say what he

likes, would go. Would a fair-minded man holding strong views, obstinate views, prejudiced views, have been capable of making this comment?...

If you take the view that this test is fulfilled, that this does come within the limits of fair comment, as I say, the proper verdict for you to bring in is a verdict for the defendants. If you were to take the view that it was so strong a comment that no fair-minded man could honestly have held it, then the defence fails.

In this case, imputations of corrupt or dishonourable motives being alleged, the central issue is whether they rendered the comment unfair. That question, and the line to be drawn between freedom of speech and unfair comment, is discussed by *Gatley on Libel and Slander,* 7th ed., para. 725, as follows:

(b) *Imputation of Corrupt or Dishonourable Motives*

725. General principles.

An imputation of corrupt or dishonourable motives will render the comment unfair, unless such imputation is warranted by the facts truly stated or referred to, i.e. is an inference which a fair-minded man might reasonably draw from such facts, and represents to honest opinion of the writer.

"A line must be drawn between criticism upon public conduct and the imputation of motives by which that conduct may be supposed to be actuated; one man has no right to impute to another, whose conduct may be fairly open to ridicule or disapprobation, base, sordid and wicked motives unless there is so much ground for the imputation that a jury shall find, not only that he had an honest belief in the truth of his statements, but that his belief was not without foundation... It is said that it is for the interests of society that the public conduct of public men should be criticised without any other limit than that the writer should have an honest belief that what he writes is true. But it seems to me that the public have an equal interest in the maintenance of the public character of public men; and public affairs could not be conducted by men of honour, with a view to the welfare of the country, if we were to sanction attacks upon them, destructive of their honour and character and made without any foundation. I think, the fair position in which the law may be settled is this: that where the public conduct of a public man is open to animadversion, and the writer who is commenting upon it makes imputations on his motives which arise fairly and legitimately out of his conduct so that a jury shall say that the criticism was not only honest, but also well founded, an action is not maintainable." [*Per* Cockburn C.J. in *Campbell v. Spottiswoode* (1863), 3 B. & S. at pp. 776, 777.]

The motive attributed to the plaintiffs was to spread "their particular brand of political venom", which the writer implies was communism. Each of the plaintiffs was known as a socialist. Assuming that the writer only meant to imply that they were more interested in advancing socialist theories than in dealing with local problems and furthering the orderly progress of the community, was that imputation warranted by the facts? Could a fair-minded person reasonably draw that inference from the facts?

Firstly, I will deal with Miss Masters. She was a member of the New Democratic Party, and she had written strong letters to the editor about Social Credit and Social Crediters. But she was not known in the community primarily as a political activist. Her deep concern and, indeed, outside her employment, her sole interest was in environmental matters. It was obvious that was why she was running for office and no fair-minded person could reasonably infer that, as a candidate, she was expressing that interest only to conceal a partisan political motive.

Mr. Von Fuchs was a socialist who advocated "replacement" of the capitalist system. He was not a communist, and no fair-minded person could think that he was — unless such person perceived all socialists to be communists. He was known as an activist in the sense that prominent press coverage had been given to the leading role played by him in the October 14, 1976 "Day of Protest". He was also an avid author of letters to the editor, and his socialist views were well-known. However, he was an active member of about 12 non-political voluntary community organizations and spent an enormous amount of time and energy in connection with them. He was obviously dedicated to matters of local concern, and to the orderly progress of the community. He did not make any secret of his political beliefs (and, I expect, antagonized many with his candour). There was no basis whatsoever for implying that he had a hidden motive for running, namely, to advance communism, socialism, or some other political cause and that he was attempting to achieve this objective under the guise of community interest.

Characterizing the man as a "full time career lay about" was not a comment at all. It falls within the category described by Gatley in para. 712 of his work, in the following language:

> But if a writer chooses to publish an expression of opinion which has no relation by way of criticism to any fact before the reader, then such an expression of opinion depends upon nothing but the writer's own authority, and stands in the same position as an allegation of fact. It cannot be protected by a plea of fair comment.

In my view, that alleged opinion should be regarded as a statement of fact, and it was false. It is true that Mr. Von Fuchs has had a variety of jobs but he has a record of almost continuous employment. At one time he was a field worker for the British Columbia Civil Liberties Association, and worked from an office located in his home. To that extent someone, not knowing the facts, may have assumed that he was temporarily unemployed. But to label him as a "full time career lay about" could not be justified upon any reasonable view of the facts. The statement has a special connotation and goes far beyond what any fair-minded person would infer from a period of temporary unemployment. It connotes a permanent state, and deliberate pursuit of that state.

I have concluded, therefore, that the defence of fair comment must fail.

Although it is not necessary to my decision to do so, I should say that the plaintiffs have alleged but, in my opinion, have not established malice.

There was some evidence to consider in respect to the defendant Fox because he had levelled another attack upon Mr. Von Fuchs a year earlier. But the evidence is insufficient upon which to base a finding of malice.

There was no evidence whatsoever of malice on the part of the newspaper. It is clear that it printed letters for and against candidates for office, and letters expressing strong opinions on both sides of a subject. The newspaper sought to provide a forum in which members of the public could "let off steam". What they did here was to let the matter get out of hand, and to fail to implement their announced policy of editing a letter which they ought to have recognized as being defamatory. It is contended that they showed malice because one of their columnists expressed satisfaction at the defeat of Mr. Von Fuchs. In my view that was an opinion that the columnist was entitled to express, and his opposition to the candidate has not in any way been connected to the publication of the letter in question.

...The defendants are therefore liable, and I turn now to assess damages.

The factors which counsel for the plaintiffs asks me to take into account in assessing damages, and which seem to be relevant, are:

1. The author of the libel was a well-known former policeman in the community, and the newspaper asserted that it did not print libel, that is, false statments. The letter would have greater weight by reason of that sponsorship.

2. The community was small, and the circulation of the newspaper was large. Thus the libel would reach a significant portion of the population, and many people with whom the plaintiffs came into daily contact.

3. The allegation that the plaintiffs could not be trusted might affect the plaintiff Masters in her occupation as an occasional trustee of estates, and might affect the plaintiff Von Fuchs in the eyes of his employer and of his union.

4. The refusal of the defendants to apologize was an aggravation of the libel.

The factors which may make the matter appear less serious are:

1. The author of the libel was known to be extremely partisan, and regularly wrote in strong terms. The letter was published in a corner of the newspaper nicknamed by local residents as "Kooks' Corner". It would not, therefore, be taken as seriously as if it had been otherwise published.

2. It was published in the heat of an election campaign, and would be assessed by the readers as being partisan and not objective.

3. Both of the plaintiffs were, and still are, regarded in this relatively small community as concerned, dedicated but sometimes controversial citizens — that is, their reputations have not been seriously affected.

Damages are assessed at $3,500 to each of the plaintiffs. The defendants will be jointly and severally liable for payment of the award, and will pay the costs of the plaintiffs to be taxed.

Judgments for plaintiffs.

5.2.3.1.2.12 *Vogel* v. *CBC* (1982), 21 C.C.L.T. 105, at 165

ESSON, J.: ... The position of CBC at trial was that such errors of fact were insignificant, that the programme came close enough because, after all, Rigg and Vogel were friendly acquaintances. To insist upon literal accuracy is mere nit-picking which makes it excessively difficult to get the message across. That attitude is not in accordance with the law. Where, as here, the "message" sought to be conveyed is that a person in public life has been guilty of serious wrong-doing, the facts offered in support of that message must be literally true as well as fairly stated.

Note: If the plaintiff can show that the defendant was motivated by malice, the defence of fair comment will be lost. As this is also true with respect to the defence of qualified privilege, the meaning of malice is dealt with in the next section.

5.2.3.1.3 Privilege

The defence of privilege is conceptually different from the other defences.

5.2.3.1.3.1 *Shultz* v. *Porter and Block Brothers Ltd.* (1979), 9 A.R. 381 (Alta. S.C.)

WAITE, J.: The law relating to qualified privilege remains unchanged since the leading case in 1834 of *Toogood v. Spryng,* 1 Cr. M. & R. 181, 149 E.R. 1044, wherein Parke B, for the court stated the defence of qualified privilege in the following passage at pp. 1049-50:

"In general, an action lies for the malicious publication of statements which are false in fact, and injurious to the character of another (within the well-known limits as to verbal slander), and the law considers such publication as malicious, unless it is fairly made by a person in the discharge of some public or private duty, whether legal or moral, or in the conduct of his own affairs, in matters where his interest is concerned. In such cases, the occasion prevents the inference of malice, which the law draws from unauthorized communications, and affords a qualified defence depending upon the absence of actual malice. If fairly warranted by any reasonable occasion or exigency, and honestly made, such communications are protected for the common convenience and welfare of society; and the law has not restricted the right to make them within any narrow limits."

The gravamen of defamation is malice. Ordinarily malice is inferred from the publication of defamatory words, but if the publication occurs on a privileged occasion that inference is rebutted and malice must then be proven expressly by the plaintiff. In the defence of qualified privilege as defined by Parke B., it is the occasion which is privileged so as to protect the publication with immunity unless the plaintiff establishes express or actual malice.

As Lord Macnaghten for the Privy Council in *Macintosh v. Dun,* [1908] A.C. 390, said at p. 399, after quoting with approval the passage aforesaid from *Toogood v. Spyring:*

"The underlying principle is 'the common convenience and welfare of society' — not the convenience of individuals or the convenience of a class, but, to use the words of Erle C.J. in *Whiteley v. Adams* (1863), 15 C.B.N.S. 392 at 418, 143 E.R. 838, 'the general interest of society'."

In *Halls v. Mitchell,* [1928] S.C.R. 125, [1928] 2 D.L.R. 97, Duff J., speaking for a majority of the court after referring to *Macintosh v. Dun* and the cases therein cited, said at p. 133:

"The defamatory statement, therefore, is only protected when it is fairly warranted by some reasonable occasion or exigency, and when it is fairly made in discharge of some public or private duty, or in the conduct of the defendant's own affairs in matters in which his interests are concerned. The privilege rests not upon the interests of the persons entitled to invoke it, but upon the general interests of society, and protects only communications '*fairly* made' (the italics are those of Parke B. himself) in the legitimate defence of a person's own interests, or plainly made under a sense of duty, such as would be recognized by 'people of ordinary intelligence and moral principles'."

He followed it with a summary of his reasons on p. 147 in the following terms:

"To summarize my reasons for thinking that the conditions have not in this case been satisfied in which the law protects privileged communications that otherwise would be actionable as defamatory. 'The underlying principle' upon which that protection is founded is 'the common convenience and welfare of society' — not the interests of individuals or of a class, but 'the general interest of society.' The court must consider whether the communication was made plainly under a duty — and a sense of that duty — which in all the circumstances would be 'recognized by people of ordinary intelligence and moral principle': and in considering that, the court will take into account the origin of the matter of the communication and 'every circumstance connected with the publication' of it: and must 'hold the balance and looking at who published the libel, and why, and to whom, and in what circumstances' must say 'whether it is for the welfare of society that such a communication honestly made should be protected by clothing the occasion of the publication with privilege'."

The principle enunciated in *Toogood v. Sprying* has been repeated in cases too numerous to mention, the few citations above being but examples of its application and confirmation. The only change in the development of the principle of qualified privilege is that in its initial stages it was the communication that was privileged, while the later expressions of the rule place the privilege on the occasion itself within which the communication was made so as to protect with immunity the publication of what would otherwise be defamatory.

5.2.3.1.3.2 Absolute Privilege

5.2.3.1.3.2.1 Ontario Libel and Slander Act, R.S.O. 1980, c.237, s.4

Report of proceedings in court

4. (1) A fair and accurate report without comment in a newspaper or in a broadcast of proceedings publicly heard before a court of justice, if published in the newspaper or broadcast contemporaneously with such proceedings, is absolutely privileged unless the defendant has refused or neglected to insert in the newspaper in which the report complained of appeared or to broadcast, as the case may be, a reasonable statement of explanation or contradiction by or on behalf of the plaintiff.

Improper matter

(2) Nothing in this section authorizes any blasphemous, seditious or indecent matter in a newspaper or in a broadcast. R.S.O. 1960, c.211, s.4.

5.2.3.1.3.2.2 Notes in Other Provincial Statutes

Section 11 of Saskatchewan's Libel and Slander Act, R.S.S. 1978, c.L-14 is almost identical to this provision. The importance of s.3 of British Columbia's Libel and Slander Act, R.S.B.C. 1979, c.234 is much the same although not as specific:

> (1) a fair and accurate report in a public newspaper or other periodical publication or in a broadcast of proceedings publicly heard before a court exercising judicial authority if published contemporaneously with the proceedings, is privileged.
>
> (2) this section does not authorize the publication of blasphemous or indecent matter.

For the most part, however, the provincial defamation statutes, and the Uniform Defamation Act, have adopted the following provisions:

> (1) A fair and accurate report, published in a newspaper or by broadcasting, of proceedings publicly heard before a court is absolutely privileged if
>
> (a) the report contains no comment,
>
> (b) the report is published contemporaneously with the proceedings that are the subject matter of the report, or within 30 days thereafter, and
>
> (c) the report contains nothing of a seditious, blasphemous or indecent nature.
>
> (2) Subsection (1) does not apply if
>
> (a) in the case of publication in a newspaper, the plaintiff shows that the defendant has been requested to insert in the newspaper a reasonable letter or statement of explanation or contradiction by or on behalf of the plaintiff, and the defendant fails to show that he has done so, or

(b) in the case of publication by broadcasting, the plaintiff shows that the defendant has been requested to broadcast a reasonable statement of explanation or contradiction by or on behalf of the plaintiff, and the defendant fails to show that he has done so, from the broadcasting stations from which the alleged defamatory matter was broadcast, on at least 2 occasions on different days and at the same time of day as the alleged defamatory matter was broadcast or at a time as near as possible to that time.

(3) For the purposes of this section, every headline or caption in a newspaper that relates to a report therein shall be deemed to be a report.

(Defamation Act, R.S.A. 1980, c.D-6, s.11; The Defamation Act, R.S.M. 1970, c.D-20, s.11, as amended by 1980, c.30, s.4; Defamation Act, R.S.N.B. 1973, c.D-5, ss.10 and 11; Defamation Act, S.N. 1983, c.63, ss.13 and 14; Defamation Act, C.S.N.S. 1979, c.D-3, ss.13 and 14; Defamation Act, R.S.P.E.I. 1974, c.D-3, s.11; Defamation Ordinance, R.O.N.W.T. 1974, c.D-1, ss.11 and 12; Defamation Ordinance, R.O.Y.T. 1975, c.D-1, ss.11 and 12; and Uniform Defamation Act, ss.11 and 12.)

The privilege may be lost if the report is not fair and accurate.

5.2.3.1.3.2.3 Tedlie v. *Southam*, [1950], 4 D.L.R. 415 (Man. K.B.)

MONTAGUE J.: — This action for defamation was tried before me without a jury.

A bad collision had occurred at 9.44 p.m. on September 1, 1947, at Dugald, when the westbound C.N.R. special train from Minaki crashed head-on into the regular eastbound passenger train standing on the main track waiting for the other train to take the siding. At the time of the accident the plaintiff was the operator on duty at Dugald and in charge of train orders and signals. He was apprehended under a coroner's warrant the next day and detained at Headingly Gaol until released on bail.

The Board of Transport Commissioners for Canada (hereinafter referred to as the "Board") ordered a public inquiry as to the causes of the wreck. Under the *Railway Act,* R.S.C. 1927, c.170, and the *Transport Act,* 1938 (Can.), c.53, the Board is a Court of record and, as respects all matters necessary or proper for the exercise of its jurisdiction, has all the powers, rights and privileges of a Superior Court. The Board's inquiry commenced at the law Courts in Winnipeg on September 23rd, and the next morning the baggageman, the rear trainman of the special, the assistant superintendent of the division (who was travelling on it), and the plaintiff, gave evidence. Their evidence, as transcribed by the Board's official reporter, was, by agreement of counsel, read in as evidence at the trial.

The Winnipeg Tribune, a daily newspaper published by the defendants, carried, on September 24th, a report of the Board's proceedings. On the front page, in large type covering seven columns, were, in two lines, the following headlines: "SPECIAL HAD GREEN LIGHT, OPERATOR TELLS HEARING"; and below this, in smaller types, covering two columns, were the following lead headlines:

"Train Reported 'Under Control' ",

"The Minaki campers special had a green light, or 'proceed' signal in its favor, at the time of the Dugald train wreck, according to testimony given today at the Board of Transport Commissioners inquiry in the law courts building."

After two further paragraphs there followed, in one-column width on pp.1 and 7 of the paper, an extensive report of the proceedings before the Board.

The plaintiff alleged that the headline and lead headlines above quoted were falsely and maliciously published of and concerning him in the way of his trade or occupation as a telegraph operator. In paras. 15 and 16 of the statement of claim, innuendoes were pleaded ascribing the meaning of the words complained of. The essential parts of these paragraphs were:

"The defendants meant and imputed and were understood to mean and impute thereby that the plaintiff while on duty as aforesaid had displayed the wrong signal, which misled the Minaki Campers's Special train resulting in the said accident, and therefore the plaintiff was incompetent and negligent in the performance of his work and duties."

Further:

"The defendants meant and imputed and were understood to mean and impute thereby that the plaintiff had been criminally negligent at the time of the said accident and had thereby caused and was therefore responsible for the said accident."

The hearing before me was the third trial of this action and at this point I shortly refer to its prior history. At the first trial which was with a jury, the action was dismissed on a motion for a nonsuit. The Court of Appeal's judgment allowing the appeal from this and directing a new trial is reported in *Tedlie* v. *Southam Co.,* [1949] 3 D.L.R. 185. It is sufficient for my purpose to say that in the majority judgment of the Court delivered by Dysart J.A. he construed, at p. 195, ss.(3) of s.11 of the *Defamation Act,* 1946, c.11, which reads as follows: "For the purposes of this section, every headline or caption in a newspaper that relates to any report therein shall be deemed to be a report."

And at p. 196 it was held: "In my opinion the subsection *must* be taken in its literal sense; and as its language is clear and unambiguous, each headline *must* 'be deemed to be a report' independent of every other headline and of the published detailed report of the testimony."

At p. 198 it was held: "The heading: 'Train reported under control' is based upon that published answer, and is, of course, not strictly accurate. But for the purposes of the plaintiff's case, that omission is not really serious, because the actual operating 'control' of the Minaki Special could not in any sense be attributed to the plaintiff. The responsibility for that 'control' lay solely with the train's crew, and no dereliction of duty in that respect could reasonably be attributed to the plaintiff by the heading."

At p. 201 it was held that certain issues of the paper prior to that of September 24th were admissible in evidence. In the next paragraph it was held: "On the whole case, I think that the words complained of are independent reports; that they are not fair and accurate reports; that they are capable of the defamatory meaning ascribed to them; and that consequently the case should have gone to the jury."

At the second trial, which was with a jury, the verdict was for the defendants. The Court of Appeal's judgment allowing the appeal from this and directing a new trial is reported in *Tedlie* v. *Southam Co.,* [1950] 1 W.W.R. 1009. Richards J.A. delivered the majority judgment of the Court at p. 1012. I refer to the third paragraph on p. 1013 where it was held that s.10 of the *Defamation Act* was inapplicable to the case (and it appears that this was the opinion of McPherson C.J.M. expressed in his dissenting judgment on the first appeal: see [1949] 3 D.L.R. at p. 186).

On p. 1015 it was held: "*The Defamation Act* constitutes a code and, in so far as it deals with a matter, the previous law is inapplicable."

And at p. 1016: "*The Defamation Act* was intended to be complete and exhaustive as to the subjects with which it deals."

At the trial before me there was no new evidence adduced which could possibly affect the judgments of the Court of Appeal on the matters I have referred to above, and while *ex abundanti cautela,* I now formally hold in these reasons the same as the Court of Appeal has held on the matters, my opinion is that it is not open to me to reconsider any of them.

In England the rule is that the decisions of the Court of Appeal upon questions of law must be followed by Courts of first instance and the decision of the Court of Appeal on questions of fact is, as between the parties, binding: 19 Hals., 2nd ed., pp. 254-5. In *McIntosh* v. *Parent,* [1924] 4 D.L.R. 420 at p. 422, 55 O.L.R. 552 at p. 555, Middleton J.A. said: ''When a question is litigated, the judgment of the Court is a final determination as between the parties and their privies. Any right, question, or fact distinctly put in issue and directly determined by a Court of competent jurisdiction... cannot be re-tried.... The right, question, or fact, once determined, must, as between them, be taken to be conclusively established so long as the judgment remains.''

In *Western Can. Power Co.* v. *Bergklint* (1916), 34 D.L.R. 467 at p. 477, 54 S.C.R. 285 at p. 299, an employer's liability case, Duff J. said: ''There is some authority indicating that where a Court of appeal in granting a new trial decides a substantive question in the litigation, that question for the purposes of that litigation is to be taken to have been conclusively determined as between the parties.''

The learned Judge stated that the point was not taken or argued before the Court and he himself thought the appeal should be allowed on other grounds. He had, however, referred to the Privy Council's decision in *Badar Bee* v. *Habib Merican Noordin,* [1909] A.C. 615, which was an appeal from the Straits Settlements' Supreme Court in a case involving the construction of a will which had been construed by that Court many years before. In this case Lord Macnaghten, delivering the judgment, at p. 623 said: ''It is not competent for the Court, in the case of the same question arising between the same parties, to review a previous decision not open to appeal.''

These authorities convince me that the decisions of our Court of Appeal on the matters referred to above are binding on me.

The first question to be dealt with is whether the words complained of were published, and if so, were they published by the defendants. On the evidence I would instruct a jury affirmatively on these points, and, performing the function of a jury, I find that the words in fact were published by the defendants.

Then, discharging my duties as a Judge, I must determine whether the words complained of are capable of the meaning ascribed to them by the innuendoes: *Sturt* v. *Blagg* (1847), 10 Q.B. 906, 116 E.R. 343; *Capital & Counties Bk.* v. *Henty & Sons* (1882), 7 App. Cas. 741 at p. 744; *Nevill* v. *Fine Art & Gen'l Ins. Co.*, [1897] A.C. 68 at p. 72; 20 Hals, 2nd ed., p. 433. I hold and determine that the words complained of, other than ''Train Reported Under Control'', are so capable and that I would so instruct a jury.

Hereafter when I use the expression ''words complained of'', it will be understood that I am referring to the words complained of in the statement of claim, other than ''Train Reported Under Control''.

Next, it is my duty, discharging that of a jury, to determine whether the words complained of and published by the defendants in the circumstances established by the evidence were, in fact, defamatory of the plaintiff.

A defamatory statement is a statement which, if published of and concerning a person, is calculated to expose him to hatred, contempt or ridicule, or to convey an imputation on him disparaging or injurious to him in his trade, business, calling or office: 20 Hals, 2nd ed., p. 384. The true test is whether, in the circumstances in which the statement was published, reasonable men to whom the publication was made would understand it in a defamatory sense. Sometimes that test may be satisfied from the mere words of the statement: *ibid.*, p. 396.

The words complained of by the plaintiff are not defamatory in their natural and ordinary meaning. They do not specify the plaintiff as the person to whom they applied. Accordingly, the onus lay on the plaintiff to prove that there were facts known to persons to whom the words were published which might reasonably lead them to understand the words in the sense alleged in the innuendoes.

This brings me to the evidence of four witnesses called by the plaintiff at the trial. To each of them the foundation question, set out in Gatley on Libel & Slander, 3rd ed., p. 619, was, in fact or effect, put. Each of them deposed to facts and circumstances within his knowledge at the time he read the headlines of the paper, which I hold entitled him to state what he understood by them.

John Renwick Brown said that he read the headlines when he got home from work. They were the first thing that caught his attention: "My first impression from these headlines was that the operator may have made a grave mistake in giving the wrong light to the westbound train. It looked as if he had given the westbound train a proceed signal to come west on the main line, which could not be possible. Order 338 gave the train rights to the east switch only; its only possible thoroughfare to proceed was through the siding."

At the end of his examination-in-chief he said: "My impression from reading the headlines was that the operator had made a mistake and in my opinion would be responsible."

This witness is a C.N.R. telegraph operator. He was one of the bondsmen for the plaintiff's bail. He is the chairman of the local branch of the Railway Telegraphers Order and as such he represented the plaintiff at the investigation held by the railway's officials. Despite these facts he did not impress me as biased.

Mr. John L. Ross, K.C., an experienced defence counsel, was the next witness. He read the paper of September 24th; remembered reading the headlines — it was because of such that he picked up the paper. According to my notes he said that "when he read the headlines his first reaction was, surely that headline cannot be correct, because if it was, then Mr. Tedlie was in a very embarrassing position under the Criminal Code for some charge of criminal negligence. If the headline was true, then Tedlie was the man responsible for this wreck. He took it from the headline reading. 'Special Had Green Light', etc., that the paper was reporting a certain set of facts. The balance of the report did not seem to support the headline". "He was definitely confused about the different signals."

Mr. H. P. Clubine has been a practising barrister since leaving the Air Force in 1946. He has never met the plaintiff. He read the paper of September 24th some time after 5.30 that evening. To him a green light meant "go ahead". The meaning he took from the headlines was that the plaintiff had either made a terrible mistake which caused the accident or he had been negligent and forgotten to change the light.

Counsel, cross-examining this witness, took him over much of the report proper as contained in the paper. Witness said he had not looked at the article since he first read it. A paragraph from the report of the testimony of the witness Cloutier at the Board's hearing was read to the witness:

"Q. Is it your understanding that if you saw the main track clear you could have gone on the main track on order 338? A. According to the rule book, no."

And the witness said in his evidence: "I read that but it did not change the opinion I formed on that headline."

He was read the following part of the paper's report: "Mr. Nicholls testified he knew of order 338. The train should have taken the siding at Dugald. He knew of no reason why it was not done."

And the witness then said: "At the time I read it I believed the light should have been changed to red."

The last witness was John A. Barbour, a clergyman. He knew what "green light" signified to him as a motorist and swore the headline implied to him that Tedlie had been guilty of a dereliction of duty. "That is the impression I got from the headline. It seemed the special had the right to go into the station."

This witness was subjected to considerable cross-examination based on parts of his evidence at the second trial, but all of such, in my opinion, was irrelevant to the matter I am now considering and I accept his evidence as to the meaning he took from the headlines.

No evidence was given contradicting the evidence of the above four witnesses as to the understanding they obtained — the impressions they got — from reading the headline and lead paragraph in question. In *R.* v. *Covert* (1916), 34 D.L.R. 662 at pp. 673-4, 28 Can. C.C. 25 at p. 37, 10 A.L.R. 349, Beck J., of the Alberta Appellate Division, laid down as fairly established, by the principles of the cases to which he referred, the following proposition:

"It cannot be said without limitation that a Judge can refuse to accept evidence. I think he cannot, if the following conditions are fulfilled: —

"(1) That the statements of the witness are not in themselves improbable or unreasonable;

"(2) That there is no contradiction of them;

"(3) That the credibility of the witness has not been attacked by evidence against his character;

"(4) That nothing appears in the course of his evidence or of the evidence of any other witness tending to throw discredit upon him; and

"(5) That there is nothing in his demeanour while in Court during the trial to suggest untruthfulness."

The evidence of the plaintiff's witnesses, who impressed me as reasonable and fair-minded men, complied fully with the requirements laid down in the *Covert* case, *supra,* and I accept such evidence. It has satisfied me, discharging the duties of a jury, that the words complained of were reasonably understood by those proven to have read them, in the meanings attributed to them in the innuendoes, or at least some of them, *viz.,* that the plaintiff had displayed the wrong signal, was negligent in performing his duties and was responsible for the accident. Again, the evidence has led me to the conclusion that the words would naturally be understood by other reasonable and fair people who read them as conveying the meanings attributed to them and specified by me. Finally, the evidence has satisfied me that the words, in their attributed meanings so specified by me, conveyed imputations disparaging and injurious to the plaintiff in his occupation as a railway telegraph operator and were, in fact, defamatory of him.

I come now to the question of privilege. Although the statement complained of be defamatory of the plaintiff and untrue, yet if the occasion of its publication be privileged the statement is absolutely or conditionally protected, according as the occasion of the publication is one of absolute or qualified privilege: 20 Hals., 2nd ed., pp. 459-60. The word "privilege" is used to denote the fact that conduct which under ordinary circumstances would subject the actor to liability, under particular circumstances does not subject him thereto: Restatement of the Law of Torts, vol. 1, p. 19.

For newspapers the *Defamation Act* creates privilege and absolute privilege in ss.10 and 11 respectively. The source of these sections is found in ss.4 and 3 respectively of the English statute, the Law of Libel Amendment Act, 1888, 51-52 Vict., c.64. See 20 Hals., 2nd ed., pp. 484-5, and 10 Hals., Stat. of Eng., p. 418. No case is cited in either of these references which suggests that s.4 of the English statute is applicable to proceedings in Court. I note that in Odgers on Libel & Slander, 6th ed., p. 268, it is stated that the words "absolutely privileged" were included in s.3 of the bill as originally introduced, but "absolutely" was omitted in the Act.

I hold that the Board of Transport Commissioners was sitting as a Court of Record on September 24, 1947, when the proceedings publicly heard before it were reported by the newspaper.

I further hold that s.11 of the *Defamation Act* applies to the case at bar. This, in part, provides:

"11 (1) A fair and accurate report, published in a newspaper or by broadcasting, of proceedings publicly heard before any court shall be absolutely privileged if,

"(*a*) the report contains no comment."

No evidence made ss.(2) applicable.

Subsection (3), providing that each headline constitutes a report, has been set out earlier in these reasons. It is unnecessary for me to stress the importance of this new subsection construed by Dysart J.A.

The report must be an impartial and accurate account. Its accuracy must not be judged by the standard of a professional law reporter. A substantially fair account of what took place in Court is enough: Odgers, 6th ed., pp. 259-60. The reporter must add nothing of his own: *ibid.,* p. 263.

In considering whether the words complained of are fair and accurate reports, they are, of course, to be tested by the testimony given before the Board and made evidence at the trial. None of this reflected in any way on the plaintiff. I find that he had faithfully and strictly complied with the rules and regulations of his employment and had properly performed his duties on the night in question. He was not in any way responsible for the negligence in the switch not being thrown or the train stopped.

I find that the headline report reading "Special Had Green Light, Operator Tells Hearing" was not true in itself and that the operator did not make that statement. His evidence, and that of all other witnesses, was that the Special was not operating on signal lights but on train orders. The published headline was not fairly or substantially accurate; it was a voluntary statement and comment by the paper; it was not a fair and accurate report.

Then as regards the paragraph following the headline "Train Reported Under Control" and reading: "The Minaki campers special had a green light or 'proceed' signal in its favor, at the time of the Dugald train wreek, according to testimony given today" etc., this refers only to the testimony of the witness Nicholls. His evidence in this connection is found on p. 87 of ex. 3. Asked if he had seen the train order board, he answered, "I saw it before the accident, yes". To the question "What did the train order board indicate", he answered, "it was in the green or proceed position". Then this follows:

"Q. Did that fact that the train order board was in green or in proceed position have any significance in relationship to the necessity of the extra taking the siding? A. No, sir.

"COMMISSIONER STONEMAN: Q. I think that is exactly the same understanding that the trainmen had, that in any event it was necessary for you to take that siding? A. Quite. Q. In spite of the fact the order board was green? A. That is right, sir."

What Nicholls said in his evidence about the "green" or "proceed" position was very much different from the paragraph published by the defendants, which was quite misleading. All of the evidence given at the Board's hearing and read in at the trial was to the effect that the indication of the order board, whatever it might be at the time had no bearing upon what the Minaki Special should do at the east switch. The green light only indicated that the Minaki Special could enter the block at the west switch after proceeding along the passing track. The green light would not become operative until the Special had taken the siding. I find that the paragraph published by the defendants was their own statement or comment and that it was not a fair and accurate report.

As I have found that the above headline and lead paragraph complained of were not fair and accurate reports, the defendants are not within the protection accorded by s.11 of the Act. The reports in question were not privileged.

5.2.3.1.3.3 Qualified Privilege

5.2.3.1.3.3.1 'Anne Skarsgard, 'Freedom of the Press'', pp. 303-307

Qualified privilege affords protection from tort liability for defamation if it is deemed that, on a particular occasion, society's interest in having the communication made outweighs the possibility of it turning out to be wrong. This privilege is "qualified"; it is available only if the person making the statement acts without malice, that is, in good faith and without improper motive. It is well established that "the circumstances that constitute a privileged occasion can themselves never be catalogued and rendered exact." In *Adam* v. *Ward* Lord Atkinson defined an occasion of qualified privilege:

> ...a privileged occasion is, in reference to qualified privilege, an occasion where the person who makes the communication has an interest or a duty, legal, social or moral, to make it to the person to whom it is made, and the person to whom it is so made has a corresponding interest or duty to receive it. This reciprocity is essential.

The problem is that very often one does not know whether the occasion is privileged or not. The bona fide belief of the maker of the statement that the occasion is privileged is irrelevant. If defendant pleads qualified privilege, it is the judge who decides whether the occasion was a privileged one. This principle has been criticized by Weiler who claims it to be completely irrational to grant only a partial privilege by making the subjective appreciation of the truth decisive but not that of the existence of a privileged occasion.

> Either it is sufficiently in the social interest to encourage these communications that it is not wrongful to take a chance of their being false, or it is not. If it is, and society wishes one to act, it can only ask that this conduct be in accordance with a reasonable perception of the facts as they appeared at the relevant time to the actor.

The law as it stands now promotes uncertainty which discourages the media from publishing statements which may or may not come under the privilege.

If the defence of qualified privilege is available to the media, it usually comes under the category of "statements made in the performance of a duty". The law recognizes that the press has a duty to report fairly and accurately parliamentary and court proceedings and the public has a corresponding interest to receive this information. As a result such reports are protected by the defence. The question is whether the press can claim the privilege when it is not just acting as a conduit relaying statements made on a privileged occasion, but when publishing original news stories and commentaries on matters of public interest.

b) The usefulness of qualified privilege to the press:

The position in England is that under certain circumstances the press does have a duty to make the communication and consequently the defence is available. Said Pearson J. in *Webb* v. *Times Publishing Co.*:

> There may be occasions where a communication to the public at large is protected by qualified privilege, provided the public at large has a legitimate interest in the subject matter of the communication.

In *Davis* v. *London Express Newspaper Ltd.* an inquiry by a newspaper as to share-pushing was held to be a privileged occasion. Said the court:

> There is now a trend towards wider recognition of the various circumstances which might create a social or moral duty in one person to make a communication to another about a third person...

It should be pointed out that in this case publication did not occur in the paper, but consisted of a newspaper editor showing a defamatory letter to a third person. The letter informed the paper that a property to which it had referred in two articles was being used for the fraudulent pushing of shares. The writer continued by saying:

> It is imperative to expose the activities of these people before the 3rd prox. ... on which date a meeting is to take place which, if no contradictory report appears in a responsible national newspaper, will enable them to rake in a good many thousands of pounds from the public who have read the various notices about this charlatan Professor Herzog.

The court held that the occasion was privileged; the newspaper editor had a duty to make the communication.

The defence was made available to the press in other English cases as well, notably in the leading case of *Adam* v. *Ward*. Here plaintiff defamed a general in Parliament, and the Army Council published a letter in the press vindicating the general and defaming the plaintiff. The House of Lords held that the occasion was a privileged one. In the words of Lord Atkinson, a man who makes a statement on the floor of the House of Commons makes it to all the world. Therefore it is the duty of the heads of the service to which the defamed individual belongs to publish his vindication to the whole world. Although the newspaper was not sued, it is safe to conclude that it too had a duty to publish the letter and therefore was protected by the privilege. Said Buckley L.J.: "If the matter is of public interest and the party who publishes it owes a duty to communicate it to the general public, the publication is privileged."

In *Duncombe* v. *Daniell* the court endorsed the principle that it was justifiable for an elector to communicate to the constituency any matter affecting the character of the candidate which he bona fide believed to be true and material to the election. Under the circumstances the privilege was defeated because of unjustifiably wide publication in the Letters to the Editor column of a newspaper, as the paper's circulation extended well beyond the boundaries of the constituency. One would assume then that such a letter would be protected if it addressed itself, for example, to the character of the national leader of the party. In such a case there would be reciprocity of interest between the letter writer and the general public. The reciprocity of interest would give rise to the privilege and the newspaper, acting as a conduit for disseminating the letter, would be protected by the privilege as well.

Until the middle of this century Canadian courts were even more liberal than the English courts in making the defence available to the media. In *Showler* v. *MacInnes*, the court held that a radio broadcast about labour organization was under the privilege because of the "vital concern of the whole citizenship of Vancouver" in the matter. Both *Dennison* v. *Sanderson* and *Drew* v. *Toronto Star Ltd. and Atkinson* decided on the trial level that election remarks published in a newspaper were privileged and these holdings were not overturned on appeal. Shortly after the second decision Drew's counsel, Mr. Cartwright, was elevated to the Supreme Court of Canada. He soon saw to it that the law was changed in the area. He held in *Douglas* v. *Tucker* that public officials were not under the qualified privilege when making statements in the mass media.

The last-mentioned decision was ambiguous enough to allow two Ontario trial judges and the Ontario Court of Appeal to hold in two subsequent decisions that the defence of qualified privilege was available to the media. In *Boland* v.*Globe and Mail Ltd.* the trial judge said:

> ...a Federal Election in Canada is an occasion upon which a newspaper has a public duty to comment on the candidates, their campaigns and their platforms or policies, and Canadian citizens have a very honest and very real interest in receiving their comments, and therefore this is an occasion of qualified privilege.

When the case reached the Supreme Court, Cartwright J. reversed the decision and stated:

> I am of the opinion that this is an erroneous statement of the law... With respect it appears to me that, in the passage quoted above, the learned trial judge has confused the right which the publisher of a newspaper has, in common with all Her Majesty's subjects, to report truthfully and comment fairly upon matters of public interest with a duty of the sort which gives rise to an occasion of qualified privilege.

Again in *Banks v. Globe and Mail Ltd.* the trial judge stated that

> The class of cases to which the defence of qualified privilege extends, has, during the course of recent years, been extended, and that extension will cover editorial comment by a metropolitan newspaper on matters of public interest. It is difficult to conceive of a matter in which the public would be more interested in the year 1957 than the most important topic of industrial relations... There is no more efficient organ for informing the public and disseminating to the public intelligent comment on such matters than a great metropolitan newspaper... The members of the public have a real, a vital — I may go so far as to say — a paramount interest in receiving those comments.

Again, Cartwright J. reversed the decision and held that the press is not under a qualified privilege. He quoted Mr. Justice (later President, then Chief Justice) Taft in *Post Publishing Co.* v. *Hallam* to the effect that if public men were to be subjected to falsities of fact, good men could not be found to hold public office. It should be noted that this was a nineteenth century controversial American decision. Since then, of course, the American position has drastically changed. The expanded *New York Times* rule denies a cause of action in defamation to public officials and public figures unless they can prove knowledge of the falsity of the statement or reckless disregard whether the statement was true or false. Even then only special damages are recoverable. *Rosenbloom* v. *Metromedia* extended the *Times* rule to any matter of public or general interest, but the Supreme Court retreated somewhat in the *Gertz* case where it was decided that if a private citizen rather than a public official or a public figure was the plaintiff in a matter of public interest, each state could impose its own standard of liability so long as strict or absolute liability was not imposed. In other words, in the United States not even private individuals can succeed in a defamation action against the media unless they show either negligence or reckless disregard for truth, depending on where they sue. The American position is that strict liability in defamation contravenes the freedom of speech provision of the First Amendment.

This is a far cry from the Canadian situation since Mr. Justice Cartwright took away the defence of qualified privilege from the media in the *Boland* and *Banks* decisions. In *Banks* Cartwright J. justified his stand by saying that the press did not need the defence of qualified privilege as the interest of free speech was sufficiently protected by the defence of fair comment.

5.2.3.1.3.3.2 Ontario Libel and Slander Act, RSO 1980, c.237, s.3; and Notes on Statutes in Other Provinces; Qualified privilege may arise from a statute

Privileged reports

3. (1) A fair and accurate report in a newspaper or in a broadcast of any of the following proceedings that are open to the public is privileged, unless it is proved that the publication thereof was made maliciously:

1. The proceedings of any legislative body or any part or committee thereof in the British Commonwealth that may exercise any sovereign power acquired by delegation or otherwise.
2. The proceedings of any administrative body that is constituted by any public authority in Canada.
3. The proceedings of any commission of inquiry that is constituted by any public authority in the Commonwealth.
4. The proceedings of any organization whose members, in whole or in part, represent any public authority in Canada.

Idem

(2) A fair and accurate report in a newspaper or in a broadcast of the proceedings of a meeting *bona fide* and lawfully held for a lawful purpose and for the furtherance of discussion of any matter of public concern, whether the admission thereto is general or restricted, is privileged, unless it is proved that the publication thereof was made maliciously.

Publicity releases

(3) The whole or a part or a fair and accurate synopsis in a newspaper or in a broadcast of any report, bulletin, notice or other document issued for the information of the public by or on behalf of any body, commission or organization mentioned in subsection 1 or any meeting mentioned in subsection 2 is privileged, unless it is proved that the publication thereof was made maliciously.

Decisions, etc., of certain types of association

(4) A fair and accurate report in a newspaper or in a broadcast of the findings or decision of any of the following associations, or any part or committee thereof, being a finding or decision relating to a person who is a member of or is subject, by virtue of any contract, to the control of the association, is privileged, unless it is proved that the publication thereof was made maliciously:

1. An association formed in Canada for the purpose of promoting or encouraging the exercise of or interest in any art, science, religion or learning, and empowered by its constitution to exercise control over or adjudicate upon matters of interest or concern to the association, or the actions or conduct of any persons subject to such control or adjudication.
2. An association formed in Canada for the purpose of promoting or safeguarding the interests of any trade, business, industry or profession, or of the persons carrying on or engaged in any trade, business, industry or profession, and empowered by its constitution to exercise control over or adjudicate upon matters connected with the trade, business, industry or profession.
3. An association formed in Canada for the purpose of promoting or safeguarding the interests of any game, sport or pastime to the playing or exercising of which members of the public are invited or admitted, and empowered by its constitution to exercise control over or adjudicate upon persons connected with or taking part in the game, sport or pastime.

Improper matter

(5) Nothing in this section authorizes any blasphemous, seditious or indecent matter in a newspaper or in a broadcast.

Saving

(6) Nothing in this section limits or abridges any privilege now by law existing or protects the publication of any matter not of public concern or the publication of which is not for the public benefit.

When defendant refuses to publish explanation

(7) The protection afforded by this section is not available as a defence in an action for libel if the plaintiff shows that the defendant refused to insert in the newspaper or to broadcast, as the case may be, a reasonable statement of explanation or contradiction by or on behalf of the plaintiff. R.S.O. 1960, c.211, s.3.

Similar provisions can be found in the defamation legislation of all the common law provinces and territories. The wording of the Acts of Newfoundland, Nova Scotia, Prince Edward Island, the Northwest Territories and the Yukon Territory is very close to that of the Ontario statute (Defamation Act, S.N. 1983, c.63, s.12; Defamation Act, C.S.N.S. 1979, c.D-3, s.12; Defamation Act, R.S.P.E.I. 1974, c.D-3, s.9: Defamation Ordinance, R.O.N.W.T. 1974, c.D-1, s.10; and Defamation Ordinance,

R.O.Y.T. 1975, c.D-1, s.10), while the provisions of the Defamation Acts of Alberta, Manitoba, New Brunswick, and the Uniform Defamation Act, take the following form:

(1) A fair and accurate report published in a newspaper or by broadcasting of
(a) a public meeting,
(b) proceedings
(i) in the Senate or House of Commons of Canada,
(ii) in the Legislative Assembly of Alberta or any other province, or
(iii) in a committee of those bodies,
except where neither the public nor any reporter is admitted,
(c) a meeting of commissioners authorized to act by or pursuant to statute or other lawful warrant or authority, or
(d) a meeting of a municipal council, school board, board of education, board of health, or of any other board or local authority formed or constituted under a public Act of Canada or of Alberta or any other province, or of a committee appointed by any such board or local authority,
is privileged, unless it is proved that the publication was made maliciously.

(2) The publication in a newspaper or by broadcasting, at the request of a government department, bureau or office or public officer, of a report, bulletin, notice or other document issued for the information of the public is privileged, unless it is proved that the publication was made maliciously.

(3) Nothing in this section applies to the publication of seditious, blasphemous or indecent matter.

(4) Subsections (1) and (2) do not apply when
(a) in the case of publication in a newspaper, the plaintiff shows that the defendant has been requested to insert in the newspaper a reasonable letter or statement of explanation or contradiction by or on behalf of the plaintiff, and the defendant fails to show that he has done so, or
(b) in the case of publication by broadcasting, the plaintiff shows that the defendant has been requested to broadcast a reasonable statement of explanation or contradiction by or on behalf of the plaintiff, and the defendant fails to show that he has done so, from the broadcasting stations from which the alleged defamatory matter was broadcast, on at least 2 occasions on different days and at the same time of day as the alleged defamatory matter was broadcast or at a time as near as possible to that time.

(5) Nothing in this section limits or abridges any privilege now by law existing, or applies to the publication of any matter not of public concern or the publication of which is not for the public benefit.

(Defamation Act, R.S.A. 1980; c.D-6, s.10; The Defamation Act, R.S.M. 1970, c.D-20, s.10; Defamation Act, R.S.N.B. 1973, c.D-5, s.9; and Uniform Defamation Act, s.10.)

Section 4 of the British Columbia Libel and Slander Act, R.S.B.C. 1979, c.234, and s.10 of Saskatchewan's Libel and Slander Act, R.S.S. 1978, c.L-14 both provide:

(1) A fair and accurate report published in a public newspaper or other periodical publication or in a broadcast of the proceedings of a public meeting, or, except where neither the public nor a news reporter is admitted, of a meeting of a municipal council,

school board, board or local authority formed or constituted under any Act, or of a committee appointed by any of the above mentioned bodies, or of a meeting of commissioners authorized to act by letters patent, Act or other lawful warrant or authority, or select committees of the Legislative Assembly, and the publication at the request of a government office or ministry, or a public officer, of a notice or report issued for the information of the public, is privileged, unless it is proved that the report or publication was published or made maliciously.

(2) This section does not authorize the publication of blasphemous or indecent matter; and the protection intended to be afforded by this section is not available as a defence in proceedings if it is proved that the defendant has been requested to insert in the newspaper or other periodical publication, or to broadcast in the same manner as that, in which the report or other publication complained of appeared, a reasonable letter or statement by way of contradiction or explanation of the report or other publication and has refused or neglected to insert it.

(3) This section does not limit or abridge a privilege now existing by law, or protect the publication of matter not of public concern and the publication of which is not for the public benefit.

Quebec rejects the defence in the case of a public meeting (see Press Act, R.S.Q. 1977, c.P-19, s.10).

5.2.3.1.3.3.3 *Cook* v. *Alexander and Others*, [1973], 3 All E.R. 1037 (Eng. C.A.).

LORD DENNING MR. This case raises a point of considerable importance. It is about the reporting of proceedings in Parliament. It has not come up for full discussion in the courts for over 100 years; that is, since *Wason v. Walter*.

In 1967 the plaintiff, Mr. Cook, was a teacher on the staff of the Court Lees approved school. It is near Godstone in Surrey. On 2nd and 7th March 1967 Mr. Cook wrote letters to the Guardian newspaper in which he criticised severely the way in which the school was conducted. He said that the boys were punished with excessive severity. He did not give his name. He was afraid of repercussions on him if he did so. So his letters appeared anonymously. The Guardian published them. The Daily Mail re-published them. They were very convincing. They had an impact on the public at large. So much so that the Home Secretary ordered an inquiry. It was held by Mr. Brian Gibbens, a Queen's Counsel. At the inquiry the headmaster was represented by lawyers. So was Mr. Cook. In due course Mr. Gibbens made his report. He found that some — not all — of the charges made by Mr. Cook were true. Four out of 11, I believe. The consequences were far-reaching. The Home Secretary made an order closing the Court Lees approved school. The boys were sent elsewhere. The staff lost their employment.

Many people were very concerned at these developments. So much so that Earl Jellicoe on 25th October 1967, in the House of Lords, rose to draw attention to the closure of the Court Lees school and to move for papers. He criticised the Home Secretary's handling of the case. He said that the school managers had been treated roughly and that injustice had been done to the headmaster and his deputy. Lord Stonham, speaking for the government, justified the closure. He said that, in the light of the report, it was the proper thing to have done. There was a debate in which 11 speakers took part. It took over three hours and filled 94 columns of Hansard. One speech in particular caused a considerable stir. It was the speech of the Bishop of Southwark, Dr. Stockwood. He criticised Mr. Cook in strong terms. In answer, Lord Longford said the bishop's speech was a monument of unfairness.

Next day, 26th October 1967, the Daily Telegraph reported the debate in the House of Lords. It reported it fully on one of the inside pages. It filled three columns of the newspaper and gave extracts — either in direct speech or in oblique speech — from all 11 speakers. The teacher, Mr. Cook, makes no complaint of that full report. He could not justly do so, because it is a fair and accurate summary of the debate.

On the back page there was one column about the debate. It is what journalists call a 'Parliamentary sketch'. It gave a commentary describing the main impression made on those who were present. It is said to be a libel on Mr. Cook. I must therefore read it. It starts with a head-line in bold letters: 'Bishop attacks Court Lees ''crusader''.' Then follows: 'By Andrew Alexander, Westminster, Wednesday.'

Then comes the sketch itself:

> 'Critics in the Lords of the Home Office's handling of the Court Lees approved school case today found a staunch ally on the progressive Left in Dr. Mervyn Stockwood, Bishop of Southwark. He launched a scathing attack on Mr. Ivor Cook, the master whose revelations prompted the inquiry. [Debate — P27]. Dr. Stockwood's own startling revelation was that Dr. Cook had sent more boys to the headmaster for discipline — which usually meant corporal punishment — than any other master.'

Then follows the sub-heading in bigger type:

'CHARGES READ OUT
House amused'

Then these words follow:

> 'Between 1963 and the time of the inquiry, Mr. Cook had issued 110 of the ''yellow tickets'' which signified that a boy required special punishment. ''I know this because they are in my possession.'' He then read out some of the charges involved, to the amusement of the House. One boy had spat in a public place; another swept drain debris across Mr. Cook's clean shoes; a third had worn socks in bed. ''This is the apostle in the crusade against corporal punishment,'' he commented with scorn.'

Then follows the sub-heading in bigger type:

'INQUIRY DEMANDED
Longford's rejection'

Then the words follow:

> 'The Bishop added his plea to those of others in the debate who demanded a full and public inquiry. But the Government was not in a conciliatory vein. Lord Longford, Leader of the House, dismissed the comments on Mr. Cook as ''a monument of unfairness''. But others in the House were impressed. Lord Dilhorne, in an unscheduled intervention, added his plea for a full inquiry, in which the dismissed headmaster would have a chance to defend himself properly. He took up a point by Baroness Serota (Lab.) and asked why — since the first inquiry had appeared to reveal serious brutality — there had been no criminal charges. Lord Longford, in what was a rather bumbling reply, became involved in exchanges with Peers when he insisted that the headmaster had not been dismissed. The school had merely been closed down. That did not involve dismissal, which was an ''ignominious'' termination of employment.'

Then follows a sub-heading in bigger type:

'HEAD CRITICISED
Recent beatings'

> 'But perhaps few things in the debate illustrated more clearly the unsatisfactory state of affairs now than the speech by Lord Annan (Ind.). Criticising the headmaster, he spoke of recent beatings for very slight sexual misbehaviour by boys. Lord Aberdare (Con.) summing up for the Opposition, said according to his information the offences in question were of a distinctly serious nature, involving the bullying of small boys in this respect. Lord Annan quickly rose to say perhaps this was so: he was only going on the ''rumour'' he had heard.'

Then there is a final sub-heading: 'Lords Debate — P27'.

That is what journalists call a Parliamentary sketch. It does not give a full report of Parliamentary proceedings but only an impression of the debate as the reporter heard and saw it. The important question is whether and to what extent such a sketch is the subject of privilege — qualified privilege. The judge stated the law to the jury in these words:

> '...it is to the advantage of the country as a whole that proceedings in our courts and in Parliament should be fairly reported. To any such report a qualified privilege attaches; and that, privilege is that, so long as the report is fair and accurate, it cannot be the subject of defamation proceedings unless it was published maliciously.'

He noted that there was no evidence of malice. So he withdrew that issue from the jury. He told the jury that the 'prime question — almost the sole question — is: Is the report as a whole a fair one? Is it an honest one?'

After retiring for two hours and 20 minutes, the jury came back with this note:

> 'We are unable to reach unanimous decision. (1) Total agreement has been reached on the question that the flavour of the debate is not contained in the [column on the back page]. (2) A majority feel that [that column] is not a fair report. (3) Although the majority feel that [the column] is not fair some are not sure it is defamatory.'

The judge gave a further direction to the jury. He told them they could decide by a majority of ten to two. He also told them the accepted definitions of defamation. Then after 53 minutes they came back. They found for Mr. Cook by a majority of 11 to one and awarded £1.000 damages. Now there is an appeal by the newspaper, the Daily Telegraph.

Seeing that a Parliamentary sketch has not come up for consideration in the courts before, it may be helpful if I quote the evidence of the journalists about it. Mr. Andrew Alexander was the one who wrote this sketch. He was on the Parliamentary staff of the Daily Telegraph. He said:

> '...the reader to whom this is directed is the man who cannot be present in the House of Lords to listen to the debate but wants to know what was the thing which apparently made an impact in a debate of this type... I aimed as usual to convey the flavour and feel of the occasion, and in this particular case the most salient feature of the debate was the very surprising development of Dr. Stockwood coming out with an attack upon Mr. Cook, which surprised so many people in the House of Lords. I tried to convey to the reader some idea of the strength of the attack and the feeling it aroused in the Lords and how it was received.'

Mr. Green, the editor of the Daily Telegraph, was asked: 'What guidance... do you give to the sketch writer, whoever produces the sketch?' He answered:

> 'The things which obviously make an impact in the House. A sort of short picture which will give a real impression of what was actually happening... he is allowed to make some sort of comment on... the quality of the speeches, whether people are clear or obscure, whether they made an impression on the House... To some extent to comment on the arguments.'

The Parliamentary sketch is thus a different thing from a report of proceedings in Parliament. A report of proceedings in Parliament, as usually understood, is a report of the words spoken in the debate, summarised so as to fit into the space available. In short, a précis. Such a report was considered in 1868 in *Wason v. Walter*. The court then held that such a report was privileged if it was a fair and honest report of what had taken place, 'published simply with a view to the information of the public, and innocent of all intention to do injury to the reputation of the party affected'. The reason for the privilege was said to be because —

> 'it is of paramount public and national importance that the proceedings of the houses of parliament shall be communicated to the public, who have the deepest interest in knowing what passes within their walls, seeing that on what is there said and done, the welfare of the community depends.'

It more than counterbalances the detriment to individuals of being defamed in the course of it.

Ever since that case it has been settled that, in a report of proceedings in Parliament, there is a privilege — a qualified privilege — in the reporter. If his report is fair and honest, then he is not liable to an action. It may be that a speaker in the debate got his facts entirely wrong or was actuated by the most express malice; nevertheless, the reporter is entitled to report what he said. Neither the reporter nor the newspaper is liable as long as the report was fair and the reporter himself was not actuated by malice. Take one instance in this very case. It appears that the Bishop of Southwark was mistaken when he said that sending a boy to the headmaster usually meant corporal punishment. We are told that it did not do so. It was for the headmaster to decide what the punishment was to be. The reporter would not be responsible for the mistake of the bishop.

I would add that, not only is the report of the proceedings privileged, but also the reporter of the newspaper can make any fair comment on it. That follows inexorably from the fact that the proceedings are presumed conclusively to be of public interest; and accordingly that fair comment can be made on it; see *Wason v. Walter* and *Mangena v. Wright*.

Such being the position of a report of proceedings in Parliament, what is the position of a Parliamentary sketch? When making a sketch, a reporter does not summarise all the speeches. He selects a part of the debate which appears to him to be of special public interest and then describes it and the impact which it made on the House. I think that a Parliamentary sketch is privileged if it is made fairly and honestly with the intention of giving an impression of the impact made on the hearers. In these days the debates in Parliament take so long that no newspaper could possibly report the debates in full, nor give the names of all the speakers, nor even summarise the main speeches. When a debate covers a particular subject-matter, there are often some aspects which are of greater public interest than others. If the reporter is to give the public any impression at all of the proceedings, he must be allowed to be selective and to cover those matters only which appear to be of particular public interest. Even then, he need not report it verbatim, word for word or letter by letter. It is sufficient if it is a fair presentation of what took place so as to convey to the reader the impression which the debate itself would have made on a hearer of it. Test it this way. If a member of the House were asked: 'What happened in the debate? Tell me about it.' His answer would be a sketch giving in words the impression it left on him, with more emphasis on one thing and less emphasis on another, just as it stuck in his memory. Such a sketch is privileged, whether spoken at the dinner table afterwards, or reported to the public at large in a newspaper. Even if it is defamatory of some one, it is privileged because the public interest in the debate counterbalances the private interest of the individual.

Applying that in the present case, when the reporter said that the Bishop of Southwark 'launched a scathing attack on Mr. Ivor Cook' he was recording the impact made on him by the bishop's remarks. When he said 'House amused', he was giving the reaction of the members of the House of Lords as he saw it. When he spoke of Lord Longford 'in what was a rather bumbling reply', he was giving his impression of Lord Longford's manner. Such a sketch, which gives the impression on the hearer, so long as it is fairly done, seems to me to be the subject of privilege — qualified privilege — for which the reporter is protected unless he is actuated by malice.

I would emphasise that it has to be fair. Here I come to the point particularly made by Mr. Cook. He said it was unfair to give such large prominence to what the bishop had said and such little prominence to the rebuttal by Lord Longford, and it was unfair to describe Lord Longford as 'bumbling' and so forth. But fairness in this regard means a fair presentation of what took place as it impressed the hearers. It does not mean fairness in the abstract as between Mr. Cook and those who were attacking him. Applying that test, it seems to me that this Parliamentary sketch is protected by the qualified privilege. It gives a fair presentation of the impression on the hearers of the bishop's speech. It made much impression on them: so it was given particular prominence. If it had been unfairly distorted, it would not have been a fair presentation. If Lord Longford's rebuttal had been omitted, it would not have been a fair presentation. But, looking at it as a whole, there is only one reasonable conclusion to which a reasonable jury could come, and that is that it was a fair presentation of what took place.

There is one further point. The column on the back page — which contained the Parliamentary sketch — gave specific references to the inner pages of the paper where there was a full report of the whole debate. I should have thought that any reader who was sufficiently interested in the case to take particular notice of what was said about Mr. Cook, would have turned to the inner page where he could have read the full report. The two together, beyond all doubt, are protected by privilege.

In my opinion, therefore, the verdict of this jury should be set aside on the ground that it was a verdict which a reasonable jury could not reasonably come to. It should be set aside. That was done in this court in *Hope v. W. C. Leng & Co. (Sheffield Telegraph) Ltd.* and we should do the same. We should set aside the verdict and order judgment to be entered for the defendants. I would allow the appeal accordingly.

BUCKLEY L.J. I agree. We are here concerned, as Lord Denning M.R. has explained, with a report of proceedings in the House of Lords. There can be no doubt that the plaintiff, Mr. Cook, is entitled to complain of such a report if it contains matter which is defamatory of him and is not a fair and accurate report insofar as it relates to him and to the defamatory matter. Mr. Cook, who (if I may be allowed to say so, has presented his argument I think very fairly and with great ability and courtesy before us) has contended that for such a report to be fair and accurate, it must really be of the nature of a précis of the whole proceedings or debate in order that it may have that quality of fairness which will bring before the reader the points and arguments that have been put forward on either side. I do not myself think that the report has to have that characteristic of being in the nature of a précis. The reporter or editor of the newspaper in which the report appears, as the case may be, is entitled in my judgment to select some part or parts of the debate or proceedings which he considers to be of particular public importance or otherwise likely to be of particular interest to the public — not on scandalous grounds or other unworthy grounds of that kind, but on the ground that the subject-matter is of genuine public interest; and he is I think entitled to report on the proceedings or that part of it which he selects in a manner which fairly and faithfully gives an impression of the events reported and will convey to the reader what he himself would have appreciated had he been present during the proceedings. Now, Mr. Cook has suggested that this report — and by that term I refer to what has been called the Parliamentary sketch which appeared on the back page of the relevant issue of the Daily Telegraph — is so selective that it does not fairly present a picture of that part of the proceedings to which the report relates. I do not feel able to accept that view. It appears to me that the report, which is admittedly a selective report concentrating on one particular aspect of the debate to which it relates, is not so tendentious or otherwise so slanted as to make it a distorted report of that part of the proceedings to which it relates; and I agree with Lord Denning M.R. in thinking that it is all the more difficult to come to the conclusion that it can be criticised in that way because the sketch itself contains two explicit references to the full Parliamentary report contained elsewhere in the same issue of the paper. On these grounds and for the reasons that Lord Denning M.R. has elaborated more fully in the judgment which he has delivered, I do not think that the conclusion at which the jury arrived was one at which on the material before them they could have properly arrived giving the matter proper consideration in the light of the proper principles; and accordingly I agree that this appeal must succeed.

Lawton L.J. For over two centuries the public in these islands have been interested in what goes on in Parliament and during that long period the Press has done what it could to keep them informed. The methods of doing so have changed from time to time. There are fashions in journalism just as there are fashions in other activities of life. Up until about 1939, if my recollection serves me rightly, most of the Press produced fairly detailed Parliamentary reports. During the war years, perhaps because of the shortage of newsprint, that kind of reporting fell into disuse, and in recent years, except for three newspapers, The Times, the Daily Telegraph and the Guardian, the practice had been not to publish the précis type of reports of Parliamentary proceedings. It may be the reason has been that the newspapers have found that the public are not interested in that kind of report. As a result, most newspapers have what has come to be called amongst journalists the Parliamentary sketch; and the three newspapers I have mentioned by name have Parliamentary sketches as well as the précis type of report. The problem which has arisen in this case is whether the Parliamentary sketch enjoys the same kind of privilege as the traditional Parliamentary précis. The Parliamentary sketch, from its very nature, cannot go into the detail which the Parliamentary précis does. At one stage in his argument I understood Mr. Cook to be saying that the Parliamentary sketch, if it is to attract the privilege which Parliamentary reports do enjoy, must have much the same balance and much the same content as a Parliamentary report of the traditional kind.

What is the basis for the qualified privilege which newspapers have in reporting Parliamentary debates? In reporting Parliamentary debates there may be occasions when the newspapers repeat defamatory statements which have been made in Parliament. The law has decided that in the public interest the repeating of such defamatory statements may be allowed provided that the newspaper carrying the report has been neither unfair nor inaccurate. What then is meant by 'unfair'? That is the sole question in this case. No question has arisen about the accuracy of the defendants' report. 'Unfair' must mean unbalanced, as Mr. Cook said. It is important to remember, however, that the balance must be in relation to the plaintiff's reputation. The plaintiff is bringing the action. He is saying that the Parliamentary sketch was defamatory — and I use the usual words of the pleader — of and concerning him. The Parliamentary sketch may be unfair to the government: it may be unfair to the opposition; it may be unfair to the speakers. But that is irrelevant for the purpose of an action for defamation in which the sole question is, was it unfair to the plaintiff?

The reporter represents the public in Parliament: he is their eyes and ears; and he has to do his best, using his professional skill, to give them a fair and accurate picture of what went on in either the House of Lords or the House of Commons. He cannot report everything that happened; he must, from the very nature of things, be selective; and what he may very well find himself doing is answering the question: Well, if I were a fair-minded, reasonable member of the public, what would I have remembered about this debate? He is, in my judgment, entitled to set out what he remembers.

In every debate the speakers are of varying quality. Some are memorable: some should be forgotten as soon as possible. It is the speakers who are memorable who leave impressions on reasonable members of the public; and the Parliamentary correspondent in this respect represents the public. He must, however, behave like a fair and reasonable man; and if in the course of the debate a good impression is made by a particular speaker and that impression is dissipated either wholly or in part by less memorable speeches, then that must be reflected in the published impression. The problem in this case was this: what was the memorable feature about the Court Lees debate? From the public's point of view it was the Bishop of Southwark's speech. The topic under debate had been before the public for about two months. The Bishop of Southwark brought some new, somewhat surprising facts — some of them not accurate — to the attention of the House of Lords. Others in the debate, including Lord Longford, cast doubt on the facts put forward and the conclusions, if any, to be drawn from them. That had to be reflected in the Parliamentary sketch made by the first defendant in this case. Were those criticisms of, and comments on, the bishop's speech properly reflected? In my judgment they were and no reasonable minded jury properly directed could have come to any other conclusion.

For those reasons I too would allow the appeal.

5.2.3.1.3.3.4 Hefferman v. *Regina Daily Star* [1930], 3 W.W.R. 656 (Sask. K.B.)

TAYLOR, J. (oral) — I still have the matters of law reserved to deal with before I can give my decision; and I think perhaps I may as well dispose of the matter now, so that you may have the benefit of the conclusion I have arrived at now.

It was argued before me that I should not leave the question of whether this was a public meeting, and whether it was a privileged occasion, to the jury generally. I reserved my decision on that argument; and then, with the concurrence of counsel, left the question to the jury as if it was solely a question of fact for them with a direction of law on the matter, the direction which I gave them.

Now, I may say that I have arrived at the conclusion that it is the duty of the Judge to determine whether in this case the publication in the newspaper was on a privileged occasion. I am influenced to that conclusion by the cases cited in the 6th edition of *Fraser,* 1925, at p. 220 — after reading those cases and the earlier cases there referred to. It is on the earlier cases that reliance is placed for a contrary view in the citations in *Gatley* and *Fraser* referred to by counsel. Authority for that same opinion is also to be found in the article in *Halsbury*. There is disagreement in the text-books. It will be seen that in *Fraser* the opinion is expressed that the cases relied on by the other learned writers must now be taken to be overruled.

One cannot weigh the authority of text writers, and the only way to deal with the matter is to read the cases and endeavour, I should say, to disregard the fact that there is a dispute between the text-book writers on the subject. And reading those cases, it seems to me, as a matter of law, that the Court is undoubtedly bound to accept the law to be as it is stated in the judgment of the Lord Chancellor, Finlay, and Lords Dunedin and Shaw, in *Adam v. Ward* [1917] A.C. 309, 86 L.J.K.B. 849. In the language of the Lord Chancellor:

> It is for the Judge, and the Judge alone, to determine as a matter of law whether the occasion is privileged, unless the circumstances attending it are in dispute, in which case the facts necessary to raise the question of law should be found by the jury.

Since delivering this judgment the Law Journal report of *Minter v. Priest* (1930) 99 L.J.K.B. 391, is to hand, in which Viscount Dunedin repeats his observations in *Adam v. Ward, supra,* and the House of Lords unanimously confirmed his view.

Now, in this case, the facts tending to establish the privileged occasion were entirely advanced by the defence, and, taking everything that was there advanced, and resolving every inference that could be drawn in favour of the defence, in my opinion, as a matter of law, it could not be held that they had satisfied the onus of establishing publication upon a privileged occasion. The question arises — I think it is a question of law — as no facts are in dispute, as to whether this was or was not a public meeting. I do not think that this meeting could be held to be a public meeting.

We must observe, in interpreting the statute in question, the law at the time it was passed, and the purpose for which it was passed. We must remember in interpreting the statute that it constitutes an inference, that it purports to authorize an interference with an existing cause of action and abolish that right of action. It is not therefore to be extended beyond its reasonable intention.

I would conclude that a public meeting must be one having in it some element of public control, not simply a meeting such as a lecture to which admission is charged, entirely under the control of the lecturer. The primary purpose of this meeting was for gain, 50 cents admission being charged to every person, and attendance was confined to those who were prepared to pay that admission. Further than that, while there was a list of the subjects to be discussed, really these could not be called discussions, because everything to be raised was to be dealt with by the lecturer. It does appear that questions could be asked, but there was nothing in the nature of discussion. It was a speech from the one person, or from persons permitted to speak by him. Now, having in view such cases as that one to which I referred where it was held that a religious service — although open to any of the public who might want to attend — was not a public meeting within the meaning of the Act, because it is confined practically to the religious sect, if that is not a public meeting, it could not possibly be held that this meeting under the control of Maloney was a public meeting. When one considers the purpose of the statute too, and the extent of the privilege which would be afforded to the newspapers, were it to be held that this was a public meeting, it seems to me that is a cogent reason for limiting it; because it would be possible for a person to hire a hall, call a meeting, publish notice of it in a newspaper, and naming certain public subjects, utter therein defamatory matter, for the publication of which action would lie. Yet if the law permitted repetition, any newspaper confining itself to a fair and accurate report would be privileged and excused from the publication; and that does not seem to me within the contemplation of the statute at all. No such licence could, in my view, have been intended.

I find no real dispute on the facts going to the issue as to whether this was or was not a public meeting. On that issue there is no controversy. As I conclude that it was not a public meeting, the statute which the defendant sets up does not apply.

Not only that, but perhaps I should express my view as to whether the publication of this particular matter which was published of and concerning the plaintiff was of a matter of public concern, the publication whereof was for the benefit of the public. I cannot agree with the defendant's contention that a case has been made out to support his contention on either of these matters. I have not time now to fully review the cases. In my address to the jury I pointed out the matters, the extent to which the plaintiff's conduct as a magistrate, and the criticism of the Government had been made matters of public concern; but I think it is absolutely clear that this matter introduced by Maloney was not germane or relevant to the discussion that had previously taken place. It was absolutely new, a charge of misconduct which had not theretofore been referred to in any way at all. It was a matter concerning Maloney himself and the plaintiff, and the charge so made by Maloney against the plaintiff and this former servant of his had not been made a matter of public concern therefore. Surely the utterances by a lecturer at a meeting, even if it were a public meeting, of a personal accusation of crime against an individual, against any person, cannot, by the very utterance by that lecturer be made a matter of public concern. Nor can I see the contention that the publication of it would be for the public benefit. Indeed, it seems to me that directly the contrary would be the case, because there is a procedure provided by law whereby prosecutions for criminal offences are to be followed. That very procedure would be interfered with if newspapers could broadcast charges before proceedings were taken to enforce them in the criminal courts by the proper criminal procedure. There is the further observation that it is the duty of every man to assist in the enforcement of the criminal law, and if a crime were committed such as Maloney said had been committed, then it would have been his duty — not to hire a hall and publish it in the hope of publication in a newspaper — it would have been his duty to lay a charge before a magistrate and have it prosecuted in the proper procedure required by law. And if, by way of argument, it were suggested that a substitute for that time-honoured procedure by publication in newspapers were permitted, I think it would constitute a very serious interference with the safety of persons accused of criminal offences; it would be a very serious departure from the proper proof of criminal charges. The nature of the charge leaves me further to conclude that it was not a matter, the publication of which was for the public benefit. As I say, it was a charge made by Maloney personally against the plaintiff. As stated in the cases to which reference was made by counsel this was a libellous matter of private concern, and I find it difficult to appreciate the contention that its publication could be for the public benefit.

To quote from *Gatley,* 2nd ed., p. 364:

> It was never intended that an editor might publish a report of anything said, however defamatory and however irrelevant to the subject of the meeting. Editors, no doubt, are under great difficulties, but they must take care not to publish foul accusations against individuals, entirely irrelevant and introduced only for the purpose of libelling them *** it was never intended that such irrelevant attacks should be published, nor can the publication of such attacks be for the public benefit. If a newspaper chooses to publish defamatory matter about anybody, though actually uttered at a public meeting but which has nothing to do with the objects of the meeting, then it cannot shield itself behind the *Law of Libel Amendment Act.*

So, therefore, I hold that the evidence was not sufficient to establish the defence of privilege and that those words were published under the protection of the Act in question. My conclusion, therefore, in that respect, is in accord with the findings of the jury, and there will, therefore, be judgment for the plaintiff for the amount of the damages found by the jury and costs.

5.2.3.1.3.3.5 Banks v. *Globe and Mail* (1961), 28 D.L.R. (2d) 343 (S.C.C.)

Note: An important question is whether the relationship between the media and the public, in respect of matters of public interest, should be regarded as giving rise to a privilege. The traditional view, as presented in *Banks* v. *Globe and Mail,* emphatically rejected such an idea.

CARTWRIGHT, J.: — This is an appeal, brought pursuant to leave granted by the Court of Appeal for Ontario, from a judgment of that Court, dismissing an appeal from a judgment of Spence, J., whereby the appellant's action was dismissed with costs.

The action was for damages for libel.

The appellant is a vice-president of the Seafarers' International Union of North America; he resides in the town of Pointe Claire in the Province of Quebec. The corporate respondent is the proprietor of a daily newspaper published under the name of "The Globe and Mail", of which the individual respondent is the editor and publisher.

The words complained of were published as the leading editorial in the issue of "The Globe and Mail" dated Monday, November 11, 1957, and are as follows:

MISSION ACCOMPLISHED

> It would seem in retrospect that Mr. Harold C. Banks, Canadian director of the Seafarers' International Union, was brought to this country for the specific purpose of scuttling Canada's deep sea fleet. If this was indeed the case, he has succeeded admirably. With the decision by Canadian National Steamships to strike its eight vessels on West Indian service from Canadian registry, Canada is left with only three ocean-going merchant ships — as against the hundred or more it had when Mr. Banks took over the SIU eight years ago.
>
> Considering his record of criminal offenses in the United States, which he diversified and extended after coming to Canada, this country has done rather well by Mr. Banks. He

enjoys great power and considerable wealth, his salary being a reported $12,000 a year. Unlike most other union leaders in Canada, he does not have to go through the irritating business of getting himself re-elected at periodic intervals; indeed, he was never elected in the first place. And he has influential friends; when he applied for Canadian citizenship this year, who should show up to vouch for him but such people as Mr. Claude Jodoin, president of the Canadian Labor Congress, and Mr. Frank Hall, head of the Brotherhood of Railway Clerks.

But if Canada has done well by Mr. Banks, it cannot be said that Mr. Banks has done well by Canada. It is true that, by his forcible demands on shipowners he has made Canada's ocean-going seamen the most highly paid in the world. But in so doing, he has put virtually all of them out of employment. With Mr. Banks directing the SIU, almost every Canadian-owned deep sea ship has been transferred to a foreign flag, and is being worked by a foreign crew.

This will now be the case with the eight West Indies vessels of CNS, which are to be registered in Port of Spain, Trinidad. The eight ships have been tied up since last July, owing to a strike called by Mr. Banks. At the time, he demanded a 30 per cent wage increase for the SIU members working them; CNS offered 10 per cent, which it later raised to 15 per cent — not reasonable considering that the West Indian service has run at a heavy loss for the last seven years. This latter offer was rejected by Mr. Banks even when CNS warned him that rejection would mean the registry transfer, and consequent unemployment of all the crew members concerned.

Mr. Banks' application for citizenship is still, apparently, before the Canadian Government, which has reached no final decision in the matter. We suggest, in the light of the CNS fiasco, that the application be turned down, and Mr. Banks be sent back to the U.S. He came here to preside over the dissolution of the Canadian Merchant Marine; the Canadian Merchant Marine has been dissolved. Why, then, should he remain? His mission has been accomplished, his work is done.

The action was commenced on December 3, 1957.

In the statement of claim it is alleged that the defendants falsely and maliciously published this editorial of and concerning the plaintiff and that in its plain and ordinary meaning it is defamatory of him and of and concerning him in the way of his office as vice-president of his union. In para. 6, thirteen innuendoes are alleged. In para. 7 it is alleged that notice of complaint was served on the defendants on November 21, 1957.

In the statement of defence publication is admitted. The defences pleaded are, (i) that the words complained of in their natural and ordinary meaning are no libel, (ii) that the said words do not bear and were not understood to bear and are incapable of bearing or being understood to bear the meaning alleged in the statement of claim, (iii) a plea of qualified privilege and (iv) a plea of the defence of fair comment.

The plea of qualified privilege is contained in paras. 3 and 4 of the statement of defence as follows:

3. The Defendants say that the words complained of were published under the following circumstances —

The said words were published following the decision by Canadian National Steamships to transfer its eight vessels on West Indian service from Canadian Registry to a Foreign Registry on the 9th of November, 1957. In July 1957 the Seafarers' International Union, of which the Plaintiff is the Canadian Director, called a strike which tied up the said eight vessels. After more than four months the strike was still not settled and the vessels were transferred to Foreign Registry as aforesaid, all of which was the subject of discussion and comment in the House of Commons and in the Public Press.

> 4. By reason of such circumstances it was the duty of the Defendants to publish, and in the interests of the public to receive communications and comments with respect to the strike and the resultant transfer of eight vessels from Canadian Registry and by reason of this the said words were published under such circumstances and upon such occasion as to render them privileged.

The plea of the defence of fair comment is set out in paras 6 and 8 of the statement of defence as follows:

> 6. Insofar as the said words consist of statements of fact the said words are in their natural and ordinary meaning, and without the meanings alleged in paragraph 6 of the Statement of Claim, true in substance and in fact; and insofar as the said words consist of expressions of opinion they are fair comment made in good faith and without malice upon the said facts which are a matter of public interest in the circumstances stated in paragraph 3.
>
> 8. In the alternative if any of the said words are capable of the meanings alleged in paragraph 6 of the Plaintiff's Statement of Claim then they are fair comment made in good faith and without malice on a matter of public interest. The said comment was based upon the transfer by Canadian National Steamships of eight vessels from Canadian Registry to Foreign Registry in the circumstances referred to in paragraph 3.

The action was tried in June, 1958. Counsel for the appellant called two witnesses, the plaintiff and a Mr. Leonard McLaughlin who was the secretary-treasurer of the Seafarers' International Union of North America, Canadian District. Counsel then read some questions and answers from the examination for discovery of the respondent Dalgleish and closed his case.

Counsel for the respondents then moved, in the absence of the jury, for the dismissal of the action on the ground that the words complained of were published on an occasion of qualified privilege and that there was no evidence of malice to go to the jury.

It appears that before commencing his argument on this motion, counsel for the respondents had announced his decision not to call any evidence. Shortly after counsel for the appellant had commenced his argument on the motion the learned trial Judge called attention to this as follows:

> HIS LORDSHIP: May I interrupt you for a moment. I think it is only proper, Mr. Walker, that I should ask you, when you commenced your argument, the thing which I did ask you in chambers and therefore I omitted to ask for the record. Is it the intention of counsel for the defendants to adduce evidence?
>
> MR. WALKER: No, my lord, I am calling no evidence.

At a later stage of his argument on this motion counsel for the plaintiff admitted that the strike and the resultant transfer of the ships involved to foreign registry constituted a matter of public interest; but, as I read the record, counsel did not admit that the statements and comments made about the plaintiff were made on a matter of public interest. This accords with the position taken by counsel in his opening to the jury in the course of which he said:

> We shall also contend throughout this trial that what was said about Mr. Banks was not said on a matter of public interest; that it was substantially a personal attack and not mere comment or expressions of opinion on a matter of public interest.

These circumstances have a bearing on the submission of counsel for the respondents, to be mentioned later, that counsel for the plaintiff at the trial had in effect admitted that the editorial was published on an occasion of qualified privilege.

At the conclusion of the argument on the motion the learned trial Judge ruled that the editorial was published on an occasion of qualified privilege but that there was evidence of malice to go to the jury.

In his charge the learned trial Judge made it clear to the jury that they had the right to bring in a general verdict but he invited them to answer a number of questions and the jury followed this course. The questions and answers are as follows:

1. Were the statements complained of and set out in Exhibit 1 under the circumstances in which they were used, defamatory of the plaintiff? Answer "Yes" or "No". Answer: Yes.

2. (a) Insofar as the statements are of fact were they all true? Answer "Yes" or "No". Answer: No. (b) Insofar as the statements are expressions of opinion did they exceed the limit of fair comment? Answer "Yes" or "No". Answer: Yes.

3. Do the words complained of and set out in Exhibit 1 mean —

(a) that the plaintiff came from the United States to Canada for the specific purpose of ending the existence of Canadian ships at sea, contrary to the interests of members of his Union and the people of Canada? Answer "Yes" or "No". Answer: Yes.

(b) that the plaintiff committed a substantial number of criminal offences in the United States? Answer "Yes" or "No". Answer: Yes.

(c) that the plaintiff has committed a substantial number of criminal offences of diverse kinds after coming to Canada? Answer "Yes" or "No". Answer: No.

(d) that the plaintiff is a dictatorial and irresponsible union officer not subject to removal or re-election by the membership of his Union? Answer "Yes" or "No". Answer: Yes.

(e) that the plaintiff has used threats of force in making demands upon Canadian ship owners? Answer "Yes" or "No". Answer: No.

(f) that the plaintiff has caused loss of employment to be suffered by most or all of Canada's ocean-going seamen? Answer "Yes" or "No". Answer: Yes.

(g) that the plaintiff, on his own initiative and without the authority of the membership of his Union, called a strike against Canadian National Steamships? Answer "Yes" or "No". Answer: No.

(h) that the plaintiff, on his own initiative and without reference to the membership of his Union demanded a 30 per cent wage increase for such members. Answer "Yes" or "No". Answer: No.

(i) that the plaintiff, on his own initiative and without reference to the membership of his Union, rejected an offer of a 10 per cent wage increase? Answer "Yes" or "No". Answer: No.

(j) that the plaintiff, while posing as a representative of working seamen, was indifferent or hostile to their interests? Answer "Yes" or "No". Answer: No.

(k) that the plaintiff deliberately used an office of trust held by him to cause injury and loss to the membership of his Union by whom he was employed? Answer "Yes" or "No". Answer: No.

(l) that the plaintiff is an unfit person to be granted Canadian citizenship? Answer "Yes" or "No". Answer: Yes.

(m) that the plaintiff is an unfit person to be permitted to reside in Canada? Answer "Yes" or "No". Answer: Yes.

4. If you have answered "Yes" to any of the sub-questions in 3 above, does such meaning exceed the limit of fair comment? Answer "Yes" or "No". Answer: Yes.

5. When the defendants published this statement were they actuated by any motive other than their duty to publish communications and comments on a matter of public interest? Answer "Yes" or "No". Answer: No.

6. At what amount do you assess the damages of the plaintiff? $3500.00 (Thirty-five hundred dollars).

Upon these answers the learned trial Judge directed judgment to be entered dismissing the action with costs.

The appellant appealed to the Court of Appeal. The first ground set out in the notice of appeal was: "That the learned trial Judge erred in holding that the words complained of were protected by the defence of qualified privilege." Laidlaw, J.A., who delivered the unanimous judgment of the Court of Appeal, in summarizing the grounds of appeal presented in argument before that Court described the first of those grounds as follows:

> First, that the decision of the learned trial Judge that the occasion was one of qualified privilege, was erroneous, or, in the alternative, that the learned Judge ought to have found that part of the published article was within the privilege and part of it was not within the privilege.

I have reached the conclusion that the learned trial Judge and the Court of Appeal were in error in holding that the occasion on which the editorial was published was one of qualified privilege and consequently do not find it necessary to consider the other grounds urged by Mr. MacKinnon in support of the appeal.

The reasons of the learned trial Judge for holding that the occasion was privileged are as follows:

> The first branch of the application may be disposed of very shortly. I think it is quite evident by consideration of the cases cited by counsel for the defendant, particularly *Jenoure v. Delmege* [1891] A.C. 73; *Pittard v. Oliver,* [1891] 1 Q.B. 474; *Mangena v. Wright,* [1909] 2 K.B. 958; *Adam v. Ward,* [1917] A.C. 309; *Showler v. MacInnes* (1937), 51 B.C.R. 391; *Dennison et al. v. Sanderson,* [1946], 4 D.L.R. 314, O.R. 601; and *Drew v. Toronto Star Ltd. & Atkinson,* [1947], 4 D.L.R. 221, O.R. 730; that the class of cases to which the defence of qualified privilege extends have, during the course of recent years, been extended, and that that extension will cover editorial comment by a metropolitan newspaper upon matters of public interest. It is difficult to conceive a matter in which the public would be much more interested in the year 1957 than the most important topic of industrial relations, when added to that there is the topic of the continued existence of a deep-sea fleet under Canadian registry. The latter topic, in fact, had so interested the public that it was included in a reference of matters to a Royal Commission, the report of which had not yet been rendered at the time of this alleged libel.
>
> There is no more efficient organ for informing the public and for disseminating to the public intelligent comment on such matters of public interest, than a great metropolitan newspaper, which the plaintiff has proved the defendant to be. The members of the public have a real, a vital — I might go so far as to say — a paramount interest in receiving those comments.
>
> The decision of Mr. Justice Manson in *Showler v. MacInnes* has been criticized but I feel that his words are most applicable to the particular situation which existed here, and I propose to adopt those words in this case where he said (51 B.C.R. at p. 395):
>
> "The whole citizenhood of Vancouver has and had at the time of the address in question a vital concern in the matter of industrial relations in the community and in knowing under what circumstances strikes might be called."
>
> adding the comment that for "all the citizens of Vancouver" I would insert "citizens of Canada".

The statement of the rule as to the burden of proof where a defence of qualified privilege is set up, contained in *Gatley on Libel & Slander,* 4th ed., p. 282 (stated in the same words in the 5th ed., of that work at p. 270) was approved by this Court in *Globe &*

Mail Ltd. v. Boland, 22 D.L.R. (2d) 277 at p. 279, [1960] S.C.R. 203 at p. 206, and is as follows:

> "Where a defence of qualified privilege is set up, it is for the defendant to allege and prove all such facts and circumstances as are necessary to bring the words complained of within the privilege, unless such facts are admitted before or at the trial of the action. Whether the facts and circumstances proved or admitted are or are not such as to render the occasion privileged is a question of law for the judge to decide."

In the case at bar the evidence of the plaintiff showed that the strike referred to in the editorial had commenced in July, 1957 and that it had no been settled at the date of the trial. His evidence in cross-examination continued:

> Q. So that when the defendant says in the Statement of Defence that after four months the strike was still not settled, that is correct. A. That is correct. Q. And you also told us that the vessels were transferred to foreign registry. Now, Mr. Banks, I suppose you read the newspapers, do you? A. Occasionally. Q. And was there considerable newspaper publicity with reference to this strike and with reference to the transfer of the vessels? A. There was. Q. And was there discussion in the House of Commons with reference to the strike and the transfer of the vessels? A. There was.

It has already been mentioned that counsel for the plaintiff admitted that the strike and the transfer of the ships involved to foreign registry constituted a matter of public interest.

I do not find it necessary to consider whether the allegations of fact on which the plea of qualified privilege was founded were sufficiently proved. If it be assumed for the purposes of argument that all the facts and circumstances alleged in paras. 3 and 4 of the statement of defence were proved it is my opinion that they were not such as to render the occasion privileged.

With the greatest respect it appears to me that in his reasons quoted above the learned trial Judge has fallen into the same error as was pointed out in the judgment of this Court in *Globe & Mail Ltd. v. Boland,* at p. 280 D.L.R., p. 207 S.C.R., and has confused the *right* which the publisher of a newspaper has, in common with all Her Majesty's subjects, to report truthfully and comment fairly upon matters of a public interest, with a *duty* of the sort which gives rise to an occasion of privilege. It is not necessary to refer again to the authorities discussed in the case last cited, but I think it desirable to recall the passage from the judgment of Lord Shaw in *Arnold v. The King Emperor* (1914), 30 T.L.R. 462 at p. 468:

> The freedom of the journalist is an ordinary part of the freedom of the subject, and to whatever lengths the subject in general may go, so also may the journalist, but, apart from statute-law, his privilege is no other and no higher. The responsibilities which attach to his power in the dissemination of printed matter may, and in the case of a conscientious journalist do, make him more careful; but the range of his assertions, his criticisms, or his comments is as wide as, and no wider than, that of any other subject. No privilege attaches to his position.

The following statement in *Gatley on Libel & Slander,* 5th ed., pp. 322-3 is, in my opinion, accurate:

> The defence of fair comment must also be distinguished from that of qualified privilege. In the defence of fair comment the right exercised by the defendant is shared by every member of the public. "Who is entitled to comment? The answer to that is 'everyone.' A newspaper

> reporter or a newspaper editor has exactly the same rights, neither more nor less, than every other citizen.'' In that of qualified privilege the right is not shared by every member of the public, but is limited to an individual who stands in such relation to the circumstances that he is entitled to say or write what would be libellous or slanderous on the part of anyone else. ''For instance, if a master is asked as to the character of a servant, and he says that the servant is a thief, he has a privilege which no one else would have.'' ''A privileged occasion is one on which the privileged person is entitled to do something which no one who is not within the privilege is entitled to do on that occasion. A person in such a position may say or write about another person things which no other person in the kingdom can be allowed to say or write. But, in the case of a criticism upon [a matter of public interest whether it be the conduct of a public man or] a published work, every person in the kingdom is entitled to do, and is forbidden to do exactly the same things, and therefore the occasion is not privileged.''

The judgments given at trial in the cases of *Dennison et al. v. Sanderson, supra,* and *Drew v. Toronto Star Ltd. & Atkinson, supra,* relied on by the learned trial Judge, in so far as they deal with the question of qualified privilege, must be regarded as having been overruled by the judgments of this Court in *Douglas v. Tucker,* [1952], 1 D.L.R. 657, 1 S.C.R. 275 and in *Globe & Mail Ltd. v. Boland, supra.* The judgment in *Showler v. MacInnes,* 51 B.C.R. 391, is, in my opinion, inconsistent with the two last-mentioned judgments of this Court and with our judgment in the case at bar and ought not to be followed. The other decisions referred to in the reasons of the learned trial Judge are all distinguishable on their facts from the case at bar.

There are of course many cases in which publication of defamatory matter in a newspaper may be privileged either by statute or at common law; examples are to be found in the *Libel and Slander Act,* R.S.O. 1950, c.204, ss.9 and 10 [now R.S.O. 1960, c.211, ss.3 and 4], and in such cases as *Adam v. Ward,* [1917] A.C. 309 and *Allbutt v. Gen'l Council of Medical Education & Registration* (1889), 23 Q.B.D. 400. In the first of these it was held that the Army Council owed a duty to publish to the whole world a letter vindicating a General who had been falsely accused before the same audience of discreditable conduct and that publication in the press was therefore privileged; in the second it was held that publication in the press of an accurate report of proceedings within the jurisdiction of the General Medical Council erasing the name of the plaintiff from the medical register was privileged on the ground, *inter alia,* that it was the duty of the Council to give the public accurate information as to who is on the register and if a person's name is erased accurate information of the cause of its erasure.

The decision of the learned trial Judge, in the case at bar, quoted above, appears to involve the proposition of law, which in my opinion is untenable, that given proof of the existence of a subject-matter of wide public interest throughout Canada without proof of any other special circumstances any newspaper in Canada (and *semble* therefore any individual) which sees fit to publish to the public at large statements of fact relevant to that subject-matter is to be held to be doing so on an occasion of qualified privilege.

Having reached the conclusion that the learned trial Judge was in error in deciding that the editorial complained of was published on an occasion of qualified privilege, it is not necessary to consider what judgment should have been given on the answers of the jury had the ruling of the learned trial Judge been upheld; but I do not wish to be understood as agreeing that even in that event the action should have been dismissed;

while the plea of qualified privilege and the answer of the jury negativing express malice would, on the hypothesis mentioned, have afforded a defence to the action in so far as it was based on the publication of defamatory statements of fact there remained the finding of the jury that the comment (and the editorial consisted partly of comment) was unfair. However, I do not pursue this question further.

It remains to consider what order should be made. Counsel for the respondent argued that if we should hold the publication was not made on an occasion of qualified privilege a new trial should be directed; this argument was based in part on the submission that at the trial counsel for the plaintiff had admitted that the occasion was one of qualified privilege. I have read all the record with care and cannot find that any such admission was made. Doubtless both counsel at the trial were familiar with the ruling which had been made by the learned trial Judge a short time before in the case of *Globe & Mail Ltd. v. Boland, supra,* and, perhaps for that reason, counsel for the plaintiff concentrated his argument on the submission that even if the occasion was one of privilege the bounds of the privilege had been exceeded. The following passage at the end of the argument of the motion, and particularly the words I have italicized, would be inconsistent with the view that the learned trial Judge considered that any such admission had been made.

> Mr. Jolliffe: Therefore the gist of my submission is that *even if the Court holds the occasion to be a privileged one,* the editorial ...
>
> His Lordship: In short, *even if the Court holds it is qualified privilege,* qualified privilege only exists for the purpose for which the privilege is set up.
>
> Mr. Jolliffe: Exactly, my lord.
>
> His Lordship: And if the motive goes beyond that, it is evidence of malice to go to the jury.
>
> Mr. Jolliffe: Exactly, my lord. That is what I am attempting to say.
>
> His Lordship: I understand that.

I am unable to find any sufficient ground for directing a new trial; I have given my reasons for holding that the defence of qualified privilege fails; the answers of the jury negatived the defence of fair comment; the error in law which, in my respectful opinion, was made by the trial Judge was not one which would cause the jury to increase the amount of the damages or would otherwise prejudice the position of the respondents.

I would allow the appeal, set aside the judgment of the Court of Appeal and that of the learned trial Judge and direct that judgment be entered for the plaintiff for $3,500 with costs throughout.

5.2.3.1.3.3.6 Stopforth v. *Goyer* (1978), 4 C.C.L.T. 265 (Ont. H.C.)

13th April 1978. LIEFF J.: — This is an action for damages for libel tried at Ottawa on 6th, 7th, 8th, 9th and 10th March 1978, without a jury, counsel having consented thereto pursuant to s.59 of The Judicature Act, R.S.O. 1970, c.228. Counsel consented to this procedure after a jury had been empanelled but before any evidence had been led.

The alleged defamatory remarks were said to have been spoken by the defendant of the plaintiff to reporters of the printed and electronic news media who were present in the Government lobby in the Parliament Buildings in Ottawa on 1st June 1976.

Shortly before that the defendant had emerged from the chamber of the House of Commons at the conclusion of the question period. The words admittedly spoken by the defendant were as follows:

"I will stand for my officials and I accept responsibility for errors of judgment, mistakes made in good faith. But I do not believe that ministerial responsibility extends to cases of misinformation or gross negligence. Why should I pay for misinformation."

It is settled law that where a person speaks defamatory words to the press with the intention or knowledge that they will be republished, the speaker is responsible in libel rather than in slander.

When a politician of experience speaks to the press he impliedly, if not expressly, authorizes republication of his communication and is thus responsible for any libel. This point was not put in issue by counsel for the defendant.

The story was carried on the Canadian Press wire service and the words sued upon were the focus of front page stories in the London Free Press, the Globe and Mail, the Montreal Gazette and the Ottawa Journal, all major Canadian newspapers of wide circulation. I therefore find as a fact that the words sued upon were widely circulated in the printed media.

At this point it may be useful to set out briefly the events which led up to the incident at which the words sued upon were spoken. A more detailed review of the facts may be more conveniently made when I deal with the defence of justification.

In 1972 the Department of National Defence (DND) determined to acquire some 18 long-range patrol aircraft (LRPA). In order to co-ordinate the LRPA acquisition a project office was established in the summer of 1972 composed of employees of DND, the Department of Supply and Services (DSS), the Department of Industry, Trade and Commerce and the Department of Regional Economic Expansion, The plaintiff, an employee of DSS, was at all material times deputy manager of the project office. The defendant was at all material times Minister of DSS.

Supervision of the project office was achieved through a bureaucratic mechanism called the Senior Management Board. This Board was composed of an assistant deputy minister from each of the four ministries involved in the project office. The assistant deputy minister from each ministry reported to his deputy minister who, in turn, reported to the minister. The DSS member of the Senior Management Board was Mr. Eric Booth, now deceased, and the Deputy Minister of Supply to whom Booth reported was Mr. Jacques DesRoches.

On 12th November 1975, when it was apparent that DND had a budgetary shortfall of some $375 million on the LRPA project, the manager of the project office, General T.S. Allan, telephoned the then competing bidders on the LRPA project, the Boeing Aircraft Corporation and the Lockheed Aircraft Corporation, to inquire as to the feasibility of the manufacturers providing bridge financing for the DND shortfall. Both manufacturers replied that such was feasible.

On 27th November 1975, Cabinet chose the Lockheed LRPA proposal over that of Boeing, which decision was approved by Treasury Board on the same date subject to two conditions:

(1) that permission would be obtained to take the specifications and plans for the P-3 Orion airplanes to be manufactured by Lockheed for the LRPA project out of the United States; and,

(2) that a specified quantum of the industrial benefits of the contract would accrue to Canada.

Neither Cabinet nor Treasury Board provided any direction as to how the LRPA project was to be paid for, even though both bodies were aware of the DND shortfall and the cost of financing it by virtue of submissions prepared for their consideration by the project office. The defendant sat as a member of both Cabinet and the Treasury Board at all material times.

On 2nd December 1975, the defendant signed a telex to Lockheed accepting its proposal subject to the two conditions dictated by Treasury Board. The acceptance was not made conditional upon Lockheed providing bridge financing for the DND shortfall.

On 17th December 1975, Lockheed informed DSS that it was not possible for it to finance the DND shortfall. The result of this information was that there were insufficient funds in DND's budget to carry out the project according to plan.

By March 1976, and through the spring of that year, debate in Parliament intensified as to how the government could have become involved in a contract without first ensuring that the project was properly and adequately funded or financed.

By May 1976, the defendant was facing frequent questioning in the House of Commons over the LRPA project. General Allan's conversation with Lockheed concerning the provision of bridge financing was of particular interest to the interlocutor during question period in the House. These questions were particularly directed at the defendant who had signed the telex accepting Lockheed's proposal without including bridge financing as a condition of the acceptance. The defendant's reply was consistent, namely, that neither he, his deputies nor his representative at the project office, the plaintiff, knew of any agreement by Lockheed to provide bridge financing before 2nd December 1975.

On 18th May 1977, the Minister of DND advised the House of the termination of the Lockheed contract on the LRPA project.

Under the pressure of intensifying debate, the defendant called the plaintiff to a meeting in his office on 19th May 1976, to confirm the information he had been providing to the House.

The evidence relating to this meeting is as follows:

(1) that the defendant explained to the plaintiff his need for precise information concerning General Allan's agreement with Lockheed and the extent of the plaintiff's knowledge as to any agreement prior to 2nd December 1975, the date on which the telex was signed; and

(2) the defendant's recollection was that the plaintiff denied any knowledge of an agreement by Lockheed to provide bridge financing for the DND shortfall, saying he (the plaintiff) did not learn of it until mid-December.

The defendant's account of this meeting with the plaintiff was confirmed by the Deputy Minister of Supply, Mr. DesRoches, who was present for most of the meeting.

The plaintiff's account of the 19th May 1976, meeting with the defendant is different from the defendant's in one material respect. The plaintiff says that:

(a) he told the defendant that he was not aware of any agreement by Lockheed to provide bridge financing but he was aware that General Allan had conferred with Lockheed on the subject and Lockheed had either agreed that such an arrangement was feasible or to look into the feasibility of such an arrangement;

(b) he told the defendant that he was not privy to General Allan's conversation with Lockheed but learned a few days afterwards that it had taken place; and

(c) it was not until mid-December 1975, when the omission of the condition of bridge financing from the 2nd December 1975, telex became important, that he first learned or heard that Lockheed had actually agreed to provide the financing.

In effect what the plaintiff is saying is that it was not until Lockheed said it could not finance the project that he formed the impression that there never could have been an actual agreement as distinguished from a study of feasibility. The defendant on the other hand asked about *a conversation which resulted in an agreement;* this the plaintiff denied.

On the basis of his meeting with the plaintiff the defendant continued to deny knowledge, on his part or on the part of his aides, of an agreement by Lockheed to provide bridge financing of the DND shortfall.

On 31st May 1976, in preparation for a "late show" (which is a continuation of question period after the close of the day's other parliamentary business), on the LRPA project the defendant became aware that the plaintiff knew of General Allan's conversation with Lockheed concerning bridge financing before 2nd December 1975. According to the defendant the implications of this revelation were very serious for it meant he had been misleading the House and this troubled him very much. The defendant testified that he consulted with the Prime Minister and other senior parliamentarians as to whether he should resign.

On 1st June 1976, the defendant made the following statement to the House (Ex. 12). During his examination-in-chief the defendant read it all into the record. It is reproduced in full:

"June 1, 1976
3:00 p.m.

"STATEMENT BY THE HONOURABLE JEAN-PIERRE GOYER

"Mr. Speaker:

"I wish to correct a statement that I made in the House yesterday in response to a question from the Honourable Member from Victoria (McKinnon). This question was in relation to whether a representative from my department on the LRPA project team was aware before December 2, 1975 that Lockheed had given verbal assurance that it could provide financing to meet DND's cash shortfall in the first three years of the project.

"But first, I would like to reiterate two points which I have repeatedly stressed both in this House and outside Parliament, namely that

"(1) The financing of any contract entered upon by the Department of Supply and Services is the prime and exclusive responsibility of the customer Department, in this case the Department of National Defence.

"(2) On December 2, 1975, when a telex was sent to Lockheed confirming the government's intention to purchase 18 Orion aircrafts, neither myself, nor my Deputy-Minister was made aware, directly or indirectly, of a telephone conversation held between an official of the DND and a representative of Lockheed to the effect that Lockheed would furnish the financing for the LRPA project.

"In any case, I repeat, not obtaining a written agreement from Lockheed was a serious error. It is elementary that an agreement involving a loan of millions of dollars should have been confirmed in a written document.

"This was not done. Furthermore, the offer never did materialize. In this respect, I refer to the statements of my colleague, the Minister of National Defence, which appear in the Hansard dated March 30, 1976, on page 12265 and March 26, 1976, page 12177.

"Personally, I might add that it was also a very serious mistake that the minister responsible for negotiating the agreement with Lockheed was not informed of the basic funding difficulties before December 2, 1975 and that the proposed solution rested upon a verbal agreement.

"Now, the statement I made yesterday was that neither myself nor my deputy nor my representative in the LRPA project office was aware of the possibility of Lockheed furnishing the financing for the LRPA project. The factual statement is that neither myself nor my deputy nor, as I stated in the House on May 25, 1976, on page 13794 of Hansard, the representative of my department on the management committee was aware of the possibility of that financial arrangement. For your information the representative on the LRPA management committee was my former Assistant Deputy Minister, Mr. Eric Booth. The portion of the statement that I wish to clarify concerns Mr. L.H. Stopforth who as my representative on the LRPA project group I now find was aware of financing discussions held between DND and Lockheed in mid-November 1975.

"During the past months, Mr. Speaker, I repeatedly attempted to ascertain whether or not any officials of my Department were aware of the financing negotiations held between the DND and Lockheed, prior to December 2, 1975. I repeatedly was assured that no one had prior knowledge of this problem and I conveyed this information to the House.

"On May the 19th, in view of the numerous questions raised by Members of the House, I personally met in the presence of my Deputy-Minister with Mr. L.H. Stopforth who assured me that he had no prior information concerning the financial negotiations between DND and Lockheed. Ministers, acting on the representations and advice from their civil servants, must rely on the information they receive on these matters on the basis of trust.

"Last evening, however, and it was confirmed to me this morning, I learned that Mr. L.H. Stopforth had modified his version to state that while he had not been privy to conversations between DND and Lockheed, he was aware of the financing discussions with Lockheed in November 1975.

"I take my Ministerial responsibilities very seriously with regard to the policies and administrative practices of my department.

"Accordingly, *I will stand by my officials, and I accept to take responsibility for errors of judgment, mistakes made 'in good faith', inadvertent errors, but I do not believe that ministerial responsibility extends to cases of misinformation or gross negligence*. In this case, a serious error was committed: not only was I nor my Deputy-Minister not informed of financial negotiations between the DND and Lockheed, prior to December 2, but subsequently, when I personally checked on this situation I remained misinformed. This is unacceptable.

"My view is that while ministerial responsibility is of prime importance, every public servant regardless of his interest in politics, also holds the public trust to some extent. Every public servant is in a position of responsibility and the responsibility here was to ensure that the Minister, the House and the public be correctly informed.

"I feel very strongly about officials who misinform their Minister. While I am not against any man or any organization I believe that preserving the integrity and the efficiency of our system of government comes first. The public must believe that the system serves it well. The public must respect the public service. My ministerial responsibility, in this case, is to see that these rights are preserved.

"Consequently, Mr. L.H. Stopforth has been removed from his function as Deputy Head of the project office." [The italics are mine.]

After making his statement to the House of Commons the defendant left the chamber and was passing through the Liberal lobby when he was encountered by the press to whom he made the statement sued upon. Mary Louise Janigan, parliamentary correspondent for the Toronto Star was present in the press gallery of the House when the defendant made his statement and was also present in the government lobby when the defendant spoke to the press and made the statement sued upon. She testified that the defendant spoke these words in response to questions by reporters concerning his reasons for demoting the plaintiff. According to her the defendant also said that the plaintiff would be transferred to another post if he chose to stay with DDS and "I don't have any confidence in him".

Exhibit No. 17 is an extract of the original "copy" of Ms. Janigan's story on the events in question typed by her on the evening of 1st June 1976, from notes she made on that day. It confirms her account of the additional statement made by the defendant. Counsel for the plaintiff relies on it as an aggravation of the statement sued upon. Such evidence is admissible for that purpose.

Deputy Minister of Supply, Mr. DesRoches, testified that:

(1) it was as a result of the events leading up to the defendant's statement to the House on 1st June 1976, that he decided to remove the plaintiff from his assignment as deputy manager of the project office;

(2) he had wanted to dismiss the plaintiff outright, but decided against it;

(3) he asked the plaintiff for his resignation which the plaintiff refused to provide;

(4) it was his own decision to remove the plaintiff from the project office; and

(5) the defendant did not direct his decision in any way.

The plaintiff testified that since the events in question his status and prestige as a senior civil servant have, in essence, been entirely stripped from him. The plaintiff has, however, suffered no cut in salary and, in fact, has had a modest pay increase since June 1976.

Exhibit No. 4 is a copy of a letter dated 8th June 1976, from counsel for the plaintiff to the defendant requesting a published retraction of the words sued upon. The defendant acknowledged receipt of Exhibit No. 4 and stated that he made no retraction.

The defendant pleaded four primary defences: fair comment, absolute privilege, qualified privilege and justification.

...

III. *QUALIFIED PRIVILEGE*

Qualified privilege attaches to statements made on a privileged occasion. One such occasion, and the one on which the defendant relies, is where the statement is made in pursuance of a moral, social or legal duty to communicate the information contained in the statement. Concommitant with the duty to speak there must also be an interest or duty in the hearer to receive the communication.

This reciprocity is essential: see *Adam v. Ward,* [1917] A.C. 309 (H.L.) per Lord Atkinson at p. 334.

The importance of the duty to speak on the occasion sued upon was dismissed in the recent cases of *Littleton v. Hamilton* (1974), 4 O.R. (2d) 283, 47 D.L.R. (3d)

663 (C.A.). In that case the defendants tried to invoke the defence of qualified privilege regarding the publication of a history of the Company of Young Canadians. The defendants relied on the fact that the organization was one of public interest, funded with public money and highly publicized across the country. Dubin J.A., who delivered the judgment of the Court, stressed that the existence of a duty to communicate is essential to the defence of qualified privilege. At p. 285 he said:

"In order to hold that words are published on an occasion of qualified privilege, something more is necessary than the mere fact that the words are being addressed to a matter of public interest. Before an individual can be said to have published words on an occasion of qualified privilege, some circumstances must be shown from which it can be concluded for valid social reasons that an individual can with impunity publish defamatory statements of others provided he does so without malice. Although it has been stated that there is no confined catalogue of such occasions, it is clear that the mere fact that the publication relates to matters of public interest is not sufficient."

The burden of proof of establishing the defence of qualified privilege, of showing both that there was a duty to speak on the occasion sued upon and a reciprocal interest or duty in the hearer to receive the information, is upon the defendant: see Button, Principles of the Law of Libel and Slander, pp. 134-5.

Having considered the substance of the communication and all the other circumstances surrounding it, I find that the defendant has failed to make out the defence of qualified privilege for two reasons:

(a) he had no duty to speak on the occasion sued upon. He had just delivered a statement to the House of Commons on an occasion of absolute privilege of the same substance and to the same effect as that for which he has been sued. Any duty he had to make the statement sued upon was thereby discharged. Statements made in the House of Commons are a matter of public record. They are recorded in Hansard and reported by the news media. The defendant added nothing when he spoke to the press in the Government lobby. Indeed, the defendant testified that he spoke to the press on this occasion to explain his view of ministerial responsibility, not because he felt he had a duty to do so;

(b) the defendant has also failed to establish the reciprocal interest or duty in the press, or the Canadian public through the press, to receive the statement sued upon. While it was a matter of public interest to learn what occurred in the DND-Lockheed transaction to cause it to be cancelled, there was no public interest in receiving the plaintiff's identity or the plaintiff's personal blameworthiness, if any.

The statement in question in this action referred to the plaintiff. It was made in response to questions concerning the plaintiff by reporters of the news media.

It is a long-standing convention of parliamentary democracy and the doctrine of ministerial responsibility which it encompasses that civil servants are to remain faceless to the public. Civil servants are responsible to their ministers. Ministers, as elected officials, are responsible to the public.

The reasoning of Kenneth Kernaghan in his recent article "Politics, policy and public servants: political neutrality revisited" (1976), 19 Can. Public Administration 432 commends itself to me. At p. 451 it reads:

"The traditional model of political neutrality requires that public servants provide forthright advice to their political superiors in private and in confidence. In return, political executives protect the anonymity of public servants by publicly accepting responsibility for departmental decisions. In a parliamentary system of government, the anonymity of public servants depends in large measure on the vitality of the doctrine of ministerial responsibility. According to this doctrine, a minister is personally responsible to Parliament both for his own actions and for those of his administrative subordinates. Thus, public servants are not directly answerable to Parliament and their minister protects their anonymity."

Kernaghan also observes that while the convention of ministerial responsibility which requires a minister's resignation for maladministration in his department is in a weakened state "[t] he convention of ministerial defence of public service anonymity is in a comparatively healthy state".

Furthermore, it is my view that no matter how advanced the state of erosion of public service anonymity (which according to Kernaghan is still rather healthy), a minister should not be able to blame or castigate personally any civil servant of a department under his control in public and then fall back upon the legal defence of qualified privilege. If that were the case and the civil servant were defamed he would be in the peculiar position of being prevented from obtaining vindication for spurious allegations by a minister. It is for this further reason that there can be no interest or duty in the public to receive information containing defamatory allegations, directed at a particular civil servant. Consequently the defence of qualified privilege fails.

Before leaving this topic, may I say that in *R. v. Morgan,* [1976] A.C. 182 (H.L.) Lord Edmond-Davies at pp. 230-31 made liberal use of academic writings. In *R. v. Fane Robinson Ltd.,* [1941] 2 W.W.R. 235, 76 C.C.C. 196 at 200, [1941] 3 D.L.R. 409 (Alta. C.A.) Ford J.A. did the same thing.

5.2.3.1.3.3.7 Stopforth v. *Goyer* (1979), 23 O.R. (2d) 696 (Ont. C.A.)

The learned trial Judge did not give effect to the defence pleaded of qualified privilege. That defence is succinctly stated in 24 Hals., 3rd ed., pp. 56-7:

> 100. ... An occasion is privileged where the person who makes a communication has an interest or a duty, legal, social or moral, to make it to the person to whom it is made, and the person to whom it is so made has a corresponding interest or duty to receive it.
>
> ...
>
> 101. ... A reason for holding any occasion privileged is the common convenience or the welfare of society, and it is not easy to mark off with precision those occasions which are from those which are not privileged or to define what kind of social or moral duty or what measure of interest will make the occasion privileged .... The trend of the modern decisions is in the direction of a more liberal application or interpretation of the rule.

In my opinion the electorate, as represented by the media, has a real and *bona fide* interest in the demotion of a senior civil servant for an alleged dereliction of duty. It would want to know if the reasons given in the House were the real and only reasons for the demotion. The appellant had a corresponding public duty and interest in satisfying that interest of the electorate. Accordingly, there being no suggestion of malice, I would hold that the alleged defamatory statements were uttered on an occasion of qualified privilege.

In denying that defence the learned trial Judge was influenced by what he found to be a convention of the House of Commons that Ministers of the Crown must accept responsibility for the acts of subordinates in their Departments and yet preserve in the House the anonymity of such subordinates. Assuming the trial Judge could take judicial notice of such a convention as a viable one, it does not seem to me it can be permitted the effect of either enlarging or abridging the law of defamation. The respondent was named by the appellant in the House. If that was a breach of convention he and his party were subject to all the disciplines of the House. However, the fact that the respondent was named in the House would create the interest of the electorate and invoke the corresponding interest of the appellant to satisfy that created interest.

The learned trial Judge disallowed the defence of justification. Before us it was very persuasively argued that such defence was made out with respect to the allegation of misinformation. However, neither before the trial Judge nor in this Court was it argued that the allegation of gross negligence was justified. Rather the appellant argued that he did not intend to impute gross negligence to the respondent. However, as the learned trial Judge noted, the test is not of intent but rather what reasonable persons would understand from the allegedly defamatory words. In the result, I agree with the learned trial Judge that the defence of justification must fall and with it falls the defence of fair comment.

Because I think the occasion was one of qualified privilege I do not deal with the argument that it was also one of absolute privilege.

In the result, I would allow the appeal with costs, set aside the judgment below and dismiss the action with costs.

5.2.3.1.3.3.8 Parlett v. *Robinson* (1986), 30 D.L.R. (4th) 247 (B.C.C.A.)

HINKSON J.A.: — The plaintiff brought action against the defendant for defamation arising out of statements made by the defendant at a news conference on December 11, 1981, at the constituency office of the defendant in Burnaby and at an interview later that day on television station CKVU in Vancouver.

In 1981 the plaintiff was a psychologist holding the position of Regional Manager of Education and Training, Pacific Region, for the Correctional Service of Canada. As such, the plaintiff was the functional supervisor of all educational and vocational programmes at federal penitentiaries in the Province of British Columbia, including Matsqui Institution.

From May, 1979, the defendant was the federal Member of Parliament representing the British Columbia constituency of Burnaby. In 1981 the defendant was the official spokesperson in the House of Commons for the New Democratic Party on the Ministry of the Solicitor-General. That ministry includes the Correctional Service. As well, the defendant was a member of the House of Commons Standing Committee on Justice and Legal Affairs.

The plaintiff was a collector of violins. He met one Morfitt, a repairer and restorer of violins, and engaged him to do some work. The plaintiff and Morfitt subsequently became friends. In 1977 Morfitt set up the Doyen Violin Shop in which he repaired, restored and sold violins. The plaintiff frequently had violins restored or repaired, some of which were consigned for sale at Doyen. From the sale of those violins the plaintiff shared the profits with Doyen on a percentage basis which varied from sale to sale. The plaintiff was the biggest customer of Doyen.

In late 1979 the plaintiff met a prisoner at Matsqui named Li and observed that he was a skilled wood carver. In late 1980 the plaintiff asked Li to carve chin rests from rosewood, which chin rests were purchased by the plaintiff. At that time within Matsqui

Institution there was a programme called ''Concraft Enterprises''. This was an entrepreneurial activity for inmates. They purchased materials and produced articles which were then sold by Concraft Enterprises. The purchase price for such articles was paid to Concraft Enterprises. Depending on the type of work being performed by the inmate, it was described as ''custom work'', ''hobby work'' or ''contract work''. ''Custom work'' was work performed by an inmate for prison personnel. It was not contemplated that such items would be resold by prison personnel for a profit. ''Contract work'' was work done for a retail outlet, which in turn would add a mark-up to the price paid to the inmate before sale to the public.

The plaintiff paid Li approximately $7.50 per chin rest. The plaintiff delivered some 200 chin rests to Doyen, where they were offered for sale. By the date of trial all but approximately 10 of the chin rests had been sold.

In May, 1981, the defendant learned of the activity of the plaintiff in supplying chin rests to Doyen from one Hill, a constituent of the defendant. The defendant had met Hill previously when they both attended the University of British Columbia. From May to November, 1978, Hill was employed at Doyen as a violin restorer. Hill met the plaintiff when the latter visited the shop. After completing his education degree at the University of British Columbia in June, 1979, Hill obtained a six-month contract of employment at Matsqui Institution in September, 1979. Hill left this employment in February, 1980.

Hill learned that the plaintiff was supplying chin rests manufactured at Matsqui Institution to Doyen. In May, 1981, Hill approached the defendant and informed him of a scheme involving the plaintiff and Morfitt pursuant to which they planned to use inmate labour to produce violin parts cheaply for their personal benefit. Hill informed the defendant that the chin rests were to be sold for $56 each. Hill also informed the defendant that Morfitt and the plaintiff were sharing the profits on the sale of violins of the plaintiff. Hill later told the plaintiff that he had been asked by the plaintiff in February, 1980, to instruct inmates in Matsqui to make violin parts and that the plaintiff had told him he could arrange to get around any difficulties that might prevent this being done.

On June 8, 1981, the defendant wrote to Mr. D. R. Yeomans, Commissioner of Corrections, with respect to the policy of the Correctional Service of Canada on ''custom work'' being done for persons on staff of the service or other persons employed with the Ministry of the Solicitor-General or its agencies. After requesting information on any outstanding guidelines, the defendant wrote:

> I would furthermore seek your assurance that the C.S.C. would view as completely unethical (and very likely, illegal) to have prisoners producing goods or services inside your institutions which are later re-sold outside, resulting directly or indirectly in a profit to staff members or other persons referred to above...

At that stage the defendant was focussing his inquiry on what has been described as ''custom work''. Ultimately, when he was able to obtain documentation from the Office of the Commissioner of Corrections, it became apparent that he was dealing with what was known within the service as ''contract work''. It was not until December 4, 1981, when Ms. Marjorie David, the Director General of Inmate Employment, wrote to him enclosing documents he had requested that the defendant became aware that Concraft Enterprises also engaged in ''contract work''. Earlier, on November 26, 1981, the defendant attended a meeting of the Standing Committee on Justice and

Legal Affairs in Ottawa at which both Mr. Yeomans and the Solicitor-General, Mr. Kaplan, were in attendance. He raised, in general terms, his concern about the absence of effective controls over possible abuse of inmate labour and referred to such abuse possibly taking place in the Pacific Region and involving a senior corrections official. At that meeting, the Commissioner of Corrections, Mr. Yeomans, stated that there were no problems whatsoever with the existing system of controls. The Solicitor-General urged the defendant to make his allegations specific by naming the individual involved. The defendant did not then name the plaintiff. Following the meeting of the Justice Committee, the Union of Solicitor-General Employees also wrote to the defendant, urging him to name publicly the individual to whom he was referring.

Following the November meeting of the Justice Committee, the defendant spoke to Hill and urged him to double-check the selling price of the Li chin rests at Doyen. Hill again confirmed the sale price at $56. The defendant telephoned Doyen at that time and spoke with an employee who stated that the sale price of the Li chin rest was $50. The defendant also telephoned the owner of another violin shop in the City of Vancouver and spoke to him about the circumstances of production and sale of Li chin rests and understood that the asking price of $50 was not out of line.

On December 4, 1981, the defendant met with Ms. Marjorie David, the National Director of Inmate Employment, and received the extensive documentation from the Pacific Region to which I have already made reference. This documentation included the employment records of Li, showing the plaintiff as a major customer. Thereafter, on December 4th, the defendant telephoned the plaintiff from Ottawa and, in a conversation which lasted over an hour, questioned him on the chin rest matter without revealing in any way the source of his information. During the conversation, the plaintiff denied any personal profit from the sale of chin rests and denied any interest in Doyen.

Following that telephone conversation, the defendant telephoned other individuals, including Hill, Morfitt and Li. It was necessary to speak to Li through an interpreter. Li informed him that he was quite content with the arrangement whereby he received an average price of $7.50 for the chin rests he carved and sold to the plaintiff.

Between December 7 and 9, 1981, the defendant again met with Ms. David and discussed in detail the allegations he had made earlier at the Justice Committee meeting and divulged the name of the plaintiff. Following that meeting, the defendant met with the Solicitor-General and urged him to initiate an inquiry into his allegations. The Minister, although familiar with the details of the defendant's allegations, refused any form of inquiry.

On December 11, 1981, the defendant held a press conference in his constituency office. He expressed his concern over the absence of any form of effective controls or regulations on use of inmate labour by correctional service officials. Statements made by the plaintiff at the press conference and again on the television programme are, in substance, allegations that the plaintiff sold chin rests, made a personal profit out of the sale of chin rests and abused his position in so doing, made a profit directly or indirectly out of an inmate's labour, and exploited inmate labour for his own profit.

The trial judge found that the plaintiff did try to sell chin rests and, therefore, concluded that the defendant had made out the defence of justification with respect to the allegation that the plaintiff had tried to sell chin rests. The trial judge also found that the defence of justification had not been made out with respect to other allegations, all of which were defamatory.

Following the press conference and the appearance on the television programme by the defendant, he wrote to the Solicitor-General, outlining in detail his concerns and urged the Minister to order a public inquiry. In January, 1982, the Minister did order a board of inquiry. The results were made public on March 4, 1982, together with a press release by the Solicitor-General.

At trial, as I have indicated, the learned trial judge held that some of the statements made by the defendant were defamatory of the plaintiff and awarded $20,000 for general damages. The trial judge accepted the evidence of the plaintiff and Morfitt where it was in conflict with Hill's evidence. As a result, a large portion of the testimony of Hill was rejected.

The defendant advanced three grounds of appeal, as follows:

(1) The learned trial judge erred in rejecting the evidence of Hill;

(2) The learned trial judge erred in failing to hold that the defence of qualified privilege applied to the statements made at the press conference and on the television programme on December 11, 1981; and

(3) The award of damages was excessive in the circumstances.

In my view, it is necessary only to consider the defence of qualified privilege. The learned trial judge made some significant findings. Firstly, he held [33 C.C.L.T. 161 at p. 176]:

> The matter upon which the defendant commented, conduct of a Corrections officer in purchasing products manufactured by an inmate and making a profit on their sale and that this was an abuse of the inmate's labour, was clearly a matter of public interest.

Secondly, the learned trial judge held [at p. 177]:

> Robinson did not refer to the plaintiff's denying that he made a profit and to Li being content with what he received for the chin rests in the news conference and TV broadcast. Nevertheless I concluded that Robinson honestly believed that Li's labour was being abused and that Parlett was making a profit from his labour.

Next, the learned trial judge held [at p. 178]:

> I accept the defendant's evidence that his purpose was to focus attention on what he considered to be abuse by Corrections Staff of inmates' labour and the absence of any controls over such situations.
>
> In order for the plaintiff's counsel's submission to succeed, I must find that Robinson's predominant purpose was something other than to publicize what he considered to be the plaintiff's abuse of an inmate's labour. I find that he made these statements publicly because he had an honest belief in them. His eagerness to go to the media was consistent with his wish to expose what he thought was an abuse. I am unable to find that he did so in order to enhance his own reputation by producing a sensational story rather than drawing attention to what he thought was wrong. I reject the submission that he was actuated by any improper motive and was guilty of malice.

However, the learned trial judge rejected the defence of qualified privilege. He made reference to the decision of the Supreme Court of Canada in *Jones v. Bennett* (1968), 2 D.L.R. (3d) 291 [1969] S.C.R. 277, 66 W.W.R. 419, and held [at p. 181]:

> In my opinion the statements made by the defendant at the news conference and on the TV broadcast were made "to the world". For these reasons the defence of qualified privilege is not available to the defendant. Accordingly, the action for libel succeeds.

On the appeal, counsel for the plaintiff contended that with respect to this ground of appeal, the issue was whether or not the publication was, in the circumstances, too broad. In *Arnott v. College of Physicians & Surgeons of Saskatchewan,* [1955] 1 D.L.R. 1, [1954] S.C.R. 538, Estey J. discussed the defence of qualified privilege. He said at p. 7 (D.L.R.):

> The defence of qualified privilege is fully discussed in *Halls v. Mitchell,* [1928] 2 D.L.R. 97 at pp. 102-3, S.C.R. 125 at p. 133, where, after referring to certain of the English authorities, Duff J., speaking for the majority of this Court, stated: "The defamatory statement, therefore, is only protected when it is fairly warranted by some reasonable occasion or exigency, and when it is fairly made in discharge of some public or private duty, or in the conduct of the defendant's own affairs in matters in which his interests are concerned. The privilege rests not upon the interests of the persons entitled to invoke it, but upon the general interests of society, and protects only communications '*fairly* made' (the italics are those of Parke, B. himself) in the legitimate defence of a person's own interests, or plainly made under a sense of duty, such as would be recognized by "people of ordinary intelligence and moral principles."
>
> Lindley L.J., speaking with respect to the duty, stated as follows: "I take moral or social duty to mean a duty recognized by English people of ordinary intelligence and moral principle, but at the same time not a duty enforceable by legal proceedings, whether civil or criminal": *Stuart v. Bell* [1891] 2 Q.B. 341 at p. 350.

The defendant contends that, as a Member of Parliament, having received a communication from a constituent suggesting impropriety on the part of the plaintiff as an offical in the employ of the Correctional Service of Canada, he was under a duty to communicate with the appropriate minister and that when he failed to persuade the Minister to investigate the matter by way of a public inquiry to then take steps which would result in exerting sufficient public pressure upon the Minister to persuade him to order such an inquiry.

R. v. Rule, [1937] 2 K.B. 375, was a case where the appellant had written to the Member of Parliament for his constituency two letters containing defamatory statements about a police officer and a justice of the peace for the place where he lived. He was charged with publishing defamatory libels. He pleaded that the libels were published on a privileged occasion. The trial judge ruled that the occasion was not privileged and the appellant had accordingly been convicted. In the Court of Criminal Appeal, Lord Hewart C.J. said at p. 380:

> The discussion has covered a wide field, but it will not be necessary for this Court to express any opinion as to the rights and duties generally of Members of Parliament. It is sufficient for the purpose of this case to say that in our judgment a Member of Parliament to whom a written communication is addressed by one of his constituents asking for his assistance in bringing to the notice of the appropriate Minister a complaint of improper conduct on the part of some public official acting in that constituency in relation to his office, has sufficient interest in the subject-matter of the complaint to render the occasion of such publication a privileged occasion. When once it is seen that a decision favourable to the appellant requires not more than this limited assertion of the interest of a Member of Parliament in the welfare of his constituents, it appears to us impossible to resist the conclusion that the conviction cannot be supported.

That passage was cited with approval by Geoffrey Lane J. (as he then was) in *Beech et al. v. Freeson,* [1972] 1 Q.B. 14. In that case the defendant, a Member of Parliament, wrote a letter to the Law Society and an identical one to the Lord Chancellor, saying that he had been specifically requested by a constituent to refer the plaintiffs' solicitors' firm to the Law Society for investigation. He set out the constituent's complaints and stated that contrary to his usual practice he had complied with the request because he had received complaints from other constituents in the past concerning the plaintiffs' firm. The plaintiffs brought action against him for libel. The defendant contended that the publication was on an occasion of qualified privilege. The plaintiffs denied the existence of a privilege and replied that in any event the defendant was actuated by express malice. That submission was rejected. It was held that such complaints made by a Member of Parliament to the Law Society at the behest of a constituent, acting as the constituent's agent to make the complaint, are made on an occasion of qualified privilege.

Geoffrey Lane J. stated at p. 24:

> The judge must, accordingly, do his best in the light of such evidence as he has, coupled with his own views as to what the defendant's duties, moral or social, were in the circumstances. Doing the best I can on those principles, it seems to me that it certainly was incumbent upon the defendant to inform the Law Society of his previous experiences through his constituents of this particular firm. As appears from the letters of Mr. Leach at the Law Society, to which I need not make a detailed reference, the Law Society is concerned to determine, amongst other things, whether a complaint is an isolated incident of casual negligence or is part of a course of conduct likely to bring the profession into disrepute if it is allowed to continue. Although the defendant may have only imperfectly realised that fact, if indeed he realised it at all, nevertheless his instinct to write as he did was a proper one. Even if the defendant had simply reiterated to the Law Society the complaints of Mr. Gold and had added nothing of his own, knowing that at the same time Mr. Gold was, himself, complaining to the Law Society, privilege would, I think, attach to such communication. That, however, is not the question here. He did have something to add which he genuinely believed to be worthy of investigation and he would have been falling short in his duty to his constituent and, indeed, his duty to the public, if he had not written in the manner in which he did. It will be a sad day when a Member of Parliament has to look over his shoulder before ventilating, to the proper authority, criticisms about the work of a public servant or a professional man who is holding himself out in practice for the benefit of the public which he honestly believes to merit investigation.
>
> When the defendant communicated with the Solicitor-General, the plaintiff contended, he had performed his duty and he was not thereafter entitled to hold a press conference or appear on a television programme to ventilate his concerns to the electorate when the Solicitor-General had declined to order a public inquiry. Further, the plaintiff contended, the defendant could have raised the matter during question period in the House of Commons. In these circumstances, the plaintiff contended, no privilege should be held to attach to the course of conduct chosen by the defendant to ventilate his concerns.

At trial the defendant responded to the suggestion that he could have raised the matter during question period in the House of Commons by answering that in his judgment that would not have been an effective way to communicate his concerns to the public and it was only if there was a public demand for an inquiry that the Solicitor-General would take steps to order such an inquiry.

As I have indicated, the defendant is the official spokesperson for his party on the Ministry of the Solicitor-General. In my opinion, the course he followed up to December 11, 1981, in seeking to persuade the Minister to order a public inquiry into the matter was an entirely proper course for him to follow. When he failed to persuade the Minister to order the inquiry, if he held an honest belief that there had been impropriety within the Correctional Service with respect to taking advantage of the work of inmates, then it was the duty of the defendant to ventilate his concerns in a way that would persuade the Minister to have an investigation conducted into the matter.

In addition to the duty of the defendant to declare his concern in this matter, it appears to me that the electorate in Canada have an interest in knowing whether the administration of the Correctional Service is being properly conducted by the officials in the Department of the Solicitor-General.

Thus we come to the issue framed by the plaintiff in this appeal, namely, whether or not the publication was too broad in the circumstances.

...

The learned trial judge quoted [from *Stopforth* v. *Goyer*] in his reasons for judgment and observed that the Ontario Court of Appeal did not cite any authority for its statement. Then the learned trial judge continued [at p. 180]:

> In my opinion the *Stopforth* case is concerned with the very special circumstances of a Minister repeating the precise statement he had made inside the House of Commons to the media immediately upon leaving the House of Commons. At p. 179 Jessop [*sic*], J.A. noted that the fact that the respondent was named in the House would create the interest of the electorate and invoke the corresponding interest of the appellant to satisfy that created interest. Those circumstances or similar circumstances do not prevail in the case at Bar.

In my respectful opinion, the learned trial judge erred in seeking to distinguish the decision in *Stopforth* on so narrow a basis. I fail to appreciate why a statement would enjoy qualified privilege when made to the media first the statement was made in the House of Commons where it would enjoy an absolute privilege. It is not the making of the statement in the House of Commons that creates the interest of the electorate but rather the subject-matter of the statement. Thus if the Member of Parliament has a duty to ventilate the subject-matter and the electorate has an interest in knowing of the matter, then the only remaining question is whether or not, in the circumstances, the publication "to the world" was too broad.

In my opinion, the statements to the media and on the television programme which were reported in newspapers and through the media cannot be said to have been unduly wide. That is because the group that had a *bona fide* interest in the matter was the electorate in Canada. Hence the privilege was not lost.

For these reasons, I would allow the appeal and dismiss the action.

Appeal allowed; plaintiff's action dismissed.

5.2.3.1.3.3.9 Camporese v. *Parton* (1983), 150 D.L.R. (3d) 208 (B.C.S.C.)

This is a libel action. The plaintiffs allege that an article written by the defendant Parton exposed them to the hatred and contempt of the public and of their business associates and injured them in their trade. They claim damages.

...

Mrs. Parton then called Mr. Camporese. She did not identify herself but rather posed as a consumer. She said she had seen the advertisement and inquired whether there were lids available and if they were Metro lids. He acknowledged they were Metro lids. She then asked him why he was selling the lids through an advertisement. Mr. Camporese said that there was too much red tape; the stores rip you off. She inquired: "Do they seal well?", to which he replied, "Yes". She then identified herself and asked him why he was selling the lids in this manner. Mr. Camporese became very emotional and said he would go ''belly up'' if he did not sell them; that he could not afford a $60,000 loss. She formed the opinion he was attempting to dump a defective product, at a cut-rate price, without drawing attention to the public that they were Metro lids. Mr. Camporese said the lids he was selling were different from the lids that had been tested by C.A.C. and he pleaded with her to test the lids. Mrs. Parton construed this as a ''stalling tactic'' commonly used by a person in Mr. Camporese's position.

Mrs. Parton then began to telephone resource people to ascertain the consequences of canning with faulty lids. It was getting late in the afternoon and her usual reference sources had left their offices. She called a former acquaintance, Donna Aldous, at Kelowna. Mrs. Aldous had been a home economist for Environment Canada whom Mrs. Parton had previously consulted. As a consequence of Mrs. Aldous' advice that faulty seals could result in the formation of the deadly toxin clostridium botulinum, Mrs. Parton considered the story had changed from one which concerned possible food spoilage to one which concerned possible death if the public used defective canning lids. The news value of this latter viewpoint was obviously of great import. Accordingly, she wrote the column in a different manner, deleting reference to the first person, putting the strongest facts first and a ''kicker'' at the close of the article.

Mrs. Parton acceded her knowledge of botulism was superficial but she felt she could safely consult with Donna Aldous and rely upon her opinion in view of her professional training and experience, being a home economist for Environment Canada.

The newspaper deadline for filing the story was early evening. Mrs. Parton said she considered that the interest of the public in immediately receiving the information outweighed the interest of Mr. Camporese in her withholding it until further checks could be made. She considered further testing would take some weeks and it was already close to the end of the canning season. She was aware of many consumers who had lost hundreds of dollars of food as a result of using the defective lids and now she had been advised by Mrs. Aldous, a home economist, that botulism was a concern where faulty lids were involved in that clostridium botulinum spores could enter a jar with a leaky lid and then germinate and produce a deadly toxin. Accordingly, she decided there was an urgency that the article be published immediately. She filed it that evening for publication on the city side of the paper next day. Her admitted purpose in so doing was to alert consumers to what she conceived to be a potential danger associated with using canning lids that failed to seal and to stop Mr. Camporese from selling the Metro lids.

While Mrs. Parton did not write the headline for the article — ''Importer Pushes Canning Lids That Could Spell Death'' — she considered it to be appropriate, pointing out that the purpose of the headline was to get people to read the article; presumably its accuracy as reflecting the thrust of the article being of secondary significance.

My impression of Mrs. Parton, formed from my observation of her responses to questions put to her by counsel, is that of an intelligent, opinionated person, who continually argued her case in a most biased way, directed to justifying her failure to research the article with greater care before rushing it to publication. Her statement, that: ''No reporter should take into account the suffering or impact upon the parties'' who are the subject of her columns, perhaps explained her haste in publishing the article with a paucity of accurate information about such an emotional and frightening subject-matter — well aware that the article could cause the plaintiffs some $60,000 loss as well as the censure of the business community and the public generally.

To write and publish an article on a matter of such public importance based solely upon a short impromptu comment made by Mrs. Aldous in the course of a telephone conversation and without questioning its accuracy, in my opinion, is reporting of a careless and reckless nature. Certainly Mrs. Aldous' comment raised concern and justified an immediate in-depth investigation into its accuracy and a complete report to the public of what such investigation revealed. It did not, in my opinion, justify immediately publishing the comment directed solely to Mr. Camporese and the canning lids he was selling. I must state, however, that I find Mrs. Parton accepted Mrs. Aldous' comments as accurate and held an honest belief that they were true at the time she wrote the article and caused it to be published.

(f) *Consequence of the publication*

As a result of the article, the public and members of the business community with whom Mr. Camporese dealt, reacted adversely, refusing to do further business with him. There is no doubt that as a result of the article he lost the respect of those persons who would normally be trading with him and his companies. I find, however, that the failure of Mr. Camporese to sell the canning lids in 1977 and thereafter was, in the main, due to the critical report of the C.A.C. and the complaints filed with "Action Line", compounded by the fact that the market was fully supplied by known brand lids in 1977. Accordingly, I find the plaintiffs have not established the loss, due to the failure to sell the canning lids, was attributable to the Province article of August 25, 1977.

(g) *Can defective seals on canning lids result in the formation of clostridium botulinum toxin in the jars of home-canned produce?*

The plaintiffs called the following experts: Dr. Skura, an expert in the field of food services, a microbiologist with the Department of Food Science at the University of British Columbia; Mr. Shkurhan, a lecturer of microbiology in the Department of Basic Health Services at the British Columbia Institute of Technology; Dr. Zottola, Professor of Food Microbiology at the Department of Food Science and Nutrition at the University of Minnesota, a man of wide experience with home canning problems; Dr. E.J. Bowman, a retired microbiologist who had an impressive background of experience in research related to clostridium botulinum studies.

The defendant called Dr. J. J. R. Campbell, bacteriologist and Professor of Microbiology at the University of British Columbia.

All these eminent gentlemen agreed on many aspects of clostridium bolutinum such as; it is one of the most toxic bacteria known the man — one gram could kill 500,000,000 people; the toxin affects the nervous system and produces asphyxiation; it will not grow in the presence of oxygen; it is a microscopic organism whose habitat is soil dust and marine environments; the spore, given the right conditions, can germinate and grow into an active cell at which time the toxin develops and accumulates in the cell; active growing cells can be killed by heat, salt, curing, etc.; the spore will not germinate in a high acid environment — pH below 4.6; it is one of the most heat-resistant spores known and hence has to be exposed to high temperatures for a prolonged period best accomplished by processing the jars in a pressure-cooker.

The experts also agree there has been no recorded case of a botulinum spore being aspirated into a home-canned jar, by reason of a leaky lid, with death or illness resulting. On this issue home canning cannot be compared to commercial canning; they are quite different processes. Most cases of botulinum contamination of home-canned produce have been attributed to insufficient heat treatment of the produce during the canning process. No research has been conducted to determine the number, if any, of botulinum spores that are airborne in the atmosphere in British Columbia. Furthermore, there is no scientific data available, or research done, to determine whether a botulinum spore aspirated into a home-canning jar could find an anaerobic condition which would permit it to grow and produce toxin. It must be kept in mind that in most investigations of the presence of clostridium botulinum bacteria in home-canned pruduce the lid has been removed so that it is impossible to say, with exactitude, whether the active spores were there because of inadequate heat treatment during canning process or whether they were aspirated into the jar after proper canning procedures had been carried out.

Generally speaking the issue upon which the experts differ is as to the probability of a botulinum spore being aspirated into a jar of food as a result of a leaky lid.

Dr. Campbell expresses the opinion that in the cooling process air will be drawn into jars through a faulty seal and such air could contain dust particles carrying botulinum spores. On storage the spores could germinate, grow and form toxin which if ingested by people may be fatal. Dr. Bowers considers this to be an over-statement of the probabilities but would accept the statement if the word ''might'' replaced the word ''could'' in the passage. Dr. Zottola takes issue with Dr. Campbell's report and finds it difficult to envisage that air leaking into a jar would encourage growth of an anaerobic bacteria and he considers that transportation of botulinum spores through the air is virtually impossible. He points out that none of the scientific literature suggests that leaking canning lids could be a cause of clostridium botulinum contamination of home-canned produce and he states that, while anything is possible, such an eventuality is highly unlikely.

In view of the complete absence of any scientific data demonstrating contamination of home-canned produce by clostridium botulinum aspirating into the jars as a result of leaky lids, I can only conclude this hypothesis to be completely speculative and I accept Dr. Zottola's opinion that while ''anything is possible, this result is highly improbable''.

Summarizing this lengthy review of the evidence I find:

1. That the ''gist'' or ''sting'' of the article was that the plaintiffs were allegedly attempting to sell canning lids to the public that could cause death;
2. That the article defamed the plaintiffs, Camporese and the associated company C.F.B. Trading Co. Ltd., in the way of their trade. No mention was made in the article of C. K. & G. Management Ltd. and A. & A. Food Importers and the readers would not consider the article referred to those two companies;
3. That the plaintiff sought the assistance of the media, in particular the Province newspaper and the Ministry of Consumer Services, to assist him in the marketing of Metro lids imported from Taiwan;
4. That the lids were defective in that many buckled and failed to seal when used under pressure for home-canning purposes;
5. That the consumer complaints about the inadequacy of the lids, the C.A.C. testing which demonstrated their inadequacy, and the increased availability of brand-name lids, resulted in the loss of any potential market for Metro lids in

1977 and 1978. The plaintiffs have not established that the article of August 25, 1977, contributed to that loss of market for the Metro lids;

6. That Nicole Parton wrote the article of August 25, 1977, without adequate research into the accuracy of the opinion expressed therein concerning the possibility of contamination of the canned foods by the ingestion of clostridium botulinum spores through leaking lids with the consequent possibility of their causing death;
7. That Nicole Parton honestly believed the opinions and facts set forth in the article;
8. That while contamination of home-canned produce by clostridium botulinum through leaky canning lids is a hypothesis which is theoretically possible, it is highly unlikely or improbable. There is no scientific data or research supporting such an occurrence;
9. That the article of August 25, 1977, did not reflect the improbable aspect of food contamination resulting from leaky canning lids and did imply that Mr. Camporese was "pushing" the sale of defective lids in order to avoid economic loss and that, in so doing, he was completely indifferent to the health hazard he was creating for the unsuspecting consumer.

Defamation of the plaintiff

I have previously found that the article of August 25, 1977, and, in particular, the headline "Importer Pushes Canning Lids That Could Cause Death", was defamatory of Mr. Camporese and C.F.B. Trading Co. Ltd. in the way of their trade in that it would and did diminish the esteem, respect, goodwill and confidence in which they were held by their business associates and members of the public.

Qualified privilege

The applicable legal principle has been succinctly expressed by *Gatley on Libel and Slander,* 8th ed. (1981), pp. 239-40, para. 562, in these words:

> The publication of defamatory matter in a newspaper will be privileged where the matter published is of general public interest and it is the duty of the defendant to communicate it to the general public. If the matter is a matter of public interest, *and* the party who publishes it owes a duty to communicate it to the general public, the publication is privileged.

See also *Banks v. Globe & Mail Ltd. et al.* (1961), 28 D.L.R. (2d) 343 at pp. 349-50, [1961] S.C.R. 474 at pp. 482-3.

It is self-evident that the matter of possible food contamination of home-canned produce by clostridium botulinum spores entering the jars through leaking canning lids was of vital concern to the general public of British Columbia. The question to be answered is whether the defendants stood in such a relationship to their readers in the circumstances that prevailed that it imposed upon them a duty to communicate to their readers the facts and opinions contained in the August 25, 1977 article.

In the circumstances I find that Mrs. Parton, her publishers and the readers had a legitimate common interest in the adequacy and performance characteristics of the Metro lids being sold by Mr. Camporese.

The particular circumstances purportedly giving rise to a special duty on the part of the defendants to communicate Mrs. Parton's opinions to those who read the Province were:

(a) that she had originally, upon the importuning of Mr. Camporese, written a column commending his canning lids to her readers;
(b) that she had advised her readers of the C.A.C. test indicating the inadequacy of the Metro canning lids and of Mr. Camporese's response to that testing;
(c) that she had become aware of the complaints of home canners contained in their correspondence with "Action Line";
(d) that Mr. Camporese actually sought and obtained the support of the media and the Ministry of Consumer Services in the marketing of Metro canning lids;
(e) that she concluded, upon reasonable grounds, that Mr. Camporese was trying to unload at cut-rate prices, upon an unsuspecting public, canning lids which he knew to be inadequate and he was seeking to do this through the channel of private advertisements;
(f) that she honestly believed the sale of such defective lids could result in clostridium botulinum contamination.

In my view, having at the plaintiffs' behest written a column commending the Metro lids to her reading public, it was Mrs. Parton's duty, upon becoming aware of any adverse characteristic of the Metro lids, to communicate such information to her readers.

Malice

This occasion of privilege entitling the defendants to write what would be libelous if written by others is qualified and may be lost by the plaintiffs adducing evidence establishing, on a balance of probabilities, express malice on the part of the defendants. That is, it is for the plaintiffs to establish that the defendants have abused the occasion by using it for an improper purpose, personal spite or ill will, or by excessive or irrelevant publication, or by a lack of belief in the truth of what was written.

I have found that Nicole Parton honestly believed the facts and opinions expressed in the article of August 25, 1977, to be true. Counsel for the plaintiffs contends, however, that an honest belief is not sufficient by itself to negative a finding of express malice and asserts that the defendants misused the occasion and exceeded the privilege. He points to the reckless manner in which the article was researched and written by Mrs. Parton; the lack of adequate inquiry into, or verification of, the accuracy of such an emotional and contentious subject-matter; the rush to make a deadline because of the newsworthy aspect of the subject-matter; the complete lack of concern over the consequences of the publication, economic or otherwise, upon the plaintiffs and the avowed objective of stopping the sale of Metro lids by Mr. Camporese. All of this, counsel submits, demonstrates that Mrs. Parton wrote the article recklessly, not caring whether it was true or false, and, accordingly, misused the occasion and lost the benefit of any privilege which the occasion would have otherwise provided.

I consider the remarks of Lord Diplock in *Horrocks v. Lowe,* [1975] A.C. 135, to be most pertinent to this submission. He stated at p. 150:

> Apart from those exceptional cases, what is required on the part of the defamer to entitle him to the protection of the privilege is positive belief in the truth of what he published or, as it is generally though tautologously termed "honest belief." If he publishes untrue defamatory matter recklessly, without considering or caring whether it be true or not, he is in this, as in other branches of the law, treated as if he knew it to be false. But indifference to the truth of what he publishes is not to be equated with carelessness, impulsiveness or irrationality in arriving at a positive belief that it is true. The freedom of speech protected by the law of

qualified privilege may be availed of by all sorts and conditions of men. In affording to them immunity from suit if they have acted in good faith in compliance with a legal or moral duty or in protection of a legitimate interest the law must take them as it finds them. In ordinary life it is rare indeed for people to form their beliefs by a process of logical deduction from facts ascertained by a rigorous search for all available evidence and a judicious assessment of its probative value. In greater or in less degree according to their temperaments, their training, their intelligence, they are swayed by prejudice, rely on intuition instead of reasoning, leap to conclusions on inadequate evidence and fail to recognise the cogency of material which might cast doubt on the validity of the conclusions they reach. But despite the imperfection of the mental process by which the belief is arrived at it may still be "honest," that is, a positive belief that the conclusions they have reached are true. The law demands no more.

While I have found Mrs. Parton wrote the article of August 25, 1977, without adequate research and with untimely haste in the circumstances, I do not consider this conduct was so unreasonable as to displace or rebut Mrs. Parton's honest belief in the subject-matter of the article or to vary the primary purpose for which she wrote the article; that is, to inform her readers of her concern for the risks, including botulism poisoning, which she believed were associated with the use of defective Metro canning lids. Accordingly, I find that the plaintiffs have failed to prove the privileged occasion upon which the article was published was abused by the defendants in a manner which would constitute "express malice" and so destroy the privilege. I find that the defendants are entitled to the protection of the privilege.

In light of the conclusion I have reached on this issue it is preferable that I do not rule on the other issues raised by the defendants.

The plaintiffs' claim must be dismissed with costs payable to the defendants.

Action dismissed.

Note: See also *Wooding* v. *Little* (1982) 24 C.C.L.T. 37

5.2.3.1.3.3.10 Shultz v. *Porter and Block Brothers* (1979), 9 A.R. 381 (S.C.)

Note: The defence may be lost if the plaintiff can prove that the statement was actuated by malice. This principle also applies where the defence raised is fair comment.

WAITE, J.: Assuming, however, that the defence of qualified privilege was found to exist, the evidence taken in its entirety clearly establishes the presence of actual or express malice on the part of the defendant Porter so as to entitle the plaintiff to judgment in any event.

Malice includes not only the general or popular definitions of that word as denoting ill-will or spite. It includes the question of an improper motive by the defendants. Excessive language in itself is insufficient to establish express or actual malice. The term is generally discussed by Lord Diplock in *Horrocks v. Lowe* at pp. 669-70 in the following terms:

"So, the motive with which the defendant on a privileged occasion made a statement defamatory of the plaintiff becomes crucial. The protection might, however, be illusory if the onus lay on him to prove that he was actuated solely by a sense of the relevant duty or a desire to protect the relevant interest. So he is entitled to be protected by the privilege unless some other dominant and improper motive on his part is proved. 'Express malice' is the term of art descriptive of such a motive. Broadly speaking, it means malice in the popular sense of a desire to injure the person who is defamed and this is generally the motive which the plaintiff sets out to prove. But to destroy the privilege the desire to injure must be the dominant motive for the defamatory publication; knowledge that it will have that effect is not enough if the defendant is nevertheless acting in accordance with a sense of duty or in bona fide protection of his own legitimate interests.

"The motive with which a person published defamatory matter can only be inferred from what he did or said or knew. If it be proved that he did not believe that what he published was true this is generally conclusive evidence of express malice, for no sense of duty or desire to protect his own legitimate interests can justify a man in telling deliberate and injurious falsehoods about another...

"...what is required on the part of the defamer to entitle him to the protection of the privilege is positive belief in the truth of what he published or, as it is generally though tautologously termed, 'honest belief'. If he publishes untrue defamatory matter recklessly, without considering or caring whether it be true or not, he is in this, as in other branches of the law, treated as if he knew it to be false. But indifference to the truth of what he publishes is not to be equated with carelessness, impulsiveness or irrationality in arriving at a positive belief that it is true....

"Even a positive belief in the truth of what is published on a privileged occasion — which is presumed unless the contrary is proved — may not be sufficient to negative express malice if it can be proved that the defendant misused the occasion for some purpose other than that for which the privilege is accorded by the law. The commonest case is where the dominant motive which actuates the defendant is not a desire to perform the relevant duty or to protect the relevant interest, but to give vent to his personal spite or ill-will towards the person he defames. If this be proved, then even positive belief in the truth of what is published will not enable the defamer to avail himself of the protection of the privilege to which he would otherwise have been entitled. There may be instances of improper motives which destroy the privilege apart from personal spite. A defendant's dominant motive may have been to obtain some private advantage unconnected with the duty or the interest which constitutes the reason for the privilege. If so, he loses the benefit of the privilege despite his positive belief that what he said or wrote was true...

Qualified privilege would be illusory, and the public interest that it is meant to serve defeated, if the protection which it affords were lost merely because a person, although acting in compliance with a duty or in protection of a legitimate interest, disliked the person whom he defamed or was indignant at what he believed to be that person's conduct and welcomed the opportunity of exposing it. It is only where his desire to comply with the relevant duty or to protect the relevant interest plays no significant part in his motives for publishing what he believes to be true that 'express malice' can properly be found."

The most recent decision on the question of qualified privilege is the decision of the Supreme Court of Canada in *McLoughlin v. Kutasy* (1979), 8 C.C.L.T. 105, wherein Ritchie J. on behalf of the majority of the court said in part at pp. 112-13:

"...the elements requisite to sustain the defence of qualified privilege are discussed in the case of *Netupsky v. Craig,* [1973] S.C.R. 55 at 61-62, 28 D.L.R. (3d) 742, where the following paragraph occurs in the judgment of this Court:

" 'The determination of this appeal in my opinion, turns on the question of whether there was any extrinsic or intrinsic evidence that the respondents were motivated by malice in writing the letter which is complained of. There can be little doubt that if there is evidence proving that the statements complained of are false to the knowledge of the person who makes them, they are taken to have been made maliciously, but this statement must be read in light of the language used by Lord Atkinson in *Adam v. Ward,* [1917] A.C. 309 at p. 339, where he said:

""""...a person making a communication on a privileged occasion is not restricted to the use of such language merely as is reasonably necessary to protect the interest or discharge the duty which is the foundation of his privilege; but that, on the contrary, he will be protected, even though his language should be violent or excessively strong, if, having regard to all the circumstances of the case, he might have honestly and on reasonable grounds believed that what he wrote or said was true and necessary for the purpose of his vindication, though in fact it was not so.""""

The plaintiff has affirmatively established actual or express malice. There can be no doubt that the statements complained of by the plaintiff were false to the knowledge of Porter. I am satisfied on a consideration of all of the evidence that Porter did not — indeed, could not — honestly believe that the plaintiff had been guilty of misrepresentation. I am satisfied that Porter was motivated by a dishonest, improper or wrong motive, being the protection of himself and his principals against the consequences of what was clearly a negligent breach of duty by the defendants to their own client, Feltham. The offending letter of 22nd June was a calculated attempt to extricate the vendor from a transaction that was improvident and that had been entered into in such circumstances as would have entitled the vendor to an appropriate action for damages against the defendants.

5.2.3.1.3.3.11 Farrell v. *St. John's Publishing Co.* (1986), 58 Nfld. & P.E.I.R. 66 (Nfld. C.A.)

MORGAN, J.A.:

I *Initial Publication*

[45] The mere publication of defamatory words is presumed to be malicious. In this context, however, malicious, sometimes referred to as malice at law, merely means that the words were published without lawful excuse. For the plaintiff to rely on express malice there must be evidence to establish that the defendant had an improper motive for publishing the words and that the improper motive was the sole or dominant motive **(Horrocks v. Lowe,** [1975] A.C. 135).

[46] In this case the appellants contended that, having satisfied themselves that the police report was authentic, they were concerned throughout that no action was being taken to implement that report. In this regard, the trial judge made contradictory findings. He stated:

> "Mr. Herder's evidence confirms my conclusion and the evasive manner in which he answered some of the questions asked him further confirms it, that what really happened in this case was that he and others responsible at The Evening Telegram became very concerned at the delay in making a report to the authorities by those investigating the fire and an inordinately long time elapsing before anything was made public regarding the cause of the fire. They suspected that a cover-up was underway by people in high places and that the plaintiff, a former cabinet minister and still a member of the legislature sitting on the government side, was being shielded from action being taken; was being protected by higher-ups. Mr. Herder

admitted in his evidence that he did indeed have such concerns, and even if he had not admitted such, the evidence would inevitably lead me to that conclusion."

[47] Later, in his judgment, however, the trial judge stated:

"I am not suggesting that Mr. Herder had some particular spite against the plaintiff or any underhanded motive for the actions taken in this matter. Rather, he operated from what must have been, in his opinion, the loftiest of motives, that being to see that the plaintiff be punished for his crime. If he were to be protected by people in high places from prosecution for his crime, then The Evening Telegram would see to it that he was tried in the court of public opinion. His rights as a citizen of this country were not important; The Evening Telegram found him guilty."

[48] The first conclusion reached by the trial judge (supra) was that the appellants published the police reports out of concern over the government's delay in investigating the cause of the fire and their suspicion of a cover-up. That, in my view, is not an improper motive. His second conclusion appears to be that the appellants were motivated solely by a desire to injure the respondent, notwithstanding that he had prefaced his remarks by stating that "he was not suggesting that Mr. Herder had some particular spite against the plaintiff or any underhanded motive for the actions taken in this matter". If Mr. Herder had no personal spite against the respondent nor any underhanded motive for his actions, how can it be said that he was conducting a personal vendetta against the respondent? In my view, the evidence is not supportive of the trial judge's second conclusion and, with respect, it cannot be accepted as evidencing an improper motive.

II *Failure to Apologize*

[49] It is well-established that the failure to apologize combined with a persistence in a plea of justification are not necessarily evidence of malice. In this regard I adopt the following statement of Sellars, L.J., in *Broadway Approvals Ltd. v. Odhams Press Ltd.*, [1965] 2 All E.R. 523, at 533:

"The failure to apologize or retract and persistence in a plea of justification are in themselves not evidence of malice. They may be in certain circumstances, but more frequently they would show sincerity and belief in what had been said and establish the best reason for the publication."
(See also **Horrock v. Lowe,** supra, at 154.)

[50] There may be cases where, after publication, a defendant obtains proof that what he said was untrue. In such circumstances a failure to retract a serious charge may provide evidence that at the time of the original publication, he was actuated by malice.

[51] It should be noted that, in February 1979, the appellants published a report of Magistrate LeClair's reasons for dismissing the charge of arson brought against the respondent. That report was headed "Magistrate outlines why arson charge dismissed" with a sub-head of even greater prominence **"Evidence was 'virtually worthless'".** Contrary to the submission of counsel for the respondent that that report was in itself defamatory of the respondent, I am of the opinion that it contained a fair summary of the magistrate's reasons for dismissing the charge against the respondent and would leave no doubt in the mind of right-thinking members of society that the crime of arson had not been established, which was the underlying reason for dismissl of the charge. The report also contained the magistrate's criticism of the media for publishing the police report, including his observation that "the coverage of the report by the news media gave credence to the assumption of guilt". Any injury to the respondent's reputation occasioned by the earlier publication would, in my view, have been ameliorated by that publication. That is not to say that the appellants did not owe the plaintiff an apology for the injury to his reputation by the unwarranted publication of the police report. A proper apology is almost certain to reduce the injury to the plaintiff's feelings and may well lessen the damages to his reputation. An absence of apology in this case, however, is at best tenuous evidence of malice, but may properly be considered in aggravation of damages.

III *Justification and Fair Comment*

[52] The mere fact that a defendant has placed a plea of justification on the record is not in itself evidence of malice even though he does not attempt to establish it at the trial. Furthermore, if a defendant has raised a plea of fair comment, the mere fact that he has also raised a plea of justification cannot be used as evidence of malice to destroy the defence. That defence, if proper, can only be destroyed by proof of malice. (Gatley, **Libel and Slander** (7th Ed.), para. 1264).

[53] The defence of justification is, of course, a dangerous one, for an unsuccessful attempt to establish it may be treated as an aggravation of the original injury. If the plea is made recklessly and the defendant persists at the trial in an imputation that he knows to be unfounded or cross-examines the plaintiff with a view to showing that he is guilty of that which he has been acquitted, malice can properly be inferred. There was no such conduct in the case at bar.

[54] The appellants pleaded justification for the sole purpose of establishing the authenticity of the police report published by them and that their reproduction of that report was fair and accurate. The fact that such proof would not avail them as a defence to libel does not make the placing of the plea on the record a malicious act and form the basis of retributive damages.

IV *Honest Belief*

[55] An honest belief in the truth of the statement published is not to be held malicious merely because the defendant was hasty in reaching that conclusion. In determining whether such honest belief did in fact exist in a given case, the trial judge, or a jury as the case may be, is entitled to take into consideration the ground on which it is founded. "The ground upon which an honest belief was founded is a most important test of its reality" (**Derby v. Peck** (1889), 14 App. Cas. 369).

[56] In this case the trial judge appears to have accepted the appellants' belief in the truthfulness of the police report but, for some undisclosed reason, he seems to find that it was not an honest belief and hence it was malicious. With respect, he should have directed his mind to the established fact that the publication, on which the libel action was based, was the reproduction of a genuine police report that resulted from their investigation into the cause of the fire. That report, as the evidence disclosed, was based on the honest belief of the investigating officers. Furthermore, as a result of that report, the respondent was subsequently charged with arson. How then can malice be imputed to the appellants for believing its contents?

V *Failure to Disclose Source*

[57] The trial judge also found that malice was to be imputed by reason of the appellants' failure to disclose the source of the police reports.

[58] The source of the alleged defamatory statement was the police reports as disclosed in the publications complained of. How that report came into the hands of the appellants was, in my view, totally irrelevant to the issue before the trial judge.

VI *Repetition*

[59] It will be a matter of aggravation if the defendant has persistently and deliberately given publicity to the defamation complained of. Whether or not malice will be inferred from such conduct, however, will depend on the defendant's motive for repeating the libel. In this case I accept the trial judge's finding that the appellants' motive for publishing the defamatory statement and hence its republication, was their concern over the delay on the part of the authorities in pursuing the investigation into the cause of the fire. That motive, in my view, is not indicative of malice. Continued repetition is of course an aggravating factor.

[60] The trial judge appears to have dealt with the issues raised as though the appellants were the originators, and not just repeators, of the statement found to be defamatory. The offence committed by the appellants was in publishing a confidential police report in which the investiating officers had expressed the opinion, for the reasons given by them, that a fire in the respondent's apartment had been deliberately set and that it had been set by the respondent. As I have already stated, the fact that the appellants were not the authors of the statement, but only published it by way of repetition, is no defence to an action of libel. It is, however, a factor to be taken into consideration when assessing damages, as evidence of the appellant's state of mind, which is always material to the question of damages. It is a somewhat less malicious act to repeat rather than to originate a defamatory statement.

[61] For all the above reasons, I am of the opinion that the factors, considered by the trial judge as evidencing malice, do not substantiate that conclusion.

5.2.3.1.3.3.12 *Vogel* v. *CBC* (1982), 21 C.C.L.T. 105, at 132, 133 and 193

At trial there was some discussion as to what, if any, significance there is to the adjective "investigative". The CBC witnesses tended to downplay it and to emphasize that all reporters must investigate to some degree. While that may be so, the word connotes a real distinction which was expressed by Mr. Waters who said, "an investigative reporter is simply a reporter who gets stories that nobody wants you to have". The distinction is with the routine business of reporting the events of a given day as set out in press releases, wire reports or as they are observed by a reporter attending, or talking to those who have attended, the fire, accident, city council meeting or whatever other event is the subject of the report.

Another distinguishing feature of investigative reporting is that, when it succeeds, the resulting story is an exclusive — a "scoop". The reporter, by his digging, brings the story to light and he and his paper or station or network get the credit. The potential rewards, in fame and fortune, are great. That is a fact of which we have seen some striking examples in recent years, of which the Watergate matter is perhaps the most famous. It is reasonable to assume that the lesson of that was not lost upon those ambitious to make their mark in the world of news reporting, including some of those responsible for the programmes which are the subject of this action.

...

A further ground upon which the defence of fair comment must fail is that the allegations were not made in good faith and without malice. There was, on the contrary, express malice.

That is not to say that the defendants were motivated by personal spite or ill will towards the plaintiff. What the law regards as malice is any indirect motive other than a sense of duty: Gatley, op. cit., p. 326. The purported motive of the defendants was to serve the public interest by exposing corruption in high places but the real motive was to enhance their own reputations by producing a sensational programme. Their concern was not as to whether the allegations were true or as to whether the public interest was served. It was, rather, to give to allegations of scandal the appearance of truth to the extent necessary to succeed in achieving their goal. That attitude, in law, is malice.

5.2.3.1.4 Consent

5.2.3.1.3.4.1 Syms *v.* Warren *(1976), 71, D.L.R. (3d) 558 (Man. Q.B.)*

HAMILTON, J.: — Plaintiff seeks damages for defamation. The plaintiff is the Chairman of the Manitoba Liquor Control Commission and the Liquor Licensing Board. Defendant Warren is the host of a radio programme and the corporate defendant is the owner of the radio station.

In December, 1974, rumours were circulating among employees of the Liquor Commission, among some members of the press, and presumably in other circles as well, that plaintiff had been charged with impaired driving but had arranged to have the proceedings quashed. There was a suggestion that the rumour was mentioned on the defendants' programme and then refuted by Warren. There is, however, no evidence that this was the source of the rumour and in any event plaintiff does not put the December programme in issue.

On January 15, 1975, Warren telephoned plaintiff, said he had investigated the rumour and was satisfied it was groundless, and asked the plaintiff if he would speak on his radio programme the next morning to deny the alleged charge and cover-up. Plaintiff agreed. Plaintiff had listened to this particular radio programme for a number of years, was aware that it was a programme where Warren expressed opinions on subjects and then discussed them with listeners who telephoned in. Plaintiff was also of the opinion that at times persons appearing on the programme, and even those who refused to appear, were subjected to what he considered to be unfair comment. The next morning, January 16th, as previously arranged, Warren telephoned plaintiff at his residence. While plaintiff was listening Warren gave a résumé of the rumours and the allegations against the plaintiff, said that he had investigated and was satisfied the rumours were incorrect. He then asked the plaintiff for his comment and the plaintiff, in an exchange of questions and answers, denied the truth of the allegations. Plaintiff said he felt that at the conclusion of the conversation the topic was closed and that he would hear nothing further. Several minutes later Warren received a telephone call from a woman identified only as "D". He spoke to her off the air and was aware she wished to comment on the interview with plaintiff and I infer Warren was aware she wished to disagree with what the plaintiff had said. The woman then came on the air and said that what the plaintiff had said by way of denial of the rumours was untrue and that she was satisfied from information she had received that the rumours were in fact correct.

Portions of the conversation with the woman are as follows:

> I just heard Frank Syms on the line this morning.
> I'm not dealing with rumors, Madame.
> No, it's not a rumor.
> What's not a rumor?
> About Frank Syms being picked up for drunken driving.
> It is a rumor.
> It's not, it's true.
> ...
> Well, he does have a history of drunken driving.
> He does not.
> Yes he does.
> No he doesn't.
> ...
> Well, I haven't met Mr. Syms personally and I know he likes his drink.

Warren invited the woman to check with her sources and suggested she would find that the story was gossip and that her informant had received the information from someone else. There is no evidence the woman ever telephoned back and there is no evidence of any further reference to the rumour on the radio programme.

The evidence showed that all calls received on the programme went from the telephone onto a tape and were then broadcast on the air with a time lapse of 10 seconds. Warren thus had the ability to censor calls and stop all or any portion of any call being broadcast.

There is no question that many of the remarks made by Warren during his conversation with plaintiff and the remarks he permitted the woman to make, and then published by permitting them to be broadcast, are defamatory. The only question is whether the plaintiff assented to the publication of the defamatory matter. If the plaintiff did assent to the publication, he has no cause of action. The principle was referred to by MacPherson, J., in *Jones v. Brooks et al.* (1974), 45 D.L.R. (3d) 413, [1974] 2 W.W.R. 729. In that case, two detectives with concealed tape recorders spoke to the defendant for the purpose of inducing the defamatory remarks and having them recorded. The learned trial Judge found the defence of *volenti non fit injuria* was available as there was an implied consent to the publication of the defamatory material. In the case at bar, the consent of the plaintiff does not have to be inferred. Plaintiff did in fact consent to, and participated in, a discussion of the defamatory matter.

In *Whitney et al. v. Moignard* (1890), 24 Q.B.D. 630, on a motion to strike out certain pleadings, Huddleston, B., commented at p. 631:

> The law is thus stated, and I think correctly stated, in Odgers on Libel and Slander, 2nd ed., page 168: "Where there is evidence that the defendant, though he spoke only to A., intended and desired that A. should repeat his words, or expressly requested him to do so; here the defendant is liable for all the consequences of A.'s repetition of the slander; for A. thus becomes the agent of the defendant."

Chapman v. Lord Ellesmere et al., [1932] 2 K.B. 431, dealt with the publication of defamatory matter in a periodical selected by the parties and in other newspapers. It was alleged the plaintiff had administered a drug to a horse. The decision of the racing stewards actually was that the plaintiff was merely guilty of a dereliction of duty and there was no finding that he had himself drugged a horse or caused it to be drugged. One defence was that the plaintiff, as a condition of his licence, agreed to the publication of the results of the stewards' decision and cannot be heard to complain of a tort to which he himself has assented. Slesser, L.J., considered this defence to be based on the doctrine of *volenti non fit injuria*. He said at pp. 463-4:

> ... for if the plaintiff assented to a report of the decision of the stewards, and they used words which were not a report of that decision, Sir Patrick Hastings' argument would have great weight; but if, on the other hand, in fact, they did report the actual decision, but in such a way that the jury say that it was to be understood to mean something other than the actual decision, that is a risk which the plaintiff, by agreeing to a report of the decision, has elected to run.

He concluded at p. 465:

> His case is that the words in their natural meaning are defamatory and so not a true report of the decision; but, for myself, for the reasons I have given, I think the case can only be based on innuendo, and, applying the doctrine of *volenti non fit injuria,* I hold that the plaintiff must fail in respect of the publication in the Racing Calendar by reason of his assent thereto.

In *Jones v. Brooks, supra,* MacPherson, J., also adopted some American precedents, particularly the comments of Justice Halpern of the Appellate Division of the Supreme Court of the State of New York in *Teichner v. Bellan* (1959), 181 N.Y.S. 2d 842 at p. 846:

> Consent is a bar to a recovery for defamation under the general principle of *volenti non fit injuria* or, as it is sometimes put, the plaintiff's consent to the publication of the defamation confers an absolute immunity or an absolute privilege upon the defendant.

In that case, the question was whether defamatory remarks in answer to a doctor's account, sent through a collection agency, amounted to a publication, whether there was consent and whether the occasion was privileged.

I am satisfied that as far as the initial conversation between the plaintiff and Warren is concerned, the plaintiff did assent to the publication of the defamatory matter. He was fully aware of the topic to be discussed, that the defamatory matter would be repeated during the conversation, and that the conversation would be published to the listening audience.

I am equally satisfied that the plaintiff did not consent to a continuation of the discussion of the rumour. The consent of the plaintiff extended only to such publication as was necessary to fulfil the purpose indicated by Warren, that is, to participate in the programme to deny the rumour and the comments of Warren that would be made in regard thereto. Even if plaintiff was aware that topics discussed on the programme were often subsequently discussed with listeners who telephoned the programme, I can find nothing in the consent of the plaintiff or in any of the evidence to indicate that the plaintiff agreed to Warren opening the topic for public discussion.

I have considered whether plaintiff's initial assent implied a consent to any and all subsequent discussion of the dafamatory material by Warren. In my opinion there is a heavy onus upon a radio broadcaster to have a person's permission before making defamatory statements about him. If the broadcaster publishes defamatory material he must assume the risk of being able to justify the publication. In this case, the broadcaster has failed in that obligation as far as the discussion with the woman is concerned. Consent is a narrow defence to defamation, one not often seen and one where the consent must be clearly established. Consent must be given or be able to be inferred with respect to each publication of defamatory material. Were it otherwise, consent to the merest publication would open the door to wide dissemination that might be very damaging and never intended to be authorized by the person giving the initial consent. The defendants have failed to satisfy me that they had the authority of plaintiff to continue to discuss the defamatory material relating to plaintiff after Warren's conversation with him ended.

Warren's support of plaintiff does not excuse the publication. *Gatley on Libel and Slander,* 7th ed. (1974), p. 121:

> 264. *Expressions of doubt at the time of republication.* The fact that the defendant expressed a doubt or disbelief as to the truth of the slander at the time will make no difference to his liability. "No character or reputation would be safe, if a mere statement of a person's disbelief of a rumour which the speaker was engaged in circulating could be made to defeat the right of recovery for the slander." (*Per* Du Relle J. in Nicholson v. Merritt (1900) 109 Kentucky R. 369 at p. 371.)

Section 3 of the *Defamation Act,* R.S.M. 1970, c.D20, provides that where defamation is proved, damage shall be presumed. Section 5 provides that an apology may mitigate damages. No apology was made in this case as defendants believed that if they had published any defamatory matter, they were justified due to the assent of the plaintiff. A public apology, in the circumstances of this case, would have required some repetition of the defamatory matter and would only have aggravated the situation. Similarly, Warren's support of plaintiff would have made an apology less meaningful than if he had been attacking the plaintiff. For these reasons I neither increase nor decrease the damages due to the lack of an apology.

Plaintiff's relationship with his employer, in effect the Government of Manitoba, requires examination when assessing damages. In December, 1974, after hearing the rumours, the Attorney-General and Egon Frech, an executive assistant to the Premier of Manitoba, joined in a telephone call to plaintiff asking if the rumours were correct. Plaintiff said the allegations in the rumours were untrue and the callers accepted that report. Plaintiff's employment has not been affected and his appointments to the Liquor Commission and Board were renewed for 1975 and 1976. Plaintiff testified he was shaken by the telephone call from the Attorney-General. He nevertheless, subsequently, agreed to participate in a discussion of the rumours on defendants' programme. On January 16th, Mr. Frech heard the portion of the programme when the woman and Warren were in conversation. He immediately telephoned plaintiff, indicated concern, and suggested plaintiff refer the matter to his solicitors. It appears to me plaintiff was not embarrassed or concerned up to that time, but was caused to act by this suggestion. On the other hand, he was embarrassed by this second telephone call from Mr. Frech and I consider this to be damage flowing from the publication of the defamatory matter during the conversation with the woman. The evidence disclosed that, like Mr. Frech, some listeners heard only a portion of each programme.

There was evidence from others who heard the programme, but none indicating any lessening of their respect for the plaintiff either as a result of the programme as a whole, or as a result of the conversation with the woman in particular.

Damages then result primarily due to s.3 of the *Defamation Act*. Damages are presumed, but there is no evidence of aggravated damages that would warrant a substantial award.

In my opinion, plaintiff must assume most of the responsibility for any damage he did suffer. If he had not participated in the discussion of the defamatory rumours, they would not have been widely disseminated. If he had not consented to the initial discussion with Warren, the woman would likely not have made her remarks or Warren might not have felt it permissible for her to make those remarks on the programme. If he had not participated in the further discussion, his superiors would not again have shown concern. Plaintiff's involvement does not excuse defendants for their publication of the defamatory remarks during Warren's discussion with the woman, but it substantially reduces the amount of damages to be awarded. Considering the extensive publication for which defendants are not liable, as opposed to the lesser publication that fixes liability, the damages I award are not substantial.

There will be judgment for the plaintiff against both defendants, jointly and severally, in the amount of $2,000 plus costs. I considered awarding costs on a solicitor-and-client basis. If I had done that, the $2,000 figure would have been substantially lower.

5.2.4 Remedies

The basic remedy in all tort actions is the award of an amount of money as damages. Since libel exists as an action through which individuals seek to protect their reputations, an award of damages will be made as compensation for an unlawful injury to reputation. How many dollars is someone's reputation worth? Alternatively, a plaintiff may seek an injunction in order to prevent the publication of a libel.

5.2.4.1 Damages

5.2.4.1.1 *Munro* v. *Toronto Sun* (1982), 21 C.C.L.T. 261, at 294

Damages in libel actions are "at large" and rest upon a consideration of the injury to the plaintiff, the conduct of the defendant and the plaintiff and, in some cases, the deterrent effect sought to be accomplished. Except to the extent that they are intended to be a deterrent, they are compensatory and not punitive. Such damages may be aggravated by the particular circumstances of the case, including the defendant's conduct, both before and after the libel, and the added detrimental effect on the plaintiff. As well, such may be considered in mitigation. Injury to reputation is assumed when libel is proved.

5.2.4.1.2 *Walker and Walker Brothers Quarries Ltd.* v. *CFTO Ltd. et al.* (1987), 19 O.A.C. 10 (Ont. C.A.)

ROBINS J.A.:

1. *Were the compensatory damages of $883,000 awarded to Walker Brothers excessive?*

The defendants' submission is that the verdict of $883,000 in favour of Walker Brothers is so grossly excessive and manifestly unreasonable that it must be set aside. In considering this submission, I first remind myself of the principles applicable to appellate review of jury awards in defamation cases. Here, general or compensatory damages, and those terms can be used interchangeably, are clearly "at large" and their amount, as is so often said, is "peculiarly the province of the jury". An appellate court is not entitled to substitute its own judgment on the proper amount of damages for the judgment of the jury. The question is not whether the court would have awarded a smaller sum than was awarded by the jury; nor is the question whether the size of the verdict was merely too great. The question is whether the verdict is so inordinately large as obviously to exceed the maximum limit of a reasonable range within which the jury may properly operate or, put another way, whether the verdict is so exorbitant or so grossly out of proportion to the libel as to shock the court's conscience and sense of justice.

Applying that strict test to this case, I am nevertheless of the opinion that the verdict cannot stand. Two dominating reasons compel me to this conclusion: first, the jury used an arbitrary yardstick in measuring these damages and could not have directed its mind to the considerations properly applicable to an award of compensatory damages for a corporate plaintiff; and second, the award, viewed most favourably to the plaintiff, bears no reasonable relationship to either the circumstances of the case or the injury inflicted on the company by the defendants' tort. Before considering these reasons, some brief general observations about compensatory damages in libel actions may be helpful.

Defamation is an invasion of a person's interest in his or her reputation, and compensatory damages are imposed primarily to compensate for the harm caused to the person's reputation by the defamatory publication. In libel actions damages are at large in the sense that the award is not limited to a pecuniary loss that can be specifically proved; damages are presumed from the publication of the libel itself and need not be established by proof of actual loss. Damages may include intangible or subjective elements; they cannot be measured by any objective monetary scale and are not capable of precise calculation.

A libelled plaintiff is, of course, entitled to special damages (as distinct from general damages) to cover the actual pecuniary loss which has resulted from the wrong. Such a plaintiff is entitled also to compensatory or general damages for both: (a) the injury sustained as a result of the lessening ot the esteem in which he or she is held in the eyes of the community because of the defamatory statements; and (b) the injury caused to his or her feelings by the defamatory statements. The damages may be aggravated by the manner in which, or the motives with which, the statement was made or persisted in. Where the defendant is guilty of insulting, high-handed, spiteful, malicious or oppressive conduct which increases the mental distress — the humiliation, indignation, anxiety, grief, fear and the like — suffered by the plaintiff as a result of being defamed, the plaintiff may be entitled to what has come to be known as "aggravated damages". Aggravated damages are damages which take into account the additional harm caused to the plaintiff's feelings by such reprehensible or outrageous conduct on the part of the defendant. Their purpose is compensatory and, being compensatory, they properly form part of a general damage award. Aggravated damages, it should be underscored, are not punitive — punishment is not the function of a compensatory award. They must be distinguished from "punitive" or "exemplary" damages (to which I shall come later) which are non-compensatory and have as their object punishment and deterrence.

Thus, a compensatory damage award in a defamation action should represent the judge or jury's estimate of the amount necessary in all the circumstances of the case: (i) to vindicate the plaintiff's reputation; and (ii) to compensate him for his wounded feelings.

5.2.4.1.3 *Farrell* v. *St. John's Publishing Co.* (1986) 58 Nfld. & P.E.I.R. 66 (Nfld. C.A.)

MORGAN, J.A.:

[72] The large subjective element in an action for defamation, where damages are said to be 'at large', makes it impossible to advance any objective standards by which to gauge the right figure in any given case and creates difficulty in drawing a fair comparison with awards in other types of action.

[73] By three judgments delivered on January 19, 1978, sometimes referred to as the "trilogy", the Supreme Court of Canada placed an upper limit of $100,000.00 on awards for non-pecuniary damages in personal injury claims. (**Andrews v. Grant & Toy Alberta Ltd.,** [1978] 2 S.C.R. 229; 19 N.R. 50; 8 A.R. 182; [1978] 1 W.W.R. 557; 83 D.L.R. (3d) 452; 3 C.C.L.T. 225; **Thornton v. Board of School Trustees of School District No. 57 (Prince George),** [1978] 2 S.C.R. 267; 19 N.R. 552; [1978] 1 W.W.R. 607; 83 D.L.R. (3d) 480; **Teno v. Arnold,** [1978] 2 S.C.R. 287; 19 N.R. 1; 83 D.L.R. (3d) 609; 3 C.C.L.T. 372.

[74] In these cases the court expressed concern over the significant increase in the size of awards, under the head of non-pecuniary loss, in personal injury claims and took the opportunity of establishing a rough upper limit where very serious and debilitating injuries had been sustained. In putting a maximum monetary value of these kinds of injury, the court recognized that it was attempting to "equate the incommensurable". In the **Andrews** case, Dickson, J., as he then was, speaking for the court stated at page 261 S.C.R.:

> "... There is no medium of exchange for happiness ... The monetary evaluation of non-pecuniary losses is a philosophical and policy exercise more than a legal or logical one. The award must be fair and reasonable, fair being gauged by earlier decisions; but the award must also of necessity be arbitrary or conventional. No money can provide true restitution."

[75] There is authority for the proposition that awards for defamation should not be disproportionate to awards for serious personal injuries. In **McCarey** (supra), Diplock, L.J., stated at p. 960:

> "'I do not believe that the law today is more jealous of a man's reputation than of his life or limb. That is the scale of values of the duel. Of course, the injuries in the two kinds of case are very different, but each has as its main consequences pain or grief, annoyance or unhappiness, to the plaintiff ... But I do not accept that that higher scale of values in defamation cases is sanctioned by the law. It is, I think, legitimate as an aid to considering whether the award of damages by a jury is so large that no reasonable jury would have arrived at that figure if they had applied proper principles, to bear in mind the kind of figures which are proper, and have been held to be proper in cases of disabling physical injury.'"
> (See also **Groom v. Crocker,** [1938] 2 All E.R. 394, at 419, and **Broadway Approvals Ltd. v. Oldham's Press Ltd.,** [1965] 2 All E.R. 523, at 536).

[76] In **Munro v. Toronto Sun** (1982), 21 C.C.L.T. 261, J. Holland, J., accepted the strictures established by the "trilogy" as applicable in assessing damages arising from libel and that the policy considerations which led the Supreme Court of Canada to impose the upper limit as expressed in the "trilogy" apply equally to any non-pecuniary award, including the "at large" award in a libel action.

[77] With respect, I am not satisfied that the upper limit in personal injury claims, established by the "trilogy", was meant to apply in actions for defamation. I do, however, recognize the desirability of having such an upper limit established to ensure some degree of consistency and hopefully to provide a rational approach to the assessment of damages for defamation. In the final analysis, whatever the strictures that may be established in the cases of defamation, if any, "the award must be fair and reasonable, fairness being gauged by earlier decisions, but the award must also of necessity be arbitrary of conventional". (Per Dickson, J., supra) What is meant to be a just award is not in fact just if the amount awarded bears no relation at all to what is awarded to another plaintiff for a similar injury.

5.2.4.1.4 Julian Porter, Q.C., "Tangents", *Canadian Lawyer,* April 1981, p. 24

The magic of libel is that damages are at large and a jury can give whatever it sees fit.

Essentially, damages in libel are on the basis of compensation, not punishment. But you are allowed to refer to the conduct of the defendant or his counsel down to the time of the jury address, which is rather unique. You can comment on lack of apology, persistence of a plea of justification, a possibility of malice, the nature of the pleadings and even defence counsel's tactics plus the humiliation your client has suffered. Because of this there is a good shot of raising the damages to a higher scale than in a personal injury action although such discrepancy is frowned upon by the courts.

*Windeyer, J. said in **Uren** v. **John Fairfax & Sons Pty. Ltd.** (1967) 117 CLR 118 at 150.*

> "It seems to me that, properly speaking, a man defamed does not get compensation for his damaged reputation. He gets damages because he was injured in his reputation, that is simply because he was publicly defamed. For this reason, compensation by damages operates in two ways — as a vindication of the plaintiff to the public and as consolation to him for a wrong done. Compensation is here a solatium rather than a monetary recompense for harm measurable in money."

This is why it is not necessarily fair to compare awards of damages in this field with damages for personal injuries. Quite obviously, the award must include factors for injury to the feelings, the anxiety and uncertainty undergone in the litigation, the absence of apology, or the reaffirmation of the truth of the matters complained of, or the malice of the defendant. The bad conduct of the plaintiff himself may also enter into the matter, where he has provoked the libel, or where perhaps he has libelled the defendant in reply. What is awarded is thus a figure which cannot be arrived at by any purely objective computation. This is what is meant when the damages in defamation are described as being "at large".

*In **McCarey** v. **Associated Newspapers Ltd.** (No. 2) Pearson, L.J. (1965) 2.B. 86 at 104, dealt with the various elements in compensatory damages as follows:*

> They may also include the natural injury to his feelings — the natural grief and distress which he may have felt at having been spoken of in defamatory terms, and if there has been any kind of high-handed, oppressive, insulting or contumelious behaviour by the defendant

which increases the mental pain and suffering caused by the defamation and may constitute injury to the plaintiff's pride and self-confidence, those are proper elements to be taken into account in a case where the damages are at large.

I believe plaintiff jury addresses in libel actions are different than in other cases. Counsel must be melodramatic.

There is a tendency by judges to dislike libel cases with their technical pitfalls and as a result they do try to force settlement or view it all as a trifling matter. I remember a judge, now deceased, who indicated to the jury that a statement widely publicized that "the Chief of Police is a member of the Mafia" was 'a tempest in a teapot'. Consequently counsel must adopt a baroque attitude with tears if possible. One must abandon and gush with vibrato. My view is that unlike other cases a plaintiff's counsel can ill afford to be cheery or chirp witty asides to a jury. A jury must be slowly and continually persuaded that the worst ailment on this earth is to be buried with a sullied name. All speeches should dwell on the illusory balm of money and the eternal pain of losing the quality of life that has been wrenched away by the monstrous libel. The great area to exploit is that damages are at large and that actual damages needn't be proved. Also, one is entitled to refer to mental pain and suffering of the plaintiff.

I would recommend referring to a judgment (it is hard for a judge to interfere if you don't try to quote a specific law — but damages can be so general).

***Youssoupoff** v. **Metro-Goldwyn Mayer Pictures Limited** (1934) The Times Law Reports, 581 at 584 and 586 reads as follows:*

> What have the jury to do? They have to give a verdict of amount without having any proof of actual damage. They need not have proof of actual damages. They have to consider the nature of the libel as they understand it, the circumstances in which it was published, and the circumstances relating to the person who publishes it, right down to the time they give their verdict, whether the defence made is true, and, if so, whether that defence has ever been withdrawn — the whole circumstances of the case. It is not the judge who has to decide the amount. The constitution has thought, and I think there is great advantage in it, that the damages to be paid by a person who says false things about his neighbor are best decided by a jury representing the public, who may state the view of the public as to the action of the man who makes false statements about his neighbor, the plaintiff.

5.2.4.1.5 Factors Related to the Plaintiff

5.2.4.1.5.1 *Barltrop* v. *CBC* (1978), 25 N.S.R. (2d) 637 (N.S.C.A.)

Summary:

This case arose out of the plaintiff's claim against the defendant for damages for defamation. The plaintiff, who was a physician of high stature and reputation, appeared as an expert witness for 2 refining companies in a public hearing on alleged lead pollution by the companies, which was a hot public issue. The physician received $1,000.00 a day and expenses from the companies while so appearing. The C.B.C. broadcast a program in which it was stated that the physician was an example of an expert hired to give an opinion favourable to the interest paying him. The physician brought an action against the C.B.C. for damages for defamation.

The Nova Scotia Supreme Court, Trial Division, in a judgment reported at paragraphs 61 to 99 below, dismissed the physician's action. The Trial Division held that, although the statements were defamatory, the C.B.C.'s defence of fair comment prevailed. The physician appealed.

MacKEIGAN, C.J.N.S.: ...The appellant asks us to assess damages, which, since this was not a jury trial, we have undoubted power to do. The respondent urges that we direct a new trial on that issue, or, if we have power to do so (which I very much doubt — Civil Procedure Rule 62.23), refer it to the trial judge for assessment of damages. I do not think a trial judge would have any special advantage as to damages arising from seeing and hearing the witnesses in this case; it is not suggested that the attitudes displayed at the trial by the parties or their witnesses would have influenced the damages to be awarded.

The law allows general damages for sullied reputation. Such damages are "at large" because they are not susceptible to any exact monetary calculation.

Fleming, supra, at p. 521, states:

> Damages for loss of reputation may be either ordinary, aggravated or exemplary. The first two look to the injury done, the last to the conduct of the injurer. Among the factors to be taken into consideration in appraising the extent of the injury are the area of dissemination of the libel, the credence given to it by those to whom it was published and whether the plaintiff had furnished any ground for the aspersion, acted provocatively or in disregard for the feelings and reputation of others.

A good name proverbially is rather to be chosen than great riches, but its loss may require heavy financial solace. *Fleming, idem,* says:

> Reputation seems to be considered of much greater value than life or limb, dishonour an infinitely greater injury than agonizing and protracted physical suffering.

Pearson, L.J., in *McCarey v. Associated Newspapers,* [1965] 2 Q.B. at pp. 104-105 said:

> Compensatory damages... may include not only actual pecuniary loss and anticipated pecuniary loss or any social disadvantages which result, or may be thought likely to result, from the wrong which has been done. They may also include the natural injury to his feelings — the natural grief and distress which he may have felt at having been spoken of in defamatory terms, and if there has been any kind of high-handed, oppressive, insulting or contumelious behaviour by the defendant which increases the mental pain and suffering caused by the defamation and may constitute injury to the plaintiff's pride and self-confidence, these are proper elements to be taken into account in a case where the damages are at large.

The courts have frequently allowed very large sums as damages where widely published defamation has seriously slurred a fine reputation, even where no loss could actually have been suffered, financially or otherwise.

Thus in *Youssoupoff v. Metro-Goldwyn-Mayer Pictures, Limited* (1934), 50 T.L.R. 581 (C.A.), an award of 25,000 pounds was not disturbed where a motion picture, widely distributed, had shown a woman, whom viewer knowing her might identify as Princess Youssoupoff, as having been seduced or raped by Rasputin. Greer, L.J., at p. 586 said:

> No doubt the damages are very large for a lady who lives in Paris, and who has not lost, so far as we know, a single friend and who has not been able to show that her reputation has in any way suffered from the publication of this unfortunate picture play, but, of course, one must not leave out of account a great many other things. One of them is that it is very difficult to value the reputation of any human being. It is very difficult to put a money figure upon

the mental pain and suffering that is necessarily undergone by a good and delicate woman who has been foully libelled in the presence of large numbers of people.
See *McGregor on Damages* (13th Ed.), paras. 1299-1301.

Injury to feelings may warrant heavy damages even where reputation was not affected. In *Fielding v. Variety Inc.*, [1967] 2 Q.B. 841 (C.A.), a theatrical producer was alleged to have had ''a disastrous flop'' in respect of a highly successful play, an allegation which obviously no one would believe. Salmon, L.J., at p. 855 said:

It seems fairly obvious to me that that article cannot have had any really serious effect upon Mr. Fielding's reputation. Nevertheless he is entitled to be compensated, as I say, for the anxiety and annoyance which he very naturally felt at the time. For my part I consider that the sum of 5,000 pounds under that head was out of all proportion to the compensation justly payable to Mr. Fielding, and I agree with my Lords that the right figure under that head is 1,500 pounds.

Hall, J., for a majority of the Supreme Court of Canada in *McElroy v. Cowper-Smith and Woodman,* [1967] S.C.R. 425, at p. 426 said:

I would not, in any way, underestimate or discount the damage that can be done to a lawyer or to an insurance executive by false allegations of misconduct and dishonesty. Defamation of a professional man is a very serious matter and ordinarily would be visited with an award of substantial damages, including punitive or exemplary damages if the circumstances so warrant.

He went on, however, to disallow an award of $25,000 damages on the ground that the defendant was temperamentally unstable and prone to make extravagant statements and that reasonable businessmen, the usual clientele of the plaintiffs, a solicitor and an insurance executive, would not likely be affected by the libels. He directed a new trial as to damages. Spence, J., dissenting, would have maintained the award.

In *Hubert et al. v. DeCamillis et al.* (1964), 41 D.L.R. (2d) 495 (B.C.S.C., Aikens, J.) damages of $15,000 were awarded a music teacher and dealer in respect of libel in letters to his students and others alleging fraud and false pretenses. The plaintiff showed no loss of specific business, but did show a general falling off of his business which he attributed to the libel.

An article published in the Canada edition of Time falsely accused a career army officer of being a member of a dope smuggling group in Viet Nam and stated he was going to be charged with smuggling: *Platt v. Time International of Canada Ltd.* (1964), 44 D.L.R. (2d) (Ont. H.C.). Chief Justice McRuer awarded him $35,000 as punitive damages. He stated (pp. 25-27):

Quite apart from the criminality of trafficking in narcotic drugs it is conduct of such a loathsome and reprehensible character as to be revolting to all right-thinking people. A false imputation that the plaintiff was charged with being one of a group, four of whom had been found guilty of trafficking in narcotic drugs gravely reflected his good name.

...

In assessing damages I must take into consideration all the circumstances of the case. These include the conduct of the plaintiff, his position and standing in the community in which he lived, the nature of the libel, the mode and extent of the publication, whether there was a proper retraction or apology and the whole conduct of the defendant from the time the libel was published down to the close of the trial. I also take into consideration the conduct of the defendant before and after the action and in Court at the trial of the action: *Gatley on Libel & Slander*, 5th Ed., p. 625.

> At no time from the publication of the offending article has the defendant expressed regret that the language used may have caused injury to the plaintiff's reputation in the community in which he lived.
>
> ...
>
> During the course of the trial counsel for the defendant made it quite clear that he was not contending that the plaintiff was implicated in smuggling opium but at no time was regret expressed for the publication of the article if it was held to be defamatory. In fact the defendant displayed throughout a measure of defiant arrogance.

Although in the present case no attempt has been made to apologize or to retract the irresponsible imputation of professional dishonesty, and although one should expect higher standards and more balanced and responsible journalism from a national programme of the national broadcasting corporation, the circumstances in my view do not quite call for exemplary or punitive damages. I think the defendant's acts and attitude fall short of the kind of defamation requiring that penalty, and do not constitute "conscious, contumelious and calculated wrongdoing" characterized by intention to inflict the injury or by reckless indifference to consequences: *Australian Consolidated Press v. Uren* (1969), 117 C.L.R. 185. (I accept the proposition that the principles of *Rookes v. Barnard,* [1964] A.C. 1129, whereby in England the scope for punitive damages is now greatly limited, do not apply in Canada and that the test here is like that in Australia. See *McElroy v. Cowper-Smith and Woodman, supra,* per Spence, J., at p. 432; *Fleming, supra* at pp. 521-522; and *Fridman: Punitive Damages in Tort* (1940), 48 Can. Bar Rev. 373.)

The very factors which, if more pronounced, might have warranted punitive damages may, however, aggravate and increase the general damages which should be awarded to compensate the plaintiff for the injury to his reputation and feelings. So it is here. The prestige and apparent authority with which the defendant's programme falsely condemned the plaintiff, and its wide dissemination, without apology or explanation, throughout the northern half of North America greatly magnified the derogatory impact on Dr. Barltrop's reputation and pride. Cf. *Jones v. Bennett, supra,* where aggravated, but not punitive, damages of $15,000 were awarded and *Ross v. Lamport* (1957), 9 D.L.R. (2d) 585 (Ont. C.A.), where the mayor of Toronto was assessed $25,000 damages for arrogantly defaming in newspapers a man who had appealed a refusal of a taxicab licence and for failing to apologize.

The respondent argued strenuously that the appellant should in any event receive no more than nominal damages — that he proved no loss in the practice of his profession, that he would have been unlikely to receive paediatric references from Canada, least of all from Atlantic Canada, and that he had not proven any actual or potential loss of consultancy business resulting from the broadcasts. The cases to which I have referred show the fallacy in that argument. Serious damage to reputation requires heavy compensation, even if no specific loss is or can be shown. Here, a man of international reputation is vilified in the eyes of his professional confreres. He thus suffers greatly, though he may not lose a single dollar.

Even if many of his professional equals might well not believe or be influenced by the radio defamation, we cannot assume that laymen, such as industrialists, legislators, aldermen and other non-experts called upon to investigate or determine questions as to industrial pollution, would not be affected if they heard or read of the programme. Surely no lawyer wishing to impress a body of such laymen would risk presenting as an expert a man whose expertise and honesty had been so seriously impugned.

Dr. Barltrop could not prove positively that he had lost any specific consulting business in North America. He produced Dr. Panke, a member of a special advisory board formed in Idaho in 1976, who testified that he understood Dr. Barltrop had not been appointed to that board because the health authorities objected, apparently, because of the "Toronto mess". This was, however, partly denied or qualified by a Dr. Bax who selected the board and stated that he had not heard of the broadcast when he had left off Dr. Barltrop and, indeed, also Dr. Epstein, because they were respectively objected to by some environmentalists and by some companies.

Dr. Barltrop showed, however, that since the broadcast he had received no new retainers as a consultant in North America, and that his income from that source, previously substantial, had now disappeared. Like the plaintiff in *Hubert et al. v. DeCamillis et al., supra,* he has in my opinion shown probable financial loss, possibly substantial although not susceptible to any exact calculation.

Taking into account all the factors to which I have referred, considering Dr. Barltrop's professional eminence, the extreme defamation, the source whence it came, the extent of its dissemination, and the absence of apology or explanation, and considering the probable effect on Dr. Barltrop's practice and income, and making the best judgment I can in the light of all the evidence, I would award Dr. Barltrop as general damages the sum of $20,000.00.

I would allow the appeal with costs here and in the Court below.

Appeal allowed.

5.2.4.1.5.2 *Leonhard* v. *Sun Publishing* (1956) 4 D.L.R. (2d) 514 (B.C.S.C.)

LORD J.: — The defendant publishes a daily newspaper known as the Vancouver Sun. On December 28, 1955, following its usual practice of giving a résumé of top newspaper stories of the year, it published the following words under the heading "Police Probe Story Tops With Newsmen":

"The drug war — which followed the British Empire Games as second place story in last year's Sun poll — was an easy choice for number three spot in 1955.

"Its ugly pattern began to shape before the year was two months old.

"A booby trap bomb exploded in the car of drug king Jacob Leonard. Pusher Thomas Kinna's legs were broken on False Creek flats in June. August brought a major drug conspiracy roundup. September saw trafficker Eddie Scosky jump bail. This month, Kinna's assailants got heavy raps."

The plaintiff alleged that the defendant meant by these words that the plaintiff was in effect the head of an illegal drug syndicate operating in Vancouver, and had in consequence been seriously injured in his character, credit and reputation and had been brought into scandal, odium and contempt.

In its statement of defence the defendant admits the publication and does not seek to justify it, and specifically does not deny that the innuendo as pleaded is correct.

As already indicated the libel was published on December 28, 1955, the writ was issued on January 6, 1956, and on January 10, 1956, the defendant published the following apology:

"FACTS NOT CORRECT IN JACOB LEONARD REPORT

"Our attention has been drawn to our issue of Dec. 28, 1955, in which a story appeared entitled 'Police Probe Story Tops with Newsmen' in which reference was made to one Jacob Leonard.

"We have now ascertained that there is no foundation for the allegations contained in the story, and we take the earliest opportunity of correcting our error and of tendering to Mr. Jacob Leonard our sincere apologies.

"We trust he will accept this expression of our very great regret for any pain or annoyance that our reference may have caused him or his family."

The defendant brought into Court the sum of $501 in satisfaction of the plaintiff's cause of action.

In mitigation of damages the defendant denied that the plaintiff had been seriously injured in his character, credit and reputation and gave notice that under O. 36, r.37, of the Rules of the Supreme Court it would give particulars to the plaintiff of the matters intended to be given in evidence. These particulars were filed on May 18, 1956, and, in general, gave notice that it intended to adduce evidence of the general bad reputation of the plaintiff prior to the publication of the libel.

Several clippings from each of the three Vancouver daily newspapers, including the Vancouver Sun, published in March, 1955, were submitted in evidence not as proof of any statements contained therein but as evidence of the general bad reputation of the plaintiff. Some of these clippings had such headlines as "Leonard Named City Drug King"; "Bomb Blast Broke Up City Drug Ring"; "Police Near To Smashing City Drug Peddling Ring", with a subhead "Bombing Victim Named Boss"; "Undercover Agent Tags Bomb Victim As Leader of Local Narcotics Ring".

The words "Bomb Victim" refer to an explosion which occurred when the plaintiff endeavoured to start his car one morning at his home which resulted in serious injuries to himself.

The newspaper clippings were admitted in evidence subject to the objection of counsel for the plaintiff. In Wigmore on Evidence, 3rd ed., vol. I, p. 492, the learned author says: "Whether in an action for *defamation* the defendant may use the *plaintiff's poor reputation* (or lack of reputation) *to mitigate the damages* has been one of the most controverted questions in the whole law."

The classic case in England would seem to be the judgment of Cave J. in *Scott* v. *Sampson* (1882), 8 Q.B.D. 491, where he said at p. 503:

"Speaking generally the law recognizes in every man a right to have the estimation in which he stands in the opinion of others unaffected by false statements to his discredit; and if such false statements are made without lawful excuse, and damage results to the person of whom they are made, he has a right of action. The damage, however, which he has sustained must depend almost entirely on the estimation in which he was previously held. He complains of an injury to his reputation and seeks to recover damages for that injury; and it seems most material that the jury who have to award those damages should know if the fact is so that he is a man of no reputation....

"On principle, therefore, it would seem that general evidence of reputation should be admitted, and on turning to the authorities previously cited it will be found that it has been admitted in a great majority of those cases, and that its admission has been approved by a great majority of the judges who have expressed an opinion on the subject."

Mr. Wigmore points out at p. 493, vol. I that the meat of the argument (in favour of acceptance of such evidence) is that a person should not be paid for the loss of that which he never had. I think that the clippings are admissible in evidence in this sense — that the words of the libel complained of, or words of similar import referring to the plaintiff as "drug king Jacob Leonard" had been published some few months before by all the Vancouver daily newspapers. If the plaintiff had been damaged in his character and reputation by the libel sued upon, then surely his character and reputation had already been damaged by the earlier publications, accompanied as they were with large headlines, as compared with a single line contained in an article dealing with other news items. It transpired during the course of the trial that no proceedings were taken by the plaintiff respecting such publications. He gave no evidence at the trial — he did not see fit to come into Court and seek to protect his name and reputation. But he admitted on examination for discovery that he had suffered damage in this respect before the publication of the libel:

"Q. 109. Is it fair to say that before December of last year you had pretty well decided what you have just stated, that you would have to leave town or dig a hole and pull it in after you? A. And it was — I was doing all right before your paper started to blast me.

"Q. 110. When did you read this —? A. Oh, I went to the loan company, and I was going to make an effort to build some houses, and they told me they wouldn't give me any credit no more. So I can't get any credit. I may as well not work around here.

"Q. 111. That was last year, was it? A. No. This just — I was going to start building houses this summer.

"Q. 112. I see. A. And this happened just a little — prior to the summer I went away to — when I found out I couldn't get any credit here, I went to another part of the town here. I have a business man, he is in the manufacturing business and electrical business, and I figure he could overlook certain things. And he told me, he said, 'You are on your own'. They even hear it down there, and I have to go and start with — just work for a living now, because I have to do something that nobody else wants to do."

Further with respect to general reputation, he admitted on discovery using other names:

"Q. 212. Have you ever used any names other than those that I gave you at the beginning, Leonhard, Leonard Stone? A. Oh, have you ever checked into a hotel? If you go incognito somewhere —

"Q. 213. I don't think the purpose of the examination is to question me, but incidentally the answer is no, I have not. A. Maybe I did, but how do I know what I do?

"Q. 214. How many names other than those I gave you have you used? A. I don't know.

"Q. 215. A dozen? A. I got two for sure, I will tell you.

"Q. 216. What two? A. Jacob Leonard and Stone.

"Q. 217. I see. You were known in town in 1954 by a number of people as Jacob Stone? A. All these — everybody that was in prison — I was in prison under Jack Stone."

It is also quite clear from the excerpts from examination for discovery that he knew and associated with underworld characters both in gambling places and in prison.

With this background can it be said that the plaintiff had any reputation to be injured? He admits damage to reputation as the result of the publications prior to the libel complained of; he fails to appear at his trial to give evidence; he admits using names other than his own, and one might ask, if he had a fair name, why use others? He admits being in prison, and associating with underworld characters in gambling clubs.

The apology, given much more prominence than the libel complained of, must of course, be given consideration in mitigation of damages.

In my estimation the plaintiff has no reputation capable of being injured. I assess damages in the nominal amount of one dollar ($1).

The plaintiff is entitled to costs up to the time of payment in. The defendant shall have costs from the time of payment in, the plaintiff's costs to be set off against the defendant's.

There will be an order for payment out of Court the amount of $500, being the excess paid in.

Judgment for plaintiff.

5.2.4.1.5.3 *Walker and Walker Brothers Quarries Ltd.* v. *CFTO Limited et al.* (1987), 19 O.A.C. 10 at 16 (Ont. C.A.)

ROBINS J.A.: To this point, I have been speaking of the elements of a compensatory award applicable in the case of a defamed individual. There is, however, a distinguishing factor in the present case. Here, the plaintiff whose compensatory award is under attack is a corporation. Unlike a natural person, a corporation is an artificial entity and as such has no reputation in the personal sense which can be defamed by words which would affect the purely personal reputation of an individual.

A company, however, does have a business reputation and statements which cast aspersions upon that reputation may be actionable. If so, then the law will presume damages from the publication of the libel itself and, as in the case of an individual, the action will be maintainable without proof of special damages.

A company whose business character or reputation (as distinct from the character or reputation of the persons who compose it) is injuriously affected by a defamatory publication is entitled, without proof of damage, to a compensatory award representing the sum necessary to publicly vindicate the company's business reputation. But a company has no feelings and, therefore, as Lord Reid noted in *Lewis* v. *Daily Telegraph, Ltd. et al.*, [1963] 2 All E.R. 156 (H.L.) at p. 156, "[a] company cannot be injured in its feelings, it can only be injured in its pocket". Hence, unlike an individual, a company is not entitled to compensation for injury to hurt feelings or, it follows, to compensation by way of aggravated damages for a loss of this nature.

5.2.4.1.6 Factors Related to the Defendant

5.2.4.1.6.1 *Vogel* v. *CBC* (1982) 21 C.C.L.T. 105, at 198

The identity of the accuser is an important factor. The accusation might have [been] made by some nasty little tabloid scandal sheet and have done no harm. Strident scandal mongering is the stock in trade of certain publications and, because it is, they have little or no effect upon the opinions of anyone whose good opinion matters. To their ugly accusations, it is a sufficient response to say: "Regard the source".

Such a response is not available when defamed by CBC. In terms of prestige, power and influence, it is at the opposite end of the spectrum from the sleazy scandal sheet. Created and maintained by Parliament to inform the Canadian public, its news services are accorded great respect throughout Canada. They have a well-merited reputation for reliability. For that very reason, CBC has an enormous capacity to cause damage. The general run of right thinking people tend to think that "it was on the CBC News, so it must be so."

5.2.4.1.6.2 *Baxter* v. *CBC* (1980), 30 N.B.R. (2d) 102, at 121-2

Although I am reluctant to interfere with a trial judge's award of damages, in my opinion, in the instant case, the trial judge failed to consider as a relevant factor in awarding damages *the extent of the publication*. In Duncan and Neill in their text on Defamation, 8th Ed., p. 136, par. 18.14, it is said:

> 18.14 In many cases an important factor in the assessment of damages will be the extent of the publication. Thus whereas a limited publication to one or two individuals may lead to a very modest award of damages, particularly if the publishers are not influenced by the publication or may disbelieve it, a publication in a national newspaper or by means of television or radio may lead to a very substantial award because the defamatory material is likely to come to the notice of a very large number of people including many who are friends or acquaintances of the plaintiff. On the other hand the gravity of the matter cannot always be assessed by reference to the extent of the publication and certainly not in any direct ratio to the number of persons to whom the defamatory material is published. Thus a publication by letter to an employer or to a limited circle of the plaintiff's friends may be no less damaging than the publication of similar material in an article in a newspaper. Moreover, where a true innuendo is relied upon, or where only persons with knowledge of special facts would identify the plaintiff, it is submitted that the jury should be warned that the only relevant publication is to the persons with the special knowledge.

In view of the fact the program was telecast to about 980,000 Canadian viewers, some of whom no doubt were friends and acquaintances of Mr. Baxter, I would increase the award of general damages from $1,000.00 to $10,000.00.

5.2.4.1.6.3 *Munro* v. *Toronto Sun* (1982), 21 C.C.L.T. 261, at 306

There remains the claim for punitive or exemplary damages to be considered. Such damages are awarded by the Court to reflect its outrage, disapproval and aversion of conduct, so as to punish and make an example of a defendant so that it will be known that such conduct will not be tolerated by our Courts. They are not to be added compensation for the injury suffered by the plaintiff — but rather are received by the plaintiff as a windfall because of the defendant's conduct. I need not consider whether or not deliberate intention to harm the plaintiff is an essential ingredient to support an award of punitive damage, because on the evidence before me I have no difficulty in concluding that both Ramsay and Reguly did deliberately intend harm to Mr. Munro. The language of Ramsay, "I've got that f.....g Munro", the article published on March 27, the lack of care as to accuracy of the story and the falsity of the contents, and the language in the memorandum made by Reguly (set out above) particularly to that "Sleaze Munro" all satisfy me that both Ramsay and Reguly were out to "get" Mr. Munro. It is accordingly an appropriate case in which to award punitive damages against Ramsay and Reguly and to provide that the corporate defendant be vicariously liable therefor. For reasons previously given I do not find that the actions of the other defendants were such as to attract a punitive award. I assess these damages payable by Ramsay, Reguly and the Toronto Sun Publishing Corporation at $25,000 in the hope that this amount will be an effective deterrent to the Sun and to all who contemplate similar actions.

5.2.4.1.6.4 *Vogel* v. *CBC* (1982) 21 C.C.L.T. 105, at 202-9

The circumstances of this case, taken together, require an award of damages at the highest end of the scale. Those circumstances include the seriousness of the libel, the breadth of its publication, the extent of the demonstrable damage, the deliberate malice shown by the defendants in the preparation of the programme and in continuing to trial a course of action calculated to inflict upon the plaintiff the maximum hurt and damage.

The plaintiff places particular reliance upon *Broome v. Cassell* as having some similarity in its pattern of facts as they bear upon damages. A book written by one defendant, and published by the other, placed the blame for one of the great naval disasters of World War II on the plaintiff, then a retired naval officer, and made serious imputations on his conduct and courage. The author, in making those imputations, had known what he was doing and persisted in spite of authoritative warnings that the passages were defamatory. In a letter to the publisher, he said that it would be possible to say, "some pretty near the knuckle things" about Captain Broome and others, and "if one says it in a clever enough way, they cannot take action." The attitude displayed by Messrs. Waters, King and Bird could be described in the same words. In *Broome v. Cassell,* the defendants were motivated by the desire for gain, a motive which is not materially different from CBC's desire to improve its ratings and attract attention and Mr. Bird's desire to make his reputation as an investigative reporter.

In some important respects, *Broome v. Cassell* was less serious. By its nature, a book could not have the immediate and shattering impact of a special feature on prime time television. The libel against Captain Broome was cruel and hurtful but, coming as it did some years after his retirement from the navy, it could not affect his career. The claim for compensatory damages was, for that and other reasons, weaker than that in this case. The principal similarity is in the conduct of the defendants and therefore in the basis for punitive damages. In that case, the jury award, which was not disturbed on appeal, was £15,000 for compensatory damages and £25,000 for punitive damages.

Platt v. Time Int., supra, is in some respects comparable. The plaintiff was a career army officer who had served for a time with the International Control Commission in Vietnam. A number of Canadian servicemen were court marshalled for taking part in an opium smuggling ring and some were convicted. A story reporting on those matters ended with the sentence: "This week the only officer in the group, Major W.A. Platt, 48, takes his turn in court."

In its context, that sentence was held to imply falsely that the plaintiff was a member of the opium smuggling ring and was to be tried for that offence. In view of some of the positions taken by CBC in this case, it is of interest to note that the sentence was literally correct in that Major Platt was the only officer in the group of people referred to in the story and he was scheduled to take his turn in Court. What the story did not say was that the charge against him was of the much less serious offence of smuggling gold and that he had not been involved in smuggling opium. It is the false implication that he was so involved which was the basis of the judgment. That is worthy of mention because it seems clear that those responsible for producing the programme had the misapprehension that defamation consists only of saying that which is untrue in the literal sense and that the law will not have regard to context where defamatory meanings are merely implied.

The libel against Major Platt may be considered more serious than that against Mr. Vogel in that it imputed to him criminal conduct of a most reprehensible kind. The conduct of the defendant had important points of similarity. The imputation was made notwithstanding knowledge by *Time's* editors that Major Platt had not been charged with smuggling opium and was done to "add colour to the article" by suggesting that an officer was involved. It was held that the publication, if not deliberate, was done with a reckless indifference to any injury that might be done.

In other respects it was a less serious case. The allegation, although serious, was specific in its nature and thus capable of being effectively rebutted. The number of viewers of the CBC news programmes was far greater than the total circulation of the Canadian edition of Time. There is no indication that public opinion was turned against Major Platt in the same way that it was turned against Mr. Vogel. That distinction is important because what makes this case almost unique is the degree of severity of the impact upon the plaintiff in his professional and personal life.

In making any comparison to earlier damage awards, it is of course now necessary to have regard to the effects of inflation. The present equivalent to an award of $35,000 in 1964 would be an amount two to three times as large.

In considering the appropriate scale of damages, the amounts awarded in *Broome v. Cassell* and other English cases are of limited assistance because, historically, the level of defamation awards in England appears to have been consistently higher than in Canada.

The defendants submit that *Snyder v. Montreal Gazette* should be disregarded as a guide because of differences between the law of Quebec and that of British Columbia. There may not be much difference in the basic principles to be applied — I note that Deschenes C.J.S.C. relied on many decisions from provinces other than Quebec. The most important difference of substance which appears in the reasons is one which affords no comfort to these defendants. By the law of Quebec, no punitive damages can be awarded (87 D.L.R. (3d) at p. 14). Were a comparison to be made, it would be necessary to bear in mind that the publication in *Snyder* came five years before, and the judgment four years before, the equivalent dates in this case. An equivalent award, after adjusting for inflation over that period, could be $175,000 or more. Furthermore, *Snyder* was a less serious case in many ways. There are points of similarity in the position of the plaintiff and the nature of the defamation but it does not appear that there were any of the elements of deliberate attack or dramatic overemphasis which were present here. The source of the libel was hearsay testimony before the Quebec Police Commission. The *Montreal Gazette,* in publishing the story, was apparently saying the same thing that was being said almost simultaneously by other members of the media. The action against the *Gazette* was one of eight brought by the plaintiff but was apparently the first to get to trial (87 D.L.R. (3d) at p. 12).

Nevertheless, I put that case out of consideration as a basis for comparison because it is still subject to appeal.

In assessing compensatory damages, the element of aggravation resulting from the defendant's conduct must be taken into account:

> "In awarding 'aggravated' damages the natural indignation of the court at the injury inflicted on the plaintiff is a perfectly legitimate motive in making a generous rather than a more

moderate award to provide an adequate solatium. But that is because the injury to the plaintiff is actually greater and as the result of the conduct exciting the indignation demands a more generous solatium."
Broome v. Cassell, [1972] A.C. at p. 1073, [1972] 1 All E.R. at pp. 825-6.

Clearly, that applies here. The injury to Mr. Vogel was greater because of the reckless and deliberately damaging actions of the defendants: see *Robitaille v. Vancouver Hockey Club Ltd.* (1981), 30 B.C.L.R. 286 at 310-13, 16 C.C.L.T. 225, 20 C.P.C. 293, 124 D.L.R. (3d) 228 (C.A.).

Compensatory damages are not confined in their scope to pecuniary losses:

"[Defamation] actions involve a money award which may put the plaintiff in a purely financial sense in a much stonger position than he was before the wrong. Not merely can he recover the estimated sum of his past and future losses, but, in case the libel, driven underground, emerges from its lurking place at some future date, he must be able to point to a sum awarded by a jury suffient to convince a bystander of the baselessness of the charge."
Broome v. Cassell, at p. 1071 A.C.; at p. 824 All E.R.

For the reasons which I have already given, I consider that adequate compensation to the plaintiff for the injury to his reputation by being publicly defamed should be fixed at $100,000.

The remaining matter to be considered is whether any additional amount should be awarded as punitive or exemplary damages. (The terms are synonymous.)

Rookes v. Barnard, [1964] A.C. 1129, [1964] 1 All E.R. 367 (H.L.), has not been accepted as stating the law in this country insofar as it restricts exemplary damages to cases falling within three specified categories it is, nevertheless, authoritative on other aspects of the law of damages so carefully considered therein. I refer particularly to the following:

"In a case in which exemplary damages are appropriate, a jury should be directed that if, but only if, the sum which they have in mind to award as compensation (which may of course be a sum aggravated by the way in which the defendant has behaved to the plaintiff) is inadequate to punish him for his outrageous conduct, to mark their disapproval of such conduct and to deter him from repeating it, then they can award some larger sum."
[1964] A.C. at p. 1228, [1964] 1 All E.R. at p. 411, quoted in *Broome v. Cassell,* [1972] A.C. at p. 1059, [1972] 1 All E.R. at p. 814.

In this province, exemplary damages may be granted in all cases where the conduct of the defendant has been such as to merit the condemnation of the Court: *Robitaille v. Vancouver Hockey Club Ltd.*, supra, at p. 310 [B.C.L.R.]. That initial test is clearly met by the facts of this case. At that point, the other matters mentioned by Lord Devlin are useful in deciding whether such damages should be awarded. If punishment is not necessary for the purpose of deterrence, the case for awarding exemplary damages is weaker.

In relation to this question, the position of the two defendants must be considered separately. Mr. Bird's circumstances in life are such that, if any amount of damages would serve to deter him from a repetition of his conduct, the appropriate amount for that purpose would be less than the amount of compensatory damages. While his conduct merits the disapproval of the Court, the amount of compensatory damages is also sufficient to signify that disapproval. Mr. Bird's conduct was in the course of his employment as a reporter. Had his employer exercised a reasonable degree of editorial judgment and control, that conduct would have caused no harm to anyone.

The damage came, not from the investigation, but from the publication. The responsibility for deciding whether to publish rested with those above Mr. Bird. The most seriously reprehensible conduct was their abdication of responsibility. That was an abdication, not by individuals, but by an organization possessing a unique degree of influence and power.

CBC is one of the great corporations of Canada. It has massive means at its disposal. There is evidence that total income in the most recent fiscal year was $656,000,000 of which $515,000,000 came from its parliamentary grant. In this action, the corporation showed no sign of feeling any real concern about the harm caused by the irresponsible abuse of its great power. Its management shares Mr. Bird's view of what is important. Mr. Lauk said that, because "we live in an increasingly secretive society", it would be wrong for him "to hindsight the newsroom".

This is not the first, although it is the most serious, case disclosing what may be a tendency on the part of CBC in some of its programmes to proclaim its view of the truth with righteous zeal but scant regard for the facts and for the reputations of those of whose conduct it disapproves. In *Barltrop v. C.B.C.* (1978), 5 C.C.L.T. 88, 36 A.P.R. 637, 86 D.L.R. (3d) 61, 25 N.S.R. (2d) 637 (N.S. C.A.), the radio programme "As It Happens" said of the plaintiff that, in testifying as a medical expert at a public inquiry into lead poisoning, he had given untruthful and misleading evidence and had done so in wanton disregard for public health. As in this case, the defence of fair comment was raised and failed. MacKeigan C.J.N.S., for the Court, said at p. 78 [D.L.R.] that there had been an "irresponsible imputation of professional dishonesty" and that "... one should expect higher standards and more balanced and responsible journalism from a national programme of the national broadcasting corporation...."

In *Thomas v. C.B.C.*, supra, it was imputed to the plaintiff in a series of radio broadcast that he had improperly performed his duties to the extent that there had been a "betrayal of public faith" which resulted in a fatal explosion. Disbery J., at p. 337 [W.W.R.], pointed out that CBC's reporter had been in possession of a great deal of information favourable to the plaintiff and inconsistent with the thrust of the programme but that the broadcast had contained not "even the shadow of a whisper" of such matters. He went on so say:

> "The repeated juxtapositioning of plaintiff's misconduct, explosion and death promoted sensationalism. How drab in comparison would the story have been if it had merely related that due to somebody's negligence on the drill ship the gas separator had not been connected and in use thus allowing gas to accumulate which, becoming ignited, exploded and caused MacKay's death. 'Man bites dog' is newsworthy, 'dog bites man' is not. These unsensational and unnewsworthy matters were, in my opinion, omitted from the broadcasts in order to be able to present to the public the more sensational story of a low level official giving quick approval to the request of a well known multinational oil corporation that even the government could not control. To only give the public a look at the side of the coin supportive of their comments and opinions and not to show the facts to the contrary on the other side of the coin is to deal in half-truths, and comments made in this way are neither fair nor made in good faith."

The broadcast in those two cases took place in 1974 and 1977 respectively. I know of no case in recent years in which any other member of the Canadian "communications media" has been subjected to similarly harsh criticism.

The question then arises whether CBC, by reason of its size and power, is immune to deterrence by any monetary award which would not be unthinkable by the moderate standards which prevail in Canada. That would be so only if the irresponsible attitude which allowed the Vogel story to be published is an established one in the controlling minds of the corporation. Such a conclusion would not be warranted in view of the general reputation for excellence of CBC's news services. There must be weighed, against the few demonstrated examples of irresponsibility and unfairness, the countless broadcasts which have shown a high standard of balanced and responsible jounalism.

The circumstances of the case call for the award of an additional amount against CBC as exemplary damages. That amount should not depart from the tradition of moderate awards but should be sufficient to mark the Court's disapproval of the conduct of CBC and provide some element of deterrence from similar conduct. That amount I fix at $25,000.

5.2.4.1.6.5 *Walker and Walker Brothers Quarries Ltd.* v. *CFTO Limited et al.* (1987), 19 O.A.C. 10 at 16 (Ont. C.A.)

ROBINS J.A.: Accepting the gravity of the libel here and viewing the circumstances in a manner most favourable to the company's position, the award of $883,000 is so inordinately large as to bear no reasonable relationship to the defamatory publication or the consequences flowing from it. While any libel by a national television network must be treated as serious, I am constrained to say that counsel's description of the program as "the most wicked libel imaginable" is insupportable. In my opinion, no jury applying the right principles and a reasonable scale of values could reach the conclusion that the defamatory statements in question are such as to warrant an award far exceeding any award ever made in a defamation action in Canada. We are told that the highest award to date was made in *Vogel* v. *Canadian Broadcasting Corporation, supra,* where $100,000 general damages and $25,000 exemplary damages were granted to a Deputy Attorney General for a defamatory allegation that he had improperly influenced the course of justice. In that case, aggravated damages compensating for such items as the shock and stress caused to the plaintiff by the defamatory broadcasts and their effect on him physically and on his family and professional life formed a significant part of the general damage assessment. And there, of course, the plaintiff was not a company.

As a general proposition, it can be fairly stated that where a defendant has engaged in some form of reprehensible conduct the scale of damages appropriate to the case of a defamed individual can reasonably be expected to be higher than the scale appropriate to the case of a defamed company. In the latter case, there can be no question of compensation for injured feelings or compensation by way of aggravated damages for increased injury to such feelings, both patently important elements in an individual's general damage claim. Furthermore, in this case, there is no question of any pecuniary loss. All that has to be compensated for here is the injury to Walker Brothers' corporate reputation. The figure set by this jury as being the amount necessary to vindicate that reputation in the eyes of right thinking people in the community goes far beyond the maximum limit of any range that can conceivably be regarded as fair or reasonable compensation for this company in these circumstances. It is so exorbitant and irrational a sum that it should not be allowed to stand.

5.2.4.1.6.6 *Gerald M. Snyder* v. *The Montreal Gazette Ltd.*
(1988) Supreme Court of Canada (unreported)

BEETZ J.: I have had the benefit of reading the reasons for judgment of my brother Lamer and I adopt his statement of the facts, the judgments of the courts below and the points at issue.

Like Lamer J., I consider that the reasons given by the majority of the Court of Appeal for concluding that the compensation awarded by the jury was unreasonable are vitiated by error.

With respect for the contrary view, however, I am unable to say that this compensation is unreasonable on other grounds.

Although the compensation seems high and is not necessarily what I would have determined, respondent did not persuade me that the trial judge erred in ruling as follows:

> This Court is not prepared to say that the jury's estimate is so grossly inflated as to be branded as unreasonable, in the light of all the circumstances of the case.
> ([1987] C.S. 628, at pp. 635-636.)

I concur in substance with the reasons of L'Heureux-Dubé J.A., dissenting in the Court of Appeal, and in particular with the following:

> [TRANSLATION]...I would not look for bases of comparison in this matter in France, the United States or even the Commonwealth countries. Custom, usage and the law are so different there that, in my opinion, such comparisons cannot serve as useful guides for our courts.
> ([1983] C.A. 604, at p. 623.)

For these reasons I would allow the appeal, reverse the judgment of the Court of Appeal and restore the Superior Court judgment, including the order to publish the aforesaid judgment unless appellant waives this order, the whole with costs throughout.

LAMER J. (dissenting): ... Is the compensation awarded nonetheless unreasonable on other grounds? The jury concluded that appellant had proven no pecuniary loss as a result of the defamation and he therefore received nothing in this regard. The $135,000 awarded to appellant thus represent only non-pecuniary loss suffered by him. These damages are offered to the victim to compensate for the humiliation, suffering, scorn, embarrassment and ridicule he was subjected to as a result of the defamation. As in principle compensation cannot be made in kind, it generally consists of a sum of money. It is far from easy to do justice in this area. The amount awarded is necessarily arbitrary, in view of the difficulty of measuring objectively such loss in pecuniary terms, especially when it concerns someone else's reputation. It is precisely because this exercise is based on empirical considerations rather than on a mathematical and scientific operation that extravagant claims for this type of loss should not be allowed by the courts.

The Court of Appeal's judgment indicates its concern to restrain the compensation awarded for non-pecuniary loss. In support of his opinion that the verdict was unreasonable, Owen J.A. referred to the upper limit established by this Court in 1978 in the "trilogy": *Andrews v. Grand & Toy Alberta Ltd., supra; Thornton v. Board of School District No. 57 (Prince George),* [1978] 2 S.C.R. 267; *Arnold v. Teno,* [1978] 2 S.C.R. 287. In those cases Dickson J., as he then was, established that a maximum of $100,000 may be awarded as compensation for non-pecuniary loss resulting from physical injuries.

According to Owen J.A., the amounts awarded for non-pecuniary loss in a defamation case also should not exceed this limit. Such a comparison is certainly conceivable, as both cases involve non-pecuniary loss which is difficult to determine objectively. However, Owen J.A. gives no reason for applying this upper limit to compensation for an attack on reputation. Should a ceiling be placed on non-pecuniary loss for defamation in Quebec law?

Under the Quebec civil law, the general rule for the assessment of damages is contained in the axiom *restitutio in integrum*. In other words, compensation must be made in full, that is, it must place the victim in the same position he would have been if the incident had not occurred. He is entitled to compensation both for his non-pecuniary and pecuniary loss. As compensation must cover all the loss sustained, the concept of an upper limit is inconsistent with the principle of full compensation. Clearly compensation cannot be denied for part of the loss sustained nor can the amount of money awarded for pecuniary loss, which is objectively calculated once the damage has been proven, be limited. Similarly, non-pecuniary loss must be compensated in full, even if it is not as easy to assess as pecuniary loss. However, as the determination of the award for non-pecuniary loss falls within the realm of the arbitrary and subjective, a reference level should be established to facilitate the determination of this amount. Such a judicial policy decision does not in my opinion impair the principle *restitutio in integrum* rule.

It should be emphasized that I do not propose to impose an upper limit that would prevent the courts from compensating the total non-pecuniary loss actually proven. The objective rather is to set parameters to which judges may refer in determining the monetary compensation to be awarded. In such an arbitrary matter, guidelines have to be established to ensure equal treatment of plaintiffs.

To this end I think that in practice, the circumstances in which a victim of defamation will have to be paid more than $50,000 in order to be fully compensated for his non-pecuniary loss will be extremely rare. Naturally, as we must determine the reasonableness of the verdict at the time of the trial judgment, this amount is expressed in 1978 dollars. At the present time, allowing for inflation, it corresponds to approximately $100,000 (Statistics Canada, All-Items Consumer Price Index, December 1987).

The Court is not here adopting the upper limit of the trilogy established under the common law system. I wish however to point out that I am not deciding whether it is appropriate to adopt a reference level in cases of non-pecuniary loss resulting from physical injuries. I simply consider that it is desirable to set reference points in Quebec law to guide the courts in assessing non-pecuniary damages resulting from a defamation.

In fixing a sum of money to compensate a defamation victim for his pain and suffering, the court is undeniably making a purely arbitrary decision. Can the judge objectively place a price on pain, humiliation and anguish? As such a determination is not based on any mathematical calculation, he can easily get carried away and award compensation beyond all accepted limits. Although the victim is entitled to full compensation, the court must still ensure that he is not over-compensated. Compensation should not be a means of enriching him at the expense of the offending party.

I am in any case inclined to be wary of high amounts designed to compensate for non-pecuniary loss, as it is hard to know whether such amounts do not to some extent conceal a punitive aspect. Apart from certain exceptional cases such as s.49 of the *Charter of Human Rights and Freedoms,* R.S.Q. 1977, c.C-12, Quebec civil law does not recognize the award of punitive damages:

> [TRANSLATION] The damages awarded to a victim of an offence or quasi-offence are intended solely as compensation. The indemnity is calculated so as to take account of the loss actually suffered and the gain lost. It must be determined in light of the compensation owed, not the penalty for wrongful or reckless conduct by the offender. In theory, therefore, there can be no question of punitive or exemplary damages. The voluntary or involuntary nature of the act causing the damage is also not a factor. This rule, applied by the Quebec courts, has been approved by a judgment of the Supreme Court of Canada.
> J.-L. Beaudoin, *La responsabilité civile délictuelle* (1985), p. 108, No. 187.

However, among the criteria relied on by the Quebec courts in estimating the non-pecuniary loss in defamation cases are the seriousness of the act, the good or bad faith and the intent of the offender, and these are all criteria with a punitive connotation: C. Bissonnette, La diffamation civile en droit québécois (Thèse de maîtrise en droit, Université de Montréal, 1985), p. 400. In general if these factors are present the court is prepared to increase this item of damage: see Baudouin, op. cit., at pp. 160-161. There is thus reason to think that the higher the amount of the indemnity, the more likely it is to have a punitive aspect. In my opinion this aspect should disappear from our system, where the rule is to compensate the victim, not to punish the offending party.

Additionally, the non-pecuniary loss suffered by a victim of defamation is in general temporary, since the suffering he experiences diminishes with the passage of time. However serious the defamation, people eventually forget the humiliating remarks made or written about the victim and the pain he has suffered gradually loses its edge. This temporary quality is a further reason which, to me, justifies the award of a maximum of $50,000 as full compensation for the damages caused in this regard.

Moreover, a person defamed who sues successfully obtains a judgment which restores his reputation; the publicity surrounding both the trial and its outcome and the possible publication of the judgment, which is authorized by the *Press Act,* are all means of providing partial or total compensation for the non-pecuniary loss. In other words, a court action allows the victim to cleanse his honour and applies a balm to his pain and suffering.

It can also be seen from the case law that Quebec courts have traditionally exercised restraint in assessing non-pecuniary damages for defamation. They have generally awarded amounts ranging from $500 to $5,000: *L'imprimerie Populaire Limitée c. L'Honorable L.A. Taschereau* (1922), 34 K.B. 554 — $1,000, or publication of the judgment and $500; *Langlois c. Drapeau,* [1962] Q.B. 277 — $2,000; *Flamand c. Bienvenue,* [1971] R.P. 49 (C.S.) — $2,000; *Lachapelle c. Véronneau,* [1980] C.S. 1136 — $2,000; *Blanchet c. Corneau,* [1985] C.S. 299 — $4,500; *Trahan c. Imprimerie Gagné Ltée,* J.E. 87-1146 (S.C.) — $2,000. Moreover, the highest awards rarely exceed $20,000: *Flamand c. Bonneville,* [1976] C.S. 1580 — $12,000 (appealed; settled out of court); *Desrosiers c. Les Publications Claude Daigneault Inc.,* [1982] C.S. 613 — $20,000; *Goupil c. Les Publications Photo-Police Inc.* [1983] C.S. 875 — $15,000 (appealed; settled out of court); *Poirier c. Leblanc,* [1983] C.S. 1214 — $10,000; *Côté c. Le Syndicat des travailleuses et des travailleurs municipaux de la Ville de Gaspé,* J.E. 87-720 (S.C.) — $10,000; *McGregor c. The Montreal Gazette,* [1982] C.S. 900 — $50,000 (appealed; settled out of court); *Dimanche-Matin Ltée c.*

Fabien, J.E. 83-971 (C.A.) — $35,000. Apart from rare exceptions, the amounts awarded fall within a quite limited range. As the assessment of non-pecuniary loss is arbitrary, judges seem to instinctively recognize a limit which they are not prepared to exceed. This limit is generally quite low.

At common law, however, the courts have shown greater generosity. In the case at bar the trial judge reviewed the amount awarded by the courts in defamation cases. In addition to Quebec and France precedents, he consulted the case law of the United Kingdom and the other Canadian provinces. In my opinion, he should have limited himself to compensation awarded by Quebec courts, since different factors are used to determine non-pecuniary damages at common law. In addition to compensatory damages the common law allows the award of aggravated and punitive damages (Gatley, *Gatley on Libel and Slander* (7th ed. 1974), at pp. 1356-61). As we have seen, at civil law damages have a purely compensatory purpose. As the indemnity is often awarded in the form of a lump sum, it is impossible in a judgment rendered under the common law to know what portion of that sum is compensatory or punitive. Any comparison between the two systems is accordingly difficult to make.

Though it is a secondary consideration, there is one other factor that must be taken into account in defamation cases. These often involve newspapers, press agencies and radio or television stations. In coming to the rescue of a defamation victim, the courts must not overlook the fact that the written and spoken press is indispensable and is an essential component of a free and democratic society. Moreover, both the Quebec and Canadian Charters recognize the importance of the press (s.3 of the *Charter of Human Rights and Freedoms* and s.2 of the *Canadian Charter of Rights and Freedoms*). If information agencies are ordered to pay large amounts as the result of a defamation the danger is that their operations will be paralyzed or indeed, in some cases, that their very existence may be endangered. Although society undoubtedly places a great value on the reputation of its members that value, as it is subjective, cannot be so high as to threaten the functioning or the very existence of the press agencies which are essential to preserve a right guaranteed by the Charters.

In sum, in view of the arbitrary nature of the compensation awarded for non-pecuniary loss, the risk that it may have a punitive aspect, the temporary nature of the loss suffered, the compensatory effect of the judgment obtained and the moderation displayed by Quebec courts, I think that aside from truly exceptional cases it will not be necessary to award an amount greater than $50,000 (now $100,000) to compensate in full for the non-pecuniary loss resulting from an attack on reputation. Certainly, Quebec courts have never awarded compensation for non-pecuniary loss in a defamation case which comes even close to this limit. However, the concern for moderation should not lead us to underestimate the intrinsic value of reputation. There are many people who would prefer to suffer heavy pecuniary losses rather than to be lowered in the esteem of their friends. The reference level set by this judgment accordingly seems to me to be fair and reasonable because, while it may serve to prevent the award of extravagant claims, it is sufficiently high to encourage the courts to take into consideration the undoubted importance of reputation.

As the $135,000 award in the case at bar is well above the reference level, namely $50,000 in 1978, the Court is bound to conclude that the jury's verdict was clearly unreasonable. I accordingly consider that the trial judge made an error in affirming this verdict. The errors made by the trial judge and the Court of Appeal accordingly provide a basis for this Court to substitute its conclusions for those of the jury in determining the reasonable amount to which appellant is entitled.

5.2.4.1.6.7 Ontario Libel and Slander Act, R.S.O. 1980, c.237, ss.5(2), 5(3), 8, 9, 19, and 22 as am. 1984, c.11, s.191(2)

Note: An apology can substantially reduce the sum awarded.

Where plaintiff to recover only actual damages

5. (2) The plaintiff shall recover only actual damages if it appears on the trial.

(*a*) that the alleged libel was published in good faith;

(*b*) that the alleged libel did not involve a criminal charge;

(*c*) that the publication of the alleged libel took place in mistake or misapprehension of the facts; and

(*d*) that a full and fair retraction of any matter therein alleged to be erroneous,

(i) was published either in the next regular issue of the newspaper or in any regular issue thereof published within three days after the receipt of the notice mentioned in subsection (1) and was so published in as conspicuous a place and type as was the alleged libel, or

(ii) was broadcast either within a reasonable time or within three days after the receipt of the notice mentioned in subsection (1) and was so broadcast as conspicuously as was the alleged libel.

Case of candidate for public office

(3) This section does not apply to the case of a libel against any candidate for public office unless the retraction of the charge is made in a conspicuous manner at least five days before the election. R.S.O. 1970, c.243, s.5.

Publication of name of publisher, etc.

8. (1) No defendant in an action for a libel in a newspaper is entitled to the benefit of sections 5 and 6 unless the names of the proprietor and publisher and the address of publication are stated either at the head of the editorials or on the front page of the newspaper.

Copy of newspaper to be *prima facie* evidence

(2) The production of a printed copy of a newspaper is admissible in evidence as *prima facie* proof of the publication of the printed copy and of the truth of the statements mentioned in subsection (1).

Where ss.5, 6 not to apply

(3) Where a person, by registered letter containing his address and addressed to a broadcasting station, alleges that a libel against him has been broadcast from the station and requests the name and address of the owner or operator of the station or the names and addresses of the owner and the operator of the station, sections 5 and 6 do not apply with respect to an action by such person against such owner or operator for the alleged libel unless the person whose name and address are so requested delivers the requested information to the first-mentioned person, or mails it by registered letter addressed to him, within ten days from the date on which the first-mentioned registered letter is received at the broadcasting station. R.S.O. 1970, c.243, s.8.

Newspaper libel, plea in mitigation of damages

9. (1) In an action for a libel in a newspaper, the defendant may plead in mitigation of damages that the libel was inserted therein without actual malice and without gross negligence and that before the commencement of the action, or at the earliest opportunity afterwards, he inserted in such newspaper a full apology for the libel or, if the newspaper in which the libel appeared is one ordinarily published at intervals exceeding one week, that he offered to publish the apology in any newspaper to be selected by the plaintiff.

Broadcast libel, plea in mitigation of damages

(2) In an action for a libel in a broadcast, the defendant may plead in mitigation of damages that the libel was broadcast without actual malice and without gross negligence and that before the commencement of the action, or at the earliest opportunity afterwards, he broadcast a full apology for the libel. R.S.O. 1970, c.243, s.9.

Evidence in mitigation of damages

10. In an action for a libel in a newspaper or in a broadcast, the defendant may prove in mitigation of damages that the plaintiff has already brought action for, or has recovered damages, or has received or agreed to receive compensation in respect of a libel or libels to the same purport or effect as that for which such action is brought. R.S.O. 1970, c.243, s.10.

Apologies

22. In an action for libel or slander where the defendant has pleaded a denial of the alleged libel or slander only, or has suffered judgment by default, or judgment has been given against him on motion for judgment on the pleadings, he may give in evidence, in mitigation of damages, that he made or offered a written apology to the plaintiff for such libel or slander before the commencement of the action, or, if the action was commenced before these was an opportunity of making or offering such apology, that he did so as soon afterwards as he had an opportunity. R.S.O. 1970, c.243, s.22.

Plaintiff's character or circumstances of publication

22a. In an action for libel or slander, where the statement of defence does not assert the truth of the statement complained of, the defendant may not give evidence in chief at trial, in mitigation of damages, concerning the plaintiff's character or the circumstances of publication of the statement, except,

(a) where the defendant provides particulars to the plaintiff of the matters on which he intends to give evidence, in the statement of defence or in a notice served at least seven days before trial; or

(b) with leave of the court.

5.2.4.1.6.8 Notes on Statutes in Other provinces

The above sections are typical of legislation adopted in all the common law provinces. For provisions similar to ss.5(2) and 5(3) see Defamation Act, R.S.A. 1980, c.D-6, s.16; Libel and Slander Act, R.S.B.C. 1979, c.234, ss.7 and 8; The Defamation Act, R.S.M. 1970, c.D-20, s.17; Defamation Act, R.S.N.B. 1973, c.D-5, s.17; Defamation Act, S.N. 1983, c.63, s.19; Defamation Act, C.S.N.S. 1979, c.D-3, s.21; Defamation Act, R.S.P.E.I. 1974, c.D-3, s.17; Defamation Ordinance,, R.O.N.W.T. 1974, c.D-1, s.18; Defamation Ordinance, R.O.Y.T. 1975, c.D-1, s.18; Uniform Defamation Act, s.18; and Libel and Slander Act, R.S.S. 1978, c.L-14, s.8 which states that in the case of a candidate for public office the retraction must be made at least *15* days before the election.

Sections resembling s.8 of the Ontario Act are, Alberta, ss.17 and 18; British Columbia, s.12; Manitoba, s.18; Nova Scotia, s.22; Newfoundland, s.20; Prince Edward Island, s.18; Northwest Territories, s.19; Yukon Territory, s.19; and Saskatchewan, s.16 which adds:

> (3) Service of the writ of summons may be made upon the proprietor or publisher of the paper by serving the writ upon any adult person at such address.

Sections 6 of the British Columbia Libel and Slander Act, 16(1) of Manitoba's Defamation Act, 18(1) of Newfoundland's Defamation Act and 7 of the Libel and Slander Act of Saskatchewan are identical to s.9 of the Ontario Act. Alberta's Defamation Act, s.15(1), adds:

> (b) broadcast the retraction and apology from the broadcasting stations from which the alleged defamatory matter was broadcast on at least two occasions on different days and at the same time of day as the alleged defamatory matter was broadcast or at a time as near as possible to that time,

as does New Brunswick, s.16(1); Nova Scotia, s.20(1); Prince Edward Island, s.16(1); Northwest Territories, s.17(1); Yukon Territory, s.17(1); and Uniform Defamation Act, s.17(1).

For provisions similar to s.10 of Ontario's Libel and Slander Act see, Alberta, s.15(2); British Columbia, s.11; Manitoba, s.16(2); New Brunswick, s.16(2); Newfoundland, s.18(2); Nova Scotia, ss.5 and 20(2); Prince Edward Island, s.16(2); Saskatchewan, s.17; Northwest Territories, s.17(2); Yukon Territory, s.17(2); and Uniform Defamation Act, s.17(2).

Section 22 of Ontario's Libel and Slander Act resembles Alberta, s.4; British Columbia, s.10; Manitoba, s.5; Newfoundland, s.5; Nova Scotia, s.4; Prince Edward Island, s.4; Saskatchewan, s.4; Northwest Territories, s.5; Yukon Territory, s.5; and Uniform Defamation Act, s.4. No other province has yet adopted s.22a.

The Nova Scotia legislation dealing with apologies is unique in that it provides for a detailed procedure dealing with offers of amends:

15. (1) A person who has published words alleged to be defamatory of another person may, if he claims that the words were published by him innocently in relation to that other person, make an offer of amends under this Section; and in any such case,

(a) if the offer is accepted by the party aggrieved and is duly performed, no proceedings for defamation shall be taken or continued by that party against the person making the offer in respect of the publication in question (but without prejudice to any cause of action against any other person jointly responsible for that publication);

(b) if the offer is not accepted by the party aggrieved, then, except as otherwise provided by this Section, it shall be a defence, in any proceedings by him for defamation against the person making the offer in respect of the publication in question, to prove that the words complained of were published by the defendant innocently in relation to the plaintiff and that the offer was made as soon as practicable after the defendant received notice that they were or might be defamatory of the plaintiff, and has not been withdrawn.

(2) An offer of amends under this Section must be expressed to be made for the purposes of this Section, and must be accompanied by an affidavit specifying the facts

relied upon by the person making it to show that the words in question were published by him innocently in relation to the party aggrieved; and for the purposes of a defence under clause (b) of subsection (1) no evidence, other than evidence of facts specified in the affidavit, shall be admissible on behalf of that person to prove that the words were so published.

(3) An offer of amends under this Section shall be understood to mean an offer,

(a) in any case, to publish or join in the publication of a suitable correction of the words complained of, and a sufficient apology to the party aggrieved in respect of those words;

(b) where copies of a document or record containing the said words have been distributed by or with the knowledge of the person making the offer, to take such steps as are reasonably practicable on his part for notifying persons to whom copies have been so distributed that the words are alleged to be defamatory of the party aggrieved.

(4) Where an offer of amends under this Section is accepted by the party aggrieved,

(a) any question as to the steps to be taken in fulfilment of the offer as so accepted shall in default of agreement between the parties be referred to and determined by the Trial Division of the Supreme Court or a Judge thereof, whose decision thereon shall be final;

(b) the power of the Court or judge [Judge] to make orders as to costs in proceedings by the party aggrieved against the person making the offer in respect of the publication in question, or in proceedings in respect of the offer under clause (a) of this subsection, shall include power to order the payment by the person making the offer to the party aggrieved of costs on an indemnity basis and any expenses reasonably incurred or to be incurred by that party in consequence of the publication in question;

and if no such proceedings as aforesaid are taken, the Court or judge [Judge] may, upon application made by the party aggrieved, make any such order for the payment of such costs and expenses as aforesaid as could by [be] made in such proceedings.

(5) For the purposes of this Section words shall be treated as published by one person (in this subsection referred to as the publisher) innocently in relation to another person if and only if the following conditions are satisfied, that is to say:

(a) that the publisher did not intend to publish them of and concerning that other person, and did not know of circumstances by virtue of which they might be understood to refer to him; or

(b) that the words were not defamatory on the face of them, and the publisher did not know of circumstances by virtue of which they might be understood to be defamatory of that other person;

and in either case that the publisher exercised all reasonable care in relation to the publication; and any reference in this subsection to the publisher shall be construed as including a reference to any servant or agent of his who was concerned with the contents of the publication.

(6) Clause (b) of subsection (1) shall not apply in relation to the publication by any person of words of which he is not the author unless he proves that the words were written by the author without malice.

Quebec has chosen to deal with the problem in yet another way. The Press Act, R.S.Q. 1977, c.P-19 provides:

Retraction

4. If the newspaper fully retracts and establishes good faith, in its issue published on the day following the receipt of such notice or on the day next after such day, only actual and real damages may be claimed.

Publication

5. Such retraction must be published by the newspaper *gratis* and in as conspicuous a place in the newspaper as the article complained of.

Paper not a daily

6. Whenever the newspaper is not a daily, the rectification must at the choice of the party who deems himself injured, and at the newspaper's expense, be published in a newspaper of the judicial district or of a neighbouring judicial district, as well as in the next issue of the newspaper itself.

Reply

7. The newspaper shall also publish at its expense any reply which the party who deems himself injured may communicate to it provided that same be *ad rem,* be not unreasonably long and be couched in fitting terms.

No prosecution

8. Whenever the party who deems himself injured has both obtained a retraction and exercised the right to reply, no prosecution may issue if the newspaper publishes such retraction and reply without further comment.

Exceptions

9. No newspaper may avail itself of the provisions of this act in the following cases:

Crime

(*a*) When the party who deems himself injured is accused by the newspaper of a criminal offence;

Election

(*b*) When the article complained of refers to a candidate and was published within the three days prior to the nomination-day and up to the polling-day in a parliamentary or municipal election.

5.2.4.1.6.9 *Hoste* v. *Victoria Times Publishing Co.* (1889) 1 B.C.R. (Pt.2) 365

BEGBIE C.J.B.C.: That is surely not sufficient. It is not the offer nor even the publication of an apology at all, but an offer to offer an apology. And even in terms, it seems to reserve to the defendant a right of judging whether the plaintiff is reasonable in demanding any particular form e.g., it offers to make such an apology as the defendant thinks fit. Such an apology as merely 'beg your pardon', or 'sorry for it', is not sufficient in a case of libel. The defendant should admit that the charge was unfounded, that it was made without proper information, under an entire misapprehension of the real facts, etc., and that he regrets that it was published in his paper....

You should not offer to make, but actually make and publish at once, and unconditionally, such an apology, expressing sorrow, withdrawing the imputation, rehabilitating the plaintiff's character as well as you can; not stipulating that the plaintiff is to accept it; not making any terms but publishing it in the interests of truth, and because you are anxious to undo whatever harm which may have accrued from a wrong which you find you have been the unconscious instrument of inflicting.

5.2.4.1.6.10 *Brannigan* v. *S.I.U.* (1964), 42 D.L.R. (2d) 249 (B.C.S.C.)

On p. 12 of the issue of December 13, 1961, of the Canadian Sailor under the heading in bold type "WE HAVE BLUNDERED" appears this statement:

> In the August 23rd, 1961, edition of the "Canadian Sailor", we published a photograph of the May Day, 1960 Communist parade in Vancouver, in which we erroneously identified a Communist banner holding Canadian Brotherhood of Railway and Transport Workers as one, William Brannigan. The standard bearing Communist supporter however was William Mozdir, Vice-President of Local 400, Canadian Brotherhood of Railway and Transport Workers. In order to set the record straight we apologise to Mr. William Brannigan for confusing two pictures and thereby embarrassing Mr. Brannigan by not showing him as he also proudly held aloft a placard in support of the policies of the Communist Party — in the same Parade, but a few squads back.
>
> In a further effort to placate the ruffled feelings of Mr. Brannigan, we publish below both pictures, with the proper identification. Again, to Mr. Brannigan, we tender our sincerest apologies and make this retraction with the hope that he will feel that satisfaction has been achieved.
>
> Before anybody else seizes the opportunity to do so, we also make another correction in that the Communist Parade in question took place in 1960 and not 1961.

Following this statement and on the same page are two pictures — one is the picture which appeared in the issue of August 23rd accompanied by a notation similar to that below the picture in the earlier edition but identifying the man on the right carrying the banner in these words:

> ...the banner waving Communist sympathizer is none other than William Mozdir, (Arrow), who was vice-president of Local 400, Canadian Brotherhood of Railway and Transport Workers at the time.

On the same page is another picture of a small group of eight men marching in the same parade, each carrying separate placards. At the side of that picture is the following heading: "PICTURE THAT SHOULD HAVE APPEARED" and underneath the statement:

> The picture on left shows Mr. Brannigan, former Financial Secretary of Local 400, Canadian Brotherhood of Railway and Transport Workers, (Arrow) as he proudly carries a placard in support of the Communist party in the same Communist May Day Parade in Vancouver of 1960.

In my view it is also evident from the form and wording of the so-called apology that it is a deliberate and intended reiteration or emphasizing of the defamatory statement made in the earlier issue of the Canadian Sailor, the truth of which the defendant has asserted throughout but has failed to establish. That apology, rather than mitigating the damage caused to the plaintiff, as urged on behalf of the defendant, would, in my opinion, tend to aggravate the damage done by the libel. That the manner of an apology may tend to increase rather than diminish the damages, see *Mayne & McGregor on Damages,* 12th ed., para. 894 and the cases there cited.

Note: If the defendant was motivated by malice or was guilty of gross negligence in publishing the defamatory material, then the benefits of making an apology will be lost. See *Snider* v. *Calgary Herald* (1985), 34 C.C.L.T. 27.

5.2.4.1.6.11 John G. Fleming, "Retraction and Reply; Alternative Remedies for Defamation", (1978) 12 *U.B.C. Law Review* 15

I. DAMAGES

The preoccupation of our law of defamation with damages has been a crippling experience over the centuries. The damages remedy is not only singularly inept for dealing with, but actually exacerbates, the tension between protection of reputation and freedom of expression, both equally important values in a civilized and democratic community. A defamed plaintiff has a legitimate claim to vindication in order to restore his damaged reputation, but a settlement for, or even a court award of, damages is hardly the most efficient way to attain that objective. In either case, the refutation of the libel is not attended with much publicity, if any, and, if resisted by the defendant, occurs long after the libel has spread its poison. Plaintiffs sometimes settle on condition that the defendant make an apology in open court, but there is no law that actually requires a defendant to do so even after he has lost a verdict. So far as the plaintiff is concerned, damages offer him a pot of gold which he may not even desire, but since this is all that the law provides him as a token of vindication, it is still widely regarded as necessary for honourable men to demand a large sum of damages lest it be misinterpreted as a tacit admission that one's reputation was not worth more. A curious inflation has thus come to prevail by which damages for libel especially to public figures often far exceed awards for the most searing personal injuries; and this remains true whether they parade under the label of "punitive" or "aggravated" damages. In times of acute social stress, damage awards are frequently used by juries to wreak vengeance on political enemies, so well illustrated by the American experience of the Civil Rights struggle in the South which prompted the intervention of the United States Supreme Court in 1964 based on the First Amendment.

Not that the link with damages invariably favours plaintiffs. For on occasions where free speech should not be chilled by the spectre of damages, the law saw no alternative to creating an immunity and thereby depriving the defamed of any right to vindication. This covers the area of privilege, absolute and qualified, including privileged reports, and the defence of fair comment. Even from a free speech point of view, those defences are hardly impeccable because, while encouraging the free flow of information and opinion, they do nothing to promote correction of falsehoods. Moreover, the system also has an undesirable countervailing effect inasmuch as our law has been understandably very reluctant to extend such immunities when its price for individual reputation is so high. This tendency has resulted in a strictness of the law of defamation which is widely felt — and not only by the media — to be incompatible with the free flow of information, especially on matters of public concern, in a modern democratic society.

The dilemma is well illustrated by recent American experience. In the celebrated case of *New York Times Company v. Sullivan* the United States Supreme Court for the first time imposed constitutional restrictions on state libel law, based on the First Amendment guarantee that no law shall abridge "freedom of speech and of the press." The reason prompting this intervention was, then and in several subsequent cases, outrageously large awards of both compensatory and punitive damages against liberal Eastern newspapers by hostile Southern juries. But instead of focussing on the *control* of damages, the Court followed the conventional path of enlarging the area of privilege.

The new constitutional privilege disqualified public officials from all remedy for libel on matters relating to their official duties, in the absence of proof of "actual malice," defined as knowledge of falsity or recklessness in that respect. This privilege went far beyond the defence of fair comment, as understood in Anglo-Canadian law and hitherto the majority of American Jurisdictions, in that it covered false statements of fact no less than any comment based thereon. In subsequent cases, the privilege was extended to libel of all "public figures" and for a time even to "all matters of public or general interest." That last extension, however, reactivated concern that private persons who, unlike public figures could not count on the same measure of access to the media for refutation and who had not voluntarily exposed themselves to public scrutiny, should thus for all practical purposes lose all opportunity for public vindication. Instead, the Court at last turned its attention on the remedies for defamation. Besides requiring that no liability for defamation could be based on less than fault, it also prohibited the award of damages for other than "actual injury," thereby abandoning the common law doctrine of *presumed* injury to reputation, and probably even punitive damages in cases of malice.

These restrictions on damage assessment reflect increasing concern over the vagaries of jury awards, a concern which may also have played a part in the House of Lords decision against punitive damages. Here we are confronted with a puzzling paradox. In England, as in some other Commonwealth countries, the civil jury has been virtually eliminated — except in actions for defamation. Whether that moratorium was prompted by historical nostalgia (back when 18th Century libel juries figured as watchdogs of democratic rights against Government) or because it was felt that the administration of libel law in any event needed a large infusion of public sentiment to remain viable, is not clear. At all events, contemporary criticism of the law of defamation dwells even more on the erratic assessment of damages by juries than on the substantive law of libel. In the U.S., the right of trial by jury is of course sacrosanct, but elsewhere there is no such peremptory impediment to reform. The Faulks Committee (1975) in England took a characteristically cautious step in that direction by recommending that the jury's role regarding damages be limited to indicating whether they should be substantial, moderate, nominal or contemptuous. The new federal Law Reform Commission of Australia, on the other hand, went all the way in proposing that juries be stripped of all function in relation to sanction for libel.

Another, perhaps even more profitable, reorientation is to explore alternative remedies to damages. I do not propose to consider here, let alone, advocate, either criminal prosecutions or injunctions because to the extent that they survive at all, their crushing impact on free speech precludes any wider role than in the most exceptional situations. Rather, I wish to share with you some thoughts about the Right of Reply and Retraction.

II. RIGHT OF REPLY

...The right of reply is firmly established in Continental law, under the inspiration of a French model dating back to 1820. But its generic label hides several important differences, especially as regards coverage and means of enforcement. Those differences help us to identify crucial issues relevant to an appraisal of the remedy.

From the plaintiff's point of view, it is of course not exactly the most ideal form of undoing the wrong done to him. For it is a commonplace in the experience of Anglo-American law that the truth never catches up with the lie; if it were, we would not have needed a law of defamation. In particular, reply lacks the persuasive force of retraction, but is arguably more effective in clearing the plaintiff's name than a money judgment. Moreover, it provides a possible remedy in situations of so-called "privilege" where we have long thought it preferable to deny damages because of the chilling effect on free speech and the plaintiff is therefore denied all means of public vindication.

How does the right of reply compare with retraction? The most important difference is undoubtedly that in its most common formulation the right of reply is not conditioned at all on proof that the charge levied against the plaintiff was false. Although this feature subjects the media to greater exposure than traditional defamation remedies do, which are based on a minimum of falsity, it dispenses with the administrative burden of litigating the truth. It is therefore peculiarly apt to rebut offensive statements of *opinion,* which by their very nature are really unamenable to a judicial determination of validity. Parenthetically, American law has at last reached the position that "[u]nder the First Amendment there is no such thing as a false idea. However pernicious an opinion may seem, we depend for its correction not on the conscience of judges and juries but on the competition of other ideas." This postulate does not appear confined to the expression of opinion only on matters of public concern. Accordingly, the Restatement, Second, Torts §566 now reads that "[a] defamatory communication [in the form of an opinion] is actionable only if it also expresses, or implies the assertion of, a false and defamatory fact which is not known or assumed by both parties to the communication."

By comparison, under Anglo-Canadian law not only can an opinion constitute a defamatory libel, but the defence of fair comment protects only defamatory opinions on matters of public interest based on true (or privileged) facts. One might well ponder therefore whether a right of reply should not be conferred at least on plaintiffs who are now barred from all relief under the defence of fair comment. Indeed, one might go further and suggest extending the same remedy in lieu of damages to honest (fair) comment on matters of public interest even if the comment is based on untrue facts. If such false facts are actually stated, it is debatable whether a right of retraction regarding such facts (though not the opinion based thereon) should not be allowed at least as an alternative to damages.

Is there a role for the right of reply in other situations? Continental experience certainly suggests that it may be invoked against defamatory statements of fact, indeed regardless of whether these are false or not. Without going to quite that length, I raised earlier the possibility of applying it to privileged occasions where the plaintiff under present law lacks all opportunity of vindication. The federal Law Reform Commission of Australia whose Discussion Paper Number One has just launched some high-flying kites for reform of the law of defamation expressed itself against any right of correction in these situations on the plausible ground that "the defaming persons will not normally be in the communication business, many not in business at all; some will have scant resources. The proof of the statement may require considerable enquiries and a lengthy trial. It is one thing to impose that burden on a media organ which has published to a wide audience, generally for commercial motives, the defamation; quite another to impose it on private persons or organizations in a reasonable manner for the purpose of giving relevant information to a person believed to have an interest in receiving it."

The Australian Commission does, however, suggest a right of reply in two other situations: first, it would apply it to all fair reports of a statement made by another named person and published for the information of the public or the advancement of education. You will notice that this proposal would extend the protection of fair reports far beyond the present limited categories, but make the defence conditional on the defendant affording the plaintiff a right of reply. The second, more controversial proposal, would substitute a right of reply for the existing remedy of general damages for loss of reputation where "the defendant, on reasonable grounds and after making all enquiries reasonably open to him in the circumstances, in fact believed the truth of all statements of fact contained in, or assumed by, the matter published." I will return to this matter later.

The Australian proposals prompt a brief word concerning the sanctioning of the right of reply. The Commission followed the model of Anglo-American retraction statutes, *i.e.* creating a defence to a claim for damages conditional on the defendant affording the plaintiff an opportunity to reply. One cannot therefore truly call this a *right* of reply, since its exercise depends on the defendant's willingness to submit to it. The Continental pattern, on the other hand, allows enforcement even against the defendant's wishes, since the plaintiff may apply for administrative or civil sanctions to force the defendant to open his pages or broadcast facilities to him. This difference may betray a cultural contrast between the deeply-rooted Anglo-American preference for attaining desirable objectives by rewards rather than force and the Continental tradition which has come to view the right of reply as an individual right, in a few countries even enshrined in their Constitution, as a necessary protection against excesses of the media. Perhaps not surprisingly, therefore, the English Faulks Committee objected to compelling a right of reply because it would create "new criminal offences and punishments." Besides this fear which Continental observers would regard as rather imaginary, the Faulks Committee also thought "objectionable a principle which entitles a person, who may be without merits, to compel a newspaper to publish a statement extolling his non-existing virtue." To this charge one can make two replies: first, there are, as we have seen, several instances in which the right of reply could be deployed without incurring this objection; secondly, it views the right of reply as a sanction against proven falsehoods rather than as giving a defamed person an opportunity to put his side of the case and letting the public rather than the court be the final arbiter of the controversy. Oddly enough, the Committee's conclusion happens to come out on the same side as the United States Supreme Court's, but whereas the Committee baulked over the plaintiff's possibly unclean hands, the American Court's concern was solely over governmental interference with editorial judgment.

III. RETRACTION

Retraction of defamatory allegations by a defendant has become a more familiar feature of our law of defamation than a right of reply. Its undoubted advantage to the plaintiff consists in the greater persuasive effect of having his reputation vindicated out of the defendant's mouth rather than his own. But against this must be set certain inherent limitations. First, retraction (especially compulsory retraction) is not really appropriate for expressions of opinion if we believe that there is no objective standard for determining the validity of opinions and that the public interest is better served by continuing debate through rebuttal rather than by compulsorily bringing it to an end. Moreover, it may also be felt as invidious to be forced to recant opinions still honestly held compared with having to correct allegations of fact proven to be false. By contrast, reply is an appropriate remedy for both types of expression and, because of the well-known difficulty of distinguishing between fact and opinion, deserves to be seriously considered as the only remedy for defamation on matters of public interest, now broadly covered by 'fair comment.'

The second limitation is that retraction can really be countenanced only with respect to statements of fact which have been shown to be false. This invites litigation; moreover, it is largely ineffective unless the defendant is faced with the alternative of having to pay damages in case he loses his plea of justification, since otherwise he would have little incentive to recant prior to a long-delayed judicial determination of truth. Hence the standard retraction statute which relieves the defendant of liability *if* he has made a suitable and prompt correction. In other words, retraction cannot very well stand on its own feet, as can reply, and needs the crutch of a continuing threat of damages to be effective.

Retraction has thus remained a voluntary alternative. Should compulsory retraction by court order be added to the judicial armoury, as in many Continental countries? This is strongly favoured by the Australian Commission as a complete substitute for *all* damages in the case of group defamation and defamation of a dead person; as a substitute for *general* (but not special) damages in the case of defamatory statements which the defendant reasonably believed to be true; and as an *addition* to general damages in case of defamatory statements not reasonably believed to be true as well as of statements which would have been privileged but for the defendant's unreasonable conduct (a substitute for malice)...

Compulsory Correction

It was mentioned earlier that our retraction statutes merely give the defendant an option between correction and general damages. Alternatively, the court could direct the defendant to retract. This system of the stick rather than the carrot is alien to our common law culture. It was rejected on rather flimsy grounds by the English Faulks Committee but appealed to the afore-mentioned Law Reform Commission of Australia which commended this procedure in several cases additional to general damages, as in the case of defamatory statements which the defendant did not reasonably believe to be true and in cases where qualified privilege was forfeited by unreasonable conduct (malice). In several other instances court-directed correction would be the only remedy, as in the case of group defamation or defamation of a dead person.

IV. CONCLUSION

To sum up, I commend the widest deployment of Reply and Retraction to help break the traditional deadlock faced by the law of defamation between the individual's interest in his reputation and the general concern in the free flow of accurate information. That deadlock is largely a product of the damages remedy for injury to reputation. Its all-or-nothing aspect necessarily entails subordinating completely the one interest to the other, to the ultimate detriment of both; rather reminiscent of such other puritanical common law blunders as the all-or-nothing rule of contributory negligence and the rule against contribution among tortfeasors. In contrast, Reply and Retraction as remedies for libel assist rather than impede the dissemination of correct information without imposing more than a negligible burden on the media. As the Draft Convention on Freedom of Information, passed at the 1948 United Nations Conference in Geneva, article 4 resolved: "The Contracting States recognize that the right of reply is a corollary of freedom of information." That burden the media should cheerfully bear in token of the social responsibility which accompanies their pivotal role in modern society.

5.2.4.1.7 Notes on damages: Appendix to *Snyder* v. *Montreal Gazette Ltd.* (1978), 87 D.L.R. (3d) 5 (Que. S.C.)

Appendix "A"

Quebec cases	*Moral damages*
1882- *Arthabaska*. Award fixed by Judge. *Levi v. Reed* (1881), 6 S.C.R. 482. Action for slander between two doctors. Award fixed by the Judge at $1,000, reduced by the Court of Appeal to $500 but restored by the Supreme Court of Canada.	$ 1,000.00
1888- *Montreal*. Award fixed by Judge. *City of Montreal v. Brown,* Montreal, No. 67, January 27, 1888 (unreported). Libel on the occasion of municipal proceedings. Award of $12,000. Reduced to $7,500 by Court of Appeal. Appeal to Privy Council followed by a desistment.	$ 7,500.00
1889- *Montreal*. Award fixed by jury. *Mail Printing Co. v. The Honourable Rodolphe Laflamme* (1888), 4 M.L.R. (Q.B.) 84; modified by Supreme Court of Canada, February 5, 1889 (unreported). Action by a former Minister of Justice of Canada against a Toronto newspaper. Award by the jury: $10,000, confirmed by the Court of Review and by the Court of Appeal where two dissenting Judges would have reduced the award to $5,000. Appeal to Supreme Court of Canada which fixed the award at $6,000 conditional upon plaintiff's acceptance, otherwise new trial to be held.	$ 6,000.00
1890- *Montreal*. Award fixed by Judge. *Cossette v. Dun et al.* (1890), 18 S.C.R. 222: Action in damages on the basis of a false credit report supplied by defendant to plaintiff's suppliers. Award fixed at $2,000, reduced to $500 by the Court of Appeal and restored by the Supreme Court of Canada.	$ 2,000.00
1896- *Quebec*. Award fixed by Judge. *Angers v. Pacaud* (1896), 5 Que. Q.B. 17. Former Lieutenant-Governor is charged by a newspaper with having abused his duties and accepting a bribe. Award fixed at $5,000, reduced to $2,000 by Court of Review, but restored by Court of Appeal.	$ 5,000.00

1907-	*Montreal*. Award fixed by Court of Appeal. *Shallow v. Gazette Printing Co.* (1907), 17 Que. K.B. 309. Action in damages by a reporter against a newspaper which commented on a suit between that reporter and a third newspaper. Action dismissed by the trial Judge but maintained by the Court of Appeal which fixes damages at $250.	$ 250.00
1922-	*Quebec*. Award fixed by Judge. *Imprimerie Populaire Ltée v. l'Honourable L.A. Taschereau* (1922), 34 Que. K.B. 554. Action by the Prime Minister of Quebec against a newspaper (Le Devoir) which had alleged misbehaviour against the Attorney-General. Award fixed at $1,000 (amount of the claim) and confirmed by the Court of Appeal.	$ 1,000.00
1937-	*Chicoutimi*. Award fixed by Judge. *Duhaime v. Talbot* (1937), 64 Que. K.B. 386. Action by a Crown Prosecutor against the Mayor of Chicoutimi for slanderous statements during a Council meeting. Award fixed at $200 and confirmed by the Court of Appeal.	$ 200.00
1955-	*Pontiac*. Award by Supreme Court of Canada. *Chaput v. Romain et al.* (1955), 1 D.L.R. (2d) 241, [1955] S.C.R. 834, 114 C.C.C. 170. Action by a Jehovah's witness as a result of the breaking of a religious meeting by the Quebec Provincial Police on grounds of sedition. Action dismissed by the Superior Court and the Court of Appeal, but maintained by the Supreme Court of Canada which establishes the damages at $2,000.	$ 2,000.00
1957-	*Montreal*. Award fixed by Judge. *Robbins v. Canadian Broadcasting Corp. (Que.)* (1957), 12 D.L.R. (2d) 35. Action by a doctor against C.B.C. for harassment encouraged during a television programme. Damages assessed at $3,000.	$ 3,000.00
1962-	*Montreal*. Award fixed by Judge. *Langlois v. Drapeau et Plante,* [1962] Que. Q.B. 277. Actions for libellous statements contained in certain pleadings against the two plaintiffs who, both lawyers, later became Mayor and Director of Police of Montreal. Award fixed in each case at $7,000, but reduced in each case to $2,000 by the Court of Appeal.	$ 2,000.00
1971-	*Quebec*. Award fixed by Judge. *Flamand v. Bienvenue,* [1971] Que. P.R. 49. Action for slander between two members of the Quebec Legislature, as a result of speeches during a political meeting. Award fixed at $2,000.	$ 2,000.00
1976-	*Trois-Rivières*. Award fixed by Judge. *Yvette Melasco et Foyer Joseph-Denys Inc. v. Le Nouvelliste Ltée et Radio Trois-Rivières Ltée C.H.L.N. et al.*, Trois-	

Rivières, No. 400-05-000679-74, June 14, 1976 (unreported).
Action by a sister-nurse against a newspaper and a radio station which enjoy a wide regional audience, as a result of charges of a criminal offence and of general bad behaviour. Award fixed at $20,000, including $10,000 for moral damages. $10,000.00

1976- *Sherbrooke*. Award fixed by jury.
Boutin v. Bachand, St-François, No. 400-05-001049-74, June 16, 1976 (unreported).
Action by a candidate to provincial elections as a result of libellous statements in a political speech of his opponent. Award fixed by the jury at $8,000. $ 8,000.00

1976- *Rouyn*. Award fixed by Judge.
Flamand v. Bonneville et Caouette et al., [1976] Que. S.C. 1580.
Action by a candidate to provincial elections as a result of a libellous television speech and various newspaper reports. Award fixed by the Judge at $20,500, including $12,000 for moral damages. $12,000.00

1977- *Rouyn*. Award fixed by Judge.
Larouche v. Bonneville et La Frontière Inc., Rouyn-Noranda, No. 11,440, March 5, 1974; Court of Appeal, No. 200-09-000170-743, November 16, 1977 (unreported).
Action by a lawyer against a newspaper (circulation: 8,000). Award fixed at $15,000 and confirmed by the Court of Appeal. $15,000.00

Appendix "B"

Canadian cases (outside Quebec) *Moral damages*

1955- *Vancouver, British Columbia*. Award fixed by British Columbia Court of Appeal.
MacKay et al. v. Southam Co. Ltd. et al. (1955), 1 D.L.R. (2d) 1, 114 C.C.C. 204, 17 W.W.R. 183.
Eight jurors sue a newspaper for a column charging them with "murder". Each one gets $ 500.00

1957- *Toronto, Ontario*. Award fixed by jury.
Ross v. Lamport (1956), 2 D.L.R. (2d) 225, [1956] S.C.R. 366 [ordering new trial as to amount of damages; affd] 9 D.L.R. (2d) 585, [1957] O.R. 402.
Taxi-owner sues Mayor of Toronto for public defamatory statements. A jury awards $40,000. The Court of Appeal of Ontario and the Supreme Court of Canada find the award exaggerated and direct a new trial on the issue of damages. A second jury awards $25,000 which the Court of Appeal confirms. $25,000.00

1963-	*Vancouver, British Columbia*. Award fixed by Judge. *Brannigan v. Seafarers' Int'l Union of Canada* (1963), 42 D.L.R. (2d) 249. Inter-union dispute. Charge of communism in a paper having a 15,000 circulation against a member of rival union.	$ 5,000.00
1964-	*Ottawa, Ontario*. Award fixed by Judge. *Platt v. Time International of Canada Ltd.* (1964), 44 D.L.R. (2d) 17, [1964] 2 O.R. 21; [affd] 48 D.L.R. (2d) 508*n*, [1965] 1 O.R. 510*n*. A major in the Canadian Army charged by Time Magazine (289,000 circulation in Canada) with drug smuggling in Viet Nam. Award fixed at $35,000 and confirmed by Court of Appeal.	$35,000.00 (including unknown punitive damages)
1967-	*Alberta*. Award fixed by Judge. *McElroy v. Cowper-Smith and Woodman* (1967), 62 D.L.R. (2d) 65, [1967] S.C.R. 425, 60 W.W.R. 85. A lawyer and an insurance executive sue for libel in various documents addressed to the Premier of Alberta and other persons. The trial Judge awards each plaintiff $25,000. The Court of Appeal of Alberta confirms the awards. The Supreme Court of Canada finds, however, the awards inordinately high and directs a new trial on the issue of damages.	$25,000.00 (but over-ruled)
1968-	*Victoria, British Columbia*. Award by Judge. *Jones v. Bennett* (1968), 2 D.L.R. (3d) 291, [1969] S.C.R. 277, 66 W.W.R. 419. Action for slander by the chairman of the British Columbia Purchasing Commission against the Prime Minister of British Columbia. The trial Judge awards $15,000. The Court of Appeal dismisses the action. The Supreme Court of Canada restores the condemnation.	$15,000.00
1969-	*Vancouver, British Columbia*. Award fixed by Judge. *Lawson v. Thompson* (1969), 5 D.L.R. (3d) 550, 69 W.W.R. 304. Suit by the president of the Joint Council of Teamsters of British Columbia for slander due to public utterances of fraud. Award fixed at $3,500 and confirmed by Court of Appeal.	$ 3,500.00
1972-	*Vancouver, British Columbia*. Award fixed by Judge. *Bennett et al. v. Sun Publishing Co. Ltd. et al.* (1972), 29 D.L.R. (3d) 423, [1972] 2 W.W.R. 643. The two sons of Premier Bennett sue a newspaper (circulation: 221, 464) for its allegation of corrupt practices. Each plaintiff is allowed.	$ 8,000.00
1973-	*Calgary, Alberta*. Award fixed by Judge. *Sykes v. Fraser* (1973), 39 D.L.R. (3d) 321, [1974] S.C.R. 526, [1973] 5 W.W.R. 484.	

	Suit by a lawyer against the Mayor of Calgary for statements alleging breach of faith in business dealings. Award of $10,000 confirmed by the Court of Appeal and the Supreme Court of Canada.	$10,000.00
1974-	*New Westminster, British Columbia.* Award fixed by Judge. *Lawson v. Chabot* (1974), 48 D.L.R. (3d) 556, [1974] 3 W.W.R. 711. Suit against the Minister of Labour of British Columbia by plaintiff who is president of the Teamsters' Joint Council of British Columbia and a member of the Senate of Canada. Allegation that plaintiff would lead the teamsters to defy the law. Award of $4,000.	$ 4,000.00
1974-	*Toronto, Ontario.* Award fixed by jury. *Littleton v. Hamilton et al.* (1974), 47 D.L.R. (3d) 663, 4 O.R. (2d) 283. Action arising out of a book dealing with the Company of Young Canadians. (1,500 sold out of 4,000.) Award by jury: $7,500, but action dismissed by trial Judge on ground of privilege. Court of Appeal overrules the judgment and restores the award.	$ 7,500.00
1974-	*Vancouver, British Columbia.* Award fixed by Judge. *Lawson v. Burns et al.* (1974), 56 D.L.R. (3d) 240, [1975] 1 W.W.R. 171. Suit against a radio station, etc., by plaintiff who is president of the Teamsters' Joint Council of British Columbia and a member of the Senate of Canada. Allegation that plaintiff had sought approval of Jimmy Hoffa, who was in jail, before accepting appointment to the Senate. Award: $10,000.	$10,000.00
1974-	*Vancouver, British Columbia.* Award fixed by Judge. *O'Neal v. Pulp, Paper & Woodworkers of Canada et al.*, [1975] 4 W.W.R. 92. During a war between two unions, a leaflet of one (circulation to workers: 5,500) accused the vice-president of the other of betraying the cause of the workers. Award: $5,000, of which $1,000 punitive.	$ 5,000.00 (including $1,000 punitive)
1976-	*British Columbia.* Award fixed by Judge. *Neeld et al. v. Western Broadcasting Co. Ltd. et al.* (1976), 65 D.L.R. (3d) 574. Suit by a young hockey player and his parents against a radio station (audience: 39,200). Award fixed at $2,750.	$ 2,750.00
1976-	*Kamloops, British Columbia.* Award fixed by Judge. *Thomson v. NL Broadcasting Ltd. and PILZ (Harrison)* (1976), 1 C.C.L.T. 278. The Mayor of Kamloops sues a radio broadcaster for charges of misbehaviour in office made over four radio stations, the	$10,000.00

largest audience being that of Kamloops (population: 50,000 to 60,000 people). Award: $10,000 of which $2,500 punitive.	(including $2,500 punitive)

Note: In 1978 the Supreme Court of Canada decided three personal injury cases, now known as the "trilogy", which placed an upper limit of $100,000 on awards for non-pecuniary damages in personal injury claims. The application of the trilogy limit in defamation cases has recently been questioned in *St. John's Publishing Co. Ltd. et al.* v. *Farrell.* In that case, Mr. Justice Morgan of the Newfoundland Court of Appeal suggested that, although the $100,000 ceiling may not apply, some sort of upper limit is desirable "to ensure some degree of consistency and hopefully to provide a rational approach to the assessment of damages for defamation". Mr. Justice Morgan did not indicate what that upper limit should be. Until such is established, he added, damages should be assessed on the basis of earlier decisions in favour of previous plaintiffs with similar injuries.

5.2.4.2 Injunctions

5.2.4.2.1 *Canada Metal Co. Ltd.* v. *CBC* (1974), 44 D.L.R. (3d) 329 (Ont. H.C.)

HOLLAND, J.: — There are two applications presently before me in the above style. The first is an application on behalf of the defendants for an order dissolving or rescinding the *ex parte* injunction granted by Mr. Justice Wilson on January 29, 1974, which restrained the defendants and each of them from alleging or implying by broadcasting on television or otherwise publicizing, that the plaintiffs and/or either of them have bought misleadingly favourable medical evidence and concealed material evidence from medical experts and from mis-stating the amounts the plaintiffs are spending to install pollution control systems. The second is brought on behalf of the plaintiffs for an order effective until the date of trial or other final disposition of the action, continuing the injunction granted by Mr. Justice Wilson aforesaid and expanding the relief therein granted by restraining the defendants from broadcasting or otherwise disseminating and from advertising or otherwise publicizing any part or portion of a programme entitled "Dying of Lead" or any part or portion of the script thereof or, alternatively, from publicizing certain portions of such script.

Originally, there was a third motion pending before me on behalf of the plaintiffs for an order committing the defendants Mark Starowicz and Max Allen to the common jail for breach of the injunction granted by Mr. Justice Wilson aforesaid and also for an order committing E. S. Hallman, Gary Perly, Graham Fraser and James L. Cooper to jail for knowingly acting in contravention of the said injunction. Mr. Hallman is apparently a vice-president of the Canadian Broadcasting Corporation and general manager of English Language Services for such corporation based in Toronto. Mr. Fraser was apparently the author of a news article appearing in the Globe and Mail, a Toronto newspaper, of which Mr. Cooper is the president and publisher. Mr. Perly apparently is the national chairman of the Canadian Liberation Movement, which published a pamphlet dealing with the subject of the injunction.

The three motions originally came on before me for hearing together and were adjourned to permit Mr. Perly to cross-examine on certain of the affidavits filed on behalf of the plaintiffs. When the motions came on again for hearing an application was made by Mr. Perly for a further adjournment of the third motion so that he could issue a subpoena for the purpose of examining Mr. Outerbridge, who is a solicotor in the office of the solicitors for the plaintiffs, and who also appeared as counsel on behalf of the plaintiffs on the motions. I granted the adjournment of this third motion to permit the issue of the subpoena but without in any way dealing with the propiety of such examination, which matter may well be dealt with by the Master of this Court. I then proceeded with the hearing of the first two motions which are the motion to continue and expand on the one hand, and the motion to dissolve on the other.

The plaintiffs operate secondary lead smelters in the City of Tôronto and the activities of the plaintiffs have been the subject of certain publicity in recent months. For example, a stop order was issued by the director of the Air Management Branch of the Ontario Ministry of the Environment, dated October 26, 1973, directing the Canada Metal Company Limited to stop their plant from emitting or discharging into the natural environment lead and lead compounds. This order was reviewed under the provisions of the *Judicial Review Procedure Act,* 1971 (Ont.), Vol. 2, c.48, by Mr. Justice Keith and at the conclusion of the hearing Mr. Justice Keith made an immediate order setting aside such stop order basically on the ground that the director exercised a power granted to him under the Act arbitrarily and not judicially.

In the morning edition of the Toronto Globe and Mail for Tuesday, January 29, 1974, there appeared an article under the heading "Television" with the subheading "Special on Lead Poisoning Fine Investigative Journalism".

This article read, in part, as follows:

> Tonight at 7, CBC Radio's As It Happens does a one-hour special on lead poisoning which, at least on the basis of reading a transcript, seems to be a definitive and terrifying show — and investigative journalism at its best.
>
> The program was sparked by the controversy over lead emissions and illness around two Toronto smelters. It includes claims that medical experts can be bought to give evidence that favors lead companies and plays down the danger. A doctor from Cleveland says that doctors who minimize the significance of high lead emissions are hired by the firms to say so.
>
> ...
>
> Doctors on the program claim that excessive lead levels can turn children into vegetables. One doctor says "all they escape is death" — and some do die. The cost of each child turned into a vegetable — just the financial cost and not including emotional torture — was set at $500,000.
>
> The cost of pollution controls at one of the Toronto lead smelters is estimated at $60,000.
>
> A doctor whose evidence helped to get a court to allow a smelter to stay in operation despite apparent lead poisoning in three nearby residents admits on the program that evidence that might have made her change her stand was concealed from her.

On the same day, the plaintiffs issued a writ in this action and applied for an *ex parte* injunction before Mr. Justice Wilson. In support of the application was filed an affidavit sworn by Michael Sigel, secretary-treasurer of the plaintiff Toronto Refiners and Smelters Limited, and an affidavit sworn by Carleton Smith, president and general manager of the Canada Metal Company Limited, by which affidavits the deponents swore that at no time had they or any member of their executive staff, or any other person at their request or with their knowledge, attempted to influence or influenced in any way by money, the expert opinions of Drs. Sachs and Barltrop, who were the two medical experts retained on behalf of their companies. In addition, Mr. Sigel swore that Toronto Refiners and Smelters is now in the final stages of installing a pollution control system at a cost to the company in excess of $150,000 and Mr. Smith swore that Canada Metal Company Limited is now in the final stages of installing a pollution control system at a cost to the company in excess of $300,000.

On the basis of the above affidavits Mr. Justice Wilson granted the *ex parte* injunction above referred to. The defendants were given notice of the injunction after the programme in question had already been broadcast in the Maritime Provinces and a short time before the broadcast was due to commence in Ontario and Quebec.

After consultation with counsel, two portions of the broadcast, which had been carried in the Maritime Provinces, were deleted from the broadcast to the other Provinces and Territories...

Defamatory words in a broadcast shall be deemed to be published and constitute libel: the *Libel and Slander Act,* R.S.O. 1970, c.243, s.2. In deciding a matter such as this the Court should always bear in mind the principle of freedom of the press. This principle, fortunately, has always existed in Canada, and this existence is specifically recognized by s.1 of the *Canadian Bill of Rights.* One must bear in mind that this particular programme, a so-called public affairs programme, dealt generally with an area of considerable public concern. This freedom of the press is, of course, a freedom governed by law and is not a freedom to make untrue defamatory statements: see *Reference re Alberta Statutes,* [1938] S.C.R. 100 at p. 133, [1938] 2 D.L.R. 81 at p. 107 (affirmed [1938] 4 D.L.R. 433, [1939] A.C. 117, [1938] 3 W.W.R. 337].

The Court in a case of this type will only interfere with a publication of an alleged libel in the very clearest of cases. The Court must be satisfied that the words are beyond doubt defamatory, are clearly untrue so that no defence of justification would succeed and, where such defence may apply, are not fair comment on true or admitted facts.

The jurisdiction of the Court in cases of this type has been described as "of a delicate nature". The Master of the Rolls in *William Coulson & Sons v. James Coulson & Co.* (1876), 3 T.L.R. 846:

> It was for the jury and not for the Court to construe the document, and to say whether it was a libel or not. To justify the Court in granting an interim injunction it must come to a decision upon the question of libel or no libel, before the jury decided whether it was a libel or not.... It ought only to be exercised in the clearest cases, where any jury would say that the matter complained of was libellous, and where if the jury did not so find the Court would set aside the verdict as unreasonable. The Court must also be satisfied that in all probability the alleged libel was untrue... It followed ...that the Court could only on the rarest occasions exercise their jurisdiction.

See also *Collard v. Marshall,* [1892] 1 Ch. 571.

Certainly one of the leading cases is *Bonnard v. Perryman,* [1891] 2 Ch. 269. An alleged defamatory article was printed and an application was brought on behalf of the plaintiffs for an interim injunction restraining the defendants from publishing the article. In support of the application the plaintiffs made affidavits to show that the statements in the article of which they complained were untrue. The defendant made an affidavit in the following terms [at p. 272]:

> "The whole of the allegations in the article entitled 'the *Fletcher Mills of Providence, Rhode Island,*' complained of by the Plaintiffs, are true in substance and in fact, and I shall be able to prove the same at the trial of this action by subpoenaing witnesses and by cross-examination of the Plaintiffs, and by other evidence which I cannot, and which I submit I ought not to have to, produce on an interlocutory application."

Chief Justice Coleridge gave the majority judgment, in which Lord Esher, M.R., and Lindley, Bowen and Lopes, L.JJ., concurred. Lord Justice Kay dissented but really on the effect of the affidavit and not on the principles of law to be applied to the case. Lord Coleridge, at p. 284, said this:

> But it is obvious that the subject-matter of an action for defamation is so special as to require exceptional caution in exercising the jurisdiction to interfere by injunction before the trial of an action to prevent an anticipated wrong. The right of free speech is one which it is for the public interest that individuals should possess, and, indeed, that they should exercise without impediment, so long as no wrongful act is done; and, unless an alleged libel is untrue, there is no wrong committed; but on the contrary, often a very wholesome act is performed in the publication and repetition of an alleged libel. Until it is clear that an alleged libel is untrue, it is not clear that any right at all has been infringed; and the importance of leaving free speech unfettered is a strong reason in cases of libel for dealing most cautiously and warily with the granting of interim injunctions. We entirely aprove of and desire to adopt as our own, the language of Lord *Esher,* M.R., in *Coulson v. Coulson,* 3 Times L.R. 846 — "To justify the Court in granting an interim injunction it must come to a decision upon the question of libel or no libel, before the jury have decided whether it was a libel or not. Therefore the jurisdiction was of a delicate nature. It ought only to be exercised in the clearest cases, where any jury would say that the matter complained of was libellous, and where, if the jury did not so find, the Court would set aside the verdict as unreasonable." In the particular case before us, indeed, the libellous character of the publication is beyond dispute, but the effect of it upon the Defendant can be finally disposed of only by a jury, and we cannot feel sure that the defence of justification is one which, on the facts which may be before them, the jury may find to be wholly unfounded; nor can we tell what may be the damages recoverable.

As I see it there are four main areas of complaint concerning the programme, they are:

(1) an allegation that the plaintiffs are polluting the area surrounding their factories with lead and that such pollution is causing lead poisoning with serious risk of illness and even death;

(2) an alleged innuendo that witnesses on behalf of the plaintiffs and in particular Drs. Barltrop and Sachs are prepared to offer their evidence for sale and that they will give untruthfully favourable evidence provided that they are paid;

(3) an alleged innuendo that the plaintiffs or their solicitors have concealed material evidence from a medical expert called on their behalf, and

(4) that the amounts of money, by implication being spent by one or other of the plaintiffs, to combat pollution has been mis-stated.

I will deal with these four allegations in order and in each case must decide whether the allegation or alleged innuendo was clearly defamatory, was clearly untrue and, where such defence may apply, was clearly not fair comment...

Dealing then with the first allegation, that is that the plaintiffs polluted the area with lead, which resulted in lead poisoning to individuals, I have no doubt that such an allegation is defamatory. The term defamatory has been defined as any imputation that may tend to lower the plaintiff in the estimation of right-thinking members of society in general or to expose the plaintiff to hatred, contempt or ridicule. Can I be satisfied that such an allegation is clearly untrue? I think not. The material filed before me is in conflict and surely if this were an action for damages for libel the matter would have to be left to the jury.

I now turn to the second allegation which is the alleged innuendo that witnesses on behalf of the plaintiff are prepared to offer their evidence for sale, in that they will give untruthfully favourable evidence provided they are paid. It was argued before me that based upon the transcript of the programme such an innuendo cannot be drawn as against the plaintiffs. In my view, such an innuendo could be drawn from the transcript as against the plaintiffs but not necessarily so. A Judge at a trial in a defamation action might well decide that the words complained of were capable of conveying a defamatory meaning but it would still be a question for the jury whether the words did in fact convey a defamatory meaning. I do not think that a jury would necessarily come to the conclusion that the words complained of were in fact defamatory of these plaintiffs. The fact of the matter is that expert witnesses are paid and the Drs. Barltrop and Sachs were paid. The affidavit material before me indicates that they were paid, or were promised to be paid, their usual fee — whatever that is. The defence of fair comment may also apply in connection with the words complained of in the programme.

I will now deal with the alleged innuendo that the plaintiffs or their solicitors have concealed material evidence from medical experts. On reading the transcript it appears quite clear to me that no such innuendo could be drawn against the plaintiffs. The allegation, if such can be said to have been made, is against the Ministry of the Environment.

I now turn to the fourth allegation which is that the amounts of money, by implication being spent by one or other of the plaintiffs, to combat pollution has been misstated. It may be that in the context of the programme such a misstatement would be defamatory. It was argued before me that the reference to the sum of $60,000 was not necessarily in connection with the operation of one or other of the plaintiffs. I would have thought that it was. However, I am of the opinion that there is sufficient doubt about it that again, should there be an action for damages for libel, it would be left to the jury. I do not think that a jury would necessarily find that such a statement was defamatory of the plaintiffs although they could well do so.

I do not think that the fact that there is a pending action for damages against Toronto Refiners and Smelters Company Limited is of any consequence. In the recent case of *Attorney-General v. Times Newspapers Ltd.*, [1973] 3 All E.R. 54, the House of Lords dealt with newspaper articles which urged a litigant to reconsider its position and which produced evidence to show that the litigant had not exercised due care in the manufacture and sale of thalidomide. The House of Lords held that the article setting out evidence was a clear case of contempt because it created a real risk that the fair trial of the action would be prejudiced and the publication thereof should be restrained by injunction. In the present case, the broadcast was a comment on a matter of general public interest and was not directed toward the litigation in progress. At p. 75 of the judgment in *Attorney-General v. Times Newspapers Ltd.* Lord Diplock states that discussion, however strongly expressed on matters of general public interest, is not to be stifled merely because there is litigation pending arising out of particular facts to which the general principles being discussed would be applicable. I think that is the rule that should be applied here. It is always open to move to strike out the jury notice in the action pending against one of the present plaintiffs. Lord Reid notes at p. 63 that it can be assumed that a publication of this sort would not affect the mind of a professional Judge.

Therefore, I have come to the conclusion that this is not a case in which the Court should interfere because, as I have said before, the Court will only interfere by way of injunction to prevent publication of alleged libel in the very clearest of cases. There are serious issues of fact which, in my view, could only be satisfactorily resolved by the hearing of evidence before Judge and jury.

It was argued before me that no order should be made for an injunction because damages would be a sufficient remedy. Should the plaintiffs commence an action for damages for libel such damages would be at large, which means, that it would not be necessary for the plaintiffs to prove any particular or special damages: see *South Hetton Coal Ltd. v. North-Eastern News Ass'n Ltd.*, [1894] 1 Q.B. 133 at p. 139. The fact that the defendant, the Canadian Broadcasting Corporation, would be in a position financially to pay any award is certainly a consideration.

The fact that I am ordering that the injunction granted by Mr. Justice Wilson be dissolved should not be taken in any way as being critical of his order. When the application was brought on before him he had only the original article, referred to earlier, appearing in the Globe and Mail and the affidavits deposing that certain of the statements therein were untrue. The programme was about to be broadcast in Ontario and, in fact, had already been broadcast to the eastern Provinces. There was no time to give the defendants notice of the application before him.

For the above reasons the motion to continue and expand the injunction will be dismissed and the motion to dissolve the injunction will be allowed. The injunction granted by Mr. Justice Wilson will therefore be dissolved. In all the circumstances the costs of the application will be costs in the cause in both motions.

Order accordingly.

Note: An appeal by Canada Metal Co. Ltd. to the Divisional Court of the High Court of Justice was dismissed: (1975), 55 D.L.R. (3d) 42.

5.2.4.2.2 Robert Martin, "Interlocutory Injunctions in Libel Actions" (1982), 20 *U.W.O. Law Review* 129

A. Introduction

In this essay I will seek first to set out the existing law with respect to the making of interlocutory injunctions in libel proceedings. Second, certain questions concerning the constitutionality of interlocutory injunctions in such circumstances will be analyzed. I will conclude with a discussion of the desirability of retaining the interlocutory injunction as a remedy in libel. I do not propose to deal with permanent injunctions. A permanent injunction may be granted after a judge or jury has determined that the matter in issue is libellous in order to prevent its further publication. This practice does not, for reasons which should become apparent below, raise the same problems as are encountered with interlocutory injunctions.

B. The Existing Law

The most complex Canadian case arose from a radio documentary. This documentary, an investigative report, led to a great deal of litigation. A brief recitation of the saga will be helpful.

The report was called "Dying of Lead"; it was an hour long; and it was to be broadcast over the CBC network on the programme *As It Happens* beginning at 7:00 p.m. EST on January 29, 1974. A column in the Toronto *Globe and Mail* that morning made reference to the programme and indicated that it contained allegations concerning "... lead emissions and illness around two Toronto smelters." On discovering this, two companies which operated smelters in Toronto, Toronto Refiners and Smelters Limited and Canada Metal Company Limited, sought an injunction to prevent the programme, or certain portions of it, being broadcast. An application was made *ex parte* on behalf of the companies to Mr. Justice Wilson of the Supreme Court of Ontario. The application was made at 5:15 p.m. and at 6:00 p.m. Wilson J. made an interim order in these terms:

> Ex parte injunction granted to plaintiffs restraining defendants, and each of them from alleging or implying by broadcasting on television or otherwise publicising that the plaintiffs and/or either of them, have bought misleadingly favourable medical evidence from medical experts, and from misstating the amounts the plaintiffs are spending to install pollution control systems.

This order was to be binding for ten days. At 6:20 p.m. the firm representing the smelter companies informed the CBC of the injunction by telephone and at 6:45 p.m. it was served on the CBC.

A CBC lawyer was actually in the studio. It was the practice with *As It Happens* to have all controversial programmes ''lawyered'' before they were broadcast with a view to removing libellous material. The fact of the injunction gave a special urgency to this procedure. The producers and the lawyer went over the script of ''Dying of Lead'' to see what could be salvaged. In the event the programme was broadcast at 7:00 p.m., but with three changes in the original script. Two passages from the programme as originally taped were deleted, with an electronic tone carried on air to indicate the deletions. In addition the order issued by Wilson J. was read over the air.

The plaintiff companies were apparently not happy with this behaviour. They applied to have the executive producer and the story editor for ''Dying of Lead'' committed for contempt on the ground that they had breached the terms of the injunction. Mr. Justice O'Leary found the producer and story editor guilty of contempt and fined them each $700.00. An appeal to the Court of Appeal was dismissed. This was by no means the end of the litigation.

Applications were made, first, by the CBC, to have the injunction issued by Wilson J. rescinded, and, secondly, by the two smelter companies, to continue the original interim injunction. The companies now sought the issuance of an order that would have been binding until the merits of their claim had been determined at trial.

Mr. Justice Holland, in a carefully reasoned judgment, dissolved the original injunction. An appeal from this decision to the Divisional Court was dismissed.

The injunction which had been granted in Ontario came too late to prevent the unexpurgated version of ''Dying of Lead'' being broadcast in Atlantic Canada; it was, in fact, being aired in that region at the very moment Wilson J. was making his order. The programme raised certain questions as to the probity of a Dr. Barltrop, a British physician who had testified on behalf of Canada Metal Company at a public hearing. Barltrop sued the CBC in the Nova Scotia courts for libel. He lost at trial, but on appeal was awarded $20,000.

A trial was never held on the merits of Canada Metal's claim against the CBC. The matter was finally settled in 1980.

What does this incident tell us about interlocutory injunctions? First, that an injunction may be granted to restrain the publication of allegedly libellous matter before a court has reached a definite conclusion as to whether the matter is libellous or whether a recognized defence has been successfully made out.

Secondly, that while the general principles regarding the making of injunctions will apply, they are to be supplemented by certain special rules which are applicable only in libel actions. These rules appear to be as follows:

a. the jurisdiction of the courts to make an interlocutory injunction is of a delicate nature and should only be exercised in the clearest of cases;
b. there must be no doubt that the material in issue is libellous of the plaintiff. Indeed the material before the court must be so evidently libellous that any jury would find it to be so, and that were a jury to find otherwise its verdict would be set aside as unreasonable;
c. an injunction will not be granted when the defendant indicates an intention to raise one of the recognised defences, unless such defence is, in the circumstances of the case, manifestly without foundation.

If the result finally reached in *Canada Metal Co. Ltd.* v. *CBC* were to be accepted as an accurate expression of the law in Canada, one could feel fairly confident that the standard to be met before an interlocutory injunction would be issued was very high, so high indeed that such orders would seldom be made. Unfortunately, there have been two other recent Canadian cases which suggest contrary approaches. The first of these cases may simply reflect different emphases given to certain principles by the British Columbia courts on the one hand and the Ontario courts on the other. The second exemplifies the real threat which interlocutory injunctions in libel actions pose to freedom of speech; a threat which, in this instance, manifested itself with disastrous consequences.

The B.C. case was *Church of Scientology* v. *Radio NW Ltd.* It is widely known that the Church [sic] of Scientology, in both Canada and the United States, has not been slow to resort to the law of libel whenever it has encountered public criticism of its unusual ideas. Radio NW, a Vancouver-based operation, had broadcast one programme about Scientology and planned to produce others as part of a series. The first programme had some uncomplimentary things to say about the Scientologists who were, as a result, seeking an injunction to prevent the broadcasting of the rest of the series. The case as a whole is most unsatisfactory because it appears that the respondents made no effort to defend themselves. They did not contradict the allegations made by the applicant and they did not file any material with the court on which they might have based a defence. It may be that under the circumstances the court had little choice but to issue an injunction. An application of the approach enunciated in *Canada Metal* v. *CBC* could well have led to the same result. But the reasoning of the B.C. court was different. It betrayed an unfortunate eagerness to issue an injunction and in the process took the law beyond the limits established in *Canada Metal* v. *CBC*. The court suggested that once the applicant had established a *prima facie* case of libel and shown "a probability of a repetition," an injunction would issue. I cannot make up my mind whether the court fully appreciated that special rules are supposed to govern libel actions and that these rules differ substantially from those which apply to "ordinary" applications for interlocutory injunctions. The court talked about these rules at the beginning of its judgment, but at the conclusion simply enunciated the standard that must be met before an injunction will issue in ordinary proceedings.

The second case was *Lorcon Inc.* v. *Kozy Insulation Specialists Ltd., Watling and Clover*. The facts are a bit unclear as the decisions given in the various stages of litigation have not been reported. The following brief statement is taken from Stuart M. Robertson, *Courts and the Media:*

> The action was commenced by an application for an injunction and a claim for damages, as a result of the intimidating threats of the defendant to publish a libellous document containing 71 pages on the subject of the plaintiffs and their products. The document contained a number of statements and articles from different sources.

The plaintiff's product was urea-formaldehyde foam insulation. On February 14, 1979, Maloney J. of the Ontario High Court granted an interim injunction *ex parte* to operate until February 27, 1979. In addition to enjoining the publication of the 71-page document referred to above, the order also prohibited "...*any other statement intended to cast into doubt the safety or acceptability as insulation of urea-formaldehyde foams made from products of the Plaintiff.*" On February 26, 1979, Labrosse J. extended this injunction until "further order," which is to say, until the merits of the applicant's claim had been determined. Mr. Justice Eberle made the injunction permanent and awarded damages on September 25, 1979, in a proceeding at which the defendants chose not to appear. Indeed, the ambit of the order was extended so that it applied not only to the defendants, but to "...any other person to whom knowledge of the order shall come." Robertson, from the evidence of his book, appears to me to be a careful and meticulous commentator. He observed:

> The terms of the injunction in *Lorcon* make impossible the publication of any reports by government or an independent body produced in the interest of public safety and consumer protection. The order assumes that any statement made, even if based on research, would cause irreparable harm to the plaintiff, even though the statement might be in the public interest. This is an assumption which extends beyond the resolution of the dispute between the parties, and operates to curb freedom of speech and of the press.

There is nothing on the record to indicate that either the judge who issued the original injunction, or the judge who extended it, accepted that there were special considerations to be observed when dealing with applications for interlocutory injunctions in libel actions.

The third general point to stress about interlocutory injunctions in libel actions is that they may be issued as the result of an application made *ex parte*. An interim injunction issued under such circumstances will, as in *Canada Metal* and *Lorcon,* be temporary. The basic problem with issuing such injunctions *ex parte* is that they make much of the law on the subject meaningless. The rule, at least as stated in *Canada Metal,* is that if the respondent avers that he plans at trial to attempt to make out one of the recognized defences, there will be no injunction. But if the respondent is not present at the time the application is made, how is the judge to make a finding on this question? It would seem that if the courts do indeed regard the making of such injunctions as a "sensitive" matter, they should simply refuse as a matter of practice to issue them *ex parte*.

Finally, it must be stressed that violation of both the letter and the spirit of an injunction can be punishable as either contempt of court or the offence of disobeying an order made by a court. Mr. Justice O'Leary in deciding to commit certain accused for contempt as a result of the "Dying of Lead" programme made it clear that a very strict standard of observance of injunctions was demanded. The court, he said, would not accept as a defence that the accused's conduct was reasonable or that due care and attention, based on legal advice, was exercised in order to avoid breaching the injunction. Indeed, the court stated that the proper course for the CBC under the circumstances would have been to postpone the programme entirely. What is perhaps most striking about O'Leary J.'s judgment is the notion that the very act of reading the terms of the injunction over the air constituted a contempt. It should be recalled that contempt is the only non-statutory crime enforceable in Canada and that as a result the punishment awarded in a particular case is a matter for the discretion of the presiding judge.

D. Conclusion

Whether or not it is constitutionally permissible to make interlocutory injunctions in libel actions, I would argue that this is a most undesirabel remedy in such proceedings. In his dissenting judgment in *Cherneskey* v. *Armadale Publishers,* Mr. Justice Dickson of the Supreme Court of Canada stated the problem clearly enough: "The law of defamation must strike a fair balance between the protection of reputation and the protection of free speech...." The objection to interlocutory injunctions is that this balance is destroyed: free speech gives way to the protection of reputation.

Three contrary arguments may be advanced. The first can be easily disposed of. It would simply be said that while my objection may be well-founded, we really shouldn't worry because few applications are made for injunctions in these circumstances, even fewer are granted, and the injunctions actually granted are, by their nature as interlocutory orders, temporary. While such an assertion is factually accurate, it misses the point. In my view, interlocutory injunctions are unacceptable as a matter of principle. It is surely not, from such a perspective, an adequate justification for the existence of a legal remedy to assert that it is seldom invoked.

The second reply is more difficult. Here it would be conceded that there is a problem, but that the courts are fully cognizant of it. It is certainly true that one can find statements in the cases which stress "...the importance of leaving free speech unfettered." And it is largely in order to protect freedom of speech that the jurisdiction to issue interlocutory injunctions is exercised with great caution. Recent official studies of the law of defamation in Australia, New Zealand, and the U.K. have all recommended against any change in the law in this area. In each instance the basis for this conclusion was confidence in the ability of the courts to exercise their jurisdiction properly. But the argument is misconceived. As the "Dying of Lead" saga suggests, this confidence in the courts is exaggerated. Legitimate criticism of the activities of Canada Metal Company was stifled; what the *Globe and Mail* called "investigative journalism at its best" was perverted. The *Lorcon* incident reinforces this view. It is now clear that ureaformaldehyde foam insulation was neither "safe" nor "acceptable." Lorcon Incorporated attempted to make the media generally aware of the injunction granted on February 14, 1979. There can be little doubt that this knowledge inhibited subsequent reporting about urea-formaldehyde foam insulation. The unavoidable fact remains that the jurisdiction to make interlocutory injunctions, no matter how delicate the courts may claim it to be, has been exercised in the past and will no doubt be exercised in the future.

Finally, it might be said that to eschew interlocutory injunctions would amount to creating a general licence to defame. On its face this view is untenable. The right of individuals to claim damages when they have been libelled exists independent of any interlocutory remedy. On further investigation the view becomes even more doubtful. Assume a potential plaintiff who, by one means or another, discovers that a potential defendant is about to publish something libellous about her. She, being a reasonable person, contacts the potential defendant and suggests that the material in question is inaccurate or unfair and explains why. A prudent potential defendant would be well-advised to take such a communication seriously. For, if the matter is eventually litigated, recalcitrant behaviour on the part of the defendant could either be evidence of malice, thereby negativing the defences of fair comment and qualified privilege, or aggravate the damages awardable.

If we are committed to the widest possible freedom of discourse on matters of public concern, the jurisdiction to make interlocutory injunctions, this undeniable judicial censorship, cannot, on principle, be accepted. The view taken by the courts in the United States is preferable, as well as being simpler and more straightforward: "...equitable relief does not extend that far... it will not restrain the commission of a libel or slander, for that is prior censorship — a basic evil denounced by the constitutions of the United States and California in protecting freedom of speech and press."

5.2.5 Procedural Questions

5.2.5.1 Ontario Libel and Slander Act, R.S.O. 1980, c.237, s.51

There are special time limits within which a libel action must be commenced:

Notice of action

5. (1) No action for libel in a newspaper or in a broadcast lies unless the plaintiff has, within six weeks after the alleged libel has come to his knowledge, given to the defendant notice in writing, specifying the matter complained of, which shall be served in the same manner as a statement of claim or by delivering it to a grown-up person at the chief office of the defendant.

5.2.5.2 Notes on Procedures in Other Provinces

The above provision is unique. Most of the other provincial defamation acts provide:

(1) No action lies unless the plaintiff has, within 3 months after the publication of the defamatory matter has come to his notice or knowledge, given to the defendant, in the case of a daily newspaper, 7, and in the case of any other newspaper or when the defamatory matter was broadcast, 14 days' notice in writing of his intention to bring an action, specifying the defamatory matter complained of.

(2) The notice shall be served in the same manner as a statement of claim.

(Defamation Act, R.S.A. 1980, c.D-6, s.13; The Defamation Act, R.S.M. 1970, c.D-20, s.14; Defamation Act, R.S.N.B. 1973, c.D-5, s.13; Defamation Act, S.N. 1983, c.63, s.16; Defamation Act, C.S.N.S. 1979, c.D-3, s.17; Defamation Act, R.S.P.E.I. 1974, c.D-3, s.13; and Uniform Defamation Act, s.14.)

Section 5 of the British Columbia Libel and Slander Act, R.S.B.C. 1979, c.234, however, states:

In an action for libel contained in a public newspaper or other periodical publication or in a broadcast, one clear day must be allowed to elapse between the cause of action complained of and the issue of the writ on the libel.

In Quebec:

2. Every person who deems himself injured by an article published in a newspaper and who wishes to claim damages must institute his action within the three months following the publication of such article, or within three months after his having had knowledge of such publication, provided, in the latter case, that the action be instituted within one year from the publication of the article complained of.

3. No such action may be brought against the proprietor of the newspaper, unless, personally or through his attorney, the party who deems himself injured gives a previous notice thereof of three days, not being holidays, at the office of the newspaper or at the domicile of the proprietor, so as to allow such newspaper to rectify or retract the article complained of.

(Press Act, R.S.Q. 1977, c.P-19.)

Pursuant to s.15 of The Saskatchewan Libel and Slander Act, R.S.S. 1978, c.L-14:

> No action shall lie for a libel contained in a newspaper unless the plaintiff has given to the defendant, in the case of a daily newspaper, five, and in the case of a weekly newspaper, fourteen, clear days notice in writing of his intention to bring the action, such notice to distinctly specify the language complained of.

And both the Defamation Ordinance of the Northwest Territories, R.O.N.W.T. 1974, c.D-1, s.14 and The Yukon Territory Defamation Ordinance, R.O.Y.T. 1975, c.D-1, s.14 provide:

> (1) No action lies unless the plaintiff has, within three months after the publication of the defamatory matter has come to his notice or knowledge, given to the defendant fourteen days' notice in writing of his intention to bring an action.
> (2) A notice under subsection (1) shall specify the language complained of and shall be served on the defendant in the same manner as a statement of claim.

5.2.5.3 *Grossman* v. *CFTO* (1983), 139 D.L.R. (3d) 618, at 625-626 (Ont. C.A.)

CORY J.A.: From the foregoing it may be appropriate to list a few general conclusions as to the notice required by the Act.

Clearly, the notice provisions contained in the *Libel and Slander Act* are mandatory and if notice is not given then a libel action cannot be maintained.

The notice may have beneficial results both for the prospective plaintiff and publisher. It gives the publisher the opportunity to once again review the matter complained of and determine whether a correction, apology or retraction are called for, and if so, to see that they are made within the time-limits prescribed by the Act. The benefits a plaintiff receives from a prompt correction, retraction or apology may be far more valuable than an award in damages.

The Act does not specify any particular form of notice. It will always be more difficult to frame a notice complaining of a matter contained in a television broadcast than of statements contained in a newspaper, magazine article or book.

A more liberal interpretation of the notice required for a broadcast is justified in light of the 1958 amendment which referred to the "matter" complained of rather than the "statement" complained of.

An appropriate test to determine whether the notice complaining of a television broadcast is adequate might be as follows: Does the notice identify the plaintiff and fairly bring home to the publisher the matter complained of? Since the Act prescribes no particular form, the court in answering this question can consider all the relevant circumstances.

The longer and more frequent the broadcasts are, the greater the particularity that may be required of the notice. Similarly, the more numerous the possible heads of complaint are, the more detailed the notice must be. The pleadings in a libel action are technical and they provide a wide variety of defences to a publisher. So long as the broadcaster is made clearly aware of the matter of which the plaintiff complains of, then there is no reason why the case, as defined by the pleadings, should not be determined on its merits.

5.2.5.4 Crown Liability Act, R.S.C. 1985, c.C-50, s.23

Procedure

Notice of claim in provincial court

23. (1) Except in the case of a counterclaim, no proceedings shall be commenced under this Part unless the claimant has at least ninety days before the commencement of the proceedings served on the Deputy Attorney General of Canada or sent to him by registered post a notice of the claim together with sufficient details of the facts upon which the claim is based to enable him to investigate it.

Proceedings in name of Attorney General or Crown agency

(2) Proceedings against the Crown under this Part may be taken in the name of the Attorney General of Canada or, in the case of an agency of the Crown against which proceedings are by Act of Parliament authorized to be taken in the name of the agency, in the name of that agency.

Service of writ

(3) Where proceedings under this Part are taken against the Crown in the name of the Attorney General of Canada the writ of summons or other instrument originating the proceedings shall be served on the Crown by serving it on, or sending it by registered mail to, the Deputy Attorney General of Canada, and where proceedings under this Part are taken against the Crown in the name of an agency of the Crown, the writ of summons or other instrument originating the proceedings shall be served on the Crown by serving it on, or sending it by registered mail to, the chief executive officer of the agency. R.S., c.C-38, s.10.

5.2.5.5 Ontario Libel and Slander Act, R.S.O. 1980, c.237, ss.6, 7, 8

Limitation of action

6. An action for a libel in a newspaper or in a broadcast shall be commenced within three months after the libel has come to the knowledge of the person defamed, but, where such an action is brought within that period, the action may include a claim for any other libel against the plaintiff by the defendant in the same newspaper or the same broadcasting station within a period of one year before the commencement of the action. R.S.O. 1970, c.243, s.6.

Application of ss.5(1), 6

7. Subsection 5(1) and section 6 apply only to newspapers printed and published in Ontario and to broadcasts from a station in Ontario. R.S.O. 1970, c.243, s.7.

Publication of name of publisher, etc.

8. (1) No defendant in an action for a libel in a newspaper is entitled to the benefit of sections 5 and 6 unless the names of the proprietor and publisher and the address of publication are stated either at the head of the editorials or on the front page of the newspaper.

Copy of newspaper to be *prima facie* evidence

(2) The production of a printed copy of a newspaper is admissible in evidence as *prima facie* proof of the publication of the printed copy and of the truth of the statements mentioned in subsection (1).

Where ss.5, 6 not to apply

(3) Where a person, by registered letter containing his address and addressed to a broadcasting station, alleges that a libel against him has been broadcast from the station and requests the name and address of the owner or operator of the station or the names and addresses of the owner and the operator of the station, sections 5 and 6 do not apply with respect to an action by such person against such owner or operator for the alleged libel unless the person whose name and address are so requested delivers the requested information to the first-mentioned person, or mails it by registered letter addressed to him, within ten days from the date on which the first-mentioned registered letter is received at the broadcasting station. R.S.O. 1970, c.243, s.8.

5.2.5.6 Notes on Statutes in Other Provinces

The three-month limitation period in s.6 of Ontario's Libel and Slander Act is unique. All of the other common law provinces which specifically mention limitations set the period at six months. The New Brunswick Defamation Act, R.S.N.B. 1973, c.D-5, s.14 is typical:

> An action against the proprietor or publisher of a newspaper, or the owner or operator of a broadcasting station, or any officer, servant or employee of such newspaper or broadcasting station, for defamation contained in the newspaper or broadcast from the station shall be commenced within six months after the defamation has come to the notice or knowledge of the person defamed; but an action brought and maintainable for defamation published within that period may include a claim for any other libel against the plaintiff by the defendant in the same newspaper or the same broadcasting station within a period of one year before the commencement of the action.

(See also Defamation Act, S.N. 1983, c.63, s.17; Defamation Act, C.S.N.S. 1979, c.D-3, s.18 which adds "Notwithstanding the Statute of Limitations" to the beginning of the section; Defamation Act, R.S.P.E.I. 1974, c.D-3, s.14; Libel and Slander Act, R.S.S. 1978, c.L-14, s.14; which states that such an action may include a claim for any other libel published against the plaintiff by the defendant in the same newspaper within a period of *two* years before the commencement of the action; Defamation Ordinance, R.O.N.W.T. 1974, c.D-1, s.15; Defamation Ordinance, R.O.Y.T. 1975, c.D-1, s.15; and Uniform Defamation Act, s.15. Alberta, British Columbia, Manitoba and Quebec have not adopted such a provision.)

No other provincial Defamation Act has a provision similar to s.7 of Ontario's Libel and Slander Act.

For section similar to Ontario's s.8, see p. 482.

5.2.5.7 Ontario Legal Aid Act R.S.O. 1980, c.234, s.15

Where legal aid not to be given

15. A certificate shall not be issued to a person,
(*a*) in proceedings wholly or partly in respect of defamation or loss of service of a female in consequence of rape;
(*b*) in relator actions;
(*c*) in proceedings for the recovery of a penalty where the proceedings may be taken by any person and the penalty in whole or in part may be payable to the person instituting the proceedings; or
(*d*) in proceedings relating to any election. R.S.O. 1970, c.239, s.15, *revised.*

Note: There is no legal aid in libel actions.

5.2.5.8 Notes: on the Use of Juries in Civil Proceedings in the Common Law Provinces

A. Number of Jurors

In the majority of the common law provinces, a jury in a civil proceeding consists of six jurors. (See Jury Act, C.S.A. 1985, c.J-2.1, s.12; Jury Act, S.M. 1982-83-84, c.69, s.32(1), pursuant to s.32(3) there may be a trial by five jurors if the parties to the action or issue or their counsel agree; Courts of Justice Act, S.O. 1984, c.11, s.121(4); Jury Act, R.S.S. 1978, c.J-4.1, s.14; Jury Ordinance, R.O.N.W.T. 1974, c.J-2, s.25; and Jury Ordinance, C.O.Y.T. 1978, c.J-2, s.25). In New Brunswick, Nova Scotia and Prince Edward Island, seven jurors are required (Jury Act, C.C.S.N.B. 1985, c.J-3.1, s.24(1); Juries Act, C.C.S.N.S. 1979, c.12, s.14(1) and Jury Act, R.S.P.E.I. 1974, c.J-5, s.20). In British Columbia the number of jurors needed for a civil jury is eight (Jury Act, R.S.B.C. 1979, c.210, s.18); while in Newfoundland it is nine (Jury Act, S.N. 1980, c.41, s.20(2).)

B. Qualifications of Jurors

All of the common law provinces require that jurors be resident in that province, Canadian citizens, and of the age of majority. Each provincial jury statute also has its own specific list of persons disqualified from serving as jurors in that province. (See, Alberta, s.4; British Columbia, ss.3 and 4; Manitoba, ss.3 and 4; New Brunswick, s.3; Newfoundland, ss.5 and 6; Nova Scotia s.4; Ontario ss.3 and 4; Prince Edward Island, s.4; Saskatchewan, s.4; Northwest Territories, ss.6 and 7; and Yukon Territory, ss.6 and 7). The British Columbia Jury Act is typical:

<u>Disqualification</u>

3. (1) A person is disqualified from serving as a juror who is:
(a) not a Canadian citizen;
(b) not a resident in the Province;
(c) under the age of majority;
(d) a member or officer of the Parliament of Canada or of the Privy Council of Canada;
(e) a member or officer of the Legislature or of the Executive Council;
(f) a judge, justice or court referee;

(g) an employee of the Department of Justice of the Solicitor General of Canada;
(h) an employee of the Ministry of the Attorney General of the Province;
(i) a barrister or solicitor;
(j) a court official;
(k) a sheriff or sheriff's officer;
(l) a peace officer;
(m) a warden, correctional officer or person employed in a penitentiary, prison or correctional institution;
(n) blind, deaf or has a mental or physical infirmity incompatible with the discharge of the duties of a juror;
(o) a person convicted within the previous 5 years of an offence for which the punishment could be a fine of more than $2,000 or imprisonment for one year or more, unless he has been pardoned;
or
(p) under a charge for an offence for which the punishment could be a fine of more than $2,000 or imprisonment for one year or more.

...

Disqualification because of language difficulty

4. Where the language in which a trial is to be conducted is one that a person is unable to understand, speak or read, he is disqualified from serving as a juror in the trial.

Certain provinces also exclude spouses of those persons referred to in s.3(1)(d)-(m) above (New Brunswick, Newfoundland, Ontario and Saskatchewan); clergymen (New Brunswick, Nova Scotia, and the Territories); "Members of religious orders vowed to live only in a convent, monastery or other like religious community" (New Brunswick); medical practitioners (New Brunswick, Nova Scotia, Ontario and the Territories); dental practitioners (New Brunswick, Nova Scotia, and the Territories); veterinarians (New Brunswick and Ontario); coroners (Ontario and Saskatchewan); firefighters (New Brunswick and the Territories); druggists and nurses in active practice (the Territories); persons confined in an institution (Alberta and Saskatchewan); telegraph, telephone and radio operators and post masters (the Territories); members of the council of a municipality or members of a board of trustees of a school district or school division (Alberta and Saskatchewan); reeves, councillors and mayors (Saskatchewan); officers and men of the Canadian Forces on active service (Nova Scotia and the Territories); consuls and consular agents (New Brunswick); "Persons actually engaged in the operation of (i) railway trains and steamships, (ii) plants producing electricity for public consumption, and (iii) water distribution systems distributing water for public consumption" (Yukon Territory); and "every person who is under subpoena or is likely to be called as a witness in a civil or criminal proceeding or has an interest in an action is ineligible to serve as a juror at any sittings of a court at which such proceeding or action might be tried" (Ontario).

C. Verdicts

Majority verdicts, in one form or another, may be returned by civil juries in all the common law provinces. The relevant legislation in most of the provinces provides:

> Any five of the jury may return a verdict or answer a question submitted to the jury by the judge, and the verdict or answer given by the five jurors has the same effect as a verdict or answer given by six jurors.

(Alberta Jury Act, s.12(2). See also Manitoba Jury Act, ss.32(1) and (2); Ontario Courts of Justice Act, s.121(6); Saskatchewan Jury Act; ss.14(a) and (b); Northwest Territories Jury Ordinance, s.25(1), and Yukon Territory Jury Ordinance, s.25(1).) In the other common law provinces majority verdicts may be received only where the jury is unable to agree in all respects on a verdict within a specified period of time. (See British Columbia Jury Act, s.19(1) which states that the verdict of 75 percent of the jurors will be acceptable if the jury was unable to reach a unanimous verdict after three hours of deliberation; pursuant to s.30(1) of New Brunswick's Jury Act, the verdict of five of the seven jurors will be binding if the entire jury was unable to agree on a verdict within three hours; under s.31 of Newfoundland's Jury Act, seven of the nine jurors may return a verdict if the jury failed to reach a unanimous decision after three hours; the verdict of five of the seven jurors will be allowed where the entire jury failed to agree on a verdict after four hours under s.14(1) of Nova Scotia's Juries Act; and s.36(1) of the Jury Act of Prince Edward Island provides that the decision of five of the seven jurors will be acceptable if the seven jurors were unable to reach a unanimous decision after deliberating for one hour.)

Unanimous verdicts, however, are required in certain circumstances. For example, where one of the jurors dies or is discharged because of illness during the course of the trial, some of the provincial Jury Acts specify that the verdict of the remaining jurors will be valid only if unanimous. (See Alberta, s.12(4); Ontario Courts of Justice Act, s.121(8); Prince Edward Island, s.22; Saskatchewan, s.15; Northwest Territories, s.30; and Yukon Territories, s.28(1). Section 16 of Nova Scotia's Juries Act states that if five of the remaining six jurors concur, their verdict will be valid.) And in Manitoba, where a five juror trial has been agreed upon, s.32(3) of the Jury Act requires that the verdict must be unanimous.

D. Juries in Defamation Actions

The circumstances under which there will be a jury in a civil trial differ slightly from province to province. The general rule in defamation actions, however, is that there will be trial by jury unless this requirement is waived by all parties. (Jury Act, C.S.A. 1985, c.J-2.1, S.16(1); The Court of Queen's Bench Act, R.S.M. 1970, c.280, s.6691); County Court Act, R.S.N.S. 1967, c.64, ss.27 [am. S.N.S. 1978, c.41, s.7; 1981, c.18, s.2]; 56(1) and 56(2) [repealed and re-enacted S.N.S. 1978, c.41, s.9]; Jury Ordinance, R.O.N.W.T. 1974, c.J-2, s.3; and Jury Ordinance, C.O.Y.T. 1978, c.J-2, s.3).

In some jurisdictions the parties to the action must request a jury (Jury Act, S.N. 1980, c.41, s.28(1) [am. S.N. 1983, c.63, s.21(1))]; and Jury Act, R.S.S. 1978, c.J-4.1, s.16(1)). The Judicature Act of Prince Edward Island, R.S.P.E.I. 1974, c.J-3, s.31(1)(b) prohibits waiver by the parties. And in other provinces a judge may override the rule in some circumstances. For example, pursuant to s.16(2) of Alberta's Jury Act:

> on a motion for directions or on a subsequent application it appears that the trial might involve
> (a) a prolonged examination of documents or accounts, or
> (b) a scientific or long investigation

that in the opinion of a judge cannot conveniently be made by a jury, the judge may, notwithstanding that the proceeding has been directed to be tried by a jury, direct that the proceeding be tried without a jury.

(See also Newfoundland's Jury Act, s.32 and Saskatchewan's Jury Act, s.20.)

Jury trials for defamation actions are no longer mandatory in Ontario (Courts of Justice Act, s.121).

5.2.5.9 Ontario Libel and Slander Act, R.S.O. 1980, c.237, s.15; Notes on Other Provinces

15. On the trial of an action for libel, the jury may give a Verdicts general verdict upon the whole matter in issue in the action and shall not be required or directed to find for the plaintiff merely on proof of publication by the defendant of the alleged libel and of the sense ascribed to it in the action, but the court shall, according to its discretion, give its opinion and directions to the jury on the matter in issue as in other cases, and the jury may on such issue find a special verdict, if they think fit so to do, and the proceedings after verdict, whether general or special, shall be the same as in other cases. R.S.O. 1970, c.243, s.15.

Note: This section is typical of the legislation found in almost every common law province (See Defamation Act, R.S.A. 1980, c.D-6, s.6; Defamation Act, R.S.M. 1970, c.D-20, s.7; Defamation Act, R.S.N.B. 1973, c.D-5, s.6; Defamation Act, S.N. 1983, c.63, s.8; Defamation Act, C.S.N.S. 1979, c.D-3, s.7; Defamation Act, R.S.P.E.I. 1974, c.D-3, s.6; Libel and Slander Act, R.S.S. 1978, c.L-14, s.5; Defamation Ordinance, R.O.N.W.T. 1974, c.D-1, s.7 which, along with Defamation Ordinance, R.O.Y.T. 1975, c.D-1, s.7, adds, "(2) where an action for defamation is tried by a judge without a jury, the judge may make such pending of a general or special nature as he sees fit"; and Uniform Defamation Act, s.6. Quebec's Press Act does not contain any similar provision.)

5.2.5.10 *McLoughlin* v. *Kutasy* (1979), 26 N.R. 242 (S.C.C.)

SPENCE, J., *dissenting:* It must be remembered that this is an appeal in an action for libel tried by a jury in which trial the jury awarded the appellant a verdict. In Ontario, from which province this appeal comes, actions for damage for libel or slander must be tried with a jury unless the parties consent to the dispensation of the jury: *Judicature Act,* R.S.O. 1970, c.228, s.59. Moreover, the Ontario *Libel and Slander Act,* R.S.O. 1970, c.243, in s.15 provides:

> on a trial of an action for libel, the jury may give a general verdict upon the whole matter in issue in the action...

and ss.66 and 67 of the *Judicature Act* providing that the judge may require the jury to give a special verdict are expressly made inapplicable to libel actions.

It is a well established principle of law that a jury's verdict must be given all deference and full weight and effect given thereto except in the most unusual circumstance. I need only cite one authority for this. Chief Justice Duff said, in *McCannell v. McLean,* [1937] S.C.R. 341, at p. 343:

> The principle has been laid down in many judgments of this Court to this effect, that the verdict of a jury will not be set aside as against the weight of evidence unless it is so plainly

unreasonable and unjust as to satisfy the Court that no jury reviewing the evidence as a whole and acting judicially could have reached it. That is the principle on which this Court has acted for at least thirty years to my personal knowledge and it has been stated with varying terminology in judgments reported and unreported.

Further, I am in accord with Nesbitt, J. when he said in *Jamieson v. Harris* (1905), 35 S.C.R. 625, at p. 631:

> Answers by the jury to questions should be given the fullest possible effect, and if it is possible to support the same by any reasonable construction, they should be supported.

And Wells J., as he then was, expressed the same view very well in *Usher v. Smith*, [1948] O.W.N. 526, at p. 527, when he said:

> Jurymen and laymen are not accustomed to state matters with the particularity and clarity which more trained men might exhibit, and it is, I apprehend, the duty of the Court to give effect to their findings in a broad way when there is evidence to justify them...

I am further of the opinion that this course must be followed very strictly in considering the jury's answers to questions in a libel action in view of the fact that the legislature has directed that such actions must be tried with a jury and that the jury may, in its sole discretion, refuse to answer specific questions and give a general answer. Every effort must be exerted to understand and give a reasonable construction to the jury's answers remembering that jurors "are laymen who are not accustomed to state matters with the particularity and clarity which more trained men might exhibit".

5.2.5.11 *Burnett* v. *CBC (No. 2)* (1981), 48 N.S.R. (2d) 181, at 196-7 (S.C. Trial Div.)

GRANT J.: Most cases of defamation of this province are tried by a judge sitting with a jury. As I understand the law and practice, there are clearly defined roles for each to play. I am sitting as both judge and jury and I consider that I should make my findings and rulings on fact and law in each instance.

Whether there was in fact a publication of certain words, I understand is a question of fact for the jury with the burden of proof being on the plaintiffs.

Whether the words or images complained of refer to the plaintiffs is a question of fact for the jury with the burden of proof being on the plaintiffs.

Whether the words or images or sounds complained of are reasonably capable of a defamatory meaning in their natural and ordinary meaning, that is, of being defamatory, is a question of law for the judge.

Whether the words, images or sounds complained of in their natural and ordinary meaning, under the existing facts and circumstances are defamatory of the plaintiffs is a question of fact for the jury.

Whether the words, images or sounds complained of are capable of being interpreted by right thinking members of society in the meaning attributed to them by the plaintiffs in their pleadings, is a question of law for the judge.

Whether the words, images or sounds complained of under the peculiar existing facts and circumstances bear the meaning attributed to them by the plaintiffs in their pleadings (the innuendo pleaded), that is, whether they are defamatory of the plaintiffs, is a question of fact for the jury.

Relating to the defence of justification whether a fact is substantially true in substance and in fact is a question of fact for the jury.

Relating to the defence of fair comment whether the words are capable of being comment is a question of law for the judge. Whether they are in fact comment is a question of fact for the jury. If they are comment it is a question of fact for the jury to determine if they are fair comment or not.

The question of public interest is a question of law for the judge to determine.

Whether the occasion of publication is one enjoying a qualified privilege is a question of law for the judge. If the surrounding facts are in issue then these facts are for the jury to decide.

If there is evidence of malice then the question of whether the defendant was actuated by malice is a question of fact for the jury.

The standard of proof is that of a preponderance of evidence or a balance of probabilities.

5.2.5.12 Crown Liability Act, R.S.C. 1985, c.C-50, s.26

No jury trials

26. In any proceedings against the Crown under this Part, trial shall be without a jury.

Note: A libel action against the CBC may not be tried by a jury.

5.2.5.13 Ontario Libel and Slander Act, R.S.O. 1980, c.237, s.16

16. An agreement for indemnifying any person against civil liability for libel is not unlawful. R.S.O. 1970, c.243, s.16.

Note: Libel insurance in Ontario is permissible; no other province has such a provision.

5.2.5.14 Notes on Libel Insurance

Libel insurance is designed to protect newspaper publishers and broadcasters from financial losses that are the consequence of injuries caused by their publications and broadcasts.

Despite the need for this kind of insurance, the number of companies able to provide appropriate coverage is extremely limited. Only two companies offer libel insurance to Canadian newspaper publishers — Mutual Insurance Company Limited of Bermuda and the Kansa Insurance Company. The majority of Thomson newspapers are insured by Kansa. Coverage limits, insurance deductibles and premium rates vary from newspaper to newspaper. It is believed that the *Toronto Star* is insured for $1 million of liability in excess of $100,000 and has large deductibles in the range of $25,000-$50,000. Kansa also ensures weeklies and community newspapers, some of which are independent publications.

The policy that is currently covering the greatest number of Thomson newspapers expired in mid-1986, and Kansa has decided not to renew its contract. Companies who continue to ensure broadcasters and publishers have described their problem in explicit terms. Chubb Insurance Company, a Toronto-based firm which ensures broadcasters, claims that it has been "clobbered in losses". Mutual Insurance Company, which insures clients through membership with the American Newspaper Publishers Association stated in a letter to its ANPA members that, in the last thirteen years, the Company received gross libel insurance premiums of $8.6 million yet paid losses and loss adjustment premiums in excess of $26 million, while over 1,700 of their cases currently remained open. The cost of libel litigation, and especially legal fees, accounts for the major portion of claims paid by an insurance company. Mutual Insurance Company's President, R.D. Spurling, declared to ANPA members that the cost of libel litigation since 1975 was best described "as an uncontrolled fire storm". Southam Newspapers are currently insured through the Mutual Insurance Company, although they initially sought a Canadian insurer. Southam stated that the availability of libel and slander insurance has decreased drastically: rates have increased, capacity has shrunk, and many insurers and reinsurers have ceased their operations.

Libel insurance that is available to publishers and broadcasters is expensive. The cost of insuring a newspaper depends largely upon its circulation. The greater its circulation, the more costly the process becomes for a publisher. The current cost of libel insurance for a major Canadian newspaper is in the range of U.S. $14,500 annually, with yearly increases dependent upon the number of claims processed, past loss history, and the current inflation rate. It is contended that, amongst other things, the profusion of libel cases in the United States has amplified insurers' losses and caused insurance rates to rise. Mutual Insurance, in an attempt to curtail some of its losses, significantly increased their premiums to ANPA members (as of August 1, 1984). Its new policy includes provisions which oblige insured parties to:

a. pay 20% of defence costs in excess of its stated deductible costs, and;
b. give the Company prompt notice when such payments approach or exceed the stated deductible amount.

The cost of libel insurance can only be expected to increase significantly. The Employers Reinsurance Corporation, a large libel insurance carrier in the United States, is considering entering the Canadian libel insurance market. The Corporation claims to have a reliable and stable market in the United States. The Thompson [*sic*] chain, in considering libel policy coverage from the Employers Reinsurance Corporation, must regard the quality of insurance that can be provided, and premium rates that must be expected to appreciate.

5.2.5.15 Ontario Supreme and District Court Practice, Rule 49

Note: Certain levers are placed in the hands of the defendant.

OFFER TO SETTLE
WHERE AVAILABLE

49.02 (1) A party to a proceeding may serve on any other party an offer to settle any one or more of the claims in the proceeding on the terms specified in the offer to settle (Form 49A).

(2) Subrule (1) and rules 49.03 to 49.14 do not apply to motions, but nothing in this subrule prevents a party from making a proposal for settlement of a motion or the court from taking the proposal into account in making an order in respect of costs.

TIME FOR MAKING OFFER

49.03 An offer to settle may be made at any time, but where the offer to settle is made less than seven days before the hearing commences, the costs consequences referred to in rule 49.10 do not apply.

WITHDRAWAL OR EXPIRY OF OFFER
Withdrawal

49.04 (1) An offer to settle may be withdrawn at any time before it is accepted by serving written notice of withdrawal of the offer on the party to whom the offer was made.

(2) The notice of withdrawal of the offer may be in Form 49B.

Offer Expiring after Limited Time

(3) Where an offer to settle specifies a time within which it may be accepted and it is not accepted or withdrawn within that time, it shall be deemed to have been withdrawn when the time expires.

Offer Expires when Court Disposes of Claim

(4) An offer may not be accepted after the court disposes of the claim in respect of which the offer is made.

EFFECT OF OFFER

49.05 An offer to settle shall be deemed to be an offer of compromise made without prejudice.

DISCLOSURE OF OFFER TO COURT

49.06 (1) No statement of the fact that an offer to settle has been made shall be contained in any pleading.

(2) Where an offer to settle is not accepted, no communication respecting the offer shall be made to the court at the hearing of the proceeding until all questions of liability and the relief to be granted, other than costs, have been determined.

ACCEPTANCE OF OFFER
Generally

49.07 (1) An offer to settle may be accepted by serving an acceptance of offer (Form 49C) on the party who made the offer, at any time before it is withdrawn or the court disposes of the claim in respect of which it is made.

(2) Where a party to whom an offer to settle is made rejects the offer or responds with a counter-offer that is not accepted, the party may thereafter accept the original offer to settle, unless it has been withdrawn or the court has disposed of the claim in respect of which it was made.

Payment into Court or to Trustee as Term of Offer

(3) An offer by a plaintiff to settle a claim in return for the payment of money by a defendant may include a term that the defendant pay the money into court or to a trustee and the defendant may accept the offer only by paying the money in accordance with the offer and notifying the plaintiff of the payment.

Payment into Court or to Trustee as a Condition of Acceptance.

(4) Where a defendant offers to pay money to the plaintiff in settlement of a claim, the plaintiff may accept the offer with the condition that the defendant pay the money into court or to a trustee and, where the offer is so accepted and the defendant fails to pay the money in accordance with the acceptance, the plaintiff may proceed as provided in rule 49.09 for failure to comply with the terms of an accepted offer.

Costs

(5) Where an accepted offer to settle does not provide for the disposition of costs, the plaintiff is entitled,

(a) where the offer was made by the defendant, to his or her costs assessed to the date the plaintiff was served with the offer; or

(b) where the offer was made by the plaintiff, to his or her costs assessed to the date that the notice of acceptance was served.

Incorporating into Judgment

(6) Where an offer is accepted, the court may incorporate any of its terms into a judgment.

Payment out of Court

(7) Where money is paid into court under subrule (3) or (4), it may be paid out on consent or by order.

COSTS CONSEQUENCES OF FAILURE TO ACCEPT
Plaintiff's Offer

49.10 (1) Where an offer to settle,

(a) is made by a plaintiff at least seven days before the commencement of the hearing;

(b) is not withdrawn and does not expire before the commencement of the hearing; and

(c) is not accepted by the defendant,

and the plaintiff obtains a judgment as favourable as or more favourable than the terms of the offer to settle, the plaintiff is entitled to party and party costs to the date the offer to settle was served and solicitor and client costs from that date, unless the court orders otherwise.

Defendant's Offer

(2) Where an offer to settle,

(a) is made by a defendant at least seven days before the commencement of the hearing;

(b) is not withdrawn and does not expire before the commencement of the hearing; and

(c) is not accepted by the plaintiff,

and the plaintiff obtains a judgment as favourable as or less favourable than the terms of the offer to settle, the plaintiff is entitled to party and party costs to the date the offer was served and the defendant is entitled to party and party costs from that date, unless the court orders otherwise.

5.2.5.16 Ontario Libel and Slander Act, R.S.O. 1980, c.237 ss.12-14

Consolidation of different actions for same libel

12. (1) The court, upon an application by two or more defendants in any two or more actions for the same or substantially the same libel, or for a libel or libels the same or substantially the same in different newspapers or broadcasts, brought by the same person or persons, may make an order for the consolidation of such actions so that they will be tried together, and, after such order has been made and before the trial of such actions, the defendants in any new actions instituted by the same person or persons in respect of any such libel or libels are also entitled to be joined in the common action upon a joint application being made by such new defendants and the defendants in the actions already consolidated.

Assessment of damages and apportionment of damages and costs

(2) In a consolidated action under this section, the jury shall assess the whole amount of the damages, if any, in one sum, but a separate verdict shall be taken for or against each defendant in the same way as if the actions consolidated had been tried separately, and, if the jury finds a verdict against the defendant or defendants in more than one of the actions so consolidated, the jury shall apportion the amount of the damages between and against the last-mentioned defendants, and the judge at the trial, in the event of the plaintiff being awarded the costs of the action, shall thereupon make such order as he considers just for the apportionment of the costs between and against such defendants.

Application

(3) This section does not apply where the libel or libels were contained in an advertisement. R.S.O. 1970, c.243, s.12.

Security for costs

13. (1) In an action for a libel in a newspaper or in a broadcast, the defendant may, at any time after the delivery of the statement of claim or the expiry of the time within which it should have been delivered, apply to the court for security for costs, upon notice and an affidavit by the defendant or his agent showing the nature of the action and of the defence, that the plaintiff is not possessed of property sufficient to answer the costs of the action in case judgment is given in favour of the defendant, that the defendant has a good defence on the merits and that the statements complained of were made in good faith, or that the grounds of action are trivial or frivolous, and the court may make an order for the plaintiff to give security for costs, which shall be given in accordance with the practice in cases where a plaintiff resides out of Ontario, and the order is a stay of proceedings until the security is given.

Where libel involves a criminal charge

(2) Where the alleged libel involves a criminal charge, the defendant is not entitled to security for costs under this section unless he

satisfies the court that the action is trivial or frivolous, or that the circumstances which under section 5 entitle the defendant at the trial to have the damages restricted to actual damages appear to exist, except the circumstances that the matter complained of involves a criminal charge.

Examination of parties

(3) For the purpose of this section, the plaintiff or the defendant or their agents may be examined upon oath at any time after the delivery of the statement of claim.

When order of judge respecting security final

(4) An order made under this section by a judge of the Supreme Court is final and is not subject to appeal, but, where the order is made by a local judge, an appeal therefrom lies to a judge of the Supreme Court whose order is final and is not subject to appeal. R.S.O. 1970, c.243, s.13.

Place of trial

14. An action for a libel in a newspaper or in a broadcast shall be tried in the county where the chief office of the newspaper or broadcasting station is, or in the county where the plaintiff resides at the time the action is brought; but, upon the application of either party, the court may direct the action to be tried, or the damages to be assessed, in any other county if it appears to be in the interests of justice or that it will promote a fair trial, and may impose such terms as to the payment of witness fees and otherwise as seem proper. R.S.O. 1970, c.243, s.14.

5.2.5.17 Notes on Statutes in Other Provinces

Provisions similar to sections 12(1), 12(2) and 14 can be found in the defamation legislation of all the common law provinces, and the Uniform Defamation Act. See Defamation Act, R.S.A. 1980, c.D-6, ss.7(1), 7(2), 8(1), 8(2) and 14; Libel and Slander Act, R.S.B.C. 1979, c.234, ss.15, 16, and 18; The Defamation Act, R.S.M. 1970, c. D-20, ss.8, 9, and 15; Defamation Act, R.S.N.B. 1973, c.D-5, ss.7, 8(1), 8(2), and 15; Defamation Act S.N. 1983, c.63, ss.9(1), 9(2), 10 and 7 which states: "An action for defamation shall be tried in the trial division before a judge or before a judge and jury". Defamation Act, C.S.N.S. 1979, c.D-3, ss.10, 11 and 19; Defamation Act, R.S.P.E.I. 1974, c.D-3, ss.7, 8, and 15; Libel and Slander Act, R.S.S. 1978, c.L-14, ss.6(1), 6(2), and 14; Defamation Ordinance, R.O.N.W.T. 1974, c.D-1, ss.8, 9, and 16; Defamation Ordinance, R.O.Y.T. 1975, c.D-1, ss.8, 9, and 16; and Uniform Defamation Act, ss.7, 8(1), 8(2), and 16.

Only Saskatchewan's Act includes a provision similar to Ontario's s.12(3). Section 16(3), R.S.S. 1978, c.L-14 states:

> For the purposes of this section "article" includes anything appearing in a newspaper as an editorial or as correspondence or otherwise than as an advertisement.

The Libel and Slander Acts of British Columbia and Saskatchewan, and Quebec's Press Act are the only statutes which provide for security for costs in defamation actions. Section 12 of Saskatchewan's legislation is identical to the Ontario Libel and Slander Act, s.13. Section 19 of the British Columbia statute differs slightly from Ontario's legislation in not including a provision similar to s.13(4). Section 11 of Quebec's Press Act is unique in its brevity:

The judge may, during a suit for defamation against a newspaper, order the plaintiff to furnish security for costs, provided that the defendant himself furnishes security to satisfy the judgment. The amount of security in each instance shall be left to the sole discretion of the judge.

5.2.6 General Questions

Robert Martin, "Libel and Class" (1983) 9 *Canadian Journal of Communication* 1.

Introduction

The law of libel contains a number of provisions, both substantive and procedural, which limit the ability of poor and working-class plaintiffs to obtain redress for injury to reputation. In what follows I will set out these provisions using the Ontario law as an illustration, and venture some analysis of them. My aim in doing so is not to expound legal doctrine in the fashion of the traditional article. Indeed, I assume a basic familiarity with libel law on the part of the reader. The purpose rather is to take note of certain well-established principles and practices and then attempt to order them from a social perspective. My premise, to adopt the words of a research study prepared for the Royal Commission on Newspapers (Kent Commission), is that libel law "...is not very accessible to the average litigant" (Wright, 1981, 49).

Legal Representation

The Legal Aid Act (R.S.O. 1980, c.234) is an appropriate starting point. The Act provides in section 15 that:

A certificate shall not be issued to a person,

(a) in proceedings wholly or partly in respect of defamation or loss of service of a female in consequence of rape;

The effect of the section is that legal aid is expressly denied in two sorts of civil proceeding.

Prior to the 1980 revision of the Statutes of Ontario, three additional actions — breach of promise of marriage, alienation of affections, and criminal conversation — were mentioned in s.15 (R.S.O. 1970, c.239, s.15). The words "or seduction" also appeared after the word "rape". It is not clear why these five actions had been excluded, nor why defamation was lumped together with the others.

On the first point, the exclusion appeared initially in the voluntary legal aid scheme which the Law Society of Upper Canada established in 1951 (Joint Committee on Legal Aid, 1965). The Joint Committee on Legal Aid noted the exclusion in its 1965 Report, but recommended that it be retained (111). The Report gave no reason for this recommendation. It was simply stated that "no representations at any time were made to the Committee that there should be any change in these exclusions under any extended legal aid plan" (Joint Committee, 1965, 59). No question was raised about the matter in the Ontario Legislature when the Bill arising from the Report was debated (Legislative Assembly, 1966, 5201).

Concerning the other point one can only speculate. It might have been thought that the four other actions were archaic or obsolete, or that they tended in practice to be frivolous and vexatious. The fact that the three actions which no longer appear in s.15

were statutorily abolished in 1977 and 1978 tends to support these views. I find it difficult, however, to see how either view could plausibly be advanced with respect to defamation proceedings. Whatever may have been the reasons for it, the provision quoted above first became law in 1966 (R.S.O. 1966, c.80, s.15).

Slightly more than a quarter of all legal aid expenditures in Ontario go towards fees and disbursements in civil actions (Law Society, 1981, 38-40). The most expensive category is divorce or other domestic matters, which in 1980-81 accounted for $9,185,678 out of $11,284,765 spent on civil actions. Given that a relatively small part of the legal aid budget goes for non-domestic matters anyway, it seems difficult on strictly financial grounds to justify the exclusion of defamation proceedings.

Since legal aid is denied, a potential plaintiff will have to finance the action out of his or her own pocket. Libel actions are expensive. Further, a plaintiff will have difficulty finding a lawyer who knows much about libel. Libel is usually not dealt with in Torts courses offered in Ontario Law schools (Wright, 1981, 49-50) and does not receive specific treatment in the Bar Admission Course. A lawyer in a small general practice will seldom handle a libel action. A plaintiff will have to seek counsel from among those practitioners who specialize in libel action. Such practitioners are usually found in large firms. Their time is valuable. Of course, if the defendant is a newspaper in a chain or a network television station, it will be able to call on the services of a skilled and experienced libel lawyer. In addition, libel actions are normally tried by a jury. This tends to make libel actions even more costly.

Retraction and Apology

The ability which the law gives to defendants to mitigate damages by retraction or apology can place severe pressure on an impecunious plaintiff. Common law recognised that an apology could operate to mitigate the defendant's damages. The Libel and Slander Act (R.S.O. 1980, c.37) has retained this principle, but has both clarified and expanded it. A written apology, tendered at an early opportunity, may be pleaded in mitigation by defendants generally (s.22). Where the defendant is a newspaper or broadcaster, and the libel was originally published without malice or gross negligence, an apology made at the earliest opportunity will have a like effect (s.9). Section 5 of the Libel and Slander Act is significant. If the defendant is a newspaper or broadcaster and makes a "full and fair" retraction within three days of the plaintiff giving notice that he or she believes himself or herself to have been libelled, the amount recoverable in subsequent proceedings is reduced to "actual damages".

Now the law is in fact somewhat more complicated than this brief recitation would suggest. Thus, there must be a *real* apology or retraction and not simply a republication of the libel (Brannigan v. S.I.U., 1964; Platt v. Time, 1964). There are also certain differences in effect between an apology and a retraction. For example, justification may be pleaded as a defense where there has been a retraction (New Era v. Toronto Star (1963), but not in conjunction with an apology (Williams, 1976, 108). The general result of an apology or retraction, however, is that the plaintiff will be unlikely to collect more than "actual" or "special" damages — direct pecuniary loss attributable to the libel. The award of damages for injury to reputation is largely precluded. The plaintiff does have the satisfaction, for what it may be worth, of an apology. He or she will have to be very determined, or very rich, to continue to seek the added solace of a judgment by a court.

Payment Into Court

If the defendant has retracted or apologized and the plaintiff still persists, then the coup de grace, a payment into court, may be administered. This step should be sufficient to dissuade any but the wealthiest or most foolhardy of plaintiffs. The effect of payment in is well known. If the plaintiff refuses to accept the money paid into court and persists in pursuing his or her claim, she or he will be penalized by having to pay the costs of the action incurred subsequent to the date of the payment in, unless the amount of money which is eventually awarded as damages exceeds the amount of the payment in. This device is generally available to defendants in civil actions (Rules of Practice, 1980, Reg. 540, Rule 306), but there are special provisions applicable only to libel actions. First, in the case of a newspaper or a broadcaster, the libel must have been published in good faith or without malice or gross negligence (Libel and Slander Act, s.11). Secondly, and more important, the fact that payment into court has been made may be brought to the attention of the judge or jury (Ontario Rule 317). The screws on the plaintiff are tightened another turn.

Security for Costs

The defendant in a libel action may ask that the plaintiff give security for costs (Libel and Slander Act, ss.13, 20. Also Ontario Rule 373). To obtain an order to this effect the defendant must show by affidavit:

a. the nature of the action and of the defence;
b. that the plaintiff is not possessed of property sufficient to answer the costs of the action in case judgment is given in favour of the defendant;
and
c. either (i) that the defendant has a good defence on the merits, or (ii) that the grounds of action are trivial or vexatious.

If the plaintiff is unable to comply with such an order, the proceedings are to be stayed until the required security is given. There are, however, cases where an impecunious plaintiff with a bona fide cause of action has, at the discretion of the court, been required to post only a nominal sum as security of costs. This discretion has been exercised when the circumstances are such that to order the plaintiff to give full security for costs would deprive him or her of a cause of action.

Measure of Damages

Assuming that a plaintiff actually manages to have his or her libel action proceed to trial, he or she will discover that, when it comes to injury to reputation, some people are more equal than others. I do not propose here to discuss the general difficulties involved in quantifying, in an amount of money, injury to reputation; nor shall I consider the entire range of factors, in particular the conduct of the defendant, which are supposed to be considered in determining the amount to be awarded. I am concerned only with the way in which, and the extent to which, the social and economic status of the plaintiff will enter into the computation of damages.

In the first place, libel actions are usually tried by a jury (Judicature Act, R.S.O. 1980, c.223, s.57). Juries ordinarily give general verdicts and they never give reasons. The award of a particular sum of money is simply announced. Accepting this, it seems to me inconceivable that a jury would not be influenced by the various indicia of class

— dress, speech, mannerisms — which the plaintiff exhibits. This speculative view is fortified by the statements of judges and commentators who assert that social status is definitely among the factors to be weighed when arriving at an assessment of damages.

The general approach has been expressed by Professor Jeremy Williams: "...the position of the plaintiff or his occupation may well affect the award of damages" (1976, 140). The cases use similar language, referring to such matters as "...the position of the parties in society and their standing in the community" (Stopforth v. Goyer, 1978), the "position and standing" of the plaintiff (Paletta v. Lethbridge Herald, 1978; Baxter v. C.B.C., 1980; See also McKewen and Lewis, 1974, 177-178), "...the actual standing and reputation of the plaintiffs in the community" (Neeld v. Western Broadcasting Co. Ltd., 1976; Vogel v. C.B.C., 1982). The justification advanced for this view runs roughly as follows. The higher the plaintiff's position or standing in society, the greater the reputation the plaintiff will have. The greater the reputation, the more serious the injury caused to it by a libel. And it must be the case that the more serious the injury, the larger the amount awarded as damages (Neeld v. Western Broadcasting Co. Ltd., 1976). For example, Chief Justice Deschenes of the Quebec Superior Court stated the following in 1978 concerning the principles to be observed in assessing damages where the plaintiff was a politician.

> If society wants, as it should, that its best citizens turn to public affairs, it must show the high esteem in which it holds them; and those who would imprudently risk, by a stroke of the pen, to destroy the reputation of such dedicated men ought to be prepared to pay the high price that such a misdeed deserves (Snyder v. Montreal Gazette, 1978).

The decision of the Nova Scotia Court of Appeal in *Barltrop v. C.B.C.* (see also Tataryn, 1981) is also illustrative. Briefly, Dr. Barltrop, an English physician, had appeared as an expert witness for two refining companies at a public hearing into allegations that the companies were causing lead pollution. Barltrop received $1,000 a day and expenses from these companies while appearing. In a subsequent documentary on the radio programme "As It Happens", the C.B.C. broadcast the following statement by an American pathologist:

> Dr. Barltrop is a paid consultant to the lead industry. He is paid to say what he has just said.

The Court of Appeal held that this statement, and, indeed, the programme as a whole, was libellous and proceeded to assess damages against the C.B.C. While the court accepted that Barltrop had not proven the loss of any consulting business as a result of being libelled, it nonetheless awarded substantial damages. The major factor the court considered in arriving at this conclusion was Dr. Barltrop's "professional eminence".

The moral seems clear. A person who is socially significant is deemed to have a good reputation and one who libels another will pay heavily. An ordinary person cannot have much of a reputation and will be unlikely to collect much in the way of damages from someone who libels him or her.

Conclusion

Let me briefly recapitulate. If a poor or working-class person gets libelled and wants to sue, something roughly like this will happen. He or she will be denied legal aid and will retain a lawyer who is neither knowledgeable nor experienced in libel matters. Conversely, if the defendant is a large newspaper or a broadcaster, it will very likely have available the services of an experienced libel lawyer. After the libel notice is issued, the defendant may retract. At this point the plaintiff's lawyer will likely advise acceptance of the retraction. If the plaintiff is determined to proceed despite this advice, the defendant may make a payment into court. If that is not sufficient, the defendant might ask that the plaintiff be ordered to give security for costs. Assume that the plaintiff is undeterred, presses on and receives judgment against the defendant. He or she will then discover that, contrary to whatever one may think about oneself, he or she has no reputation to speak of. He or she will be awarded a token sum as damages. This sum will be less than the amount paid into court and the plaintiff will be presented with an enormous bill for costs. Indeed, that may not be the end of the matter. The defendant may decide to appeal. The appellate court judges may not give the plaintiff even the courtesy which he or she received from the jury. If that which seemed reasonable to the jury does not appear in the same light to a bench of appellate judges they may set aside the trial court's judgment (See for example, the Supreme Court of Canada's decision in McLoughlin v. Kutasy, 1979).

Now it may well be objected that the foregoing is somewhat fanciful since poor or working-class people do not, in the existing scheme of things, get libelled very often. This, up to a point, is true. The media prefer to comment on the doings of the rich, the famous, and the powerful. But it is not the case that poor or working-class people are never libelled.

When this happens, the law is expressly biased against the plaintiff. This is anomalous. The central ideological feature of bourgeois legal systems is that, formally at least, they treat all people as equals. The law may affect people unequally, but each person confronts the legal system as the national equal of all others. But not in the law of libel.

5.2.6.2 Robert Martin, Does Libel Have a "Chilling Effect" in Canada?

Introduction

It is a commonplace in U.S. media circles to speak of the "chilling effect"[1] of libel actions against newspapers and broadcasters. The suggestion is that the fear of a possible libel action may operate as an implicit prior restraint; that newspapers and broadcasters may refrain from publishing significant information in order to avoid being sued. I do not know if the law of libel in the United States does in fact have a "chilling effect" on their mass media. I do know that many people in the Canadian media seem to think our libel law must have a "chilling effect" on our mass media. This has been made particularly evident in recent months with the exaggerated claims made by the *Ottawa Citizen* about the general threat to press freedom posed by an apparently groundless libel against it.[2] The aims of this essay are to critically examine that assumption and, at the same time, suggest ways people working in the media may avoid libel actions.

In the course of the essay I will be discussing certain specific features of libel law in Canada. Before doing that, I want to make two general observations.

When Canadians profess to be concerned with the "chilling effect" of libel law they are simply falling victim to a disturbing, but perhaps inevitable, feature of Canadian life. This is the habit of imagining that we live in the United States. While the error may be excusable, it is still an error.

Our major sources of information, and what some might call ideas, are the U.S. mass media, especially television. Thus, to take an especially prominent example, we become so immersed in the violent crime which is a constant presence in U.S. life that we begin to believe similar dangers lurk in Canadian streets.

There are some important distinctions between Canadian society and U.S. society which are relevant here. First, the social roles of the mass media in the two countries are different. The oracular role played by mass media in the U.S. is reflected in the special legal protection afforded to them. As Frederick Schauer put it:

> Because the press is in an abnormally strong position in American affairs and because it occupies a pre-eminent position in influencing public decisions, it commands more weight in the balancing process that creates the rules of the law of defamation.[3]

Secondly, and I admit to making an unscientific assumption based on my own experience of cultural differences between Canada and the U.S., Canadians seem to have different notions of the importance of reputation. The difference is bound to be reflected in Canadian libel law. Again, Schauer:

> ...the law of defamation in a society reflects, to a large extent, the assumptions of that society respecting the relative importance of an untarnished reputation, on the one hand, and an uninhibited press on the other.[4]

This is similar to the way Mr. Justice Dickson of the Supreme Court of Canada put the matter in *Cherneskey* v. *Armadale Publishers Limited:*

> The law of defamation must strike a fair balance between the protection of reputation and the protection of free speech....[5]

The proper and acceptable balance is bound to vary from society to society and, indeed, within the same society over time. The simple point about libel law is that the way it is applied in any society will be peculiar to that society.

There are other relevant differences between the U.S. and Canada. The most important is that Americans are incomparably more litigious than Canadians. The cultural inclination to sue is markedly weaker in Canada. This is reinforced by the fact that the potential economic benefits of a libel suit are vastly less attractive in this country. As we shall see, awards of damages to successful plaintiffs are far lower than in the U.S. A plaintiff, or a plaintiff's lawyer where contingent fees are permitted, simply has less to gain.

Having, I hope, got the United States out of the way, we can now turn to the second preliminary consideration. It is this. Whatever may be the actual extent of the "chilling effect" of libel on the Canadian mass media, it is of small consequence when compared to the exceedingly frigid effects which the proprietary rights of media owners have.

While broadcasting frequencies remain, by law, "public property",[6] the rights of the owners of newspapers are the same as the rights of the owners of soap factories or used car lots. This has three important implications for freedom of expression.

First, the owner has absolute authority to determine, with the possible exception of a newspaper's advertising content,[7] what is to be published and what is not. If the owner does not want to see certain stories covered, they will not be covered. If the owner wants a particular bias maintained, it will be maintained. Press councils, it is often suggested, have the effect of limiting these proprietary rights. Since press councils have no real power to enforce their decisions, this claim is inaccurate and misleading.[8]

The second is that owners have, within the limits of provincial employment laws and any collective agreement, complete control over the hiring and firing of reporters and editors. This means that owners can decide to hire only those people who view the world in a particular way. It also means that owners can sack journalists who express uncongenial opinions in the pages of the newspaper or even outside the workplace.[9]

Finally, and most important of all, owners have absolute authority over all financial matters affecting newspapers. They determine how much money is to be spent on hiring, training, and providing necessary support for editorial staff.

Newspapers can be closed or merged at the whim of owners. Newspapers, which provide an excellent cash flow, can be milked to finance other, unrelated, ventures within a conglomerate empire.[10]

The point about the power and authority of media owners is made simply in order to put the ''chilling effect'' of libel in perspective. To whatever extent the law of libel may inhibit free expression, it is not the most significant inhibiting factor.

I will now turn to the application of Canadian libel law to the media. My argument is that competent, professional journalists who do good, thorough jobs of reporting and editing have little to fear from libel actions. They may get sued, but the law offers defences which should provide adequate shelter for properly done stories.

I am not suggesting there can never be problems. I will, therefore, look at some of the defences available in a libel action to highlight areas where difficulties may arise. I will then look at awards of damages and the problem of interlocutory injunctions. Some observations will be made about the role of lawyers. Having determined whether Canadian libel law does or does not have a ''chilling effect'', I will make some observations on whether it would be desirable to constitutionalise our libel law as has happened in the U.S.

Justification

Justification is the name lawyers give to the defence of truth. The law of the various provinces does not recognise a general right to privacy.[11] Thus, apart from the quite injustified protection afforded to judges,[12] there is, in Canada, little you may not say about other people provided it is true.[13]

In a libel action any factual assertions which the plaintiff claims to be defamatory are assumed to be false. If the newspaper or broadcaster which made the assertions wishes to defend them, it must prove their truth. Since libel is a civil action, it is, in theory anyway, only necessary that the truth of the allegations be established ''on a balance of probabilities'', not, as in a criminal proceeding, beyond a reasonable doubt.

For professional, responsible journalists this should cause few, if any, problems. If the reporter assigned to a given story does a careful job of reporting, then the facts should be correctly ascertained. If the editor who handles the reporter's copy does a proper and competent job of editing, the story as it appears in its finished form should not be libellous. Good reporting and good editing are generally reliable ways of avoiding a libel action.

Sources can lead to problems with the defence of justification. The first of those can be broadly characterised as the ''disappearing source''. The difficulty is this. In the Canadian legal system the predominant method of proving facts in a courtroom is through the oral testimony of live witnesses. This is complemented by the hearsay rule. In essence, the hearsay rule says the only person who can testify as to the existence of a fact is someone who has direct knowledge of that fact through his or her own senses. This means a defendant in a libel action who is trying to prove the truth of allegedly libellous statements can do so only through the testimony of sources who have direct knowledge of the true facts. If a source is unavailable for the trial or tells a different story in the witness-box from the one which was first told to the reporter, the defence of justification goes out the window.

This seems, with a bit of reading between the lines, to have been the problem in *Roberge* v. *Tribune Publishers Limited,*[14] a New Brunswick case. A newspaper reported that a physician had been ''ousted'' from the Board of Directors of a hospital. The physician sued and the newspaper raised the defence of justification. The defence was rejected. The court concluded that the plaintiff had not been ''ousted'', but simply ''not reappointed'' to the board. The court read ''ousted'' as conveying an implication that the plaintiff had been got rid of because there was, presumably, something undesirable about him. On reading the decision, I could not avoid the sense of there being more to it than met the eye, and that the newspaper had had a source of additional information who refused to tell his story in court.

The second difficulty relates to the credibility of sources. In *Drost* v. *Sunday Herald Ltd.*[15] a Newfoundland newspaper published a story about an incident of alleged police brutality. The paper's source was a convicted criminal who said that he had been beaten up by two R.C.M.P. officers. The officers denied this and claimed the source had been resisting arrest. The story had the ring of truth to it. Nonetheless, the court rejected the testimony of the source, whom the paper had obviously believed, and accepted instead the testimony of the two police officers.

The only precaution reporters and editors can take against things like these happening is to make a substantial effort to satisfy themselves as to the reliability, veracity, and credibility of a source before publishing a particularly tendentious story. It is useful to have more than one source.

A problem related to sources, which can be avoided, arises when a source attempts to manipulate a reporter to achieve his or her own ends. A classic example is *Vogel* v. *CBC*.[16] A disgruntled civil servant sought to use a reporter in order to attack his administrative superior. The reporter, who seems to have been both too ambitious and too credulous, accepted the information he was fed by the civil servant. The reporter failed to make the critical assessment the story required. There was a breakdown of the reporting function. This was compounded by a complementary failure of the editing function. The reporter accepted what he was told by the source and the reporter's supervisor accepted what he was told by the reporter. As a result, the C.B.C. paid $125,000.00 in damages.

When the performance of both the reporting and editing functions breaks down, no defence is possible. This happened in *Munro* v. *Toronto Sun*.[17]

The *Sun* hired an individual and gave him the title ''investigative reporter''. (This is dangerous and should be avoided). This reporter then claimed to have information showing that John Munro had used his position as a federal minister to benefit a company in which he had an interest. The story, it turned out, was a work of fiction.

An older reporter was assigned to work with the investigative reporter on the story. He came to believe in the truth of the story. Various editors were persuaded to accept the story without personally checking the identity, or even existence, of sources or the reliability or authenticity of documents. The *Sun,* thanks to some excellent lawyering on its behalf at the trial, managed to escape with only $75,000.00 in damages.

The trial judge, Mr. Justice Holland of the Ontario High Court of Justice, suggested some rules reporters and editors should follow.

(a) The great power and influence possessed by the media is an important factor in moulding public opinion and its exercise requires great care to be taken as otherwise great harm can result.
(b) There must be a separation of functions between the reporter and the editor, it being the responsibility of the editor to confirm the accuracy of the contents of a story before publication.
(c) Where important documentation has been obtained it is good practice to put it in a safe place and to thereafter work from a copy.
(d) There must be constant supervision maintained by the editor over the reporter, with a regular reporting requirement.
(e) It is the editor's responsibility to know in detail before publication, the documentation to support the story and the reliability of the sources and so ensure its accuracy.
(f) When the story is prepared — and the paper has the "goods" on the person targetted in the story — it is basic and necessary that that person be confronted with the story so that his reaction be obtained. This could cause the story to be discarded and could also enable the newspaper to add those comments should publication take place. A sound reason (there are others) for this to be established practice, is that it prevents the newspaper from publishing an incorrect story with all the attendant problems which that would generate.[18]

These rules, with the possible exception of (f), which may be controversial, are really only a lawyer's way of stating the essentials of good reporting and good editing. If they are observed, there should be no reason to fear a libel action. Unfortunately, even with good reporting and editing problems can remain. This final category of problem has to do largely with judges.

Canadian judges have shown a decided lack of sympathy for investigative reporting. As a consequence, they have often demanded a very high standard of those who seek to defend investigative pieces.

The cases show two ways in which this can be done. The first is to give a strict interpretation to the allegedly defamatory statement and then require the defendant to prove the literal truth of that interpretation. *Baxter* v. *CBC*.[19] is an excellent example.

This case had to do with a report broadcast on "The Fifth Estate" in April 1977 about certain activities of John Baxter, a former Minister of Justice in New Brunswick. Rumours had been circulating in the province about kickbacks being made to a secret Conservative Party fund. The R.C.M.P. began an investigation, but, according to the CBC were ordered by Baxter to desist. The crucial words from the script were:

> In an internal police memo written in September, 1973, an R.C.M.P. sergeant reported that a man under investigation for another matter makes many references to kickbacks to a Conservative Party fund, The police wanted to follow that lead, but then a week later they were stopped by the then Minister of Justice, John Baxter, and their own superiors.

So the CBC said that Baxter as Minister of Justice had stopped an R.C.M.P. investigation of *kickbacks* to his own party. Baxter sued. The C.B.C. relied on the defence of justification. They lost.

The New Brunswick Court of Appeal concluded that the R.C.M.P. had been directed to stop investigating *political contributions* to the Conservative Party. Political contributions are not the same as kickbacks. The CBC's story was not, therefore, true and the defence of justification failed.

A moment's reflection reveals the inadequacy of the court's reasoning. Political parties do not keep separate accounts for kickbacks; special receipts marked ''kick-back'' are not given. A kickback is, on its face, a lawful political contribution. It is only after investigation that an ostensibly lawful contribution may be revealed as a kickback. Thus, an order to stop investigating lawful political contributions will have the effect of frustrating the investigation of kickbacks.

The point is that the statement broadcast by the CBC expressed the inevitable result of the order which Baxter, it was conceded, actually gave to the police. But because the matter was not stated with absolute precision, the defence of justification failed.

Secondly, some courts in dealing with investigative reporting have had difficulty in understanding and applying the civil standard of proof. As I have noted, facts in civil cases need only be proven ''on a balance of probabilities''. This is supposed to mean that a fact is taken to be proven if a court accepts it as being more likely than not. I understand this to mean that a court exercising civil jurisdiction need only be 51 percent satisfied before accepting an allegation as true.

So what is one to make of the following statement?

> ...in my opinion the work of the investigative reporter must meet the test of absolute reliability.[20]

This is strange. There are two interpretations which can be put on this passage, both of which are disturbing and wrong in law.

To begin with, while I do not know exactly what ''absolute reliability'' means, it suggests a standard considerably higher than ''on a balance of probabilities''. Indeed, it suggests a standard higher even than ''beyond a reasonable doubt''.

Secondly, the passage also suggests that investigative journalism is to be separated out from ordinary journalism and judged, at least in libel actions, according to more rigorous standards.

Despite the reservations and qualifications I have expressed, justification remains a valuable defence. It provides an almost foolproof shield.

As can be seen from cases like *Munro* and *Vogel,* justification will offer little comfort to writers of fiction, but this is, surely, as it should be and is not something which could be accurately described as a ''chilling effect''.

Fair Comment

Justification is used to defend assertions of fact. Fair comment is for expressions of opinion.

In *Pearlman* v. *CBC* it was said of the plaintiff that he had ''...no morals, principles or conscience''.[21] This was held to be fair comment. Since it is difficult to imagine anything worse that could be said about someone, it should be evident that fair comment can be used to defend almost any opinion.

And this is the essence of fair comment. If the defendant is honestly expressing his real opinion, the defence should prevail. As was said in the leading English decision:

> Every latitude must be given to opinion and to prejudice....Mere exaggeration, or even gross exaggeration, would not make the comment unfair. However wrong the opinion may be in point of truth, or however prejudiced the writer, it may still be within the prescribed limits.[22]

The crucial thing with fair comment is that the opinion expressed must be based on facts and the facts, unless they are notorious, must be correctly stated. However, if the facts are right, then one should be able to express one's opinion freely and still be within the limits of fair comment.

But, as with justification, there can be problems with fair comment. Two are worth noting.

First, since fair comment defends expressions of opinion and justification is for assertions of fact, a court hearing a libel action must decide which category a given statement fits in. This can cause problems. For, if a statement is categorised as being an assertion of fact, it can ordinarily only be defended by proving its truth.

The distinction between ''facts'' and ''opinions'' is, from the point of view of epistemology, meaningless. Nonetheless, it is one which judges must make. It is in the nature of the distinction that there are few objective criteria to assist judges. The result is that a judge who is not sympathetic to a particular story or defendant may decide that something which looks like an ''opinion'' is, in fact, a ''fact''.

This is what happened in *Vander Zalm* v. *Times Publishers*.[20] The current premier of British Columbia was, at the time, the province's Minister of Human Resources. He had, in that office, demonstrated the reactionary views which later propelled him to the premiership. In response, the Victoria *Times* printed an editorial page cartoon about Vander Zalm. It showed him

> ... smiling, seated at a table, and engaged in plucking the wings from a fly. Other flies, without wings, were shown moving on the table. On the plaintiff's lapel were inscribed the words ''Human Resources''.[24]

The trial judge found for the plaintiff. He rejected the defence of fair comment on the ground that the cartoon was an assertion of a fact — that Vander Zalm was ''...a person with a love of cruelty who enjoys causing suffering to defenceless creatures''. The B.C. Court of Appeal showed an understanding of the nature of editorial cartoons. The notion that an editorial cartoon could be anything but an expression of opinion was dismissed.

Barltrop v. *CBC*[25] raised a similar difficulty. The CBC, on the programme ''As It Happens'', aired an investigative piece about emissions from two metal refineries in Toronto. Some attention focussed on a Dr. Barltrop, a physician who had acted as a consultant to one of the refining companies. He had developed a reputation as someone who was willing to publicly attempt to minimize the dangers of industrial pollution. A U.S. physician was quoted on the programme saying the following about Barltrop.

> Dr. Barltrop is a paid consultant to the lead industry. He is paid to say what he has just said.[26]

Now, it is obvious the first sentence is an assertion of fact, but what about the second? If it is an opinion, it is defensible as fair comment. If it is an assertion of fact, the defendant will have to prove it is true, which, given the nature of the statement, would not be easy.

The courts thought the statement was an assertion of fact and the CBC lost.

The issue is simple. The outcome of a lawsuit may turn on a highly questionable and totally subjective distinction. This may not have a ''chilling effect'', but it does suggest the need for careful attention being given to making it clear to readers or listeners or viewers which statements are expressions of opinion and which are assertions of fact. This may still not satisfy a court. In libel actions a defendant's intentions are generally irrelevant and it may still be held that something which was sincerely intended as an expression of opinion is, nevertheless, an assertion of fact.

The second problem has to do with malice. If the plaintiff can establish that the defendant was motivated by malice in making the allegedly defamatory statements, the defence of fair comment will be lost. What is malice in this sense?

Malice has to do with motive. The question turns on whether the defendant's "dominant motive" in publishing the material was to injure the plaintiff. Thus, if the defendant was motivated by personal spite or ill-will, fair comment will not succeed as a defence.[27]

Well, once again, there should be no "chilling effect" here. Good reporting and good editing demand that there should never be a suggestion of malice about a story. But one decision does suggest a possible problem. In *Vogel* v. *CBC* the trial judge came very close to saying that investigative reporting amounted, by its nature, to malice.

> A further ground upon which the defence of fair comment must fail is that the allegations were not made in good faith and without malice. There was, on the contrary, express malice. That is not to say that the defendants were motivated by personal spite or ill will towards the plaintiff. What the law regards as malice is any indirect motive other than a sense of duty. The purported motive of the defendants was to serve the public interest by exposing corruption in high places but the real motive was to enhance their own reputations by producing a sensational programme. Their concern was not as to whether the allegations were true or as to whether the public interest was served. It was, rather, to give to allegations of scandal the appearance of truth to the extent necessary to succeed in achieving their goal. That attitude, in law, is malice.[28]

Damages

What happens if everything goes wrong and despite the best efforts of reporters and editors a libellous story does somehow get published? All is by no means lost. A timely apology can be relied upon to reduce the amount of money awarded as damages. And even if an apology is not tendered, damage awards in Canadian libel cases have traditionally been modest.

The Ontario Libel and Slander Act,[29] which is similar to legislation in the other common law provinces, gives substantial benefits to media defendants. When the alleged libel has been published in a newspaper or broadcast over radio or television, the person libelled has six weeks within which to issue a libel notice to the newspaper or broadcaster. This period is strictly enforced. As soon as the libel notice is received the potential defendant has three days to decide what to do. If an apology is printed or broadcast within this period, the amount of money which can be awarded in a subsequent libel action is reduced to "actual damages". This means a plaintiff can only recover for direct pecuniary loss caused by the libel. There will be no damages for injury to reputation or as a solace for wounded feelings. In most cases this means there will be no damages at all.

The practical effect of this provision is that a potential media defendant gets a second chance. Three days are provided within which to review the story, re-check the sources, and consult with a lawyer. If it turns out that something did, inexplicably, go wrong, an apology can be offered and that should be the end of the matter.

Now no-one likes to publicly admit to an error. And to be legally adequate the apology must contain a bit of grovelling.[30] Still, it seems exaggerated to talk about a "chilling effect" when the law says you can actually libel someone and then wriggle off the hook. And even if a defendant fails for some reason to apologize within the magic three day period, an apology made at any time prior to judgment being given for the plaintiff will have the effect of reducing the amount of money awarded.[31]

The most striking distinction between Canadian and U.S. libel law is found in the size of awards given to plaintiffs. The amounts of money given as general damages — compensation for injury to reputation and solace for hurt feelings — awarded in Canadian courts, have been, by U.S. standards, miserly.

This is not to say that plaintiffs have not been willing to ask for the moon. It is to say that they haven't been given it. For example, the same radio programme that led to Dr. Barltrop's suit against the CBC, also induced two refining companies to sue. Canada Metal Company asked for $14 million in 1974. In 1980 the action was settled for $10,000.00.[32]

The largest award in a Canadian libel case is probably the $135,000.00 given in *Snyder* v. *Montreal Gazette*.[33] An Ontario trial court recently awarded $883,000.00 in *Walker and Walker Brothers Quarries* v. *CTV*. The Court of Appeal viewed this award as seriously out of line and ordered that a new trial be held to reassess the damages.[34]

There have been occasional suggestions that the courts should fix an upper limit on the amount of damages which can be awarded as a solace or in respect of injury to reputation. In 1978 the Supreme Court of Canada decided three personal injury cases (the trilogy).[35] It was laid down that the maximum amount which a plaintiff could recover for non-pecuniary loss was $100,000.00. There has been discussion in subsequent cases as to whether the trilogy limit should apply to libel actions.[36] In only one case[37] has a court decided that it did.

In 1988 the Supreme Court of Canada had an opportunity to apply the trilogy limit to libel. The opportunity was declined and no reasons were given for doing so.[38]

Injunctions

Interlocutory injunctions in libel actions *do* have a "chilling effect". Under certain circumstances a court may be persuaded to issue an injunction to prevent the publication of an expected libel. This is prior restraint, pure and simple.

The best known Canadian case is *Canada Metal Company* v. *CBC*.[39] It involved an investigative radio report. The report was called "Dying of Lead"; it was an hour long; and it was to be broadcast on the programme "As It Happens" beginning at 7:00 p.m. EST on 29 January 1974. A column in the Toronto *Globe and Mail* that morning referred to the programme and said it contained allegations concerning "... lead emissions and illness around two Toronto smelters". On discovering this, two companies which operated smelters in Toronto, Toronto Refiners and Smelters Limited and Canada Metal Company Limited, sought an injunction to prevent the programme, or certain portions of it, being broadcast. An application was made ex parte to Mr. Justice Wilson of the Supreme Court of Ontario. The application was made at 5:15 p.m. and at 6:00 p.m. the judge made this interim order:

> Ex parte injunction granted to plaintiffs restraining defendants, and each of them from alleging or implying by broadcasting on television or otherwise publicising that the plaintiffs and/or either of them, have bought misleadingly favourable medical evidence from medical experts, and from misstating the amounts the plaintiffs are spending to install pollution control systems.

The order was to be binding for ten days. At 6:20 p.m. the firm representing the smelter companies informed the CBC of the injunction by telephone and at 6:45 p.m. it was served on the CBC.

A CBC lawyer was in the studio. It was the practice with ''As It Happens'' to have all controversial programmes lawyered before they were broadcast to remove libellous material. The fact of the injunction gave an urgency to this procedure. The producers and the lawyer went over the script of ''Dying of Lead'' to see what could be salvaged. The programme aired at 7:00 p.m., but with the three changes in the script. Two passages from the programme as originally taped were deleted, with an electronic tone carried on air to indicate the deletions. The order issued by Wilson J. was also read over the air.

The refining companies were not happy. They applied to have the executive producer and the story editor for ''Dying of Lead'' committed for contempt on the ground that they had breached the terms of the injunction. Mr. Justice O'Leary found the producer and story editor guilty of contempt and fined them each $700.00. An appeal to the Court of Appeal was dismissed. This was not the end of the litigation.

Applications were made, first by the CBC, to have the injunction issued by Wilson, J. rescinded, and, secondly, by the two smelter companies, to continue it. The companies now sought an order that would have been binding until a trial was held. Mr. Justice Holland dissolved the original injunction. An appeal from this decision to the Divisional Court was dismissed.

The technical law about interlocutory injunctions in libel actions is complicated and not of direct concern here.[40] If properly applied, the law should make it difficult for anyone to be successful in getting an injunction to restrain the publication of a libel. Unfortunately, this is not always the case and from time to time injunctions are made.

There is only one solution acceptable in a democracy. A court must rule that the issuance of interlocutory injunctions in libel actions is an unjustifiable limitation on the ''freedom of expression'' guaranteed in s.2(b) of the Canadian Charter of Rights and Freedoms. This would remove a significant anomaly from our legal system. Unfortunately, a recent Supreme Court of Canada decision makes this unlikely.[41]

Lawyers

In Toronto, Montreal, Ottawa, and Vancouver there are some excellent and experienced lawyers who know a great deal about libel law. These lawyers tend, apart from the CBC legal department, to be found in prestigious and expensive firms. They give advice to large media clients. They give excellent advice.

When we move away from these firms, the picture is not so bright. The simple fact is that most lawyers know little about libel law. There are good reasons for this. Libel is a highly specialized area of the law. Libel cases just don't come along that often. There is not enough libel work to enable a sole practitioner or a lawyer in a smaller firm to become knowledgeable. And there is often no theoretical awareness upon which a practitioner might build. Libel is usually not covered in Canadian law schools or professional training courses.

The result is that a newspaper or broadcaster located outside of one of the major media centres may have difficulty finding an experienced libel lawyer. An unskilled lawyer may well have a ''chilling effect''.

Lawyers are taught to keep their clients out of trouble. Their natural professional inclination is towards caution. If a media client asks for assistance with a potentially libellous story, there is one form of advice which the lawyer can give that will be foolproof, that can never lead to trouble for the client. That advice is: kill the story. But this is not the advice the newspaper or broadcaster wants to hear. The advice they want is on how to run the story and get away with it.

There is a ''chilling effect'' here, but it is an effect caused by lawyers, not by the law itself. Reporters and editors should be aware of this and, at the very least, demand of their lawyers that cautious advice be rigourously justified.

The Constitution

In 1964, in *New York Times* v. *Sullivan,*[42] the Supreme Court of the United States transformed that country's libel law. It was held that the First Amendment's protection of freedom of speech and of the press applied to libel actions. When an alleged libel involves the public conduct of a public official, a plaintiff can only succeed by proving actual malice on the part of the defendant. This is supposed to make things more difficult for plaintiffs. Debate continues in the United States over whether *New York Times* v. *Sullivan* was a good thing.[43]

Since the adoption of the Canadian Charter of Rights and Freedoms in 1982 we have had a constitutional guarantee of ''freedom of expression, including freedom of the press and other media of communication''. Should this guarantee be used as the basis for constitutionalising Canadian libel law?[44]

The question, in fact, breaks down into a number of elements. First, and most important, is it necessary to radically alter Canadian libel law? This brings us back to the central question posed in this essay. Does our libel law really have a ''chilling effect'' on our mass media. My answer to that question should, by now, be obvious. Apart from the egregious case of interlocutory injunctions, I do not believe that libel law inhibits the freedom of expression of responsible, professional journalists. Put another way, I believe our libel law does strike a reasonable and acceptable balance between encouraging free expression and protecting reputation. I do not see any necessity for adopting a *New York Times* v. *Sullivan* approach, or some variant of it, in Canada.

But others may disagree. The next issue to be addressed is whether the Charter would even apply to libel actions. A simple answer to this question is that it hasn't, yet. That is, there has so far been no reported libel case in which a defendant has sought to rely on the Charter.

Despite this the recent decision of the Supreme Court of Canada in *Retail, Wholesale and Department Store Union, Local 580* v. *Dolphin Delivery Limited*[45] may have largely precluded resort to the Charter in libel actions. The court held that the Charter has no direct application in purely ''private'' disputes. The Charter applies to the ''legislative, executive and administrative branches of government'' and, therefore, there must be some element of ''government action'' before the Charter can be invoked in litigation. The implication of this decision is that when the state acts to limit freedom of expression, persons may challenge that action; but when a non-state body, such as a corporation, interferes with freedom of expression, there is no legal recourse.

The result in *Dolphin Delivery* is especially strange if one considers the decision in relation to interlocutory injunctions in libel actions, the one area where, in my opinion, the existing law seriously compromises freedom of expression. *Dolphin Delivery* involved an injunction prohibiting secondary picketing in a labour dispute. The injunction was, in the opinion of the court, an interference with freedom of expression. But, because the injunction had been issued in the course of private litigation, the court refused to intervene.

On closer examination, however, the decision is less clear and more equivocal than the last paragraph would suggest. The court also held that the Charter would apply to rules of common law (which is where we find the main body of libel law). But, said the court, the Charter would only apply directly in litigation where one party was the state. The court did, however, stipulate that

> ... the judiciary ought to apply and develop the principles of the common law in a manner consistent with the fundamental values enshrined in the Constitution.

Thus, while there could be no "Charter causes of action or Charter defences between individuals", "... the Charter is far from irrelevant to private litigants whose disputes fail to be decided at common law".

What, if anything, does this mean? A newspaper or broadcaster cannot defend a libel action by relying directly on the Charter, but can argue that the existing defences should be interpreted in a manner consistent with the Charter.

To the extent that elements of libel law are found in legislation, that legislation will, as a clear state act, be subject to the Charter. As a practical matter this will be of little benefit to media defendants. The various provincial statutes dealing with defamation generally have amended the common law so as to confer benefits on defendants. The restrictions, if any, on freedom of expression are found in the common law, not in the statutes.

Even if the Charter were held to apply generally in libel actions, its effect would be limited. The reason for this is to be found in the structure of Charter litigation.

Charter cases have two stages. In the first stage the party relying on the Charter must establish the infringement or denial of a Charter right. Is libel law, apart from interlocutory injunctions, an interference with freedom of expression? To answer this question fully would require repeating most of this essay. Suffice it to say the answer is not immediately obvious.

If the defendant could persuade a court that current libel law was in some way an infringement of freedom of expression, it would then be necessary to move to the second stage of Charter litigation. Section 1 of the Charter permits infringement of guaranteed rights so long as the infringement is reasonable, prescribed by law, and can be justified in a free and democratic society. The plaintiff, then, would have the responsibility of satisfying the court that the existing law of libel was justified in a free and democratic society.

How do courts decide what is or is not justified? Obviously, this is a highly subjective decision. The Supreme Court of Canada laid down an approach to this question in *R.* v. *Oakes*.[46] It involves an assessment of both means and ends. The court attempts to determine whether the objective sought through the limitation is legitimate and whether the methods employed are proportionate to the objective. I assume that courts would regard the objective of libel law — protecting the reputation of individuals — as legitimate. The issue of means is less clear. Does libel law interfere with freedom of expression to any greater degree than is necessary in order to protect reputation? My opinion is that it does not.

The Charter is not likely to have much of an effect on libel law. It is probably not applicable and even if it were held to apply, would not lead to substantive change in the law.

Conclusion

I do not think libel law *should* have a "chilling effect" on the mass media. The fear of a libel action may have some effect. This fear can be displaced through knowledge of libel law and through realising that a libel suit, in fact, holds few terrors for thorough and competent journalists.

Notes

1. *Dombrowski* v. *Pfister* (1965) 380 U.S. 479.
2. See Davis, "The Robert Coates Libel Case", *Ottawa Citizen,* 11 June 1988, p. A4.
3. "Social Foundations of the Law of Defamation: A Comparative Analysis" (1980) 1 *Journal of Media Law and Practice* 3 at p. 19.
4. *Ibid.* at p. 3.
5. (1979) 90 D.L.R. (3d) 321 at p. 342.
6. Broadcasting Act, R.S.C. 1970, c.B-11, s.3(a).
7. See, as one illustrative decision, *R.* v. *Telegram Publishing Co.* (1960) 25 D.L.R. (2d) 471.
8. Martin, "Press Councils: Watchdogs with no bite", (1986) 28 *Bulletin of the Centre for Investigative Journalism* 30.
9. MacFarlane and Martin, "Political Activity and the Journalist: A Paradox", (1984) 10 *Canadian Journal of Communication,* no. 2, 1.
10. See Kent, "The Significance of Corporate Structure in the Media", (1985) 23 *The University of Western Ontario Law Review* 151.
11. See *Silber and Value Industries Ltd.* v. *B.C.T.V. et al.* [1986] 2 W.W.R. 609.
12. In Ontario, at least, this protection has ended. *R. v. Kopyto* (1987) 61 C.R. (3d) (Ont. C.A.).
13. This is probably an overstatement. Such Criminal Code offence as defamatory libel or wilfully promoting hatred might be applied.
14. (1977) 20 N.B.R. (2d) 381.
15. (1976) 11 Nfld & P.E.I.R. 342.
16. (1982) 21 C.C.L.T. 105.
17. (1982) 21 C.C.L.T. 261.
18. *Ibid.,* at pp. 292-293.
19. (1980) 30 N.B.R. (2d) 102.

20. *Munro* v. *Toronto Sun,* note 14 at 294.
21. (1982) Man. L.R. (2d) 1 at p. 21.
22. *Merivale* v. *Carson* (1887) 20 Q.B.D. 275 at pp. 280-281.
23. (1980) 18 B.C.L.R. 210.
24. *Ibid.*
25. (1978) 25 N.S.R. (2d) 637.
26. *Ibid.* at p. 650. This statement had, as a result of an injunction, been deleted from the programme as broadcast in central and western Canada. The statement had already been aired in Atlantic Canada.
27. See the discussion in *Shultz* v. *Porter and Block Brothers* (1979) 9 A.R. 381.
28. Note 13 at p. 193.
29. R.S.O. 1980, c.237, s.5(2).
30. *Hoste* v. *Victoria Times Publishing Co.* (1889) 1 B.C.R. (Pt. 2) 365.
31. *Munro* v. *Toronto Sun,* note 14.
32. Tataryn, ''A 'Watershed' Court Case Could Cramp Investigations'', (1981) 13 *Bulletin of the Centre for Investigative Journalism* 10.
33. (1978) 87 D.L.R. (3d) 5.
34. (1987) 19 O.A.C. 10.
35. *Andrews* v. *Grand and Toy Alberta Ltd.* [1978] 2 S.C.R. 229. *Thornton* v. *Board of School Trustees of School District No. 57 (Prince George)* [1978] 2 S.C.R. 267; *Temo* v. *Arnold* [1978] 2 S.C.R. 287.
36. *Farrell* v. *St. John's Publishing Co.* (1986) 58 Nfld. & P.E.I.R. 66.
37. *Munro* v. *Toronto Sun,* note 14.
38. *Snyder* v. *Montréal Gazette,* unreported.
39. See (1974) 44 D.L.R. (3d) 329; (1975) 55 D.L.R. (3d) 42; (1974) 48 D.L.R. (3d) 641; and (1975) 65 D.L.R. (3d) 231.
40. Martin, ''Interlocutory Injunctions in Libel Actions'', (1982) 20 *The University of Western Ontario Law Review* 139.
41. See reference below to *Dolphin Delivery* case.
42. 376 U.S. 254. A useful analysis and re-evaluation of this case is found in the various articles in (1984) 25 *William and Mary Law Review,* no. 5.
43. See the thoughtful discussion by Dworkin in *The New York Review of Books,* 26 February 1987, p. 27.
44. The U.S. law and its relevance to Canada are discussed in Raymond E. Brown, *The Law of Defamation in Canada,* Toronto, 1987, ch. 27.
45. [1986] 2 S.C.R. 573.
46. [1986] 1 S.C.R. 103.

5.3 The Right to Privacy

Note: The following materials seek to determine whether a right to privacy exists in Canada and, if so, what its limits are.

5.3.1 The Charter

5.3.1.1 Section 7, The Canadian Charter of Rights and Freedoms

Legal Rights

Life, liberty and security of person

7. Everyone has the right to life, liberty and security of the person and the right not to be deprived thereof except in accordance with the principles of fundamental justice.

5.3.1.2 *R.* v. *Nicolucci and Papier* (1985) 22 C.C.C. (3d) 207 (Que. S.C.)

BOILARD J.: The right to privacy is one enjoyed by all citizens living in Canada and it has been enshrined in the *Canadian Charter of Rights and Freedoms*. Section 8 of the Charter protects not only against unreasonable search and seizure of one's home or business premises but also against unreasonable interceptions of private communications.

5.3.2 Privacy at Common Law

5.3.2.1 *Robbins* v. *CBC*, (1957), 12 D.L.R. (2d) 35 (Que. S.C.)

W. B. SCOTT ASSOC. C.J.: — This is an action for damages brought by the plaintiff against the defendant arising under the following circumstances:

From paras. 1 and 2 of plaintiff's declaration (which are admitted by the defendant), it appears that the plaintiff is a member of the College of Physicians & Surgeons of the Province of Quebec and has been practising as a physician in the Cities of Montreal and Outremont and vicinity for upwards of 40 years and is consulting physician to the Montreal General Hospital, Chief of the Medical Department of the Reddy Memorial Hospital and Chairman of the Medical Board of the Reddy Memorial Hospital; and that the defendant is a body corporate carrying on a radio broadcasting and television service throughout Canada and has a monopoly of the television service in Canada except for a few cities therein.

For some time prior to February 1, 1956, the defendant had been televising and broadcasting throughout Eastern Canada a programme entitled "Tabloid". It was put on at 7 p.m. and lasted for one-half hour.

It may be stated parenthetically that the delay in hearing this action is due to the fact that an earlier action taken by the plaintiff was dismissed because the defendant invoked s.10 of the *Crown Liability Act*, 1952-53 (Can.), c.30, which requires a prior 90-day notice to the Deputy Attorney-General of Canada with particulars of the claim before a suit can be brought. Thus this is a second suit, instituted after due compliance with this provision of the statute.

From the evidence given by Ross McLean, who was Producer at that time, the programme was what he called a "provocative" one. On January 16, 1956 plaintiff wrote a letter to the Producer of Tabloid, CBC Television Studios, Toronto, on a letterhead reading "5770 Durocher Avenue, Outremont, P.Q." Dr. Robbins says that it was posted in an envelope bearing his name as a doctor. The letter reads as follows (ex. P-4):

"5770 Durocher Ave.,
"Outremont, P.QUE.
"January 16th, 1956.

"The Producer
"TABLOID
"CBC Television Studios
"Toronto
"Sir,

"I am enclosing a clipping from the Montreal Star which I trust you will read and in turn pass it along to the EASY M.C. and his partners in on TABLOID.

"It is indeed fortunate that Mr. W. O'Hearn did not see some of the past performances in which the script called for MacDougal and Saltzman to put on the most infantile acts one could imagine.

"It would be interesting to know what our American Viewers think of this production, but probably they do as many here do, SHUT it off as soon as the weather is over.

"The weather is the only redeeming feature of the show and I must congratulate Mr. Saltzman on his clear talks on this subject.

"Our only hope is that Tabloid like LIVING in the past will die a natural death.

"I wonder if the Tabloid Quartette will read this letter along with some of the others they get from Viewers.

"Yours

"(Sgd.) E. E. Robbins."

With this letter plaintiff enclosed a clipping from the Montreal Star of an article by Mr. Walter O'Hearn containing criticisms of the Tabloid programme (ex. P-5). It appears from the evidence that Mr. Walter O'Hearn is a drama critic and television critic for the Montreal Star.

Plaintiff complains that on Wednesday, February 8, 1956, the defendant in its programme broadcast and televised the newspaper article and plaintiff's letter to the viewers and listeners of Tabloid, with its own comments thereon and requested its viewers and listeners to write or telephone to the plaintiff to "cheer" him up.

From the evidence it appears that the Master of Ceremonies, one Dick MacDougal (since deceased), read the script prepared for him in advance by the Producer, Ross McLean, and added his own comments.

In para. 3 of its defence defendant states that MacDougal said on that occasion: "Well, I guess we might have skipped Mr. Robbins' letter if he hadn't added that last paragraph, because frankly it's not a very pleasant addition to tonight's program. Now then, when we quoted from similar letters in the past, some of you have written to us — people write to us to kind of cheer us up. That's been very kind of you, but this time, perhaps the person you really should cheer up is Mr. Robbins himself, so if you'll get a pencil and some paper handy we're going to give you his address. Here it is:"

It has become common ground after hearing the evidence that plaintiff's name and address, as appearing on his letterhead, were flashed twice on the screen; the second occasion being after an interval of time between the first flashing of the name and address.

In substance plaintiff complains that the defendant and its employees or agents who prepared or conducted the television and broadcast and the said request to its listeners and viewers committed serious fault and negligence: that they were actuated by resentment of this criticism and by vindictiveness and malice towards the plaintiff, that the defendant and its employees know, or ought to have known, that the said television and broadcast and request would be a damaging invasion of the plaintiff's privacy and would be seen and heard by many thousands of people in Eastern Canada and the United States and that a large number of them would respond to the said request and subject the plaintiff to abuse and insults and prejudice and humiliation and would cause loss and damage to the plaintiff; also that the television and broadcast and the said request constituted an incitement to the public to cause loss and damage to the plaintiff, and did cause loss and damage.

There is some contradiction in the testimony adduced before the Court as to whether the Master of Ceremonies, MacDougal, did or did not ask listeners to telephone to the plaintiff on that occasion. McLean, the Producer, going back in his memory of what took place some 22 months ago, is of the opinion that MacDougal did ask people to write to plaintiff and gave the postage rate for a letter from Montreal and what it would be on a letter from outside of Montreal. He has no recollection of any invitation to telephone the plaintiff.

On the other hand, Dr. Robbins and his wife and Mrs. Sears, who were following the programme on that occasion, all testified that MacDougal asked people to telephone as well as to write.

The Court, after seeing Dr. Robbins and his wife and Mrs. Sears in the witness-box, is satisfied that they have proved that there was an invitation to telephone as well as write. In any event, it is reasonable to say that the natural result of this invitation by MacDougal to the viewers and listeners would, in the normal course of events, result in people using the telephone, that is to say, the people living in and around Montreal. The City of Outremont is a prosperous and well-known suburban municipality adjoining the City of Montreal. All anybody would have to do would be to look up the Montreal telephone book where Dr. Robbins' name and address appeared. He was listed as Dr. E. E. Robbins, 5770 Durocher. Moreover it is far easier for people to telephone even if they are not invited to telephone than it is to take time to sit down and write a letter.

Plaintiff's allegation in para. 5 that the defendant and its employees knew that this invitation would be seen and heard by many thousands of people in Eastern Canada is borne out by the proof. The first witness plaintiff called was one Jean Leveille who is a Research Director of International Surveys Ltd. This company is employed by the CBC itself to furnish estimates of the numbers of listeners and viewers on CBC programmes, including Tabloid, and on that night he estimated that in Montreal and within a radius of 50 miles from Montreal, some 66,000 homes were watching the television programme of Tabloid. His estimate is that the average number of viewers per home is 3 persons.

In Toronto on that same evening his estimate is that 90,000 people in Toronto and within a radius of 50 miles were viewing the Tabloid programme. It is also admitted by Mr. McLean this morning that the programme could be seen and heard at distances beyond 50 miles, though sometimes with more difficulty. He said, however, that it could be seen in Ottawa, which is established by one of the letters filed in the sheaf of 102 letters as ex. P-3, as there is a letter from Billings Bridge which is not far from Ottawa.

There is no need to elaborate too much on these figures as there is evidence that there was a vast number of viewers and listeners and the defendant corporation is continually being furnished with the estimates by people employed by them; so they know approximately how many people would hear this invitation expressed by MacDougal.

Although MacDougal, as McLean said, "adlibbed" on the programme prepared for him in advance by the Producer, the deliberateness of this action by the CBC was made manifest by the fact that practically all of the language used was prepared by Ross McLean himself in advance. When asked by the Court yesterday afternoon whether he prepared the name and address of E. E. Robbins flashed on the screen, he said he did not do it himself but admitted that the graphic arts department, which was one branch of the CBC set-up in Toronto, had prepared it at his request.

The law governing the subject is simply stated in art. 1053 of the *Civil Code,* which reads as follows:

"1053. Every person capable of discerning right from wrong is responsible for the damage caused by his fault to another, whether by positive act, imprudence, neglect or want of skill."

And Article 1054 says:

"1054. He is responsible not only for the damage caused by his own fault, but also for that caused by the fault of persons under his control and by things he has under his care;...

"Masters and employers are responsible for the damage caused by their servants and workmen in the performance of the work for which they are employed."

It was neither alleged nor proved that the law of Ontario differs from our own law in this respect, so that for the purposes of this case the Court must assume that the law of Ontario is the same as our own.

Now the first question to be decided is this: Did the defendant and his servants and employees violate the provisions of art. 1053 and art. 1054 of our *Civil Code?* The Court has no hesitation whatever in holding that the defendant is responsible for an actionable wrong committed by its employees and servants. Defendant says in its plea that the letter of criticism did not mention that the plaintiff was a practising physician. It does not matter whether or not the plaintiff was a physician, because all citizens are protected by the above two articles of the Civil Code.

Both counsel have frankly admitted that they have not been able to find any case in the books similar to the one that is now before us. As far as I am concerned, I am very happy they were not able to find any such case, because in the opinion of the Court what the Producer and the "Easy Master of Ceremonies", the late Dick MacDougal, did on that occasion constituted a grievous positive wrongful act against Dr. Robbins, making the defendant corporation responsible for the damages flowing from such wrongful act.

There is no need to attempt any precise definition of this fault which the defendant's servants committed. By no stretch of the imagination can it be held that when Dr. Robbins wrote this letter on January 16th criticizing this programme, he invited the Producer to incite the listeners to "cheer him up" for daring to criticize the programme.

It can be quite properly held from the language used by the plaintiff that he wanted this letter merely to be read, not only by the Producer but by the quartette who appeared on the programme.

Even if it can be inferred that he wished to have his criticism and that of Mr. O'Hearn read out to the viewers and listeners to give them something to think about, never in this wide world can it be deduced that the Producer and Master of Ceremonies were invited to "set the dogs on Dr. Robbins" for having dared to criticize.

The defendant corporation very wisely have not submitted that any such power was given to them by Parliament in the charter of the CBC which appears in R.S.C. 1952, c.32, because I can find nothing in that charter which in any shape or form would be or could be construed as parliamentary approval to persecute or incite persecution of a private citizen who dared to criticize any programme.

Interesting and instructive evidence was given by Dr. Krauser, yesterday afternoon. He is a graduate of McGill University. He had 5 years in general practice and for the last five years has been specializing in psychiatry. He is attached to the Montreal General Hospital and is a demonstrator in psychiatry at McGill University.

He said that with such a large audience of viewers and listeners there was bound to be a large number who were just marginal in their ability to control themselves, and that when such people received an invitation to get after somebody, in the way in which it was done on this programme, it was inevitable that a certain percentage of these marginal people would take that as an invitation to abuse the person whose name and address were given them. He made it clear that this was a fact which would or should be known to people conducting a system of mass communication such as that carried on by the defendant, the Canadian Broadcasting Corp.

No contradiction whatever of his testimony was attempted by the defendant, not even by Mr. Ross McLean. And the evidence of Dr. Krauser is corroborated first by what the plaintiff told us as to what happened at his house within 15 minutes after the invitation to "cheer up" plaintiff was given, when his telephone started ringing and continued until late that evening when he and his wife had to take the telephone off the receiver to get some peace. Further, it so continued for three days, until the situation became so intolerable at his home that he had to go to the telephone company and have them disconnect his number and give him another number. His Telephone Answering Service was also swamped with calls. Plaintiff spoke about the hostile messages he had received. Some of the language was so crude he did not want to repeat it in Court.

It should be added that this inciting invitation was followed by people who decided to "cheer up" the plaintiff by sending C.O.D. food parcels to his house. Some other person or persons apparently telephoned in his name and ordered taxis to go to his home. The first one came to the door and there were half a dozen others waiting out on the street. There was no contradiction whatever to this evidence.

Dr. Krauser's testimony was also fully corroborated by the 102 letters which the doctor received both from the Province of Quebec and from Ontario, and as far away as North Troy, Vermont.

Not all those letters were written in terms of abuse. Yesterday counsel for defendant read out two quite mild ones saying they did not agree with the plaintiff but a great many of the remainder are disgusting and abusive — so much so that I shall not repeat them here.

It is noteworthy to find how many of them are written by women who signed their names.

The uncontradicted testimony of the plaintiff stands as to what happened to him.

The only reasonable inference to draw from all this is that the Producer and the Master of Ceremonies knew this was likely to happen.

On the whole the Court holds that neither the defendant nor its employees had the right to select for treatment such as that given to plaintiff any citizen who had written a letter criticizing one of its programmes.

Now as to the quantum of damages to which the plaintiff is entitled. There is a claim for loss of income from his private practice at his home. This is apart from the income he received for consultations and treatments at the Reddy Memorial Hospital and apart from the salary he receives as Registrar for which he is making no claim.

Plaintiff estimates he is losing $300 a month. But he had brought no books with him nor cards nor income tax returns which would enable this statement to be tested by cross-examination. It is quite clear, however, that for a doctor, 76 years of age, it is a serious matter to have one's telephone cut off for a whole month.

Counsel for defendant agreed, with the consent of plaintiff's counsel, that for purposes of this case the defence would admit that there had been a diminution in the income of plaintiff following this episode.

The next item of damage appearing in para. 11 of the declaration is impairment of Dr. Robbin's health. On that we have the evidence of Dr. Shister who examined the plaintiff shortly after February 8, 1956. He said Dr. Robbins was suffering from severe emotional disturbance, which I consider would be a most natural consequence. There was no evidence to the contrary.

Dr. Shister added that for the first few weeks following this episode the plaintiff was in no condition to practise and he considered this situation lasted for two or three months. The general effect of the testimony was that it had not done the doctor any good — especially for a man of that age. Dr. Robbins testified to the same effect.

Mrs. Robbins gave evidence as to the insomnia from which the doctor suffered following February 8th.

This evidence was not contradicted.

Plaintiff also has a claim for humiliation and invasion of privacy. What was done was a form of malicious mischief or a premeditated way of causing a public nuisance to the doctor.

Before proceeding to assess and fix the damages, allusion should be made to the fact that on February 13th the CBC, on the television News programme at 6:45 p.m., referred to this incident. McLean had no record of that reference. However, from the evidence given by plaintiff, which was not contradicted, the CBC employees in charge of that programme referred to the letter of regret and apology written by Mr. Dilworth, Director of Programmes for Ontario, to plaintiff on February 10th, *i.e.,* three days before this News broadcast on Monday, February 13th. Mr. Dilworth's letter (ex. P-1) reads as follows:

"CANADIAN BROADCASTING CORPORATION

"354 Jarvis Street,
"Toronto, Ontario,
"February 10th, 1956.

"*Airmail*
"*Special Delivery.*
"Dr. E. E. Robbins,
5770 Durocher Avenue,
Montreal, Quebec.

"Dear Dr. Robbins,

"I wish to tell you how very deeply I regret the incident which occurred on our 'Tabloid' program last Wednesday evening. I offer you my personal apologies and the apologies of the Corporation.

"I assure you that we have gone beyond regretting the incident and have acted very quickly to bring proper and very severe disciplinary action to bear upon the people responsible for this unfortunate incident.

"Yesterday morning I issued a statement to the press. I am enclosing a copy for your information and interest.

"Yours sincerely.

"(Sgd.) Ira Dilworth
Director for the Province
of Ontario."

Apparently there was some sort of internal conflict within the ranks of the CBC — that is to say, the employees in charge of the News programme were apparently not following the stand taken by Mr. Dilworth. I mention this because what was shown and said on that News programme resulted in a further invasion of the private life of the plaintiff.

On February 10th, Mr. E. W. Robbins, son of the plaintiff, wrote to Mr. David Dunton, Chairman of the CBC, telling of the trouble caused to his father and saying that "many people have suggested my Father should seek redress through legal channels".

On February 16th, six days later, Mr. Dunton replied as follows (ex. P-2):

"CANADIAN BROADCASTING CORPORATION

"OFFICE OF THE CHAIRMAN

140 Wellington Street,
Ottawa, Ontario,
February 16th, 1956.

"Mr. E. W. Robbins,
"26 Ballantyne Avenue, South,
"Montreal West, P.Q.

"Dear Mr. Robbins,

"May I begin by saying that all of us, in the Corporation are extremely sorry about the 'Tabloid' incident which involved your father and caused him so much inconvenience.

"By now you will have learned of the apology the Corporation made and the action taken in relieving the producer of his post on this program. Naturally you have my assurance that the Corporation is determined that there shall be no recurrence of any invasion of a citizen's privacy and right to criticism.

"In Dr. Dilworth's apology he referred to the incident as 'a grave error of judgment and good taste'. It was indeed a very serious matter even though I am sure there was no malicious intent.

"The Corporation has received a great number of letters and phone calls protesting the disciplinary action taken with regard to the producer. Nevertheless, I can assure you that we will continue to take a firm stand whenever the listeners' rights are in any way jeopardized by CBC actions. No better example of the power of the television medium can possibly be found. In this country CBC has been charged with the responsibility of developing this powerful medium to suit the desires and needs of Canadians. This responsibility is a great one and its fulfilment cannot be interrupted by incidents such as the one in question.

"Thank you again for your comments. I hope that our program efforts in future will inspire commendation rather than the justifiable criticism of your last letter.

"Yours sincerely,
"(Signed) A. D. Dunton."

Taking the Chairman's letter and Mr. Dilworth's letter together it would appear that there is an admission of fault on the part of the employees of the defendant as alleged in para. 9 of the declaration. I take this opportunity of saying that Mr. Dunton's letter is that of a gentleman and so is that of Mr. Dilworth.

There is one more thing to mention. The position taken by the Chairman of the Board and Mr. Dilworth with regard to plaintiff appears to be at complete variance with the defence filed by the Canadian Broadcasting Corp. in this case. If Mr. Dunton were giving the instructions there would be a confession of judgment as to liability and either a tender into Court or a request to the Court to assess the damages. But not a bit of it. The only witness called by the defendant in this case is the Producer of Tabloid, Ross McLean, who was in the witness-box not only yesterday but again this morning, and he was the one who was suspended by his superior officers for three weeks for what he and MacDougal had done. He has sat here throughout this trial. He has heard the evidence of Dr. Robbins and his wife, who are respectable, decent citizens. He has heard the evidence of the two doctors called by the plaintiff. He has heard in open Court the letters of the Chairman and Mr. Dilworth. But not one note of regret was anywhere expressed by Mr. McLean in his testimony saying "We are sorry this happened". He did not apologize, neither when he was in the box yesterday nor today. So it would still appear that there was some conflict going on between the different departments of the defendant.

I have gone into this matter at some length because we have had no similar case in Canada of which I am aware, and in view of the fact that there is such a large "fan" audience of viewers and listeners of CBC programmes the public is entitled to have the views of this Court in some detail.

Sitting as both Judge and jury, it remains now to assess the damages which the plaintiff should receive. In assessing damages I have followed the principles laid down by the Supreme Court of Canada in the case of *Chaput* v. *Romain,* 1 D.L.R. (2d) 241, 114 Can. C.C. 170, [1955] S.C.R. 834.

After taking everything into consideration I have reached the conclusion that the fair and proper compensation for the plaintiff will be the total sum of $3,000.

WHEREFORE the Court doth condemn the defendant to pay to plaintiff the sum of $3,000 with interest from date of service of the action and costs.

Judgment for plaintiff.

5.3.2.2 *Krouse* v. *Chrysler Canada* (1973), 1 O.R. (2d) 225 (Ont. C.A.)

Appellant automobile manufacturer distributed a device bearing the names and numbers of all professional football players which was designed to assist people who watched professional football on television to identify the players and which also advertised appellant's automobiles. On the device there was an action photograph of a football game which focused attention on respondent player who was identifiable by the number on his uniform provided that the user of the device recognized the uniform and thus realized which team's player list to examine. The player had not consented to the use of the photograph. The player recovered damages in an action on the basis that something of commercial value to him had been misappropriated by the manufacturer and on the basis that there was a passing-off.

On appeal, *held,* the appeal should be allowed. There was no passing-off. The player and the manufacturer were not in a common field of endeavour and the buying public would not be led to believe that the manufacturer's products, or the advertising device itself, had been designed or manufactured by the player. Nor was the device in competition with a similar product marketed by the player. There was no implication that the player endorsed the product, as there might have been had he been shown sitting in or standing by one of the manufacturer's vehicles. While the common law does contemplate a concept which may be broadly classified as an appropriation of one's personality for commercial purposes, appellant had not committed this wrong. Exposure through the publication of photographs and information is the life-blood of professional sport. Some minor loss of privacy and even some loss of potential for commercial exploitation must be expected to occur as a by-product of the express or implied licence to publicize the institution of the game itself. Appellant manufacturer had sought a trade advantage through association with the game of football generally, and it was the game of professional football rather than the personality of the respondent which had been deliberately incorporated in the advertising device.

5.3.2.3 *Burnett* v. *The Queen in Right of Canada* (1979) 23 O.R. (2d) 109 (Ont. H.C.)

Question 5: Is there such a thing as a tort of "invasion of privacy"?
The plaintiff's statement of claim reads in part:

45. The plaintiff further states that during the programme "Connections" he was at various times depicted on the screen driving his automobile, a 1973 Rolls Royce. Pictures of the plaintiff driving his vehicle were taken at a time or times known to the defendants but unknown to the plaintiff and by person or persons known to the defendants and unknown to the plaintiff but at all material times without his consent or knowledge. The defendants did also during the course of the programme "Connections" portray on the screen a picture of his house and a picture of his offices. These pictures were taken at time or times known to the defendants and unknown to the plaintiff and by a person or persons known to the defendants and unknown to the plaintiff but at all material times without his consent or knowledge.

46. The plaintiff states that such pictures were taken through the use of hidden cameras by persons attending from time to time at his offices and by persons following him as he drove in his vehicle. The plaintiff states that in attending at his residence and offices, in following him in his vehicle and filming him with hidden cameras, the defendants have violated his right to be free from invasion of his privacy and free from unlawful interference in the enjoyment of his property and security of his person.

47. The plaintiff further states that the broadcast of the programme "Connections" throughout Canada and the publication of the defamatory words and images contained thereon was a further violation of his right to be free from invasion of his privacy and free from unlawful interference in the enjoyment of his property and security of his person.

48. The plaintiff further states that the defendants and person or persons unknown to the plaintiff and known to the defendants conspired each with the other to cause injury and harm to the plaintiff, namely to publish words and images defamatory of the plaintiff, to publish malicious falsehoods, invade his right of privacy and interfere in the lawful enjoyment of his property and the security of his person.

...

51. The plaintiff pleads and relies upon The Bill of Rights, R.S.C. 1970, appendix 111 and the provisions thereof.

...

52.(c) Damages in the amount of $5,000,000.00 for invasion of privacy;

Counsel for the defendants submits that there is no such tort known to law and, therefore, requests that I strike out the plaintiff's statement of claim under the provisions of Rule 126.

Counsel have referred me to the following authorities:

(1) *Krouse v. Chrysler Canada Ltd. et al.*, [1970] 3 O.R. 135 at p. 136, 12 D.L.R. (3d) 463 at p. 464, 1 C.P.R. (2d) 218, *per* Parker, J. (as he then was):

> Although this Court has inherent jurisdiction to strike out a statement of claim on the ground that it discloses no reasonable cause of action or stay an action, such power should be sparingly exercised and only when there is no doubt that no cause of action exists. Neither counsel was able to submit any decided case on this point that has been tried in this jurisdiction so it would appear that the matter has not been considered and judicially decided. It may be that the action is novel, but it has not been shown to me that the Court in this jurisdiction would not recognize a right of privacy. The plaintiff therefore has the right to be heard, to have the issue decided after trial.

(2) *Krouse v. Chrysler Canada Ltd. et al.*, [1972] 2 O.R. 133, 25 D.L.R. (3d) 49, 5 C.P.R. (2d) 30. Haines, J., at trial, specifically refrained from deciding whether there was such a common law right to privacy; Haines, J., decided the case on the basis of ''passing-off''.

(3) *Krouse v. Chrysler Canada Ltd. et al.* (1973), 1 O.R. (2d) 225 at pp. 233-4 and 237-8, 40 D.L.R. (3d) 15 at pp. 23-4 and 27-8, 13 C.P.R. (2d) 28, *per* Estey, J.A., discussed the right to privacy but did not state that no such cause of action existed in the Province of Ontario.

(4) *Motherwell et al. v. Motherwell* (1976), 73 D.L.R. (3d) 62, [1976] 6 W.W.R. 550, Alberta Appellate Division, *per* Clement, J.A. In this case a plaintiff was successful in an action for breach of the right to privacy.

(5) Section 381(1)(*c*), (*e*) and (*f*) of the *Criminal Code* of Canada.

In my view, having regard to the present state of the law in this Province, the words of Parker, J. (as he then was), are most apt and this part of the defendants' application will be dismissed.

5.3.2.4 *Motherwell* v. *Motherwell* (1976), 73 D.L.R. (3d) 62 (Alta. S.C.)

CLEMENT, J.A.: — The defendant appellant Elizabeth Motherwell is the daughter of the plaintiff respondent William Motherwell, and the sister of the plaintiff respondent John Motherwell who is the husband of the plaintiff respondent Dorothy Motherwell. I will designate the respondents respectively as the father, the brother, and the sister-in-law.

This appeal is from the judgment of Kirby, J., in two actions which were consolidated for trial. The allegations in the statement of claim of the brother and the sister-in-law with which these appeals are particularly concerned are that the appellant had on numerous occasions ''contacted the plaintiffs by telephone, making false accusations and statements against the plaintiffs and refuses to cease making such allegations and false statements'', and ''written letters to the plaintiffs making unfounded statements and accusations concerning the affairs of the plaintiffs''. The appellant persisted in this conduct despite demands that she cease, which the plaintiffs assert to be an invasion of their privacy, and a nuisance, and pray for nominal damages and

> ...an interim and a permanent injunction against the Defendant or anyone acting on her behalf enjoining her or anyone else acting on her behalf from contacting, telephoning, writing, visiting or in any other way communicating with the Plaintiffs or their children.

The defence of the appellant with which we are concerned is that ''no action lies by the plaintiffs or either of them to restrain her lawful communications with the plaintiffs''.

In his statement of claim against the appellant, the father alleges that the appellant had on numerous occasions

> ... communicated with the plaintiff by telephone and has continuously made false accusations and statements against the plaintiff's son and daughter-in-law, John and Dorothy Motherwell, and against the plaintiff's housekeeper, and the defendant continues to communicate ceaselessly in this fashion with the plaintiff and to make such allegations and false statements, and to harangue the plaintiff.

He also alleges that the appellant persisted in this conduct despite demands that she cease, and asserts this to be an invasion of his privacy, and a nuisance. He further alleges that

> ... the constant harassment of him by the defendant causes him great strain and mental anguish. The plaintiff is 90 years of age. The said nuisance by the defendant is dangerous and injurious to the mental and physical health of the plaintiff.

The prayer is for nominal damages and an injunction enjoining the appellant from ''molesting, harassing, or in any way interfering with the plaintiff and from communicating with him by telephone, personal contact, letter, or in any other way''. The relevant defence of the appellant is that

> ... she has committed no actional wrong giving rise to the cause for an injunction as alleged in the statement of claim herein or at all and that as the daughter of the plaintiff she has an inalienable right to lawfully communicate with and visit her father.

Additional allegations in each statement of claim sound in trespass in the traditional sense and do not require review. The appeals are directed to the alleged harassment by telephone and letter. In each action Kirby, J., granted, *inter alia,* nominal damages and an injunction in the terms prayed for. It is from these orders that this appeal is taken. There was also consolidated with the two actions a petition by the father pursuant to the *Mentally Incapaciated Persons Act,* R.S.A. 1970, c.232, upon which Kirby, J., declared the appellant is, through mental infirmity, a person who is incapable of managing her affairs, and committed the custody and management of her estate to the Public Trustee. This order is not in appeal.

The appellant lives in Calgary. Her mental condition is the cause of the matters complained of by the plaintiffs. It is diagnosed as a paranoid condition accompanied by some thought disorder, which appeared initially about 1970 and grew in intensity. It is concerned with the family relationships and related matters, and manifests itself by a conviction that the sister-in-law, and the housekeeper referred to in the statement of claim of the father, are influencing the brother and father against her. The medical testimony is that she has no malice towards the brother and the father, for whom she appears to have some concern, but that she bears malice towards the sister-in-law and the housekeeper as a concomitant of her paranoid condition.

The father also lives in Calgary. He had injured his leg in December, 1973, and has been in hospital or nursing homes at intervals since then. His wife, the appellant's mother, died in December, 1974. The telephone calls of which he complains commenced some time prior to then and were made to him when he was at home. His evidence was that after his wife's death they increased in frequency and were made continuously (which I take to mean to be of a daily nature) up to a dozen times a day. He was harassed by these calls to the point where he was afraid to answer the telephone as he found them to be very upsetting. The gist of them was a tirade against his daughter-in-law and his housekeeper. In his weak condition he found it upsetting physically as well as emotionally, and is unable to stand such "harassment" as he describes it. It is to be inferred that he asked the appellant to desist but she did not do so and he obtained an interim injunction. He also received some letters of the kind received by the brother, which I will shortly refer to, but this part of his complaints does not loom large.

The brother is highly placed in the executive management of three business and commercial enterprises in Calgary. His home is in Calgary where he lives with his wife, the sister-in-law, and their three children aged 15, 10, and 8 years, respectively. For the purposes of his business he has an office in his home and there is a telephone used in part for business purposes. He also has an office downtown served by a telephone. The telephone calls from the appellant, of which he complains, commenced about 1972. Not to labour the point, they increased in frequency, particularly from the spring of 1974 onwards, to as many as 60 calls in one day and were made as well to his office as to his home. The gist of them was abuse of the sister-in-law, whom the appellant called a "crook" and a "gold-digger" and maligned her in a manner which the brother described as vindictive and vitriolic. Calls to the home were made in the middle of the night and first thing in the morning, amongst other times. In 1974 the brother installed an answering device on his home telephone and a diary kept for the purpose shows that on one occasion in the space of an hour, the appellant made as many as 30 calls. This was the maximum capacity of the device. The purpose was to avoid the calls from the appellant but provide a record so that the brother could call back other persons who were trying to reach him. As the appellant was plugging the answering device, the brother obtained an unlisted telephone number for his home and spent a good deal of time and money informing his friends and business associates of the new number. Unfortunately, the appellant, by a fortuitous circumstance, learned the new number and her calls immediately started again. He obtained another unlisted number but it was not known to his friends and business associates, many of whom were unable to reach him. He then applied to the Trial Division of this Court and obtained an interim injunction against the appellant, and reverted to his original listed telephone number after the order was granted. It appears that the appellant has been in contempt of the order. He testified that by reason of this harassment his health has suffered and he has lost 26 lbs. in weight. He also said that the calls had been terribly hard on his children, who on occasion answered the telephone, but no details are given. He feels that the appellant has some vindictiveness towards him as well as towards others.

The evidence of the sister-in-law is to the same effect. It is probably best summarized in this testimony of the effect of the calls:

> Well, they have created a fantastic tension within the home with the children, all members of the family, and at one point when we were receiving so many calls I would say, ''George, you answer it this time'', nobody wants to answer the phone because they know that it was going to probably be Elizabeth on the other end.

As to the letters the brother testified that he had received in his mail ''a whole briefcase full of them''. Those that were put in evidence appear to be incoherent, tedious, and abusive. He did not read all of them. As I have noted, the father gave evidence of the receipt of similar letters from the appellant, but they seemed to contribute little to his feeling of harassment.

It is desirable to make clear the limitation on the legal considerations that arise in this appeal on the foregoing facts. They are confined to the common law. It was not contended in argument that s.31 of the *Alberta Government Telephones Act,* R.S.A. 1970, c.12, of itself gives rise to civil remedies:

> 31. A person who uses profane, obscene or abusive language while talking on a telephone or over a telecommunication wire or by other means interferes with the use or enjoyment of the system is guilty of an offence and liable on summary conviction to a fine of not more that $100 or to imprisonment for not more than six months.

While that issue is not before this Court, nevertheless the section has a place in the context of an aspect to which I will presently come. The matters of complaint are unwanted communications made to the respondents. If such acts are properly within the concept of ''invasion of privacy'' they occupy a niche of their own, distinct from such matters as surveillance, the clandestine gathering and use of personal information by various means, the interception of private communications, and unwanted publicity, discussed by Peter Burns in ''The Law of Privacy: The Canadian Experience'', 54 *Can. Bar Rev.* (No. 1, March, 1976), p. 1. In this opinion I will use the phrase only as a convenient designation of the acts of the appellant I have described upon which these actions are founded. In considering the authorities I will leave aside those which deal with the other concepts and are usually influenced by considerations that are not applicable here.

The arguments in appeal advanced by the appellant draw a distinction between nuisance and invasion of privacy. It is said that invasion of privacy does not come within the principle of private nuisance, and that it is a species of activity not recognized as remedial by the common law. It is urged that the common law does not have within itself the resources to recognize invasion of privacy as either included in an existing category or as a new category of nuisance, and that it has lost its original power, by which indeed it created itself, to note new ills arising in a growing and changing society and pragmatically to establish a principle to meet the need for control and remedy; and then by categories to develop the principle as the interests of justice make themselves sufficiently apparent. For these propositions the appellant relies on a passage in the judgment of Dixon, J., in *Victoria Park Racing & Recreation Grounds Co. Ltd. v. Taylor et al.* (1937), 58 C.L.R. 479, of which it is sufficient to reproduce only the following at p. 505:

> There is, in my opinion, little to be gained by inquiring whether in English law the foundation of a delictual liability is unjustifiable damage or breach of specific duty. The law

> of tort has fallen into great confusion, but, in the main, what acts and omissions result in responsibility and what do not are matters defined by long-established rules of law from which judges ought not wittingly to depart and no light is shed upon a given case by large generalizations about them.

The obsolescence of this view in the field of negligence is made apparent by Lord Reid in *Dorset Yacht Co. Ltd. v. Home Office,* [1970] A.C. 1004 at pp. 1026-7:

> About the beginning of this century most eminent lawyers thought that there were a number of separate torts involving negligence, each with its own rules, and they were most unwilling to add more. They were of course aware from a number of leading cases that in the past the courts had from time to time recognized new duties and new grounds of action. But the heroic age was over; it was time to cultivate certainty and security in the law; the categories of negligence were virtually closed. The Attorney-General invited us to return to those halcyon days, but, attractive though it may be, I cannot accede to his invitation.
>
> In later years there has been a steady trend towards regarding the law of negligence as depending on principle so that, when a new point emerges, one should ask not whether it is covered by authority but whether recognized principles apply to it. *Donoghue v. Stevenson* [1932] A.C. 562 may be regarded as a milestone, and the well-known passage in Lord Atkin's speech should I think be regarded as a statement of principle. It is not to be treated as if it were a statutory definition. It will require qualification in new circumstances. But I think that the time has come when we can and should say that it ought to apply unless there is some justification or valid explanation for its exclusion.

This passage, and more, was adopted by Spence, J., as part of his reasons in delivering the majority judgment of the Supreme Court of Canada in *O'Rourke et al. v. Schacht* (1974), 55 D.L.R. (3d) 96, [1976] 1 S.C.R. 53, 3 N.R. 453. And in *Haig v. Bamford et al.* (1976), 72 D.L.R. (3d) 68, 27 C.P.R. (2d) 149, 9 N.R. 43, Dickson, J., speaking for the majority of the Court noted anew the effect growth and change in society has in enlarging the scope of the duty of care: the neighbour concept.

But it is not only in the field of negligence that the common law demonstrates its continuing ability to serve the changing and expanding needs of our present society. In *Canadian Aero Service Ltd. v. O'Malley et al.* (1973), 40 D.L.R. (3d) 371, 11 C.P.R. (2d) 206, [1974] S.C.R. 592, the Supreme Court of Canada examined the reltionship which gives rise to a fiduciary duty, and the scope of that duty. In giving the judgment of the Court Laskin, J. (as he then was), reviewed the progression of authorities and said, p. 384 D.L.R., p. 610 S.C.R.: "What these decisions indicate is an updating of the equitable principle whose roots lie in the general standards that I have already mentioned...".

In the context of contract Lord Simonds vigorously expressed similar views in *British Movietonews Ltd. v. London & District Cinemas Ltd.,* [1952] A.C. 166 at p. 188: "It is no doubt essential to the life of the common law that its principles should be adapted to meet fresh circumstances and needs." In the same spirit Morden, J., approached the principle of restitution in *James More & Sons Ltd. v. University of Ottawa* (1974), 49 D.L.R. (3d) 666, 5 O.R. (2d) 162. He referred to the widening of the principle apparently effected by *County of Carleton v. City of Ottawa* (1965), 52 D.L.R. (2d) 220, [1965] S.C.R. 663, and said at p. 676:

> I mention this to indicate that where a Court, on proper grounds, holds that the doctrine of restitution is applicable, it is not necessary to fit the case into some exact category, apparently established by a previous decision, giving effect to the doctrine. Just as the categories of negligence are never closed, neither can those of restitution. The principles take precedence over the illustrations or examples of their application.

It is worth recalling the salutary passage from the speech of Lord Macmillan in *M'Alister (or Donoghue) v. Stevenson,* [1932] A.C. 562 at p. 619, which Morden, J., here applies to the principle of restitution: "The criterion of judgment must adjust and adapt itself to the changing circumstances of life. The categories of negligence are never closed." The developing principle of restitution, or unjust enrichment to distinguish a somewhat different conceptual approach, is discussed by G.H.L. Fridman in his valuable article "Reflections on Restitution" in 8 Ottawa Law Review 156 (1976), at p. 162, in which he points out "... that while the historical categories are still important, and cannot be ignored, the operation of the law is not confined to those categories".

The application of this spirit of the common law is apparent in other cases of importance. The issues in appeal must be approached in the same spirit.

Let me observe here that I do not wish to be entrapped in semantics or nomenclature. For the present purposes I will employ the term *principle* as a general concept of legal rights and duties in an aspect of human activities in which some common element is to be found: Lord Atkin in *Donoghue v. Stevenson* at p. 580; and I will employ the term *categories* as the application of a principle to particular circumstances, discernible in precedents, which have been found to come within the principle. The scope of the principle of private nuisance, as well as its established categories, require consideration in the issues in appeal.

The rule of *stare decisis* operates, as it seems to me, to regulate the application of precedents to cases which can be said to fall within a category. When the circumstances of a case do not appear to bring it fairly within an established category, they may lie sufficiently within the concept of a principle that consideration of a new category is warranted. The scope of a category may in time be broadened by a trend in precedents which reflect judicial considerations going beyond the disciplines of *stare decisis*. Those same considerations, arising from adequately demonstrated social need of a continuing nature, may lead, when necessary to maintain social justice, to a new category or the review of a principle. The considerations I refer to were termed public policy by Lord Wright in *Fender v. St. John-Mildmay,* [1938] A.C. 1 At p. 38 he said:

> In one sense every rule of law, either common law or equity, which has been laid down by the Courts, in that course of judicial legislation which has evolved the law of this country, has been based on ... public ... policy.

That case arose out of a claim by a woman founded on a breach of promise of marriage made to her by a man who had at that point obtained only a decree *nisi* of divorce from his wife. Lord Atkin addressed himself to the principle of public policy and delivered a caution in respect of the establishment of new categories in terms which bear repeating here. He referred to *Janson v. Driefontein Consolidated Mines, Ltd.,* [1902] A.C. 484, and went on to say at pp. 11-2:

> In the same case Lord Halsbury indeed appeared to decide that the categories of public policy are closed, and that the principle could not be invoked anew unless the case could be brought within some principle [*sic,* category] of public policy already recognized by the law. I do not find, however, that this view received the express assent of the other members of the House; and it seems to me, with respect, too rigid. On the other hand, it fortifies the serious warning illustrated by the passages cited above that the doctrine should only be invoked in clear cases in which the harm to the public is substantially incontestable, and does not depend upon the idiosyncratic inferences of a few judicial minds. I think that this should be regarded as the true guide.

I have gone on at this length because of the course taken in argument, and I thought that I should express my own views as clearly as possible. Whether the approach is to review a principle, or to determine the need to broaden an existing category, or to determine whether the circumstances of the case warrant the recognition of a new category, the considerations are basically similar although the required urgencies may differ in degree. Assuming the circumstances of a case fall within a relevant principle, their categorization will depend on the analysis of the Judge. I now turn to the principle of nuisance.

Much has been written by authors of distinction on the principle of nuisance. For example *Clerk & Lindsell on Torts,* 13th ed. (1969), p. 780, para. 1391, opens the subject in this way: "The essence of nuisance is a condition or activity which unduly interferes with the use or enjoyment of land." As the text of the paragraph shows, this definition of principle may be unduly restrictive in respect of public nuisance by confining its operation to the use or enjoyment of land, but that is not in issue here. In respect of private nuisance this is said:

> Nuisance is an act or omission which is an interference with, disturbance of or annoyance to a person in the exercise or enjoyment of ... (b) his ownership or occupation of land or of some easement, profit, or other right used or enjoyed in connection with land ...

And at p. 781, para. 1393, this is said:

> A private nuisance may be and usually is caused by a person doing on his own land something which he is lawfully entitled to do. His conduct only becomes a nuisance when the consequences of his acts are not confined to his own land but extend to the land of his neighbour by ...

There follows a statement of three categories in which it has been recognized that the principle is applicable. It is the third that is relevant here: "(3) unduly interfering with his neighbour in the comfortable and convenient enjoyment of his land". A number of the illustrations given of this category support the view that it is not necessary to attract the application of the principle that the matter complained of should emanate from the defendant's land, no more than it is for public nuisance. As pointed out in many texts, the maxim *sic utere tuo ut alienum non laedas* is frequently invoked in the cases and when this is done the maxim is employed as a statement of the principle of nuisance. The maxim is certainly of sufficient vintage to warrant such employment. It is attributed to Lord Coke and translated and defined in the Dictionary of English Law by Earl Jowitt, vol. 2, p. 1639, in these terms: "(9 Co. Rep. 59) (Use your own property so as not to injure your neighbour's) Use your own rights so that you do not interfere with those of another." The definition in brackets speaks of property, not land. The second definition is even broader and gives full support to those cases that do not confine the principle to emanations from land, nor even to the use by the defendant of his "property" (in the narrow sense) in creating the matter complained of.

The Latin maxim was criticized as a statement of principle by Lord Wright in *Sedleigh-Denfield v. O'Callaghan et al.,* [1940] A.C. 880 at p. 903:

> This, like most maxims, is not only lacking in definiteness but is also inaccurate. An occupier may make in many ways a use of his land which causes damage to the neighbouring land-owners and yet be free from liability.

With respect, it seems to me that Lord Wright is here treating the categories as the principle itself. It is out of the principle that the categories have come to be recognized: In *Clerk & Lindsell,* p. 784, para. 1395, this is said:

> The acts complained of as constituting the nuisance, such as noise, smells or vibration, will usually be lawful acts which only become wrongful from the circumstances under which they are performed, such as the time, place, extent or the manner of performance.

Support for this statement may be found in *St. Helen's Smelting Co. v. Tipping* (1865), 11 H.L.C. 642, 11 E.R. 1483. The protean aspect of the principle is apparent from the many cases and texts. I think that of it, equally with its relative, negligence, the categories are never closed. The cases on watching and besetting are particularly in point. It seems to me that the frequent reference in the cases to nuisance emanating from the land of the defendants reflects only the circumstances of the particular facts before the Court, not an intentional limitation on the scope of the principle. This is acknowledged in the third passage above taken from *Clerk & Lindsell.* In saying this, I am aware of the dictum of Lord Wright in *Sedleigh-Denfield v. O'Callaghan* [at p. 903]: "The ground of responsibility is the possession and control of the land from which the nuisance proceeds." But, with respect, I am in agreement with the interpretation put on it by Wilson, C.J.S.C., in *Newman et al. v. Conair Aviation Ltd. et al.* (1972), 33 D.L.R. (3d) 474 at pp. 479-80, [1973] 1 W.W.R. 316 at p. 322 (B.C.), that Lord Wright did not intend it to be read restrictively.

In *J. Lyons & Sons v. Wilkins,* [1899] 1 Ch. 255, members of a trade union on strike picketed the plaintiff's works and the works of a subcontractor of the plaintiff. This was found to amount to watching and besetting. Lindley, M.R., said at pp. 267-8:

> The truth is that to watch or beset a man's house with a view to compel him to do or not to do what is lawful for him not to do or to do is wrongful and without lawful authority unless some reasonable justification for it is consistent with the evidence. Such conduct seriously interferes with the ordinary comfort of human existence and ordinary enjoyment of the house beset, and such conduct would support an action on the case for a nuisance at common law: see *Bamford v. Turnley* 3 B. & S. 62, *Broder v. Saillard* 2 Ch. D. 692, 701, per Jessel M.R., *Walter v. Selfe* 4 De G. & Sm. 315, and *Crump v. Lambert* L.R. 3 Eq. 409.

Chitty, L.J., held the same view. He said at pp. 271-2:

> But further, the acts of watching or besetting here proved in reference to the 4th subsection, and done with the view mentioned, were acts in themselves unlawful at common law, and are not made lawful by the Legislature. In my opinion they constitute a nuisance at common law. True it is that every annoyance is not a nuisance; the annoyance must be of a serious character, and of such a degree as to interfere with the ordinary comforts of life. To watch or beset a man's house for the length of time and in the manner and with the view proved would undoubtedly constitute a nuisance of an aggravated character.

The acts of watching and besetting were not, of course, carried on within premises occupied by the defendants. They were carried on, I infer, on property to which the public had access. The right of the defendants to be on a public place was so abused to the detriment of the plaintiffs that it was held they had committed a common law nuisance, as well as a breach of s.7 of the *Conspiracy, and Protection of Property Act, 1875*. The point is dealt with specifically by Devlin, J. [at trial], in *Esso Petroleum Co. Ltd. v. Southport Corp.,* [1956] A.C. 218 at p. 224:

> I think that it is convenient to begin by considering whether there is a cause of action in nuisance. It is clear that to give a cause of action for private nuisance the matter complained of must affect the property of the plaintiffs. But I know of no principle that it must emanate from land belonging to the defendant.

[See also [1953] 2 All E.R. 1204 at p. 1207 (Q.B.), revd [1954] 2 Q.B. 182 (C.A.).] He then referred to *Cunard et al. v. Antifyre, Ltd.*, [1933] 1 K.B. 551, and went on to say [at pp. 224-5]:

> It is clear from that statement of principle that the nuisance must affect the property of the plaintiff; and it is true that in the vast majority of cases it is likely to emanate from the neighbouring property of the defendant. But no statement of principle has been cited to me to show that the latter is a prerequisite to a cause of action; and I can see no reason why, if land or water belonging to the public, or waste land, is misused by the defendant, or if the defendant as a licensee or trespasser misuses someone else's land, he should not be liable for the creation of a nuisance in the same way as an adjoining occupier would be.

That case arose out of the discharge of oil from a vessel into a river, in consequence of which damage ensued to the adjoining foreshore. The case went on to the House of Lords but their Lordships took the view that the case turned on negligence and did not discuss the principle of nuisance.

More recently, Stamp, J., commented on common law nuisance in *Torquay Hotel Co. Ltd. v. Cousins et al.*, [1968] 3 W.L.R. 540. The defendants had picketed the plaintiff's hotel in the course of a trade dispute. Amongst other issues was that of nuisance on which Stamp, J., said in part at p. 554:

> I turn to consider picketing. In view of my decision that what was done by the defendants in relation to the plaintiff company was not done in contemplation or furtherance of a trade dispute, the defendants had no statutory protection for any tort which they may commit in this regard. At common law a plaintiff is entitled to the lawful use and enjoyment of his property, and a substantial interference with that use and enjoyment is a nuisance. In my judgment picketing outside the entrance of a plaintiff's hotel, if persisted in, for the purpose of persuading tradesmen and their employees from delivering supplies vital to the running of the hotel in order to compel the plaintiffs to submit to the defendants' demand is thus, prima facie, a common law nuisance.

For this he drew support from *J. Lyons & Sons v. Wilkins, supra.*

The nature of the activities which may constitute a private nuisance were considered by Lord Evershed, M.R., in *Thompson-Schwab et al. v. Costaki et al.*, [1956] 1 All E.R. 652, in a case in which the complaint of the plaintiff was that the defendant's adjoining premises were used for purposes of prostitution. At pp. 653-4 he adopted the third passage from *Clerk & Lindsell* above quoted and went on to say:

> The forms which activities constituting actionable nuisance may take are exceedingly varied, and there is the highest authority for saying that they are not capable of precise or close definition. If the principle is rightly stated in the passage which I have read, then it must depend on the facts of each particular case whether the conditions, which I have stated as required to constitute a nuisance, are satisfied; and in considering whether they are satisfied or not the count must apply to the matter the usages of civilised society as they may be at the relevant date.
>
> In *Sedleigh-Denfield v. O'Callaghan* ([1940] 3 All E.R. 349) LORD WRIGHT said (ibid., at p. 364):
>
> "It is impossible to give any precise or universal formula, but it may broadly be said that a useful test is perhaps what is reasonable according to the ordinary usages of mankind

> living in society, or, more correctly, in a particular society. The forms which nuisance may take are protean."

And Romer, L.J., said, at p. 656:

> The second point on which the defendants rely is that nothing can constitute a private nuisance at law unless it affects the reasonable enjoyment of other premises in a physical way. This is only an interlocutory application, and at the trial no doubt that point will be taken again and may be argued at greater length, but my present impression is that it is unsound. It appears to be an unwarrantable gloss on the law on the subject as formulated in the text-books, and, what is perhaps more important, it appears to be inconsistent with the judgments of this court in *J. Lyons & Sons v. Wilkins* ([1899] 1 Ch. 255) which was the picketing case.

Parker, L.J., concurred with both. This authority and others were followed by Wilson, C.J.S.C., in *Newman et al. v. Conair Aviation Ltd., supra,* which involved noise and vibration from a low flying aircraft.

It is clear to me that the protracted and persistent harassment of the brother and the father in their homes, and in the case of the brother as well in his office, by abuse of the telephone system is within the principle of private nuisance as it has been recognized in the authorities I have referred to. The question is whether the calls amounted to undue interference with the comfortable and convenient enjoyment by the plaintiffs of their respective premises. I can conceive that persistent and unwanted telephone calls could become an harassment even if the subject-matter is essentially agreeable. The deliberate and persistent ringing of the telephone cannot but affect the senses in time, and operate on the nervous system as the evidence discloses. No special damage is required to support an injunction: it is the loss of the amenities of the premises in substantial degree that is involved.

I think that the interests of our developing jurisprudence would be better served by approaching invasion of privacy by abuse of the telephone system as a new category, rather than seeking by rationalization to enlarge the third category recognized by *Clerk & Lindsell.* We are dealing with a new factor. Heretofore the matters of complaint have reached the plaintiff's premises by natural means; sound through the air waves, pollution in many forms carried by air currents, vibrations through the earth, and the like. Here, the matters complained of arise within the premises through the use by the appellant of communication agencies in the nature of public utilities available to everyone, which the plaintiffs have caused to serve their premises. They are non-selective in the sense that so long as they are employed by the plaintiffs they have no control over the incoming communications. Nevertheless there are differences between the two agencies of telephone and mail and it does not necessarily follow from their similarities that both should be accepted into a new category.

The telephone system is so much the part of the daily life of society that many look on it as a necessity. Its use is certainly taken as a right at least in a social sense. It virtually makes neighbours not only of the persons close at hand, but those in distant places, other cities, other countries. It is a system provided for rational and reasonable communication between people, and its abuse by invasion of privacy is a matter of general interest within the meaning given the phrase by Lord Atkin in *Fender v. St. John-Mildmay,* [1938] A.C. 1. It is essential to the operation of such a system that a call from someone be signalled to the intended receiver by sound such as the ringing of a bell. The receiver cannot know who is calling him until he answers. Calls must be answered if the system is to work. There are not many who would assert that protection against invasion of privacy by telephone would be a judicial idiosyncrasy. Further than that, the people of this Province through the Legislature have expressed a public interest in the proper use of the system in enacting s.31 of the *Alberta Government Telephones Act*.

In *Clerk & Lindsell*, p. 785, para. 1396, this is said: "A nuisance of this kind, to be actionable, must be such as to be a real interference with the comfort or convenience of living according to the standards of the average man." This statement is amply supported by authority and I take it to be applicable to invasion of privacy. The proof here of real interference is well nigh overwhelming. All of these considerations lead me to accept the statement of Townley, J., in *Stoakes et al. v. Brydges*, [1958] Q.W.N. 9 at p. 10:

> It is quite a lawful use of his premises to use the instrument installed thereon for the purpose for which it was quite obviously intended. But there are numerous cases in the books which clearly show that although a person may be using his premises for the conduct of some operation perfectly lawful in itself, he must not so conduct that operation as to interfere materially with the health or comfort of other persons in the ordinary enjoyment of their premises. I do not think that this restriction is to be confined merely to interference with the health and comfort of neighbouring occupiers or owners strictly so called. I think any person who comes within the ambit of the operation and whose health or comfort in the ordinary enjoyment of his premises is interfered with to the requisite degree may take action to restrain that interference. The category of nuisances, particularly by such potentially noxious things as noise, is not closed and, it seems to me, will never be closed whilst human ingenuity is still attempting to devise fresh means of communicating or disseminating sound. Suppose a public address or Tannoy system is used under such conditions as to interfere materially with the sleep or rest of persons living in the vicinity I apprehend that it is not only the occupiers of those premises which immediately adjoin the source of the noise who may take action but also those whose premises though not immediately adjoining that source, nevertheless are situated within the radius of its effect.

I am of opinion that the brother and the father have established a claim in nuisance by invasion of privacy through abuse of the system of telephone communications.

There remains the question whether the sister-in-law herself has a right of action in nuisance against the appellant. The injunction against telephone calls to the matrimonial home will, of course, benefit her and the children: *Broder v. Saillard* (1876), 2 Ch.D. 692 at p. 703; but that is not the point. She claims in her own right. For the appellant it is urged that at least as far as the sister-in-law is concerned it is the substance of the calls, not their frequency, that is the real matter of complaint, and that nuisance extends only to harassment of the senses, not to sensibilities. The evidence on which this submission is made is based on one question and answer in cross-examination, and in the context of the whole of her evidence it is apparent that the subject-matter of the telephone calls was an added irritant in the harassment. In any event, I do not think there is any validity in this attempted fine distinction. I have pointed out above that in my opinion there may be harassment even although the subject-matter of the telephone calls would otherwise be agreeable in nature.

The texts rely on *Malone v. Laskey et al.*, [1907] 2 K.B. 141, as authority denying a right of action to a wife, and this is invoked on behalf of the appellant. In that case the defendant owner had let premises to a tenant, Witherby & Co., and this tenant had sublet the premises to a company. Malone was the manager of the subtenant company and occupied a part of the premises apparently as part of the consideration for his services. The plaintiff was his wife. The defendant created vibrations by the operation of machinery in its adjoining property, in consequence of which a water tank in the premises became insecure and fell on the plaintiff, to her injury. In respect of her claim in nuisance Sir Gorell Barnes, P., said, at p. 151:

> Many cases were cited in the course of the argument in which it had been held that actions for nuisance could be maintained where a person's rights of property had been affected by the nuisance, but no authority was cited, nor in my opinion can any principle of law be formulated, to the effect that a person who has no interest in property, no right of occupation in the proper sense of the term, can maintain an action for a nuisance arising from the vibration caused by the working of an engine in an adjoining house.

And Fletcher Moulton, L.J., said, at pp. 153-4:

> A person in the position of the plaintiff, who was in the premises as a mere licensee, had no right to dictate to Witherby & Co. [*i.e.*, the tenant of the premises] which course they should take, and they seem to have voluntarily permitted the vibration to continue... But, whether that be so or not, it was a matter entirely for the tenant, and a person who is merely present in the house cannot complain of a nuisance which has in it no element of a public nuisance.

I take it from this that he would not have allowed recovery by the husband, either, if he had also sustained injuries: he too was a mere licensee according to the facts. Beyond that it is rather light treatment of a wife, at least in today's society where she is no longer considered subservient to her husband.

In *Cunard et al. v. Antifyre, Ltd.*, [1933] 1 K.B. 551, the plaintiff and his wife occupied a flat on the third floor of a building. He was in possession by virtue of a monthly sublease granted by the tenant of that and other floors of the building. The tenant was the lessee of the defendant. The wife was personally injured in circumstances that amounted to a nuisance on the part of the defendant, if it were actionable by her. She claimed in both nuisance and negligence and recovered on negligence. The claim in nuisance was treated cursorily. Counsel for the wife argued that *Malone v. Laskey* was distinguishable because there the husband was not a tenant and had no estate whatever in the premises. Talbot, J., at p. 557 disposed of the issue shortly, saying that: "... it would manifestly be inconvenient and unreasonable if the right to complain of such interference extended beyond the occupier...". For this he relied on *Malone v. Laskey*.

In *Metropolitan Properties, Ltd. v. Jones,* [1939] 2 All E.R. 202, the position of a wife was not involved at all. Goddard, L.J., treated *Malone v. Laskey* as authority that an occupier must have some legal interest in the land which he claims to have been affected by nuisance. He said [at p. 205]:

> I am bound by *Malone v. Laskey,* in which the Court of Appeal appear to me to have laid down in terms that, unless the plaintiff in an action for nuisance has legal interest in the land which is alleged to be affected by the nuisance, he has no cause of action.

For myself, I do not read *Malone v. Laskey* as being so explicit. The judgments did not recognize any right of occupancy by the husband as against the tenant Witherby & Co., and of course his wife would be in no better position. In the case at bar the brother is, as I infer, the owner of the premises he occupies with his wife, the sister-in-law, and their family.

There is authority that a claim in nuisance is not necessarily restricted to an occupier who has some legally demonstrable and enforceable right of occupation. In *Foster v. Warblington Urban Council,* [1906] 1 K.B. 648, a substantial *de facto* occupation was recognized as sufficient. There, the plaintiff sued on nuisance affecting his oyster pond which he had used for many years for the storage of oysters. There was much controversy over his legal right of occupancy, and after discussing this Vaughan Williams, L.J., said at pp. 659-60:

> But, even if title could not be proved, in my judgment there has been such an occupation of these beds for such a length of time — not that the length of time is really material for this purpose — as would entitle the plaintiff as against the defendants, who have no interest in the foreshore, to sustain this action for the injury which it is alleged has been done by the sewage to his oysters so kept in those beds.

Thus, a distinction is drawn between one who is "merely present" and occupancy of a substantial nature. In the latter case it is the fact of the occupation that supports the action, although admittedly the legal aspect of an occupation may well have an influence on the conclusion. I would not think trespass, even if persisted in, would ground an action in nuisance.

Here we have a wife harassed in the matrimonial home. She has a status, a right to live there with her husband and children. I find it absurd to say that her occupancy of the matrimonial home is insufficient to found an action in nuisance. In my opinion she is entitled to the same relief as is her husband, the brother.

As to the unwanted mail, the evidence does not show that the plaintiffs have been unduly disturbed in their enjoyment of their respective premises. In such circumstances, to discuss further the use of the mails as a possible vehicle of harassment would be only *obiter*.

In the result the judgment roll should be varied by limiting para. 2(b) to harassment by telephone, and by personal contact which I take it refers to trespass to the person. Undoubtedly the major point in the appeal is invasion of privacy by telephone communications, and the appellant has failed on this issue. I would dismiss the appeal, save as to the variation above noted in the judgment roll, with costs to the respondents on the fifth column.

Appeals dismissed, with variations of trial judgments.

5.3.2.5 *Capan* v. *Capan* (1981) 14 C.C.L.T. 191 (Ont. H.C.)

OSLER J.: — This was a motion on behalf of the defendant for an order striking out the statement of claim and dismissing the action on the ground that the statement of claim discloses no reasonable cause of action.

The action was commenced by a generally endorsed writ, claiming "damages for continuing mental and physical harassment and invasion of privacy". The plaintiff and defendant were married on April 22, 1972, and separated from September 1977, until May 1978, at which time the plaintiff returned to the matrimonial home in order to be with her infant son. After a brief period of reconciliation, the plaintiff and defendant separated September 1978, and have not lived together since that time.

For purposes of this motion, the parties accepted, as they must, the facts as set out in the statement of claim, and it is common ground that I should not strike out the statement of claim or dismiss the action unless I must conclude that the plaintiff's action could not possibly succeed and that it is beyond doubt that no reasonable cause of action has been shown.

Paragraph 4 of the statement of claim states that during the later years of cohabitation and during the periods of separation "the defendant has incessantly and unlawfully persisted in molesting, annoying and harassing the plaintiff, invading her privacy, and interfering with her right to establish a separate life of her own". Particulars are given of the alleged abuse...

It is stated that, as a result of the behaviour described, the plaintiff lives in a state of nervous tension and that her sleep, her appetite and her work have been interfered with and her life made miserable "by the jealous scrutiny and interference of the defendant". She therefore claims damages "for harassment and invasion of privacy".

Counsel for the defendant submitted before me that a plaintiff should normally join all known causes of action and that, by limiting herself to the claim as above described, the defendant will be unable to rely at trial upon any of the nominate torts which might be applicable to certain of the conduct described, such as trespass, nuisance or assault. Counsel for the plaintiff submitted that this was a risk she was fully and deliberately prepared to run and that, while one or more of the nominate torts might well have been enumerated, the cumulative effect of the defendant's actions amounted to something more than the sum of all those actions and, together, they amounted to what could be described as a continuing intent and attempt to change the quality of the defendant's life.

While the allegations in the statement of claim included harassment and invasion of privacy, the latter concept founded the arguments before me and it is principally with that claim that I shall deal in these reasons.

It might be enough to state, as I do, that I have been referred to no reported case in Ontario that has decided that a right to privacy will not be protected by the Courts of this province. This very finding was made by Parker J. as he then was, on a motion similar to this one in *Krouse v. Chrysler Can. Ltd.*, [1970] 3 O.R. 135 at 136, 1 C.P.R. (2d) 218, 12 D.L.R. (3d) 463, where he stated:

> "...It may be that the action is novel, but it has not been shown to me that the Court in this jurisdiction would not recognize a right of privacy."

He went on to state that the plaintiff had the right to have the issue decided after trial. There has been, in my view, no real development of the law in that respect in this province since that judgment of Parker J. was reported. At trial [reported at [1972] 2 O.R. 133, 5 C.P.R. (2d) 30, 25 D.L.R. (3d) 49], Haines J. decided that the plaintiff had a claim that should be supported, based on passing-off. He specifically declined to rule on the issue of whether there is a common law right to privacy in Ontario.

On appeal, Estey J.A., as he then was, for the Court of Appeal, in 1 O.R. (2d) 225, 13 C.P.R. (2d) 28, 40 D.L.R. (3d) 15, found that there was not, on the facts, a passing-off established and the action was dismissed. In so finding, Estey J.A. found it unnecessary to deal with the concept of the right to privacy and the question of whether such alleged right will be protected by our Courts. At p. 229 [O.R.], there is a plain finding that:

> "In argument before us the respondent did not found his claim in the common law action of passing-off or, indeed, in any alleged right of privacy,..."

The action was really founded upon a claim that the plaintiff had commercial rights flowing from the use of his picture and that it was such right, described by Estey J.A. as "the right to realize upon this potential" that was allegedly injured by the unauthorized use of the defendant's photograph.

The only case cited from the Ontario decisions, therefore, if it was concerned with privacy at all, had no bearing upon the sort of invasion complained of in the present instance.

Two cases of more relevance are found in Quebec and in Alberta. In *Robbins v. C.B.C. (Que.),* [1958] Que S.C. 152, 12 D.L.R. (2d) 35, Scott A.C.J. found that in a television programme originating in Toronto, viewers were asked to telephone and write to the plaintiff who lived in the Montreal area. As a result, the plaintiff's telephone began ringing and continued to ring late into the evening and continued thus for three succeeding days until he had his telephone number changed. Chief Justice Scott had no difficulty in finding that, under Quebec law, art. 1053 of the Civil Code made the defendant responsible for the conduct complained of and that it "constituted a grievous, positive, wrongful act against Dr. Robbins, making the defendant corporation responsible for the damages flowing from such wrongful act". He assumed, for the purposes of his judgment, that the law of Ontario was the same as that of Quebec.

More closely in point is *Motherwell v. Motherwell,* [1976] 6 W.W.R. 550, 1 A.R. 47, 73 D.L.R. (3d) 62 (C.A.). Clement J.A. who delivered the judgment of the Court, reviewed the allegations upon which an injunction had been granted, concentrating upon the claims that the defendant had contacted the plaintiffs by telephone with false accusations and, with respect to one plaintiff, had subjected him to constant harassment by telephone. He set out that the arguments advanced by the appellant drew a distinction between nuisance and invasion of privacy. It was submitted that invasion of privacy does not come within the principle of private nuisance and that it is a species of activity not recognized as remediable by the common law. At p. 67 [D.L.R.] is found the following:

> "...It is urged that the common law does not have within itself the resources to recognize invasion of privacy as either included in an existing category or as a new category of nuisance, and that it has lost its original power, by which indeed it created itself, to note new ills arising in a growing and changing society and pragmatically to establish a principle to meet the need for control and remedy; and then by categories to develop the principle as the interests of justice make themselves sufficiently apparent."

At p. 70, reference is made to Clerk and Lindsell on Torts (13th ed., 1969), where nuisance is defined as "a condition or activity which unduly interferes with the use or enjoyment of land" [p. 780, para. 1391] and the learned Justice of Appeal concentrates upon a specific category discussed by that text under the description of "unduly interfering with his neighbour in the comfortable and convenient enjoyment of his land".

At p. 71, Clement J.A. quotes from one definition in Jowitt's dictionary of law [Dictionary of English Law, vol. 2, p. 1639] in these terms, "Use your own rights so that you do not interfere with those of another." The judgment goes on to draw distinctions between various illustrations that have been given in the texts and in the cases, apparently with a view to underlining that not all conduct that has been enjoined by virtue of its being characterized as a private nuisance has in fact affected the use of land. In the end, however, Clement J.A. seems to find that abuse of privacy by use of the telephone is properly characterized as a form of nuisance. At p. 74 is found the following:

> "I think that the interest of our developing jurisprudence would be better served by approaching invasion of privacy by abuse of the telephone system as a new category, rather than seeking by rationalization to enlarge the third category recognized by *Clerk & Lindsell.*"

At p. 75, after observing that, "There are not many who would assert that protection against invasion of privacy by telephone would be a judicial idiosyncrasy," a further quotation from Clerk and Lindsell [p. 785, para. 1396] is set out in the following terms, "A nuisance of this kind, to be actionable, must be such as to be a real interference with the comfort or convenience of living according to the standards of the average man."

The conduct of the defendant here, assuming the statement of claim to be factual, comes well within that description. It is, therefore, entirely possible, as stated at the outset, that the Judge trying the action will find that nuisance, trespass or assault describes every part of the conduct objected to. As I apprehend the argument of counsel for the plaintiff, however, it is submitted that upon analysis all claims of trespass or nuisance are founded upon the use of land and the right thereto. What is complained of here is, in its very essence, an abuse of personal rights to privacy and to freedom from harassment. The common law, developing as it did from property concerns, speaks vaguely or not at all of personal rights.

As pointed out above, it has not been demonstrated that the rights referred to will not be recognized by our Courts nor that their infringement will not found a cause of action. In my view, it would not be right, on a motion of this kind, for the Court to deprive itself of the opportunity to determine, after hearing the evidence, whether such right exists and whether it should be protected.

In the course of argument, extensive reference was made to cases in various jurisdictions within the United States of America in which these matters have been considered. I cite one of these judgments not only for the colourful nature of its language but as a succinct, if possibly oversimplified, statement of the question. In *Fergerstrom v. Hawaiian Ocean View Estates* (1968), 441 P. 2d 141, Levinson Justice for the Supreme Court of Hawaii, sitting in appeal, let fall the following:

> "The defendant contends that since the ancient common law did not afford a remedy for invasion of privacy, and there is no case in Hawaii recognizing such a right, only the legislature can provide for such a cause of action. The magnitude of the error in the defendant's position approaches Brobdingnagian proportions. To accept it would constitute more than accepting a limited view of the essence of the common law. It would be no less than an absolute annihilation of the common law system. This spectre of judicial self-emasculation has pervaded one case in which the court accepted this line of argument."

The Court goes on to state, at p. 143 that:

> "...The common law system would have withered centuries ago had it lacked the ability to expand and adapt to the social, economic, and political changes inherent in a vibrant human society."

I cannot conclude that the plaintiff may not succeed at trial. The application must therefore be dismissed with costs to the plaintiff-respondent, in the cause.

Application dismissed.

5.3.2.6 *Saccone* v. *Orr* (1982), 19 C.C.L.T. 37 (Ont. Co. Ct.)

September 11, 1981. JACOB CO. CT. J. (orally): — In the matter of Augustine Saccone, plaintiff, and Robert Orr, defendant, I will try to be as cohesive as I possibly can in giving this judgment orally, because I realize that as a result of this action, we may be trespassing on some new law.

Let me say at the outset, for the purpose of the record, that at the opening of trial the defendant, through his counsel, admitted the allegations in paras. 1, 2, and 3 of the plaintiff's statement of claim, and also the allegation in para. 4 only as regards to the taping of the telephone conversation as stated in the first two lines of that paragraph. Paragraph 5 is also admitted by the defendant, through his counsel, as is all of para. 6 as set out on pp. 2-6 inclusive, that is, to the top of p. 6 of the statement of claim.

Also at the opening of trial, the plaintiff, through his counsel, withdraws his action as stated in para. 12 of the statement of claim as to libel and slander and the Criminal Code, R.S.C. 1970, c.C-34. And at the request of plaintiff's counsel and upon the consent of defendant's counsel, para. 13(a) of the statement of claim was amended to read: "Damages in the sum of $7,500.00 against the defendant Orr for invasion of privacy with malice." The words "defamation of character" are expunged from para. 13(a).

Also at the commencement of trial, defendant's counsel, Mr. Crowe, moved that the action be dismissed, mainly on the grounds that there is no such [cause of] action as "invasion of privacy" known to the common law and insofar as this province particularly is concerned.

In defence of that motion, plaintiff's counsel cited to me several cases, most of which I have read and attempted to digest. One of those was *Krouse v. Chrysler Can. Ltd.*, [(1973), 1 O.R. (2d) 225, 40 D.L.R. (3d) 15, 13 C.P.R. (2d) 28, reversing] [1972] 2 O.R. 133, 25 D.L.R. (3d) 49, 5 C.P.R. (2d) 30, motion to strike out claim dismissed [1970] 3 O.R. 135, 1 C.P.R. (2d) 218, 12 D.L.R. (3d) 463 (C.A.). Mr. Justice Haines, at p. 140 [[1972] 2 O.R.] of that case stated:

> "I specifically decline to rule on the issue of whether there is a common law right to privacy in Ontario."

And again on p. 140, after having cited and referred to several other cases, he went on to say:

> "Courts do have the power, and must exercise the power, of adapting the common law to the facts of the day."

And then, further on the page, he went on to say [pp. 140-141]:

> "...where the making of a fundamental pronouncement of law is not essential to the resolution of a lawsuit, this type of necessary and proper judicial law-making should be left to a higher Court. Were it necessary to the resolution of the dispute, I would have no hesitation in making a determination of the issue."

The pleadings in the case at Bar, having been amended as I stated in my opening remarks, actually leave no other issue before me than that upon which I must decide as to whether an action exists with regard to invasion of privacy.

The case in the Alberta Court of Appeal of *Motherwell v. Motherwell,* [1976] 6 W.W.R. 550, 1 A.R. 47, 73 D.L.R. (3d) 62, was actually decided on the question of nuisance, as I read the case. But there were some very pertinent observations made in the judgment of Clement J.A., who gave judgment for the Court in that case. One of those is on p. 70 [D.L.R.] where he said:

> "Whether the approach is to review a principle, or to determine the need to broaden an existing category, or to determine whether the circumstances of the case warrant the recognition of a new category, the considerations are basically similar although the required urgencies may differ in degree. Assuming the circumstances of a case fall within a relevant principle, their categorization will depend upon the analysis of the Judge."

And having said that, he went on to discuss private nuisance, and the judgment turned on that issue.

In the case of *Burnett v. R.* (1979), 23 O.R. (2d) 109, 9 C.P.C. 310, 94 D.L.R. (3d) 281 (H.C.), Mr. Justice O'Driscoll refused to strike out the part of the plaintiff's claim for damages for invasion of privacy, as did Mr. Justice Parker in the *Krouse* [case], supra.

In *Krouse* at p. 136 [[1970] 3 O.R.] Mr. Justice Parker (as he then was), said this:

> "Although this Court has inherent jurisdiction to strike out a statement of claim on the ground that it discloses no reasonable cause of action or stay an action, such power should be sparingly exercised and only when there is no doubt that no cause of action exists. Neither counsel was able to submit any decided case on this point that has been tried in this jurisdiction so it would appear that the matter has not been considered and judicially decided. It may be that the action is novel, but it has not been shown to me that the Court in this jurisdiction would not recognize a right of privacy. The plaintiff therefore has the right to be heard, to have the issue decided after trial."

The remarks of Mr. Justice Parker (as he then was) were quoted with approval by Mr. Justice O'Driscoll in the *Burnett* case, supra. And I tend to go along with Mr. Justice Haines' observations in the *Krouse* case that [p. 154 [1972] 2 O.R.]:

> "Our Courts, and law in general, have an obligation to protect those who for whatever reason cannot protect themselves ... [because] In a very real sense the law belongs to the people and ... they must have access to the forum of their choice without fear that even though vindicated in principle they will suffer financially."

The latter part of those remarks was, of course, dealing with the issue of costs, to which I will address myself at the conclusion of my findings.

In this case, the facts are relatively simple: the defendant, Orr, recorded a private conversation with the plaintiff, that is, a conversation which took place over the telephone. These men were good friends. The plaintiff subsequently found out about the tape, went to the defendant's office and, Mr. Orr not being there, told a girl in the office that Mr. Orr was not to use the tape of their conversation on the phone. According to the plaintiff Saccone, he received a call from the defendant Orr that same evening and Mr. Orr denied to Mr. Saccone the existence of the tape, to which the plaintiff replied: "If you have a tape, don't use it or I'll have to sue you." This evidence is not denied and I accept it.

Nevertheless, Mr. Orr did play the taped conversation at a council meeting, apparently to vindicate himself of an accusation made by a fellow councillor and, as so very often happens in controversial issues of this nature, the tape was printed in The Niagara Falls Review publication and an editorial resulting from the episode was written, both of which are exhibits in this case. The editorial explains the situation very adequately and I feel that I need not elaborate on that any further.

Mr. Saccone stated that a few days after the publication he met Mr. Orr, who apologized for using the tape, to which the plaintiff Saccone replied it was in his lawyer's hands and there [were], on the evidence given before me, no public apologies in the press.

The plaintiff's evidence in chief was that people continued to question him as to what was going on and he reached the point where he didn't want to talk to people, he "just wanted to hide", in his words. He said also as a result he became ill, missed a lot of work as a result of which he lost his job, and that he was under the impression that people seemed cool to him because he wasn't to be trusted, and he felt that Mr. Orr was trying to clear his credibility by damaging Mr. Saccone's credibility.

Now in cross-examination I recall, in answer to a question by Mr. Crowe, defence counsel, Mr. Saccone actually agreed that it was just his impression. I must state that no other persons were called in evidence and the only evidence before me is that of Mr. Saccone.

Mr. Saccone stated in chief as well that he was not claiming special damages on any out-of-pocket expenses. Really, all he's claiming is the embarrassment which he feels he suffered.

He further stated that after the incident he worked for one year with the Niagara Falls Junior-A Club hockey team, with which he had been a long time affiliated or in which he was interested. Again, on cross-examination by Mr. Crowe, he admitted that what was printed was in fact his own words and that what was printed was true insofar as what he said was concerned. He stated that he told Mr. Orr he didn't want to get involved with Mr. Orr and his problems within the council. He further admitted to defendant's council that in 1976 he was ill before he lost his job, and that he really lost so much time that he referred to in chief because of the illness which, in his words, was some disease which flares up now and again as a lung and glandular disorder, and that it resulted in his being in a wheelchair, if I remember his evidence correctly, for some five years prior to 1971. And that the real reason he was laid off from his work was because he lost so much time due to that illness. He admitted that he collected disability insurance and that he had told the Unemployment Insurance Commission that the reason that he lost his job was because of his illness which had caused him to miss so much time off work. He further admitted that he had not lost anything in terms of dollars and cents or damages because of the publication.

As I said, no other witnesses were called in relation to the question of damages and the defendant called no evidence.

The whole case of the plaintiff therefore falls on a question of invasion of privacy in the plane [sic] of a recorded private telephone conversation between the plaintiff and the defendant. There is no doubt that the telephone conversation was recorded without the plaintiff's knowledge or consent. There was also no doubt that Orr denied the existence of the tape, after which he played it at a council meeting despite being told by the plaintiff that if the tape existed he wasn't to use it, and that if he did use it, he would be sued.

It also appears to me quite clear that the defendant's purpose was to vindicate himself and to prove that he was not a liar and the he didn't break confidences. But in fact, as it turns out, he broke the confidence of Mr. Saccone, firstly [by] taping the conversation without Mr. Saccone's knowledge, and secondly by denying the existence of the tape.

Although the plaintiff's evidence as to damages is very weak, I find that he did not lose his job because of this article or the printing of the conversation, nor did he suffer any material loss as a result. His complaint, insofar as the result of the publication of the conversation is concerned, is that he was embarrassed and felt that his confidence had been betrayed.

Be that as it may, it's my opinion that certainly a person must have the right to make such a claim as a result of a taping of a private conversation without his knowledge, and also as against the publication of the conversation against his will or without his consent.

Certainly, for want of a better description as to what happened, this is an invasion of privacy, and despite the very able argument of defendant's counsel that no such action exists, I have come to the conclusion that the plaintiff must be given some right of recovery for what the defendant has in this case done.

It was suggested by plaintiff's counsel that because Mr. Orr denied the existence of the tape and then went on to have it played to council, as a result of which it became published, that that in itself was an action of malice, and he asked me to find that there was an invasion of privacy with malice. I don't accept that argument. I find that the defendant did not act with malice but was really reacting to an allegation by another member of council which he felt obligated to rebut and that his action was not directed intentionally toward harming the plaintiff. I mention that because certainly, on principle, this would have a bearing on the quantum of damages. As I have previously stated, the proven damages are minimal.

As a result of what I have said, I am awarding damages to the plaintiff in the amount of five hundred dollars.

Counsel have already addressed me on the issue of costs on the day of the trial. I spoke to them again this morning with regard to the question of costs, and in that regard, I felt that in this type of action, where there is no indication that the action was in itself frivolous or that it unduly took up the time of the Courts, that costs should perhaps follow the event and not the amount that has been awarded. I am mindful that this is a County Court action. I am also mindful that the award which has been given to the plaintiff is on the Small Claims Court scale.

As I previously quoted from Mr. Justice Haines in the *Krouse* case, a person must have access or should have access to the forum of their choice without fear that, even though vindicated in principle, they will suffer financially. Now, keeping that principle in mind, I realize that if the plaintiff were awarded his costs, they would be taxed on a County Court scale and as a round figure, not being a Taxing Officer, I would assume that that would be somewhere in the neighbourhood of twelve to fifteen hundred dollars. I feel that that would be excessive in light of the circumstances of this case in particular.

On the other hand, I know that it will be argued by defendant's counsel that the award is on a Small Claims Court scale and that costs should be awarded on that scale, which would be probably in costs something around one hundred dollars, which I feel [is] far too little in a case of this kind.

I am, therefore, going to take it upon my self, and I will listen to counsel if they so want to address themselves later, to fix the costs to be paid to the plaintiff by the defendant at five hundred dollars.

Judgment for the plaintiff.

5.3.2.7 Annotation to *Saccone* v. *Orr*, 19 C.C.L.T. 191 (Ont. H.C.)

In this case, once all the plaintiff's more familiar causes of action had been abandoned, Judge Jacob found himself unavoidably confronted with this stark question: Did a paragraph in the statement of claim, alleging "invasion of privacy... with malice," disclose a viable cause of action at common law? In the event, the learned Judge, with becoming trepidation, decided that it did, and awarded general damages of $500 plus costs under this rubric.

As Judge Jacob well realized, authority for such a bold step — the announcement, in effect, of a new common law tort — is both meagre and oblique. He cited certain leading Ontario authorities: the judgment of O'Driscoll J. in *Burnett v. R.* (1979), 23 O.R. (2d) 109, 9 C.P.C. 310, 94 D.L.R. (3d) 281 (H.C.) [a motion to strike out an "invasion of privacy" claim], and those of Parker J. and Haines J., at respectively the interlocutory and trial stages of *Krouse v. Chrysler Can. Ltd.* (1973), 1 O.R. (2d) 225, 40 D.L.R. (3d) 15, 13 C.P.R. (2d) 28, reversing [1972] 2 O.R. 133, 25 D.L.R. (3d) 49, 5 C.P.R. (2d) 30, motion to strike out claim dismissed [1970] 3 O.R. 135, 1 C.P.R. (2d) 218, 12 D.L.R. (3d) 463 (C.A.), all indicate an unwillingness to reject such a new head of liability out of hand. He could, one might note, have added as the most recent authority to that effect, the decision of Osler J., also of the Ontario High Court, in *Capan v. Capan* (1981), 14 C.C.L.T. 191, again merely deciding upon a motion to strike out a claim there, for "harassment and invasion of privacy", but again declining to accede to such a motion.

Stronger, some would say, is the judgment of Henry J. in *Athans v. Can. Adventure Camps Ltd.* (1977), 17 O.R. (2d) 425, 4 C.C.L.T. 20, 34 C.P.R. (2d) 126, 80 D.L.R. (3d) 583 (H.C.) where the plaintiff actually received a remedy in damages. Similar is the recent decision of Montgomery J., in *Heath v. Weist-Barron School of T.V. (Can.) Ltd.* (1981), 18 C.C.L.T. 129, but in fact decided some five weeks later than our present case, in which the learned Judge again declined to strike out, as manifestly unarguable, a statement of claim founded inter alia upon breach of the plaintiff's right to privacy.

Against such hopeful pointers, there is really no contrary authority. Admittedly, the plaintiff in *Krouse,* supra, ultimately lost his action in the Court of Appeal, but in that Court, as Estey J.A. for the Court was careful to point out, the concept of privacy was not relied upon by the plaintiff.

The possible emergence of a new tort of "invasion of privacy" has of course attracted voluminous and sometimes lively academic discussion. While I would not claim to be a completely impartial critic, I would refer readers in particular to a valuable recent book: Aspects of Privacy Law; Essays in Honour of John M. Sharp (1980), Professor R.D. Gibson ed. Covering as it does so many of the varied perspectives of the subject, and in such depth, I consider that it absolves me from making any more fulsome commentary in this annotation than the following list of observations:

(i) The existence or non-existence of a common law tort of invasion of privacy is not an issue which will trouble all Canadian jurisdictions these days. That is because of the enactment of Privacy Acts in the provinces of British Columbia [Privacy Act, R.S.B.C. 1979, c.336], Manitoba [The Privacy Act, 1970 (Man.), c.74 (also C.C.S.M., c.P125)], and Saskatchewan [The Privacy Act, R.S.S. 1978, c.P-24], statutes which (though so far they have engendered very little litigation) empower the Judges in very general terms to evolve tort protection for individual privacy. A particularly valuable discussion of these three statutes is to be found in an essay by Professor P.H. Osborne (Gibson, op. cit., c.4). (See also D. Vaver *What's mine is not yours: Commercial Appropriation of Personality under the British Columbia, Manitoba and Saskatchewan Privacy Acts* (1981), 15 U.B.C.L. Rev. 241.) In addition, the position in Quebec, regarding the delictual protection of privacy, is perceptively analyzed by Professor H.P. Glenn, in an essay forming c.3 of the above-mentioned book.

(ii) The support to be derived from dicta in *Krouse,* even when reinforced by observations in the *Athans* and *Heath* cases, supra, is, as Judge Jacob doubtless realized, not of the strongest. For these cases, if indeed they are properly considered under the heading of "privacy" at all, are *special* privacy cases, cases of "appropriation of personality". That fascinating issue I have analyzed in great, possibly even tiresome detail, elsewhere (J. Irvine *The Appropriation of Personality,* Gibson, op. cit., c.7), so I will spare readers a re-hash of the very conservative thesis developed there. As I there point out, the subsumption of this topic under the heading of "privacy" may owe rather more to tradition, and to the history and format of American privacy treatises, than to any compelling logical analysis. Nonetheless, given the fact that privacy in our law is still a young and malleable "green twig", it is difficult to understand the dogmatic and agitated vehemence of such writers as R. Wacks (cf., e.g., (1981), 97 L.Q.R. 663 at 664) in insisting that appropriation of personality "lies well beyond the land of privacy". One would have thought that there was at least a familial resemblance between the interests invaded in cases like *Athans,* and the pristine concept of privacy.

(iii) The slowness of Canadian Courts — and English ones too — in developing a nominate tort of invasion of privacy, may reflect not so much a distrust of the concept, as a simple lack of need for such a creation. The privacy interest in its myriad forms has long been protected from an equally varied series of affronts and invasions, by the imaginative use of more familiar nominate torts. A good example is the way the tort of private nuisance was pressed into service by the Alberta Courts in *Motherwell v. Motherwell,* [1976] 6 W.W.R. 550, 1 A.R. 47, 73 D.L.R. (3d) 62 (C.A.), an authority cited by Judge Jacob in our present case. This piecemeal but not ineffective approach to what are really privacy suits, has been carefully analyzed by Professor P. Burns, first in his well-known essay in (1976), 54 Can. Bar Rev. 1, and again in a useful revision of that paper in Gibson, op. cit., c.2.

(iv) It might at first seem that on its facts the present case could have been decided under one of those more familiar extant causes of action, namely an action for "breach of confidence", a tort of equitable origin which traces its roots back to the cases, superficially similar to the present, of *Prince Albert v. Strange* (1849), 1 Mac & G. 25, 41 E.R. 1171, and *Argyll v. Argyll,* [1967] Ch. 302, [1965] 1 All E.R. 611. Most cases under this rubric nowadays relate to the disclosure of business information (though see the recent case of *Damien v. O'Mulvenny,* post, p. 48). However, the key to all of these cases (save perhaps the *Argyll* case) is, as Lord Denning M.R. said in a leading case

> "...the broad principle of equity that he who has received information in confidence shall not take unfair advantage of it. He must not make use of it to the prejudice of him who gave it without obtaining [his] consent": *Seager v. Copydex Ltd.,* [1967] 1 W.L.R. 923, [1967] 2 All E.R. 415 at 417.

That suggests that a remedy will be extended only where the initial information was obtained in confidence. There is nothing in the facts of our present case of *Saccone v. Orr* to suggest such a circumstance, the initial taping having been enveloped not so much in confidentiality as in stealth. It is difficult to see how, when once the tape had been obtained, the subsequent strictures of the plaintiff not to make use of it could somehow give rise to a duty to preserve confidentiality. Perhaps, however, I take too narrow a view of this difficult cause of action: see the expert analyses of P.M. North (1972), 12 J.S.P.T.L. 149, and of Professor H.J. Glasbeek, Gibson, op. cit., c.8. Certainly one cannot blame Judge Jacob for feeling that this avenue of decision was closed to him like the others, so that only by frankly acknowledging a tort of invasion of privacy could a remedy be extended.

(v) Should this new tort take root in Ontario law, some obvious and difficult questions will have to be settled at an early stage, concerning the essential nature of the newcomer. First, is "malice", as Judge Jacob seems to suggest, an irrelevance? If so, in what sense is "malice" here used? Secondly, is the new tort a form of action on the case, or is it not? On that academic question may devolve the more practical one, of whether damage is an essential ingredient of any claim for even nominal damages, or whether this tort is actionable per se. In our present case, the plaintiff receives $500 in damages for damages which are in essence (as Judge Jacob points out) no more tangible than "embarrassment". Is this then a tort actionable per se? Certainly, there is nothing in this case which offends common sense, nor is the interest of the plaintiff, here protected, any more fanciful than that familiarly protected by defamation. But one would appreciate early clarification of these issues, if the new tort takes a firm hold on life.

Then again, what are the limits of liability? When will disclosures, such as that perpetrated here, be regarded as privileged? One cannot blame Judge Jacob for declining to address such questions on this occasion. But it will be interesting to see, now that one Judge has finally grasped the nettle and proclaimed the new tort, how his brother Judges receive and develop it.

John Irvine.

5.3.2.8 Notes on Photographs and Rights of Privacy

The law about taking and publishing photographs is largely an aspect of the law of privacy. There is as yet no recognized common law right of privacy as such in the Commonwealth. In Canada, however, constitutional and statutory changes and some recent extensions of traditional tort principles have resulted in the protection of various privacy-related interests. But, until privacy is recognized as a distinct right, photographs may be freely taken and published as long as no established tort or other wrong is committed.

The following illustrates the ways in which photographs may be taken and published without committing a recognized tort.

A. *Taking Photographs*

"... no one possesses a right of preventing another person photographing him any more than he has a right of preventing another person giving a description if not libellous or otherwise wrongful. These rights do not exist." (*Sports and General Press Agency, Ltd.* v. *"Our Dogs" Publishing Co. Ltd.*, [1916] 2 K.B. 880, at 884.)

1. *Interference with the Plaintiff's Land*

a. Trespass to Land.

"Trespass" has been defined as "a wrongful disturbance of another's possession of grounds or land" (*CED*, 3rd, vol. 32, s.1, pp. 142-15). For an action in trespass to land to lie there must be actual physical penetration of the plaintiff's airspace, sub-soil or surface (unless the defendant's acts arose out of unreasonable use of a public thoroughfare). The plaintiff must also prove that he is the occupier of the affected land. Damage need not be proven; but if no real damage is established, only nominal damages will generally be awarded.

To enter another person's airspace, sub-soil or surface without that person's permission and take photographs, then, is an actionable trespass. But, if the photographer remains outside the plaintiff's boundary, there can be no cause of action in trespass. For example, in *Bernstein of Leigh (Baron)* v. *Skyviews and General Ltd.* ([1978] 1 Q.B. 479) the court held that no actionable trespass occurred when the defendant repeatedly flew over the plaintiff's land taking photographs of the plaintiff and his home, which were later offered to him for sale. The plaintiff's right to the airspace above his land was found to extend only to such height necessary for the ordinary use and enjoyment of land and the structures upon it. The defendant's flights were well above the ground and they did not interfere with any use to which the plaintiff might have wished to put his land.

In discussing whether photographing of the plaintiff and his estate was an invasion of privacy, Mr. Justice Griffith stated:

> There is, however, no law against taking a photograph, and the mere taking of a photograph cannot turn an act which is not a trespass into the plaintiff's air space into one that is a trespass. (p. 485).

More recently, in *Belzberg* v. *BCTV Broadcasting System Ltd.* (B.C.S.C. 1981 (unreported)) an action in trespass was brought against a television news reporter and his cameraman for taking photographs of the front of the plaintiff's house, without permission, in the course of visiting the plaintiff's house to seek an interview. In dismissing the action, Mr. Justice Macfarlane stated that if he were in error in holding that there had been no trespass, the trespass was so insignificant in the circumstances that only nominal damages would be merited.

The latter reasoning was followed in *Silber* v. *BCTV Broadcasting System Ltd.* ((1985), 69 B.C.L.R. 34 (S.C.)). A news reporter and his cameraman were held to have committed a trespass in filming a strike occurring in the plaintiff's parking lot after the plaintiff told them he did not want them on the premises. Although the court held that the plaintiff had a right to exclude trespassers (because the property was private), only nominal damages were awarded. It was the court's view that "the real substance of the claim was for violation of privacy."

Trespass to land is a limited cause of action. It has rarely been successfully invoked against individuals taking photographs. The cases will probably become rarer as modern techniques make it possible to take photographs at greater and greater distances.

b. Private Nuisance.

A private nuisance has been described as any "real interference with the comfort or convenience of living according to the standards of the average man" (*Motherwell*

v. *Motherwell* (1976), 73 D.L.R. (3d) 62 (Alta. C.A.)). The tort of private nuisance is not limited to physical intrusions on a plaintiff's land. And even those who are occupiers of land may have standing to bring an action in private nuisance.

Nevertheless, the tort of private nuisance offers only modest protection. As Mr. Justice Griffith said in *Bernstein:*

> The present action is not founded in nuisance for no court would regard the taking of a single photograph as an actionable nuisance. But if the circumstances were such that a plaintiff was subjected to harassment of constant surveillance of his house from the air, accompanied by the photographing of his every activity, I am far from saying that the court would not regard such a monstrous invasion of his privacy as an actionable nuisance for which they would give relief (p. 489).

2. *Interference with the Plaintiff's Person*

Although the torts falling under this head are rarely invoked with success against photographers, their existence should not be ignored.

a. Battery.

A battery is any intentional harmful or offensive contact with the person of another. The offensive contact must have been intended or known to be substantially certain to result before it will constitute an actionable battery. Even the least touching of another in anger is actionable. (*Cole* v. *Turner* (1705), 87 E.R. 907 (N.P.))

b. Assault.

Intentionally creating in another person an apprehension of imminent harmful or offensive contact is an actionable assault. Physical contact itself is not necessary to form an action in assault. All that is required is the intent to arouse apprehension of physical contact. Accordingly, the use of a flash camera in a menacing way might be actionable.

c. Intentional Infliction of Mental Suffering.

If a photographer takes a picture with the intent of causing emotional distress in another, and in consequence causes physical harm through mental distress, an action may lie. (*Wilkinson* v. *Downton,* [1897] 2 Q.B. 57). Accordingly, even the use of a photograph in an advertisement or its publication without consent could render a publisher or advertiser liable for any emotional distress it causes if there is some tangible physical injury as evidence of the nervous shock. The practical application of the tort of intentional infliction of mental suffering against unwanted photography is severely limited by the requirement that accompanying physical harm be proved.

B. *Using Photographs*

1. *Use of Photographs for Commercial Purposes*

a. Breach of Contract, Confidence and Copyright.

Publishing photographs without the consent of the individual photographed may be actionable under various torts. For example, in *Pollard* v. *Photographic Co.* ((1888),

40 Ch.D. 345) the plaintiff had her picture taken by the defendant and commissioned copies for herself. The defendant made extra copies for himself, intending to sell them and exhibit one as an example of his work. The court granted an injunction restraining the sale or exhibition of the pictures, finding an implied term of the contract that no copies be made or used beyond what had been expressly agreed by the parties. It was also held that an individual, sitting for a photographer, had, in effect, created a relationship of confidence in which the photographer could not, without consent, use the photographs for his own advantage.

And in *Tuck* v. *Priester* ((1887), 19 Q.B.B. 639) the plaintiffs agreed to have the defendant make a number of photographic copies of a painting which they owned. The defendant made extra copies for himself and offered them for sale, in competition with the plaintiffs. An injunction was granted prohibiting the defendant from selling these copies and damages were awarded to the plaintiffs because the court found it to be an implied contractual term that the defendant would not make or use extra copies of the painting. The same result may flow from a breach of copyright. (*Williams* v. *Settle,* [1960] 1 W.L.R. 1072 (C.A.))

Even in the absence of a breach of a contractual term, a court will restrain the publication of a photograph, or information, which has been obtained in confidence (cf. *Argyll* v. *Argyll,* [1965] 2 W.L.R. 780; *Prince Albert* v. *Strange* (1849), 41 E.R. 1171). The cases establish that no proprietary interest need be proven by the plaintiff and the defendant need not have been a party to the confidence, as long as he knew that the information or material was originally obtained in confidence.

b. Passing Off and Appropriation of Personality.

A defendant commits the tort of passing off by claiming that the goods he is offering are those created or manufactured by the plaintiff. Thus, Kellogg's can sue me if I put my own concoction in a cardboard box and try to market it as "Kellogg's Corn Flakes". Neither actual deception nor resulting damage need be proven. All that is required is evidence that the defendant's practice was likely to mislead the public and involved a substantial risk of detriment to the plaintiff's business activities. This tort may also enable an individual whose image, or name, or voice is used by another with the intention of deceiving to obtain an injunction, damages, or an accounting of profits.

In *Krouse* v. *Chrysler Ltd.* ((1974) 40 D.L.R. 15 (Ont. C.A.)) an enhanced photograph of the respondent, a professional football player, was printed without his consent in a promotional brochure put out by the appellant company which contained a list of football players and their team numbers. Mr. Justice Estey held that a case of passing off had not been made out "because the buying public would not buy the products of the appellant on the assumption that they had been designed or manufactured by the respondent ... [and] the spotter was not produced by the appellants to be passed off on the public in competition with a similar product marketed by the respondent" (p. 25). However, in *Falconbridge Nickel Mines Ltd.* v. *Falconbridge Land Dev. Co. Ltd.* ([1974] 5 W.W.R. 385) the British Columbia Supreme Court followed the New Zealand case of *Henderson* v. *Rodeo Corporation Pty. Ltd.* ([1960] S.R.N.S.W. 576 (S.C.)) and held that overlapping business activity is not a necessary requirement of the tort of passing off.

Since the *Krouse* decision, in order to succeed in an action for passing off, in Ontario at least, the plaintiff must be engaged in a business which is similar to, or overlaps with, the business of the defendant. It has also been held that the plaintiff must establish that the relevant segments of the public would be likely to confuse the business of the plaintiff with that of the defendant. (*Athans* v. *Canadian Adventure Camps Ltd.* (1977) 17 O.R. (2d) 425 (H.C.))

The unauthorized use of a person's picture, or name, in aid of advertising or other commercial purpose, may also be actionable under the newly emerging tort of appropriation of personality. (*Heath* v. *Weist-Barron School of Television (Canada) Ltd.* (1981) 18 C.C.L.T. 129 (H.C.)) An action for misappropriation of another's ''image'' for commercial purposes was successful in *Athans* although a claim in passing off was dismissed. In that case, Mr. Justice Henry applied the reasoning in *Krouse* to award damages to a water skier, famous in the sport, whose enhanced photograph had been used in an advertisement of the defendant's summer camps. The court rejected liability based on appropriation of personal identity because the plaintiff was not well known to the public and his identity was, therefore, not being used as a ''drawing card'' for the defendant's camp. However, the court held for the plaintiff on the ground that his *image* had been wrongfully appropriated because the photograph showed him in a distinctive pose which he ''used as an essential component in the marketing of his personality'' (p. 34).

Similarly, in *Heath,* the court declined to strike out a claim based on misappropriation. The plaintiff in that case was a six-year old professional actor who had appeared extensively in television commercials. The defendant used the plaintiff's photograph and name in various advertisements for the advancement of the defendant's private vocational school without the plaintiff's authority.

Because appropriation of personality is such a new area of tort liability, several questions remain unanswered. The present law in Ontario seems to protect an individual from the unauthorized publication of his personality for the commercial benefit of a third party. Beyond this the law does not go.

2. *Defamation*

In *Palmer* v. *The National Sporting Club Ltd.* ((1906) MacGillvray's Copyright Cases, 1905-1910, p. 55), the court would not grant an injunction to a boxer to prevent the showing of photographs of a fight in which he was defeated. The plaintiff's argument that the showing of the pictures would damage his reputation and cause much personal annoyance and indignity was unsuccessful because the court was of the opinion that the photographs were a ''truthful representation of the context.''

There have been successful suits in defamation with respect to the publication of photographs. In *Tolley* v. *J. S. Fry and Sons Ltd.* ([1931] A.C. 333) a chocolate company issued an advertisement depicting Tolley, an amateur golfer, playing golf with one of their chocolate bars protruding from his pocket. The plaintiff did not receive notice of the defendant's intention to use his likeness, and brought an action for unlawful use of his caricature for commercial benefit. The English Court of Appeal found for the plaintiff on the basis of defamation by innuendo, reasoning that the public seeing the advertisement would undoubtedly believe the plaintiff to have prostituted his amateur status through a commercial promotion of the defendant's product. The plaintiff would not have been successful, however, if he had been either a professional or an ordinary golfer, as no damage to his reputation would have occurred.

There are other cases in the reports. An action in defamation prevented an advertising agency from using a photograph of a former policeman, without his permission, to advertise a cure for sore feet. (*Plumb* v. *Jeyes' Sanitary Compounds Co. Ltd., The Times,* 15 April, 1937) An actress was able to prevent the use of her toothless photograph as an advertisement for a dentist. (*Finston* v. *Pearson, The Times,* 12 March, 1915) and the publishing of a man's photographed head imposed on the picture of a body of an old fop was found to be an actionable defamation. (*Dunlop Rubber Co. Ltd.* v. *Dunlop* [1921] 1 A.C. 3678).

Plaintiffs have also succeeded in defamation actions in cases concerning the publication of their photographs in newspapers. For example: where a photograph of a girl appeared with the caption ''The Whitsun Girl'', the innuendo being that the girl could be picked up at Whitsuntide (*Wallis* v. *London Mail (Ltd.), The Times,* 20 July 1917).

5.3.3 Privacy Statutes

5.3.3.1 Notes on Provincial Privacy Acts

British Columbia, Manitoba, Newfoundland, and Saskatchewan are the only common law provinces to have enacted legislation creating statutory torts for wrongful invasions of privacy (Privacy Act, R.S.B.C. 1979, c.336; The Privacy Act, S.M. 1970, c.74 — Cap. P-24; The Privacy Act, S.N. 1981, c.6; and The Privacy Act, S.S. 1974, c.P-24). The four statutes are essentially the same. Each one creates a right of action for invasions of privacy *per se,* without the necessity of the plaintiff proving any damage.

Although ''privacy'' is not defined in any of the Acts, every provincial Privacy Statute sets out various ways in which privacy may be invaded — eavesdropping, surveillance, wire-tapping, use of personal documents, and appropriation, to name a few. All of the acts list specific defences (or ''exceptions'' under the British Columbia Act) including consent (express or implied in Manitoba), acting under legal authority, and publishing a matter of public interest, a fair comment on a matter of public interest, or that which would be privileged under the law of defamation. And before the court can conclude that an actionable invasion of privacy has occurred, each statute requires that the claimed privacy interest be assessed ''in all the circumstances''.

In addition, the British Columbia, Newfoundland and Saskatchewan acts list specific factors for the court to consider in determining whether there has been a violation of privacy: the nature, incidence and occasion of the act or conduct, for example. The Manitoba, Newfoundland and Saskatchewan statutes also outline particular remedies which the court may grant in an action for violation of privacy — damages and injunctive relief. Under the British Columbia, Newfoundland and Saskatchewan legislation privacy is considered to be a personal right which is extinguished by the death of the person whose privacy is alleged to have been violated. And both the Newfoundland and Saskatchewan Privacy Acts shift the burden of proving innocence to the defendant and impose limitation periods on actions for the violation of privacy. The Newfoundland statute sets the time at two years from the date the alleged violation became known or should have become known by the aggrieved individual or, ''in any case, after the expiration of seven years from the date on which the violation of privacy occurred''. (s.10). The Saskatchewan legislation simply states that the action must be commenced within two years from the time the alleged violation was discovered by the injured party (s.9).

There are certain distinctive features of each of the provincial privacy statutes. The British Columbia Act creates two heads of tortious liability, providing for general protection of privacy as well as a separate tort of misappropriation of another person's name or likeness for commercial purposes without consent. Under the Manitoba statute a violation of privacy need not be intentional to be actionable. The Newfoundland Privacy Act deems itself paramount where there is a conflict between one of its provisions and a provision of any other Newfoundland statute. And the legislation in Saskatchewan creates a new defence for the news media. Section 4(1)(e) provides that an act, conduct or publication of a person involved in news gathering for the media will not be a violation of privacy under the Act if it was reasonable and necessary for or incidental to ordinary news gathering.

Although the privacy legislation should provide more protection for privacy than that available only indirectly under the common law, this is not the case. No litigation has occurred under either the Newfoundland or Saskatchewan statutes to date, and what little case law there has been under the British Columbia and Manitoba Acts has not been encouraging to plaintiffs. For example, no invasion of privacy was held to exist in *Davis* v. *McArthur* ((1970) 17 D.L.R. (3d) 760 (B.C.C.A.)) where the plaintiff was watched and followed at home and at work by the defendant private investigator, hired by the plaintiff's wife in order to uncover proof of his adultery (which was never found). In *Wooding* v. *Little* ((1982) 24 C.C.L.T. 37 (B.C.S.C.)) a newspaper publication of an individual's confidential medical reports was found not to constitute a tort under the British Columbia Privacy Act because the publication was privileged under the law of defamation. The defence of public interest defeated actions for invasions of privacy resulting from television broadcasts in both *Belzberg* v. *BCTV Broadcasting System Ltd.* ([1981] W.W.R. 85 (B.C.S.C.)) and *Silber* v. *BCTV Broadcasting System Ltd.* ((1986 69 B.C.L.R. 35 (S.C.)). And in *Bingo Enterprises Ltd., Vic and Joe Enterprises Ltd. and Buffalo Ventures Ltd.* v. *Price Waterhouse* ((1985) 36 Man. R. (2d) 249 (Q.B.)) financial information, which the plaintiff corporation voluntarily gave to a Commission of Inquiry, was disclosed to a prosecutor by one of the Commission's accountants when he was subpoened to testify at the trial when criminal charges were laid against one of the plaintiffs and its principals. The court dismissed the plaintiffs' claim for invasion of privacy holding that although the accountant's conduct fell within one of the examples of violation of privacy listed in the Manitoba Act, the violation was not "substantial and unreasonable", as required by the statute.

A claim for invasion of privacy has succeeded in only one decision to date. In *I.C.B.C.* v. *Somosh* ((1983) 51 D.C.L.R. (S.C.)) a credit investigator phoned Somosh's place of employment and asked the receptionist questions about him involving his personal habits, morality, and which bars he frequented. The court found these questions, and the manner in which they were asked, to be an invasion of privacy. However, only nominal damages were awarded.

The provincial privacy statutes have not provided much protection against invasions of privacy. Unfortunately, the federal legislation is even less satisfactory. The Privacy Act (S.C. 1982, c.111), enacted as part of the Access to Information Act, does not actually create a right to privacy. Rather, it creates a right in an individual to apply to obtain personal information held by the State about himself or herself. And the so-called "Protection of Privacy Act" is an amendment to the Criminal Code (S.C. 1973-4, c.50; 1976-7, c.53) which purports to protect personal privacy by making it an indictable offence to wilfully intercept private communications by electromagnetic, acoustic, mechanical or other devices (s.178.11(1)). Various exceptions to the prohibitions are set out in the legislation. The major one allows certain state officials to apply for and obtain authorization to intercept private communications. Such interceptions are almost always admitted into evidence. Under the federal ''Protection of Privacy Act'', the protection of privacy seems to be subordinate to the desire to obtain evidence of criminal acts.

5.3.3.2 Privacy Act R.S.C. 1985, c.P-21

PROTECTION OF PERSONAL INFORMATION

7. Personal information under the control of a government institution shall not, without the consent of the individual to whom it relates, be used by the institution except

(*a*) for the purpose for which the information was obtained or compiled by the institution or for a use consistent with that purpose; or

(*b*) for a purpose for which the information may be disclosed to the institution under subsection 8(2).

8. (1) Personal information under the control of a government institution shall not, without the consent of the individual to whom it relates, be disclosed by the institution except in accordance with this section.

(2) Subject to any other Act of Parliament, personal information under the control of a government institution may be disclosed

(*a*) for the purpose for which the information was obtained or compiled by the institution or for a use consistent with that purpose;

(*b*) for any purpose in accordance with any Act of Parliament or any regulation made thereunder that authorizes its disclosure;

(*c*) for the purpose of complying with a subpoena or warrant issued or order made by a court, person or body with jurisdiction to compel the production of information or for the purpose of complying with rules of court relating to the production of information;

(*d*) to the Attorney General of Canada for use in legal proceedings involving the Crown in right of Canada or the Government of Canada;

(*e*) to an investigative body specified in the regulations, on the written request of the body, for the purpose of enforcing any law of Canada or a province or carrying out a lawful investigation, if the request specifies the purpose and describes the information to be disclosed;

(*f*) under an agreement or arrangement between the Government of Canada or an institution thereof and the government of a province, the government of a foreign state, an international organization of states or an international organization established by the governments of states, or any institution of any such government or organization, for the purpose of administering or enforcing any law or carrying out a lawful investigation;

(*g*) to a member of Parliament for the purpose of assisting the individual to whom the information relates in resolving a problem;

(*h*) to officers or employees of the institution for internal audit purposes, or to the office of the Comptroller General or any other person or body specified in the regulations for audit purposes;

(*i*) to the Public Archives for archival purposes;

(*j*) to any person or body for research or statistical purposes if the head of the government institution

(i) is satisfied that the purpose for which the information is disclosed cannot reasonably be accomplished unless the information is provided in a form that would identify the individual to whom it relates, and

(ii) obtains from the person or body a written undertaking that no subsequent disclosure of the information will be made in a form that could reasonably be expected to identify the individual to whom it relates;

(*k*) to any association of aboriginal people, Indian band, government institution or part thereof, or to any person acting on behalf of such association, band, institution or part thereof, for the purpose of researching or validating the claims, disputes or grievances of any of the aboriginal peoples of Canada;

"Indian band" means

(*a*) a band, as defined in the *Indian Act;* or

(*b*) a band, as defined in the *Cree-Naskapi (of Quebec) Act.*"

(*l*) to any government institution for the purpose of locating an individual in order to collect a debt owing to Her Majesty in right of Canada by that individual or make a payment owing to that individual by Her Majesty in right of Canada; and

(*m*) for any purpose where, in the opinion of the head of the institution,

(i) the public interest in disclosure clearly outweighs any invasion of privacy that could result from the disclosure, or

(ii) disclosure would clearly benefit the individual to whom the information relates.

(3) Subject to any other Act of Parliament, personal information under the control of the Public Archives that has been transferred to the Public Archives by a government institution for archival or historical purposes may be disclosed in accordance with the regulations to any person or body for research or statistical purposes.

(4) The head of a government institution shall retain a copy of every request received by the government institution under paragraph (2)(*e*) for such period of time as may be prescribed by regulation, shall keep a record of any information disclosed pursuant to the request for such period of time as may be prescribed by regulation and shall, on the request of the Privacy Commissioner, make such copies and records available to the Privacy Commissioner.

(5) The head of a government institution shall notify the Privacy Commissioner in writing of any disclosure of personal information under paragraph (2)(*m*) prior to the disclosure where reasonably practicable or in any other case forthwith on the disclosure, and the Privacy Commissioner may, if the Commissioner deems it appropriate, notify the individual to whom the information relates of the disclosure.

9. (1) The head of a government institution shall retain a record of any use by the institution of personal information contained in a personal information bank or any use or purpose for which such information is disclosed by the institution where the use or purpose is not included in the statements of uses and purposes set forth pursuant to subparagraph 11(1)(*a*)(iv) and subsection 11(2) in the index referred to in section 11; and shall attach the record to the personal information.

"(1.1) Subsection (1) does not apply in respect of information disclosed pursuant to paragraph 8(2)(*e*)."

(2) For the purposes of this Act, a record retained under subsection (1) shall be deemed to form part of the personal information to which it is attached.

(3) Where personal information in a personal information bank under the control of a government institution is used or disclosed for a use consistent with the purpose for which the information was obtained or compiled by the institution but the use is not included in the statement of consistent uses set forth pursuant to subparagraph 11(1)(*a*)(iv) in the index referred to in section 11, the head of the government institution shall

(*a*) forthwith notify the Privacy Commissioner of the use for which the information was used or disclosed; and

(*b*) ensure that the use is included in the next statement of consistent uses set forth in the index.

PERSONAL INFORMATION BANKS

10. (1) The head of a government institution shall cause to be included in personal information banks all personal information under the control of the government institution that

(*a*) has been used, is being used or is available for use for an administrative purpose; or

(*b*) is organized or intended to be retrieved by the name of an individual or by an identifying number, symbol or other particular assigned to an individual.

(2) Subsection (1) does not apply in respect of personal information under the control of the Public Archives that has been transferred to the Public Archives by a government institution for archival or historical purposes.

PERSONAL INFORMATION INDEX

11. (1) The designated Minister shall cause to be published on a periodic basis not less frequently than once each year, an index of

(*a*) all personal information banks setting forth, in respect of each bank,

(i) the identification and a description of the bank, the registration number assigned to it by the designated Minister pursuant to paragraph 71(1)(*b*) and a description of the class of individuals to whom personal information contained in the bank relates,

(ii) the name of the government institution that has control of the bank,

(iii) the title and address of the appropriate officer to whom requests relating to personal information contained in the bank should be sent,

(iv) a statement of the purposes for which personal information in the bank was obtained or compiled and a statement of the uses consistent with such purposes for which the information is used or disclosed,

(v) a statement of the retention and disposal standards applied to personal information in the bank, and

(vi) an indication, where applicable, that the bank was designated as an exempt bank by an order under section 18 and the provision of section 21 or 22 on the basis of which the order was made; and

(*b*) all classes of personal information under the control of a government institution that are not contained in personal information banks, setting forth in respect of each class,

(i) a description of the class in sufficient detail to facilitate the right of access under this Act, and
(ii) the title and address of the appropriate officer for each government institution to whom requests relating to personal information within the class should be sent.

(2) The designated Minister may set forth in the index referred to in subsection (1) a statement of any of the uses and purposes, not included in the statements made pursuant to subparagraph (1)(*a*)(iv), for which personal information contained in any of the personal information banks referred to in the index is used or disclosed on a regular basis.

(3) The designated Minister shall cause the index referred to in subsection (1) to be made available throughout Canada in conformity with the principle that every person is entitled to reasonable access to the index.

ACCESS TO PERSONAL INFORMATION

Right of Access

12. (1) Subject to this Act, every individual who is a Canadian citizen or a permanent resident within the meaning of the *Immigration Act, 1976* has a right to and shall, on request, be given access to
(*a*) any personal information about the individual contained in a personal information bank; and
(*b*) any other personal information about the individual under the control of a government institution with respect to which the individual is able to provide sufficiently specific information on the location of the information as to render it reasonably retrievable by the government institution.

(2) Every individual who is given access under paragraph (1)(*a*) to personal information that has been used, is being used or is available for use for an administrative purpose is entitled to
(*a*) request correction of the personal information where the individual believes there is an error or omission therein;
(*b*) require that a notation be attached to the information reflecting any correction requested but not made; and
(*c*) require that any person or body to whom such information has been disclosed for use for an administrative purpose within two years prior to the time a correction is requested or a notation is required under this subsection in respect of that information
(i) be notified of the correction or notation, and
(ii) where the disclosure is to a government institution, the institution make the correction or notation on any copy of the information under its control.

(3) The Governor in Council may, by order, extend the right to be given access to personal information under subsection (1) to include individuals not referred to in that subsection and may set such conditions as the Governor in Council deems appropriate.

Requests for Access

13. (1) A request for access to personal information under paragraph 12(1)(*a*) shall be made in writing to the government institution that has control of the personal information bank that contains the information and shall identify the bank.

(2) A request for access to personal information under paragraph 12(1)(*b*) shall be made in writing to the government institution that has control of the information and shall provide sufficiently specific information on the location of the information as to render it reasonably retrievable by the government institution.

14. Where access to personal information is requested under subsection 12(1), the head of the government institution to which the request is made shall, subject to section 15, within thirty days after the request is received,

(*a*) give written notice to the individual who made the request as to whether or not access to the information or a part thereof will be given; and

(*b*) if access is to be given, give the individual who made the request access to the information or the part thereof.

15. The head of a government institution may extend the time limit set out in section 14 in respect of a request for

(*a*) a maximum of thirty days if

(i) meeting the original time limit would unreasonably interfere with the operations of the government institution, or

(ii) consultations are necessary to comply with the request that cannot reasonably be completed within the original time limit, or

(*b*) such period of time as is reasonable, if additional time is necessary for translation purposes,

by giving notice of the extension and the length of the extension to the individual who made the request within thirty days after the request is received, which notice shall contain a statement that the individual has a right to make a complaint to the Privacy Commissioner about the extension.

16. (1) Where the head of a government institution refuses to give access of any personal information requested under subsection 12(1), the head of the institution shall state in the notice given under paragraph 14(*a*)

(*a*) that the personal information does not exist, or

(*b*) the specific provision of this Act on which the refusal was based or the provision on which a refusal could reasonably be expected to be based if the information existed,

and shall state in the notice that the individual who made the request has a right to make a complaint to the Privacy Commissioner about the refusal.

(2) The head of a government institution may but is not required to indicate under subsection (1) whether personal information exists.

(3) Where the head of a government institution fails to give access to any personal information requested under subsection 12(1) within the time limits set out in this Act, the head of the institution shall, for the purposes of this Act, be deemed to have refused to give access.

Access

17. (1) Subject to any regulations made under paragraph 77(1)(*o*), where an individual is to be given access to personal information requested under subsection 12(1), the government institution shall

(*a*) permit the individual to examine the information in accordance with the regulations; or

(*b*) provide the individual with a copy thereof.

(2) Where access to personal information is to be given under this Act and the individual to whom access is to be given requests that access be given in a particular official language, as declared in the *Official Languages Act,*

(*a*) access shall be given in that language if the personal information already exists under the control of a government institution in that language; and

(*b*) where the personal information does not exist in that language, the head of the government institution that has control of the personal information shall cause it to be translated or interpreted for the individual if the head of the institution considers a translation or interpretation to be necessary to enable the individual to understand the information.

EXEMPTIONS

Exempt Banks

18. (1) The Governor in Council may by order designate as exempt banks certain personal information banks that contain files all of which consist predominantly of personal information described in section 21 or 22.

(2) The head of a government institution may refuse to disclose any personal information requested under subsection 12(1) that is contained in a personal information bank designated as an exempt bank under subsection (1).

(3) An order made under subsection (1) shall specify

(*a*) the section on the basis of which the order is made; and

(*b*) where a personal information bank is designated that contains files that consist predominantly of personal information described in subparagraph 22(1)(*a*)(ii), the law concerned.

Personal Information

26. The head of a government institution may refuse to disclose any personal information requested under subsection 12(1) about an individual other than the individual who made the request, and shall refuse to disclose such information where the disclosure is prohibited under section 8.

27. The head of a government institution may refuse to disclose any personal information requested under subsection 12(1) that is subject to solicitor-client privilege.

28. The head of a government institution may refuse to disclose any personal information requested under subsection 12(1) that relates to the physical or mental health of the individual who requested it where the examination of the information by the individual would be contrary to the best interests of the individual.

REPORTS TO PARLIAMENT

38. The Privacy Commissioner shall, within three months after the termination of each financial year, submit an annual report to Parliament on the activities of the office during that financial year.

39. (1) The Privacy Commissioner may, at any time, make a special report to Parliament referring to and commenting on any matter within the scope of the powers, duties and functions of the Commissioner where, in the opinion of the Commissioner, the matter is of such urgency or importance that a report thereon should not be deferred until the time provided for transmission of the next annual report of the Commissioner under section 38.

(2) Any report made pursuant to subsection (1) that relates to an investigation under this Act shall be made only after the procedures set out in section 35, 36 or 37 have been followed in respect of the investigation.

40. (1) Every report to Parliament made by the Privacy Commissioner under section 38 or 39 shall be made by being transmitted to the Speaker of the Senate and to the Speaker of the House of Commons for tabling in those Houses.

(2) Every report referred to in subsection (1) shall, after it is transmitted for tabling pursuant to that subsection, be referred to the committee designated or established by Parliament for the purpose of subsection 75(1).

REVIEW BY THE FEDERAL COURT

41. Any individual who has been refused access to personal information requested under subsection 12(1) may, if a complaint has been made to the Privacy Commissioner in respect of the refusal, apply to the Court for a review of the matter within forty-five days after the time the results of an investigation of the complaint by the Privacy Commissioner are reported to the complainant under subsection 35(2) or within such further time as the Court may, either before or after the expiry of those forty-five days, fix or allow.

42. The Privacy Commissioner may

(*a*) apply to the Court, within the time limits prescribed by section 41, for a review of any refusal to disclose personal information requested under subsection 12(1) in respect of which an investigation has been carried out by the Privacy Commissioner, if the Commissioner has the consent of the individual who requested access to the information;

(*b*) appear before the Court on behalf of any individual who has applied for a review under section 41; or

(*c*) with leave of the Court, appear as a party to any review applied for under section 41.

43. In the circumstances described in subsection 36(5), the Privacy Commissioner may apply to the Court for a review of any file contained in a personal information bank designated as an exempt bank under section 18.

70. (1) This Act does not apply to confidences of the Queen's Privy Council for Canada, including, without restricting the generality of the foregoing, any information contained in

(*a*) memoranda the purpose of which is to present proposals or recommendations to Council;
(*b*) discussion papers the purpose of which is to present background explanations, analyses of problems or policy options to Council for consideration by Council in making decisions;
(*c*) agenda of Council or records recording deliberations or decisions of Council;
(*d*) records used for or reflecting communications or discussions between Ministers of the Crown on matters relating to the making of government decisions or the formulation of government policy;
(*e*) records the purpose of which is to brief Ministers of the Crown in relation to matters that are before, or are proposed to be brought before, Council or that are the subject of communications or discussions referred to in paragraph (*d*); and
(*f*) draft legislation.

(2) For the purposes of subsection (1), ''Council'' means the Queen's Privy Council for Canada, committees of the Queen's Privy Council for Canada, Cabinet and committees of Cabinet.

(3) Subsection (1) does not apply to
(*a*) confidences of the Queen's Privy Council for Canada that have been in existence for more than twenty years; or
(*b*) discussion papers described in paragraph (1)(*b*)
(i) if the decisions to which the discussion papers relate have been made public, or
(ii) where the decisions have not been made public, if four years have passed since the decisions were made.

71. (1) Subject to subsection (2), the designated Minister shall
(*a*) cause to be kept under review the manner in which personal information banks are maintained and managed to ensure compliance with the provisions of this Act and the regulations relating to access by individuals to personal information contained therein;
(*b*) assign or cause to be assigned a registration number to each personal information bank;
(*c*) prescribe such forms as may be required for the operation of this Act and the regulations;
(*d*) cause to be prepared and distributed to government institutions directives and guidelines concerning the operation of this Act and the regulations; and
(*e*) prescribe the form of, and what information is to be included in, reports made to Parliament under section 72.

(2) Anything that is required to be done by the designated Minister under paragraph (1)(*a*) or (*d*) shall be done in respect of the Bank of Canada by the Governor of the Bank of Canada.

(3) Subject to subsection (5), the designated Minister shall cause to be kept under review the utilization of existing personal information banks and proposals for the creation of new banks, and shall make such recommendations as he considers appropriate to the heads of the appropriate government institutions with regard to personal information banks that, in the opinion of the designated Minister, are underutilized or the existence of which can be terminated.

(4) Subject to subsection (5), no new personal information bank shall be established and no existing personal information banks shall be substantially modified without approval of the designated Minister or otherwise than in accordance with any term or condition on which such approval is given.

(5) Subsections (3) and (4) apply only in respect of personal information banks under the control of government institutions that are departments as defined in section 2 of the *Financial Administration Act*.

(6) The designated Minister may authorize the head of a government institution to exercise and perform, in such manner and subject to such terms and conditions as the designated Minister directs, any of the powers, functions and duties of the designated Minister under subsection (3) or (4).

72. (1) The head of every government institution shall prepare for submission to Parliament an annual report on the administration of this Act within the institution during each financial year.

(2) Every report prepared under subsection (1) shall be laid before the Senate and the House of Commons within three months after the financial year in respect of which it is made or, if Parliament is not then sitting, on any of the first fifteen days next thereafter that Parliament is sitting.

(3) Every report prepared under subsection (1) shall, after it is laid before the Senate and the House of Commons, under subsection (2), be referred to the committee designated or established by Parliament for the purpose of subsection 75(1).

73. The head of a government institution may by order designate one or more officers or employees of that institution to exercise or perform any of the powers, duties or functions of the head of the institution under this Act that are specified in the order.

74. Notwithstanding any other Act of Parliament, no civil or criminal proceedings lie against the head of any government institution, or against any person acting on behalf or under the direction of the head of a government institution, and no proceedings lie against the Crown or any government institution, for the disclosure in good faith of any personal information pursuant to this Act or for any consequences that flow from such disclosure, or for the failure to give any notice required under this Act if reasonable care is taken to give the required notice.

5.3.3.3 *Silber and Value Industries Ltd.* v. *British Columbia Television Broadcasting System Ltd., Hicks and Chu* [1986] 2 W.W.R. 609 (B.C.S.C.)

LYSYK J.: The plaintiff Arnold Silber was then and is now the president and sole shareholder of the plaintiff Value Industries Ltd. (''Value''), the owner of Staceys. The defendants Dale Hicks and Ken Chu were at all material times employed by the defendant British Columbia Television Broadcasting System Ltd. (''B.C.T.V.''). On the date of the events giving rise to this action, 25th November 1980, Hicks and Chu were operating as a news reporting team. Hicks was the on-camera journalist who delivered the commentary and Chu was the cameraman.

The facts, in outline, are these. Since May of 1980 the teamsters' union had been on strike against Collingwood Services Ltd. The latter, a company associated with the corporate plaintiff, Value, and controlled by the plaintiff Silber, performed delivery services for Staceys. It was a bitter strike. There had been a number of incidents in the months prior to 25th November, some of which resulted in court proceedings and some of which attracted coverage in the local press. B.C.T.V. decided to run a story on the strike and Mr. Hicks received the assignment.

About 10:00 a.m. on 25th November Mr. Hicks attended at Staceys and met with Mr. Silber to discuss the proposed news story. Mr. Silber declined to be interviewed on camera, although he said he would be prepared to grant an interview after the strike was over. According to his testimony, he was concerned that publicity would deter customers from patronizing the store. After learning that Hicks was expecting a cameraman to join him, Silber told Hicks that he did not want the B.C.T.V. team on the premises and he made it clear that the prohibition extended to Staceys' parking lot. Hicks left the store after indicating that he was not prepared to postpone the news report to a later date. Shortly afterwards Silber observed Hicks and Chu filming from a vantage point across the street. Silber did nothing at this time, he testified, because they were not on Staceys' property.

Around 1:00 p.m., a Staceys employee informed Silber that the B.C.T.V. team was filming on Staceys' parking lot. Silber went to the store entrance doors facing the lot. Outside these doors there is a platform with a few steps down to the parking lot. As he came out onto the platform, Silber saw Hicks some 10 to 20 feet from the foot of the steps, facing away from the store and holding a microphone. Chu was a few feet beyond that, his camera trained on Hicks with Staceys in the background. Silber testified that he heard his name mentioned by Hicks as the latter spoke into a microphone.

Some of what happened next was captured on film. For the most part, however, events must be reconstructed from the accounts of the participants. That their recollections differ in detail, after a lapse of five years, is not surprising. Taken as a whole, however, the evidence provides a reasonably clear picture of what transpired.

Silber moved quickly toward Hicks, saying something to the effect that he thought he had told Hicks to stay off the property. He tried to wrest the microphone away from Hicks and to block the camera, which Chu continued to operate. Silber told the Staceys manager, Mr. Schuck, who had followed him out of the store, to call the police. As Silber struggled with Hicks for possession of the microphone, he called out to his son, Stuart Silber, and a Staceys security guard to get Chu's camera, or to get the film from it. This they attempted to do, but Chu broke free and ran away from the building toward the exit from the parking lot. Chu was tackled there and the struggle for the camera resumed. In response to a call from Hicks for assistance for Chu, a teamster picket joined the fray. Shortly thereafter the R.C.M.P. arrived, the camera was handed over to one of the officers and the altercation came to an abrupt end.

Later that afternoon B.C.T.V. recovered the film from the police. The film was edited and Mr. Hicks prepared a commentary to accompany it. The film was shown on news broadcasts at 6:00 p.m. and 11:00 p.m. that evening, and probably at noon the next day, over B.C.T.V.'s Vancouver television station, channel 8. According to the testimony of Mr. Bell, B.C.T.V.'s news director, the total viewing audience for these news programs would average 400,000 or more. The film clip aired included the somewhat dramatic conclusion brought to Hicks' parking lot commentary by Silber's sudden entry upon the scene.

The statement of claim alleges that: ''The broadcast of this tape has upset Silber and caused him concern and anguish and furthermore has been a source of embarrassment for both Silber and Value''. The plaintiffs say that, as a result of the television broadcasts, Staceys' business dropped off and remained lower than would otherwise have been the case for the next several months. They seek compensation for such financial loss.

The claim for violation of privacy in the case at hand presents two elements. First, was Mr. Silber's privacy violated by the circumstances of the filming on Staceys' parking lot? Second, was it violated by subsequent publication through the television news broadcasts? I am of the view that both of these questions must be answered in the negative for the following reasons.

The nature and degree of privacy to which a person is entitled, s.1(2) of the Act tells us, is ''that which is reasonable in the circumstances, due regard being given to the lawful interests of others''. This is elaborated upon in subs. (3), which directs that regard shall be given, among other things, to ''the nature, incidence and occasion of the act or conduct'' said to constitute a violation of privacy.

Insofar as the events in the parking lot are concerned, the ''act or conduct'' relevant to the claim for violation of privacy was the filming. The nature and degree of privacy to which Mr. Silber was entitled was that which was reasonable in the circumstances having regard, in particular, to the ''occasion'' of the filming. The salient feature here, in my view, is the location in which the filming took place. Events transpiring on this parking lot could hardly be considered private in the sense of being shielded from observation by the general public. They occurred in the middle of the day, on a site open to unobstructed view from an adjoining heavily travelled thoroughfare, in a busy commercial neighbourhood. The property was private in the sense that the plaintiffs had the right to exclude trespassers from it, but Mr. Silber could hardly expect to enjoy a right of privacy with respect to what happened there because that was open for anyone happening by to see.

In *Harrison v. Carswell,* [1976] 2 S.C.R. 200, [1975] 6 W.W.R. 673, 75 C.L.L.C. 14,286, 235 C.C.C. (2d) 186, 62 D.L.R. (3d) 68, 5 N.R. 523 [Man.], a trespass case concerning picketing in the common areas of a shopping centre, Laskin C.J.C., in dissenting reasons, made some observations about the character of such areas which, I believe, are pertinent to the claim for violation of privacy here (albeit, in view of the result, not to the claim in trespass). He stated (at pp. 207-208):

''The considerations which underlie the protection of private residences cannot apply to the same degree to a shopping centre in respect of its parking areas, roads and sidewalks. Those amenities are closer in character to public roads and sidewalks than to a private dwelling. All that can be urged from a theoretical point of view to assimilate them to private dwellings is to urge that if property is privately owned, no matter the use to which it is put, trespass is as appropriate in the one case as in the other and it does not matter that possession, the invasion of which is basic to trespass, is recognizable in the one case but not in the other. There is here, on this assimilation, a legal injury albeit no actual injury. This is a use of theory which does not square with economic or social fact under the circumstances of the present case.'' In citing this passage, the only point I wish to make is that the character of the property where the act or conduct complained of took place is highly relevant to the question of what constitutes a reasonable expectation of privacy.

On this point, the decision of the California Supreme Court, in Bank, in *Gill v. Hearst Publishing Co.,* 253 P. 2d 441 (1953), is instructive. The defendant had published an unauthorized photograph of the plaintiffs taken by the defendants' employee while the plaintiffs were seated in an affectionate pose at their place of business, a confectionary and ice cream concession in the Farmers' Market in Los Angeles. This photograph was used to illustrate an article entitled "And so the World Goes Round", a short commentary reaffirming "the poet's conviction that the world could not revolve without love". Apparently the picture had no particular news value but was designed to serve the function of entertainment, there treated as a matter of legitimate public interest. The character of the property in which the plaintiffs' place of business was situated was commented upon in the following passage from the majority reasons (at p. 444):

"In considering the nature of the picture in question, it is significant that it was not surreptitiously snapped on private grounds, but rather was taken of plaintiffs in a pose voluntarily assumed in a public market place. So distinguishable are cases such as Barber v. Time, Inc.,... where the picture showed plaintiff in her bed at a hospital, which circumstance was held to constitute an infringement of the right of privacy. Here plaintiffs, photographed at their concession allegedly 'well known to persons and travelers throughout the world' as conducted for 'many years' in the 'worldfamed' Farmers' Market, had voluntarily exposed themselves to public gaze in a pose open to the view of any persons who might then be at or near their place of business. By their own voluntary action plaintiffs waived their right of privacy so far as this particular public pose was assumed... for 'There can be no privacy in that which is already public.'" [citations omitted]

It was held, reversing the decision at trial, that the plaintiffs could not succeed.

Staceys' parking lot was, assuredly, private property. But what transpired there was observable by anyone in the vicinity, on or off the property. Mr. Silber could have no reasonable expectation of privacy there.

The second question is whether the plaintiffs' privacy was violated by broadcast of the film in the television news broadcasts. In a passage following immediately after the above quotation from the *Hearst Publishing* decision, the California court reasoned as follows (at pp. 444-45):

"The photograph of plaintiffs merely permitted other members of the public, who were not at plaintiffs' place of business at the time it was taken, to see them as they had voluntarily exhibited themselves. Consistent with their own voluntary assumption of this particular pose in a public place, plaintiffs' right to privacy as to this photographed incident ceased and it in effect became a part of the public domain, Brandeis-Warren Essay, 4 Harvard Law Rev. 193, 218; Melvin v. Reid, supra... as to which they could not later rescind their waiver in an attempt to assert a right of privacy. Cohen v. Marx... In short, the photograph did not disclose anything which until then had been private, but rather only extended knowledge of the particular incident to a somewhat larger public than had actually witnessed it at the time of occurrence...

"Plaintiffs have failed to cite, and independent research has failed to reveal, any case where the publication of a mere photograph under the circumstances here prevailing — a picture (1) taken in a pose voluntarily assumed in a public place and (2) portraying nothing to shock the ordinary sense of decency or propriety — has been held an actionable invasion of the right of privacy. To so hold would mean that plaintiffs 'under all conceivable circumstances had an absolute legal right to [prevent publication of] any photograph of them taken without their permission. If every person has such a right, no [periodical] could lawfully publish a photograph of a parade or a street scene. We are not prepared to sustain the assertion of such a right.'" [citations omitted]

In brief, the view there taken appears to have been that where there is an implied waiver of the right to privacy by reason of the public character of the property on which the photographed behaviour occurred, subsequent publication of the photograph will not give rise to a right of action for invasion of privacy. I need not decide whether that reasoning is applicable under the Privacy Act because there is another reason why the terms of that enactment stand in the way of recovery by the plaintiffs.

The relevant provision in the Privacy Act is s.2(2), and it will be convenient to set out the material portion again:

"(2) A publication of a matter is not a violation of privacy if

"(*a*) the matter published was of public interest or was fair comment on a matter of public interest...

"but this subsection does not extend to any other act or conduct by which the matter published was obtained if that other act or conduct was itself a violation of privacy."

With reference to the latter part of the subsection, I have already found that the act or conduct by which the matter published was obtained — by filming — was not itself a violation of privacy.

Was the matter published through the television newscasts one of public interest? In the first section of these reasons reference was made to the long and bitter strike which had brought the plaintiffs into confrontation with the teamsters' union. There were court proceedings and these, as well as the incidents themselves, had attracted press coverage. The plaintiff's own conduct to some extent invited attention to the labour dispute. Staceys, for example, displayed a large banner which read "Striking for Lower Prices". Also, a former Staceys outlet in Surrey reopened under the name of "Union Furniture", and it displayed signs, symbols and slogans commonly associated with trade unions. Organized labour was not amused. The opening of Union Furniture attracted a rally attended by representatives from a number of unions. These and related events were duly reported in the local press: Ex. 14, B.C.T.V. was intrigued. According to the evidence, these were all factors contributing to newsworthiness and to B.C.T.V.'s decision to run a story. The portion of the film broadcast which recorded Mr. Silber's intervention must be seen in that context. If nothing else, it illustrated the volatility and high feelings which appeared to be characteristic of this labour dispute.

I have no difficulty in concluding that broadcast of the film was of public interest within the meaning of s.2(2) of the Act.

Counsel for the plaintiffs submitted that they were entitled to succeed on the basis that the film presented the plaintiff to the public in a false light. The television commentary accompanying the film made no mention of the fact that Mr. Silber had directed Hicks to stay off the premises, including the parking lot. It did not say that Hicks and Chu were trespassers. As a result, it was argued, the viewing audience could draw the conclusion that Mr. Silber engaged in intemperate or violent behaviour, entirely without justification.

Publicity placing a person in a false light in the public eye has been recognized as one form of invasion of privacy in the United States: see, e.g., Prosser and Keeton on The Law of Torts, 5th ed. (1984), at p. 863 ff., and Restatement of the Law, Second, Torts 2d, vol. 3, p. 394, para. 652E. To establish this cause of action it must be shown that the defendant published false facts about the plaintiff which, while not necessarily defamatory, would be highly objectionable to an ordinary reasonable person under the circumstances.

On this branch of the argument the plaintiffs in the present case are confronted by two obstacles. The first is that s.2(2) of the Act provides that publication "is not a violation if the matter published was of public interest". I have found that the matter was of public interest. Secondly, even if s.2(2) does not provide a complete answer to the claim, an essential element of the "false light" doctrine is the publication as fact of something which is false. Prosser states (at p. 865):

"Recovery for an invasion of privacy on the ground that the plaintiff was depicted in a false light makes sense only when the account, if true, would not have been actionable as an invasion of privacy. In other words, the outrageous character of the publicity comes about in part by virtue of the fact that some part of the matter reported was false and deliberately so."

Counsel for the plaintiffs here does not point to anything in the broadcast as untrue. He is driven to argue that it was misleading due to its incompleteness. Even if the Privacy Act leaves room for the "false light" doctrine, which is doubtful, I do not read the American authorities relied upon in argument as extending to circumstances such as those of the present case.

I conclude that the plaintiffs' claim for violation of privacy cannot succeed.